VOLATILITY

New Estimation Techniques for Pricing Derivatives

VOLATILITY

New Estimation Techniques for Pricing Derivatives

Edited by Robert Jarrow

RISK BOOKS

Published by Risk Books, a specialist division of Risk Publications.
104–112 Marylebone Lane
London W1M 5FU
Tel: +44 (0)171 487 5326
Fax: +44 (0)171 487 0760

ISBN 1 899332 41 3 (hardback)
ISBN 1 899332 46 4 (softback)

British Library Cataloguing in Publication Data
A catalogue record for this book is available from the British Library

Risk Books Commissioning Editor: Sue Grayling
Typesetter: Miles Smith-Morris

Printed and bound in Great Britain by Bookcraft (Bath) Ltd, Somerset.

The introduction to each section and Chapters 29, 30 and 31 are published here for the first time. The remaining chapters are slightly revised versions of articles previously published in the following journals:

Chapter 1 *Journal of Economic Surveys*, Vol. 7 (1993), Chapter 2 *Journal of Econometrics*, Vol. 52 (1992), Chapter 3 *Mathematical Finance*, Vol. 4 (1994), Chapter 4 *Papers and Proceedings of the American Statistical Association*, 1995, Chapter 5 *Review of Derivatives Research*, Vol. 1 (1997), Chapter 6 *Journal of Business & Economic Statistics*, Vol. 15 (1997), Chapter 7 *Applied Economics Letters*, Vol. 3 (1996), Chapter 8 *Journal of Banking & Finance*, Vol. 20 (1996), Chapter 9 *The Journal of Derivatives*, Winter 1993, Chapter 10 *The Review of Financial Studies*, Vol. 4 (1991), Chapter 11 *Journal of Financial and Quantitative Analysis*, Vol. 29 (1994), Chapter 12 *The Journal of Derivatives*, Winter 1993, Chapter 13 *The Review of Financial Studies*, Vol. 6 (1993), Chapter 14 *The Review of Financial Studies*, Vol. 6 (1993), Chapter 15 *The Review of Financial Studies*, Vol. 10 (1997), Chapter 16 *Journal of Business, Finance & Accounting*, Vol. 5 (1995), Chapter 17 *The Financial Review*, Vol. 32 (1997), Chapter 18 *Pacific-Basin Finance Journal*, Winter 1996, Chapter 19 *Journal of Banking & Finance*, Vol. 21 (1997), Chapter 20 *Journal of Economics and Business*, Vol. 48 (1996), Chapter 21 *Review of Quantitative Finance and Accounting*, Vol. 4 (1994), Chapter 22 *The Review of Financial Studies*, Vol. 4 (1991), Chapter 23 *The Review of Financial Studies*, Vol. 6 (1993), Chapter 24 *Mathematical Finance*, Vol. 5 (1995), Chapter 25 *The Journal of Derivatives* Summer 1996, Chapter 26 *The Journal of Derivatives*, Summer 1997, Chapter 27 *The Journal of Derivatives*, Summer 1995, Chapter 28 *The Journal of Derivatives*, Winter 1993.

FOREWORD

This book of readings is entitled *Volatility: New Estimation Techniques for Pricing Derivatives.* This title is descriptive. This book is a collection of readings on stochastic volatility for stocks, stock indexes, foreign currencies, interest rates, and commodities. It is a collection of readings on new techniques - that is, techniques beyond the standard Black-Scholes framework. And its focus is on pricing derivatives and managing financial portfolios. This focus can best be understood by considering each of these uses in more detail.

Pricing derivatives means more than simply determining a fair or arbitrage-free price. It also includes the issue of hedging - the synthetic replication of the derivative using either static or dynamic trading strategies in the underlying asset or assets. When this synthetic replication is possible, the market is "complete". With stochastic volatility, markets can take one of three different forms. The first two are when the market for the derivative is complete in a single underlying, called the stock for simplicity, and riskless investment (one) or not (two). These two classes of models are discussed in Sections V and VI. The third form is when the market for the derivative is complete with trading in the stock, riskless investment and a collection of call options (all strikes and maturities), a class discussed in Section VII. This third class of models is the most useful for pricing exotics on the underlying assets and includes the other two classes as special cases.

There are many different factors to consider in managing financial portfolios under stochastic volatilities. The most obvious, perhaps, is the issue of portfolio diversification. This involves the construction of mean-variance efficient portfolios, taking advantage of an asset's time varying mean, variance and correlation with other assets. Of course, the better the stochastic model for modelling the evolution of these assets' returns and covariances, the more precise the quantification is for diversification. The first three sections of this book discuss new techniques and useful applications - *Making Garch Work: Tests, Refinements and Applications*; *Exploring Volatility Patterns over Time* and *Forecasting Volatilities with Implied Volatilities*. These models can also be used for the determination of capital requirements, using quantities such as value-at -risk (VAR). After all, if an asset's mean return and covariance changes over time in a stochastic manner, these changes need to be incorporated in a firm' s VAR computation.

The second use of these techniques for managing portfolios is for speculation. Speculation, for us, is defined as the formation of a portfolio (or trading strategy) to take advantage of special views on the movements of an asset's price or volatility. Stochastic volatility models can be useful here. Indeed, the better that volatilities and returns can be predicted, the easier it is to tailor a portfolio to match its owner's views of the future. These issues are discussed in Sections III and VII.

These readings represent the knowledge and experiences of a diverse set of outstanding scholars. Many different topics are discussed, from many different perspectives. The hope, in bringing these readings together, was to generate a single source of knowledge that can be used to help resolve any question in the area of stochastic volatility. I'm pleased with the outcome and I hope you are as well. Good reading!

Robert Jarrow

Professor of Finance and Economics, Johnson Graduate School, Cornell University

June 1998

CONTENTS

IV. INTERRELATED INTERNATIONAL MARKETS: PRICE AND VOLATILITY SPILLOVERS

V. STOCHASTIC VOLATILITY MODELS: THE NEXT GENERATION?

VI. SMILES, SKEWS AND STOCHASTIC VOLATILITIES

VII. A PRACTITIONER'S PERSPECTIVE: WHAT'S AHEAD?

AUTHORS

Kaushik Amin is currently a senior vice president and head of the emerging markets derivatives group at Lehman Brothers. Previously, he was head of the mortgage swaps desk at Lehman. He joined the firm in 1994 after five years as a finance professor at the University of Michigan. He has published over a dozen articles in leading academic finance journals on the pricing and hedging of derivative securities. He obtained his PhD in finance from Cornell University in 1989.

Anil Bera is a professor of economics at the University of Illinois, Urbana-Champaign. He has contributed to the development of a number of test statistics, such as the Bera-Jarque test for normality and the Bera-McAleer test for linear–non-linear models. Currently, his main research interests include testing under misspecified models, spatial econometrics and non-linear time-series models. He is an associate editor of the *Journal of Business and Economic Statistics* and *Econometric Review* and a guest editor of the *Journal of Statistical Planning and Inference*. He received his PhD from the Australian National University. Before joining Illinois, he was a CORE Fellow at the Université Catholique de Louvain. He has been a visiting faculty member at a number of academic institutions, including the University of Western Ontario, Indiana University, Monash University, the University of Melborne, the Indian Statistical Institute, the University of Hawaii and Tilburg University, Holland.

Tim Bollerslev is the Commonwealth Professor of Economics at the University of Virginia. His research on the modelling and forecasting of financial market volatility has been particularly influential. The Garch methodology he originally developed is now routinely used by economists and finance practitioners all over the world. He received his PhD in economics at the University of California, San Diego, in 1986. Before joining the University of Virginia in 1996, he taught at the JL Kellogg Graduate School of Management at Northwestern University. He currently serves on the editorial boards of nine academic journals.

G. Geoffrey Booth is a professor of finance at Louisiana State University and holds the Union National Life Insurance Company Endowed Professorship in insurance. His current research interests focus on financial markets, risk and risk management. He has published numerous articles in leading academic journals and serves in an editorial capacity for several finance, economics and statistics journals. He received his PhD in finance at the University of Michigan, and has also served on the faculty of Syracuse University and the University of Rhode Island.

Galen Burghardt is senior vice president at Carr Futures in Chicago. He received his PhD from the University of Washington in Seattle. Before joining Carr Futures, he was senior vice president for Dean Witter Institutional Futures and executive vice president for Discount Corporation of New York Futures. He was formerly vice president, financial research, at the Chicago Mercantile Exchange, has taught economics at Amherst College, and served in the research division of the Federal Reserve Board in Washington DC. He launched, and is a regular contributor to, Carr Futures research note series. He teaches an MBA course on financial futures, swaps and options for the University of Chicago.

Linda Canina is an assistant professor of finance at Cornell University's School of Hotel Administration, where she has been since 1993. She holds a PhD in finance from the Stern School of Business, New York University. Prior to joining Cornell, she was an assistant professor of finance at Brown University. She has developed and teaches academic courses in hospitality financial management, financial economics, corporate finance, investments and empirical finance. In addition to her teaching, she conducts research in finance and relates that research to the hospitality industry. Currently, she is involved in developing and analysing a lodging property total return index (LPI) with other members of the Cornell faculty, the American Hotel and Motel Association and the Industry Real Estate Finance Advisory Council. The LPI will be computed and analysed on a regular basis. She has published in academic journals on the areas of options and index arbitrage. Other research interests include corporate finance and empirical asset pricing.

Peter Carr is a vice-president in the quantitative equity department of Morgan Stanley. Prior to joining Morgan Stanley, he was a professor of finance at Cornell University, having received his PhD in finance from UCLA in 1989. He has published articles in the *Journal of Finance*, the *Review of Financial Studies* and various other finance journals. He is currently an associate editor for five academic journals, including the *Journal of Computational Finance*. His research interests are primarily in the field of derivative securities, especially American-style and exotic derivatives. He has consulted for several firms and has given numerous talks at both practitioner and academic conferences.

Kalok Chan is an assistant professor with the department of finance at the Hong Kong University of Science and Technology. His areas of specialisation include linkages between derivatives and spot markets, liquidity and trading costs in financial markets, and asset prices in international markets. He has published articles in the *Journal of Finance*, *Journal of Financial Economics*, *Review of Financial Studies* and *Journal of Financial and Quantitative Analysis*. He has reviewed papers for more than 20 journals, and is co-editor of the *Pacific-Basin Finance Journal*. He obtained his PhD in finance from Ohio State University, and taught at Arizona State University before joining the HKUST.

K.C. Chan is currently professor and head of the department of finance at the Hong Kong University of Science and Technology. He is also the associate dean of its business school. He received his BA in economics from Wesleyan University in 1979. He then entered the Graduate School of Business at the University of Chicago, and received his MBA in 1981, and PhD in finance in 1989. From 1984 to 1993, he taught at Ohio State University. His research interests include the pricing of financial assets, and regulatory issues dealing with the efficiency of financial markets.

Ray Y. Chou is an associate research fellow at the Institute of Economics, Academia Sinica, the leading research institute in Taiwan. Previously, he was an assistant professor of economics at the Georgia Institute of Technology. He received a PhD in economics from the University of California, San Diego, in 1988. His professional expertise is in financial econometrics. He has published numerous articles in major professional journals on the statistical modelling of financial risks. He has received several research awards from the National Science Council. He teaches at several national universities in Taiwan, serves as an advisor at the Taiwan Economic Research Institute, and is on the editorial boards of several academic journals in Taiwan.

Mustafa Chowdhury is director of interest rate risk management at the Federal Home Loan Mortgage Corporation. He received his PhD in economics at the University of California, San Diego. He is an expert in options and fixed income securities and is routinely involved in pricing complex options. Prior to joining Freddie Mac, he was an assistant professor of finance at Louisiana State University. His academic research has been published in several finance and economics journals.

Neil A. Chriss is a portfolio manager and researcher in the quantitative research group at Goldman Sachs Asset Management in New York. He is also director of the program for mathematics in finance at the Courant Institute of Mathematical Sciences at New York University. He is author of *Black-Scholes and Beyond: Option Pricing Models*.

Andreas Christofi is an assistant professor and chair of the department of economics and finance at Monmouth University, New Jersey. He has published papers in *Financial Management*, the *Journal of Fixed Income*, *Journal of Portfolio Management*, *Management International Review* and *Financial Review*. His research interests include: modelling volatility, pricing of risky assets, and the term structure of interest rates. He holds a degree from Pennsylvania State University.

Charles Corrado is associate professor of finance at the University of Missouri-Columbia. He received his BA in Asian Studies from the University of Maryland-College Park, his PhD in economics from the State University of New York-Albany, and his PhD in finance from the University of Arizona-Tucson. He teaches in the general area of investments and his research currently focuses on financial derivatives.

Theodore E. Day, associate professor of finance at the University of Texas at Dallas, teaches courses in corporate finance and portfolio management. He has a BA from the University of Oklahoma and PhD from Stanford University. He has taught at Vanderbilt University and the University of North Carolina.

His research includes papers on the effects of inflation on stock returns, the term structure of interest rates, and the volatility of derivative asset markets. His work has been published in professional journals including the *Journal of Econometrics*, the *Journal of Finance*, the *Journal of Political Economy* and the *Review of Financial Studies*. His recent research examines discrimination in mortgage lending and the adequacy of margin requirements in futures markets.

Emanuel Derman is a managing director at Goldman Sachs, where he is head of the quantitative strategies group. He has a PhD in theoretical physics from Columbia University. Prior to joining Goldman Sachs in 1985, he worked for Bell Laboratories and held a number of academic positions while doing research in particle physics. At Goldman Sachs he directs the valuation modelling and the development of risk management strategies and systems. He publishes research into option trading strategies and consults with clients on volatility and modelling issues.

Monique W.M. Donders holds a masters degree and PhD in finance from Erasmus University, Rotterdam. She was an assistant professor at the department of finance at Erasmus and a consultant to the European Options Exchange. She has published in the *Journal of Banking and Finance* and *Statistica Neerlandica*. She is currently employed as a senior derivatives researcher at the Institute for Research and Investment Services, a joint venture between Rabobank and Robeco Group.

Jin-Chuan Duan currently teaches at the department of finance at the Hong Kong University of Science and Technology. Prior to this post, he was an associate professor at McGill University. He received his PhD in finance from the University of Wisconsin-Madison. His general research interests are derivative security pricing, time-series econometrics and banking. His current research primarily focuses on extensions of, and the computational issues related to, the Garch option pricing theory pioneered by him.

Michael Dueker is a senior economist at the Federal Reserve Bank of St Louis. He has published articles concerning time-series analysis of stock market volatility, fractional cointegration, and monetary policy rules. He also shares responsibility for briefing the bank president on monetary policy matters. He received his PhD in economics from the University of Washington-Seattle, and BS in mathematics from the University of Oregon.

Bruno Dupire heads the quantitative research team at Nikko Financial Products, where he develops pricing and arbitrage models. Prior to the last ten years in finance, he entered the Ecole Normale Superieure in mathematics, obtaining a masters degree in artificial intelligence and PhD in numerical analysis. He later became involved in biology modelling and neural networks, which he applied to finance as early as 1988. After leading the derivatives research teams at Société Générale and Paribas, he joined Nikko in September 1997. He is best known for his research into stochastic volatility, the pricing of exotic options in the presence of volatility smiles, and improvements to Monte Carlo simulations.

Larry Eisenberg is president of the Risk Engineering Company. Previously, he has traded on the CBOE, modelled and traded exotic equity options at Salomon and foreign exchange options at Lehman Brothers. Other work as a practitioner includes modelling and calibrating term-structure models for Bermudan interest rates in yen, dollars and European currencies. He has served on the finance faculty at the University of Illinois, and on the editorial board of the *Journal of Financial Engineering*. His derivatives publications include articles on exotic options and foreign exchange options as well as stochastic volatility. He has also developed models of systemic risk.

Robert F. Engle holds the Chancellor's Associates Chair in economics at the University of California, San Diego. He graduated from William's College in 1964 and received a PhD in economics from Cornell University in 1969. He was an assistant professor at Massachusetts Institute of Technology before moving to UCSD in 1977. He was chair of the department of economics from 1990 to 1994. He now lectures widely to both academic and practitioner audiences. He is an expert on time series analysis with a long-standing interest in the analysis of financial markets. His research has produced such innovative statistical methods as Arch, cointegration, band spectrum regression, common features, and most recently the ACD model with its procedures for modelling transaction data. Altogether he has published over one hundred papers and three books.

Stephen Figlewski is a professor of finance and Yamaichi Faculty Fellow at the New York University Leonard N. Stern School of Business, where he has been since 1976. He holds a BA degree in economics from Princeton and a PhD in economics from the Massachusetts Institute of Technology. He has published extensively in academic journals, especially in the area of financial futures and options. He is the founding editor of the *Journal of Derivatives* and an associate editor of several other journals. He is the editor of the Financial Economics Network's two "Derivatives" series published over the Internet, and is an associate editor of another recently launched Internet journal, *Net Exposure*. In addition to his academic career, he has also worked on Wall Street as a vice president at the First Boston Corporation, in charge of research on equity derivative products, and he has been a member of the New York Futures Exchange and a Competitive Options Trader at the New York Stock Exchange, trading for his own account as a market maker in stock index futures and options.

Gerald A. Hanweck, Jr is vice president for research for JP Morgan Futures in Chicago. He received his PhD in managerial economics and decision science from the Kellogg Graduate School of Management at Northwestern University in 1994, and holds an AB in mathematics from Princeton University. He has taught finance courses at Kellogg and at the University of Chicago. Prior to joining JP Morgan, he held positions in financial research at Discount Corporation of New York Futures and as a software developer at Microsoft Corporation.

Steven L. Heston is assistant professor of finance at the John M Olin School of Business, Washington University in St Louis, where he specialises in options, fixed income and investments. Previously, he taught at the School of Organization and Management at Yale University and was a visiting assistant professor at Columbia Business School. He holds a BA from the University of Maryland, College Park, and MS and PhD from Carnegie Mellon University.

Matthew L. Higgins is an assistant professor in the department of economics at Western Michigan University. His research concentrates on the specification error testing of non-linear time series models. He has also investigated problems in the econometrics of rational expectations and the dynamic properties of interest rates. He received his PhD in economics from the University of Illinois. He has previously taught at the University of Wisconsin-Milwaukee and at the University of Illinois.

Robert Jarrow is the Ronald P and Susan E Lynch Professor of Investment Management at the Johnson Graduate School of Management, Cornell University. He is also managing director and director of research at Kamakura Corporation. He is the 1997 IAFE/SunGard Financial Engineer of the year. A graduate of Duke University, Dartmouth College and the Massachusetts Institute of Technology, he is renowned for his pioneering work on the Heath-Jarrow-Morton model for pricing interest rate derivatives. His current research interests include the pricing of exotic interest rate options and credit derivatives, as well as investment management theory. His publications include four books, *Options Pricing*, *Finance Theory*, *Modelling Fixed Income Securities* and *Interest Rate Options and Derivative Securities*, as well as over 65 publications in leading finance and economic journals. He is currently editor of *Mathematical Finance* and an associate editor of the *Journal of Financial and Quantitative Analysis*, *The Review of Derivatives Research*, *Journal of Fixed Income*, *The Financial Review*, the *Journal of Derivatives* and *The Review of Futures Markets*. He is an advisory editor for *Financial Engineering and the Japanese Markets*.

Emel Kahya is an assistant professor of accounting in the School of Business, Rutgers University, and serves as the treasurer of the Multinational Finance Society. Her research interests are in prediction and forecasting methods, business failures, alternative income measurement and accounting systems, and financial markets. She has published articles in a number of journals, including *The Financial Review*, *Journal of Business Finance & Accounting*, and the *Journal of Multinational Financial Management*.

Alex Kane is professor of finance and economics at the Graduate School of International Relations and Pacific Studies, University of California, San Diego, with research interests in portfolio management, capital markets, and corporate finance. He has been a research associate at the National Bureau of Economic Research and visiting professor at the University of Tokyo and Harvard.

Iraj Kani is president of Martingale Technologies. Prior to that he was a vice president in the quantitative strategies group of Goldman Sachs and also spent some time in the fixed income division of Bankers Trust. He has a PhD in theoretical particle physics from Oxford University (in conjunction with Harvard University), and is an associate editor of the *International Journal of Theoretical and Applied Finance*.

Andrew Karolyi joined the Richard Ivey School of Business at the University of Western Ontario in 1996. He previously taught at Ohio State University. He received his BA in economics from McGill

University in 1983, and went on to spend several years in the research department at the Bank of Canada. He holds MBA and PhD degrees from the University of Chicago. His research focuses on international finance, global financing and investing strategies, and Pacific-Basin capital markets. He has published numerous articles in the *Journal of Finance*, *Journal of Financial Economics*, *Review of Financial Studies*, and *Journal of Financial and Quantitative Analysis*, and is currently assistant editor of the *Journal of Empirical Finance* and *Pacific-Basin Finance Journal*.

Gregory Koutmos is an associate professor of finance at Fairfield University. His current research interests are in the areas of risk modelling and risk management. He has published numerous articles in such journals as *The Journal of Futures Markets*, *The Journal of Economics and Business*, the *Journal of International Money and Finance*, the *Journal of Business Finance and Accounting*, *The Financial Review* and *The Journal of International Financial Markets, Institutions and Money*. He has served as associate editor for *The Financial Review* and the *Multinational Finance Journal*.

Ken Kroner is a managing director at Barclays Global Investors, where he is responsible for all asset allocation research, including tactical and global asset allocation. He was previously an associate professor in the finance and economics department at the University of Arizona. His research interests include asset allocation, volatility modelling and forecasting correlations. He has published many papers in academic and practitioner journals, and serves on the editorial board of *Studies in Nonlinear Dynamics and Econometrics*. He received his PhD in economics from the University of California, San Diego.

Chris Lamoureux is an associate professor of finance at the University of Arizona. He has previously taught at Louisiana State University and Washington University (in St. Louis). His research generally examines empirically the dynamic properties of asset prices. Most recently he has used Bayesian econometrics and the Gibbs sampler to model predictability of stock returns and the term structure of interest rates.

William D. Lastrapes is an associate professor of economics at the University of Georgia. He received his BS in finance from Louisiana State University in 1980 cum laude and his PhD in Economics from the University of North Carolina at Chapel Hill in 1986. He served on the faculty of Louisiana State University from 1985 to 1990, and was recently a visiting lecturer at the Jean Moulin University in Lyon, France. His research expertise is in the fields of monetary, macro and financial economics, and he has published articles in scholarly journals such as *The Review of Economics and Statistics*, *The Journal of Finance*, *The Journal of Money, Credit and Banking*, and *The Journal of Business and Economic Statistics*.

Tae-Hwy Lee is an assistant professor of economics at the University of California, Riverside. His research interests are time series econometrics, applied finance and macroeconometrics, and his articles have appeared in leading economic and statistics journals. He received his PhD in economics at the University of California, San Diego, and later taught at Louisiana State University. He held an ASA/NSF/BLS Senior Research Fellowship in 1995-6.

Unro Lee is an associate professor of finance in the Eberhardt School of Business at the University of the Pacific in Stockton, California. His research interests include the intertemporal behaviour of asset prices, the interaction of market variables and stock returns, and econometric analysis of the Pacific Rim securities markets. His papers have been published in numerous finance journals. He has an undergraduate degree in economics from the University of California in Los Angeles, and a masters degree in economics from Indiana University and a PhD in economics, with emphasis on econometrics and finance, from Purdue University, West Lafayette, Indiana.

Craig M. Lewis is associate professor of management at the Owen Graduate School of Management at Vanderbilt University. He holds a BS from Ohio State University and MS and PhD degrees from Wisconsin CPA. He has recently conducted research on the use of convertible debt and stock market responsiveness to analyst forecasts. He has published numerous papers on derivative securities, market volatility and corporate finance, in journals such as *The Journal of Econometrics*, the *Journal of Finance*, the *Journal of Financial and Quantitative Analysis* and the *Review of Financial Studies*. A former accountant with Arthur Young and Co, he teaches courses in corporate value management, portfolio management and derivative securities valuation.

Dilip B. Madan is professor of finance at the University of Maryland. He received his PhD in economics in 1971, and his PhD in mathematics in 1975, both from the University of Maryland. He then taught econometrics and operations research at the University of Sydney, Australia. His research focuses on the applications of the theory of stochastic process to the field of mathematical finance. He has published extensively in such journal as the *Journal of Business*, the *Review of Financial Studies*, *Mathematical Finance* and *Finance and Stochastics*. He is associate editor of *Mathematical Finance* and executive secretary of the Bachelier Finance Society.

Teppo Martikainen is a professor of accounting at the University of Vaasa, Finland. He holds a PhD in accounting and finance from the same university. His current interest areas are international financial markets and financial statement analysis. He has published numerous articles in leading academic journals, has written two books on financial markets and serves on the editorial boards of many journals. He was elected the Outstanding Young Person of Finland by the Junior Chamber of Finland in 1996, and is currently a consultant to several financial institutions and firms.

Victor Ng is vice president and manager of econometric modelling and trading strategies at Goldman Sachs and Co. He is responsible for building equilibrium term structure models and statistical models for yield curve and volatility trading in the major treasury and swap markets. He is also responsible for building spline models for treasury markets around the world and the US corporate market. Prior to Goldman Sachs, he was an economist at the International Monetary Fund and on the finance faculty at the University of Michigan at Ann Arbor. He received his PhD in economics from the University of California, San Diego.

Jaesun Noh received his PhD in economics from University of California, San Diego in 1993. He taught time series econometrics and finance at University of California at Irvine and also developed time series programs for EViews. Since September 1997, he has been with the risk management division of the Canadian Imperial Bank of Commerce. His research interests are in financial econometrics such as stochastic volatility and option price modelling, market risk and credit risk modeling, and statistical inference for non-stationary stochastic processes.

Joshua V. Rosenberg is an assistant professor of finance at New York University's Stern School of Business. Previously, he managed the equity models group at BARRA. He received his PhD in economics from the University of California, San Diego. His undergraduate degree is from Oberlin College, in mathematics and religion.

Elias M. Stein is the Albert Baldwin Dod Professor of Mathematics at Princeton University. He is the author of over a hundred articles and several books in the field of analysis, including the recent *Harmonic Analysis*. In 1993, he was named the first winner of the Schock Prize in mathematics, awarded by the Swedish Academy of Arts and Sciences. He is also a long-standing member of the US National Academy of Science.

Jeremy C. Stein is the JC Penney Professor of Management at MIT's Sloan School of Management. He has written on a wide range of topics in finance and economics, including options pricing, stock market trading, corporate investment and financing decisions, risk management, banking and monetary policy. He has served as an associate editor of several leading journals, including the *American Economic Review*, the *Journal of Finance*, and the *Quarterly Journal of Economics*. He is also a four-time winner of the Sloan School's Excellence in teaching award.

Tie Su is assistant professor of finance with the School of Business at the University of Miami-Coral Gables. He received his BS in statistics from Beijing University and PhD in finance from the University of Missouri-Columbia in 1995. He specialises in financial derivatives and investments, and his current research focuses on option pricing models and general valuation methods.

Stephen Taylor is a professor of finance at Lancaster University. Since 1995, he has been head of the department of accounting and finance, a department rated in the "most prestigious" category in the 1996 UK research ratings exercise. His numerous publications over 20 years of research include the book *Modelling Financial Time Series*, in which he presented the first description of stochastic volatility models and a pioneering analysis of Garch models. He continues to research a wide range of volatility issues. He has taught his own advanced financial econometrics course in England, Austria, Belgium, Hong Kong and Australia. He obtained his MA and PhD degrees from Lancaster University, following his BA in mathematics from Cambridge University.

Peter Theodossiou is an assistant professor of finance at Rutgers University, New Jersey. His interests are in international financial markets, financial distress and acquisitions, statistical financial techniques, neural networks and mathematical financial methods. He has published several articles in top business and statistics journals, such as *The Financial Review*, *Journal of Business*, *Finance and Accounting*, *Journal of Banking and Finance*, *Managerial and Decision Economics*, *Management Science* and the *Journal of the American Statistical Association*. He is the founding president of the

Multinational Finance Society, managing editor of the *Multinational Finance Journal*, co-editor of *Ekonomia* and an associate editor of *The Financial Review*.

Yiuman Tse is an assistant professor of finance at Binghamton University, the state university of New York. He received his PhD at Louisiana State University in 1994. He holds an MBA from Binghamton University and BA (mechanical engineering) from the University of Hong Kong. His research interests include international financial markets, time series analysis, investment, and China trade business. His articles have appeared in *Management Science*, the *Journal of Banking and Finance* and the *Journal of International Money and Finance*.

Ton Vorst holds a chair in finance and econometrics at Erasmus University, Rotterdam. His current research interests are mainly in derivative instruments and financial risk management, and he has acted as a consultant on this topic for major financial institutions in the US and Netherlands. He has published articles in a number of publications, including the *Journal of Banking and Finance*, the *Journal of Finance*, the *Journal of Financial and Quantitative Analysis*, *Risk* and the *Handbook of Exotic Options*. He is associate editor of several journals, including the *Journal of Derivatives*, the *International Review of Financial Analysis* and the *European Financial Review*. He holds a doctorate in mathematics from the University of Utrecht, and masters degrees from the University of Utrecht and Erasmus University.

Robert E. Whaley is the T Austin Finch Foundation Professor of Business Administration at the Fuqua School of Business, Duke University, and director of the Futures and Options Research Center (FORCE). He holds a Bachelor of Commerce degree from the University of Alberta and an MBA and PhD from the University of Toronto. His current research interests are in the areas of predictability of market volatility, market microstructure, valuation of exotic options stock splits, executive stock option valuation and volatility futures and option contracts. He has recently published three books, and his work has been printed in top academic and practitioner journals. He holds a number of editorial positions including co-editor of *The Review of Futures Markets*, and associate editor of the *Journal of Financial Economics*, *Journal of Finance* and the *Journal of Derivatives*.

Gary Xu is a senior lecturer in accounting and finance at the University of Manchester, where he teaches investment analysis and capital market theory. His research interest are in volatility modelling and forecasting, the efficiency of financial futures and options markets, and empirical tests of asset pricing models. Three innovative papers were published from his PhD thesis on exchange rate volatility, including important contributions about the term structure and smile properties of implied volatilities. He obtained his BSc from Beijing University, his MBA from Aston University and his PhD from Lancaster University.

MAKING GARCH WORK: TESTS, REFINEMENTS AND APPLICATIONS

Introduction

Robert Jarrow

This section contains a collection of papers that study two key questions. One, what are Arch (Garch) and their refinements? And two, do they work? That is, do they better model financial security returns (in-sample estimation)? And can they be used to better forecast future volatilities (out-of-sample estimation)?

The first paper, by Anil Bera and Matthew Higgins, addresses the first question on the meaning of Arch (autoregressive conditional heteroskedasticity). This is a complete and readable primer on the mathematics of Arch models. It provides an excellent review of their statistical properties, estimation and hypothesis testing procedures, and discusses the following univariate Arch models:

- ❑ Arch(q),
- ❑ Garch(p,q) – Generalised Arch,
- ❑ Aarch – Augment Arch,
- ❑ Qarch – Quadratic Arch,
- ❑ Narch – Nonlinear Arch,
- ❑ Egarch – Exponential Garch,
- ❑ Tarch – Threshold Arch,
- ❑ Qtarch – Qualitative Tarch,
- ❑ Igarch – Integrated Garch, and
- ❑ Arch-M – Arch in the mean.

Bera and Higgins start by explaining the various models, and provide expressions for their various moments and autocorrelations. Issues relating to temporal aggregation and conditional density functions (non-normal) are covered. The mathematics of forecasting with Arch is reviewed, with extensions to multivariate Garch processes and related mathematics. They also cover estimation procedures, including maximum likelihood estimation, quasi-maximum likelihood estimation (QMLE), semiparametric and nonparametric methods, and the generalised method of moments (GMM). Finally, the hypothesis testing methods are reviewed – their logical structure, sampling distributions, benefits and limitations. The paper also has an exhaustive bibliography. An excellent first stop to understanding Arch models.

Tim Bollerslev, Ray Chou and Kenneth Kroner also address the first question on the meaning of Arch. But they consider the second as well, by providing an excellent review of "Arch Modelling in Finance". This paper brings the beginner up to speed with the terminology, tools, issues and it also provides an overview of the known results, both statistical and their applications to finance.

The authors start by defining an Arch model and then discuss general maximum likelihood estimation. At first, this is done for the univariate case. Various special cases are also classified and discussed:

- ❑ linear Arch (q),
- ❑ linear Garch(p,q),
- ❑ non-normal conditional densities,
- ❑ maximum likelihood (ML), quasi-maximum likelihood (QLM) and generalised method of moments (GMM),
- ❑ non-linear Arch, in particular Egarch(p,q),
- ❑ Arch-in-means or Arch-M, and
- ❑ Igarch(p,q).

Bollerslev, Chou and Kroner then show how to extend this analysis to the multivariate case. They finish with a summary of the literature on the applications of these techniques to financial data, with particular reference to equity price data, term structure of interest rates data, and foreign currency data.

There is overwhelming evidence of the importance of these techniques in providing more accurate estimation in financial modelling. The relevance of Arch models to portfolio theory, capital asset pricing models (risk premium) and derivatives is discussed. This paper also has an excellent bibliography.

The Arch models reviewed so far are all discrete time models. Prices (or returns) are modelled as observable at discrete time intervals – a day or a week, for example. In contrast, the literature on the pricing of derivatives almost exclusively uses continuous time models. This is the case, for example, with the Black–Scholes formula. Trading takes place continuously in these option pricing models, so that dynamic hedging can occur. The purpose of Stephen Taylor's paper "Modelling Stochastic Volatility: A Review and Comparative Study" is to compare these discrete time Arch models with the discrete time approximations of the stochastic volatility models used in the option pricing literature, known as ARV models. He studies whether there is a difference between the two approaches for pricing options.

Taylor provides an analytic comparison of four volatility models: the information counting model, the discrete approximation to diffusion models (ARV), Garch(1,1), and Exponential Arch(1,0). Not surprisingly, the ARV models are shown to have similar characteristics (moments, autocorrelations, and so on) to the Arch models. Given their theoretical similarity, an empirical analysis is provided to distinguish the models.

First, a comparison of the Garch(1,1) and Exponential Arch(1,0) models is made using three different conditional density functions (normal, t distribution, and the generalised error distribution (GED)). For daily returns on the Deutschmark/dollar exchange rate over December 1977–November 1990, the Exponential Arch(1,0) model with the GED distribution provides the best (in sample) fit. Next, the ARV model is fitted to this same data base. The ARV and Arch models are shown to provide similar estimates of persistence in volatilities. Both the Arch and ARV models give similar option prices (when the model parameters are appropriately matched). In essence, Taylor shows that these two models yield observational equivalent approaches to pricing options. Thus, with respect to the pricing of options, these two approaches are not really different. To distinguish the techniques on other grounds, he notices that numerical procedures for computing option prices are faster for ARV, but estimation is simpler for Arch.

An interesting and unresolved question, not explicitly addressed yet, is whether multivariate Garch is necessary in the modelling of financial data. Kenneth Kroner and Victor Ng study this issue by considering the conditional heteroskedasticity of the covariance matrix of returns. Are there spillover effects across different stocks due to stochastic volatility? Kroner and Ng demonstrate that the answer to this question is yes.

Their paper "Multivariate Garch Modelling of Asset Returns" develops a new model called the Asymmetric Dynamic Covariance Matrix Model (ADC) for conditional heteroskedasticity in the covariance matrix. Kroner and Ng also develop a robust test for testing asymmetric effects in return covariance matrices. This new test is used to compare the ADC model empirically with four standard univariate models – the VECH model, the BEKK model, the FAC model, and the CCOR model (these terms are defined in the paper). Using weekly returns on both a small firm and a large firm portfolio over July 1962–December 1988, they show that the four standard models are misspecified (with respect to their covariance matrix). In contrast, the new model appears not to be misspecified.

In addition, the new insights obtained on return covariances are that:

❑ bad news on large firm returns causes increased volatility in both large and small firm returns,

❑ bad news on large firm returns causes the conditional covariance between large and small firm returns to increase, and

❑ news about small firms has little impact on large firm variances or covariances.

This is an important paper, especially because of its implications for portfolio management and VAR computations. Ignoring these spillover effects in return covariance matrices will provide both inefficient portfolios (in a dynamic setting) and biased VAR estimates. The extent of this bias, however, awaits subsequent research.

One of the key uses of stochastic volatility models is to speculate on option price movements. So the accuracy of the forecasts implied by Arch models is crucial. This is the issue studied by the two remaining papers in this section, an issue known as out of sample estimation. Each of the papers takes a different approach to answering this question.

Robert Engle, Alex Kane and Jaesun Noh compare the forecasting ability of Arch volatility models versus historical moving averages. The criteria for judging a model's forecasting ability is the profit earned from trading on the forecasts using options (straddles in particular). The options employed are on the NYSE index using daily observations of the NYSE index over the period June 1968–December 1991.

Five different volatility forecasting methods are compared: Garch(1,1), Garch(1,1)-D (adjusted for weekends and holidays), Garch(1,1)–I (adjusted for the Hull and White stochastic volatility option price), Garch(1,1)–DI (adjusted for both weekends and holidays and the Hull and White model), and MA (moving average of historic volatilities). The MA model is the "strawman", the standard approach against which the Arch models are compared.

Engle, Kane and Noh use a clever procedure for generating option prices. Instead of using actual market prices, they construct a simulated market, with hypothetical traders trading against each other (using forecasts 1–5 above). Traders (pairwise) buy or sell straddles at the average of their bid-ask prices, based on their different forecasts (using the Black–Scholes prices or the Hull and White formula, where applicable). This simulated market avoids the typical problems associated with actual option prices – non-simultaneous observations between the index and the options. Perhaps not surprisingly, the Garch(1,1)–DI model (traders) did the best, while the MA forecast did the worst. These results confirm the in-sample results reported by the other papers in this section.

The last paper in this section, by Michael Dueker, studies the forecasting ability of Garch with respect to implied volatilities, using a new Garch model developed within the paper. This model introduces a Markov switching process into the framework, allowing for discrete shifts in the conditional volatility. In all, four new switching models are formulated: Garch-DF (switching in degrees of freedom), Garch-NF (switching in the normalisation factor), Garch-UV (switching in the unconditional variance), and Garch-K (switching in the conditional kurtosis).

These models differ with respect to which parameters in the underlying Garch model follow the Markov switching process. The conditional density for all these models is the t distribution. Using daily S&P500 index returns from January 1982 to December 1991, Dueker estimates these four models, plus an Arch model with switching, and an ordinary Garch(1,1) model, added for purposes of comparison. A goodness of fit test is provided for both an in-sample and out-of-sample tests.

The results are mixed. All models are rejected in sample, except for the Garch-DF model. Surprisingly, all models are rejected out of sample. There are two likely reasons for this – a more refined testing procedure is used, and the additional parameters probably overfit the noise within the in-sample data period. This is not an uncommon problem in multiple parameter estimation.

To get a sense of the economic significance of this new Garch model (the ability to generate better profits by speculation), an out-of-sample forecast of implied volatilities is studied. The implied volatilities are those from S&P100 options, as measured by the CBOE volatility index (VIX). Dueker forecasts the implied volatilities with the six models. Consistent with the previous results, the best forecasts were obtained with the Garch-DF and Garch-K models. However, these forecasts provide a significant improvement, confirming the economic importance of the new Garch switching model.

In summary, these two papers, both with a different testing procedure, confirm the usefulness of Garch models in forecasting future volatilities. A consistent story unfolds, useful in answering the questions formulated at the beginning of this brief review. These papers have shown us that Garch models do work better than the standard historical moving average techniques in modelling financial data, both in and out of sample.

A Survey of Arch Models:

Properties, Estimation and Testing*

Anil K. Bera and Matthew L. Higgins
University of Illinois at Urbana-Champaign; Western Michigan University

The aim of this chapter is to provide an account of some of the important developments in the autoregressive conditional heteroskedasticity (Arch) model since its inception in a seminal paper by Engle (1982). This model takes account of many observed properties of asset prices and therefore various interpretations can be attributed to it. We start with the basic Arch models and discuss their different interpretations. Arch models have been generalised in different directions to accommodate more and more features of the real world. We provide a comprehensive treatment of many of the extensions of the original Arch model. Next we discuss estimation and testing for Arch models and note that these models lead to some interesting and unique problems. There have been numerous applications and we mention some of these as we present different models. This chapter includes a glossary of the acronyms for the models we describe.

The history of Arch models is indeed a very short one for Robert Engle introduced Arch only a decade ago. Within this brief period, however, the Arch literature has grown in a spectacular fashion. The numerous applications of Arch models defy observed trends in scientific advancements. Usually, applications lag theoretical developments, but Engle's original Arch model and its various generalisations have been applied to numerous economic and financial data series of many countries, while it has seen relatively fewer theoretical advancements.

The concept of Arch might be only a decade old but its roots go far into the past – possibly as far as Bachelier (1900), who was the first to conduct a rigorous study of the behaviour of speculative prices. There was then a period of long silence. Mandelbrot (1963a, b; 1967) revived interest in the time series properties of asset prices with his theory that "random variables with an infinite population variance are indispensable for a workable description of price changes" (cf 1963b, p 421). His observations – such as unconditional distributions have thick tails, variances change over time and large (small) changes tend to be followed by large (small) changes of either sign – are "stylised facts" for many economic and financial variables. Figures 1, 2 and 3 present three typical data series on price changes. These are, respectively, the weekly rate of return on the US dollar/British pound exchange rate, changes in the three-month Treasury bill rate and the growth rate of the NYSE monthly composite index. The first noticeable thing is that, for all three series, the means appear to be constant, whereas the variances change over time. In particular, for the Treasury bill rate, there is a dramatic increase in the variance in the late 1970s and early 1980s. Sample

* *This paper was first published in the* Journal of Economic Surveys, *Vol. 7 no. 4 (1993). It is reprinted with the permission of Blackwell Publishers. We are grateful to three anonymous referees and editor Leslie Oxley for many helpful suggestions and detailed comments on the earlier version of the paper. Thanks are also due to Ken Kroner for his comments. However, we retain the responsibility for any remaining errors. Financial support from the Research Board of the University of the Illinois is gratefully acknowledged.*

1. Weekly rate of return on the dollar/pound exchange rate

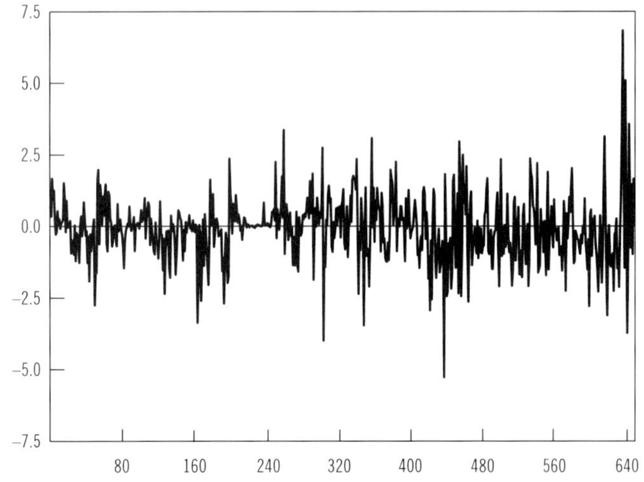

2. First difference of the three-month treasury bill rate

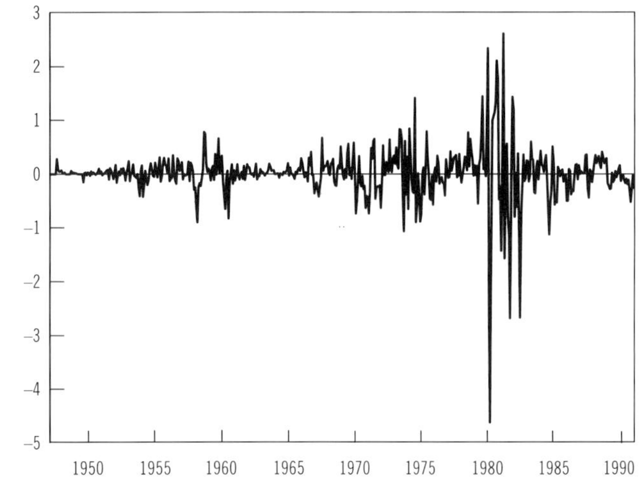

3. Monthly rate of return on the NYSE composite index

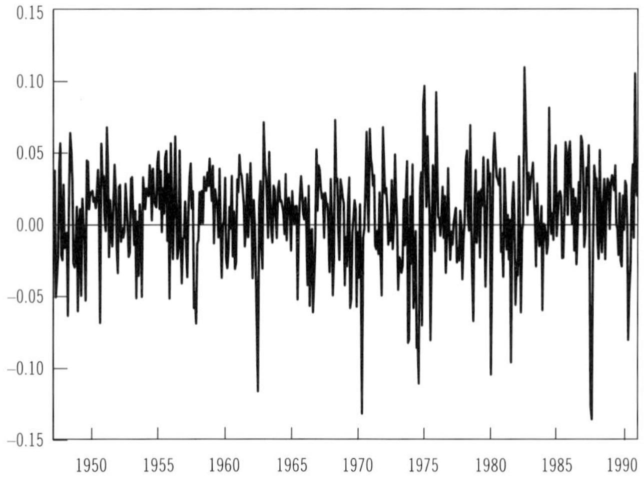

statistics from these series overwhelmingly support Mandelbrot's other stylised facts.

Prior to the introduction of Arch, researchers were very much aware of changes in variance but used only informal procedures to take account of this. For example, Mandelbrot (1963a) used recursive estimates of the variance over time and Klien (1977) took five period-moving variance estimates about a 10-period moving-sample mean. Engle's (1982) Arch model was the first formal model that seemed to capture the stylised facts mentioned above.

The Arch model is useful not only because it captures some stylised facts, but also because it has applications to numerous and diverse areas. For example, it has been used in asset pricing to test the CAAPM, the I-CAPM, the CCAPM and the APT; to develop volatility tests for market efficiency and to estimate the time varying systematic risk in the context of the market model. It has been used to measure the term structure of interest rates; to develop optimal dynamic hedging strategies; to examine how information flows across countries, markets and assets; to price options and to model risk premia. In macroeconomics, it has been successfully used to construct debt portfolios of developing countries, to measure inflationary uncertainty, to examine the relationship between exchange rate uncertainty and trade, to study the effects of central bank interventions, and to characterise the relationship between the macroeconomy and the stock market.

The literature on Arch is so vast that it is almost impossible to provide a comprehensive review. There are already a few survey papers on this topic. In particular, we would refer the readers to Engle and Bollerslev (1986) and Bollerslev, Chou and Kroner (1992). The latter paper noted several hundred papers that apply the Arch methodology to various financial markets. Some recent references to the very rapidly growing bibliography include Bekaert (1992), Bollerslev and Hodrick (1992), Duffee (1992), Koedijk, Stork and De Vries (1992) and Ng and Pirrong (1992), just to name a few. The purpose of this review paper is rather modest. Our aim is to provide an informal account of recent theoretical advances and their impact on applied work. It should be mentioned that our use of the term "Arch" does not refer to Engle's original model. By Arch, we mean the phenomenon of conditional heteroskedasticity in general and all models that capture this phenomenon.

The plan of the paper is as follows. The basic Arch models are described below. As these models capture various stylised facts, they can be given different interpretations and these are also discussed. It has been found that the basic Arch models are unable to capture all observed phenomena, such as the leverage effect, excess kurtosis and the high degree of non-linearity. Generalisations of the basic Arch models to capture these phenomena are then discussed, and we then consider forecasting with Arch models. The following sections review further generalisations, such as multivariate Arch and Arch-in-mean (Arch-M) models. Finally, we discuss estimation and testing of Arch models. The paper concludes with a few remarks. At the end of the paper, we include a complete glossary of the acronyms for the Arch models that we describe in the survey.

Autoregressive conditional heteroskedasticity

In this section, we introduce the Engle's (1982) original Arch model. We begin by defining the Arch process, and heuristically describe its properties. We emphasise the properties of the Arch model that make it appealing for modelling the volatility of economic time series. We subsequently introduce the generalised Arch (Garch) model of Bollerslev (1986), which provides a parsimonious parameterisation for the conditional variance. The properties of the Arch process are then formally characterised by describing its unconditional moments. We also discuss how aggregating an Arch process over time affects the moments of the process.

DEFINITION OF THE PROCESS

An Arch process can be defined in a variety of contexts. We will define it in terms of the distribution of the errors of a dynamic linear regression model. The dependent variable y_t is assumed to be generated by

$$y_t = x_t'\xi + \varepsilon_t, \quad t = 1,\ldots,T, \tag{1}$$

where x_t is a $k \times 1$ vector of exogenous variables, which may include lagged values of the dependent variable, and ξ is $k \times 1$ vector of regression parameters. The Arch model characterises the distribution of the stochastic error ε_t conditional on the realised values of the set of variables $\psi_{t-1} = \{y_{t-1}, x_{t-1}, y_{t-2}, x_{t-2}, \ldots\}$. Specifically, Engle's (1982) original Arch model assumes

$$\varepsilon_t \big| \psi_{t-1} \sim N(0, h_t) \tag{2}$$

where

$$h_t = \alpha_0 + \alpha_1\varepsilon_{t-1}^2 + \cdots + \alpha_q\varepsilon_{t-q}^2, \tag{3}$$

with $\alpha_0 > 0$ and $\alpha_0 \geq 0$, $i = 1,\ldots,q$, to ensure that the conditional variance is positive. Note that since $\varepsilon_{t-i} = y_{t-i} - x_{t-i}'\xi$, $i = 1,\ldots,q$, h_t is clearly a function of the elements of ψ_{t-1}.

The distinguishing feature of the model (2) and (3) is not simply that the conditional variance h_t is a function of the conditioning set ψ_{t-1}, but rather it is the particular functional form that is specified. Episodes of volatility are generally characterised as the clustering of large shocks to the dependent variable. The conditional variance function (3) is formulated to mimic this phenomenon. In the regression model, a large shock is represented by a large deviation of y_t from its conditional mean $x_{t-i}'\xi$, or equivalently, a large positive or negative value of ε_t. In the Arch regression model, the variance of the current error ε_t, conditional on the realised values of the lagged errors $\varepsilon_{t-i}, i = 1,\ldots,q$ is an increasing function of the magnitude of the lagged errors, irrespective of their signs. Hence, large errors of either sign *tend* to be followed by a large error of either sign. Similarly, small errors of either sign *tend* to be followed by a small error of either sign. The order of the lag q determines the length of time for which a shock persists in conditioning the variance of subsequent errors. The larger the value of q, the longer the episodes of volatility will tend to be.

A linear function of lagged squared errors, of course, is not the only conditional variance function that will produce clustering of large deviations. Any monotonically increasing function of the absolute values of the lagged errors will lead to such clustering. However, since variance is expected squared deviation, a linear combination of lagged squared errors is a natural measure of the recent trend in variance to translate to the current conditional variance h_t. Alternative formulations of the conditional variance function have been found to be useful and these formulations will be discussed in depth below.

To illustrate the characteristic appearance of Arch data, we generate artificial samples from (2). An explicit generating equation for an Arch process is

$$\varepsilon_t = \eta_t\sqrt{h_t}, \tag{4}$$

where $\eta_t \sim \text{IID } N(0,1)$ and h_t is given by (3). Since h_t is a function of the elements of ψ_{t-1}, and is therefore fixed when conditioning on ψ_{t-1}, it is clear that ε_t as given in (4) will be conditionally normal with $E(\varepsilon_t | \psi_{t-1}) = \sqrt{h_t}E(\eta_t | \psi_{t-1}) = 0$ and $Var(\varepsilon_t | \psi_{t-1}) = h_t Var(\eta_t | \psi_{t-1}) = h_t$. Hence, the process specified by (4) is identical to the Arch

4. Simulated Gaussian white noise

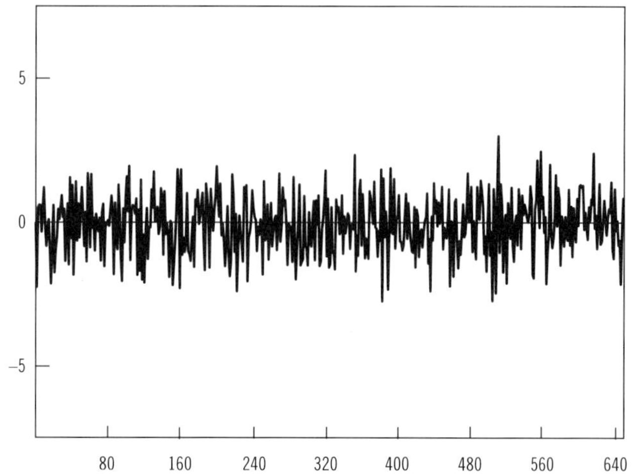

5. Simulated Arch(1) data

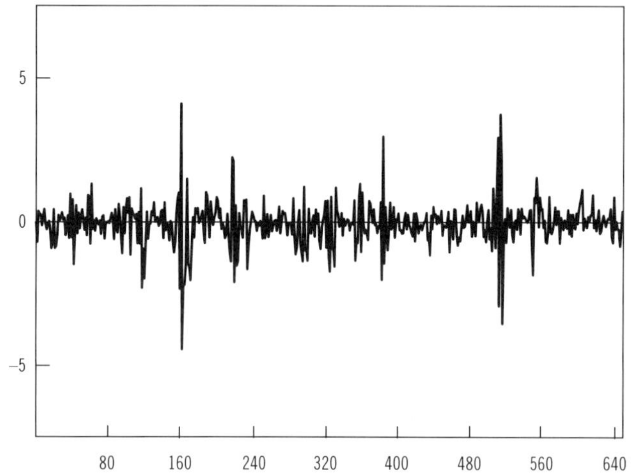

6. Simulated Arch(4) data

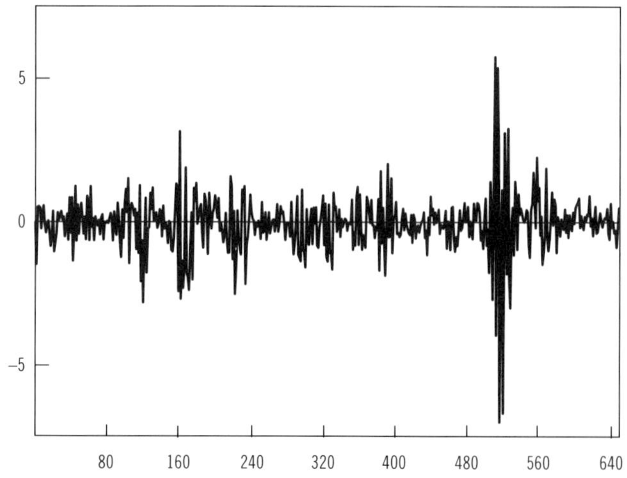

process (2). The generating equation (4) reveals that Arch rescales an underlying Gaussian innovation process η_t by multiplying it by the conditional standard deviation, which is a function of the information set ψ_{t-1}. First, for comparison when Arch is not present in the data, in Figure 4 we present a plot of 500 realisations of $\varepsilon_t = \eta_t$, setting $h_t = 1$ by imposing $\alpha_0 = 1$ and $\alpha_i = 0$ for $i = 1,\ldots,q$. The displayed data are simply Gaussian white noise, the process usually assumed for the errors in a linear model. Then, using the same η_ts shown in Figure 4, Figures 5 and 6 are plots of $\varepsilon_t = \eta_t\sqrt{h_t}$ for which the h_ts are respectively

$$h_t = 0.1 + 0.9\varepsilon_{t-1}^2, \tag{5}$$

and

$$h_t = 0.1 + 0.36\varepsilon_{t-1}^2 + 0.27\varepsilon_{t-2}^2 + 0.18\varepsilon_{t-3}^2 + 0.09\varepsilon_{t-4}^2. \tag{6}$$

To make the scale of the data comparable in all three figures, the parameter values in (5) and (6) were chosen to make the unconditional variances of the Arch processes equal to 1. Later it will become clear why the conditional variance functions (5) and (6) imply that the unconditional variances of the processes are 1. We do not notice any clustering of the observations in Figure 4. Figures 5 and 6, however, have close resemblance to our earlier Figures 1, 2 and 3. In particular, the closeness of Figures 2 and 6 is quite striking. Comparing Figures 5 and 6 we also note that, as expected, the episodes of volatility are longer for Arch(4).

GENERALISED AUTOREGRESSIVE CONDITIONAL HETEROSKEDASTICITY

In the first empirical applications of Arch to the relationship between the level and the volatility of inflation, Engle (1982, 1983) found that a large lag q was required in the conditional variance function. This would necessitate estimating a large number of parameters subject to inequality restrictions. To reduce the computational burden, Engle (1982, 1983) parameterised the conditional variance as

$$h_t = \alpha_0 + \alpha_1 \sum_{i=1}^{q} w_i \varepsilon_{t-i}^2,$$

where the weights

$$w_i = \frac{(q+1)-i}{\frac{1}{2}q(q+1)},$$

decline linearly and are constructed so that

$\Sigma_{i=1}^{q} w_i = 1$. With this parameterisation, a large lag can be specified and yet only two parameters are required to be estimated in the conditional variance function. Although linearly declining weights are plausible, the formulation does put undue restrictions on the dynamics of the Arch process.

Bollerslev (1986) proposed an extension of the conditional variance function (3), which he termed generalised Arch (Garch), which has proven to be very useful in empirical work. The Garch model was also independently proposed by Taylor (1986), who used a different acronym. They suggested that the conditional variance be specified as

$$h_t = \alpha_0 + \alpha_1\varepsilon_{t-1}^2 + \cdots + \alpha_q\varepsilon_{t-q}^2 + \beta_1 h_{t-1} + \cdots + \beta_p h_{t-p}, \quad (7)$$

where the inequality restrictions

$$\alpha_0 > 0$$
$$\alpha_i \geq 0 \text{ for } i = 1,\ldots,q \quad (8)$$
$$\beta_i \geq 0 \text{ for } i = 1,\ldots,p$$

are imposed to ensure that the conditional variance is strictly positive. A Garch process with orders p and q is denoted as Garch (p,q). The motivation of the Garch process can be seen by expressing (7) as

$$h_t = \alpha_0 + \alpha(B)\varepsilon_t^2 + \beta(B)h_t,$$

where $\alpha(B) = \alpha_1 B + \cdots + \alpha_q B^q$ and $\beta(B) = \beta_1 B + \cdots + \beta_p B^p$ are polynomials in the backshift operator B. If the roots of $1 - \beta(Z)$ lie outside the unit circle, we can rewrite (7) as

$$h_t = \frac{\alpha_0}{1-\beta(1)} + \frac{\alpha(B)}{1-\beta(B)}\varepsilon_t^2 = \alpha_0^* + \sum_{i=1}^{\infty}\delta_i\varepsilon_{t-i}^2 \quad (9)$$

where $\alpha_0^* = \alpha_0/(1 - \beta(1))$ and the coefficient δ_i is the coefficient of B^i in the expansion of $\alpha(B)[1 - \beta(B)]^{-1}$. Hence, expression (9) reveals that a Garch (p,q) process is an infinite order Arch process with a rational lag structure imposed on the coefficients. The generalisation of Arch to Garch is similar to the generalisation of an MA process to an Arma process. The intention is that Garch can parsimoniously represent a high order Arch process.

Although the restrictions (8) are sufficient to ensure that the conditional variance of a Garch (p,q) process is strictly positive, Nelson and Cao (1992) demonstrated that weaker sufficient conditions can be found (see also Drost and Nijman (1993)). They pointed out that from the inverted representation of h_t in (9)

$$\alpha_0^* > 0 \text{ and } \delta_i \geq 0, \quad i = 1,\ldots,\infty \quad (10)$$

are sufficient to ensure the conditional variance is strictly positive. Expressing α_0^* and the δ_is in terms of the original parameters of the Garch model, Nelson and Cao showed that (10) does not require all the inequalities in (8) to hold. For example, in a Garch(1,2) process, $\alpha_0 > 0$, $\alpha_1 \geq 0$, $\beta_1 \geq 0$ and $\beta_1\alpha_1 + \alpha_2 \geq 0$ are sufficient to guarantee that $h_t > 0$. Therefore, in the Garch(1,2) model, α_2 may be negative. They presented general results for Garch(1,q) and Garch(2,q), but suggest a derivation for Garch processes with $p \geq 3$ is difficult. Nelson and Cao cited several empirical studies, such as French, Schwert and Stambaugh (1987), Baillie and Bollerslev (1989), and Engle, Ito and Lin (1990), which reported negative coefficients and yet satisfy the conditions for a positive conditional variance based on (10). They concluded that the inequality restrictions (8) should not be imposed in estimation, as violation of these inequalities does not necessarily imply that the conditional variance function is misspecified.

UNCONDITIONAL MOMENTS OF ARCH

We described the properties of Arch above and illustrated the visual appearance of Arch with computer-generated data. The unconditional moments of the Arch process formally characterise these properties. Engle (1982) gave expressions for many of the moments, and stated necessary and sufficient conditions for the existence of the moments for the original linear Arch process (3). Milhoj (1985) provided additional moments. Subsequently, Bollerslev (1986) extended these results to the Garch process.

The derivation of the unconditional moments of the Arch process is possible through extensive use of the following important probability result:

Law of iterated expectations: let Ω_1 and Ω_2 be two sets of random variables such that $\Omega_1 \subseteq \Omega_2$. Let y be a scalar random variable. Then $E(y|\Omega_1) = E[E(y|\Omega_2)|\Omega_1]$.

In the context of this chapter, Ω_1 and Ω_2 are information sets available at different periods in time. A special case of the law is frequently employed to find the moments of the Arch process. If $\Omega_1 = \varnothing$ is the empty set, then $E(y) = E[E(y|\Omega_2)]$. This expression is useful because it relates an unconditional moment to a conditional moment. Since the Arch model is specified in terms of its conditional moments, it provides a method for deriving unconditional moments.

Using the law of iterated expectations, we can

easily derive the fundamental properties of an Arch process. First, consider the unconditional mean of a Garch(p,q) error ε_t with conditional variance (7). Applying the law of iterated expectations, $E(\varepsilon_t) = E[E(\varepsilon_t | \Psi_{t-1})]$. However, because the Garch model specifies that $E(\varepsilon_t | \Psi_{t-1}) = 0$ for all realisations of Ψ_{t-1}, it follows that $E(\varepsilon_t) = 0$. Thus, the Garch process has mean zero.

Next, consider the unconditional variance of the Garch(p,q) process. Although the variance of ε_t can be evaluated in general, for simple illustration, we consider the Garch(1,1) process. Using (7), with $p = q = 1$, and the law of iterated expectations

$$\begin{aligned} E(\varepsilon_t^2) &= E\left[E\left(\varepsilon_t^2 | \Psi_{t-1}\right)\right] \\ &= E(h_t) \\ &= \alpha_0 + \alpha_1 E(\varepsilon_{t-1}^2) + \beta_1 E(h_{t-1}) \\ &= \alpha_0 + (\alpha_1 + \beta_1) E(\varepsilon_{t-1}^2), \end{aligned}$$

which is a linear difference equation for the sequence of variances. Assuming the process began infinitely far in the past with a finite initial variance, the sequence of variances converge to the constant

$$\sigma_\varepsilon^2 = E(\varepsilon_t^2) = \frac{\alpha_0}{1 - \alpha_1 - \beta_1}$$

if $\alpha_1 + \beta_1 < 1$. For the general Garch(p,q) process, Bollerslev (1986) gave the necessary and sufficient condition

$$\alpha(1) + \beta(1) = \sum_{i=1}^{q} \alpha_i + \sum_{i=1}^{p} \beta_i < 1 \qquad (11)$$

for the existence of the variance. When this condition is satisfied, the variance is

$$\sigma_\varepsilon^2 = E(\varepsilon_t^2) = \frac{\alpha_0}{1 - \alpha(1) - \beta(1)}.$$

Although the variance of ε_t conditional on Ψ_{t-1} changes with the elements of the information set, unconditionally the Arch process is *homoskedastic*. Considering Figures 5 and 6 again, the visual appearance of the generated data conveys the impression that the unconditional variance changes with time. This false perception results from the clustering of large deviations. A major contribution of the Arch literature is the finding that apparent changes in the volatility of economic time series may be predictable and result from a specific type of nonlinear dependence rather than exogenous structural change in the variance.

The nature of the unconditional density of an Arch process can be analysed by the higher order moments. As ε_t is conditionally normal, for all odd integers m, $E(\varepsilon_t^m | \Psi_{t-1}) = 0$. The skewness coefficient is immediately seen to be zero. Since ε_t is continuous, this implies that the unconditional distribution is symmetric. Higher moments indicate further properties of the Arch process. An expression for the fourth moment of a general Garch(p,q) process is not available, but Engle (1982) gave it for the Arch(1) process and Bollerslev (1986) generalised it to the Garch(1,1) case. Engle's result for the Arch(1) case requires that $3\alpha_1^2 < 1$ for the fourth moment to exist. Simple algebra then reveals that the kurtosis is

$$\frac{E(\varepsilon_t^4)}{\sigma_\varepsilon^4} = 3\left(\frac{1 - \alpha_1^2}{1 - 3\alpha_1^2}\right)$$

which is clearly greater than 3, the kurtosis coefficient of the normal distribution. Therefore, the Arch(1) process has tails heavier than the normal distribution. This property makes the Arch process attractive because the distributions of asset returns frequently display tails heavier than the normal distribution. Although no known closed form for the unconditional density function of an Arch process exists, Nelson (1990b) demonstrated that, under suitable conditions, as the time interval goes to zero, a Garch(1,1) process approaches a continuous time process whose stationary unconditional distribution is a Student's t. Nelson's result indicates why heavy-tailed distributions are so prevalent with high-frequency financial data.

That the parameterisation of the Arch process does not *a priori* impose the existence of unconditional moments is an important characteristic of the model. It has long been suggested, at least as early as Mandelbrot (1963b), that the distribution of asset returns is such that the variance may not exist. In empirical applications of Garch, estimated parameters frequently do not satisfy (11). The fact that the Arch model admits an infinite variance is desirable because such behaviour may be a characteristic of the data-generating process that should be reflected in the estimated model. Also, fortunately, as will be noted later, even for Garch models with infinite variances, standard results on consistency and asymptotic normality might still be valid.

Above we considered the univariate distribution of a single ε_t. The moments of the joint distribution of the ε_ts also reveal important properties of the Arch process. For $k \geq 1$, the autocovariances of the Garch(p,q) process are

$$\begin{aligned} E(\varepsilon_t\varepsilon_{t-k}) &= E\left[E\left(\varepsilon_t\varepsilon_{t-k}|\Psi_{t-1}\right)\right] \\ &= E\left[\varepsilon_{t-k}E\left(\varepsilon_t|\Psi_{t-1}\right)\right] \\ &= 0. \end{aligned}$$

Since the Garch process is serially uncorrelated, with constant mean zero, the process is weakly stationary if the variance exists, that is if (11) holds. A remarkable property of a Garch process, first demonstrated by Nelson (1990a) for Garch(1,1), is that it may be strongly stationary without being weakly stationary. Bougerol and Picard (1992) extended Nelson's result to the Garch(p,q) process and stated necessary and sufficient condition for strong stationarity. These conditions are very technical and will not be described here. That the Garch process may be strongly stationary without being weakly stationary stems from the fact that weak stationarity requires that the mean, variance and autocovariances be finite and time invariant. Strong stationarity requires that the distribution function of any finite set of ε_ts is invariant under time translations. Finite moments are not required for strong stationarity. The results of Nelson (1990a) and Bougerol and Picard (1992) show that the unconditional variance may be infinite and yet the Garch process may still be strongly stationary.

The lack of serial correlation is an important characteristic of the Arch process, which makes it suitable for modelling financial time series. The efficient-market hypothesis asserts that past rates of return cannot be used to improve the prediction of future rates of return. In (1), suppose y_t is the rate of return on an asset and that $\xi = 0$ so that there is no regression component in the model. Then y_t is identical to ε_t and becomes a pure Garch process. The optimal prediction of the return y_t is the expectation of the return conditional on any available information. As the Garch model specifies $E(y_t | \psi_{t-1}) = E(y_t) = 0$, the past observations on y_t contained in ψ_{t-1} do not alter the optimal prediction of the rate of return. Therefore, the presence of Arch does not represent a violation of market efficiency.

Of course, the lack of serial correlation does not imply that the ε_t are independent. Above, we suggested that the qualitative appearance of data generated from an Arch process arises from the particular type of dependence. Bollerslev (1986) gave a representation for the Garch(p,q) process that reveals the nature of the dependence. Letting $v_t = \varepsilon_t^2 - h_t$, the squared error can be written as

$$\begin{aligned} \varepsilon_t^2 &= h_t + v_t \\ &= \alpha_0 + \sum_{i=1}^{m}(\alpha_i+\beta_i)\varepsilon_{t-i}^2 - \sum_{i=1}^{p}\beta_i\left(\varepsilon_{t-i}^2 - h_{t-i}\right) + v_t \\ &= \alpha_0 + \sum_{i=1}^{m}(\alpha_i+\beta_i)\varepsilon_{t-i}^2 - \sum_{i=1}^{p}\beta_i v_{t-i} + v_t \end{aligned} \qquad (12)$$

where $m = \max(p,q)$, $\alpha_i = 0$, and $i > q$ and $\beta_i = 0$ for $i > p$. As $E(v_t | \psi_{t-1}) = 0$, the law of iterated expectations reveals that v_t has mean zero and is serially uncorrelated. Therefore, from (12), we see that ε_t^2 has an ARMA(m,p) representation. The autocorrelation and partial autocorrelation functions of the squared process ε_t^2 will have the familiar patterns of those from an ARMA process. Bollerslev (1988) has suggested that these autocorrelation functions of ε_t^2 may be used to identify the orders p and q of the Garch process. In practice, the identification of the order of a Garch(p,q) has not posed much of a problem, at least in comparison with the earlier modelling experience with ARMA(p,q) processes. In applied work, it has frequently been demonstrated that the Garch(1,1) process is able to represent the majority of financial time series. A data set that requires a model of order greater than Garch(1,2) or Garch(2,1) is very rare.

ILLUSTRATIVE EXAMPLE WITH THE WEEKLY DOLLAR/POUND EXCHANGE RATE

The Arch model has been widely applied to the study of the dynamics of the rate of return on holding foreign currencies (see Bollerslev, Chou and Kroner (1992), pp. 37–46, for a survey of applications). In this section, we illustrate the properties of conditionally heteroskedastic data by estimating Arch and Garch models for the weekly rate of return in the US/British currency exchange market. The data are the weekly spot exchange rate from January 1973 to June of 1985. There are 651 observations. Let s_t denote the spot price of the British pound in terms of the US dollar. We then analyse the continuously compounded percentage rate of return, $r_t = 100 \cdot \log(s_t/s_{t-1})$, from holding the British pound one week. These are the data plotted in Figure 1.

We begin by identifying and estimating an AR process for the mean of r_t. The autocorrelation and partial autocorrelation functions of r_t suggest the data can be represented by an AR(3) process. The estimated model is given by

$$\underset{(0.04)}{r_t = -0.07} + \underset{(0.04)}{0.27r_{t-1}} - \underset{(0.04)}{0.08r_{t-2}} + \underset{(0.04)}{0.10r_{t-3}}$$

$$l(\hat{\theta}) = -971.70,$$

Table 1. Summary statistics for the standardised residuals from AR, Arch and Garch models for the rate of return on the weekly US/British exchange rate

	Autocorrelations of squared residuals								Skewness	Kurtosis
	1	2	3	4	5	6	7	8		
AR(3)	0.16	0.14	0.22	0.15	0.06	0.05	0.11	0.00	0.22	6.78
AR(3) + Arch(6)	0.01	–0.02	–0.01	0.01	–0.04	–0.02	–0.02	0.02	–0.45	6.40
AR(3) + Garch(1,1)	0.02	0.00	–0.02	0.00	–0.05	0.01	–0.03	–0.02	–0.41	6.21

Note: (1) the asymptotic standard error of the autocorrelations of the squared standardised residuals is $1/\sqrt{T} = 0.04$. (2) the asymptotic standard errors of the skewnss and kurtosis coefficients are respectively 0.096 and 0.192.

where the standard errors are shown in parentheses and $l(\hat{\theta})$ is the value of the maximised log likelihood function assuming the data are normally distributed. Box-Pierce statistics computed from the residuals indicate that the AR(3) process adequately accounts for the serial correlation in the data. The higher order moments of the residuals, however, reveal that non-linearity is present in the data and that the unconditional distribution is non-normal. In Table 1, we present the skewness and kurtosis coefficients of the residuals, and the autocorrelations of the squared residuals. If the errors of the AR process are independent, the autocorrelations of the squared residuals should be approximately zero. From Table 1, the autocorrelations at lags 1, 2, 3, 4 and 7 exceed twice their asymptotic standard errors, suggesting the presence of non-linear dependence in the data. The skewness coefficient conveys some evidence of asymmetry in the unconditional distribution. The kurtosis coefficient is significantly greater than 3, which indicates that the unconditional distribution of the data has much heavier tails than a normal distribution.

As emphasised earlier, non-linear dependence and heavy-tailed unconditional distributions are characteristic of conditionally heteroskedastic data. We maintain the AR(3) specification for the conditional mean of r_t, but now specify the error as an Arch(q) process. The autocorrelations of the squares of the AR residuals suggest dependence through order 7. Therefore, we initially estimated an Arch(7) model, but found α_7 to be insignificant. We respecify the errors as Arch(6) and estimate the model by the maximum likelihood method to obtain

$$r_t = \underset{(0.03)}{-0.06} + \underset{(0.05)}{0.27}r_{t-1} - \underset{(0.05)}{0.03}r_{t-2} + \underset{(0.04)}{0.07}r_{t-3}$$

$$l(\hat{\theta}) = -919.72,$$

$$h_t = \underset{(0.06)}{0.42} + \underset{(0.06)}{0.23}\varepsilon_{t-1}^2 + \underset{(0.06)}{0.21}\varepsilon_{t-2}^2 + \underset{(0.04)}{0.05}\varepsilon_{t-3}^2 + \underset{(0.04)}{0.05}\varepsilon_{t-4}^2 + \underset{(0.04)}{0.07}\varepsilon_{t-5}^2 + \underset{(0.05)}{0.12}\varepsilon_{t-6}^2.$$

The Arch parameters α_1, α_2 and α_6 are highly significant. The Arch model also produces a significant increase in the value of the log likelihood. A likelihood ratio test easily rejects the null of an AR(3) process with independent Gaussian errors against the alternative of an AR(3) process with conditionally normal Arch(6) errors. Notice that the coefficient of r_{t-2} loses its significance. Frequently, after Arch is accounted for, the initial specification of the mean must be re-evaluated.

The Arch(6) model can apparently explain the non-linear dependence in the residuals. In Table 1, we present the autocorrelations of the squared standardised residuals $\hat{\eta}_t^2 = \hat{\varepsilon}_t^2/\hat{h}_t$. None of the first eight autocorrelations are significant at any reasonable significance level. The skewness coefficient of the standardised residuals is different in sign from the AR residuals and larger in magnitude, but still not excessively big. The sample kurtosis coefficient of the standardised residuals is smaller than the coefficient for the AR residuals, but is still significantly greater than 3. This suggests that the unconditional distribution of the conditionally normal Arch process is not sufficiently heavy tailed to account for the excess kurtosis in the data. The rejection of the conditional normality assumption is frequently encountered in applications of the Arch model. As will be discussed below, there are ways to take account of this excess kurtosis.

We have demonstrated how the Garch model can provide a parsimonious parameterisation of a high-order Arch process. To illustrate this, we estimate an AR(3) model for r_t with the conditional variance of the errors specified as Garch(1,1). Maintaining the conditional normality assumption, the estimated model is

$$r_t = \underset{(0.04)}{-0.05} + \underset{(0.05)}{0.27}r_{t-1} - \underset{(0.05)}{0.03}r_{t-2} + \underset{(0.04)}{0.08}r_{t-3}$$

$$h_t = \underset{(0.03)}{0.09} + \underset{(0.04)}{0.17}\varepsilon_{t-1}^2 + \underset{(0.05)}{0.77}h_{t-1}.$$

$$l(\hat{\theta}) = -920.02,$$

The estimates of the AR parameters are similar to the estimates for Arch(6) errors, with only the coefficient of r_{t-2} changing sign and becoming even less significant. The autocorrelations of the squares of the Garch(1,1) standardised residuals, shown in Table 1, are insignificant and similar in magnitude to those for the Arch(6) standardised residuals. This indicates that the Garch(1,1), which requires estimating only three conditional variance parameters, can account for the non-linear dependence as well as the Arch(6) model, which requires the estimation of seven conditional variance parameters. The skewness and kurtosis coefficients of the standardised Garch(1,1) residuals, also given in Table 1, are almost identical to the coefficients for the standardised Arch(6) residuals. The value of the maximised Arch(6) log likelihood is marginally greater than the value of the Garch(1,1) log likelihood. But any model selection criterion, such as AIC or BIC, which penalises a model for additional parameters, would select the Garch(1,1) specification over the Arch(6) specification. Finally, in Figure 7 we present a plot of the estimates of the conditional variances, h_t, from the Garch(1,1) model. The conditional variances show considerable variation over time. Comparing the plot of the weekly returns in Figure 1 with the plot of the conditional variances in Figure 7, it is clear that a clustering of large deviations, of either sign, in the returns is associated with a rise in the conditional variance.

TEMPORAL AGGREGATION OF ARCH PROCESSES

One of the important issues in time series modelling is temporal aggregation. It is well known that a high frequency (eg fitted to daily data) ARMA process aggregates to a low frequency (fitted to say, weekly data) ARMA process. A natural question is whether Arch models also possess this property. Drost and Nijman (1993) considered this issue in detail and we follow their analysis. Let us consider the Arch model (2) and (3) with q = 1, ie

$$\varepsilon_t | \psi_{t-1} \sim N(0, h_t) \quad (13)$$

where

$$h_t = E(\varepsilon_t^2 | \psi_{t-1}) = \alpha_0 + \alpha_1 \varepsilon_{t-1}^2, \quad t = 1,2,...,T. \quad (14)$$

Suppose we want to find the corresponding model for ε_t, when t = 2,4,...,T. The information set will consist of only $\{y_{t-2}, x_{t-2}, y_{t-4}, x_{t-4}, ...\}$ and we will denote it by $\psi_{t-(2)}$. Drost and Nijman showed that

7. Conditional variance of the dollar/pound weekly return

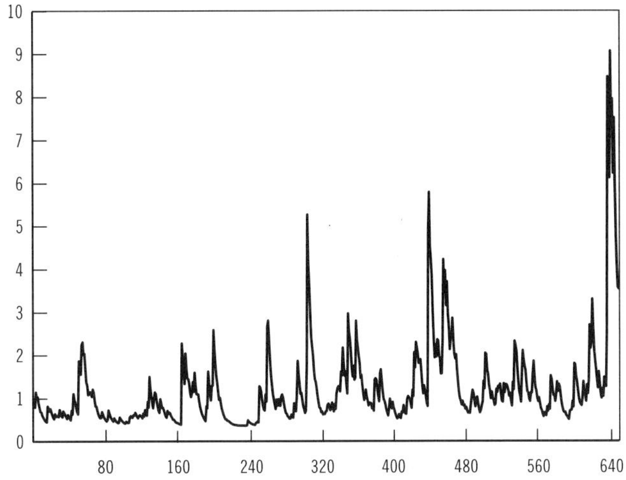

$$E(\varepsilon_t | \psi_{t-(2)}) = 0$$
$$E(\varepsilon_t^2 | \psi_{t-(2)}) = \alpha_0(1+\alpha_1) + \alpha_1^2 \varepsilon_{t-2}^2, \quad t = 2,4,...,T$$
$$= h_{t(2)},$$

say. In general, if we consider t = m,2m,...,T, then

$$E(\varepsilon_t | \psi_{t-(m)}) = 0$$
$$E(\varepsilon_t^2 | \psi_{t-(m)}) = \alpha_0 \frac{1-\alpha_1^m}{1-\alpha_1} + \alpha_1^m \varepsilon_{t-m}^2.$$

Therefore, in terms of the first two moments, an Arch process is closed under temporal aggregation and we have an algebraic relationship between the parameters corresponding to high- and low-frequency data. It is interesting to note that as m → ∞, $E(\varepsilon_t^2 | \psi_{t-(m)}) \to \alpha_0/(1-\alpha_1)$ so that, in the limit, the aggregate process behaves like a conditional homoskedastic model as pointed out by Diebold (1988). If we consider the reverse operation of going from a low frequency model to a higher one, in the limit the process will have an integrated Arch structure as noted by Nelson (1990b).

Now let us consider the distributional part of the specification (13), which can be stated as

$$\varepsilon_t / \sqrt{h_t} | \psi_{t-1} \sim IID\ N(0,1) \quad t = 1,2,...,T. \quad (15)$$

We need to check the conditional distribution of $\varepsilon_t^* = \varepsilon_t/\sqrt{h_{t(2)}}$, t = 2,4,...,T. Drost and Nijman (1993) showed that

$$E(\varepsilon_t^{*4} | \psi_{t-(2)}) = 3 + 6\left[\frac{\alpha_0}{h_{t(2)}} - 1\right]^2.$$

The conditional moments of ε_t^* therefore depend

on the information set and hence the conditional distribution of ε_t^* does not have the IID structure (15). Moreover, the distribution is no longer normal. So, from a distributional point of view, an Arch process is not closed under aggregation.

For practical purposes, if we specify an Arch model only in terms of moments, it is possible to estimate the low-frequency parameters from the estimation of a high frequency model and vice versa. Drost and Nijman (1993) demonstrated this using the empirical results of Baillie and Bollerslev (1989), who fitted a Garch(1,1) model to several exchange rates. For the Swiss franc, the estimates of α_1 and β_1 from the daily data were 0.073 and 0.907. Using the relationship between the parameters of high and low frequency data, Drost and Nijman showed that the implied weekly estimates are 0.112 and 0.792. Baillie and Bollerslev's estimates using the actual weekly data were 0.121 and 0.781. Except for the Japanese yen, Drost and Nijman found that direct estimates were very close to the implied weekly estimates.

Interpretations of Arch

Apart from its simplicity, the main reason for the success of Arch models is that they take account of the many observed features of the data, such as thick tails of the distribution, clustering of large and small observations, non-linearity and changes in our ability to forecast future values. It is not surprising therefore that these models can be interpreted in a number of ways, and we discuss some of these interpretations in this section.

RANDOM COEFFICIENT INTERPRETATION

In the last section, we noted that Arch takes account of the clustering of large and small errors and fatness of the tail part of the distribution (excess kurtosis) as observed in many financial data series. One of the major considerations for introducing Arch by Engle (1982, p 989) was that econometricians' ability to predict the future varies from one period to another. Predictions are usually made by using a conditional mean model. Uncertainty about the conditional mean can be expressed by a random coefficient formulation. Consider a random coefficient AR(1) process

$$y_t = \phi_t y_{t-1} + \varepsilon_t$$

where $\phi_t \sim (\phi, \alpha_1)$ and $\varepsilon_t \sim (0, \alpha_0)$ are independent. Then $E(y_t \mid \psi_{t-1}) = \phi y_{t-1}$ as with the fixed AR(1) process; however, now $\text{Var}(y_t \mid \psi_{t-1}) = \alpha_0 + \alpha_1 y_{t-1}^2$ which has the same form as (3). To obtain a general Arch(q) model in our regression context from a random coefficient framework, we need to start with the following set up:

$$y_t = x_t'\xi + \varepsilon_t \qquad (16)$$

$$\varepsilon_t = \sum_{i=1}^{q} \phi_{it}\varepsilon_{t-i} + u_t$$
$$= \sum_{i=1}^{q} (\phi_i + \eta_{it})\varepsilon_{t-i} + u_t \qquad (17)$$

where $\eta_t = (\eta_{1t}, \ldots, \eta_{qt})' \sim (0, A_{q\times q})$ and $u_t \sim (0, \sigma_u^2)$ are independent. It immediately follows that

$$E(\varepsilon_t \mid \psi_{t-1}) = \phi'\underline{\varepsilon}_{t-1},$$

where $\phi = (\phi_1, \ldots, \phi_q)'$ and $\underline{\varepsilon}_{t-1} = (\varepsilon_{t-1}, \ldots, \varepsilon_{t-q})'$, and that

$$\text{Var}(\varepsilon_t \mid \psi_{t-1}) = \underline{\varepsilon}_{t-1}' A \underline{\varepsilon}_{t-1} + \sigma_u^2. \qquad (18)$$

If $A = ((\alpha_{ij}))$ is a diagonal matrix with $A = \text{diag}(\alpha_1, \ldots, \alpha_q)$ and $\sigma_u^2 = \alpha_0$ then

$$\text{Var}(\varepsilon_t \mid \psi_{t-1}) = \alpha_0 + \sum_{i=1}^{q} \alpha_i \varepsilon_{t-i}^2$$

as we have in (3). A non-diagonal "A" specifies an Arch process with additional cross-product terms between the past errors. The intuition behind the inclusion of the cross-product terms is that they take account of the effect of the interaction between the lagged residuals on the conditional variance. White's (1980) test for heteroskedasticity has a similar feature, which includes the cross-products of the regressors as the test variables while the operational form of the Breusch and Pagan (1979) test does not. The model (18) was discussed in detail by Bera, Higgins and Lee (1992), which they called the augmented Arch (Aarch) model (see also Tsay (1987)). If we add linear terms of $\underline{\varepsilon}_{t-1}$ in (18), we obtain the quadratic Arch (Qarch) model of Sentana (1991). Bera, Higgins and Lee (1996) extended the framework (16) and (17) to give the Garch(p,q) model a random coefficient interpretation. It can immediately be seen that, unlike Arch, Aarch is not symmetric in the sense that the conditional variance depends on the sign of the individual lagged ε_ts.

In their empirical analysis of exchange rate data, Cheung and Pauly (1990) found that many of the off-diagonal elements of "A" were significantly different from zero and concluded that a random coefficient formulation provided a richer formulation of time varying volatility than did the standard Arch characterisation. Bera, Higgins and Lee (1996) also noted similar results when they reconsidered Engle's (1983) model for measuring variability of US inflation. They found that the estimate of the coefficient of the augmented Arch term $\varepsilon_{t-4}\varepsilon_{t-7}$ was -0.195 with a *t*-statistic of 4.89. Their resulting specification of an AR-Aarch model passed the specification tests and diagnostic checks they performed, while Engle's original Arch model had some unexplained serial correlation and conditional heteroskedasticity. An empirical application in Sentana (1991) with a century of daily US stock returns provided support for his Qarch model. Coefficients of all of the cross-product terms were highly significant.

Bera and Lee (1993) established the connection between random coefficients and Arch in a somewhat indirect way. They applied White's (1982) information matrix (IM) test to a linear regression model with autocorrelated errors. The IM test had six distinct components and a special case of one component, which corresponded to the autocorrelation parameter ϕ, was found to be identical to Engle's (1982) Lagrange multiplier (LM) test for Arch. Given Chesher's (1984) interpretation of the IM test as a test for parameter variation, it can be said that, as far as the test is concerned, the presence of Arch is "equivalent" to random variation in the autocorrelation coefficient. In our analysis above, we noted that both Arch and the random coefficient model lead to the same first two conditional moments. Under the additional assumption of conditional normality, all the moments, and hence the two processes themselves, are identical.

One by-product of the random coefficient representation of the Arch model is that standard results from the time series literature can be used to derive the necessary and sufficient conditions for stationarity. Andel (1976), Nicholls and Quinn (1982) and Ray (1983) stated simple conditions for second-order stationarity of the AR process with random coefficients. We noted above that the stationarity condition for an Arch(q) process in the absence of autocorrelation is $\Sigma_{i=1}^{q}\alpha_i < 1$. As demonstrated in Bera, Higgins and Lee (1996), presence of autocorrelation leads to a different stationarity condition. For example, the stationarity condition for an Arch(q) process in the presence of first order serial correlation is

$$\frac{1}{1-\phi_1^2}\sum_{i=1}^{q}\alpha_i < 1.$$

In the absence of autocorrelation, $\Sigma_{i=1}^{q}\alpha_i < 1$ is sufficient for weak stationarity. This clearly demonstrates that the presence of autocorrelation can make a stationary Arch process non-stationary.

A CONDITIONAL MIXTURE MODEL INTERPRETATION

Following the work of Clark (1973) and Tauchen and Pitts (1983), Gallant, Hsieh and Tauchen (1991) provided an interesting rationale for the presence of conditional heteroskedasticity and heterogeneity in the higher-order moments of asset prices. Let us write the observed price change y_t as

$$y_t = \mu_t + \sum_{i=1}^{I_t}\zeta_i \qquad (19)$$

where $\zeta_i \sim \text{IID } N(0,\tau^2)$. Here μ_t can be viewed as the forecastable component, the ζ_is are the incremental changes and I_t is the number of times new information comes to the market in period t. I_t is a serially dependent unobservable random variable and is independent of $\{\zeta_i\}$. Because of the randomness of I_t, y_t is not normally distributed; it is in fact a mixture of normal distributions. Here we can view y_t as a subordinated stochastic process, where $y_t - \mu_t$ is subordinate to ζ_i, and I_t is the directing process. Equation (19) can be written as

$$y_t = \mu_t + \tau I_t^{1/2} v_t \qquad (20)$$

with $v_t \sim N(0,1)$. Then, conditional on the information set ψ_{t-1} and I_t, we have the conditional heteroskedastic normal distribution

$$y_t|\psi_{\tau-1}, I_t \sim N(\mu_t, \tau^2 I_t). \qquad (21)$$

Since I_t is not observable, in practice we can work only with the conditional distribution $y_t|\psi_{t-1}$. From the general result that if a random variable is conditionally (on I_t) normal, unconditionally it must be non-normal, and a realistic distribution for $y_t|\psi_{t-1}$ would be conditionally heteroskedastic and non-normal.

Framework (21) is very general, and a variety of interesting cases can be derived from this. When I_t is a constant c, we have

$$y_t|\psi_{\tau-1} \sim N(\mu_t, c\tau^2),$$

which is our standard homoskedastic model. If our information set ψ_{t-1} also includes I_t, then

$$y_t|\psi_{\tau-1} \sim N(\mu_t, \tau^2 I_t).$$

This is a conditional heteroskedastic-normal model. However, the assumption about the knowledge of I_t is not realistic. For the general case (21) the first four moments are

$$E\left[(y_t - \mu_t)|\psi_{\tau-1}\right] = 0$$

$$E\left[(y_t - \mu_t)^2|\psi_{\tau-1}\right] = \tau^2 E\left[I_t|\psi_{\tau-1}\right]$$

$$E\left[(y_t - \mu_t)^3 \middle| \psi_{\tau-1}\right] = 0$$
$$E\left[(y_t - \mu_t)^4 \middle| \psi_{\tau-1}\right] = \tau^4 3E\left[I_t^2 \middle| \psi_{\tau-1}\right].$$

Hence, the conditional kurtosis

$$\frac{E\left[(y_t - \mu_t)^4 \middle| \psi_{\tau-1}\right]}{E\left[(y_t - \mu_t)^2 \middle| \psi_{\tau-1}\right]^2} = \frac{3E\left[I_t^2 \middle| \psi_{\tau-1}\right]}{E\left[I_t \middle| \psi_{\tau-1}\right]^2} \tag{22}$$

exceeds 3. Therefore, it is not surprising that in many empirical studies the normal-Arch model could not capture most of the excess kurtosis in the data, whereas a conditional t or some non-normal Arch models worked somewhat better (see, for example, Engle and Bollerslev (1986), Baillie and Bollerslev (1989), Bollerslev (1987), Hsieh (1989), Gallant, Hsieh, Tauchen (1991), Gallant and Tauchen (1989), Lee and Tse (1991)). Conditional t or other non-normal distributions do not of course solve all the problems, since the quantity in (22) is not necessarily time invariant. The conditional t distribution, for example, although it allows kurtosis to exceed 3, assumes constant conditional kurtosis. Note that the kurtosis in (22) will be time invariant if I_t and ψ_{t-1} are independent. To take account of the time-varying higher moments, Hansen (1992) generalised the conditional t model by expressing the corresponding shape parameter (the degrees of freedom) as a function of the information set. We will discuss this model below.

Bera and Zuo (1996) suggested a specification test for Arch models that examines the constancy of the kurtosis of the standardised residuals of an estimated Arch model. They call it a test for heterokurtosis. The test is derived using the information matrix test principle and hence is a test for heterogeneity of the Arch parameters. As we discussed earlier, conditional heteroskedasticity can be viewed as a randomness of the AR parameters. Conditional heterokurtosis is related to the heterogeneity of the Arch parameters. Mizrach (1990) used a generalisation of the Arch model that allowed for time-varying coefficients in the conditional variance equation and found the model to perform better than the standard Garch model in an exchange-rate application.

At this point a question could be raised: why, in many empirical applications, do Arch models work remarkably well? To explain this, we again follow Gallant, Hsieh and Tauchen (1991). As noted before, the conditional variance is

$$E\left[(y_t - \mu_t)^2 \middle| \psi_{\tau-1}\right] = \tau^2 E\left[I_t \middle| \psi_{\tau-1}\right].$$

Denoting $y_t - \mu_t = \tau I_t^{1/2} v_t$ as the error ε_t, we have

$$\begin{aligned}\mathrm{Cov}\left(\varepsilon_t^2, \varepsilon_{t-j}^2\right) &= \tau^4 \ \mathrm{Cov}\left(I_t v_t^2, I_{t-j} v_{t-j}^2\right) \\ &= \tau^4 \ \mathrm{Cov}\left(I_t, I_{t-j}\right).\end{aligned}$$

If the I_ts are serially dependent, which seems plausible at the outset, this will introduce correlation in the squared errors. The Arch methodology tries to capture this correlation.

Using the US daily stock return data, Lamoureux and Lastrapes (1990a) provided empirical evidence in support of the hypothesis that Arch is a manifestation of the time dependence in the rate of information arrival to the market. They assumed that I_t in (19) is serially correlated and expressed it as

$$I_t = \gamma_0 + \gamma(B) I_{t-1} + u_t, \tag{23}$$

where γ_0 is a constant, $\gamma(B)$ is a lag polynomial and u_t is white noise. Defining $\Omega_t = E[(y_t - \mu_t)^2 \mid I_t] = \tau^2 I_t$ and using (23), we have

$$\Omega_t = \tau^2 \gamma_0 + \gamma(B)\Omega_{t-1} + \tau^2 u_t,$$

which has a similar structure to that of a Garch model. Since I_t is not observable, Lamoureux and Lastrapes used daily trading volume, V_t, as a proxy for the daily information that flows into the market. When V_t was included as an extra variable in the Garch(1,1) model (7), its coefficient was highly significant for the 20 stocks they considered. Moreover, inclusion of V_t in h_t made the Arch effects (coefficients α_1 and β_1) become negligible for most of the stocks. To summarise, this empirical work supports the view that Arch in daily stock returns is an outcome of the time dependence in the news that flows into the market.

To evaluate the role of news in the determination of volatility in the foreign exchange markets, Engle, Ito and Lin (1990) provided a test of two hypotheses – heat waves and meteor showers. The heat wave hypothesis states that the major sources of disturbances come from within a market, whereas the meteor shower hypothesis states that disturbances come from spillovers between markets. They used the intra-daily yen/dollar exchange rate in the Tokyo, European, New York and Pacific markets. To test the two hypotheses they included the squared innovations from the other markets in the specification of each h_t. Coefficients of all of these variables were found to be highly significant, thus lending support to the meteor shower hypothesis. In fact, they found that the foreign news was more important than the past domestic news. In particular, Japanese news had the greatest impact on the volatility of all markets except the Tokyo market.

NON-LINEAR MODEL INTERPRETATION

It is clear that one of the essential features of the Arch model is $Cov(\varepsilon_t^2, \varepsilon_{t-j}^2) \neq 0$, although $Cov(\varepsilon_t, \varepsilon_{t-j}) = 0$ for $j \neq 0$. In other words, Arch postulates a non-linear relationship between ε_t and its past values. There are many non-linear time series models such as the bilinear, threshold autoregressive, exponential autoregressive and non-linear moving average models that can also exhibit this property (see Tong 1990). For simplicity, we concentrate on the bilinear model and its relation to the Arch model. A time series $\{\varepsilon_t\}$ is said to follow a bilinear model if it satisfies (see Granger and Andersen 1978 and Tong 1990)

$$\varepsilon_t = \sum_{i=1}^{p} \phi_i \varepsilon_{t-i} + \sum_{j=1}^{r} \sum_{k=1}^{s} b_{jk} \varepsilon_{t-j} u_{t-k} + u_t, \qquad (24)$$

where u_t is a sequence of IID $(0, \sigma_u^2)$ variables. The first two conditional moments for this process are

$$E(\varepsilon_t | \psi_{t-1}) = \sum_{i=1}^{p} \phi_i \varepsilon_{t-i} + \sum_{j=1}^{r} \sum_{k=1}^{s} b_{jk} \varepsilon_{t-j} u_{t-k}$$
$$Var(\varepsilon_t | \psi_{t-1}) = \sigma_u^2.$$

These conditional moments contrast with those of an Arch process in which the conditional mean is, in general, a constant, but the conditional variance is time varying. Their unconditional moments, however, might be similar. For example, the bilinear model

$$\varepsilon_t = b_{21} \varepsilon_{t-2} u_{t-1} + u_t,$$

has $E(\varepsilon_t) = 0$ and $Cov(\varepsilon_t^2, \varepsilon_{t-2}^2) = b_{21}^2 \sigma_u^2$. As this process is autocorrelated in squares, it will exhibit temporal clustering of large and small deviations like an Arch process. In fact, a bilinear model is quite similar to an Arch model in that it can also be represented as a varying coefficient model. Equation (24) can be written as

$$\varepsilon_t = \sum_{j=1}^{m} \left[\phi_j + A_j(t)\right] \varepsilon_{t-j} + u_t = \sum_{j=1}^{m} \phi_{jt} \varepsilon_{t-j} + u_t, \qquad (25)$$

say, where $m = max(p, r)$ and $A_j(t) = \Sigma_{k=1}^{s} b_{jk} u_{t-k}$ with $\phi_i = 0$, $i \geq p + 1$, $b_{jk} = 0$, $j \geq r + 1$ (see Tong 1990, p 114). The basic difference between (17) and (25) is that, in the former, the coefficients are purely random, whereas in (25), the varying coefficient part $A_j(t)$ has a structure that is a linear function of the lagged innovations u_t.

There is yet another way of looking at the similarities and differences between Arch and bilinear models. Although both models take account of non-linear dependence, Arch represents the dependence in a multiplicative fashion

$$\varepsilon_t = u_t \cdot f_1(\varepsilon_{t-1}, \varepsilon_{t-2}, \ldots; u_{t-1}, u_{t-2}, \ldots) = u_t \cdot f_{1t}, \qquad (26)$$

say, whereas a bilinear model postulates an additive structure

$$\varepsilon_t = f_2(\varepsilon_{t-1}, \varepsilon_{t-2}, \ldots; u_{t-1}, u_{t-2}, \ldots) + u_t = f_{2t} + u_t, \qquad (27)$$

say, where $f_1(\cdot)$ and $f_2(\cdot)$ are some well-defined non-linear functions. Hsieh (1989) exploited these differences to discriminate between the two types of non-linearities. Bera and Higgins (1997) suggested a Cox non-nested procedure to test these two models against each other. From a practical point of view, these models have different implications. Using a bilinear model we can improve the point forecast over standard ARMA modelling but cannot assess the accuracy of the forecast interval. On the other hand, the Arch specification makes it possible to forecast the conditional variance without any additional gain in point forecastability. It is quite possible that the data may be represented by a joint Arch-bilinear model such as the one suggested by Weiss (1986b). Higgins and Bera (1989, 1991) developed simple procedures for detecting the joint presence of Arch and bilinearity.

The empirical results on this topic are somewhat mixed. Hsieh (1989) finds that the Arch model is able to account for the non-linearities in the daily Deutschmark, Canadian dollar and Swiss franc, but not in the British pound nor the Japanese yen. The Arch standardised residuals exhibited substantial non-linearity for the latter two currencies and, for the British pound, more non-normality (excess kurtosis) than the raw data. Diebold and Nason (1990) addressed the issue of whether conditional heteroskedasticity actually exists in exchange rate data or whether it is just a reflection of some misspecification in the conditional mean of the model. They tackled the problem by estimating the conditional mean through a non-parametric regression and testing the residuals for the presence of Arch. Arch was found in the non-parametric residuals, implying that conditional heteroskedasticity was not due to misspecification of the mean. Bera and Higgins (1997) applied the Cox test to three series. When the Garch model was taken as the null hypothesis, they failed to reject it for all the data series. When bilinearity is taken as the null, however, it was rejected in two cases. Moreover, an out-of-sample forecasting exercise showed that the Garch model is superior. The results, therefore, indicate a strong preference for the Garch model.

Lastly, we should mention an inherent problem in using a non-linear conditional mean specification to model financial data. For a non-linear conditional mean model to explain the sort of volatility observed in practice, the variation in the conditional first moment would have to be enormous, implying huge unexploited profit opportunities for the traders. Possibly because of this reason, models that are non-linear in the mean have not become as popular in analysing financial data. The Arch models do not have this drawback because changes in volatility are represented by changes in the conditional variance, linking volatility to a natural measure of risk.

OTHER INTERPRETATIONS

Continuing with the question of why Arch is so prevalent in empirical studies, there are a number of other interesting explanations, such as Mizrach's (1990) learning model and Stock's (1988) time deformation hypothesis. Mizrach (1990) developed a model of asset pricing and learning in which Arch disturbances evolve out of the decision problem of economic agents. He showed that errors made by the agents during the learning process are highly persistent, and that the current errors are dependent on all past errors. This leads the conditional variance to have an Arch like structure with a long lag.

Stock (1988) established the link between time deformation and Arch models. Any economic variable, in general, evolves on an "operational" timescale, whereas, in practice, it is measured on a "calendar" time scale. And this inappropriate use of a calendar timescale may lead to volatility clustering as, relative to the calendar time, the variable may evolve more quickly or slowly (see Diebold 1986a). Stock (1988) showed that a time deformation model of a random variable ε_t can be approximated by

$$\varepsilon_t = \rho_t \varepsilon_{t-1} + v_t, \quad v_t \big| \psi_{t-1} \sim N(0, h_t),$$

where $h_t = \alpha_0 + \alpha_1 \varepsilon_{t-1}^2$. Stock also established that when a relatively long segment of operational time has elapsed during a unit of calendar time, ρ_t is small and h_t is large, the time varying autoregressive parameter is inversely related to the conditional variance.

A number of researchers investigated the empirical relationship between autocorrelation and volatility, see for example Kim (1989), Sentana and Wadhwani (1991), Oedegaard (1991) and LeBaron (1992). Oedegaard found that the first-order autocorrelation of the Standard and Poor's (S&P) 500 daily index decreased over time, which he attributed to the introduction of new financial markets, such as options and futures on the index. However, when Arch was explicitly introduced into the model, the evidence of time-varying autocorrelation became very weak. The other papers detected the simultaneous presence of autocorrelation and Arch, and found them to be inversely related. LeBaron (1992) used the following model

$$y_t = a + f(h_t) y_{t-1} + \varepsilon_t$$
$$\varepsilon_t \big| \psi_{t-1} \sim N(0, h_t)$$
$$f(h_t) = b_0 + b_1 e^{-h_t/b_2}, \qquad (28)$$

where h_t was specified as a Garch(1,1) model. The function $f(\cdot)$ took account of the changing autocorrelation parameter. For estimation, LeBaron set b_2 to the sample variances of the various series he considered. Since

$$\frac{df(h_t)}{dh_t} = -\frac{b_1}{b_2} e^{-h_t/b_2},$$

the coefficient b_1 measures the influence of volatility on autocorrelation. For the S&P 500 composite daily index from January 1928 to May 1990, the estimate of b_1 was 0.36 with a t-value of 11.70. When the sample was divided into three subsamples, the estimate of b_1 did not change very much. For other data series, he used the weekly return for the S&P 500 index, the Center for Research and Securities Prices (CRSP) value weighted index, the Dow index and IBM returns. The general result was that lower correlations were connected with periods of high volatility. As possible explanations, LeBaron mentioned non-trading and the accumulation of news. Some stocks do not trade close to the end of the day and information arriving during that period is reflected on the next day's trading. This induces serial correlation. At the same time, non-trading results in overall lower trade volume, which has a strong positive relationship with volatility. When new information reaches the market very slowly, for traders, the optimal action is to do nothing until enough information is accumulated. This leads to low trade volume and high correlation. Finding the exact causes of serial correlation and its relationship with volatility is still an open empirical problem. The relationship noted in (28) requires further investigation and some other models need to be examined.

Extensions of the model

In the original exposition of the Arch model, it was natural for Engle (1982) to assume that the conditional variance function was linear in the squared errors and that the conditional distribution was normal. He acknowledged, however, that the linearity and conditional normality assumptions may not be appropriate in particular applications. Subsequent empirical work has borne this out. In this section, we survey alternative formulations of the conditional variance function and conditional distribution, which have proven useful in applied research.

NON-LINEAR CONDITIONAL VARIANCE

One of the first difficulties encountered with the linear Arch model was that the estimated α_i coefficients were frequently found to be negative. To avoid this problem Geweke (1986) and Milhoj (1987a) suggested the log Arch model (see also Pantula 1986).

$$\log(h_t) = \alpha_0 + \alpha_1 \log(\varepsilon_{t-1}^2) + \cdots + \alpha_q \log(\varepsilon_{t-q}^2). \qquad (29)$$

Taking the exponential of both sides of (29), $h_t = e^{(\cdot)}$ is strictly positive, and therefore, no inequality restrictions are required for the α_is to ensure that the conditional variance is strictly positive. To determine whether the linear model (3) or the logarithmic model (29) provided a better fit to actual data, Higgins and Bera (1992) proposed a non-linear Arch (Narch) model, which still requires non-negativity restrictions, but includes linear Arch as a special case and log Arch as a limiting case. They specified the conditional variance as

$$h_t = \left[\phi_0(\sigma^2)^\delta + \phi_1(\varepsilon_{t-1}^2)^\delta + \cdots + \phi_q(\varepsilon_{t-q}^2)^\delta\right]^{1/\delta}, \qquad (30)$$

where $\sigma^2 > 0$, $\phi_i \geq 0$, $\delta > 0$ and the ϕ_is are such that $\Sigma_{i=0}^{q}\phi_i = 1$. The motivation of the Narch model can be seen by rearranging (30) to give

$$\frac{h_t^\delta - 1}{\delta} = \phi_0\frac{(\sigma^2)^\delta - 1}{\delta} + \phi_1\frac{(\varepsilon_{t-1}^2)^\delta - 1}{\delta} + \cdots + \phi_q\frac{(\varepsilon_{t-q}^2)^\delta - 1}{\delta}, \qquad (31)$$

from which it is evident that the Narch model is a Box-Cox power transformation of both sides of the linear Arch model. It is apparent that when $\delta = 1$, (31) is equivalent to the linear Arch model and that as $\delta \to 0$, (31) approaches the log Arch model (29). Higgins and Bera (1992) estimated (30) with weekly exchange rates and found that δ was typically significantly less than 1 and much closer to zero, indicating that the data favoured the logarithmic rather than the linear Arch model. Extensions of the above functional forms to the Garch process are straightforward.

A possible limitation of the functional forms described above is that the conditional variance function h_t is symmetric in the lagged ε_ts. Nelson (1991) suggested that a symmetric conditional variance function may be inappropriate for modelling the volatility of returns on stocks because it cannot represent a phenomenon known as the "leverage effect", which is the negative correlation between volatility and past returns. In a symmetric Arch model, h_t is not affected by the sign of ε_{t-i} and therefore h_t is uncorrelated with past errors. To rectify this, Nelson began by defining $\varepsilon_t = \eta_t\sqrt{h_t}$, where η_t is independent and identically distributed with $E(\eta_t) = 0$ and $Var(\eta_t) = 1$. He suggested that in the general Arch formulation

$$h_t = h(\eta_{t-1},\ldots,\eta_{t-q},h_{t-1},\ldots,h_{t-p}), \qquad (32)$$

h_t can be viewed as a stochastic process in which η_t serves as the forcing variable for both the conditional variance and the error. He then chose $h(\cdot)$ in (32) to produce the desired dependence. To avoid non-negativity restrictions on parameters, Nelson maintained the logarithmic specification (29) and proposed

$$\log(h_t) = \alpha_0 + \sum_{i=1}^{q}\alpha_i g(\eta_{t-i}) + \sum_{i=1}^{p}\beta_i \log(h_{t-i}), \qquad (33)$$

where

$$g(\eta_t) = \theta\eta_t + \gamma\left[|\eta_t| - E|\eta_t|\right]. \qquad (34)$$

The conditional variance (33), with (34), is known as exponential Garch (Egarch). It is easy to see that the sequence $g(\eta_t)$ is independent with mean zero and constant, if finite, variance. Therefore, (33) represents a linear ARMA model for $\log(h_t)$ with innovation $g(\eta_t)$. The properties of the Egarch model are determined by the careful construction of the function (34). These properties are:

- The innovation to the conditional variance is piecewise linear in η_t with slopes $\alpha_i(\theta + \gamma)$ when η_t is positive and $\alpha_i(\theta - \gamma)$ when η_t is negative. This produces the asymmetry in the conditional variance.
- The first term in (34) allows for correlation between the error and future conditional variances. For example, suppose that $\gamma = 0$ and that $\theta < 0$. Then a negative η_t will cause the error to

be negative and the current innovation to the variance process to be positive.

❑ The second term in (34) produces the Arch effect. Suppose that $\theta = 0$ and $\gamma > 0$. Whenever the absolute magnitude of η_t exceeds its expected value, the innovation $g(\eta_t)$ is positive. Large shocks therefore increase the conditional variance.

Nelson (1991) fitted the Egarch model to the excess daily return on the CRSP value-weighted stock-market index from July 1962 to December 1987. The estimate of θ was -0.118 and had a standard error of 0.008, confirming a highly significant negative correlation between the excess return and subsequent volatility. For other applications of the Egarch model see, for example, Pagan and Schwert (1990) and Taylor (1990).

Building on the success of the Egarch model to represent asymmetric responses in the conditional variance to positive and negative errors, a series of papers have proposed other Arch models, which allow a very general shape in the conditional variance function. Although these models are parametric and estimated by maximum likelihood, they are non-parametric in spirit because the shape of the conditional variance function is largely determined by the data themselves. Glosten, Jagannathan and Runkle (1991) and Zakoian (1990) independently suggested a conditional standard deviation of the form

$$\sqrt{h_t} = \alpha_0 + \sum_{i=1}^{q} \alpha_i^+ \varepsilon_{t-i}^+ - \sum_{i=1}^{q} \alpha_i^- \varepsilon_{t-i}^-, \qquad (35)$$

where $\varepsilon_t^+ = \max\{\varepsilon_t, 0\}$ and $\varepsilon_t^- = \min\{\varepsilon_t, 0\}$. The parameters are constrained by $\alpha_0 > 0$, $\alpha_i^+ \geq 0$, and $\alpha_i^- \geq 0$ for $i = 1,\ldots,q$ to ensure that the conditional standard deviation is positive. Zakoian referred to this formulation as a threshold Arch (Tarch) model because the coefficient of ε_{t-i} changes when ε_{t-i} crosses the *threshold* of zero. When $\varepsilon_{t-i} > 0$, the conditional standard deviation is linear in ε_{t-i} with slope α_i^+ and when $\varepsilon_{t-i} < 0$, the conditional standard deviation is linear in ε_{t-i} with slope $-\alpha_i^-$. This allows for asymmetry in the conditional variance in the fashion of Egarch.

Gourieroux and Monfort (1992) proposed that a step function over the support of the conditioning error vector $\underline{\varepsilon}_{t-1} = (\varepsilon_{t-1},\ldots,\varepsilon_{t-q})'$ can approximate a highly non-linear conditional variance function. Let $A_1,\ldots,A_m$ be a partition of the support of ε_t. Gourieroux and Monfort considered a conditional variance of the form

$$h_t = \alpha_0 + \sum_{i=1}^{m} \sum_{j=1}^{q} \alpha_{ij} 1_{A_i}(\varepsilon_{t-j}), \qquad (36)$$

where $1_A(\varepsilon_t)$ is the indicator function of the set A, which takes the value of 1 when $\varepsilon_t \in A$ and zero otherwise. They describe (36) as a qualitative Tarch (Qtarch) model because the conditional variance is determined by the region in R^q in which $\underline{\varepsilon}_{t-1}$ lies, rather than by the continuous values of the elements of $\underline{\varepsilon}_{t-1}$.

Engle and Ng (1991) provided a summary of asymmetric Arch models and introduced several new models of their own. They concentrated on the Garch(1,1) process and the functional relationship $h_t = h(\varepsilon_{t-1})$, which they term the "news impact curve". They proposed the parametric models

$$h_t = \alpha_0 + \alpha_1(\varepsilon_{t-1} + \gamma)^2 + \beta h_{t-1} \qquad (37)$$

$$h_t = \alpha_0 + \alpha_1(\varepsilon_{t-1} / h_{t-1}^{1/2} + \gamma)^2 + \beta h_{t-1} \qquad (38)$$

$$h_t = \alpha_0 + \alpha_1(\varepsilon_{t-1} + \gamma h_{t-1}^{1/2})^2 + \beta h_{t-1}. \qquad (39)$$

In the standard Garch(1,1) model, while holding h_{t-1} constant, h_t is a parabola in ε_{t-1} that takes its minimum at $\varepsilon_{t-1} = 0$. In the conditional variance function (37), the introduction of the parameter γ shifts the parabola horizontally so that the minimum occurs at $\varepsilon_{t-1} = -\gamma$. This produces asymmetry because if, for example, $\gamma < 0$, then $h_t = h(-\varepsilon_{t-1})$ exceeds $h_t = h(\varepsilon_{t-1})$ for $\varepsilon_{t-1} > 0$. The model (38) is similar to (37), except that the conditional variance is quadratic in the standardised error $\varepsilon_{t-1}/h_{t-1}^{1/2}$. In (39), the minimum of h_t occurs at $-\gamma h_{t-1}^{1/2}$, which varies with the information set. Engle and Ng (1991) also proposed a very flexible functional form, which is similar to the Qtarch model but is piecewise linear over the support of ε_{t-1} rather than a step function as in (36). They characterised this model as "partially non-parametric" (PNP). They partitioned the support of ε_{t-1} into intervals, where the boundaries of the intervals are $\{\tau_{m^-},\ldots,\tau_{-1},0,\tau_1,\ldots,\tau_{m^+})$, and m^- is the number of intervals below zero and m^+ is the number of intervals above zero. Engle and Ng then specified

$$h_t = \alpha + \sum_{i=0}^{m^+} \theta_i P_{it}(\varepsilon_{t-1} - \tau_i) + \sum_{i=0}^{m^-} \delta_i N_{it}(\varepsilon_{t-1} - \tau_{-i}) + \beta h_{t-1} \qquad (40)$$

where the variables P_{it} and N_{it} are defined as

$$P_{it} = \begin{cases} 1 & \text{if } \varepsilon_{t-1} > \tau_i \\ 0 & \text{otherwise} \end{cases}$$

and

$$N_{it} = \begin{cases} 1 & \text{if } \varepsilon_{t-1} < \tau_{-i} \\ 0 & \text{otherwise} \end{cases}.$$

From (40), h_t will be linear with a different slope over each interval. For example, if ε_{t-1} is positive and lies in the interval (τ_i, τ_{i+1}), then the slope coefficient is $\theta_1 + \cdots + \theta_i$. Engle and Ng chose the τ_is to be multiples of the unconditional standard deviation of the series.

Engle and Ng (1991) also conducted an experiment to compare the ability of asymmetric Arch models to represent the conditional variance of stock returns. Using daily observations on the Japanese Topix stock index from January 1980 to September 1987, Engle and Ng fitted Garch(1,1) versions of the Egarch and Tarch models, and the models given by (37), (38) and (39). All of the fitted models confirmed the presence of the leverage effect but, using a series of diagnostic tests that we describe below, Engle and Ng concluded that the simple parametric models (37), (38) and (39) significantly underestimated the volatility produced by large negative errors. The Egarch and Tarch models, however, adequately represented this "negative size" effect. Engle and Ng also estimated the PNP model and used the fitted conditional variance function as a baseline by which to compare the other asymmetric Arch models. Relative to the prediction of the PNP model, the three models given in (37), (38) and (39), again underpredicted volatility for large negative ε_{t-1} and overpredicted volatility for large positive ε_{t-1}. The fitted conditional variance functions of the Egarch and Tarch model were very close to the PNP's but the Egarch significantly overstated volatility for extremely large negative ε_{t-1}. Although based on only one data set, Engle and Ng's results indicate that, for a parsimonious and highly parametric model, Egarch can represent an asymmetric conditional variance remarkably well. Whether any inadequacies in the Egarch functional form for representing the volatility of stock returns justifies the additional computational effort of estimating a more flexible model like the Tarch, Qtarch or PNP models, may largely depend on the peculiarities of the individual data set and the ultimate purpose of the empirical analysis.

In the context of estimating risk premia, Pagan and Hong (1991) suggested that no parametric functional form is sufficiently general to represent the diverse types of data that display conditional heteroskedasticity. Using data from French, Schwert and Stambaugh (1987) and Engle, Lilien and Robins (1987), Pagan and Hong (1991) used a non-parametric kernel estimator of the conditional variance and demonstrated that the non-parametric estimators give different conclusions about the effect of the risk premium on asset returns than do the standard parametric Arch models. Below, we will briefly discuss the non-parametric approach suggested in Pagan and Hong (1991). Undoubtedly, as research on the Arch phenomenon continues, new empirical regularities of conditional heteroskedasticty will be discovered and new functional forms will be put forward to model these regularities.

NON-NORMAL CONDITIONAL DISTRIBUTION

As described above an attractive feature of the Arch process is that, even though the conditional distribution of the error is normal, the unconditional distribution is non-normal with tails thicker than the normal distribution. In spite of this property, early empirical work with Arch models for daily exchange rates indicated that the implied unconditional distributions of estimated Arch models were not sufficiently leptokurtic to represent the distribution of returns. In the linear regression model with conditionally normal Arch errors, suppose that $\hat{\varepsilon}_t$ and $\hat{h}_t$ are estimates of the error and conditional variance. Then the standardised residuals $\hat{\varepsilon}_t/\hat{h}_t^{1/2}$ should be approximately $N(0,1)$. Hsieh (1988, 1989), McCurdy and Morgan (1988) and Milhøj (1987b), however, demonstrated for a variety of currencies that the sample kurtosis coefficient of the standardised residuals often exceeded 3.

The frequent inability of the conditionally normal Arch model to pass this simple diagnostic test has lead to the use of conditional distributions more general than the normal distribution. Let $\eta_t = \hat{\varepsilon}_t/h_t^{1/2} = (y_t - x_t'\xi)/h_t^{1/2}$ be the standardised error. In this approach, the conditional distribution of η_t is specified as

$$\eta_t \big| \psi_{t-1} \sim f(\eta, \theta), \tag{41}$$

where θ is a low dimension parameter vector whose value determines the shape of the conditional distribution of η_t. In the conditionally normal Arch model, θ is absent and $f(\eta)$ is simply the $N(0,1)$ density. Bollerslev (1987) was the first to adopt this approach and specified $f(\eta,\theta)$ as a conditional t distribution, where θ, a scalar, is the degrees of freedom of the distribution. The conditional t distribution allows for heavier tails than the normal distribution and, as the degrees of freedom go to infinity, includes the normal distribution as a limiting case. Bollerslev suggested that a test for conditional normality could be conducted by testing that the reciprocal of the degrees of freedom equals zero. Using the daily rate of return in the spot market for the Deutschmark and the British pound from March 1980 to January 1985, Bollerslev estimated Garch(1,1) models with conditional t distributions and rejected the hypothesis of conditional normality. The sample kurtosis coefficients of the standardised residuals were very close to the kurtosis coefficients of the t distribution evaluated at the estimated parameters. With the Deutschmark, for example, the sample kurtosis coefficient of the standardised residuals was 4.63, whereas the implied kurtosis of the fitted t distribution was 4.45, suggesting that the conditional t distribution adequately accounted for the excess kurtosis in the unconditional distribution. Bollerslev presented similar results for the daily rate of return on five S&P stock indexes. Engle and Bollerslev (1986), Baillie and Bollerslev (1989) and Hsieh (1989) also found that employing a conditional t distribution helped account for the excess kurtosis in daily exchange rates. Spanos (1991) demonstrated that if the observed data are assumed to have an uncorrelated multivariate t distribution, the conditional distribution of the error also has a t distribution, with an Arch structure for the variance.

Other specifications of the conditional distribution of the Arch process have been suggested. Nelson (1991) employed a generalised error distribution (Ged) with his Egarch model. The Ged encompasses distributions with tails both thicker and thinner than the normal, and includes the normal as a special case. For a stock price index, Nelson found evidence of non-normality in the conditional distribution, but concluded that tails of the estimated Ged were not sufficiently thick to account for a large number of outliers in the data. Lee and Tse (1991) suggested that the conditional distribution not only be leptokurtotic but also asymmetric. They argued that for rates of return that cannot be negative, such as nominal interest rates, the conditional distribution should be skewed to the right. They used a distribution based on the first three terms of the Gram-Charlier series, which allows for both thick tails and skewness. Using interest rates from the Singapore Asian dollar market, Lee and Tse estimated their model but failed to find any evidence of skewness.

As with parametric specifications of the conditional variance function, no single parametric specification of the conditional density (41) appears to be suitable for all conditionally heteroskedastic data. Applications in which none of the above conditional distributions appear to be appropriate are often encountered. For example, Hsieh (1989) found that a Garch(1,1) model with either a conditional t or a conditional Ged distribution could not adequately represent daily returns on the British pound nor the Japanese yen. Hansen (1992) recently suggested an approach to allow more flexibility in the conditional distribution within a parametric framework. While conventional Arch models allow the mean and variance to be time varying, Hansen argues that other properties of the conditional distribution, such as skewness and kurtosis, should also be time varying and a function of the current information set. More formally, Hansen proposed that the conditional distribution (41) should be generalised to

$$\eta_t | \psi_{t-1} \sim f(\eta, \theta_t), \tag{42}$$

where the parameters θ_t, which determine the shape of the conditional density, are themselves a function of the elements of the information set ψ_{t-1}. Hansen refers to (42) as an autoregressive conditional density (ARCD) model.

To illustrate the use of an ARCD model, Hansen estimated a Garch model with a conditional t distribution and time-varying degrees of freedom for the monthly excess holding yield on short-term US Treasury securities. To allow the tail thickness of the conditional distribution to be determined by the information set, the degrees of freedom were parameterised as logistic transformation of a quadratic function of the lagged error and the difference between the one-month yield and the instantaneous yield. A likelihood ratio test rejected a conditional t distribution with constant degrees of freedom in favour of the ARCD model. A time plot of the estimated degrees of freedom revealed that the degrees of freedom varied considerably over time, with a mean of about 5, but frequently reaching 30 and 2.1, the upper and lower bounds imposed by the logistic transformation.

Forecasting with Arch models

A very important use of Arch models is the evaluation of the accuracy of forecasts. In standard time series methodology, which uses conditionally homoskedastic ARMA processes, the variance of the forecast error does not depend on the current information set. If the series being forecast displays Arch, the current information set can indicate the accuracy with which the series can be forecasted. Below, we demonstrate how this is possible. Engle and Kraft (1983) were the first to consider the effect of Arch on forecasting. Baillie and Bollerslev (1992) extended many of their results. The discussion below draws heavily from these two papers.

MEASUREMENT OF FORECAST UNCERTAINTY

We illustrate the effects of Arch on the measurement of forecast uncertainty in the context of predicting a univariate linear time series. Consider the ARMA(k,l) process

$$\phi(B)y_t = \theta(B)\varepsilon_t \qquad (43)$$

where $\phi(B) = 1 - \phi_1 B - \dots - \phi_k B^k$, $\theta(B) = 1 + \theta_1 B + \dots + \theta_l B^l$, B is the backshift operator and ε_t is a Garch(p,q) process. We consider forecasting the value of the process s periods from an origin t, which is given by

$$y_{t+s} = \sum_{i=1}^{k} \phi_i y_{t+s-i} + \sum_{i=1}^{l} \theta_i \varepsilon_{t+s-i} + \varepsilon_{t+s}.$$

The optimal predictor is the mean of y_{t+s} conditional on the available information up to period t, ψ_t. Because $E(\varepsilon_{t+s} | \psi_t) = 0$, the optimal predictor is

$$E(y_{t+s}|\psi_t) = \sum_{i=1}^{k} \phi_i E(y_{t+s-i}|\psi_t) + \sum_{i=1}^{l} \theta_i E(\varepsilon_{t+s-i}|\psi_t), \qquad (44)$$

where:

- ❑ $E(y_{t+s-i} | \psi_t)$, for $i < s$, is given recursively by (44)
- ❑ $E(y_{t+s-i} | \psi_t) = y_{t+s-i}$, for $i \geq s$
- ❑ $E(\varepsilon_{t+s-i} | \psi_t) = 0$, for $i < s$
- ❑ $E(\varepsilon_{t+s-i} | \psi_t) = \varepsilon_{t+s-i}$, for $i \geq s$.

Expression (44) is the standard recursive relation for the optimal point forecast of the conventional ARMA process, which can be found for example in Box and Jenkins (1976, p 129). The presence of Arch does not therefore affect the way in which the point forecast is constructed. This is because Arch introduces dependence in high order moments and only affects the uncertainty in the point forecast.

To consider the effect of Arch on the uncertainty of the point forecast, we require an expression for the forecast error. Assuming the roots of $\phi(B) = 1 - \phi_1 B - \dots - \phi_k B^k$ lie outside the unit circle, the ARMA process (43) can be inverted to give

$$y_{t+s} = \sum_{i=0}^{\infty} \gamma_i \varepsilon_{t+s-i}, \qquad (45)$$

where γ_i is the coefficient of B^i in the expansion of $\phi(B)^{-1}\theta(B)$. Using the moving average representation, the optimal predictor is

$$E(y_{t+s}|\psi_t) = \sum_{i=0}^{\infty} \gamma_i \varepsilon_{t+s-i}. \qquad (46)$$

Let $e_{t,s}$ be the forecast error from origin t with forecast horizon s. Subtracting (46) from (45), the forecast error

$$e_{t,s} = y_{t+s} - E(y_{t+s}|\psi_t) = \sum_{i=0}^{s-1} \gamma_i \varepsilon_{t+s-i} \qquad (47)$$

is seen to be a linear combination of the innovations from $t + 1$ to the horizon $t + s$. The uncertainty in a forecast can be measured by the variance of the forecast error conditional on the information ψ_t used to construct the forecast. Using (47), the variance of the forecast error is

$$Var(e_{t,s}|\psi_t) = \sum_{i=0}^{s-1} \gamma_i^2 (\varepsilon_{t+s-i}^2|\psi_t). \qquad (48)$$

Expression (48) reveals how Arch affects the conditional variance of the forecast error. When Arch is present, $E(\varepsilon_{t+s-i}^2 | \psi_t)$ will depend on the elements of ψ_t and will, in general, be time varying. In contrast, for a conditionally homoskedastic model, in which $E(\varepsilon_{t+s-i}^2 | \psi_t) = \sigma_\varepsilon^2$, the variance of the forecast error reduces to

$$Var(e_{t,s}|\psi_t) = \sigma_\varepsilon^2 \sum_{i=0}^{s-1} \gamma_i^2.$$

In this case, the variance of the forecast error does not depend upon the elements of the information set ψ_t, but only on the length of the forecast horizon s.

To make (48) operational, for constructing prediction intervals, for example, it is necessary to evaluate the expectations $E(\varepsilon_{t+s-i}^2 | \psi_t)$. This can be done by using the ARMA(m,p) representation of the square of a Garch(p,q) process (see equation (12)):

$$\varepsilon_{t+s}^2 = \alpha_0 + \sum_{i=1}^{m} (\alpha_i + \beta_i)\varepsilon_{t+s-i}^2 - \sum_{i=1}^{p} \beta_i v_{t+s-i} + v_{t+s}.$$

The conditional expectation is then seen to be

$$E(\varepsilon_{t+s}^2|\psi_t) = \alpha_0 + \sum_{i=1}^{m} (\alpha_i + \beta_i) E(\varepsilon_{t+s-i}^2|\psi_t) - \sum_{i=1}^{p} \beta_i E(v_{t+s-i}|\psi_t), \qquad (49)$$

where:

- ❑ $E(\varepsilon_{t+s-i}^2 | \psi_t)$, for $i < s$, is given recursively by (49)
- ❑ $E(\varepsilon_{t+s-i}^2 | \psi_t) = \varepsilon_{t+s-i}^2$, for $i \geq s$
- ❑ $E(v_{t+s-i} | \psi_t) = 0$, for $i < s$
- ❑ $E(v_{t+s-i} | \psi_t) = v_{t+s-i}$, for $i \geq s$.

The expression for $E(\varepsilon^2_{t+s} \mid \psi_t)$ in (49) is completely analogous to the optimal predictor $E(y_{t+s} \mid \psi_t)$ in (44).

As an example of constructing estimates of the variance of the forecast, consider the stationary AR(1) process

$$y_t = \phi_1 y_{t-1} + \varepsilon_t, |\phi_1| < 1,$$

where ε_t is a Garch(1,1) process. The optimal point forecasts follow the recursion

$$E(y_{t+s}|\psi_t) = \phi_1 E(y_{t+s-1}|\psi_{t-1})$$

where the first period forecast is $E(y_{t+1} \mid \psi_t) = \phi_1 y_t$. Inverting the AR(1) process, the coefficients in (46) are seen to be $\gamma_i = \phi_1^i$. Therefore, from (48), the variance of the forecast error is

$$\text{Var}(e_{t,s}|\psi_t) = \sum_{i=0}^{s-1} \phi_1^{2i} E(\varepsilon^2_{t+s-i}|\psi_t), s \geq 1,$$

where the expectations can be computed recursively by

$$E(\varepsilon^2_{t+s}|\psi_t) = \alpha_0 + (\alpha_1 + \beta_1)E(\varepsilon^2_{t+s-1}|\psi_t), s > 1,$$

with the initial expectation $E(\varepsilon^2_{t+1} \mid \psi_t) = \alpha_0 + \alpha_1\varepsilon^2_t + \beta_1 h_t$.

To further demonstrate the effect of Arch on the construction of forecast intervals, in Figure 8 we present prediction intervals for the generated Arch(4) data that were displayed in Figure 6. Since the process has a constant conditional mean of zero, the optimal point forecast of the series is simply zero. The prediction intervals are then $\pm 2E(\varepsilon^2_{t+s} \mid \psi_t)^{1/2}$, where $E(\varepsilon^2_{t+s} \mid \psi_t)$ is given in (49). The information sets ψ_{100} and ψ_{400} on which the intervals are based were chosen because $t = 100$ was a tranquil period for the series and $t = 400$ was a volatile period. Notice that for ψ_{100}, the prediction intervals increase monotonically, indicating that uncertainty increases with the forecast horizon, whereas for ψ_{400}, the intervals decrease, indicating that certainty in the point forecast increases with the forecast horizon. Although at first sight it may seem peculiar that the accuracy of a forecast can increase as we forecast further into the future, this phenomenon is very plausible in the context of Arch models. If the forecast is constructed in a highly volatile period, an Arch model will convey that volatility is likely to persist for several periods. But as the forecast horizon increases, the volatility is likely to return to its typical level and therefore the expected accuracy of the point forecast actually increases as we forecast further ahead. Also notice that, for both information sets, the intervals converge to $\pm 2\sigma_\varepsilon$, where σ_ε is the unconditional standard deviation of the process. In an important class of Arch models, the conditional variances of the forecast errors may not converge to the unconditional variance of the process. We characterise this class of models in the next section.

8. Two standard error prediction intervals

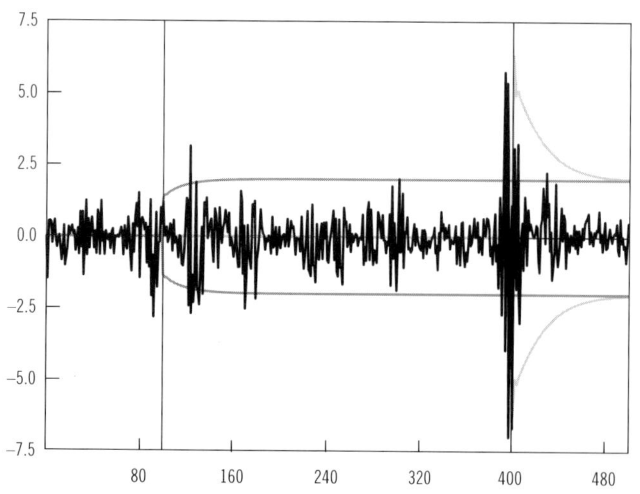

PERSISTENCE IN VARIANCE

When Arch is present, current information is useful for assessing the accuracy by which a process can be forecast. It is interesting to consider how the available information ψ_t affects the forecast uncertainty as the forecast horizon s increases. For $s > p$, the conditional variance (49) of the innovation to the forecast error reduces to

$$E(\varepsilon^2_{t+s}|\psi_t) = \alpha_0 + \sum_{i=1}^{m}(\alpha_i + \beta_i)E(\varepsilon^2_{t+s-i}|\psi_t), \quad (50)$$

which is a linear difference equation for the sequence $\{E(\varepsilon^2_{t+s} \mid \psi_t)\}^\infty_{s=p+1}$. If the roots of $1-(\alpha_1+\beta_1)Z - \dots - (\alpha_m+\beta_m)Z^m = 1 - \alpha(Z) - \beta(Z)$ lie outside the unit circle, the solution sequence of (50) converges to

$$\lim_{s\to\infty} E(\varepsilon^2_{t+s}|\psi_t) = \frac{\alpha_0}{1-\alpha_1 - \dots - \alpha_q - \beta_1 - \dots - \beta_p},$$

which is the unconditional variance of the innovation. In this case, as the forecast horizon becomes very large, the conditioning set provides no information about the variance of ε_{t+s}. If, however, the roots of $1 - \alpha(Z) - \beta(Z)$ lie on or inside the unit circle, this will not be the case. For example, consider a Garch(1,1) process with $1 - \alpha(Z) - \beta(Z)$ having a unit root, implying $\alpha_1 + \beta_1 = 1$. Then (50) reduces to

$$E(\varepsilon^2_{t+s}|\psi_t) = \alpha_0 + E(\varepsilon^2_{t+s-1}|\psi_t)$$

which has the solution

$$E(\varepsilon^2_{t+s}|\psi_t) = s\alpha_0 + E(\varepsilon^2_t|\psi_t).$$

Therefore, when $\alpha_1 + \beta_1 = 1$, the conditional variance grows linearly with the forecast horizon and the dependence on the information set persists through $E(\varepsilon^2_t | \psi_t)$.

Engle and Bollerslev (1986) were the first to consider Garch processes with $\alpha(1) + \beta(1) = 1$ as a distinct class of models, which they term integrated Garch (Igarch). They pointed out the similarity between Igarch processes and processes that are integrated in the mean. For a process that is integrated in the mean - one that must be differenced to induce stationarity - a shock in the current period affects the level of the series into the indefinite future. In an Igarch process, a current shock persists indefinitely in conditioning the future variances. The Igarch model is important because a remarkable empirical regularity, repeatedly observed in applied work, is that the estimated coefficients of a Garch conditional variance sum close to 1. For example, Baillie and Bollerslev (1989) estimated Garch(1,1) models for six US exchange rates and found $\hat{\alpha}_1 + \hat{\beta}_1$ ranging between 0.94 and 0.99 for the six series. Bollerslev and Engle (1989) considered multivariate Igarch processes and defined a concept of co-integration in variance that they termed co-persistence. A set of univariate Igarch processes is co-persistent if there exists a linear combination of the processes that is not integrated in variance. Nelson (1990a) has cautioned that drawing an analogy with processes that are integrated in the mean may be somewhat misleading. As described above, Nelson demonstrated that although Igarch models are not weakly stationary, because they have infinite variances, they could be strongly stationary. Processes that are integrated in the mean are not stationary in any sense.

The consistent finding of very large persistence in variance in financial time series is perplexing because currently no theory predicts that this should be the case. Lamoureux and Lastrapes (1990b) argued that large persistence may actually represent misspecification of the variance and result from structural change in the unconditional variance of the process, as represented by changes in α_0 in (7). A discrete change in the unconditional variance of a process produces clustering of large and small deviations, which may show up as persistence in a fitted Arch model. To illustrate this possibility, Lamoureux and Lastrapes used 17 years of daily returns on the stocks of 30 randomly selected companies and estimated Garch(1,1) models holding α_0 constant and allowing α_0 to change discretely over sub-periods of the sample. For the restricted model, in which α_0 is constant, the average estimate of $\alpha_1 + \beta_1$ for the 30 companies was 0.978, while for the unrestricted model, in which α_0 is allowed to change, the average estimate fell to 0.817. Lamoureux and Lastrapes also present Monte Carlo evidence that demonstrated that the MLE of $\alpha_1 + \beta_1$ has a large positive bias when changes in the unconditional variance are ignored.

Multivariate Arch models

As economic variables are interrelated, generalisation of univariate models to the multivariate and simultaneous set-up is quite natural - this is more so for Arch models. Apart from possible gains in efficiency in parameter estimation, estimation of a number of financial "coefficients" such as the systematic risk (beta coefficient) and the hedge ratio requires sample values of covariances between relevant variables. The motivation for multivariate Arch also stems from the fact that many economic variables react to the same information and hence have non-zero covariances conditional on the information set. For simplicity, we concentrate on two variables, and using our earlier notation as in (20), let

$$\begin{aligned} y_{1t} &= \mu_{1t} + \tau_1 I_t^{1/2} v_{1t}, \\ y_{2t} &= \mu_{2t} + \tau_2 I_t^{1/2} v_{2t}, \end{aligned} \qquad (51)$$

where y_{1t} and y_{2t} are two time series, driven by the same directing process I_t and

$$\begin{pmatrix} v_{1t} \\ v_{2t} \end{pmatrix} \sim N\left[\begin{pmatrix} 0 \\ 0 \end{pmatrix}, \begin{pmatrix} 1 & c_{12} \\ c_{12} & 1 \end{pmatrix}\right].$$

Then we have

$$\begin{pmatrix} y_{1t} \\ y_{2t} \end{pmatrix} \Big| \psi_{t-1}, I_t \sim N\left[\begin{pmatrix} \mu_{1t} \\ \mu_{2t} \end{pmatrix}, I_t \begin{pmatrix} \tau_1^2 & c_{12}\tau_1\tau_2 \\ c_{12}\tau_1\tau_2 & \tau_2^2 \end{pmatrix}\right]. \qquad (52)$$

This is the bivariate counterpart of (21) and provides a rationale behind higher dimensional Arch processes. As discussed above, several special cases can be derived from (52).

Let us now consider an $N \times 1$ vector time series $y_t = (y_{1t}, \ldots, y_{Nt})'$. We can express a general form of the multivariate Garch model as

$$y_t | \psi_{t-1} \sim N(\mu_t, H_t),$$

where μ_t is an $N \times 1$ vector and H_t is an $N \times N$ matrix. Of course, the conditional distribution could be something other than normal. As in the univariate case, one main problem is the specification of H_t. In fact we will soon realise that the problem is more serious here. Even if we confine ourselves to linear specifications for multivariate Arch, there are many choices.

To express H_t in a vector form, we use the "vech" notation, which stacks the lower triangular elements of a symmetric matrix in a column. A somewhat general form of H_t can be written as

$$\text{vech}(H_t) = \text{vech}(\Sigma) + \sum_{i=1}^{q} A_i \,\text{vech}(\varepsilon_{t-i}\varepsilon'_{t-i}) + \sum_{i=1}^{q} B_i \,\text{vech}(H_{t-i}), \quad (53)$$

where $\varepsilon_t = (\varepsilon_{1t},\ldots,\varepsilon_{Nt})'$, Σ is an $N \times N$ positive definite matrix and A_i and B_i are $N(N + 1)/2 \times N(N + 1)/2$ matrices. This is a direct generalisation of our earlier univariate Garch(p,q) model given in equation (7). Representation (53) is called the "vech representation" of a multivariate Arch model. For $N = 2$ and $p = q = 1$, (53) takes the form

$$\text{vech}(H_t) = \begin{bmatrix} h_{11,t} \\ h_{12,t} \\ h_{22,t} \end{bmatrix} = \begin{bmatrix} \sigma_{11} \\ \sigma_{12} \\ \sigma_{22} \end{bmatrix} + \begin{bmatrix} a_{11} & a_{12} & a_{13} \\ a_{21} & a_{22} & a_{23} \\ a_{31} & a_{32} & a_{33} \end{bmatrix} \begin{bmatrix} \varepsilon^2_{1,t-1} \\ \varepsilon_{1,t-1}\varepsilon_{2,t-1} \\ \varepsilon^2_{2,t-1} \end{bmatrix} + \begin{bmatrix} b_{11} & b_{12} & b_{13} \\ b_{21} & b_{22} & b_{23} \\ b_{31} & b_{32} & b_{33} \end{bmatrix} \begin{bmatrix} h_{11,t-1} \\ h_{12,t-1} \\ h_{22,t-1} \end{bmatrix}. \quad (54)$$

The two main problems concerning the specification of H_t are that it should be positive definite for all possible realisations and some exclusion restrictions should be imposed so that number of parameters to be estimated is not very large. Formulation (53) will be difficult to estimate, for it has $[N(N + 1)/2]\ [1+ [N(N + 1)/2](p + q)]$ parameters, which for the special bivariate case (54) amounts to 21 parameters - still too large.

Engle, Granger and Kraft (1986) published the first paper on multivariate Arch models. They considered a bivariate Arch model, which was (54), without the lagged h_t components. For that model, they showed necessary conditions for H_t to be positive definite are

$$\begin{gathered} \sigma_{11} > 0, \sigma_{22} > 0, \sigma_{11}\sigma_{22} - \sigma^2_{12} > 0, \\ a_{11} \geq 0, a_{13} \geq 0, a_{31} \geq 0, a_{33} \geq 0, \\ a_{11}a_{33} - a^2_{22} \geq 0, \\ a_{11}a_{13} - \tfrac{1}{4}a^2_{12} \geq 0, a_{11}a_{31} - a^2_{21} \geq 0, \\ a_{31}a_{33} - \tfrac{1}{4}a^2_{32} \geq 0, a_{13}a_{33} - a^2_{23} \geq 0. \end{gathered} \quad (55)$$

Note that in (53) and (54), each $h_{ij,t}$ depends on lagged squared residuals and past variances of all the variables in the system. One simple assumption that could be made to reduce the number of parameters is to specify that a conditional variance depends only on its *own* lagged squared residuals and lagged values. The assumption amounts to taking A_i and B_i to be diagonal matrices. In that case, conditions in (55) reduce to

$$\begin{gathered} \sigma_{11} > 0, \sigma_{22} > 0, \sigma_{11}\sigma_{22} - \sigma^2_{12} > 0, \\ a_{11} \geq 0, a_{33} \geq 0, a_{11}a_{33} - a^2_{22} \geq 0. \end{gathered} \quad (56)$$

From (53), the "diagonal representation" for $p = q = 1$ can be expressed as

$$h_{ij,t} = \sigma_{ij} + a_{ij}\varepsilon_{i,t-1}\varepsilon_{j,t-1} + b_{ij}h_{ij,t-1} \quad i,j = 1,2,\ldots,N. \quad (57)$$

This form was used by Bollerslev, Engle and Wooldridge (1988) for their analysis of returns on bills, bonds and stocks, and by Baillie and Myers (1991) and Bera, Garcia and Roh (1991) for hedge ratio estimation in commodity markets.

The diagonal representation appears to be too restrictive and, at the same time, positive definiteness of the resulting H_t, in general, is not easy to check and also difficult to impose at the estimation stage (see (56)). Baba, Engle, Kraft and Kroner (1990) suggested the following parameterisation, known as the "BEKK representation", which is almost guaranteed to be positive definite (see also Engle and Kroner (1995))

$$H_t = \Sigma + \sum_{i=1}^{q} A_i^{*\prime} \varepsilon_{t-1}\varepsilon'_{t-1}A_i^* + \sum_{i=1}^{p} B_i^{*\prime} H_{t-i}B_i^*, \quad (58)$$

where A_i^* and B_i^* are $N \times N$ matrices. If Σ is positive definite, then so is H_t. For $N = 2$ and $p = q = 1$, (58) will have only 11 parameters compared to the 21 parameters of the vech representation (54), as (58) now takes the form

$$\begin{bmatrix} h_{11,t} & h_{12,t} \\ h_{12,t} & h_{22,t} \end{bmatrix} = \begin{bmatrix} \sigma_{11} & \sigma_{12} \\ \sigma_{21} & \sigma_{22} \end{bmatrix} + \begin{bmatrix} a^*_{11} & a^*_{12} \\ a^*_{21} & a^*_{22} \end{bmatrix}' \begin{bmatrix} \varepsilon^2_{1,t-1} & \varepsilon_{1,t-1}\varepsilon_{2,t-1} \\ \varepsilon_{1,t-1}\varepsilon_{2,t-1} & \varepsilon^2_{2,t-1} \end{bmatrix} \times \begin{bmatrix} a^*_{11} & a^*_{12} \\ a^*_{21} & a^*_{22} \end{bmatrix} + \begin{bmatrix} b^*_{11} & b^*_{12} \\ b^*_{21} & b^*_{22} \end{bmatrix}' \begin{bmatrix} h_{11,t-1} & h_{12,t-1} \\ h_{12,t-1} & h_{22,t-1} \end{bmatrix} \begin{bmatrix} b^*_{11} & b^*_{12} \\ b^*_{21} & b^*_{22} \end{bmatrix}. \quad (59)$$

By taking the vech of (58), it can be shown that under certain non-linear restrictions on A_i^*, B_i^*, A_i and B_i, (53) and (58) are equivalent (see Baba, Engle, Kraft and Kroner 1990). The relationship is easily seen by comparing the special cases (54) and (59).

Bollerslev (1990) introduced an attractive way to simplify H_t. He assumed that the conditional correlation matrix of $\varepsilon_t = (\varepsilon_{1t},\ldots,\varepsilon_{Nt})'$ is constant and expressed H_t as

$$H_t = \mathrm{diag}\left(\sqrt{h_{11,t}},\ldots,\sqrt{h_{NN,t}}\right)R \\ \mathrm{diag}\left(\sqrt{h_{11,t}},\ldots,\sqrt{h_{NN,t}}\right) \quad (60)$$

where R is the time invariant correlation matrix. When N = 2, this representation takes the form

$$H_t = \begin{bmatrix} \sqrt{h_{11,t}} & 0 \\ 0 & \sqrt{h_{22,t}} \end{bmatrix} \begin{bmatrix} 1 & \rho \\ \rho & 1 \end{bmatrix} \begin{bmatrix} \sqrt{h_{11,t}} & 0 \\ 0 & \sqrt{h_{22,t}} \end{bmatrix}, \quad (61)$$

where $|\rho| < 1$ is the correlation coefficient between ε_{1t} and ε_{2t}, and the individual variances $h_{11,t}$ and $h_{22,t}$ are assumed to be standard univariate Arch(p,q) processes, for example

$$h_{11,t} = \sigma_{11} + \sum_{i=1}^{q} \alpha_{1i}\varepsilon^2_{1,t-i} + \sum_{i=1}^{p} \beta_{1i}h_{11,t-i}. \quad (62)$$

For positive definiteness of H_t in this constant correlation representation, we need $\sigma_{ii} > 0$, $\alpha_{ij} \geq 0$, $\beta_{ik} \geq 0$, $i = 1,\ldots,N$, $j = 1,\ldots,q$, $k = 1,\ldots,p$. Many of the recent applications of bivariate Arch use this representation (see, for example, Baillie and Bollerslev (1990); Baillie and Myers (1991); Bera, Garcia and Roh (1990); Bollerslev (1990); Kroner and Claessens (1991) and Kroner and Sultan (1991)). However, it is quite obvious that constant correlation is a strong assumption. Bera and Roh (1991) suggested a test for the constant correlation hypothesis and found that the null hypothesis is rejected for many financial data series (see also Bera and Kim (1998)).

None of the above forms take account of the motivation behind multivariate Arch discussed earlier. Diebold and Nerlove (1989) were the first to exploit the theory that only a few factors influence all the variables $(y_1,\ldots,y_N)$ and their conditional variances. They suggest a one-factor multivariate Arch model represented as

$$y_t = \lambda F_t + \eta_t, \quad (63)$$

where $\eta_t = (\eta_{1t},\ldots,\eta_{Nt})$, $\eta_{it} \sim (0,\sigma_{ii})$, $i = 1,\ldots,N$ and the unobservable factor F_t is conditionally distributed as $F_t | \psi_{t-1} \sim N(0,h_t)$. Then

$$\mathrm{Var}(y_t|\psi_{t-1}) = h_t\lambda\lambda' + \mathrm{diag}(\sigma_{11},\ldots,\sigma_{NN}) \quad (64)$$

and we can specify a univariate Garch process for h_t. The effect of the common factor F_t on y_i is measured by $\lambda_i (i = 1,\ldots,N)$. Their application of this model to seven weekly exchange rate series gave superior results compared to seven separate univariate Arch models.

Harvey, Ruiz and Sentana (1992) presented a more general unobserved component model that includes (63) as a special case and allows for richer dynamics in the mean of y_t. They consider the model

$$y_t = Z_t\alpha_t + \Lambda\eta_t + \eta^*_t,$$

in which α_t is a $m \times 1$ state vector that evolves according to the transition equation

$$\alpha_t = T_t\alpha_{t-1} + \Gamma\varepsilon_t + \varepsilon^*_t,$$

where T_t and Z_t are observable matrices, and the $m \times 1$ vector ε^*_t and the $N \times 1$ vector η^*_t are conditionally homoskedastic. Conditional heteroskedasticity is introduced through the scalar processes ε_t and η_t, which are assumed to follow univariate Arch processes. The state space formulation provides a convenient representation for estimation and prediction by means of a Kalman filter. Higgins and Majin (1992) applied a univariate version of this model to measure the time-varying volatility of both the latent *ex ante* real interest rate and the market's forecast errors of inflation from the observable *ex post* real interest rate.

To discuss Engle's (1987) multivariate Arch model with a k-factor structure, we start with a slight generalisation of the BEKK representation (58), namely

$$H_t = \Sigma + \sum_{j=1}^{k}\left[\sum_{i=1}^{q} A^{*\prime}_{ij}\varepsilon_{t-i}\varepsilon'_{t-i}A^*_{ij} + \sum_{i=1}^{p} B^{*\prime}_{ij}H_{t-i}B^*_{ij}\right], \quad (65)$$

where A^*_{ij} and B^*_{ij} are $N \times N$ matrices and $k << N$. Engle obtained a very parsimonious structure for H_t by restricting the rank of A^*_{ij} and B^*_{ij} to 1 (see also Lin 1992). More specifically, he assumed that these matrices have the same left and right eigenvectors, g_j and f_j, ie

$$A^*_{ij} = \alpha_{ij}f_jg'_j \quad \text{and} \quad B^*_{ij} = \beta_{ij}f_jg'_j$$

with

$$f_jg'_l = \begin{cases} 0 & \text{for } j \neq l \\ 1 & \text{for } j = l \end{cases}$$

where f_j and g_l are $N \times l$ vectors, $j,l = 1,2,\ldots,N$. Using these expressions for A^*_{ij} and B^*_{ij} in (65), we have the k-factor Garch(p,q) model

$$H_t = \Sigma + \sum_{j=1}^{k} g_jg'_j\left[\sum_{i=1}^{q}\alpha^2_{ij}f'_j\varepsilon_{t-i}\varepsilon'_{t-i}f_j + \sum_{i=1}^{p}\beta^2_{ij}f'_jH_{t-i}f_j\right]. \quad (66)$$

In the Diebold and Nerlove model, the factor is an unobserved latent variable, whereas in the k-factor Garch model, the jth factor, F_{jt}, is a linear combination of the residuals, namely $F_{jt} = f'_j\varepsilon_t$. Therefore

$$\mathrm{Var}(F_{jt}|\psi_{t-1}) = f'_jH_tf_j = h^*_{jt} \quad (67)$$

(say). Substituting (66) into (67), we have

$$h^*_{jt} = f'_j \Sigma f_j + \sum_{i=1}^{q} \alpha^2_{ij} F^2_{j,t-i} + \sum_{i=1}^{p} \beta^2_{ij} h^*_{j,t-i}.$$

Therefore, each h^*_{jt} has a Garch(p,q) structure, $j = 1,\ldots,k$. This enables us to express (66) as

$$H_t = \Sigma + \sum_{j=1}^{k} g_j g'_j \left[h^*_{jt} - f'_j \Sigma f_j\right] = \Sigma^* + \sum_{j=1}^{k} g_j g'_j h^*_{jt}, \quad (68)$$

where

$$\Sigma^* = \Sigma - \sum_{j=1}^{k} g_j g'_j f'_j \Sigma f_j.$$

Expression (68) demonstrates that the conditional variance of ε_t is regulated completely by the conditional variance of the k factors. For $k = 1$, we can see the similarities between (64) and (68). Engle (1987), Kroner (1988), Lin (1992) and Engle, Ng and Rothschild (1990) discussed other interesting properties of the k-factor Garch model. Two notable applications of this model are Engle, Ng and Rothschild (1990) to explain the excess return for Treasury bills and Ng, Engle and Rothschild (1992) to study the behaviour of stock returns.

Lin (1992) examined the finite sample properties of various estimators, such as maximum likelihood and two-stage estimators, for the factor Garch(1,1) model through simulation. Estimators were found to be, in general, unbiased and, as predicted by asymptotic theory, the maximum likelihood estimators were most efficient. The major problems in estimation are devising methods for finding the number of factors and the factor weights.

Arch-M models

It is reasonable to expect that the mean and variance of a return move in the same direction. Denoting the mean by μ_t, we can express this idea as

$$\mu_t = \xi_0 + \delta g(h_t),$$

where $g(h_t)$ is a monotonic function of the conditional variance h_t, with $g(\alpha_0) = 0$. In finance models, $\delta g(h_t)$ represents the risk premium, that is, the increase in the expected rate of return due to an increase in the variance of the return. Existence of risk premia in foreign exchange markets and the term structure of interest rates have been studied extensively. Most of the earlier studies concentrated on detecting a constant risk premium. Arch in the mean (Arch-M) models, first proposed by Engle, Lilien and Robbins (1987), provide a new approach by which we can test for and estimate a time varying risk premium. In the regression set-up, an Arch-M model is specified as

$$y_t = x_t'\xi + \delta g(h_t) + \varepsilon_t, \quad (69)$$

where

$$\varepsilon_t | \psi_{t-1} \sim N(0, h_t)$$

and h_t is an Arch or Garch process. The presence of h_t in the conditional mean is the distinctive feature of this model.

To examine the properties of the Arch-M model, we consider a simple version of (69), namely

$$y_t = \delta h_t + \varepsilon_t,$$

where

$$\varepsilon_t | \psi_{t-1} \sim N(0, h_t)$$

and

$$h_t = \alpha_0 + \alpha_1 \varepsilon^2_{t-1}.$$

We can then write

$$y_t = \delta\alpha_0 + \delta\alpha_1 \varepsilon^2_{t-1} + \varepsilon_t,$$

where ε_t follows an Arch(1) process. From this expression, and using $E(\varepsilon^2_{t-1}) = \alpha_0/(1 - \alpha_1)$, it immediately follows that

$$E(y_t) = \delta\alpha_0 \left(\frac{\alpha_0}{1-\alpha_1}\right),$$

which can be viewed in finance models as the unconditional expected return for holding a risky asset. Similarly

$$\mathrm{Var}(y_t) = \frac{\alpha_0}{1-\alpha_1} + \frac{(\delta\alpha_1)^2 2\alpha_0^2}{(1-\alpha_1)^2(1-3\alpha_1^2)}.$$

In the absence of a risk premium $\mathrm{Var}(y_t) = \alpha_0/(1 - \alpha_1)$. Therefore, the second component of $\mathrm{Var}(y_t)$ is due to the presence of a risk premium which makes y_t more dispersed. Finally, the Arch-M effect makes y_t serially correlated, since (see Hong 1991).

$$\rho_1 = \mathrm{Corr}(y_t, y_{t-1}) = \frac{2\alpha_1^3\delta^2\alpha_0}{2\alpha_1^2\delta^2\alpha_0 + (1-\alpha_1)(1-3\alpha_1^2)}$$

$$\rho_k = \mathrm{Corr}(y_t, y_{t-k}) = \alpha_1^{k-1}\rho_1, \ k = 2,3,\ldots.$$

From the expressions for ρ_1 and ρ_2, it is easily seen that the admissible region for (ρ_1, ρ_2) will be very restrictive. Bollerslev (1988) obtained similar results for the Garch process. Arch-M models introduce some interesting problems in terms of estimation and testing, which will be discussed in the following sections.

In most applications, $g(h_t) = \sqrt{h_t}$ has been

used (see, for example, Domowitz and Hakkio (1985) and Bollerslev, Engle and Wooldridge (1988)), although Engle, Lilien and Robins (1987) found that $g(h_t) = \log(h_t)$ worked better in their estimation of the time-varying risk premia in the term structure. Pagan and Hong (1991) commented that the use of $\log(h_t)$ is problematic since for $h_t < 1$, $g(h_t)$ will be negative and also when $h_t \to 0$, the effect on y_t will be infinite. It would be an interesting problem to investigate the appropriate function form for $g(h_t)$.

Estimation

The most commonly used estimation procedure for Arch models has been the maximum likelihood approach. The log likelihood function of the standard Arch regression model

$$y_t | \psi_{t-1} \sim N(x_t'\xi, h_t)$$

is given by

$$l(\theta) = \frac{1}{T}\sum_{t=1}^{T} l_t(\theta),$$

where

$$l_t(\theta) = \text{const.} - \frac{1}{2}\log(h_t) - \frac{e_t^2}{2h_t}, \qquad (70)$$

and $\theta = (\xi', \gamma')'$. Here ξ and γ denote the conditional mean and conditional variance parameters respectively. One attractive feature of this normal likelihood function is that the information matrix is block diagonal between the parameters ξ and γ. To see this, note that the (i,j)th element of the off-diagonal block of the information matrix can be written as

$$\frac{1}{T}\sum_{t=1}^{T} E\left[\frac{\partial^2 l_t}{\partial \xi_i \partial \gamma_j}\right] = \frac{1}{T}\sum_{t=1}^{T} E\left[\frac{1}{2h_t^2}\frac{\partial h_t}{\partial \xi_i}\frac{\partial h_t}{\partial \gamma_j}\right]. \qquad (71)$$

If h_t is a symmetric function of the lagged errors in the sense of Engle (1982), then the last expression in square brackets is anti-symmetric and, therefore, has expectation zero. The Arch, Garch, log Arch and Narch models given in (3), (7), (29) and (30) respectively, are all symmetric according to the definition of Engle (1982).

The advantage of having this block diagonality is that, under the likelihood framework, estimation and testing for the mean and variance parameters can be carried out separately (see Engle (1982, p. 996); Bollerslev (1986, p. 317) and Higgins and Bera (1992, p. 996)). Most of the applied work on Arch models uses the Berndt, Hall, Hall and Hausman (1974) algorithm (BHHH) to maximise $l(\theta)$. Starting from estimates of the rth iteration, the (r + 1)th step of the BHHH algorithm can be written as

$$\xi^{(r+1)} = \xi^{(r)} + \left[\sum_{t=1}^{T}\left(\frac{\partial l_t}{\partial \xi}\right)\left(\frac{\partial l_t}{\partial \xi}\right)'\right]^{-1}\sum_{t=1}^{T}\frac{\partial l_t}{\partial \xi}$$

and

$$\gamma^{(r+1)} = \gamma^{(r)} + \left[\sum_{t=1}^{T}\left(\frac{\partial l_t}{\partial \gamma}\right)\left(\frac{\partial l_t}{\partial \gamma}\right)'\right]^{-1}\sum_{t=1}^{T}\frac{\partial l_t}{\partial \gamma},$$

where the derivatives are evaluated at $\xi^{(r)}$ and $\gamma^{(r)}$. The block diagonality of the information matrix no longer holds for the Arch-M model in (69) and the asymmetric models like Aarch in (18) and Egarch in (33). For these models, the BHHH algorithm needs to be carried out jointly for both the conditional mean and variance parameters.

For most applications, it is very difficult to justify the conditional normality assumption in (70). Therefore, the log likelihood function $l(\theta)$ may be misspecified. However, we can still obtain estimates of ξ and γ by maximising $l(\theta)$ and such estimators are called quasi maximum likelihood estimators (QMLE). Weiss (1986a) was the first to study the asymptotic properties of the QMLE of Arch models. His important finding was that as long as the first two conditional moments are correctly specified, ξ and γ will be consistently estimated even if the conditional normality assumption is violated. To state the asymptotic distribution of the QMLE $\hat{\theta} = (\hat{\xi}', \hat{\gamma}')'$, let us denote

$$A = -\frac{1}{T}E\left[\frac{\partial^2 l(\theta_0)}{\partial\theta\,\partial\theta'}\right] \text{ and}$$

$$B = \frac{1}{T}E\left[\left(\frac{\partial l(\theta_0)}{\partial\theta}\right)\left(\frac{\partial l(\theta_0)}{\partial\theta}\right)'\right], \qquad (72)$$

where θ_0 is the true value of the parameter. Then under certain regularity conditions

$$\sqrt{T}\left(\hat{\theta} - \theta_0\right) \xrightarrow{L} N(0, A^{-1}BA^{-1})$$

and consistent estimators of A and B are given by

$$\hat{A} = -\frac{1}{T}\sum_{t=1}^{T}\frac{\partial^2 l_t(\hat{\theta})}{\partial\theta\,\partial\theta'} \text{ and}$$

$$\hat{B} = \frac{1}{T}\sum_{t=1}^{T}\left(\frac{\partial l_t(\hat{\theta})}{\partial\theta}\right)\left(\frac{\partial l_t(\hat{\theta})}{\partial\theta}\right)'.$$

Robust inference about θ can be achieved using this result. If the normality assumption is correct,

$A = B$ and valid inference can be drawn using either $\hat{A}^{-1}$ or $\hat{B}^{-1}$ as the covariance matrix estimator. Bollerslev and Wooldridge (1992) generalised the univariate Arch results of Weiss (1986a) to the multivariate Garch case under a different set of regularity conditions. Although the specification of a univariate Arch model in Weiss (1986a) was very general, he assumed a finite fourth moment of the error term. As an example, for the Arch(2) model this condition requires (see Bollerslev 1986)

$$3\alpha_1^2 + 3\alpha_2^2 - 3\alpha_2^3 + 3\alpha_1^2\alpha_2 + \alpha_2 < 1,$$

which might be difficult to justify in practice. For higher order Arch and Garch models, the condition will restrict models to a small part of the parameter space. Bollerslev and Wooldridge (1992) did not assume finiteness of the fourth moment, but instead, they required $l_t(\theta)$ and its derivatives to satisfy a uniform weak law of large numbers, which are not easy to verify. Lumsdaine (1991a) established the consistency and asymptotic normality of the QMLE of the Garch(1,1) and Igarch(1,1) models under a different set of assumptions. Her basic conditions are

$$E\left[\frac{\partial h_t}{\partial \theta} h_t^{-1}\right] < \infty \quad \text{and} \quad E\left[\left(\frac{\partial h_t}{\partial \theta}\right)\left(\frac{\partial h_t}{\partial \theta}\right)' h_t^{-2}\right] < \infty$$

and these are easy to verify. For simplicity, consider an Arch(1) model

$$h_t = \alpha_0 + \alpha_1 \varepsilon_{t-1}^2.$$

Then

$$E\left[\left(\frac{\partial h_t}{\partial \alpha_1}\right)^2\right] = E\left(\varepsilon_{t-1}^4\right)$$

might not exist, and yet

$$E\left[\left(\frac{\partial h_t}{\partial \alpha_1}\right)^2 h_t^{-2}\right] = E\left[\frac{\varepsilon_{t-1}^4}{\alpha_0^2 + \alpha_1^2\varepsilon_{t-1}^4 + 2\alpha_0\alpha_1\varepsilon_{t-1}^2}\right]$$

may exist because here both the numerator and the denominator grow at the same rate. In terms of the standarised variable $\varepsilon_t^* = \varepsilon_t/\sqrt{h_t}$, Lumsdaine's assumptions are that ε_t^* is IID and drawn from a symmetric and unimodal density with 32 finite moments. Lee and Hansen (1991) obtained similar results under the somewhat weaker condition that ε_t^* is stationary and ergodic with a bounded fourth conditional moment. Lumsdaine (1991a) and Lee and Hansen (1991) showed that the QMLE for the Igarch(1,1) model has the same asymptotic distribution as that of the Garch(1,1) model. This result is important because it establishes that the difficulties of the unit root model is not encountered with Igarch.

Lee (1991) extended all these asymptotic distribution results to the Garch(1,1)-M and Igarch(1,1)-M models. As discussed in Lee, these models pose additional difficulties because unlike the Garch model, the conditional variance of a Garch-M model is a non-linear difference equation. To see this, note from (69) that for a Garch(1,1)-M model

$$\begin{aligned} h_t &= \alpha_0 + \alpha_1\varepsilon_{t-1}^2 + \beta_1 h_{t-1} \\ &= \alpha_0 + \alpha_1\left[y_{t-1} - x_t'\xi - \delta g(h_{t-1})\right]^2 + \beta_1 h_{t-1}. \end{aligned}$$

To avoid the difficulties associated with non-linear difference equations, Lee (1991) used the fact that at the true parameter value, h_t is a linear difference equation.

Engle and González-Rivera (1991) pointed out that although the QMLE is consistent and asymptotically normal, it can be inefficient. They demonstrated that the loss of efficiency due to misspecification could be severe when the true distribution is asymmetric and a normal quasi likelihood function is used. They suggested a semiparametric approach in which one maximises the log likelihood function $l(\theta) = 1/T\Sigma_t l_t(\theta)$, where the non-constant part of $l_t(\theta)$ in (70) is replaced by

$$-\tfrac{1}{2}\log(h_t) + \log\left(g\left(\varepsilon_t / h_t^{1/2}\right)\right). \qquad (73)$$

Engle and González-Rivera (1991) used a nonparametric method to estimate the function $g(\cdot)$. To do this, they started with an initial estimator of θ, obtained $\hat{\varepsilon}_t/\hat{h}_t^{1/2}$, used these values to estimate $g(\cdot)$ and then maximised $l(\theta)$ to get a revised estimate of θ. The procedure was repeated until it converged. Their Monte Carlo results indicated that there is substantial gain in efficiency from using the semiparametric method over QMLE.

Another attractive way to estimate Arch models without assuming normality is to apply the generalised method of moments (GMM) approach as advocated by Rich, Raymond and Butler (1991) (see also Sabau (1987), (1988)). For simplicity, consider an Arch(1) model and define the following two errors

$$\begin{aligned} \varepsilon_t &= y_t - x_t'\xi \\ v_t &= \varepsilon_t^2 - \alpha_0 - \alpha_1\varepsilon_{t-1}^2 \\ &= \left(y_t - x_t'\xi\right)^2 - \alpha_0 - \alpha_1\left(y_{t-1} - x_{t-1}'\xi\right)^2. \end{aligned}$$

Then the GMM estimator is obtained from the

following two moment conditions

$$E(\varepsilon_t|Z_t) = 0 \text{ and } E(v_t|Z_t) = 0,$$

where z_t is a set of predetermined variables. The asymptotic distribution of the GMM estimator follows directly from the general formula in Hansen (1982).

Weiss (1986a) and Pantula (1988) studied the asymptotic properties of least squares estimators, which also do not require a normality assumption. They proved the consistency and asymptotic normality of such estimators. However, as can be expected, least squares estimators are less efficient than GMM estimators and MLEs with a correct likelihood function. It would be interesting to compare the finite sample properties of all of these estimators.

We previously mentioned the importance of correct specification of the conditional variance function h_t. All the forms of h_t we discussed above are fully parametric. Pagan and Hong (1991) argued that the existing parametric forms are not very convincing due to the lack of optimising theory in their formulation. They advocated non-parametric estimation of h_t, as originally suggested by Pagan and Ullah (1988). They even recommended estimating both the conditional mean, m_t, and the conditional variance, h_t, non-parametrically since misspecification in the conditional mean might exaggerate the variation in h_t. In the statistics literature, many non-parametric techniques are available. For their empirical application, Pagan and Hong (1991) used the kernel method and the Fourier series approximation of Gallant (1982). These procedures estimate the first two conditional moments by relating them to the past values of y_t. If r lags of y_t are chosen, then m_t and h_t can be estimated by using the formulae

$$\hat{m}_t = \sum_{\substack{i=1 \\ i \neq t}}^{T} \omega_{it} y_i, \text{ and } \hat{h}_t = \sum_{\substack{i=1 \\ i \neq t}}^{T} \omega_{it} y_i^2 - \hat{m}_t^2,$$

where ω_{it} are the kernel weights. For the Gaussian kernel

$$\omega_{it} = \frac{\kappa_{it}}{\sum_{\substack{i=1 \\ i \neq t}}^{T} \kappa_{it}},$$

where $\kappa_{it} = \exp\{-\tfrac{1}{2}\Sigma_{s=1}^{r} h_s^{-2}(y_{i-s} - y_{s-t})^2\}$, h_s being the bandwidth (for details see Pagan and Hong (1991), p 60). The empirical applications of Pagan and Hong (1991) showed the advantages of the non-parametric approach. They plotted the non-parametric $\hat{h}_t$ against y_{t-1} and found a high degree of non-linearity, which would be difficult to capture by simple parametric models. Cox non-nested tests for parametric versus non-parametric models also rejected the Engle, Lilien and Robins (1987) specification of the Arch-M model for excess holding yields on Treasury bills. The non-parametric method does require much larger data sets. Fortunately, we do have large data sets for economic and financial variables where Arch models are generally applied. Of course, results from non-parametric analysis are not as easily interpretable in terms of response coefficients as those obtained from a parametric method. However, at the very least, non-parametric methods can point out deficiencies in the existing parametric models and offer some guidance for modification.

Not much is known about the finite sample distribution of the different estimators discussed above. Engle, Hendry and Trumble (1985), Bollerslev and Wooldridge (1992) and Lumsdaine (1991b) reported some Monte Carlo results on the QMLE. For the Garch(1,1) model, Bollerslev and Wooldridge (1992) found the QMLE of α_1 to be biased upward, the QMLE of β_1 to be biased downward, and the overall estimate of $\alpha_1 + \beta_1$ to be slightly biased downward. This was consistent with the Arch(1) results of Engle, Hendry and Trumble (1985). Lumsdaine (1991b) reported that in small samples, QMLEs are not normally distributed and rather skewed. For example, she found $\hat{\beta}_1$ to be skewed to the right. This is similar to the downward bias observed by Bollerslev and Wooldridge (1992). Lumsdaine (1991b) also observed some pile-up for the estimator of β_1. Surprisingly, the pile-up was at the zero boundary. In most applications β_1 seems to take values above 0.5, so this may not be taken as a small sample effect.

Geweke (1988a,b, 1989) argued that a Bayesian approach, rather than the classical one, might be more suitable for estimating Arch models due to two distinct features of these models. First, as we noted earlier, some inequality restrictions must be imposed on the parameters to ensure positivity of the conditional variance h_t. In the classical estimation framework, these restrictions are somewhat impractical to impose. However, under the Bayesian paradigm, diffuse priors can incorporate these inequalities. Second, most of the time the main interest is not in the individual parameters, but rather in h_t, which is a function of the parameters. Exact posterior distributions and means of h_t can be obtained quite easily using Monte Carlo integration with importance sampling. The recent introduction of Gibbs sampling to the Bayesian econometrics literature might make the task even easier. Geweke's successful application to inflation and stock price data demonstrated the viability of the Bayesian approach for estimating Arch models. Unfortunately, other researchers have not pursued this approach.

Testing

The introduction of Arch to econometrics has led to many interesting testing problems. The basic test for the Arch model is testing for the presence of Arch – ie a test for the null hypothesis H_0: $\alpha_1 = \alpha_2 = \ldots = \alpha_q = 0$ in (3). Engle (1982) derived the LM statistic for testing H_0, which is computed as TR^2, where T is the number of observations and R^2 is the coefficient of multiple determination from the regression of $\hat{\varepsilon}_t^2$ on a constant and $\hat{\varepsilon}_{t-1}^2,\ldots,\hat{\varepsilon}_{t-q}^2$, $\hat{\varepsilon}_t$s being the OLS residuals from the model (2.1). Under H_0, the LM statistic asymptotically follows a χ_q^2 distribution. The structure of the test is the same as that of the Breusch and Pagan (1979) and Godfrey (1978) "static" heteroskedasticity test in the regression model. As noted in Bera and Lee (1993), this test is also a special case of the IM test applied to the regression model (1) with an AR(q) error structure and can be viewed as a test for randomness of the AR parameters $\phi_1,\ldots,\phi_q$.

A convenient way of looking at a general test for Arch is to give it a moment test interpretation, the moment condition being

$$E\left(\frac{\varepsilon_t^2}{\alpha_0} - 1 \middle| z_t\right) = 0, \tag{74}$$

where z_t is some vector of variables. For Engle's test, $z_t = (1,\varepsilon_{t-1}^2,\varepsilon_{t-2}^2,\ldots,\varepsilon_{t-q}^2)$. If the alternative model is Garch, as given in (7), then z_t would be specified as $z_t = (1,\varepsilon_{t-1}^2,\varepsilon_{t-2}^2,\ldots,\varepsilon_{t-q}^2,h_{t-1},\ldots,h_{t-p})$. When estimated under H_0, z_t becomes $z_t = (1,\hat{\varepsilon}_{t-1}^2,\hat{\varepsilon}_{t-2}^2,\ldots,\hat{\varepsilon}_{t-q}^2,\hat{\alpha}_0,\ldots,\hat{\alpha}_0)$. Therefore, the last p elements of $\hat{z}_t$ are redundant and a test for no conditional heteroskedasticity against an Arch(q) or an Garch(p,q) will be identical (see Bollerslev (1986) and Lee (1991)). For the Aarch model (18), $z_t = (1,\varepsilon_{t-1}^2,\varepsilon_{t-2}^2,\ldots,\varepsilon_{t-q}^2,\varepsilon_{t-1}\varepsilon_{t-2},\ldots,\varepsilon_{t-1}\varepsilon_{t-q})$ and the test is carried out by running a regression of $\hat{\varepsilon}_t^2$ on a constant and the squares and cross products of $\hat{\varepsilon}_{t-i}, i = 1,2,\ldots,q$ (see Bera and Lee (1993) and Bera, Higgins and Lee (1992,1996)).

A complication arises when H_0 is tested against an Arch-M model given in (69). The conditioning set z_t is the same as in the Arch case, namely $z_t = (1,\varepsilon_{t-1}^2,\varepsilon_{t-2}^2,\ldots,\varepsilon_{t-q}^2)$. However, we note that when the null hypothesis of no Arch is imposed on the model, the nuisance parameter δ is not identified. This renders the information matrix to be singular under H_0, and thereby invalidates the standard distribution of the LM test. However, note that for a given value of δ, say δ^*, the LM statistic is perfectly well behaved and has the form (see Domowitz and Hakkio 1985)

$$LM(\delta^*) = \frac{1}{2+\delta^{*2}}$$

$$\gamma' Z\left[Z'Z - \frac{\delta^{*2}}{2+\delta^*} Z'X(X'X)^{-1}X'Z\right]^{-1} Z'\gamma, \tag{75}$$

where γ is a $T \times 1$ vector with tth element $\gamma_t = (\hat{\varepsilon}_t^2/\hat{\alpha}_0 - 1) + (\delta^*\hat{\varepsilon}_t/\hat{\alpha}_0)$. The second component of this LM test is due to the non-block diagonality of the information matrix between the conditional mean and variance parameters. It is clear that when $\delta^* = 0$, $LM(\delta^*)$ reduces to Engle's test for Arch. Any arbitrary choice of δ will lead to a suboptimal test.

The same problem is faced for the Narch model (30). When $\alpha_1 = \alpha_2 = \cdots = \alpha_q = 0$ in (30), the parameter δ becomes unidentified. For a fixed value of δ, again say δ^*, the LM statistic $S(\delta^*)$ can be computed as TR^2, where the R^2 is obtained by a regression of $\hat{\varepsilon}_t^2$ on an intercept and

$$\frac{(\hat{\varepsilon}_{t-i}^2)^{\delta^*} - 1}{\delta^*}, i = 1,2,\ldots,q.$$

Therefore, in our conditional moment test framework

$$z_t = \left[1, \frac{(\varepsilon_{t-1}^2)^{\delta^*} - 1}{\delta^*}, \ldots, \frac{(\varepsilon_{t-q}^2)^{\delta^*} - 1}{\delta^*}\right],$$

which is the Box-Cox transformation of the lagged squared residuals. It is obvious that when $\delta^* = 1$, z_t reduces to the conditioning set of Engle's test. To overcome the non-identification of δ, Bera and Higgins (1992) followed the procedure of Davies (1977, 1987) and suggested basing the test on a critical region of the form

$$\left\{S = \sup_{\delta^*} S(\delta^*) > \omega\right\}, \tag{76}$$

where ω is a suitably chosen constant. However, unlike $S(\delta^*)$, S does not have an asymptotic χ_q^2 distribution under the null hypothesis. It is clear that if χ_q^2 critical values are used, the type-I error probability of the test will be too high. Davies (1987) provided an approximation to the p-value of the test as

$$\Pr\left[\chi_q^2 > S\right] + V\frac{e^{-S/2}S^{(p-1)/2}}{2^{p/2}\Gamma p/2}, \qquad (77)$$

where V measures the variation in $\sqrt{S(\delta)}$ over values of δ corresponding to different alternative hypotheses. This V can be estimated by

$$V = \sum_{j=1}^{R}\left|\sqrt{S(\delta_j)} - \sqrt{S(\delta_{j-1})}\right|,$$

where δ_0 and δ_R are the lower and upper bounds for δ, and $\delta_1,\delta_2,\ldots,\delta_{R-1}$ are the turning points of $\sqrt{S(\delta)}$. The second component in (77) can be viewed as the correction factor to the standard χ^2 p-value due to the scanning across a range of values of δ. Monte Carlo results and an empirical illustration presented in Bera and Higgins (1992) suggest that the above procedure is more powerful than the standard LM test for Arch when the true process has $\delta \neq 1$. Bera and Ra (1995) applied the same technique to the Arch-M model and obtained similar results. Hansen (1991) developed a simulation approach, which approximates the asymptotic null distribution of statistics that have the structure of S. Andrews and Ploberger (1992) also considered the general problem of testing when a nuisance parameter exists only under the alternative hypothesis and derived asymptotically optimal tests in terms of weighted average power in the class of all tests with a given significance level. Andrews (1993) used this latter approach for testing the presence of conditional heteroskedasticity with Garch(1,1) as the alternative model.

One drawback of using the LM test principle in testing H_0: $\alpha_1 = \alpha_2 = \ldots = \alpha_q = 0$ is that it does not take account of the one-sided nature of the alternative hypothesis – ie that the α_is cannot take negative values. We can expect some loss of power due to this omission, although the two-sided LM test will have the correct size asymptotically. Demos and Sentana (1991) and Lee and King (1991) suggested some one-sided versions of the LM test. Demos and Sentana's version of the one-sided LM test can be obtained as the sum of the squared t-ratios associated with the positive coefficients of the OLS regression of $\hat{\varepsilon}_t^2$ on $1,\hat{\varepsilon}_{t-1}^2,\ldots,\hat{\varepsilon}_{t-q}^2$, while Lee and King's version is based on the sum of the scores $\partial l(\theta)\partial/\alpha_i$, $i = 1,\ldots,q$. Lee and King (1991) carried out a Monte Carlo study of the finite sample power properties of the two-sided and their one-sided LM statistics, and found that the one-sided version of the test has better power.

In the moment condition (74), the term $\varepsilon_t^2/\alpha_0 - 1$ is essentially a result of the normality assumption. If we consider a general log-density function of the form (73), then $\varepsilon_t^2/\alpha_0 - 1$ could be replaced by $\phi(\varepsilon_t/\sqrt{\alpha_0})\cdot\varepsilon_t/\sqrt{\alpha_0} - 1$, where $\phi = -g'/g$ is the score function. For the normal distribution, $\phi(\varepsilon_t/\sqrt{\alpha_0}) = \varepsilon_t/\sqrt{\alpha_0}$. As in Engle and González-Rivera (1991), the score function can be estimated non-parametrically. As a general test for Arch under non-normality, we can think of running a regression of $\phi_t\varepsilon_t$ on z_t. In our discussion above of the TR^2-type test statistics, we noted various tests by changing the independent variable set z_t with the same dependent variable $\hat{\varepsilon}_t^2$. Now we can think of different dependent variables corresponding to various non-normal distributions. For example, if we assume a double exponential distribution, we need to run the regression of $|\hat{\varepsilon}_t|$ on z_t. This is known as the Glejser (1969) test for heteroskedasticity. In the context of testing static heteroskedasticity and autocorrelation in the regression model, Bera and Ng (1991) successfully used such non-parametric tests and these could easily be adapted to Arch models (see also Pagan and Pak (1991)).

Any general test for non-linear dependence may also detect conditional heteroskedasticity. The BDS test of Brock, Dechert and Scheinkman (1987) is frequently used in empirical work with Arch models (see for example Hsieh (1989); Gallant, Hsieh and Tauchen (1991) and Bera and Higgins (1992)). The BDS test measures non-linearity by the proportion of "m-histories", $y_t^m = \{y_t, y_{t+1},\ldots,y_{t+m-1}\}$, which lie in within a specified distance of one another. Hsieh (1989) and Brock, Hsieh and LeBaron (1991) demonstrated by Monte Carlo experiments that the BDS test has good power against Arch alternatives.

All of the above tests are only for detection of the possible presence of conditional heteroskedasticity and do not provide any information regarding the form of the conditional variance function h_t. As we mentioned earlier, correct specification of h_t is very important. The accuracy of forecast intervals depends on selecting an h_t which correctly relates the future variances to the current information set. Also Pagan and Sabau (1987a) showed that an incorrect functional form for h_t can result in inconsistent maximum likelihood estimates of the conditional mean parameters. This is more likely to happen when h_t is asymmetric or for the Arch-M models. Most of the empirical papers indirectly test for the correct specification of h_t and other accompanying assumptions by studying the properties of the standardised residuals $\hat{\varepsilon}_t^* = \hat{\varepsilon}_t/\hat{h}_t^{1/2}$. The basis of considering ε_t^* is that under our setup

$$\varepsilon_t^* = \frac{\varepsilon_t}{h_t^{1/2}} | \psi_{t-1} \sim N(0,1).$$

Therefore, if the model is correctly specified, $\hat{\varepsilon}_t^*$ should behave as white noise. The various diagnostic checks that are commonly used include testing the normality of $\hat{\varepsilon}_t^*$ and considering the sample autocorrelations of $\hat{\varepsilon}_t^*$. These diagnostics are helpful in detecting certain misspecifications, but we cannot expect them to be very powerful tests.

Using the Newey (1985) and Tauchen (1985) principle of moment tests, Pagan and Sabau (1987b) suggested a consistency test for Arch models. The test is based on the moment condition $E[h_t(\varepsilon_t^2 - h_t)] = 0$. Therefore, the test could be carried out by regressing $\hat{\varepsilon}_t^2 - \hat{h}_t$ on a constant and $\hat{h}_t$, and testing whether the coefficient of $\hat{h}_t$ is zero. However, if h_t is symmetric and the model is not of the Arch-M type, then misspecificaton of h_t will not lead to inconsistency and consequently the test will not have any power.

In most Arch models, misspecification may not lead to inconsistency, but it might make likelihood-based inference invalid. In that case, misspecification can be tested through the IM equality, ie by testing $A = B$, which is defined in equation (72). Bera and Zuo (1996) suggested such a test. One component of the IM test can be calculated by running a regression of $\hat{\varepsilon}_t^{*4} - 6\hat{\varepsilon}_t^{*2} + 3$ on the cross products of $\hat{\varepsilon}_{t-i}^{*2}$, where $\hat{\varepsilon}_t^* = \hat{\varepsilon}_t/\hat{h}_t^{1/2}$ is as above. This is essentially a test for heterokurtosis, and it can also be viewed as a test for randomness of the parameters in the specified h_t.

Another simple test for an estimated Arch model like (3) is derived in Higgins and Bera (1992). The relevant null hypothesis for this is H_0: $\delta = 1$ in the Narch model (30). The LM statistic for testing H_0 can be calculated by running a regression of $\hat{\varepsilon}_t^2$ on z_t, where

$$z_t = \left(1, \hat{\varepsilon}_{t-1}^2, \ldots, \hat{\varepsilon}_{t-q}^2, \pi_t - \hat{h}_t \log\left(\hat{h}_t\right)\right)$$

with

$$\pi_t = \sum_{i=1}^{q} \hat{\alpha}_i \hat{\varepsilon}_{t-i}^2 \log\left(\hat{\varepsilon}_{t-i}^2\right).$$

The test can be viewed as a diagnostic check of the adequacy of the Arch model (3) after it has been estimated. Starting from a different alternative model, Hall (1990) derived a simple LM test for an estimated Arch model. The alternative distribution for his heteroskedastic normal model is that the distribution is a member of the family with semiparametric probability density functions considered by Gallant and Tauchen (1989). His test is based on the possible correlations of $\hat{\varepsilon}_t/\hat{h}_t$ and $\hat{\varepsilon}_t^2/\hat{h}_t^2$ with the information set. Simulation results reported in his paper indicate that the LM test, which uses all the information under the null hypothesis, has good finite sample properties in moderate to large samples.

Engle and Ng (1991) proposed a battery of tests designed to detect misspecification of a maintained conditional variance function. Let S_t^- be a dummy variable that takes the value 1 when ε_{t-1} is negative, and zero otherwise. Similarly, let S_t^+ be a dummy variable that takes the value 1 when ε_{t-1} positive, and zero otherwise. Engle and Ng suggested standardising the residual with the null h_t, regressing $\hat{\varepsilon}_t^{*2}$ on an intercept, S_t^-, $S_t^-\hat{\varepsilon}_{t-1}$ and $S_t^+\hat{\varepsilon}_{t-1}$ and testing that the coefficients on the three constructed regressors are zero using an F or TR^2 statistic. The first regressor, S_t^-, represents the *sign bias test*, which is intended to detect an asymmetric influence by the lagged negative and positive errors on the conditional variance, which may not be incorporated in the conditional variance function specified under the null hypothesis. The second regressor, $S_t^-\hat{\varepsilon}_{t-1}$, should be significant if the impact of large negative errors versus small negative errors on the conditional variance is different from the impact implied by the null h_t. This component of the regression is called the *negative size bias test*. The third regressor, $S_t^+\hat{\varepsilon}_{t-1}$, represents the *positive size bias test* and should detect different impacts of large positive errors versus small positive errors on the conditional variance. Engle and Ng point out that the components of the test can be conducted individually if a particular form of misspecification is suspected.

The introduction of conditional heteroskedasticity in econometrics also leads to another interesting problem. Diebold (1986b) demonstrated that the presence of Arch invalidates the standard asymptotic distribution theory of the sample autocorrelations, and hence of the Box-Pierce and Box-Ljung test statistics for serial correlation. For simplicity, consider the test for $\phi_1 = 0$ in

$$\begin{aligned} y_t &= x_t\xi + \varepsilon_t \\ \varepsilon_t &= \phi_1\varepsilon_{t-1} + u_t, \end{aligned} \tag{78}$$

where $u_t \sim (0, \sigma_u^2)$ and $\text{Var}(\varepsilon_t | \psi_{t-1}) = \alpha_0 + \alpha_1\varepsilon_{t-1}^2$. As we noted, having Arch of the above form is equivalent to ϕ_1 being random or u_t being heteroskedastic. Then the problem is equivalent to testing for the significance of a regression coefficient under heteroskedasticity. We know that the use of White's (1980) consistent estimator for the variance-covariance matrix provides asymptotically valid inference in the presence of an unknown form of heteroskedasticity. Therefore, a robust way to test $\phi_1 = 0$ is to run a regression of the OLS residuals $\hat{\varepsilon}_t$ on x_t and $\hat{\varepsilon}_{t-1}$, and test the significance of the coefficient of $\hat{\varepsilon}_{t-1}$ using White's standard error. Wooldridge (1990) suggested exactly this procedure for testing autocorrelation in the presence of Arch (see also Davidson and MacKinnon (1985), Bollerslev and Wooldridge (1992) and MacKinnon (1992)). Note that the standard LM approach for testing first order autocorrelation is to regress $\hat{\varepsilon}_t$ on x_t and $\hat{\varepsilon}_{t-1}$ and use a TR^2 statistic. The robust procedure involves two regressions:

❑ Run $\hat{\varepsilon}_{t-1}$ on x_t and save the residuals as $\tilde{\varepsilon}_{t-1}$.
❑ Compute TR^2 from running 1 on $\hat{\varepsilon}_t\tilde{\varepsilon}_{t-1}$.

The statistic TR^2 asymptotically follows a χ^2_1 distribution under the null hypothesis of no serial correlation. Steps 1. and 2. are equivalent to using White's consistent variance-covariance matrix estimator as mentioned above. Monte Carlo results reported in Bollerslev and Wooldridge (1992) indicate that the size of the robust version of the LM test is much closer to the nominal size than the size of the standard LM test. Bera, Higgins and Lee (1992, 1996) derived LM tests for autocorrelation that take account of specific forms of Arch disturbances. Of course, validity of such tests depend on the correct specification of the Arch process. In practice, the tests could be very useful by specifying different forms of conditional heteroskedasticity and then testing for serial correlation. Being fully parametric, this test could be expected to have higher power when h_t is specified correctly.

Epilogue

Research on modelling conditional first moments started many decades ago, and this field is still very active. The problems currently being investigated, just to name a few, are structural change, different kinds of non-linearities, cointegration and finite sample properties of estimators and test statistics. It is safe to say that most of the problems encountered in modelling the first moment also transmits to Arch, ie conditional second moment modelling. In this survey paper, we have provided a brief account of these problems. For years to come, researchers will be occupied with topics like structural change in Arch, co-persistence, asymptotic and finite sample statistical inference for Arch, and procedures robust in the presence of Arch. We have also noted that Arch models have their own unique problems, which are not present in modelling the conditional mean. Gradually, we will also see more rigorous economic foundations for Arch models than those currently available. The frontiers of Arch will therefore keep on moving further, though possibly not at the spectacular rate we observed in its first decade of existence. The success of Arch might even tempt researchers to model higher order moments – the third and fourth – in a systematic way. From that we might learn more about the behaviour of speculative prices, and economic variables in general, a tradition started by Louis Bachelier almost a century ago.

Appendix

GLOSSARY

Aarch: Augmented autoregressive conditional heteroskedasticity.

ARCD: Autoregressive conditional density.

Arch: Autoregressive conditional heteroskedasticity.

Arch-M: Autoregressive conditional heteroskedasticity in the mean.

Egarch: Exponential autoregressive conditional heteroskedasticity.

Garch: Generalised autoregressive conditional heteroskedasticity.

Igarch: Integrated generalised autoregressive conditional heteroskedasticity.

Narch: Non-linear autoregressive conditional heteroskedasticity.

PNP Arch: Partially non-parametric autoregressive conditional heteroskedasticity.

Qarch: Quadratic autoregressive conditional heteroskedasticity.

Qtarch: Qualitative threshold autoregressive conditional heteroskedasticity.

Tarch: Threshold autoregressive conditional heteroskedasticity

BIBLIOGRAPHY

Andel, J., 1976, "Autoregressive series with random parameters", *Mathematische Operationsforschung und Statistik, Series Statistics* 7, 736-41.

Andrews, D.W.K., 1993, "An introduction to econometric applications opf empirical process theory for dependent random variables, *Economic Reviews* 12, pp. 183-216.

Andrews, D.W.K., and W. Ploberger, 1992, "Optimal tests when a nuisance parameter is present only under the alternative", Cowles Foundation Discussion Paper, No 1015.

Baba, Y., Engle, R.F., Kraft, D.F. and Kroner, K. F., 1990, "Multivariate simultaneous generalized Arch", Mimeo, Department of Economics, University of California, San Diego.

Bachelier, L., 1900, Théorie de la spéculation, *Annales de l'Ecole Normale Supérieure* 17, pp. 21-86.

Baillie, R.T., and T. Bollerslev, 1989, "The message in daily exchange rates: a conditional variance tale", *Journal of Business and Economic Statistics*, 7, pp. 297-305.

Baillie, R.T., and T. Bollerslev, 1990, "A multivariate generalized Arch approach to modelling risk premia in forward foreign exchange rate markets", *Journal of International Money and Finance*, 16, pp. 109-24.

Baillie, R.T., and T. Bollerslev, 1992, "Prediction in dynamic models with time-dependent conditional variances", *Journal of Econometrics*, 52, pp. 91-113.

Baillie, R. T., and R. J. Myers, 1991, "Bivariate Garch estimation of optimal commodity futures hedge", *Journal of Applied Econometrics*, 16, pp. 109-24.

Bekaert, G., 1992, "The time-variation of expected returns and volatility in foreign exchange markets", Mimeo, Northwestern University.

Bera, A.K., P. Garcia and J.-S. Roh, 1991, "Estimation of time-varying hedge ratios for agricultural commodities: Bgarch and random coefficient approaches", Mimeo, Department of Economics, University of Illinois at Urbana-Champaign.

Bera, A.K. and M.L. Higgins, 1992, "A test for conditional heteroskedasticity in time series models", *Journal of Time Series Analysis*, 13, pp. 501-19.

Bera, A.K. and M.L. Higgins, 1997, "Arch and bilinearity as competing models for nonlinear dependence", *Journal of Business and Economic Statistics*, 15, pp. 43-50.

Bera, A.K., M.L. Higgins, and S. Lee, 1992, "Interaction between autocorrelation and conditional heteroskedasticity: a random coefficient approach", *Journal of Business and Economic Statistics*, 10, pp. 133-42.

Bera, A.K., and S-W. Kim, 1998, "Testing constancy of correlation with an application to international equity returns", paper presented at the Econometric Society winter meeting, January 1998, Chicago.

Bera, A.K., M.L. Higgins, and S. Lee, 1996, "On the formulation of a general structure for conditional heteroskedasticity", *Sankhya* 58, pp. 199-220.

Bera, A.K. and S. Lee, 1993, "Information matrix test, parameter heterogeneity and Arch: a synthesis", *Review of Economic Studies* 60, pp. 229-40.

Bera, A.K. and P.T. Ng, 1991, "Robust tests for heteroskedasticity and autocorrelation using score functions", Mimeo, Department of Economics, University of Illinois at Urbana-Champaign.

Bera, A.K. and S.S. Ra, 1995, "A test for conditional heteroskedasticity within the Arch-M model", *Econometric Reviews* 14, pp. 473-85.

Bera, A. K. and J.-S. Roh, 1991, "A moment test of the constancy of the constancy of the correlation coefficient in the bivariate Garch model", Mimeo, Department of Economics, University of Illinois at Urbana-Champaign.

Bera, A.K. and X. Zuo, 1996, "Specification test for a linear regression model with Arch process", *Journal of Statistical Planning and Inference* 50, pp. 283-308.

Berndt, E.K., B.H. Hall, R.E. Hall and J. Hausman, 1974, "Estimation and inference in nonlinear structural models", *Annals of Economic and Social Measurement* 4, pp. 653-65.

Bollerslev, T., 1986, "A Generalized Autoregressive Conditional Heteroskedasticity", *Journal of Econometrics* 31, pp. 307-27.

Bollerslev, T., 1987, "A conditionally heteroskedastic time series model for speculative prices and rates of return", *Review of Economics and Statistics* 69, pp. 542-7.

Bollerslev, T., 1988, "On the correlation structure of the generalized autoregressive conditional heteroskedastic process". *Journal of Time Series Analysis* 9, pp. 121-31.

Bollerslev, T., 1990, "Modelling the coherence in short-run nominal exchange rates: a multivariate generalized Arch approach", *Review of Economics and Statistics* 72, pp. 498-505.

Bollerslev, T., and R. F. Engle, 1989, "Common persistence in conditional variances", *Econometrica* 61, pp. 167-86.

Bollerslev, T., and R. J. Hodrick, 1992, "Financial market efficiency tests", Kellogg Graduate School of Management Working Paper, No 132.

Bollerslev, T., and J. M. Wooldridge, 1992, "Quasi-maximum likelihood estimation and inference in dynamic models with time-varying covariances", *Econometric Reviews* 11, pp. 143-79.

Bollerslev, T., R. Y. Chou and K. F. Kroner, 1992, "Arch modelling in finance: a review of the theory and empirical evidence", *Journal of Econometrics* 52, pp. 5-59; reprinted as Chapter 2 of the present volume.

Bollerslev, T., R. F. Engle and J. M. Wooldridge, 1988, "A capital asset pricing model with time-varying covariances", *Journal of Political Economy* 96, pp. 116-131.

Bougerol, P., and N. Picard, 1992, "Stationarity of Garch processes and of some nonnegative time series", *Journal of Econometrics* 52, pp. 115-27.

Box, G., and G. Jenkins, 1976, *Time Series Analysis, Forecasting and Control,* revised edition, Holden-Day, San Francisco.

Breusch, T.S., and A.R. Pagan, 1979, "A simple test for heteroscedasticity and random coefficient variation", *Econometrica,* vol 47, pp. 239-53.

Brock, W., W.D. Dechert, and J. Scheinkman, 1987, "A test for independence based on the correlation dimension", Mimeo, University of Wisconsin-Madison.

Brock, W., D.A. Hsieh and B. LeBaron, 1991, *Nonlinear Dynamics, Chaos and Instability,* MIT Press, Cambridge.

Chesher, A.D. 1984, "Testing for neglected heterogeneity", *Econometrica* 52, pp. 865-71.

Cheung, Y-W. and P. Pauly, 1990, "Random coefficient modelling of conditionally heteroskedastic processes: short run exchange rate dynamics". Paper presented at the International Conference on Arch Models, June 1990, Paris.

Clark, P. K., 1973, "A subordinated stochastic process model with finite variance for speculative prices", *Econometrica* 41, pp. 135-156.

Davidson, R. and J.G. MacKinnon 1985, "Heteroskedasticity-robust tests in regression directions", *Annales de INSEE* 59/60, pp. 183-218.

Davies, R.B., 1977, "Hypothesis testing when a nuisance parameter is present only under the alternative", *Biometrika* 64, pp. 247-54.

Davies, R.B., 1987, "Hypothesis testing when a nuisance parameter is present only under the alternative", *Biometrika* 74, pp. 33-43.

Demos, A., and E. Sentana, 1991, "Testing for Garch effects: a one-sided approach", Mimeo, Financial Market Group, London School of Economics.

Diebold, F.X, 1986a, "Modelling the persistences of conditional variances: a comment", *Econometric Reviews* 5, pp. 51-6.

Diebold, F.X, 1986b, "Testing for serial correlation in the presence of heteroskedasticity", *Proceedings of the American Statistical Association, Business and Economic Statistics Section*, pp. 323-8.

Diebold, F.X, 1988, *Empirical modelling of exchange rate dynamics*, Springer Verlag, New York.

Diebold, F.X., and J.A. Nason, 1990, "Non-parametric exchange rate prediction", *Journal of International Economics* 28, pp. 315-32.

Diebold, F. X., and M. Nerlove, 1989, "The dynamics of exchange rate volatility: a multivariate latent factor Arch model", *Journal of Applied Econometrics* 4, pp. 1-21.

Domowitz, I., and C.S. Hakkio, 1985, "Conditional variance and the risk premium in the foreign exchange market", *Journal of International Economics* 19, pp. 47-66.

Drost, F.C. and T.E. Nijman, 1993, "Temporal aggregation of Garch processes", *Econometrica* 61, pp. 909-27.

Duffee, G.R., 1992, "Reexamining the relationship between stock returns and stock return volatility", Federal Reserve Board Finance and Economics Discussion Series, No 191.

Engle, R.F., 1982, "Autoregressive conditional heteroscedasticity with estimates of the variance of UK inflation", *Econometrica* 50, pp. 987-1008.

Engle, R.F., 1983, "Estimates of the variance of US inflation based upon the Arch model", *Journal of Money, Credit, and Banking* 15, pp. 286-301.

Engle, R.F., 1987, "Multivariate Arch with factor structures - cointegration in variance", Discussion paper no 87-27, University of California San Diego.

Engle, R.F. and T. Bollerslev, 1986, "Modelling the persistence of conditional variances", *Econometric Reviews* 5, pp. 1-87.

Engle, R.F. and G. González-Rivera, 1991, "Semiparametric Arch models", *Journal of Business and Economic Statistics* 9, pp 345-359.

Engle, R.F. and D. Kraft, 1983, "Multiperiod forecast error variances of inflation estimated from Arch models", in A. Zellner (ed.), *Applied Time Series Analysis of Economic Data,* Bureau of the Census, Washington DC.

Engle, R.F. and V.K. Ng, 1991, "Measuring and testing the impact of news on volatility", Mimeo, Department of Economics, University of California San Diego.

Engle, R.F., C.W.J. Granger and D. Kraft, 1984, "Combining competing forecasts of inflation using a bivariate Arch model", *Journal of Economic Dynamics and Control* 8, pp. 151-65.

Engle, R.F., D. Hendry and D. Trumble, 1985, "Small-sample properties of Arch estimates and tests", *Canadian Journal of Economics* 18, pp. 66-93.

Engle, R.F., T. Ito and W-L. Lin, 1990, "Meteor showers or heat waves? Heteroskedastic intra-daily volatility in the foreign exchange market", *Econometrica* 58, pp.525-42.

Engle, R.F., D.M. Lilien and R.P. Robins, 1987, "Estimating time varying risk premia in the term structure: the Arch-M model", *Econometrica* 55, pp. 391-407.

Engle, R.F., V. Ng and M. Rothschild, 1990, "Asset pricing with a FACTOR-ARCH covariance structure: empirical estimates for treasury bills", *Journal of Econometrics* 45, pp. 213-37.

French, K.R., G.W. Schwert, and R.F. Stambaugh, 1987, "Expected stock returns and volatility", *Journal of Financial Economics* 19, pp. 3-30.

Gallant, R., 1982, "Unbiased determination of production technologies", *Journal of Econometrics* 20, pp. 285-323.

Gallant, A.R., and G. Tauchen, 1989, "Seminonparametric estimation of conditionally constrained heterogeneous processes: asset pricing applications", *Econometrica* 57, pp. 1091-129.

Gallant, A. R., D. A. Hsieh and G. Tauchen, 1991, "On fitting a recalcitrant series: the pound/dollar exchange rate, 1974-1983", in Barnett, W. A., J. Powell. and G. Tauchen (eds) *Non-parametric and Semiparametric Methods in Econometrics and Statistics,* Cambridge University Press, Cambridge.

Geweke, J., 1986, "Modelling the persistence of conditional variances: comment", *Econometric Reviews* 5, pp. 57-61.

Geweke, J., 1988a, "Comments on Poirier: operational Bayesian methods in econometrics", *Journal of Economic Perspectives* 2, pp. 159-66.

Geweke, J., 1988b, "Exact inference in models with autoregressive conditional heteroskedasticity", in Berndt, E., H. White, and W. Barnett (eds) *Dynamic Econometric Modeling,* Cambridge University Press, Cambridge.

Geweke, J., 1989, "Exact predictive densities in linear models with Arch disturbances", *Journal of Econometrics* 44, pp. 307-25.

Glejser, H. 1969, "A new test for heteroskedasticity", *Journal of the American Statistical Association* 64, pp. 316-23.

Glosten, L.R., R. Jagannathan, and D. Runkle, 1991, "Relationship between the expected value and the volatility of the nominal excess return on stocks", Mimeo, Northwestern University.

Godfrey, L.G. 1978, "Testing for multiplicative heteroskedasticity", *Journal of Econometrics* 8, pp. 227-36.

Gourieroux, C. and A. Monfort 1992, "Qualitative threshold ARCH models", *Journal of Econometrics* 52, pp. 159-99.

Granger, C.W.J., and A.P. Andersen, 1978, *An Introduction to Bilinear Time Series Models,* Vandenhoeck & Ruprecht, Göttingen.

Granger, C.W.J., R.P. Robins and R.F. Engle, 1984, *Wholesale and Retail Prices: Bivariate Time Series Modelling with Forecastable Error Variances,* in D. A. Belsley and E. Kuh (eds), Model Reliability, MIT Press, Cambridge.

Hall, A., 1990, "Lagrange multiplier tests for normality against semiparametric alternatives", *Journal of Business and Economic Statistics* 8, pp. 417-26.

Hansen, B.E., 1991, "Inference when a Nuisance Parameter is not Identified under the Null Hypothesis", Rochester Center for Economic Research, Working Paper, No 296.

Hansen, B.E., 1992, "Autoregressive Conditional Density Estimation", Rochester Center for Economic Research Working Paper, No 332.

Hansen, L.P., 1982, "Large sample properties of the method of moment estimators", *Econometrica* 50, pp. 1029-54.

Harvey, A., E. Ruiz and E. Sentana, 1992, "Unobserved component time series models with Arch disturbances", *Journal of Econometrics* 52, pp. 129-57.

Higgins, M.L., and A.K. Bera, 1989, "A joint test for Arch and bilinearity in the regression model", *Econometric Reviews* 7, pp. 171-81.

Higgins, M.L., and A.K. Bera, 1992, "A class of nonlinear ARCH models", *International Economic Review* 33, pp.137-58.

Higgins, M.L., and S. Majin, 1992, "Measuring the volatility of the ex ante real interest rate: a structural Arch approach", Mimeo, University of Wisconsin-Milwaukee.

Hong, P.Y., 1991, "The autocorrelation structure for the Garch-M process", *Economic Letters* 37, pp. 129-32.

Hsieh, D.A., 1988, "The statistical properties of daily foreign exchange rates: 1974-1983", *Journal of International Economics* 24, pp. 129-45.

Hsieh, D.A.,1989, "Testing for nonlinear dependence in daily foreign exchange rate changes", *Journal of Business* 62, pp.339-68.

Kim, C. M., 1989, "Volatility effect on time series behaviour of exchange rate changes", Working Paper, Korea Institute for International Economic Policy.

Klien, B., 1977. "The demand for quality-adjusted cash balances: price uncertainty in the US demand for money function", *Journal of Political Economy* 85, pp. 692-715.

Koedijk, K.G., P. A. Stork and C.G. De Vries, 1992, "Conditional heteroskedasticity, realignments and the European monetary system", Mimeo, Katholieke Universiteit Leuven.

Kroner, K. F., 1988, "Estimating and testing for factor Arch", Mimeo, University of Arizona.

Kroner, K.F., and S. Claessens, 1991, "Optimal currency composition of external debt: applications to Indonesia and Turkey", *Journal of International Money and Finance* 10, pp. 131-148.

Kroner, K. F., and J. Sultan, 1991, "Exchange rate volatility and time varying hedge ratios", in Rhee, S. G. and R. P. Change (eds), Pacific-Basin Capital Markets Research, Vol. II, North-Holland, Amsterdam.

Lamoureux, G.C., and W.D. Lastrapes, 1990a, "Heteroskedasticity in stock return data: volume versus Garch effects", *The Journal of Finance* 45, pp. 221-29.

Lamoureux, G.C., and W. D. Lastrapes, 1990b, "Persistence in variance, structural change, and the Garch model", *Journal of Business Economic Statistics* 8, pp. 225-34.

LeBaron, B., 1992, Some relations between volatility and serial correlations in stock market returns, *Journal of Business* 65, pp. 199-219.

Lee, J. H., and M.L. King, 1991, "A locally most mean powerful based score test for Arch and Garch regression disturbances", Working Paper, No 9/91, Department of Economics, Monash University.

Lee, S-W., 1991, "Asymptotic properties of the maximum likelihood estimator of the Garch-M and Igarch-M models", Mimeo, Department of Economics, University of Rochester.

Lee, S-W., and B.E. Hansen, 1991, "Asymptotic properties of the maximum likelihood estimator and test of the stability of parameters of the Garch and Igarch models", Mimeo, Department of Economics, University of Rochester.

Lee, T.K.Y., and Tse, Y.K., 1991, "Term structure of interest rates in the Singapore Asian dollar market", *Journal of Applied Econometrics* 6, pp. 143-152.

Lin, W-L. 1992, "Alternative estimators for factor Garch models - a Monte Carlo comparison", *Journal of Applied Econometrics* 7, pp. 259-79.

Lumsdaine, R.L., 1991a, "Asymptotic properties of the quasi-maximum likelihood estimator in Garch(1,1) and IGarch(1,1) models", Mimeo, Department of Economics, Princeton University.

Lumsdaine, R. L., 1991b, "Finite sample properties of the maximum likelihood estimator in Garch(1,1) and Igarch(1,1) models: a Monte Carlo investigation". Mimeo, Department of Economics, Princeton University.

MacKinnon, J.G., 1992, "Model specification tests and artificial regression", *Journal of Economic Literature* 30, pp. 102-46.

Mandelbrot, B., 1963a, "The variation of certain speculative prices", *Journal of Business* 36, pp. 394-419.

Mandelbrot, B., 1963b, "New methods in statistical economics", *Journal of Political Economy* 71, pp. 421-40.

Mandelbrot, B., 1967, "The variation of some other speculative prices", *Journal of Business* 40, pp. 393-413.

McCurdy, T.H., and I. Morgan, 1988, "Testing the martingale hypothesis in Deutschemark futures with models specifying the form of the heteroskedasticity", *Journal of Applied Econometrics* 3, pp. 187-202.

McLeod, A.I., and W.K. Li, 1983, "Diagnostic checking ARMA time series models using squared-residual autocorrelations", *Journal of Time Series Analysis* 4, pp. 269-73.

Milhoj, A., 1985, "The moment structure of Arch processes", *Scandinavian Journal of Statistics* 12, pp. 281-92.

Milhoj, A., 1987a, "A multiplicative parameterization of Arch models". Research Report, No 101, Institute of Statistics, University of Copenhagen.

Milhoj, A., 1987b, "A conditional variance model for daily observations of an exchange rate", *Journal of Business and Economic Statistics* 5, pp. 99-103.

Mizrach, B., 1990, "Learning and conditional heteroskedasticity in asset returns", Mimeo, Department of Finance, The Wharton School, University of Pennsylvania.

Nelson, D.B., 1990a, "Stationarity and persistence in the Garch(1,1) model", *Econometric Theory* 6, pp. 318-34.

Nelson, D.B., 1990b, "Arch models as diffusion approximations", *Journal of Econometrics* 45, pp. 7-38.

Nelson, D.B., 1991, "Conditional heteroskedasticity in asset returns: a new approach", *Econometrica* 59, pp. 347-70.

Nelson, D.B., and C.Q. Cao, 1992, "Inequality constraints in the univariate Garch model", *Journal of Business and Economic Statistics* 10, pp. 229-35.

Newey, W., 1985, "Maximum likelihood specification testing and conditional moment tests", *Econometrica* 53, pp. 1047-70.

Ng, V.K. and S.C. Pirrong, 1992, "Disequilibrium adjustment, volatility, and price discovery in spot and futures markets", Mimeo, University of Michigan.

Ng, V.K., R.F. Engle and M. Rothschild, 1992 "A multi-dynamic-factor model for stock returns", *Journal of Econometrics* 52, pp. 245-66.

Nicholls, D.F. and B.G. Quinn 1982, *Random Coefficient Autoregressive Models: An Introduction*, Springer-Verlag, New York.

Oedegaard, B. A., 1991, "Empirical tests of changes in autocorrelation of stock index returns", Mimeo, Graduate School of Industrial Administration, Carnegie Mellon University.

Pagan, A.R., and Y.S. Hong, 1991, "Non-parametric estimation and the risk premium", in Barnett, W. A., J. Powell and G. Tauchen (eds) *Non-parametric and Semiparametric*

Methods in Econometrics and Statistics, Cambridge University Press, Cambridge.

Pagan, A.R., and Y. Pak, 1991, "Tests for heteroskedasticity", Mimeo, Department of Economics, University of Rochester.

Pagan, A.R., and H. Sabau, 1987a, "On the inconsistency of the MLE in certain heteroskedastic regression models", Mimeo, Department of Economics, University of Rochester.

Pagan, A.R., and H. Sabau, 1987b, "Consistency tests for heteroskedastic and risk models", Mimeo, Department of Economics, University of Rochester.

Pagan, A.R., and G.W. Schwert, 1990, "Alternative models for conditional stock volatility", *Journal of Econometrics* 45, pp. 267–90.

Pagan, A.R., and A. Ullah, 1988, "The econometric analysis of models with risk terms", *Journal of Applied Econometrics* 3, pp 87–105.

Pantula, S.G., 1986, "Modelling the persistence of conditional variances: comment", *Econometric Reviews* 5, pp. 79–97.

Pantula, S.G., 1988, "Estimation of autoregressive models with Arch errors", *Sankhya: The Indian Journal of Statistics* 50, Series B, pp. 119–38.

Ray, D., 1983, "On the autoregressive model with random coefficients", *Calcutta Statistical Association Bulletin* 32, pp. 135–42.

Rich, R.W., J. Raymond and J. S. Butler, 1991, "Generalized instrumental variables estimation of autoregressive conditional heteroskedastic models", *Economics Letters* 35, pp. 179–85.

Sabau, H.C.L., 1987, "The structure of GMM and ML estimators in conditionally heteroskedastic models", Working Paper No 153, Faculty of Economics, Australian National University.

Sabau, H.C.L., 1988, "Some Theoretical Aspects of Econometric Inference with Heteroskedastic Models", Unpublished Ph.D. dissertation, Australian National University.

Sentana, E., 1991, "Quadratic Arch models: a potential reinterpretation of Arch models", Mimeo, Department of Economics and Financial Markets Group, London School of Economics.

Sentana, E., and S. Wadhwani, 1991, "Feedback traders and stock returns autocorrelations: evidence from a century of daily data", *Economic Journal* 58, pp. 547–63.

Spanos, A., 1991, "A parametric approach to dynamic heteroskedasticity: the Student's t and related models", Mimeo, Department of Economics, Virginia Polytechnic Institute and State University.

Stock, J.H., 1988, "Estimating continuous-time processes subject to time deformation", *Journal of the American Statistical Association* 83, pp. 77–85.

Tauchen, G., 1985, "Diagnostic testing and evaluation of maximum likelihood models", *Journal of Econometrics* 30, pp. 415–43.

Tauchen, G., and M. Pitts, 1983, "The price variability-volume relationship on speculative markets", *Econometrica* 51, pp.485–505.

Taylor, S.J., 1986, *Modelling Financial Time Series,* John Wiley, Chichester.

Taylor, S.J., 1990, "Modelling stochastic volatility: a review and comparative study", *Mathematical Finance* 4, 2 pp. 183–204; reprinted as Chapter 3 of the present volume.

Tong, H., 1990, *Non-linear Time Series, Dynamical System Approach.* Clarendon Press, Oxford.

Tsay, R.S., 1987, "Conditional heteroscedastic time series models", *Journal of the American Statistical Association* 82, pp. 590–604.

Weiss, A.A., 1986a, "Asymptotic theory for Arch models: estimation and testing". *Econometric Theory* 2, pp. 107–31.

Weiss, A.A., 1986b, "Arch and bilinear time series models: comparison and combination", *Journal of Business and Economic Statistics* 4, pp. 59–70.

White, H., 1980, "A heteroscedastic-consistent covariance matrix and a direct test for heteroscedasticity", *Econometrica* 48, pp. 421–48.

White, H., 1982, "Maximum likelihood estimation of misspecified models", *Econometrica* 50, pp. 1–25.

Wooldridge, J.M., 1990, "A unified approach to robust regression-based specification tests", *Econometric Theory* 6, pp. 17–43.

Zakoian, J.-M., 1990, "Threshold heteroskedastic model", Mimeo, INSEE, Paris.

2

ARCH Modelling in Finance

A review of the theory and empirical evidence*

Tim Bollerslev, Ray Y. Chou and Kenneth F. Kroner
University of Virginia; Academica Sinica; Barclays Global Investors

Although volatility clustering has a long history as a salient empirical regularity characterising high-frequency speculative prices, it was not until recently that applied researchers in finance have recognised the importance of explicitly modelling time-varying second-order moments. Instrumental in most of these empirical studies has been the Autoregressive Conditional Heteroskedasticity (Arch) model introduced by Engle (1982). This paper contains an overview of some of the developments in the formulation of Arch models and a survey of the numerous empirical applications using financial data. Several suggestions for future research, including the implementation and tests of competing asset pricing theories, market microstructure models, information transmission mechanisms, dynamic hedging strategies, and the pricing of derivative assets, are also discussed.

Uncertainty is central to much of modern finance theory. According to most asset pricing theories the risk premium is determined by the covariance between the future return on the asset and one or more benchmark portfolios; for example, the market portfolio or the growth rate in consumption. In option pricing the uncertainty associated with the future price of the underlying asset is the most important determinant in the pricing function. The construction of hedge portfolios is another example where the conditional future variances and covariances among the different assets involved play an important role.

While it has been recognised for quite some time that the uncertainty of speculative prices, as measured by the variances and covariances, are changing through time (see, for example, Mandelbrot (1963) and Fama (1965)), it was not until recently that applied researchers in financial and monetary economics have started explicitly modelling time variation in second- or higher-order moments. One of the most prominent tools that has emerged for characterising such changing variances is the Autoregressive Conditional Heteroskedasticity (Arch) model of Engle (1982) and its various extensions. Since the introduction of the Arch model several hundred research papers applying this modelling strategy to financial time series data have already appeared. In this paper we survey those contributions that we consider to be the most important and promising

* *This paper was first published in the* Journal of Econometrics, *Vol. 52, (1992). It is reprinted with permission of Elsevier Science. An earlier version by T. Bollerslev, R. Chou, N. Jayaraman and K. Kroner was entitled: "ARCH Modeling in Finance: A Selective Review of the Theory and Empirical Evidence, with Suggestions for Future Research". The authors would like to thank colleagues who helped supply the references cited in this survey, especially Buz Brock, John Campbell, Ray DeGennaro, Frank Diebold, Rob Engle, Martin Evans, Gikas Hardouvelis, Ravi Jagannathan, Narayanan Jayaraman, J. Huston McCulloch, Tom McCurdy, Dan Nelson, Adrian Pagan, Peter Robinson, Bill Schwert, Stephen Taylor, participants at the Conference on Statistical Models of Financial Volatility at UCSD on April 6–7, 1990, and an anonymous referee for very helpful and detailed comments on an earlier draft. Tim Bollerslev, Ray Chou, and Ken Kroner would like to acknowledge financial support from NSF #SES90-22807, the Georgia Tech Foundation, and the Karl Eller Center at the University of Arizona, respectively.*

in the formulation of Arch-type models and their applications in the modelling of speculative prices. Several interesting topics in empirical finance awaiting future research are also discussed.

The plan of this paper is as follows. We begin with a brief overview of some of the important theoretical developments in the parameterisation and implementation of Arch-type models, and continue with applications of the Arch methodology to stock return data. The next sections cover the modelling of interest rates and foreign exchange rates, respectively. A detailed bibliography is given at the end of the paper.

Arch

Following the seminal paper by Engle (1982) we shall refer to all discrete time stochastic processes (ε_t) of the form

$$\varepsilon_t = z_t\sigma_t, \qquad (1)$$

$$z_t \text{ i.i.d., } E(z_t) = 0, \ \text{var}(z_t) = 1, \qquad (2)$$

with σ_t a time-varying, positive, and measurable function of the time $t - 1$ information set, as an Arch model. For now ε_t is assumed to be a univariate process, but extensions to multivariate settings are straightforward as discussed below. By definition ε_t is serially uncorrelated with mean zero, but the conditional variance of ε_t equals σ_t^2, which may be changing through time. In most applications ε_t will correspond to the innovation in the mean for some other stochastic process, say $\{y_t\}$, where

$$y_t = g(x_{t-1};b) + \varepsilon_t, \qquad (3)$$

and $g(x_{t-1};b)$ denotes a function of x_{t-1} and the parameter vector b, where x_{t-1} is in the time $t - 1$ information set. To simplify the exposition, in most of the discussion below we shall assume that ε_t is itself observable.

Let $f(z_t)$ denote the density function for z_t, and let θ be the vector of all the unknown parameters in the model. By the prediction error decomposition, the log-likelihood function for the sample $\varepsilon_T, \varepsilon_{T-1}, \ldots, \varepsilon_1$ becomes, apart from initial conditions,[1]

$$L(\theta) = \sum_{t=1}^{T}\left[\log f\left(\varepsilon_t\sigma_t^{-1}\right) - \log \sigma_t\right]. \qquad (4)$$

The second term in the summation is a Jacobian term arising from the transformation from z_t to ε_t. Note that (4) also defines the sample log-likelihood for $y_t, y_{T-1}, \ldots, y_1$ as given by (3). Given a parametric representation for $f(z_t)$, maximum likelihood estimates for the parameters of interest can be computed directly from (4) by a number of different numerical optimisation techniques.

The setup in (1) and (2) is extremely general and allows for a wide variety of models. At the same time, the economic theory explaining temporal variation in conditional variances is very limited. Consequently, in the remainder of this section we shall concentrate on some of the more successful time series techniques that have been developed for modelling σ_t^2. These models for the temporal dependence in conditional seconds moments bear much resemblance to the time series techniques for conditional first moments popularised in the early 1970s. Just as the integration of time series techniques for the conditional mean into structural econometric model building has led to a much deeper and richer understanding of the underlying dynamics, similar results have already started to emerge in the modelling of conditional variances and covariances.

THE LINEAR ARCH(Q) MODEL

As Engle (1982) suggests in his seminal paper, one possible parameterisation for σ_t^2 is to express σ_t^2 as a linear function of past squared values of the process,

$$\sigma_t^2 = w + \sum_{i=1}^{q}\alpha_i\varepsilon_{t-i}^2 = \omega + \alpha(L)\varepsilon_t^2, \qquad (5)$$

where $\omega > 0$ and $\alpha_i \geq 0$, and L denotes the lag operator. This model is known as the linear Arch(q) model. With financial data it captures the tendency for volatility clustering, ie for large (small) price changes to be followed by other large (small) price changes, but of unpredictable sign. In order to reduce the number of parameters and ensure a monotonic declining effect of more distant shocks, an ad hoc linearly declining lag structure was often imposed in many of the earlier applications of the model; ie $\alpha_i = \alpha(q + 1 - i)/(q(q + 1))$ as in Engle (1982, 1983).

For z_t normally distributed, the conditional density entering the likelihood function in (4) takes the form

$$\log f\left(\varepsilon_t\sigma_t^{-1}\right) = -0.5 \log 2\pi - 0.5\varepsilon_t^2\sigma_t^{-2}. \qquad (6)$$

Maximum likelihood (ML)-based procedures for the Arch class of models under this distributional assumption are discussed in Engle (1982) and Pantula (1985). Although the likelihood function is highly non-linear in the parameters, a simple scoring algorithm is available for the linear Arch(q) model defined in (5). Furthermore, a Lagrange Multiplier (LM) test for $\alpha_1 = \ldots = \alpha_q = 0$ can be calculated as TR^2 from the regression of ε_t^2 on $\varepsilon_{t-1}^2, \ldots, \varepsilon_{t-q}^2$, where T denotes the sample size. This same test is generally valid using consistently estimated residuals from the model given in (3). An alternative but asymptotically equivalent testing procedure is to subject ε_t^2 to standard tests for serial correlation based on the autocorrelation structure, including conventional portmanteau tests as in Ljung and Box (1978). In addition, Gregory (1989) suggests a non-parametric test for Arch(q) derived from a finite state Markov chain approximation, while Robinson (1991) presents an LM test for very general serially dependent heteroskedasticity. The small sample performance of some of these estimators and test statistics have been analysed by Engle, Hendry, and Trumble (1985), Diebold and Pauly (1989), Bollerslev and Wooldridge (1991), and Gregory (1989). Interestingly, the well-known small sample downward bias for the parameter estimates in autoregressive models for the mean carries over to the estimators for $\alpha_1, \ldots, \alpha_q$ also.[2]

As an alternative to ML estimation, Arch-type models can also be estimated directly with Generalised Method of Moments (GMM). This was suggested and implemented by Mark (1988), Bodurtha and Mark (1991), Glosten, Jagannathan, and Runkle (1991), Simon (1989), and Rich, Raymond, and Butler (1990a, b), and in a closely related context by Harvey (1989) and Ferson (1989). A comparison of the efficiency of exact ML, Quasi Maximum Likelihood (QML), and GMM estimates using different instrument sets would be interesting. Bayesian inference procedures within the Arch class of models are developed in a series of papers by Geweke (1988, 1989a, b), who uses Monte Carlo methods to determine the exact posterior distributions.

An observationally equivalent representation for the model in (1), (2), and (5) is given by the time-varying parameter MA(q) model,

$$\varepsilon_t = w_t + \sum_{i=1}^{q} a_{ti}\varepsilon_{t-i},$$

where $w_t, a_{t1}, \ldots, a_{tq}$ are i.i.d. with mean zero and variance $\omega_t, \alpha_1, \ldots, \alpha_q$, respectively. This relationship between the time-varying parameter class of models and the linear Arch(q) model has been further studied by Tsay (1987), Bera and Lee (1989, 1991), Kim and Nelson (1989), Wolff (1989), Cheung and Pauly (1990), and Bera, Higgins, and Lee (1991). Similarly, in Weiss (1986b) and Higgins and Bera (1989a) comparisons to the bilinear time series class of models are considered.

THE LINEAR GARCH(P, Q) MODEL

In many of the applications with the linear Arch(q) model a long lag length q is called for. An alternative and more flexible lag structure is often provided by the Generalised Arch, or Garch(p, q), model in Bollerslev (1986),[3]

$$\sigma_t^2 = \omega + \sum_{i=1}^{q}\alpha_i\varepsilon_{t-i}^2 + \sum_{i=1}^{p}\beta_i\sigma_{t-i}^2 = \omega + \alpha(L)\varepsilon_t^2 + \beta(L)\sigma_t^2. \quad (7)$$

To ensure a well-defined process all the parameters in the infinite-order AR representation $\sigma_t^2 = \phi(L)\varepsilon_t^2 = (1 - \beta(L))^{-1}\alpha(L)\varepsilon_t^2$ must be non-negative, where it is assumed that the roots of the polynomial $\beta(\lambda) = 1$ lie outside the unit circle; see Nelson and Cao (1991) and Drost and Nijman (1991). For a Garch(1,1) process this amounts to ensuring that both α_1 and β_1 are non-negative. It follows also that ε_t is covariance stationary if and only if $\alpha(1) + \beta(1) < 1$.[4] Of course, in that situation the Garch(p, q) model corresponds exactly to an infinite-order linear Arch model with geometrically declining parameters.

An appealing feature of the Garch(p, q) model concerns the time series dependence in ε_t^2. Rearranging terms, (7) is readily interpreted as an ARMA model for ε_t^2 with autoregressive parameters $\alpha(L) + \beta(L)$, moving average parameters $-\beta(L)$, and serially uncorrelated innovation sequence $\{\varepsilon_t^2 - \sigma_t^2\}$. Following Bollerslev (1988), this idea can be used in the identification of the orders p and q, although in most applications $p = q = 1$ is found to suffice.[5]

Much of modern finance theory is cast in terms of continuous time stochastic differential equations, while virtually all financial time series are available at discrete time intervals only. This apparent gap between the empirically motivated Arch models and the underlying economic theory is the focus of Nelson (1990b), who shows that the discrete time Garch(1,1) model converges to a continuous time diffusion model as the sampling interval gets arbitrarily small.[6] Along similar lines, Nelson (1992) shows that if the true model is a diffusion model with no jumps, then the discrete time variances are consistently estimated by a weighted average of past residuals as in the Garch(1,1) formulation. Another possible reason for the success of the Garch(p, q) models in estimating conditional variances is discussed in Brock, Hsieh, and LeBaron (1991). They show that if ε_t^2 is linear in the sense of Priestly (1981), the Garch(p, q) representation may be seen as a parsimonious approximation to the possibly infinite Wold representation for ε_t^2.

While aggregation in conventional ARMA models for the conditional mean is straightforward, temporal aggregation within the Arch class of models is not obvious. However, in an insightful paper, Drost and Nijman (1991) show that the class of Garch(p, q) models is closed under temporal aggregation, appropriately defined in terms of best linear projections. Also, Diebold (1986b, 1988), using a standard central limit theorem type argument, shows convergence towards normality of a martingale process with Arch errors under temporal aggregation.

NON-NORMAL CONDITIONAL DENSITIES

At the same time that high-frequency financial data exhibit volatility clustering, it is also widely recognised that the unconditional price or return distributions tend to have fatter tails than the normal distribution; for some of the earliest evidence see Mandelbrot (1963) and Fama (1965). Although the unconditional distribution for ε_t in the Garch(p, q) model with conditional normal errors as given by (1), (2), (6), and (7) have fatter tails than the normal distribution (see Milhøj (1985) and Bollerslev (1986)), for many financial time series it does not adequately account for the leptokurtosis. That is, the standardised residuals from the estimated models, $\hat{z}_t = \hat{\varepsilon}_t\hat{\sigma}_t^{-1}$, often appear to be leptokurtic.[7]

Following White (1982), asymptotic standard errors for the parameters in the conditional mean and variance functions that are robust to departures from normality have been derived by Weiss (1984, 1986a). Bollerslev and Wooldridge (1991) present a consistent estimator for this robust variance-covariance matrix in the Arch framework that requires only first derivatives, together with an illustration of the small sample performance of the estimator and the properties of the robust TR^2 Lagrange Multiplier tests in Wooldridge (1988, 1990). It is found that the conventional standard errors based on the outer product of the quasi-gradient obtained under the assumption of conditional normality tend to understate the true standard errors for the parameters in the conditional variance equation when conditional leptokurtosis is present. These ideas are also illustrated empirically in Baillie and Bollerslev (1991).[8]

While the QML based inference procedures are straightforward to implement, fully efficient maximum likelihood estimates may be preferred in some situations. In addition to the potential gains in efficiency, the exact form of the error distribution also plays an important role in several important applications of the Arch model, such as option pricing and the construction of optimal forecast error intervals; see Engle and Mustafa (1992) and Baillie and Bollerslev (1992). Bollerslev (1987) suggests using the standardised Student-t distribution with the degrees of freedom being estimated.[9] Other parametric densities that have been considered in the estimation of Arch models include the normal-Poisson mixture distribution in Jorion (1988), the power exponential distribution in Baillie and Bollerslev (1989), the normal-lognormal mixture distribution in Hsieh (1989a), and the generalised exponential distribution in Nelson (1990c). In a related context, McCulloch (1985) suggests the use of an infinite variance leptokurtic stable Paretian distribution in the maximum likelihood estimation of the so-called Adaptive Conditional Heteroskedasticity, or ACH, model.

As an alternative to maximum likelihood, a semiparametric density estimation technique could be used in approximating $f(z_t)$. Following Gallant and Nychka (1987), in Gallant and Tauchen (1989), Gallant, Hsieh, and Tauchen (1989), and Gallant, Rossi, and Tauchen (1990), $f(z_t)$ is replaced by a polynomial expansion, whereas Engle and Gonzalez-Rivera (1991) suggest a density estimator originally developed by Tapia and Thompson (1978).[10] By avoiding any specific distributional assumption, semiparametric density estimation gives an added flexibility in the specification. Of course, compared to full information maximum likelihood with a correctly specified density, the semiparametric approach invariably involves a loss in asymptotic efficiency. However, with markedly skewed distributions the efficiency of the semiparametric estimator compares favourably with the QML estimates obtained under the assumption of conditional normality; see Engle and Gonzalez-Rivera (1991).

NON-LINEAR AND NON-PARAMETRIC ARCH

In the Garch(p, q) model (7) the variance only depends on the magnitude and not the sign of ε_t. As discussed below, this is somewhat at odds with the empirical behaviour of stock market prices where leverage effects may be present. In the Exponential Garch(p, q), or Egarch(p, q), model introduced by Nelson (1990c), σ_t^2 is an asymmetric function of past ε_ts as defined by (1), (2), and

$$\log \sigma_t^2 = \omega + \sum_{i=1}^{q} \alpha_i \left(\phi z_{t-i} + \gamma \left[|z_{t-i}| - E|z_{t-i}| \right] \right) + \sum_{i=1}^{p} \beta_i \log \sigma_{t-i}^2. \tag{8}$$

Unlike the linear Garch(p, q) model in (7), there are no restrictions on the parameters α_i and β_i to ensure non-negativity of the conditional variances. Thus, the representation in (8) resembles an unrestricted ARMA(p, q) model for log σ_t^2. If $\alpha_i\phi < 0$, the variance tends to rise (fall) when ε_{t-i} is negative (positive) in accordance with the empirical evidence for stock returns discussed below. Assuming z_t is i.i.d. normal, it follows that ε_t is covariance stationary provided all the roots of the autoregressive polynomial $\beta(\lambda) = 1$ lie outside the unit circle. The Egarch model is closely related to the logarithmic parameterisation discussed by Geweke (1986) and Pantula (1986) and the Multiplicative Arch model suggested by Milhøj (1987b, c),

$$\log \sigma_t^2 = \omega + \sum_{i=1}^{q} \alpha_i \log z_{t-i}^2 + \sum_{i=1}^{p} \beta_i \left(\log z_{t-i}^2 - \log \sigma_{t-i}^2 \right).$$

Many other alternative parametric Arch formulations have been considered in the literature, including power transformations of ε_t^2 as in the Non-linear Arch model of Higgins and Bera (1989b) and Bera and Higgins (1991) and a threshold Arch model as in Zakoian (1990); see also Engle and Bollerslev (1986). In the threshold model, the σ_t^2 is a linear piecewise function, thereby allowing different reactions of volatility to different signs and magnitudes of the shocks. A related model, based on a Markov chain approach, is proposed by Gourieroux and Monfort (1992). Also, Harvey, Ruiz, and Sentana (1992) have recently proposed an unobserved components time series model in which Arch disturbances are placed on both the state and updating equations. A more formal comparison of these many alternative formulations would be informative.

Instead of relying on a parametric representation for σ_t^2, a non-parametric estimation technique could be used in approximating the conditional variance. Following Robinson (1987a, b), several authors, including Pagan and Ullah (1988), Robinson (1988), Whistler (1988), Pagan and Hong (1990), and Sentana and Wadhwani (1989), have advocated kernel methods in which σ_t^2 is estimated as a weighted average of ε_t^2, $t = 1, 2, \ldots, T$, such that ε_t^2s for which the conditioning set (defined in terms of lagged information) "close" to that of ε_t receives the highest weight.[11] Several different weighting schemes are possible, but the most frequent in the estimation of Arch models have been Gaussian kernels. Very little is known about the infinite sample properties of these techniques in the present context.

An alternative non-parametric estimation strategy involves approximating the unknown conditional variance function by a series expansion where the number of terms in the expansion is an increasing function of the sample size. For instance, in the Flexible Fourier Form introduced by Gallant (1981), σ_t^2 is approximated by a function of polynomial and trigonometric terms in lagged values of ε_t. In the semi-non-parametric approach in Gallant and Nychka (1987) the basic idea is to multiply the normal density in (6) by a polynomial expansion. For increasing orders of this expansion, under weak conditions the maximum likelihood estimates found using this method have the same classical properties as non-parametric estimates. In applications of this idea very-low-order polynomial approximations have typically been used; see, for example, Pagan and Hong (1988), Gallant and Tauchen (1989), and Gallant, Hsieh, and Tauchen (1989).

A good illustration and comparison of some of the different parametric and non-parametric methods discussed in this subsection is given in Pagan and Schwert (1990).

ARCH-IN-MEAN MODELS

In the Arch-in-Mean, or Arch-M, model introduced by Engle, Lilien, and Robins (1987), the conditional mean is an explicit function of the conditional variance of the process, as given by (1), (2), and

$$y_t = g\left(x_{t-i}, \sigma_t^2; b\right) + \varepsilon_t. \tag{9}$$

In this model, an increase in the conditional variance will be associated with an increase or a decrease in the conditional mean of y_t depending on the sign of the partial derivative of $g(x_{t-1}, \sigma_t^2; b)$ with respect to σ_t^2. Many theories in finance involve an explicit tradeoff between the risk and the expected return. The Arch-M model is ideally suited to handling such questions in a time series context where the conditional variance may be time-varying. The most common choices for the functional form of $g(x_{t-1}, \sigma_t^2; b)$ have involved linear or logarithmic functions of σ_t^2 or σ_t.

Formally, estimation of the Arch-M model

poses no added difficulties. However, in the absence of Arch-M effects, the information matrix obtained between the auxilliary assumption of conditional normality is block diagonal between the parameters in the conditional mean and variance functions of the model. This is no longer true for the Arch-M model. Thus, unlike the linear Garch model in (7) where consistent estimates of the parameters in the function $g(x_{t-1}; b)$ can be obtained even in the presence of misspecification in σ_t^2, consistent estimation in the Arch-M model requires that the full model be correctly specified. This parallels the results for asymmetric variance formulations such as the Egarch model in (8), where correct specification of the full model is generally required in order to guarantee consistency; see Pagan and Sabau (1987a) and Pagan and Hong (1990). Diagnostic tests for the variance specification therefore become very important before interpretations are made about the parameter estimates. The consistency tests outlined in Pagan and Sabau (1987b) form the basis for one such set of diagnostics.

PERSISTENCE IN VARIANCE

A common finding in much of the empirical literature using high-frequency financial data concerns the apparent persistence implied by the estimates for the conditional variance functions. In the linear Garch(p, q) model in (7) that is manifested by the presence of an approximate unit root in the autoregressive polynomial; ie $\alpha_1 + \ldots + \alpha_q + \beta_1 + \ldots + \beta_p = 1$. Engle and Bollerslev (1986) refer to this class of models as Integrated in variance, or Igarch.[12] As in the martingale model for conditional means, current information remains important for forecasts of the conditional variance for all horizons.[13] To illustrate, in the simple Igarch(1,1) model with $\alpha_1 + \beta_1 = 1$, the minimum mean square error forecast for the conditional variance s steps ahead is equal to $\omega(s-1) + \alpha_{t+1}^2$.[14]

Consequently, the unconditional variance for the Igarch(1,1) and the general Igarch(p,q) model does not exist. The idea of an infinite unconditional variance distribution in characterising financial data is not new to the Igarch class of models, however. Mandelbrot (1963) and Fama (1965) both suggest the stable Paretian class of distributions with characteristic exponent less than two as providing a good description of the distributional properties of speculative prices.

While the Igarch class of models bears much resemblance to the well-known ARIMA class of models for conditional first moments in terms of the optimal forecasts of the process, the analogy is far from complete. As shown in Nelson (1990a) and Bougerol and Picard (1992), the Igarch model is strictly stationary and ergodic, though not covariance stationary. Asymptotic theory for Arch models is notoriously difficult. However, in an important paper, Lumsdaine (1991) shows that standard asymptotically-based inference procedures are generally valid even in the presence of Igarch effects, though the Monte Carlo evidence presented in Hong (1988) suggests that the sample sizes must be quite large for the asymptotic distributions to provide good approximations.

Whereas many financial time series may exhibit a high degree of persistence in the variance of their univariate time series representations, this persistence is likely to be common among different series, so that certain linear combinations of the variables show no persistence. In that situation the variables are defined to be co-persistent in variance. This has important implications for the construction of optimal long-term forecasts for the conditional variances, and covariances which are essential in many asset pricing relationships; see Bollerslev and Engle (1990) for further discussion along these lines.

MULTIVARIATE ARCH

The models discussed in the preceding sections have all been univariate. However, many issues in asset pricing and portfolio allocation decisions can only be meaningfully analysed in a multivariate context. Thus, now let $\{\varepsilon_t\}$ denote an $N \times 1$ vector stochastic process. Then any process that permits the representation

$$\varepsilon_t = z_t \Omega_t^{1/2}, \tag{10}$$

$$z_t \text{ i.i.d.}, E(z_t) = 0, \text{var}(z_t) = I, \tag{11}$$

where the time-varying $N \times N$ covariance matrix Ω_t is positive definite and measurable with respect to the time $t-1$ information set, is naturally referred to as a multivariate Arch model. Inference in the multivariate Arch model proceeds as for the univariate model in (1) and (2) discussed above.[15]

The general multivariate definition in (10) and (11) opens up a wide variety of possible representations, but only a few parameterisations have been found particularly useful. In the multivariate linear Arch(q) model in Kraft and Engle (1983), Ω_t is given by a linear function of the contemporaneous cross-products in the past squared errors; ie $\text{vech}(\varepsilon_{t-1}\varepsilon'_{t-1}), \ldots, (\varepsilon_{t-q}\varepsilon'_{t-q})$ where $\text{vech}(\cdot)$ denotes the operator that stacks the lower portion of an $N \times N$ matrix as an $(N(N+1)/2) \times 1$ vector. This model was subsequently generalised to the multivariate linear Garch(p, q) model in Bollerslev, Engle, and Wooldridge (1988).

$$\text{vech}(\Omega_t) = W + \sum_{i=1}^{q} A_i \,\text{vech}(\varepsilon_{t-i}\varepsilon'_{t-i}) + \sum_{i=1}^{p} B_i \,\text{vech}(\Omega_{t-i}). \tag{12}$$

Here W denotes an $(N(N+1)/2) \times 1$ vector, and A_i and B_i are $(N(N+1)/2) \times (N(N+1)/2)$ matrices. Several properties of this model, including sufficient conditions for this parameterisation to ensure that Ω_t are positive definite, have been derived in Baba, Engle, Kraft, and Kroner (1991). The number of unique parameters in (12) equals $\tfrac{1}{2}N(N+1)[1 + N(N+1)(p+q)/2]$, so in practice for moderately sized N some simplifying assumptions must be imposed. For instance, in the diagonal Garch(p, q) model employed by Bollerslev, Engle, and Wooldridge (1988), the A_i and B_i matrices are all taken to be diagonal. A simple parameterisation for the diagonal Garch(p, q) model guaranteed to be positive definite is given in Attanasio and Edey (1988) and in Baba, Engle, Kraft, and Kroner (1991).

Motivated by the commonality in volatility clustering across different assets, Diebold and Nerlove (1989) have proposed a multivariate latent factor Arch model. Identification in the context of this model is discussed in Sentana (1990), but the presence of an unobserved latent variable in the covariance matrix renders exact inference in the latent factor Arch model extremely complicated. Alternatively, in the K-factor Arch representation suggested by Engle (1987),

$$\text{vech}(\Omega_t) = W + \sum_{k=1}^{K} \text{vech}(f_k f'_k)\sigma^2_{tk}, \tag{13}$$

where the f_ks denote $N \times 1$ vectors and σ^2_{tk} the time-varying variance of the kth factor. Of course, to complete this representation an explicit form for the σ^2_{tk}s is needed. In the K-factor Garch(p, q) model, the σ^2_{tk}s are given by the conditional variance of K independent linear combinations of ε_t, each of which has a univariate Garch(p,q) representation; ie $\sigma^2_{tk} = \omega_k + \alpha_k(L)(g'_k\varepsilon_t)^2 + \beta_k(L)\sigma^2_{tk}$, where $g'_i g_j = g'_i f_j = 0$ for $i \neq j$. Low-order factor Garch models have been estimated by Engle, Granger, and Kraft (1984), Kroner (1987), Engle, Ng, and Rothschild (1989, 1990), and Engle and Ng (1990). The small sample behaviour of various estimators in the one-factor Garch(1,1) model has been analysed by Lin (1991).

Other multivariate representations include the constant conditional correlation model put forward in Bollerslev (1990). In this representation the conditional covariance matrix Ω_t is time-varying, but the conditional correlations are assumed to be constant. This assumption greatly simplifies the inference procedures, and several studies have found it to be a reasonable empirical working hypothesis; see, for instance, Cecchetti, Cumby, and Figlewski (1988), Kroner and Claessens (1991), McCurdy and Morgan (1991a), Ng (1991), Kroner and Lastrapes (1991), Brown and Ligeralde (1990), Baillie and Bollerslev (1990), and Schwert and Seguin (1990).

ALTERNATIVE MEASURES OF UNCERTAINTY

Several alternative measures to the Arch model defined above have been employed in characterising volatility in speculative prices. One such alternative involves the construction of variance estimates by averaging the squared errors obtained with models for the conditional mean estimated over finer horizons. For instance, following Merton (1980), several authors, including Poterba and Summers (1986), French, Schwert and Stambaugh (1987), Schwert (1989a, 1990a, b), and Schwert and Seguin (1990), construct monthly stock return variance estimates by taking the average of the squared daily returns within the month,[16] whereas Pindyck (1988) and Harris (1989) use this idea in calculating annual standard deviations of returns. To asses the temporal dependence, standard time series models are subsequently estimated for these variance estimates. Obviously, this procedure does not make efficient use of all the data. Furthermore, following Pagan (1984, 1986), the conventional standard errors from the second-stage estimation may not be appropriate. If the information matrix for the full model is not block diagonal between the parameters in the mean and variance, the actual parameter estimates may also be inconsistent; see Pagan and Ullah (1988). Further, as argued by Chou (1988) and Attanasio (1988), the two-stage procedure may result in misleading conclusions about the true underlying dependence in the second-order moments of the data. This is formally documented by the Monte

Carlo evidence in Attanasio and Wadhwani (1989), where the estimates for the Arch-in-Mean parameters are found to be biased towards zero. Nonetheless, the computational simplicity of the two-stage procedure makes it an appealing tool for preliminary data analysis.

In a second alternative to the Arch models discussed above, ARMA-type models are estimated for the conditional standard deviation, as measured by the absolute value of the errors from some first-step estimates for the conditional mean. Schwert (1989a) uses this strategy in determining the underlying causes of movements in conditional stock market volatility. This two-stage alternative remains subject to the same errors-in-variables type problem discussed by Pagan and Ullah (1988) and, as argued by Schwert (1989a), the resulting test statistics, including tests for persistence in the variance, have to be carefully interpreted.

Another popular method for assessing volatility in financial data is based on the implied volatility from options prices. Under the assumption of a constant variance, the lack of arbitrage leads us to the well-known Black and Scholes (1973) formula; for some of the first empirical evidence along these lines, see Black and Scholes (1972). The possibility of a stochastic volatility process within this framework is explicitly considered by Hseih and Manas-Anton (1988), Jorion (1988), Lyons (1988), Engle and Mustafa (1992), Day and Lewis (1992), and Engle, Hong, and Kane (1992). Even though this method potentially could lead to estimates superior to Arch-type alternatives, not all assets of interest have actively traded options. Also, several complications arise in the theory of option pricing with stochastic volatility; see, for instance, Melino and Turnbull (1990) among others.

The use of inter-period high and low prices constitutes yet another method for assessing the variability. Under the assumption that the logarithm of speculative prices takes the form of a continuous time random walk with a constant instantaneous variance, the exact distribution of the high/low price ratio follows from the theory of range statistics. As shown by Parkinson (1980), the moments of this high/low price distribution are functions of the underlying variance of the process, suggesting an estimator of the variance based on the realised interperiod highs and lows; see Taylor (1987) and Schwert (1990a). With a time-variant conditional variance, the efficiency of this alternative estimator compares favourably with the conventional estimator given by the sample analogue of the mean adjusted squared returns over fixed time intervals. The generalisation of these ideas to other stochastic processes allowing for time-varying variances is not straightforward, although the Arch diffusion approximation in Nelson (1990b) may prove constructive. Furthermore, high and low prices are not readily available for many assets.

Building on the theoretical developments in Glosten and Milgrom (1985), where the variance of the asset price is proportional to the square of the bid-ask spread, the magnitude in the spread could also be used in extracting estimates of volatility. This idea has been pursued by Brock and Kleidon (1990).

Cross-sectional dispersion in survey data forms the basis for a measure of uncertainty. For example, the dispersion in experts earnings forecasts has been used as an estimate of the systematic risk for a stock by Cragg and Malkiel (1982) and Weston (1986) among others. Similarly, the dispersion in forecasts among experts has been suggested as a measure of inflation uncertainty by Carlson (1977) and Levi and Makin (1979), among others, though Rich, Raymond, and Butler (1990b) find only limited evidence of a relationship between forecast dispersion and Arch measures of uncertainty. Also, Frankel and Froot (1987) and Froot and Frankel (1989) provide an interesting use of survey data in modelling expectations formation and in interpreting tests of the unbiasedness hypothesis in the forward foreign exchange rate market. However, survey measures only provide an indicator of the heterogeneity in expectations, which may not be a good approximation of the fundamental underlying uncertainty depending on the homogeneity of expectations. In addition, the availability of survey data pertaining to speculative prices is very limited.

A related measure often used in quantifying the uncertainty of inflation is derived from relative contemporaneous prices. As discussed by Pagan, Hall, and Trivedi (1983), the validity of this method depends on the homogeneity of the different markets, assets or agents; see also Pagan and Ullah (1988). This is the same idea underlying the relative return dispersion measure across different stocks recently put forward by Amihud and Mendelson (1989) and Cutler (1989) as a means for quantifying overall market volatility, and is related to the use of cross-sectional dispersion of asset returns as a measure of uncertainty in the traditional event studies literature. A formal characterisation of conditions under which heterogeneity in cross-sectional returns could be used as a measure of return uncertainty would be interesting.

A utility-based comparison of some of these alternative statistical models for volatility in terms of the willingness of an investor with a mean-variance utility function to pay for one variance forecast rather than another is given in West, Edison, and Cho (1991). Very interestingly, on using weekly exchange rate data the authors find that the Garch(1,1) formulation in (7) tends to outperform the alternative methods investigated, and they argue "... that an investment advisor whose only specialised tool is Garch may be as worthy of her hire as are professionals currently on Wall Street". Alternative profit driven evaluations have been suggested by Brock, Lakonishok, and LeBaron (1990) and Engle, Hong, and Kane (1992). Engle, Hong, and Kane, for example, compare the difference in profits arising from pricing one-day options on the NYSE portfolio on the basis of alternative variance forecasts. The Garch(1,1) model is again found to outperform MA and ARMA formulations for the squared residual returns. This is consistent with the direct forecast-based comparison of implied options variances and Garch(1,1) estimates in Lamoureux and Lastrapes (1991) and Day and Lewis (1992).

A more conventional statistically-based mean squared error comparison of statistical volatility models is conducted by Pagan and Schwert (1990), who find that non-parametric methods may be superior for stock returns. They conclude that the extension of parametric models in the non-parametric direction (by adding on Fourier terms, for example) is likely to be the best modelling strategy. Further comparisons of these many alternatives to Arch-based methods for assessing the uncertainty in different speculative prices seem worthwhile.

SOURCES OF ARCH

While serial correlation in conditional second moments is clearly a property of speculative prices, a systematic search for the cause of this serial correlation has only recently begun. One possible explanation for the prominence of Arch effects is of course the presence of a serially correlated news arrival process, as discussed by Diebold and Nerlove (1989) and Gallant, Hsieh, and Tauchen (1989).[17] In a detailed empirical analysis, Engle, Ito, and Lin (1990a, b) find support for this hypothesis, although any satisfactory explanation for this dependence in the underlying news arrival process is notably lacking.[18] This is also related to Stock's (1987, 1988) notion of time deformation in which economic and calendar time proceed at different speeds. In a related context Bollerslev and Domowitz (1991) have shown how the actual market mechanisms may themselves result in very different temporal dependence in the volatility of transactions prices, with a particular automated trade execution system inducing a very high degree of persistence in the variance process. Some other preliminary theoretical results on the foundation of Arch models together with some interesting empirical evidence for the significance of various exogenous forcing variables in the variance equation have been obtained by Domowitz and Hakkio (1985), Smith (1987), Diebold and Pauly (1988a), Hsieh (1988b), Lai and Pauly (1988), Ng (1988), Thum (1988), Backus, Gregory, and Zin (1989), Giovannini and Jorion (1989), Hodrick (1989), Schwert (1989a), Attanasio and Wadhwani (1989), Engle and Susmel (1990), and Brock and Kleidon (1990) among others. Further developments concerning empirical specifications for the observed heteroskedasticity remains a very important area for future research. At the same time, the direct implementation of such more structural models over short time intervals, such as daily or weekly, is likely to be hindered by the unavailability of data.

Applications of Arch to stock return data

Volatility clustering in stock return series has many important theoretical implications, so it is not surprising that numerous empirical applications of the Arch methodology in characterising stock return variances and covariances have already appeared. In the following sections, a review of this literature will be presented.

ARCH EFFECTS AND MODEL SPECIFICATION

Arch effects have generally been found to be highly significant in equity markets. For example, highly significant test statistics for Arch have been reported for individual stock returns by Engle and Mustafa (1992), for index returns by Akgiray (1989), and for futures markets by Schwert (1990a).[19] As in the specification of ARMA(p, q) models for the conditional mean, most empirical implementations of Garch(p, q) models adopt low orders for the lag lengths p and q. Typically, Garch(1,1), Garch(1,2), or Garch(2,1) models are adopted. It is interesting to note that such small numbers of parameters seem sufficient to model the variance dynamics over very long sample periods. For instance, French, Schwert, and Stambaugh (1987) analyse daily S&P stock index data for 1928-1984 for a total of 15,369 observations and require only four parameters in the conditional variance equation.

Exceptions to this low-order rule in the Arch specification include Bodurtha and Mark (1991) and Attanasio (1991) where Arch(3) models are employed in analysing portfolios of monthly NYSE stock returns and monthly excess returns on the S&P 500 index, respectively. It is possible that this seasonality may be explained by the clustering effect for firms in the quarterly announcements of dividends and earnings. If variances of stock returns are systematically evoked by these announcements, then a monthly stock index return may exhibit such a seasonal pattern in conditional variances. This hypothesis is yet to be tested, but it illustrates the importance of understanding the generating forces behind the Arch effects, as discussed below. Similarly, the well-known weekend effect, according to which the variance of returns tends to be higher on days following closures of the market, could also lead to the finding of high-order Arch models. This effect, as documented by French and Roll (1986) using daily unconditional variances, remains significant in the low-order Arch models for the daily index returns presented in French, Schwert, and Stambaugh (1987), Nelson (1989, 1990c), and Connolly (1989), and a failure to take proper account of such deterministic influences might lead to a spurious seasonal Arch effect.[20]

The importance of adjusting for Arch effects in the residuals from conventional market models has been analysed in a series of papers by Morgan and Morgan (1987), Bera, Bubnys, and Park (1988), Diebold, Im, and Lee (1990), Connolly (1989), and Schwert and Seguin (1990), where it is argued that inferences can be seriously affected by ignoring the Arch error structure. For instance, Morgan and Morgan (1987), in a study of the small firm effect, find that correcting for the conditional variance in returns from portfolios long in small and short in large firms reduces the estimate of market risk and increases the estimate of abnormal return.

Related to the specification of Arch models, it is also worth noting the results in the recent literature on deterministic chaos as a form of non-linearities in stock returns. On applying the correlation integral-based test statistic in Brock, Dechert, and Scheinkman (1987) (BDS), which has power against both deterministic chaos and non-linear dependencies, most studies tend to find that once Arch effects are removed the BDS test on standardised residuals exhibits very little of non-linear dependence.[21] Hence most of the seemingly chaotic non-linearities work through the conditional variance. For examples, see Schwert (1989b) or Scheinkman and LeBaron (1989) for individual firms' returns, LeBaron (1989) for daily and weekly returns of the S&P 500 index, and Hsieh (1990) for a series of different weekly returns, including size-ranked portfolios. The BDS statistic has also been used as a diagnostic tool in the specification of multivariate Arch models for equity returns by McCurdy and Stengos (1992).

NON-NORMAL CONDITIONAL DENSITIES

Stock returns tend to exhibit non-normal unconditional sampling distributions, in the form of skewness but more pronounced in the form of excess kurtosis (see, for example, Fama (1965)). As described above, the conditional normality assumption in Arch generates some degree of unconditional excess kurtosis, but typically less than adequate to account fully for the fat-tailed properties of the data. One solution to the kurtosis problem is the adoption of conditional distributions with fatter tails than the normal distribution. In Baillie and DeGennaro (1990) and de Jong, Kemna, and Kloeck (1990), the assumption of conditionally t-distributed errors together with a Garch(1,1) model for the conditional variance is adopted, and it is found that failure to model the fat-tailed property can lead to spurious results in terms of the estimated risk-return tradeoff. Other attempts to model the excess conditional kurtosis in stock return indices include the estimates of the Egarch model with a generalised exponential distribution in Nelson (1989) and the jump-diffusion process with Arch errors in Jorion (1988).

An alternative to the explicit assumption of conditionally leptokurtic distributions is the semi-non-parametric method discussed above. Using this method, Gallant and Tauchen (1989) report significant evidence of both conditional heteroskedasticity in the direction of Arch and conditional non-normality for the daily NYSE value-weighted index for two separate periods, 1959–78 and 1959–84. A variant of the semi-non-parametric method in which the leading term is an Arch-type formulation is also used in Gallant,

Hansen, and Tauchen (1989) in estimating the density function for monthly stock returns. Similarly, Engle and Gonzalez-Rivera (1991) employ non-parametric density estimation with a Garch(1,1) specification for the conditional variance to model the daily stock returns for some small firms. They note that the skewness as well as kurtosis are important in characterising the conditional density function of returns on many small firm stocks.

NON-LINEAR ARCH AND THE LEVERAGE EFFECT

In addition to the leptokurtic distribution of stock return data, Black (1976) has noted a negative correlation between current returns and future volatility. A plausible economic explanation suggested by Black (1976), and further investigated by Christie (1982), is the so-called leverage effect. According to the leverage effect, a reduction in the equity value would raise the debt-to-equity ratio, hence raising the riskiness of the firm as manifested by an increase in future volatility. As a result, the future volatility will be negatively related to the current return on the stock. The linear Garch(p, q) model is not able to capture this kind of dynamic pattern since the conditional variance is only linked to past conditional variances and squared innovations, and hence the sign of returns plays no role in affecting the volatilities. This limitation of the standard Arch formulation is one of the primary motivations for the Egarch model in (8) developed by Nelson (1990c). In this class of Arch models, the volatility depends not only on the magnitude of the past surprises in returns but also on their corresponding signs. Empirical support for this specification of the Arch model is documented in Nelson (1989, 1990c).

Discussion of the leverage effect can also be found in Kupiec (1990) where the leverage effect is tested within the context of a linear Garch(p,q) model by introducing a stock price level in the variance equation. The coefficient is insignificant though this may be a result of a failure to adjust for the strong trend in the price level. However, recent empirical evidence in Gallant, Rossi, and Tauchen (1990) using semi-non-parametric estimation techniques suggest that when conditioning on past trading volume together with past returns, the leverage effect in the daily NYSE index is no longer statistically significant. One possible explanation for this finding could be that the estimated leverage effect is attributable to a few outliers which become less influential in a bivariate setting or with a fat-tailed distribution; see also French (1990). Further empirical work along these lines, including individual stock returns, could be very informative.

It is also worth noting that the leverage effect can only partially explain the strong negative correlation between current return and current volatility in the stock market; see Black (1976) and Christie (1982), for example. In contrast to the causal linkage of current return and future volatility explained by the leverage effect, the fundamental risk-return relation predicts a positive correlation between future returns and current volatilities in stock prices. This issue is discussed in the following subsection. However, an alternative explanation is the volatility feedback effect, studied in French, Schwert, and Stambaugh (1987) and Campbell and Hentschel (1990).

ARCH-M AND ASSET PRICING MODELS

The importance of Arch models in finance comes partly from the direct association of variance and risk and the fundamental tradeoff relationship between risk and return. Three of the most prominent theories in asset pricing, the CAPM of Sharpe (1964), Lintner (1965), Mossin (1966), and Merton (1973), the consumption-based CAPM of Breeden (1979) and Lucas (1978), and the APT of Ross (1976) and Chamberlain and Rothschild (1983), have all found empirical implementations using Arch. We will discuss these empirical papers in this and the next subsection.

Building on the intertemporal CAPM in Merton (1973), Merton (1980) provides an approximate linear relationship between the return and variance of the market portfolio. The Arch-M model developed by Engle, Lilien, and Robins (1987), discussed above, provides a natural tool for estimation of this linear relationship. The parameter measuring the impact of the conditional, variances on the excess returns corresponds to the coefficient of relative risk aversion.

Applications of this model to different stock index returns have been reported by numerous authors. Examples include French, Schwert, and Stambaugh (1987) for the daily S&P index, Chou (1988) for the weekly NYSE value-weighted returns along with different temporal aggregations of the daily returns, Attanasio and Wadhwani (1989) for monthly and annual returns for both US and UK stock indices, and Friedman and Kuttner (1988) for quarterly US stock indices; see also Pindyck (1984, 1988) and

Poterba and Summers (1986). In a related study on dividend-price ratio and volatility-measured discount factors, Campbell and Shiller (1989) estimate the relative risk aversion parameter using annual data on the Cowles/S&P for 1871–1986 and a value-weighted index for the NYSE for the 1926–86 period.

Interestingly, in all the above papers the estimates of the risk aversion parameter are unanimously positive and fall within a fairly small range, from 1 to 4.5. Furthermore, with the exception of Campbell and Shiller (1989), all of these point estimates are significantly different from zero at the usual 5% level. This is in sharp contrast to the literature reporting the many alternative structural-based estimates of the risk aversion parameter, where very imprecise and often plausible point estimates are reported; see, for example, Grossman, Melino, and Shiller (1987) in the context of a Consumption CAPM and Engel and Rodrigues (1989) using international data in a multivariate CAPM model.

Some evidence of the sensitivity of the parameter estimate in the Arch-M model with respect to different model specification is given in Baillie and DeGennaro (1990) using both daily and monthly portfolio returns. By changing the conditional distribution from normal to Student-t, the parameter for the conditional variance entering the mean equation changes from significantly positive at the 5% level to insignificant and of either sign. Similar results are found in Bollerslev and Wooldridge (1991) using robust standard errors; see also French, Schwert, and Stambaugh (1987) and Cocco and Paruolo (1990). Furthermore, Glosten, Jagannathan, and Runkle (1991) show that the sign of the Arch-M coefficient is sensitive to the instruments which are added to the mean and variance equations of the model; see also Gallant, Rossi, and Tauchen (1990) for similar results in a semi-non-parametric framework.

The constancy of the linear relationship between the expected return and the conditional variance in the simple Arch-M model has also been called into question by various authors. For example, on introducing additional instruments over the past squared residuals in estimating the conditional variance, Harvey (1989) reports the coefficient to be significantly time-varying of either sign, depending on the stage of the business cycle. This constancy is also challenged by Chou, Engle, and Kane (1992), who generalise the standard Arch-M model to allow the parameter of the conditional variance in the mean equation to be time-varying through a state-space formulation. They also found instability, which they credit to Roll's (1977) critique; see also Ferson, Kandel, and Stambaugh (1987) and Ng (1991). Including various proxies for the omitted "non-stock" risky assets is found to help establish the constancy of the parameter. This empirical evidence against the validity of a simple linear relationship between the expected return and the volatility of stock indices are corroborated by the theoretical results in Backus and Gregory (1988) and Gennotte and Marsh (1987).[22]

In a related context, Attanasio and Wadhwani (1989) find that the predictability of stock returns given lagged dividend yields reported in Fama and French (1988), among others, can be explained by a risk measure using Arch. The evidence of this finding is stronger for the US than for the UK. However, other explanatory variables, including lagged nominal interest rates and inflation rates, remain significant in explaining the movement of expected returns in addition to the influence of their own conditional variance. Attanasio (1991) extends the Arch-M model to incorporate both the static and the consumption CAPM in a nested formulation. His result confirms the evidence in Mankiw and Shapiro (1986) and many others, that the static CAPM performs better, from an empirical point of view, than the consumption providing a poor measure of the fundamental consumption risk. See also Lee and Yoon (1990) and Sentana and Wadhwani (1989).

It is apparent that the final words have not been said on the empirical relationship between expected market return and volatility. However, it is also clear that in the framework of conditional models, any satisfactory model must incorporate the temporal variation in volatility. Empirically the explicit Arch-M formulations or the semi-non-parametric methods both hold promise of further interesting insights into this important issue. Nonetheless, the use of the Arch-M model as an implementation of Merton's (1973) CAPM is not without criticism. As noted by Pagan and Ullah (1988) and discussed above, in the Arch-M model the estimates for the parameters in the conditional mean equation are not asymptotically independent of the estimates of the parameters in the conditional variance, hence any misspecification in the variance equation generally leads to biased and inconsistent estimates of the parameters in the mean equation.

In a related context the implications of most

contingent claims pricing models also depend crucially on the variance of the underlying asset; see Rubinstein (1987) for a review of theoretical models for the pricing of derivative assets. We shall not attempt a detailed survey of the empirical literature here, but as discussed above, the Arch methodology has already been successfully applied to the pricing of individual stocks and stock index options by Jorion (1988), Engle, Hong, and Kane (1992), Day and Lewis (1992), Lamoureux and Lastrapes (1991), and Choi and Wohar (1990) among others.

MULTIVARIATE ARCH, FACTOR ARCH, AND ASSET PRICING MODELS

While the papers discussed in the previous section use univariate analysis, many interesting questions in finance can only be meaningfully answered within a multivariate framework. In Bollerslev, Engle, and Wooldridge (1988) a multivariate Garch(1,1)-M formulation is used in the implementation of a CAPM model for a market portfolio consisting of three assets – stocks, bonds, and bills. The model estimates suggest a significant positive mean variance tradeoff among the three broadly defined asset categories. However, while the trivariate model seems superior to the corresponding three univariate Garch(1,1)-M models, there is also some evidence that the growth rate in aggregate consumption expenditures and lagged excess returns may have additional explanatory power over the non-diversifiable risk as measured by the time-varying conditional covariance with the market.

A similar approach has been used in a series of papers in analysing the mean-variance tradeoff across both domestic and international equity markets. A partial list of these studies includes Bodurtha and Mark (1991), Hall, Miles, and Taylor (1988), Kaplan (1988), Engel, Frankel, Froot, and Rodrigues (1989), Engel and Rodrigues (1989), Giovannini and Jorion (1989), Ng (1991), De Santis and Sbordone (1990), French (1990), Giovannini and Jorion (1990), Harvey (1991), and McCurdy and Stengos (1992). Without attempting a detailed discussion of this extensive literature, a common thread in most of these studies concerns the finding of a time-varying risk premium, while at the same time the restrictions implied by the CAPM are formally rejected. It is important to recognise that the relationships that hold with the conditional CAPM will not hold with unconditional moments; see Bollerslev, Engle, and Wooldridge (1988). Thus, earlier rejections of the unconditional CAPM do not have any direct bearing on these results.

As discussed above, computational difficulties are of major concern in applications of multivariate Arch models. In addition to the diagonal parameterisation and the constant correlations structure used in the applications above, the factor Arch model in (13) provides an alternative simplifying structure on the covariance matrix. A factor Arch model is used by Engle, Ng, and Rothschild (1989) for 10 size-ranked portfolios. Interestingly, one of the empirically identified factors is found to load onto a January dummy variable, while the other is related to the bond risk premium. Hence the well-known small firm effect is explained in this model as a response to time-varying covariances.

A factor Arch approach is also employed in King, Sentana, and Wadhwani (1990) in an international asset pricing model to study the link between international stock markets. This linkage is investigated further by Hamao, Masulis, and Ng (1990a), who examine the issue of volatility spillovers among international stock markets using an Arch-M model on daily open and close prices. Some evidence is provided for spillovers of volatility from New York to Tokyo and London to Tokyo, but not from Tokyo to either New York or London. Using cross-correlations among standardised residuals from Garch(1,1) models, these results are confirmed in Cheung and Ng (1990). Interestingly, these spillovers are shown in Hamao, Masulis, and Ng (1990b) to have been magnified following the October 1987 crash. A similar approach is taken in Engle and Susmel (1990), where a significant spillover between the US and UK stock markets is found, and in Ng, Chang, and Chu (1991), where spillovers are found among the Pacific Rim countries.

Other studies concerning the transmission of volatility include Chan, Chan, and Karolyi (1990), where the relationship between the S&P 500 stock index and the stock index futures market is investigated using five-minute data from 1984-1986 for a total of 36,500 observations. Consistent with the notion that futures trading tends to increase the volatility in the cash market, a causal relationship from the futures market to the cash market is documented. Interestingly, however, a reverse transmission of volatility from the cash market to the futures market is also evident. The transmission of volatility within the stock market is studied by Conrad, Gultekin, and Kaul (1990), who find that volatility, or news, is incorporated into security prices in a unidirectional manner from the largest to smallest firms.

Future work along these lines seems promising and might help in further understanding the linkage and transmission of stock return volatility.

VOLATILITY PERSISTENCE

An interesting property of stock market volatility relates to the persistence of shocks to the variance. Poterba and Summers (1986) argue that for multiperiod assets like stocks shocks have to persist for a long time for a time-varying risk premium to be able to explain the large fluctuations observed in the stock market. If volatility changes are only transitory, no significant changes in the discount factor or the price of a stock as determined by the net present value of the future expected cash flow will occur.[23]

Poterba and Summers (1986), on using a two-step procedure, argue that shocks to the US stock market are only short-lived, with a half-life of less than six months. As a result, they reject Malkiel's (1979) and Pindyck's (1984) hypothesis that shocks to the investment environment during the early and mid-1970s were the most important factor in explaining the market plunge during the mid-1970s. However, on using a Garch(1,1)-M model, Chou (1988) reports a very different result on the persistence of volatility, with the average half-life for volatility shocks being about one year, consistent with the changing risk premium hypothesis; see also Campbell and Hentschel (1990). These markedly different findings are most likely due to the difference in estimation methodology; see above for a critique of the two-step estimation method.

Indeed, formal tests for a unit root in a variance have been performed by several authors, and the null hypothesis of a unit root is typically not rejected. For example, French, Schwert, and Stambaugh (1987) find a unit root in the variance of the S&P daily index, Chou (1988) finds one in the variance of the NYSE value-weighted index, Pagan and Schwert (1990) find one in the variance of US stocks, and Schwert and Seguin (1990) find one in the variance of monthly size-ranked portfolios. Interestingly, Schwert and Seguin also find evidence of a common source of time-varying volatility across the disaggregated stock portfolios, suggesting the portfolios might be co-persistent in the sense of Bollerslev and Engle (1990). Furthermore, this finding of a unit root seems robust to the parameterisation of the Arch model chosen. For example, Nelson (1989, 1990c) finds evidence of persistence using an Egarch formulation, and Gallant, Rossi, and Tauchen (1990) find evidence using semi-non-parametric methods.

The degree of persistence in volatility shocks is also investigated in Engle and Mustafa (1992), who combine the Black-Scholes option pricing formula with a stochastic variance process modelled by an Arch process. The Garch(1,1) model for the volatility of the underlying security, inferred from the observed option prices written on the security, indicates very strong persistence of the conditional variances. However, a markedly lower persistence is reported after the October 1987 crash. A qualitatively similar result is given by Schwert (1990a), who finds that the stock volatility returned to pre-crash levels by early 1988. However, this short-lived property for volatility shocks due to a market crash is not observed for any of the smaller market downturns prior to 1987. Along these lines, Friedman and Laibson (1989) modify the Arch model such that outliers, or extremely large shocks, are allowed to have different dynamic effects than "ordinary" shocks. Interestingly, and in contrast to the Kearns and Pagan (1990) results on Australian data, "ordinary" shocks tend to persist longer than outliers, so Garch models, which do not distinguish outliers from ordinary shocks, therefore tend to underestimate the persistence of "ordinary" shocks.[24] Also, Engle and Gonzalez-Rivera (1991) report that the persistence in variance seems to be related to the size of the firm, with small firms having a lower persistence than the larger firms studied in the paper by Engle and Mustafa (1992). This is also in accordance with the results for size ranked portfolios reported in Schwert and Seguin (1990).

Lamoureux and Lastrapes (1990a) argue that the high degree of persistence in Garch models might be due to a misspecifications of the variance equation. By introducing dummy variables for deterministic shifts in the unconditional variances, they discover that the duration of the volatility shocks is substantially reduced. A similar point is raised by Diebold (1986a), who conjectures that the apparent existence of a unit root as in the Igarch class of models may be the result of shifts in regimes which affect the level of the unconditional variances. The same critique of standard tests for unit roots in the conditional mean has recently been put forward by Perron (1989). The identification of the timing of shifts in the unconditional variance and the degree of dependence of conditional variances remain areas for useful research. Generalisations of Hamilton's (1989) model of stochastic regime shifting may prove helpful along these lines; see Schwert (1989b) and Pagan and Schwert (1990). However, it should be noted that even if Igarch with a constant ω is generating the data, then dummy variables for "deterministic" shifts in regime will probably show up as being significant.

These somewhat mixed empirical results, together with the important economic implications of the volatility persistence issue, suggest the need for further research in this area. Such investigations may shed light on linkages between the different modelling dichotomies employed in previous studies, the outliers versus ordinary shocks as in Friedman and Laibson (1989), the distinction between recession association and non-recession associated or financial crises associated and non-financial crises associated persistence in Schwert (1989a), large versus small firm persistence as in Engle and Gonzalez-Rivera (1991), the identification of deterministic shifts in the unconditional variances verus persistent conditional variances as in Lamoureux and Lastrapes (1990a), and the possible co-persistence in variance across different stocks and portfolios in Schwert and Seguin (1990). Further, a distinction between permanent versus temporary shocks, as is common in the literature about issues pertaining to unit roots in the mean, may also help in analysing whether conditional variances are positively related to the expected stock returns. It is possible that the overall variance can be decomposed into two components, one of which is "priced" and the other of which is "non-priced".

It would also be interesting to use different data sets to further assess the degree of persistence in stock return volatility. With very few exceptions, most current studies use data from the US stock market. More insights may be provided by using data from the other US markets, such as the options market and futures markets, together with international stock market data. Some existing examples are given by Attanasio's (1988) study on the UK market, Kearns and Pagan's (1990) study on Australian data, Hamao, Masulis, and Ng's (1990a) study on volatility spillovers among three international stock markets, de Jong, Kemna, and Kloeck's (1990) study on the Dutch stock market, and the international CAPM model by Engel and Rodrigues (1989).

ARCH AND EVENT STUDIES

The significant Arch effects in individual firm's stock returns has important implications for the conventional event study methodology frequently applied in empirical studies of corporate finance. In fact, the importance of recognising time-varying variances in the context of event studies has already been pointed out by many researchers in finance; see, for example, Brown and Warner (1985). It is intuitively clear that in assessing the abnormal returns, it is essential to get a correct estimate of the standard error for the purpose of statistical inferences. This is especially true, since it is frequently documented that "events" are associated with changes in the variabilities of the underlying stock returns. However, the current treatment of changing variances in the literature is mostly ad hoc, and a systematic approach using the Arch methodology seems clearly attractive.

Several empirical works have appeared which apply the Arch methodology to event studies; Connolly and McMillan (1988) on capital structure changes, Poon (1988) on stock splits, and de Jong, Kemna, and Kloeck (1990) on the option expiration effect. De Jong, Kemna, and Kloeck (1990), for example, show that ignoring the fat tails and the time-varying variances could lead to spurious detection of abnormal returns.

In all of the above studies, the dynamic patterns of the conditional variances and the betas have not been modelled simultaneously. However, the link between time-variation in beta and the time-varying conditional variance of a firm can further be exploited as in the CAPM model of Bollerslev, Engle, and Wooldridge (1988) discussed above in which the beta is given by the ratio for the time-varying covariance of the individual firm's return to the variance of the market return. In particular, by assuming a constant conditional correlation structure as in Bollerslev (1990), the dynamics of beta are completely specified by the firm's own variances and the variance of the market. This model seems more plausible than an Arch variance coupled with a constant beta or a beta process independent of the error variances.

THE ARCH EFFECT AND ECONOMIC INTERPRETATIONS

The widespread existence of Arch effects and the persistence of stock return volatility have led researchers to search for its origin(s). The Garch(p,q) model can be viewed as a reduced form of a more complicated dynamic structure for the time-varying conditional second-order moments. Thus interpretations and explanatory variables for the observed Arch effects have been proposed both on the micro and the macro level. On the micro level, Lamoureux and Lastrapes (1990b) argue that the Arch effect is a manifestation of clustering in trading volumes. By introducing the contemporaneous trading volumes in the variance equation of a Garch(1,1) model for individual firm's returns, they discover that the lagged squared residuals are no longer significant. A simultaneity problem may seriously bias their results, as contemporaneous correlations between volume and price data have been documented by various authors, including Karpoff (1987) among others. Indeed, using lagged volume as an instrument for the contemporaneous volume does not "remove" the standard Arch effect. This joint relation of lagged volume and lagged returns to stock return volatility is explored using semi-non-parametric results in Gallant, Rossi, and Tauchen (1990) for the value-weighted NYSE index. In addition to the positive correlation between conditional volatility and volume, the Gallant, Rossi, and Tauchen study also finds that large price movements are followed by high volume.

On the macroeconomic level, relevant economic variables driving stock volatilities have also been proposed by various researchers. For example, both Campbell (1987) and Glosten, Jagannathan, and Runkle (1991) have found that nominal interest rates are significant determinants of volatility. In addition, Glosten, Jagannathan, and Runkle (1991) show that entering the interest rate into the Garch formulation leads to a decrease in persistence as measured by the conventional linear Garch parameters, suggesting copersistence between the interest rate and returns. Other related studies include Attanasio (1991) and Attanasio and Wadhwani (1989), who report a significant role for dividend yields in driving stock volatilities. Engel and Rodrigues (1989) show that the variance of stock returns depends on the M1 money supply and an oil price index, while Schwert (1989a) identifies a linkage to the business cycle and financial crises. By using US stock returns for 1834–1987, Schwert finds that stock volatility tends to be higher during recessions and reacts strongly to banking crises.

A related and much debated issue concerns the impact of changes in margin requirements on stock volatilities. Hardouvelis (1990b) finds a significant negative relationship between return volatility and margin requirements in the US and Japanese markets, respectively. However, Hsieh and Miller (1990) and Schwert (1989b, c) argue that this result is likely to be spurious because of the high degree of persistence in volatility shocks; see also Kupiec (1990) and Seguin (1990). In fact, these studies find that changes in margin requirements tend to follow increases in volatility, but not vice versa.

It is unlikely that the determinants of the Arch effect, or more generally the duration of fluctuations, is exhausted by the variables suggested in the above list of studies. While exploring a larger set of variables is certainly a worthwhile exercise, a more fruitful strategy for future research in this area might involve the construction of structural models that can explain the empirical findings. The recent evidence in Brock and Kleidon (1990) documenting the widening bid-ask spread around opening and closing, possibly related to peak load pricing, might be interesting. Also, further developments along the lines of Admati and Pfleiderer (1988) among others, that simultaneously determine the price and the volume of stock returns in accordance with the documented empirical regularities, could prove informative.

Applications of Arch to interest rate data

The relationship between long- and short-term interest rates and the importance of a risk premium in explaining the term structure have received much attention during the last decade. For instance, Shiller (1979) and Singleton (1980) have both argued that long-term interest rates are too volatile to be established by the rational expectations theory of the term structure and a constant liquidity premium. This is also consistent with other studies that have found the estimators of future interest rates derived from the term structure under the assumption of rational expectations and a time-variant risk premium to be biased. Subsequent attempts by Shiller, Campbell, and Schoenholtz (1983) and Mankiw and Summers (1984) among others to model particular forms of irrational expectations have largely been unsuccessful. However, as the degree of uncertainty for the different rates varies through time, so will the compensation required by a risk-averse investor, and a time-varying risk premium might therefore reconcile these findings with market efficiency.[25] In the following sections, we shall discuss some of the papers which use Arch techniques to model time-varying conditional second-order moments and risk premia in the term structure of interest rates.

MODEL SPECIFICATION AND VOLATILITY PERSISTENCE

Modelling volatility clustering in interest rate data goes back at least to Fama (1976). However, the first explicit Arch formulation is given in Weiss (1984), who estimates Arch models on a set of sixteen different macroeconomic time series, including monthly data on AAA corporate bond yields. Very significant Arch effects are evident. These findings have been confirmed in many subsequent studies, and as for stock returns the actual parameter estimates obtained from many of these models are indicative of high persistence in the volatility shocks, or Igarch behaviour. For instance, Hong (1988), on estimating a Garch(1,1) model on the excess return of three-month Treasury bills over one-month Treasury bills, finds $\hat{\alpha}_i + \hat{\beta}_i = 1.073$. Similar results are reported in Engle, Lilien, and Robins (1987) using a linear Arch(12) specification on quarterly data for the excess holding yield of six-month Treasury bills over three-month Treasury bills. At the same time, the estimates for 20-year AAA corporate bonds suggest that for the longer end of the term structure, volatility shocks may be somewhat less persistent. A formal investigation of this issue would be interesting. Note also that the results in Engle, Ng, and Rothschild (1990) indicate that the underlying forces behind the volatility shocks for the shorter end of the term structure are common across the different rates, indicative of co-persistence in variance.

Whereas the simple Arch models with conditionally normal errors have been found inadequate in capturing all the excess kurtosis for stock return and foreign exchange rates, less evidence along these lines is currently available for interest rates. Some exceptions include the studies by Lee and Tse (1991), who find significant evidence against conditional normality in the Singapore Asian dollar market using conditional t and Gram-Charlier distributions, and McCulloch (1985), who finds significant departures from conditional normality in US data using the Adaptive Conditional Heteroskedasticity formulation. Also, most studies involving interest rates have adopted linear Garch(p,q) specifications. However, as with the leverage effect for stock return data discussed above, it is certainly possible that non-linear dependencies exist in the conditional variance for interest rates. A more systematic investigation of both of these issues would be interesting.

ARCH-M AND TIME-VARYING RISK PREMIA

In Engle, Lilien, and Robins (1987) the ARCH-M model is applied to quarterly data on the excess holding yield of six-month over three-month Treasury bills from 1960 to 1984. After experimenting with different functional forms a significant time-varying risk premium as proxied by the logarithm of the conditional variance is found to provide the best fit for the data. On average the term premium is only 0.14 quarterly per cent, but it varies in a systematic way through the sample.[26] Interestingly, with the notable exception of the yield spread, variables which had previously been found successful in forecasting excess returns generally are no longer significant when a function of the conditional variance is included as a regressor. Similar results are reported in Baba (1984). However, the empirical findings for the six-month Treasury bill data have been called into question by Pagan and Sabau (1987b) who, on using several different tests for consistency, argue that the Arch(12) variance equation is misspecified, resulting in inconsistent parameter estimates for the risk premium term.

The usefulness of the Arch-M model for providing a good measure of risk has also been challenged on more theoretical grounds by Backus, Gregory, and Zin (1989). By generating data from an artificial Mehra and Prescott (1985) representative agent dynamic exchange economy in which the risk premia are known functions of the state, it is shown that in this economy the Arch effects are more closely related to forecast errors than to the risk premium. This issue is pursued further in Backus and Gregory (1988), who show that there need be no relationship between the risk premium and conditional variances in their theoretical economy. In contrast, Morgan and Neave (1989) derive a theoretical model in which the return of a futures contract is linearly determined by its own conditional standard deviation. Using Treasury bill futures and Eurodollar futures contracts, the explicit Arch-M specification suggested by the theory is generally supported empirically, although other variables such as day-of-the-week effects and the level of short-term interest rates are also found to be important. Among other extensions, more theoretical work along these lines could prove insightful. Also, the application of an Arch-M framework might help shed light on the recently debated issue of the relationship between term structure and the Federal Reserve System; see Mankiw, Miron, and Weil (1987, 1990), Hardouvelis (1988), and Fishe and Wohar (1990).

MULTIVARIATE ARCH AND THE TERM STRUCTURE

As discussed above, the theoretical motivation for the significant univariate ARCH-M relationships observed with short-term interest rates is somewhat lacking. Most asset pricing theories call for an explicit tradeoff between the expected returns and the conditional covariance(s) with some benchmark portfolio(s). For instance, according to the standard CAPM the expected returns are proportional to the covariance of the returns with the market portfolio. As discussed above, Bollerslev, Engle, and Wooldridge (1988) use a trivariate Garch(1,1)-M model to implement a CAPM with time-varying covariances, assuming the market consists of only bills, bonds, and stocks. Interestingly, the non-diversifiable risk as measured by the time-varying conditional covariance with the market is found to provide a better explanation for the term premia than does the own conditional variance from the corresponding univariate Garch(1,1)-M models. The implied betas for both bills and bonds are also found to be time-varying and forecastable. Similarly, Evans (1989) employs a multivariate Arch-M approach in estimating and testing an intertemporal CAPM in which the betas are allowed to change through time, and finds that the ICAPM is not rejected if the benchmark portfolio is taken to include both stocks and real estate.

The pricing of the short end of the term structure is studied in Engle, Ng, and Rothschild (1990) using data on two-month through 12-month Treasury bills. Interestingly, on applying both one- and two-factor versions of the factor Arch model, an equally-weighted bill portfolio is found to be effective in predicting both the volatility and the risk premium across the different maturities. Engle and Ng (1990) use a similar model to study the shape of the yield curve through time and the effect of yield shocks on volatility; see also the empirical evidence in Steeley (1990) pertaining to UK data. Among many other promising extensions, future work for the longer end of the term structure would be desirable.

In a different application, Evans and Wachtel (1990) investigate the effects of movements of output and inflation on interest rates based on a generalised Fisher equation derived from the consumption CAPM. Using monthly data and an indirect two-step estimation procedure, Evans and Wachtel (1990) argue that, in contrast to the standard Fisher equation, the consumption-based CAPM generalisation with time-varying conditional covariances and time-varying coefficients adequately explains the dynamics of short-term interest rates.

DYNAMIC HEDGING

The traditional estimate of the risk-minimising hedge ratio is found by regressing the instrument being hedged on the hedging instrument, corresponding to an estimate of the unconditional covariance divided by the unconditional variance. This is also the approach taken in the study by Park and Bera (1987), where estimates for the risk-minimising hedge ratio with spot and futures mortgage rates (GNMA) are presented. Park and Bera (1987) find that, when cross-hedging is involved, the regression residuals are characterised by Arch, and more efficient estimates of the hedge ratio are obtained by explicitly modelling the heteroskedasticity using a simple linear Arch(1) model; see also Bera, Park, and Bubnys (1987).

However, the systematic temporal variation observed in the conditional second-order moments for the most high-frequency financial time series, including interest rates and interest rate futures, means that the hedge ratios which involve functions of the conditional variances and covariances will generally not be time-invariant. The multivariate Arch model is ideally suited to addressing this question. This is the approach taken by Cecchetti, Cumby, and Figlewski (1988), where a bivariate linear Arch(3) model with constant conditional correlations is estimated for monthly 20-year Treasury bonds and Treasury bonds futures. Both the estimates for the risk-minimising hedge ratio and the utility optimising hedge ratio, obtained under the assumption of log utility, are found to exhibit substantial variation through the sample period, ranging between 0.52 and 0.91. Among other interesting extensions, the same ideas could be used in the analysis of immunisation and portfolio insurance strategies.

Applications of Arch to foreign exchange rate data

The characterisation of exchange rate movements, including second-order dynamics, have important implications for many issues in international finance. In addition to international asset pricing theories along the lines discussed in the previous two sections for domestic assets, international portfolio management obviously depends on expected exchange rate movements through time. Several policy-oriented questions relating to the impact of the exchange rate on different macroeconomic variables also require an understanding of the exchange rate dynamics.

ARCH EFFECTS AND MODEL SPECIFICATION

As for other speculative prices, traditional time series models have not been able to capture the stylised facts of short-run exchange rate movements such as their contiguous periods of volatility and stability together with their leptokurtic unconditional distributions; see, for example, Mussa (1979) and Friedman and Vandersteel (1982). As discussed above, the Arch class of models is ideally suited to modelling such behaviour. Whereas stock returns have been found to exhibit some degree of asymmetry in their conditional variances, the two-sided nature of the foreign exchange market makes such asymmetrics less likely. In the absence of any structural model for the conditional variances, the linear Garch(p,q) model in (7) therefore is a natural candidate for modelling exchange rate dynamics.

For example, using daily data on five different nominal US dollar rates, Hsieh (1988a) argues that the conditional distributions of the daily nominal returns are changing through time, as evidenced by the significant autocorrelations for the squared returns, but that an Arch(12) model with linearly declining lag structure captures most of the non-linear stochastic dependencies present; see also Milhøj (1987a), Diebold (1988), and Diebold and Nerlove (1989).[27] These findings are corroborated in the later papers by Hsieh (1989a, b) using Garch(1,1) type formulations.[28] Interestingly, judged on the basis of the BDS test for the standardised squared residuals, the simple Garch(1,1) model does better in describing the data than the Arch(12) model estimated in Hsieh (1988a). Similar conclusions are reached in the studies by Taylor (1986), McCurdy and Morgan (1988), Kugler and Lenz (1990), and Papell and Sayers (1990).

Of course, as for other speculative prices, it is possible that the significant Arch effects could be due to misspecified first-order dynamics resulting in dependence in the higher-order conditional moments. However, if such non-linear dependence is present in the conditional mean it should be exploitable for forecasting purposes. Interestingly, in a detailed non-parametric analysis using locally-weighted regression techniques for 10 weekly US dollar exchange rates. Diebold and Nason (1990) find that forecasts based on these non-parametric estimates lead to no improvement in forecast accuracy when compared to the forecasts from a simple martingale model, consistent with the idea that any significant dependencies in short-run exchange rate movements work through the conditional variance and higher even-ordered conditional moments only. Similar conclusions are reached in the studies by Meese and Rose (1991) and Kim (1989), though Taylor (1990b) surprisingly argues that the conditional mean can be predicted well enough to obtain net trading profits.

While Arch effects are highly significant with daily and weekly data, both Diebold (1988) and Baillie and Bollerslev (1989) have noted that Arch effects tend to weaken with less frequently sampled data. For example, in Baillie and Bollerslev (1989) the average Ljung-Box portmanteau test for the first ten autocorrelations for the squared logarithmic first difference of the exchange rates averaged across the six currencies decreases gradually from a highly significant 130.6 for daily data to an insignificant 10.6 for data sampled monthly. This is in accordance with the asymptotic results in Diebold (1986b, 1988), and as shown in Drost and Nijman (1991) the actual parameter estimates obtained by Baillie and Bollerslev (1989) for the Garch(1,1) models with less frequently sampled data may also be explained by aggregation effects. For most domestic assets the empirical evidence pertaining to temporal aggregation is less clear, possibly due to compounding higher-order non-linear dependencies. A detailed empirical study of these issues across different asset categories seems worthwhile.

NON-NORMAL CONDITIONAL DENSITIES

While the simple symmetric linear Garch(1,1) model may provide a good description of the second-order dynamics for most exchange rate series over the post-1973 free float, the assumption of conditional normality does not capture all the excess kurtosis observed in daily or weekly data; see McCurdy and Morgan (1987), Milhøj (1987a), Hsieh (1989a), and Baillie and Bollerslev (1989). As discussed above the resulting QML estimates obtained under the assumption of conditional normality are generally consistent and asymptotically normally distributed but the asymptotic covariance matrix of the parameter estimates will have to be appropriately modified. However, in many applications, including options pricing, a complete characterisation of the distribution for the spot rates and not just the conditional variance are of interest.

Following the discussion in the previous sections, several alternative conditional error distributions have consequently been employed in the literature. Baillie and Bollerslev (1989) find that the Student-t distribution compares favourably to the power exponential and captures the excess kurtosis for most of the rates. The Student-t distribution is also estimated by Hsieh (1989a), together with the generalised error distribution, a normal-Poisson, and a normal-lognormal mixture distribution. It is also worth noting the results in Jorion (1988), where the jump-diffusion Arch(1) model discussed above is estimated for weekly data on the Deutschmark/dollar rate for the 1974–85 period. Based on a standard likelihood ratio test, both the jump process parameters and the Arch parameters are jointly significant, consistent with the presence of excess kurtosis in the standardised residuals from conventional Arch models.

In a related context, Lastrapes (1989) finds, not surprisingly, that including dummy variables in the conditional variance to allow for changes in the policy of the FED reduces the degree of leptokurtosis in the standardised residuals.[29] Similarly, McCurdy and Morgan (1988) find that departures from conditional normality tend to be associated with a few specific policy events. Further work trying to determine endogenously the timing of major exchange rate movements and changes in regimes would be interesting and could help explain part of the remaining leptokurtosis; see also Engel and Hamilton (1990).

NON-LINEAR AND NON-PARAMETRIC ARCH

As discussed in the previous section, several authors have noted deviations from normality in the standardised residuals from estimated linear Garch(p,q) models, and successfully proceeded to characterise these deviations by some parametric leptokurtic density. Alternatively, following the discussion above, a non-parametric procedure could be employed. This is the approach taken by Gallant, Hsieh, and Tauchen (1989), where the semi-non-parametric techniques of Gallant and Tauchen (1989) is used in estimating a model for the "recalcitrant" sterling/dollar rate analysed in Hsieh (1989a). The leading term in the expansion for the conditional density resembles the conventional linear Arch model, and contrary to other speculative prices, the response of the conditional variance to negative and positive surprises is virtually symmetric. However, the estimated conditional density has interesting hump-shaped tails. This same shape is also evident in the results reported in Engle and Gonzalez-Rivera (1991), where non-parametric density estimation is used in characterising the distribution of the standardised residuals from a Garch(1,1) model for the same rate and sample period. It is likely that this particular pattern is influenced by a few observations, and therefore peculiar to the given period. In fact, Bollerslev (1987) and Baillie and Bollerslev (1989) on analysing data for sterling for 1980–85, ie excluding data from the 1970s, find little evidence against the simple Garch(1,1) model with t-distributed errors.

SOURCES OF INTERMARKET AND INTRAMARKET VOLATILITY

Maintaining market efficiency, the pronounced Arch effects present with high-frequency data could be due to the amount of information or the quality of the information reaching the market in clusters, or from the time it takes market participants to process the information fully; see, for example, Diebold and Nerlove (1989) and Gallant, Hseih, and Tauchen (1989). In order to show that information processing is the source of the volatility clustering, Engle, Ito, and Lin (1990a) define four separate market locations: Europe, New York, Pacific, and Tokyo. If the information arrivals in one market are uncorrelated with the information arrivals in any other market, a test of whether increased volatility in one market causes an increase in volatility in another market is in effect a test of information processing as the source of volatility clustering. The results in Engle, Ito, and Lin (1990a) with intraday observations on the yen/dollar rate show that, except for the Tokyo market, each market's volatility is significantly affected by changes in volatility in the other markets, so that volatility is transmitted through time and different market locations as a "meteor shower", lending support to the information processing hypothesis. Information processing as the main determinant behind the volatility spillovers is also consistent with the evidence reported in Engle, Ito, and Lin (1990b), who rule out the influence of stochastic policy coordination on the basis of equally important volatility spillover in the early 1980s, a period known for little international policy coordination. Lin (1989) on applying a multivariate factor Arch model reaches a similar conclusion.

Using hourly data on four major US currencies during the first half of 1986, Baillie and Bollerslev (1991) also examine the causal relationship between returns and volatility. Significant evidence for the "meteor shower" hypothesis is again evident. Interestingly, however, Baillie and Bollerslev (1991) also report some evidence for market-specific volatility, after taking account of deterministic patterns across the trading day. Furthermore, the volatility during the day is found to exhibit a very distinct and remarkably similar pattern for all four rates, with increases occurring around the opening and closing of each of the three major world markets, ie London, New York, and Tokyo. Consistent with the findings in Whistler (1988), the US market is overall the most volatile, followed by the European market.

The implementation and tests of more structural models consistent with the empirical findings discussed above would clearly be of interest and could help in gaining some further understanding about the underlying market micro structure theories at work. The empirical analysis of higher-frequency data, such as the continuously recorded bid and ask quotations described in Goodhart (1990), also hold the promise of important insights along these lines.

VOLATILITY PERSISTENCE

In accordance with the findings for stock returns and interest rates, the persistence of volatility shocks in the foreign exchange market is also very high. For instance, Engle and Bollerslev (1986), on estimating a Garch(1,1) model for weekly data on the US data vis à vis the Swiss franc, finds $\alpha_1 + \beta_1 = 0.996$, providing a motivation for the Integrated Garch, or Igarch, class of models discussed above. Very similar results are reported in Bollerslev (1987), McCurdy and Morgan (1987, 1988), Hsieh (1988a), Kim (1989), Baillie and Bollerslev (1989), Hsieh (1989a), and Taylor (1990a).[30]

Even though many different currencies may exhibit Igarch-type behaviour, it is certainly possible that this persistence is common across different rates.[31]

The presence of such co-persistence among the variances has many important practical implications (for example, in optimal portfolio allocation decisions involving a trade-off between future expected returns and the associated risk). The empirical relevance of this idea has been illustrated within the context of a bivariate Garch(1,1) model by Bollerslev and Engle (1990), where it is found that most of the persistence in the conditional covariance matrix for the Deutschmark and the sterling/dollar rates derives from some common set of underlying forcing variables, and that the corresponding bilateral sterling/Deutschmark rate has much less persistent volatility shocks. In addition to further theoretical work along these lines, extensions of the limited empirical evidence to other currencies and asset categories would be desirable.

ARCH-M MODELS AND THE RISK PREMIUM

A growing body of literature has found that the forward rate is not an unbiased predictor of the corresponding future spot rate; see, for example, Hakkio (1981), Hsieh (1984), Baillie (1989), and McCurdy and Morgan (1991a). Assuming that expectations are rational, a risk premium can reconcile this observation with market efficiency, and several theoretical models have been formulated which generate risk premia in foreign exchange markets.[32] Examples include Hodrick and Srivastava (1984), Domowitz and Hakkio (1985), Diebold and Pauly (1988a), and Kendall (1989). According to most of these theories, the risk premium depends on some function of the conditional probability distribution of the future spot rate. Given the evidence in the previous sections pertaining to the time-varying nature of the conditional distribution of spot exchange rates, this may therefore result in a time-varying risk premium. Several different specifications and proxies for this risk premium have been used empirically, many of which depend directly on the conditional variance of the spot rate; see Hodrick (1987) for an excellent survey of this literature.

The first attempts by Domowitz and Hakkio (1985) and Diebold and Pauly (1988a) at modelling such a time-varying risk premium in the forward foreign exchange market within a univariate Arch-M framework were largely unsuccessful. Several explanations for this are possible. For example, the problem of determining who is compensated for risk in an exchange economy might argue against the constancy of the Arch-M parameter, leading to insignificant results.[33] An alternative explanation is that both studies use monthly data, which as above generally shows only minimal Arch effects, thereby leading to insignificant findings.[34]

Indeed, Kendall and McDonald (1989) on using weekly data for the Australian dollar/US dollar and a Garch(1,1)-M model obtain a significant estimate for the Arch-M parameter. Conversely, the results in McCurdy and Morgan (1988) with daily and weekly futures data, and in Kendall (1989) with weekly spot data do not support a significant simple mean-variance tradeoff. However, since the conditional variance merely serves as a proxy for the risk premium, a more structural based multivariate approach is likely to be superior from a theoretical perspective.

Before we turn to a discussion of the implementation of such multivariate models, it is worth noting the analysis in Hodrick (1989), where an Arch-M model is used to examine how the exchange rate is affected by the uncertainty in the inflation rate, monetary policy, and income growth. A two-step procedure is employed in which the exogenous conditional variances are estimated from a set of linear Arch(1) models, and subsequently used as regressors to explain the monthly movements in the US exchange rate for Japan, West Germany, and the United Kingdom. As the conditional variance estimates again show little temporal variation on a monthly basis, the results for the formal monetary cash-in-advance model are somewhat disappointing, but holds the promise of important future insight. Of course, from a more technical point of view, the indirect two-step procedure is subject to the same criticism as discussed above.

MULTIVARIATE ARCH MODELS AND ASSET PRICING

Several authors have speculated that the weak results that have been found in the foreign exchange market using univariate Arch-M models to estimate time-varying risk premia might be due to the conditional variances being poor proxies for risk; see, for example, Domowitz and Hakkio (1985), McCurdy and Morgan (1987, 1988), Diebold and Pauly (1988a), Lee (1988), Thomas and Wickens (1989), and Baillie and Bollerslev (1990). In particular, the premium might be better approximated by a function of the time-varying cross-currency conditional covariances as opposed to the own conditional variance.

Indirect support for this hypothesis is provided by Lee (1988), who finds that the conditional covariance between the Deutschmark and the yen/dollar spot rates, as modelled by a bivariate Arch(12) model, helps explain the weekly movements in the yen/US dollar rate. The results in Baillie and Bollerslev (1990) with weekly data and a four-dimensional Garch(1,1) model for the one-month-forward rate forecast error for four European currencies also indicate highly significant contemporaneous correlations. However, the time-varying conditional covariances do not yield any improvement in forecast accuracy beyond the MA(4) correlation structure in the overlapping forward rate forecast errors implied from a simple martingale model for the spot rates.

More formal tests for mean-variance efficiency and alternative pricing formulations have also found their implementation in the foreign exchange market. Attanasio and Edey (1988), Mark (1988), Engel and Rodrigues (1989), and Giovannini and Jorion (1989) all estimate and test specifications of the international CAPM in Frankel (1982), while explicitly allowing for a time-varying conditional covariance matrix. Modelling the temporal dependence in the second-order moments generally leads to significantly better performance of the model and a more precise estimate of the coefficient of relative risk aversion. Nonetheless, both Engel and Rodrigues (1989) using five-monthly US exchange rates and Giovannini and Jorion (1989) with weekly data on three US currencies and a stock market index, formally reject the restrictions implied by the CAPM. An alternative structural based approach is taken by Kaminsky and Peruga (1990), who estimate a version of the intertemporal consumption-based CAPM in which the risk premium is a function of the time-varying conditional covariances between the future spot rate and consumption. Using monthly data together with a multivariate Arch(1) formulation little support for the model is forthcoming. Of course, the model may still provide a good description over shorter time intervals than one month, but the availability of data complicates such an analysis; see McCurdy and Morgan (1991a). In fact using weekly foreign exchange rates, McCurdy and Morgan (1991b) find evidence of a significant time-varying risk premium in deviations from uncovered interest rate parity, where the risk premium is given by the conditional covariance with a benchmark portfolio set equal to the return on a worldwide equity index.

While the studies discussed above have highlighted the importance of accounting for short-lived temporal variation in both conditional variances and covariances, a completely satisfactory model for the time-varying risk premium in the forward foreign exchange market has yet to be formulated.

MULTIVARIATE ARCH MODELS, POLICY ANALYSIS, AND DYNAMIC HEDGING

Multivariate ARCH models have also been useful in addressing various policy issues related to the foreign exchange market. For instance, Diebold and Pauly (1988b) and Bollerslev (1990) study the effect on short-run exchange rate volatility following the creation of the European Monetary System (EMS). Both studies find an increase in the conditional variances and covariances among the different European rates after the 1979 inception of the EMS. At the same time, Bollerslev (1990), on estimating a multivariate Garch(1,1) model with constant conditional correlations, argues that the coherence also increased over the EMS period, possibly as a result of the increased policy coordination among the member countries.

In a series of recent papers, the effect of central bank interventions on foreign exchange dynamics have been analysed in the context of a Garch formulation by Connolly and Taylor (1990), Humpage and Osterbert (1990), and Mundaca (1990). A common finding across these studies concerns the positive correlation between current intervention and exchange rate volatility. However, further analysis regarding the simultaneous determination of exchange rates and intervention policies seems warranted.

Other macroeconomic motivated applications include Kroner and Lastrapes (1991), who use a multivariate Garch(1,1)-M model to show that exchange rate uncertainty significantly affects the level and the price of trade in the economy. In a related context, Kroner and Claessens (1991) present a dynamic multiple hedging model based on the intertemporal CAPM in which the optimal hedging portfolio is a function of the time-varying variances and covariances. Using a multivariate Garch(1,1) model, the optimal debt portfolios for Indonesia are estimated.

Given the substantial increase in international portfolio diversification by many investors and institutions in recent years coupled with the complex second-order dynamics of short-run exchange rate movements, it would be very interesting to extend the analysis in Kroner and Claessens (1991) and Cecchetti, Cumby, and Figlewski (1988), discussed above, to optimal dynamic hedging strategies for the currency risk involved with direct short-term investment in foreign assets. The results in Kroner and Sultan (1991) pertaining to the yen and Baillie and Myers (1991) for different commodities are encouraging.

Conclusion

Volatility is a key variable which permeates most financial instruments and plays a central role in many areas of finance. For example, volatility is crucially important in asset pricing models and dynamic hedging strategies as well as in the determination of options prices. From an empirical standpoint, it is therefore of utmost importance to model carefully any temporal variation in the volatility process. The Arch model and its various extensions have proven very effective tools along these lines. Indeed, by any yardstick, the literature on Arch has expanded dramatically since the seminal paper by Engle (1982). However, many interesting research topics remain to be examined, some of which are discussed above and others of which the reader will undoubtedly glean upon reading this survey. It is our hope that this overview of the extensive Arch literature may serve as a catalyst in fostering further research in this important area.

1 *Throughout this paper, the dependence of* ε_t *and* σ_t *on the parameter vector* θ *are suppressed for notational convenience.*

2 *It is also worth noting that in the presence of Arch(q) effects, standard tests for serial correlation in the mean will lead to overrejections, see Weiss (1984), Taylor (1984), Milhøj (1985), Diebold (1987), and Domowitz and Hakkio (1987) for further discussion.*

3 *The simple Garch(1,1) model was independently suggested by Taylor (1986).*

4 *In an interesting paper, Hansen (1990) derives sufficient conditions for near epoch dependence and the application of standard asymptotic theory in a Garch(1,1) model.*

5 *As pointed out in Milhøj (1990) within the context of the Arch(1) model, the asymptotic standard error for the autocorrelations and the partial autocorrelations for* ε_t^2 *exceeds* $1/\sqrt{T}$ *in the presence of Arch, thus leading to potentially lower power of such tests.*

6 *See also the comparison in Taylor (1990a) of the statistical properties of the Garch(1,1) and autoregressive random variable (ARV) models motivated by diffusion formulations.*

7 *It follows from Jensen's inequality that with a correctly specified conditional variance, the excess kurtosis in* $\varepsilon_t\sigma_t^{-1}$ *cannot exceed the excess kurtosis in* ε_t*; see Hsieh (1989a).*

8 *At the same time, abstracting from any inference, Nelson (1990d) has shown that the normal quasi-likelihood increases with more precise volatility estimates (appropriately defined), while this is not generally true for non-normal likelihood functions.*

9 *In the continuous conditionally normal Garch(1,1) diffusion approximation discussed in Nelson (1990b), the innovations observed over short time intervals are*

approximately t-*distributed.*

10 *The fact that the information matrix is not block diagonal between the "density parameters" and the Arch parameters complicates the adaptive estimation of the Arch parameters, as suggested by Engle and Gonzalez-Rivera (1991).*

11 *To guard against the influence of outliers, the "leave-one-out" estimator is often adopted; ie* $\tau \neq t$.

12 *One possible explanation for the empirical Igarch behaviour is provided by the diffusion approximations in Nelson (1990b). In the diffusion limit for the Garch(1,1) model,* $\alpha_1 + \beta_1$ *converges to one as the sampling frequency diminishes.*

13 *An unobserved component alternative to the Igarch model has recently been proposed by Shephard (1990).*

14 *The IGARCH(1,1) model with* $\omega = 0$ *is closely related to the ACH formulation in terms of absolute errors proposed by McCulloch (1985).*

15 *In terms of the log-likelihood function in (4), the Jacobian term* $-\log |\Omega_t^{1/2}|$ *replaces* $-\log \sigma_t$ *and* $\varepsilon_t \Omega_t^{-1/2}$ *replaces* $\varepsilon_t \sigma_t^{-1}$.

16 *The monthly variance estimate is often adjusted by adding two times the first-order daily sample serial correlation coefficient in order to account for any negative autocorrelation possibly induced by non-synchronous trading.*

17 *Bookstaber and Pomerantz (1989) arrive at a compound Poisson process for volatility by assuming a linear relation to the underlying information arrival process..*

18 *Following Tauchen and Pitts (1983) such serial correlation in the news arrival process would likely induce a strong contemporaneous relationship between volume and volatility as well, thus explaining the Lamoureux and Lastrapes (1990a) results.*

19 *Schwert (1990a) finds that futures returns tend to be slightly more volatile than cash returns, possibly because futures react more quickly to news due to lower transactions costs and because they price the underlying bundle of securities simultaneously.*

20 *Interestingly, Baillie and DeGennaro (1989) have argued that by including a proxy for variations in delivery and payment terms, the effect of the holding period in the conditional variance becomes much less important.*

21 *As shown in Brock, Hsieh, and LeBaron (1991) both analytically and through Monte Carlo methods, a correction factor is required when applying the BDS statistic to standardised residuals from estimated Garch models. Failure to do so would lead to overrejections, ie, finding non-linear dependence, too often.*

22 *In discussing the Arch-in-Mean relationship it is also worth noting the recent empirical findings in Sentana and Wadhwani (1991) where, motivated by a noise trading model in which some traders follow feedback strategies, it is found that the constancy of the serial correlation parameter is affected by the level of volatility. Similarly, LeBaron (1989) argues that the magnitude of the serial correlation is inversely related to the volatility, consistent with non-synchronous trading being more severe when volatility and volume are both low.*

23 *Attanasio (1991), however, argues that if volatility is high enough, then it does not have to persist in order to affect returns.*

24 *This could be because large outliers might be the result of large doses of measurement error, which would not be expected to persist.*

25 *Allowing for a unit root in the short rate could also explain the apparent excess volatility; see Campbell and Shiller (1991).*

26 *Amsler (1985) uses the liquidity premium estimated by Engle, Lilien, and Robins (1987) in deriving the implied variance bound for the long versus short rate. Including this time-varying liquidity premium is found to widen the variance bound and weaken Shiller's (1979) conclusion of excess volatility.*

27 *Tsay (1987), on using a generalisation of the time-varying parameter formulation of the standard linear Arch(q) model as discussed above, finds that when allowing for cross-parameter correlations the estimates from this model with weekly data on the sterling/ dollar exchange rate are very close to the results obtained with a conventional linear Arch(12) model.*

28 *Only for sterling, as analysed further in Gallant, Hsieh, and Tauchen (1989) using semi-non-parametric methods, is there any substantial evidence against the Garch(1,1) model including deterministic vacation effects in the conditional variance as a simple parsimonious representation of the daily nominal rates.*

29 *Also, the degree of persistence in the conditional variance is diminished.*

30 *Somewhat puzzling, for the hourly Garch(24,1) models with hourly dummy variables in the conditional variances reported by Baillie and Bollerslev (1991), the estimates indicate much less persistence, with* $\hat{\alpha}_1 + \hat{\alpha}_{24} + \hat{\beta}_1$ *between 0.374 and 0.771 only.*

31 *For example, in a study similar to Lamoureux and Lastrapes (1990a), Connolly (1990) finds that using contemporaneous volume in the conditional variance equation for the yen/dollar spot rate tends to decrease the measured persistence, suggesting a common forcing variable for volume and volatility.*

32 *An alternative explanation consistent with market efficiency would be the restriction imposed by limit moves. However, in a detailed empirical analysis, Kodres (1990) finds little support for this hypothesis.*

33 *Also, Frankel (1986) argues that the risk premium must be small because it is determined by the conditional variance of the difference between the change in the spot rate*

and the forward discount, which is bounded by the unconditional variance. However, as Pagan (1988) points out, this argument is not true if the conditional variance is changing through time. Thus as noted in Frankel (1988), only the average risk premium must be small.

34 *In contrast, Pagan and Ullah (1988) find strong support for the presence of a time-varying risk-premium in the Canadian dollar/US dollar market with monthly data over the earlier time period from 1970–78. The risk premium here is proxied by a simple linear function of a non-parametric estimate for the conditional variance obtained from a normal kernel. However, this might be driven by the influence of the Quebec crisis.*

BIBLIOGRAPHY

Admati, A.R., and P. Pfleiderer, 1988, "A theory of intraday patterns: Volume and price variability", *Review of Financial Studies* 1, pp. 3–40.

Akgiray, V., 1989, "Conditional heteroskedasticity in time series of stock returns: Evidence and forecasts", *Journal of Business* 62, pp. 55–80.

Amihud, Y., and H. Mendelson, 1989, "Market microstructure and price discovery on the Tokyo Stock Exchange", *Japan and the World Economy* 1, pp. 341–70.

Amsler, C., 1985, "Including time varying liquidity premia in term structure variance bounds", Unpublished manuscript, Michigan State University.

Attanasio, O.P., 1988, "A note on the persistence of volatility and stock market fluctuations", Unpublished manuscript, London School of Economics.

Attanasio, Orazio P., 1991, "Risk, time varying second moments and market efficiency", *Review of Economic Studies* 58, pp. 479–94.

Attansio, O.P., and M. Edey, 1988, "Non-constant variances and foreign exchange risk: An empirical study", Unpublished manuscript, London School of Economics.

Attansio, O.P., and S. Wadhwani, 1989, "Risk and the predictability of stock market returns", Unpublished manuscript, Stanford University.

Baba, Y., 1984, "Estimation of the effect of uncertainty: Theory and empirical studies", Unpublished Ph.D. dissertation, University of California, San Diego.

Baba, Y., R.F. Engle, D.F. Kraft, and K.F. Kroner, 1991, "Multivariate simultaneous generalised ARCH", Unpublished manuscript, University of California, San Diego.

Backus, D.K., and A.W. Gregory, 1988, "Theoretical relations between risk premiums and conditional variances", Unpublished manuscript, Federal Reserve Bank of Minneapolis.

Backus, D.K., A.W. Gregory, and S.E. Zin, 1989, "Risk premiums in the term structure: Evidence from artificial economics", *Journal of Monetary Economics* 24, pp. 371–99.

Baillie, R.T., 1989, "Econometric tests of rationality and market efficiency", *Econometric Reviews* 8, pp. 151–86.

Baillie, R.T., and T. Bollerslev, 1989, "The message in daily exchange rates: A conditional variance tale", *Journal of Business and Economic Statistics* 7, pp. 297–305.

Baillie, R.T., and T. Bollerslev, 1990, "A multivariate generalised ARCH approach to modeling risk premia in forward foreign rate markets", *Journal of International Money and Finance* 9, pp. 309–24.

Baillie, R. T., and T. Bollerslev, 1991, "Intra day and inter market volatility in foreign exchange rates", *Review of Economic Studies* 58, pp. 565–85.

Baillie, R.T., and T. Bollerslev, 1992, "Conditional forecast densities from dynamic models with GARCH innovations", *Journal of Econometrics* 52, 1-2, pp. 91–113.

Baillie, R.T., and R.P. DeGennaro, 1989, "The impact of delivery terms on stock return volatility", *Journal of Financial Services Research* 3, pp. 55–76.

Baillie, R.T., and R.P. DeGennaro, 1990, "Stock returns and volatility", *Journal of Financial and Quantitative Analysis* 25, pp. 203–14.

Baillie, R.T., and R.J. Myers, 1991, "Modelling commodity price distributions and estimating the optimal futures hedge", *Journal of Applied Econometrics* 6, pp. 109–124.

Bera, A.K., and M. L. Higgins, 1991, "A test for conditional heteroskedasticity in time series models", Unpublished manuscript (Department of Economics, University of Illinois, Champaign, IL).

Bera, A.K., and S. Lee, 1989, "On the formulation of a general structure for conditional heteroskedasticity", Unpublished manuscript, University of Illinois.

Bera, N.K., and S. Lee, 1991, "Information matrix test, parameter heterogeneity and ARCH: A synthesis", Unpublished manuscript, University of Illinois.

Bera, A. K., E. Bubnys, and H. Park, 1988, "Conditional heteroskedasticity in the market model and efficient estimates of betas", *Financial Review* 23, pp. 201–14.

Bera, A.K., M.L. Higgins, and S. Lee, 1991, "Interaction between autocorrelation and conditional heteroskedasticity: A random coefficient approach", Unpublished manuscript, University of Illinois.

Bera, A.K., H. Park, and E. Bubnys, 1987, "The ARCH effects and efficient estimation of hedge ratios: Stock index futures", Unpublished manuscript, University of Illinois.

Black, F., 1976, "Studies in stock price volatility changes", *Proceedings of the 1976 Business Meeting of the Business and Economic Statistics Section, American Statistical Association*, pp. 177-81.

Black, F., and M. Scholes, 1972, "The valuation of option contracts and a test of market efficiency", *Journal of Finance* 37, pp. 399-417.

Black, F., and M. Scholes, 1973, "The pricing of options and corporate liabilities", *Journal of Political Economy* 81, pp. 637-59.

Bodurtha, J.N., and N. C. Mark, 1991, "Testing the CAPM with time varying risks and returns", *Journal of Finance* 46, pp. 1485-505.

Bollerslev, T., 1986, "Generalised autoregressive conditional heteroskedasticity", *Journal of Econometrics* 31, pp. 307-27.

Bollerslev, T., 1987, "A conditional heteroskedastic time series model for speculative prices and rates of return", *Review of Economics and Statistics* 69, pp. 542-7.

Bollerslev, T., 1988, "On the correlation structure for the generalised autoregressive conditional heteroskedastic process", *Journal of Time Series Analysis* 9, pp. 121-31.

Bollerslev, T., 1990, "Modelling the coherence in short-run nominal exchange rates: A multi-variate generalised ARCH approach", *Review of Economics and Statistics* 72, pp. 498-505.

Bollerslev, T., and I. Domowitz, 1991, "Price volatility, spread variability and the role of alternative market mechanisms", *Review of Futures Markets*.

Bollerslev, T., and R.F. Engle, 1990, "Common persistence in conditional variance: Definition and representation", Unpublished manuscript (J.L. Kellogg Graduate School, Northwestern University, Evanston, IL).

Bollerslev, T., and J.M. Wooldridge, 1991, "Quasi maximum likelihood estimation and inference in dynamic models with time varying covariances", *Econometric Reviews*.

Bollerslev, T., R.F. Engle, and J. M. Wooldridge, 1988, "A capital asset pricing model with time varying covariances", *Journal of Political Economy* 96, pp. 116-31.

Bookstaber, R.M., and S. Pomerantz, 1989, "An information based model of market volatility", *Financial Analysis Journal* Nov/Dec, pp. 37-46.

Bougerol, P., and N. Picard, 1992, "Stationarity of GARCH processes and of some nonnegative time series", *Journal of Econometrics* 52, 1-2, pp. 115-27.

Breeden, D.T., 1979, "An intertemporal asset pricing model with stochastic consumption and investment opportunities", *Journal of Financial Economics* 7, pp. 265-96.

Brock, W.A., and A.W. Kleidon, 1990, "Exogenous demand shocks and trading volume: A model of intraday bids and asks", Unpublished manuscript, University of Wisconsin.

Brock, W.A., W.D. Dechert, and J.A. Scheinkman, 1987, "A test for independence based on the correlation dimension", Unpublished manuscript, University of Wisconsin.

Brock, W.A., D.A. Hsieh, and B. LeBaron, 1991, "Nonlinear dynamics, chaos and instability", (MIT Press, Cambridge, MA).

Brock, W.A., J. Lakonishok, and B. LeBaron, 1990, "Simple technical trading rules and the stochastic properties of stock returns", Unpublished manuscript, University of Wisconsin.

Brown, B.W., and A.V. Ligeralde, 1990, "Conditional heteroskedasticity in overlapping prediction models", Unpublished manuscript, Rice University.

Brown, S.J., and J.B. Warner, 1985, "Using daily stock returns: The case of event studies", *Journal of Financial Economics* 14, pp. 3-31.

Campbell, J.Y., 1987, "Stock returns and the term structure", *Journal of Financial Economics* 18, pp. 373-99.

Campbell, J.Y., and L. Hentschel, 1990, "No news is good news: An asymmetric model of changing volatility in stock returns", Unpublished manuscript, Princeton University.

Campbell, J.Y., and R.J. Shiller, 1989, "The divided price ratio and expectations of future dividends and discount factors", *Review of Financial Studies* 1, pp. 175-228.

Campbell, J.Y., and R.J. Shiller, 1991, "Yield spreads and interest rate movements: A bird's eye view", *Review of Economics Studies* 58, pp. 479-94.

Carlson, J.A., 1977, "A study of price forecasts", *Annals of Economic and Social Measurement* 6, pp. 27-56.

Cecchetti, S.G., R.E. Cumby, and S. Figlewski, 1988, "Estimation of the optimal futures hedge", *Review of Economics and Statistics* 70, pp. 623-30.

Chamberlain, G., and M. Rothschild, 1983, "Arbitrage, factor structure and mean-variance analysis on large asset markets", *Econometrica* 51, pp. 1281-304.

Chan, K., K.C. Chan, and G.A. Karolyi, 1990, "Intraday volatility in the stock index and stock index futures markets", Unpublished manuscript, Ohio State University.

Cheung, Y-W. and L.K. Ng, 1990, "The causality in variance test and its application to the US/Japan stock markets", Unpublished manuscript, University of Texas.

Cheung, Y-W. and P. Pauly, 1990, "Random coefficient modeling of conditionally heteroskedastic processes: Short run exchange rate dynamics", Unpublished manuscript, University of Pennsylvania.

Choi, S., and M.E. Wohar, 1990, "Volatility implicit in options markets", Unpublished manuscript, University of Missouri.

Chou, R.Y., 1988, "Volatility persistence and stock valuations: Some empirical evidence using GARCH", *Journal of Applied Econometrics* 3, pp. 279-94.

Chou, R.Y., R.F. Engle, and A. Kane, 1992, "Estimating risk aversion with a time-varying price of volatility", *Journal of Econometrics*, 52, 1-2, pp. 201-24.

Christie, A.A., 1982, "The stochastic behavior of common stock variances: Value, leverage and interest rate effects", *Journal of Financial Economics* 10, pp. 407-32.

Cocco, F., and P. Paruolo, 1990, "Volatility persistence and the Italian risk premium: Parametric and non-parametric evaluation", Unpublished manuscript, Università di Bologna.

Connolly, R.A., 1989, "An examination of the robustness of the weekend effect", *Journal of Financial and Quantitative Analysis* 24, pp. 133-69.

Connolly, R.A., 1990, "Volume and GARCH effects in conditional exchange rate volatility models", Unpublished manuscript, University of North Carolina.

Connolly, R.A, and H. McMillan, 1988, "Time conditional variances and event studies: The case of capital structure changes", Unpublished manuscript, University of California.

Connolly, R.A., and W.A. Taylor, 1990, "The impact of central bank interventions on spot foreign exchange market volatility", Unpublished manuscript, University of North Carolina.

Conrad, J., Mustafa, N. Gultekin, and G. Kaul, 1990, "Asymmetric assimilation of information across securities", Unpublished manuscript, University of North Carolina.

Cragg, J., and B. Malkiel, 1982, "Expectations in the structure of share prices", NBER monograph, University of Chicago Press, Chicago, IL.

Cutler, D., 1989, "Stock market volatility cross-sectional volatility and stock returns", Unpublished manuscript, MIT.

Day, T.E., and C.M. Lewis, 1992, "Stock market volatility and the information content of stock index options", *Journal of Econometrics*.

de Jong, F., A. Kemna, and T. Kloek, 1990, "The impact of option expirations on the Dutch stock market", Unpublished manuscript, Erasmus University.

De Santis, G., and A.M. Sbordone, 1990, "A CAPM with a multivariate generalised ARCH process: An empirical analysis of the Italian financial market", Unpublished manuscript, University of Chicago.

Diebold, F.X., 1986a, "Modeling the persistence of conditional variances: A comment", *Econometric Reviews* 5, pp. 51-6.

Diebold, F.X., 1986b, "Temporal aggregation of ARCH models and the distribution of asset returns", Unpublished manuscript, Federal Reserve Board.

Diebold, F.X., 1987, "Testing for serial correlation in the presence of ARCH", *Proceedings from the American Statistical Association, Business and Economic Statistics Section*, pp. 323-28.

Diebold, F.X., 1988, *Empirical modeling of exchange rate dynamics*, Springer Verlag, New York.

Diebold, Francis, X., and James M. Nason, 1990, "Nonparametric exchange rate prediction", *Journal of International Economics* 28, pp. 315-32.

Diebold, F.X., and M. Nerlove, 1989, "The dynamics of exchange rate volatility: A multivariate latent factor ARCH model", *Journal of Applied Econometrics* 4, pp. 1-21.

Diebold, F.X., and P. Pauly, 1988a, "Endogenous risk in a portfolio balance rational expectations model of the Deutschmark-dollar rate", *European Economic Review* 32, pp. 27-53.

Diebold, F.X., and P. Pauly, 1988b, "Has the EMS reduced member country exchange rate volatility?", *Empirical Economics* 13, pp. 81-102.

Diebold, F., X., and P. Pauly, 1989, "Small sample properties of asymptotically equivalent tests for autoregressive conditional heteroskedasticity", *Statistische Hefte* 30, pp. 105-31.

Diebold, F.X., J. Im, and C. Jevons Lee, 1990, "Conditional heteroskedasticity in the market", *Journal of Accounting, Auditing and Finance*.

Domowitz, I., and C.S. Hakkio, 1985, "Conditional variance and the risk premium in the foreign exchange market", *Journal of International Economics* 19, pp. 47-66.

Domowitz, I. and C.S. Hakkio, 1987, "Testing for serial correlation and common factor dynamics in the presence of heteroskedasticity", Unpublished manuscript, Northwestern University.

Drost, F.C., and T.E. Nijman, 1991, "Temporal aggregation of GARCH processes", Unpublished manuscript, Tilburg University.

Engle, C., and J.D. Hamilton, 1990, "Long swings in the dollar: Are they in the data and do markets know it?" *American Economic Review* 80, pp. 869-713.

Engle, C., and A.P. Rodrigues, 1989, "Tests of international CAPM with time varying covariances, *Journal of Applied Econometrics* 4, pp. 119-38.

Engle, C., A.A. Fraenkel, K.A. Froot, and A. Rodrigues, 1989, "Conditional mean variance efficiency of the US stock market", Unpublished manuscript, University of Virginia.

Engle, R.F., 1982, "Autoregressive conditional heteroskedasticity with estimates of the variance of UK inflation", *Econometrica* 50, pp. 987-1008.

Engle, R.F., 1983, Estimates of the variance of U.S. inflation based on the ARCH model", *Journal of Money, Credit and Banking* 15, pp. 286-301.

Engle, R.F., 1987, "Multivariate GARCH with factor structures - Cointegration in variance", Unpublished manuscript, University of California, San Diego.

Engle, R.F., and T. Bollerslev, 1986, "Modelling the persistence of conditional variances", *Econometric Reviews* 5, 1-50, pp. 81-87.

Engle, R.F., and G. Gonzalez-Rivera, 1991, "Semiparametric ARCH models", *Journal of Business and Economic Statistics* 9, pp. 345-60.

Engle, R.F., and C. Mustafa, 1992, "Implied ARCH models from options prices", *Journal of Econometrics*, 52, 1-2, pp. 289-311.

Engle, R.F., and V.K. Ng, 1990, "An examination of the impact of volatility shocks on the short end of the term structure based on a factor-ARCH model for treasury bills", Unpublished manuscript, University of Michigan.

Engle, R.F., and R. Susmel, 1990, "Intraday mean and volatility relations between US and UK stock market returns", Unpublished manuscript, University of California, San Diego.

Engle, R.F., C.W.J. Granger, and D.F. Kraft, 1984, "Combining competing forecasts of inflation using a bivariate ARCH model", *Journal of Economic Dynamics and Control* 8, pp. 151-165.

Engle, R.F., D.F. Hendry, and D. Trumble, 1985, "Small sample properties of ARCH estimators and tests", *Canadian Journal of Economics* 18, pp. 66-93.

Engle, R.F., T. Hong, and A. Kane, 1992, "Valuation of variance forecasts with simulated options markets", Unpublished manuscript, University of California, San Diego.

Engle, R.F., T. Ito, and W-L. Lin, 1990a, "Meteor showers or heat waves? Heteroskedastic intra daily volatility in the foreign exchange market", *Econometrica* 58, pp. 525-42.

Engle, R,F., T. Ito, and W-L. Lin, 1990b, "Where does the meteor shower come from? The role of stochastic policy coordination", Unpublished manuscript, University of Wisconsin.

Engle, R.F., D.M. Lilien, and R.P. Robins, 1987, "Estimating time varying risk premia in the term structure: The ARCH-M model", *Econometrica* 55, pp. 391-407.

Engle, R.F., V. Ng, and M. Rothschild, 1989, "A factor ARCH model for stock returns", Unpublished manuscript, University of California, San Diego.

Engle, R.F., V. Ng, and M. Rothschild, 1990, "Asset pricing with a factor ARCH covariance structure: Empirical estimates for Treasury bills", *Journal of Econometrics* 45, pp. 213-38.

Evans, M.D.D., 1989, "Interpreting the term structure using the intertemporal capital asset pricing model: An application of the non-linear ARCH-M model", Unpublished manuscript, New York University.

Evans, M.D.D., and P. Wachtel, 1990, "A modern look at asset pricing and short-term interest rates", Unpublished manuscript, NBER working paper no. 3245.

Fama, E.F., 1965, "The behavior of stock market prices", *Journal of Business* 38, pp. 34-105.

Fama, Eugene F., 1976, "Inflation, uncertainty and expected returns on Treasury bills", *Journal of Political Economy* 84, pp. 427-48.

Fama, E.F., and K.R. French, 1988, "Dividend yields and expected stock returns", *Journal of Financial Economics* 22, pp. 3-26.

Ferson, W.E., 1989, "Changes in expected security returns, risk and the level of interest rates", *Journal of Finance* 44, pp. 1191-218.

Ferson, W.E., S. Kandel, and R.F. Stambaugh, 1987, "Tests of asset pricing with time varying risk premiums and market betas", *Journal of Finance* 42, pp. 201-20.

Fishe, R.P., and M. Wohar, 1990, "Did the Federal Reserve System really represent a regime change 1914?", *American Economic Review* 80, pp. 968-76.

Frankel, J.A., 1982, "In search of the exchange risk premium: A six currency test assuming mean-average optimisation", *Journal of International Money and Finance* 1, pp. 255-74.

Frankel, J.A., 1986, "The implications of mean-variance optimisation for four questions in international macroeconomics", *Journal of International Money and Finance* 5, Suppl., S53-75.

Frankel, J.A., 1988, "Recent estimates of time-variation in the conditional variance and in the exchange risk premium", *Journal of International Money and Finance* 7, pp. 115-25.

Frankel, J.A., and K.A. Froot, 1987, "Using survey data to test standard propositions regarding exchange rate expectations", *American Economic Review* 77, pp. 133-53.

French, K.R., and R. Roll, 1986, "Stock return variances: The arrival of information and the reaction of traders", *Journal of Financial Economics* 17, pp. 5-26.

French, K.R., G.W. Schwert, and R.F. Stambaugh, 1987, "Expected stock returns and volatility", *Journal of Financial Economics* 19, pp. 3-30.

French, M.W., 1990, "Multivariate asset pricing models",

Unpublished manuscript, Federal Reserve Board.

Friedman, B.M., and K.N. Kuttner, 1988, "Time varying risk perceptions and the pricing of risky assets", Unpublished manuscript, Harvard University.

Friedman, B.M., and D.I. Laibson, 1989, "Economic implications of extraordinary movements in stock prices", *Brookings Papers on Economic Activity* 2, pp. 137-89.

Friedman, D., and S. Vandersteel, 1982, "Short-run fluctuations in foreign exchange rates", *Journal of International Economics* 13, pp. 171-86.

Froot, K.A., and J.A. Frankel, 1989, "Forward discount bias: Is it an exchange risk premium?" *Quarterly Journal of Economics* 103, pp. 139-61.

Gallant, A.R., 1981, "On the bias in flexible functional forms and an essentially unbiased form: The Fourier flexible form", *Journal of Econometrics* 15, pp. 211-44.

Gallant, A.R., and D.W. Nychka, 1987, "Seminonparametric maximum likelihood estimation", *Econometrica* 55, pp. 363-90.

Gallant, A.R, and G. Tauchen, 1989, "Semi non-parametric estimation of conditionally constrained heterogeneous processes: Asset pricing applications", *Econometrica* 57, pp. 1091-120.

Gallant, A.R, L.P. Hansen, and G. Tauchen, 1989, "Using conditional moments of asset payoffs to infer the volatility of intertemporal marginal rates of substitution", Unpublished manuscript, Duke University.

Gallant, A.R., D.A. Hsieh, and G. Tauchen, 1989, "On fitting a recalcitrant series: The pound/dollar exchange rate 1974-82", Unpublished manuscript, Duke University.

Gallant, A.R., P.E. Rossi, and G. Tauchen, 1990, "Stock prices and volume", Unpublished manuscript, Duke University.

Gennotte, G., and T. Marsh, 1987, "Valuations in economic uncertainty and risk premiums on capital assets" Unpublished manuscript, University of California, Berkeley.

Geweke, J., 1986, "Modeling the persistence of conditional variance: A comment", *Econometric Reviews* 5, pp. 57-61.

Geweke, J., 1988, "Exact inference in models with autoregressive conditional heteroskedasticity, in: E. Berndt, H. White, and W. Barnett, eds, *Dynamic econometric modeling* (Cambridge University Press) pp. 73-104.

Geweke, J., 1989a, "Exact predictive densities in linear models with ARCH disturbances", *Journal of Econometrics* 44, pp. 307-25.

Geweke, J., 1989b, "Bayesian inference in econometric models using Monte Carlo integration", *Econometrica* 57, pp. 1317-39.

Giovannini, A., and P. Jorion, 1989, "The time variation of risk and return in the foreign exchange and stock markets", *Journal of Finance* 44, pp. 307-25.

Giovannini, A. and P. Jorion, 1990, "Time-series tests of a non-expected utility model of asset pricing", Unpublished manuscript, Columbia University.

Glosten, L.R., and P. Milgrom, 1985, "Bid, ask and transactions prices in a specialist market with heterogeneously informed traders", *Journal of Financial Economics* 14, pp. 71-100.

Glosten, L.R., R. Jagannathan, and D. Runkle, 1991, "Relationship between the expected value and the volatility of the nominal excess return on stocks", Unpublished manuscript, Northwestern University.

Goodhart, C., 1990, "News and the foreign exchange market", Unpublished manuscript, London School of Economics.

Gourieroux, C., and A. Monfort, 1992, "Qualitative threshold ARCH models", *Journals of Econometrics* 52, 1-2, pp. 159-99.

Gregory, A.W., 1989, "A non-parametric test for autoregressive conditional heterskedasticity: A Markov-chain approach", *Journal of Business and Economic Statistics* 7, pp. 107-15.

Grossman, S., A. Melino, and R.J. Shiller, 1987, "Estimating the continuous time consumption based asset pricing model", *Journal of Business and Economic Statistics* 5, pp. 315-27.

Hakkio, C.S., 1981, "Expectations and the forward exchange rate", *International Economic Review* 22, pp. 663-78.

Hall, S.G., D.K. Miles, and M. Taylor, 1988, "A multivariate GARCH in mean estimation of the capital asset pricing model", Unpublished manuscript, London School of Economics.

Hamao, Y., R.W. Masulis, and V.K. Ng, 1990a, "Correlations in price changes and volatility across international stock markets", *Review of Financial Studies* 3, pp. 281-307.

Hamao, Y., R.W. Masulis, and V.K. Ng, 1990b, "The effect of the stock crash on international financial integration", Unpublished manuscript, University of California, San Diego.

Hamilton, J.D., 1989, "A new approach to the economic analysis of nonstationary time series and the business cycle", *Econometrica* 57, pp. 357-84.

Hansen, B.E., 1990, "GARCH(1,1) processes are near epoch dependent", Unpublished manuscript, University of Rochester.

Hardouvelis, G., 1988, "The predictive power of the term structure during recent monetary regimes", *Journal of*

Finance 43, pp. 339-56.

Hardouvelis, G., 1990a, "Margin requirements, volatility and the transitory component of stock prices", *American Economic Review* 80, pp. 736-63.

Hardouvelis, G., 1990b, "Do margin requirements stabilize the market? The case of Japan", Unpublished manuscript, Rutgers University.

Harris, L., 1989, "S&P 500 cash stock price volatilities", *Journal of Finance* 4, pp. 1155-75.

Harvey, A., E. Ruiz, and E. Sentana, 1992, "Unobserved component time series models with ARCH disturbances", *Journal of Econometrics*, 52, 1-2, pp. 129-58.

Harvey, C., 1989, "Is the expected compensation for market volatility constant through time?", Unpublished manuscript, Duke University.

Harvey, C., 1991, "The world price of covariance risk", *Journal of Finance* 46, pp. 111-57.

Higgins, M.L., and A.K. Bera, 1989a, "A joint test for ARCH and bilinearity in the regression model", *Econometric Reviews* 7, pp. 171-81.

Higgins, M.L., and A. K. Bera, 1989b, "A class of nonlinear ARCH models", Unpublished manuscript, University of Illinois.

Hodrick, R.J., 1987, *The empirical evidence on the efficiency of forward and futures foreign exchange markets*, (Scientific and Technical Book Service, New York).

Hodrick, R.J., 1989, "Risk, uncertainty, and exchange rates", *Journal of Monetary Economics* 23, pp. 433-59.

Hodrick, R.J., and S. Srivastava, 1984, "An investigation of risk and return in forward foreign exchange rates", *Journal of International Money and Finance* 3, pp. 5-29.

Hong, C-H., 1988, "The integrated generalized autoregressive conditional heteroskedastic model: The process, estimation and Monte Carlo experiments", Unpublished manuscript, University of California, San Diego.

Hsieh, D.A., 1984, "Tests of rational expectations and no risk premium in forward exchange markets", *Journal of International Economics* 24, pp. 129-45.

Hsieh, D.A., 1988a, "The statistical properties of daily foreign exchange rates: 1974-1983", *Journal of International Economics* 24, pp. 129-45.

Hsieh, D.A., 1988b, "A nonlinear stochastic rational expectations model of exchange rates", Unpublished manuscript, University of Chicago.

Hsieh, D.A., 1989a, "Modeling heteroskedasticity in daily foreign exchange rates", *Journal of Business and Economic Statistics* 7, pp. 307-17.

Hsieh, David A., 1989b, "Testing for nonlinear dependence in daily foreign exchange rate changes", *Journal of Business* 62, pp. 339-68.

Hsieh, D.A., 1990, "Chaos and nonlinear dynamics: Application to financial markets", Unpublished manuscript , Duke University.

Hsieh, D.A., and L. Manas-Anton, 1988, "Empirical regularities in the Deutschmark futures options", Unpublished manuscript, University of Chicago.

Hsieh, D.A., and M.H. Miller, 1990, "Margin regulation and stock market volatility", *Journal of Finance* 43, pp. 3-29.

Humpage, O.S., and W.P. Osterbert, 1990, "Intervention and the foreign exchange risk premium: An empirical investigation of daily effects", Unpublished manuscript, Federal Reserve Bank of Cleveland.

Jorion, P., 1988, "On jump processes in the foreign exchange and stock markets", *Review of Financial Studies* 1, pp. 427-45.

Kaminsky, G.L., and R. Peruga, 1990, "Can a time varying risk premium explain excess returns in the forward market for foreign exchange?" *Journal of International Economics* 28, pp. 47-70.

Kaplan, P.D., 1988, "Risk and return: An asset pricing model with time varying conditional second moments", Unpublished manuscript, Northwestern University.

Karpoff, J.M., 1987, "The relation between price changes and trading volume: A survey", *Journal of Financial and Quantitative Analysis* 22, pp. 399-408.

Kearns, P., and A.R. Pagan, 1990, "Australian stock market volatility: 1875-1987", Unpublished manuscript (University of Rochester, Rochester, NY).

Kendall, J.D., 1989, "Role of exchange rate volatility in U.S. import price pass-through relationships", Unpublished Ph.D. dissertation, University of California, Davis.

Kendall, J.D., and A.D. McDonald, 1989, "Univariate GARCH-M and the risk premium in a foreign exchange market", Unpublished manuscript, University of Tasmania, .

Kim, C-J., and C.R. Nelson, 1989, "The time varying parameter model for modeling changing conditional variance: The case of the Lucas hypothesis", *Journal of Business and Economic Statistics* 7, pp. 433-40.

Kim, C.M., 1989, "Volatility effect on time series behavior of foreign exchange rate changes", Unpublished manuscript, University of Chicago.

King, M.A., E. Sentana, and S.B. Wadhwani, 1990, "A heteroskedastic factor model for asset returns and risk premia with time-varying volatility: An application to sixteen world stock markets", Unpublished manuscript, London School of Economics.

Kodres, L.F., 1990, "Tests of unbiasedness in the foreign exchange futures markets: An examination of price limits and conditional heteroskedasticity", Unpublished manuscript, University of Michigan.

Kraft, D.F., and R.F. Engle, 1983, "Autoregressive conditional heteroskedasticity in multiple time series", Unpublished manuscript, University of California, San Diego.

Kroner, K.F., 1987, "Estimating and testing for factor ARCH", Unpublished manuscript, University of California, San Diego.

Kroner, K.F., and S. Claessens, 1991, "Optimal currency composition of external debt: Applications to Indonesia and Turkey", *Journal of International Money and Finance* 10, pp. 131-48.

Kroner, K.F., and W.D. Lastrapes, 1991, "The impact of exchange rate volatility on international trade: Estimates using the GARCH-M model", Unpublished manuscript, University of Arizona.

Kroner, K.F., and J. Sultan, 1991, "Foreign currency futures and time varying hedge ratios, in: S. Ghon Rhee and Rosita P. Change, eds.", *Pacific-basin Capital Markets Research,* Vol. II, North-Holland, Amsterdam, pp. 397-412.

Kugler, P., and C. Lenz, 1990, "Chaos, ARCH and the foreign exchange market: Empirical results from weekly data", Unpublished manuscript, Volkswirtschaftliches Institut, Zurich.

Kupiec, P.H., 1990, "Initial margin requirements and stock returns volatility: Another look", *Journal of Financial Services Research* 3, pp. 287-301.

Lai, K-S., and P. Pauly, 1988, "Time series properties of foreign exchange rates re-examined", Unpublished manuscript, University of Pennsylvania.

Lamoureux, C.G., and W.D. Lastrapes, 1990a, "Persistence in variance, structural change and the GARCH model", *Journal of Business and Economic Statistics* 8, pp. 225-34.

Lamoureux, C.G., and W.D. Lastrapes, 1990b, "Heteroskedasticity in stock return data: Volume versus GARCH effects", *Journal of Finance* 45, pp. 221-29.

Lamoureux, C.G., and W.D. Lastrapes, 1991, "Forecasting stock return variance: Toward an understanding of stochastic implied volatilities", Unpublished manuscript, Washington University, St. Louis.

Lastrapes, W.D., 1989, "Weekly exchange rate volatility and U.S. monetary policy regimes: An application of the ARCH model", *Journal of Money, Credit and Banking* 21, pp. 66-77.

LeBaron, B., 1988, "Stock return nonlinearities: Comparing tests and finding structure", Unpublished manuscript, University of Wisconsin.

LeBaron, B., 1989, "Some relations between volatility and serial correlation in stock market returns", Unpublished manuscript, University of Wisconsin.

Lee, B-S., and Y.J. Yoon, 1990, "An intertemporal consumption based capital asset pricing model with time varying risk", Unpublished manuscript, University of Minnesota.

Lee, T.K., 1988, "Does conditional covariance or conditional variance explain time varying risk premia in foreign exchange returns?" *Economics Letters* 27, pp. 371-3.

Lee, T.K., and Y. K. Tse, 1991, "Term structure of interest rates in the Singapore Asian dollar market: ARCH-M modelling with autocorrelated non-normal errors", *Journal of Applied Econometrics* 6, pp. 143-52.

Levi, M.P., and J.M. Makin, 1979, "Fisher, Phillipps, Friedman and the measured impact of profits on returns", *Journal of Finance* 34, pp. 35-152.

Lin, W-L., 1989, "The sources of intra daily volatility in the foreign exchange market: A multivariate factor GARCH approach", Unpublished manuscript, University of Wisconsin.

Lin, W-L., 1991, "Alternative estimators for factor GARCH models: A Monte Carlo comparison", Unpublished manuscript, University of Wisconsin.

Lintner, J., 1965, "The valuation of risky assets and the selection of risky investments in stock portfolios and capital budgets", *Review of Economics and Statistics* 47, pp. 13-37.

Ljung, G. M., and G.E.P. Box, 1978, "On a measure of lag of fit in time series models", *Biometrika* 67, pp. 297-303.

Lucas, R.E. Jr., 1978, "Asset prices in a production economy", *Econometrica* 46, pp. 1429-45.

Lumsdaine, R.L., 1991, "Asymptotic properties of the maximum likelihood estimator in GARCH(1,1) and IGARCH(1,1) models", Unpublished manuscript, Princeton University.

Lyons, R.K., 1988, "Tests of the foreign exchange risk premium using the expected 2nd moments implied by option pricing", *Journal of International Money and Finance* 7, pp. 91-108.

Malkiel, B., 1979, "The capital formation problem in the United States", *Journal of Finance* 34, pp. 291-306.

Mandelbrot, B., 1963, "The variation of certain speculative prices", *Journal of Business* 36, pp. 394-419.

Mankiw, N. Gregory and M.D. Shapiro, 1986, "Risk and return: Consumption versus market beta", *Review of Economics and Statistics* 68, pp. 452-9.

Mankiw, N. Gregory, and Lawrence H. Summers, 1984, "Do long-term interest rates overreact to short-term interest rates?", *Brookings Papers on Economic Activity*, pp. 223-42.

Mankiw, N. Gregory, J. Miron, and D. Weil, 1987, "The adjustment of expectations to a change in regime: A study on the founding of the Federal Reserve", *American Economic Review* 77, pp. 358–74.

Mankiw, N. Gregory, J. Miron, and D. Weil, 1990, "The adjustment of expectations to a change in regime: A reply", *American Economic Review* 80, pp. 977–9

Mark, N., 1988, "Time varying betas and risk premia in the pricing of forward foreign exchange contracts", *Journal of Financial Economics* 22, pp. 335–54.

McCulloch, J.H., 1985, "Interest-risk sensitive deposit insurance premia - Stable ARCH estimates", *Journal of Banking and Finance* 9, pp. 137–56.

McCurdy, T.H., and I. Morgan, 1987, "Tests of the martingale hypothesis for foreign currency futures with time varying volatility", *International Journal of Forecasting* 3, pp. 131–48.

McCurdy, T.H., and I.Morgan, 1988, "Testing the martingale hypothesis in Deutschmark futures with models specifying the form of the heteroskedasticity", *Journal of Applied Econometrics* 3, pp. 187–202.

McCurdy, T.H., and I. Morgan, 1991a, "Evidence of risk premia in foreign currency futures markets", *Review of Financial Studies*.

McCurdy, T.H., and I. Morgan, 1991b, "Tests for systematic risk components in deviations from uncovered interest rate parity", *Review of Economic Studies* 58, pp. 587–602.

McCurdy, T.H., and T. Stengos, 1992, "A comparison of risk-premium forecasts implied by parametric versus nonparametric conditional mean estimators", *Journal of Econometrics* 52, 1-2, pp. 225–44.

Meese, R.A., and A.K. Rose, 1991, "An empirical assessment of nonlinearities in models of exchange rated determinations", *Review of Economic Studies* 58, pp. 603–19.

Mehra, R., and E. Prescott, 1985, "The equity premium: A puzzle", *Journal of Monetary Economics* 15, pp. 145–61.

Melion, A., and S. Turnbull, 1989, "Pricing foreign currency options with stochastic volatility", *Journal of Econometrics* 45, pp. 239–66.

Merton, R.C., 1973, "An intertemporal capital asset pricing model", *Econometrica* 41, pp. 867–87.

Merton, R.C., 1980, "On estimating the expected return on the market", *Journal of Financial Economics* 8, pp. 323–61.

Milhøj, A., 1985, "The moment structure of ARCH processes", *Scandinavian Journal of Statistics* 12, pp. 281–92.

Milhøj, A., 1987a, "A conditional variance model for daily observations of an exchange rate", *Journal of Business and Economic Statistics* 5, pp. 99–103.

Milhøj, A., 1987b, "A multiplicative parameterization of ARCH models", Unpublished manuscript, University of Copenhagen.

Milhøj, A., 1987, "Simulation and application of MARCH models", Unpublished manuscript, University of Copenhagen.

Milhøj, A., 1990, "Distribution of empirical autocorrelations of a square first order ARCH process", Unpublished manuscript, University of Copenhagen.

Morgan, A., and I. Morgan, 1987, "Measurement of abnormal returns from small firms", *Journal of Business and Economic Statistics* 15, pp. 121–29.

Morgan, I.G., and E.H. Neave, 1989, "Pricing treasury bills and futures contract: Theory and tests", Unpublished manuscript, Queen's University.

Mossin, J., 1966, "Equilibrium in a capital asset market", *Econometrica* 34, pp. 768–83.

Mundaca, B.G., 1990, "Intervention decisions and exchange rate volatility in a target zone", Unpublished manuscript, Norges Bank, Oslo.

Mussa, M,, 1979, "Empirical regularities in the behavior of exchange rates and theories of the foreign exchange market", in: K. Brunner and A. H. Meltzer, eds, *Carnegie-Rochester Conference Series on Public Policy* Vol. 11, North-Holland, Amsterdam.

Nelson, D.B., 1989, "Modeling stock market volatility changes", 1989 *Proceedings of the American Statistical Association, Business and Economic Statistics Section*, pp. 93–8.

Nelson, D.B., 1990a, "Stationarity and persistence in the GARCH(1,1) model", *Econometric Theory* 6, pp. 318–34.

Nelson, D.B., 1990b, "ARCH models as diffusion approximations", *Journal of Econometrics* 45, pp. 7–38.

Nelson, D.B., 1990c, "Conditional heteroskedasticity in asset returns: A new approach", *Econometrics* 59, pp. 347–70.

Nelson, D.B., 1990d, "A note on the normalized residuals from ARCH and stochastic volatility models", Unpublished manuscript, University of Chicago.

Nelson, D.B., 1992, "Filtering and forecasting with misspecified ARCH models I: Getting the right variance with the wrong model", *Journal of Econometrics* 52, 1-2, pp. 61–90.

Nelson, D.B., and C.Q. Cao, 1991, "A note on the inequality constraints in the univariate GARCH model", *Journal of Business and Economic Studies*.

Ng, L., 1991, "Tests of the CAPM with time varying covariances: A multivariate GARCH approach", *Journal of Finance*

46, pp. 1507-21.

Ng, V., 1988, "Equilibrium stock return distributions in a simple log-linear factor economy", Unpublished manuscript, University of California, San Diego.

Ng, V., R.P. Chang, and R. Chou, 1991, "An examination of the behavior of international stock market volatility," in: S. Ghon Rhee and Rosita P. Chang, eds, *Pacific-basin Capital Markets Research* Vol II, North-Holland, Amsterdam, pp. 245-60.

Pagan, A.R., 1984, "Econometric issues in the analysis of regressions with generated regressors", *International Economics Review* 25, pp. 221-47.

Pagan, A.R., 1986, "Two stage and related estimators and their applications", *Review of Economic Studies* 53, pp. 517-38.

Pagan, A.R., 1988, "A note on the magnitude of risk premia", *Journal of International Money and Finance* 7, pp. 109-10.

Pagan, A.R., and Y.S. Hong, 1990, "Non-parametric estimation and the risk premium," in: W. Barnett, J. Powell, and G. Tauchen, eds., *Semiparametric and nonparametric methods in econometrics and statistics*, Cambridge University Press.

Pagan, A.R., and H.C.L. Sabau, 1987, "On the inconsistency of the MLE in certain heteroskedastic regression models", Unpublished manuscript, University of Rochester.

Pagan, A.R., and H.C.L. Sabau, 1988, "Consistency tests for heteroskedasticity and risk models", Unpublished manuscript, University of Rochester.

Pagan, A.R., and G.W. Schwert, 1990, "Alternative models for conditional stock volatility", *Journal of Econometrics* 45, pp. 267-90.

Pagan, A.R., and A. Ullah, 1988, "The econometric analysis of models with risk terms", *Journal of Applied Econometrics* 3, pp. 87-105.

Pagan, A.R., A.D. Hall, and P.K. Trivedi, 1983, "Assessing the variability of inflation", *Review of Economic Studies* 50, pp. 585-96.

Pantula, S.G., 1985, "Estimation of autoregressive models with ARCH errors", Unpublished manuscript, North Carolina State University.

Pantula, S.G., 1986, "Modeling the persistence of conditional variances: A comment", *Econometric Reviews* 5, pp. 71-4.

Papell, D.H., and C,L. Sayers, 1990, "Nonlinear dynamics and exchange rate frequency", Unpublished manuscript, University of Houston.

Park, H.Y., and A.K. Bera, 1987, "Interest rate volatility, basis risk and heteroskedasticity in hedging mortgages", *AREUEA Journal* 15, pp. 79-97.

Parkinson, M., 1980, "The extreme value method for estimating the variance of the rate of return", *Journal of Business* 53, pp. 61-5.

Perron, P., 1989, "The great crash, the oil price shock, and the unit root hypothesis", *Econometrica* 57, pp. 1361-401.

Pindyck, R., 1984, "Risk, inflation and the stock market", *American Economic Review* 74, pp. 335-51.

Pindyck, R., 1988, "Risk aversion and determinants of stock market behavior", *Review of Economics and Statistics* 70, pp. 183-90.

Poon, P., 1988, "Three essays on price volatility and trading volume in financial markets", Unpublished PhD dissertation, Louisiana State University.

Poterba, J., and L. Summers, 1986, "The persistence of volatility and stock market fluctuations", *American Economic Review* 76, pp. 1142-51.

Priestley, M.B., 1981, *Spectral analysis and time series*, Academic Press, New York.

Rich, R.W., J. Raymon, and J.S. Butler, 1990a, "Generalized instrumental variables estimation of autoregressive conditionally heteroskedastic models", *Economics Letters*.

Rich, R.W., J. Raymond, and J.S. Butler, 1990b, "The relationship between forecast dispersion and forecast uncertainty: Evidence from a survey data - ARCH model", Unpublished manuscript, Vanderbilt University.

Robinson, P.M., 1987a, "Adaptive estimation of heteroskedastic econometric models", *Revista de Econometrica* 7, pp. 5-28.

Robinson, P.M., 1987b, "Asymptotically efficient estimation in the presence of heteroskedasticity of unknown form", *Econometrica* 55, pp. 875-91.

Robinson, P.M., 1988, "Semiparametric econometrics: A survey", *Journal of Applied Econometrics* 3, pp. 35-51.

Robinson, P.M., 1991, "Testing for strong serial correlation and dynamic conditional heteroskedasticity in multiple regression", *Journal of Econometrics* 47, pp. 67-84.

Roll, Richard, 1977, "A critique of asset pricing theory tests, Part 1", *Journal of Financial Economics* 4, pp. 129-76.

Ross, S.A., 1976, "The arbitrage theory of capital asset pricing", *Journal of Economic Theory* 13, pp. 341-60.

Rubenstein, M., 1987, "Derivative asset analysis", *Journal of Economics Perspective* 1, pp. 73-93.

Scheinkman, J.A., and B. LeBaron, 1989, "Nonlinear dynamics and stock returns", *Journal of Business* 62, pp. 311-37.

Schwert, G.W., 1989a, "Why does stock market volatility change over time?", *Journal of Finance* 44, pp. 1115-53.

Schwert, G.W., 1989b, "Business cycles, financial crises, and stock volatility", *Carnegie-Rochester Conference Series on Public Policy* 39, pp. 83-126.

Schwert, G.W., 1989c, "Margin requirements and stock volatility", *Journal of Financial Services Research* 3, pp. 153-64.

Schwert, G.W., 1990a, "Stock volatility and the crash of 87", *Review of Financial Studies* 3, pp. 77-102.

Schwert, G.W., 1990b, "Indexes of United States stock prices from 1802 to 1987", *Journal of Business* 63, pp. 399-431.

Schwert, G.W., and P.J. Seguin, 1990, "Heteroskedasticity in stock returns", *Journal of Finance* 45, pp. 1129-55.

Seguin, P.J., 1990, "Stock volatility and margin trading", *Journal of Monetary Economics* 26, pp. 101-21.

Sentana, E., 1990, "Identification and estimation of multivariate conditionally heteroskedasticity latent factor models", Unpublished manuscript, London School of Economics.

Sentana, E., and S. Wadhwani, 1989, "Semi-parametric estimation and the predictability of stock market returns: Some lessons from Japan", Unpublished manuscript, London School of Economics.

Sentana, E., and S. Wadhwani, 1991, "Feedback traders and stock returns autocorrelations: Evidence from a century of daily data", *Review of Economic Studies* 58, pp. 547-63.

Sharpe, W.F., 1964, "Capital asset prices: A theory of market equilibrium under conditions of market risk", *Journal of Finance* 19, pp. 425-42.

Shephard, N.G., 1990, "A local scale model: An unobserved component alternative to integrated GARCH processes", Unpublished manuscript, London School of Economics.

Shiller, R.J., 1979, "The volatility of long-term interest rates and expectations models of the term structure", *Journal of Political Economy* 87, pp. 1190-219.

Shiller, R.J., J.Y. Campbell, and K.L. Schoenholtz, 1983, "Forward rates and future policy: Interpreting the term structure of interest rates", *Brookings Papers on Economic Activity*, pp. 173-217.

Simon, D.P., 1989, "Expectations and risk in the treasury bill market: An instrumental variables approach", *Journal of Financial and Quantitative Analysis* 24, pp. 357-66.

Singleton, K.J., 1980, "Expectations models of the term structure and implied variance bounds", *Journal of Political Economy* 88, pp. 1159-76.

Smith, G.W., 1987, "Endogenous conditional heteroskedasticity and tests of menu-cost pricing theory", Unpublished manuscript, Queen's University.

Steeley, J.M., 1990, "Modelling the dynamics of the term structure of interest rates", Unpublished manuscript, University of Keele.

Stock, J.H., 1987, "Measuring business cycle time", *Journal of Political Economy* 95, pp. 1240-61.

Stock, J.H., 1988, "Estimating continuous time process subject to time deformation", *Journal of the American Statistical Association* 83, pp. 77-85.

Tapia, R.A., and J.R. Thompson, 1978, *Nonparametric probability density estimation*, Johns Hopkins University Press.

Tauchen, G.E., and M. Pitts, "The price variability -volume relationship on speculative markets", *Econometrica*, 51, pp. 485-505.

Taylor, S.J., 1984, "Estimating the variances of autocorrelations calculated from financial time series", *Journal of Royal Statistical Association, Series C (Applied Statistics)* 33, pp. 300-08.

Taylor, S.J., 1986, *Modelling financial time series,* Wiley, New York.

Taylor, S.J., 1987, "Forecasting the volatility of currency exchange rates", *Journal of International Forecasting* 3, pp. 159-70.

Taylor, S.J., 1990a, "Modelling stochastic volatility", Unpublished manuscript, University of Lancaster.

Taylor, S.J., 1990b, "Efficiency of the yen futures market at the Chicago Mercantile Exchange", in: B.A. Gross, ed, *Rational expectations and efficiency in futures markets*, Routledge.

Thomas, S.H., and M.R. Wickens, 1989, "International CAPM: Why has it failed?" Unpublished manuscript , University of Southampton.

Thum, F., 1988, "Economic foundations of ARCH exchange rate processes", Unpublished manuscript, University of Texas.

Tsay, R.S., 1987, "Conditional heteroskedastic time series models", *Journal of the American Statistical Association* 82, pp. 590-604.

Weiss, A.A., 1984, "ARMA models with ARCH errors", *Journal of Time Series Analysis* 5, pp. 129-43.

Weiss, A.A., 1986a, "Asymptotic theory for ARCH models: Estimation and testing", *Econometric Theory* 2, pp. 107-31.

Weiss, A.A., 1986b, "ARCH and bilinear time series models: Comparison and combination", *Journal of Business and Economic Statistics* 4, pp. 59-70.

West, K.D., H.J. Edison, and D. Cho, 1991, "A utility

based comparison of some models of foreign exchange volatility", Unpublished manuscript, University of Wisconsin.

Weston, J., 1986, "Industry characteristics and earnings estimates", Unpublished manuscript, University of California, Los Angeles.

Whistler, D., 1988, "Semi-parametric ARCH estimation of intra daily exchange rate volatility", Unpublished manuscript, London School of Economics.

White, H., 1982, "Maximum likelihood estimation of misspecified models", *Econometrica* 50, pp. 1-25.

Wolff, C.C.P., 1989, "Autoregressive conditional heteroskedasticity: A comparison of ARCH and random coefficient models", *Economics Letters* 27, pp. 141-3.

Wooldridge, J.M., 1988, "Specification testing and quasi maximum likelihood estimation", Unpublished manuscript, MIT.

Wooldridge, J.M., 1990, "A unified approach to robust regression based specification tests", *Econometric Theory* 6, pp. 17-43.

Zakoian, J-M., 1990, "Threshold heteroskedastic model", Unpublished manuscript, INSEE.

Zandamela, R.L., 1989, "Wage indexation, openness and inflation uncertainty - The case of Italy", *Journal of Applied Economics* 21, pp. 651-57.

Zin, S.E., 1986, "Modelling the persistence of conditional variances: A comment", *Econometric Reviews* 5, pp. 75-80.

3

Modelling Stochastic Volatility:

A Review and Comparative Study*

Stephen J. Taylor
Lancaster University

Diffusion models for volatility have been used to price options while Arch models predominate in descriptive studies of asset volatility. This paper compares a discrete-time approximation of a popular diffusion model with Arch models. These volatility models have many similarities but the models make different assumptions about how the magnitude of price responses to information alters volatility and the amount of subsequent information. Several volatility models are estimated for daily Deutschmark/dollar exchange rates from 1978 to 1990.

Volatility changes occur for all classes of assets and have been reported in numerous stock, currency, and commodity studies. Important issues in volatility research include, first, the implications for option pricing, second, volatility estimation, and, third, whether volatility shocks persist indefinitely. These issues have been addressed using different models and methodologies. First, the finance literature contains diffusion models for a stochastic volatility variable which permit the rigorous valuation of options for such models (eg Hull and White 1987a; Chesney and Scott 1989; Heston 1993). The diffusion models have not been motivated by data analysis, and inferences about any mean reversion in volatility have been drawn primarily from studies of implied volatilities (eg Merville and Pieptea 1989, Stein 1989). Second, a very substantial econometric literature has focused on discrete-time Arch models displaying conditional heteroskedasticity, following the path-breaking paper by Engle (1982). Maximum likelihood estimates for Arch models permit a direct evaluation of the mean reversion issue.

The motivation for this paper is the opinion that an understanding of both Arch and other models for volatility is more beneficial than knowledge of only one way to model volatility. For example, it is possible to value options numerically without recourse to Arch methods (Chesney and Scott 1989; Melino and Turnbull 1990) or to do this solely using Arch methods (Engle and Mustafa 1992; Duan 1995), but a methodology which takes advantage of both non-Arch and Arch methods provides more satisfactory results. Details are provided later.

This paper reviews, compares, and estimates the volatility models studied in options and econometric research. Nelson (1990) and Bollerslev, Chou, and Kroner (1992) have respectively published important theoretical results and an excellent review of Arch literature. This paper, however, provides a more comprehensive comparison of the various volatility models deserving serious consideration. Four models are considered in detail. These are an information counting model (Tauchen and Pitts 1983), an autoregressive simplification of a diffusion model, here called the ARV model (Taylor 1986), the Garch(1,1) model (Bollerslev 1986), and the exponential Arch(1,0) model (Nelson 1991). All four models can explain, first, the high kurtosis and small autocorrelations of daily returns and, second, the statistically significant positive autocorrelations of squared daily returns.

* *This paper was first published in* Mathematical Finance, *Vol. 4, No.2 (1994) and is reprinted and updated with permission of Blackwell Publishers. The author thanks all those who have helped to clarify the arguments presented here, including participants at the 1990 European Finance Association meeting, the 1992 French Finance Association meeting, and seminars held at the European Institute for Advanced Studies in Management, Lancaster University, Monash University, Reading University, Stockholm School of Economics, and Warwick University.*

The paper is organised as follows. The terms stochastic volatility and conditional variance are often used, and they are defined precisely below. An information counting model is used to show that these two mathematical quantities are in general not functions of each other. I then review the continuous-time volatility models that have been used for option pricing. Certain discrete-time simplifications of a popular diffusion model define an AR(1) model for the logarithm of volatility and hence an autoregressive random variance (ARV) model for returns. A summary of the model's moments is provided. I consider generalised and exponential autoregressive conditional heteroskedasticity (Arch) models and their moments. The next section summarises theoretical comparisons for the ARV and Arch models. There are many statistical similarities but different economic principles relate volatility to information and prices. I then compare Arch and ARV parameter estimates for daily observations of the Deutschmark/dollar exchange rate from December 1977 to November 1990. The results from fitting several Arch models support mean reversion in Deutschmark/dollar volatility for this period and two subperiods. I note that both ARV and Arch models can contribute constructively to the calculation of fair option prices, and finally present our conclusions.

Definitions

Let $P(t)$ denote the price of some asset at time t. Assuming no dividends, define the return from an integer time $t-1$ to time t by

$$X_t = \ln[P(t)/P(t-1)].$$

The word volatility in finance literature is frequently associated with a quantity σ and prices described by the familiar stochastic differential equation

$$d(\ln P) = \mu\ dt + \sigma\ dW$$

with $W(t)$ a standard Wiener process. When μ and σ are constants, X_t has a normal distribution and

$$X_t = \mu + \sigma U_t \text{ with } U_t \sim N(0,1). \qquad (1)$$

Furthermore, the U_t are independent and identically distributed (i.i.d.).

STOCHASTIC VOLATILITY

Equation (1) may be generalised by replacing σ by a positive random variable σ_t to give

$$X_t = \mu + \sigma_t U_t \text{ with } U_t \text{ i.i.d. and } U_t \sim N(0,1). \qquad (2)$$

Whenever the returns process $\{X_t\}$ can be represented by (2), I will call σ_t the stochastic volatility for period t. A normal distribution for $(X_t - \mu)/\sigma_t$ is an essential component of the definition of stochastic volatility adopted here.[1]

The stochastic process $\{\sigma_t\}$ will generate realised volatilities $\{\sigma_t^*\}$, which are in general not observable. For any realisation σ_t^*,

$$X_t \mid \sigma_t = \sigma_t^* \sim N(\mu, \sigma_t^{*2}).$$

A mixture of these conditional normal distributions defines the unconditional distribution of X_t, which has excess kurtosis whenever σ_t has positive variance and is independent of U_t.

CONDITIONAL VARIANCE

Capital letters will often be used to denote random variables, and their outcomes will be represented using the corresponding lowercase letters. Given a set of observed returns, $I_{t-1} = \{x_1, x_2, \ldots, x_{t-1}\}$, the conditional variance for period t is

$$h_t = \text{var}(X_t \mid I_{t-1}).$$

It is important to note that the random variable H_t which generates the observed conditional variance h_t is not in general equal to σ_t^2. I have $H_t \neq \sigma_t^2$ both for the models favoured in option pricing literature and for Arch models having non-normal conditional distributions.

AN INFORMATION COUNTING MODEL

The easiest way to use economic theory to motivate changes in volatility assumes that returns are defined by a stochastic number of intraperiod price revisions, as in Clark (1973), Tauchen and Pitts (1983), Harris (1987), Lamoureux and Lastrapes (1990), Gallant, Hsieh, and Tauchen (1991), and Andersen (1996). Suppose there are N_t price revisions during trading day t, each caused by unpredictable information. Let event i on day t change the price logarithm by ω_{it}, with

$$X_t = \mu + \sum_{i=1}^{N_t} \omega_{it}.$$

Finally suppose that the ω_{it} are i.i.d. and that they are independent of the random variable N_t, with $\omega_{it} \sim N(0, \sigma_\omega^2)$. Then

$$\sigma_t^2 = \sigma_\omega^2 N_t \text{ and } H_t = \sigma_\omega^2 E[N_t | I_{t-1}]. \qquad (3)$$

Thus, squared volatility is proportional to the amount of price information for this model. Furthermore, $\sigma_t^2 = H_t$ only if the unrealistic assumption is made that price information up to time $t-1$ determines the quantity of information during period t.

Models used to price options

CONTINUOUS-TIME SPECIFICATIONS

Option pricing models have been published for general price processes, in which the asset price $P(t)$ and the volatility $\sigma(t)$ each follow a diffusion process. Several authors give numerical options results for specific processes. Scott (1987, 1991), Wiggins (1987), and Chesney and Scott (1989) suppose the logarithm of the volatility follows the Ornstein-Uhlenbeck (O-U) process, as follows:

$$dP/P = \alpha\,dt + \sigma\,dW_1, \tag{4}$$

$$d(\ln\sigma) = \lambda(\xi - \ln\sigma)dt + \gamma\,dW_2, \tag{5}$$

and

$$dW_1\,dW_2 = \delta\,dt \tag{6}$$

with α, λ, ξ, γ, and δ constant parameters and $(W_1(t), W_2(t))$ a two-dimensional standard Wiener process.

At least four other processes for $\sigma(t)$ have been investigated. These are

$$d\sigma = \lambda(\xi - \sigma)dt + \gamma\,dW_2, \tag{7}$$

$$d\sigma = \lambda\sigma(\xi - \sigma)dt + \gamma\sigma\,dW_2, \tag{8}$$

$$d\sigma = \lambda\sigma\,dt + \gamma\sigma\,dW_2, \tag{9}$$

and

$$d\sigma = \sigma^{-1}(\xi - \lambda\sigma^2)dt + \gamma\,dW_2. \tag{10}$$

Stein and Stein (1991) and Heston (1993) give closed-form option valuation formulas, respectively, for (7) and (10). Hull and White (1987a) give results for (8), Hull and White (1987b) and Johnson and Shanno (1987) consider (9), and Hull and White (1988) evaluate pricing biases for (10).

Bailey and Stulz (1989) and Scott (1992) give general equilibrium results for (10), with stochastic α in (4) and stochastic interest rates. Both papers show that the choice of volatility model can have economic implications for fair option values. Finally, replacing σ in (4) by $vP^{(\beta/2)-1}$ and letting $\ln(v)$ follow the O-U process, as in (5), gives the interesting model of Melino and Turnbull (1990), when their price drift parameter α is zero.

It is notable that these models have been motivated by convenience and intuition rather than by studies of observed prices.

DISCRETE-TIME SPECIFICATIONS

Parameter estimates can be obtained for particular discrete-time approximations of the most popular continuous-time model, defined by (4)-(6). Wiggins (1987), Chesney and Scott (1989), and Duffie and Singleton (1989) choose to work with

$$\ln(P_t) = \ln(P_{t-1}) + \mu + \sigma_{t-1}U_t \tag{11}$$

and

$$\ln(\sigma_t) = \alpha + \phi\left[\ln(\sigma_{t-1}) - \alpha\right] + \theta\eta_t, \tag{12}$$

with t now restricted to integer values. Here, μ, α, ϕ, and θ are constants, the pairs (U_t, η_t) are i.i.d. and bivariate normal, and the standard normal variables U_t and η_t have correlation δ. The volatility logarithm follows a stationary, Gaussian, AR(1) process when $-1 < \phi < 1$ and a random walk when $\phi = 1$; also the price logarithm follows a random walk with time-varying conditional innovation variance.

The lagged volatility σ_{t-1} appears in (11) because this equation is the Euler approximation to (4). Consequently σ_{t-1} (not σ_t) is then the stochastic volatility for period t. However, it can be argued that a more natural simplification of (4) is simply

$$\ln(P_t) - \ln(P_{t-1}) = X_t = \mu + \sigma_t U_t. \tag{13}$$

The special case defined by (12), (13), and $\delta = 0$ can be found in Taylor (1986). This special case is almost compatible with the equilibria-counting model presented above, providing we ignore the fact that σ_t and the count N_t are, respectively, continuous and discrete random variables.

The words autoregressive random variance model (ARV) are used to describe these models and the additional adjectives lagged and contemporaneous are used to select (11) and (13), respectively.

The two innovations (U_t, η_t) in the ARV model prevent observation of the sample values of $\{\sigma_t\}$; we can only observe prices. Furthermore, the variance of a return, conditional upon past returns, is an intractable function for ARV models, unlike the simple functions we will see for Arch models.

KALMAN FILTERING

Scott (1987) and Harvey, Ruiz, and Shephard (1994) have shown that estimates of $\ln(\sigma_t)$ can be obtained by applying the Kalman filter to the logarithms of absolute (mean-adjusted) returns, $L_t = \ln(|X_t - \mu|)$. For the contemporaneous ARV model, from (12) and (13),

$$L_t = \ln(\sigma_t) + \ln(|U_t|) \tag{14}$$

and

$$\ln(\sigma_t) = \alpha(1-\phi) + \phi\ln(\sigma_{t-1}) + \theta\eta_t. \tag{15}$$

The variable $\ln(|U_t|)$ has mean -0.63518 … and variance $\pi^2/8$ (Scott 1987), and this variable is uncorrelated with η_t whatever the value of δ (Harvey, Ruiz, and Shephard 1994). It is straightforward to estimate the three parameters α, ϕ, and θ by maximising the quasi-likelihood function of data $\{l_t = \ln|x_t - \bar{x}|\}$. A refinement of the above Kalman filter specification, which uses the additional information provided by the series $\{\mathrm{sign}(x_t - \bar{x})\}$, can be used to obtain an estimate of δ (Harvey and Shephard 1993).

MOMENTS

Parameter estimates for the ARV model have often been obtained by matching sample and population moments; consequently, these are described in some detail. The ARV model is stationary if and only if $-1 < \phi < 1$ and then $\ln(\sigma_t)$ has mean α and variance $\beta^2 = \theta^2/(1-\phi^2)$. Initially, consider the stationary, lagged ARV model. The unconditional distribution of the return X_t is a lognormal mixture of normal distributions, as in Clark (1973) and Tauchen and Pitts (1983). As U_t is independent of σ_{t-1}, the mean return is μ, $E[|X_t - \mu|^r] < \infty$ for all $r > 0$ and

$$E[|X_t - \mu|] = (2/\pi)^{1/2} e^{\alpha+\beta^2/2}, \tag{16}$$

$$\mathrm{var}(X_t) = e^{2\alpha+2\beta^2}, \tag{17}$$

and

$$\mathrm{kurtosis}(X_t) = 3e^{4\beta^2}. \tag{18}$$

Clearly the distribution of X_t is leptokurtic and the kurtosis can be arbitrarily large.

The autocorrelations of returns are trivially zero at all positive lags. Using ρ to represent autocorrelation and two subscripts to denote the lag and process, $\rho_{\tau,X} = 0$ for all positive τ. The dependence in the volatility process implies $S_t = (X_t - \mu)^2$ and $L_t = ½\ln(S_t)$ both define autocorrelated processes. Straightforward algebra shows the autocorrelation of the squares S_t are

$$\rho_{\tau,S} = \frac{\left[1 + 4\delta^2\theta^2\phi^{2(\tau-1)}\right]e^{4\beta^2\phi^\tau} - 1}{3e^{4\beta^2} - 1}, \quad \tau > 0.$$

For small β and/or large ϕ^τ, there is the following approximation when δ is zero (Taylor 1986):

$$\rho_{\tau,S} = A(\beta)\phi^\tau, \; A(\beta) = \left(e^{4\beta^2} - 1\right)/\left(3e^{4\beta^2} - 1\right). \tag{19}$$

As L_t has an ARMA(1,1) representation, it can be proved that

$$\rho_{\tau,L} \approx B(\beta)\phi^\tau, \; B(\beta) = 8\beta^2/\left(8\beta^2 + \pi^2\right), \; \tau > 0. \tag{20}$$

Often β is approximately estimated to be 0.4 in currency studies and then the constants in (19) and (20) are $A(\beta) = 0.191$ and $B(\beta) = 0.115$.

The parameter δ is proportional to the covariance of X_{t-1} with both $L_t - \phi L_{t-1}$ (Chesney and Scott 1989) and $|X_t - \mu|$ (Melino and Turnbull 1990).

Second, consider the stationary, contemporaneous ARV model. Equations (16)-(20) can be used when δ is zero, because the lagged and contemporaneous versions then have identical multivariate distributions. When δ is not zero, the return X_t is μ plus the product of correlated variables σ_t and U_t which ensures more complicated results for the moments than before. For example, the mean return no longer equals μ and the returns are not uncorrelated.

As researchers prefer models that have tractable moments, the lagged version will be assumed for the remainder of this paper whenever $\delta \neq 0$, while $\delta = 0$ will be assumed whenever the contemporaneous version is discussed.

PARAMETER ESTIMATES

The stationary ARV model has five parameters: the mean return μ, the mean α, the standard deviation β and autoregressive coefficient ϕ of the process $\{\ln(\sigma_t)\}$, and the correlation δ between the two innovation terms. Estimates of ϕ are particularly interesting as they provide information about the persistence of volatility shocks. This parameter has been estimated using simple moment-matching methods (Taylor 1986), the generalised method of moments (Duffie and Singleton 1989; Melino and Turnbull (1990), and ARMA methodology applied to $l_t = \ln|x_t - \bar{x}|$ (Chesney and Scott 1989; Scott 1991), assuming $|\phi| < 1$. The quasi-likelihood maximisation method noted above (Harvey, Ruiz, and Shephard 1994) only assumes $|\phi| \leq 1$. Almost all of the estimates of ϕ in these six studies of daily returns are greater than 0.95 and a substantial proportion of the estimates are greater than 0.99. Bayesian probability intervals for ϕ can be found in Jacquier, Polson, and Rossi (1994).

Models for Conditional Heteroskedasticity

GENERAL SPECIFICATIONS

Arch models describe the conditional variance h_t of the return X_t by a simple function of information known at time $t-1$. The general structure considered here involves a constant expected return μ, a function f which converts the information in previous returns into conditional variances, an i.i.d. sequence $\{Z_t\}$ and a family of distributions $D(\mu,\sigma^2)$ satisfying the condition $Y \sim D(\mu,\sigma^2)$ implies $(Y-\mu)/\sigma \sim D(0,1)$. The general structure can be summarised by the equations

$$X_t = \mu + H_t^{1/2} Z_t, \quad H_t = f(X_{t-1}, X_{t-2}, \ldots), \quad Z_t \text{ i.i.d.}, \quad Z_t \sim D(0,1). \tag{21}$$

The autocovariances of the returns are zero at all positive lags because the conditional mean of X_t does not depend on the information I_{t-1} about previous returns. The comprehensive review papers by Bollerslev, Chou, and Kroner (1992) and Bollerslev, Engle, and Nelson (1994) survey the above class of models and many extensions.[2]

GARCH SPECIFICATIONS

The Garch(p, q) model developed by Bollerslev (1986) has conditional variance

$$h_t = a_0 + \sum_{i=1}^{q} a_i (x_{t-i} - \mu)^2 + \sum_{j=1}^{p} b_j h_{t-j}. \tag{22}$$

The parameters $a_0, \ldots, a_q, b_1, \ldots, b_p$ are all non-negative. Most researchers find that the special case $p = q = 1$ is satisfactory.

EXPONENTIAL ARCH SPECIFICATIONS

The typical term $a_i(x_{t-i} - \mu)^2$ appearing in (22) is a symmetric function of $x_{t-i} - \mu$. However, an asymmetric function will be appropriate if there is an asymmetric relationship between volatility and price news. Campbell and Hentschel (1992) refine this idea by developing an economic model. Following Nelson (1991), asymmetry can be modelled by using the following function, $g(z_t)$, of the standardised returns, $z_t = (x_t - \mu)/h_t^{1/2}$, as the residuals of an ARMA(p, q) process for the logarithm of the conditional variance:

$$g(z_t) = \omega z_t + \gamma\{|z_t| - E[|Z_t|]\}. \tag{23}$$

An important example is the AR(1) specification

$$\ln(h_t) - \alpha_t = \Delta[\ln(h_{t-1}) - \alpha_{t-1}] + g(z_{t-1}), \tag{24}$$

which will be referred to as the exponential Arch(1,0) model. The α_t are constants which are typically used to model weekend and holiday effects.

THE CONDITIONAL DISTRIBUTION

When Arch model parameters are replaced by maximum likelihood estimates the standardised variables z_t usually display excess kurtosis which is a theoretical prediction of the information counting model (Gallant, Hsieh and Tauchen (1991)). Thus, non-normal conditional distributions are required.

One plausible conditional distribution is a scaled t-distribution. The density function $f(z)$ for $D(0,1)$ depends on the degrees-of-freedom (d.o.f.) parameter v, as follows:

$$f(z) = \pi^{-1/2}(v-2)^{-1/2} \Gamma\left[\frac{v+1}{2}\right]\Gamma\left[\frac{v}{2}\right]^{-1}\left\{1 + \frac{z^2}{v-2}\right\}^{-(v+1)/2} \tag{25}$$

for $v > 2$.

Another plausible conditional distribution is the generalised error distribution (GED) described by Box and Tiao (1973). The density function then depends on a single tail-thickness parameter v:

$$f(z) = \frac{v \exp\left[-\frac{1}{2}|z/\lambda|^v\right]}{\lambda 2^{1+1/v}\Gamma[1/v]}, \quad v > 0, \tag{26}$$

with

$$\lambda = \left\{\frac{2^{-2/v}\Gamma[1/v]}{\Gamma[3/v]}\right\}^{1/2}.$$

When $v = 2$, $Z_t \sim N(0,1)$, while for $v < 2$ the distribution has thicker tails than the normal. In particular, $v = 1$ gives the double exponential distribution.[3]

STOCHASTIC VOLATILITY

A t-distribution is a mixture of normal distributions having different variances. From Praetz (1972) and Bollerslev (1987) there is a mixing variable M_t, distributed as inverted gamma, for which

$$X_t - \mu = H_t^{1/2} Z_t = H_t^{1/2} M_t^{1/2} U_t, \quad \text{with } E[M_t] = 1 \text{ and } U_t \sim N(0,1). \tag{27}$$

Then

$$X_t|I_{t-1} \sim D(\mu,h_t) \text{ and } X_t|I_{t-1}, m_t \sim N(\mu,m_th_t). \quad (28)$$

Equations (27) and (28) also apply for a conditional GED when $1 \le v < 2$ (Hsu 1982). Unfortunately, the distribution of the mixing variable M_t, which depends on the tail-thickness parameter v, appears to be very complicated for the GED; some diagrams are given by Hsu (1980).

Comparing (27) with (2) shows the stochastic volatility for an Arch model with conditional t or GED distributions is

$$\sigma_t = (M_tH_t)^{1/2}. \quad (29)$$

The distinction between H_t and σ_t^2 can be ascribed to uncertainty about the amount of news revealed during period t. This effect is measured by M_t. When $m_t > 1$, price volatility during period t exceeds the value h_t expected at time $t - 1$, and vice versa. Neither m_t nor the realised value of σ_t can be observed; only h_t is observable.

LIKELIHOODS

The considerable interest shown in Arch models is due to their descriptive successes and the availability of maximum likelihood estimates. The likelihood L of returns $\{x_1, x_2, \ldots, x_n\}$, for initial values I_0 and a model parameterised by a vector θ, is the product of conditional densities defined by conditional distributions $D(\mu,h_t)$, with the h_t being functions of the data, I_0 and θ. When $f(z)$ is the density function of $D(0,1)$, which can depend on a subset of θ, the log-likelihood is

$$\ln L(\theta) = \sum_{t=1}^{n} -\frac{1}{2}\ln\left[h_t(\theta)\right] + \ln\left[f(z_t|\theta)\right]. \quad (30)$$

Likelihood calculations can be used to compare model specifications and distributions and to test if an integrated model is appropriate. Examples are given later. Quasi-ML estimates are given by assuming $D(\ )$ is normal. These estimates are asymptotically consistent for any $D(\ )$ and robust standard errors can be calculated, providing certain regularity conditions are satisfied (Bollerslev and Wooldridge 1992).

PARAMETER ESTIMATES

Bollerslev, Chou, and Kroner (1992) provide a review of parameter estimates. Some innovative stock studies are Akgiray (1989), Baillie and DeGennaro (1990), Schwert and Seguin (1990), all of which involve a Garch specification, and Nelson (1991) which uses exponential Arch. Two important currency studies are Engle and Bollerslev (1986) and Hsieh (1989). The half-lives of volatility shocks implied by Arch parameter estimates vary considerably for the studies mentioned, from about two months to several years. It may be expected for daily returns that $a + b$ and Δ are greater than 0.95, respectively, for Garch(1,1) and exponential Arch(1,0) estimates.

AUTOCORRELATIONS

These are helpful for illustrating similarities with the ARV models described earlier. First, consider the Garch(1,1) model. Let $a = a_1$, $b = b_1$ with $a, b > 0$. When $a + b < 1$, the model is covariance stationary, $E[X_t] = \mu$ and $var(X_t) = a_0/(1-a-b)$. The X_t have finite kurtosis if and only if

$$k_Z = E[Z_t^4] < \infty \text{ and } (a + b)^2 + a^2[k_Z - 1] < 1.$$

Providing the X_t have finite kurtosis, the squares have autocorrelations

$$\rho_{\tau,S} = C(a,b)(a + b)^{\tau}, \ \tau > 0,$$

with

$$C(a,b) = \frac{a(1 - ab - b^2)}{(a + b)(1 - 2ab - b^2)}.$$

Second, consider the exponential Arch(1,0) model. This model is strictly stationary if $|\Delta| < 1$ and the α_t in (24) are the same for all t; all the moments of returns are then finite if $D(0,1) \sim GED$ and $v > 1$ (Nelson (1991)). Formulas for the moments of the squares are extremely complicated. The autocorrelations of

$$L_t = \ln(|X_t - \mu|) = 0.5\ln(H_t) + \ln(|Z_t|)$$

follow from the linear model for $\ln(H_t)$. When $D(\ )$ is symmetric,

$$\rho_{\tau,L} = F(\gamma,\Delta,f)\Delta^{\tau}, \ \ \tau > 0,$$

with $F(\gamma,\Delta,f)$ a constant which depends on the density function $f(z)$ of $D(0,1)$, providing these autocorrelations exist; F is positive when γ and Δ are both positive.

Comparisons

SIMILARITIES

The ARV models described earlier have many similarities with particular Arch models. These similarities are most obvious for the contemporaneous ARV and exponential Arch(1,0) models. The two models both state that $X_t - \mu$ is the product of an i.i.d., standardised process (either

U_t in (3) or Z_t in (21)) and a second process whose logarithm is linear and first-order autoregressive (either σ_t defined by (12) or $H_t^{1/2}$ defined by (24)). The only obvious difference between the two models is that the product involves processes which are independent of each other for the contemporaneous ARV model but not for the exponential Arch model.

Stationary ARV, Garch(1,1) and exponential Arch(1,0) models can all explain the following "stylised facts" for samples of daily returns:

- they have excess kurtosis compared with the normal distribution,
- they have small autocorrelations, and
- the autocorrelations of squared returns are (i) positive, (ii) statistically significant, (iii) generally smaller as the time-lag increases, and (iv) noticeably larger than the respective autocorrelations of returns for several time lags. The population autocorrelations are very similar for all the models. All models have $\rho_{\tau,X} = 0$ for all positive τ, while the squares $S_t = (X_t - \mu)^2$ have

$$\rho_{\tau,S} \approx A(\beta)\phi^{\tau}$$

for the ARV model, and

$$\rho_{\tau,S} = C(a, b)(a + b)^{\tau}$$

for Garch(1,1), when $\tau > 0$, with $A,C > 0$. Also the variables $L_t = ½\ln(S_t)$ have

$$\rho_{\tau,L} = B(\beta)\phi^{t}$$

for the ARV model, and

$$\rho_{\tau,L} = F(\gamma,\Delta,f)\Delta^{\tau} \text{ for exp. Arch(1,0)}, \tau > 0,$$

with $B,F > 0$ (assuming $\gamma,\Delta > 0$ and symmetric conditional distributions). The preceding autocorrelations are those of ARMA(1,1) models. It follows that any application of standard identification methods to autocorrelations, partial autocorrelations, and/or spectral densities of the squares or their logarithms cannot provide information about the relative validity of the ARV and Arch models. This conclusion is a natural consequence of a theorem proved by Nelson (1990), which shows that a particular sequence of exponential Arch(1,0) models converges to the bivariate diffusion process for price and volatility which motivates the ARV model (4)-(6)).[4]

DISCUSSION

Although the ARV and exponential Arch(1,0) models are approximations to the same continuous-time process, it does not follow that the approximations are of equal value for describing prices observed at discrete moments in time. It is difficult to decide which model provides the best discrete-time approximation, either theoretically or by studying data. At present it is unknown if this uncertainty matters.

A probabilistic distinction between the models makes use of the idea of a reversible stochastic process. Kelly (1979, p. 5) writes of such a process: "... when the direction of time is reversed the behaviour of the process remains the same..."[5] A Gaussian AR(1) process is reversible. Consequently the contemporaneous ARV model is reversible, because it is the product of stochastically independent reversible processes. However, the exponential Arch(1,0) model is not reversible. This model has characteristics which are different when it is studied backwards through time.[6]

IMPLICATIONS FOR THE INFORMATION COUNTING MODEL

A first impression is that prices cause volatility in Arch models but not in the contemporaneous ARV model. As volatility is a function of information for the equilibria-counting model outlined earlier, it is tempting to conclude that prices cause the number of future information flows for Arch models but not for the ARV model.

To be more precise, first consider the volatility residuals for the ARV model:

$$\varepsilon_t = \ln(\sigma_t) - \phi\ln(\sigma_{t-1}) - (1-\phi)\alpha,$$

with ϕ possibly equal to 1. Then ε_t is independent of the returns history I_{t-1}. This implies that prices cannot "cause" volatility. Second, for the exponential Arch(1,0) model consider

$$\varepsilon_t^* = \ln(\sigma_t) - \Delta\ln(\sigma_{t-1}) - 0.5(1-\Delta)\alpha_E,$$

with Δ possibly equal to 1. Using (24) and (29) it then follows that

$$2\varepsilon_t^* = g(Z_{t-1}) + \ln(M_t) - \Delta\ln(M_{t-1}).$$

Consequently, the adjustment ε_t^* depends on the information set I_{t-1}. Thus prices partially "cause" volatility for this model, through the term Z_{t-1} which is a function of the entire history of returns. For conditional normal distributions, $M_t = 1$ so that ε_t^* is then a deterministic function of past prices.

Suppose we now accept that the intraperiod price revision model is appropriate. Then the information count N_t is proportional to σ_t^2. It follows that the number of information items absorbed by the market during a period is a function of the previous period's number and a count residual term which is independent of past prices for the ARV model but dependent on past prices for the exponential Arch model (but only conceptually as N_t is discrete while σ_t^2 is a continuous random variable). To conclude:

❑ Prices change when information becomes available to a market,

❑ The contemporaneous ARV model states that, given N_{t-1}, how much the price has changed in period $t-1$ is irrelevant for determining future volatility and the number of future information items (N_t only depends on constants, N_{t-1} and ε_t),

❑ In contrast, Arch models imply that the magnitude of price changes partially determines future volatility and the number of future information items (N_t depends on N_{t-1}, I_{t-1}, M_{t-1}, and M_{t-1}).

Results for the Deutschmark/dollar exchange rate

DATA

Model parameters have been estimated for a selection of Arch models and the contemporaneous ARV model, permitting a comparison of the results from different models and estimation methods. The results are for daily Deutschmark/dollar returns covering the 13 years from December 1977 to November 1990. These changes in the price logarithm are calculated from the closing prices of June and December futures contracts traded in Chicago. Six months of prices are used for each contract, commencing with prices from December 1977 to May 1978 for the June 1978 contract.[7] Models have been estimated for the complete time series of futures returns (3,283 observations) and also for two subsets (Dec. 1977–Dec. 1983, 1,533 observations and Jan. 1984–Nov. 1990, 1,750 observations).

ARCH METHODOLOGY

An appraisal of calendar dummy variables showed that seven are required. Variables for Mondays and holidays are included in the conditional variance equations because returns measured over more than 24 hours have higher variances than 24-hour returns. Five additional variables define the conditional means, one for each day of the week (cf. McFarland, Pettit, and Sung 1982).

The Arch models are fitted to returns minus their conditional means. A non-seasonal conditional variance h_t^* is defined to be the conditional variance h_t divided by any relevant dummy variable, thus:

$$
\begin{aligned}
h_t/h_t^* &= 1 \text{ if close } t \text{ is 24 hours after close } t-1,\\
&= M \text{ if } t \text{ falls on a Monday and } t-1 \text{ on a Friday},\\
&= V \text{ if a holiday (vacation) occurs between close } t \text{ and close } t-1.
\end{aligned}
$$

Nonseasonal Arch models for h_t^* combined with the above definition of h_t/h_t^* define appropriate seasonal models for h_t.

Only one initial value is required in the calculations for most of the models fitted here, namely h_1, or equivalent h_1^*. We have used all the observations to define h_1^* to be the appropriate estimate of the unconditional, non-seasonal variance.

ARCH RESULTS

Comparisons are first made between the Garch(1,1) model and the symmetric exponential Arch(1,0) model and between the three most popular conditional distributions: the normal, the scaled-t, and the GED. Table 1 presents the results for the complete series from fitting the six combinations of Arch specification and conditional distribution.

The results show that the GED is superior to the t-distribution for describing the conditional distributions of Deutschmark/dollar returns during the period studied. The maximum log-likelihood is 10.51 more for Garch-GED than for Garch-t and it is 9.34 more for exp.-Arch-GED than for exp.-Arch-t. The differences range from 3.91 to 4.40 for the two subperiods.[8] Conditional normal distributions are unacceptable. The exponential Arch(1,0) model then has a maximum log-likelihood which is 73.27 less than the figure for a conditional GED specification. As the normal distribution is the GED with $v = 2$, doubling the difference to 146.54 and comparing with X_1^2 makes it clear that a non-normal conditional distribution is essential.

Comparing the maximum log-likelihoods for Garch with exponential Arch reveals that the latter fits slightly better with log-likelihood differences of 5.01 and 6.18, respectively, for the GED and t-distribution specifications. The differences range from 0.77 to 1.76 for the subperiods. The estimates of M and V are approximately 1.4 and 1.7, respectively, and are greater than the comparable stock estimates in French and Roll (1986) and Nelson (1991). The choice of initial value of h_1 does not matter much. Letting h_1 be an additional parameter increases the maximum log-likelihood by only 0.33 for Garch-t and 0.11 for exp.-Arch-GED.

Table 1. Parameter estimates for Garch(1,1) and exponential Arch(1,0) models

	Garch estimates			Exponential Arch estimates		
Parameter	Normal	t	GED	Normal	t	GED
a	0.0990	0.0892	0.0935			
γ				0.1983	0.1805	0.1885
(s.e.)[a]	(0.0117)	(0.0137)	(0.0141)	(0.0199)	(0.0231)	(0.0239)
[r.s.e.][b]	[0.0165]			[0.0295]		
a + b	0.9702	0.9790	0.9737			
Δ				0.9607	0.9702	0.9658
(s.e.)	(0.0083)	(0.0092)	(0.0098)	(0.0076)	(0.0080)	(0.0087)
[r.s.e.]	[0.0111]			[0.0117]		
$10^5 a_0/(1 - a - b)$	5.270	5.707	5.283			
α_E				−9.827	−10.013	−10.071
(s.e.)	(0.703)	(1.384)	(0.954)	(0.086)	(0.096)	(0.095)
[r.s.e.]	[0.860]			[0.111]		
1/v		0.155			0.158	
v	2		1.321	2		1.317
(s.e.)	(0)	(0.018)	(0.047)	(0)	(0.018)	(0.046)
M	1.407	1.430	1.423	1.389	1.415	1.406
(s.e.)	(0.085)	(0.105)	(0.106)	(0.086)	(0.106)	(0.107)
[r.s.e.]	[0.109]			[0.109]		
V	1.519	1.731	1.643	1.550	1.792	1.695
(s.e.)	(0.198)	(0.283)	(0.271)	(0.206)	(0.294)	(0.283)
[r.s.e.]	[0.250]			[0.237]		
max.ln(L)	11,738.49	11,798.46	11,808.97	11,740.71	11,804.64	11,813.98

Maximum likelihood estimates and the maxima of the log-likelihood function for Arch models fitted to 3,283 daily DM/$ returns (December 1977 to November 1990). The Arch models contain seasonal dummy variables M and V for Mondays and vacations. The conditional distribution is either normal, Student's t, or generalised error. Five day-of-the-week conditional mean terms are included in the models. The estimates of these parameters are not given here.

Models for the conditional variance h_t: $h_t = h_t^*$, Mh_t^*, or Vh_t^*; $x_t^* = x_t - E[X_t \mid I_{t-1}]$;

Garch(1,1) $h_t^* = a_0 + a(x_{t-1}^*)^2 + bh_{t-1}^*$.

Exp.Arch(1,0) $\ln(h_t^*) = \alpha_E + \Delta[\ln(h_{t-1}^*) - \alpha_E] + \gamma(|x_{t-1}^*| / \sqrt{h_{t-1}} - \text{cst.})$.

[a] s.e. refers to the standard error. These are calculated using the Hessian and numerical second derivatives.
[b] r.s.e. refers to the robust standard error calculated from numerical first derivatives using the formulas in Bollerslev and Wooldridge (1992).

FURTHER EXPONENTIAL-ARCH-GED RESULTS

The best model from Table 1, namely the symmetric exponential Arch(1,0)-GED model, is now taken to be a benchmark against which other models can be compared.[9] The adjusted log-likelihood for an alternative model, denoted AL, is defined to be the maximum log-likelihood for that model minus the comparable value for the benchmark model.

First, consider whether an integrated model is credible. Letting $\Delta = 1$ in (24) gives a driftless random walk for $\ln(H_t)$. Fitting this model (with $\omega = 0$) and allowing H_1 to be a parameter gives AL = -19.11. Including a further parameter for any drift in the random walk for $\ln(H_t)$ leaves AL unchanged. The likelihood ratio test using −2AL as the test statistic very probably has size greater than the significance level and is therefore unreliable, but a robust Wald test for a unit root in the volatility process appears to be reliable (Lumsdaine 1995, 1996). The test statistic can be calculated from quasi-ML estimates and formulas given by Bollerslev and Wooldridge (1992) and Engle and Gonzalez-Rivera (1991). From Table 1, the robust Wald statistic is $t = (\hat{\Delta} - 1)/\text{s.e.}(\hat{\Delta}) = (0.9607-1)/0.0117 = -3.36$, which is to be compared with N(0,1).[10] It is concluded that Deutschmark volatility was mean-reverting during the period from 1978 to 1990. The data support this conclusion for both subperiods using a 5% significance level (t = -2.96, 1978-83; t = -2.34, 1984-90).

Second, consider alternative specifications for the volatility residual $g(z_{t-1})$. The benchmark model has $\omega = 0$ in the equation

$$g(z_{t-1}) = \omega z_{t-1} + \gamma\left(|z_{t-1}| - E\left[|Z_{t-1}|\right]\right). \tag{31}$$

Specification (31) and

$$g(z_{t-1}) = \omega z_{t-1} + \gamma\left(z_{t-1}^2 - 1\right), \tag{32}$$

respectively, have AL = 0.55 and AL = -10.51. Thus the kinked function (31) helps to describe DM returns better than the smooth function (32). Considering (31) further, the estimated values of ω and γ are 0.0119 and 0.1883, respectively, and the small value of AL clearly supports the hypothesis $\omega = 0$. The estimated ratio ω/γ is only 0.06 compared with the US stock values of -0.76 in Nelson (1991) and -0.39 in Brock, Lakonishok, and LeBaron (1992). The result here is not surprising: there are plausible theories for a negative ω in stock models but none for a non-zero ω in currency models.

Third, consideration of exponential Arch (p,q)

Table 2. Exponential Arch(1,0) estimates for subperiods

Parameter	Complete dataset (Dec 1977-Nov 1990; 3283 observations)	First subperiod (Dec 1977-Dec 1983; 1,533 observations)	Second subperiod (Jan 1984–Nov 1990; 1,750 observations)
γ	0.1885	0.2659	0.1368
(s.e.)[a]	(0.0239)	(0.0424)	(0.0267)
Δ	0.9658	0.9478	0.9628
(s.e.)	(0.0087)	(0.0167)	(0.0128)
α_E	−10.071	−10.337	−9.871
(s.e.)	(0.095)	(0.132)	(0.101)
v	1.317	1.304	1.357
(s.e.)	(0.046)	(0.066)	(0.066)
M	1.406	1.735	1.180
(s.e.)	(0.107)	(0.191)	(0.122)
V	1.695	2.054	1.414
(s.e.)	(0.283)	(0.497)	(0.324)
Mean return $\times 10^4$			
Monday	-6.26	-7.94	-4.86
(s.e.)	(2.63)	(3.44)	(3.68)
Tuesday	-2.20	-4.18	0.23
(s.e.)	(2.12)	(2.73)	(3.03)
Wednesday	4.43	5.16	2.76
(s.e.)	(2.18)	(2.19)	(3.46)
Thursday	-4.57	-9.37	2.20
(s.e.)	(2.21)	(2.99)	(3.47)
Friday	-4.26	-6.00	-2.67
(s.e.)	(2.35)	(3.06)	(3.10)
max ln(L)	11,813.98	5,683.58	6,146.94

Maximum likelihood estimates and the maxima of the log-likelihood function for exponential ARCH(1,0) models fitted to daily DM/$ returns for various periods. The ARCH models contain seasonal dummy variables M and V for Mondays and vacations. Five day-of-the-week conditional mean terms are included in the models. The conditional distribution is generalised error with tail-thickness parameter v.

Model for the conditional variance h_t: $h_t = h_t^*$, Mh_t^*, or Vh_t^*; $x_t^* = x_t - E[X_t \mid I_{t-1}]$,

$$\ln(h_t^*) = \alpha_E + \Delta[\ln(h_{t-1}^*) - \alpha_E] + \gamma(|x_{t-1}^*| / \sqrt{h_{t-1}} - \text{cst.}).$$

[a] s.e. refers to the standard error. These are calculated using the Hessian and numerical derivatives.

models with $(p,q) \neq (1,0)$ shows that they have nothing extra to offer. For example, $(p,q) = (2,1)$ has AL equal to only 0.55.

Table 2 presents subperiod estimates for the benchmark model. The subperiod estimates and their standard errors suggest there may have been significant changes in the

- Magnitude of volatility shocks ($\hat{\gamma}$ decreases from 0.27 to 0.14, t-ratio -2.58)
- Long-run level of volatility ($\hat{\alpha}_E$ increases from -10.34 to -9.87, t-ratio 2.80)
- Weekend volatility effect ($\hat{M}$ decreases from 1.74 to 1.18, t-ratio -2.45)
- Thursday conditional mean term (t-ratio 2.53).

Quasi-ML estimates and their robust standard errors give similar t-ratios for the estimated parameter changes: -1.96 for $\hat{\gamma}$, 2.13 for $\hat{\alpha}_E$, -2.49 for $\hat{M}$, and 2.70 for the Thursday mean.

The point estimates of α_E, M, and V imply that the median annualised volatility is 10% for the first subperiod and 12% for the second period. Fitting models in which α_E depends linearly on the time t, so $\alpha_E = \alpha_0 + \alpha_1 t$, gives $\hat{\alpha}_1 > 0$ for the complete dataset but $\hat{\alpha}_1 < 0$ for each subperiod. There is therefore little evidence for an upward drift in Deutschmark/dollar volatility.

ARV ESTIMATES

Seasonal effects are included in the ARV model by writing $\ln(\sigma_t) - \ln(\sigma_t^*) = 0$, $0.5\ln(M)$, or $0.5\ln(V)$, as appropriate, and then supposing that $\{\ln(\sigma_t^*)\}$ is a Gaussian, AR(1) process having mean α, standard deviation β, and autoregressive parameter ϕ. Many methods for estimating α, β, and ϕ were noted previously. Some of these methods are used here. Other methods, including GMM, are the subject of continuing research.

The estimation methods make use of adjusted returns x_t^*, defined by $x_t^* = x_t - \bar{x}$, $(x_t - \bar{x})/M^{1/2}$, or $(x_t - \bar{x})/V^{1/2}$, as appropriate, with $M = 1.406$ and $V = 1.695$ from Table 1. Matching the mean absolute deviation and the variance of $\{x_t^*\}$, using (16) and (17), gives $\hat{\alpha} = -5.153$ and $\hat{\beta} = 0.415$. Alternatively, β can be estimated by matching the kurtosis using (18) and, on this occasion, a similar estimate is obtained: $\hat{\beta} = 0.412$.

The autoregressible parameter ϕ has been estimated in three ways. Fitting the function $K\phi^\tau$ to the first 50 autocorrelations of the absolute adjusted returns, $|x_t^*|$, by ordinary least squares, gives $\hat{K} = 0.114$ and $\hat{\phi} = 0.969$. Second, fitting a linear ARMA(1,1) model to the variables $l_t = \ln(|x_t^*|)$ gives $\hat{\phi} = 0.972$ with an estimated standard error of 0.026. The standard error of $\hat{\phi}$ is more than twice as large as the comparable Arch standard errors and a simple test of the unit-root hypothesis $\phi = 1$ would accept the possibility that the volatility was not mean reverting. A Type II error would then occur according to the Arch test described above. Third, maximising the quasi-likelihood function of the series $\{l_t\}$, using the Kalman filter specification given by (14)-(15), gives $\hat{\phi} = 0.938$ and also $\hat{\alpha} = -5.193$ and $\hat{\beta} = 0.404$. Subperiod estimates show an increase in $\hat{\alpha}$ and a decrease in $\hat{\beta}$ from the first to the second subperiod, approximately comparable to the changes in the estimates of the exponential Arch parameters α_E and γ.

COMPARISONS OF VOLATILITY PERSISTENCE ESTIMATES

The sum $a + b$, for a Garch(1,1) model, is a measure of the persistence of volatility shocks, likewise Δ for the exponential Arch(1,0) model and ϕ for the ARV model. Table 3 presents seven estimates of these persistence measures for the complete dataset and seven estimates for each of the two subperiods. It can be seen that six of the full-period estimates are similar but the Kalman filter estimate is somewhat smaller, although all the estimates are similar for the subperiods. In six of the rows in Table 3 both the subperiod estimates are slightly less than the full-period estimate, which may reflect one or more changes in the unconditional variance as noted earlier.

An estimate of a + b, Δ, or ϕ equal to 0.9669 (the average figure in Table 3 for all 13 years) implies a half-life h of 30 calendar days by solving the equation $(0.9669)^{252h/365} = 0.5$. For an estimate equal to 0.9610 (the subperiod average figure), the half-life is 25 calendar days.

Option pricing implications

The ARV and exponential Arch(1,0) models provide fair option prices which are almost identical when the model parameters are matched appropriately. Nevertheless, both the ARV and Arch models are constructive when valuing options.

Numerical valuation methods are much quicker for the ARV model because it typically requires integration of the Black-Scholes function multiplied by the probability density of the average variance during the life of the option, if it is assumed that

❑ volatility risk is not priced and

❑ price and volatility innovations are uncorrelated (Hull and White 1987a).

Integration over a variance distribution is much faster than the Arch alternative which requires integration over a price distribution with respect to a risk-neutral measure, if similar assumptions about risk and the innovations are made (Duan 1995; Engle and Mustafa 1992). These integrals have been evaluated using Monte Carlo methods enhanced by the antithetic variable and control-variate methods. Approximately 2,000 option prices can be calculated from the ARV model in the time taken to calculate one option price from the exponential Arch(1,0) model to the same accuracy, when the volatility parameters are similar to the Deutschmark/dollar estimates.

Model estimation and validation is simpler when Arch models are used. These models permit robust tests for a unit root in the volatility process and tests of the assumption that price and volatility residuals are uncorrelated, as illustrated here. Comparisons of different Arch specifications provide guidance about a suitable volatility process. The results given here show exponential Arch(1,0) describes the Deutschmark/dollar returns best within the Arch family and hence the ARV model is a credible choice when the distribution of the average variance is required. An initial variance is needed when the average variance is simulated. Arch equations provide an appropriate value for this initial variance.

Table 3. Persistence estimates for Deutschmark/dollar volatility

		Complete dataset (Dec 1977–Nov 1990; 3,283 observations)	First Subperiod (Dec 1977–Dec 1983; 1,533 observations)	Second Subperiod (Jan 1984–Nov 1990; 1,750 observations)
Model[a]	Parameter	Estimate	Estimate	Estimate
ARV	ϕ^b	0.9384	0.9574	0.9519
Exp-Arch-GED	Δ	0.9658	0.9478	0.9628
ARV	ϕ^c	0.9688	0.9667	0.9583
Exp-Arch-t	Δ	0.9702	0.9558	0.9656
ARV	ϕ^d	0.9719	0.9646	0.9666
Garch-GED	a + b	0.9737	0.9645	0.9581
Garch-t	a + b	0.9790	0.9728	0.9612
Average		0.9669	0.9613	0.9606

Estimates of persistence parameters for Arch and ARV models fitted to daily DM/$ returns. The Arch estimates are maximum likelihood estimates. The order of the rows in the table is determined by the magnitude of the persistence estimates for the complete dataset.

[a] Exp-Arch refers to exponential Arch(1,0), Garch to Garch(1,1), GED to conditional generalised error distributions, t to conditional Student's t-distributions, and ARV to the contemporaneous autoregressive random variance model.
[b] Estimates obtained by the Kalman filter method of Harvey, Ruiz, and Shephard (1994).
[c] Estimates obtained by matching autocorrelations, as in Taylor (1986).
[d] Estimates obtained by the ARMA fitting method of Chesney and Scott (1989).

Conclusions

The theoretical results summarised above, theorems proved by Nelson (1990), and the empirical results reported here and elsewhere all support an important conclusion: a discrete-time approximation to a stochastic volatility model used to price options in theoretical studies (here called the ARV model) is very similar to the best Arch models identified in descriptive studies of asset prices. For the exchange rates considered, a methodology which uses both ARV and Arch models permits the very quick calculation of options values based upon stochastic processes which are empirically credible. A fundamental difference between the two types of models can be identified when volatility is a function of the quantity of information incorporated into prices: variation in this quantity exclusively explains changes in volatility for the ARV model while past prices are the primary determinant of volatility changes for Arch models.

1 *Andersen (1992) offers volatility definitions which avoid distributional assumptions.*

2 *These include multivariate models and models that make use of further information, for example, interest rates related to the stock market's settlement process (Baillie and DeGennaro (1989), trading volume (Lamoureux and Lastrapes 1990), option implied volatilities (Day and Lewis 1992), and FED policy change dummy variables (Lastrapes 1989).*

3 *The expectation of* $|Z_t|$ *equals* $(2/\pi)^{1/2}$ *when* D( ) *is normal,* $\Gamma[2/v]/[\Gamma[1/v]\Gamma[3/v]]^{1/2}$ *when* D( ) *is the GED, and* $2(v-2)^{1/2}\Gamma((v+1)2)/[\pi^{1/2}(v-1)\Gamma(v/2)]$ *when* D( ) *is a scaled-t distribution.*

4 *The theorem suggests methods for estimating the parameters of the diffusion model. For example, the correlation* δ *between the price and volatility differential in (6) can be estimated by fitting (23) and (24), with conditional normal distributions, because* $\delta \approx \text{sign}(\omega)[1+(\gamma/\omega)^2(1-2/\pi)]^{-1/2}$.

5 *A stochastic process is reversible if and only if the likelihood function has* $L(x_{t+1}, x_{t+2}, \ldots, x_{t+n}) = L(x_{t+n}, x_{t+n-1}, \ldots, x_{t+1})$ *for all* $n, t, x_{t+1}, \ldots, x_{t+n}$.

6 *Simulations have shown there are several such characteristics when the conditional distribution is normal but the results to date are not constructive when the conditional distribution is double exponential (the GED with* $v = 1$*).*

7 *Every return is calculated using two prices for the same contract. On a few occasions the futures prices reported by the market are not transaction prices because of the limit rules operated until May 1985. Consequently, 28 futures prices have been replaced by equivalent forward prices; 17 of these replacements are needed in 1978.*

8 *It is not possible to deduce immediately that the GED is preferable, because the likelihood functions are not nested. Estimation of an exp-Arch model in which* Z_t *has density* $pf_1(z) + (1-p)f_2(z)$, *with* f_1 *the* t *density and* f_2 *the GED density, provides no evidence to reject* $p = 0$ *but obviously rejects* $p = 1$. *Our differences conflict with the claim made by Baillie and Bollerslev (1989) that the* t*-distribution gives substantially higher maximum log-likelihoods than the GED for their currency data. However, the term* $-\frac{1}{2}\ln(\pi)$ *is missing from their log-likelihood function for the* t*-distribution.*

9 *The standardised residuals for this model are compatible with the model assumptions. The average values of* z_t, $z_t^2 - 1$, z_t^3, $z_t z_{t+\tau}$ *and* $(z_t^2-1)(z_{t+\tau}^2-1)$, $1 \le \tau \le 10$, *are all close to zero as required.*

10 $t = -2.68$ *for the Garch(1,1) specification.*

BIBLIOGRAPHY

Akgiray, V., 1989, "Conditional heteroskedasticity in time series of stock returns: evidence and forecasts", *Journal of Business* 62, pp. 55-80.

Andersen, T.G., 1992, "Volatility", Working paper, Kellogg Graduate School of Management, Northwestern University.

Andersen, T.G., 1993, "Return volatility and trading volume: an information flow interpretation of stochastic volatility", *Journal of Finance* 51, pp. 169-204.

Bailey, W., and R.M. Stulz, 1989, "The pricing of stock index options in a general equilibrium model", *Journal of Financial and Quantitative Analysis* 24, pp. 1-12.

Baillie, R.T., and T. Bollerslev, 1989, "The message in daily exchange rates: a conditional-variance tale", *Journal of Business and Economic Statistics* 7, pp. 297-305.

Baillie, R.T., and R.P. DeGennaro, 1989, "The impact of delivery terms on stock return volatility", *Journal of Financial Services Research* 3, pp. 55-76.

Baillie, R.T., and R.P. DeGennaro, 1990, "Stock returns and volatility", *Journal of Financial and Quantitative Analysis* 25, pp. 203-14.

Bollerslev, T., 1986, "Generalized autoregressive conditional heteroskedasticity", *Journal of Econometrics* 31, pp. 307-27.

Bollerslev, T., 1987, "A conditionally heteroskedastic time series model for security prices and rates of return data", *Review of Economic Statistics* 59, pp. 542-7.

Bollerslev, T., R.Y. Chou, and K.F. Kroner, 1992, "Arch modeling in finance: a review of the theory and empirical evidence", *Journal of Econometrics* 52, pp. 5-59; reprinted as Chapter 2 of the present volume.

Bollerslev, T., R.F. Engle, and D.B. Nelson, 1993, "Arch models," in *The Handbook of Econometrics* vol. IV, North-Holland, pp. 2959-3038.

Bollerslev, T., and J.M. Wooldridge, 1992, "Quasi-maximum likelihood estimation and inference in dynamic models with time varying covariances", *Econometric Review* 11, pp. 143-72.

Box, G.E.P., and G.C. Tiao, 1973, *Bayesian Inference in Statistical Analysis*. Reading, MA: Addison-Wesley.

Brock, W., J. Lakonishok, and B. LeBaron, 1992, "Simple Technical Trading Rules and the Stochastic Properties of Stock Returns", *Journal of Finance* 47, pp. 1731-64.

Campbell, J.Y., and L. Hentschel, 1992, "No news is good news: an asymmetric model of changing volatility in stock returns", *Journal of Financial Economics* 31, pp. 281-318.

Chesney, M., and L.O. Scott, 1989, "Pricing European currency options: a comparison of the modified Black-Scholes model and a random variance model", *Journal of Financial and Quantitative Analysis* 24, pp. 267-84.

Clark, P.K., 1973, "A subordinated stochastic process model with finite variance for speculative prices", *Econometrica* 41, pp. 135-55.

Day, T.E., and C.M. Lewis, 1992, "Stock market volatility and the information content of stock index options", *Journal of Econometrics* 52, pp. 267-87.

Duan, J.-C., 1995, "The GARCH option pricing model", *Mathematical Finance* 5, pp 13-32; reprinted as Chapter 24 of the present volume.

Duffie, D., and K.J. Singleton, 1989, "Simulated moments estimation of Markov models of asset prices", Unpublished manuscript, Graduate School of Business, Stanford University; conference paper, London School of Economics.

Engle, R.F., 1982, "Autoregressive conditional heteroskedasticity with estimates of the variance of U.K. inflation", *Econometrica* 50, pp. 987-1008.

Engle, R.F., and T. Bollerslev, 1986, "Modelling the persistence of conditional variances", *Econometric Reviews* 5, pp. 1-50.

Engle, R.F., and G. Gonzalez-Rivera, 1991, "Semi-parametric Arch models", *Journal of Business and Economic Statistics* 9, pp. 345-59.

Engle, R.F., and C. Mustafa, 1992, "Implied ARCH models from options prices," *Journal of Econometrics* 52, pp. 289-311.

French, K.R., and R. Roll, 1986, "Stock return variances: the arrival of information and the reaction of traders", *Journal of Financial Economics* 17, pp. 5-26.

Gallant, A.R., D. Hsieh, and G.E. Tauchen, 1991, "On fitting a recalcitrant series: the pound/dollar exchange rate, 1974-83", in *Nonparametric and Semiparametric Methods in Econometrics and Statistics*, eds. W. A. Barnett, J. Powell, and G. E. Tauchen. Cambridge, UK: Cambridge University Press.

Harris, L., 1987, "Transaction data tests of the mixture of distributions hypothesis", *Journal of Financial and Quantitative Analysis* 22, pp. 127-41.

Harvey, A.C., E. Ruiz, and N.G. Shephard, 1994, "Multivariate stochastic variance models," *Review of Economic Studies* 61, pp. 247-264.

Harvey, A.C., and N.G. Shephard, 1993, "The econometrics of stochastic volatility", Working paper, Department of Statistical and Mathematical Sciences, London School of Economics.

Heston, S.L., 1993, "A closed-form solution for options with stochastic volatility with applications to bond and currency options", *Review of Financial Studies* 6, pp. 327-43; reprinted as Chapter 23 of the present volume.

Hsieh, D.A., 1989, "Modelling heteroskedasticity in daily foreign-exchange rates", *Journal of Business and Economic Statistics* 7, pp. 307-17.

Hsu, D.-A., 1980, "Further analyses of position errors in navigation", *Journal of Navigation* 33, pp. 452-74.

Hsu, D.-A., 1982, "A Bayesian robust detection of shift in the risk structure of stock market returns", *Journal of the American Statistical Association* 77, pp. 29-39.

Hull, J., and A. White, 1987a, "The pricing of options on assets with stochastic volatilities", *Journal of Finance* 42, pp. 281-300.

Hull, J., and A. White, 1987b, "Hedging the risks from writing foreign currency options", *Journal of International Money Finance* 6, pp. 131-52.

Hull, J., and A. White, 1988, "An analysis of the bias in option pricing caused by a stochastic volatility", *Advances in Futures and Options Research* 3, pp. 29-61.

Jacquier, E., N.G. Polson, and P.E. Rossi, 1994, "Bayesian analysis of stochastic volatility models" (with discussion), *Journal of Business and Economic Statistics*, 12, pp. 371-417.

Johnson, H., and D. Shanno, 1987, "Option pricing when the variance is changing", *Journal of Financial and Quantitative Analysis* 22, pp. 143-52.

Kelly, F.P., 1979, *Reversibility and Stochastic Networks*, Chichester, UK: Wiley.

Lamoureux, C.G., and W.D. Lastrapes, 1990, "Heteroskedasticity in stock return data: volume versus GARCH effects", *Journal of Finance* 45, pp. 221-9.

Lastrapes, W.D., 1989, "Weekly exchange rate volatility and US monetary policy regimes: an application of the ARCH model", *Journal of Money, Credit & Banking* 21, pp. 66-77.

Lumsdaine, R.L., 1995, "Finite sample properties of the maximum likelihood estimator in GARCH(1,1) and IGARCH(1,1) models: a Monte Carlo investigation", *Journal of Business and Economic Statistics* 13, pp. 1-10.

Lumsdaine, R.L., 1996, "Consistency and asymptotic properties of the quasi-maximum likelihood estimator in IGARCH(1,1) and covariance stationary GARCH(1,1) models," *Econometrica* 64, pp. 575-96.

McFarland, J.W., R.R. Pettit, and S.K. Sung, 1982, "The distribution of foreign exchange price changes: trading day effects and risk management", *Journal of Finance* 37, pp. 693-715.

Melino, A., and S.M. Turnbull, 1990, "Pricing foreign currency options with stochastic volatility", *Journal of Econometrics* 45, pp. 239-65.

Merville, L.J., and D.R. Pieptea, 1989, "Stock price volatility, mean-reverting diffusion, and noise," *Journal of Financial Economics* 24, pp. 193-214.

Nelson, D.B., 1990, "ARCH models as diffusion approximations," *Journal of Econometrics* 45, pp. 7-38.

Nelson, D.B., 1991, "Conditional heteroskedasticity in asset returns: a new approach," *Econometrica* 59, pp. 347-70.

Praetz, P.D., 1972, "The distribution of share price changes", *Journal of Business* 45, pp. 49-55.

Schwert, G.W., and P.J. Seguin, 1990, "Heteroskedasticity in stock returns", *Journal of Finance* 45, pp. 1129-55.

Scott, L.O., 1987, "Option pricing when the variance changes randomly: theory, estimation, and an application", *Journal of Financial and Quantitative Analysis* 22, pp. 419-38.

Scott, L.O., 1991, "Random variance option pricing: empirical tests of the model and delta-sigma hedging", *Advances in Futures and Options Research* 5, pp. 113-35.

Scott, L.O., 1992, "Stock market volatility and the pricing of index options: an analysis of implied volatilities and the volatility risk premium in a model with stochastic interest rates and volatility", Working paper, Department of Finance, University of Georgia.

Stein, E.M., and J.C. Stein, 1991, "Stock price distributions with stochastic volatility: an analytic approach", *Review of Financial Studies* 4, pp. 727-52; reprinted as Chapter 22 of the present volume.

Stein, J.C., 1989, "Overreactions in the options market", *Journal of Finance* 44, pp. 1011-23.

Tauchen, G.E., and M. Pitts, 1983, "The price variability-volume relationship on speculative markets", *Econometrica* 51, pp. 485-505.

Taylor, S.J., 1986, *Modelling Financial Time Series*. Chichester, UK: Wiley.

Wiggins, J.B., 1987, "Option values under stochastic volatility: theory and empirical estimates", *Journal of Financial Economics* 19, pp. 351-72.

Multivariate Garch Modelling of Asset Returns*

Kenneth F. Kroner and Victor K. Ng
Barclays Global Investors; Goldman Sachs

This paper studies asymmetric responses of covariances to return shocks. Asymmetric/leverage effects have been found in variances but few studies have examined such effects in covariances, even though they might have important implications for portfolio management and hedging. We propose a robust conditional moment test to detect the presence of such asymmetric effects in the covariances. We also introduce a general dynamic covariance matrix model, which nests many of the existing multivariate Garch models and addresses covariance asymmetries. To illustrate the tests and the new model, we apply them to weekly returns from a large firm and a small firm portfolio. Our results suggest that bad news about large firms can cause volatility in both small firm returns and large firm returns. The conditional covariance between large firm returns and small firm returns will also increase following bad news about large firms. In contrast, news about small firms has a minimal effect on variances and covariances.

Recent studies on the time series properties of stock return volatility find that volatility is predictable and is affected by the magnitude and direction of past return shocks. See Bollerslev, Chou and Kroner (1992) for a survey. Specifically, large return shocks lead to high subsequent volatility, with negative return shocks inducing higher subsequent volatility than positive return shocks of the same magnitude (See Black (1976); French, Schwert and Stambaugh (1987); Nelson (1991); Pagan and Schwert (1990); Engle and Ng (1993)). To capture such empirical regularities, many volatility models have been developed in the literature and used in the valuation of assets. For instance, Kuwahara and Marsh (1992) use the Garch and Egarch models to price Japanese equity warrants, and Amin and Ng (1994) compare the performance of several Garch models in pricing individual stock options. These papers generally find that the asymmetric/leverage effects in volatility is important in option valuation.

While relatively few studies have examined the existence of asymmetric effects in the covariances, it is conceivable that such effects might exist, possibly for similar reasons as for volatility asymmetries. For instance, if the asymmetry in volatility is caused by a leverage effect – an increase in the riskiness of the stock due to an increase in the debt/equity ratio of the firm following a price drop – then the change in financial leverage in the firm might also change the degree of comovement between its stock return and other stock returns. As another possibility, if the asymmetric effect in volatility is caused by an increase in the amount of information flow following bad news, then the covariance between stock returns will also be affected because there would be a different relative rate of information flow across firms. Furthermore, since covariances play an important role in portfolio selec-

* *This paper was first published in the* Papers and Proceedings of the American Statistical Association, Business and Economics Section *(1995). It is reprinted with permission of the American Statistical Association. We are grateful to Robin Brenner, Gautam Kaul and Richard Harjes for helpful suggestions. We also thank Gautam Kaul, Jennifer Conrad and Mustafa Gultekin for providing the data used in this paper.*

tion, risk management and the pricing of derivative assets, these effects could have important investment implications.

This paper has three contributions. First, given the lack of diagnostic tests for multivariate models with time varying variances and covariances, we introduce a robust conditional moment test to detect the presence of such asymmetric effects in covariances. Second, we introduce a general model which nests the four most popular time varying covariance models: the VECH model of Bollerslev, Engle, and Wooldridge (1988), the constant correlation model of Bollerslev (1990), the factor Arch model of Engle, Ng, and Rothschild (1990), and the BEKK model of Engle and Kroner (1995). Third, we work out a natural generalisation of this encompassing model to allow for asymmetric/leverage effects in variances and covariances. This asymmetric dynamic covariance matrix model nests various asymmetric extensions of the four existing models.

To illustrate the models and the new tests, we apply them to the bivariate system of weekly large firm and small firm portfolio returns used in Conrad, Gultekin and Kaul (1991). The sample period is from July 1962 to December 1988, for a total of 1,371 weekly observations. We find that all four existing models are misspecified, especially in the dynamics of the covariances. Using our proposed model, we find that bad news about large firms causes increased volatility in both small firm and large firm returns. The conditional covariance between small and large firm returns also increases after bad news about large firms. In contrast, news about small firms has a minimal effect on variances and covariances.

Time varying covariance models

In an extension of the capital asset pricing model to allow for time varying betas, Bollerslev, Engle and Wooldridge (1988) model the time varying variances and covariances of asset returns with a Box-Jenkins ARMA type specification for the squares and cross products of unexpected asset returns. This specification is named the VECH model in the literature. It has also been applied by Giovannini and Jorion (1989) to study foreign exchange volatility, by Bodurtha and Mark (1991) to re-evaluate the Capital Asset Pricing Model using US equity market data, and by Baillie and Myers (1991) to compute optimal hedge ratios in commodity spot and futures markets.

Let R_{it}, $i = 1,\ldots,N$, be the rates of return of asset i at time t. Let ψ_{t-1} be an information set containing the history of all variables up to time $t-1$. Since investors know ψ_{t-1} when they make their investment decision at time $t-1$, the relevant measures of expected return, return variability and comovement are the mean returns, the variances, and the covariances or correlations conditional on ψ_{t-1}. Let $\mu_{it} \equiv E_{t-1}R_{it}$, $h_{iit} \equiv var_{t-1}(R_{it})$, and $h_{ijt} \equiv cov_{t-1}(R_{it},R_{jt})$, where $E_{t-1}(\cdot)$ is the conditional expectation operator, $var_{t-1}(\cdot)$ is the conditional variance operator, and $cov_{t-1}(\cdot)$ is the conditional covariance operator. Further, let $H_t \equiv [h_{ij,t}]$ be the conditional covariance matrix of asset returns at time t. Under the VECH model, H_t is modelled as follows:

$$h_{ij,t} = \omega_{ij} + \beta_{ij}h_{ij,t-1} + \alpha_{ij}\varepsilon_{i,t-1}\varepsilon_{j,t-1} \qquad (1)$$

for all $i,j = 1,\ldots,N$, where $\varepsilon_{i,t-1} \equiv R_{i,t-1} - \mu_{i,t-1}$ is the stock return shock to asset i at time $t-1$.

To ensure the positive definiteness of the estimated variance-covariance matrix of asset returns, restrictions have to be imposed on the parameters to ensure that $h_{ii,t}(\cdot)$ is a positive function and the conditional correlation

$$\rho_{ij,t} = h_{ij,t} / \sqrt{h_{ii,t}h_{jj,t}}$$

is a bounded function in the interval $(1,-1)$. A sufficient condition is that $\omega_{ii} > 0$, $\beta_{ii} \geq 0$, $\alpha_{ii} \geq 0$,

$$\omega_{ij} \leq \sqrt{\omega_{ii}\omega_{jj}},\ \beta_{ij} \leq \sqrt{\beta_{ii}\beta_{jj}} \text{ and } \alpha_{ij} \leq \sqrt{\alpha_{ii}\alpha_{jj}}.$$

Because the number of restrictions increases exponentially with the number of assets, it is hard to keep track of all the parameter values, even for relatively small systems, that guarantee positive definiteness of the estimated variance covariance matrix.

To overcome this problem, Engle and Kroner (1995) propose using quadratic forms to model the variance and covariance functions. Their model, called the BEKK model, has been applied to model the time varying variances and covariances of different size-based stock portfolios by Conrad, Gultekin and Kaul (1991), of international stock returns by Chan, Karolyi and Stulz (1992), and of spot and futures returns by Baillie and Myers (1991).

Let $\varepsilon_{t-1} = (\varepsilon_{1t-1},\ldots,\varepsilon_{Nt-1})$ be the vector of return shocks at time $t-1$, and let C, A, and B be $N \times N$ matrices. The BEKK model takes the form

$$H_t = C'C + B'H_{t-1}B + A'\varepsilon_{t-1}\varepsilon'_{t-1}A. \qquad (2)$$

This model allows the conditional covariance matrix of asset returns to be determined by the outer product matrices of the vector of past return shocks. Given that each term on the right hand side of (3) is expressed as a quadratic form, the positive definiteness of the conditional covariance matrix of asset returns is guaranteed provided that the null spaces of C and B intersect only at the origin (Engle and Kroner, [1995]). A sufficient condition for this to hold is that either C or B be full rank.

While the positive definiteness of the estimated conditional covariance matrix is ensured, the number of parameters in the BEKK model is large especially for a system with many asset return series. Alternatives which guarantee positive definiteness and fewer parameters have therefore been proposed. One is the Factor ARCH model (FAC) of Engle (1987), Engle, Ng and Rothschild (1990) and Ng, Engle and Rothschild (1992). Let Ω be an $N \times N$ positive definite symmetric matrix, λ and w be $N \times 1$ vectors, and α and φ be scalars. The specification for a one-factor ARCH model is

$$H_t = \Omega + \lambda\lambda'\left[\varphi \cdot w'H_{t-1}w + \phi\left(w'\varepsilon_{t-1}\right)^2\right]. \quad (3)$$

This can be viewed as a special case of the BEKK model, in which the A and B matrices are rank 1 and share an eigenvector. Essentially, the Factor ARCH model assumes that the conditional variances and covariances of the asset returns are functions of the conditional variances of a portfolio return which follows a GARCH type process. Let $R_{pt} \equiv w'R_t$, where $R_t = (R_{1t},\ldots,R_{Nt})'$, be the returns to a portfolio formed with a weight vector w. The time $t-1$ return shock of this portfolio is $\varepsilon_{pt-1} = w'\varepsilon_{t-1}$ and the time t conditional variance of this portfolio is $h_{pt} = w'H_tw$. The one factor ARCH model can be rewritten in the following alternative form:

$$h_{ijt} = \sigma_{ij} + \lambda_i\lambda_j \cdot h_{pt} \quad (4a)$$

for all $i,j = 1,\ldots,N$.

$$h_{pt} = \omega_p + \varphi \cdot h_{p,t-1} + \phi\varepsilon^2_{p,t-1} \quad (4b)$$

where Ω_{ij} is the (i,j)th element of Ω, $\omega_p \equiv w'\Omega w$, and $\sigma_{ij} \equiv \Omega_{ij} - \lambda_i\lambda_j\omega_p$.

In Schwert and Seguin (1990) and the one factor case in Ng, Engle and Rothschild (1992), R_{pt} is taken to be the market return. In other words, the entire conditional covariance matrix of asset returns is driven by the conditional variance of the market portfolio. Like the BEKK model, the estimated conditional covariance matrix of asset returns is positive definite as long as the constant part of the conditional covariance matrix is positive definite.

A second way to model the time series behaviour of the conditional covariance matrix of asset return parsimoniously is the constant correlation model (CCOR) suggested by Bollerslev (1990). This model restricts the conditional covariance between two asset returns to be proportional to the product of the conditional standard deviations of the asset returns. In this way the conditional correlation coefficient of the two asset returns is time invariant. Specifically, the model is:

$$h_{iit} = \omega_{ii} + \beta_{ii}h_{ii,t-1} + \alpha_{ii}\varepsilon^2_{i,t-1} \quad \forall i = 1,\ldots,N \quad (5a)$$

$$h_{ijt} = \rho_{ij} \cdot \sqrt{h_{iit}h_{jjt}} \quad \forall i \neq j. \quad (5b)$$

Bollerslev (1990) applies this model to study time varying volatility in exchange rates. Ng (1991) applies this model to study a conditional CAPM with time varying variances and covariances, and Kroner and Claessens (1991) and Kroner and Sultan (1993) apply this model to obtain better hedge ratios in currency markets. Chan, Chan, and Karolyi (1991) use a modified version of this model to study the volatility relationship between stock index spot and futures markets.

To analyse the asymmetric properties of time varying covariance matrix models systematically, we define the following effects, where ${}_k\varepsilon_{t-1}$ is the $(N-1) \times 1$ vector of return shocks at time $t-1$, excluding $\varepsilon_{k,t-1}$:

OWN VOLATILITY ASYMMETRY
A covariance matrix function $H_t = Q(\varepsilon_{t-1},H_{t-1}) = [q_{ij}(\varepsilon_{t-1},H_{t-1})]$ exhibits own volatility asymmetry if for some i, $q_{ii}({}_i\varepsilon_{t-1},\varepsilon_{i,t-1},H_{t-1}) \neq q_{ii}({}_i\varepsilon_{t-1},-\varepsilon_{i,t-1},H_{t-1})$.

CROSS VOLATILITY ASYMMETRY
A covariance matrix function $H_t = Q(\varepsilon_{t-1},H_{t-1}) = [q_{ij}(\varepsilon_{t-1},H_{t-1})]$ exhibits cross volatility asymmetry if for some i and for some $j \neq i$, $q_{ii}({}_j\varepsilon_{t-1},\varepsilon_{j,t-1},H_{t-1}) \neq q_{ii}({}_j\varepsilon_{t-1},-\varepsilon_{j,t-1},H_{t-1})$.

COVARIANCE ASYMMETRY
A covariance matrix function $H_t = Q(\varepsilon_{t-1},H_{t-1}) = [q_{ij}(\varepsilon_{t-1},H_{t-1})]$ exhibits covariance asymmetry if for some i and for some $j \neq i$, $q_{ij}({}_j\varepsilon_{t-1},\varepsilon_{j,t-1},H_{t-1}) \neq q_{ij}({}_j\varepsilon_{t-1},-\varepsilon_{j,t-1},H_{t-1})$.

In simple terms, own variance asymmetry means that the conditional variance of an asset is affected by the sign of the asset's own return shock. Cross variance asymmetry means that the conditional variance of an asset is affected by the sign of the return shock of another asset. Cross variance asymmetry is in fact an extension of the

Table 1. Model summaries

Model	Own-variance asymmetry	Cross-variance asymmetry	Covariance asymmetry
VECH	no	no	yes
BEKK	yes	yes	yes
FAC	yes	yes	yes
CCOR	no	no	no

idea of volatility spillovers in Hamao, Masulis, and Ng (1990) and Chan, Chan, and Karolyi (1991), with good or bad news about one asset having different effects on the volatility of another asset. Finally, covariance asymmetry means that the covariance between two assets is affected by the sign of the return shock of at least one of the two assets. The properties of the four time varying covariance matrix models with respect to these asymmetric effects are summarised in the Table 1.

To describe these differences between the models further, we define "news impact surfaces," which are three-dimensional graphs of the current conditional covariance (variance) plotted against trailing large and small firm shocks, holding the past conditional variances and covariances constant at their in-sample averages. The graph is a bivariate generalisation of the news impact curve in Engle and Ng (1993). More precisely, let q_{t-1} be the vector of inputs (known at time t – 1) into h_{ijt}, excluding $e_{i,t-1}$, and let Q be the unconditional mean of q_{t-1}. The news impact surface for h_{ijt} is the three-dimensional graph of

$$h_{ijt} = h_{ij}\left(\varepsilon_{i,t-1}, \varepsilon_{j,t-1} \middle| q_{t-1} = Q\right).$$

Variance news impact surfaces reveal own variance asymmetry and cross variance asymmetry, while covariance news impact surfaces reveal covariance asymmetry.

Figure 1 shows the effects of return shocks of different sign and magnitude on the covariance between large and small firm portfolios implied by these four models.[1] The figures clearly illustrate that the different models imply different news impact surfaces for the covariance, even though the models are fitted to the same dataset. For example, the CCOR model implies that bad news to the small firm coupled with good news to the large firm causes increased covariance, while the VECH model implies that this causes decreased covariance. These kinds of differences have important implications on the computation of the optimal portfolio weights, optimal hedge ratios, and the betas of the securities in asset pricing problems. Therefore, we must question which, if any, of these models correctly specify the covariances or equivalently which, if any, of the covariance news impact surfaces are good descriptions of the data.

1. Covariance news impulse response surfaces from the four basic models

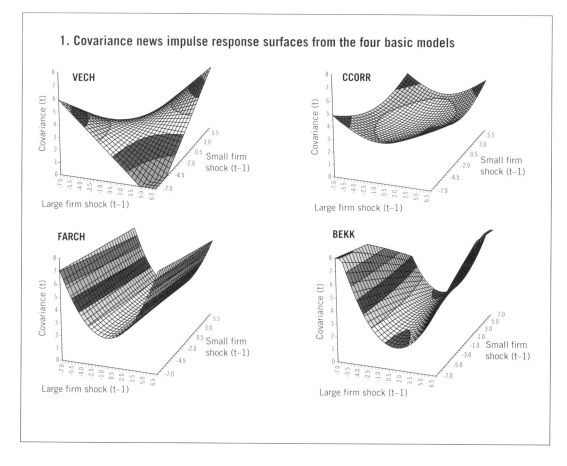

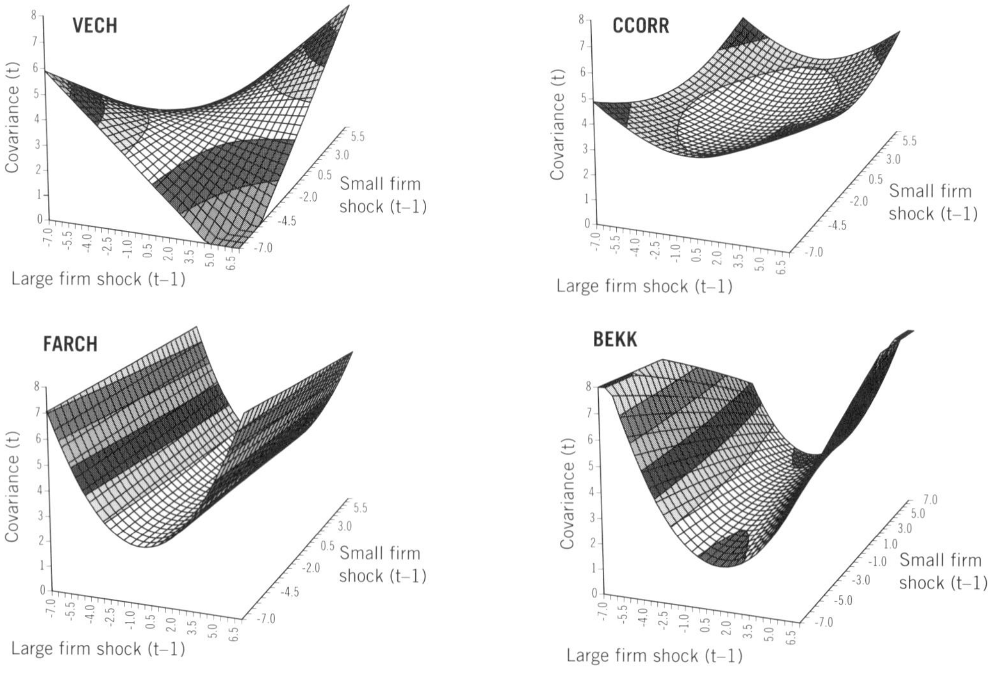

Robust conditional moment tests

To test the validity of a model, we propose to use robust conditional moment tests[2] (Wooldridge (1990)) to study how well the implied news response surfaces match the data. Conditional moment tests are distributed χ^2_k under the null hypothesis that the "generalised residual" has mean zero, conditional on k "misspecification indicators". The generalised residual can be any function with mean zero if the model is correct, and the misspecification indicator is the direction(s) in which the test has maximum power. For our purposes, the generalised residual is the distance between the implied news impact surface and the realised data. Specifically, it is $u_{ij,t} = \varepsilon_{it}\varepsilon_{jt} - h_{ijt}$ if we are examining the covariance news impact surface. It is impractical to define misspecification indicators that test if each point on the surface is correct, so we propose to use indicators that examine only a limited set of points on the news impact surface. For most empirical applications, if the news impact surface is the wrong height somewhere, it is likely to be reflected in one of the following directions (see Engle and Ng (1993)).

SIGN MISSPECIFICATION INDICATORS

The model might systematically over or underpredict covariances (variances) after good news or bad news. If so, the misspecification indicators

$$m_1^i = I(\varepsilon_{i,t-1} < 0),$$

where $I(\cdot)$ is the indicator function which takes the value 1 if the argument in parentheses is true, should be significant.

QUADRANT MISSPECIFICATION INDICATORS

The model might systematically over or underpredict covariances (variances) in any of the four quadrants $(\varepsilon_1 > 0, \varepsilon_2 > 0),\ldots,(\varepsilon_1 < 0, \varepsilon_2 < 0)$. If so, at least one of the misspecification indicators

$$m_2^{-,-} = I(\varepsilon_{1,t-1} < 0, \varepsilon_{2,t-1} < 0)$$
$$m_2^{+,-} = I(\varepsilon_{1,t-1} > 0, \varepsilon_{2,t-1} < 0)$$
$$m_2^{-,+} = I(\varepsilon_{1,t-1} < 0, \varepsilon_{2,t-1} > 0)$$
$$m_2^{+,+} = I(\varepsilon_{1,t-1} > 0, \varepsilon_{2,t-1} > 0)$$

should be significant.

SIZE-SIGN MISSPECIFICATION INDICATORS

The model might systematically over or underpredict covariances (variances) following unexpectedly large or small return shocks of different signs. A set of misspecification indicators which

Table 2. Robust conditional moment tests

	VECH	CCOR	BEKK	FAC
m_1^1	4.85	5.17	4.85	4.91
m_1^2	16.22	17.63	16.27	16.34
$m_2^{-,-}$	5.88	10.95	6.45	6.40
$m_2^{-,+}$		6.84		
$m_2^{+,-}$			4.10	
$m_2^{+,+}$	11.09	10.46	12.67	12.06
m_3^{11}				
m_3^{12}	3.99	6.45	5.54	5.01
m_3^{21}		4.03	5.40	4.24
m_3^{22}	4.41	4.95	6.29	5.11

tests for this is

$$m_3^{ii} = \varepsilon^2_{i,t-1} I(\varepsilon_{i,t-1} < 0)$$
$$m_3^{ij} = \varepsilon^2_{i,t-1} I(\varepsilon_{j,t-1} < 0)$$
$$m_3^{ji} = \varepsilon^2_{j,t-1} I(\varepsilon_{i,t-1} < 0)$$
$$m_3^{jj} = \varepsilon^2_{j,t-1} I(\varepsilon_{j,t-1} < 0).$$

Table 2 reports the robust conditional moment test results for misspecification in the covariances from the four standard covariance models discussed above. The first variable in the model is the small firm portfolio returns, and the second variable is the large firm portfolio returns. Blank entries in the table mean that the test was insignificant from zero at the 5% level.

The covariance equations from all four basic models are misspecified because they are unable to capture asymmetric effects in the covariances. Both sign misspecification indicators (m_1^1 and m_1^2) are different from zero for all the models, suggesting that bad news (negative residuals) have different effects on covariances than good news (positive residuals). This is corroborated by the sign-size misspecification indicators (m_3^{ij}), though the insignificant m_3^{11} implies that the model does not misspecify how small firm returns affect covariances when the small firm news is bad. Finally, the significance of $m_2^{-,-}$ and $m_2^{+,-}$ means that the models misspecify how covariances respond to bad news about the large firm portfolio, independent of the sign of the news to the small firm portfolio.

New models

These test results strongly suggest the existence of asymmetric effects in the covariances and variances that none of the existing models can account for. A more general model is needed that can explicitly capture the asymmetries. Instead of working on extensions for each of the four models and then comparing the large number of possible extensions, we follow a more structured approach. First, we will introduce a general dynamic covariance matrix model that can nest all four models. Then, we will generalise this model to include asymmetric effects. The resulting asymmetric covariance matrix model encompasses various asymmetric extensions of the four models. The specification of the basic encompassing model is as follows:

GENERAL DYNAMIC COVARIANCE (GDC) MATRIX MODEL

Let a_i and b_i be $N \times 1$ vectors. The GDC model is

$$h_{ij,t} = \begin{cases} \theta_{ij,t} & \text{if } i = j \\ \phi_{ij}\theta_{ijt} + \rho_{ij}\sqrt{\theta_{iit}\theta_{jjt}} & \text{if } i \neq j \end{cases}$$

where

$$\theta_{ijt} \equiv \omega_{ij} + b_i' H_{t-1} b_j + a_i' \varepsilon_{i,t-1} \varepsilon_{j,t-1}' a_j.$$

In matrix notation, this is

$$H_t = \Omega + \Phi \circ A' \varepsilon_{t-1} \varepsilon_{t-1}' A + B' H_{t-1} B + \Lambda_{t-1} C \Lambda_{t-1},$$

where A and B are $N \times N$ matrices with columns a_i and b_i, $i = I,\ldots,N$, respectively, Φ is a symmetric $N \times N$ matrix with ones along the diagonal and ϕ_{ij} off the diagonal, C is a diagonal matrix with zeros on the diagonal and ρ_{ij} off the diagonal, and

$$\Lambda_{t-1} \equiv \text{diag}\left\{\sqrt{h_{11,t}},\ldots,\sqrt{h_{NN,t}}\right\}.$$

Parameter restrictions necessary to ensure that variances are positive and correlations are between -1 and 1 are that $\rho_{ij} \in (-1,1)$ for all $i \neq j$ and that $|\phi_{ij}| \leq 1 - |\rho_{ij}|$. See Kroner and Ng (1995) for proof.

It is straightforward to show that this model nests the BEKK, CCOR and FAC covariance models. For example, if $\phi_{ij} = 0$ for all i and j, the model reduces to a CCOR model in which the coefficients are restricted to be positive. Similarly, if $\rho_{ij} = 0$ and $\phi_{ij} = 1$ for all i and j, the model reduces to the BEKK model. And as discussed above, further restrictions on the BEKK model will yield the FAC model. Furthermore, the GDC model nests a positive definite form of the VECH model. Specifically, if $\rho_{ij} = 0$ for all $i \neq j$ and if $a_i = \alpha_i \tau_i$ and $b_i = \beta_i \tau_i$ where τ_i is the ith column of an $N \times N$ identity matrix and α_i and β_i are scalars, then the GDC model is a special case of the diagonal VECH model in which the parameters are restricted to ensure positive definiteness. See Kroner and Ng (1995) for further discussion and proof of these special cases.

To generalise the above model to allow for asymmetric effects in the variances and covariances, we follow the direction of Glosten, Jagannathan, and Runkle (1993) and Zakoian (1994). In particular, we add new terms related to $\min(\varepsilon_{i,t-1},0)$. The model is defined as follows:

ASYMMETRIC DYNAMIC COVARIANCE (ADC) MATRIX MODEL

The ADC model is similar to the GDC model, except that the definition of θ_{ijt} is replaced with

$$\theta_{ijt} \equiv \omega_{ij} + b_i' H_{t-1} b_j + a_i' \varepsilon_{i,t-1} \varepsilon_{j,t-1}' a_j + f_i' \eta_{i,t-1} \eta_{j,t-1}' f_j.$$

where $\eta_{t-1} \equiv (\eta_{1,t-1},\ldots,\eta_{N,t-1})$ and $\eta_{i,t-1} \equiv \min(\varepsilon_{i,t-1},0)$.

The asymmetric dynamic covariance matrix model nests some natural extensions of the four models that allows for asymmetry in variances and covariances.

To check the performance of this model, we apply it to our large and small firm return series. The estimation results are reported in Table 3.[3] Notice that since ρ is significantly different from zero, the model cannot be simplified into the VECH, FAC or BEKK forms. Also, since ϕ and most of the covariance parameters are non-zero, the model cannot reduce to the CCOR model.

To check for misspecification, we apply the set of robust conditional moment tests to the model. With one exception, all the conditional moment tests, for both the variances and covariances, are insignificant. The exception is the test associated with the sign of $\varepsilon_{2,t-1}$ (the large firm residual) in the covariance equation, which is significant at the 2% level. Overall, we find minimal evidence of misspecification for the model.

Figure 2 plots the news impact surfaces implied by the ADC model. Interestingly, Panel A shows that the covariance between large and small firm returns is higher following a negative

Table 3. ADC model estimates

	Estimate	Standard error
ω_{11}	0.218	0.040
ω_{12}	–0.595	0.436
ω_{22}	0.027	0.019
α_{11}	0.217	0.015
α_{12}	–0.083	0.025
α_{21}	–0.070	0.057
α_{22}	0.254	0.033
f_{11}	0.075	0.041
f_{12}	–0.008	0.037
f_{21}	0.436	0.044
f_{22}	0.373	0.048
ρ_{12}	0.381	0.151
ϕ_{12}	0.626	0.163
β_{11}	0.868	0.014
β_{12}	0.495	0.241
β_{22}	0.884	0.015

shock to the large firm portfolio, while it is almost unaffected by shocks to the small firm portfolio. Next, Panel B shows that the variance of the large firm portfolio is unaffected by small firm shocks, whether these shocks represent good news or bad news. This confirms the results of Conrad, Gultekin and Kaul (1991) who concluded that small firm news does not affect large firm volatility. On the other hand, volatility of the large firm portfolio increases after any news to the large firm, but especially after bad news. This could simply be a leverage effect. Finally, Panel C indicates that the small firm portfolio has a dominant impact on small firm variances. This supports the findings of Conrad, Gultekin and Kaul (1991), who also show that large firm news spills over to small firm volatility. But it provides the additional insight that it is only the bad news that spills over, and not the good news.

2. News impulse response surfaces for the ADC model

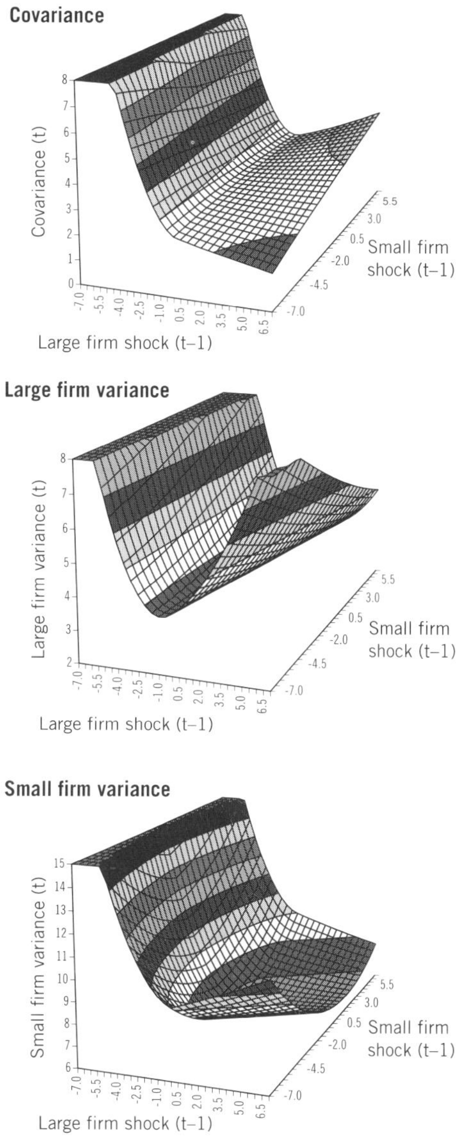

Conclusion and summary

Several different multivariate Garch models have been used in financial modelling. Each of these models has different implications about how past news impacts future variances and covariances. Caution must therefore be exercised when selecting a multivariate volatility model. We propose a set of misspecification indicators which can aid in this decision. We also show that the existing models misspecify the covariances of large firm and small firm equity portfolios. We therefore propose a more general model that nests most of the existing models, which passes most of the specification tests. Our model reveals that bad news to the large firm portfolio spills over to the small firm portfolio, but no other volatility spillovers exist.

1 *Since our main focus is on the effect of last period's return shocks on current volatility, we simply model the mean of the return vector as a 10th order vector autoregression (VAR) with 10 lags of a threshold term. The threshold term is added to make sure that any asymmetry found in the variances and covariances is not caused by a misspecification in the mean. We do the estimation in two steps: first we estimate the mean equation to get the residuals, then we estimate the conditional covariance matrix parameters jointly using maximum likelihood, treating the residuals as observable data. The block diagonality of the information matrix guarantees that consistency is not lost in such a procedure. The estimation results (not reported) are available from the authors.*

2 *See Kroner and Ng (1995) for a detailed discussion of robust conditional moment tests in the Multivariate GARCH context.*

3 *In this model, we replaced the term* $b_i'H_{t-1}b_j$ *with* $b_{ij}h_{ij,t-1}$.

BIBLIOGRAPHY

Amin, K., and V.K. Ng, 1994, "A Comparison of Predictable Volatility Models using Option Data". Unpublished manuscript, IMF Research Department.

Baillie, R.T., and R. J. Myers, 1991, "Modeling Commodity Price Distributions and Estimating the Optimal Futures Hedge," *Journal of Applied Econometrics* 6, pp. 109-24.

Black, F., 1976, "Studies in Stock Price Volatility Changes," *Proceedings of the 1976 Business Meeting of the Business and Economic Statistics Section, American Statistical Association*, pp. 177-81.

Bodurtha, J. and N. Mark, 1991, "Testing the CAPM with Time Varying Risks and Returns," *Journal of Finance* 46, pp. 1485-1505.

Bollerslev, T., 1990, "Modeling the Coherence in Short-Run Nominal Exchange Rates: A Multivariate Generalized ARCH Approach," *Review of Economics and Statistics* 72, pp. 498-505.

Bollerslev, T., R. Engle and J. Wooldridge, 1988, "A Capital Asset Pricing Model with Time Varying Covariances," Journal of Political Economy 96, pp. 116-31.

Bollerslev, T., R. Chou and K. Kroner, 1992, "ARCH Modeling in Finance: A Selective Review of the Theory and Empirical Evidence," *Journal of Econometrics* 52, pp. 5-59; reprinted as Chapter 2 of the present volume.

Chan, K., K.C. Chan and G.A. Karolyi, 1991, "Intraday Volatility in the Stock Index and Stock Index Futures Markets," *Review of Financial Studies* 4, pp. 657-83.

Chan, K.C., G.A. Karolyi and R. Stulz, 1992, "Global Financial Markets and the Risk Premium on U.S. Equity," *Journal of Financial Economics* 32, pp. 137-67.

Conrad, J., M. Gultekin and G. Kaul, 1991, "Asymmetric Predictability of Conditional Variances," *Review of Financial Studies* 4, pp. 597-622.

Engle, R., 1987, "Multivariate GARCH with Factor Structures - Cointegration in Variance," unpublished manuscript, UC San Diego.

Engle, R.F. and K.F. Kroner, 1995, "Multivariate Simultaneous Generalized ARCH," *Econometric Theory* 11, pp. 122-50.

Engle, R. and V. Ng, 1993, "Measuring and Testing the Impact of News on Volatility," *Journal of Finance* 48, pp. 1749-78.

Engle, R., V. Ng and M. Rothschild, 1990, "Asset Pricing with a Factor ARCH Covariance Structure: Empirical Estimates for Treasury Bills," *Journal of Econometrics* 45, pp. 213-38.

French, K., G. W. Schwert and R. Stambaugh, 1987, "Expected Stock Returns and Volatility," *Journal of Financial Economics* 19, pp. 3-29.

Giovannini, A. and P. Jorion, 1989, "The Time Variation of Risk and Return in the Foreign Exchange and Stock Market," *Journal of Finance* 44, pp. 307-25.

Glosten, L., R. Jagannathan and D. Runkle, 1993, "Relationship Between the Expected Value and the Volatility of the Nominal Excess Return on Stocks," *Journal of Finance* 48, pp. 1779-801.

Hamao, Y., R. Masulis and V. Ng, 1990, "Correlations in Price Changes and Volatility Across International Stock Markets," *Review of Financial Studies* 3, pp. 281-307.

Kroner, K.F. and S. Claessens, 1991, "Optimal Dynamic Hedging Portfolios and the Currency Composition of External Debt," *Journal of International Money and Finance* 10, pp. 131-48.

Kroner, K.F. and V.K. Ng, 1995, "Modeling the Time-Varying Comovement of Asset Returns," unpublished manuscript, University of Arizona.

Kroner, K.F. and J. Sultan, 1993, "Time Varying Distributions and Dynamic Hedging with Foreign Currency Futures," *Journal of Financial and Quantitative Analysis* 28, pp. 535-51.

Kuwahara, H., and T. Marsh, 1992, "The Pricing of Japanese Equity Warrants," *Management Science* 38, 11, p. 1610.

Nelson, D., 1991, "Conditional Heteroskedasticity in Asset Returns: A New Approach," *Econometrica* 59, pp. 347-70.

Ng, L., 1991, "Tests of the CAPM with Time Varying Covariances: A Multivariate GARCH Approach," *Journal of Finance* 46, pp. 1507-21.

Ng, V., R. Engle, and M. Rothschild, 1992, "A Multi Dynamic Factor Model for Stock Returns," *Journal of Econometrics* 52, pp. 245-66.

Pagan, A. and G.W. Schwert, 1990, "Alternative Models for Conditional Stock Volatility," *Journal of Econometrics* 45, pp. 267-90.

Schwert, G. W. and P. Seguin, 1990, "Heteroskedasticity in Stock Returns," *Journal of Finance* 45, pp. 1129-55.

Zakoian, J., 1994, "Threshold Heteroskedasticity Model," *Journal of Economic Dynamics and Control* 18, pp. 931-55.

5

Index-Option Pricing with Stochastic Volatility and the Value of Accurate Variance Forecasts*

Robert F. Engle, Alex Kane and Jaesun Noh
University of California, San Diego; Canadian Imperial Bank of Commerce

In pricing primary-market options and in making secondary markets, financial intermediaries depend on the quality of forecasts of the variance of the underlying assets. Hence, pricing of options provides the appropriate test of forecasts of asset volatility. New York Stock Exchange index returns over the period 1968–91 suggest that pricing index options of up to 90-days maturity would be more accurate when the following conditions apply: using Arch specifications in place of a moving average of squared returns; using Hull and White's (1987) adjustment for stochastic variance in the Black and Scholes formula; accounting explicitly for weekends and the slowdown of variance whenever the market is closed.

When distributions of asset returns are time varying, forecasts of asset return variance are valuable. Even passive investors need periodic variance forecasts to calibrate asset allocation. More critically, financial intermediaries who must offer competitive bids on primary-market options, or make market in outstanding options, need continuous updating of variance forecasts.

Since the variance of the underlying asset return is the only unobserved variable in the Black and Scholes (1973) valuation formula for options,[1] updates of variance are the major contestable input to valuation of contingent contracts by direct parties or financial intermediaries.

Emphasis on improved variance forecasts also calls for a corresponding adaptation of the pricing model that will explicitly account for stochastic volatility. When variance risk is not priced[2] and the return distribution can be well approximated by a diffusion process, Hull and White's (1987) model is acceptable. Operationally, we must average the would-be Black-Scholes prices for all possible variance rates over the life of the option, using a variance forecasting algorithm to generate the probability distribution of future variance rates. Another nuisance with stochastic volatility is that we cannot invert observed option prices to obtain the correct implied volatility – a widely used practice since Schmalensee and Trippi (1978).

A natural criterion for choosing between any pair of competing methods to forecast the variance of the rate of return on an asset would be the expected incremental profit from replacing the lesser forecast with the better one. We used this principle in Engle, Hong, Kane and Noh (1993) to estimate the profit from improving variance forecasts in pricing one-day index options (see also an application by Muller (1991) at

* *This paper was first published in the* Review of Derivatives Research, *Vol. 1, (1997). It is reprinted with permission of Kluwer Academic Publishers. The authors acknowledge helpful comments from two anonymous referees and Menachem Brenner.*

BARRA), and reported that the evidence favoured Garch forecasts.[3] Obviously, implications that apply to trading options of only one day maturity have little practical use. The role of variance forecasts in pricing options of longer maturity is the focus of this paper.

When daily variance forecasts are used to price options of longer maturities, the persistence of changes in the variance rate affects the economics of pricing options in two ways: first, the greater the volatility of the variance rate over the life of the option, the more acute the need for an option-pricing model that accounts for stochastic volatility. Moreover, a significant correlation of changes in the variance rate with economic factors will worsen the accuracy of the Black–Scholes model, and reduce the remedial potential of the Hull-White adjustment. Second, the greater the volatility and persistence of changes in the variance rate, the greater the benefits from using one-day forecasts for longer maturity options. Put another way, if changes in the variance do not persist, then the value of one-day forecasts for longer horizons will deteriorate quickly.

In this paper we measure the economic value of two innovations in forecasting daily variance rates: first, we use Garch forecasts as an alternative to a moving average of squared returns; second, we introduce a weekend calendar variable to the estimation and forecasting algorithm to account for how long the market is closed, and the degree of slow-down of the variance rate during the time the market is closed. We also measure the value of using the Hull–White algorithm with the Black–Scholes option-pricing model to account for stochastic volatility in conjunction with the improved variance models.

We start by describing the variance forecasts for the NYSE index that are used in the exercise. We then use Hansen and Hodrick's (1980) method to compute critical t-ratios for means of overlapping returns, to account for the extreme case where traders take the same position (long or short) during the life of each straddle. In the next section we use the return history of the NYSE index over the period 1968–91 to determine the realised payoffs to hypothetical options of various maturities on the NYSE index. We use these payoffs to examine the profitability of various index-option trading strategies related to variance forecasts.

The variance-forecast algorithms

Engle, Hong, Kane, and Noh (1993, EHKN) develop a market in simulated options on the NYSE index to test the relative accuracy of forecasts of the NYSE-return variance. In this simulated market, hypothetical traders use different forecast algorithms to price, in real time, hypothetical options on the actual NYSE. Each trader is allowed to choose to write or purchase such options, depending on the difference between his reservation prices (based on his variance forecast) and those of the other traders. The accumulated profit/loss of each agent from the cash settlements (computed from the actual NYSE index upon maturity of each of the traded options), enumerates the economic value of the relative accuracy of the forecast algorithm used by the agent. This set-up allows for the valuation of NYSE-index variance forecasts without the need to observe actual option prices, avoiding the perennial problems with observed actual option prices.

EHKN used 12 different specifications to generate alternative daily forecasts for the variance of the returns on the NYSE index and applied these forecasts to price one-day options on $1 shares of the NYSE index. They operated the simulated market in these options as follows. Each day, differences in the variance forecasts of the twelve algorithms resulted in different reservation prices for one-day options on the underlying index. These differences triggered trades in the options among 12 hypothetical agents, each using one of the forecast algorithms. An agent with a higher variance forecast had a higher reservation price for the one-day option. Hence this agent would buy (sell) a straddle (one call and one put option) on a $1 share of the NYSE index from any of the other eleven agents with lower (higher) forecast/reservation prices. The exercise price for these one-day straddles was set daily at $\$e^r$ (where r is the continuously compounded risk-free rate), and a trade between two agents was executed at the average of the reservation prices of the two agents, that is, at the average of the bid/ask prices. Upon expiration of each one-day straddle over the period 1962-1990, the realised daily returns on the NYSE were used to compute the profit from each daily trade between each pair of agents. Overall, Arch models produced the highest profits, suggesting that Arch forecasts were the most useful. A moving-average of 300 squared residuals was the nearest competitor to Arch forecasts.

In this paper we extend the setting by supposing that every day, agents trade at-the-money straddles with maturities ranging from one day to one year. Positions are held to maturity, when profits/losses are credited/debited to agents from cash settlements based on the realised NYSE index. Consequently, traders must forecast volatilities up to one year ahead, and account for uncertain volatility in pricing the straddles. We consider several models. Based on the EHKN results, we use the 300-day moving-average of squared daily returns (MA) as a benchmark variance estimate for all horizons. Of the Arch family of specifications first introduced by Engle (1982) and surveyed in Bollerslev, Chou, and Kroner (1992), we use the Garch(1,1) specification for the NYSE return series:

$$R_t = a_0 + \varepsilon_t$$
$$h_t = b_0 + b_1\varepsilon_{t-1}^2 + b_2 h_{t-1}. \qquad (1)$$

In order to generate variance forecasts of horizons from one day up to T days, the most recent 1,000 daily observations are first used to estimate the parameters a_0, b_0, b_1, b_2, in (1). The forward volatility forecasts are then computed from:

$$h_{t,t+1} = b_0 + b_1\varepsilon_t^2 + b_2 h_t$$
$$h_{t,t+k} = b_0 + b_1 E\left[\varepsilon_{t+k-1}^2 \middle| \omega_t\right] + b_2 h_{t,t+k-1}$$
$$= b_0 + (b_1 + b_2)h_{t,t+k-1},\ k = 2,\ldots,T \qquad (2)$$

where $h_{t,t+k}$ is the prediction of h_{t+k} at time t. The average volatility is $(1/T)\Sigma_{k=1}^{T} h_{t,t+k}$. We denote this forecast as Garch.

We expect the mean and variance of the return from market close to close to be affected by calendar time, that is, mean and variance from Friday close to Monday close are expected to be greater than, say, from Wednesday close to Thursday close, and more so for long weekends. However, French and Roll (1986) showed that the variance rate slows down significantly in days when the market is closed. In an attempt to capture this phenomenon, we modify (1) and (2) multiplicatively as follows.

$$h_t = d_t^{\delta}\left[b_0 + d_{t-1}^{-\delta}\left(b_1\varepsilon_{t-1}^2 + b_2 h_{t-1}\right)\right]$$
$$h_{t,t+1} = d_{t+1}^{\delta}\left[b_0 + d_t^{-\delta}\left(b_1\varepsilon_t^2 + b_2 h_t\right)\right]$$
$$h_{t,t+k} = d_{t+k}^{\delta}\left\{b_0 + d_{t+k-1}^{-\delta}\left[b_1 E\left(\varepsilon_{t+k-1}^2 \middle| \omega_t\right) + b_2 h_{t,t+k-1}\right]\right\}$$
$$= d_{t+k}^{\delta}\left\{b_0 + d_{t+k-1}^{-\delta}\left[(b_1 + b_2)h_{t,t+k-1}\right]\right\},$$
$$k = 2,\ldots,T \qquad (3)$$

where d_t is a calendar-day variable that gives the number of calendar days between the close of the previous trading day $(t - 1)$ and the close of the trading day t. As explained below, d_t in the variance equation is raised to the power δ which measures the average speed of the variance rate over the d_t calendar days of trading day t. As before, $h_{t,t+k}$ is the variance forecast made at date t for date $t + k$. We denote the Garch forecast adjusted for marked closures by Garch-D.

Assuming the variance surprises are independent of economic factors, we can use the Hull-White modification to the Black-Scholes formula. In order to test the potential economic value of the Hull-White modification we use (2) as follows. For each date $t + k$; $k = 1,\ldots,T$, we generate 1,000 sets of $\varepsilon_{t+k}(j)$; $j = 1,\ldots,1000$, from a standard normal distribution. For each j we calculate the average daily variance rate over the $k = 1,\ldots,T$ days to maturity of the option, and use this variance rate to calculate a price which is contingent on the jth path. The average of these prices (over $j = 1,\ldots,1000$ iterations) is the Hull and White's (1987) modified price. We denote these integrated prices by Garch-I. A forecast that uses weekend dummies throughout the integration will be denoted Garch-DI. Thus we have four alternative Garch forecasts: Garch, Garch-D, Garch-I and Garch DI to compete with MA.

t-ratios for means of overlapping returns

Suppose that the Garch trader were to come up with consistently lower variance forecasts, every day, for the entire life of a one-year option. Accordingly, the Garch trader would take short positions in all trades, while the MA trader takes the long positions. In this case, the Garch trader's sequence of returns from the year-long position in that option (from 365 days to maturity down to one day to maturity) would amount to a series of overlapping returns. Thus, in the extreme case, were this to happen through the entire sample period, the traders' returns would be highly serially correlated. To err on the conservative side, we compute critical t-ratios for the traders' expected returns under this extreme hypothesis to better evaluate the results. In this section we demonstrate these calculations.

Two methods to compute standard errors for overlapping observations are available: Hansen and Hodrick (1980) and Richardson and Stock (1989). They differ in the assumption about the stationarity of the daily return series.

Let $R_{m,t}$ be the mth agent's one-day return from options trading, assumed to be unpredictable from past values, except for a constant μ. That is,

$$R_{m,t} = \mu + \varepsilon_t \qquad (4)$$

where $E[\varepsilon_t | \varepsilon_{t-1}, \varepsilon_{t-2}, \ldots, \varepsilon_1] = 0$, and $E[(1/T) \Sigma_{k=1}^{T} E[\varepsilon_t^2 | \varepsilon_{t-1}, \varepsilon_{t-2}, \ldots, \varepsilon_1] \rightarrow \sigma^2$ as $T \rightarrow \infty$ by assumption. Also, assume that $\sup_t E[\varepsilon_t^4] < \infty$.[4]

Consider the following J-period returns

$$X_{t+j}(J) = \sum_{i=0}^{J-1} R_{m,t+J-i}, \quad t = 0, \ldots, T-J$$

and the regression

$$X_{t+j}(J) = \beta(J) Z_t(J) + \eta_{t+j}(J), \tag{5}$$

where, in our case, $Z_t(J) = 1$ (this case is not considered by Richardson and Stock (1989), but the analysis is similar).

The null hypothesis that we are interested in is $H_0: \beta(J) = 0$. Testing whether $\beta(J)$ is zero requires an estimate of the standard error of $\beta(J)$. Asymptotic justification of the conventional computation of a standard error in the ordinary least squares (OLS) estimator for $\beta(J)$ requires that the errors be serially uncorrelated. Consequently, one strategy is to define the sampling interval to be equal to the return interval, the J-period. In such non-overlapping samples, the number of observations would be small, even though the raw sample is large. If the frequency of the observations is greater than the forecast frequency, we must consider the resulting serial correlation in the errors. Hansen and Hodrick (1980) propose a variance estimator using specific weights on sample autocovariances of errors and regressors. They assume that the overlap in the data (denoted by J) is fixed as $T \rightarrow \infty$ so that $J/T \rightarrow \infty$. If we assume, as in Richardson and Stock (1989), that $J/T \rightarrow \psi$, then the conventional t-ratios of the coefficients in the regression have different asymptotic distributions. The OLS estimate of the coefficient of the regression in (5),

$$\hat{\beta}(J) = \frac{1}{T-J} \sum_{t=0}^{T-J} X_{t+J}(J), \tag{6}$$

diverges as $T \rightarrow \infty$, and $\hat{\beta}(J)/\sqrt{T}$ has a limiting distribution given as a functional of Brownian motions (see Appendix).

Hansen and Hodrick's (1980) variance estimator of (J) is computed as follows,

$$\hat{\omega}^2(J) = \frac{1}{T} \sum_{i=-(J-1)}^{J-1} \frac{T-|i|}{T} \hat{\gamma}_u^2(I) \tag{7}$$

where

$$\hat{\gamma}_u^2(i) = \frac{1}{T+J-|i|}$$

$$\sum_{t=|i|}^{T-J} \left[X_{t+j}(J) - \hat{\beta}(J)\right]\left[X_{t+J-|i|}(J) - \hat{\beta}(J)\right] \tag{8}$$

also converges to a functional of Brownian motion, as $T \rightarrow \infty$ and $J/T \rightarrow \psi$ (see Appendix).

THEOREM 1

(See Appendix for proof). Under the assumptions in Phillips (1987), the conventional t-ratio, $t_{\hat{\beta}}$ converges, not to a normal, but to a functional of a Brownian motion, as $T \rightarrow \infty$ and $J/T \rightarrow \psi$,

$$t_b = \frac{\beta(J)}{\sqrt{\hat{\omega}^2(J)}} \Rightarrow \frac{\frac{1}{1-\psi}\int_0^{1-\psi} \{W(s+\psi) - W(s)\} ds}{\left[\int_{-\psi}^{\psi} \Gamma_u(\rho,\psi) d\rho\right]^{1/2}} \tag{9}$$

where

$$\Gamma_u(\rho,\psi) = (1-|\rho|)\frac{1}{1-\psi-|\rho|}$$

$$\int_{|\rho|}^{1-\psi} U_\psi(s+\psi) U_\psi(s+\psi-|\rho|) ds \tag{10}$$

$$U_\psi = W(\lambda) - W(\lambda-\psi) - \frac{1}{1-\psi}$$

$$\int_0^{1-\psi} \{W(\lambda) - W(\lambda-\psi)\} d\lambda \tag{11}$$

and $W(\lambda)$ is a Brownian motion on the unit interval, $\lambda \in [0,1]$.

Since the distribution of $t_{\hat{\beta}}$ does not follow the student t-distribution, we compute the critical values from Monte Carlo simulations shown in Table 1. These can be used to test hypotheses for different values of $\psi = J/T$ and will give better finite- sample critical values.

Table 1. Distribution of the t-statistic (6,000 Monte Carlo simulations)*

				Percentile			
	2.5%	5%	10%	50%	90%	95%	97.5%
$\delta = 1/200$	–1.99	–1.67	–1.26	0.02	1.32	1.70	2.04
$\delta = 1/100$	–2.02	–1.69	–1.28	0.01	1.34	1.74	2.08
$\delta = 1/40$	–2.10	–1.77	–1.34	0.02	1.37	1.78	2.17
$\delta = 1/20$	–2.34	–1.91	–1.45	0.03	1.48	1.96	2.40

* δ is a measure of dependence of the series. As δ increases, the t-ratio statistic follows a heavier tailed distribution.

Estimation of the value of variance forecasts with a simulated market in index-options of various maturities

The objective is to estimate the potential profit from improving the variance forecast when pricing options of various maturities. By using a simulated option market instead of observing actual index-option prices, we are able to circumvent perennial difficulties that plague empirical studies of option prices: non-synchroneity of option and stock-prices, market depth, the wildcard delivery option, and dividend protection as well as limited maturity dates and strikes. Thus, with a simulated index-option market, the Black–

Scholes model need only be reconciled with the fact the variance is stochastic.

We observe NYSE-index returns excluding dividends, thus creating in effect a hypothetical option market on a non-dividend paying index of the underlying NYSE stocks. Relative to the variance of the daily capital gains, the variance of the dividend yield is negligible. It is safe to suppose that an algorithm that predicts better the variance of the daily rate of capital gains, will do better in predicting the total NYSE return. Moreover, in this way we circumvent the issue of incorporating dividends in the option-valuation formula which is quite separate from the issue of stochastic volatility.

Table 2 shows average straddle prices that were written every day between 1968–91 on one dollar's worth of the NYSE index, with an exercise price of $\$e^r$, where r is the risk-free rate for the life of the option. These average prices are categorised by maturity (in calendar days) for the alternative forecasting methods: MA, Garch, Garch-I, Garch-D and Garch-DI. Table 2 shows that Garch prices are slightly lower than MA prices for maturities shorter than 90 days, and slightly greater for longer maturities. Figure 1 plots the daily straddle prices produced by the MA and Garch agents for 30-day and 365-day maturities over the entire sample period. The plots show that for both long and short maturities there are no systematic biases.

For maturities up to 50 days, integration over alternative Garch forecasts, shown by the Garch-I column, produced higher average straddle prices than the Garch. However, for maturities in the range of 60–365 days, integration produced smaller average straddle prices.[5] Finally, adjusting Garch and Garch-I variance forecasts to account for weekends increase average straddle prices for maturities up to 13 days and decreases average straddle prices for maturities greater than 14 days, compared to Garch prices.

Table 3 overleaf shows the annualised rate of return from a daily investment in straddles on the NYSE index by two hypothetical agents one using MA and the other using Garch variance forecasts. Each day, each agent invests one dollar in each maturity (1 to 365 days) of straddles. The transaction price is the average of the reservation prices of the agents based on their private variance forecasts. The position in each straddle is held to maturity, and the agent who takes the short position in a given maturity (due to a lower variance forecast), invests the $1 proceeds from writing the straddle plus the $1 endowment in

Table 2. Average straddle price (June 20, 1968–December 31, 1991)*

Day	Obs	MA300	Garch	Garch-I	Garch-D	Garch-DI
1	5921	0.00685	0.00660	0.00660	0.00658	0.00658
2	5921	0.00906	0.00875	0.00889	0.00880	0.00894
4	5921	0.01157	0.01120	0.01140	0.01134	0.01156
6	5921	0.01380	0.01337	0.01361	0.01343	0.01369
8	5921	0.01652	0.01603	0.01630	0.01599	0.01627
10	5921	0.01833	0.01780	0.01808	0.01781	0.01811
12	5921	0.01973	0.01919	0.01946	0.01923	0.01953
14	5921	0.02131	0.02074	0.02102	0.02067	0.02097
18	5921	0.02427	0.02368	0.02394	0.02365	0.02395
20	5921	0.02537	0.02477	0.02503	0.02471	0.02501
22	5921	0.02694	0.02633	0.02658	0.02621	0.02650
24	5921	0.02809	0.02748	0.02771	0.02738	0.02766
26	5921	0.02902	0.02841	0.02863	0.02835	0.02861
28	5921	0.03011	0.02950	0.02971	0.02935	0.02961
30	5921	0.03144	0.03083	0.03103	0.03067	0.03092
40	5921	0.03600	0.03540	0.03553	0.03524	0.03543
50	5921	0.04039	0.03983	0.03988	0.03956	0.03968
60	5921	0.04415	0.04362	0.04360	0.04334	0.04339
90	5921	0.05393	0.05354	0.05330	0.05312	0.05296
270	5921	0.09352	0.09392	0.09283	0.09289	0.09192
365	5921	0.10874	0.10952	0.10815	0.10823	0.10699

* Day is the number of days till maturity of straddles. Obs is the total number of trading days. The third column through the seventh column show the average straddle price over different maturities for each method.

1. Option prices

Daily straddle price of the MA300 and Garch methods for 30-day and 365-day maturities over the sample period June 1968–December 1991

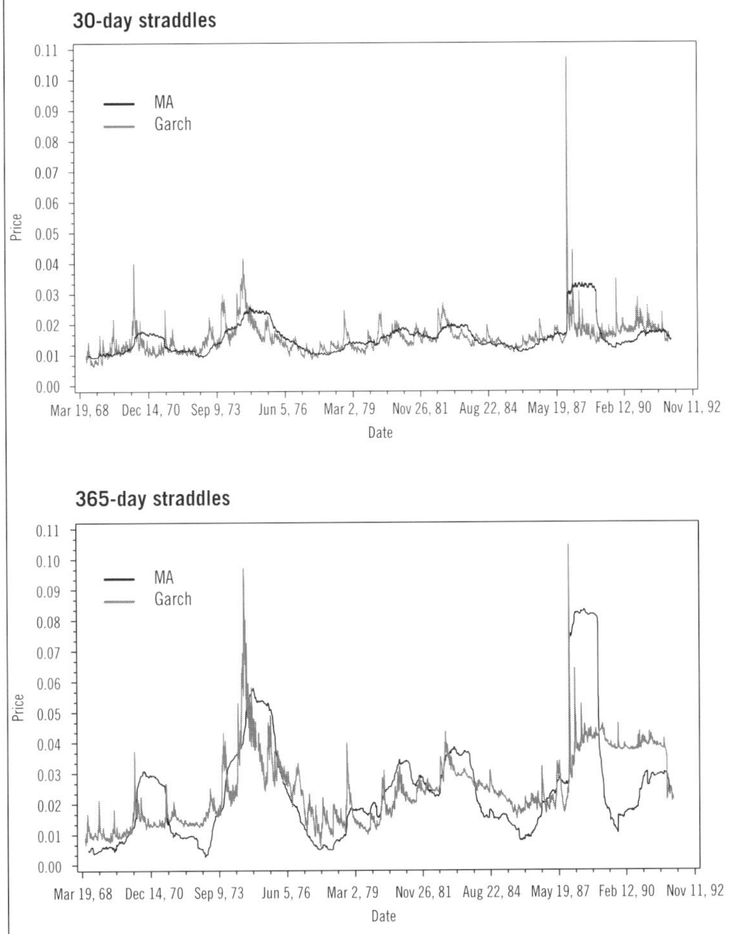

Table 3. Annualised average rate of return in decimals from daily trade of $1 worth of straddles per day, Garch vs MA300 (June 20, 1968–December 31, 1991)*

Day	Obs	Garch over MA300	MA300 R_m	Garch R_m	MA300 Total	Garch Total	Garch t-ratio
1	5921	18.962(2.726)	0.046(0.023)	0.063(0.019)	−18.916(2.728)	19.025(2.726,2.726)	6.98
2	5921	19.122(3.916)	0.081(0.048)	0.113(0.037)	−19.031(3.923)	19.225(3.916,3.021)	4.91
4	5921	9.992(2.335)	0.041(0.036)	0.076(0.027)	−9.951(2.342)	10.068(2.335,1.643)	4.31
6	5921	4.799(1.355)	0.044(0.027)	0.052(0.021)	−4.755(1.360)	4.851(1.355,0.802)	3.58
8	5921	4.052(1.225)	0.065(0.029)	0.068(0.023)	−3.988(1.230)	4.120(1.226,0.640)	3.36
10	5921	3.580(1.036)	0.053(0.027)	0.056(0.021)	−3.527(1.041)	3.636(1.037,0.483)	3.51
12	5921	2.831(0.962)	0.054(0.026)	0.050(0.021)	−2.777(0.965)	2.880(0.962,0.433)	2.99
14	5921	2.337(0.846)	0.065(0.026)	0.055(0.022)	−2.271(0..847)	2.391(0.848,0.372)	2.82
18	5921	1.722(0.712)	0.062(0.025)	0.048(0.022)	−1.660(0.711)	1.770(0.713,0.292)	2.48
20	5921	1.553(0.671)	0.064(0.025)	0.050(0.022)	−1.489(0.669)	1.603(0.672,0.267)	2.39
22	5921	1.213(0.601)	0.064(0.024)	0.051(0.022)	−1.149(0.598)	1.264(0.602,0.229)	2.10
24	5921	0.956(0.591)	0.065(0.024)	0.051(0.022)	−0.891(0.587)	1.007(0.592,0.218)	1.70
26	5921	0.745(0.571)	0.063(0.025)	0.050(0.023)	−0.682(0.568)	0.795(0.572,0.208)	1.39
28	5921	0.545(0.524)	0.066(0.024)	0.048(0.022)	−0.479(0.521)	0.594(0.525,0.182)	1.13
30	5921	0.426(0.494)	0.066(0.023)	0.047(0.022)	−0.360(0.490)	0.472(0.495,0.165)	0.95
40	5921	0.326(0.448)	0.070(0.023)	0.041(0.023)	−0.256(0.443)	0.368(0.450,0.129)	0.82
50	5921	0.207(0.372)	0.074(0.023)	0.041(0.023)	−0.133(0.366)	0.249(0.374,0.101)	0.67
60	5921	0.150(0.355)	0.074(0.022)	0.039(0.023)	−0.076(0.349)	0.189(0.358,0.086)	0.53
90	5921	0.072(0.313)	0.077(0.022)	0.036(0.023)	0.006(0.308)	0.108(0.318,0.057)	0.34
270	5921	0.230(0.162)	0.073(0.027)	0.043(0.019)	−0.157(0.157)	0.274(0.162,0.019)	1.69
365	5921	0.243(0.159)	0.070(0.027)	0.049(0.019)	−0.174(0.152)	0.292(0.151,0.014)	1.93

* Day is the number of days till maturity of straddles. Obs is the total number of trading days. The third column shows the return for an agent using Garch in trading straddles with an agent using MA300. MA 300 R_m (Garch R_m) shows the return from a $1 endowment in the NYSE-index portfolio when an agent using MA300 (Garch) takes a short position. MA300 Total (Garch Total) is the sum of the return from trading straddles and the return from the NYSE-index portfolio for an agent using MA 300 (Garch Total). Numbers in parentheses from the third column to the sixth column are Hansen-Hodrick standard errors. Numbers in parentheses in the seventh column are Hansen-Hodrick standard error and ordinary standard error, respectively. The last column is the t-ratio of Garch Total based on Hansen-Hodrick standard error.

the NYSE-index portfolio for the life of the straddle. Upon maturity each position is settled according to the actual level of the NYSE index on the maturity date. Because the agents trade every day straddles of various maturities, holding periods overlap. The straddles are always written on one dollar's worth of the NYSE index, with an exercise price of $\$e^r$ where the risk- free rate is taken from one month T-bill yields. The trades are executed at the average of the variance-forecast driven reservation prices of the two agents.

The first column of Table 3 shows the maturity of the traded straddles; there are 5,921 observations for each maturity. The third column in Table 3 shows the time weighted annualised rate of return to the Garch agent from the cash flows received from, and paid to, the MA agent in lieu of settlements of the maturing straddles - based on the history of the NYSE index over the period 1968–91. The fourth and fifth columns in Table 3 enumerate the annualised rate of return to the MA and the Garch agents from investing in the NYSE-index portfolio on days when they took short positions. The sixth and seventh columns show the total annualised rate of return of the MA and the GARCH agents from the entire trading activity. Because the investment in the NYSE index augments the short positions, the competition between the agents is not a zero sum game.

The Hansen-Hodrick standard errors are given in parenthesis next to the average rate of return and in the seventh column ordinary standard errors are given in the same parenthesis as well. The difference between these two standard errors is growing as the maturity increases. For one-year straddles, the Hansen-Hodrick standard error is ten times greater than the ordinary standard error! The eighth column computes t-ratios for the total annualised rates of return of the Garch agents in the seventh column using the Hansen-Hodrick standard errors. Those that are significant at 5% can be chosen by the critical values of Table 1 in the previous section.

Table 3 shows enormous rates of return to the Garch agent (at the expense of the MA agent) from trades of short term straddles: 1,903% for one-day straddles. The rates of return are monotone decreasing with maturity up to 90 days and then increase again. While at 22 days maturity the 126% annualised return is statistically and economically significant, it is obvious that the apparent advantage of the Garch forecasts over the MA forecasts is fading with the forecast horizon. Above 22 days maturity, the average rate of return is still considerable (96% for 24 days), but is no longer statistically significant. Note that the average rates of return to the Garch agents are positive for all maturities, and are still at 29% for a one-year maturity, and statistically significant by the critical values of Table 1.

The return from investing short position proceeds in the market are not too different for both agents, indicating that none specialised in short positions. While the higher average straddle price (up to 90-days) from MA variance forecasts (Table 2) would have us expect that the MA agent would take less short positions, proceeds from investing short positions show that the variance in straddle prices swamps the mean difference between the methods, and that the MA and Garch agents' short/long positions are similarly distributed. The bottom line is that the Garch forecasts are economically, and statistically, significantly better than the MA forecasts in pricing options of up to 22 days maturity, for which the Garch agent earned an average return of 126% from the MA agent.

Tables 4–6 present results from repeating the straddle trading exercise replacing the Garch agents of Table 3 with improved Garch forecasts. Table 4 presents results from integrating the straddle price from the Black-Scholes formula over the Garch forecasts based on the distributions of forecasting errors from past forecasts to implement the Hull and White correction. The rates of return earned by the Garch-I agent are markedly better than those earned from the MA agent by the Garch agent. In Table 5, the Garch-D agent accounts for the weekend effect by using (3). For short maturities, the rates of return earned by the Garch-D agent from the MA agent are better than those earned by the Garch agent. The improvement in the forecasts fades with maturity, and becomes insignificant for maturities over 20 days. Table 6 shows the results from incorporating the weekend effect into the integrated Garch forecasts. The average annualised return for a 20-days maturity is 112% for the Garch-DI agent, compared with 59% for the Garch agent, and is statistically significant.

Similar tests (not reported here) show that Garch-DI forecasts are superior against both Garch and Garch-I for maturities of up to 90 days.

Figure 2 overleaf plots the cumulative percentage returns to the Garch and Garch-DI agents from the MA agent by maturity. The graphs show the economically significant improvement that can be obtained by integrating the forecast with the Hull-White method and by accounting for the weekend effect.

A few issues come to mind when evaluating the applicability of these results:

Table 4. Annualised average rate of return in decimals from daily trade of $1 worth of straddles per day, Garch-I vs MA300 (June 20, 1968–December 31, 1991)*

Day	Obs	Garch-I over MA300	MA300 R_m	Garch-I R_m	MA300 Total	Garch-I Total	Garch-I t-ratio
1	5921	18.962(2.726)	0.046(0.023)	0.063(0.019)	−18.916(2.728)	19.025(2.726,2.726)	6.98
2	5921	25.110(3.938)	0.091(0.049)	0.104(0.036)	−25.019(3.946)	25.214(3.938,3.001)	6.40
4	5921	14.774(2.385)	0.046(0.037)	0.073(0.026)	−14.728(2.393)	14.847(2.385,1.636)	6.22
6	5921	7.256(1.391)	0.049(0.028)	0.048(0.020)	−7.207(1.396)	7.304(1.391,0.794)	5.25
8	5921	5.926(1.248)	0.071(0.030)	0.062(0.022)	−5.855(1.253)	5.988(1.248,0.630)	4.80
10	5921	4.917(1.043)	0.056(0.027)	0.053(0.020)	−4.861(1.048)	4.970(1.043,0.476)	4.77
12	5921	3.882(0.936)	0.059(0.027)	0.053(0.020)	−3.824(0.938)	3.927(0.935,0.427)	4.20
14	5921	3.248(0.837)	0.068(0.027)	0.053(0.021)	−3.180(0.839)	3.301(0.838,0.366)	3.94
18	5921	2.310(0.731)	0.064(0.026)	0.047(0.021)	−2.246(0.730)	2.357(0.731,0.287)	3.22
20	5921	1.984(0.688)	0.064(0.026)	0.050(0.022)	−1.920(0.688)	2.034(0.689,0.263)	2.95
22	5921	1.563(0.614)	0.066(0.025)	0.049(0.021)	−1.498(0.613)	1.613(0.614,0.226)	2.63
24	5921	1.412(0.608)	0.066(0.026)	0.049(0.022)	−1.346(0.607)	1.461(0.608,0.215)	2.40
26	5921	1.180(0.585)	0.065(0.026)	0.048(0.022)	−1.115(0.584)	1.228(0.585,0.205)	2.10
28	5921	1.008(0.534)	0.068(0.024)	0.047(0.021)	−0.940(0.532)	1.055(0.534,0.180)	1.98
30	5921	0.926(0.509)	0.066(0.024)	0.047(0.021)	−0.860(0.507)	0.972(0.508,0.163)	1.91
40	5921	0.703(0.450)	0.066(0.024)	0.045(0.022)	−0.637(0.447)	0.748(0.451,0.128)	1.66
50	5921	0.512(0.385)	0.069(0.023)	0.046(0.023)	−0.442(0.382)	0.558(0.386,0.100)	1.44
60	5921	0.307(0.375)	0.071(0.022)	0.042(0.023)	−0.236(0.372)	0.349(0.378,0.086)	0.92
90	5921	0.150(0.326)	0.076(0.022)	0.038(0.024)	−0.075(0.321)	0.188(0.330,0.057)	0.57
270	5921	0.227(0.160)	0.070(0.027)	0.047(0.020)	−0.157(0.155)	0.274(0.159,0.019)	1.72
365	5921	0.234(0.155)	0.067(0.028)	0.051(0.020)	−0.166(0.147)	0.285(0.147,0.014)	1.94

* Day is the number of days till maturity of straddles. Obs is the total number of trading days. The third column shows the return for an agent using Garch-I in trading straddles with an agent using MA300. MA 300 R_m (Garch-I R_m) shows the return from a $1 endowment in the NYSE-index portfolio when an agent using MA300 (Garch-I) takes a short position. MA300 Total (Garch-I Total) is the sum of the return from trading straddles and the return from the NYSE-index portfolio for an agent using MA 300 (Garch-I Total). Numbers in parentheses from the third column to the sixth column are Hansen-Hodrick standard errors. Numbers in parentheses in the seventh column are Hansen-Hodrick standard error and ordinary standard error, respectively. The last column is the t-ratio of Garch-I Total based on Hansen-Hodrick standard error.

Table 5. Annualised average rate of return in decimals from daily trade of $1 worth of straddles per day, Garch-D vs MA300 (June 20, 1968–December 31, 1991)*

Day	Obs	Garch-D over MA300	MA300 R_m	Garch-D R_m	MA300 Total	Garch-D Total	Garch-D t-ratio
1	5921	19.950(2.714)	0.021(0.023)	0.089(0.019)	–19.930(2.716)	20.039(2.713,2.713)	7.39
2	5921	16.250(3.801)	0.057(0.047)	0.137(0.037)	–16.193(3.810)	16.388(3.800,2.990)	4.31
4	5921	9.397(2.331)	0.034(0.036)	0.084(0.027)	–9.363(2.339)	9.481(2.332,1.627)	4.07
6	5921	5.228(1.394)	0.049(0.027)	0.048(0.021)	–5.180(1.398)	5.276(1.395,0.801)	3.78
8	5921	3.905(1.252)	0.063(0.029)	0.069(0.023)	–3.842(1.256)	3.975(1.252,0.639)	3.17
10	5921	3.492(1.041)	0.052(0.026)	0.057(0.021)	–3.439(1.046)	3.549(1.041,0.481)	3.41
12	5921	2.836(0.978)	0.054(0.027)	0.050(0.021)	–2.783(0.980)	2.886(0.978,0.431)	2.95
14	5921	2.281(0.858)	0.063(0.026)	0.057(0.022)	–2.219(0..859)	2.339(0.859,0.372)	2.72
18	5921	1.530(0.727)	0.058(0.025)	0.052(0.022)	–1.471(0.726)	1.581(0.728,0.291)	2.17
20	5921	1.366(0.686)	0.062(0.025)	0.052(0.022)	–1.304(0.684)	1.418(0.687,0.267)	2.06
22	5921	1.102(0.609)	0.061(0.024)	0.054(0.022)	–1.040(0.606)	1.156(0.609,0.229)	1.90
24	5921	0.884(0.603)	0.061(0.025)	0.054(0.023)	–0.823(0.600)	0.939(0.604,0.218)	1.55
26	5921	0.728(0.583)	0.061(0.025)	0.051(0.023)	–0.667(0.579)	0.780(0.583,0.207)	1.34
28	5921	0.556(0.536)	0.064(0.024)	0.051(0.022)	–0.492(0.532)	0.606(0.536,0.182)	1.13
30	5921	0.450(0.501)	0.064(0.023)	0.048(0.022)	–0.386(0.497)	0.499(0.501,0.165)	0.99
40	5921	0.378(0.445)	0.069(0.023)	0.042(0.023)	–0.308(0.440)	0.420(0.447,0.129)	0.94
50	5921	0.246(0.375)	0.074(0.023)	0.041(0.023)	–0.172(0.369)	0.288(0.377,0.101)	0.76
60	5921	0.125(0.361)	0.075(0.022)	0.038(0.023)	–0.050(0.355)	0.163(0.365,0.086)	0.45
90	5921	0.118(0.311)	0.077(0.022)	0.036(0.023)	–0.041(0.305)	0.154(0.316,0.058)	0.49
270	5921	0.228(0.163)	0.072(0.027)	0.044(0.020)	–0.155(0.158)	0.272(0.162,0.019)	1.68
365	5921	0.243(0.160)	0.069(0.028)	0.049(0.019)	–0.174(0.152)	0.292(0.152,0.014)	1.92

* Day is the number of days till maturity of straddles. Obs is the total number of trading days. The third column shows the return for an agent using Garch-D in trading straddles with an agent using MA300. MA 300 R_m (Garch-D R_m) shows the return from a $1 endowment in the NYSE-index portfolio when an agent using MA300 (Garch-D) takes a short position. MA300 Total (Garch Total) is the sum of the return from trading straddles and the return from the NYSE-index portfolio for an agent using MA 300 (Garch-D Total). Numbers in parentheses from the third column to the sixth column are Hansen-Hodrick standard errors. Numbers in parentheses in the seventh column are Hansen-Hodrick standard error and ordinary standard error, respectively. The last column is the t-ratio of Garch-D Total based on Hansen-Hodrick standard error.

Table 6. Annualised average rate of return in decimals from daily trade of $1 worth of straddles per day, Garch-DI vs MA300 (June 20, 1968–December 31, 1991)*

Day	Obs	Garch- DI over MA300	MA300 R_m	Garch-DI R_m	MA300 Total	Garch-DI Total	Garch-DI t-ratio
1	5921	19.950(2.714)	0.021(0.023)	0.089(0.019)	–19.930(2.716)	20.039(2.713,2.713)	7.39
2	5921	22.675(3.828)	0.067(0.048)	0.128(0.036)	–22.607(3.838)	22.802(2.829,2.973)	5.96
4	5921	14.182(2.343)	0.039(0.037)	0.080(0.026)	–14.142(2.351)	14.262(2.343,1.619)	6.09
6	5921	7.430(1.396)	0.049(0.028)	0.048(0.020)	–7.381(1.401)	7.487(1.395,0.790)	5.36
8	5921	5.884(1.251)	0.069(0.030)	0.064(0.022)	–5.815(1.255)	5.948(1.251,0.629)	4.76
10	5921	4.862(1.031)	0.054(0.027)	0.056(0.020)	–4.807(1.035)	4.917(1.030,0.474)	4.78
12	5921	4.168(0.946)	0.056(0.027)	0.048(0.021)	–4.112(0.949)	4.216(0.945,0.425)	4.46
14	5921	3.113(0.833)	0.065(0.026)	0.055(0.021)	–3.048(0.834)	3.168(0.833,0.366)	3.80
18	5921	2.209(0.735)	0.062(0.026)	0.048(0.022)	–2.147(0.734)	2.258(0.735,0.287)	3.07
20	5921	1.941(0.696)	0.063(0.026)	0.052(0.022)	–1.879(0.695)	1.993(0.696,0.263)	2.86
22	5921	1.567(0.613)	0.065(0.025)	0.050(0.021)	–1.502(0.611)	1.617(0.613,0.226)	2.64
24	5921	1.344(0.603)	0.064(0.025)	0.052(0.022)	–1.280(0.602)	1.396(0.603,0.215)	2.31
26	5921	1.238(0.595)	0.064(0.026)	0.049(0.022)	–1.174(0.593)	1.287(0.595,0.204)	2.16
28	5921	1.072(0.540)	0.066(0.025)	0.049(0.021)	–1.006(0.538)	1.120(0.540,0.180)	2.08
30	5921	0.956(0.509)	0.065(0.024)	0.048(0.021)	–0.891(0.507)	1.004(0.509,0.163)	1.97
40	5921	0.760(0.453)	0.066(0.024)	0.045(0.022)	–0.694(0.450)	0.806(0.454,0.128)	1.77
50	5921	0.494(0.381)	0.071(0.023)	0.044(0.023)	–0.422(0.377)	0.538(0.382,0.100)	1.41
60	5921	0.382(0.372)	0.073(0.023)	0.040(0.023)	–0.309(0.367)	0.422(0.374,0.086)	1.13
90	5921	0.163(0.325)	0.075(0.022)	0.038(0.024)	–0.088(0.319)	0.201(0.328,0.057)	0.61
270	5921	0.223(0.160)	0.070(0.027)	0.047(0.020)	–0.153(0.155)	0.269(0.159,0.019)	1.69
365	5921	0.232(0.156)	0.067(0.028)	0.052(0.038)	–0.166(0.147)	0.284(0.148,0.014)	1.92

* Day is the number of days till maturity of straddles. Obs is the total number of trading days. The third column shows the return for an agent using Garch-DI in trading straddles with an agent using MA300. MA 300 R_m (Garch-DI R_m) shows the return from a $1 endowment in the NYSE-index portfolio when an agent using MA300 (Garch DI) takes a short position. MA300 Total (Garch-DI Total) is the sum of the return from trading straddles and the return from the NYSE-index portfolio for an agent using MA 300 (Garch-DI Total). Numbers in parentheses from the third column to the sixth column are Hansen-Hodrick standard errors. Numbers in parentheses in the seventh column are Hansen-Hodrick standard error and ordinary standard error, respectively. The last column is the t-ratio of Garch-DI Total based on Hansen-Hodrick standard error.

RISK AND RETURN

The forecasting errors in all cases are uncorrelated with the NYSE returns and their betas are practically zero. Similar results are found for the rates of return earned by the various forecasters. The proceeds invested by the short positions in the index are too small relative to the returns from trades to induce any positive correlation with the index, or a positive beta on it. Hence, there is no question of any systematic risk associated with the returns from trade on variance forecasts in this sample.

TRANSACTION COSTS

Transaction costs do not play a role in this experiment since we only ask which algorithm would be preferred to use in pricing options of various maturities. Traders using different algorithms would be subject to similar transaction costs and there is no reason to suspect that any one algorithm would be inferior in that respect.

CRASHES AND JUMPS

Any study involving a return interval that includes the crash is subject to question. While excluding the week of the crash in this large number study didn't affect the results, the issue of jumps, in general seems compelling.

In a recent working paper, Kane, Lehmann and Trippi (1996) examine S&P 500 and TSE returns over the period 1970–94 and find that return variances and risk premiums exhibit discontinuous behaviour following jumps of magnitudes exceeding three standard deviations. This finding raises serious questions about the use of mechanical forecast algorithms that do not address jumps, a phenomenon that traders surely do not generally ignore. The present study neglects this important issue which is left to a subsequent investigation.

USING A SHORTER INTERVAL IN THE MA VARIANCE ESTIMATES

Using a benchmark such as MA300 naturally raises the question whether it is appropriate. Our choice was based on the EHKN study which found MA300 marginally to outperform longer estimation intervals of 1000 and 5000 days. It was suggested to us that perhaps a shorter interval would in fact be a superior benchmark.

Table 7 reports the results from repeating the experiment with Garch-DI using MA30 as benchmark, that is, a 30 day estimation interval. The results are indistinguishable in the magnitude of the returns and their t-ratios. Thus we can conclude that the quality of MA estimates is quite similar in a very broad range of 30-5,000 days.

2. Cumulative profits (against the MA300 method)

Cumulative percentage returns for the Garch and Garch-DI methods in trading straddles with the MA300 method over the period June 1968–December 1991

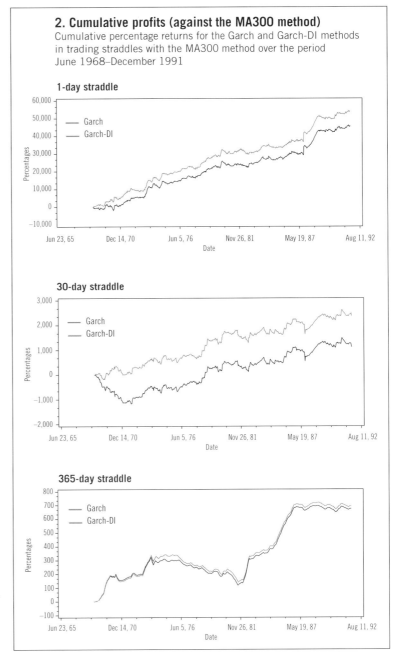

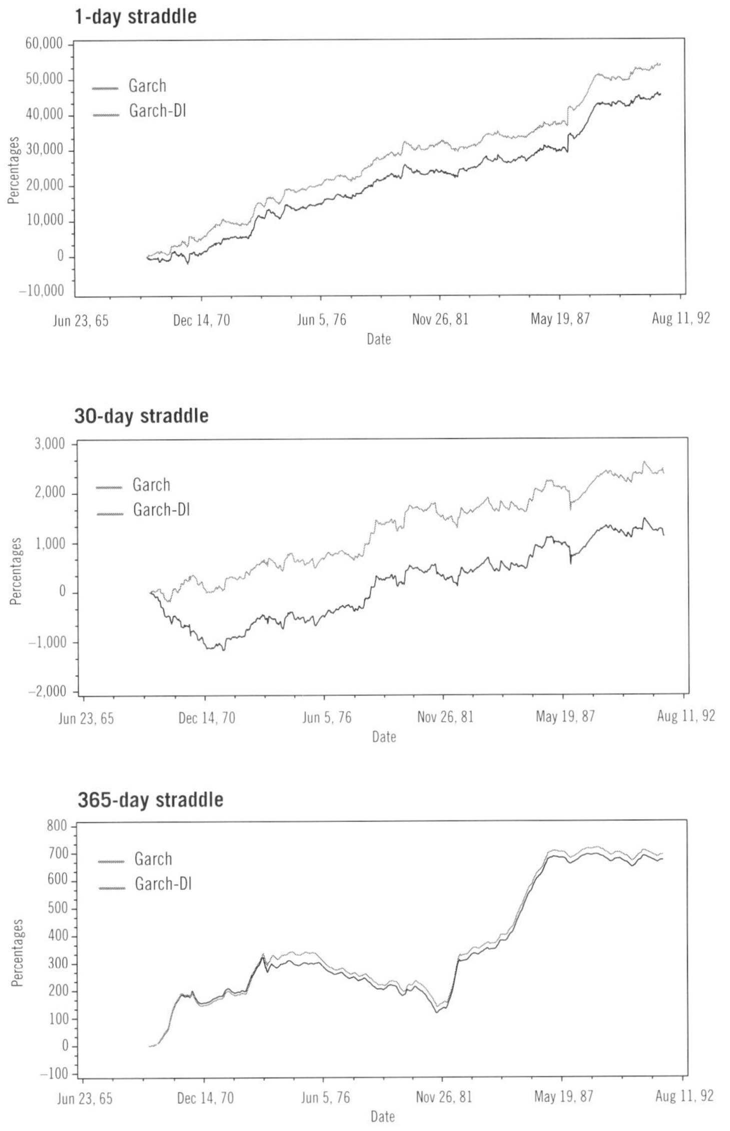

THE SENSIBILITY OF USING OVERLAPPING OBSERVATIONS

The large sample used in the study raises the question of whether the statistical complexity that is necessitated by the use of overlapping observations is justified. Why not use a smaller, but perhaps sufficient, number of non-overlapping intervals?

The fact of the matter is that the number of observations simply falls too fast when we restrict the experiment to non-overlapping observations. For one-month options, the number of observations falls from 5,921 to less than 200, and so on. While average returns are similar, the t-ratios are

Table 7. Annualised average rate of return in decimals from daily trade of $1 worth of straddles per day, Garch-DI vs MA30 (June 20, 1968–December 31, 1991)*

Day	Obs	Garch- DI over MA30	MA30 R_m	Garch-DI R_m	MA30 Total	Garch-DI Total	Garch-DI t-ratio
1	5921	14.078(2.754)	0.038(0.023)	0.072(0.018)	−14.040(2.756)	14.149(2.754,2.754)	5.14
2	5921	15.517(3.950)	0.064(0.048)	0.131(0.036)	−15.453(3.960)	15.648(3.950,3.018)	3.96
4	5921	12.073(2.364)	0.042(0.037)	0.078(0.026)	−12.031(2.371)	12.151(2.363,1.622)	5.14
6	5921	6.316(1.385)	0.046(0.028)	0.051(0.020)	−6.270(1.391)	6.367(1.385,0.786)	4.60
8	5921	5.479(1.266)	0.067(0.030)	0.066(0.022)	−5.412(1.271)	5.545(1.266,0.620)	4.38
10	5921	4.416(1.033)	0.054(0.027)	0.056(0.020)	−4.363(1.038)	4.472(1.032,0.466)	4.33
12	5921	3.774(0.949)	0.053(0.027)	0.051(0.021)	−3.722(0.952)	3.826(0.948,0.416)	4.04
14	5921	3.027(0.850)	0.063(0.027)	0.058(0.021)	−2.964(0.853)	3.085(0.850,0.358)	3.63
18	5921	2.255(0.737)	0.057(0.026)	0.053(0.021)	−2.198(0.738)	2.309(0.737,0.279)	3.13
20	5921	1.967(0.700)	0.060(0.027)	0.054(0.022)	−1.907(0.701)	2.021(0.701,0.255)	2.88
22	5921	1.600(0.629)	0.061(0.026)	0.054(0.021)	−1.539(0.629)	1.654(0.629,0.219)	2.63
24	5921	1.432(0.617)	0.062(0.026)	0.054(0.022)	−1.371(0.618)	1.486(0.617,0.208)	2.41
26	5921	1.247(0.604)	0.062(0.027)	0.051(0.022)	−1.185(0.604)	1.298(0.604,0.198)	2.15
28	5921	1.112(0.545)	0.063(0.025)	0.051(0.021)	−1.049(0.546)	1.163(0.546,0.174)	2.13
30	5921	1.014(0.521)	0.062(0.025)	0.050(0.021)	−0.951(0.520)	1.064(0.521,0.157)	2.04
40	5921	0.816(0.471)	0.062(0.025)	0.050(0.022)	−0.754(0.470)	0.865(0.473,0.123)	1.83
50	5921	0.540(0.400)	0.067(0.024)	0.049(0.023)	−0.473(0.398)	0.589(0.401,0.097)	1.47
60	5921	0.429(0.384)	0.069(0.024)	0.044(0.023)	−0.360(0.382)	0.473(0.387,0.083)	1.22
90	5921	0.199(0.328)	0.071(0.023)	0.042(0.023)	−0.128(0.324)	0.241(0.332,0.055)	0.73
270	5921	0.203(0.141)	0.074(0.026)	0.043(0.019)	−0.130(0.132)	0.246(0.142,0.018)	1.73
365	5921	0.226(0.145)	0.072(0.027)	0.046(0.019)	−0.154(0.134)	0.272(0.138,0.013)	1.97

* Day is the number of days till maturity of straddles. Obs is the total number of trading days. The third column shows the return for an agent using Garch-DI in trading straddles with an agent using MA30. MA 30 R_m (Garch-DI R_m) shows the return from a $1 endowment in the NYSE-index portfolio when an agent using MA30 (Garch DI) takes a short position. MA30 Total (Garch-DI Total) is the sum of the return from trading straddles and the return from the NYSE-index portfolio for an agent using MA 30 (Garch-DI Total). Numbers in parentheses from the third column to the sixth column are Hansen-Hodrick standard errors. Numbers in parentheses in the seventh column are Hansen-Hodrick standard error and ordinary standard error, respectively. The last column is the t-ratio of Garch-DI Total based on Hansen-Hodrick standard error.

smaller, although always significant for less than 30-day maturities. Using overlapping observations suggest that Garch forecasts are economically and statistically superior for longer periods.

Conclusion

The return history of the NYSE suggests that the choice of variance forecasts for pricing index options can make a significant economic difference to investors. The impact on investment in index options from choosing between different forecast methods is important for option maturities up to one year and is significant at a 5% level for options of maturity of up to one month. An important step in improving variance forecasts is to make Hull and White's (1987) modification to Black and Scholes' (1973) formula. Moreover, incorporating the weekend effect into the parameter estimation and forecast specification is also important.

Using simulated option markets has circumvented the problems of market depth, price synchroneity, dividend protection and delivery options. Thus these results are not subject to objections grounded in problems that plague empirical work with actual option prices.

Appendix

PROOF OF THEOREM 1

Let

$$S_\tau = \sum_{t=1}^{\tau} \varepsilon_t, \quad \tau = 1,2,\ldots,T$$

and set $S_0 = 0$. The functional central limit theorem (FCLT)[6] states that the random function $\{(1/\sigma\sqrt{T})S_{[T\lambda]}\}$, $\lambda \in [0,1]$, weakly converges to a standard Brownian motion process on the unit interval, $W(\lambda)$: as $T \to \infty$,

$$S_{[T\lambda]} \Rightarrow W(\lambda) \tag{A1}$$

From the continuous mapping theorem, as $T \to \infty$,

$$T^{-3/2}\frac{1}{\sigma}\sum_{t=1}^{[T\lambda]} S_t \Rightarrow \int_0^\lambda W(s)ds \tag{A2}$$

and

$$T^{-2}\frac{1}{\sigma^2}\sum_{t=1}^{[T\lambda]} S_t^2 \Rightarrow \int_0^\lambda W(s)ds. \tag{A3}$$

Since the J-period return was defined as

$$X_{t+j}(J) = \sum_{i=0}^{J-1} R_{m,t+J-i}, \quad t = 0,\ldots,T-J,$$

the OLS estimate of the regression (5) above can

be rewritten as follows,

$$\hat{\beta}(J) = \frac{1}{T-J}\sum_{t=0}^{T-J} x_{t+J}(J)$$
$$= \frac{1}{T-J}\sum_{t=0}^{T-J}\left\{\sum_{i=0}^{t+J} R_{m,i} - \sum_{i=0}^{t} R_{m,i}\right\}. \quad (A4)$$

Using equations (A1), (A2) and (A3), the following holds, as $T \to \infty$ and $J/T \to \psi$,

$$\frac{1}{\sqrt{T}}\hat{\beta}(J) \Rightarrow \sigma\frac{1}{1-\psi}\int_0^{\psi}\{W(s+\psi) - W(s)\}ds. \quad (A5)$$

Also, the following holds, as $T \to \infty$•, $J/T \to \psi$, and $i/T \to \rho$,

$$\frac{1}{T}\hat{\gamma}_u^2(i) = \frac{1}{T}\frac{1}{T-J-|i|}\sum_{t=|i|}^{T-J}\left(x_{t+J}(J) - \hat{\beta}(J)\right)$$
$$\left(x_{t+J-|i|}(J) - \hat{\beta}(J)\right)$$
$$\Rightarrow \sigma^2\left(1-|\rho|\right)\frac{1}{T-\psi-|\rho|}$$
$$\int_{|\rho|}^{1-\psi} U_\psi(s+\psi)U_\psi\left(s+\psi-|\rho|\right)ds \quad (A6)$$

where $U_\psi(\lambda)$ is defined in the text.

Hence, Hansen and Hodrick's (1980) variance estimator of $\hat{\beta}(J)$ converges to a functional of Brownian motion, as $T \to \infty$ and $J/T \to \psi$,

$$\frac{1}{T}\hat{\omega}^2(l) = \frac{1}{T^2}\sum_{i=-(J-1)}^{J-1}\frac{T-|i|}{T}\gamma_u^2(i)$$
$$\Rightarrow \sigma^2\int_{-\psi}^{\psi}\Gamma_u(\rho,\psi)d\rho \quad (A7)$$

where $\Gamma_u(\rho,\psi)$ is defined in the text.

Therefore, the conventional t-ratio, $t_{\hat{\beta}}$ converges to a functional of Brownian motion, as $T \to \infty$ and $J/T \to \psi$,

$$t_{\hat{\beta}} = \frac{\hat{\beta}(J)}{\sqrt{\hat{\omega}(J)}}$$
$$\Rightarrow \frac{\frac{1}{1-\psi}\int_0^{1-\psi}\{W(s+\psi) - W(s)\}ds}{\left[\int_{-\psi}^{\psi}\Gamma_u(\rho,\psi)d\rho\right]^{1/2}}.$$

1 *However, as Brenner and Galai (1986) observe, it is not all that clear which asset should be observed to obtain the risk-free rate in the Black-Scholes formula.*

2 *The volatility of the variance of an underlying asset will not be priced if it is non-systematic. When the variance is priced, the Black-Scholes formula in the Hull and White's (1987) model must be amended to account for a deficiency in the asset risk premium. See McDonald and Siegel (1984) and Heston (1992).*

3 *We compared Garch(1,1) to three versions of a moving average of squared residuals. Each forecast algorithm was used to provide a rolling daily forecast of the NYSE-index return variance. We used three alternative lengths of past observations to estimate the parameters: 300 days, 1,000 days and 5,000 days. The 12 time series of forecasts were used to price and hypothetically trade one-day options. The Garch forecasts were decidedly superior in the NYSE sample for 1962-90. Using an estimation interval of 1,000 days was slightly better than either 300 or 5,000 days.*

4 *By assumption, the returns are allowed to be conditionally heteroskedastic. However, an Igarch process violates the assumption that* $\sup_t E[\varepsilon_t^4] < \infty$. *See Engle and Bollerslev (1986).*

5 *The Hull-White method for stochastic volatility is expected to generate a smaller variance rate and hence lower straddle prices, yet Table 2 shows that the average Garch-I price exceeds the average price from simple Garch for maturities up to 50 days. While a strict interpretation of the Garch process requires that the forecast error for day 1 be zero, we take the daily Garch process as an approximation to a diffusion process and hence generate the series of variance-forecast errors as of day one. Since the forecast errors are squared, this procedure increases the variance rate. As maturities rise, the importance of day-1 forecast errors declines and the overall convexity of the Hull-White expectation takes over.*

6 *See Billingsley (1968) or Hall and Heyde (1980) or Herndorff (1984) for the FCLT and continuous mapping theorem. For applications of the FCLT and continuous mapping theorem, see Phillips (1987).*

BIBLIOGRAPHY

Billingsley, P., 1968, *Convergence of probability measure*. New York, NY: Wiley.

Black, F., and M. S. Scholes, 1973, "The pricing of options and corporate liabilities", *Journal of Political Economy* 81, pp. 637-59.

Bollerslev, T., R. Chou, and K.F. Kroner, 1992, "ARCH modelling in finance: A review of the theory and empirical evidence", *Journal of Econometrics* 52, pp. 5-59; reprinted as Chapter 2 of the present volume.

Brenner, M., and D. Galai, 1986, "Implied interest rates", *Journal of Business* 59, no. 3, pp. 493-508.

Engle, R.F., 1982, "Autoregressive conditional heteroskedasticity with estimates of the variance of UK inflation", *Econometrica* 50, pp. 987-1008.

Engle, R.F., and T. Bollerslev, 1986, "Modelling the persistence of conditional variances," *Econometric Reviews* 5, pp. 1-50, 81-7.

Engle, R.F., T. Hong, A. Kane, and J. Noh, 1993,

"Arbitrage valuation of variance forecasts", *Advanced Futures and Options Research* 6, pp. 393-415.

French, K.G., and R. Roll, 1986, "Stock return variance: the arrival of information and the reaction of traders", *Journal of Financial Economics* 17, no. 1, pp. 5-26.

Hall, P., and C. C. Heyde, 1980, *Martingale limit theory and its application*. New York, NY: Academic Press.

Hansen, L.P., and R.J. Hodrick, 1980, "Forward exchange rates as optimal predictors of future spot rates: An econometric analysis", *Journal of Political Economy* 88, pp. 829-53.

Herndorff, N., 1984, "A functional central limit theorem for weakly dependent sequences of random variables", *Annals of Probability* 12, pp.141-53.

Heston, S., 1992, "Option pricing with stochastic volatility",Working paper, Yale University.

Hull, J., and A. White, 1987, "The pricing of options on assets with stochastic volatility, *Journal of Finance* 42, pp. 281-300.

Kane, A., B. Lehmann and R. Trippi, 1996, "Regularities in volatility and the price of risk following large stock market movements in the US and Japan", UCSD Working Paper, July.

McDonald, R.L., and D. Siegel, 1984, "Option pricing when the underlying asset earns a below-equilibrium rate return", *Journal of Finance* 39, pp. 261-5.

Muller, 1991, BARRA newsletter.

Phillips, P.C.B., 1987, "Times series regression with a unit root", *Econometrica* 55, pp. 226-301.

Richardson, M., and J.H. Stock, 1989, "Drawing inferences from statistics based on multiyear asset returns", *Journal of Financial Economics* 25, pp. 323-48.

Schmalensee, R., and R.R. Trippi, 1978, "Common stock volatility expectations implied by option prices", *Journal of Finance* 33, pp. 129-147.

6

Markov Switching in Garch Processes and Mean-Reverting Stock Market Volatility*

Michael J. Dueker
Federal Reserve Bank of St Louis

This paper introduces four models of conditional heteroskedasticity that contain Markov-switching parameters to examine their multi-period stock market volatility forecasts as predictions of options-implied volatilities. The volatility model that best predicts the behaviour of the options-implied volatilities allows the student-t degrees-of-freedom parameter to switch such that the conditional variance and kurtosis are subject to discrete shifts. The half-life of the most leptokurtic state is estimated to be a week, so expected market volatility reverts to near-normal levels fairly quickly following a spike.

Volatility clustering is a well-documented feature of financial rates of return: price changes that are large in magnitude tend to occur in bunches rather than with equal spacing. A natural question is how long financial markets will remain volatile, because volatility forecasts are central to calculating optimal hedging ratios and options prices. Indeed we can study the behaviour of options-implied stock-market volatilities to find stylised facts that parametric volatility models should aim to capture. Two stylised facts that conventional volatility models, notably generalised autoregressive conditional heteroskedasticity (Garch), (Bollerslev (1986)), find hard to reconcile are:

- conditional volatility can increase substantially in a short amount of time at the onset of a turbulent period;
- the rate of mean reversion in stock market volatility appears to vary positively and non-linearly with the level of volatility. In other words, stock market volatility does not remain persistently two to three times above its normal level the same way it can persist at 30–40% above normal.

Hamilton and Susmel (1994) and Lamoureux and Lastrapes (1993) highlight the forecasting difficulties of conventional Garch models by showing that they can provide worse multi-period volatility forecasts than constant-variance models. In particular, multi-period Garch forecasts of the volatility are too high in a period of above-normal volatility. Friedman and Laibson (1989) address the forecasting issue by not allowing the conditional variance in a Garch model to respond proportionately to "large" and "small" shocks. In this way, the conditional variance is restrained from increasing to a level from which volatility forecasts would be undesirably high. One drawback of this approach is that in such a model the conditional volatility might understate the true variance by not responding sufficiently to large shocks and thereby never be pressed to display much mean reversion. Thus, such "threshold" models do not necessarily address the two stylised facts listed above: sharp upward jumps in volatility, followed by fairly rapid reversion to near-normal levels.

* *This paper was first published in the* Journal of Business & Economic Statistics, *Vol. 15, No. 1 (1997) and is reprinted with permission of the American Statistical Association.* *The content is the responsibility of the author and does not represent official positions of the Federal Reserve Bank of St. Louis or the Federal Reserve System.* *The author thanks James Hamilton and Bruce Hansen for sharing their programs and Barbara Ostdiek and Robert Whaley for the VIX data.*

This paper endeavours to craft a volatility model that can address these two stylised facts from within the class of Garch models with Markov-switching parameters. Markov-switching parameters ought to enable the volatility to experience discrete shifts and discrete changes in the persistence parameters.

Partly in response to Lamoureux and Lastrapes (1990), who observed that structural breaks in the variance could account for the high persistence in the estimated conditional variance, Hamilton and Susmel (1994) and Cai (1994) introduced Markov-switching parameters to Arch models and we extend the approach to Garch models, since the latter are more flexible and widely used. The next section presents tractable methods of estimating Garch models with Markov-switching parameters. The third section describes four specifications that are estimated and provides in-sample and out-of-sample goodness-of-fit test results. The fourth section uses the estimated models to generate multi-period forecasts of stock market volatility and compares the forecasts with options-implied volatilities to see which of the Garch/Markov switching models best explains the two stylised facts described above.

Garch/Markov switching volatility models

Each of the volatility-model specifications will assume a student-t error distribution with n_t degrees of freedom in the dependent variable y:

$$y_t = \mu_t + \varepsilon_t \tag{1}$$

$\varepsilon_t \sim$ student-t (mean $= 0, n_t, h_t$), $n_t > 2$. In all of the models, the conditional mean, μ_t, is allowed to switch according to a Markov process governed by a state variable, S_t: $\mu_t = \mu_l S_t + \mu_h(1-S_t)$, $S_t \in \{0,1\}$ $\forall t$,

$$\Pr(S_t = 0 \mid S_{t-1} = 0) = p$$
$$\Pr(S_t = 1 \mid S_{t-1} = 1) = q. \tag{2}$$

The unconditional probability of $S_t = 0$ equals $(1-q)/(2-p-q)$. The variance of ε_t is denoted σ_t^2 and is a function of n_t and h_t in all of the models considered such that $\sigma_t^2 = f(n_t, h_t)$, where the specific function f varies across the models. In all cases, however, h is assumed to be a Garch(1,1) process with Markov-switching parameters also governed by S, so that a general form for h is

$$h_t(S_t, S_{t-1}, \ldots, S_0) = \gamma(S_t) + \alpha(S_{t-1})\varepsilon_{t-1}^2 + \beta(S_{t-1})h_{t-1}(S_{t-1}, \ldots, S_0). \tag{3}$$

Note that the presence of lagged h on the right side of (3) causes the Garch variable to be a function of the entire history of the state variable. If h were an Arch(p) process, then h would depend only on the p most recent values of the state variable, as in Cai (1994) and Hamilton and Susmel (1994). Here I discuss how methods described in Kim (1994) can be applied to make estimation feasible for Garch processes subject to Markov switching.

Clearly it is not practical to examine all of the possible sequences of past values of the state variable when evaluating the likelihood function for a sample of more than 1,000 observations, as the number of cases to consider exceeds 1,000 by the time $t = 10$. Kim (1994) addresses this problem by introducing a collapsing procedure that greatly facilitates evaluation of the likelihood function at the cost of introducing a degree of approximation that does not appear to distort the calculated likelihood by much. The collapsing procedure, when applied to a Garch process, calls for treating the conditional dispersion, h_t, as a function of at most the most recent M values of the state variable S. For the filtering to be accurate, Kim notes that when h is p-order autoregressive, then M should be at least $p + 1$. In the Garch(1,1) case $p = 1$, so we would have to keep track of M^2 or four cases, based on the two most recent values of a binary state variable. Thus, h_t is treated as a function of only S_t and S_{t-1}: $h_t^{(i,j)} = h_t(S_t = i, S_{t-1} = j)$.

Denoting φ_t as the information available through time t, we keep the number of cases to four by integrating out S_{t-1} before plugging lagged h into the Garch equation:

$$h_t^{(i)} = \sum_{j=0}^{1} \Pr\left(S_{t-1} = j \middle| S_t = i, \varphi_t\right) h_t^{(i,j)}. \tag{4}$$

This method of collapsing of $h_t^{(i,j)}$ onto $h_t^{(i)}$ at every observation gives us a tractable Garch formula which is approximately equal to the exact Garch equation from equation (3):

$$h_t^{(i,j)} = \gamma(S_t = i) + \alpha(S_{t-1} = j)\left(\varepsilon_{t-1}^{(j)}\right)^2 + \beta(S_{t-1} = j)h_{t-1}^{(j)}. \tag{5}$$

Note that the collapsing procedure integrates out the first lag of the state variable, S_{t-1}, from the Garch function, h_t, at the right point in the filtering process to prevent the conditional density from becoming a function of a growing number of past values of the state variable.

From this general framework, we choose specifications that differ according to the parameters that switch and the relationship between the Garch process, h, and the variance σ^2. In several specifications, the Garch processes are functions of lagged values of the state variable, but not the contemporaneous value, S_t. For these, we treat h_t as a function of only S_{t-1}, so we only need to keep track of two cases: $h^{(j)} = h(S_{t-1} = j)$. Furthermore, after integrating out S_{t-1}, we are left with a scalar in the collapsing process:

$$\hat{h}_t = \Pr\left(S_{t-1} = 0 \middle| \varphi_t\right) h_t^{(0)} + \Pr\left(S_{t-1} = 1 \middle| \varphi_t\right) h_t^{(1)}. \quad (6)$$

A tractable Garch equation is then an even simpler version of equation

$$h_t^{(j)} = \gamma + \alpha(S_{t-1} = j)\left(\varepsilon_{t-1}^{(j)}\right)^2 + \beta(S_{t-1} = j)\hat{h}_{t-1}. \quad (7)$$

Another feature of this Garch/Markov switching framework is that the state variable implies a connection between the mean stock return and the variance and possibly kurtosis. If the mean stock return is lower in the high-volatility state, then the model can explain negatively skewed distributions, both unconditional and conditional on available information. The student-t distributions have zero skewness only when conditional on particular values of the state variables, which are unobservable.

Four specifications and estimation results

The first specification is a Garch analogue to Cai's (1994) Arch model with Markov switching in γ. The variance is assumed to follow a Garch process so that $\sigma_t^2 = h_t$ and the only parameter in h_t subject to Markov switching is γ. This type of switching is tantamount to allowing shifts in the unconditional variance, since the unconditional variance of the ordinary, constant-parameter Garch (1,1) process is $\gamma/(1 - \alpha - \beta)$. For this model, the Garch variance takes the form

$$h_t^{(i,j)} = \gamma(S_t = i) + \alpha\left(\varepsilon_{t-1}^{(j)}\right)^2 + \beta h_{t-1}^{(j)}, \quad (8)$$

with constant α and β. We denote this model as the Garch-UV model for Garch with switching in the unconditional variance. In practice, we parameterise $\gamma(S_t)$ as $g(St)\gamma$, where $g(S = 1)$ is normalised to unity.

The second specification is a Garch analogue to Hamilton and Susmel's (1994) Arch model with Markov switching in a normalisation factor g, where the variance $\sigma_t^2 = g_t h_t$. In this case, the Garch equation (5) takes the form

$$h_t^{(j)} = \gamma + \frac{\alpha}{g(S_{t-1} = j)}\left(\varepsilon_{t-1}^{(j)}\right)^2 + \beta\hat{h}_{t-1}, \quad (9)$$

where γ and β are constant and $g(S = 1)$ is normalised to unity. We denote this model as the Garch-NF model for Garch with switching in the normalisation factor, g. Note that in the Garch-NF model the Garch process in equation (9) is not a function of S_t, so estimation is somewhat simplified.

The third specification is a Markov-switching analogue to Hansen (1994), where the variance follows a Garch process ($\sigma_t^2 = g_t h_t$) and the student-t degrees-of-freedom parameter is allowed to switch. Hansen (1994) introduces a model in which the student-t degrees-of-freedom parameter, n_t is allowed to vary over time as a probit-type function of variables dated up to time $t - 1$. Because Hansen's (1994) specification is not conducive to multi-period forecasting, however, we chose to make n_t follow a Markov process governed by S_t: $n_t = n_l S_t + n_h(1 - S_t)$. Although n_t does not enter the Garch equation (7) in this specification, the Garch process is still a function of the state variable, because state-switching in the mean implies that ε is a function of the state variable:

$$h_t^{(j)} = \gamma + \alpha\left(\varepsilon_{t-1}^{(j)}\right)^2 + \beta\hat{h}_{t-1}. \quad (10)$$

Because the kurtosis of a student-t random variable equals $3(n_t - 2)/(n_t - 4)$ and is uniquely determined by n_t, we call this the Garch-K model for Garch with switching in the conditional kurtosis.

The fourth specification is similar to the Garch-K model except the variance is assumed to be

$$\sigma_t^2 = h_t n_t / (n_t - 2) \quad (11)$$

rather than $\sigma_t^2 = h_t$. In this model, the Garch process h_t scales the variance of ε_t for a given value of the shape parameter n_t. Here it is convenient to define $v_t = 1/n_t$, so that $(1 - 2v_t) = (n_t - 2)/n_t$ and the Garch equation (7) becomes

$$h_t^{(j)} = \gamma + \alpha\left(1 - 2v_{t-1}^{(j)}\right)\left(\varepsilon_{t-1}^{(j)}\right)^2 + \beta\hat{h}_{t-1}. \quad (12)$$

We denote this specification as the Garch-DF model for Garch with switching in the degrees-of-freedom parameter. As in the Garch-NF and Garch-K models, h is a function of S_{t-1}, but not S_t, in the Garch-DF model. The Garch-DF model shares two features with the Garch-NF model: the variance is subject to discrete shifts and the lagged squared residuals are endogenously downweighted in states where σ^2/h is large. With the

Garch-K model, the Garch-DF model shares the feature of time-varying conditional kurtosis, so that conditional fourth moments are not assumed to be constant.

We also report results on the usual Garch(1,1) model with Markov switching in the mean and a model of switching Arch with a leverage effect (Swarch-L), as in Hamilton and Susmel (1994). The Swarch-L model has switching in a normalising factor in the variance: $\sigma_t^2 = g_t h_t$, where h_t follows an Arch(2) process with a leverage effect:

$$h_t^{(j,k)} = \gamma + \frac{\left(\alpha_1 + \delta D_{t-1}^{(j)}\right)}{g(S_{t-1} = j)} \left(\varepsilon_{t-1}^{(j)}\right)^2 + \frac{\alpha_2}{g(S_{t-2} = k)} \left(\varepsilon_{t-2}^{(k)}\right)^2, \qquad (13)$$

where $D_{t-1}^{(j)}$ is dummy variable that equals 1 when $\varepsilon(S_{t-1} = j)_{t-1} < 0$. The leverage effect posits that negative stock returns increase debt-to-equity ratios, making firms riskier initially. Hence the leverage-effect parameter δ is expected to have a positive sign.

The log-likelihood function for the Garch-DF model, for example, is

$$\ln L_t^{(i,j)} = \ln\Gamma\left(.5\left(n_t^{(i)} + 1\right)\right) - \ln\Gamma\left(.5n_t^{(i)}\right) - .5\ln\left(\pi n_t^{(i)} h_t^{(j)}\right) - .5\left(n_t^{(i)} + 1\right) \times \ln\left(1 + \frac{\left(\varepsilon_t^{(i)}\right)^2}{h_t^{(j)} n_t^{(i)}}\right), \qquad (14)$$

where $i \in \{0,1\}$ corresponds with $S_t \in \{0,1\}$, $j \in \{0,1\}$ corresponds with $S_{t-1} \in \{0,1\}$ and Γ is the gamma function.

The function maximised is the log of the expected likelihood or

$$\sum_{t=1}^{T} \ln\left(\sum_{i=0}^{1}\sum_{j=0}^{1} \Pr\left(S_t = i, S_{t-1} = j \middle| \varphi_{t-1}\right) L_t^{(i,j)}\right) \qquad (15)$$

as in Hamilton (1990).

ESTIMATION RESULTS

The four Garch/Markov switching volatility models, the usual Garch(1,1) model, and the Swarch-L model are applied to daily percentage changes in the S&P 500 index from January 6, 1982 to December 31, 1991. Observations from the post-1991 period are reserved for evaluation of the out-of-sample fit.

Some interpretation of the parameter estimates in Table 1 follows. The Garch-DF model shows switching in the student-t degrees-of-freedom parameter between the values of 2.64 and 8.28. This implies that conditional fourth moments do not exist in one state, whereas the conditional kurtosis is $3(n-2)/(n-4) = 4.4$ in the other state. The weight given to lagged squared residuals in the Garch process is shown to be $\alpha(1 - 2v(S_{t-1}))$ in equation (12), and this weight shifts with the state variable between .009 and .027. In this way, shocks drawn from the low degree-of-freedom state do not affect the persistent Garch dispersion process proportionately. Most importantly, shifts in the degrees-of-freedom parameter bring potentially large discrete shifts in the variance. A shift out of the low degree-of-freedom state causes the variance to decrease by about 68%, holding the dispersion constant:

$$\left(\frac{\dfrac{n_h}{n_h - 2}}{\dfrac{n_l}{n_l - 2}}\right) = .32.$$

The unconditional probability of being in the low degree-of-freedom state is about 10% with a half-life of five trading days. The unconditional value for the degrees-of-freedom parameter is about 6.8. The Garch-DF model also suggests that stock returns are negatively skewed, because the mean stock return is below normal in the high-volatility state when $S_t = 0$. In fact, all of the models find negative skewness except the conventional Garch model.

The Garch-NF model finds an estimate of the variance inflation factor $g(S = 0) = 12.59$ with a large standard error. The effective sample from which to estimate this parameter is small, because the unconditional probability of $S_t = 0$ is only about 1%.

The factor $g(S = 0)$ raises γ by a significant multiple of 5.7 in the Garch-UV model, but the unconditional probability of being in that state is only 11%. The state with $g(S = 1)$ is extremely persistent with $q = .995$.

The Garch-K model estimates that the degrees-of-freedom parameter switches between 10.7 and 4.2, with an unconditional value of about 6. Both states are highly persistent with nearly identical transition probabilities. Two states for the mean stock return are better defined in the Garch-K model than in the conventional Garch model with switching in the mean. Table 1 shows that in the usual Garch(1,1) model, the mean stock return, μ, is virtually identical in both states. Hence the two states are not well identified and the calculation of standard errors for the transition probabilities failed.

Using daily data, the weights attached to lagged squared residuals are not significant in the Swarch-L model, with the borderline exception of the leverage-effect parameter, δ. The normalising factor, g, is estimated to raise the variance by a multiple of 3.78 in the high-volatility state, which has unconditional probability 0.13. The high degree of persistence of both states suggests that low and high volatility states constitute regimes, as opposed to short-lasting episodes. The Garch-DF model, on the other hand, finds relatively short-lasting low-degree-of-freedom states.

If we were certain that significant state switching occurred in the mean, then likelihood ratio tests of state switching in the degrees-of-freedom parameters and g would be appropriate. But, the Garch model suggests that switching in the mean cannot be taken for granted, so likelihood ratio tests cannot assume that the transition probabilities are identified under the null of no state switching in v or g. Hansen (1992) has discussed simulation methods to derive critical values for such likelihood ratio tests with non-standard distributions. The critical values are computationally burdensome to calculate, however, so we do not pursue that strategy here. Instead, we follow Vlaar and Palm (1993) by using a goodness-of-fit test that is valid for data that are not identically distributed. We perform the test over the in-sample period (1982–91) and an out-of-sample period (1992–September 1994). We divide the observations into 100 groups based on the probability of observing a value smaller than the actual residual. If the model's time-varying density function fits the data well, these probabilities should be uniformly distributed between 0 and 1. Following Vlaar and Palm (1993),

$$n_i = \sum_{t=1}^{T} I_{it},$$

where

$$I_{it} = 1 \text{ if } \frac{(i-1)}{100} < EF(\varepsilon_t, \hat{\theta}) \leq \frac{i}{100}$$
$$= 0 \text{ otherwise.} \qquad (16)$$

The expected value of the cumulative density function, F, is taken across the states that might have held at each time. The goodness-of-fit test statistic equals $100/T \sum_{i=1}^{100} (n_i - T/100)^2$ and is distributed X^2_{99} under the null.

Table 2 provides results from the goodness-of-fit tests. Only the Garch-DF model is not rejected on an in-sample basis, with a .57 probability value. All six models are rejected out of sample, however.

Table 1. Garch/Markov-switching models applied to daily percentage changes in S&P 500 index

Parameter	Garch-DF	Garch-NF	Garch-UV	Garch-K	Garch	Swarch-L
Log-likelihood	−3294.3	−3294.1	−3292.7	−3295.3	−3301.0	−3311.5
$\mu(S_t = 0)$	.0107	−1.333	−.0971	.0158	.0542	.0366
	(.1431)	(1.487)	(.1287)	(.0219)	(.1287)	(.0884)
$\mu(S_t = 1)$	.0619	.0576	.0636	.0803	.0556	.0585
	(.0207)	(.0164)	(.0169)	(.0224)	(.0890)	(.0168)
$v(S_t = 0)$	.3787	.1478	.1762	.0931	.1860	.1833
	(.0480)	(.0209)	(.0090)	(.0323)	(.0195)	(.0198)
$v(S_t = 1)$	.1208	.1478	.1762	.2393	.1860	$\delta = .041$
	(.0272)	(.0209)	(.0090)	(.0270)	(.0195)	(.025)
γ	.0105	.0109	.0124	.0233	.0228	.6912
	(.0035)	(.0038)	(.0033)	(.0066)	(.0064)	(.0372)
α	.0360	.0334	.0138	.0328	.0344	$\alpha_1 = 1.3E-4$
	(.0076)	(.0060)	(.0046)	(.0074)	(.0077)	(.0083)
β	.9466	.9537	.9554	.9307	.9394	$\alpha_2 = .0192$
	(.0102)	(.0082)	(.0090)	(.0323)	(.0121)	(.0139)
$g(S_t = 0)$	na	12.59	5.703	na	na	3.782
	na	(6.414)	(1.882)	na	na	(.4780)
$g(S_t = 1)$	na	1	1	na	na	1
p	.8544	.7479	.9602	.9978	.9144	.9849
	(.0961)	(.1644)	(.0173)	(.0021)		(.0076)
q	.9842	.9980	.9950	.9986	.9420	.9977
	(.0148)	(.0017)	(.0018)	(.0013)		(.0012)

Note: standard errors are in parentheses.

Table 2. Chi-squared goodness-of-fit tests for Garch/Markov-switching models

In-sample period: 1982–91; Out-of-sample period: 1992–Sept 1994

Model	In-sample	Out-of-sample
Garch-DF	96.65	152.1
	(.577)	(4.8E-4)
Garch-NF	193.7	208.1
	(.000)	(.000)
Garch-UV	136.6	188.4
	(.007)	(.000)
Garch-K	235.4	294.3
	(.000)	(.000)
Garch	140.0	228.4
	(.004)	(.000)
Swarch-L	231.0	307.9
	(.000)	(.000)

Note: probability values are in parentheses.

To examine the source of failure in models other than Garch-DF in the goodness-of-fit test, Figures 1 and 2 overleaf plot the distribution of the in-sample observations across the 100 groups. Figure 1 shows that the Garch-DF observations are roughly uniformly distributed across the groups, whereas the Garch-NF observations have a hump-shaped distribution in Figure 2. Too many Garch-NF residuals are near the centre of the cumulative density, which implies that the model's conditional densities are overly peaked – that is, are too leptokurtic. By not allowing the conditional kurtosis to change, the Garch-NF model apparently fits a constant conditional kur-

1. Distribution of Garch-DF residuals into 100 groups based on cumulative density function

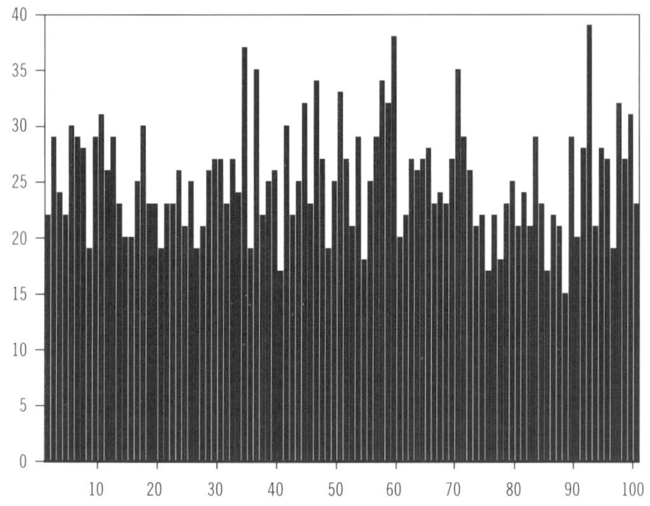

2. Distribution of Garch-NF residuals into 100 groups based on cumulative density function

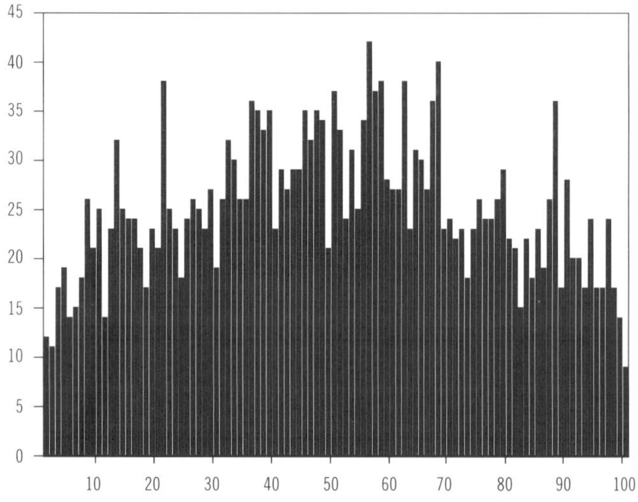

3. Distribution of Garch-K residuals into 100 groups based on cumulative density function

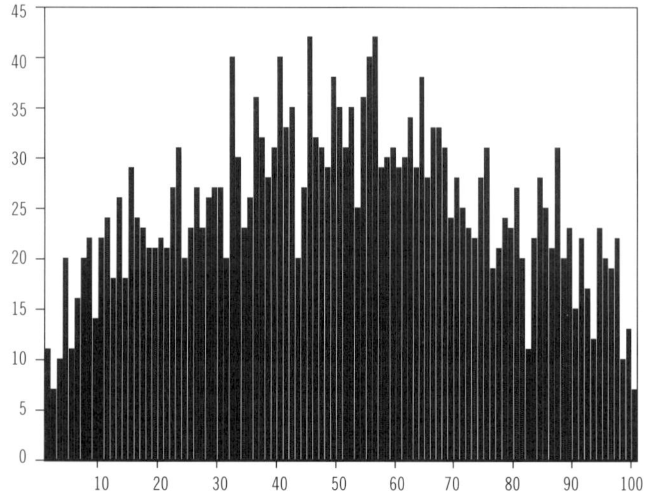

tosis that is too high. If time-varying kurtosis is an important feature of stock returns, then it is worth studying the distribution of the observations in the Garch-K model also. Figure 3 shows that the Garch-K model also provides conditional densities that are too leptokurtic on average, despite its provision for time-varying kurtosis. The reason might be that the Garch-K model has a very persistent state in which fourth moments do not exist, because $q = .9986$. It is possible that the Garch-K model overstates the persistence of periods of fat-tailed stock returns distributions: they might be better described as episodes than regimes, as the Garch-DF model suggests.

Predicting options-implied volatilities

As an economic test of the Garch/Markov switching models, we use them to predict the next day's opening level of the volatility index (VIX) compiled by the Chicago Board Options Exchange. The VIX is derived from an options-pricing model and is not a direct observation of market expectations. Nevertheless, many financial market participants are interested in options-implied volatilities in their own right. The VIX attempts to represent, as closely as possible, the implied volatility on a hypothetical at-the-money option on the Standard & Poor (S&P) 100 with 30 calendar days (22 trading days) to expiration. Details on the construction of the VIX from near-the-money options prices were given by Whaley (1993). The implied volatility on an option reflects beliefs about average volatility over the life of the option. Thus, the constant 22-day horizon of the VIX implies that we must use the Garch/Markov switching volatility models to create multi-period forecasts of volatility for all periods between one and 22 days ahead. In other words, to predict the VIX index well, the Garch/Markov switching models need to provide good multi-period forecasts for a full range from one to 22 trading days ahead.

Daily data on the VIX index were available from 1986–92. Because the VIX data are based on the S&P 100 and the stock market data are S&P 500 returns, the mean of the VIX index is slightly higher than the average volatility forecast from the Garch models. The broader S&P 500 index is somewhat less volatile than the S&P 100. For this reason, we normalise each volatility measure with its 1986–92 sample mean. Hence a value of 1.5 means that volatility is expected to be one-and-a-half times its normal level in the coming month. Details on the construction of

Table 3. Predicting options-implied volatility with Garch/Markov-switching models, 1986–92

Model	Forecast-error variance
Garch-DF	.0365 (.86)
Garch-NF	.0548 (1.33)
Garch-UV	.0589 (1.43)
Garch-K	.0399 (.97)
Garch	.0413 (1.00)
Swarch-L	.0956 (2.31)

Note: size of forecast-error variance relative to Garch in parentheses.

multi-period forecasts from the Garch/Markov switching models are set out in the Appendix.

This paper uses a minimum forecast error variance criterion to measure the closeness of the model-implied and options-implied monthly volatilities. If we denote the options-implied volatility as VIX and the monthly average of the model-predicted volatilities as $\bar{\sigma}$, then the criterion is

$$\frac{1}{T}\sum_{t=1}^{T}(\bar{\sigma}_t - VIX_t)^2.$$

Note that $\bar{\sigma}_t$, for a Wednesday, for example, is calculated using information available through Tuesday, whereas VIX_t is the data from Wednesday's opening quotes. In this sense, we are using the Garch/Markov switching models to predict the options-implied volatilities.

Table 3 shows that only the Garch-DF and Garch-K models predict the options-implied volatility index better than the conventional Garch model, and the Garch-DF model achieves a notable 14% reduction in the forecast error variance.

Figures 4–6 depict the 22-day average volatility forecasts for all the models and the VIX volatility in the aftermath of the October 1987 stock market crash. As described by Schwert (1990), for several days after October 19, 1987 options markets became very thin and the options written contained extremely large risk premia - that is, implied volatilities. Figures 4–6 show that the VIX reached about eight times its normal level immediately following the crash but returned to less than two times normal by the end of October 1987. The Garch-DF model best predicts the VIX index throughout November and early December 1987. The switch to $n(S_t = 0) = 2.64$

4. VIX options-implied and three model-implied volatilities, autumn 1987

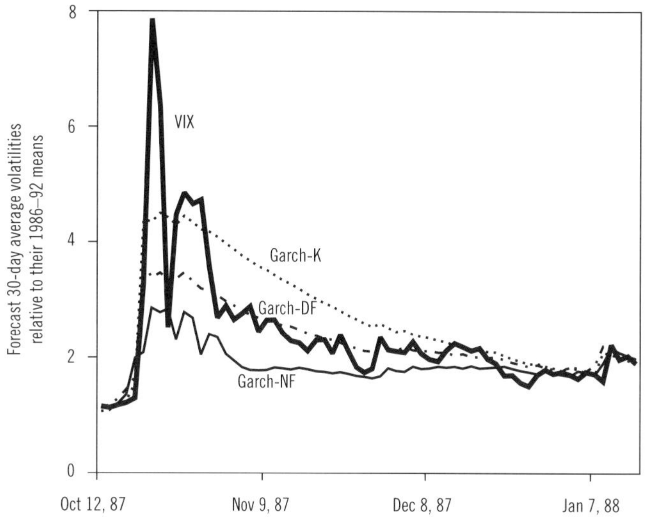

5. VIX options-implied and two model-implied volatilities, autumn 1987

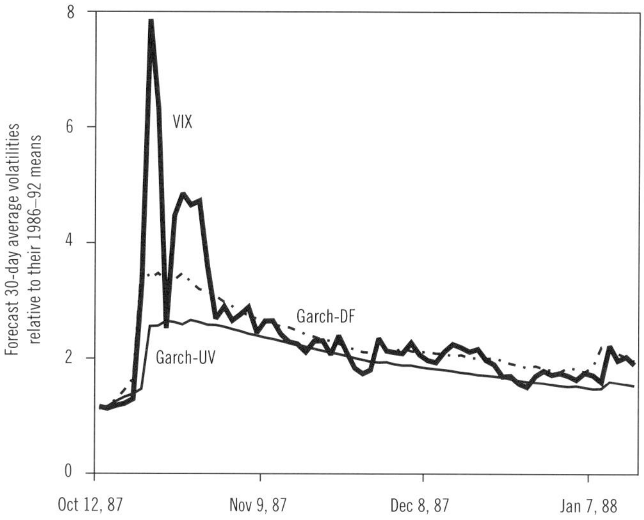

6. VIX options-implied and model-implied volatilities with Swarch, autumn 1987

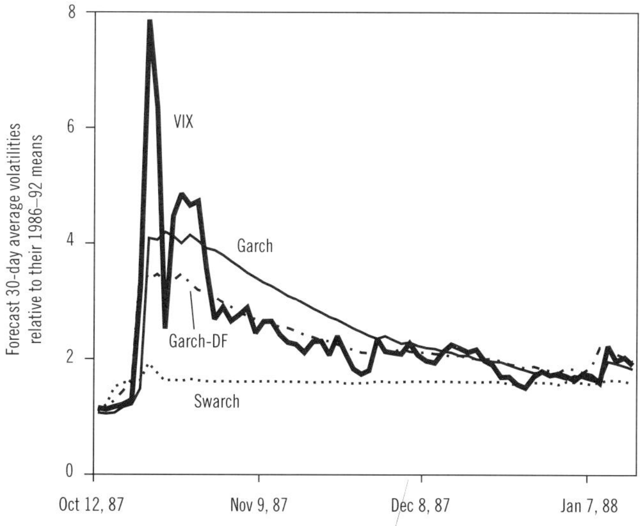

7. VIX options-implied and three model-implied volatilities, autumn 1989

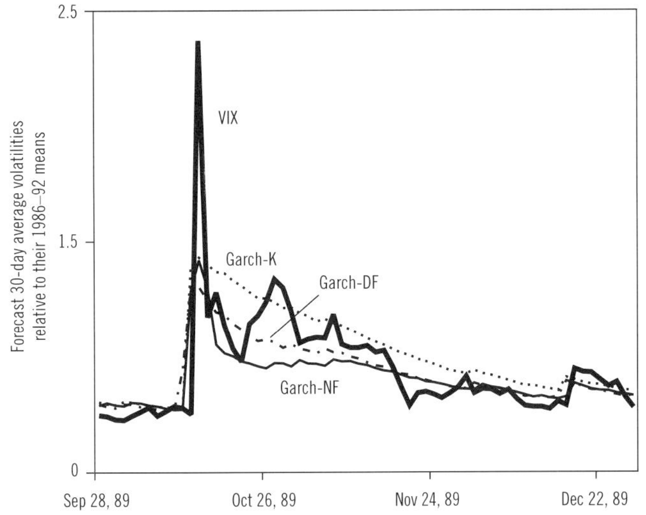

8. VIX options-implied and two model-implied volatilities, autumn 1989

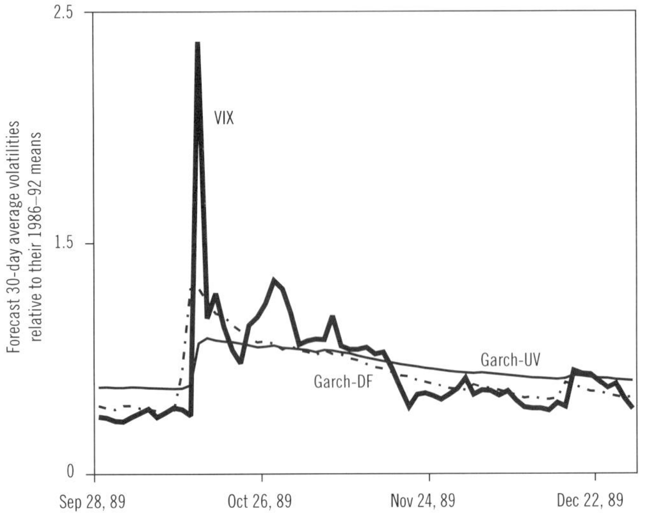

9. VIX options-implied and model-implied volatilities with Swarch, autumn 1989

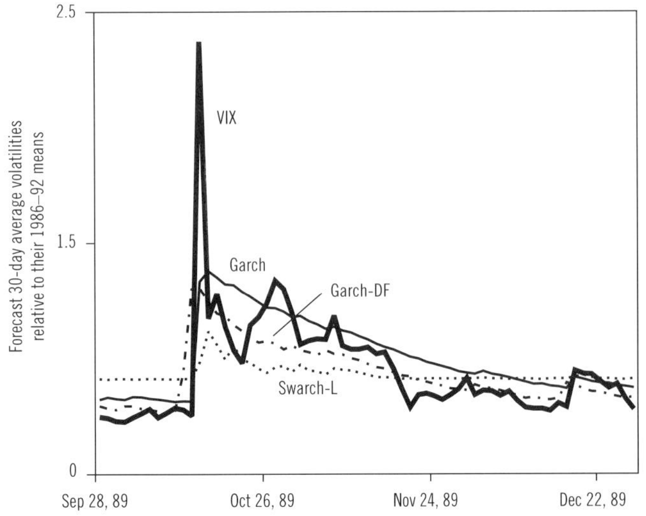

led to a downweighting, from .027 to .009, of the lagged squared residuals in the persistent Garch process. Furthermore, the conditional variance temporarily shifted discretely upward for as long as $n(S_t = 0)$ was expected to persist.

The volatility implied by the Garch-K model in Figure 4, in contrast, overpredicts the VIX index for about six weeks, beginning at the end of October 1987. The variance in the Garch-K model is a Garch process, so it displays the same over-persistence that characterises the conventional Garch model, shown in Figure 6. In fact, the forecasts from the conventional Garch model and the Garch-K model look very similar.

The Garch-NF model in Figure 1, on the other hand, underpredicts volatility following the crash. The Garch-NF model quickly switched to the state where $g(S_t = 1) = 12.59$, so the squared residuals were given little weight in the Garch process and h did not increase much. The variance, $\sigma_t^2 = g_t h_t$ did increase with $g = 12.59$, but the increase was never projected to last long with $p = .75$. Consequently the forecast average volatility for the month never increased to more than three times the normal level in the Garch-NF model. In Figure 5, the Garch-UV model badly underpredicts the VIX in late October 1987, but does fairly well in November and December 1987. The Garch-UV model estimates a constant and relatively low weight, α, on the lagged squared residuals in the Garch process, so the conditional variance never increases to more than three times normal, in contrast to the spike in the VIX. In this sense, the Garch-UV does not necessarily describe the rate of mean reversion in stock market volatility well, since it does not capture the initial volatility spike. In Figure 6, the Swarch-L model shows a good deal of persistence, but does not put enough weight on lagged squared residuals to lift the conditional variance to the levels necessary to match the spike in the VIX index either.

Figures 7–9 focus on a milder volatility spike in October 1989, when the VIX peaked at about 2.5 times its normal level. Again, the Garch-DF tends to split through the middle of oscillations of the VIX better than the other model-implied volatilities, although the improvement is less marked than in Figures 4–6. The same general patterns hold in Figure 7–9 as in Figure 4–6, with the Garch-K and Garch models tending to overpredict volatility and the Garch-UV and Swarch-L models showing persistence, but failing to yield sufficiently dramatic initial increases in volatility.

Conclusions

This paper introduces a tractable framework for adding Markov-switching parameters to conditional variance models. Four different specifications of Markov-switching volatility models are estimated, and the addition of Markov-switching parameters is found to have a variety of effects on the behaviour of the conditional volatility, relative to the model without switching. The specification found to predict options-implied expectations of stock market volatility best is the one in which the student-t degrees-of-freedom parameter switches so as to induce substantial discrete shifts in the conditional variance. This model allows for two sources of mean reversion in the wake of large shocks that are not available in a standard model: a switch out of the fat-tailed state is estimated to induce a 68% decrease in volatility for a given level of dispersion, and the weight given to the most recent shock decreases by two-thirds when the fat-tailed state pertains, thereby reducing the influence and persistence of large shocks.

Another novel feature of this model is that it relates stock returns to the degree of leptokurtosis in the conditional returns distribution. Traditional models, in contrast, assume constant conditional kurtosis and relate expected returns to the conditional variance. The point estimates support the hypothesis that stock returns are generally lower in the more fat-tailed state.

We also draw economically relevant comparisons between the behaviours of options-implied volatilities and the conditional variances from the volatility models studied. Because options-implied volatilities serve as useful proxies for market expectations of volatility, it is interesting to observe that the conditional variance from one of the switching-in-the-variance models reverts to normal about as quickly as the options-implied volatility following large shocks, such as the stock market crash of October 1987. The conventional volatility model, in contrast, has a conditional variance that remains above normal with considerably greater persistence. Thus, Markov switching in the variance is shown to add a realistic degree of mean reversion to the conditional variance. In addition, the description of time-varying stock return skewness and kurtosis provided by these models could prove useful in analysing options prices on the S&P 500 index.

An interesting extension would be to model the transition probabilities of the Markov process as time-varying functions of conditioning variables in order to test whether transitions into and out of fat-tailed states could be better predicted using more information.

Appendix

MULTI-PERIOD VOLATILITY FORECASTS

Forecasts of the volatility m periods ahead are based on the well-known relationship between Garch models and autoregressive, moving-average representations of the squared disturbances. A Garch(1,1) process,

$$h_t = \gamma + \alpha\varepsilon_{t-1}^2 + \beta h_{t-1}, \qquad \text{(A1)}$$

implies that the squared residuals obey an Arma(1,1) process:

$$\varepsilon_t^2 = \gamma + (\alpha+\beta)\varepsilon_{t-1}^2 - \beta\left(\varepsilon_{t-1}^2 - h_{t-1}\right) + \left(\varepsilon_t^2 - h_t\right), \qquad \text{(A2)}$$

where $\varepsilon_t^2 - h_t$ is a mean zero error that is uncorrelated with past information. In forecasting the squared residuals m periods ahead with the Garch-DF model, for example, we define $H_t = \varepsilon_t^2(1 - 2v_t)$. In this case H has an Arma(1,1) representation,

$$H_t = \gamma + (\alpha+\beta)H_{t-1} - \beta\left(H_{t-1} - \hat{h}_{t-1}\right) + \left(H_t - h_t\right), \qquad \text{(A3)}$$

where

$$E_t\left[H_{t+1} \middle| H_t\right] = h_{t+1} = \gamma + \alpha H_t + \beta\hat{h}_t. \qquad \text{(A4)}$$

Because the sample size is large, longer-range forecasts can be built from the asymptotic forecasting equation for first-order autoregressive processes, so that for $m > 1$

$$E_t\left[H_{t+m} \middle| H_t\right] = (\alpha+\beta)^{m-1} h_{t+1} + \left[1 - (\alpha+\beta)^{m-1}\right]\frac{\gamma}{1-\alpha-\beta}. \qquad \text{(A5)}$$

It remains to integrate out the unobserved states:

$$E_t\varepsilon_{t+m}^2 = \sum_{i=0}^{1}\sum_{j=0}^{1} \Pr\left(S_{t+m} = i, S_t = j \middle| \varphi_t\right) \times E_t\left[H_{t+m} \middle| S_t = j\right]\frac{1}{1 - 2v_{t+m}^{(i)}}. \qquad \text{(A6)}$$

where $H_t(S_t = j) = (\varepsilon_t^{(j)})^2(1 - 2v_t^{(j)})$. The expected average variance over the next 22 trading days is then taken as

$$\overline{\sigma_t^2} = \frac{1}{22}\sum_{m=1}^{22} E_t\varepsilon_{t+m}^2. \qquad \text{(A7)}$$

Similar forecasts are drawn for the other models

with H defined such that $H_t = \varepsilon_t^2/g_t$ in the Garch-NF model and $H_t = \varepsilon_t^2 - \gamma_t$ in the Garch-UV model.

For the Swarch-L model, the multi-period forecasts are derived by recursive substitution as in Hamilton and Susmel (1994).

BIBLIOGRAPHY

Bollerslev, T., 1986, "Generalized Autoregressive Conditional Heteroscedasticity", *Journal of Econometrics* 31, pp. 307-27.

Cai, J., 1994, "A Markov Model of Switching-Regime ARCH", *Journal of Business and Economic Statistics* 12, pp. 309-16.

Friedman, B.M., and D.I. Laibson, 1989, "Economic Implications of Extraordinary Movements in Stock Prices", *Brookings Papers on Economic Activity* 2, pp. 137-89.

Hamilton, J.D., 1990, "Analysis of Time Series Subject to Changes in Regime", *Journal of Econometrics* 45, No. 1/2, 39-70.

Hamilton, J.D., and R. Susmel, 1994, "Autoregressive Conditional Heteroskedasticity and Changes in Regime", *Journal of Econometrics* 64, pp. 307-33.

Hansen, B.E., 1992, "The Likelihood Ratio Test under Nonstandard Conditions: Testing the Markov Switching Model of GNP", *Journal of Applied Econometrics* 7, S61-82.

Hansen, B.E., 1994, "Autoregressive Conditional Density Estimation", *International Economic Review* 35, pp. 705-30.

Kim, C.J., 1994, "Dynamic Linear Models with Markov Switching", *Journal of Econometrics* January/February, pp. 1-22.

Lamoureux, C., and W. Lastrapes, 1990, "Persistence in Variance, Structural Change, and the GARCH Model", *Journal of Business and Economic Statistics* 8, pp. 225-34.

Lamoureux, C., and W. Lastrapes, 1993, "Forecasting Stock-Return Variance: Toward an Understanding of Stochastic Implied Volatilities", *Review of Financial Studies* 5, pp. 293-326; reprinted as Chapter 14 of the present volume.

Schwert, G.W., 1990, "Stock Volatility and the Crash of '87", *Review of Financial Studies* 3, pp. 77-102.

Vlaar, P.J., and F.C. Palm, 1993, "The Message in Weekly Exchange Rates in the European Monetary System: Mean Reversion, Conditional Heteroscedasticity, and Jumps," *Journal of Business and Economic Statistics* 11, pp. 351-60.

Whaley, R.D., 1993, "Derivatives on Market Volatility: Hedging Tools Long Overdue", *Journal of Derivatives* 1, pp. 71-84; reprinted as Chapter 28 of the present volume.

EXPLORING VOLATILITY PATTERNS OVER TIME

Introduction

Robert Jarrow

The intraday and interday predictability of volatilities are important for risk management purposes, such as computing value-at-risk, or for speculating with options. This section contains papers which study important questions related to this issue. Do volatilities differ across times, within a day or between days? Do they differ before and after scheduled news announcements? Or do they vary before and after random news events occurring at random times within a day?

It is commonly believed that stock returns are more volatile when the market is open than when it is closed (overnight, or for weekends and holidays). The first paper by G. Geoffrey Booth and Mustafa Chowdhury confirms this, using data from the Frankfurt Stock Exchange (FSE). Due to institutional changes in the exchange, a unique experiment could be conducted. On January 15, 1990 the FSE extended the trading day from two to three hours. Booth and Chowdhury consider the impact of this change on stock return variances, analysing 28 DAX stocks using intradaily prices for the years 1989 and 1990. Historical daily return variances are computed in various ways: open-close, close-open, close-close and open-open. All computations confirm the increase in the variance of returns over trading versus non-trading times.

Trading versus non-trading differences is the first question that might be asked about predictable patterns in intraday volatilities. The next is whether volatilities differ before and after scheduled news announcements? This issue is considered in the next two papers.

Monique Donders and Ton Vorst investigate the influence of scheduled news announcements on Black-Scholes implied volatilities. As American options are employed, the implied volatility is obtained from the Roll-Geske-Whaley extension of the Black-Scholes European options model. A deterministic volatility specification is utilised, with a jump at the event date. The time period covered is June 1991-December 1992, using 23 firms and 96 scheduled announcements for stocks listed on the Amsterdam Stock Exchange. The options are traded on the European Options Exchange.

In order to allow for changes in market-wide volatilities, Donders and Vorst use both a market index of implied volatility and a control group of stocks. Their results show that implied volatilities increase prior to a news release, reach a maximum on the announcement date, and return to the long run level thereafter.

Galen Burghardt and Gerald Hanweck, Jr. study the same question, but in a different way. They start by surveying account executives' beliefs about the impact of the release of 20 different economic statistics on volatilities. They find that the account executives definitely believe that information releases increase volatility, and that they rank non-farm payroll as the most important statistic. Perhaps surprisingly, the producer price index (PPI), the consumer price index (CPI) and retail sales were viewed as less important.

Burghardt and Hanweck then perform a statistical study using Deutschmarks, Eurodollars, S&P 500, and Treasury Bond futures data from January 1986 to October 1992 to confirm their findings. Volatility is measured using daily historical returns and estimated with maximum likelihood procedures (based on lognormal returns). The economic statistics considered were non-farm payroll, the PPI, the CPI, and retail sales. The announcement dates of these statistics are known in advance.

The statistical analysis confirms the results of the survey; payroll announcements are the most important statistic in their influence on volatility, and estimated volatilities for both Eurodollars and Treasury bond futures prices increase on the payroll announcement date. Less of an impact is seen for both the Deutschmark and S&P futures prices, while the PPI appears to affect Treasury bond futures volatilities. The other statistics contribute little to the various volatilities.

The paper also outlines a technique for adjusting volatilities in the Black-Scholes model to account for these changing volatilities, based on what they call calendar days. Essentially, calendar days rescale time differently, according to whether information is released on that day or not. Days with information announcements are counted more (perhaps equal to three ordinary days). The importance of this technique for more accurate option pricing awaits subsequent research.

Both these studies show that scheduled news announcements increase volatilities. But what about random news announcements? Do they increase volatilities as well? The simplest of these announcements are price changes of a related asset (not a macroeconomic statistic) at random times. The next paper, by Kalok Chan, K.C. Chan and Andrew Karolyi, shows that the answer to this question is yes.

This paper studies the relation between the intraday volatility of the S&P500 stock index and the S&P500 index futures prices over the period August 1984–December 1989. In order to compute intraday volatilities, Chan, Chan and Karolyi partition returns into five minute intervals. (The MMI (Major Market Index) over July 1984–June 1985, is also studied, but more on this later).

Simple computations of autocorrelations and cross correlations between the two markets show that lead/lag relationships exist for returns and changes in volatilities across the two markets. To capture this dependence, a bivariate AR(1)-Garch(1,3) model is fitted to the joint cash and futures stock index return processes. Standard maximum likelihood estimation with a conditional normal density function is employed.

The bivariate Garch model fits the data well. As expected from previous studies, the estimates are consistent with futures prices leading cash prices. Perhaps more importantly, however, the evidence shows that the futures volatility affects the cash market volatility, and vice versa. Tests using the MMI confirm these results, indicating that this interdependence is not due to asynchronous trading.

In summary, these four papers all demonstrate that there are predictable time series patterns in volatilities, either within the day or across days. Volatilities are predictable based on trading versus non-trading hours, open-middle-close hours, at regularly scheduled news announcement times, and after related market volatilities (cash versus futures) change. In an efficient market, these predictable patterns should be reflected in option prices. Of the papers considered so far, only Donders and Vorst shows that this is the case. For the other patterns, this demonstration awaits subsequent research.

The last paper in this section, by Xinzhong Xu and Stephen Taylor, studies the interday time series properties of implied volatilities and the term structure (in maturity) of implied volatilities as obtained from the Black-Scholes formula. Two different estimation procedures are considered – a standard regression procedure and Kalman filtering. Foreign currency options on the Deutschmark, Japanese yen, Swiss franc, and pound sterling are used. Daily closing prices are obtained from the Philadelphia Stock Exchange over the time period January 1985 to November 1989. To compute implied volatilities, since the options are American, the Barone-Adesi-Whaley approximation is employed, using only the "nearest" at-the-money options.

The regression results show that persistence in implied volatilities exists. An initial shock (increase) in the implied volatility suggests that subsequent implied volatilities will also be larger than average. More interesting, however, is the evidence on the term structure of the implied volatilities. Two different implied volatilities were studied, a long- and short-term volatility. Perhaps surprisingly, both the long- and short-term implied volatilities are random (non-constant), often crossing – the long term is not always greater than the short term. Further, as might be expected, the short-term volatility is more variable than the long-term volatility. The more sophisticated Kalman filtering model also confirms these results.

Xu and Taylor's analysis provides evidence inconsistent with the Black-Scholes model. Indeed, the Black-Scholes model assumes (at most) that volatilities are deterministic. This hypothesis is obviously rejected by the data in their study for foreign currency options. But these results are of more use than for model selection alone. As market prices are in a one-to-one correspondence with implied volatilities, these patterns can still be useful for speculation and hedging. Even with a misspecified model, if implied volatilities can be predicted, then market prices can be predicted as well.

7

Information Noise and Stock Return Volatility:

Evidence from Germany*

G. Geoffrey Booth and Mustafa Chowdhury
Louisiana State University, Federal Home Loan Mortgage Corporation

Using data from the Frankfurt Stock Exchange, this paper investigates the impact of an increase in trading hours (from two to three on January 15, 1990) on the variance of stock returns. The results confirm those of most earlier studies that report that trading time volatility is significantly larger than non-trading time volatility. In addition, the results are consistent with the private and public information hypotheses with regard to stock return volatility, but they do not support the noise trading hypothesis.

It is now a stylised fact that stock returns are more volatile when the market is open than when it is closed. Public information, private information, and noise trading "stories" have been given to explain this phenomenon. Using New York Stock Exchange data, however, French and Roll (1986) reject the flow of public information story. In a similar study of the Tokyo Stock Exchange, Barclay, Litzenberger and Warner (1990) reject both public information and noise trading stories. Both these studies, however, support the private information explanation. The purpose of this paper is to continue this research agenda using data from the Frankfurt Stock Exchange (FSE). It confirms that stock return variances are larger during trading hours than during non-trading hours, and it provides evidence consistent with the private and public information and against the noise trading explanations.

Institutional environment and data

Before January 15, 1990, the FSE opened for floor trading at 11:30am and closed at 1:30pm (Frankfurt time). On January 15, the two-hour trading day was extended to three hours by opening the FSE at 10:30am. The impact of the change in trading hours is investigated by comparing stock return volatilities as measured by variances. Twenty-eight stocks in the Deutscher Aktienindex (DAX) for both 1989 and 1990 are considered. Nine of these stocks are also traded on the International Stock Exchange (ISE) in London, which is open from 10:00am to 6:00pm (Frankfurt time). The data are intradaily prices for the 488 trading days in 1989 and 1990. Open-close, close-open, close-close, and open-open return variances for each stock are calculated. For the three-hour trading day, the open–11:30am and 11:30am–close variances are also calculated, the latter being analogous to the open–close variance in the two-hour period. In all cases, return is defined as the natural logarithm of the price relatives.

Theory and empirical implications

The theory with regard to the sources of volatility is neither conclusive nor clear cut. Kyle (1985) suggests a sequential auction model where privately informed traders incorporate their information into the price, with volatility reflecting the rate at which this incorporation takes place. Assuming risk-neutral market makers, a change in the level of noise trading does not affect volatility because there is an offsetting

* *This paper was first published in* Applied Economics Letters, *Vol. 3 (1996). It is reprinted with permission of Routledge Publishing.*

change in the level of information trading. Kyle's (1985) model has been extended by Admati and Pfleiderer (1988), Bhushan (1991) and Chowdhury and Nanda (1991). None of these models suggests that noise trading itself causes any change in the volatility of stock returns. Subrahmanyan (1991), however, shows that when informed traders are risk averse, noise trading raises price volatility because these traders respond less aggressively to an increase in noise trading than do risk-neutral informed traders. Further, De Long, Scheifer, Summers and Waldman (1990) suggest that presence of a certain type of noise traders, "positive feedback traders", may lead to an increase in volatility. This occurs when informed speculators, rather than taking positions opposite to the positive feedback traders, reinforce the market price movement (away from its fundamental value).

There are three implications of the above models that are testable with the available FSE data. First, the trading hours increased by 50%, while non-trading hours decreased by 4.5%. Since an important hour was taken away from the non-trading hours, the close-open variance is expected to decline by more than 4.5%. Further, if the rate of public information flow is uniform throughout the trading day, the open–close variance is expected to increase by less than 50%. These expectations are based on the notion that trading time variances are generated by public information, private information, and noise trading but non-trading time variances are only attributable to public information. Therefore, an increase in the flow of public information is likely to increase the total variance by a smaller amount, assuming that rate of flow of public information is the same during the two-year period. It is, however, possible that 1990 contained much more information than 1989 because of such unusual events as the reunification of Germany and the Gulf War. One way to control for this possibility is to compare the variance associated with the first hour of trading to the variance of the remaining two hours of trading. The variance ratios should not exceed one-half if the change in overall variance is consistent with the public information story.

Second, if the total amount of private information is constant and if informed traders release their information gradually, some of the variability associated with private information shifts from the 11:30am to 1:30pm period to 10:30am to 11:30am period. Kyle's model, however, suggests that open–close variance does not change because of the extra hour of trading. Nevertheless, for the stocks that are traded on the FSE and ISE, there is a private information related increase in open–close variance. This occurs because part of private information is released through London trading. Therefore, what was the close–open return includes this private information, which is now shifted to open-close returns. This suggests that there is a larger decline in close–open variance for FSE and ISE traded stocks than FSE-only traded stocks.

Finally, if increased trading hours attract additional noise trading and the informed traders are risk averse, there may be an increase in open–close variances and an increase in the negative correlation (or a decrease in positive correlation) between open–close and close–open returns. This occurs because part of the increased volatility during the open-close period is a result of mispricing. If this mispricing in the open–close period is corrected during the subsequent close-open period, the correlation is negative (Summers, 1986).

Empirical results

Table 1 presents the average of the ratio of open–close, close–open and close–close variances of the three-hour trading period to the corresponding variances of the two-hour trading period. The figures in parentheses in Table 1 are the median signed Levene W10 statistics (Brown and Forsythe, 1974). Prior to calculating the variances, the returns are adjusted either by removing the sample mean and or by eliminating the market effect via the market model (an equally weighted portfolio proxies the market). Both the mean-adjusted and market-adjusted returns are considered because it is often assumed that the variance generated by private information tends to be firm specific while the variance generated by noise trading tends to be marketwide. The

Table 1. Three-hour to two-hour trading day variance ratios

	Open–close	Close–open	Close–close
Mean-adjusted returns			
Stocks traded	2.43	0.65	1.16
on FSE only	(19.3)	(–0.13)	(3.25)
Stocks traded	2.96	1.20	1.65
on FSE and ISE	(26.12)	(4.31)	(12.66)
Market-adjusted returns			
Stocks traded	1.87	0.91	1.27
on FSE	(14.0)	(–0.84)	(2.65)
Stocks traded	2.13	1.37	1.44
on FSE and ISE	(5.79)	(.58)	(3.50)

Median signed Levene's W10 statistics are in parentheses and are distributed as F(1,485), with the 5% critical value being 3.84.

variance generated by publicly available information, however, may be either.

The statistical results in the first column of Table 1 indicate that stocks traded on the FSE only and traded on the FSE and ISE experienced a significant increase in both the total and the firm-specific variance of open–close returns. For both groups of stocks, the increase in the total variance is, however, somewhat higher than the increase in the firm-specific variance. In the case of the stocks traded on the FSE only, the close–open variance declines in both cases, but not significantly so. Nevertheless, the decline is sufficient to make the change in the close–close variance not significantly different from zero. One reason that the decline is not significant, albeit sufficient to offset the increase in open–close variance, is that the percentage decrease in the close–open hours is relatively small compared to the percentage increase in open–close hours. That the close–close variances do not change significantly suggests that any increase in variance is not due to noise trading.

The close–open and close–close variance ratios for the mean-adjusted returns for those stocks traded on the FSE and ISE are different from those that are traded on the FSE only. The variance ratio results for the market-adjusted returns for the stock groups are similar. In particular, the variance of the mean-adjusted close–close returns of the those stocks that are traded on both exchanges increases. Since the firm-specific close–close variances do not change significantly, this increase can be attributed to either an increase in noise trading or an increase in the flow of marketwide public information during the three-hour trading period. Two additional factors support the public information hypothesis. First, the close–close variances for market indices in the US and the UK whose markets did not experience a change in trading hours, increased. For instance, the S&P 500 and the FTSE-30 close–close variance ratios are 1.40 and 1.37, respectively. Second, the FSE and ISE traded firms tend to be significantly larger in capitalisation than those only traded on the FSE and have above the median FSE trading volume. This is consistent with the notion that these firms tend to be relatively more affected by the global and national events.

One of the implications of the noise trading hypothesis is that a change in price during a trading session is offset, at least partially, by a price movement in the opposite direction overnight. The presence of this phenomenon, as pointed out by Lo and MacKinlay (1988), is able to be detected by variance ratio tests. Only variance ratios for mean-market adjusted returns are considered because of the conjecture that noise is market determined. These tests and the relevant variance ratios are presented in Table 2. The first and the second columns contain the ratio of the variance of close–close returns to the sum of close–open and subsequent open–close variances for the two-hour and three-hour trading days, respectively. The third and the fourth columns contain a similar variance ratio but the numerator is the variance of the open–open returns instead of the variance of the close–close returns. The magnitude of these ratios are determined by the covariance between close-open returns and open-close returns. If the close–open returns are independent of the open–close returns, these variance ratios equal one. An increase in noise trading is consistent with a decrease in these ratios. An examination of the close–close variance ratios indicates this did not happen when the FSE extended its hours. In the case of the open–open variance ratios, the amount of positive autocorrelation decreased but this decrease is not significant at the 5% level, assuming that the variance ratios are normally distributed and independent (see Lo and MacKinlay, 1989). Thus, there is no evidence of increased mispricing corrections, which is non-supportive of the noise trading hypothesis.

Table 2. Dependency ratios

	Close–close		Open–open	
	Two-hour trading day	Three-hour trading day	Two-hour trading day	Three-hour trading day
Mean-adjusted returns				
Stocks traded	.93	1.01	1.12	1.11
on FSE only	(.03)	(.02)	(.02)	(.02)
Stocks traded	1.03	1.06	1.16	1.13
on FSE and ISE	(.03)	(.02)	(.02)	(.03)

Standard errors are in parentheses.

Conclusion

This paper studies the effect of an increase in trading hours on return variance using FSE data. It confirms the results of most of the earlier studies that report that trading time volatility is significantly higher than non-trading time volatility. The increase in volatility brought about by adding an extra trading hour can be partially explained by the shift of privately informed trading to this hour from other trading hours and by more public information being released during this hour compared to average non-trading hour. The noise trading explanation is not supported.

BIBLIOGRAPHY

Admati, A., and P. Pfleiderer, 1988, "A theory of intraday trading patterns: volume and price variability", *Review of Financial Studies* 1, pp. 3-40.

Barclay, M. J., R. Litzenberger and J.B. Warner, 1990, "Private information, trading volume and stock return variances", *Review of Financial Studies* 3, pp.233-53.

Bhushan, R., 1991, "Trading costs, liquidity and asset holdings", *Review of Financial Studies* 4, pp.343-60.

Brown, M., and A. Forsythe, 1974, "Robust tests for equality of variances", *Journal of the American Statistical Association* 69, pp. 364-67.

Chowdhury B., and V. Nanda, 1991, "Multimarket trading and market liquidity", *Review of Financial Studies* 4, pp. 483-511.

De Long, J.B., A. Scheifer, L.H. Summers, and R.J. Waldman, 1990, "Noise trader risk in financial markets", *Journal of Political Economy* 98, pp. 703-38.

French, K.R., and R. Roll, 1986, "Stock return variances: The arrival of information and the reaction of traders", *Journal of Financial Economics* 17, pp. 5-26.

Kyle, A., 1985, "Continuous auctions and insider trading", *Econometrica* 53, pp. 1315-35.

Lo, A. W., and C. A. MacKinlay, 1988, "Stock market prices do not follow random walks: evidence from a simple specification test", *Review of Financial Studies* 1, pp. 41-66.

Lo, A. W., and C. A. MacKinlay, 1989, "The size and power of the variance ratio test in finite samples: a Monte Carlo investigation", *Journal of Econometrics* 40, pp. 203-38.

Subrahmanyan, A., 1991, "Risk aversion, market liquidity, and price efficiency", *Review of Financial Studies* 4, pp. 17-51.

Summers, L. H., 1986, "Does the stock market rationally reflect fundamental values?", *Journal of Finance* 41, pp. 591-600.

8

The Impact of Firm-Specific News on Implied Volatilities*

Monique W.M. Donders and Ton C.F. Vorst
Institute for Research and Investment Services, Rotterdam; Department of Finance, Erasmus University, Rotterdam

We study the implied volatility behaviour of call options around scheduled news announcement days. Implied volatilities increase significantly during the pre-event period and reach a maximum on the eve of the news announcement. After the news release, implied volatility drops sharply and gradually moves back to its long-run level. Only on the event date are movements in the price of the underlying significantly larger than expected. These results confirm the theoretical results of Merton (1973).

This paper examines the behaviour of implied volatilities of call option prices around scheduled news announcements. In an efficient securities market we expect stock prices to adjust to new information very quickly. Patell and Wolfson (1984) find an initial price reaction to earnings and dividend announcements within a few minutes on the New York Stock Exchange (NYSE), but disturbances in the variance persist for several hours. Ederington and Lee (1993) examine the impact of scheduled macroeconomic news on interest rate and foreign exchange futures. They find that volatility is substantially higher than normal for roughly 15 minutes after the news release and slightly elevated for several hours.

There are different ways to model a volatility process that incorporates large movements in the asset price. The most well-known models describing changing volatilities over time are the autoregressive conditional heteroskedasticity (Arch) models, originally introduced by Engle (1982) and extended to generalised Arch (Garch) models by Bollerslev (1986) and exponential Garch (Egarch) models by Nelson (1990). Bollerslev et al (1992) provide an excellent survey on the theory and evidence of these models for financial time series. One important characteristic of this family of models, however, is that a period of high volatility is assumed to follow a large movement in the price of the asset, whereas in an efficient market we expect uncertainty to decrease after new information is released. Although predictable volatility models like the Garch family are useful in valuing derivative instruments, it is not clear that the implications for option values of these one shot increases in volatility due to scheduled news announcements are covered by the standard forms of these models. However, we show that Garch models with an additional structural break in volatility might better describe these implications.[1]

A jump diffusion process might better describe the shock in the price of the underlying stock on the earnings announcement day. Merton (1976) and Amin (1993) consider the valuation of options under this kind of process. However, in a jump diffusion process the exact time of a

* *This paper was first published in the* Journal of Banking & Finance, *Vol. 20 (1996). It is reprinted with kind permission of Elsevier Science NL, Sara Burgerhartstraat 25, 1055 KV Amsterdam, The Netherlands. We acknowledge the helpful comments and suggestions of Werner de Bondt, Frank de Jong, Frank Kleibergen, Teun Kloek, Eva Liljeblom, Michael Rockinger and two anonymous referees as well as participants in the May 1994 Workshop on Empirical Research in Securities Markets at EIASM, the 1994 AFFI, EFA and NFA conferences, the INQUIRE 1994 meeting, the 15th AMEX Options and Derivatives Colloquium and the Fifth Annual Derivatives Conference at Cornell University. We thank the EOE-Optiebeurs for providing the data and Marco Lavooi for excellent research assistance. The usual disclaimer applies.*

jump in the stock price is unknown, whereas scheduled news announcement dates are, by definition, known in advance.

Markets' expectations of future volatility are reflected in the implied volatilities of option prices. According to Merton (1973), the implied volatility of a European option is equal to the average volatility over the remaining life of the option if volatility is a deterministic function of time. Heynen et al (1994) show that the same result approximately holds for at-the-money options if volatility is stochastic or follows an Egarch process. For these models, the implied volatility is equal to the average expected volatility of the asset over the remaining life of the option.

If investors sense more uncertainty about the stock price on the eve of a news release than on other days, the average expected volatility, and hence the implied volatility, should increase during the pre-announcement period. After the stock price adjusts to the new information, volatility will drop to its normal level.

We use the event study methodology to study the influence of scheduled news announcements on implied volatilities. We find that implied volatility rises during the pre-announcement period, reaches a maximum just before the news release and drops sharply afterward. This result holds both for the raw data as well as for implied volatilities that are adjusted for general market movements in volatility. Furthermore, we examine the behaviour of the variance of returns of the underlying assets and conclude that, except for the event day itself, this volatility is not significantly different from its normal level in the period surrounding an announcement. This means that the increase in implied volatility cannot be explained by higher variance of stock returns before the news announcement.

1. Average volatility and Garch volatility around announcement days

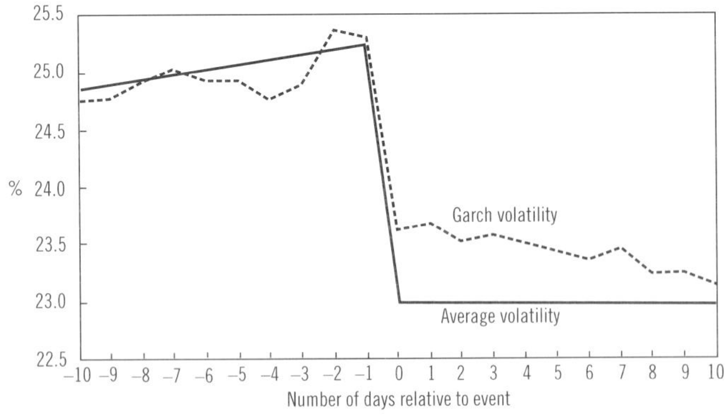

Parameter values for the simulated Garch process are $\alpha_0 = 0.000015$, $\alpha_1 = 0.8$, $\alpha_2 = 0.1$, $\kappa = 0.5$, $r = 0.05$, $\lambda = 0.05$ and $\beta_u = 5/4$, $\beta_d = 5/9$. Simulation for asset prices starts at 110 days before the event day at a fixed asset price and the stationary volatility, which is 0.231869 for these parameter values. At-the-money options with maturity date 40 days after the event have been used; 10,000 Monte Carlo simulations are used to compute the Garch option prices and from these prices implied volatilities are calculated for the Black–Scholes formula. This simulation is repeated 50 times to compute the average implied volatilities around the event day.

We find one important difference between the theoretical and empirical patterns in implied volatilities: the implied volatility 10 days before an announcement is lower than expected. We test a trading strategy using call options and the underlying asset that may profit from this "overreaction" in implied volatilities and find that, when taking transactions costs into account, it does not yield significant returns. The market seems to be efficient in the sense that large shocks in the stock price coincide with large reductions in future volatility.

This paper is organised as follows. The following section presents a model on the behaviour of implied volatilities around scheduled news announcements. We continue by discussing the test methodology and the data. The empirical analysis follows together with a discussion of the empirical results.

Theory

In this chapter we concentrate on "scheduled news", for which the disclosure date is known in advance but the information content is not. In the Black and Scholes (1973) pricing model for European type options it is assumed that the volatility of the underlying stock is constant over time. However, if volatility is a deterministic function of time, Merton (1973) shows that the Black-Scholes formula still holds if we replace the volatility by the average volatility until expiration. Daily stock price returns are random variables that might be independently and identically distributed on normal days. During scheduled news announcement days, however, a higher volatility is expected. If volatility on a normal day is σ^2_{normal} and on unexpected news announcement day is equal to σ^2_{high}, then average volatility AV_x over the remaining life of the option if the announcement has not occurred yet is defined as

$$AV_x = \sqrt{\frac{(x-1)}{x}\sigma^2_{normal} + \frac{1}{x}\sigma^2_{high}} \qquad (1)$$

where x is the number of days until the expiration date of the option. After the news announcement day, the average volatility drops to σ^2_{normal} (assuming there are no other scheduled information releases before expiration). With this simple model the implied volatility, as a function of the time until and after the expected news announcement, can be described by the function depicted by the solid line in Figure 1.

It is well known that volatilities are not constant over time and the assumption that the volatility is constant except for scheduled news announcement days does not seem very realistic. However, Heynen et al (1994) show that for the option-pricing model of Hull and White (1987), which is based on a stochastic volatility process, the implied volatility in option prices is approximately equal to average expected volatility until the expiration date. They also show that the same result holds under the assumption that stock prices follow a Garch or Egarch process and option prices are based on the model developed by Duan (1995). If the volatility during non-announcement days can be described by, for example, a Garch model and if the peaks in volatility on scheduled news announcement days are large compared to the fluctuations due to the Garch specification, we can use the following extension, which exhibits a structural break in volatility in the news announcement date:

$$\ln\left(\frac{X_{t+1}}{X_t}\right) = r + \lambda\sigma_{t+1} - \frac{1}{2}\sigma_{t+1}^2 + \sigma_{t+1}\varepsilon_{t+1}, \quad (2)$$

$$\sigma_{t+1}^2 = \left[\alpha_0 + \alpha_1\sigma_t^2 + \alpha_2\sigma_t^2(\varepsilon_t - \kappa)^2\right]$$
$$\left[1 + \chi_{t+1=t^*}\beta_u - \chi_{t+1=t^*+1}\beta_d\right]^2 \quad (3)$$

with X_t, the underlying stock price, r the riskless interest rate, λ the market price of risk, σ_t the volatility, ε_{t+1}, conditional on the time t information, a standard normal random variable, t^* the event date and χ an indicator function. α_0, α_1, α_2, β_u and β_d are constants. If we set $\beta_u = \beta_d = 0$ in Equation (3), the non-linear asymmetrical Garch model of Engle and Ng (1993) results. The parameters β_u and β_d determine the magnitude of the increase and decrease in volatility around the event day.

Invoking the local risk-neutralisation principle of Duan (1995), theoretical option prices and hence implied volatilities can be calculated with respect to the risk-neutral probability measure.

To illustrate the properties of this model, the behaviour of implied volatility around event days for this model is depicted by the dotted line in Figure 1 for a certain set of parameter values. It is clear that the extended Garch model and our simple average volatility model yield basically the same patterns. Although there are some differences, both lines basically reveal the same pattern in implied volatilities.

The solid line in Figure 1 describes the hypothesis about implied volatilities that is tested in this paper. In addition to the pattern in implied volatilities we also test the assumption that the underlying asset has a significantly higher volatility only on the scheduled news announcement day and not in the pre- and post-event periods. As changes in returns and (implied) volatilities of individual stocks might not only result from firm specific circumstances but can also be caused by general market trends, we correct for these market wide changes in (implied) volatility.

Methodology

DATA

Announcements The announcement sample contains 96 scheduled news disclosures released by 23 firms during the period June 1991–December 1992. During this period, stocks of these firms were listed on the Amsterdam Stock Exchange (ASE) and options on the stocks were listed on the European Options Exchange (EOE).

We used *Beursplein 5* (a weekly information bulletin of the ASE) to identify scheduled news announcement dates. Using the *Financieele Dagblad (FD)*, we checked whether on these dates a news item on the particular event did indeed occur. Of the initial 143 announcements, 47 did not appear in FD.[2] The average number of days between the official publication of the announcement day and the actual information release is 78.5 days. As the announcements frequently concern quarterly (28), semi-annual (43) or annual (22) earnings disclosures, and as most listed firms have a fiscal year ending in December, the announcements are clustered in time.

Implied volatilities Daily records for each traded call option were obtained from the EOE for the period June 18, 1991 through December 30, 1992. We only include records that satisfy the following criteria:

❑ the option has at least ten days to maturity

❑ the option has a bid price and an ask price that are both larger than zero

❑ the average of the bid price and the ask price is greater than or equal to f0.20.

We impose these criteria for the following reasons. De Jong et al (1992) find a slight reduction in volatility around expiration days. To avoid this effect, we eliminate very short maturity calls.

The minimum tick size on the EOE is f0.10. As the influence of rounding errors in option prices smaller than f0.20 is too large to make accurate estimates of implied volatilities, we eliminate these. To avoid the effect of bid-ask bouncing on consecutive days, we use the average of the bid price and the ask price as an estimate for the "true" price of an option. Both prices must therefore be larger than zero. For every day and each option class we follow Beckers (1981) by selecting only the option with the shortest time to maturity and the smallest absolute moneyness to calculate the implied volatility. We define moneyness as the ratio of the stock price net of the present value of dividends to be paid during the life of the option to the present value of the exercise price minus 1. To incorporate the early exercise premium due to dividend payments we apply the Roll-Geske-Whaley formula (Hull, 1993) for American options on dividend paying stocks. This formula is valid because our sample does not contain any options with more than one dividend payment during the remaining life of the option. We use a Newton Raphson iterative search to calculate the implied volatilities.

The interest rate used is the Amsterdam Interbank Offered Rate (Aibor) with maturity closest to the maturity of the option. These Aibor rates are obtained from Datastream. Dividend data are collected from EOE publications, the *Effectengids* and the *Officiële Prijscourant*. We use actual dividends instead of market expectations. Since we only use options with a relative short time to maturity, we assume that there is no uncertainty regarding the amount of dividend paid. The recorded stock price is the price from the last transaction in that stock on the ASE.

We control for market wide changes in volatility in two different ways. First, for every implied volatility, we subtract the implied volatility of the EOE index option with the same time to maturity as the stock option. This index consists of 25 stocks, including the 23 stocks studied in this chapter. A second way to correct for market-wide changes in volatility, following Sheikh (1989), is using control stocks. For every trading day, betas for all stocks are estimated by an OLS regression of the previous 120 daily total returns on the returns of the EOE index. Five groups of stocks[3] of comparable betas and standard deviations are formed. For every control group we calculate the implied volatility on each day as being the average of the implied volatilities of stocks that do not have an announcement in the 10 days preceding or following this day. The control groups are formed in such a way that, for every day, there is at least one such stock for every control group.

TESTS

We are interested in comparing cross-sectional volatilities and implied volatilities during the periods around the scheduled news announcements to the volatilities and implied volatilities during normal periods. To see whether these differences are significant, a number of tests are used that are described below and are based on section 16.5 of Davidson and MacKinnon (1993). Let

$$r_{jt} = \ln S_{jt} - \ln S_{jt-1} \quad (4)$$

be the logarithmic return for stock j during day t and define the extra return R_{jt} as

$$R_{jt} = r_{jt} - \frac{1}{T}\sum_{t=1}^{T} r_{jt} \quad (5)$$

where T is the length of the total observation period. Let

$$V_{jt} = \sqrt{R_{jt}^2}$$

be the so-called "volatility on day t". For each event we distinguish four periods:

I_{j1}: the period from T_1 to 1 day before the event date - the pre-event period;

I_{j2}: the event day;

I_{j3}: the period from 1 day to T_3 days after the event - the post-event period;

I_{j4}: the control period, all days not included in an I_{j1}, I_{j2} or I_{j3} period, T_4 days.

We define the excess volatility of stock j on day t as

$$EV_{jt} = V_{jt} - \frac{1}{T_4}\sum_{t \in I_{j4}} V_{jt} \quad (6)$$

and dummy-variables x_1, x_2, and x_3:

$$x_{j1t} = \begin{cases} 1 & \text{if } t \in I_{j1} \\ 0 & \text{otherwise} \end{cases}$$
$$x_{j2t} = \begin{cases} 1 & \text{if } t \in I_{j2} \\ 0 & \text{otherwise} \end{cases}$$
$$x_{j3t} = \begin{cases} 1 & \text{if } t \in I_{j3} \\ 0 & \text{otherwise} \end{cases}. \quad (7)$$

To test for heteroskedasticity we use a GMM regression with Newey-West standard errors to estimate

$$EV_{jt} = c + \alpha_1 x_{j1t} + \alpha_2 x_{j2t} + \alpha_3 x_{j3t} + \varepsilon_{jt} \forall j, t. \quad (8)$$

The t-values of the coefficients α_1, α_2 and α_3 indicate whether the volatilities in the three sub-periods are statistically different from those in the control period.

We use the same regression equation to test for heteroskedasticity in implied volatilities by replacing V_{jt} with the implied volatilities. EIV_{jt} is the excess implied volatility.

Results

STOCK RETURN VOLATILITIES

For the simple model of implied volatilities in (1) to hold, the standard deviation of stock returns should only be different from their control-period level on the event day and not in the pre- and post-event periods. To test this hypothesis, we apply the regression in Equation 8 to both raw stock return volatilities (Equation 9a) and EOE index-adjusted returns (Equation 9b); t-values are in brackets:

$$EV_{jt} = 0.00015 + \underset{(2.62)}{0.00108}x_{j1t} + \underset{(10.16)}{0.01256}x_{j2t} + \underset{(1.42)}{0.00058}x_{j3t} + \varepsilon_{jt}, \quad (9a)$$

$$EV_{jt} = 0.00012 + \underset{(1.28)}{0.00046}x_{j1t} + \underset{(12.11)}{0.01312}x_{j2t} + \underset{(1.98)}{0.00071}x_{j3t} + \varepsilon_{jt}. \quad (9b)$$

The pre-event and post-event periods consist of 10 days.

Although the coefficient for x_{j1t} in Equation 9a is slightly significant, it is of a different order of magnitude from the coefficient for x_{j2t}. Both Equation 9b and Figure 2 show that the (EOE index-adjusted) volatility of stock returns during the pre-event period and the post-event period does not differ significantly from the volatility during periods without scheduled news announcements. It is clear, however, that the volatility on the event day differs significantly from the volatility during other periods. Results for control-group adjusted volatilities do not differ significantly from those for EOE index-adjusted volatilities and are available from the author upon request. We conclude that the underlying assumptions of the models as described above seem to hold.

IMPLIED VOLATILITIES

Figure 3 gives the (EOE index-adjusted) average implied volatilities (IV) in the period from 10 days before the event until 10 days after the event. On each day this average is calculated as the sum of the implied volatilities of the individual announcements divided by the number of announcements. The horizontal solid lines in the graphs give the long-run level of the implied volatility. This long-run level of the implied volatility is the weighted average of implied volatilities of the 23 stocks over the control period. Each stock is weighted with the number of events for that stock.

2. Stock return volatilities around event days

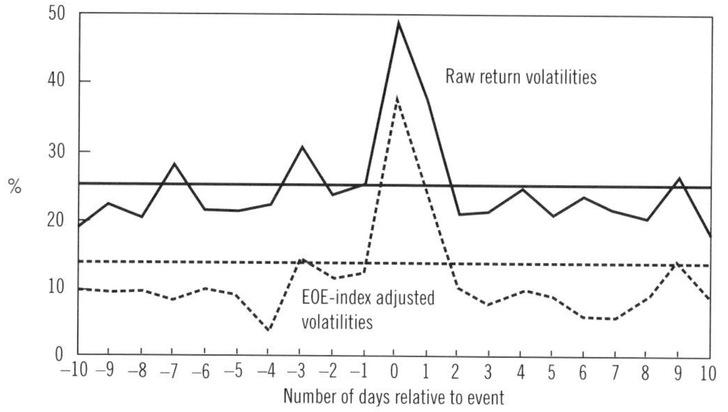

3. Implied volatility around event days

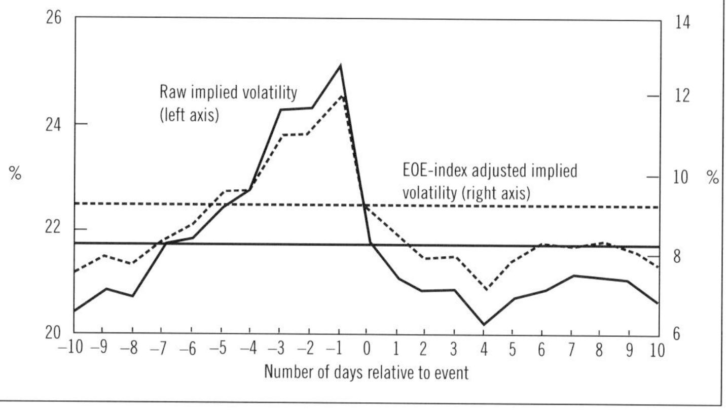

Both graphs peak just before the scheduled news announcement date. After the announcement, the implied volatility is sharply lower.

The decline in implied volatilities from approximately 25% to 22% means a price drop of 13% for a typical option in our sample. For implied volatilities, we slightly adjust (8). Instead of one dummy variable for the pre-event period, we introduce a trend variable $x^*_{j1t} = (T_1 + 1 + t)$ $\forall t \in [-T_1,\ldots,-1]$, which increases as the number of days till the event declines. The regression equation is given by (t-values in brackets):

$$EIV_{jt} = -0.00405 + \underset{(6.03)}{0.00509}x^*_{j1t} + \underset{(1.30)}{0.00987}x_{j2t} + \underset{(0.30)}{0.00079}x_{j3t} + \varepsilon_{jt}, \quad (10a)$$

$$EIV_{jt} = -0.00379 + \underset{(6.25)}{0.00468}x^*_{j1t} + \underset{(1.32)}{0.00889}x_{j2t} - \underset{(-0.44)}{0.00100}x_{j3t} + \varepsilon_{jt}. \quad (10b)$$

Table 1. Changes in implied volatilities of option prices around announcement dates*

Days	Events	N+	N−	Median % change	Wilcoxon
Panel A. Post-event period average IV as compared to pre-event period average IV					
10	85	23	62	−6.99	−4.879
9	87	21	66	−7.67	−5.350
8	87	21	66	−8.54	−5.896
7	87	19	68	−9.74	−6.222
6	88	18	70	−9.77	−6.453
5	88	17	71	−10.45	−6.612
4	89	15	74	−9.87	−6.499
3	90	13	77	−9.66	−6.460
2	92	21	71	−8.23	−5.506
1	92	20	72	−8.51	−4.984
Panel B. Post-event period average IV as compared to pre-event period average IV, using EOE-index adjusted IVs ($IV_i - IV_{EOE\text{-}index}$)					
10	85	26	59	−5.94	−3.227
9	87	27	60	−18.55	−3.496
8	87	25	62	−21.16	−4.101
7	87	24	63	−21.71	−4.160
6	88	24	64	−24.65	−4.148
5	88	25	63	−26.15	−4.369
4	89	23	66	−27.89	−4.433
3	90	19	71	−30.68	−4.912
2	92	27	65	−27.75	−3.773
1	92	26	66	−18.80	−2.566
Panel C. Post-event period average IV as compared to pre-event period average IV, using control-group adjusted IVs ($IV_i - IV_{control\text{-}group}$)					
10	85	30	55	−35.74	−2.890
9	87	33	54	−29.14	−2.607
8	87	35	52	−23.71	−1.955
7	87	32	55	−33.32	−2.476
6	88	33	55	−33.29	−2.401
5	88	32	56	−31.21	−1.789
4	89	32	57	−40.02	−2.318
3	90	33	57	−33.82	−1.978
2	92	32	60	−32.23	−2.083
1	92	32	60	−25.17	−2.403

* The changes are for 95 announcements of "scheduled" news over the period June 18, 1991 through December 30, 1992. In Panel A we use IVs calculated from call option prices. In Panels B and C we subtract the IVs of the EOE index and the average implied volatility of the group of control stocks respectively. "Days" is the number of days in the pre-event and post-event period. N− (N+) denotes the number of events for which the average IV in the post-event period was smaller (larger) than the average IV in the pre-event period. "Median % change" gives the median percentage change between the post-event period IV and pre-event period IV, averaged over all events. "Events" gives the number of events for which IVs could be calculated for every day in the pre-event and post-event period. "Wilcoxon" is the Wilcoxon signed-rank statistic for the hypothesis that the sum of the plus ranks equals the sum of the minus ranks.

As in (9a), the pre-event and post-event periods consist of 10 days. Equations (10a) and (10b) show that during the pre-event period the rise in (EOE index-adjusted) implied volatility is highly significant, whereas in the post-event period the implied volatility is not significantly different from that in the control period. Control group-adjusted implieds yield similar results. These results are comparable to those found by Patell and Wolfson (1979).

In Panel A of Table 1 the implied volatilities of individual stocks are compared for the pre- and post-event period. For each stock the average implied volatility over a fixed number of days before the event is compared with the average implied volatility of the same number of days, including the event date, after the event. N− gives the number of events for which the post-event average implied volatility is lower and N+ gives the number of events for which the post-event average implied volatility is higher. For example, in the period of three days before the event the implied volatility was higher than for the period of three days after the event in 77 out of 90 cases. Also, the median percentage change in implied volatilities for all stocks is given. In Panel B and C the same numbers are given for the index-adjusted and control-group adjusted implied volatilities respectively.

From Table 1 and the cross-sectional regressions (10a) and (10b), we may conclude that Figure 3 is in many respects similar to the theoretical Figure 1. The drop in implied volatilities on the event day is significant (the last row of every panel in Table 1). Before the news announcement the implied volatility is significantly higher than the implied volatility in the period after the event.

Figures 1 and 3 differ with respect to the first days in the pre-event period. Since the exact dates of the news releases are known well in advance, the empirical implied volatility for these days are lower than theoretically expected. Furthermore, the implied volatility drops below its long-run level in the four days (t-statistic: -1.987) after the event, which is not explained by the model.

EVENT-DAY RETURNS AND IMPLIED VOLATILITIES

To determine whether a large shock in the price of the underlying asset at the event day coincides with a large reduction in uncertainty about future stock price returns, we regress the absolute value of market model residual returns on an event day on the differences in implied volatility on the event day and the pre-event day. The following equation results:

$$|R_{j0}| = 0.0169 - \underset{(-2.001)}{0.0024} DIV_j + \varepsilon_j \qquad (11)$$

with $|R_{j0}|$ the absolute value of the market model adjusted return for stock j on the event day and $DIV_j = IV_{j,0} - IV_{j,-1}$ the difference between the implied volatility on the event day and the implied volatility on the pre-event day. Since the estimated coefficient is significant, we conclude that large price shocks are correlated with large reductions of uncertainty.

Alternatively, the market predicts large shocks by significantly increasing the implied volatility before an announcement.

TRADING STRATEGY

As noticed before, Figure 3 exhibits roughly the same shape as Figure 1. Hence, the hypothesis in (1) seems to hold. Options have a higher implied volatility before the event because average expected volatility is higher and hence the replication costs increase. There is one remarkable difference between Figure 3 and Figure 1, however. Both raw implied volatilities and adjusted implied volatilities are approximately at their long-run level 10 days before and 10 days after the event. Figure 1 predicted the result for 10 days after the event. The average implied volatility 10 days before the event is too low compared to the model in Figure 1, however. Although the hypothesis in the "theory" section of this chapter seems to hold, there might also be a secondary effect in the market that can explain the difference with Figure 1. Just before a scheduled news announcement there are market participants who speculate on a large increase in the stock price. Instead of buying stocks, investors buy call options because of the higher leverage of these instruments and the limited downside risk in case the stock price falls in reaction to the new information. There is hence a higher demand for call options. This increases the price and the implied volatility. Thus, the observed implied volatility might be higher than the theoretical implied volatility in Figure 1.

We consider a trading strategy that profits from this overreaction. Ten days before the event we buy a call option and short the underlying stock to obtain a delta-neutral portfolio. Each trading day the stock position is adjusted to changes in the hedge ratio of the option. Daily trading profits and losses are assumed to yield the AIBOR rate. The portfolio is liquidated on the day before the event day, when the implied volatility, and with that the call-option value, reach a maximum.

The average return over all events for this strategy is 49.69% (Wilcoxon signed-rank statistic 3.27) of the initial option value. Of course, this strategy involves both implicit and explicit transaction costs. Since explicit transaction costs such as commissions and fees differ dramatically across investors, we only consider implicit transaction costs due to the bid–ask spread. Quoted bid and ask prices for all options are in the dataset. Unfortunately, there are no quoted spreads available for ASE stocks. Interviews with brokers, however, indicate that, on a normal trading day, these spreads vary from f0.10 (the minimum ticksize) for the stocks with the highest liquidity to f0.50 for smaller stocks. Taking the bid–ask spread for both options and stocks into account, we find a return on the delta-neutral position of –2.34% (Wilcoxon signed-rank statistic 1.12). Hence, this trading strategy does not yield economically significant returns, indicating that the European Options Exchange functions efficiently.[4]

Conclusion

This chapter studied the implied volatility of options around scheduled news announcement days of the underlying stock. Implied volatilities increase when the event day approaches. After the news announcement, the implied volatility drops sharply for a few days. It even drops below its long-run level. The volatility of the underlying stock is not different from its control period level during both the pre-event and the post-event period.

On the event date itself, however, volatility seems to be higher. If we use a standard (E)Garch or a stochastic volatility process to model the behaviour of the underlying stocks, we do not detect this one-day increase in volatility. Jump diffusion option pricing models are also not suited to describe this kind of phenomenon as these models usually assume that the jumps appear at random. However, the adjusted Garch model described in Equations 2 and 3 indicates a direction for further research to combine a Garch model with exogenous shocks in volatility due to earnings announcements.

The simple model for the volatility of the underlying asset around scheduled news announcements produces a time-dependence in implied volatilities that seems to agree with the pattern we find in the options market. However, the market seems to react too strongly. This overreaction might be caused by trading by investors who speculate on changes in the price of the underlying stock, causing an excess demand for call options before the event. We find a trading strategy that profits from these overreactions. This strategy yields economically insignificant returns when transaction costs are taken into account, indicating that the European Options Exchange functions efficiently.

1 *This approach was suggested by an anonymous referee.*

2 *There were also 45 news items in* Financieele Dagblad *that did not appear in* Beursplein 5 *as announcements. These news items most frequently concern annual stockholder meetings and publication of annual reports. Since we cannot be sure that these news items are "scheduled news" we do not include these in our sample.*

3 *As discussed before, the events are strongly clustered in time. As pre-event and post-event periods of the announcement stock and the control stock must be non-overlapping, in many cases it is not possible to match an announcement stock with a single control stock.*

4 *We also tried a similar trading strategy to profit from the drop of the implied volatility below the long run level four days after the event. This strategy was not profitable even without transaction costs.*

BIBLIOGRAPHY

Amin, K., 1993, "Jump Diffusion Option Valuation in Discrete Time", *Journal of Finance* 48, pp. 1833-63.

Beckers, S., 1981, "Standard Deviations in Option Prices as Predictors of Future Stock Price Variability", *Journal of Banking and Finance* 5, pp. 363-82.

Black, F., and M.J. Scholes, 1973, "The Pricing of Options on Corporate Liabilities", *Journal of Political Economy* 81, pp. 637-59.

Bollerslev. T., 1986, "Generalized Autoregressive Conditional Heteroskedasticity", *Journal of Econometrics* 31, pp. 307-27.

Bollerslev, T., R. Chou and K. Kroner, 1992, "Arch Modelling in Finance: a Review of Theory and Empirical Evidence", *Journal of Econometrics* 52, pp. 5-59; reprinted as Chapter 2 of the present volume.

Davidson, R., and J. G. MacKinnon, 1993, *Estimation and Inference in Econometrics*, New York, Oxford University Press.

De Jong, F., A.G.Z. Kemna and T. Kloek, 1992, "A Contribution to Event Study Methodology with an Application to the Dutch Stock Market", *Journal of Banking and Finance* 16, pp. 11-36.

Duan, J.C., 1995, "The Garch Option Pricing Model", *Mathematical Finance* 5, pp. 13-32; reprinted as Chapter 24 of the present volume.

Ederington, L.H., and J.H. Lee, 1993, "How Markets Process Information: News Releases and Volatility", *Journal of Finance* 48, pp. 1161-91.

Engle, R., 1982, "Autoregressive Conditional Heteroskedasticity with Estimates of the Variance of UK Inflation", *Econometrica* 50, pp. 987-1008.

Engle, R., and V.K. Ng, 1993, "Measuring and Testing the Impact of News on Volatility", *Journal of Finance* 48, pp. 1749-78.

Heynen, R., A. Kemna and T. Vorst, 1994, "Analysis of the Term Structure of Implied Volatilities", *Journal of Financial and Quantitative Analysis* 29, pp. 31-56.

Hull, J., 1993, *Options, Futures and Other Derivative Securities*, Englewood Cliffs, Prentice-Hall.

Hull, J., and A. White, 1987, "The Pricing of Options on Assets with Stochastic Volatilities", *Journal of Finance* 42, pp. 281-300.

Merton, R.C., 1973, "The Theory of Rational Option Pricing", *Bell Journal of Economics and Management Science* 4, pp. 141-83.

Merton, R.C., 1976, "Option Pricing when Underlying Stock Returns are Discontinuous", *Journal of Financial Economics* 3, pp. 125-44.

Nelson, D., 1990, "Conditional Heteroskedasticity in Asset Returns: A New Approach", *Econometrica* 59, pp. 347-70.

Patell, J.M., and M.A. Wolfson, 1979, "Anticipated Information Release Reflected in Call Option Prices," *Journal of Accounting and Economics* 1, 2, pp. 107-40.

Patell, J.M., and M.A. Wolfson, 1984, "The Intraday Speed of Adjustment of Stock Prices to Earnings and Dividend Announcements," *Journal of Financial Economics* 13, pp. 223-52.

Sheikh, A.M., 1989, "Stock Splits, Volatility Increases and Implied Volatilities", *Journal of Finance* 44, pp. 1361-72.

9

Calendar-Adjusted Volatilities*

Galen Burghardt and Gerald A. Hanweck, Jr.
Carr Futures; JP Morgan

Price variability depends on the flow of information into the market, which does not occur smoothly over time. Announcement-day results for an important economic statistic are more volatile than those on an ordinary business day, which are in turn more volatile than on a weekend day. We examine volatility for Deutschmark, Eurodollar, S&P 500 Index, and Treasury bond futures and find significant information release and weekend effects. Eurodollar and T-bond futures are particularly influenced by the release of non-farm payroll and unemployment statistics, while a weekend day contributes almost no volatility for any of the four contracts. Treating all calendar days alike produces misleading estimates of time decay and spurious jumps in implied volatilities. We propose the concept of "economic days," based on the price volatility on each day, as an alternative way of measuring the effective time to maturity of an option. "Implied" economic days corresponding to a particular information event can be derived from the behaviour of implied volatilities in options prices. For example, during the first half of 1993, the Eurodollar futures market valued a payroll announcement at 10.69 economic days, while the market delivered the volatility equivalent of 5.64 economic days.

You don't have to be Stephen Hawking to know that not all spans of time are equally important in the life of an option. Some days, or even moments, can be loaded with events that cause the underlying price to swing widely in one direction or the other. For example, the few seconds surrounding the announcement of an important economic statistic at 7:30 in the morning (Chicago time) are much more important to the fate of an option than the several hours during which the sun is passing over the Pacific Ocean.

In this paper, we show that of all the various economic releases, the announcement of the non-farm payroll and unemployment numbers - typically on the first Friday of each month - has been the richest and most reliable source of interest rate volatility in recent years. As a result, the passing of a payroll announcement day should matter more than the passing of other days, and the rate of time decay should be larger.

One way to handle such a difference is to distinguish among calendar days, business days and "economic" days. We show how to do this and draw out the implications for reckoning implied volatilities. Our "calendar-adjusted volatilities" for options on bond futures suggest that time decay in these options tracks the passing of their reckoning of economic days better than it does the passing of business days.

We also show how to determine the implied economic day value that the options market places on various key announcements and how these can be compared with their historical values. For example, we found that over the first half of 1993, the bond options market considered a payroll announcement to be the equivalent of more than three business days, while the historical volatility associated with these announcements suggests they have been worth only slightly less than two. The Eurodollar market has valued the non-farm payroll announcements at more than ten regular business days, while the historical volatility associated with these

This paper was first published in The Journal of Derivatives, *Winter (1993). Reprinted (with minor amendments) with permission from Institutional Investor, Inc. To order a subscription, or for other information, please call (212) 224 3185.*

announcements has been the equivalent of only slightly more than five.

Variable volatility and option prices

The price of a European-style option depends chiefly on the expected distribution of the underlying's price at the end of the option's life. So does the price of an American-style option, although the paths leading to the distribution can influence the price as well.

In either case, for any given starting price of the underlying commodity, the expected distribution of the underlying's price at the end of the option's life depends on two things:

❑ How changeable the underlying's price is expected to be whenever it has an opportunity to change.

❑ How many opportunities it is given to change.

The first of these is what option traders call volatility. The second is the time left in the option's life. When viewed this way, a piece of news can affect the price of an option in either of two ways. One is by increasing or decreasing the underlying's price. The second is by increasing or decreasing people's beliefs or expectations about how volatile the underlying price is likely to be.

Opportunities for a change in the price of the underlying are afforded by the passing of time. This is why time plays such as important role in the life of an option. If time is not allowed to pass, the underlying price has no opportunity to change, and an option will have no value apart from whatever intrinsic or exercise value it may have.

For those who are long options, time passes all too quickly, because the passing of time robs the optionholder of potentially valuable chances to experience a large and favourable change in the underlying price. For those who are short options, time cannot pass quickly enough.

Conventional option pricing models reckon the time left in an option's life as fractions of years. How one calculates these fractions, however, reveals a great deal about how one views the passing of time. Those who calculate the time remaining in an option's life by dividing the number of calendar days left by 365 exhibit complete indifference about what kind of time is passing. A weekday is given the same weight as a Saturday or Sunday.

Option traders are far from indifferent, however, about the kind of time that passes. Weekends, for example, are viewed as relatively worthless, so that by the close of business on Friday, option prices typically have fallen to levels at which they are expected to open at the beginning of the next week. In such a world, it makes more sense to calculate the time remaining in an option's life by dividing the number of business days left by the number of business days in a year.

Because of differences in holidays around the world, there is a considerable latitude in the choice of business days in a year, and the number can range between 250 and 260. We use 253 in this paper to allow for normal holidays in the United States.

Even this more enlightened approach to the passing of time may fall short of the mark by giving equal weight to all business days. In practice, we know that the days on which important economic statistics are released can be relatively valuable. Thus, an option might exhibit a relatively greater rate of time decay over the course of an announcement day than on a normal business day.

The difference between the way option traders think of weekends and announcement days reflects a perfectly reasonable view of the world when prices are driven by important economic events and when more of these events are likely to occur on some days than on others.

How important is the problem?

To get an idea of how important it can be to have a refined sense of the passing of time, we did two things. First, we conducted a survey of our account executives. Then we estimate the incremental effect of various announcements on the historical volatility of four key futures contracts – Deutschmarks, Eurodollars, the S&P 500, and Treasury bonds.

SURVEY RESULTS

In our survey, we asked our institutional futures account executives to rank the announcement effects of twenty different key economic statistics on the volatility of the Eurodollar, Treasury bond, S&P 500, and Deutschmark futures prices. The statistics that we asked them to rank ranged from auto sales through retail sales. The full list is shown in Table 1.

Our survey produced a number of interesting results. For example, our account executives consistently ranked non-farm payroll as the announcement that produced the greatest market volatility. They also indicated that the consumer price index (CPI), producer price index (PPI), and jobless claims announcements were important for the interest rate markets. Gross domestic product (GDP) and retail sales announcements were thought to contribute to the volatility of S&P 500 futures prices. The consumer confidence announcement was thought to have an effect on currency price volatilities.

A number of our account executives remarked on shifting fashions in the market's sensitivity to various announcements. Trade balance announcements used to wreak havoc in currency markets, for example, but now can pass without leaving a trace.

EMPIRICAL RESULTS

To lend concreteness to experience, we estimated the announcement effects of the four leading contenders - non-farm payroll, PPI, CPI, and retail sales - on daily price changes of four lead futures contracts.[1] Specifically, we analysed Deutschmarks, Eurodollars, S&P 500, and Treasury bonds using data from January 2, 1986, through October 23, 1992. While we were at it, we also estimated two day-of-the-week effects, one for Friday and one for the weekend.

We isolated Friday as a special day of the week because so many payroll announcements are made on Fridays, and payroll announcements seemed to be consistent producers of volatility. Thus, we wanted to isolate the effect of the announcements from anything else that might have made Fridays different from other days of the week. What we call the weekend effect is simply the result of comparing volatility from Friday's close to Monday's close with volatilities from close to close for the other four business days.

Volatility is calculated in most cases by maximum likelihood, assuming lognormal returns and using dummy variables to measure the announcement and calendar effects. "Base volatility," is the fitted volatility with all dummies set equal to 0.[2]

THE IMPORTANCE OF NON-FARM PAYROLL ANNOUNCEMENTS

Our survey results are borne out by the data fairly well, especially for the two interest rate contracts. As shown in Table 2, Eurodollar and bond volatilities were much higher on payroll announcement days than on other days. Eurodollar futures were 1.7 times as volatile on payroll announcement days as on other days, while bond futures were 1.5 times as volatile. In contrast, payroll announcement days were indistinguishable from other days for the Deutschmark and S&P futures markets.

Table 1. Key economic releases

Auto sales
Beige Book
Consumer confidence (University of Michigan)
Consumer credit
Consumer price index
Durable goods
Factory orders
Gross domestic product
Housing starts
Jobless claims
Johnson Redbook
Leading indicators
Merchandise trade balance
Money supply
Non-farm payroll/unemployment
Personal income
Producer price index
Purchasing Managers' Report (Chicago)
Purchasing Managers' Report (US)
Retail sales

PASSING FANCIES

Even though the payroll announcement has been a consistent contributor to Eurodollar and bond volatilities, the effect of the announcement has varied from year to year. As shown in Table 3, payroll announcement days were, in most years, more volatile than non-payroll days. During 1987, however, payroll announcement days were actually quieter than other business days. Then again, in 1988, payroll announcement days were more than twice as volatile as non-payroll days.

Table 2. Effect of payroll announcements on lead futures contract volatility (annualised volatility, Jan 2, 1986–Oct 23, 1992)

Futures	Non-Payroll Day (1)	Payroll Day (2)	Ratio (2)/(1)
Deutschmarks	12.3	12.9	1.0
Eurodollars	19.0	32.4	1.7
S&P 500	23.4	22.4	1.0
Treasury Bonds	11.2	17.1	1.5

Table 3. Changing importance of the payroll announcement on lead futures contracty volatility (annualised volatility)

	Eurodollars			Treasury Bonds		
Year	Non-Payroll Day (1)	Payroll Day (2)	Ratio (2)/(1)	Non-Payroll Day (3)	Payroll Day (4)	Ratio (4)/(3)
1986	16.5	31.2	1.9	15.7	23.1	1.5
1987	26.8	16.9	0.6	15.3	10.9	0.7
1988	13.8	33.2	2.4	10.0	24.9	2.5
1989	18.6	30.5	1.6	7.9	14.3	1.8
1990	15.0	22.7	1.5	9.8	16.4	1.7
1991	16.8	27.0	1.6	8.0	14.4	1.8
1992	22.3	50.2	2.3	8.2	11.0	1.4
Avg.	18.5	30.2	1.7	10.7	16.4	1.6

Table 4. Ratio of event volatility to base volatility

Event	DM lead	Eurodollar lead	S&P lead	US lead
Base	1.0	1.0	1.0	1.0
Payroll	1.1	2.2	1.0	1.8*
PPI	1.2	1.3	1.2	1.4*
CPI	1.1	1.1	1.0	1.2
Retail sales	0.9	0.9	0.9	1.1
Weekend**	1.2*	0.8*	1.1	1.1
Friday***	1.1	0.9	1.0	1.1

* Indicates the number is significantly different from 1.0 at the 5% level
** Weekend reflects Friday's close to Monday's close.
*** Includes all Fridays.

ESTIMATED ANNOUNCEMENT EFFECTS

Table 4 summarises our empirical findings, which are shown as the ratio of event volatility (for example, the volatility on PPI days) to base volatility. Note that Table 4 differs from Table 2. In Table 4, we relate event day volatility to base volatility, while Table 2 compares payroll announcement days to all other days, including days on which other events occurred.

We find a confirmation, at least for Eurodollar and bond futures, of the volatility produced by payroll announcements. We also see that of the other three leading contenders, only the PPI announcement has had much of an effect over the past six years, and then the effect has been significant statistically only for bond futures.

The CPI and retail sales announcements have contributed comparatively little to overall volatility. The relative worthlessness of Saturday and Sunday is borne out for all four commodities, although the ratio of 1.2 is shown to be significant statistically for Deutschmark futures. And interestingly enough, the Eurodollar market seems to have been very slightly less volatile from Friday's close to Monday's close than during other business days. Finally, we see that Friday is no different from other business days, and so we can conclude safely that the payroll announcement really is important.

How to deal with time and variable volatility

The predictable relationship between volatility and various days of the week poses an interesting problem for estimating time decay in an option. The passing of Saturday and Sunday, for example, ought to have no effect on the price of an option because these days of the week are so barren when it comes to producing news that drives financial markets. The passing of a payroll announcement day, on the other hand, should have a greater than normal effect on the price of an option because such a day is an unusually rich source of market surprises.

Many people solve the weekend problem by simply ignoring Saturdays and Sundays in their reckoning of time, and assume instead that a year consists only of 250 or so business days. While this approach is fine for the weekend effect, it does not provide a way of dealing with what appear to be predictable changes in volatility from day to day.

To deal with variable volatility, we think there is merit in introducing the notion of an "economic day," which we can use to refine the distinction between a calendar day and a business day. The distinction between calendar and business days is rooted in the idea that weekend days have no economic content and that only business days are sources of market volatility. All that is missing from this application of the idea of an economic day is an allowance for the predictably and significantly higher volatilities that are associated with certain kinds of business days.

An illustration will show how time and volatility are related to one another, and how the relationship can be used to convert business days into economic days. The illustration also shows how the distinction affects the way we treat the passing of time and the way we calculate implied volatilities.

TIME AND VOLATILITY

An option's price depends mainly on the expected distribution of the price of the underlying commodity at the end of the option's life. The width of this distribution, as measured by its standard deviation, can be increased either by increasing the volatility that drives the underlying price or by extending the option's life.

For example, doubling daily price volatility will double the standard deviation of the price at option expiration. The same effect can be had by quadrupling the option's life. This is because the contribution of time to the standard deviation of the underlying's price is proportional to the square root of time.

This relationship between time and volatility provides us with a useful rule of thumb:

A doubling of price volatility has the same effect on an option's price as quadrupling its time to expiration.

Put differently, from the standpoint of an option's price:

One day at 20% volatility is worth four days at 10% volatility.

As with all rules of thumb, the relationship is

only approximate, but the approximation is very good.

IMPLICATIONS FOR VARIABLE VOLATILITY

What does this mean for a world in which volatility can vary systematically from day to day? Consider the example shown in Figure 1. In the upper portion is a two-business-day time line. On the first day, volatility is 20%. On the second day, volatility is 10%. For the purpose of pricing an option with two business days to expiration, we can use a conventional pricing model, but we have to use a single volatility, which we will call "term volatility".

1. Business days and economic days

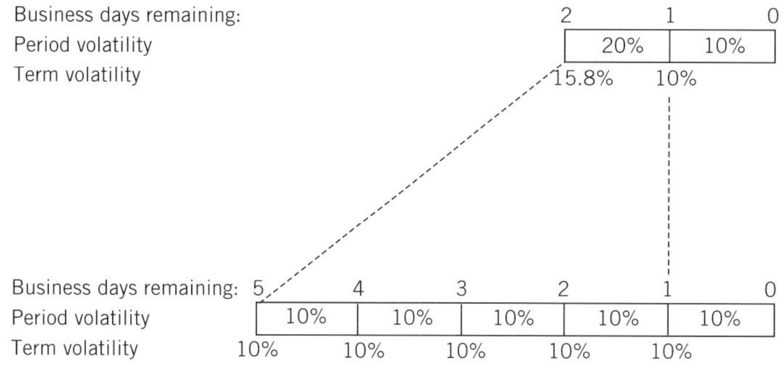

In this case, the single volatility with two days left to expiration would be 15.8%, which is calculated as:

$$\text{Term volatility} = \sqrt{\frac{20^2 + 10^2}{2}}$$

That is, to find the "average" daily volatility for the two-day term, we simply average the squared values of the daily volatilities and take the square root of the result, essentially taking the square root of the average variance of relative or percentage price changes.

A different approach would be to think of the first day of 20% volatility as if it were four hypothetical "economic" days of 10% volatility. If we take this approach, the two-day option with one day of 20% volatility and one day of 10% volatility could be thought of as a five-day option at 10% volatility for all five days.

The two approaches yield the same option price. That is, the price of a two-day option at 15.8% volatility is the same as the price of a five-day option at 10% volatility.

HANDLING THE PASSING OF TIME

We now have two ways of dealing with variable volatility and the passing of time in an option's life. The first is to allow time to pass one business day at a time. If we take this approach in a world in which volatilities are known to vary from one day to the next, however, we must take care to calculate a new term volatility each day to reflect the "average" volatility of the underlying price over the remaining term of the option's life. In our simple example, the appropriate volatility for the option with two days to expiration would be 15.8%, while one day later – with one day left to expiration – the appropriate volatility would be 10%.

The second approach is to hold base volatility constant over the life of the option but to allow economic time to pass at different speeds. In our simple example, the passing of the first business day at 20% volatility would correspond to the passing of four economic days at 10% volatility.

In either case, the drop in the option's price from the first business day to the next would be the same. In the first case, however, the drop is the combined effect of the passing of calendar time and a drop in term volatility. In the second case, the drop is entirely the result of the passing of economic time.

IMPLICATIONS FOR MEASURING TIME DECAY

Each passing day eats away at the price of an option; the standard name given this effect is "theta". In the language of options, an option's theta measures the effect of a change in time remaining to expiration on the price of the option while holding all other things constant. Among these other things is the volatility of the underlying price.

Our simple example shows that we should take some care in the way we use theta as a measure of time decay.

A working example

Suppose it is the close of business on Thursday, December 3, 1992, and that the next day is a payroll announcement day. Suppose further that bond futures are trading at 100, that normal bond futures price volatility is 8%, and that the January 1993 at-the-money option on the March 1993 futures contract has eleven business days remaining to expiration.

The results shown in Table 3 indicate that if we look just at the past four years, bond futures price volatility on payroll announcement days has been about 1.7 times as volatile as on a regular business day. Put differently, a payroll announcement day is worth about three economic days [= approximately 1.7^2].

How should we reckon the theta of a par call in such a setting?

METHOD 1: TERM VOLATILITIES

The option has 11 business days left to expiration. One of these days is a payroll day, however. If a payroll day is worth exactly three regular business days, its contribution to bond futures price volatility is 1.73 [$=\sqrt{3}$] times the normal 8%. This means that the term volatility for the full 11 business days is:

$$\text{Term volatility} = \sqrt{\frac{1\times(1.73\times 8\%)^2+10\times(8\%)^2}{11}}$$
$$= 8.69\%$$

If we load all the relevant information into an option pricing model, we would be told that:

11 business days, 8.69% volatility:

Call price	= 0.462 (or 46.2/64ths)
Theta	= 0.021 (or 2.1/64ths)
Zeta	= 0.053 (or 5.3/64ths)

where zeta (also known as vega) is the change in an option's price with respect to a change in the volatility parameter, ie in implied volatility. The theta of 2.1/64ths is the model's indication that the passing of the next day would cause the option's price to fall by 2.1/64ths to about 44/64ths.

METHOD 2: ECONOMIC DAYS

Although the option has 11 business days left to expiration, we know that the next day is a payroll day that is worth the equivalent of three economic days. As a result, we can think of the option as having 13 economic days [= 3 + 10] remaining to expiration at a constant volatility of 8%. If we load all this alternative information into an option pricing model, we would be told that:

13 economic days, 8.00% volatility:

Call price	= 0.462 (or 46.2/64ths)
Theta	= 0.018 (or 1.8/64ths)
Zeta	= 0.058 (or 5.8/64ths)

Notice that the price is the same, but that the theta and zeta values are different because we are valuing the option with more time to expiration at a lower volatility.

This approach indicates that the passing of an economic day should cost the optionholder about 1.8/64ths. Because the passing of the payroll announcement day is the equivalent of the passing of three economic days, this approach indicates that the price of the option should fall by about 5.4/64ths [= 3 × 1.8/64ths].

WHICH APPROACH IS BETTER?

Which theta provides a better measure of the time decay associated with the passing of a payroll announcement day? Check and see. By the close of business on Friday, December 4, the payroll announcement has passed and the option has 10 equally valuable business days remaining to expiration. That is, it has 10 economic days left to expiration as well. Volatility is expected to be 8% for the rest of the option's life. Now if we price the option with either approach, we would find:

10 business and economic days, 8% volatility:
Call price = 0.406 (or 40.6/64th)

which is 5.6/64ths lower than it was at the close of business on the night before. The theta provided by the economic approach [5.4/64ths = 3 × 1.8/64ths] comes closer to the mark than does the theta provided by the business day approach [2.1/64ths = 1 × 2.1/64ths].

Why is the first approach so far off? Because the passing of the Friday payroll announcement sees more than the passing of one day's time. Term volatility drops as well, from 8.69% to 8.00%, and the conventional approach to measuring theta fails to take predictable changes in volatility into account. Of course, we can always augment the conventional concept of theta by incorporating predictable changes in volatility. In this example, we expect term volatility to fall from 8.69% to 8.00%. If we had applied this anticipated decrease of 0.69 percentage points to the option's zeta of 5.3/64ths, the effect of the anticipated 0.69 percentage point drop in term volatility would have been 3.7/64ths [= 0.69 × 5.3/64ths]. If we then add this to the conventional measure of theta, the predicted drop in the option's price would be 5.8/64ths [= 2.1/64ths + 3.7/64ths], much closer to the actual drop.

Calendar-adjusted volatilities

The concept of an economic day can be helpful in understanding the time decay in an option's price. The concept also can help us in measuring implied volatilities.

Most option traders have encountered the spurious gaps in implied volatilities that seem to appear between the close of trading on Friday afternoons and the opening of trading on

Monday mornings. These gaps are the result of nothing more than treating all calendar days as if they were equally important to the value of the option, when in practice weekend days are more or less worthless.

Experienced option traders know that an option's price at the close of business on Friday has already fallen to the level at which the price is expected to open on Monday morning. No further time decay over Saturday or Sunday is expected. If one calculates the option's implied volatility on Friday, however, and then two calendar days later on Monday, implied volatility will appear to be higher on Monday morning than it was on Friday evening. This illusion is avoided by using business days as a proxy for economic days (and instead of calendar days) when calculating implied volatilities.

We find, too, that the concept of economic time works well in tracking the behaviour of implied volatilities through the course of economic announcements. Consider the usual pattern of implied volatility behaviour before and after a key economic announcement such as non-farm payroll. On Thursday evening, if the announcement is the following Friday, implied volatility will be high. Then, because most announcements convey comparatively little news, implied volatility typically will fall after the announcement, and close lower on Friday than it did on Thursday.

Our simple examples explain this behaviour. The passing of a day that is especially rich in market volatility causes the remaining "term" volatility to drop. In our first example, the passing of the 20% volatility day caused term volatility to drop from 15.8% to 10%. Similarly, in the second example, we would expect to see implied volatility drop from 8.69% with 11 business days to expiration to 8.00% with 10 business days to expiration. Thus, if we continue to use business days as our measure of time, we can expect to see predictable drops in implied volatilities following most announcements.

The alternative, of course, is to use economic days when calculating implied volatilities. In our first example, we would find an implied volatility of 10% with five economic days to expiration and again with one economic day to expiration. In the second example, we would get 8.00% implied volatilities at both 13 and 10 economic days to expiration. The advantage in this approach is that it helps us to avoid spurious changes in our readings of implied volatilities.

The application of economic days works fairly well in practice. Consider the behaviour of implied volatilities in bond options around the payroll announcements from November 1991 to November 1992. As shown in Table 5, if we use business days as our measure of time, we find that implied volatility in the lead bond option fell an average of 0.99% between Thursday's close and Friday's close.

Table 5. Effects of the passing of payroll days on implied volatilities in the expiring bond option

	Business days			Economic days		
Announcement month	Before	After	Change	Before	After	Change
Nov 91	9.85	8.77	−1.09	9.25	8.77	−0.48
Dec 91	9.28	8.56	−0.71	8.71	8.56	−0.14
Jan 92	9.79	8.85	−0.94	9.18	8.85	−0.33
Feb 92	10.78	10.22	−0.56	10.05	10.22	0.17
Mar 92	10.50	8.86	−1.63	9.85	8.86	−0.98
Apr 92	9.99	9.11	−0.88	9.32	9.11	−0.21
May 92	9.99	8.26	−1.73	8.94	8.26	−0.67
Jun 92	9.22	7.91	−1.31	8.65	7.91	−0.74
Jul 92	7.58	7.02	−0.56	7.25	7.02	−0.23
Aug 92	9.42	8.13	−1.29	8.84	8.13	−0.71
Sep 92	9.28	8.44	−0.84	8.66	8.44	−0.22
Oct 92	9.92	9.49	−0.43	9.49	9.49	0.00
Nov 92	9.31	8.38	−0.93	8.74	8.38	−0.35
Average	9.61	8.62	−0.99	8.99	8.62	−0.38

Computations use a factor of 2.5 economic days per payroll announcement day. We estimated this factor using historical price data for 1986 to 1990.

If instead we use our estimate of economic days as our measure of time, we find that implied volatility still fell on average but that the size of the decrease would have been only 0.38%, much closer to the zero that we would expect to find if we had captured completely the economic content of an announcement day.

Implied economic days

If one is willing to work with the idea that the price of an underlying commodity is driven by a base level of volatility, but that some segments of time are predictably richer or poorer sources of volatility than others, one can estimate the implied number of economic days for any economic event. This is done simply by finding the elapsed time required to keep the implied volatility in the option the same both before and after the event.

For example, how many economic days was the payroll announcement on Friday, October 2, 1992, worth for the traders of the November 1992 bond option on the December 1992 futures contract?

To answer this simple question, note first in Table 5 that implied volatility in the at-the-money options closed after the announcement (Friday's close) at 9.49%. At that time, these options had 15 business days remaining to expiration. At the

Table 6. Economic day values (January–June 1993)

Economic release	Deutschmarks	Eurodollars	S&P 500	Treasury bonds
		Implied (Historical)*		
Non-Farm Payroll	2.58 (2.39)	10.69 (5.64)	1.26 (0.72)	3.63 (1.83)
CPI	1.70 (0.09)	4.54 (10.82)	1.84 (1.41)	2.47 (1.56)
PPI/Retail Sales**	0.89 (0.37)	11.56 (5.23)	1.24 (1.20)	2.64 (2.03)

* Historical economic days in parentheses are calculated as the ratio of the sample variance of daily logarithmic returns for event days to the sample variance for non-event days.
** PPI and Retail Sales are combined because they coincided several times over the sample period.

close of the previous day, before the announcement, the options had 16 business days left to expiration, and implied volatility in the at-the-money bond options closed at 9.92%.

If we were to recalculate implied volatility for the at-the-money bond options using Thursday's closing prices but 17.5 economic days rather than 16 business days, we would get 9.49%. Thus, we can conclude that the value placed by option traders on the payroll announcement was the equivalent of 2.5 regular business days.

The information presented in Table 6 allows one to gauge how well the various markets have valued the volatility content of various economic releases. Over the first half of 1993, the Eurodollar options market, for example, valued a payroll announcement at 10.69 economic days, while the market delivered the volatility equivalent of 5.64 economic days.

Thus, in hindsight, the Eurodollar options market paid too much for the volatility content in these announcements. At the same time, given the kind of variability that one can expect when looking at only six observations, one would be hard pressed to conclude that Eurodollar options traders had done a bad job of assessing the importance of the release for the Eurodollar market.

Occasionally, implied volatilities may rise instead of fall after an announcement, producing an implied economic day value that is less than one (perhaps even negative). For example, in Table 6, the Deutschmark options market valued the PPI/Retail Sales announcements at 0.89 economic days.

An increase in implied volatility after an announcement may stem from important but unrelated news that happens to fall on the same day as the announcement. Such news could cause the markets to revise their forecasts of future volatility upward sufficiently to swamp the effect of the passing of the announcements. Or the announcement itself may greatly surprise the markets, causing them to reevaluate their volatility forecasts.

How can this information be used?

Understanding volatility is one of the keys to successful option trading. We have shown how one can assess the contributions of key economic releases to the values of various options. And, by representing these contributions in the form of implied economic days and historical economic days, we have provided a handy and effective way of seeing whether options traders have paid too much or too little for the volatility they have received.

In their own way, comparisons of implied and historical economic day values may prove as useful to options traders as the conventional comparisons of implied and historical volatilities.

1 *The lead futures contract is the contract nearest expiration.*

Intraday Volatility in the Stock Index and Stock Index Futures Markets*

Kalok Chan, K.C. Chan and G. Andrew Karolyi
Hong Kong University of Science and Technology; University of Western Ontario

This paper examines the intraday relationship between returns and returns volatility in the stock index and stock index futures markets. Our results indicate a strong intermarket dependence in the volatility of the cash and futures returns. Price innovations that originate in either the stock or futures markets can predict the future volatility in the other market. We show that this relationship persists even during periods when the dependence in the returns themselves appears to weaken. The findings are robust to controlling for potential market functions such as asynchronous trading in the stock index. Our results have implications for understanding the pattern of information flows between the two markets.

A growing theoretical and empirical literature has sought to understand the relationship between index futures markets and stock markets. The increased research interest in this area is no doubt due to the heightened public concern that the new trading strategies made possible by the existence of index futures markets have increased stock market volatility – see the Brady Commission Report (1988); the NYSE Report on Market Volatility and Investor Confidence (1990), and some recent studies by Harris (1989b), Bessembinder and Seguin (1989), Furbush (1989), Neal (1990), Harris, Sofianos, and Shapiro (1990), and Froot and Perold (1990). Another reason to study the relationship between prices of the index futures market and the stock market is to answer a fundamental question often asked in finance: "Does the same asset trading in two different markets sell at the same price at each point in time?" Strictly speaking, the assets traded in the two markets are not identical but the value of the futures contract should reflect the information about individual stocks impounded in the cash market prices. Similarly, the prices of individual stocks in the cash market should also reflect the information in the value of the futures contract. Further, index arbitrage should reinforce the informational link between the two markets since the value of the index futures contract should not deviate from the cost of buying the individual stocks that make up the index and holding them to maturity, including the transaction costs. Empirical studies, however, report a large number of instances where the index level and the futures price are so different that arbitrage might be profitable (MacKinlay and Ramaswamy (1988); Chung (1989)). Furthermore, many studies suggest that price movements in the futures markets systematically lead price movements of the underlying index in the cash markets.[1]

Uncovering lead and lag relationships in price

**This paper was first published in* The Review of Financial Studies, *Vol 4, No 4 (1991). It is reprinted with permission of Oxford University Press. The authors are grateful for comments from Ravi Jagannathan, Merton Miller, Rob Neal, Paul Seguin, Hans Stoll, editor Chester Spatt, an anonymous referee, and seminar participants at Cornell University, the University of Pittsburgh, the Northern and European Finance Associations, and Ohio State University, especially colleagues Warren Bailey, Tom George, Francis Longstaff, Dave Mavers, and René Stulz. The authors also thank the Dice Center for Financial Economics at Ohio State University for financial support. Errors remain the authors' own responsibility* changes raises an interesting possibility that the futures and cash markets are not equal in their capacity to discover new information about asset prices. Indeed, studies on this lead and lag relation suggest that the index futures market serves as a primary market of price discovery and argue that new information disseminates in the futures market before the stock market. In this article, we show that a further analysis of the intermarket dependence between the cash and futures prices does not support such a unidirectional relation. Instead, our results suggest that price innovations in either the cash or futures market may be able to predict the arrival of new information in the other market.

Our analysis focuses on the intraday relationship between price changes and price change volatility in the stock index and stock index futures markets. Thus, we extend the current studies of lead and lag relations between stock and futures price changes by allowing the volatility of price changes, as well as price changes themselves, to interact across the cash and futures markets. Our evidence from August 1984 to December 1989 for the Standard & Poor's (S&P) 500 stock index and index futures contract offers four major findings:

❑ intraday volatility patterns in both the cash and futures markets demonstrate strong persistence and predictability. That is, the intraday volatility of stock and futures price changes varies over time and in a predictable manner given the past volatility of price changes;

❑ conditional on the persistence and predictability of the intraday volatilities of price changes in their respective markets, the past volatility of futures (cash) price changes is also an important predictor of the future volatility of cash (futures) price changes. In other words, price innovations in either the cash or futures market influence the volatility in the other market;

❑ although the lead and lag relations between the price changes of the cash and futures markets appear to diminish over the sample period, the intermarket dependence of volatility grows stronger and comparably in both directions;

❑ finally, these findings are robust to controlling for the potential effects of infrequent trading of the component stocks in the index and other market frictions.

Why focus on the intraday volatility of the cash and futures price changes and not just on the price changes themselves? There are several reasons. First, if the volatility of the price changes in the cash and futures markets vary over time in a related way and if this is ignored in tests of lead and lag relations in the price changes, specification error can lead to incorrect inferences about the relationship between futures and cash prices. The lead and lag results reported in previous studies may, therefore, arise from model misspecification. Second, finding a lead or lag relation in price changes may offer only inconclusive evidence on how information flows to the two markets. Time-varying intraday conditional volatility of price changes in the cash and futures markets represents another way in which we can measure how information can flow to those two markets. Exploring this alternative measure is reasonable given studies by Clark (1973), Tauchen and Pitts (1983) and recently Ross (1989), which show that it is the volatility of an asset's price, and not the asset's simple price change, which is related to the rate of flow of information to the market. More importantly, however, this alternative measure may generate new insights. For example, from a number of existing studies that find futures prices systematically lead cash prices, a common interpretation of the result is that traders with marketwide information prefer to go to the futures market before the cash market.[2,3] When we allow for time-varying and intermarket-dependent volatility of price changes while simultaneously controlling for the lead or lag effects in price changes themselves, we uncover a strong bi-directional dependence in the intraday volatility of the cash and futures markets. That is, price innovations in either the cash or futures market not only predict the volatility of their own market but also that of the other market. Our results suggest that new information that hits either market can, in general, predict the arrival rate of information in the other market. This finding is thus inconsistent with the notion posited by some studies that information flows systematically to the futures market before the cash market.

The data are discussed in the first section of this chapter. Autocorrelations and cross-correlations of the intraday cash and futures returns are presented in the following section. These results motivate the econometric model employed, which is discussed in the third section. The estimation results are presented in the fourth section. We then focus on important econometric problems relating to asynchronous trading, index reporting delays, and other market frictions that may influence the relation between cash and futures prices. We also implement the tests on

❑ the Major Market Index contract traded on the Chicago Board of Trade; and

❑ the S&P 500 futures contract with a single heavily traded stock, IBM.

Data

STANDARD & POOR'S 500 STOCK INDEX AND STOCK INDEX FUTURES PRICES

The data used in the study are from the "Quote Capture" information provided by the Chicago Mercantile Exchange for the period August 1, 1984–December 31, 1989. The first set of data contains the time (to the nearest 10 seconds) and exact price of the S&P futures transactions whenever the price is different from the previous one. The second set of data consists of the S&P 500 index level each time it is computed and transmitted to Chicago.[4] Since the nearby contract is usually the most actively traded, only the data for the nearby futures contract are used.

The intraday time series are partitioned into five-minute intervals. During each interval, the last futures price and cash index level quotes are employed. Since the New York Stock Exchange closes at 15:00 (Central Time), 15 minutes earlier than the futures market, futures price observations after that time are removed. Futures prices recorded before the New York Stock Exchange (NYSE) opens are also excluded. Before September 30, 1985, the NYSE opened at 09:00 (Central Time) and there were 72 five-minute intervals during the trading day. After that date, the NYSE began opening at 08:30 (Central Time) and price observations increased to 78 five-minute quotes. The price observations were used to compute the five-minute intraday and overnight simple returns for the futures and cash index. The overnight return was computed from the 09:05 (08:35 after September 30, 1985) price and the 15:00 price of the previous day for both markets.[5]

MAJOR MARKET INDEX AND INDEX FUTURES PRICES

Later we shall evaluate the impact of mismeasurement of returns due to asynchronous trading of component stocks in the index on the results of the study. One way in which this problem is addressed is by replicating the results with data on the Major Market Index (MMI) and its associated futures contract traded on the Chicago Board of Trade (CBOT). Since the MMI is a price-weighted index of 20 of the largest and most actively traded NYSE stocks, the problems of asynchronous trading are likely to be mitigated. A second way in which we deal with the asynchronous problem is by modelling five-minute returns on the S&P 500 index futures contract jointly with five-minute returns computed for only IBM stock.

The MMI futures price data are supplied by the Chicago Board of Trade for the period July 23, 1984–June 30, 1985, which overlaps with the first part of the S&P 500 sample. The data file contains the time and price of futures transactions whenever the price is different from the previous one, as well as the stock index level. For the MMI futures contracts, again, only the nearby futures contract is used.

There are time lags in the index value reported by the exchanges due to computation and subsequently transmission delays.[6] The evidence in Chan (1992) suggests that these reporting lags are non-trivial. To circumvent this problem, in every five-minute interval, the MMI index value is computed using the price-weighted formula from the most recent transaction prices for each of the individual stocks recorded by the "Fitch" data obtained from Francis Emory Fitch Inc. These data consist of a time-ordered record of every transaction of the 20 component stocks of the MMI. For each transaction, the date, time, price, and number of shares traded are available. Five-minute returns series are computed as for the S&P 500 and MMI reported indexes, except the first observation in the day is arbitrarily taken as at 08:45 (Central Time) to ensure that all component stocks have opened trading. Finally, the tests using IBM and S&P 500 stock index futures use the Fitch time-stamped prices for the IBM shares.

Autocorrelations and cross-correlations of intraday returns

Tables 1 and 2 show a wide range of descriptive statistics for the stock and futures returns series for five roughly evenly divided subperiods over the 1984–89 sample. Subperiod breaks are, however, specifically chosen to;

❑ match that for the MMI results shown in below to allow comparisons; and

❑ isolate the crash period.[7] In Table 1 overleaf, the statistics reported include the mean, standard deviation, skewness, excess kurtosis for the intraday cash, and futures returns, respectively. The same statistics for the overnight returns are presented below in brackets.

The sample moments for both stock and futures returns series indicate empirical distributions with heavy tails and sharp peaks at the centre compared with the normal distribution. For most subperiods, there is negative skewness in

Table 1. Summary statistics for intraday five-minute and overnight returns on S&P 500 stock index and the S&P 500 index futures from July 1984–December 1989

	Intraday stock index returns					Intraday stock index futures returns				
Statistic	1984–85	1985–86	1986–87	1987–88	1988–89	1984–85	1985–86	1986–87	1987–88	1988–89
Sample size	16,169	20,440	22,925	18,316	22,247	16,169	20,440	22,925	18,316	22,247
	[231]	[274]	[306]	[243]	[294]	[231]	[274]	[306]	[243]	[294]
Mean	0.0010	0.0004	0.0005	0.0003	0.0003	0.0002	0.0004	0.0003	0.0001	0.0002
	[0.0306]	[0.0487]	[0.0665]	[0.0671]	[0.0639]	[0.0933]	[0.0443]	[0.0788]	[0.0868]	[0.0669]
Standard deviation	0.0442	0.0509	0.0721	0.0787	0.0538	0.0826	0.0888	0.1122	0.1198	0.0806
	[0.2234]	[0.1881]	[0.3217]	[0.4599]	[0.3135]	[0.4509]	[0.3351]	[0.4423]	[0.6322]	[0.3342]
Skewness	1.1901	−0.1582	−0.7458	0.2160	−3.3751	−0.013	−0.344	−0.328	−0.204	−1.623
	[0.1672]	[−0.1730]	[0.2559]	[−0.0281]	[0.0074]	[3.203]	[0.712]	[0.234]	[0.772]	[0.544]
Excess kurtosis	10.771	12.312	15.330	10.763	23.559	2.84	5.51	20.08	5.06	64.48
	[0.4212]	[0.1478]	[0.6226]	[2.1917]	[2.8308]	[18.13]	[3.23]	[1.45]	[9.47]	[2.19]
$\rho(r_t, r_{t-k})$										
1	0.45*	0.40*	0.33*	0.30*	0.27*	0.01	−0.01	−0.03*	−0.02	−0.01
2	0.23*	0.15*	0.05*	0.04*	0.04*	−0.03*	−0.04*	−0.03*	−0.03*	−0.04*
3	0.06*	0.04*	−0.03*	−0.01	−0.02*	−0.05*	−0.03*	−0.02*	−0.01	−0.03*
4	−0.01	−0.00	−0.03*	−0.03*	−0.03*	−0.03*	−0.00	−0.02*	−0.02*	−0.03*
5	−0.04*	−0.01	−0.03*	−0.03*	−0.02*	−0.01	−0.01	−0.02*	−0.02*	−0.01
6	−0.04*	−0.02*	−0.02*	−0.02*	−0.02*	−0.01	−0.01	−0.01	0.00	−0.00
$\rho(r_t^2, r_{t-k}^2)$										
1	0.29*	0.23*	0.19*	0.18*	0.15*	0.04*	0.05*	0.07*	0.07*	0.07*
2	0.09*	0.07*	0.07*	0.06*	0.05*	0.02*	0.03*	0.07*	0.04*	0.04*
3	0.02*	0.04*	0.04*	0.03*	0.03*	0.01	0.02*	0.04*	0.03*	0.03*
4	0.01	0.02*	0.03*	0.02*	0.02*	0.02*	0.02*	0.03*	0.03*	0.01
5	0.00	0.02*	0.02*	0.01	0.02*	−0.00	0.02*	0.03	0.03*	0.02*
6	0.01	0.02*	0.01	0.02*	0.01	−0.00	0.01	0.02*	0.03*	0.02*

Autocorrelation coefficients $\rho(r_t, r_{t-k})$, for up to k lags are computed from five-minute intraday returns beginning with the 09:05 (Central Time) price quote and ending with the 15:00 (Central Time) price quote in the market each day. These reported coefficient estimates are averages computed from the number of days in each subperiod. The kurtosis coefficient is computed in excess of 3. The alignment of futures and cash price quotations required that quotes from the futures market after 15:00 (Central Time) be removed from the sample. Corresponding statistics computed for overnight returns are given in brackets. Asymptotic standard errors for the autocorrelation coefficients can be approximated as the square root of the reciprocal of the number of observations (for example ± 0.0071 for around 20,000 observations) under the null hypothesis of zero autocorrelation. * denotes that the coefficient is at least 2.325 standard errors from zero, which approximates significance at the 1% level. The exact calendar days spanned by the subperiods are, respectively, August 1, 1984– June 30, 1985; July 1, 1985–July 31, 1986; 1 August, 1986–16 October, 1987; 13 November, 1987–31 October, 1988 and 1 November, 1988–31 December, 1989.

both stock and futures returns but a more significant effect prevails in the futures returns. Zero excess kurtosis is rejected confidently for both series in all subperiods, but especially in 1988-89.[8]

AUTOCORRELATIONS

The sample autocorrelation functions for the intraday five-minute stock and futures returns are also presented in Table 1. For each day, the autocorrelation coefficients up to the sixth order are computed for the futures and cash returns. The estimates are then averaged over the number of trading days in each subperiod. We approximate the standard error for the correlation coefficients as the square root of the reciprocal of the number of five-minute observations (around 20,000), which is about 0.0071.[9] As found in the previous studies of intraday stock returns by Stoll and Whaley (1990b), MacKinlay and Ramaswamy (1988), and Chan (1992), the autocorrelations in the stock index are positive and more than two standard errors from zero for the first and, possibly, second five-minute interval. Beyond lag 3, a negative serial correlation (although usually less than three standard errors from zero) takes over in the index returns. In contrast, the serial correlation coefficients for the futures returns appear to be negative for the second and third lags. Interestingly, the autocorrelations in the cash returns do diminish over time, as the first-order autocorrelations fall from 0.45 in 1984 to 0.27 in 1989. This finding is consistent with Froot and Perold (1990).

The autocorrelation coefficients for the squared intraday returns are also computed and displayed in Table 1. These are presented as evidence of non-linear dependence in the returns series.[10] The sample autocorrelations of the squared series for the stock index and stock index futures returns are positive and decay at a slow rate to zero. These results imply that a model for the returns generating processes in the cash and futures markets should account for higher order dependence in the returns, possibly as a result of changing conditional volatility over time. One family of models that closely approximates second-order non-linear processes, commonly known as the autoregressive conditional heteroskedastic (Arch) models, has been developed by Engle (1982). The process allows the first and second moments of the returns to depend on its past values. This paper implements such models to characterise the returns-generating process for intraday stock index and futures returns.

CROSS-CORRELATIONS

Panel A of Table 2 shows the average intraday cross-correlations between the five-minute stock and futures returns for up to six leads and lags for the five subperiods. The average contemporaneous correlation is about 0.4, more than 16 standard errors from zero. For the most part, price changes occur simultaneously in both markets. The lagged futures returns do seem to have some forecast power in explaining current stock index returns as the lags 1 to 3 have correlation coefficients at least four standard errors from zero. On the other hand, the leading cross-correlations (predictability from cash to futures) are negative but closer to zero. Both lead and lag effects appear to diminish in 1988 and 1989, particularly at the second and third lags. Stoll and Whaley (1990b) also recognise this weakening cross-market dependence in returns over time.

In Panel B, the lead and lag correlations are computed for the squared returns for each subperiod. These represent a crude measure of intermarket association of volatility. Most correlations are greater than zero by more than four standard errors contemporaneously and apparently up to three lags in the direction of futures to cash and one lag in the direction of cash to futures. An interesting contrast between Panels A and B is that the first and second lead correlations from cash to futures in the squared returns appear to increase over the same period while diminishing in the raw returns. On the other hand, the lead correlations from futures to cash of the squared returns decrease over the sample period similarly to the raw return cross-correlations. These preliminary results indicate that a lead/lag relationship may exist not only for price changes of futures and stocks, but also for the volatility of their price changes. Moreover, these relations appear to be capturing distinctly different phenomena. We utilise these findings for the modelling strategy that follows.[11]

Table 2. Sample cross-correlation coefficients between intraday S&P 500 stock index and S&P 500 stock index futures returns

Lag	1984–85	1985–86	1986–87	1987–88	1988–89
A. Cross–correlation of returns $\rho(r_{st}, r_{f,t-k})$					
–6	–0.0191*	–0.0153	–0.0179*	–0.0033	–0.0162
–5	–0.0177*	–0.0207*	–0.0248*	–0.0184*	–0.0112
–4	–0.0264*	–0.0162	–0.0206*	–0.0232*	–0.0177
–3	–0.0580*	–0.0234*	–0.0334*	–0.0214*	–0.0302*
–2	–0.0726*	–0.0595*	–0.0527*	–0.0342*	–0.0411*
–1	–0.0404*	–0.0330*	–0.0320*	–0.0323*	–0.0255*
0	0.4055*	0.3641*	0.4131*	0.4894*	0.5083*
1	0.4330*	0.4536*	0.5418*	0.4950*	0.4554*
2	0.3106*	0.2890*	0.1863*	0.1494*	0.1443*
3	0.1487*	0.1199*	0.0431*	0.0389*	0.0345*
4	0.0559*	0.0419*	0.0059	0.0044	–0.0064
5	0.0177*	0.0189*	–0.0073	–0.0173*	–0.0071
6	–0.0097	0.0125	–0.0063	–0.0099	–0.0024
B. Cross–correlation of squared returns $\rho(r^2_{st}, r^2_{f,t-k})$					
–6	–0.0164	0.0091	0.0244*	0.0225*	0.0112
–5	–0.0135	0.0152	0.0223*	0.0257*	0.0205*
–4	–0.0060	0.0079	0.0304*	0.0258*	0.0246*
–3	0.0052	0.0157	0.0402*	0.0381*	0.0267*
–2	0.0051	0.0210*	0.0475*	0.0473*	0.0411*
–1	0.0270*	0.0555*	0.0830*	0.0706*	0.0865*
0	0.2977*	0.2507*	0.3300*	0.4680*	0.4963*
1	0.3554*	0.3324*	0.4176*	0.3459*	0.2768*
2	0.1565*	0.1453*	0.1025*	0.0759*	0.0791*
3	0.0553*	0.0562*	0.0648*	0.0456*	0.0294*
4	0.0186*	0.0328*	0.0429*	0.0163	0.0256*
5	0.0154	0.0286*	0.0314*	0.0205*	0.0132
6	0.0129	0.0240*	0.0275*	0.0211*	0.0251*

Cross-correlation coefficients are computed from five-minute intraday returns beginning with the 21:05 (Central Time) price quotation and ending with the 15:00 (Central Time) price quotation in both markets each day. These coefficients are averaged over the number of days in each subperiod. The alignment of futures and cash price quotes requires that futures prices after 15:00 (Central Time) be removed from the sample. Positive lags (k) indicate cross-correlations, $\rho(r_{st}, r_{f,t-k})$, between past futures returns, $r_{f,t-k}$, and current cash returns, $r_{s,t}$. Negative lags ($k < 0$), or "leads", indicate cross-correlations between future futures returns and current cash returns. Asymptotic standard errors for the correlation coefficients can be approximated as the square root of the reciprocal of the number of observations (for example, ± 0.0071 for around 20,000 observations) under the null hypothesis of zero autocorrelation. * denotes that the coefficient is at least 2.325 standard errors from zero, which approximates significance at the 1% level. The subperiods correspond to those calendar days shown in Table 1.

The bivariate Garch model

The analysis of autocorrelations and cross-correlations suggests that a model of the dynamics of the intraday returns in the cash and futures markets should seek to capture:

❑ the time variation in the volatility of intraday stock and futures returns; and

❑ the intermarket dependence of the returns and volatility of returns between the cash and futures markets.

The analysis in this paper uses statistical models based on the autoregressive conditional heteroskedastic (Arch) family of models developed by Engle (1982) and generalised (Garch) by Bollerslev (1986). These models have been shown empirically to capture reasonably well the time variation in the volatility of daily and monthly stock returns (Bollerslev 1987; French, Schwert, and Stambaugh 1987; Schwert 1989; Nelson 1991; Akgiray 1989). Moreover, in their generalised multivariate form, such models will allow for intermarket dependence in the returns generating processes of the cash and futures markets.

We posit the following bivariate AR(1)-Garch(1,3) model for the joint processes governing the stock index and index futures returns:

$$\mathbf{r}_t = \alpha = \mathbf{d}_1 D_{1t} + \beta \mathbf{r}_{t-1} + d_3 \mathbf{r}_{t-1} D_{2t} + \eta_t,$$
$$\eta_t = (\iota + \mathbf{d}_2 D_{1t})\varepsilon_t, \qquad (1)$$

$$\varepsilon_t | \Phi_{t-1} \sim N(\mathbf{0}, H_t);$$
$$\begin{bmatrix} h_{ss,t} \\ h_{ff,t} \end{bmatrix} = \mathbf{A} + B \begin{bmatrix} h_{ss,t-1} \\ h_{ff,t-1} \end{bmatrix} + \sum_{k=1}^{3} C_k \begin{bmatrix} \varepsilon^2_{ss,t-k} \\ \varepsilon^2_{ff,t-k} \end{bmatrix}; \qquad (2)$$

$$h_{sf,t} = h_{fs,t} = \rho (h_{ss,t} h_{ff,t})^{1/2}; \qquad (3)$$

where the returns vector for the stock index and index futures series is given by $\mathbf{r}'_{qt} = [r_{s,t} r_{f,t}]$, the residual vectors by $\eta'_t = [\eta_{s,t} \eta_{f,t}]$ and $\varepsilon'_t = [\varepsilon_{s,t} \varepsilon_{f,t}]$, and the conditional covariance matrix by H_t, where $\{H_t\}_{ij} = h_{ij,t}$, for i,j = s,f. The parameter vectors and matrices are defined as $\alpha' = [\alpha_s \alpha_f]$, $\mathbf{d}'_j = [d_{s,j} d_{f,j}]$, for j = 1,2, $\mathbf{A}' = [a_s a_f]$, ι, a 2×1 vector of 1s, and $\{\beta\}_{ij} = \beta_{ij,k}$, $\{\mathbf{d}_3\}_{ij} = d_{ij,3}$, $\{\mathbf{B}\}_{ij} = b_{ij}$, $\{\mathbf{C_k}\}_{ij} = c_{ij,k}$, all for i,j = s,f, and lags k = 1,2, or 3. Φ_{t-1} is the set of all information available at time t–1, D_{1t} is a dummy variable that is set to unity for overnight returns, and D_{2t} is a dummy variable that is set to unity for the first five-minute trading interval each day.

Our bivariate model is closely related to those employed by Bollerslev, Engle, and Wooldridge (1988), Engle (1987), Baillie and Bollerslev (1987), Schwert and Seguin (1990), Engle and Kroner (1989), Engle, Ito, and Lin (1990), and Conrad, Gultekin, and Kaul (1991). Equation (1) models the security returns as an AR(1) process. This specification follows from the summary statistics in the previous section. A secondary role is to absorb the potential effects of asynchronous trading in the component stocks of the index, bid-ask bounce in the futures returns, or any other market frictions that may influence the dependence in cash and futures returns.

From the evidence in Table 1, the information shocks from overnight returns are likely to perturb the time series process of intraday returns. The model differentiates the effects of overnight returns from intraday returns for the mean returns and volatility with the dummy variables D_{1t} and D_{2t}. The first dummy variable scales the overnight return for the mean returns via $\mathbf{d}_1$ and the volatility of returns via $\mathbf{d}_2$. This approach is similar to that taken by Glosten, Jagannathan, and Runkle (1989) to deal with seasonality issues. The second dummy variable adjusts the influence of the overnight return as an independent variable in (1) on the returns of the first five-minute trading interval.

Conditional on this dependence in means, the cash and futures returns series are assumed to have a bivariate normal distribution with conditional covariance matrix H_t. Equation (2) models the diagonal elements of the conditional covariance matrix H_t as a function of the diagonal elements of the conditional covariance matrix of the past period, as well as the squared return innovations of three past periods. Following Baillie and Bollerslev (1987) and Schwert and Seguin (1990), our model imposes an assumption of a constant correlation matrix of returns over time (3). This parameterisation ensures that H_t is positive definite under reasonable conditions and also offers an efficient representation for the tests that follow.

Our model facilitates an analysis of the volatility relations between the stock index and index futures markets in two forms. First, the off-diagonal parameters in matrix $\mathbf{B}$, given by parameters $b_{s,f}$ and $b_{f,s}$, measure the dependence of the conditional return volatility in the cash market on that of the futures market and the dependence of the conditional return volatility in the futures market on that of the cash market in the last period. Second, the absolute size of price shocks originating in one market in previous periods, measured by the squared value of lagged innovations, also transmits to the current period's conditional volatility in the other market by means of the off-diagonal elements of matrices $\mathbf{C_k}$ given by parameters $c_{sf,k}$ and $c_{fs,k}$.

Note that these volatility relations are analysed holding fixed the lead and lag relations in the changes in price levels in the conditional mean returns (1), via matrix β. These predictive relations in price changes can appear because of asynchronous trading, short-sale constraints, and other market frictions that cause information already known in the futures market to be incorporated in the cash index price with a delay (Chan, 1992). If these market frictions are captured by the lead/lag relation in prices in the conditional mean equation (1), then the conditional volatility of the cash index return should not necessarily be predictable. It is possible, however, that asynchronous trading might be related to volatility so that its effect would not be captured adequately by (1). We deal with this alternative hypothesis in more detail below.

Given a sample of T five-minute returns, the parameters of the bivariate system (1)-(3) are estimated by computing the conditional log likelihood function for each time period as

$$L_t(\theta) = -\log 2\pi - \tfrac{1}{2}\log\left|\mathbf{H}_t(\theta)\right| - \tfrac{1}{2}\varepsilon_t'(\theta)\mathbf{H}_t^{-1}(\theta)\varepsilon_t(\theta), \qquad (4)$$

$$L(\theta) = \sum_{t=1}^{T} L_t(\theta), \qquad (5)$$

where θ is the vector of all parameters. Numerical maximisation of (4) and (5) following the Berndt et al (1974) algorithm yields the maximum likelihood estimates and associated asymptotic standard errors.

Results

BIVARIATE GARCH RESULTS

Table 3 shows the results of fitting the bivariate Garch model to the intraday index and futures returns. The set of parameters that measure the dependence of the current cash returns on past cash returns, given by β_{ss}, and on past futures returns, given by β_{sf}, are significantly different from zero in all subperiods except 1988–89. The attenuation in the serial dependence in the cash market for the last subperiod is, as noted earlier,

Table 3. Estimates from bivariate generalised autoregressive conditional heteroskedastic models (Garch) of intraday returns on S&P 500 stock index and S&P 500 stock index futures from August 1984–December 1989

α_s	β_{ss}	β_{sf}	a_s	b_{ss}	b_{sf}	$c_{ss,1}$	$c_{sf,1}$	$c_{ss,2}$	$c_{sf,2}$	$c_{ss,3}$	$c_{sf,3}$
α_f	β_{fs}	β_{ff}	a_f	b_{fs}	b_{ff}	$c_{fs,1}$	$c_{ff,1}$	$c_{fs,2}$	$c_{ff,2}$	$c_{fs,3}$	$c_{ff,3}$
Sample period 1984–85											
–0.0005	0.3822	0.01226	0.00004	0.9044	–0.0037	0.2349	0.0335	–0.1811	–0.0159	–0.0232	–0.0077
(–2.12)	(50.5)*	(30.6)*	(19.4)*	(159.0)*	(–13.2)*	(34.0)*	(38.8)*	(–19.9)*	(–13.7)*	(–4.75)*	(–9.91)*
–0.0019	–0.0604	–0.0021	0.00010	–0.1891	0.9728	0.0623	0.1134	–0.0308	–0.0346	0.0251	–0.0421
(–3.81)*	(–3.99)*	(–0.245)	(12.4)*	(–10.0)*	(623.0)*	(2.67)*	(15.6)*	(–1.11)	(–3.48)*	(2.53)*	(–6.69)*
ρ = .5024 (94.4)*; log likelihood = 53,602.869; Wald test A = 2405.2; Wald test B = 330.75											
Sample period 1985–96											
0.0005	0.3123	0.1456	0.00003	0.8425	0.0015	0.1509	0.0702	–0.0831	–0.0321	–0.0146	–0.0203
(2.52)*	(45.0)*	(35.4)*	(16.9)*	(138.0)*	(3.55)*	(22.7)*	(53.5)*	(–10.6)*	(–23.0)*	(–3.49)*	(–25.6)*
0.0011	–0.0219	–0.0838	0.00004	–0.2014	0.9916	0.1770	0.1187	–0.1406	–0.0237	0.0351	–0.0638
(2.76)*	(–1.79)*	(–12.6)*	(15.7)*	(–19.2)*	(1116.0)*	(8.55)*	(18.9)*	(–5.10)*	(–2.65)*	(2.02)	(–11.0)*
r = .4597 (90.7)*; log likelihood = 64,648.113; Wald test A = 4458.0; Wald test B = 395.34											
Sample period 1986–87											
0.0011	0.1648	0.2457	0.00006	0.8995	–0.0081	0.0910	0.1053	–0.0433	–0.0656	–0.0094	–0.0183
(4.04)*	(26.9)*	(53.5)*	(26.5)*	(260.0)*	(–15.0)*	(19.7)*	(53.7)*	(–8.18)*	(–31.2)*	(–2.91)*	(–17.8)*
0.0016	–0.0061	–0.0934	0.00034	–0.1915	0.9088	0.0778	0.1232	–0.0337	0.0428	0.0246	–0.0654
(3.50)*	(–0.660)	(–15.2)*	(22.9)*	(–10.2)*	(219.0)*	(4.82)*	(20.4)*	(–1.75)	(4.85)*	(2.17)	(–11.3)*
ρ = .5192 (118.0)*; log likelihood = 60,682.251; Wald test A = 4172.3; Wald test B = 457.87											
Sample period 1987–88											
0.0002	0.1301	0.2550	0.00008	0.9058	–0.0095	0.0772	0.0946	–0.0443	–0.0551	–0.0020	–0.0157
(0.621)	(16.5)*	(45.9)*	(21.4)*	(185.0)*	(–8.09)*	(14.8)*	(38.7)*	(–6.87)*	(–20.0)*	(–0.495)	(–11.3)*
–0.0014	0.0096	–0.0663	0.00047	–0.0895	0.8749	0.0669	0.1379	–0.0303	–0.0286	–0.0127	0.0031
(–2.31)	(0.78)	(–9.13)*	(18.8)*	(–3.50)*	(119.0)*	(4.12)*	(16.6)*	(–1.60)	(–2.66)*	(–1.10)	(0.409)
ρ = .5510 (123.0)*; log likelihood = 45,261.163; Wald test A = 2585.5; Wald test B = 122.36											
Sample period 1988–89											
0.0006	0.0838	0.2566	0.00006	0.8696	–0.0015	0.0674	0.1073	–0.0469	–0.0590	0.0166	–0.0248
(2.42)*	(11.3)*	(45.5)*	(24.4)*	(180.0)*	(–2.52)*	(14.9)*	(41.9)*	(–9.56)*	(21.2)*	(6.08)*	(–17.9)*
0.0001	–0.0367	–0.0372	0.00017	–0.1431	0.9371	0.1457	0.1294	–0.0920	–0.0414	–0.0133	–0.0195
(0.333)	(–3.33)*	(–5.08)*	(20.3)*	(–7.79)*	(229.0)*	(11.5)*	(20.2)*	(–5.87)*	(–4.71)*	(–1.31)	(–3.50)*
ρ = .5467 (133.0)*; log likelihood = 71,899.545; Wald test A = 2916.7; Wald test B = 83.723											

The model is

$$\mathbf{r}_t = \alpha = \mathbf{d}_1 D_{1t} + \beta\mathbf{r}_{t-1} + d_3\mathbf{r}_{t-1}D_{2t} + \eta_t,\quad \eta_t = (\iota + \mathbf{d}_2 D_{1t})\varepsilon_t,\quad \varepsilon_t\left|\Phi_{t-1}\right. \sim N(\mathbf{0},H_t),\quad \begin{bmatrix} h_{ss,t} \\ h_{ff,t} \end{bmatrix} = \mathbf{A} + B\begin{bmatrix} h_{ss,t-1} \\ h_{ff,t-1} \end{bmatrix} + \sum_{k=1}^{3} C_k \begin{bmatrix} \varepsilon^2_{ss,t-k} \\ \varepsilon^2_{ff,t-k} \end{bmatrix}, h_{sf,t} = \rho\left(h_{ss,t}h_{ff,t}\right)^{1/2}.$$

The vectors and matrices are defined as follows:

$$\mathbf{r}_t = \begin{bmatrix} r_{st} \\ r_{ft} \end{bmatrix},\ \alpha = \begin{bmatrix} \alpha_s \\ \alpha_f \end{bmatrix},\ \beta = \begin{bmatrix} \beta_{ss} & \beta_{sf} \\ \beta_{fs} & \beta_{ff} \end{bmatrix},\ \eta_t = \begin{bmatrix} \eta_{st} \\ \eta_{ft} \end{bmatrix},\ \varepsilon_t = \begin{bmatrix} \varepsilon_{st} \\ \varepsilon_{ft} \end{bmatrix},\ \mathbf{d}_1 = \begin{bmatrix} d_{s,t} \\ d_{f,t} \end{bmatrix},\ H_t = \begin{bmatrix} h_{ss,t} & h_{sf,t} \\ h_{fs,t} & h_{ff,t} \end{bmatrix},\ \mathbf{A} = \begin{bmatrix} a_s \\ a_f \end{bmatrix},\ B = \begin{bmatrix} b_{ss} & b_{sf} \\ b_{fs} & b_{ff} \end{bmatrix},\ C_k = \begin{bmatrix} c_{ss,k} & c_{sf,k} \\ c_{fs,k} & c_{ff,k} \end{bmatrix},\ d_3 = \begin{bmatrix} d_{ss,3} & d_{sf,3} \\ d_{fs,3} & d_{ff,3} \end{bmatrix}.$$

and r_{tt} is the interval t S&P 500 stock index or stock index futures return, Φ_{t-1} is the set of all information at time $t-1$, D_{1t} is the overnight dummy variable set to unity for overnight returns, and zero for intraday returns, and D_{2t} is the dummy set to unity for the first five-minute return of each training day. The model is estimated using the Berndt et al (1974) maximum likelihood algorithm. The conditional log likelihood function to be maximised is given in (4) and (5). The values in parentheses are asymptotic t-statistics with * denoting coefficient estimates at least 2.325 standard errors from zero. The dummy coefficient estimates are not reported. The number of intraday returns observations used per estimation period are the same as those given in Table 1. The Wald test for independence (zero exclusion test) in the conditional volatility system hypothesises that

Test A: $H_0 = b_{sf} = 0,\ b_{fs} = 0$ and $c_{sf,k} = 0\ \ c_{fs,k} = 0\ \ \forall k = 1,2,3,$

Test B: $H_0 = b_{sf} = 0,\ b_{fs} = 0.$

The χ^2 critical values for eight degrees of freedom are 15.5 and 20.1 and for two degrees of freedom are 5.99 and 9.21 for the 5% and 1% confidence levels, respectively.

1. Intraday volatility of S&P 500 index and S&P 500 stock index futures returns for November 1988–December 1989

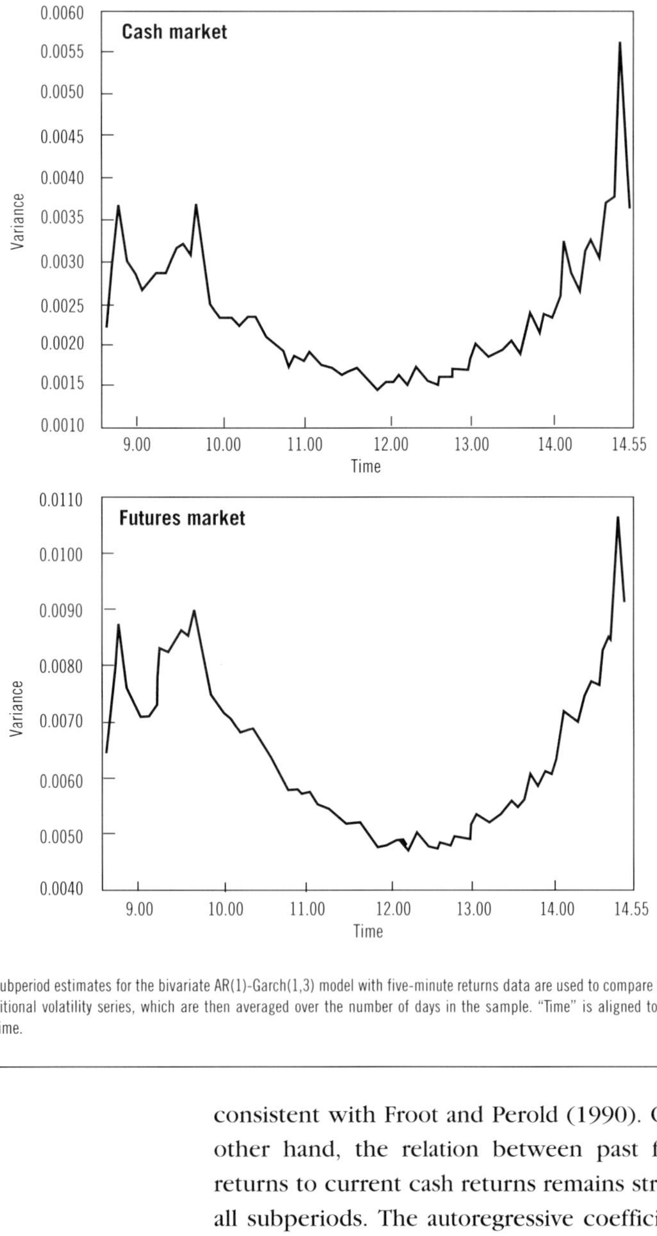

Subperiod estimates for the bivariate AR(1)-Garch(1,3) model with five-minute returns data are used to compare the conditional volatility series, which are then averaged over the number of days in the sample. "Time" is aligned to Central Time.

consistent with Froot and Perold (1990). On the other hand, the relation between past futures returns to current cash returns remains strong in all subperiods. The autoregressive coefficient of the futures returns, β_{ff}, as expected, is negative and small for the 1984–85 period, but larger thereafter. The coefficient for the lagged index returns, β_{fs}, is statistically significant and positive only for the 1984–85 period and possibly 1987–88. Overall, our strong evidence of a lead from futures to cash returns and only weak evidence of a lead from cash to futures returns is consistent with many previous studies.

The coefficients for the overnight return dummy in the volatility equation, $\mathbf{d}_2$, are not reported, but are significant in all periods with values ranging from 2.42 in 1985–86 to 5.54 in 1987–88. The implied stock index variance of the overnight return is equal to $(1 + d_{s,2})^2$ or, on average, about 20 times the variance of the five-minute return. These ratios of overnight to intraday stock return variances estimated by the Garch model are comparable to the sample statistics reported in Table 1 and reasonably consistent with French and Roll (1986). The intercept coefficients associated with the overnight dummy for the mean returns, $\mathbf{d}_1$, are significantly positive, but only for the latter subperiods. Finally, the dummy variable for the slope coefficients, d_3, for the first five-minute interval of the day are always jointly significantly different from zero. The coefficient that captures the influence of the overnight cash return on the first cash return of the trading day is consistently negative with values around -0.25. In Figure 1, the intraday volatility patterns are plotted for the cash and futures markets in the last subperiod 1988–89, although those for the other subperiods are similar. We compute the average conditional variance measure in each five-minute interval during the day over each day in the sample. The figures confirm the familiar U-shaped pattern that a number of earlier studies have uncovered, including Harris (1986).

Estimates from the joint conditional volatility processes for the cash and futures returns indicate that the volatility in each of the two markets is affected by events in its own market as well as the other market. The coefficients that measure the cross-market impact of returns shocks on the volatility, $c_{sf,k}$ and $c_{fs,k}$, for all lags k, are significant and usually positive in the first five-minute lag and negative in the second and third five-minute intervals following the return shock. For example, in the 1988–89 subperiod, the parameters $c_{sf,k}$ (equal to 0.1072, -0.0590, and -0.0248 for the three lags) transmit the past futures return innovations to the conditional variance of the cash market and, similarly, the $c_{fs,k}$ (equal to 0.1457, -0.0920, and -0.0133 for the three lags) transmit the past index return innovations to the conditional variance of the futures market. The parameters that measure the intermarket dependence in the conditional volatilities, b_{sf}, b_{fs}, are also significant and negative in all periods. Note that the generally negative signs of these cross-market coefficients of the B matrix do not imply that the conditional volatility of one market is correlated negatively with the conditional volatility of the other market in the previous period. As the latter is itself a function of the past price shocks in both markets, the best way to see how price shocks in one market affect the conditional volatility of the other market is to invert the system so that the conditional volatilities are expressed as a function of all past price shocks originating in both markets. We illustrate the dynamics of the bivariate Garch system by solving for the impulse response function coefficients in the next subsection.

Our evidence suggests that a "full-feedback" system obtains. Two tests are reported in Table 3 that evaluate the importance of intermarket dependence in the conditional volatility process for the cash and futures returns. The Wald test statistics measure the statistical significance of the off-diagonal coefficient estimates of the B and C_k matrices (Wald test A) and, separately, those of the B matrix alone (Wald test B). The hypothesis of no intermarket dependence for both tests is rejected easily in all periods.

The lead and lag relations found between the intraday volatilities of the cash and futures markets are not the same phenomena uncovered in the lead and lag relations between the returns of the two markets. We usually find some predictability from the cash to futures returns but the relation between a cash market shock to futures market volatility is stronger and more robust. In particular, in the two subperiods in which we find no significant lead from cash to futures returns, 1985–86 and 1988–89, the impact of cash market return shocks and past cash market volatility on the futures market volatility is even stronger than usual. This result for the volatility relations suggests that the pattern of new information flows to the cash and futures markets may be more symmetric than that inferred from examination of only the cash and futures returns.

Although not reported in the tables, some diagnostic tests of the residuals were performed. No indications of serious model misspecification are observed. The autocorrelations and partial autocorrelations for the squared standardised residuals for the stock index and futures returns series are all insignificantly different from zero for the bivariate AR(1)-Garch(1,3) model. This suggests that the conditional volatility process captures successfully the intertemporal dependence highlighted in the returns shown in Table 1. The fit of the bivariate model was further evaluated by examining the distributional properties of the standardised residuals. Although the normal hypothesis is rejected by the Kolmogorov–Smirnov goodness-of-fit tests, there is a substantial reduction in the excess kurtosis observed in Table 1 for the raw returns. The results provide evidence of a reasonable fit for the bivariate Garch(1,3) model.

IMPULSE RESPONSE ANALYSIS

To illustrate the dynamics of the bivariate Garch system estimated for cash and futures returns, we solve for the impulse response functions implied by the system. The impulse response coefficient, say $R_{ij,t+k}$, shows the impact of a unit returns shock (the squared return innovation) originating in market j at time t on the conditional volatility of market i at time $t + k$. These impulse responses can be computed by solving the two recursive equations in the conditional volatility (2) and (3) of the bivariate system. This type of analysis is analogous to solving a vector autoregression (VAR) system into a moving average representation (see Engle, Ito and Lin (1990)).

We plot the impulse response coefficients for the first and last subperiods for which we estimate the model, denoted Figures 2 and 3, respectively. Two important results emerge from the diagrams. First, contrasting the results for the two subperiods shows that the cross-market impulse responses are larger in the more recent subperiods, suggesting that the degree of intermarket dependence in volatility has increased over the sample period. In the first subperiod, it appears that return innovations have a larger immediate impact on their own market volatility than that of the other market, but the latter subperiod shows the opposite effect. Surprisingly, the futures market shock has greater initial impact on cash market volatility and the cash market shock has greater initial impact on futures market volatility. Referring back to Table 3 shows that this trend toward greater intermarket dependence in volatility over the sample period has been gradual. Again, it is useful to contrast this surprising finding with that of previous studies that have shown the lead and lag relations between cash and futures market returns to have attenuated over time (Stoll and Whaley, 1990b).

The second result shown in the figures is that returns shocks to cash market volatility are less persistent than returns shocks to futures market volatility. We believe this result is somewhat unexpected. Because of the effects of asynchronous trading and other market frictions that are likely to affect the returns process in the cash market, we would expect shocks should take longer to die out in the cash market volatility than in the futures market volatility. We find the opposite effect is pervasive and strong. In the next section, we attempt to control for the effects of asynchronous trading and market frictions more directly.

Overall, the results of this section indicate that

2. Impulse response functions of intraday conditional volatility of S&P 500 stock index and S&P 500 stock index futures returns for August 1984–July 1985

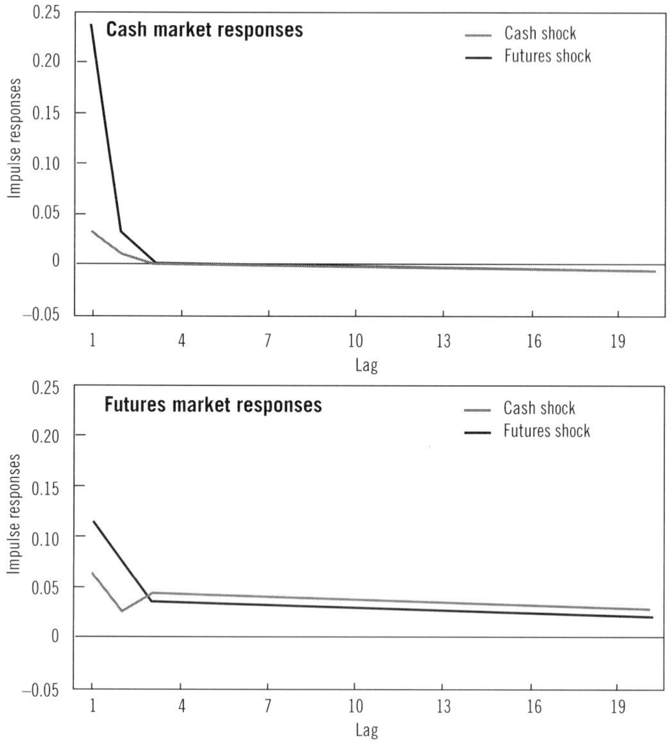

Subperiod estimates for the bivariate AR(1)-Garch(1,3) model with five-minute returns data are used to compute the impulse response coefficients following a unit return shock originating in each market.

3. Impulse response functions of intraday conditional volatility of S&P 500 stock index and S&P 500 stock index futures returns for November 1988–December 1989

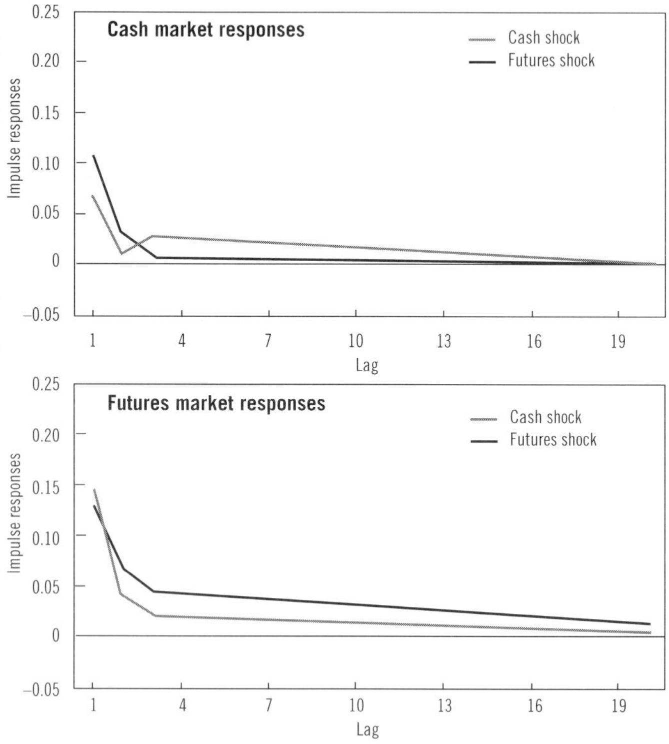

Subperiod estimates for the bivariate AR(1)-Garch(1,3) model with five-minute returns data are used to compute the impulse response coefficients following a unit return shock originating in each market.

there exists a strong intermarket dependence in the volatility processes in the cash and futures markets. This relation is robust and has, in fact, become stronger over the entire 1984–89 period, unlike the patterns of intermarket dependence captured in the returns alone.

Asynchronous trading

Asynchronous trading of the component stocks in the S&P 500 Stock Index will influence the measurement of the intermarket dependence of intraday returns and volatility of returns. In fact, the magnitude and persistence of the cash and futures market shocks on the volatility of returns in those markets demonstrated by this study may be induced spuriously by the asynchronous trading problem. We evaluate this alternative hypothesis examining results using the Major Market Index with its associated futures contract and IBM stock with the S&P 500 stock index futures contract.

TESTS USING THE MAJOR MARKET INDEX DATA

The potential dangers of asynchronous trading are likely to be greater for a large index of stocks, like the S&P 500, than for a small and highly actively traded stock index, like the Major Market Index (MMI). The Major Market Index is a price-weighted index of 20 large NYSE-traded stocks. The Chicago Board of Trade (CBOT) trades a futures contract on the MMI. All of the results obtained with the S&P 500 data are replicated for the MMI and its futures contract for the 1984-1985 subperiod for which it is available.

Table 4 shows the estimates of the bivariate Garch model on the MMI index and index futures data. Results based on the reported MMI index values and the index futures are shown in Panel A; results with the computed MMI index values are in Panel B. Recall that the index values reported to the CBOT Exchange floor may be subject to significant time delays.[12] As a result, we seek to control for this reporting delay by implementing our analysis with MMI index values computed in each five-minute interval directly from the most recent transactions prices for each of the component stocks in the index recorded on the "Fitch" data. We must restrict our analysis to the 1984-85 subperiod because of data limitations with the MMI index futures but some useful comparisons with the first subperiod of the S&P 500 results of Table 3 arise. As expected, the MMI index returns derived from the reported index have much smaller serial correlation than that found in the S&P 500 index returns. The value for β_{ss} is only 0.066 for the

Table 4. Estimates from bivariate generalised autoregressive conditional heteroskedastic models (Garch) of intraday returns on the MMI stock index and MMI stock index futures from July 23, 1984–June 30, 1985

α_s / α_f	β_{ss} / β_{fs}	β_{sf} / β_{ff}	a_s / a_f	b_{ss} / b_{fs}	b_{sf} / b_{ff}	$c_{ss,1}$ / $c_{fs,1}$	$c_{sf,1}$ / $c_{ff,1}$	$c_{ss,2}$ / $c_{fs,2}$	$c_{sf,2}$ / $c_{ff,2}$	$c_{ss,3}$ / $c_{fs,3}$	$c_{sf,3}$ / $c_{ff,3}$
A. Results based on the MMI stock index values reported to the CBOT exchange floor											
–0.0000	0.0661	0.2718	0.00019	0.8535	0.0035	0.2024	0.0787	–0.1432	–0.0177	–0.0093	–0.0403
(–0.089)	(7.88)*	(39.3)*	(7.64)*	(46.0)*	(1.65)	(31.2)*	(23.4)*	(–15.8)*	(–3.76)*	(–1.63)	(–13.1)*
–0.0008	–0.0237	–0.0186	0.00000	0.0087	0.9832	0.0672	0.1135	–0.0399	–0.0480	0.0286	–0.529
(–1.38)	(–2.18)	(–2.01)	(0.014)*	(0.857)	(1011.0)*	(5.75)*	(16.3)*	(–2.52)*	(–4.51)*	(–3.04)*	(–7.07)*
ρ = .5093 (95.4)*; log likelihood = 42,747.592											
B. Results based on the MMI stock index values computed from "Fitch" transactions prices for each component stock											
–0.0005	–0.0961	0.2136	0.00021	0.9834	–0.1248	0.0761	0.1226	0.0041	–0.0927	–0.0425	–0.0018
(–0.865)	(–10.7)*	(17.9)*	(8.70)*	(459.0)*	(–8.11)*	(10.6)*	(10.7)*	(0.382)	(–5.96)*	(–5.12)*	(–0.182)
0.0002	0.2219	0.0943	0.00022	–0.0022	0.8543	0.0559	0.1433	–0.0239	–0.0973	–0.0031	–0.0125
(0.457)	(34.1)*	(10.2)*	(11.1)*	(–1.02)	(62.7)*	(14.7)*	(22.1)*	(–5.63)*	(–12.2)*	(–1.21)	(–2.59)*
ρ = .5297 (102.0)*; log likelihood = 41,994.706											

The model is

$$\mathbf{r}_t = \alpha = \mathbf{d}_1 D_{1t} + \beta \mathbf{r}_{t-1} + d_3 \mathbf{r}_{t-1} D_{2t} + \eta_t,\ \ \eta_t = (\iota + \mathbf{d}_2 D_{1t})\varepsilon_t,\ \ \varepsilon_t | \Phi_{t-1} \sim N(\mathbf{0}, H_t),\ \ \begin{bmatrix} h_{ss,t} \\ h_{ff,t} \end{bmatrix} = \mathbf{A} + B \begin{bmatrix} h_{ss,t-1} \\ h_{ff,t-1} \end{bmatrix} + \sum_{k=1}^{3} C_k \begin{bmatrix} \varepsilon^2_{ss,t-k} \\ \varepsilon^2_{ff,t-k} \end{bmatrix}, h_{sf,t} = \rho (h_{ss,t} h_{ff,t})^{1/2}.$$

The vectors and matrices are defined as follows:

$$\mathbf{r}_t = \begin{bmatrix} r_{st} \\ r_{ft} \end{bmatrix},\ \alpha = \begin{bmatrix} \alpha_s \\ \alpha_f \end{bmatrix},\ \beta = \begin{bmatrix} \beta_{ss} & \beta_{sf} \\ \beta_{fs} & \beta_{ff} \end{bmatrix},\ \eta_t = \begin{bmatrix} \eta_{st} \\ \eta_{ft} \end{bmatrix},\ \varepsilon_t = \begin{bmatrix} \varepsilon_{st} \\ \varepsilon_{ft} \end{bmatrix},\ \mathbf{d}_1 = \begin{bmatrix} d_{s,t} \\ d_{f,t} \end{bmatrix},\ H_t = \begin{bmatrix} h_{ss,t} & h_{sf,t} \\ h_{fs,t} & h_{ff,t} \end{bmatrix},\ \mathbf{A} = \begin{bmatrix} a_s \\ a_f \end{bmatrix},\ B = \begin{bmatrix} b_{ss} & b_{sf} \\ b_{fs} & b_{ff} \end{bmatrix},\ C_k = \begin{bmatrix} c_{ss,k} & c_{sf,k} \\ c_{fs,k} & c_{ff,k} \end{bmatrix},\ d_3 = \begin{bmatrix} d_{ss,3} & d_{sf,3} \\ d_{fs,3} & d_{ff,3} \end{bmatrix}.$$

and r_{tt} is the interval t MMI stock index [reported to CBOT exchange floor (Panel A) or computed value based on "Fitch" stamped transactions prices for individual stocks from NYSE (Panel B) or stock index futures return, Φ_{t-1} is the set of all information at time $t - 1$, D_{1t} is the overnight dummy variable set to unity for overnight returns, and zero for intraday returns, and D_{2t} is the dummy variable set to unity for the first five-minute return of the training day and zero otherwise. The model is estimated using the Berndt et al (1974) maximum likelihood algorithm. The conditional log likelihood function to be maximised is given in (4) and (5). The values in parentheses are asymptotic t-statistics with * denoting coefficient estimates at least 2.325 standard errors from zero, which approximates significance at the 1% level. The dummy coefficient estimates are not reported.

MMI results in contrast with a value in excess of 0.382 for the S&P 500 results in the same 1984-85 subperiod. The magnitude and significance of the coefficients of the conditional volatility equations (2) and (3) are very similar to those reported in Table 3. For example, the impact of lagged shocks from the cash market to futures market volatility, $c_{sf,j}$, is significant at all lags with a large positive initial impact and subsequent negative values for the second and third lags. For the reverse direction, the effect of a futures market shock to cash market volatility, $c_{sf,j}$, is similar for the S&P 500 results but changes sign at the third lag for the MMI results. Finally, a comparison of the B matrix in Tables 3 and 4 shows less intermarket dependence in the MMI results where neither coefficient b_{sf} nor b_{fs} is significant. Overall, these results offer further supportive evidence that the primary results are not sensitive to the presence of asynchronous trading in the S&P 500 stock index.

The results based on the computed MMI index and the index futures are also reported in Table 4. Compared with the results on the reported index, this panel suggests that the futures returns have weaker predictive power for the MMI index returns. On the other hand, there is evidence that the index return can predict the futures return, as shown by the statistical significance of the b_{fs} coefficient estimates. These results are consistent with the findings of Chan (1992). The parameters in the conditional volatility equation are largely similar to those shown for the reported MMI index. They do show a stronger link between the past cash index price shocks and the current conditional volatility of the futures market but a slightly weaker link between the past futures price shocks and the current conditional volatility of the cash market.

In sum, the MMI results also indicate that unexpected price changes in both the cash and futures markets impact the conditional volatility of price changes in the same and the other markets. Although asynchronous trading and reporting lags may account for the transmission lag between S&P 500 index price changes and index futures price changes, these additional tests employing two different sets of MMI index data, corroborate the results found for the cash and futures conditional volatility processes using the S&P 500 data.

ADDITIONAL TESTS USING IBM AND S&P 500 STOCK INDEX FUTURES

One way to confront the asynchronous trading problem even more directly is to implement the

Table 5. Estimates from bivariate generalised autoregressive conditional heteroskedastic models (Garch) of intraday returns on IBM and the S&P 500 stock index futures from August 1984 to July 1986

α_s α_f	β_{ss} β_{fs}	β_{sf} β_{ff}	a_s a_f	b_{ss} b_{fs}	b_{sf} b_{ff}	$c_{ss,1}$ $c_{fs,1}$	$c_{sf,1}$ $c_{ff,1}$	$c_{ss,2}$ $c_{fs,2}$	$c_{sf,2}$ $c_{ff,2}$	$c_{ss,3}$ $c_{fs,3}$	$c_{sf,3}$ $c_{ff,3}$
0.0007	0.4443	−0.2033	0.00073	0.8335	0.0258	0.1438	0.1225	−0.0645	−0.0359	−0.0128	−0.0192
(1.32)	(53.5)*	(−34.3)*	(18.9)*	(126.0)*	(5.87)*	(34.9)*	(18.9)*	(−11.4)*	(−3.58)*	(−3.39)*	(−3.03)*
−0.0005	−0.0546	0.0789	0.00016	−0.0334	0.9952	0.0199	0.1057	−0.0142	−0.0269	0.0077	−0.568
(1.41)	(−8.68)*	(19.6)*	(13.4)*	(−13.8)	(827.0)*	(11.9)*	(22.9)*	(−6.72)*	(−3.94)*	(5.59)*	(−12.4)*

$\rho = .4983$ (144.0)*; log likelihood = 73,015.051

The model is

$$\mathbf{r}_t = \alpha = \mathbf{d}_1 D_{1t} + \beta \mathbf{r}_{t-1} + d_3 \mathbf{r}_{t-1} D_{2t} + \eta_t,\quad \eta_t = (\iota + \mathbf{d}_2 D_{1t})\varepsilon_t,\quad \varepsilon_t | \Phi_{t-1} \sim N(\mathbf{0}, H_t),\quad \begin{bmatrix} h_{ss,t} \\ h_{ff,t} \end{bmatrix} = \mathbf{A} + B \begin{bmatrix} h_{ss,t-1} \\ h_{ff,t-1} \end{bmatrix} + \sum_{k=1}^{3} C_k \begin{bmatrix} \varepsilon^2_{ss,t-k} \\ \varepsilon^2_{ff,t-k} \end{bmatrix}, h_{sf,t} = h_{fs,t} = \rho (h_{ss,t} h_{ff,t})^{1/2}.$$

The vectors and matrices are defined as follows:

$$\mathbf{r}_t = \begin{bmatrix} r_{st} \\ r_{ft} \end{bmatrix}, \alpha = \begin{bmatrix} \alpha_s \\ \alpha_f \end{bmatrix}, \beta = \begin{bmatrix} \beta_{ss} & \beta_{sf} \\ \beta_{fs} & \beta_{ff} \end{bmatrix}, \eta_t = \begin{bmatrix} \eta_{st} \\ \eta_{ft} \end{bmatrix}, \varepsilon_t = \begin{bmatrix} \varepsilon_{st} \\ \varepsilon_{ft} \end{bmatrix}, \mathbf{d}_1 = \begin{bmatrix} d_{s,t} \\ d_{f,t} \end{bmatrix}, H_t = \begin{bmatrix} h_{ss,t} & h_{sf,t} \\ h_{fs,t} & h_{ff,t} \end{bmatrix}, \mathbf{A} = \begin{bmatrix} a_s \\ a_f \end{bmatrix}, B = \begin{bmatrix} b_{ss} & b_{sf} \\ b_{fs} & b_{ff} \end{bmatrix}, C_k = \begin{bmatrix} c_{ss,k} & c_{sf,k} \\ c_{fs,k} & c_{ff,k} \end{bmatrix}, d_3 = \begin{bmatrix} d_{ss,3} & d_{sf,3} \\ d_{fs,3} & d_{ff,3} \end{bmatrix}.$$

and r_{st} is the interval t IBM stock index, r_{ft} is the interval t S&P 500 stock index futures return, Φ_{t-1} is the set of all information at time $t-1$, D_{1t} is the overnight dummy variable set to unity for overnight returns, and zero for intraday returns, and D_{2t} is the dummy variable set to unity for the first five-minute return of the training day and zero otherwise. The model is estimated using the Berndt et al (1974) maximum likelihood algorithm. The conditional log likelihood function to be maximised is given in (4) and (5). The values in parentheses are asymptotic t-statistics with * denoting coefficient estimates at least 2.325 standard errors from zero, which approximates significance at the 1% level. The dummy coefficient estimates are not reported.

model with intraday returns of the S&P 500 index futures and IBM stock. Clearly, just as infrequent trading is less of a problem for the MMI than for the S&P 500 stocks, it is essentially not a problem for IBM. Over the 1984-86 period, IBM averages 7.83 trades per five-minute interval and there is only a 0.5% chance that it will not trade in any given five-minute interval. Again, we focus on the earlier subperiods because the asynchronous trading problem is likely to be most serious.

Table 5 shows the results for the 1984-86 subperiod for which the "Fitch" data are available. In the conditional mean equation, predictability of price changes from S&P 500 futures to IBM and vice versa are both statistically significant, but the coefficient value for b_{fs} is lower than that of Table 4 for the computed MMI index. Similarly, the cross-market effects in the conditional volatility processes are significant, yet weaker than for the indexes.

On the whole, the results of Table 5 lend support to the claim that the main results related to the intraday patterns in conditional volatility between the futures and cash markets are not likely to be driven by either asynchronous trading of component stocks in the stock index or significant delays in reporting the stock index levels.

Conclusions

We examined the intraday relationship between price changes and price-change volatility in the stock index and stock index futures markets. Our evidence for the S&P 500 stock index and stock index futures markets from 1984-89 indicates that:

- ❑ the intraday volatility patterns in both markets demonstrate strong persistence and predictability;
- ❑ there exists strong and pervasive intermarket dependence in the volatility of their price changes, even in subperiods in which the dependence in the price changes themselves appears to be diminished; and
- ❑ these findings are robust even when the analysis controls for potential market frictions such as asynchronous trading in the stock index.

Previous studies that have found intraday futures market price changes systematically leading cash market price changes conclude that index futures markets serve as the primary market for price discovery. They argue that new information appears to disseminate in the futures market first and subsequently in the cash market. This chapter extended and generalised the findings of these existing studies by examining the intraday relations of the volatility of these markets while at the same time controlling for lead and lag relations in their price changes. We show much stronger dependence in both directions in the volatility of price changes between the cash and futures markets than that observed in the price changes alone. Information in price innovations that originate in the cash market is transmitted to the volatility of the futures market and information in price innovations that originate in the futures market is transmitted to the volatility of the cash market. Our evidence is thus consistent with the hypothesis that new market information disseminates in both the futures and stock markets and that both markets serve important price discovery roles.

1 *See Stoll and Whaley (1986, 1990b), Ng (1987), Kawaller, Koch, and Koch (1987a, 1987b, 1990), Cheung and Ng (1990), and Chan (1992). Note that Stoll and Whaley (1990b) and Chan (1992) find a leading relation from cash to futures returns, but it is much weaker than that from futures to cash returns.*

2 *A number of theoretical studies differentiate types of information that flow to the cash and futures markets. For example, Kumar and Seppi (1989), Subrahmanyam (1991), and Chan (1990) show that fixed costs of trading, budget constraints, or different expected profits cause traders in the futures market to collect more market-wide information and traders in the cash market to collect more firm-specific information.*

3 *The notion that the futures market incorporates information more rapidly than the cash market is broadly consistent with the results of Kawaller, Koch, and Koch (1987a, 1987b) and Stoll and Whaley, (1990b) that futures market prices systematically lead cash market prices, but inconsistent with the new findings of Chan (1992) and theoretical conclusions (proposition 11) of Subrahmanyam (1991). The evidence in Chan (1992) is consistent with the hypothesis that cash market frictions influence the pattern of leads and lags in market price changes. He specifically studies the effects of short-sales constraints, differential trading volume and market-wide or stock-specific news events.*

4 *Prior to June 13, 1986, the stock index was computed approximately once a minute but, since that time, it has been computed and reported approximately four times per minute.*

5 *Stoll and Whaley (1990a) show that greater volatility is observed at market open. This could result from the resolution of uncertainty in the overnight period. They attribute this result to the "one-shot auction" at the open due to the specialists' monopoly powers. Moreover, they find that the average time to first trade for NYSE stocks is 15.48 minutes from the open and only 4.98 minutes for stocks in the largest decile of the NYSE. For this reason, the main results of this paper are replicated with the opening price defined to be that prevailing half an hour after the open. The results are similar.*

6 *Stoll and Whaley (1990b) explain how the cash index value is recorded: "AMEX computes and disseminates the MMI level at 15-second intervals. The time stamps that appear on the CBOT data base are the times at which the prices are received and recorded by the CBOT."*

7 *Subperiods 3 and 4 are constructed to exclude the period of October 15, 1987 to November 13, 1987. We do not seek to analyse this highly influential and unusual subperiod. Note that we also exclude the three weeks following the crash because of a number of observed trading suspensions in the futures market during the trading days in that period. For details, see Harris (1989a).*

8 *The large excess kurtosis due to the heavy tails of the distribution observed for these intraday returns series are consistent with models of time-varying conditional heteroskedasticity, such as the Arch and Garch models of Engle (1982) and Bollerslev (1986).*

9 *The large sample size of this analysis means that the appropriate criteria for statistical significance for sample statistics and estimated coefficients are unclear. We highlight throughout the text and tables critical values at the 1% significance level or 2.325 asymptotic standard errors from zero, but caution the readers that a more conservative cut-off may be appropriate. For references, see Chapter 3.2 of Zellner (1984) or Zellner and Siow (1980).*

10 *Generally, if a process, x, is strict white noise, the process for x_t^2 is also strict white noise and intertemporally should exhibit statistical independence.*

11 *Examining the cross-correlation of the squared values of filtered 15-minute returns of the S&P index and S&P index futures, Cheung and Ng (1990) also note this bi-directional feedback. They argue that noise in the futures prices feeds into cash prices, which makes it difficult for market participants to establish profitable trading rules to exploit the well known lead-lag relation between futures and cash prices.*

12 *Studies have shown that reporting lags have exacerbated the extent of the leading relation in price changes from futures to cash. See, in particular, Chan (1992).*

BIBLIOGRAPHY

Akgiray, V., 1989, "Conditional Heteroscedasticity in Time Series of Stock Returns: Evidence and Forecasts", *Journal of Business* 62, pp. 55-80.

Baillie, R., and T. Bollerslev, 1987, "A Multivariate Generalized Arch Approach to Modelling Risk Premia in Forward Foreign Exchange Rate Markets", *Journal of International Money and Finance* 9, pp. 309-24.

Berndt, E., *et al*, 1974, "Estimation and Inference in Nonlinear Structural Models", *Annals of Economic and Social Measurement*, 3, pp. 653-65.

Bessembinder, H., and P. Seguin, 1992, "Futures-Trading, Activity and Stock Price Volatility", *Journal of Finance* 47, pp. 2015-34.

Bollerslev, T., 1986, "Generalized Autoregressive Conditional Heteroskedasticity", *Journal of Econometrics* 31, pp. 307-27.

Bollerslev, T., 1987, "A Conditionally Heteroskedastic Time Series Model of Securing Prices and Rates of Return Data", *Review of Economics and Statistics* 59, pp. 542-7.

Bollerslev, T., R. Engle and J. Wooldridge, 1988, "A Capital Asset Pricing Model with Time-Varying Covariances", *Journal of Political Economy* 96, pp. 116-31.

Chan, K., 1992, "A Further Analysis of the Lead-Lag Relationship between the Cash Market and the Stock Index Futures Market", *Review of Financial Studies* 5, pp. 123-52.

Chan, K., 1993, "Imperfect Information and Cross-Autocorrelations among Stock Returns", *Journal of Finance* 48, pp. 1211-33.

Cheung, Y., and L. Ng, 1990, The Dynamics of S&P 500 Index and S&P 500 Futures Intraday Price Volatilities, Working paper, University of California at Santa Cruz.

Chung, P., 1989, A Transactions Data Test of Stock Index Futures Market Efficiency and Index Arbitrage Profitability, Unpublished Ph.D. dissertation, Ohio State University.

Clark, P., 1973, "A Subordinate Stochastic Process Model with Finite Variance for Speculative Prices", *Econometrica* 41, pp. 135-55.

Conrad, J., B. Gultekin and G. Kaul, 1991, "Asymmetric Predictability of Conditional Variances", *Review of Financial Studies* 4, pp. 597-622.

Engle, R., 1982, "Autoregressive Conditional Heteroscedasticity with Estimates of the Variance of UK Inflation", *Econometrica* 50, pp. 987-1008.

Engle, R., 1987, Multivariate Arch with Factor Structures-Cointegration of Variance, Working paper, University of California at San Diego.

Engle, R., T. Ito, and W. Lin, 1990, "Meteor Showers or Heat Waves? Heteroskedastic Intra-daily volatility in the Foreign Exchange Market", *Econometrica* 58, pp. 525-42.

Engle, R., and K. Kroner, 1989, "Multivariate Simultaneous Generalized Arch, *Econometric Theory* 11, pp. 122-50.

French, K., and R. Roll, 1986, "Stock Return Variance: The Arrival of Information and the Reaction of Traders", *Journal of Financial Economics* 17, pp. 5-26.

French, K., W. Schwert and R. Stambaugh, 1987, "Expected Stock Returns and Volatility," *Journal of Financial Economics* 19, pp. 3-30.

Froot, K., and A. Perold, 1990, New Trading Practices and Short-run Market Efficiency, working paper, Massachusetts Institute of Technology.

Furbush, D., 1989, "Program Trading and Price Movement: Evidence from the October 1987 Market Crash", *Financial Management* 18, pp. 68-83.

Glosten, L., R. Jagannathan and D. Runkle, 1993, "Seasonal Patterns in the Volatility of Stock Index Excess Returns", *Journal of Finance* 48, pp. 1779-802.

Harris, L., 1986, "A Transactions Data Study of Weekly and Intradaily Patterns in Stock Returns", *Journal of Financial Economics* 16, pp. 99-117.

Harris, L., 1989a, "The October 1987 S&P 500 Stock-Futures Basis", *Journal of Finance* 44, pp. 77-99.

Harris, L., 1989b, "S&P 500 Cash Stock Price Volatilities", *Journal of Finance* 44, December, pp. 1155-75.

Harris, L., G. Sofianos and J. Shapiro, 1990, "Program Trading and Intraday Volatility", *Review of Financial Studies* 7, pp. 656-86.

Kawaller, I., P. Koch, and T. Koch, 1987a, "The Temporal Price Relationship between S&P 500 Futures and S&P 500 Index", *Journal of Finance* 42, pp. 1309-29.

Kawaller, I., P. Koch and T. Koch, 1987b, "Intraday Relationships between the volatility in the S&P 500 Futures Prices and the Volatility in the S&P 500 Index", *Journal of Banking and Finance* 14, pp. 373-97.

Kumar, P., and D. Seppi, 1989, Information and Index Arbitrage, Working Paper 88-89-90, Graduate School of Industrial Administration, Carnegie Mellon University.

MacKinlay, A.C., and K. Ramaswamy, 1988, "Index-Futures Arbitrage and the Behavior of Stock Index Futures Prices", *Review of Financial Studies* 1, pp. 137-58.

Neal, R., 1990, Program Trading on the NYSE: A Descriptive Analysis and Estimates of the Intraday Impact on Stock Returns, Working paper, University of Washington.

Nelson, D., 1991, "Conditional Heteroskedasticity in Asset Returns: A New Approach", *Econometrica* 59, pp. 347-71.

Ng, N., 1987, "Detecting Spot Prices Forecasts in Futures Prices Using Causality Tests," *Review of Futures Markets* 6, pp. 61-89.

Report of The Presidential Task Force on Market Mechanisms, 1988, Washington DC, US Government Printing Office.

Report for Market Volatility and Investor Confidence Panel, 1990, New York, New York Stock Exchange.

Ross, S., 1989, "Information and Volatility: The No-Arbitrage Martingale Approach to Timing and Resolution Irrelevancy", *Journal of Finance* 44, pp. 1-17.

Schwert, G.W., 1989, "Why Does Stock Market Volatility Change Over Time?" *Journal of Finance* 44, pp. 1115-53.

Schwert, G.W., and P. Seguin, 1990, "Heteroskedasticity in Stock Returns," *Journal of Finance* 45, pp. 1129-56.

Stoll, H., and R. Whaley, 1986, Expiration Date Effects of Index Options and Futures, Monograph 1986, 3, New York, Salomon Brothers Center for the Study of Financial Institutions, Graduate School of Business Administration, New York University.

Stoll, H.R., and R.E. Whaley, 1990a, "Stock Market Structure and Volatility", *Review of Financial Studies* 3, pp. 37-71.

Stoll, H., and R. Whaley, 1990b, "The Dynamics of Stock Index and Stock Index Futures Returns", *Journal of Financial and Quantitative Analysis* 25, pp. 441-68.

Subrahmanyam, A., 1991, "A Theory of Trading in Stock Index Futures," *Review of Financial Studies*, 4, pp. 17-51.

Tauchen, G., and M. Pitts, 1983, "The Price Variability-Volume Relationship on Speculative Markets," *Econometrica* 51, pp. 485-505.

Zellner, A., 1984, *Basic Issues in Econometrics*, Chicago, University of Chicago.

Zellner, A., and A. Siow, 1980, "Posterior Odds Ratios for Selected Regression Hypotheses", in J.M. Bernardo et al. (eds), Bayesian Statistics, Proceedings of the First International Meeting Held in Valencia (Spain), May 28 to June 2, 1979, pp. 585-603, Valencia, Spain, University Press.

The Term Structure of Volatility Implied by Foreign Exchange Options*

Xinzhong Xu and Stephen J. Taylor
University of Manchester; Lancaster University

This paper illustrates regression and Kalman filtering methods for estimating the time-varying term structure of volatility expectations revealed by options prices. Short- and long-term expectations are estimated for four currencies using daily PHLX options prices from 1985 to 1989. Throughout this period, there were important differences between short- and long-term expectations. The slope of the term structure changed frequently and there were significant variations in long-term volatility expectations. The expectation estimates can be used to value OTC options, to improve hedging strategies, and to test the hypothesis that the options market overreacts.

Options provide information about the expected future volatility of the underlying asset. Implied volatilities at any moment in time vary, however, for different times to option expiry T and different exercise prices X. A matrix of implied volatilities is frequently available, say with columns ordered by T and rows ordered by X. Rational expectations of the average volatility during the next T years will vary with T whenever volatility is believed to be stochastic. Thus, the rows of the implied volatility matrix may provide information about the term structure of expected future volatility. This paper describes and illustrates methods for estimating this term structure from one row of the implied volatility matrix, corresponding to nearest-the-money options.

We model both the term structure of expected volatility and the time series characteristics of the term structure. We then describe a simple specification for the term structure at one moment in time. The specification involves two "factors" representing short-term expected volatility and long-term expected volatility. Thus, the specification is more general than the single factor approach of Stein (1989). The term structure specification is particularly appropriate when a satisfactory model for asset prices is Garch(1,1). This model has often been recommended in empirical studies (see Bollerslev, Chou, and Kroner (1992)). We describe two estimation methods. A Kalman filter formulation has many advantages and allows estimation of time series models for the long-term expected volatility and the spread between short- and long-term expected volatility; examples are given for AR(1) models.

The empirical examples are for spot currency options on sterling, the Deutschmark, the yen, and the Swiss franc, quoted against the dollar.

* *This paper was first published in the* Journal of Financial and Quantitative Analysis, *Vol. 29, No.1 (1994). Xinzhong Xu was at the Financial Options Research Centre, University of Warwick, when the paper was written and revised. The authors thank Jonathan Karpoff, an anonymous referee, Les Clewlow, Gordon Gemmill, Teng-Suan Ho, Stewart Hodges, Richard Stapleton, participants at seminars held at City University, Lancaster University, Oxford University, and Warwick University, and participants at the 1992 meetings of the European and French Finance Associations for their helpful comments and advice. The authors thank the Philadelphia Stock Exchange for providing their currency options data.*

Daily implied volatilities are modelled for the five-year period from January 1985 to November 1989. The next section describes the Philadelphia Stock Exchange options data, and we then present the empirical estimates of the term structure. Volatility expectations are shown to revert from their short-term level towards their long-term level with a half-life of approximately four weeks. There are considerable fluctuations in the spread between short- and long-term expectations and frequent changes in the slope of the term structure. There are also significant changes in long-term volatility expectations, which can be modeled either by an AR(1) process or a random walk. The final section presents our conclusions.

The term structure of implied volatilities has also been discussed by Poterba and Summers (1986), Stein (1989), Franks and Schwartz (1991), Diz and Finucane (1993), and Heynen, Kemna, and Vorst (1994). Only two values of T are considered at any moment of time in these papers. Any number of T values can be studied using the estimation methods presented here and the number can vary from day to day. Time series studies involving one implied volatility per day are reported in several papers (for example, Merville and Pieptea (1989) and Day and Lewis (1992)), but such studies ignore term structure effects because T then varies from day to day. Our empirical analysis shows that it is possible to estimate interesting time series models for both short- and long-term expected currency volatility using the Kalman filter.

Stein (1989) directly examined the term structure of implied volatilities, using two daily time series on implied volatilities for S&P 100 index options over the period December 1983 to September 1987. The values of T were less than one month for the first series and between one and two months for the second series. Based on the assumption that the volatility is mean reverting, as supported by his data, Stein claimed that the elasticity of volatility changes is larger than suggested by rational expectations theory: long-maturity options tend to "overreact" to changes in the implied volatility of short-maturity options. This conclusion has been disputed by Diz and Finucane (1993) following their analysis of similar S&P 100 index data. Furthermore, Heynen, Kemna, and Vorst (1994) found that their conclusion about overreaction depended on the model used to represent changes in asset price volatility. They considered one year of European Options Exchange data and two values of T, one varying between zero and three months, the other between six and nine months.

Resnick, Sheikh, and Song (1993) have used stock options to show that investors perceive monthly differences in return variability and, hence, the implied volatility term structure is not flat. The monthly differences are economically significant.

A model for the term structure

Volatility is defined in our term structure model in the usual way and is always expressed in annual terms. Thus, the volatility for some time period is the annualised standard deviation of the change in the price logarithm during the same period of time. It is supposed that each year is divided into n smaller intervals of time. These intervals might be calendar days or they might be trading days and so they commence when a market closes on one day and end when the market next closes; alternatively the durations of the intervals might be one week.

Market agents will have expectations at time t about the volatility during future time periods. Suppose they form expectations of the quantities,

$$\mathrm{Var}\left(\ln P_{t+\tau} - \ln P_{t+\tau-1}\right), \quad \tau = 1,2,\ldots, \qquad (1)$$

where P refers to the price of the asset upon which options are traded. These expectations can be annualised by multiplying them by n. After doing this, let $\sigma_{t,t+\tau}$ denote the volatility expectation at time t for time interval $t + \tau$, so

$$\sigma^2_{t,t+\tau} = n\mathrm{Var}\left(\ln\left(P_{t+\tau} / P_{t+\tau-1}\right)\middle| M_t\right), \qquad (2)$$

where M_t is the information set used by the options market.

Our term structure model is intended to be as simple as is reasonably possible. The model supposes that the expectations $\sigma_{t,t+\tau}$ are functions of at most three parameters. The first is the short-term expectation α_t for the next time interval,

$$\alpha_t = \sigma_{t,t+1}. \qquad (3)$$

The second parameter is the long-term expectation, μ_t, given by assuming that the expectations converge for distant intervals,

$$\mu_t = \lim_{\tau\to\infty} \sigma_{t,t+\tau}. \qquad (4)$$

Expectations are assumed to revert towards the time-dependent level μ_t as τ increases. The third parameter, ϕ, controls the rate of reversion towards μ_t and ϕ is assumed to be the same for all t. It is more practical to suppose that reversion applies to variances than to standard deviations, as follows,

$$\sigma^2_{t,t+\tau} - \mu^2_t = \phi\left(\sigma^2_{t,t+\tau-1} - \mu^2_t\right),\quad \tau > 1. \qquad (5)$$

It then follows that the expectation for time interval $t + \tau$ depends upon α_t, μ_t, ϕ, and τ, thus,

$$\sigma^2_{t,t+\tau} = \mu^2_t + \phi^{\tau-1}\left(\alpha^2_t - \mu^2_t\right),\quad \tau > 0. \qquad (6)$$

Market agents have mean-reverting expectations when $0 < \phi < 1$. Stein (1989) used an equation similar to the special case of (6) given by constant μ_t. Constant expectations as t varies, consistent with the Black-Scholes paradigm, are only obtained when $\phi = 0$ or $\phi = 1$.

Our preference for a simple model only permits three shapes for a graph of $\sigma_{t,t+\tau}$ against τ. The expectations are either monotonic increasing or monotonic decreasing as τ increases, or they are the same for all τ. Graphs of the expectations cannot contain spikes, perhaps aligned with seasonal events or the anticipated release of particularly important information.

The preceding equations summarise expectations made at time t for unit time intervals commencing at later times. The expected volatility at time t for an interval of general length T, from time t to time t + T, is the square root of

$$v^2_T = \frac{1}{T}\sum_{\tau=1}^{T}\sigma^2_{t,t+\tau} = \mu^2_t + \frac{1-\phi^T}{T(1-\phi)}\left(\alpha^2_t - \mu^2_t\right), \qquad (7)$$

here assuming that subsequent asset prices, $\{P_{t+\tau}, \tau > 0\}$, follow a random walk. The numbers $v_T, T = 1,2,3,\ldots$, define the term structure of expected average volatility at time t; note the units for T are time intervals in (7), not years. We are interested in using implied volatilities from options prices to estimate the time series $\{\alpha_t\}$ and $\{\mu_t\}$ and also the mean-reversion parameter ϕ. This can be achieved because (7) shows that v^2_T is a linear function of α^2_t and μ^2_t.

Estimation methods

Two methods have been developed for estimating the term structure model. The first method seeks the best match between the model and a dataset of implied volatilities. This method makes few assumptions about the time series properties of the series $\{\alpha_t\}$ and $\{\mu_t\}$. The method is also very quick. The second method supposes that $\{\alpha_t\}$ and $\{\mu_t\}$ follow autoregressive processes (possibly with unit roots) and then uses the Kalman filter to provide estimates of both the term structure and the parameters of the models assumed for $\{\alpha_t\}$ and $\{\mu_t\}$. This method requires substantially more computer resources.

NOTATION

The time t is now supposed to count trading days. On day t, there will be implied volatility information for N_t expiry dates, supposed to be represented by a single number for each expiry date. It is a feature of our datasets that N_t varies from day to day. Let $y_{j,t}$ denote the implied volatility for option expiry date j on day t and suppose the times to expiry are $T_{j,t}$, measured in calendar days, with $T_{1,t} < T_{2,t} < \ldots < T_{N_t,t}$.

A REGRESSION METHOD

Forward implied variances $f_{j,t}$ can be calculated from the implied volatilities. At time t, the forward variance for the time interval from $t + T_{j-1,t}$ to $t + T_{j,t}$ is

$$f_{j,t} = \frac{T_{j,t}y^2_{j,t} - T_{j-1,t}y^2_{j-1,t}}{T_{j,t} - T_{j-1,t}}. \qquad (8)$$

This is an annualised number. When $j = 1$, $T_{0,t} = 0$ in (8).

The forward implied variance can be compared with the expected value for the appropriate part of the term structure. The forward expected variance $g_{j,t}$ is

$$g_{j,t} = \frac{1}{T_{j,t} - T_{j-1,t}}\left(\sum_{\tau=T_{j-1,t}+1}^{T_{j,t}}\sigma^2_{C(t),C(t)+\tau}\right), \qquad (9)$$

where C(t) is the calendar day count corresponding to the passage of t trading days and τ is measured in calendar days. From (6) it can be seen that the forward expected variance is a linear combination of α^2_t and μ^2_t. The combination is

$$g_{j,t} = \mu^2_t + x_{j,t}\left(\alpha^2_t - \mu^2_t\right), \qquad (10)$$

with

$$x_{j,t} = \frac{\phi^{T_{j-1,t}} - \phi^{T_{j,t}}}{(1-\phi)\left(T_{j,t} - T_{j-1,t}\right)}, \qquad (11)$$

assuming $\phi < 1$.

Let n now denote the number of days for which there are implied volatilities. We wish to find estimates of ϕ, $\alpha_1, \alpha_2, \ldots, \alpha_n$, $\mu_1, \mu_2, \ldots, \mu_n$, giving small values for the differences, $e_{j,t} = f_{j,t} - g_{j,t}$, $1 \le j \le N_t$, $1 \le t \le n$.

Our estimates are given by minimising sums of terms $e^2_{j,t}$ for various ϕ, followed by choosing ϕ to be the value giving the smallest sum across all times t. We could estimate α_t and μ_t using the implied volatilities for period t alone, providing $N_t \ge 2$. These estimates are rather erratic because the differences $e_{j,t}$ are nontrivial. There are many possible explanations for nontrivial differences including bid/ask spreads and nonsynchronous options and asset prices (Day and Lewis (1988)), incorrectly priced options, and misspecification of the term structure model. Less erratic estimates for period t can be obtained by using the implied volatilities for a time window t − k to t + k. This will be a reasonable method when it can be assumed that the volatility term structure is approximately constant within the time window.

The estimation method can be summarised by three steps. Step 1 involves selecting a set of plausible values for ϕ, say $\phi_1,\ldots,\phi_m$. Step 2 involves finding the best estimates $\hat{\alpha}_{i,t}$, $\hat{\mu}_{i,t}$, when $\phi = \phi_i$, $i = 1,\ldots,m$. As $g_{j,t}$ is a linear function of $x_{j,t}$, from (10), these estimates are given for period t by regressing $f_{j,s}$ on $x_{j,s}$, with $1 \le j \le N_s$ and $t - k \le s \le t + k$. From (10), the estimated intercept is $\hat{\mu}^2_{i,t}$ and the sum of the estimated slope and the estimated intercept is $\hat{\alpha}^2_{i,t}$. These estimates are obtained for $t = k + 1,\ldots,n - k$, and the sum of the squared regression errors calculated, summing over the three variables j, s, and t. Call the sum $S(\phi_i)$ when $\phi = \phi_i$. Step 3 gives $\hat{\phi}$ as the value that minimises $S(\phi_i)$, and the time series of estimates $\{\hat{\alpha}_t\}$ and $\{\hat{\mu}_t\}$ as the regression estimates when $\phi = \hat{\phi}$. When this method was implemented for our data, it was found that $\hat{\phi}$ is essentially the same for all k between 1 and 10. Consequently, results are reported below with $k = 5$.

THE KALMAN FILTER METHOD

The expected squared volatility over any period of time is a linear function of the current values of $\alpha_t^2 - \mu_t^2$ and μ_t^2, from (7). This suggests a Kalman filter method is ideal for estimating the term structure, day by day, if a set of squared implied volatilities is considered to be the expected squared volatility (from the term structure model) plus a set of measurement errors that can be attributed to option mispricing, non-synchronous observations, and other issues. The Kalman filter formulation has several attractive properties:

- it permits comparisons of models for the time series behaviour of the state variables;
- all the parameters can be obtained by maximising a quasi-likelihood function;
- the number of observations N_t can vary from day to day; and
- it can be extended to give results for several assets simultaneously, thus permitting the identification of common factors in the term structure of similar assets.

There are many ways to define the state variables and to model their time series characteristics. One credible example is presented here and further examples are evaluated below. We suppose $\{\alpha_t^2\}$ and $\{\mu_t^2\}$ are stationary processes and have the same mean value $\bar{\mu}$. The state variables are taken to be $\alpha_t^2 - \mu_t^2$ and $\mu_t^2 - \bar{\mu}$, which both have zero mean and are unlikely to be highly correlated with each other. This choice is preferred to $\alpha_t^2 - \bar{\mu}$ and $\mu_t^2 - \bar{\mu}$ because these variables will probably have substantial covariation. The simplest plausible model for each of the chosen state variables is an AR(1) process. Independence between the state variables will be assumed. This gives the following state equations,

$$S_t = \begin{pmatrix} \alpha_t^2 - \mu_t^2 \\ \mu_t^2 - \bar{\mu} \end{pmatrix}, \tag{12}$$

a 2×1 vector,

$$S_t = \begin{pmatrix} \phi_1 & 0 \\ 0 & \phi_2 \end{pmatrix} S_{t-1} + \varepsilon_t, \tag{13}$$

$$E[\varepsilon_t] = 0,\ E[\varepsilon_t \varepsilon_t'] = \begin{pmatrix} \sigma_1^2 & 0 \\ 0 & \sigma_2^2 \end{pmatrix}. \tag{14}$$

The observation equation for the Kalman filter is written as

$$Y_t = Z_t S_t + \xi_t. \tag{15}$$

Here Y_t is a $N_t \times 1$ vector of squared implied volatilities minus $\bar{\mu}$, S_t is the 2×1 vector of state variables that summarise the term structure of expected volatility, Z_t is a $N_t \times 2$ matrix of state coefficients, and ξ_t is a $N_t \times 1$ vector of measurement errors. We have

$$Y_t = \begin{pmatrix} y_{1,t}^2 - \bar{\mu} \\ \cdot \\ \cdot \\ y_{N_t,t}^2 - \bar{\mu} \end{pmatrix} \text{ and } Z_t = \begin{pmatrix} z_{1,t} & 1 \\ \cdot & \cdot \\ \cdot & \cdot \\ z_{N_t,t} & 1 \end{pmatrix}, \tag{16}$$

with

$$z_{j,t} = \frac{1 - \phi^{T_{j,t}}}{T_{j,t}(1 - \phi)} \tag{17}$$

from (7). The measurement errors are assumed to have zero means. Specification of their covariance matrix H_t is far from straightforward. Our preliminary results were based on the assumption that this matrix is diagonal with all N_t diagonal terms equal to the same number,

$$H_t = E[\xi_t \xi_t'] = \mathrm{diag}(\sigma_0^2,\ldots,\sigma_0^2). \tag{18}$$

Assuming uncorrelated measurement errors, so $E[\xi_s \xi_t'] = 0$ when $s \ne t$, concludes the specification of this particular model.

Sequential application of the Kalman filter to

increasing information sets $I_t = \{Y_1, Y_2, \ldots, Y_t\}$ yields the minimum mean square linear estimators (MMSLE) of the state variables, $E[S_t \mid I_t]$, using standard updating equations; these can be found in Harvey (1989). The MMSLE are 2×1 vectors from which can be calculated the $N_t \times 1$ prediction error vectors,

$$v_t = Y_t - Z_t \begin{pmatrix} \phi_1 & 0 \\ 0 & \phi_2 \end{pmatrix} E\left[S_{t-1} \middle| I_{t-1}\right], \qquad (19)$$

and the term structure estimates,

$$\begin{pmatrix} \hat{\alpha}_t^2 \\ \hat{\mu}_t^2 \end{pmatrix} = \begin{pmatrix} \bar{\mu} \\ \bar{\mu} \end{pmatrix} + \begin{pmatrix} 1 & 1 \\ 0 & 1 \end{pmatrix} E\left[S_t \middle| I_t\right]. \qquad (20)$$

Equations (12)–(18) specify a model having seven parameters, summarised by the vector

$$\theta = \left(\phi, \phi_1, \phi_2, \sigma_0^2, \sigma_1^2, \sigma_2^2, \bar{\mu}\right).$$

A quasi-maximum likelihood estimate of θ can be obtained because the likelihood function is the product of conditional densities $f(Y_t \mid I_{t-1})$ and these densities depend, through θ, upon the prediction errors v_t and their covariance matrices $F_t = E[v_t v_t' \mid I_{t-1}]$. Following the arguments of Harvey ((1989), p. 126), the quasi-log-likelihood function is as follows, given by assuming the prediction errors are multivariate normal,

$$\ln L(Y_1, Y_2, \ldots, Y_n) = \sum_{t=1}^{n} \ln f\left(Y_t \middle| I_{t-1}\right)$$

$$= -\frac{1}{2} \sum_{t=1}^{n} \left(N_t \ln(2\pi) + \ln(\det F_t) + v_t' F_t^{-1} v_t\right). \qquad (21)$$

This function can be maximised using standard subroutines. We used the NAG subroutine E04JAF for our optimisations.

Data and computation of implied volatility

THE MARKET

The Philadelphia currency options market is the world's leading exchange in European and American-style options on spot currencies, with markets in sterling, the Deutschmark, yen, Swiss franc, French franc, Australian dollar, Canadian dollar, and European currency unit. Total volume in these contracts represented approximately $2 billion in underlying value each trading day in 1990. The expiry months always include March, June, September, and December. Two nearby months are also traded so that $N_t = 6$ when trade occurs for all the expiry months.

DATA SOURCES

The primary source database for this study is the transaction report compiled daily by the Philadelphia Stock Exchange (PHLX). This report contains the following information for each option traded during a day: a date (the trade date before February 1987; for February 1987 onwards, the date on which the report was compiled, usually one day later), the style (call or put, European or American) and currency, expiration month, exercise price, number of trades, number of contracts traded, the opening, closing, lowest, and highest option prices, and the simultaneous spot exchange rate quotes. Only the closing option prices have been used. The database studied here contains options prices for the seven currencies mentioned above and the ECU from November 5, 1984, to November 21, 1989. However, the transaction report is not available for some trading days during the above period; for some others, the report is not complete or, in a few cases, is in some way clearly erroneous.

Prices have been collected manually from the *Wall Street Journal* (WSJ) whenever necessary. Approximately 10% of our implied volatilities are calculated from WSJ prices. The WSJ options prices and the associated spot prices are not simultaneous; we discuss the consequences of this non-simultaneity in detail below.

All the results presented in this paper are for the period commencing January 2, 1985. The prices for November and December 1984 are only used to commence the Kalman filter calculations.

The interest rates used are London euro-currency rates, collected from Datastream. This source provides overnight, seven days, one month, three months, six months, and one year interest rates. For intermediate times, we simply use linear interpolation. There is unlikely to be a simultaneity problem with the option data as the trading times are similar.

The London euro-currency interest rates were chosen because they consist of the maximum number of different maturities that we could use to make the interest rates used in calculating implied volatility as accurate as possible. Furthermore, they ensure the foreign and domestic interest rates are contemporaneous and are offered by the same institutions.

DATA SELECTION AND REVISIONS

Results have been obtained for American style options on four currencies, sterling, the Deutschmark, yen, and Swiss franc, separately for calls and puts. Results for the other three currencies have not been sought because trading was thin, in particular during the early part of the period studied.

Two essential changes have been made to the original data. First, we changed all the report compilation dates to the appropriate trading dates. Second, as the options expire on the Saturday before the third Wednesday of the expiration month but settle on the third Wednesday of that month, we have multiplied each option premium by $e^{R_d(4/365.25)}$, with R_d the relevant domestic (ie dollar) interest rate.

Several exclusion criteria were used to remove uninformative options records from the database. Five criteria are first listed and then explained. We use standard notation, with S the spot rate, X the exercise price, T the time to expiry measured in years, and R_f the foreign interest rate:

❑ Options with time to expiration less than 10 calendar days.

❑ Options violating European boundary conditions, $c < Se^{-R_fT} - Xe^{-R_dT}$, $p < Xe^{-R_dT} - Se^{-R_fT}$.

❑ Options violating American boundary conditions, $C < S - X$, $P < X - S$.

❑ Options with premia less than or equal to 0.01 cents.

❑ Options that are far in- or out-of-the-money: $X < 0.8S$ or $X > 1.2S$.

The first criterion was used to eliminate options with small times to maturity as the implied volatilities then behave erratically.

The second and third criteria eliminate options violating the boundary conditions for European and American options. As the American options could be exercised at any time up to expiration, both boundary conditions must be satisfied, otherwise a riskless arbitrage could arise. Where an option price violates a rational pricing bound, there are good reasons for suspecting that trades could not be made at this price.

The fourth criterion is used to exclude options for which the necessarily discrete market prices are particularly likely to distort calculations of implied volatility.

The final criterion is used to eliminate those options that are either deep in-the-money or deep out-of-the-money. As their implied volatilities are extremely sensitive to a small change in the option price, they could distort calculations of implied volatility. Furthermore, these options trade without much volume and are thus unrepresentative.

Preliminary calculations showed that a very small number of extreme outliers ought to be removed because of their excessive influence on the model estimates. After all the exclusions, there are at least three maturities for between 75% and 90% of the days in each of the eight datasets studied.

COMPUTATION OF IMPLIED VOLATILITY

Implied volatilities have been calculated from American model prices. The model prices are approximated by the very accurate functions derived in Barone-Adesi and Whaley (1987). The calculations of implied volatility used an interval subdivision method, which always converges to an unique solution.

It was decided to calculate the implied volatilities only from the closing prices of the nearest-the-money options; the nearest-the-money option on some day for a specific T is the option whose exercise price minimises $|S - X|$. Nearest-the-money options were chosen for two reasons. First, given the widely reported "strike bias" or "smile effect" (Shastri and Wethyavivorn (1987), Sheikh (1991), Taylor and Xu (1994)), including out-of-the-money and in-the-money options would introduce further noise into the term structure estimates; in theory, the smile effect can be a consequence of stochastic volatility (Hull and White (1987), Stein and Stein (1991)). Second, the approximation that the implied volatility of a rationally priced option will equal the mean expected volatility over the time to expiry is generally considered more satisfactory for an at-the-money option than for all other options (Stein (1989), Day and Lewis (1992), Heynen, Kemna, and Vorst (1994)).

Results

RESULTS FROM THE REGRESSION METHOD

The regression method described above produces an estimate of ϕ, the mean-reversion parameter for volatility expectations, by fitting term structures to implied volatilities within windows containing $2k + 1$ trading days. Table 1 lists the estimates of ϕ when $k = 5$. These are very similar across currencies, ranging from 0.968 to 0.980. The median of the eight ϕ estimates is 0.975 corresponding to a "half-life" of 27 calendar days by solving the equation $0.975^h = 0.5$. The call and put estimates can be seen to be very similar: the two smallest estimates are for the yen, the third and fourth in magnitude are for sterling, the fifth and sixth are for the Deutschmark, and the two largest are for the Swiss franc.

Table 1 also provides estimates of the parameter ϕ for two subperiods, the first from January

Table 1. Regression method estimates of the term structure parameter ϕ when k = 5

Options	Full sample (85.01–89.11)	Subsample 1 (85.01–87.06)	Subsample 2 (87.07–89.11)
SC	0.973	0.967	0.980
SP	0.973	0.965	0.983
DMC	0.976	0.967	0.986
DMP	0.977	0.972	0.983
JYC	0.968	0.939	0.979
JYP	0.972	0.964	0.976
SFC	0.978	0.979	0.978
SFP	0.980	0.978	0.981

SC refers to sterling calls, SP to sterling puts, etc.

1985 to June 1987 and the second from July 1987 to November 1989. Again the differences between the estimates from call and put options are very similar except for the yen in the first period. Most of the estimates of ϕ in the second period are higher than their counterparts in the first period although the differences are fairly small. The range is much greater for the first period, from 0.939 to 0.979, than for the second period, from 0.976 to 0.986. The median values are 0.967 and 0.981, respectively, for the first and second periods, corresponding to "half-lives" equal to 21 and 36 calendar days. These estimates of the "half-life" provide the important result that the market does not expect volatility shocks to persist for long, ie their effect is expected to disappear quickly.

Figure 1 summarises the term structure of volatility expectations for mark calls. Very similar numbers are obtained for mark puts as expected. Figure 1 shows the time series estimates of the 15-day expectations (from Equation (6) with $t = 15$) and the long-term expectations μ_t. The 15-day expectations (Equation 6) are very similar to the 30-day expected average volatilities (Equation 7). We chose to plot estimates for 15-day expectations rather than expectations estimates for the next day to avoid extrapolation beyond the limits implied by our data; recall $T \geq 10$ calendar days in all the calculations. Further figures, available from the authors, make clear that volatility expectations for the three European currencies have been extremely similar with the yen close to the European currencies after mid-1987.

Five conclusions are suggested by Figure 1. First, the difference between 15-day and long-term expectations is often several per cent so the implied volatilities reveal a significant term structure. Second, the estimates of the 15-day and long-term expectations frequently cross over, so

1. Estimated volatility expectations (regression method, DM calls)

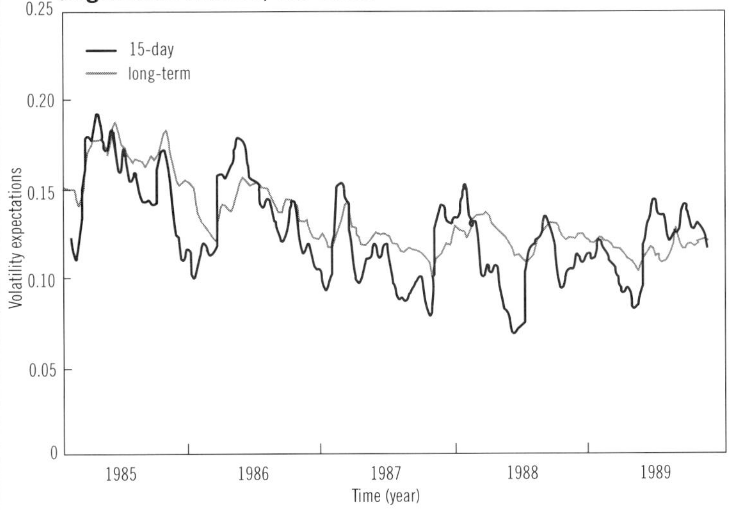

the slope of the term structure often changes. Crossovers occur, very approximately, at an average rate of once every two to three months. Third, the long-term expected volatility varies significantly. This will become clearer when the results from the Kalman filter are analysed. Fourth, as might be expected, the estimated 15-day volatility expectation is much more variable over time than the estimated long-term expectation. Finally, the implied volatility process may not have been stationary in the sense that the average level appears to have been higher in 1985 than in the later years 1986 to 1989, although historic estimates of volatility are also high in 1985.

RESULTS FROM THE KALMAN FILTER

There are seven parameters in the time-varying term structure model described above. The parameter ϕ continues to measure the rate of reversion in volatility expectations towards the long-term level. The spread between short- and long-term expected squared volatility is assumed to follow an AR(1) process with AR parameter ϕ_1, mean zero, and residual variance σ_1^2. The long-term expected squared volatility is assumed to independently follow an AR(1) process with AR parameter ϕ_2, mean $\bar{\mu}$, and residual variance σ_2^2.

The final parameter in the above section on the Kalman filter method is the variance of the measurement errors when the model is fitted to squared implied volatilities. One parameter for the measurement error variances has been found to be insufficient to give a satisfactory model for our implied volatilities data. The magnitude of the measurement errors is larger, on average, for the WSJ observations because of nonsimultaneous spot and options prices. Furthermore, we have noted that the magnitude of the measurement errors increases, on average, as T decreases, for both data sources. Our preferred model has nine parameters with three parameters (σ_P^2, σ_T^2, and σ_W^2) used to define the dispersion matrix for the measurement errors ξ_t. The following diagonal matrix is preferred,

$$H_t = E[\xi_t \xi_t'] = \mathrm{diag}\left(\sigma_S^2 + \frac{\sigma_T^2}{T_{1,t}}, \ldots, \sigma_S^2 + \frac{\sigma_T^2}{T_{N,t}}\right),$$

$$\sigma_S^2 = \sigma_P^2 \text{ for PHLX prices,}$$
$$= \sigma_W^2 \text{ for WSJ prices.} \qquad (22)$$

Results are discussed in some detail for this nine-parameter model and then for simplifications (eg, $\phi_2 = 1$) and, finally, for more general models (eg H_t is not diagonal).

The preferred model Table 2 gives the parameter estimates obtained by maximising the quasi-log-likelihood function (21) defined by the Kalman filter. Panel A presents the estimates and approximate standard errors for the complete five-year period from 1985 to 1989. The standard errors have been calculated from the information matrix using numerical second derivatives, although the reliability of the usual likelihood theory in this context is unknown to us because the matrices of state coefficients, Z_t, are time-dependent. Panel B presents the estimates for the two subperiods, from January 1985 to June 1987 and from July 1987 to November 1989.

The square root of an estimate $\bar{\mu}$ is an estimate of the median level of volatility expectations. These median estimates are smaller for the yen than for the European currencies and they decrease from the first subperiod to the second subperiod for all currencies.

The Kalman filter estimates of ϕ are very similar to the estimates for the regression method. The average of the Kalman estimate minus the regression estimate is almost zero and the differences only vary from −0.006 to 0.004. The

Table 2. Estimated parameters for the preferred term structure model

Options	ϕ	ϕ_1	ϕ_2	$\sqrt{\bar{\mu}}$	σ_P^2 (10^{-6})	σ_W^2 (10^{-6})	σ_T^2 (10^{-5})	$\sigma_1^2/(1-\phi_1^2)$ (10^{-5})	$\sigma_2^2/(1-\phi_2^2)$ (10^{-5})
*Panel A. Estimates, 1985–89**									
SC	0.9714	0.9685	0.9972	0.1279	1.14	3.82	9.03	6.39	8.53
	(0.0019)	(0.0078)	(0.0021)	(0.0281)	(0.08)	(0.59)	(0.71)	(1.47)	(6.43)
SP	0.9666	0.9631	0.9959	0.1334	2.08	8.99	6.99	7.79	8.06
	(0.0027)	(0.0087)	(0.0026)	(0.0212)	(0.12)	(0.95)	(0.77)	(1.71)	(5.08)
DMC	0.9756	0.9709	0.9934	0.1292	0.63	3.36	5.98	4.92	3.29
	(0.0012)	(0.0071)	(0.0033)	(0.0112)	(0.04)	(0.38)	(0.39)	(1.14)	(1.59)
DMP	0.9766	0.9689	0.9916	0.1280	0.37	14.16	7.26	4.77	2.65
	(0.0012)	(0.0074)	(0.0035)	(0.0089)	(0.04)	(1.25)	(0.41)	(1.06)	(1.10)
JYC	0.9717	0.9511	0.9838	0.1127	0.99	3.99	4.87	3.90	1.18
	(0.0018)	(0.0098)	(0.0053)	(0.0048)	(0.06)	(0.47)	(0.46)	(0.72)	(0.37)
JYP	0.9733	0.9524	0.9844	0.1099	0.33	2.57	5.09	3.56	0.95
	(0.0013)	(0.0083)	(0.0037)	(0.0045)	(0.03)	(0.32)	(0.32)	(0.56)	(0.21)
SFC	0.9772	0.9680	0.9773	0.1353	1.35	5.47	10.84	5.66	3.03
	(0.0018)	(0.0082)	(0.0064)	(0.0054)	(0.10)	(0.76)	(0.79)	(1.29)	(0.81)
SFP	0.9799	0.9640	0.9876	0.1309	0.53	9.02	13.24	4.82	2.26
	(0.0016)	(0.0086)	(0.0047)	(0.0065)	(0.08)	(1.18)	(0.84)	(1.04)	(0.81)
*Panel B. Subperiod estimates***									
SC Sub 1	0.9651	0.9700	0.9978	0.1248	1.46	1.56	12.00	9.08	16.46
Sub 2	0.9798	0.9737	0.9807	0.1167	0.47	7.99	6.26	4.16	0.40
SP Sub 1	0.9557	0.9652	0.9965	0.1414	2.55	8.85	8.35	14.61	12.94
Sub 2	0.9811	0.9701	0.9692	0.1173	1.30	10.66	6.23	3.69	0.57
DMC Sub 1	0.9667	0.9683	0.9921	0.1388	0.78	3.70	6.80	6.45	4.40
Sub 2	0.9832	0.9764	0.9810	0.1193	0.36	3.24	5.62	4.11	0.31
DMP Sub 1	0.9705	0.9636	0.9883	0.1384	0.42	7.74	8.45	6.21	3.22
Sub 2	0.9816	0.9768	0.9803	0.1173	0.25	17.92	6.35	3.66	0.32
JYC Sub 1	0.9474	0.9300	0.9847	0.1164	1.39	2.14	3.19	5.00	1.92
Sub 2	0.9814	0.9616	0.9826	0.1084	0.05	3.76	9.95	4.19	0.39
JYP Sub 1	0.9655	0.9443	0.9830	0.1130	0.35	2.75	5.31	3.34	1.54
Sub 2	0.9752	0.9564	0.9834	0.1065	0.32	2.62	4.67	4.04	0.30
SFC Sub 1	0.9783	0.9716	0.9648	0.1463	1.29	6.89	15.53	5.02	3.36
Sub 2	0.9770	0.9579	0.9769	0.1230	1.07	5.52	7.18	6.34	0.52
SFP Sub 1	0.9805	0.9596	0.9793	0.1409	0.51	6.82	17.98	4.37	2.42
Sub 2	0.9790	0.9737	0.9849	0.1206	0.17	11.34	10.70	5.09	0.44

* The numbers in parentheses are the estimated standard deviations of the parameter estimates calculated from the information matrix using numerical second derivatives.
** The first subsample is from January 1985 to June 1987 and the second from July 1987 to November 1989.

Kalman filter estimates of ϕ range from 0.967 to 0.980 for the full samples, with median 0.974 and "half-life" equal to 27 calendar days. The Kalman filter estimates of ϕ, like those for the regression method, are generally larger for the second subperiod. The median and "half-life" for the first subperiod are 0.966 and 20 days, with a range from 0.947 to 0.981. The corresponding figures are 0.980, 35 days, 0.975 and 0.983 for the second subperiod.

Some models for asset returns imply estimates of ϕ and ϕ_1 should be similar if expectations are formed rationally. A Garch(1,1) model for returns is one example. The estimates of ϕ_1 are nontrivially smaller than the estimates of ϕ, but the former estimates are associated with trading days and the latter estimates with calendar days. The median estimate of ϕ_1 for the full samples is 0.966, and the associated "half-life" is 20 trading days or approximately 29 calendar days, compared with 27 calendar days for ϕ. The subperiod median estimates of ϕ_1 are very similar: 0.964 and 0.972.

All the estimates of ϕ_2 exceed 0.975 for the complete datasets and half of these estimates exceed 0.99. The "half-lives" for the median estimates are 66 trading days for the complete period, 51 trading days for the first subperiod, and 36 trading days for the second subperiod.

The penultimate column of Table 2 shows estimates of $\sigma_1^2/(1-\phi_1^2)$, which is the variance of the spread term. The variation in the spread term is similar across the subperiods for three currencies but not for the pound, which has smaller values in the later subperiod. The final column gives estimates of $\sigma_2^2/(1-\phi_2^2)$, which is the variance of long-term expectations. The numbers document a substantial fall over the five years in the variability through time of these expectations. An approximate 95% probability interval for the long-term volatility expectation can be obtained from $\sigma_2^2/(1-\phi_2^2)$ and $\bar{\mu}$. An example is an interval from 10.4% to 13.3% for the Deutschmark, using the call estimates for the later subperiod. A corresponding interval for 15-day volatility expectations can be calculated by additionally using $\sigma_1^2/(1-\phi_1^2)$ and ϕ. This gives 6% to 16% for the same mark source.

The small estimated values of σ_P^2 and σ_T^2 indicate that the time-varying term structure model fits the PHLX data reasonably well. A very approximate standard deviation for the difference between an observed implied volatility ($y_{j,t}$) and the correct term structure value (v_t, Equation 7) is given by the square root of $(\sigma_P^2 + T_{j,t-1}^{-1}\sigma_T^2)/(4\bar{\mu})$ for PHLZ observations. Typical values are 0.8% for a 15-day option and 0.4% for a 180-day option (from mark calls, full sample). The relative inaccuracy of the WSJ source is confirmed by the higher estimates for σ_W^2 than for σ_P^2. The illustrative approximate standard deviations for WSJ observations increase to 1.0% and 0.8%, respectively for 15- and 180-day options.

2. Estimated 60-day average volatilities (regression vs Kalman filter, DM calls)

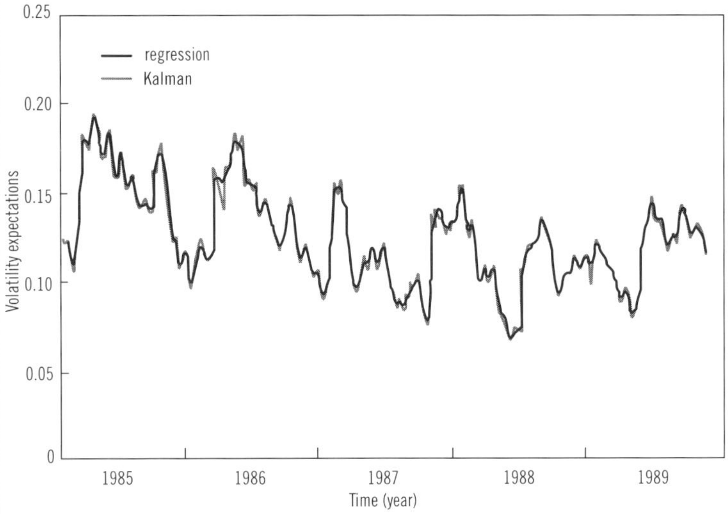

Figure 2 compares the Kalman filter estimates of volatility expectations with the regression method estimates. It can be seen that the estimates of 60-day expected average volatilities (from Equation 7) are very similar and this is also true for 15-day and long-term expectations. Further figures, not presented here, indicate that the plotted series are less smooth for the filter method, particularly for the 15-day expectations, because the regression method uses overlapping 11-day windows. Also, the differences between the expectations obtained from call and put options are more variable for the Kalman filter.

Simpler models To help evaluate certain simplifications of the preferred specification of the time-varying term structure model, we present comparisons of the maximum quasi-log-likelihoods for the nine-parameter model with the corresponding figures for special cases requiring fewer parameters. The usual likelihood-ratio tests provide some insight. Cautious interpretations of log-likelihood differences are necessary, however, not least because several model parameters may have varied during the five-year period. The results for seven simplifications are summarised in Table 3, Panel A.

To emphasise that term structure effects exist,

Table 3. Comparisons of the maximum quasi-log-likelihoods for the preferred time-varying term structure model with the figures for alternative models

		Changes in log-likelihood*		
	Parameters	Minimum	Maximum	Significant**
Panel A. Simplifications				
Flat term structures	6	–1644.81	–720.71	8
Constant long-term expectations	7	–1413.26	–579.41	8
Measurement error variance:				
Same for both sources	8	–466.56	–22.13	8
Same for all T	8	–250.64	–52.05	8
Random walks for:				
Spreads and long-term expectations	6	–19.51	–10.26	8
Long-term expectations	7	–6.80	–0.90	4
Same reversion rate in the spread and the term structure	8	–0.75	–0.01	0
Panel B. Generalisations				
Average spread not zero	10	0.05	1.21	0
State variables correlated	10	0.06	5.31	3
Correlated measurement errors	10	0.22	45.08	3
Mean long-term expectation varies with time	10	0.38	9.01	3
σ_T^2 depends on data source	10	0.01	36.33	4

The simplifications and generalisations are defined completely in the section of this paper covering Kalman filter results.
* The change in the quasi-log-likelihood function is the maximum of the function for the particular simplification or generalisation minus the maximum for the preferred nine-parameter model. Each row of the table summarises eight changes, four for pound, mark, yen, and franc call options, and four for put options.
** Number of significant test values out of eight at the 5% level. In Panel A, the test value is minus twice the change and the null hypothesis is that the preferred model is no better than the simplification. In Panel B, the test value is twice the change and the null hypothesis is that the generalisation is no better than the preferred model. Test values are compared with a chi-squared distribution with degrees-of-freedom given by the number of extra parameters in the alternative hypothesis. The test values must be interpreted with caution.

the model has been fitted with the restriction that the spread term is always zero ($\sigma_1 = \phi = \phi_1 = \alpha_0^2 - \mu_0^2 = 0$). The maximum log-likelihood then falls by more than 700 for each of the eight datasets. The possibility of constant long-term expectations through time ($\sigma_2 = \phi_2 = 0$) is also not credible as the maximum log-likelihood always falls by more than 500 for this model. Likewise, we can confidently disregard the idea that the two sources provide implied volatilities of equal accuracy ($\sigma_P = \sigma_W$), and we can reject the assumption that the model fits with the same accuracy for all times to expiry ($\sigma_T = 0$).

The joint hypothesis that both the spread between short- and long-term expectations and the long-term expectations follow random walks ($\phi_1 = \phi_2 = 1$, $\bar{\mu}$ undefined) gives likelihood-ratio test values ranging from 20.52 to 39.02, which could be compared with χ_3^2 if we trust the usual asymptotic theory. The test values strongly suggest that the joint hypothesis is doubtful. The more plausible hypothesis that the long-term expectation alone follows a random walk ($\phi_2 = 1$, $\bar{\mu}$ undefined) can be accepted for the pound and the mark using standard theory and a 5% significance level.

The hypothesis that the spread term reverts towards zero through trading time (weekdays less holidays) at the same rate as the term structure displays reversion in calendar time towards long-term expectations ($\phi_1^{4.8} = \phi_7$) is supported by all the datasets with the maximum value of the likelihood-ratio test statistic equal to 1.50.

More general models There are many ways to add a tenth parameter to the preferred model. The results for five generalisations are summarised in Table 3, Panel B, although none of them give substantial improvements for a majority of the datasets. The generalisations nearly always change the estimates of ϕ and ϕ_1 by negligible amounts. A few estimates of ϕ_2 change non-trivially, especially for the Swiss franc data.

A variation that deserves evaluation is to remove the assumption that $\{\alpha_t^2\}$ and $\{\mu_t^2\}$ have the same mean value, ie, on average, the term structure is flat. Figure 1, at first sight, suggests that, on average, the term structure slopes upwards. Defining different means for $\{\alpha_t^2\}$ and $\{\mu_t^2\}$ gives a ten-parameter model. The difference between the square root of the estimated long-term mean and the square root of the estimated short-term mean ranges from a minimum of 0.002 for yen calls to a maximum of 0.011 for pound calls, implying a positive average slope. However, the increases in the maximum quasi-log-likelihoods are all small and insignificant.

The spread innovation is assumed to be uncorrelated with the long-term innovation in (14), which implies that there is no correlation between the spread and long-term variables. Adding a parameter for correlation between the innovation terms give small correlation estimates; they vary from 0.03 to 0.28.

The covariance matrix H_t for the measurement errors is assumed to be diagonal in the preferred model. An extra parameter can be added by assuming that all the off-diagonal elements in the associated correlation matrix are equal. Except for the Swiss franc, the estimated common correlation term is very small (range -0.05 to 0.04) and the changes in the log-likelihood are unimportant. There is far more correlation between the measurement errors for the exceptional currency, 0.28 for the calls and 0.13 for the puts with large changes in the log-likelihood. Three parameters define the diagonal terms of H_t in (22). Increasing this to four, by allowing σ_T^2 to differ for the PHLX and WSJ sources improves some of the model fits but has no discernible effect upon the six parameters that do not appear in H_t.

Figure 1 and the subperiod estimates of $\bar{\mu}$ suggest that the mean of the process for long-term expectations may have declined as time progressed. Replacing $\bar{\mu}$ by $\mu_0 + \mu_1 t$ leads to negative estimates of μ_1 as expected, but the increases in the log-likelihood are not large.

Conclusion

Two methods for estimating the time-varying term structure of volatility expectations have been illustrated. These methods assume that expectations revert monotonically from a short-term value towards a long-term level as the horizon of the expectations increases. The regression method is elementary and obtains many of the conclusions provided by the technically more demanding Kalman filter method. The filter method, however, also permits estimation of time series model for volatility expectations and comparisons between models. Independent autoregressive models for long-term expectations and the spread between short- and long-term expectations are preferred for currency markets.

Our study of volatility expectations for four currencies provides five further conclusions. First, there are significant term structure effects. Fifteen-day and long-term volatility expectations often differ by several per cent, which causes implied volatilities to vary significantly across maturities. Second, the term structure sometimes slopes upwards, sometimes downwards, and its direction (up or down) frequently changes. The direction changes, on average, approximately once every two or three moths. Third, there are significant variations in long-term volatility expectations, although these expectations change more slowly than both short-term expectations and the spread between short- and long-term expectations. Fourth, the term structures of sterling, the Deutschmark, Swiss franc, and yen at any moment in time have been very similar. Finally there are nonstationary elements in the term structure in the sense that some of the parameters of the preferred autoregressive models change during the five years investigated.

The volatility expectations provide insights into how the currency options market behaves. A constant volatility assumption is not made by the market. Volatility shocks are assumed to be transitory with an estimated half-life of approximately only one month. There is no evidence that the currency options market overreacts because this half-life is indistinguishable from the half-life for the mean-reverting spread between short- and long-term expectations. This is contrary to the equity results of Stein (1989), who assumed constant long-term expectations.

The volatility term structure estimates summarise the market's beliefs about volatility for all future periods. These estimates are expected to be more informative than forecasts obtained from historic prices alone. The estimates can be used to enhance hedging strategies and to value options for all maturities T including those that are not traded at exchanges.

Day and Lewis (1992) and Lamoureux and Lastrapes (1993) have estimated Arch models for returns using implied volatility information, but disregarding term structure effects. Further research should estimate Arch models for asset returns using the information in historic returns and short- and long-term volatility expectations. The conditional variance should then depend on short-term expectations alone if the options market is efficient. Xu and Taylor (1995) use this Arch methodology and conclude that the PHLX currency options market is informationally efficient.

BIBLIOGRAPHY

Barone-Adesi, G., and R.E. Whaley, 1987, "Efficient Analytic Approximation of American Option Values," *Journal of Finance* 42, pp. 301-20.

Bollerslev, T., R.Y. Chou, and K.F. Kroner, 1992, "ARCH Modeling in Finance: a Review of the Theory and Empirical Evidence", *Journal of Econometrics* 52, pp. 5-59; reprinted as Chapter 2 of the present volume.

Day, T.E., and C.M. Lewis, 1988, "The Behaviour of the Volatility Implicit in the Prices of Stock Index Options", *Journal of Financial Economics* 22, pp. 103-22.

Day, T.E., and C.M. Lewis, 1992, "Stock Market Volatility and the Information Content of Stock Index Options", *Journal of Econometrics* 52, pp. 267-87.

Diz, F., and T.J. Finucane, 1993, "Do the Options Markets Really Overreact?" *Journal of Futures Markets* 13, pp. 299-312.

Franks, J.R., and E. S. Schwartz, 1991, "The Stochastic Behaviour of Market Variance Implied in the Prices of Index Options," *The Economic Journal* 101, pp. 1460-75.

Harvey, A.C., 1989, *Forecasting, Structural Time Series Models and the Kalman Filter.* Cambridge, UK: Cambridge University Press.

Heynen, R., A.G.Z. Kemna, and T. Vorst, 1994, "Analysis

of the Term Structure of Implied Volatilities," *Journal of Financial and Quantitative Analysis* 29, pp. 31-56.

Hull, J., and A. White, 1987, "The Pricing of Options on Assets with Stochastic Volatilities," *Journal of Finance* 42, pp. 281-300.

Lamoureux, C.G., and W.D. Lastrapes, 1993, "Forecasting Stock-Return Variance: Toward an Understanding of Stochastic Implied Volatilities," *Review of Financial Studies* 6, pp. 293-326; reprinted as Chapter 14 of the present volume.

Merville, L.J., and D.R. Pieptea, 1989, "Stock Price Volatility, Mean-Reverting Diffusion, and Noise," *Journal of Financial Economics* 24, pp. 193-214.

Poterba, J.M., and L.H. Summers, 1986, "The Persistence of Volatility and Stock Market Fluctuations," *American Economic Review* 76, pp. 1142-51.

Resnick, B.G., A.M. Sheikh, and Y. Song, 1993, "Time Varying Volatilities and Calculation of the Weighted Implied Standard Deviation," *Journal of Financial and Quantitative Analysis* 28, pp. 417-30.

Shastri, K., and K. Wethyavivorn, 1987, "The Valuation of Currency Options for Alternate Stochastic Processes," *Journal of Financial Research* 10, No. 2, pp. 283-93.

Sheikh, A.M., 1991, "Transaction Data Tests of S&P 100 Call Option Pricing," *Journal of Financial and Quantitative Analysis* 26, pp. 459-75.

Stein, E.M., and J.C. Stein, 1991, "Stock Price Distributions with Stochastic Volatility: An Analytic Approach," *Review of Financial Studies* 4, pp. 727-52; reprinted as Chapter 22 of the present volume.

Stein, J. C., 1989, "Overreactions in the Options Market," *Journal of Finance* 44, pp. 1011-23.

Taylor, S. J., and X. Xu, 1994, "The Magnitude of Implied Volatility Smiles: Theory and Empirical Evidence for Exchange Rates," *Review of Futures Markets* 13, pp.355-80.

Xu, X., and S. J. Taylor, 1995, "Conditional Volatility and the Informational Efficiency of the PHLX Currency Options Market," *Journal of Banking and Finance* 19, pp. 803-21.

FORECASTING VOLATILITIES WITH IMPLIED VOLATILITIES

Introduction

Robert Jarrow

Do implied volatilities forecast future realised (historic) volatilities better than time series procedures, such as Garch? The idea is that if markets are rational, then the implied volatility embedded in the options price provides the best forecast of the future realised volatility. Although simply stated, the answer to this question is not so simply obtained. Indeed, an estimate for an implicit volatility is linked to the particular option pricing model used, such as Black–Scholes. This means that only conditional answers can be achieved, since they are conditional upon a particular option model. As such, implied volatilities under the correct model could provide the best available forecasts, yet if the wrong model is used, a negative answer would be obtained. So when reading the papers in this section, it is important to be aware of the option pricing model employed and the market studied.

The first paper, by Theodore Day and Craig Lewis, uses the Black–Scholes model and studies crude oil futures options from November 1986 to March 1991. As these options are American, the binomial approximation to the Black-Scholes formula is employed, using daily closing prices for at-the-money options.

Day and Lewis compare these implied volatilities with Garch (historic) volatilities. Two types of tests are performed: within sample and out of sample. The within sample test uses a Garch model and includes the implied volatility into the Garch specification. The notion is that if the implied volatility uses all available information (and gives the best forecast), then the Garch model should provide no additional explanatory power. Two forms of Garch model are studied, a Garch(1,1)-M and an Egarch(1,1)-AR(1), both with maximum likelihood estimation (a discussion of these models can be found in Section I of this book). The out-of-sample test compares the forecasting power of the Garch models versus the implied volatilities.

The results of these two tests are quite interesting. For the within sample tests, the implied volatilities provide unbiased estimates, but the Garch models still contain additional information not found in the implied volatilities. However, this could be due to overfitting noise within sample (a standard concern with in-sample estimation). For the out-of-sample tests, the implied volatilities are again unbiased. In addition, the implied volatilities provide the best forecasts (much better than Garch). In fact, it is shown that the Garch model provides no additional information beyond that contained in the implied volatilities.

In summary, the Day and Lewis paper, using the Black–Scholes model and crude oil futures options, provides evidence consistent with the forecasting power of implied volatilities. For some evidence to the contrary, we turn to the paper by Linda Canina and Stephen Figlewski.

Canina and Figlewski study S&P100 index options (OEX options) using the Black–Scholes formula. They compare the implied volatility with the historic volatility, both as estimates for the future realised volatility.

Closing prices on all OEX call options from March 1983 to March 1987 are considered, excluding only very near-term, long-dated and deep in- or deep out-of-the-money options. As the OEX options are American, the binomial approximation is used for computing the implied volatilities.

The results are in contrast to those reported for oil futures options. First, Canina and Figlewski document the patterns in implied volatilities across strike and maturity. They obtain the traditional "smile" in strikes and a decreasing "sneer" in maturities. (Note that these patterns are inconsistent with the Black–Scholes model, which assumes a constant volatility across strikes.)

Secondly, they perform various regression tests to see if the implied volatilities are unbiased predictors of realised volatilties. Their tests strongly reject this hypothesis. In fact, they show that in most cases, the implied volatility has no significant correlation with the realised volatility. This evidence provides a strong rejection of the joint hypothesis of rational markets and the Black–Scholes model. Given the evidence of strike smiles in the implied volatility, it is probably the Black–Scholes model which is being rejected by the data.

We can interpret the paper by Christopher Lamoureux and William Lastrapes as providing additional evidence in this regard. Lamoureux and Lastrapes study the Hull and White stochastic volatility option pricing model and Chicago Board of Options Exchange (CBOE) stock options.

They compare implied volatilities (using a stochastic volatility option model) to historic Garch(1,1) volatilities (obtained using maximum likelihood estimation with conditional normal densities). This Garch model formulation for historic volatilities is consistent with the stock price process underlying the Hull and White stochastic volatility option pricing model.

Daily returns on 10 stocks over April 1982 to March 1984 are used. The 10 options considered pay no dividends, so although the CBOE options are American, a European formula applies. The test considers only at-the-money options.

The results are informative. First, it is shown that the Garch model provides a good fit for the 10 stocks' returns. This is consistent with the Hull and White model's formulation. Second, two tests for the forecasting ability of the implied volatility are performed: in-sample and out-of- sample.

The in-sample test includes the implied volatility into the Garch equation to see if the Garch equation has any remaining predictive power. If the markets are rational and the Hull and White model is valid, then the Garch model should have no explanatory power after the implied volatility has been included. This joint hypothesis is rejected for seven out of the 10 stocks. In this analysis, two potential biases in computing implied volatilities are controlled for non-synchronous prices and the non-linearity of the Hull and White (and Black–Scholes) formula. The evidence shows that these cannot be the reasons for the rejection. Again, in-sample tests always have the possibility of overfitting the noise in the data.

The out-of-sample test compares the forecast performance of the two different volatilities: the Garch and the implied. In eight out of the 10 companies, the Garch model did better (a lower root mean squared error). A regression test confirms this forecasting analysis. The implied variance tends to under-predict the future realised variance. Again, the joint hypothesis is rejected by the data. This evidence is inconsistent with the Hull and White option pricing model and rational markets. Since the Hull and White model assumes that volatility risk is diversifiable (not priced), this may be the reason for the rejection rather than market rationality. This conjecture awaits subsequent research.

The last paper, by Kaushik Amin and Victor Ng, studies a different market, the Eurodollar futures options market and a different model, the Heath–Jarrow–Morton (HJM) term structure model. Their evidence is more encouraging with respect to market rationality.

They study the forecasting ability of implied volatilities from five different HJM models versus standard Garch volatilities. Eurodollar futures options markets are selected due to low transaction costs and high liquidity. The time period is from January 1988 to November 1992. Daily prices (as of 8:30 am) of the Eurodollar futures options are used. All options are American, so a suitable binomial approximation procedure is employed.

Amin and Ng consider five single factor HJM volatility models: the Ho and Lee model, the Cox-Ingersoll-Ross model, the Courtadon model, the Vasicek model, and the Linear Proportional model. All of these formulations have deterministic volatilities.

Two Garch models for the spot rate's volatility are employed, both a Garch(1,1) and an adjustment to Garch (1,1) that accounts for asymmetric volatility responses due to positive and negative shocks, called the GJR model. Various interest rate level formulations were also embedded into the two preceding Garch models, resulting in four different Garch model specifications.

An in-sample test of the forecasting ability of implied volatility versus the Garch model is employed. The implied volatility is added as an extra explanatory variable in the Garch models. As in Lamoureux and Lastrapes, if the market is rational and the HJM model holds, then the Garch model should provide no additional explanatory power.

The results are encouraging. For the Vasicek and linear proportional models, one cannot reject the hypothesis that the markets are rational and these forms of the HJM model hold (even after considerations of various corrections for potential biases). The other interest rate models, however, do not perform as well.

More refined tests show that the HJM models do not capture the full interaction between rate shocks and the level of the spot rate in determining the realised volatility. These refined results suggest a more complex volatility structure in the HJM formulation (perhaps stochastic volatility) may still provide better forecasts.

In summary, the papers in this section tell a uniform story; the predictive ability of implied volatilities is highly dependent on the option pricing model selected. A misspecified model will lead to poor forecasts. This insight motivates the discussion of the new option pricing models in Section V.

12

Forecasting Futures Market Volatility*

Theodore E. Day and Craig M. Lewis
University of Texas at Dallas; Vanderbilt University

This paper compares the accuracy of different methods of forecasting the volatility of crude oil futures prices. Using daily data from November 1986 through March 1991, we examine volatilities from models of the generalised autoregressive conditional heteroscedasticity (Garch) family and contrast them with the implied volatilities from call options on crude oil futures. In-sample tests are conducted by embedding the implied volatility in Garch and Egarch models as an additional explanatory variable. The results show that both sources of volatility information contribute statistically significant explanatory power. No particular reason is found for preferring the more complex Egarch model, because there appears to be no asymmetry in the volatility response to futures price changes. In out-of-sample tests of forecasts of futures volatility over the remaining lives of both nearby and more distant option contracts, the Garch and Egarch models violate the requirements for forecast rationality, but implied volatilities do not. A naive historical volatility estimate is also examined, but its performance is not as good as implied volatility. "Encompassing regression" tests show that out-of-sample forecasts from the Garch-type models contained no information that was not impounded in implied volatilities. Bias-adjusted and combined forecasts based on the encompassing regression results do not perform as well out-of-sample as the unadjusted implied volatility.

Prediction of the future volatility of an asset's return is essential both for efficient pricing of derivative securities and for effective use of these securities in hedging the underlying asset. An advance in forecasting future volatility is the development of the class of generalised autoregressive conditional heteroscedasticity (Garch) models to describe the evolution of the volatility of asset returns over time. The Garch framework is appealing because the time series model for the volatility of the asset is estimated jointly with a time series model for asset returns. For example, the Garch-in-mean (Garch-M) model specifies that the expected return is proportional to the variance of returns.

Another frequently-used member of this class of models is the exponential Garch (Egarch) model of Nelson (1992). In this model, a logarithmic transformation of the variance is used to capture asymmetric behaviour, such as the negative correlation between asset returns and changes in volatility that has been observed in stock returns (such as Christie (1982)).

---

* *This paper was first published in* The Journal of Derivatives, *Winter (1993). Reprinted with permission of Institutional Investor, Inc. To order a subscription, or for other information, please call (212) 224 3185. This article has been presented at the Third Annual Winter Finance Conference at the University of Utah, the Fifth Annual Conference of the Financial Options Research Center at the University of Warwick, and at Vanderbilt University. The authors thank Cliff Ball, Don Chance, Andrew Karolyi, Barry Schacter, Paul Seguin, Hans Stoll, and conference participants for many helpful comments. The research was supported by a grant from the New York Mercantile Exchange and by the Dean's Fund for Faculty Research at the Owen Graduate School of Management.*

An alternative approach to forecasting volatility is based on the information contained in option prices. Merton (1973) and Hull and White (1987) show that the variance of return that is implicit in the price of a call option can be interpreted as a forecast of the average volatility of the underlying asset. Therefore, simultaneous observations of option prices and the price of the underlying asset can be used to estimate volatility that is expected over the remaining life of the option. If option prices reflect all currently available information concerning future levels of volatility and if the correct option pricing model is used to infer volatility, implied volatilities should provide better forecasts of future volatility than Garch models, which rely completely on the past series of prices to estimate volatility.

(Note that Garch and similar models describe the behaviour of the variance of returns, while the term volatility is typically used for the square root of the variance. For convenience, in this article we use variance and volatility interchangeably, leaving it to the reader to understand when it is necessary to take the square root.)

This paper examines the relative accuracy of the predictions of these alternative models for volatility using data from the crude oil futures market. We chose the crude oil futures market for two reasons. First, the underlying market for crude oil is of great importance in the economy. Second, the time period covered by our sample makes the crude oil futures market an ideal setting for evaluating the performance of alternative models for volatility.

Since the introduction of trading in options on crude oil futures contracts in 1986, the crude oil futures market has been characterised by a period of relatively stable prices, then a period of highly volatile prices following the invasion of Kuwait by Iraq. The increase in futures market volatility following the invasion of Kuwait is both more dramatic and more prolonged than the volatility of stock prices observed during the period following the stock market crash of 1987. This period of unanticipated volatility provides an opportunity to evaluate the speed with which new information is incorporated in implied volatilities relative to other forecasts of volatility.

We examine the information content of implied volatilities from call options on crude oil futures relative to the information contained in alternative models of volatility. The in-sample information content of the alternative forecasting models is examined by including implied volatility as an exogenous variable in alternative Garch models for futures market volatility. Since these in-sample tests may be biased in favour of the Garch specifications, we also compare the out-of-sample forecasting power of implied volatilities with forecasts from Garch models.

The evidence shows that the forecasts based on implied volatilities statistically dominate those extracted from alternative time series specifications. Further, we find that implied volatilities provide unbiased forecasts of future volatility while the forecasts from Garch models and naive forecasts based on historic volatility tend to underestimate future volatility during this period.

Data

The data consist of daily closing prices for call options on crude oil futures and the underlying futures contracts from the beginning of trading in the options on November 14, 1986, through March 18, 1991. The risk-free rate of interest for each option expiration series is computed for each day using the average of the bid and ask discounts for the US Treasury bill whose maturity is closest to the expiration date. Bid and ask discounts for US Treasury bills are collected daily from the *Wall Street Journal*.

In addition, the prices for the nearest to delivery futures contract from April 8, 1983, through March 18, 1991, are used to estimate a rolling series of forecasting models. The forecasts generated by these time series models are then used to make out-of-sample comparisons of relative forecasting power.

The data also are used to estimate the implied volatility of the at-the-money call option for each expiration series trading on a given date. We focus on the at-the-money options for two reasons. First, since the at-the-money call options tend to provide the most actively traded strike price for a given expiration series, this minimises the extent to which our estimates of implied volatilities are affected by noise from the non-synchronous trading of the options and their underlying futures contracts. Second, at-the-money options are the most sensitive to changes in volatility.

Estimation of implied volatility

The implied volatilities for at-the-money call options on crude oil futures contracts are estimated using a search algorithm that finds the volatility that equates the price from a binomial model to the observed market price of each futures option. Note that options on crude oil futures contracts are American options. Therefore, the pricing model used to estimate implied volatilities must account for the early exercise feature embedded in the options. Since a closed-form solution for the price of an American futures option does not exist, we estimate implied volatilities using a binomial pricing technique.[1]

The option valuation procedure begins by partitioning the time to expiration for each option into $nT = N$ time intervals, where T is the number of trading days to expiration, and n is the number of changes in the futures price each day. Given the current futures price of F_0, there are $N + 1$ possible values for the futures price at the option expiration:

$$F_{jN} = u^j F_0 \qquad (1)$$

with

$$u = e^{\sigma\sqrt{\Delta t}}$$

where F_{jN} is the futures price at expiration, j is the number of upticks minus the number of downticks that have occurred in the futures price, σ is the volatility of the futures price, and Δt is the length of a time step in fractions of a year. The expiration value of the option is C_{jN}, which is equal to $F_{jN} - X$ for each j for which the futures price exceeds the exercise price X. Otherwise the option expires worthless.

At each time t prior to expiration, the set of possible prices for the option is determined recursively using the relation

$$\hat{C}_{jt} = e^{-r\Delta t}\left[pC_{j+1t+1} + (1-p)C_{j-1t+1}\right] \qquad (2)$$

where $p = (1 - u)/(u - 1/u)$ represents the "risk-neutral" probability of an up movement in the futures price.

If at any node in the binomial tree the value for the option given by (2) is less than the proceeds from exercising the option immediately, $F_{jt} - X$, the proceeds from immediate exercise are substituted for $\hat{C}_{jt}$ before proceeding to solve recursively for the current value of the option. Therefore the value of the option at each node in the binomial lattice is given by

$$C_{jt} = \max\left[\hat{C}_{jt}, F_{jt} - X\right]. \qquad (3)$$

The implied volatility for each at-the-money futures option is estimated by solving for an updated estimate of the implied volatility using a Newton-Raphson algorithm.[2]

Table 1 presents the summary statistics for the implied volatilities from the four option contracts nearest to expiration. The data show that on average there is little difference between the implied volatilities for the two option contracts nearest to expiration. A comparison of the means and standard deviations of the implied volatilities for the two nearest expiration series with those of the two more distant expiration series shows that on average the implied volatilities from crude oil futures options tend to decrease and become less variable as the time to expiration increases.

Table 1. Summary statistics for implied volatilities from call options on crude oil futures

	Expiration date (τ)			
	τ_1	τ_2	τ_3	τ_4
Number of observations	806	995	982	860
Mean number of trading days to expiration	13.9	32.5	50.4	68.0
Mean	0.3413	0.3311	0.3183	0.2965
Standard deviation	0.2013	0.1997	0.1714	0.1520
Minimum value	0.1029	0.1242	0.1437	0.1221
Maximum value	1.8474	1.5830	1.1786	1.5648
Skewness	2.70	2.59	2.40	3.15

Notes: Summary data for the implied volatilities from call options on crude oil futures contracts. The sample covers the period from November 14, 1986, through March 18, 1991. Implied volatilities are presented for the four option contracts nearest to expiration. The sample period includes 1,086 trading days. The number of observations for each expiration date may be fewer than this since at-the-money options are excluded from the sample if: 1) there are fewer than five days to expiration, 2) the boundary conditions for early exercise are violated, or 3) fewer than 100 contracts were traded during the day. These requirements eliminate 280 observations at the nearest time to expiration, with 248 observations eliminated by requirement 1) and 32 observations eliminated by requirements 2) and 3).

This feature of the sample, which is consistent with mean reversion in the short-run volatility of futures prices, is attributable to the relatively greater impact of short-run increases in spot market volatility on the implied volatility of the near expiration options. This effect is similar to the expiration day effects noted by Day and Lewis (1988) in the market for S&P 100 call options.

Table 1 also indicates that the distributions of implied volatilities at each expiration date are highly skewed. This is primarily attributable to several dramatic increases in the volatility of the crude oil futures market during the sample period.

Panel A of Figure 1 plots the time series of implied volatilities for the crude oil futures options having the second shortest time to expiration on each day within the sample period. The two divisions on the right-hand side of Panel A (labelled Period 1 and Period 2) represent time periods of equal length and correspond respectively to the pre- and post-invasion volatility of the crude oil futures market.

These two subperiods are shown in greater detail in Panels B and C, where the difference between the volatility of the most distant expiration series and the shorter expiration series is

1. Implied volatilities of crude oil futures options

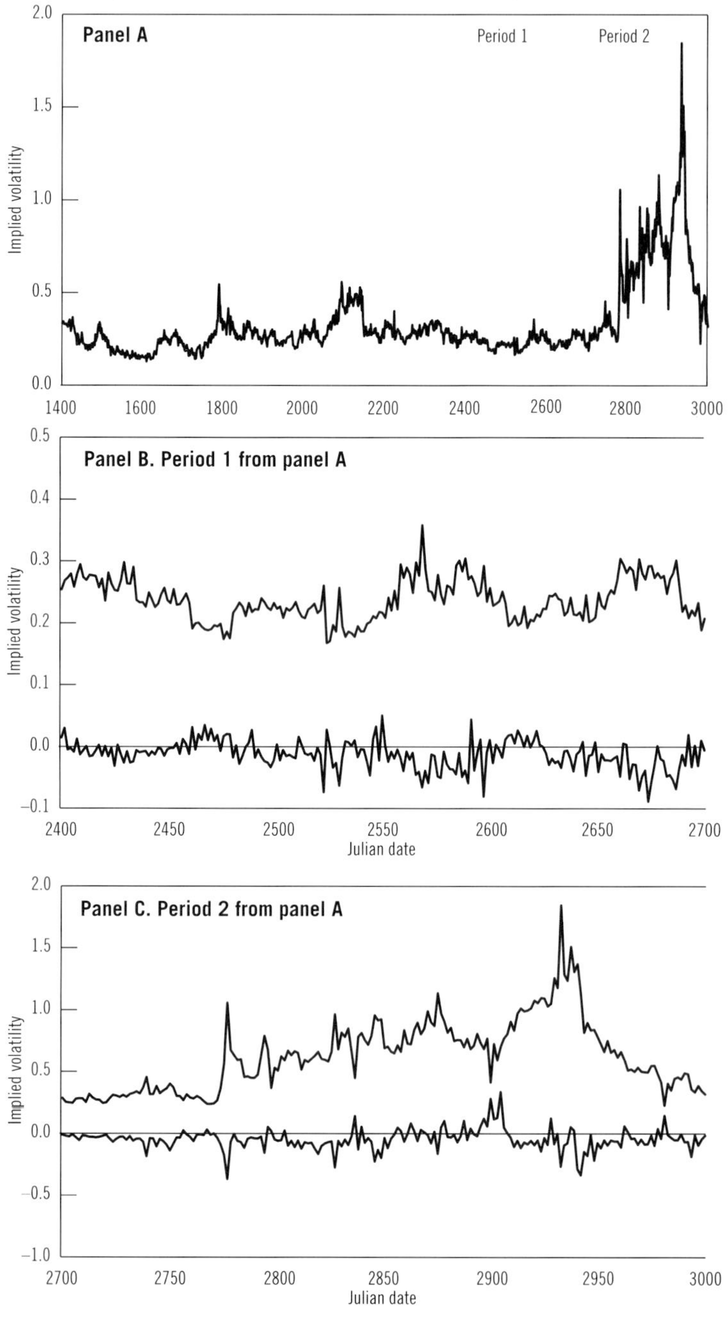

Panel A plots the time series of implied volatilities from the crude oil futures contracts that have the second shortest time to expiration (τ_2) on each day within the sample period. The divisions on the right-hand side of Panel A (labelled Period 1 and Period 2) represent time periods of equal length and correspond to pre- and post-invasion volatility. These two subperiods are shown in greater detail in Panels B and C. Panels B and C display two data series. The upper series in both panels is the implied volatility of the expiration series τ_2, while the lower series is the difference between implied volatilities from expiration series τ_4 (the most distant series) and expiration series τ_2 ie, $\sigma(\tau_4) - (\tau_2)$.

included for purposes of comparison. Panel C shows that, as should be expected, the short-run increase in the volatility of the crude oil futures market has a greater impact on the implied volatility for the near expiration series than on the implied volatility for the distant expiration. This is consistent with the summary statistics presented in Table 1.

Empirical results

This section examines the information content of implied volatilities from call options on crude oil futures relative to the information contained in alternative models for futures market volatility. First, the within-sample information content is examined by including implied volatility as an exogenous variable in alternative Garch models for futures market volatility. We also compare the out-of-sample forecasting power of implied volatilities with forecasts from Garch models. The evidence presented next shows that the forecasts based on implied volatilities dominate the forecasts that can be extracted from the alternative time series specifications.

WITHIN-SAMPLE TESTS

The within-sample information content of implied volatilities is examined by adding the implied volatility from the option having the shortest time (but at least five trading days) to expiration as an exogenous variable in a Garch model for the volatility of the daily returns on the futures contract underlying the expiring option. The Garch models are estimated using a maximum likelihood approach utilising the Berndt-Hall-Hall-Hausman algorithm.[3] These tests are conducted using both the Garch(1,1)-M and Egarch-AR(1) specifications for futures market volatility.[4]

In the Garch(1, 1)-M model, the return on the futures contract nearest to delivery is expressed as

$$R_{Ct} = \lambda_0 + \lambda_1 h_t^2 + \varepsilon_t \tag{4}$$

where h_t^2 is the variance of the return on the crude oil futures contract during period t, and ε_t is a random error term that is normally distributed with mean zero and variance h_t^2.

The variance of the futures market return for period t is given by

$$h_t^2 = \alpha_0 + \alpha_1 \varepsilon_{t-1}^2 + \beta_1 h_{t-1}^2 \tag{5}$$

where $\alpha_0 > 0$, $\alpha_1 > 0$, and $\beta_1 > 0$.

Equation (5) indicates that the variance of returns for period t is a function of a constant term, α_0, the squared value of last period's shock to the return-generating process, ε_{t-1}^2, and the variance of returns during the previous period, h_{t-1}^2. The restrictions on the parameters of the model are sufficient to assure that variance is always positive.

In the Egarch-AR(1) model, the return on the futures contract is expressed as a function of the lagged return, R_{Ct-1}, and a normally distributed residual error with a zero mean and a variance of h^2_{t-1}. That is,

$$R_{Ct} = \lambda_0 + \lambda_1 R_{Ct-1} + \varepsilon_t. \qquad (6)$$

The variance of the residual error term for the Egarch-AR(1) is given by

$$\ln\left(h_t^2\right) = \alpha_0 + \beta_1 \ln\left(h_{t-1}^2\right) + \theta\psi_{t-1} + \gamma\left(\left|\psi_{t-1}\right| - (2/\pi)^{1/2}\right) \qquad (7)$$

where ψ_{t-1} represents the residual error from the return process (Equation (6)) standardised to have unit variance, $\varepsilon_{t-1}/h_{t-1}$.

In (7), the variance for the futures market return in period t is a function of the variance of the futures market return in the previous period, h^2_{t-1}, the standardised value of last period's shock to the return process, ψ_{t-1}, and the deviation of the absolute value of ψ_{t-1} from the expected absolute value of a standardised normal variate, $(2/\pi)^{1/2}$. Including both the standardised shock and its absolute value permits the variance equation to capture any asymmetries in the relation between past returns and current futures market volatility. Since (7) is specified in terms of the logarithm of the variance, the parameter values are unrestricted.

The information content of implied volatilities can be analysed by testing the variance specifications in (5) and (7) against more general models, which include implied volatility (σ^2_{It-1}) as an exogenous variable:

$$h_t^2 = \alpha_0 + \alpha_1\varepsilon_{t-1}^2 + \beta_1 h_{t-1}^2 + \delta\sigma_{It-1}^2 \qquad (8)$$

and

$$\ln\left(h_t^2\right) = \alpha_0 + \beta_1 \ln\left(h_{t-1}^2\right) + \theta\psi_{t-1} + \gamma\left(\left|\psi_{t-1}\right| - (2/\pi)^{1/2}\right) + \delta\ln\left(\sigma_{It-1}^2\right). \qquad (9)$$

The coefficient δ can be interpreted either as a measure of how much incremental information implied volatilities contribute to the model for the change in volatility over time or as a measure of how mis-specified the respective models for volatility are when implied volatility is not included. The hypothesis that the prices of call options impound volatility information in addition to that contained in the historic series of futures returns can be tested by examining the statistical significance of δ. The null hypothesis that implied volatilities contain no additional information can be tested using a likelihood ratio test.

Tables 2 and 3 present the parameter estimates for the Garch(1,1)-M and Egarch-AR(1) specifications for futures market volatility. In each case, the estimate for the coefficient of implied volatility is positive and significantly greater than zero. In addition, likelihood ratio tests of the restrictions on the coefficient on implied volatility (ie δ = 0) in (8) and (9) reject the hypothesis that implied volatility adds no information at the 0.001 level. The respective chi-squared (χ^2) statistics are 80.62 and 101.74.

Table 2. Garch(1,1)-in-mean models for daily returns on crude oil futures contracts*

$$R_{Ct} = \lambda_0 + \lambda_1 h_t^2 + \varepsilon_t \qquad (4)$$

$$h_t^2 = \alpha_0 + \alpha_1\varepsilon_{t-1}^2 + \beta_1 h_{t-1}^2 + \delta\sigma_{It-1}^2 \qquad (8)$$

$$h_t^2 = \alpha_0 + \alpha_1\varepsilon_{t-1}^2 + \beta_1 h_{t-1}^2 \qquad (5)$$

$$h_t^2 = \alpha_0 + \delta\sigma_{It-1}^2 \qquad (10)$$

Variance specification	λ_0	λ_1	$\alpha_0 \times 10^4$	α_1	β_1	δ	Log L	χ^2**
(8)	0.001	0.542	0.000	0.084	0.605	0.349	2772.17	
	(1.35)	(0.46)	(0.00)	(1.83)	(5.55)	(3.03)		
(5)	0.001	0.699	0.081	0.170	0.830		2731.86	80.62
	(1.28)	(0.47)	(2.44)	(4.63)	(32.91)			
(10)	0.001	−0.179	0.001			1.105	2761.70	20.94
	(2.45)	(−0.45)	(0.00)			(9.69)		

* T-statistics are in parentheses. Standard errors are computed using the robust inference procedures developed by Bollerslev and Wooldridge (1988).

** χ^2 statistics are for tests of the restricted variance specifications given by Equations (5) and (10) models against the alternative given by Equation (8). The χ^2 statistics for Equations (5) and (10) are respectively distributed χ^2 with one and two degrees of freedom.

Table 3. Egarch-AR(1) models for daily returns on crude oil futures contracts*

$$R_{Ct} = \lambda_0 + \lambda_1 R_{Ct-1} + \varepsilon_t \qquad (6)$$

$$\ln\left(h_t^2\right) = \alpha_0 + \beta_1 \ln\left(h_{t-1}^2\right) + \theta\psi_{t-1} + \gamma\left(\left|\psi_{t-1}\right| - (2/\pi)^{1/2}\right) + \delta\ln\left(\sigma_{It-1}^2\right) \qquad (9)$$

$$\ln\left(h_t^2\right) = \alpha_0 + \beta_1 \ln\left(h_{t-1}^2\right) + \theta\psi_{t-1} + \gamma\left(\left|\psi_{t-1}\right| - (2/\pi)^{1/2}\right) \qquad (7)$$

$$\ln\left(h_t^2\right) = \alpha_0 + \delta\ln\left(\sigma_{It-1}^2\right) \qquad (11)$$

Variance specification	λ_0	λ_1	α_0	β_1	θ	γ	δ	Log L	χ^2**
(9)	0.001	0.006	0.300	0.703	0.000	0.002	0.345	2769.94	
	(2.02)	(0.41)	(1.25)	(5.28)	(0.02)	(1.58)	(2.28)		
(7)	0.001	0.004	0.279	1.057	0.000	0.004		2719.07	101.74
	(1.29)	(0.24)	(4.98)	(99.66)	(0.24)	(5.12)			
(11)	0.001	0.026	0.241				1.019	2762.90	14.08
	(2.30)	(0.96)	(0.45)				(15.53)		

* T-statistics are in parentheses. Standard errors are computed using the robust inference procedures developed by Bollerslev and Wooldridge (1988).

** χ^2 statistics are for tests of the restricted variance specifications given by Equations (7) and (11) models against the alternative given by Equation (9). The χ^2 statistics for Equations (7) and (11) are respectively distributed χ^2 with one and two degrees of freedom.

These results foreshadow similar findings in the out-of-sample forecast comparisons.

The estimates of λ_1 reported in Tables 2 and 3 are not statistically significant. This may be attributable in part to the limited length of the sample period. However, the estimates of the parameters for the respective variance equations are virtually identical to those that would have been obtained from other versions of the Garch and Egarch models by restricting the value of λ_1 to be zero.

The purpose of the logarithmic transformation of volatility in the Egarch model is to allow for correlation between asset returns and volatility changes, such as the negative association observed in stock returns (such as Christie (1982)). In the Egarch specification for volatility given by (7), this is captured by θ, the coefficient for the standardised residual (ψ_{t-1}) from the AR(1) specification for returns. Nelson (1992) and Day and Lewis (1992) report estimates of q that are significantly negative for Egarch models of the volatility of returns for stock market indexes, confirming Christie's finding.

Note that in Table 3 the reported estimate of θ is not significantly different from zero, which indicates that this effect is not present in the crude oil futures market. Therefore, the Egarch model may not be more useful than Garch in forecasting volatility in this market.

The question whether the Garch(1,1)-M and Egarch-AR(1) specifications for volatility contain information that is not impounded in implied volatilities can be examined by estimating (8) and (9) under the constraint that the time series parameters (α_1 and β_1 in (8) and θ, γ, and β_1 in Equation (9)) are equal to zero. In this case, the equations describing the evolution of volatility over time are given by

$$h_t^2 = \alpha_0 + \delta\sigma_{It-1}^2 \tag{10}$$

and

$$\ln\left(h_t^2\right) = \alpha_0 + \delta\ln\left(\sigma_{It-1}^2\right). \tag{11}$$

Since (10) and (11) are nested within Equations (8) and (9), a likelihood ratio test can be used to test the null hypothesis that the Garch models do not contain incremental information.

The likelihood ratios used to test the null hypothesis that the Garch(1,1)-M and Egarch-AR(1) models contain no incremental information are distributed respectively as chi-squared with two and three degrees of freedom (χ_2^2 and χ_3^2). The respective test statistics are 20.94 and 14.08, which allow the null hypotheses to be rejected at the 0.01 level. Given these results, we conclude that Garch models for volatility contain information in addition to the information contained in implied volatilities. Similar results have been found by Day and Lewis (1992) for the volatility of the S&P 100 index and by Lamoureux and Lastrapes (1993) for the volatilities of individual stocks.

The parameter estimates for (10) and (11) can also be used to test whether implied volatilities are unbiased predictors of within-sample volatility. If implied volatilities are unbiased estimates of future volatility, the parameter estimates of α_0 and δ will be close to 0 and 1.

The estimates of δ (1.105 and 1.019) presented in Tables 2 and 3 are not significantly different from 1. Similarly, the estimates for α_0 (0.0001 and 0.2407) are not significantly different from 0. The test statistics for the likelihood ratio test of the joint hypothesis that α_0 is equal to 0 and δ is equal to 1 are 2.04 for the Garch model and 5.66 for the Egarch model. Therefore, the null hypothesis that implied volatilities provide unbiased forecasts of volatility cannot be rejected at the 0.05 level.

The within-sample results demonstrate that although implied volatilities contain incremental information regarding the variability of returns, the information contained in the implied volatility series does not subsume the information contained in the time series of returns. This latter result does not hold up in the out-of-sample tests of forecasting power.

OUT-OF-SAMPLE TESTS

The previous section uses likelihood ratio tests of nested Garch models to determine which specification for volatility is most successful in explaining the within-sample changes in the volatility of the crude oil futures market. Although these results allow us to assess the relative information content of time series models and implied volatilities, they do not represent a true test of relative forecasting power, because we use the entire sample period for which implied volatilities are available to estimate the nested Garch models. Another limitation of these tests is that the Garch model has a forecast horizon of one day, while the implied volatility forecasts volatility over the time until option expiration (up to one month).

Here we explicitly examine the relative information content of out-of-sample forecasts of volatility through option expiration from implied volatilities and Garch models. The models are compared by regressing the futures market volatility actually realised on the forecasts from the alternative models.

The Garch models for futures market volatility discussed in the previous section generate forecasts of futures market volatility "one-step-ahead," which in this case represents a forecast of volatility for the next day. Since an implied volatility represents a forecast of volatility over the remaining life of the option, there is a maturity mismatch between the forecast horizon covered by Garch specifications for volatility and the forecast horizon implicit in option prices. To control for this problem, we use a procedure suggested by Lamoureux and Lastrapes (1993) to transform the daily Garch forecasts into a forecast of volatility over a horizon comparable to the forecast horizon for the implied volatilities.

On any day denoted by t, the "one-step-ahead" forecast of volatility h^2_{t+1}, can be used to generate a Garch forecast for daily volatility j days in the future. The Appendix demonstrates that for a Garch (1, 1) model this forecast can be expressed as:

$$\sigma^2_{t+j} = \left(1 - w_j\right)\bar{\sigma}^2 + w_j h^2_{t+1} \tag{12}$$

where $\bar{\sigma}^2$ is equal to $a_0/(1 - \alpha_1 - \beta_1)$, the long-run volatility of futures prices implicit in the Garch model, and w_j determines the relative importance of the one-step-ahead forecast and long-run volatility in determining the forecast of the volatility j days in the future.

In the Appendix, it is shown that w_j decreases exponentially so that as j becomes large, the forecast of daily volatility approaches $\bar{\sigma}^2$. The Garch forecasts for each of the N days until the expiration of the option can be averaged to create an average-step-ahead forecast of variance per day over the remaining life of the option;[5]

$$\sigma^2_{Ft} = \frac{1}{N}\sum_{j=1}^{N}\sigma^2_{t+j}. \tag{13}$$

The time series of average step-ahead forecasts is obtained by estimating a series of Garch models using a rolling sample period. For each date during the sample period (beginning at observation 500), the parameters for a Garch model are estimated using a constant sample size of 500 daily observations. To obtain the average step-ahead forecast for day $t + 1$, the daily futures market return for day $t - 500$ is dropped from the sample, the daily return for day t is added, and the parameters for the Garch model are re-estimated. The new parameter estimates are then used to obtain the average step-ahead forecast of volatility for day $t + 1$. This process is repeated for each day during the sample period.

The Garch forecasts and implied volatilities are used to predict the future volatility of the crude oil futures market. The realised future volatility, denoted by σ^2_{Ht+1}, is estimated by computing the variance of daily returns for the N days remaining until the expiration of the option (as of the forecast date). The daily variance of returns for the N-day period prior to the observation of implied volatility, σ^2_{Nt}, is included in our tests of forecasting power as a form of naive forecast.

The relative predictive power of the alternative forecasts of volatility over the remaining life of the options is evaluated by estimating regressions of the form

$$\sigma^2_{Ht+1} = b_0 + b_1\sigma^2_{Ft} + \eta_{t+1} \tag{14}$$

where σ^2_{Ht+1} represents the actual volatility realised during the subsequent periods until option expiration, σ^2_{Ft} is a forecast of future volatility based on the information available at the end of period t, and η_{t+1} represents the forecast error.

By decomposing realised volatility into predictable and unpredictable components, the regression methodology represented by (14) permits the predictive power of alternative forecasts to be compared. If the forecasts of volatility are unbiased, the estimate of b_0 will be approximately zero, and the estimate of b_1 will be close to 1. Consistent estimates of the regression coefficients in (14) can be obtained using ordinary least squares.

However, the regression error is a moving average process because the forecast horizon exceeds the frequency of the data. Since the forecast horizon becomes shorter as option expiration approaches, the number of lags in the moving average process for the error term decreases as expiration approaches, and then increases when the forecast horizon is matched to the expiration of the next option contract.

To control for this problem, a consistent estimator of the variance covariance matrix of the OLS estimators is obtained using a generalisation of the Hansen and Hodrick (1980) correction for autocorrelation and heteroscedasticity, which adjusts for the variable length of the forecast intervals (see also Hodrick and Srivastava (1987)). Fleming (1992) uses this procedure to control for autocorrelation in the forecast errors for the volatility of the S&P 100 index.

Table 4 presents estimates of (14) for each series of forecasts of near-term volatility. The near-term forecasts match the remaining life of

Table 4. Out-of-sample predictive power of alternative forecasts of near-term volatility

$$\sigma^2_{Ht+1} = b_0 + b_1\sigma^2_{Ft} + \eta_{t+1}$$

Forecasting model σ^2_{Ft}	b_0	b_1	R^2	χ^2_2
Historic volatility	0.008	0.607	0.392	4.51*
	(0.004)	(0.223)		
Garch	0.007	1.160	0.371	34.54**
	(0.006)	(0.529)		
Egarch	0.018	0.183	0.022	17.26**
	(0.005)	(0.198)		
Implied volatility	0.003	0.880	0.718	0.97
	(0.003)	(0.147)		

* Significant at the 0.05 level.
** Significant at the 0.01 level.
Notes: The near-term forecast horizon matches the remaining life of the call option having the second shortest time to expiration. The sample includes 995 forecasts having an average length of 32.5 trading days. The standard errors in parentheses are computed using a generalisation of the Hansen and Hodrick (1980) correction for autocorrelation and heteroscedasticity that adjusts for the variable length of the forecast intervals (eg see Hodrick and Srivastava (1987)). The Wald statistic for the test of the joint hypothesis that b_0 is equal to 0 and b_1 is equal to 1 is distributed as χ^2_2.

Table 5. Out-of-sample predictive power of alternative forecasts of distant-term volatility

$$\sigma^2_{Ht+1} = b_0 + b_1\sigma^2_{Ft} + \eta_{t+1}$$

Forecasting model σ^2_{Ft}	b_0	b_1	R^2	χ^2_2
Historic volatility	0.010	0.552	0.265	7.40*
	(0.004)	(0.230)		
Garch	0.008	1.437	0.258	86.89**
	(0.007)	(0.783)		
Egarch	0.014	0.352	0.095	16.77**
	(0.003)	(0.179)		
Implied volatility	0.006	0.829	0.489	8.16*
	(0.002)	(0.107)		

* Significant at the 0.05 level.
** Significant at the 0.01 level.
Notes: The distant-term forecast horizon matches the remaining life of the call option having the longest time to expiration. The sample includes 860 forecasts having an average length of 68.0 trading days. The standard errors in parentheses are computed using a generalisation of the Hansen and Hodrick (1980) correction for autocorrelation and heteroscedasticity that adjusts for the variable length of the forecast intervals (eg see Hodrick and Srivastava (1987)). The Wald statistic for the test of the joint hypothesis that b_0 is equal to 0o and b_1 is equal to 1 is distributed as χ^2_2.

the call option with the second shortest time to expiration. The sample includes 995 forecasts, which have an average length of 35.5 trading days.

The reported R^2s are much higher than those reported in Day and Lewis (1992) and Pagan and Schwert (1990), but are comparable to those reported by Lamoureux and Lastrapes (1993). The out-of-sample forecasts based on implied volatilities appear to have the most explanatory power, with an R^2 of 0.718. In addition, the estimated value for b_1 of 0.880 is not significantly different from 1.

The joint null hypothesis that b_0 is equal to 0 and b_1 is equal to 1 can be examined using the Wald statistic, which is distributed as χ^2_2. The Wald statistic for implied volatility forecasts has a value of 0.97, which indicates that the null hypothesis that implied volatility is an unbiased forecast of future near-term volatility cannot be rejected. These results suggest that the specification of the binomial option pricing model is adequate for deriving reasonable forecasts of near-term volatility.

The forecast power of the Garch model is little different from that of historic futures market volatility, with respective R^2s of 0.392 and 0.371. The forecasts based on the Egarch model have the least explanatory power, with an R^2 of 0.022 and a coefficient of b_1 that is not significantly different from 0.

The Wald statistic for the (naive) historic volatility forecasts, with a value of 4.51, fails to reject the null hypothesis that historic volatility is an unbiased predictor of future volatility. However, the Wald statistics for the Garch and Egarch models are respectively 34.54 and 17.26, which indicates that the Garch and Egarch forecasts have statistically significant biases.[6]

Table 5 presents estimates of (14) for the forecasts of out-of-sample volatility corresponding to the remaining life of the call option having the longest time to expiration. The sample includes 860 forecasts having an average length of 68.0 trading days.

As was the case for the near-term forecasting horizon, the out-of-sample forecasts based on implied volatilities have the most explanatory power, with an R^2 of 0.489. Although the estimated value for b_1 of 0.829 is not significantly different from 1, the Wald statistic of 8.16 permits rejection of the joint hypothesis that b_0 is equal to 0 and b_1 is equal to 1 at the 0.05 level.

The predictive power of the historic volatility and Garch forecasts is again similar, with respective R^2s of 0.265 and 0.258. As is the case for implied volatility forecasts, the null hypothesis that historic volatility provides unbiased forecasts of future volatility, which has a Wald statistic of 7.40, can be rejected at the 0.05 level for the distant-term volatility series.

The comparisons of the relative accuracy of the alternative forecasts of futures market volatility indicate that forecasts based on the implied volatilities from the options market provide better forecasts of future volatility than do either historic volatility or the Garch forecasts of volatility. However, if either historic volatility or Garch forecasts contain information that is not impounded in implied volatilities, it may be possible to obtain more accurate forecasts by incorporating this incremental information with the forecasts based on the implied volatilities.

The issue of whether one forecast contains different information from another can be addressed using encompassing tests similar to those of Fair and Shiller (1990). The extent to which the information contained in forecasts from Garch models differs from the information contained by implied volatilities and naive proxies can be examined by estimating the regression

$$\sigma^2_{Ht+1} = b_0 + b_1\sigma^2_{It} + b_2\sigma^2_{Gt} + b_3\sigma^2_{Et} + b_4\sigma^2_{Nt} + \eta_{t+1} \qquad (15)$$

where σ^2_{Ht+1} is future volatility, σ^2_{It} is the implied volatility at time t, σ^2_{Gt} is the average step-ahead Garch(1,1)-M forecast, σ^2_{Et} is the average step-ahead Egarch-AR(1) forecast, and σ^2_{Nt} is the naive forecast based on historic volatility over the previous N days. If a forecast of volatility contains independent information that is useful in predicting future volatility, the OLS regression coefficient of that forecast variable should be significantly greater than zero.

Table 6 reports the results of the encompassing tests for forecasts of near-term volatility. The results show that neither the Garch models nor historic volatility add much explanatory power to predictions of near-term volatility based on implied volatilities. The R^2s for the forecasting models that include Garch forecasts and historic volatility along with implied volatility are almost identical to those obtained using implied volatility alone. Further, none of the other forecasts has a significant regression coefficient when implied volatility is present as an explanatory variable.

These results indicate that implied volatilities subsume the information contained in other forecasts of near-term volatility. Similar results are found for the implied volatilities from the expiring option series, having an average time to expiration of 13.9 trading days.

The results of the encompassing tests for the distant horizon forecasts of volatility are reported in Table 7. As was the case for near-term volatility the Garch forecasts and historic volatilities fail to add explanatory power to the predictions based on implied volatilities. Note, however, that combining the Egarch forecasts with implied volatilities appears to improve the explanatory power of the forecasts, increasing the R^2 reported for implied volatilities in Table 5 from 0.489 to 0.600.

Table 6. Comparison of the relative information content for out-of-sample forecasts of near-term volatility

$$\sigma^2_{Ht+1} = b_0 + b_1\sigma^2_{It} + b_2\sigma^2_{Gt} + b_3\sigma^2_{Et} + b_4\sigma^2_{Nt} + \eta_{t+1}$$

Forecast comparison	b_0	b_1	b_2	b_3	b_4	R^2
I, G	0.003	0.962	–0.196			0.722
	(0.003)	(0.146)	(0.212)			
I, G, H	0.003	0.971	–0.173		–0.022	0.741
	(0.003)	(0.156)	(0.235)		(0.092)	
I, E	–0.001	0.881		0.188		0.741
	(0.003)	(0.144)		(0.120)		
I, E, H	–0.001	0.942		0.189	–0.074	0.743
	(0.003)	(0.161)		(0.119)	(0.088)	
I, H	0.003	0.938			–0.071	0.720
	(0.003)	(0.154)			(0.090)	
G, H	0.006		0.562		0.374	0.421
	(0.005)		(0.587)		(0.277)	
E, H	0.005			0.178	0.606	0.412
	(0.003)			(0.152)	(0.218)	
G, E	0.003		1.168	0.204		0.398
	(0.003)		(0.507)	(0.152)		

Notes: The near forecast horizon matches the remaining life of the call option having the second shortest time to expiration. The forecast variables I, G, E, and N, respectively, indicate forecasts based on implied volatility, a GARCH(1,1)-M model, an EGARCH-AR(1) model, and lagged historic volatility. The proxy for ex post volatility is the sample variance of the daily returns for the spot-month futures contract over the forecast period. The sample includes 806 forecasts having an average length of 32.5 trading days. The standard errors in parentheses are computed using a generalisation of the Hansen and Hodrick (1980) correction for autocorrelation and heteroscedasticity that adjusts for the variable length of the forecast intervals (eg, see Hodrick and Srivastava (1987)).

Table 7. Comparison of the relative information content for out-of-sample forecasts of distant-term volatility

$$\sigma^2_{Ht+1} = b_0 + b_1\sigma^2_{It} + b_2\sigma^2_{Gt} + b_3\sigma^2_{Et} + b_4\sigma^2_{Nt} + \eta_{t+1}$$

Forecast comparison	b_0	b_1	b_2	b_3	b_4	R^2
I, G	0.005	0.777	0.185			0.491
	(0.004)	(0.168)	(0.571)			
I, G, H	0.005	0.831	0.279		–0.100	0.494
	(0.006)	(0.181)	(1.473)		(0.314)	
I, E	–0.002	0.843		0.380		0.600
	(0.004)	(0.135)		(0.148)		
I, E, H	–0.002	0.901		0.382	–0.069	0.602
	(0.005)	(0.256)		(0.198)	(0.193)	
I, H	0.005	0.777			0.185	0.491
	(0.004)	(0.168)			(0.571)	
G, H	0.007		0.807		0.333	0.306
	(0.012)		(2.173)		(0.399)	
E, H	0.003			0.351	0.552	0.360
	(0.007)			(0.232)	(0.217)	
G, E	–0.001		1.471	0.375		0.366
	(0.007)		(0.738)	(0.178)		

Notes: The near forecast horizon matches the remaining life of the call option having the second shortest time to expiration. The forecast variables I, G, E, and N, respectively, indicate forecasts based on implied volatility, a GARCH(1,1)-M model, an EGARCH-AR(1) model, and lagged historic volatility. The proxy for ex post volatility is the sample variance of the daily returns for the spot-month futures contract over the forecast period. The sample includes 860 forecasts having an average length of 68.0 trading days. The standard errors in parentheses are computed using a generalisation of the Hansen and Hodrick (1980) correction for autocorrelation and heteroscedasticity that adjusts for the variable length of the forecast intervals (eg, see Hodrick and Srivastava (1987)).

The incremental information content of the Egarch forecasts over the longer forecast horizon may be partly attributable to the difficulties involved in estimating implied volatilities from the prices of distant expiration call options. Since distant expiration options are traded less frequently than the near expiration series, the implied volatilities for distant expiration options must contain less information. Further, estimation problems associated with larger bid-ask spreads and non-synchronous trading will cause estimates of implied volatility to contain relatively greater measurement error. The impact of these factors on the forecasting power of implied volatilities to forecast distant-term volatility is reflected in the decrease in the R^2 of the forecasting regression from 0.718 to 0.489.

The improved forecasting accuracy that comes from combining the Egarch forecasts with implied volatilities may indicate that the Egarch forecasts of daily volatility for distant points in the future more accurately reflect the long-run volatility of the crude oil futures market. The increase in the explanatory power of the Egarch model from an R^2 of 0.022 for the near-term forecast horizon to an R^2 of 0.095 over the distant forecast horizon is consistent with this explanation.

The out-of-sample forecasting comparisons indicate that implied volatilities provide better forecasts than either the average step-ahead Garch forecasts or the naive forecasts using historic volatility. The results suggest that options traders incorporate information beyond that contained in the past series of oil futures prices in their implicit predictions of the future volatility of the oil futures market.

This is in contrast to the results of Day and Lewis (1992) and Lamoureux and Lastrapes (1993), which suggest that improved forecasts of the volatility of the S&P 100 index and certain NYSE stocks may be obtained by combining implied volatilities with Garch forecasts. The results also contrast sharply with those of Canina and Figlewski (1993), who argue that the implied volatility from S&P 100 index options has virtually no correlation with future volatility.

DETERMINING THE OPTIMAL FORECAST ADJUSTMENT

The results of the simple forecast regressions indicate that implied volatilities provide better out-of-sample forecasts than any of the alternative forecasting models for volatility. In most cases, however, the competing forecasts cannot be considered to be unbiased since the Wald statistic indicates that the unbiased forecast hypothesis can be rejected at a confidence level of at least 95%. Further, the results of the encompassing tests suggest that improved forecasts can be obtained by combining the information in alternative forecasts of volatility. Here we investigate the extent to which forecasts of volatility can be improved by using the estimated parameters of the forecast and encompassing regressions to create composite forecasts of futures market volatility.

If the forecasts from a model for volatility are not unbiased, it should be possible to improve them by making an adjustment to offset the estimated biases. To investigate this possibility, we first estimate (14) for each of the alternative models of volatility using a subset of our time series of forecasts. This produces a distinct set of parameter estimates, b_0 and b_1, for each of the alternative forecast models (much as in Tables 4 and 5). These parameter estimates are then used to create adjusted out-of-sample forecasts of volatility for each of the forecasts in the holdout sample.

The adjusted forecast is given by

$$\sigma^2_{At+1} = \hat{b}_0 + \hat{b}_1\sigma^2_{Ft} \qquad (16)$$

where σ^2_{At+1} represents an adjusted forecast of the volatility for period $t+1$, σ^2_{Ft} is the raw (unadjusted) forecast of volatility available at the end of period t, and $\hat{b}_0$ and $\hat{b}_1$ are the appropriate adjustment parameters for the forecast in question.

Adjusted forecasts can also be created using alternative combinations of forecasts. The adjustment models for the combined forecasts are developed using the same procedures as above. The general encompassing regression given by (15) is first estimated for the same estimation sample as above using several combinations of implied volatility and one or more of the other forecasts. The resulting parameter estimates are then used to generate a series of adjusted out-of-sample forecasts for several alternative combinations of forecasts.

The adjusted combination of forecasts can be expressed as

$$\sigma^2_{At+1} = \hat{b}_0 + \hat{b}_1\sigma^2_{It} + \hat{b}_2\sigma^2_{Gt} + \hat{b}_3\sigma^2_{Et} + \hat{b}_4\sigma^2_{Nt} \qquad (17)$$

where $\hat{b}_0$, $\hat{b}_1$, $\hat{b}_2$, $\hat{b}_3$, and $\hat{b}_4$ are the estimated parameters for the adjustment model.

The adjustment models for near-term and distant-term forecasts of volatility are estimated using the first 845 and the first 710 forecast observations in the respective time series of forecasts, leaving in each case a holdout sample of

150 observations to be used to determine the out-of-sample forecasting accuracy of the alternative raw and adjusted forecasts. The out-of-sample forecast accuracy of these forecasts is measured using the average forecast error (ME), the root mean-squared error (RMSE), and the mean absolute forecast error (MAE).[7]

Out-of-sample comparisons of the accuracy of the adjusted and unadjusted forecasts are presented in Tables 8 and 9. The results in Table 8 show that, of the adjusted forecasts, the adjustment based on the implied volatilities provides the most accurate out-of-sample forecasts over both the near- and distant-term horizons. In each case, however, the forecast based simply on the implied volatility has less out-of-sample forecast error than does the corresponding adjusted forecast. As should be expected, the out-of-sample forecasting accuracy of implied volatilities over the near-term horizon is greater than the accuracy over the distant-term horizon.

Similar results are presented in Table 9 for several adjusted combinations of implied volatilities and the other forecasts. For the near-term forecast horizon, the adjusted combinations of implied volatilities and Garch forecasts have the least amount of error according to each of the three measures of forecasting accuracy.

A comparison of the forecast error for the adjusted combinations of implied volatilities and Garch forecasts with the forecast error for the unadjusted implied volatilities reported in Table 8 however, shows that unadjusted implied volatilities have less forecast error than any adjusted forecast or any combination of forecasts over the near-term horizon. A similar result holds for the distant-term forecast horizon. Although the combination of implied volatilities and Egarch forecasts is the best of the combined forecasts, the unadjusted implied volatilities dominate every adjusted forecast and every combination of forecasts over the distant-term forecast horizon.

Table 8. Comparison of the raw forecasts and adjusted forecasts of volatility

$$\sigma^2_{At+1} = \hat{b}_0 + \hat{b}_1\sigma^2_{Ft}$$

Forecast	Pure forecasts			Adjusted forecasts		
	ME	RMSE	MAE	ME	RMSE	MAE
			Near-term volatility			
Historic	–0.00024	0.00243	0.00176	0.00207	0.00265	0.00227
Garch	0.00215	0.00284	0.00247	0.00196	0.00257	0.00216
Egarch	0.00256	0.00305	0.00255	0.00287	0.00323	0.00287
Implied	0.00006	0.00128	0.00096	0.00092	0.00145	0.00119
			Distant-term volatility			
Historic	0.00049	0.00230	0.00199	0.00221	0.00257	0.00232
Garch	0.00271	0.00305	0.00282	0.00217	0.00252	0.00227
Egarch	0.00168	0.00218	0.00177	0.00240	0.00268	0.00241
Implied	0.00099	0.00179	0.00155	0.00190	0.00219	0.00197

Notes: The parameters used to adjust the raw forecasts of volatility, σ^2_{Ft}, are determined by estimating (14) for each of the alternative models of futures market volatility. The adjustment models for near-term forecasts of volatility are estimated using the first 845 forecast observations in the sample, leaving a holdout sample of 150 observations to be used to determine the out-of-sample forecasting accuracy of the alternative raw and adjusted forecasts. The adjustment models for distant-term volatility are estimated using the first 710 forecast observations, leaving a holdout sample of 150 observations. The accuracy of the adjusted forecasts is compared with the accuracy of the raw forecasts on the basis of the average forecast error (ME), the root mean-squared error (RMSE), and the mean absolute forecast error (MAE). (Although the parameters for the forecast adjustment models are not reported, they are available from the authors on request.)

Table 9. Comparison of the raw forecasts and adjusted combinations of volatility forecasts

$$\sigma^2_{At+1} = \hat{b}_0 + \hat{b}_1\sigma^2_{It} + \hat{b}_2\sigma^2_{Gt} + \hat{b}_3\sigma^2_{Et} + \hat{b}_4\sigma^2_{Nt}$$

	Near-term forecasts			Distant-term forecasts		
Forecast combination	ME	RMSE	MAE	ME	RMSE	MAE
I, G	0.00097	0.00145	0.00118	0.00185	0.00218	0.00199
I, G, H	0.00108	0.00149	0.00123	0.00195	0.00221	0.00198
I, E	0.00101	0.00147	0.00121	0.00181	0.00207	0.00186
I, E, H	0.00123	0.00156	0.00134	0.00199	0.00214	0.00199
I, H	0.00107	0.00149	0.00124	0.00199	0.00222	0.00200

Notes: The forecast variables I, G, E, and N, respectively, indicate forecasts based on implied volatility, a GARCH(1, l)-M model, an EGARCH-AR(1) model, and lagged historic volatility. The parameters used to compute the weighted combination of raw forecasts of volatility are determined by estimating several restricted versions of Equation (15). The adjustment models for near-term forecasts of volatility are estimated using the first 845 forecast observations in the sample, leaving a holdout sample of 150 observations to be used to determine the out-of-sample forecasting accuracy of the alternative raw and adjusted forecasts. The adjustment models for distant-term volatility are estimated using the first 710 forecast observations, leaving a holdout sample of 150 observations. The accuracy of the adjusted forecasts is compared with the accuracy of the raw forecasts on the basis of the average forecast error (ME), the root mean-squared error (RMSE), and the mean absolute forecast error (MAE). (Although the parameters for the forecast adjustment models are not reported, they are available from the authors on request.)

Conclusion

We have examined the relative power of implied volatilities and generalised autoregressive conditional heteroscedasticity models to predict volatility in the crude oil futures market. The results show that the implied volatilities from crude oil futures options have significant within-sample explanatory power.

Although implied volatilities contain information that is incremental to the information contained in time series models of volatility, we provide evidence that Garch models for volatility contain information that is not impounded by the prices of call options on crude oil futures contracts. The encompassing tests for forecasts of near-term volatility show that neither the Garch models nor historic volatility adds much explanatory power to predictions of near-term volatility based on implied volatilities. These results are confirmed by our comparisons of the forecasting accuracy of implied volatilities with the forecasting accuracy of a variety of adjusted forecasts and adjusted forecast combinations.

Consequently, market professionals interested in forecasting near-term volatility (up to two months in the future) may wish to avoid complex time series models for volatility and restrict their attention to the forecasts implicit in option prices.

Bear in mind, however, the unique character of our sample period, in which the models were called upon to produce out-of-sample forecasts for the period following the invasion of Kuwait. One strength of implied volatility as a forecast is that it can adapt more quickly to changing market conditions than can models that must be fitted statistically to the time series of past prices.

Appendix

DERIVATION OF GARCH FORECASTS OF DAILY VOLATILITY J DAYS IN THE FUTURE

Given the information available at the end of day t, the Garch forecast of the variance of returns for day t + 1 is given by

$$h^2_{t+1} = \alpha_0 + \alpha_1\varepsilon^2_t + \beta_1 h^2_t.$$

Similarly, given the information available at the end of day t + 1, the Garch forecast of the variance of returns for day t + 2 is given by

$$h^2_{t+2} = \alpha_0 + \alpha_1\varepsilon^2_{t+1} + \beta_1 h^2_{t+1}.$$

Given that h^2_{t+1} is known at the end of day t but that ε^2_{t-1} is unknown, the day t forecast of volatility for day t + 2 can be expressed as the conditional expectation

$$E\left(h^2_{t+2}\middle|h^2_{t+1}\right) = \alpha_0 + \alpha_1 E\left(\varepsilon^2_{t+1}\middle|h^2_{t+1}\right) + \beta_1 E\left(h^2_{t+1}\middle|h^2_{t+1}\right). \quad \text{(A1)}$$

By definition, the conditional expectation $E(h^2_{t+1} \mid h^2_{t+1})$ is equal to h^2_{t+1}. Since ε^2_{t+1} has a mean value of zero and a variance of h^2_{t+1}, (A1) can be expressed as

$$E\left(h^2_{t+2}\middle|h^2_{t+1}\right) = \alpha_0 + (\alpha_1 + \beta_1)h^2_{t+1}. \quad \text{(A2)}$$

By expressing the day t forecast of the volatility for day t + 3 $E(h^2_{t+3} \mid h^2_{t+1})$ in terms of $E(h^2_{t+2} \mid h^2_{t+1})$ and $E(\varepsilon^2_{t+2} \mid h^2_{t+1})$ as in (A1) and then proceeding as before, we have

$$E\left(h^2_{t+3}\middle|h^2_{t+1}\right) = \alpha_0 + \alpha_0(\alpha_1 + \beta_1) + \alpha_0(\alpha_1 + \beta_1)^2 h^2_{t+1}. \quad \text{(A3)}$$

Proceeding in this manner and letting

$$\sigma^2_{t+j} = E\left(h^2_{t+j}\middle|h^2_{t+1}\right)$$

the day t Garch forecast of volatility for day t + j can be expressed as

$$\sigma^2_{t+j} = \alpha_0 + \alpha_0(\alpha_1 + \beta_1) + \ldots + \alpha_0(\alpha_1 + \beta_1)^{j-2} + (\alpha_1 + \beta_1)^{j-1}h^2_{t+1}. \quad \text{(A4)}$$

Multiplying (A4) by $(\alpha_1 + \beta_1)$, subtracting the result from the original (A4), and rearranging shows that

$$\sigma^2_{t+j} = (1 - w_j)\bar{\sigma}^2 + w_j h^2_{t+1} \quad \text{(A5)}$$

where

$$w_j = \frac{(\alpha_1 + \beta_1)^{j-1} - (\alpha_1 + \beta_1)^j}{1 - \alpha_1 + \beta_1}$$

and $\bar{\sigma}^2$ is equal to $\alpha_0/(1 - \alpha_1 - \beta_1)$, the long-run volatility of the futures market that is implicit in the Garch model. Equation (A5) shows that given only the one-step-ahead forecast of volatility available at day t (h^2_{t+1}), the forecast of daily volatility j days in the future is a weighted average of the long-run volatility of the futures market, $\bar{\sigma}^2$, and the one-step-ahead forecast (w_j) declines geometrically as the length of the forecast increases so that as j becomes large the forecast of daily volatility for day t + j approaches $\bar{\sigma}^2$.

1 *Harvey and Whaley (1992) use a binomial approach to estimate the implied volatilities for S&P 100 index options. Another possible approach is an approximation for the price of an American futures option developed by Baroni-Adesi and Whaley (1987).*

2 *The updated estimate of the implied volatility is given by*

$$\sigma_{1t}(t) = \sigma_0(t) + \frac{C(\sigma) - C(\sigma_0)}{\frac{\partial C(\sigma_0)}{\partial \sigma}}$$

where $C(\sigma_0)$ represents the value of the futures option for an underlying futures volatility of σ_0, and $C(\sigma)$ represents the (observed) current market price. The derivative of $C(\sigma_0)$ is computed numerically using the binomial model described previously. Given an initial estimate of $\sigma_0(t)$, we iterate using (3) and the binomial valuation formula until our estimate of $\sigma_{1t}(t)$ converges to within 0.0001.

3 *The first derivatives of the likelihood function are computed numerically.*

4 *See Bollerslev, Engle, and Wooldridge (1988) and Nelson (1992) for discussions of Garch-in-mean and exponential Garch models.*

5 *For the Egarch-AR(1), the average-step-ahead forecast of*

volatility incorporates the estimate of the first-order autocorrelation of daily returns (λ_1) implicit in (4). In this case, the average-step-ahead forecast becomes

$$\sigma^2_{Ft} = \frac{1}{N}\sum_{j=1}^{N} A_j^2 \sigma^2_{t+j}$$

where A_j *is equal to* $(1 - \lambda_1^j)/(1 + \lambda_1)$.

6 *Note that for the Garch forecasting model neither of the simple null hypotheses, that* b_0 *is equal to 0 or that* b_1 *is equal to 1, can be rejected individually. However, the Wald test that both conditions hold simultaneously incorporates the additional information that the estimates of* b_0 *and* b_1 *are both greater than their values under the null hypothesis, and rejects the joint hypothesis that* b_0 *is equal to 0 and that* b_1 *is also equal to 1.*

7 *The average forecast error (ME), the root mean-squared error (RMSE), and the mean absolute forecast error (MAE) are given, respectively, by*

$$ME = \frac{1}{N}\sum_{i=1}^{N} E_i$$

$$RMSE = \left[\frac{1}{N}\sum_{i=1}^{N} E_i^2\right]^{\frac{1}{2}}$$

$$MAE = \frac{1}{N}\sum_{i=1}^{N} |E_i|$$

where the forecast error E_i *is equal to* $\sigma^2_{Ht+1} - \sigma^2_{At+1}$.

BIBLIOGRAPHY

Baroni-Adesi, G., and R.E. Whaley, 1987, "Efficient Analytic Approximation of American Option Values", *Journal of Finance* 42, pp. 301-20.

Bollerslev, T., R.F. Engle, and J.M. Wooldridge, 1988, "A Capital Asset Pricing Model with Time Varying Covariances", *Journal of Political Economy* 96, pp.116-31.

Bollerslev, T., and J.M. Wooldridge, 1988, "Quasi-Maximum Likelihood Estimation of Dynamic Models with Time-Varying Covariances", Unpublished manuscript.

Canina, L., and S. Figlewski, 1993, "The Informational Content of Implied Volatility," *Review of Financial Studies* 6, No. 3, pp. 659-82, reprinted as Chapter 13 of the present volume.

Christie, A.A., 1982, "The Stochastic Behavior of Common Stock Variances: Value, Leverage and Interest Rate Effects", *Journal of Financial Economics* 10, pp. 407-32.

Day, T.E., and C.M. Lewis, 1988, "The Behavior of the Volatility Implicit in the Prices of Stock Index Options", *Journal of Financial Economics* 22, pp. 103-22.

Day T.E., and C.M. Lewis, 1992, "Stock Market Volatility and the Information Content of Stock Index Options", *Journal of Econometrics* 52, pp. 267-87.

Fair, R.C., and R.J. Shiller, 1990, "Comparing Information in Forecasts from Econometric Models", *American Economic Review* 80, pp. 375-89.

Fleming, J., 1992, "The Rationality of Market Volatility Forecasts Implied by S&P 100 Index Option Prices," Unpublished working paper.

Hansen, L.P., and R.J. Hodrick, 1980, "Forward Exchange Rates as Optimal Predictors of Future Spot Rates: An Econometric Analysis", *Journal of Political Economy* 88, pp. 829-53.

Harvey, C.R., and R.E. Whaley, 1992, "Market Volatility Prediction and the Efficiency of the S&P 100 Index Option Market", *Journal of Financial Economics* 30, pp. 43-74.

Hodrick, R.J., and S. Srivastava, 1987, "Foreign Currency Futures", *Journal of International Economics* 22, pp. 1-24.

Hull, J., and A. White, 1987, "The Pricing of Options on Assets with Stochastic Volatilities", *Journal of Finance* 42, pp. 281-300.

Lamoureux, C.B., and W.D. Lastrapes, 1993, "Forecasting Stock Return Variance: Toward an Understanding of Stochastic Implied Volatilities", *Review of Financial Studies* 6, pp. 293-326; reprinted as Chapter 14 of the present volume.

Merton, R.C., 1973, "The Theory of Rational Option Pricing", *Bell Journal of Economics and Management* 4, pp. 141-83.

Nelson, D.B., 1992, "Conditional Heteroscedasticity in Asset Returns: A New Approach", *Econometrica* 59, pp. 347-70.

Pagan, A.R., and G.W. Schwert, 1990, "Alternative Models for Conditional Stock Volatility", *Journal of Econometrics* 45, pp. 267-90.

13

The Informational Content of Implied Volatility*

Linda Canina and Stephen Figlewski
Cornell University; Stern School of Business, New York University

Implied volatility is widely believed to be informationally superior to historical volatility, because it is the "market's" forecast of future volatility. But for S&P 100 index options, the most actively traded contract in the United States, we find implied volatility to be a poor forecast of subsequent realised volatility. In aggregate and across subsamples separated by maturity and strike price, implied volatility has virtually no correlation with future volatility, and it does not incorporate the information contained in recent observed volatility.

One of the most attractive features of the Black-Scholes option pricing model is that its parameters are almost all observable. The one input that must be forecast is the volatility of the underlying asset. Unfortunately, price volatility of most optionable securities varies considerably over time and accurate prediction is far from easy. The two basic approaches are either to compute the realised volatility over the recent past from historical price data, or to calculate the "implied volatility" (IV) from current option prices in the market by solving the pricing model for the volatility that sets the model and market prices equal.

It has become almost an article of faith in the academic finance profession that the implied volatility is the "market's" volatility forecast, and that it is a better estimate than historical volatility. Indeed, researchers often use implied volatility in other models as an *ex ante* measure of perceived asset price risk.[1] Here, we examine that proposition as it pertains to the most active options market in the United States, options on the Standard and Poor's 100 Index (frequently called by their ticker symbol, OEX options). The results we obtain from analysing over 17,000 OEX call option prices conflict sharply with the conventional wisdom.

We begin the analysis with a discussion of the logic behind the conventional wisdom and a critical examination of how it should be tested. The next section describes our data and methodology. If implied volatility is the market's prediction of actual volatility over the time remaining to an option's expiration date, daily observations on IV involve sequential forecasts for overlapping time periods. This leads to serial dependence in the time-series of forecast errors, and a statistical problem in testing the model. In addition, simultaneous trading in multiple contracts with different strike prices and overlapping expirations creates further cross-correlations if the data sample contains observations on more than one option per day. Previous studies dealt with the problem by aggregating and excluding data to create non-overlapping observations. Unfortunately, such procedures can severely reduce the power of statistical tests. Instead, we maximise the amount of information obtained from the data by adopting an estimation procedure that makes use of the entire data sample and corrects for the time dependence directly.

* *This paper was first published in* The Review of Financial Studies, *Vol.6, No.3 (1993). It is reprinted with permission of Oxford University Press. We would like to thank the Interactive Data Corporation and Yogi Thambiah for supplying the data used in this study. Helpful comments from Clifford Ball, Stephen Brown, Stephen Cecchetti, William Greene, Barry Schachter, William Silber, Bruce Tuckman, Robert Whaley, the editor, Robert Stambaugh, and an anonymous referee, as well as seminar participants at Boston College, Cornell, Duke, N.Y.U., Ohio State, and V.P.I. are gratefully acknowledged.*

We then present our estimation results. In brief, they show that for OEX index options, implied volatility is an inefficient and biased forecast of realised future volatility that does not impound the information contained in recent historical volatility. In fact, the statistical evidence shows little or no correlation at all between implied volatility and subsequent realised volatility.

Volatility forecasts and implied volatility

REALISED VOLATILITY, IMPLIED VOLATILITY AND THE MARKET'S VOLATILITY FORECAST

It is widely accepted that the implied Black-Scholes volatility computed from the market price of an option is a good estimate of the "market's" expectation of the volatility of the underlying asset, and that the market's expectation is informationally efficient.

Black and Scholes assume that the price for the underlying stock follows a logarithmic diffusion process with constant instantaneous mean and volatility. However, there is an obvious conflict in applying an approach that assumes the asset price process has a known constant volatility to a situation in which volatility must be forecast because it changes randomly over time. Investors who were fully rational in valuing options should use a pricing model that deals rigorously with the stochastic nature of volatility, as in Hull and White (1987) or Wiggins (1987). Stochastic volatility models require the investor to forecast not just a single volatility parameter, but the entire joint probability distribution for asset returns and changes in volatility, and also the market price of volatility risk. These requirements make these models significantly more difficult to implement than Black-Scholes and other constant volatility models. During the period covered by our data sample, ending in 1987, option traders had easy access to theoretical values, implied volatilities, deltas, and so on for traded options from the standard fixed volatility models, but formal stochastic volatility models were not in general use. Even today, it is common practice for option traders to make trading and hedging decisions by picking a point forecast for volatility – perhaps the implied volatility, an estimate computed from historical prices, or some subjectively determined combination of the two – and then inserting this point estimate into the Black-Scholes or binomial model. Similarly, academic investigators almost invariably use implied volatilities from standard fixed volatility models to measure the market's volatility expectations.

Thus, we consider the analysis presented in this subsection to be more valid as a description of the approach taken by many actual investors and researchers than as optimal behaviour in a world of stochastic volatility. One way to interpret our empirical work is as a test of whether the "rule of thumb" strategy of computing implied volatility from a standard fixed volatility model is an efficient way to obtain a volatility forecast.

For a series of prices $\{S_0, S_1, \ldots, S_T\}$, the realised volatility σ is defined as the annualised standard deviation of the continuously compounded returns, $\{R_1, R_2, \ldots, R_T\}$, where $R_t \equiv \ln(S_t/S_{t-1})$, $\bar{R}$ is the sample mean of the R_t, and K is the number of observation intervals in a year:[2]

$$\sigma = \left(\frac{K}{T-1} \sum_{t=1}^{T} \left(R_t - \bar{R} \right)^2 \right)^{1/2}. \tag{1}$$

In the later discussion of our empirical work, the annualised volatility that will be realised over the remaining lifetime of a τ-period option as of date t will be denoted $\sigma_t(\tau)$. In this section, we simplify the notation by suppressing the explicit dependence on t and τ.

One estimate of future volatility can be obtained from historical prices by assuming that the recent realised level of volatility will continue in the future. Another estimate comes from current option prices. Given the observable parameters and an option valuation formula, there is a one-to-one correspondence between the option price and the volatility input. Computing the implied volatility, IV, from the observed market price then gives an estimate of the "market's" volatility forecast,

$$IV = E_{MKT}[\sigma], \tag{2}$$

where $E_{MKT}[\sigma]$ denotes the market's (subjective) expectation for σ.[3]

By definition, realised volatility can be written as its expected value conditional on an information set Φ plus a zero mean random error that is orthogonal to Φ:

$$\sigma = E[\sigma|\Phi] + \varepsilon, \quad E[\varepsilon|\Phi] = 0.$$

This formulation leads to the well-established regression test for the rationality of a forecast,

$$\sigma = \alpha + \beta F(\Phi) + u, \tag{3}$$

where $F(\Phi)$ is the forecast of σ based on the information set Φ and u is the regression residual.[4] If the forecast is the true expected value of σ conditional on Φ, regressing realised values of σ on their expectations should produce regression estimates of 0.0 and 1.0 for α and β, respectively. Deviation from those values is evidence of bias and inefficiency in the forecasts.

Since the forecast error must be orthogonal to any rationally formed forecast, (3) should hold with $\alpha = 0$ and $\beta = 1$ for any Φ. Running (3) on forecasts derived from a more inclusive information set does not change the expected coefficient estimates, but a better forecast should produce a higher R^2. Further, if one regresses σ on two forecasts, $F_1(\Phi_1)$ and $F_2(\Phi_2)$, where the second is derived from a subset of the information used in forming the first ($\Phi_1 \supset \Phi_2$),

$$\sigma = \alpha + \beta_1 F_1(\Phi_1) + \beta_2 F_2(\Phi_2) + u, \qquad (4)$$

the slope coefficient of the first, β_1, should still be 1.0 and the less informed forecast should have $\beta_2 = 0$. Analysing the relative information content of two different forecasts by means of a regression like (4) is known as an "encompassing regression" test. Fair and Shiller (1990) discuss this approach in detail and use it to evaluate the forecasting performance of different macroeconomic models.

The tests we report below are based on (3) and (4), with implied volatility and historical volatility as the conditional forecasts.

Empirical evidence on implied volatility

Early studies by Latané and Rendleman (1976), Chiras and Manaster (1978) and Beckers (1981) all use the basic Black-Scholes European option model or a variant of it in computing IV's for American calls on dividend-paying stocks.[5] In the tests presented below, we derive the IV's from a binomial model that adjusts for dividends and captures the value of early exercise. This resolves the problem of analysing American options but does not address the many other issues raised by the possibility that the "market" may not be using exactly the same model we are. For example, the market's option model may allow non-lognormal price changes or price jumps. Using the wrong model violates (2): the computed IV will differ from the market's real volatility forecast.

In the early studies, stock price volatility was typically treated as if it were a constant parameter, so that the exact timing and periodicity of the data sample used in estimating it did not matter much. This tacit assumption gave rise to problems in the way the data was handled, including use of sparse monthly data spanning long time periods to estimate historical volatility, estimating "realised" volatility over periods that did not match option maturity, and in at least one case, analysing "forecasts" of volatility over periods prior to the date the forecast was made.[6] Only Beckers (1981) recognises the importance of timing, in that he uses daily data to estimate historical volatility from the previous three months of stock prices, and realised volatility over the period from the observation date to option expiration.

Recent papers by Day and Lewis (1990) and Lamoureux and Lastrapes (1993) also examine implied volatility as a source of information. Both studies find that IV contributes a statistically significant amount of information about volatility over the (short term) forecasting horizon covered by the models, but they also find that IV does not fully impound the information that the model is able to extract from historical prices. LL also examine forecasting volatility through option expiration and find that IV alone is less accurate than the models that incorporate historical prices in eight out of 10 cases.

Data and methodology

The data sample is drawn from the set of closing prices for all call options on the OEX index from March 15, 1983, shortly after index option trading opened, through March 28, 1987. We eliminated options with less than seven or more than 127 days to expiration and those that were more than 20 points in- or out-of-the-money.[7] Also, some of the recorded option prices violated the lower arbitrage boundary, that the call price should be greater than the current stock price minus the present value of the strike price plus future dividends. An option's price equals the boundary value if volatility is zero. In the case of a boundary violation, implied variance would have to be negative, so those options were also excluded from the sample. This left a total of 17,606 observations. At the outset, there were contracts traded for two expiration dates, September and December 1983. Starting in December 1983, the expiration cycle was changed so that there were always one, two, three, and four month maturities.

These are American options and the OEX index portfolio contains mostly dividend-paying stocks. To take into account the value of early exercise, we used a Binomial model with 500 time steps,[8] a very fine grid size (eg 10 steps per

Table 1. Summary statistics of implied volatility by maturity group

Maturity group (i)	Days to expiration	Number of obs	IV mean	Sample standard deviation
All		17,606	0.168	0.055
1	7–35	4,088	0.195	0.080
2	29–63	5,196	0.166	0.046
3	57–98	4,709	0.158	0.039
4	85–127	3,613	0.152	0.035

The table shows the breakdown of implied volatilities for OEX call options between March 15, 1983 and March 28, 1987, into four maturity groups corresponding to the number of contract months to expiration. For example, the first group (i = 1) contains the near-month options. The rightmost columns give the mean and the standard deviation of implied volatilities within each group.

Table 2. Summary statistics of implied volatility by intrinsic-value group

Group (j)	Intrinsic value	Number of obs	Mean	Standard deviation
All		17,606	0.168	0.055
1	–20 to –15.01	1,800	0.167	0.038
2	–15 to –10.01	2,761	0.158	0.034
3	–10 to –5.01	3,069	0.154	0.034
4	–5 to –0.01	3,093	0.155	0.036
5	0 to 5	2,907	0.158	0.043
6	5.01 to 10	2,127	0.179	0.058
7	10.01 to 15	1,230	0.209	0.082
8	15.01 to 20	619	0.263	0.121

The table shows the breakdown of implied volatilities for OEX call options between March 15, 1983 and March 28, 1987, into eight intrinsic value groups corresponding to the amount the option is in- or out-of-the-money. For example, the first group (j = 1) contains the options that are between 15 and 20 points out-of-the-money. The rightmost columns give the mean and the standard deviation of implied volatilities within each group.

1. Implied volatility vs time to expiration

OEX call options, March 15, 1983–March 27, 1987

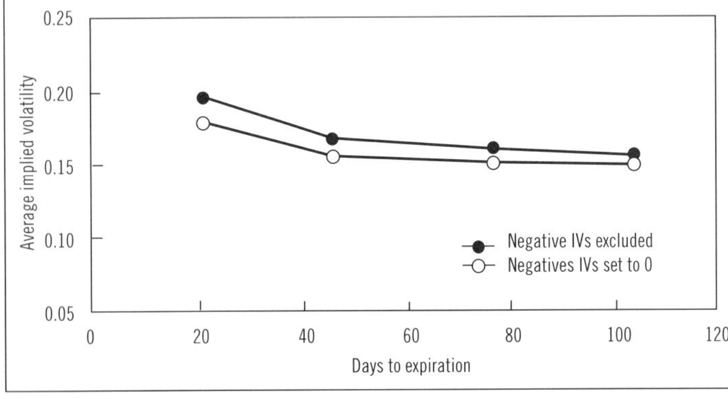

2. Implied volatility vs intrinsic value

OEX call options, March 15, 1983–March 27, 1987

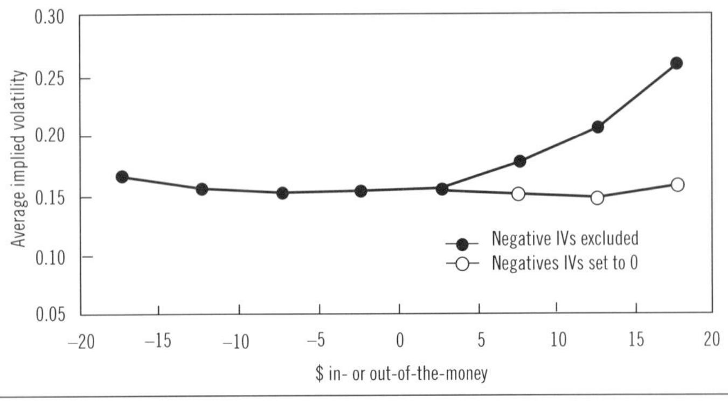

day for an option with 50 days to expiration). In selecting a measure of the riskless interest rate, we have tried to take account of both the relevant lending and borrowing rates faced by options traders. Instead of T-Bill rates, we used the average of the Eurodollar deposit rate and the broker call rate on each date. We treated dividends as if future payouts were known, and used the actual stream of dividends paid over the option's life. Annualised implied volatilities were then calculated to the nearest 0.001 by an iterative search procedure.

On each date, there are prices, and therefore implied volatilities, for many different options. We find that the IV's for OEX options observed at a given point in time vary systematically across the different strikes and maturity months, where maturity month refers to the near, second, third, and fourth month expiration dates. This regular cross-sectional structure is illustrated in Tables 1 and 2 and Figures 1 and 2 for subsamples of the data, broken up according to maturity month and the extent to which the options are in- or out-of-the-money.

The extent to which the options are in- or out-of-the-money is simply (S – X), the current level of the index minus the option's strike price. To save space we will hereafter refer to this quantity as the option's "intrinsic value," although this usage is somewhat unconventional (because it takes negative values for out-of-the-money options).

Table 1 shows that the average implied volatility in the sample is a decreasing function of time to option expiration. The mean for the entire set of 17,606 observations is 0.168, while the averages for our four maturity groups decline monotonically from 0.195 for near-month options to 0.152 for those expiring in the fourth month.

Latané and Rendleman pioneered the practice of forming a weighted average implied standard deviation (WISD) using multiple options on the same stock. This makes sense if the only reason IV's for two options on the same asset will differ is random noise in the sampling process. But with time-varying volatility, options expiring on different dates may reasonably be priced using different volatilities. Other differences are often observed, such as a regular structure of IV's across strike prices for options with a given maturity, and these constitute evidence against the hypothesis that IV is the market's fully rational volatility forecast.[9] Regularity in IV differences suggests the existence of systematic factors that lead investors to price particular options high or low relative to others.[10] It is therefore inappropriate simply to average together IVs from options with different expirations or IVs measured on different dates as if they were just multiple noisy observations on the same parameter.[11]

The most striking result in Table 2 is that deep in-the-money calls appear to have much higher IVs than at-the-money options. Beckers also finds this pattern in his study of individual stock options. In his sample, IVs for deep-in-the-money near to expiration calls are as much as ten times the IVs for the corresponding at-the-money options. One explanation for this phenomenon is that in constructing the sample, we were obliged to exclude the calls that would have negative IVs because their prices violated the lower boundary. Deep-in-the-money options are quite insensitive to volatility, meaning a large change in the implied volatility is produced by a small change in the option's price. At the same time, these options are rather illiquid and they trade less frequently than those nearer to the money, so they have wider bid-ask spreads and nonsynchronous data is a larger problem. Thus there is relatively more "noise" in the prices of these calls, and apparent boundary violations are most frequent for them. In forming our sample, we are potentially introducing a bias by keeping calls whose prices were artificially high due to trading noise but eliminating them when noise drove their prices down below the boundary.

To see how this bias might affect the results, we constructed a broader sample including the calls that violated the boundary and arbitrarily assigned them IV of 0. The second curves in Figures 1 and 2 plot the results from this procedure. Figure 2 shows how this alters the estimates of mean IVs for the deep-in-the-money calls and brings them much closer to the values observed for the other option groups. We suspect that Becker's results may also be partly due to eliminating option prices that violated the lower arbitrage boundary.

When the market prices embody a regular volatility structure that seems to reflect systematic factors other than predicted future volatility, we do not know which option's IV, if any, represents the market's true expectation. It is also clear that simply averaging different IVs together would contaminate our estimate of the market's volatility forecast with price effects relating to those other factors. Accordingly, we subdivide the sample into groups, which we analyse separately, according to maturity and intrinsic value. This allows us to test whether any one group of options, such as those that are at-the-money and near to expiration, provides a more useful IV.

The sample is broken into four maturity groups, and each of those is divided into eight intrinsic value groups. This produces 32 subsamples, which we denote as subsample (i,j), where i represents the maturity group and j, the intrinsic value group. For example, subsample (1,2) – maturity group 1 and intrinsic value group 2 – contains implied volatilities for the near-month options that are between 15 and 10 points out-of-the-money. The subsample breakpoints are displayed in Tables 1 and 2. Break points for the intrinsic value groups are set five points apart, corresponding to the contract strike prices. Since options expire on the third Friday of the delivery month, the near-month calls may have up to 35 days to expiration, while in other months, the second month options might mature in as few as 29 days.[12] Our subsamples are constructed such that each contains a maximum of one option price per day.

Equation (3) is estimated separately for each subgroup. We rewrite (3) to bring out its dependence on maturity, intrinsic value, and the time period, as

$$\sigma_t(\tau) = \alpha + \beta \cdot IV_t(i,j) + u_{t,i,j}, \qquad (5)$$

where $IV_t(i,j)$ is the implied volatility computed at time t from the option in maturity group i and intrinsic value group j, and $u_{t,i,j}$ represents the regression disturbance. The symbol $\sigma_t(\tau)$ is the realised volatility of returns over the period between t and $t + \tau$, the option's expiration date, annualised by multiplying the calculated volatility per trading day by the square root of 260. In the tests reported below, the realised volatility $\sigma_t(\tau)$ is computed over the remaining life of the option as the annualised sample standard deviation of log returns including cash dividends, that is, $\ln[(S_s + D_s)/S_{s-1}]$, for $t < s \leq t + \tau$.

As long as the regressors and disturbances are uncorrelated with one another, the least squares estimates of α and β will be unbiased and consistent. However, when daily data are used, the disturbances $u_{t,i,j}$ will be serially correlated. Since the realised volatility involves each day's return, from $t + 1$ to expiration at $t + \tau$, $\sigma_t(\tau)$ is only fully known on the day after the expiration date. The forecast errors are therefore correlated for IVs computed from any pair of options whose remaining lifetimes overlap.

Define X_n as the row vector of the independent variables for observation n in the sample, ie,

Table 3. Realised volatility over the remaining life of the option regressed on implied volatility:
Equation (5) $\sigma_t(\tau) = \alpha + \beta \cdot IV_t(i,j) + u_{t,i,j}$

	Intrinsic value							
Maturity group	−20 to −15.01 j = 1	−15 to −10.01 j = 2	−10 to −5.01 j = 3	−5 to −0.01 j = 4	0 to 5 j = 5	5.01 to 10 j = 6	10.01 to 15 j = 7	15.01 to 20 j = 8
Maturity i=1; t = 7–35								
α	0.152	0.125	0.101	0.098	0.113	0.143	0.158	0.161
SE	0.026	0.019	0.015	0.013	0.011	0.012	0.014	0.012
β	−0.063	0.065	0.205	0.229	0.138	−0.025	−0.070	−0.047
SE	0.104	0.087	0.080	0.069	0.058	0.045	0.042	0.028
R^2	0.004	0.003	0.044	0.067	0.035	0.000	0.032	0.037
N	336	611	691	697	675	513	343	222
Maturity i=2; t = 29–63								
α	0.125	0.111	0.109	0.113	0.123	0.143	0.161	0.182
SE	0.027	0.020	0.018	0.017	0.016	0.016	0.014	0.015
β	0.110	0.178	0.188	0.163	0.102	−0.020	−0.100	−0.171
SE	0.143	0.109	0.099	0.101	0.084	0.070	0.054	0.060
R^2	0.010	0.049	0.062	0.053	0.025	0.000	0.055	0.197
N	564	792	851	852	836	685	407	209
Maturity i=3; t = 57–98								
α	0.116	0.112	0.112	0.118	0.127	0.143	0.162	0.176
SE	0.024	0.024	0.021	0.018	0.017	0.017	0.013	0.009
β	0.171	0.191	0.188	0.144	0.081	−0.015	−0.108	−0.157
SE	0.138	0.143	0.125	0.110	0.093	0.080	0.053	0.070
R^2	0.038	0.062	0.070	0.046	0.019	−0.001	0.061	0.147
N	507	731	803	810	789	593	324	152
Maturity i=4; t = 85–127								
α	0.135	0.120	0.121	0.131	0.139	0.154	0.155	0.159
SE	0.026	0.022	0.019	0.017	0.016	0.016	0.015	0.010
β	0.060	0.138	0.129	0.062	0.002	−0.093	−0.075	−0.084
SE	0.155	0.136	0.121	0.109	0.102	0.072	0.046	0.044
R^2	0.002	0.033	0.035	0.009	−0.002	0.031	0.022	0.019
N	393	627	724	734	607	336	156	36

The table reports regression results from equation (5) (shown above) for OEX call options between March 15, 1983 and March 28, 1987 for each of the 32 subsamples defined by maturity and intrinsic value. The coefficients are fitted by OLS but the standard errors (labelled SE) are corrected for intercorrelation as described in the text. N is the number of observations in the subsample. $IV_t(i,j)$ is the implied volatility computed from the date t price of the call option from maturity group i (expiring at $t + \tau$), and intrinsic value group j. $\sigma_t(\tau)$ is the realized volatility of the OEX index from date t to $t + \tau$. $u_{t,i,j}$ is the regression residual. The hypothesis that $IV_t(i,j)$ is an informationally efficient forecast of $\sigma_t(\tau)$ requires $\alpha = 0.0$ and $\beta = 1.0$. The hypothesis is overwhelmingly rejected in every subsample.

$X_n = (1 \ \ IV)_n$. X is the $N \times 2$ matrix of the X_n. (X is $N \times 3$ for regressions based on equation (4)). Let u_n be the regression error for observation n and let u denote the N-vector of the u_n.

Following Hansen (1982), we compute

$$\hat{\psi} = N^{-1}\sum_{n=1}^{N}\left(\hat{u}_n\right)^2 X_n'X_n + N^{-1}\sum_{k=1}^{N}\sum_{n=k+1}^{N} Q(k,n)\hat{u}_k\hat{u}_n\left(X_n'X_k + X_k'X_n\right), \qquad (6)$$

where u_k and u_n are the fitted residuals for observations k and n from the OLS regression. Q(k,n) is an indicator function taking the value 1 if there is an overlap between the periods to expiration for the two options and 0 otherwise.

The estimated covariance matrix for the coefficients is

$$\hat{\Omega} = (X'X)^{-1}\hat{\psi}(X'X)^{-1}. \qquad (7)$$

The procedure we have just described is consistent, but a question remains as to its performance in small samples (and how large a sample has to be before it is no longer "small"). Another important question is how much statistical power is gained by making use of all available data rather than restricting the analysis to non-overlapping observations. The Appendix describes the results of a simulation study with a data sample constructed to be like the one we examine here. We find the corrected standard errors to be reasonably close to the true values. Moreover, incorporating the overlapping data points leads to a standard error on the β coefficient between one quarter and one eighth of what would be obtained with only non-overlapping data, depending on the option maturity.

The forecasting performance of implied volatility

To test the predictive power of implied volatility, the regression equation (5) was fitted separately for each of the 32 subsamples. The equations were estimated using OLS, and for hypothesis testing the consistent estimate of the coefficient covariance matrix, shown in (6) and (7), was computed.

The results are presented in Table 3, by subsample. For example, for the subsample of options that expire in the second month (i = 2) that are between \$0 and \$5 out-of-the-money (j = 4), the intercept is 0.113 and the estimated slope coefficient is 0.163, with standard errors of 0.017 and 0.101, respectively. The adjusted R^2 is 0.053. Thus, the hypothesis that $\alpha = 0$ and $\beta = 1.0$, and implied volatility is an unbiased forecast of future realised volatility, is strongly rejected for this subsample.

The results obtained for subsample (2,4) are representative of what we find generally in Table 3: in every subsample, implied volatility fails the unbiasedness test. Indeed, the slope coefficient is estimated to be significantly different from zero at the 5% significance level in only six out of the 32 subsamples, and three of these were negative. In the group of three significant positives, the coefficient on implied volatility ranged from 0.138 to 0.229 and the adjusted R^2 was between 0.035 and 0.067. Far from demonstrating that implied volatility in OEX options is an unbiased and efficient forecast of subsequent realised volatility, these results show that in most cases, implied volatility has no statistically significant correlation with realised volatility at all.

We do see that the options that are expected

to be the most efficiently priced, those that are at- or slightly out-of-the-money (intrinsic value groups 3, 4, and 5) and near to expiration (maturity group 1) do produce significant positive βs and some of the highest R^2s. Nevertheless, the results in Table 3 appear to constitute a strong rejection of the null hypothesis.

However, it could be that OEX volatility is just very hard to predict accurately. In that case, the market's information set simply contains very little useful information for predicting $\sigma_t(\tau)$ and the estimation results are dominated by the forecast errors. In order to check whether volatility is predictable at all from data available to the market, each of the regressions was estimated using a historical measure of volatility as the independent variable, in place of implied volatility:

$$\sigma_t(\tau) = \alpha + \beta \cdot VOL60_t(i,j) + u_{t,i,j} \qquad (8)$$

where $VOL60_t(i,j)$ is the annualised standard deviation of the log returns of the S&P 100 stock index portfolio over the 60-day period preceding the date of the implied volatility, for all of the dates t corresponding to implied volatility observations contained in subsample (i,j). A 60-day sample period was used for historical volatility because it was approximately equal to the average forecast horizon in our sample, but tests using historical volatilities computed from 30 and 120 days of data yielded similar results. As before, the equation was fitted using OLS and the covariance matrix was adjusted for heteroskedasticity and time dependence by using (7).

The results are reported in Table 4. The contrast with the previous table is striking. The largest slope coefficient is 0.589, all of the estimated values are positive and most are significantly different from zero at the 5% level.[13]

Table 4. Realised volatility over the remaining life of the option regressed on historical volatility:
Equation (8) $\sigma_t(\tau) = \alpha + \beta \cdot VOL60_t(i,j) + u_{t,i,j}$

	Intrinsic value							
Maturity group	−20 to −15.01 j = 1	−15 to −10.01 j = 2	−10 to −5.01 j = 3	−5 to −0.01 j = 4	0 to 5 j = 5	5.01 to 10 j = 6	10.01 to 15 j = 7	15.01 to 20 j = 8
Maturity i=1; t = 7–35								
α	0.070	0.058	0.054	0.055	0.057	0.063	0.056	0.104
SE	0.037	0.025	0.023	0.023	0.025	0.028	0.031	0.040
β	0.483	0.556	0.576	0.573	0.562	0.521	0.573	0.270
SE	0.272	0.180	0.172	0.172	0.181	0.196	0.212	0.255
R^2	0.059	0.106	0.119	0.118	0.108	0.087	0.094	0.016
N	336	611	691	697	675	513	343	222
Maturity i=2; t = 29–63								
α	0.888	0.078	0.074	0.074	0.074	0.068	0.075	0.085
SE	0.027	0.024	0.024	0.024	0.025	0.027	0.033	0.042
β	0.381	0.441	0.464	0.464	0.467	0.499	0.453	0.394
SE	0.181	0.166	0.165	0.165	0.170	0.185	0.218	0.268
R^2	0.085	0.132	0.151	0.151	0.150	0.158	0.117	0.064
N	564	792	851	852	836	685	407	209
Maturity i=3; t = 57–98								
α	0.091	0.079	0.078	0.078	0.077	0.073	0.069	0.091
SE	0.029	0.029	0.028	0.028	0.029	0.032	0.033	0.041
β	0.367	0.439	0.445	0.444	0.454	0.478	0.504	0.368
SE	0.188	0.193	0.191	0.192	0.193	0.211	0.218	0.266
R^2	0.112	0.183	0.188	0.186	0.190	0.203	0.197	0.063
N	507	731	803	810	789	593	324	152
Maturity i=4; t = 85–127								
α	0.091	0.077	0.077	0.078	0.071	0.067	0.059	0.108
SE	0.033	0.027	0.026	0.026	0.026	0.029	0.031	0.033
β	0.367	0.459	0.455	0.446	0.497	0.522	0.589	0.242
SE	0.207	0.174	0.171	0.176	0.178	0.202	0.221	0.223
R^2	0.105	0.208	0.220	0.212	0.240	0.240	0.286	0.000
N	393	627	724	734	607	336	156	36

The table reports regression results from equation (8) (shown above) for OEX call options between March 15, 1983 and March 28, 1987 for each of the 32 subsamples defined by maturity and intrinsic value. The coefficients are fitted by OLS but the standard errors (labelled SE) are corrected for intercorrelation as described in the text. N is the number of observations in the subsample. $VOL60_t(i,j)$ is the implied volatility computed from the OEX index values on dates $t - 60$ to $t - 1$. Each $VOL60_t(i,j)$ subsample is set up to match the corresponding $IV_t(i,j)$ subsample in Table 3. That is, for each IV in subsample (i,j) of Table 3, subsample (i,j) of Table 4 contains the historical volatility estimated from the previous 60 days' prices. $\sigma_t(\tau)$ is the realized volatility of the OEX index from date t to $t + \tau$. $u_{t,i,j}$ is the regression residual. The hypothesis that $VOL60_t(i,j)$ is an informationally efficient forecast of $\sigma_t(\tau)$ requires $\alpha = 0.0$ and $\beta = 1.0$. The hypothesis is rejected in every subsample.

Table 4 shows that the future volatility of the OEX index was partly forecastable using publicly available information on historical volatility. Note, though, that the historical volatility estimate also fails the rationality test. Even so, the fact that (measured) implied volatility is a less accurate forecast than historical volatility confirms that it is not informationally efficient.

Table 5 reports the results for the "encompassing regression" test. Equation (4) in this case becomes

$$\sigma_t(\tau) = \alpha + \beta_1 \cdot IV_t(i,j) + \beta_2 \cdot VOL60_t(i,j) + u_{t,i,j}. \quad (9)$$

The estimated coefficient on historical volatility in Table 5 is significantly greater than zero in most of the regressions, and its value is comparable to that in the corresponding Table 4 regression. The coefficient on IV is nowhere significantly greater than zero and is negative for 28 out of 32 subsamples. The table clearly illustrates the overall message of our tests – that implied volatility is a poor forecast of subsequent realised volatility and it does not accurately impound the information contained in a readily available historical volatility estimate.

The subsamples we have analysed so far contain a maximum of one observation per day, but the same procedure can equally well be applied to the case in which there is any number of observations per day. This allows estimation on more aggregated samples without the loss of information that occurs when the data points themselves are aggregated, as they are in forming WISDs.

We have applied this procedure to fit (5) on

Table 5. Realised volatility over the remaining life of the option regressed on implied and historical volatility:
Equation (9) $\sigma_t(\tau) = \alpha + \beta_1 \cdot IV_t(i,j) + \beta_2 \cdot VOL60_t(i,j) + u_{t,i,j}$

	Intrinsic value							
Maturity group	−20 to −15.01 j = 1	−15 to −10.01 j = 2	−10 to −5.01 j = 3	−5 to −0.01 j = 4	0 to 5 j = 5	5.01 to 10 j = 6	10.01 to 15 j = 7	15.01 to 20 j = 8
Maturity i=1; t = 7–35								
α	0.082	0.061	0.053	0.055	0.056	0.069	0.076	0.120
SE	0.039	0.023	0.022	0.023	0.024	0.025	0.031	0.039
β_1	−0.056	−0.022	0.043	0.077	0.038	−0.024	−0.063	−0.048
SE	0.097	0.087	0.106	0.100	0.070	0.041	0.038	0.027
β_2	0.478	0.567	0.488	0.488	0.522	0.521	0.554	0.275
SE	0.272	0.204	0.241	0.241	0.223	0.198	0.210	0.253
R^2	0.062	0.105	0.119	0.122	0.109	0.087	0.120	0.054
N	336	611	691	697	675	513	343	222
Maturity i=2; t = 29–63								
α	0.092	0.078	0.074	0.074	0.074	0.075	0.095	0.122
SE	0.030	0.024	0.024	0.024	0.024	0.029	0.035	0.026
β_1	−0.062	−0.010	0.001	−0.008	−0.026	−0.061	−0.100	−0.174
SE	0.142	0.122	0.106	0.097	0.080	0.050	0.045	0.052
β_2	0.423	0.451	0.473	0.473	0.492	0.529	0.451	0.416
SE	0.197	0.206	0.203	0.203	0.196	0.192	0.236	0.198
R^2	0.086	0.131	0.150	0.150	0.150	0.171	0.172	0.270
N	564	792	851	852	836	685	407	209
Maturity i=3; t = 57–98								
α	0.091	0.080	0.079	0.079	0.078	0.079	0.088	0.128
SE	0.030	0.029	0.028	0.028	0.028	0.032	0.036	0.037
β_1	−0.006	−0.040	−0.020	−0.037	−0.042	−0.066	−0.108	−0.147
SE	0.128	0.134	0.123	0.107	0.081	0.060	0.043	0.069
β_2	0.372	0.474	0.478	0.478	0.489	0.507	0.504	0.313
SE	0.208	0.224	0.230	0.230	0.217	0.216	0.228	0.259
R^2	0.110	0.184	0.188	0.187	0.193	0.218	0.260	0.191
N	507	731	803	810	789	593	324	152
Maturity i=4; t = 85–127								
α	0.099	0.080	0.079	0.082	0.076	0.081	0.072	0.118
SE	0.033	0.025	0.024	0.024	0.023	0.025	0.029	0.034
β_1	−0.146	−0.147	−0.143	−0.152	−0.163	−0.148	−0.096	−0.096
SE	0.138	0.146	0.135	0.117	0.088	0.043	0.024	0.035
β_2	0.468	0.589	0.587	0.587	0.639	0.584	0.608	0.294
SE	0.231	0.236	0.234	0.234	0.204	0.193	0.204	0.222
R^2	0.122	0.229	0.244	0.253	0.307	0.320	0.327	0.033
N	393	627	724	734	607	336	156	36

The table reports regression results from equation (9) (shown above) for OEX call options between March 15, 1983 and March 28, 1987 for each of the 32 subsamples defined by maturity and intrinsic value. The coefficients are fitted by OLS but the standard errors (labelled SE) are corrected for intercorrelation as described in the text. N is the number of observations in the subsample. $IV_t(i,j)$ is the implied volatility computed from the date t price of the call option from maturity group i (expiring at $t + \tau$), and intrinsic value group j. $VOL60_t(i,j)$ is the implied volatility computed from the OEX index values on dates $t - 60$ to $t - 1$. Each $VOL60_t(i,j)$ subsample is set up to match the corresponding $IV_t(i,j)$ subsample in Table 3. That is, for each IV in subsample (i,j) of Table 3, subsample (i,j) of Table 4 contains the historical volatility estimated from the previous 60 days' prices. $\sigma_t(\tau)$ is the realized volatility of the OEX index from date t to $t + \tau$. $u_{t,i,j}$ is the regression residual. The hypothesis that $IV_t(i,j)$ is an informationally efficient forecast of $\sigma_t(\tau)$ and that it fully impounds the information contained in $VOL60_t(i,j)$ requires $\alpha = 0.0$, $\beta_1 = 1.0$, and $\beta_2 = 0.0$. In fact, the estimate for β_1 is negative in 28 out of 32 subsamples. β_2 is significantly less than 1.0 nearly everywhere, but significantly positive in most subsamples.

more aggregated samples of our data. Using the entire data sample in one grand regression (i = 1,...,4 and j = 1,...,8) yields

$$\hat{\sigma}_t(\tau) = \underset{(0.012)}{0.136} + \underset{(0.050)}{0.022} \cdot IV_t(i,j),$$

$$N = 17{,}606,\ R^2 = 0.002$$

and Table 6 shows the results of aggregating across maturity and intrinsic value separately. In all cases, the results only confirm what was shown in the disaggregated subsamples: implied volatility is not a rational forecast of future volatility.

One final issue that we can evaluate is whether the errors in variables problem caused by nonsynchronous prices can account for the results we have seen. We obtained transactions data for the time period spanned by our sample, for options with maturities in the second month (i = 2), and have replicated the regressions reported in Table 3. Because of small differences in the dates represented in the two data sets, we formed matching samples in the following way. On each date for which there were both transactions prices and a closing price observation that was included in the Table 3 regression, we took the last recorded option transaction of the day prior to the NYSE close and matched it with the simultaneously observed level of the OEX index. Table 7 compares the results from estimating (5) on these transactions data with those obtained from closing prices, as in Table 3. We find only small differences in the estimated coefficients: the αs are almost identical and the βs tend to be lower in the regressions with transactions prices. Although the standard errors are somewhat smaller with transactions data, none of the estimated βs is significantly positive and 3 of the 8 point estimates are negative. It is evident from this table that the use of slightly nonsynchronous closing price data does not explain the negative results we obtained before.

Conclusion

It is widely accepted that an option's implied volatility is a good estimate of the "market's" expectation of the asset's future volatility, but our results from a large sample of prices for the most actively traded option contract strongly refute that view. How should one interpret what we have found?

One possibility is to point to problems in the testing procedure. However, our strong belief is that despite the potential technical criticisms, our procedures were reasonable and the results were so clear that further perfecting of the methodology would not change the basic conclusions. At the very least, we observe that if there is actually a strong correlation between IV and realised volatility but it cannot be detected with this methodology, one cannot expect the normal procedure of simply computing IVs from recorded closing option prices to give useful volatility estimates.

We also tend to reject the conclusion that options traders are irrational. Although we cannot rule out irrationality entirely without independent data on market expectations, given the enormous amount of evidence that financial markets are largely efficient, it would be surprising if options traders were clearly inferior to other investors in this regard.

The interpretation we favour is based on the fact that along with investors' volatility forecasts an option's market price also impounds the net effect of the many factors that influence option supply and demand but are not in the option model. These include liquidity considerations, interaction between the OEX option and the (occasionally mispriced) S&P 500 index futures contract, investor tastes for particular payoff patterns, and so on. Option pricing theories ignore such factors because in a frictionless market, unlimited arbitrage drives the price to the model value regardless of what trading strategies other market participants follow. In the real world, however, the arbitrage between an OEX option and the underlying index is a difficult and very costly strategy that requires continuously buying and selling 100 stocks to maintain a delta neutral hedge.[14] In practice, there is little arbitrage trading of OEX options against the underlying stocks; most hedging by professionals is said to be done using S&P 500 futures. Thus, many factors can affect the price of an OEX option without inducing arbitrage to offset them, and the implied volatility will impound the net price effect of all of them.[15]

Several conclusions and conjectures result from this interpretation. One is that how accurate implied volatility is as a forecast of future volatility should be related to how easy the arbitrage trade is. Options on futures contracts are at one extreme, since they are traded on the same trading floors as the underlying futures and transactions costs are very low.[16] At the other extreme would probably lie options on broad stock indexes like OEX and the S&P 500. In between are options on individual stocks, for which the arbitrage is possible but somewhat costly.

Another conclusion from our results is that since both IV and historical volatility fail the rationality test, neither is an appropriate volatility forecast for OEX options. To compute the true expected value of future volatility from the information contained in stock and options prices, one must treat implied volatility as an element of the information set from which the conditional expectation will be derived, and not as the conditional expectation itself. As inputs to the calculation, it is perfectly reasonable to combine both implied and historical volatilities, without regard for whether either individually passes the rationality test. Moreover, since this is the way a rational economist should use OEX index options prices in forecasting future volatility, we should expect a rational investor to do the same thing.

Table 6. Realised volatility regressed on implied volatility for samples aggregated across maturities and intrinsic values: Equation (5) $\sigma_t(\tau) = \alpha + \beta \cdot IV_t(i,j) + u_{t,i,j}$

Results by intrinsic value group for all maturities (for i = 1,...,4)

	Intrinsic value							
	−20 to −15.01 j = 1	−15 to −10.01 j = 2	−10 to −5.01 j = 3	−5 to −0.01 j = 4	0 to 5 j = 5	5.01 to 10 j = 6	10.01 to 15 j = 7	15.01 to 20 j = 8
α	0.142	0.123	0.113	0.116	0.125	0.145	0.156	0.157
SE	0.017	0.019	0.017	0.015	0.014	0.014	0.013	0.011
β	0.020	0.106	0.165	0.148	0.085	−0.030	−0.072	−0.051
SE	0.075	0.094	0.093	0.083	0.073	0.056	0.038	0.026
R^2	0.012	0.042	0.038	0.025	0.006	0.001	0.086	0.065
N	1,800	2,761	3,069	3,093	2,907	2,127	1,230	619

Results by maturity group for all intrinsic values (for j = 1,...,8)

	Maturity group			
	Near month 7–35 days i = 1	2nd month 29–63 days i = 2	3rd month 57–98 days i = 3	4th month 85–127 days i = 4
α	0.132	0.134	0.132	0.136
SE	0.009	0.015	0.017	0.017
β	0.025	0.037	0.056	0.032
SE	0.030	0.071	0.096	0.101
R^2	0.003	0.004	0.009	0.003
N	4,088	5,196	4,709	3,613

The table reports regression results from equation (5) (shown above) for OEX call options between March 15, 1983 and March 28, 1987. In the top panel each of the 8 subsamples aggregates across all maturities within the specified intrinsic value group, while the bottom panel aggregates across all intrinsic values within a specified maturity group. The coefficients are fitted by OLS but the standard errors (labelled SE) are corrected for intercorrelation as described in the text. See the notes to Table 3 for further discussion of the variables.

Table 7. Realised volatility regressed on implied volatility-comparison between closing prices and transactions prices: Equation (5) $\sigma_t(\tau) = \alpha + \beta \cdot IV_t(i,j) + u_{t,i,j}$

	Intrinsic value							
	−20 to −15.01 j = 1	−15 to −10.01 j = 2	−10 to −5.01 j = 3	−5 to −0.01 j = 4	0 to 5 j = 5	5.01 to 10 j = 6	10.01 to 15 j = 7	15.01 to 20 j = 8
Maturity i=2: closing prices								
α	0.125	0.109	0.107	0.111	0.121	0.141	0.161	0.175
SE	0.028	0.019	0.016	0.016	0.016	0.017	0.014	0.014
β	0.108	0.193	0.190	0.170	0.114	−0.007	−0.092	−0.133
SE	0.150	0.107	0.098	0.090	0.085	0.078	0.055	0.052
R^2	0.009	0.056	0.070	0.061	0.030	0.001	0.048	0.122
N	520	733	780	778	756	607	329	161
Maturity i=2: transactions prices								
α	0.129	0.119	0.121	0.126	0.133	0.142	0.163	0.172
SE	0.016	0.014	0.013	0.012	0.011	0.011	0.012	0.012
β	0.079	0.127	0.111	0.078	0.036	−0.008	−0.110	−0.116
SE	0.085	0.079	0.076	0.068	0.058	0.052	0.038	0.035
R^2	0.009	0.038	0.038	0.026	0.008	0.001	0.093	0.149
N	520	733	780	778	756	607	329	161

See the notes to Table 3. This table compares the results from estimating equation (5) on recorded closing prices for the option and the index, as in Table 3, with synchronous prices drawn from transactions data. For dates during the sample period for which both transactions data and closing prices are available, we take the last trade price for the option prior to the close of the NYSE and match it with the simultaneously observed level of the OEX index.

To measure the "market's" volatility estimate, therefore, we must not just take the implied volatility. We should attempt to compute the true conditional expectation of the future volatility from the market's information set.

Appendix

This appendix reports Monte Carlo simulation results that allow us to evaluate the performance of the estimation procedure from two perspectives. We would like to know first how close the corrected standard errors are likely to be to the true values, and second, how much additional statistical power is gained by using all of the available daily data in the estimation, rather than restricting the analysis to non-overlapping observations.

We generated random series of returns, designed to look as much like the actual data in our sample of OEX returns as possible. First the sample mean and volatility of the OEX index, μ_k and σ_k, were computed for each calendar month k in our data. Then a random series of returns R_t was created for that month using equation (A1)

$$R_t = \mu_k + \sigma_k z_t, \tag{A1}$$

where z_t represents a random draw from a standard normal distribution, and μ_k and σ_k are the mean and volatility of returns, here expressed in terms of their values per trading day. This process was repeated month by month until a return for each day in the sample had been generated. Then for each day, the "realised" volatility of the simulated series was computed from that point to the expiration date for the option maturity being considered, exactly as we did with the actual OEX returns.

The results we obtained in the analysis of actual prices suggested virtually no connection between IV and subsequent realised volatility. To create a simulated IV series with the same distributional characteristics as the actual IVs but having no correlation with the simulated volatilities, we simply chose randomly from the set of observed IVs for intrinsic value group 4 (at- to slightly out-of-the-money). To maintain the same pattern of serial correlation among the IVs as is present in the actual data, the selection was done in batches, as follows. For the first observation pertaining to a given expiration date, we randomly chose an IV for an option with the same number of days to maturity from the data sample. IVs were then taken in order from the sample of actual IVs until a new expiration date was called for, at which point another random selection was made. In essence, this procedure randomly selects about one month of observations at a time from the series of actual IVs.

The series of realised volatilities computed from the simulated returns was then regressed on the series of randomly selected implied volatilities in two ways, first with the full sample of overlapping observations as we did in the paper, and then again using only non-overlapping observations. OLS standard errors were calculated for both cases and the corrected standard errors were computed for the overlapping sample. The coefficient estimates were also recorded so that their true standard deviations across simulations could be computed. This process was repeated 10,000 times for each maturity group, $i = 1, 2, 3, 4$.

Table A1 summarises the results. For each maturity group, we show the standard errors on the two regression coefficients. The first line gives the true standard deviations of the coefficient estimates across the 10,000 regressions. For example, for the second maturity group, the true standard error of the estimate of β was 0.1174. Next we show the uncorrected OLS results, both the average values for the estimated standard errors and the sample standard deviations of those estimates in the 10,000 regressions. With no adjustment, the OLS estimates are severely biased downwards, and show very little variability across regressions. The next lines show that the corrected standard errors are much closer to the true values on average, eg 0.1031 versus the true value of 0.1174 for β in the second maturity group, although they are still slightly downward biased and also somewhat variable across regressions. These results give us confidence that the standard error correction procedure used in the paper is effective in removing the effect of cross-correlation in the residuals.

The lower portion of Table A1 reveals how much more accurate the coefficients estimated from the overlapping data are compared with those computed using only non-overlapping observations from the same data sample. To run these regressions, we took only non-overlapping data points for 18, 40, 75, and 100 days to expiration for maturity groups 1, 2, 3, and 4, respectively. Although there is little difference in the accuracy with which the regression constant is estimated, there is a large increase in the true standard errors for the slope coefficients, up to a

Table A1. Monte Carlo simulations of estimated coefficient standard errors for different procedures

Maturity	i = 1		i = 2		i = 3		i = 4	
	α	β	α	β	α	β	α	β
Overlapping sample								
True standard deviation	0.0208	0.1285	0.0186	0.1174	0.0176	0.1122	0.0153	0.1023
OLS standard errors								
Mean	0.0062	0.0377	0.0045	0.0284	0.0041	0.0262	0.0039	0.0263
Standard deviation	0.0008	0.0047	0.0006	0.0040	0.0007	0.0040	0.0006	0.0042
Corrected standard errors								
Mean	0.0202	0.1214	0.0173	0.1031	0.0159	0.0927	0.0142	0.0811
Standard deviation	0.0040	0.0237	0.0047	0.0279	0.0053	0.0310	0.0053	0.0308
Non-overlapping sample								
True standard deviation	0.0139	0.4770	0.0178	0.6989	0.0205	0.7934	0.0190	0.7840
OLS standard errors								
Mean	0.0145	0.4729	0.0181	0.6827	0.0207	0.7609	0.0193	0.7446
Standard deviation	0.0020	0.0763	0.0038	0.1463	0.0046	0.1974	0.0055	0.2496

The table presents summary results on the estimated coefficient standard errors from regressions like equation (5): $\sigma_t(\tau) = \alpha + \beta\, IV_t(i,j) + u_{t,i,j}$, for intrinsic value group 4 (at- to 5 points out-of-the-money), run on 10,000 simulated returns series. See the text for details of the sample construction. The "Overlapping sample" makes use of all simulated data points, while the "Non-overlapping sample" restricts the sample to only observations for which the periods to option expiration do not overlap. "True standard deviation" is the sample standard deviation of the estimated parameter across the 10,000 regressions. "OLS standard errors" are uncorrected for correlation in the residuals, while "Corrected standard errors" are corrected using the methodology described in the paper. "Mean" and "Standard deviation" refer to the sample average and standard deviation of the standard error estimates across the 10,000 regressions.

factor of about 8 for maturity group 4. Because there is no cross-correlation in the residuals, the OLS standard error estimates are consistent for this case, as is apparent in the table. Notice, however, that even in this case where the true slope coefficient is zero by construction and we have four years of data, the standard errors that come out of the non-overlapping regressions are so large that if the estimate of the slope coefficient turned out to be 0.0 it would still be impossible to reject the hypothesis that $\beta = 1.0$ for any but the first maturity group, and only a marginal rejection would be possible there!

1 *See Patell and Wolfson (1979, 1981) or Poterba and Summers (1986) for examples of the use of implied volatility as a proxy for the market's risk assessment. Implied volatility has also been used as a proxy for the true instantaneous price volatility of the underlying asset, as in Stein's (1989) study of the "term structure" behaviour of implied volatility.*

2 *Equation (1) is widely used as a* consistent *estimator of volatility, but while the expression in the large parentheses yields an unbiased estimate of the variance, taking the square root to obtain the volatility is a non-linear transformation that introduces a small bias in a finite sample, by Jensen's inequality. It is common practice to treat this bias as negligible.*

3 *Again, we ignore the bias in a forecast of σ obtained as the square root of an unbiased forecast of σ^2.*

4 *Theil (1966) is credited with introducing this test of forecast rationality and analysing it in detail. It has been widely applied to test the rationality of expectations, as in Pesando (1975) (for inflation expectations) or Brown and Maital (1981) (for a broad selection of economic variables).*

5 *LR, in fact, made no adjustment for dividend payout at all. CM corrected this mistake by using Merton's continuous payout European call formula. Beckers, recognising the problem posed by the possibility of early exercise, adopted an ad hoc adjustment to the European formula.*

6 *For example, in LR's study of option prices from October 1973 through June 1974, historical volatility was computed from 4 years of monthly data ending at the beginning of the sample period. This long time period with sparsely distributed monthly data contrasts with the one to six months of daily data that options traders typically use to compute historical volatility, and makes it likely that the estimates were contaminated by stale data. CM also used monthly data, but only from the 24 months immediately preceding the date of the option price. However, in trying to establish the relative forecasting accuracy of historical volatility versus implied volatility, both LR and CM computed "realised" volatility figures for time periods that did not match option maturities. In fact, one of LR's realised volatility series included stock prices observed six months prior to the first option price in their sample.*

7 *Note that the level of the OEX index was over 200 for most of the sample period, so an option with a strike price 20 points away from the current level of the index is not actually very far in- or out-of-the-money in percentage terms.*

8 *In fact, because the dividend stream on the OEX index portfolio is much less lumpy than that of an individual stock, rational early exercise is unlikely, and American option values are quite close to those derived from the dividend-adjusted Black-Scholes European option formula.*

9 *That there seems to be a systematic structure to implied volatilities is quite well known. For example, the observed "overpricing" of deep-out-of-the-money options has given rise to numerous theories and articles over the years. Rubinstein (1985) provides an extensive analysis of implied*

volatilities from individual stocks that reveals several regular patterns. A pattern that is observed in a number of markets, of IVs that are lowest at-the-money and become progressively higher the further the option is in- or out-of-the-money, is known to traders as the "smile."

10 *Using a careful analysis of transactions data, Harvey and Whaley (1992) also find several interesting regularities in the time pattern of implied volatilities drawn from OEX options, including a day of the week effect. Call IVs are low on Fridays and high on Mondays, but puts do not show the same pattern.*

11 *LR, for example computed their WISDs, one per week, and then averaged them over the whole 39 week sample period into a single IV for each stock. By contrast, Beckers found the IV drawn from a single at-the-money option to be at least as accurate a predictor of future volatility as the weighted average IV.*

12 *Technically, expiration is on the Saturday following the third Friday, but since Friday is the last date the options can be traded and their payoffs are based on Friday's closing stock prices, expiration is effectively at the close on the third Friday.*

13 *Note that since neither realised nor historical volatility is a function of option intrinsic value, the differences among the eight regressions reported for each maturity group in Table 4 are due only to the differences in the dates whose observations are included in the subsamples. Nearly identical sample composition leads to nearly identical regressions, as in subsamples (2,3) and (2,4). There is a small amount of regularity in the differences among subsamples, due to the fact that the options exchange tends not to introduce options at strikes far below the current index. This means there will only be deep in-the-money options when the market price has risen substantially after listing. This results in a lower average* t *for intrinsic value groups 7 and 8 (52.9 and 45.8 days, respectively, compared with an average* t *of between 59.8 and 61.8 for intrinsic value groups 1 to 6).*

14 *Figlewski (1989) shows in a simulation analysis that both the transactions costs and the risk borne by an arbitrageur who attempts to follow a model-based arbitrage strategy are very large, leading to wide bands around the model price within which arbitrage will not be done.*

15 *Evidence that arbitrage involving stock index options is difficult to do and that "mispricings" do not seem to be easily arbitraged away is provided by Evnine and Rudd (1985). Using intraday data, they document numerous violations of arbitrage relations, including put-call parity, for both OEX and Major Market Index options.*

16 *Both Feinstein (1989) and Park and Sears (1985) present evidence that implied volatilities from stock index futures options contain a significant amount of information about futures volatility. (However, Feinstein also finds that implied volatility from S&P 500 futures options does not pass the rationality regression test.)*

BIBLIOGRAPHY

Beckers, S., 1981, "Standard Deviations Implied in Option Prices as Predictors of Future Stock Price Variability", *Journal of Banking and Finance* 5, pp. 363-81.

Brown, B.W., and S. Maital, 1981,"What Do Economists Know? An Empirical Study of Experts' Expectations", *Econometrica* 49, pp. 491-504.

Chiras, D.P., and S. Manaster, 1978, "The Information Content of Option Prices and a Test of Market Efficiency", *Journal of Financial Economics* 6, pp. 213-34.

Day, T.E., and C.M. Lewis, 1990, "Stock Market Volatility and the Information Content of Stock Index Options", *Journal of Econometrics* 52, pp. 267-87.

Evnine, J., and A. Rudd, 1985, "Index Options: The Early Evidence", *Journal of Finance* 40, pp. 743-56.

Feinstein, S., 1989, "Bias, Forecast Efficiency, and Information in the Black-Scholes Implied Volatility," Working paper, Yale School of Management.

Figlewski, S., 1989, "Options Arbitrage in Imperfect Markets", *Journal of Finance* 44, pp. 1289-311.

Fair, R. C., and R.J. Shiller, 1990, "Comparing Information in Forecasts from Econometric Models", *American Economic Review* 80, pp. 375-89.

Hansen, L. P., 1982, "Large Sample Properties of Generalized Method of Moments Estimators," *Econometrica* 50, pp. 1029-54.

Harvey, C.R., and R.E. Whaley, 1992, "Market Volatility Estimation and the Pricing of S&P 100 Options", *Journal of Financial Economics* 31, pp. 43-73.

Hull, J., and A. White, 1987, "The Pricing of Options on Assets with Stochastic Volatilities," *Journal of Finance* 42, pp. 281-300.

Latané, H.A., and R.J. Rendleman, 1976, "Standard Deviations of Stock Price Ratios Implied in Option Prices", *Journal of Finance* 31, pp. 369-81.

Lamoureux, C.G., and W.D. Lastrapes, 1993, "Forecasting Stock-Return Variance: Toward an Understanding of Stochastic Implied Volatilities", *Review of Financial Studies*, 6, pp. 293-326; reprinted as Chapter 14 of the present volume.

Newey, W.K., and K.D. West, 1987, "A Simple, Positive Semi-Definite, Heteroskedasticity and Autocorrelation Consistent Covariance Matrix", *Econometrica* 55, pp. 703-8.

Park, H.Y., and R.S. Sears, 1985, "Estimating Stock Index Futures Volatility through the Prices of their Options," *Journal of Futures Markets* 5, pp. 223-37.

Patell, J.M., and M.A. Wolfson, 1979, "Anticipated Information Releases Reflected in Call Option Prices", *Journal of Accounting and Economics*, pp. 117–40.

Patell, J.M., and M.A. Wolfson, 1981, "The Ex Ante and Ex Post Price Effects of Quarterly Earnings Announcements Reflected in Option and Stock Prices", *Journal of Accounting Research* 2, pp. 434–58.

Pesando, J.E., 1975, "A Note on the Rationality of the Livingston Price Expectations", *Journal of Political Economy* 83, pp. 849–58.

Poterba, J.M., and L. Summers, 1986, "The Persistence of Volatility and Stock Market Fluctuations", *American Economic Review*, pp. 1142–51.

Rubinstein, M., 1985, "Nonparametric Tests of Alternative Option Pricing Models Using All Reported Trades and Quotes on the 30 Most Active CBOE Option Classes from August 23, 1976 through August 3, 1978", *Journal of Finance* 40, pp. 455–80.

Stein, J., 1989, "Overreactions in the Options Market," *Journal of Finance* 44, pp. 1011–23.

Theil, H., 1966, *Applied Economic Forecasting*, North-Holland, Amsterdam.

White, H., 1980, "A Heteroskedasticity-Consistent Covariance Matrix Estimator and a Direct Test for Heteroskedasticity", *Econometrica* 48, pp. 817–38.

Wiggins, J., 1987, "Option Values Under Stochastic Volatility: Theory and Empirical Estimates", *Journal of Financial Economics* 19, pp. 351–72.

14

Forecasting Stock-Return Variance:

Toward an Understanding of Stochastic Implied Volatilities*

Christopher G. Lamoureux and William D. Lastrapes
University of Arizona; University of Georgia

We examine the behaviour of measured variances from the options market and the underlying stock market. Under the joint hypotheses that markets are informationally efficient and that option prices are explained by a particular asset pricing model, forecasts from time-series models of the stock-return process should not have predictive content given the market forecast as embodied in option prices. Both in-sample and out-of-sample tests suggest that this hypothesis can be rejected. Using simulations, we show that biases inherent in the procedure we use to imply variances cannot explain this result. Thus, we provide evidence inconsistent with the orthogonality restrictions of option pricing models that assume that variance risk is unpriced. These results also have implications for optimal variance forecast results.

According to the Black and Scholes (1973) model of option valuation, equilibrium option prices are determined by the absence of arbitrage profits. This condition depends on the assumption that the variance of the underlying stock returns is constant over time or deterministically changing through time. The model is a powerful economic tool because market behaviour can be understood without explicitly specifying and estimating preferences of agents.

A problem with the empirical implementation of the Black-Scholes model is that the variance assumption is inconsistent with the data. Since stochastic volatility is manifest in time-series models of stock returns as well as in the empirical variances implied from the Black-Scholes model itself, models of option pricing have been developed in which the variance of the underlying asset returns varies randomly through time. Hull and White (1987) derive a closed-form solution for European call option prices under the assumption that volatility risk is unpriced. They show that, given certain conditions on the stochastic process governing underlying returns, the option price equals the expected value of the Black-Scholes price over the distribution of average variance.

While the stochastic volatility generalisation has been shown by Hull and White (1987) and others to improve the explanatory power of the Black-Scholes model, the full implications of the stochastic volatility option pricing models have not been adequately tested. In particular, a clear test of whether the strong assumption of market indifference to volatility risk is consistent with the data is missing in the empirical finance litera-

* *This paper was first published in* The Review of Financial Studies, *Vol. 6 No. 2 (1993). It is reprinted with minor amendments with the permission of Oxford University Press. We are grateful to Don Andrews, Kerry Black, Phil Dybvig, Ravi Jagannathan, Andrew Lo, Chester Spatt and an anonymous referee for numerous suggestions. But we wish to absorb all culpability.*

ture. Although this assumption may be unattractive from a theoretical perspective, it does afford simplification to both valuation and variance extraction, and the model lends itself to unambiguous empirical testing. We examine this issue by testing an important implication of the *class* of models represented by Hull and White (1987) in which volatility risk is unpriced. If option markets are informationally efficient, then information available at the time market prices are set cannot be used to predict actual return variance better than the variance forecast embedded in the option price, which represents the subjective expectation of the market. That is, the forecast error of the subjective expectation should be orthogonal to all available information.

To test this orthogonality restriction, we interpret the variance implied from equating the observed market option price to the Hull and White model price as the market's assessment of return variance. However, implying a variance from the closed-form expression of Hull and White may distort, or bias, the market forecast, even assuming that the joint null hypothesis is true since the Black-Scholes formula is nonlinear (Jensen's inequality) and the variance and stock processes may be instantaneously correlated. We carefully calibrate simulations of the stock-price and variance processes for each of the stocks in the sample to examine the extent to which such bias exists. The simulations demonstrate that this distortion is trivial for our sample of at-the-money options. Furthermore, we couch our statistical influence in the context of the simulations to account for the possible sources of distortion. This procedure enables us to refer to our empirical exercise as a formal test of an asset pricing model. If we did not control for the distribution or couch our inference in terms of this distortion, our exercise would simply be an examination of the extent to which filtering the options and stock-price data with the Black-Scholes model has information.

We test the orthogonality restriction for at-the-money call options on individual stocks by comparing the forecast performance of the implied variance from the model with time-series representations of stock-return volatility. We use a simple time-series model of serial dependence in volatility, the generalised autoregressive conditional heteroskedasticity (Garch) process of Engle (1982) and Bollerslev (1986), to capture available information that can explain the evolution of return variance. Two types of tests of the orthogonality restriction are performed: in-sample and out-of-sample. The in-sample, regression-based tests incorporate the implied variance into the Garch equation of the return process to measure the marginal predictive power of past information on variance. We then compare out-of-sample forecast performance of the implied variance with time-series models using standard measures of average forecast error and encompassing regressions. The out-of-sample encompassing analysis helps us to explore an important issue; regardless of the outcome of tests of the orthogonality restrictions, does filtering market data through the model provide information about the future evolution of return variance that is not evident in the past time series of stock returns? This issue is relevant to constructing optimal variance forecast rules.

Our research design differs from most previous tests of stochastic volatility option pricing models. Melino and Turnbull (1990), for example, test such a model for foreign exchange options. They estimate a stochastic volatility process for the underlying asset, then price options on this asset using the parameters from the process and the option pricing model. This price is found to predict the actual option price better than a constant variance price. However, they also add that current information can explain some of the model's forecast error. By testing the implications of the option pricing model in measures of variance rather than option price, we exploit different information than Melino and Turnbull to test the orthogonality restrictions. More importantly, our forecast comparisons are performed ultimately out-of-sample. Out-of-sample analysis is more natural than in-sample analysis for scrutinising models that depend on the information set of agents at any point in time, since the econometrician's conditioning set is a proper subset of the information available to the agents in the economy.

Our work in this paper complements concurrent, independent research by Day and Lewis (1992), which also compares implied volatilities from option pricing models with Garch models. Essentially four major differences occur in the papers.

❑ We broaden the data sample by using daily data in individual stocks, whereas Day and Lewis use weekly data on stock indexes.

❑ As noted, we provide simulation evidence to quantify the extent to which implying variances under Black-Scholes distorts the actual variance forecast *under the null hypothesis* for each stock in our sample. Thus, unlike Day and Lewis we interpret our analysis as a formal test of a specific asset pricing model.

❑ Given the daily frequency of data, we are better able than Day and Lewis to adjust for the inconsistencies between the forecast horizons of the time-series models and the maturity of the options in the sample.

❑ Perhaps most importantly, we take considerable care to purge problems related to measurement error by effectively using intraday data to construct the daily series. Day and Lewis, for example, use closing prices in both option and stock markets, which do not even close at the same time. To attenuate this problem, they imply the price of the underlying asset from the option price, under the assumption that the model which they are testing is true. Because our data are carefully mapped into our research design, we reduce those errors-in-variables problems substantially.

Although our empirical strategy is discussed in the context of the model developed by Hull and White (1987), we wish to emphasise that we do not attempt to test all of the implications of their model. These authors were interested in explaining the biases of the Black-Scholes restrictions when volatility is stochastic as a function of moneyness and maturity of the option. This aim requires exploiting a broader range of options than we use to infer moments beyond the mean of the subjective distribution of variance. Our strategy is to focus solely on the orthogonality restrictions implied by this *class* of models, hence our reliance on the market's expectation of return variance. In other words, we are not treating the null hypothesis that Black-Scholes is true against the stochastic variance alternative. We are treating the stochastic volatility option pricing model as a special case of more general models of asset pricing that include the possibility of pricing volatility risk.

Both the in-sample tests and the out-of-sample encompassing tests suggest that, while the implied variance helps predict future volatility, the orthogonality restriction of the joint null hypothesis is rejected. One possible reason for the rejection of the null is that volatility risk is priced. Therefore, further attempts to learn from the data should explicitly model a risk premium on the variance process, as in Heston (1993), for example. Assuming constant relative-risk aversion and using a Fourier inversion formula (Stein and Stein (1991)), Heston has obtained a closed-form expression for an option on an asset with stochastic volatility that allows for the volatility process to be priced.

In the following section, we lay out the analytical framework of the study. We describe the Hull and White (1987) model, state explicitly the orthogonality restrictions that it implies jointly with the assumption of market efficiency, and outline the general test strategy. We also characterise stochastic volatility in the data by using the Garch model, and we report simulation results to quantify certain biases in our implied variances. We then describe the options data used in this study, the specific in-sample and out-of-sample tests of the orthogonality restriction undertaken, and the results from these tests. Our conclusions are presented in the next section.

Analytical framework

THEORETICAL MODEL AND TEST STRATEGY

The framework for the empirical analysis in this article is the model developed by Hull and White (1987), which is an application of Garman (1976). The model represents the class of stochastic volatility options pricing models, including those of Scott (1987), Wiggins (1987), and Johnson and Shanno (1987), that assumes volatility risk does not affect the option price. The Hull-White (HW) model is based upon the following continuous-time process for the underlying stock:

$$dS = \phi S dt + \sqrt{V} S dw, \qquad (1)$$

$$dV = \mu V dt + \xi V dz, \qquad (2)$$

where S is the stock price, and the Brownian motions dw and dz have an instantaneous correlation of ρ. Under the assumption that volatility risk is not priced and $\rho = 0$, a call option on this stock at time t will be priced as

$$p_t = \int BS(\bar{V}_t) h(\bar{V}_t | I_t) d\bar{V}_t = E\left[BS(\bar{V}_t | I_t)\right], \qquad (3)$$

where

$$\bar{V}_t = \frac{1}{T-t}\int_t^T V_t di,$$

$h(\bar{V}_t \mid I_t)$ is the density of $\bar{V}_t$ conditional on the current I_t, T is the expiration date of the option, I_t is the information set at time t, and $BS(\cdot)$ is the Black-Scholes pricing formula. Thus, the HW price is the mean Black-Scholes price, evaluated over the conditional distribution of average variance $\bar{V}_t$.

To price options according to (3), market participants must form a subjective conditional density on $\bar{V}_t$. If these participants are rational, then the subjective density of the market equals the actual density, $h(\bar{V}_t \mid I_t)$. The focus of our study is on the mean of this distribution:

$$E(\bar{V}_t|I_t) = \int \bar{V}_t h(\bar{V}_t|I_t) d\bar{V}_t.$$

The average variance can be decomposed as

$$\bar{V}_t = E(\bar{V}_t|I_t) + \mu_t,$$

where μ_t, is orthogonal to the conditional expectation and, therefore, to any information available to agents up to time t. Thus, if option market participants are rational (in the mean sense), then the subjective mean, $E^s(\bar{V}_t \mid I_t)$, equals the actual mean, $E(\bar{V}_t \mid I_t)$, and the subjective forecast error, $\mu^s_t = \bar{V}_t - E^s(\bar{V}_t \mid I_t)$, is orthogonal to all available information. This orthogonality condition is tested in this article.

The market's conditional expectation of variance is not directly observable. But given market prices on options, the HW model implies a variance that can be used to estimate the expectation. Because the variance of the underlying asset is the only unknown argument in the Black-Scholes formula, the implied variance (discussed in more detail later) is the value of that argument that equates the market price to the theoretical Black-Scholes price. It is evident from (3) that the implied variance is not in general a good prediction of the market's evaluation of variance, since the conditional density h is unaccounted for. However, Cox and Rubinstein (1985, p. 218) show that the Black-Scholes formula is essentially a linear function of the standard deviation for at-the-money options, so that $E[BS(\bar{V}_t) \mid I_t]$ approximately equals $BS[E(\bar{V}_t) \mid I_t]$.[1] For this reason, we use a sample of at-the-money options and therefore interpret the implied variance as the market's assessment of average stock-return variance over the remaining life of the option, $E^s(\bar{V}_t \mid I_t)$, under the assumption that the HW market is valid.

We test whether the forecast error constructed from $\bar{V}_t$ and the implied variance is orthogonal to past information, using in-sample and out-of-sample tests. This orthogonality condition is based on a joint hypothesis:

- option markets are informationally efficient, so observed option prices contain all relevant, available information; and
- the HW pricing model is correct, so the implied variances are valid estimates of the subjective variance of the market.

The test design is analogous to tests in the international finance literature that examine the hypothesis that forward exchange rates are optimal predictors of future spot exchange rates (eg Hansen and Hodrick (1980)). If the foreign exchange market is informationally efficient, then the difference between the realised future spot rate and the market's subjective expectation of that rate is orthogonal to obtainable information. As with our approach, an economic model must be used to link the market's expectation to observable variables (ie market prices). Given this link, the forecast error can be measured and regressed on past information available to traders. The primary difference between the exchange rate tests and our own is that we exploit option price data to focus on the variance, not the mean, of the underlying asset.

CHARACTERISATION OF STOCHASTIC VOLATILITY

Tests of the orthogonality restrictions will lack power unless information available to the market can be used to predict return volatility. We show in this subsection that the returns in our sample are accurately characterised by the Garch process, a parametric model of persistence in conditional variance. As such the model links return volatility to the past behaviour of the return process itself, which is included in I_t. Under the null hypothesis, Garch momentum would be fully used by options traders in forming expectations of variance; thus, the Garch model will have no marginal predictive power over the implied variance.

Consider the following Garch(1,1) model for stock returns:

$$r_t = \bar{r} + \varepsilon_t, \tag{4}$$

$$\varepsilon_t | \varepsilon_{t-1}, \varepsilon_{t-2}, \ldots \sim N(0, h_t), \tag{5}$$

$$h_t = C + \alpha\varepsilon^2_{t-1} + \beta h_{t-1} + \gamma\zeta_{t-1}, \tag{6}$$

where r_t is the return over day t, $\bar{r}$, C, α, β and γ are parameters, and ζ_{t-1} is a vector of exogenous variables. In this section, we constrain γ to be zero, so (6) is the conventional Garch specification. It is easily verified that if $\alpha + \beta = 1$ there is no mean reversion in the variance. In this case, the conditional variance is integrated, and unconditional variance is undefined. Persistence of shocks to variance increases rapidly as this sum approaches unity from below. The return process is stationary if $\alpha + \beta < 1$.

The Garch model is a discrete-time approximation to the diffusion process in (1) and (2) and is therefore consistent with the HW model. We can think of the actual stock price and its variance as being generated in continuous time by (1) and (2), but with the data observed discretely (daily). It is evident that (4) is the discrete-time analogue to (1), where $\bar{r}$ approximates the drift ϕ. To see how (6) maps into (2) (assuming $\gamma = 0$), subtract h_{t-1} from both sides of (6) to obtain

$$h_t - h_{t-1} = \left[C / h_{t-1} - (1 - \alpha - \beta)\right]h_{t-1} + \alpha h_{t-1}\left(\theta_{t-1}^2 - 1\right), \qquad (7)$$

where we have used the identity $\varepsilon_t^2 = h_t\theta_t^2$, and θ is an i.i.d. standardised normal random variable. Nelson (1990) has shown that as the time interval goes to zero this expression approaches the diffusion in (2), where $C/h_{t-1} - (1 - \alpha - \beta)$ approaches $\mu\ dt$ and α approaches $\xi\sqrt{dt/2}$. This approximation is not unique, but it is consistent with our use of the Garch model in the subsequent analysis.

It is not intuitive that the continuous-time limit of the Garch process has two sources of randomness (dw and dz in (2)), whereas the discrete-time process appears to have a single source of randomness (ε is the only stochastic term in (4) to (6)). The intuition for this is as follows. By definition, the conditional variance of *next period*'s residual is not stochastic in the Garch framework. However, the (conditional) forecast of the variance over the next two periods depends on the realisation of ε_{t+1} and hence is random. Now, as the interval between time periods shrinks to its limit, the ability to distinguish between time $t + 1$ and time t is lost, which yields the second source of randomness in the limiting case.

The Garch model is estimated for a sample of daily returns for 10 individual stocks over the period April 19, 1982, to March 30, 1984 (496 trading days), except for company 10, the sample for which begins June 30, 1982. The sample is chosen to conform to our tests of the orthogonality restrictions, as discussed in the following section. The return data come from the CRSP tapes; daily returns are thus calculated as the rate of change of the last transaction price of the day.

Estimates from the Garch model are reported in Table 1, for each of the 10 companies, as model 2. Ticker symbols are provided in Table 1, and we use these in reference to particular companies. Maximum likelihood estimation of the Garch model is carried out by using a variant of

Table 1. Specifications of conditional variance

Model	$\mathcal{L}$	P (t-stat)	C (t-stat)	α (t-stat)	β (t-stat)	γ (t-stat)
A. Computer Sciences Corp (CSC) (20536310)						
1	−2281.8	0.648	590.52			
		(0.56)	(18.98)			
2	−2270.3	0.385	238.15	0.110	0.484	
		(0.33)	(1.99)	(2.04)	(2.10)	
3	−2275.0	0.000	262.62			0.576
		(0.00)	(3.53)			(3.79)
4	−2264.9	−0.034	58.85	0.058	0.612	0.237
		(−0.03)	(1.02)	(1.76)	(2.82)	(1.60)
B. Digital Equipment Corp (DEC) (25384910)						
1	−2292.0	0.484	614.71			
		(0.42)	(38.71)			
2	−2280.2	0.011	413.79	0.094	0.228	
		(0.01)	(2.44)	(1.77)	(0.74)	
3	−2292.1	0.489	613.55			0.000
		(0.42)	(9.80)			(0.00)
4	2280.2	0.008	404.80	0.095	0.230	0.157
		(0.01)	(2.45)	(1.76)	(0.70)	(0.85)
C. Datapoint (DPT) (23810020)						
1	−2511.9	0.910	492.31			
		(0.52)	(9.68)			
2	−2482.0	1.338	11.56	0.020	0.969	
		(0.88)	(2.06)	(5.00)	(138.43)	
3	−2485.6	0.583	0.00			1.629
		(0.59)	(0.00)			(9.70)
4	−2475.2	0.562	31.37	0.081	0.373	0.843
		(0.34)	(0.39)	(2.89)	(1.34)	(1.86)
D. Federal Express (FDX) (31330910)						
1	−2259.2	0.678	538.12			
		(0.65)	(20.00)			
2	−2245.3	0.474	40.18	0.056	0.869	
		(0.46)	(1.84)	(2.67)	(15.52)	
3	−2251.9	0.301	0.0			1.348
		(0.29)	(0.00)			(3.62)
4	−2243.7	0.298	0.00	0.057	0.791	0.204
		(0.28)	(0.00)	(2.36)	(8.15)	(1.46)
E. National Semiconductor (NSM) (63764010)						
1	−2464.3	1.855	1230.98			
		(1.14)	(18.40)			
2	−2450.7	1.972	55.20	0.052	0.904	
		(1.26)	(1.73)	(2.60)	(24.43)	
3	−2451.8	1.489	0.00			1.768
		(0.95)	(0.00)			(3.94)
4	−2445.8	1.274	0.00	0.050	0.678	0.480
		(0.83)	(0.00)	(1.32)	(2.63)	(1.01)
F. Paradyne (PDN) (69911310)						
1	−2492.8	−0.359	1443.24			
		(−0.21)	(29.08)			
2	−2476.5	1.599	188.51	0.089	0.783	
		(0.97)	(3.08)	(3.56)	(12.63)	
3	−2482.3	0.616	321.59			1.402
		(0.35)	(2.60)			(7.01)
4	−2477.4	0.623	230.78	0.000	0.194	1.166
		(0.34)	(1.96)	(0.00)	(0.85)	(3.28)
G. Rockwell (ROK) (77434710)						
1	−2181.0	1.558	392.10			
		(1.73)	(20.84)			
2	−2171.7	1.590	31.86	0.048	0.871	
		(1.73)	(1.33)	(2.00)	(11.02)	
3	−2175.5	1.558	161.21			1.011
		(1.77)	(2.71)			(3.74)
4	−2167.9	1.427	25.98	0.043	0.742	0.253
		(1.59)	(0.94)	(0.12)	(3.80)	(1.28)

continued overleaf

Table 1 (continued)

Model	$\mathfrak{L}$	P (t-stat)	C (t-stat)	α (t-stat)	β (t-stat)	γ (t-stat)
H. Storage Technologies (STK) (86211110)						
1	–2443.6	–1.328	1134.58			
		(–0.85)	(23.09)			
2	–2423.7	–1.548	96.26	0.079	0.836	
		(–1.09)	(3.06)	(3.76)	(19.90)	
3	–2428.2	–2.015	0.000			1.505
		(–1.34)	(0.00)			(5.57)
4	–2421.1	–1.762	0.00	0.093	0.573	0.261
		(–1.19)	(0.00)	(2.16)	(3.54)	(2.01)
I. Tandy Corp (TAN) (87538210)						
1	–2337.2	0.362	738.35			
		(0.30)	(19.11)			
2	–2311.3	–0.548	49.97	0.112	0.819	
		(–0.49)	(2.38)	(3.50)	(16.06)	
3	–2325.4	–0.248	0.00			1.350
		(–0.21)	(0.00)			(4.35)
4	–2307.9	–0.66	0.00	0.128	0.656	0.387
		(–0.59)	(0.00)	(2.72)	(4.72)	(1.39)
J. Toys R Us (TOY) (89233510)						
1	–1980.2	2.082	680.39			
		(1.63)	(20.64)			
2	–1962.2	2.086	8.14	0.040	0.946	
		(1.80)	(1.48)	(3.64)	(59.12)	
3	–1968.6	1.674	0.00			1.311
		(1.35)	(0.00)			(5.06)
4	–1961.9	–1.615	0.00	0.102	0.381	0.682
		(1.28)	(0.00)	(1.57)	(1.22)	(1.80)

Model: $r_t = \bar{r} + \varepsilon_t$
1. $\varepsilon_t \sim N(0,C)$
2. $\varepsilon_t \sim N(0,h_t)$
$h_t = C + \alpha\varepsilon^2_{t-1} + \beta h_{t-1}$
3. $\varepsilon_t \sim N(0,h_t)$
$h_t = C + \gamma\zeta_{t-1}$
4. $\varepsilon_t \sim N(0,h_t)$
$h_t = C + \alpha\varepsilon^2_{t-1} + \beta h_{t-1} + \gamma\zeta_{t-1}$
ζ_t represents the daily implied variance from minimising the sum-of-squared errors from all option midpoint quotes on day t, for the nearest to-the-money option, intermediate term to expiration. All returns are daily percentage times 1,000. t stat. represents the asymptotic Student's t statistic. This may be biased as a result of the departure from normality of $\varepsilon_t h_t^{-.5}$. $\mathfrak{L}$ represents the value of the log-likelihood function at its optimum for each model. All models are estimated using daily data from April 19, 1982 through March 30, 1984; except TOY, which starts June 30, 1982 (423 days).

the Berndt, Hall, Hall, and Hausman optimisation algorithm that constrains parameter estimates in the variance equations to be nonnegative (Biegler and Cuthrell (1985)). First derivatives are calculated numerically.[2]

The evidence in Table 1 shows that the Garch model provides a good fit for the 10 stocks in the sample. In all cases but one, the Garch parameters are statistically different from zero at small significance level, according to the asymptotic t-statistics. For DEC (Panel B), α is significant at a 10% level. For most of the stocks the sum α + β exceeds 0.9.

CHARACTERISATION OF BIAS

The interpretation of our tests relies on equating the variance implied from the data and the Black-Scholes model with the market's subjective variance of returns over the remaining life of the option. However, there are potentially important ways in which the implied variance can be expected to differ from the subjective variance, even assuming the HW model is valid and markets are efficient. In this subsection, we attempt to quantify this bias in order to determine if it affects our inferences.

The implied variance may deviate from the subjective variance as a result of measurement error in the option price and nonsynchronous stock and option prices. However, because of our careful choice and handling of the data, as discussed below, the bias from this source is likely to be trivial and will not influence our results.

Two other sources of bias, however, are potentially more serious. First, as noted, the virtual linearity of the Black-Scholes formula for at-the-money options means that the implied variance will only be an approximation of the true subjective variance. Without further analysis, however, it is not clear how good the approximation will be. Hull and White (1987), for example, indicate that large values for the standard deviation of the variance process can lead to large biases in implied variances even for at-the-money options. Second, the stock return distribution may be skewed, implying a nonzero ρ and additional bias. In order to understand the importance, *in our data*, of the linearity approximation and the assumption that ρ = 0, we perform a Monte Carlo simulation of the continuous-time process for returns in (1) and (2). The simulation allows ρ to be nonzero. The magnitude of the bias from these two sources is measured by comparing the implied variance from the simulated data with the actual variance inherent in this data.

We calibrate the simulation to be consistent with the market data used in this study. Because the Garch model approximates the diffusion process, the parameters in (1) and (2) are constructed from the Garch estimates in Table 1. For example, $\xi = \sqrt{2\alpha}$, dt is taken to be 1, and α is estimated directly from the Garch model. Sample values for ρ are obtained by estimating the sample correlation between r_t and h_t, the fitted value from the Garch equation (6).

Given these parameter values, which are grounded in the data, the simulation proceeds as follows for each company in the sample. Risk-neutral pricing and (1) and (2) are assumed to be true. Also, the sample value of ρ is assumed to be true, as are the (time-dependent) values of μ and (time-independent) values of ξ obtained from the Garch estimates. Finally, ϕ is assumed to be the average daily return on the riskless asset and takes the value 0.000245. Given these parameter values, the stock return process is simulated 1,000 times over the life of the option according to (1) and (2), where we approximate the continuous-time process by dividing the 135-day remaining life of the option into discrete, daily increments.[3] This experiment yields an estimate of the actual price for the (European) call option. Under risk-neutral valuation, this estimate is computed as the mean of the discounted terminal value of the option over the 1,000 trials. The method described below is then used to impute a variance from the simulated price and the initial value of the stock price, where stock and strike prices are chosen to be at-the-money. The simulations also define the actual mean cumulative variance over the option's remaining life, $E(\bar{V}_t \mid I_t)$. Under the null hypothesis, this conditional mean equals the subjective variance. Bias is then defined as the difference between the simulated actual mean cumulative variance and the implied variance from the model.

If there were no computational limits to the simulation, there would be no reason to generate only 1,000 replications of the process. In the limit as the number of realisations approaches infinity, the empirical distribution of $\bar{V}$ approaches its true distribution. However, given practical constraints, it is impossible to determine how many finite simulations are required to obtain a good estimate of the true distribution. Our strategy is to use 1,000 simulations to compute the option price and $E(\bar{V}_t \mid I_t)$ and to repeat this procedure 100 times. With 100 realisations of the option price (and thus the implied variance) we are able to construct a confidence interval around mean bias, which quantifies the numerical bias in the experiment.[4]

As a check on the possible numerical bias from using only 1,000 draws, the foregoing procedure is modified so that 10,000 draws of the stock and variance evolution are made (the 10,000-draw simulation is conducted independently from the 1,000-draw simulation). Here 1,000,000 draws are taken for each stock. The effect of the size of the simulation is seen by comparing the results as we go from 1,000 to 10,000 draws.

The results from the Monte Carlo experiments are contained in Table 2. Sample means and standard errors are reported over the 100 repetitions of the simulated mean cumulative variance $E(\bar{V}_t \mid I_t)$, the implied variance, and inherent bias. These values are computed and reported for

Table 2. Bias inherent in analytic approximation

Draws	V(0)	Simulated variance (std err)	Implied variance (std err)	Bias (%) (2 std err range)
A. CSC, ρ = 0.2962				
1000	438.56	589.49	593.86	–0.74
		(0.01)	(4.12)	(–2.14, 0.66)
1000	590.52	591.02	596.54	–0.93
		(0.01)	(4.14)	(–2.33, 0.47)
1000	750.52	592.84	599.52	–1.13
		(0.01)	(4.17)	(–2.53, 0.28)
10,000	590.52	591.04	592.50	–0.25
		(0.004)	(1.26)	(–.67, 0.18)
B. DEC, ρ = –0.1872				
1000	354.71	614.06	617.19	–0.51
		(0.01)	(4.29)	(0.89, –1.91)
1000	614.71	614.42	619.43	–0.81
		(0.01)	(4.14)	(–2.15, 0.53)
1000	834.71	615.36	621.98	–1.07
		(0.01)	(4.17)	(–2.43, 0.27)
10,000	614.71	614.39	614.98	–0.10
		(0.003)	(1.30)	(–0.52, 0.33)
C. DPT, ρ = 0.1059				
1000	332.31	681.07	679.87	0.18
		(0.03)	(4.81)	(–1.24, 1.59)
1000	492.31	763.05	762.97	0.01
		(0.03)	(5.49)	(–1.43, 1.45)
1000	642.31	840.19	841.14	–0.11
		(0.04)	(6.13)	(1.57, 1.35)
10,000	492.31	763.09	757.56	0.72
		(0.01)	(1.66)	(0.29, 1.16)
D. FDX, ρ = –0.0493				
1000	378.12	522.16	524.68	–0.48
		(0.02)	(3.59)	(–1.86, 0.89)
1000	538.12	536.66	540.46	–0.71
		(0.03)	(3.72)	(–2.10, 0.68)
1000	798.12	560.59	566.48	–1.05
		(0.03)	(3.91)	(–2.44, 0.34)
10,000	538.12	536.67	536.79	–0.02
		(0.01)	(1.12)	(–0.44, 0.39)
E. NSM, ρ = 0.2085				
1000	880.98	1196.00	1205.98	–0.83
		(0.10)	(9.58)	(–2.44, 0.76)
1000	1230.98	1251.91	1265.30	–1.07
		(0.11)	(10.12)	(–2.69, 0.55)
1000	1580.98	1308.22	1325.03	–1.28
		(0.11)	(10.67)	(–2.92, 0.35)
10,000	1230.98	1252.03	1254.77	–0.20
		(0.03)	(3.10)	(–0.70, 0.28)
F. PDN, ρ = –0.0408				
1000	1043.24	1457.01	1465.23	–0.56
		(0.09)	(11.58)	(–2.15, 1.02)
1000	1443.24	1476.86	1488.33	–0.78
		(0.09)	(10.20)	(–2.16, 0.60)
1000	1843.24	1497.19	1511.89	–0.98
		(0.09)	(12.05)	(–2.59, 0.63)
1000	1443.24	1476.97	1475.35	0.11
		(0.03)	(3.64)	(–0.40, 0.60)
G. ROK, ρ= 0.0360				
1000	262.10	382.61	384.55	–0.45
		(0.01)	(2.54)	(–1.78, 0.87)
1000	392.10	393.62	396.39	–0.70
		(0.01)	(2.63)	(–2.04, 0.63)
1000	522.10	404.61	408.40	–0.94
		(0.01)	(2.72)	(–2.28, 0.41)
10,000	392.10	393.60	393.83	–0.06
		(0.005)	(0.79)	(–0.46, 0.34)

continued overleaf

Table 2 (continued)

Draws	V(0)	Simulated variance (std err)	Implied variance (std err)	Bias (%) (2 std err range)
H: STK, $\rho = -0.2735$				
1000	884.58	1115.95	1114.47	0.13
		(0.09)	(8.19)	(–1.34, 1.60)
1000	1134.50	1135.74	1136.07	–0.03
		(0.09)	(8.38)	(–1.50, 1.45)
1000	1484.58	1163.81	1166.63	–0.24
		(0.09)	(8.64)	(–1.73, 1.24)
10,000	1134.58	1135.84	1127.21	0.76
		(0.03)	(2.56)	(0.31, 1.21)
I: TAN, $\rho = -0.0563$				
1000	518.35	707.59	704.63	0.42
		(0.16)	(4.82)	(–0.94, 1.78)
1000	738.35	729.40	727.98	0.19
		(0.17)	(5.01)	(–1.18, 1.57)
1000	1008.35	756.52	756.91	–0.05
		(0.18)	(5.23)	(–1.43, 1.33)
10,000	738.35	729.59	722.75	0.94
		(0.06)	(1.53)	(0.005, 1.36)
J: TOY, $\rho = 0.1518$				
1000	530.39	558.84	559.12	–0.05
		(0.09)	(3.99)	(–1.48, 1.38)
1000	680.39	625.41	626.52	–0.18
		(0.10)	(4.53)	(–1.63, 1.27)
1000	880.39	714.29	716.49	–0.31
		(0.13)	(5.26)	(–1.78, 1.16)
10,000	680.39	625.34	622.22	0.50
		(0.03)	(1.38)	(0.06, 0.94)

Model:

$$dS = \phi S dt + \sqrt{V} S dw, \qquad (1)$$

$$dV = \mu V dt + \xi V dz. \qquad (2)$$

S is the stock price. The Brownian motions dw and dz have an instantaneous correlation of ρ. Following Hull and White (1987), risk–neutral option valuation is performed by simulating the following two equations:

$$S_t = S_{t-1} \exp\left[\left(r_t - V_{t-1}/2\right)\Delta t + u_t\sqrt{V_{t-1}\Delta t}\right], \qquad (1')$$

$$V_t = V_{t-1} \exp\left[\left(\mu - \xi^2/2\right)\Delta t + \rho u \xi\sqrt{\Delta t} + \sqrt{1-\rho^2}\, v\xi\sqrt{\Delta t}\right]. \qquad (2')$$

The relevant time increment (Δt) is taken to be one day. In all cases the option expires in 135 days. (1') and (2') are simulated 1,000 times (draws), using the four-way control variate technique described in Hull and White (1987). (The simulation is repeated using 10,000 simulations, 100 times for the middle value of V(0). The results from this experiment are reported for each company – using the middle value of V(0) – below the first horizontal line.) This provides a single (market) option price (and market cumulative forecast) from which an implied volatility is computed analytically, following Black–Scholes. This will be exactly correct in those cases where Black–Scholes is exactly linear in V and where $\rho = 0$. This simulation to obtain an implied volatility is repeated 100 times to provide the mean and standard errors of the inherent bias (the source of variations is numeric, not sampling error). u and v are independent normal (0,1) random deviates. $S(0) = Xe^{-rT}$, $r_t = 0.000245$. The values of μ and ξ are derived from the Garch(1,1) estimates of the variance equation for each company (see Table 1), following Nelson (1990). The value of ρ is computed as the sample correlation between the Garch(1,1) conditional variance on day t (given information up to day t–1 and the return on day t. All variances are daily times 1 million.

three values of initial variance [V(0)]. The middle value of V(0) is the unconditional variance, V(0), taken from Table 1, specification 1. Simulations using 10,000 draws are only conducted for the middle value of V(0) and are reported last for each company in the table.

The results show that mean bias inherent in the analytic approximation using the option pricing model is never more than 1.3% of the actual variance. The variance nested in the Monte Carlo analysis appears to be trivial because standard errors of the bias are also small: two-standard-error confidence intervals around the mean bias never include 3% in absolute value. When 10,000 trials are repeated, the two-standard-error bounds are always less than 1.5% in absolute value. Note also that the mean implied volatility from the 10,000-draw simulations is always within two numerical standard errors of the 1,000-draw simulation.

From the simulation results obtained by Hull and White (1987), we might expect large bias for cases in which α is large. For example, they show that for $\xi = 3$ on an annual basis, which approximately corresponds to $\alpha = 0.11$ (as for CSC and TAN in our data), the bias of the implied variance is 20%. However, their result holds for $\mu = 0$; that is, the variance process follows a random walk. Our findings of low bias are likely due to mean reversion in the estimated discrete time variance process. Also, for companies like DPT and TOY that have strong persistence in variance, estimated α values are relatively small.

As a sensitivity check, the experiments for several companies were repeated with much higher values of ρ in absolute value. For instance, FDX with V(0) of 538.12 and ρ of -0.8 generates a mean bias of 0.59% (two-standard-error confidence interval: [-0.69, 1.86]); when ρ is set to 0.8, the mean bias becomes -1.28% (two-standard-error confidence interval: [-2.78, 0.22]). This result is representative of those for all 10 stocks. We conclude that under the HW model with risk-neutral probabilities, our variance extraction procedure appears to be insensitive to the nonlinearity assumption and skewess in the context of our data. We still refer to these results to ascertain the potential effects of the inherent bias on inferences from the forecast-based tests of the orthogonality restrictions.

Tests of the orthogonality restriction

TESTS AND DATA

We test the orthogonality restrictions in two basic ways. The first set of tests analyses the marginal predictive power of the past behaviour of the return process, given the implied variance, using in-sample regressions and classical statistical tests. We then consider results from out-of-sample tests of forecastability. We investigate the ability of implied variance to predict actual volatility out-of-sample to models using past information by comparing root mean square errors and by estimating encompassing regressions.

The implied variations used in this study are constructed from option and contemporaneous stock-price data for 10 individual stocks with publicly traded options on the Chicago Board Options Exchange (CBOE) for the period April 19, 1982, through March 31, 1984. On the floor of the CBOE there are multiple competing market makers for each of these options. A clerk records every time one of the market makers quotes a bid price that is higher than the bids of the other market makers. Similarly, the clerk records all ask quotes that are lower than extant asks. Both the bid and ask quotes at such points are posted – time-stamped to the nearest second – along with the most recent stock price to have crossed the ticker. We refer to the highest bid and lowest ask quotes as the inside spread. The best bid and best ask quotes are not necessarily from the same market maker. Our data, taken from the Berkeley options database, consist of every inside spread during each day in our sample. Each option inside spread is paired with the most recent stock price from the ticker, recorded by the clerk.

The sample of data and extraction techniques used in this study are chosen to avoid as much as possible errors in the measurement of the implied variance. The stocks in our sample paid no cash dividends from 1981 through 1985; therefore, the options are essentially European. The sample period has no special significance. It starts nine years following the inception of public trading in listed options, so market makers should be adroit at their job. It also allows isolation of non-dividend-paying stocks and is a relatively calm period (compared to, say, late 1987), so the ticket should report up-to-the-minute stock transaction prices.

Note that we are not using transaction prices from the options market. At any point in time when the market is open, the option price is assumed to be the midpoint of the inside bid-ask spread. Although actual transaction prices may include price pressure effects, and (latest) transaction prices from both markets at a fixed point in time (such as closing) will always be asynchronous, our data suffer from neither of these problems.

However, the daily return series may embody noise due to the bid-ask spread "bounce". The subset of stocks with listed options in 1982 consisted of actively traded and generally large stocks in terms of market value of equity. For these stocks, relative spreads tend to be small, and the observed price process should be an excellent instrumental variable for the latent "true" price. By the same token, the most recent stock price matched to the option from the Berkeley tapes may contain some noise. Again, to the extent that this noise is well-behaved, the procedure used to imply a single variance from the entire day's data should serve to trivialise the errors-in-variables problem.

Only those options that were closest to being at-the-money are used. Furthermore, of the three expiration dates available for most companies and most days, the intermediate-term option is used throughout the analysis. The number of quotes in a day varies significantly across the sample, but the average number of quotes per day per company is about 50 for the at-the-money, intermediate-term call option.

We construct time series of implied variances for each stock in the sample as follows. On each day, at-the-money options are isolated by choosing those options with the closest discounted (at the risk-free rate) strike price to stock price at option market close. Of these, for those options that expire at the intermediate term, a single daily implied variance is computed by minimising over variance the sum of squared errors from actual midpoint quotes to the Black-Scholes model value at that variance.[5] The model value is taken to be a function of the yield on the US Treasury bill maturing as closely as possible to the intermediate-term expiration date and the most recent transaction price of the stock from the NYSE, which is the simultaneous stock price reported on the Berkeley tape.[6] As noted, there are on average 50 quote pairs used to define a single implied variance per day. Options quote midpoints and the corresponding stock prices that violate the Black-Scholes lower boundary condition are discarded. Otherwise, all qualifying options within the day are treated equally. This procedure assumes that the variance is constant within a day.

REGRESSION-BASED TESTS

In this subsection we test the orthogonality restrictions by examining the significance of the Garch coefficients (α and β) in the conditional variance specification after accounting for option market forecasts of volatility. Hence, we define ζ_{t-1} in (6) to be the implied variance given information at time $t - 1$, and we allow γ to be a free parameter. From the discussion above, the conditional variance h_t corresponds to the instantaneous variance of the diffusion V_t. If the life of the option T is one day, then $\overline{V}_t$ and V_t are identical for the discrete-time approximation. The general conditional variance equation in (6) then can be interpreted as a regression of $\bar{V}_t$ on the subjective variance, as measured by the implied variance, and past information. The orthogonality restriction of the joint hypothesis implies that the Garch coefficients in (6) are zero (ie that the Garch variables have no marginal predictive power).

This test is subject to an obvious and important criticism. Whereas h_t is the conditional variance of daily returns, in this study ζ_{t-1} is the implied variance from an option that matures at a horizon greater than a day (between 64 and 129 trading days). Under the HW model, the implied variance represents the market's prediction of average daily volatility over the remaining life of the option. Thus, given this specification, ζ_t is not an exact predictor of the dependent variable h_t. Day and Lewis (1992) use weekly return horizons with index options that mature in a month and are thereafter subject to the same criticism. We conduct these tests as a preliminary characterisation of the orthogonality restrictions and account for this maturity mismatch problem with out-of-sample tests below.

The results of the in-sample, regression-based tests are shown in Table 1. The table contains the estimation results for the unrestricted model in (4) to (6) (specification 4) and three restricted specifications. Specification 1 is a homoskedastic model where the restriction $\alpha = \beta = \gamma = 0$ is imposed. Specification 2 is standard Garch(1,1) where γ is restricted to equal 0 (and is discussed above). Specification 3 restricts the conditional heteroskedasticity to be entirely manifest in the option market's variance forecast. A likelihood ratio test (LRT) on the restrictions imposed on specification 2 by specification 1 suggests that the null hypothesis of no Garch ($\alpha = \beta = 0$) can be rejected at the 1% level for all 10 companies, assuming conditional normality, which confirms the inferences outlined above. As discussed there, nontrivial variance clustering is an important characteristic of most of the companies.

From specification 3, we can reject the null that ζ has no explanatory power for actual daily variance for all companies except DEC, even given the maturity mismatch problem. In all other cases, this coefficient is significant and positive. The coefficient on ζ exceeds unity in eight cases.

The joint null hypothesis of informational efficiency and the HW model can be tested against the alternative that allows Garch terms to have incremental predictive ability by comparing specifications 3 and 4. Using the LRT, we reject the null hypothesis at standard significance levels for seven of the 10 companies: CSC, FDX, NSM, ROK, STK, TAN, and TOY.[7] Statistical inference for the remaining three companies is hindered by the fact that the nonnegativity constraints imposed in estimation are binding in the variance equation.[8]

Despite different sample periods, assets, horizons, and so forth, these results are consistent with those of Day and Lewis (1992) – past information improves the market forecast of volatility. However, this result must be interpreted with caution since the maturity mismatch problem may bias the test against the implied variance. In the next subsection we make adjustments for this problem in the context of out-of-sample forecast comparisons.

OUT-OF-SAMPLE TESTS

The incompatibility of forecast horizons that arises in the regression-bases tests is eliminated in this subsection by transforming Garch forecasts of daily variance to forecasts of average daily variance over the remaining life of the corresponding option. On any day t in the sample ($t = 1,...,495$), we can construct a forecast of h_t by using the fitted value of (6) with γ equal to zero. By recursive substitution of this Garch equation, the forecast for h_{t+k} can be constructed for any $k > 0$, given information at t. To obtain a Garch forecast that is directly comparable to our interpretation of the implied variances, we construct the Garch forecasts for $h_{t+1}, h_{t+2}, \ldots, h_{t+N}$ where N is the number of days left in the life of the intermediate-term option on day t. Denote the mean over these N forecasts by G_t. The forecast horizons for G_t, and the implied variance are identical by construction. The joint null hypotheses imply that G_t, is not a better predictor of N-step ahead realised return volatility than the implied variance; that is, the orthogonality restriction means that G_t cannot be used to improve the forecast in the implied variance. In this subsection, we compare the forecast performance of implied variance with the Garch forecast G and a naive forecasting model.

To ensure that forecast comparisons are not biased in favour of the time-series model, we are careful to construct the Garch forecasts by using information available to traders at the time the forecasts are made. Thus, forecast comparisons are made out-of-sample. We estimate both rolling and updating Garch models. The rolling structure uses a constant sample size of 300 observations, adding the return on day $t-1$ and deleting the return on day $t-301$ from the sample used to estimate Garch on each day t. The updating procedure simply adds information as time progresses to construct an updated forecast. Because the Garch model is estimated only from stock-return data (and is therefore not tied down to the options sample), the first sample begins 301 trading days before April 19, 1982, the first day of our implied variance sample. The Garch model is re-estimated 495 times, for each procedure, to construct out-of-sample forecasts that are up-to-date. In addition to Garch, we also consider the updated sample variance of past returns as a naive forecast of variance:

$$H_t = \frac{1}{t}\sum_{i=1}^{t}\hat{\varepsilon}_t^2,$$

where ε_t^2 is the estimated residual from (4), with $\alpha = \beta = \gamma = 0$.

Forecasting performance is judged by comparing the ability of the forecasts to predict the out-of-sample mean of the squared return residuals from (4) over the remaining life of the intermediate-term option. To be precise, assume that this option on day t has N days to maturity. Then the realised volatility over this period is given by

$$z_t = \frac{1}{N}\sum_{i=1}^{N}\hat{\varepsilon}_{t+1}^2.$$

Note that z_t is constructed to be compatible with the interpretation of the implied variance and G_t. Comparisons are based upon the out-of-sample mean error

$$ME = \frac{1}{495}\sum_{t=1}^{495}(z_t - x_t),$$

where x_t is alternatively the implied variance at time t, the two Garch forecasts, and H_t, mean absolute error

$$MAE = \frac{1}{495}\sum_{t=1}^{495}\left|z_t - x_t\right|,$$

and root mean square error

$$RMSE = \left[\frac{1}{495}\sum_{t=1}^{495}(z_t - x_t)^2\right]^{.5}.$$

The results of this exercise are contained in Table 3. The implied variance has the smallest RMSE for only two companies (DPT and TOY). For the remaining companies, the Garch and the naive forecasts have lower RMSE than the implied variance. Thus, for these companies, using past information on the stock-return process can improve the market's forecast. The following points are also evident from the table:

❑ The updating Garch outperforms rolling Garch for all 10 companies under RMSE criterion.[9]

❑ The updated sample variance has the lowest RMSE in five of 10 cases. This relative forecasting performance is at odds with the results of

Table 3. Comparisons of out-of-sample variance forecasts

	Implied variance	Updated G_t	Rolling G_t	H_t
A. CSC				
ME	33.48	–11.04	–12.14	–20.32
MAE	187.26	132.05	147.85	133.67
RMSE	232.15	150.61	169.84	150.32
B. DEC				
ME	257.00	188.80	107.23	239.22
MAE	308.37	306.09	331.32	300.41
RMSE	392.84	375.86	389.23	300.72
C. DFT				
ME	261.63	–829.87	–899.04	–327.47
MAE	402.04	905.79	1051.97	593.85
RMSE	541.84	1537.71	1719.35	670.95
D. FDX				
ME	143.41	–-22.91	–4.89	–25.89
MAE	179.12	185.86	211.14	184.84
RMSE	241.21	213.12	233.74	212.61
E. NSM				
ME	547.96	115.72	–5.66	141.25
MAE	557.17	367.14	447.95	381.81
RMSE	693.59	535.82	592.99	536.92
F. PDN				
ME	664.95	372.79	136.16	386.43
MAE	689.63	571.96	674.26	584.19
RMSE	917.84	751.40	812.22	760.52
G. ROK				
ME	177.74	–4.38	0.25	–12.99
MAE	203.28	94.51	115.09	99.67
RMSE	243.78	114.91	135.86	114.93
H. STK				
ME	434.22	115.36	59.76	–125.06
MAE	496.36	431.79	520.75	414.72
RMSE	635.48	538.00	616.10	513.18
I. TAN				
ME	203.32	–50.24	–51.02	–53.56
MAE	275.50	279.86	307.21	283.17
RMSE	389.52	350.04	393.33	343.31
J. TOY				
ME	71.15	–79.78	–136.79	–60.62
MAE	241.51	266.82	275.33	256.89
RMSE	296.57	330.84	363.50	319.96

Garch (G), historical (H), and implied variance are each being used to forecast the mean of the daily variance over the remaining life of the option. For each day in the sample, each forecast is compared to the actual mean of the daily variance. In this table, only those options with days to maturity of between 90 and 180 days are used. Only call options that are closest-to-the-money are used. The realised variable is measured as the sample average of $\varepsilon^2 = (r_t - r)^2$ over the remaining life of the option, where r is the unconditional mean of the return process.

As defined in the text, ME refers to mean forecast error, MAE refers to mean absolute error, and RMSE refers to the root mean square error. Rolling Garch forecasts use 300 days prior to the day from which the forecast is being made. Updated Garch adds an additional observation for each forecast. All returns are daily percentage times 1,000.

Akgiray (1989). Akgiray finds that Garch variance forecasts are convincingly superior to historical variance as a forecast using the RMSE criterion for stock index data. However, Akgiray uses a forecast horizon of only 20 days. We replicated his analysis with a 200-day horizon (representative of the average number of calendar days in the horizon in this study) and found that the relative rankings of historical variance and Garch were overturned, which is consistent with our results.

- The ME for implied variance is positive for all companies, which indicates that the implied variance is systematically lower than the actual volatility in this period.

As noted by Fair and Schiller (1990, pp. 375–6), simply comparing out-of-sample forecasts using RMSE has limitations. Further insights into the nature of the different forecast models can be obtained by regressing the realised mean squared residuals on the three alternative out-of-sample forecasts:

$$z_t = \beta_0 + \beta_1\zeta_t + \beta_2 G_t + \beta_3 H_t + u_t. \tag{8}$$

All variables are as defined before, except note that G_t is the updated Garch forecast, conditional on information available at time t, of the mean variance; rolling Garch is not used here because updating Garch dominates it under RMSE, and these two are highly correlated.

This regression is in the spirit of the encompassing literature (Hendry and Richard (1982)). If a forecast contains no useful information regarding the evolution of the dependent variable, we would expect the coefficient on that forecast to be insignificantly different from zero. The orthogonality restriction implies that the alternative time-series models contain no information not incorporated in the implied variance that can be used to predict realised volatility. Thus, the encompassing regressions are closely related to the in-sample regression tests. However, this design avoids the maturity mismatch problem, and the forecasts are conditioned on information available at period t. As pointed out by Fair and Schiller (1990), this test also avoids the inherent ambiguity of RMSE comparisons.[10]

Ordinary least squares (OLS) is a consistent estimator of these regression coefficients. However, because the forecast horizon exceeds the frequency of the available data, the error term will be a moving average process. Since generalised least squares is inconsistent (as the forecast errors are not strictly exogenous), we take the approach of obtaining a consistent estimator of the variance covariance matrix of the OLS estimators by generalised method of moments (GMM). An early example of this procedure is Hansen and Hodrick (1980).

To construct this consistent estimator, we use the Bartlett kernel approximation to the spectral density at frequency 0 of the residuals to weight lagged values as suggested by Newey and West (1987). As noted by Andrews (1991), the asymptotic theory for this estimator requires that the lag length used to accumulate the variance go to infinity with the sample size. Therefore, selection of lag length is not obvious. We use the method of Andrews (1991) to estimate optimally this lag length.[11]

Table 4 contains the results of the optimal forecast weighting tests. Two regressions are reported. In the first, β_3 is constrained to be 0, and the second is the unrestricted model. In the table, we report the automatic bandwidth obtained from the Andrews procedure, M^*; the t-statistics are computed by using M^* in the Newey-West weighting scheme. All tests were conducted with a bandwidth of 32, 66, and 132, as well. None of the following inferences are sensitive to the choice of bandwidth.

In general, the optimal out-of-sample forecast of mean realised volatility places a statistically significant positive weight on the implied variance from the options market, no significant weight on the Garch forecast, and a large significant negative weight on the updated sample variance. DEC, PDN, and ROK are exceptions to this pattern. Only DEC has a significantly negative coefficient on the Garch forecast. In all 10 cases the intercept is positive and statistically significant. This result is consistent with earlier evidence that during this period variance forecasts are biased downward.

These regression results suggest the importance of the point made by Fair and Schiller (1990). RMSE comparisons suppress a large amount of information about the problem of constructing an optimal forecast. Despite having the lowest RMSE in only two cases, implied variance has significant forecast weight in seven cases. Symmetrically, note that in the two cases where implied variance had the lowest RMSE (DPT and TOY), the historical variance has significant forecasting power.

The results reported in this table suggest that the joint null hypothesis of market efficiency and the HW model is rejected at standard significance levels. However, it is not the case that filtering the data with the HW model is uninformative. To an agent confronted with deriving an optimal variance forecast, the norm here is to exploit information in both the historical path of stock prices and contemporaneous option and stock prices.

An alternative regression is run, and the results are provided in Table 5. Here the dependent variable is defined as the variance measured model error; $z_t - \zeta_t$. The regressor is the updated sample variance estimate at time t. Test statistics are derived from the GMM covariance matrix as in Table 4. Except for ROK (also an outlier in the optimal forecast analysis, with an insignificant negative weight on ζ_t), the intercept in this regression is positive and significant. The coefficient on the current variance estimate is negative and significant. Note that the order of magnitude of the intercept is the same as the dependent variable itself. The r^2 values reported in Table 5 are high. In half of the cases, more than 45% of the variance measured pricing error is explained by the evolution of the current variance.

INTERPRETATION OF RESULTS

The results of the different experiments conducted are in general inconsistent with the joint hypothesis of the stochastic variance option pricing model and informational efficiency. This inference is robust across the in- and out-of-sample experimental designs. The tests uncover two facts for the 10 companies in the sample:

- Implied variance tends to underpredict realised variance (see mean error in Table 3 and the significantly positive intercept in Table 5).
- Forecasts of variance from past returns contain relevant information not contained in the market forecast constructed under the HW assumptions. The optimal weight placed on these forecasts of realised variance is negative (see Tables 4 and 5).

We refer to the results in Table 2 and ask whether these characteristics can be due solely to the bias inherent in our procedure for implying volatilities under the assumptions of zero correlation between the instantaneous rate of change in the stock price and the instantaneous variance and linearity of the pricing model. The smallest percentage bias in the data is for CSC. Here the mean error of implied variance from Table 3 is 33.48, and the level of variance is 590.52 (see Table 1, specification 1), a percentage error of 5.67. From Table 2, under the joint null, we would expect a percentage error of -0.25%; if the estimated percentage error fell between -0.67 and 0.18%, we would be unable to reject the null at an approximate 5% level of significance.[12] For Tandy, as a more representative company, the expected bias under the null is 0.94%, with a two-standard-error range of 0 to 1.36%. The bias in the data is 27.54%. In all 10 cases, the out-of-sample forecasting error lies well outside the calibrated two-standard-error confidence interval. Thus, the documented underprediction of implied variances cannot be attributed to the two potential sources of bias.

Table 4. Encompassing tests of variance forecasts

	β_0 (GMM t)	β_1 (GMM t)	β_2 (GMM t)	β_3 (GMM t)	r^2 M*
A: CSC					
	2014.269	0.276	–2.580		0.357
	(5.39)	(3.81)	(–4.32)		50
	2950.717	0.272	0.522	–4.566	0.451
	(4.72)	(3.81)	(0.98)	(–3.47)	54
B. DEC					
	981.366	0.382	–1.012		0.222
	(7.52)	(1.60)	(–3.96)		42
	1069.920	0.361	–0.890	–0.327	0.227
	(3.26)	(1.16)	(–2.49)	(–0.30)	66
C. DPT					
	445.920	0.531	0.129		0.418
	(3.18)	(1.82)	(2.92)		60
	3692.963	0.970	0.093	–2.360	0.573
	(2.64)	(3.97)	(2.12)	(–2.49)	51
D. FDX					
	1585.291	1.116	–2.641		0.304
	(3.38)	(2.35)	(–2.71)		75
	3161.79	0.831	1.736	–6.938	0.508
	(3.87)	(2.99)	(1.29)	(–2.70)	85
E. NSM					
	2084.680	1.462	–1.659		0.387
	(3.65)	(4.28)	(–2.80)		59
	4955.058	0.490	0.366	–4.093	0.839
	(9.73)	(2.21)	(1.57)	(–1.17)	73
F. PDN					
	1997.741	0.118	–0.632		0.030
	(2.96)	(0.52)	(–0.93)		184
	2388.188	0.212	1.074	–2.175	0.086
	(2.63)	(0.79)	(1.94)	(–2.34)	196
G. ROK					
	1988.790	–0.452	–3.775		0.356
	(6.69)	(–0.48)	(–5.02)		98
	2141.949	–0.100	–1.556	–2.504	0.375
	(4.81)	(–1.24)	(–0.80)	(–1.02)	119
H. STK					
	2491.690	1.300	–2.166		0.402
	(4.24)	(3.01)	(–3.27)		47
	5073.759	0.619	–0.389	–3.792	0.637
	(3.41)	(2.28)	(0.96)	(–2.54)	86
I. TAN					
	1858.705	0.748	–1.907		0.215
	(4.24)	(3.01)	(–3.27)		47
	5030.08	0.390	0.730	–6.351	0.488
	(3.41)	(2.28)	(0.96)	(–2.54)	86
J. TOY					
	824.120	1.171	–1.273		0.227
	(4.23)	(2.56)	(–2.85)		59
	4053.326	0.660	0.028	–5.999	0.555
	(4.91)	(2.57)	(–0.02)	(–4.32)	87

Model: $z_t = b_0 + \beta_1\zeta_t + \beta_2 G_t + \beta_3 H_t + u_t$

Table 5. Implied volatility forecast "errors" and the level of variance

Company	β_0 (GMM t)	β_1 (GMM t)	r^2 M*
CSC	3601.40	−5.77	0.26
	(4.36)	(−4.32)	24
DEC	905.16	−1.54	0.12
	(6.63)	(−4.39)	38
DPT	3557.52	−2.16	0.28
	(2.35)	(−2.18)	54
FDX	2869.53	−4.81	0.48
	(4.41)	(−4.43)	75
NSM	4622.75	−3.73	0.82
	(10.62)	(−9.61)	46
PDN	2381.30	−1.67	0.18
	(2.57)	(−2.11)	101
ROK	1721.33	−3.61	0.11
	(1.75)	(−1.54)	47
STK	5092.60	−4.47	0.62
	(5.68)	(−5.28)	77
TAN	4790.36	−5.74	0.48
	(5.45)	(−5.37)	29
TOY	3987.13	−6.13	0.51
	(5.56)	(−5.64)	69

Model: $z_t - \zeta_t = \beta_0 - \beta_1 H_t + u_t$
z_t is the realised mean $(r_t - \bar{r})^2$ during the period t + 1 through t + N, where t + N is the maturity date of the option, ζ_t is the implied variance from all quotes on the at-the-money, intermediate-term options (that expire at time t = N) on day t. G_t is N-step ahead (updated) Garch(1,1) variance forecast (conditional on information available at time t). H is the updated sample variance measured through day t. M* is the optimal bandwidth used to estimate the Bartlett kernel in the Newey-West variance-covariance matrix (following Andrews (1991)). GMM t refers to the Student's s t-statistic computed using this matrix. All returns are daily percentage times 1000. All variances are on a daily basis.

Also, from Table 2, we ask whether the empirical relationship between the forecast error of the implied variance and the current variance is solely a result of the approximation procedure used to imply variances. It is possible that the negative coefficient on H_t (or G_t) in the encompassing regressions picks up a tendency for the bias in implied variance, though small, to change with the level of variance. Note from Table 2 that in all 10 cases the inherent percentage bias is inversely related to the level of variance, V(0). However, the magnitude of this phenomenon is very different from that manifest in the data. Federal Express is a typical case. From the three sets of values in Table 2 (generated with 1000 draws, 100 times), the change in absolute bias divided by the change in level of variance is -0.008. From Table 5, the change in the forecast error relative to a change in historical variance is -4.81.[13] Therefore, whereas we expect a negative coefficient on historical variance, the size of this coefficient computed from actual data is too large to be the result of the inherent biases in the experimental design.

Since the biases inherent in our extraction procedure are unlikely to be the reason for the rejection of the null hypothesis, we can speculate as to the potential causes. One interpretation of the statistically significant negative effect of the updated sample variance is that market participants totally ignore the information contained in past realisations of returns. An alternative interpretation is that the market overreacts to recent volatility shocks: too much weight is placed on the recent past of the variance process. A current increase to volatility raises the sample variance, but the negative β_3 suggests that this shock is temporary. However, options traders impute a permanence to the shock, leading to an underprediction of variance (Stein (1989)).

Given informational efficiency, our results can be explained by the existence of a risk premium applied to the nontraded variance process. Recall that an assumption underlying the use of the implied variance from the model as an instrument for the market's forecast of variance is that volatility risk is unpriced. The option price is independent of risk preferences if agents are risk-neutral, or if the instantaneous variance is uncorrelated with aggregate consumption and, therefore, is uncorrelated with marginal utility of wealth. If this assumption is false, then observed option prices will include a risk premium. For example, if variance uncertainty gives negative utility to traders, the observed option price will be lower than the risk neutral price, *ceteris paribus*. When the observed price is applied to the Black-Scholes formula, the implied variance will be correspondingly lower than actual variance. As noted, we document this underprediction by the implied variance for all stocks in the sample. The negative coefficient on the current level of variance means that the risk premium is time dependent. Specifically, the implied variance rises relative to the future (realised) volatility as the stock's variance rises. Thus the variance risk premium embedded in option prices diminishes as the stock's variance increases.[14]

Melino and Turnbull (1990) use numerical methods to evaluate a partial differential equation in the spirit of Garman (1976), and they find evidence to support the notion that a nonzero risk premium on the variance process exists in the Canadian dollar–US dollar exchange rate option market. They restricted the price of variance risk to be a constant. Our results suggest that such a risk premium is time-varying in the stock market.

Our empirical analysis is confined to constructing an optimal variance forecast. Since we reject the joint null hypothesis of market efficiency and stochastic variance option pricing model-based pricing of these options, these results do not indicate that one could take the optimal variance forecasts and use them to "beat" the option market. It is plausible that the market's forecast as embodied in option prices is optimal, but that filtering the prices through the simple option pricing model distorts the forecast. Thus, if one used the "optimal forecast" from the regressions, the profits generated by that strategy would be offset by volatility risk if this trader's utility function is the same as the market's.

Although we have motivated this experiment as a test of the restrictions of an asset pricing model, the tests also provide insights into the nature of the variance process for these individual stocks. The poor out-of-sample performance of Garch at the 90- to 180-calendar-day horizons appears inconsistent with its good in-sample fit and good forecast performance at short horizons (see Akgiray (1989)). This set of results is consistent with a variance process that is subject to highly persistent shocks at low frequencies and quickly dampening shocks at high frequencies. This property of stock-return variances and its relationship to Garch has been suggested by Lamoureux and Lastrapes (1990). Theoretical analysis of this phenomenon is provided by Nelson (1992). Garch treats all innovations equally; therefore, it overstates the persistence of high-frequency shocks, which leads to excellent short-term forecasts but poor long-term forecasts.

As a final note, Back (1993) has developed an equilibrium model of informed trader behaviour in the spirit of Kyle (1985), where the monopolistically informed trader may trade with an uninformed market maker in either the stock or option market. Back shows that the only equilibrium that does not generate arbitrage opportunities for the informed trader is one in which the stock's variance is stochastic and in which the option price contains information about the future variance that is not publicly available elsewhere. Thus, the option allows a finer partition of information than is available from an information set that excludes the current option price. Empirically, this theoretical result could be rejected if, for example in our analysis, we found that the optimal forecast weight on implied variance could not be statistically distinguished from zero. For seven of the 10 companies the implied variance has a statistically positive weight. This result is consistent with Back's model.

Conclusions

We examine the joint hypothesis of a class of stochastic volatility option pricing models and informational efficiency in the options markets using a criterion function based on the variance of the underlying stock returns. To examine this hypothesis, we represent the subjective variance of the market as the implied variance from the data and the option pricing model. By utilising discrete-time simulations of the continuous-time return process, calibrated to our data, we show that potential biases between these two variance concepts are small and do not affect the inferences of our tests of the joint hypothesis.

Using both in-sample and out-of-sample tests, we reject the implication of the hypothesis that available information cannot be used to improve the market's variance forecast embedded in observable prices as measured by this class of models. This result is robust across the different test designs and to inherent measurement bias and is consistent with the results of Melino and Turnbull (1990) and Day and Lewis (1992). If the market is efficient, our results suggest that the fundamental assumptions of the model are not sufficient to account for the properties of the data. In particular, equilibrium models of option pricing that do not assume investor indifference to volatility risk appear necessary to reconcile the theory and data. The data suggest that the market premium on variance risk is time varying; it is a decreasing function of the level of the stock's variance. Results concerning the nature of this risk premium are uniform (and strikingly similar) across the 10 stocks used in our analysis.

Although the option pricing model is rejected as the price-determining market mechanism, filtering the data with the simple model does contain useful information that is not contained in the historical price process of the underlying stock for forecasting the stock's variance over a 180- to 90-calendar-day horizon. This result has normative implications for optimal variance forecast rules, even in the absence of the "correct" equilibrium option pricing model capable of explaining the data.

1 *While this linearity has normally been expressed in terms of the standard deviation, our analysis is conducted in terms of the variance. Simulations reported in the subsection on the characterisation of bias show that the linearity applies to the variance as well, for our data. Feinstein (1989) analyses implied volatilities and confirms the linearity documented by Cox and Rubinstein.*

2 *We tested all 10 companies for the presence of an AR(1) process in returns, allowing for Garch residuals. All 10 had positive first-order serial correlation, but this was significant at the 10% level for only one company (number 10). The magnitude of this serial correlation is trivial, the largest first-order serial correlation (company 10) is 0.13, the median is 0.06.*

3 *The antithetic variate technique of using each pair of draws four times, discussed in Hull and White (1987), is used in this regard. Equation (11) of that article (see notes to our Table 2), with normally distributed random variates, form the basis for the simulation.*

4 *In effect, the simulation experiment utilises 100,000 simulations (1000 realisations, 100 times) to construct estimates of bias. The comparable alternative strategy – 100,000 realisations with no repetitions – yields only one estimate of option price, so no confidence interval can be constructed. Though 100,000 simulations may be sufficient to ensure a precise estimate of the true option price and the distribution of* $\bar{V}$*, there is no way to determine this from the alternative strategy.*

5 *A quadratic hill climbing algorithm is used that has good convergence properties. This technique was suggested by Whaley (1982) and is more efficient than that used by Brenner and Galai (1987), namely, implying a variance from each option and using the daily average.*

6 *We collected daily Treasury-bill yields from the* Wall Street Journal*. For options that mature in six months or less, there is always a one-day difference in the maturity date of the Treasury bill and the option expiration date. Since 12-month bills are only auctioned every four weeks, there is sometimes an eight-day difference between the maturity of the applicable Treasury bill and the expiration of the option. There are three days in the sample period where the Treasury bill market was closed, but the NYSE and CBOE were open. In these cases, the previous day's rate data were substituted. The Berkeley database is missing data for the dates July 1, 1983, and December 23, 1983. For these dates, we use the options data from the previous day to replace the missing values.*

7 *The LRT is more appropriate than Wald tests given the potential collinearity between* ε^2_{t-1}, β_{t-1} *and* ζ_{t-1}.

8 *These constraints bind in some other cases (eg FDX), but here the constraint is binding in both specifications 3 and 4.*

9 *In a study that examines the forecast efficiency of Garch (in terms of expected utility), West et al. (1990) find that rolling Garch is superior to updating. The data in that paper are weekly foreign exchange rates.*

10 *Fair and Schiller (1990) use this empirical strategy to infer the information content of alternative models of real GNP growth. In particular, they examine the forecasting performance of a structural model and various time-series models of aggregate output. Although the economic issue in our article differs from Fair and Schiller, it is clear that the questions we ask are analogous to theirs. Thus, their methods of inference are appropriate for our analysis.*

11 *Andrews (1991) has developed the asymptotic theory to estimate the optimal lag length or bandwidth for a given sample of size* T *as a function of the autocovariance structure of the matrix* V*, where* $V = \varepsilon'X$*,* ε *is a* $T \times 1$ *vector of the OLS residuals, and* X *is the* $T \times K$ *matrix of regressors. In our case, the first column is a vector of 1s. We estimate a univariance AR(1) process for each column of* V*. The* K *AR(1) coefficients and residual variances are then used to compute* $\hat{\alpha}(1)$ *by using Equation (6.4) in Andrews (1991, p. 83–5). We use weights of 1 for* $p = 2,\ldots,K$ *and 0 for* $p = 1$ *(which Andrews notes yields scale-invariant covariance matrix, p. 834). Since we are using the triangular (Bartlett) kernel estimator as in Newey and West (1987), we obtain the optimal bandwidth by plugging* $\hat{}(1)$ *into Andrew's Equation (6.2) (p. 834). The result of this equation is equal to* $M^* + 1$*, where* M^* *is the optimal bandwidth used to compute the variance-covariance matrix, as in Newey and West.* M^* *increases with the cubed root of* T.

12 *Recognising that the unconditional variance is estimated with sampling error, add two standard errors to this estimate, and the percentage error is 5.1. The inference is unchanged.*

13 *The regression coefficient reported in Table 5 is a first derivative analogous in its interpretation to the ratio of changes reported. Although the magnitude of change in the variance level is large in Table 2 , the size and sign of the pseudo-derivative are virtually identical across companies and independent of the size of change in* $V(0)$.

14 *There is no reason to suspect* a priori *that this risk premium would be the same across stocks. It is a function of the correlation between the variance process and marginal utility. To the extent that stock variances include common factors, the risk premiums will be related.*

BIBLIOGRAPHY

Akgiray, V., 1989, "Conditional Heteroskedasticity in Time Series of Stock Returns: Evidence and Forecasts", *Journal of Business* 62, pp. 55-80.

Andrews, D.W.K., 1991, "Heteroskedasticity and Autocorrelation Consistent Covariance Matrix Estimation", *Econometrica* 59, pp. 817-58.

Back, K., 1993, "Asymmetric Information and Options", *Review of Financial Studies* 6, pp. 435-72.

Biegler, L.J., and J.E. Cuthrell, 1985, "Improved Feasible Path Optimization for Sequential Modular Simulators. II: The Optimization Algorithm", *Computers and Chemical Engineering* 9, pp. 257-67.

Black, F., and M. S. Scholes, 1973, "The Pricing of Options and Corporate Liabilities", *Journal of Political Economy* 81, pp. 637-54.

Bollerslev, T., 1986, "Generalized Autoregressive Conditional Heteroskedasticity", *Journal of Econometrics* 31, pp. 307-27.

Brenner, M., and D. Galai, 1987, "On the Prediction of the Implied Standard Deviation", in *Advances in Futures and Options Research*, JAI Press, Greenwich, Conn.

Cox, J.C., and M. Rubinstein, 1985, *Options Markets* Prentice-Hall, Englewood Cliffs, N.J.

Day, T.E., and C.M. Lewis, 1992, "Stock Market Volatility and the Information Content of Stock Index Options", *Journal of Econometrics* 52, pp. 267-87.

Engle, R.F., 1982, "Autoregressive Conditional Heteroskedasticity with Estimates of the Variance of UK Inflation", *Econometrica* 50, pp. 987-1007.

Fair, R.C., and R.J. Schiller, 1990, "Comparing Information in Forecasts from Econometric Models", *American Economic Review* 80, pp. 375-89.

Feinstein, S.P., 1989, "A Theoretical and Empirical Investigation of the Black-Scholes Implied Volatility". Unpublished thesis, Yale University.

Garman, M., 1976, "A General Theory of Asset Valuation under Diffusion State Processes". Working paper, University of California, Berkeley.

Hansen, L.P., and R.J. Hodrick, 1980, "Forward Exchange Rates as Optimal Predictors of Future Spot Rates: An Econometric Analysis", *Journal of Political Economy* 88, pp. 829-53.

Hendry, D.F., and J.F. Richard, 1982, "On the Formulation of Empirical Models in Dynamic Economics", *Journal of Econometrics* 20, pp. 3-33.

Heston, S., 1993, "A Closed-Form Solution for Options with Stochastic Volatility with Applications to Bond and Currency Options", *Review of Financial Studies* 6, pp. 327-43; reprinted as Chapter 23 of the present volume.

Hull, J., and A. White, 1987, "The Pricing of Options on Assets with Stochastic Volatilities", *Journal of Finance* 42, pp. 281-300.

Johnson, H., and D. Shanno, 1987, "Option Pricing When the Variance is Changing", *Journal of Financial and Quantitative Analysis*, pp. 143-51.

Kyle, A.S., 1985, "Continuous Auctions and Insider Trading", *Econometrica* 53, pp. 1315-35.

Lamoureux, C.G., and W.D. Lastrapes, 1990, "Persistence in Variances, Structural Change, and the GARCH Model", *Journal of Business and Economic Statistics* 8, pp. 225-34.

Melino, A., and S. Turnbull, 1990, "Pricing Foreign Currency Options with Stochastic Volatility", *Journal of Econometrics* 45, pp. 239-65.

Nelson, D.B., 1990, "ARCH Models as Diffusion Approximation", *Journal of Econometrics* 45, pp. 7-38.

Nelson, D.B., 1992, "Filtering and Forecasting with Misspecified ARCH Models. I: Getting the Right Variance with the Wrong Model", *Journal of Econometrics* 52, pp. 61-90.

Newey, W.K., and K.D. West, 1987, "A Simple, Positive Semi-Definite Heteroskedasticity and Autocorrelation Consistent Covariance Matrix", *Econometrica* 55, pp. 703-6.

Scott, L.O., 1987, "Option Pricing When the Variance Changes Randomly", *Journal of Financial and Quantitative Analysis* 22, pp. 419-38.

Stein, E.M., and J.C. Stein, 1991, "Stock Price Distributions with Stochastic Volatility: An Analytic Approach", *Review of Financial Studies* 4, pp. 727-52.

Stein, J.C., 1989, "Overreactions in the Options Market", *Journal of Finance* 44, pp. 1011-23.

West, K.D., H.J. Edison, and D. Cho, 1990, "A Utility Based Comparison of Some Models of Exchange Rate Volatility". Working paper, University of Wisconsin.

Whaley, R.E., 1982, "Valuation of American Call Options on Dividend Paying Stocks: Empirical Tests", *Journal of Financial Econometrics* 10, pp. 29-58.

Wiggins, J.B., 1987, "Option Values under Stochastic Volatility: Theory and Empirical Estimates", *Journal of Financial Econometrics* 19, pp. 351-72.

Inferring Future Volatility from the Information in Implied Volatility in Eurodollar Options:

A New Approach*

Kaushik I. Amin and Victor K. Ng
Lehman Brothers; Goldman Sachs & Co

We study the information content of implied volatility from several volatility specifications of the Heath-Jarrow-Morton (1992) (HJM) models relative to popular historical volatility models in the Eurodollar options market. The implied volatility from the HJM models explains much of the variation of realised interest-rate volatility over both daily and monthly horizons. The implied volatility dominates the Garch terms, the Glosten, Jagannathan and Runkle (1993) type asymmetric volatility terms, and the interest rate level. However, it cannot explain that the impact of interest rate shocks on the volatility is lower when interest rates are low than when they are high.

Recent studies on the information content of implied volatility yield disappointing results for implied volatility models. These include Canina and Figlewski (1993), Chiras and Manaster (1978), Day and Lewis (1992) and Lamoureux and Lastrapes (1993). For example, Canina and Figlewski (1993) report that "implied volatility has virtually no correlation with future volatility, and it does not incorporate the information contained in recent observed volatility." In Day and Lewis (1992), the coefficient of the implied volatility is barely significant in the volatility-forecast equation. These results contrast with a large body of academic literature that views implied volatility as the "market's volatility forecast" (see Schwert (1990)) and superior to historical data-based forecasts. As most of our option-pricing models depend only on the volatility of the underlying process, the lack of information content of implied volatility questions their validity.

In this article we study the information content of implied volatility by correcting for several biases in previous studies. First, existing studies are based on either OEX index options or individual stock options for which the transaction costs for arbitrage are non-trivial. As Canina and Figlewski (1993) argue, high transaction costs may permit market prices to deviate significantly from theoretical prices. Correspondingly, implied volatilities from OEX and individual stock options are not very informative with respect to future volatility. This issue therefore needs to be studied in a liquid market with low transaction costs. We choose the Eurodollar futures options market. Sophisticated institutional investors dominate this market, and the trading volume is more than

* *This paper was first published in* The Review of Financial Studies, *Vol.10, No. 2, (1997). It is reprinted with permission from Oxford University Press. Most of the work in this chapter was completed while Victor K. Ng was an economist at the International Monetary Fund. The views in this article do not represent those of Lehman Brothers, Goldman Sachs & Co, or the International Monetary Fund. We thank Yacine Ait-Sahalia, Ravi Jagannathan, Andy Morton, and participants in the June 1995 Western Finance Association Meetings and the finance workshops at New York University and Duke University for helpful comments.*

twice that in any other options market (based on both the number of contracts and underlying notional value). Further, since they are futures options, Eurodollar options carry very low transaction costs for arbitrage activity.

Second, we offer some methodological improvements to the tests used in previous studies by Day and Lewis (1992) and Lamoureux and Lastrapes (1993). These studies embed the implied volatility as an exogenous term in a Garch variance equation. However, this method implicitly includes an entire lag structure of the implied volatility through the Garch persistence terms. This structure is apparent if we rewrite the model in a distributed lag form through recursive substitution of the lagged conditional volatility. It biases both implied volatility significance and the Garch persistence parameter. We redesign the test equation to correct this bias. We also control for fat tails in the distribution for interest rate shocks.

Third, to avoid model misspecification, we study the implied volatility from several interest rate option models for pricing Eurodollar futures options. Previous studies have used only the Black-Scholes model with a lognormal distribution for the underlying price. We embed five different interest rate models within the Heath-Jarrow-Morton (1992) (HJM) framework to price interest rate claims. The HJM framework is based on the absence of arbitrage and requires only the initial term structure and the volatility of forward interest rates as inputs. Since these volatilities are the only unobservable parameters, we can use these models to infer the interest rate volatilities from the market prices of interest rate claims. We can then compare the forecast ability of our implied volatility to historic volatility models.

We focus on the volatility of the shortest maturity interest rate available from Eurodollar futures prices, hereafter called the spot interest rate. To estimate its implied volatility, we incorporate the following models in the HJM framework: Courtadon (1982), Cox, Ingersoll, and Ross (1985) (CIR), Ho and Lee (1986), Vasicek (1977) and a linear proportional volatility model studied by Amin and Morton (1994). From these models we estimate the implied volatility parameters every day. Using these implied parameters, we compute the implied volatility of the short-term Eurodollar rate from each interest rate model. We then compare the information content of the implied volatility from each model relative to historical volatility benchmarks. This approach lends insight into the validity of the HJM models and into the functional form of the volatility process.

Our historical volatility forecasts are based on both volatility persistence and interest rate levels. Since a large body of academic literature has demonstrated that economic time series exhibit volatility persistence (see the survey by Bollerslev, Chou, and Kroner (1992)), models incorporating this persistence constitute natural benchmarks to estimate volatility forecasts from time-series data. We use Bollerslev's (1986) Garch model and its extension by Glosten, Jagannathan, and Runkle (GJR) (1994), as two of our historical benchmarks. The GJR model permits an asymmetric volatility response to positive and negative shocks. This asymmetry is important in previous studies using equity data for example, GJR and Nelson (1990). The Garch and GJR models are preferable to rolling constant volatility estimates for estimating historical interest rate volatility because they optimally incorporate information decay over time through higher weighting of recent shocks.

We also include all the volatility specifications used in each of the five models used to estimate the implied volatility in our historical volatility forecasts. In addition to the Garch and GJR forecasts, historical volatility estimates are computed separately for the CIR (1985) and Courtadon (1982) volatility specifications. In these models, the volatility depends on the interest rate level. Since we focus only on the volatility of the spot interest rate, the Ho and Lee (1986), Vasicek (1977), and the linear proportional model are special cases of the Garch and Courtadon (1982) models for computing the historical volatility forecasts.[1]

Fourth, in the historical volatility forecasts, we also incorporate an interaction effect between the level and shocks to the interest rate identified by Brenner, Harjes and Kroner (1993). Interestingly, these authors find that the volatility sensitivity to past shocks depends on interest rate levels. Koedijk, Nissen, Schotman and Wolff (1994) confirm this interaction with a different sample and a different model specification. Ignoring this effect biases the sensitivity to past shocks upwards. Furthermore, our study can offer a more powerful test of this phenomenon because we also use option price data.

Most of our tests are based on single-period volatility forecasts over a daily horizon. Finally, as a robustness check, we test the ability of implied volatility to explain realised volatility over monthly horizons relative to historical forecasts.

We follow the regression approach of Canina and Figlewski (1993) by comparing future realised volatility over the following month with historical and implied volatility forecasts.

This chapter may be briefly summarised as follows. In the first section we describe our dataset. Then we describe the HJM (1992) approach to the valuation of Eurodollar futures options and the methodology used to estimate the term structure of forward rates and the implied volatilities. We also present various plausible forms for the volatility function. In the following section we estimate the historical volatility models from the time series of interest rates. Next we describe the methodology for studying the information content and forecast ability of implied volatility relative to historical volatility. We present both the standard approach used by Day and Lewis (1992) and our new approach that corrects for the potential biases under the standard approach. We go on to present results comparing historical forecasts with implied volatility forecasts of single-period realised volatility. We also examine the robustness of the single period results by comparing the multiperiod forecast ability of implied volatility relative to historical volatility estimates over monthly horizons.

Data description: Eurodollar futures and options

Eurodollar futures trade with maturities up to 10 years. Almost all the activity is in contracts that expire on the second business day before the third Wednesday of March, June, September, and December. There is significant liquidity (average trading volume greater than 1,000 contracts per day) in contracts with maturity up to five years. At maturity date T, the futures settlement price $F_T(T)$ is

$$F_T(T) = 100[100 - y(T)], \quad (1)$$

where y(T) is the three-month Libor[2] interest rate at date T. The notional amount for each futures contract is \$1 million. Since each contract covers a three-month rate (0.25 years), each 0.0001 change in the interest rate corresponds to a \$25 (= 0.0001 × 0.25 × 1,000,000) change in the futures price.

Based on Equation (1), each futures contract yields information about a three-month forward rate beginning from the maturity of the futures contract to three months after maturity. This three-month period is called the accrual period of the futures contract. Since there exists a Eurodollar futures contract with maturity every three months, the entire term structure of forward rates can be estimated using the "strip" of Eurodollar futures prices. We assume that the instantaneous forward interest rate curve is constant to the end of the accrual period of the first futures contract and between futures maturities after that. In this study we focus on the shortest maturity Eurodollar interest rate available from the futures prices. We term this rate, which is the forward rate over the accrual period of the first futures contract, the "spot rate".

The options on this contract are American, with the same maturity date as the futures. Upon exercise, the cashflow to a call option equals the difference between the current futures price and the exercise price. The owner of a put option receives the difference between the exercise price and the current futures price. Most traded options have a maturity of less than one year.

We use the dataset in Amin and Morton (1994). This covers the period from January 1, 1988 to November 10, 1992. It includes the last traded price for all Eurodollar futures and futures options contracts as of 8:30 am CST (approximately an hour after trading opens). The futures and options prices are therefore sampled intraday and are based on transaction prices. Thus they are not subject to the asynchronous trading problems of prior studies using closing prices. For summary statistics on the dataset see Amin and Morton (1994).

The HJM framework

THE BASIC MODEL

In this section we describe the HJM class of models. Let f(t,T) be the forward interest rate at date t for instantaneous and riskless borrowing or lending at date T. The spot interest rate at date t is given by r(t) = f(t,t). At each trading date t, HJM specify the simultaneous evolution of forward interest rates of every maturity T, according to the stochastic differential equation:

$$df(t,T) = a(t,T,.)dt + \sigma\big(t,T,f(t,T)\big)dW(t), \quad (2)$$

where a(t,T,.) and σ(t,T,f(t,T)) are the drift and dispersion coefficients for the forward interest rate of maturity T and W(t) is a one-dimensional standard Brownian motion. Under complete markets. HJM show the existence of a "risk-neutral" pricing measure under which the price of every security discounted by the spot interest rate is a martingale. To illustrate, fix some final horizon date, S. Let P(t,T) be the price of a discount bond at date t that matures at date T. Define

$$Z(t,T) = P(t,T)\exp\left[-\int_0^t r(u)du\right] \tag{3}$$

for $t \le T \le S$. For every discount bond of maturity $T \le S$, $Z(t,T)$ [for $0 \le t \le T$] is a martingale under the risk-neutral measure. Under this measure we can price every security as if investors are risk neutral. Therefore the security price equals the expectation of its value at any future date discounted back to today using the spot interest rate.

Applying the martingale condition to discount bond prices yields the drift coefficient for each maturity, T:

$$\alpha(t,T,.) = \sigma(t,T,f(t,T))\int_t^T \sigma(t,u,f(t,u))du. \tag{4}$$

The function $\sigma(t,T,f(t,T))$, which is the instantaneous standard deviation of the forward interest rate of maturity T at date t, constitutes the parameter input(s) to the model. Specifying $\sigma(.)$ completely specifies the model since $\alpha(.)$ is then determined from Equation (4). If $\sigma(.)$ is a constant (as a function of both time and maturity), Equation (1) reduces to the Ho and Lee (1986) model. Furthermore, by appropriately specifying $\sigma(.)$, we can treat many spot rate models as special cases. For example, if the volatility of forward interest rates is an exponential function of time to maturity, the process for the spot interest rate is the same as assumed by Vasicek (1977). If $\sigma(t,T,f(t,T)) = \sigma f(t,T)^{1/2}$, then the spot interest rate is virtually identical to that in CIR. Thus, we refer to this specification as the CIR model. Similarly, we refer to $\sigma(t,T,f(t,T)) = \sigma f(t,T)$ as the Courtadon (1982) model.

Consider the pricing of futures. Although futures prices do not equal forward prices if interest rates are stochastic (Jarrow and Oldfield, 1981), futures can be valued like any other contingent claim. The initial investment in a futures contract is zero. Therefore the expected change in the futures price under a risk-neutral measure must be zero.

Let $E_t[.]$ denote the expectation with respect to the risk-neutral measure conditional on the information set at date t. If the futures price is date t for maturity T is $F_T(t)$, and $F_T(T)$ is the terminal futures (and spot) price at maturity,

$$0 = E_t\left[F_T(T) - F_T(t)\right].$$

In other words,

$$F_T(t) = E_t\left[F_T(T)\right]. \tag{5}$$

Correspondingly, the futures price for a continuously marked-to-market futures contract is a martingale under the risk-neutral measure. Given the terminal spot price distribution under the risk-neutral measure, we can use Equation (5) to determine any prior futures price.

Similarly, a European option with a payoff C(T) at date T can be valued using the equation

$$C(t) = E_t\left[\exp\left[\int_t^T r(u)du\right]C(T)\right]. \tag{6}$$

Finally, American-style claims can be valued using a modified version of Equation (6), which accounts for early exercise. In practice, we can compute futures options prices using a path-dependent binomial-style model by discretising Equations (2) and (4) under the risk-neutral measure. For details, see Amin and Morton (1994).

HJM VOLATILITY FUNCTIONS

To minimise the possibility of model misspecification, we study five volatility models. In terms of Equation (1), these can be stated as

1. Ho and Lee (1986) model: $\sigma(t,T,f(t,T)) = \sigma_0$.
2. CIR (1985): $\sigma(t,T,f(t,T)) = \sigma_0 f(t,T)^{1/2}$.
3. Courtadon (1982): $\sigma(t,T,f(t,T)) = \sigma_0 f(t,T)$.
4. Vasicek (1977): $\sigma(t,T,f(t,T)) = \sigma_0 \exp(-\lambda(T-t))$.
5. Linear Proportional (HJM, 1992): $\sigma(t,T,f(t,T)) = [\sigma_0 + \sigma_1(T-t)]\, f(t,T)$.

Specification (3) above is identical to the "Black model" (1976) used by practitioners for pricing interest rate caps and floors - see Brace, Gatarek, and Musiela (1995) for details. Furthermore, as Eurodollar futures options are based on forward interest rates with maturity up to one year, specifications (4) and (5) permit the volatility of forward rates with maturity between 0 and 1 year to have different volatilities. However, the specific parameterisations force a unique maturity structure. By testing models that permit different maturity structures of forward rate volatilities, we can make inferences about these maturity structures.

The five separate specifications can be embedded in a unique volatility specification that nests the functions. However since we estimate parameters each day using only the small number of available option prices, this encompassing specification yields unstable parameter estimates (Amin and Morton, (1994)). Unlike an estimation exercise using historical interest rate changes, which uses a long time series, the implied estimation procedure uses only the small number of options traded on each date. Therefore, we study the volatility functions separately.

In this chapter we consider only single-factor HJM models, that is, models with a single Brownian motion (shock) in Equation (2) to determine the evolution of forward rates. We have also implemented a two-factor model. The parameter estimates in a two-factor model are unstable, however, because futures options do not contain sufficient information to infer the correlation structure embedded in a multiple-factor model. Even with over-the-counter (OTC) caps and floors,[3] this estimation exercise is fruitless. Since we use a single-factor model to determine identical volatilities, we focus our attention on the historical volatility of single rate, taken as the shortest maturity interest rate obtained from the Eurodollar futures rates. We term this rate the spot interest rate.

ESTIMATING THE TERM STRUCTURE OF FORWARD RATES AND VOLATILITY PARAMETERS

As forward rates do not equal futures rates with stochastic interest rates, we cannot estimate forward rates directly from the futures prices (rates). For each day in the data sample, we estimate the term structure of forward interest rates up to the maturity of the longest maturity option, using the futures prices and the previous day's parameter estimates to satisfy Equations (1) and (5). Under our assumptions, the term structure is unique and reprices all the futures exactly under each term-structure model. Since the forward-futures rate mapping is model dependent, the estimated daily term structure is different for each model. However, in practice, all models yield estimates within 1/100 of a basis point (10^{-6}) for the spot rate.

After estimating the forward rates, we use the interest rate model to estimate the parameters. Specifically, we minimise the sum of the squares of the errors between model and market prices of all available options. Model option prices are computed using (6) by discretising (2) and (4) on a path-dependent tree with 10 time steps. Repeating this process for each model, for each day in the sample period, yields a daily time series of implied parameter estimates and implied volatilities. For additional details on this estimation, see Amin and Morton (1994).

Before analysing the implied volatility series from each model, we must interpret the different implied volatility parameters for each date, given our model assumption that volatility parameters are constant. There are two interpretations to reconcile this apparent inconsistency. First, the daily implied volatility estimation might reflect estimation errors that lead to different values. By estimating unknown parameters on several different days, we can construct reliable statistical measures. Note that even with constant parameters, the volatility need not be constant since it can depend on the spot rate level. The forecasting exercise is therefore still informative.

A second, more plausible interpretation is that volatility varies with both interest rate levels and time. However, the implied volatility captures the market's volatility forecast during the remaining life of the option. As Amin and Morton (1994) argue, "prices in stochastic volatility models are of similar form to those in a constant volatility model, with volatility terms in the latter replaced by their conditional expected levels in the stochastic volatility environment."

Note that the bias introduced by using a model with deterministic volatility parameters from which daily implied volatilities are computed is very small relative to a model that explicitly accounts for the stochastic nature of volatility. See Lamoureux and Lastrapes (1993) for details.

HJM IMPLIED VOLATILITY

We compute the implied volatility of the spot interest rate as follows. First, we compute implied parameter values from each model, as described in the previous section. Second, using the functional form of each volatility specification, we compute the daily implied volatility of the spot interest rate, $\sigma(t,t,f(t,t))$, for each model. For example, for the CIR specification, the implied volatility of the spot interest rate is

$$\sigma\big(t,t,f(t,t)\big) = \sigma_0 f(t,t)^{1/2}, \qquad (7)$$

where we substitute the implied parameter estimate for σ_0 in the above equation. We then use the implied spot rate volatility from each model in our analysis.

Time-series models of volatility

In this section we study the volatility forecasts estimated using only historical spot interest rates. We will compare these forecasts with implied volatility forecasts in the next section.

Figure 1 provides a model-independent overview of the data. In Figure 1 we plot the daily interest rate level, the daily interest rate change (shock), and the realised 20-day moving average of daily squared spot interest rate changes. Standardising (for comparison), we subtract the sample mean for each series and then divide by the sample standard deviation. We then

1. Daily time series of rate, rate change and rolling standard deviation of rate changes

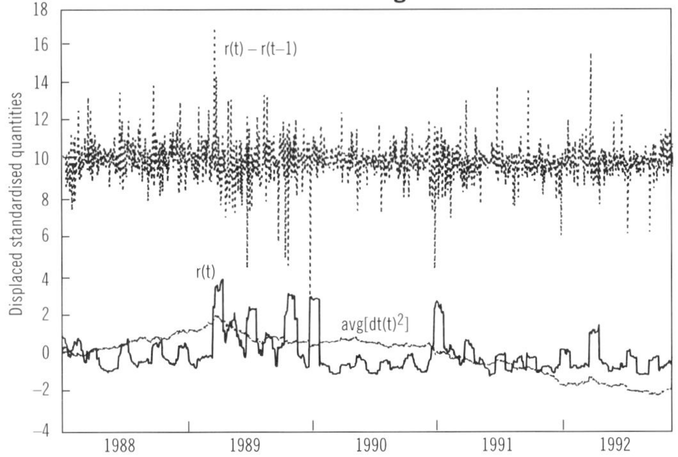

This figure plots the z-values for the three series represented by the daily spot Eurodollar interest rate level, r(t), implied from the first Eurodollar contract, the daily change in the spot interest rate (interest rate shock = r(t) – r(t–1)), and the realised 20-day moving average of the daily squared spot interest rate changes (marked as avg[dr(t)^2] on the graph). The z-values are obtained for each series by subtracting the sample mean and dividing by the sample standard deviation. The data period is January 1, 1988– November 10, 1992.

translate the standardised daily shocks series by 10 for graphic convenience. The moving average of the daily squared spot interest rate changes proxies for the realised volatility of interest rate changes.

From Figure 1 several patterns are apparent. First, volatility clustering (persistence) is more prevalent during a high interest rate period (1989). Indeed, the large shocks in 1991 and 1992, when interest rates were low, did not significantly increase volatility. Second, interest rate shocks occur at all periods and levels, even though they are more frequent during high interest rate periods. These observations affect the interest rate levels and Garch terms in our tests.

Table 1. Dynamics of the "spot rate" and adjustment for biases due to contract rollover

Mean equation representing the true interest rate process (r_t):

$$r_t - r_{t-1} = a + br_{t-1} + \varepsilon(t).$$

Observed interest rate process after adjusting for the contract rollover effect:*

$$r_t^{obs} = r_t + qSwitch_t YCslope_{t-1}.$$

Model for observed interest rate (the estimation is based on this equation):

$$r_t^{obs} - r_{t-1}^{obs} = r_t - r_{t-1} + qSwitch_t YCslope_{t-1} - qSwitch_{t-1} YCslope_{t-2}$$
$$= a + br_{t-1}^{obs} + qSwitch_t YCslope_{t-1} - (1+b)qSwitch_{t-1} YCslope_{t-2} + \varepsilon_t.$$

Parameter estimates based on daily interest rates (in %) from January 1, 1988–November 10, 1992

	a	b	q
Estimate	–0.0058	0.0004	0.1164
t-statistic	(–0.72)	(0.33)	(3.18)

Summary statistics

	Mean	Std dev	Skewness	Kurtosis	Q(5)	Q(10)
ε_t	0.0000	0.0786	–0.3526	7.7846	12.4	19.7
ε_t^2	0.0062	0.0193	9.9664	134.5258	14.8	25.8

As the spot interest rate is estimated to be the forward rate implicit in the first Eurodollar futures contract, we need to correct explicitly for expiration day effects when we switch from the expiring contract to the next contract. These two contracts differ in maturity by three months. On expiration dates, we subtract any effect due to the slope of the term structure. This effect is also estimated along with the mean equation.
The interest rate is in percent and the sample period is from January 1, 1998 to November 10, 1992. The t-statistics are White heteroskedasticity consistent t-statistics. Q(n) is the nth-order Box–Pierce statistics for serial correlation.

* Switch is a dummy variable that takes a value of 1 if a new Eurodollar futures contract is used starting at day t and $YCslope_{t-1}$ is the slope of the yield curve at time t – 1 (before the switching date). YCslope is proxied by the observed spread between the one-year forward rate and the one-month forward rate.

Before applying our formal statistical tests we must adjust spot interest rates for the effect of futures expiration dates. On the expiration date we switch from the expiring contract to the next maturity contract to estimate the spot interest rate. This contract switching leads to spurious shocks to the "spot" rate. With an upward sloping yield curve we would experience a spurious increase in rates the day after a futures expiration date.

Let r(t) be the spot interest rate at date t and r^{obs} be the interest rate observed from the first futures contract each day. We assume these two rates are related by

$$r^{obs}(t) = r(t) + qSwitch(t)YCslope(t-1), \quad (8)$$

where q is the regression coefficient, Switch(t) is the indicator function for a contract switching date, and YCslope(t – 1) is the slope of the term structure on date t – 1. The one year/one month forward rate proxies for the slope. We then assume a simple mean reversion for the spot rate:

$$r(t) - r(t-1) = a + br(t-1) + \varepsilon(t), \quad (9)$$

where ε(t) is the shock to the interest rate at date t. Based on Equations (8) and (9), we derive the observed spot rate process:

$$r^{obs}(t) - r^{obs}(t-1) = a + br^{obs}(t-1) + qSwitch(t)YCslope(t-1) - (1+b)qSwitch(t-1)YCslope(t-2) + \varepsilon(t). \quad (10)$$

By estimating q in Equation (10), we can construct r(t) from $r^{obs}(t)$ in Equation (8). This estimation also yields the time-series estimates for the interest rate shocks, ε(t).

Table 1 provides daily volatility estimates and diagnostic statistics. A significant q parameter indicates a contract switching effect. The Box–Pierce statistic for serial correlation for ε(t) does not show any evidence of misspecification in the mean equation. However, the same statistic for $\varepsilon^2(t)$ indicates significant serial correlation, which indicates time-varying volatility.

We now consider the historical volatility models. First, we consider Garch models. These models offer a natural benchmark for assessing the information content of the implied volatility. For examples of these models, see Brenner, Harjes and Kroner (1993), Engle, Lilien and Robins (1987), Engle, Ng and Rothschild (1990), Koedijk et al (1994), and Longstaff and Schwartz (1992).

Let $h(t)$ be the variance of $r(t) - r(t-1)$ conditional on all information available at time $t-1$. In a typical Garch(1,1) model, $h(t)$ is specified as

$$h(t) = \omega + \beta h(t-1) + \alpha\varepsilon^2(t-1), \qquad (11)$$

where ω, β, and α are parameters of the model. In this equation the shock effect, or dependence on past interest rate shocks, contrasts with the "level effect" in many interest rate models (including the CIR, Courtadon, and HJM linear proportional models) where volatility depends only on past interest rate levels.

In addition to the Garch(1,1) model, we also consider the Garch model due to Glosten et al. (1993) (the GJR model), which incorporates an asymmetric volatility response due to positive and negative shocks. Several studies have found that stock return volatility increases more after negative shocks than after positive shocks. This difference may represent involuntary liquidation of positions due to margin calls, stop-loss strategies, or other market frictions following significant price drops. Volatility dependence on the direction of rate moves can also create an asymmetric effect. To incorporate this asymmetry, GJN specify the volatility equation as

$$h(t) = \omega + \beta h(t-1) + \alpha\varepsilon^2(t-1) + \alpha\_\eta^2(t-1), \quad (12)$$

where $\eta(t-1) = \max[0, -\varepsilon(t-1)]$. Here $\eta(t-1)$ represents the asymmetric negative shock to the interest rate. A positive (negative) $\alpha\_$ coefficient implies that the volatility increase is larger (smaller) after a negative shock than after a positive one.

To estimate the volatility equations, we take the estimate residual, $\varepsilon(t)$, from Equation (10) as a predetermined variable and then use maximum likelihood to estimate the variance equation. This procedure follows the two-step estimation approach of Pagan and Schwert (1990) and Gallant, Rossi, and Tauchen (1993).

The diagnostic statistics in Table 1 indicate that the distribution of $\varepsilon(t)$ is fat tailed. Therefore, we assume a t-distribution (versus normal) for $\varepsilon(t)$ for more precise statistical inference (Bollerslev, (1987)). To ensure convergence of the estimates, we assume that the degrees of freedom parameter of the t-distribution is given by a logistic function dependent on a parameter, θ, which is unrestricted. Specifically we assume

$$df(t\text{-distribution}) = 5 + 30\left[1 - \frac{1}{1+\exp[-10(\theta-0.5)]}\right]. \quad (13)$$

This transformation bounds the degrees of freedom of the t-distribution between 5 and 35. The lower bound ensures a finite fourth moment of the t-distribution, while the upper bound ensures that we do not have to compute very high-order factorials when evaluating the gamma function in the t-distribution density. The other parameter values in the logistic function ensure a smooth transition to the upper and lower bounds. These parameter values mainly affect the speed of convergence of the maximum likelihood estimation. When θ is negative, the degree of freedom of the t-distribution is very close to 35, providing a virtually normal distribution. Therefore a significantly positive θ indicates a rejection of normality. In our estimations θ is significantly positive (around 1.8). The corresponding asymptotic t-statistic is always significantly greater than 2.0. For conciseness, these values are not reported.

In Table 2 we report the estimation results for the Garch and GJR specifications (Equations (11) and (12)) and the level effect models. As expected, the coefficient of $\varepsilon^2(t-1)$ is significant in the Garch equation. Further, the coefficient of the asymmetric response term in the GJR specification is significantly negative. Therefore interest rate volatility increases more after an interest rate increase than after a decrease. This finding parallels the finding that return volatility increases by a larger amount after negative return shocks than after positive return shocks (see Engle and Ng (1993); Nelson (1991)). Both results are consistent if viewed in price terms since bond prices decrease as interest rates increase. Therefore price decreases lead to higher volatility in both the stock and fixed-income markets.

To study historical volatility models based on rate levels we estimate the Courtadon (1982) and CIR (1985) models. The Courtadon (1982) model mimics the linear proportional model if we focus on a single rate. Further, the Ho and Lee (1986) and Vasicek (1977) models reduce to a constant volatility model, which is a special case of the Garch model.[4] Specifically, the estimated models are

$$h(t) = \gamma\, r(t-1), \text{ (Courtadon);} \qquad (14)$$

$$h(t) = \gamma \sqrt{r(t-1)}, \text{ (CIR).} \qquad (15)$$

Using only historical data, these models cannot capture the persistence in the volatility that the Garch and GJR models capture. Therefore their log-likelihood is significantly lower. Including an additional constant term in Equations (14) and (15) does not significantly affect the estimates for γ or the log-likelihood.

We now incorporate interest rate levels in the Garch and GJR models to explain volatility. Further, we also test the interaction between rate levels and the Garch-type volatility clustering found by Brenner, Harjes and Kroner (1993) and Koedijk et al (1994). Specifically, these authors find that the impact of shocks to volatility is lower when interest rates are low than when they are high. One explanation is as follows. At low rates, if a large shock were to cause a large and persistent (through the Garch term $h(t)$) increase in volatility, the probability of negative interest rates would be very high. In fact, a criticism of Garch-type models for interest rate volatility is that they do not preclude negative interest rates. The interaction term scales the squared shocks by the level of interest rates. Therefore it incorporates Garch-type effects in the determination of interest rate volatility without permitting a very high probability of negative interest rates.

On the economic side, it is also likely that investors react differently under different interest rate regimes. For example, many investors maintain a duration target for their asset portfolio. As rates change, these investors rebalance their bond portfolio to maintain their duration target. Since bond prices are convex functions of interest rates, an interest rate increase will decrease the duration of a bond portfolio. Therefore the investor will buy long-term bonds and sell short-term bonds. This rebalancing will counter the initial rate shocks, as he will be buying (selling) the short end following a short rate increase (decrease). Furthermore, since bond prices are more convex at low rate levels, the counteraction effect will be stronger when rates are low. Hence, following large shocks, we are less likely to see high volatility at low rates.

Ignoring the interaction of rate levels and shocks can lead to significantly wrongly estimated parameters (Brenner, Harjes and Kroner, 1993). For example, the power parameter for the volatility sensitivity to the rate level as estimated by Chan et al. (1992) is almost three times as high without making allowances for the interaction.

To address this interaction, we consider four combinations of the shock and level effects by combining the Garch and GJR models individually with the Courtadon and CIR volatility specifications. For consistency with the term incorporating the interest rate level, we define the interaction term as $J(t-1) = r(t-1)\varepsilon^2(t-1)$ for the Courtadon model and

$$C(t-1) = \sqrt{r(t-1)}\,\varepsilon^2(t-1)$$

for the CIR model. The resulting equations are

1. Mixed Garch and Courtadon model:

$$h(t) = \omega + \beta h(t-1) + \alpha\varepsilon^2(t-1) + \phi J(t-1) + \gamma r(t-1). \qquad (16)$$

2. Mixed Garch and CIR model:

$$h(t) = \omega + \beta h(t-1) + \alpha\varepsilon^2(t-1) + \phi C(t-1) + \gamma\sqrt{r(t-1)}. \qquad (17)$$

3. Mixed GJR and Courtadon model:

$$h(t) = \omega + \beta h(t-1) + \alpha\varepsilon^2(t-1) + \phi J(t-1) + \gamma r(t-1) + \alpha\_\eta^2(t-1). \qquad (18)$$

4. Mixed GJR and CIR model:

Table 2. Alternative volatility models (historical estimates)

Garch models (based on past interest rate shocks)

Garch(1,1)

	log L	Constant	h_{t-1}	ε^2_{t-1}
Coefficient	1553.2	0.000	0.937	0.035
t-statistic		2.5	59.8	4.0

Glosten-Jagannathan-Runkle $[\eta_{t-1} = \max(0, -\varepsilon_{t-1})]$

	log L	Constant	h_{t-1}	ε^2_{t-1}	η^2_{t-1}
Coefficient	1557.1	0.000	0.921	0.071	−0.051
t-statistic		2.7	52.9	4.0	−2.9

Models based on the level of interest rates

Cox-Ingersoll-Ross (CIR)

	log L	$\sqrt{r_{t-1}}$
Coefficient	1535.7	0.002
t-statistic		21.9

Courtadon

	log L	r_{t-1}
Coefficient	1539.5	0.001
t-statistic		22.1

Hybrid models

Mixed Garch(1,1) and Courtadon $(J_{t-1} = r_{t-1}\varepsilon^2_{t-1})$

	log L	Constant	h_{t-1}	ε^2_{t-1}	J_{t-1}	r_{t-1}
Coefficient	1557.4	0.001	0.809	−0.118	0.025	0.000
t-statistic		5.9	17.8	−8.8	5.9	−1.7

Mixed Garch(1,1) and CIR $(C_{t-1} = \sqrt{r_{t-1}}\varepsilon^2_{t-1})$

	log L	Constant	h_{t-1}	ε^2_{t-1}	C_{t-1}	$\sqrt{r_{t-1}}$
Coefficient	1560.7	0.000	0.890	−0.096	0.054	0.000
t-statistic		1.5	30.7	−1.8	2.4	−0.3

Mixed GJR and Courtadon

	log L	Constant	h_{t-1}	ε^2_{t-1}	J_{t-1}	r_{t-1}	η^2_{t-1}
Coefficient	1561.9	0.000	0.891	0.009	0.007	0.000	−0.034
t-statistic		1.5	26.7	0.3	1.7	0.8	−1.8

Mixed GJR and CIR

	log L	Constant	h_{t-1}	ε^2_{t-1}	C_{t-1}	$\sqrt{r_{t-1}}$	η^2_{t-1}
Coefficient	1562.8	0.000	0.906	−0.065	0.047	0.000	−0.037
t-statistic		1.9	38.3	−1.3	2.5	−0.9	−2.2

This table reports the maximum likelihood parameter estimates for several historical volatility models, with volatility dependent on both interest rate levels and past shocks to the interest rate. For each model, the date t volatility, h_t is assumed to be linear in the specified variables with a conditional t-error distribution. The degree of freedom parameter of the t distribution (not reported) is estimated jointly with the other parameters. The sample period is from January 1, 1988–November 10, 1992; r_t is the spot interest rate; ε_t is the interest rate shock and h_t is the volatility at date t.

$$h(t) = \omega + \beta h(t-1) + \alpha\varepsilon^2(t-1) + \phi C(t-1) + \gamma\sqrt{r(t-1)} + \alpha\_\eta^2(t-1). \quad (19)$$

Table 2 presents the estimates for these hybrid volatilities. Interestingly, the interaction terms J(t – 1) and C(t – 1) swamp both interest rate level effects and the Garch-type terms. The GJR asymmetric response term is still significant after incorporating the interaction, although it is much weaker.

To contrast the Garch/GJR, level effect, and hybrid models, we plot the volatility h(t) against the shock ε(t – 1) at selected interest rate levels r(t – 1). These plots are a two-dimensional extension of the news impact curve of Engle and Ng (1993). Figure 2 represents the GJR model. It shows that a positive shock (an unexpected increase in the interest rate) causes a higher volatility than a negative shock of the same magnitude. Note that the model does not permit the lagged interest rate level to affect the volatility. Figure 3 represents the CIR model. It shows a flat graph along the axis for ε(t – 1) since the model does not permit a shock (Garch) effect. Finally, Figure 4 of the mixed GJR and CIR models shows the interaction effect. For a shock of the same magnitude, volatility is impacted less by rate shocks at low rates than at high rates.

Implied HJM volatility and historical volatility based on Garch and GJR models

In this section we compare the relative forecast ability of the implied HJM volatilities to the historical volatility models studied in the previous section.

TEST FRAMEWORK

One way to test the individual significance of historical and implied volatility is to test the nested form:

$$h(t) = \kappa h_{historical}(t) + \delta\sigma_1^2(t), \quad (20)$$

where $h_{historical}(t)$ is the conditional volatility based on past returns and shocks (from a Garch-type model) and $\sigma_1^2(t)$ is the implied (HJM) volatility from traded options. If κ is significant, but δ is not, then implied volatility provides no additional information about the actual volatility. Similarly, if δ is significant but κ is not, then the historical volatility contains no additional information.

In a Garch historical volatility model, k is multiplied by each coefficient in the Garch variance

2. GJR volatility as a function of lagged shock and rate level

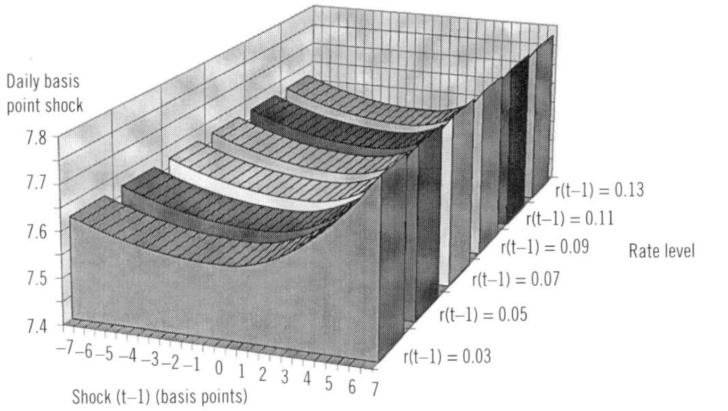

This figure plots the next period's forecast volatility for the spot rate interest rate based on the previous period's interest rate shock and rate level, using the GJR volatility model. The parameters of the GJR model are estimated using maximum likelihood with the daily time series of the spot rates (3-month Eurodollar interest rate implied from the first Eurodollar futures contract) during January 1, 1988–November 10, 1992.

3. CIR volatility as a function of lagged shock and rate level

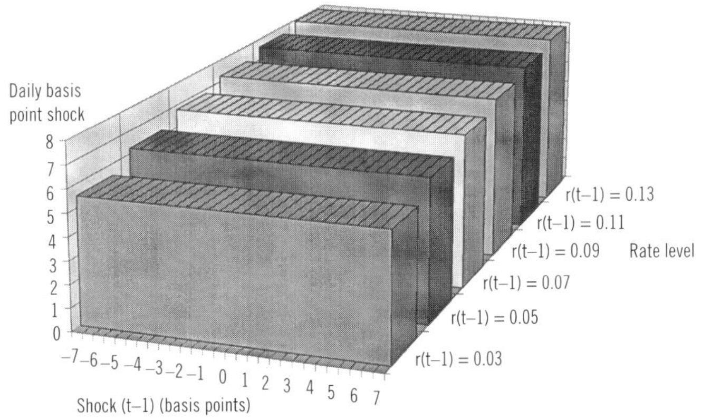

This figure plots the next period's forecast volatility based on the previous period's interest rate shock and rate level, based on the Cox, Ingersoll and Ross (1985) volatility model. The spot rate volatility is proportional to the square root of the spot interest rate. The proportionality parameter is estimated using maximum likelihood with the daily time series of the spot rates (3-month) Eurodollar interest rate implied from the first Eurodollar futures contract) during January 1, 1988– November 10, 1992.

4. Hybrid GJR and CIR volatility as a function of lagged shock and rate level

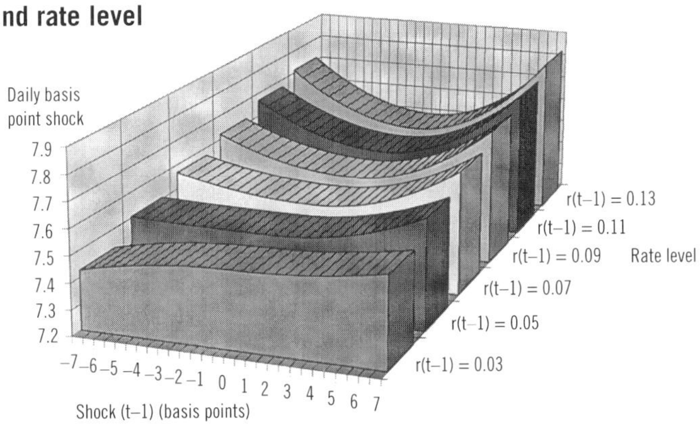

This figure plots the next period's forecast volatility based on the previous period's interest rate shock and rate level, based on the hybrid GJR and CIR volatility model. The parameters are estimated using maximum likelihood with the daily time series of the spot rates (3-month) Eurodollar interest rate implied from the first Eurodollar futures contract) during January 1, 1988–November 10, 1992.

equation. Thus it cannot be identified. In this case the significance of κ is equivalent to the significance of some Arch/Garch coefficients. Thus, unless we study non-linear historical volatility models, the relevant form is

$$h(t) = h_{garch}(t) + \delta\sigma_t^2(t). \tag{21}$$

Further, the implied volatility estimation yields $\sigma_1(t)^2$ to be the expectation of the average volatility between time t and the options expiration (Amin and Morton, 1994). However, the above equation is justifiable for two reasons. First, exchange-traded options are near to-the-money options whose price is almost linear in the expected average volatility. Second, if the volatility follows a simple mean reversion model (an AR(1)) such as

$$\sigma^2(t) = \kappa + \theta\sigma^2(t-1) + v(t),$$

where $v(t)$ is i.i.d. with a zero mean, then the time t expectation of the average volatility between time t and a later time T is just a simple linear function of $\sigma(t)^2$. Thus, if an AR(1) model approximates the volatility dynamics, $\sigma_1(t)^2$ is a reasonable substitute for $\sigma(t)^2$.

To test for the information effect of implied volatility, we first include the current implied volatility, $\sigma_1^2(t)$, in Equation (21). Since $\sigma_1^2(t)$ contains current information, this specification yields a strong test. Furthermore, the significance of $\varepsilon^2(t-1)$ in the testing equation provides a strong rejection of the informational efficiency of the implied volatility under all the maintained assumptions. Secondly, we construct a predictive test, including the lagged implied volatility, $[\sigma_1^2(t-1)]$, in Equation (21). The statistical significance of δ in the predictive test indicates the implied volatility's forecast ability relative to historical forecasts.

A NEW TESTING APPROACH

Day and Lewis (1992) and Lamoureux and Lastrapes (1993) implement a version of Equation (21) by embedding the implied volatility in a Garch equation.

$$h(t) = \omega + \beta h(t-1) + \alpha\varepsilon^2(t-1) + \delta\sigma_1(t)^2. \tag{22}$$

However, Equation (22) implies significantly different restrictions from Equation (21). Recursively substituting out the lagged conditional volatility in Equation (22), we find that

$$h(t) = \frac{\omega}{1-(\alpha+\beta)} + \alpha\sum_{i=0,t-1}(\alpha+\beta)^i v(t-1-i)$$
$$+\delta\sigma_1^2(t) + \delta\sum_{i=1,t-1}(\alpha+\beta)^i\sigma_1^2(t-i). \tag{23}$$

Notice that in a standard Garch(1,1) model

$$h(t) = \omega + \beta h(t-1) + \alpha\varepsilon^2(t-1)$$
$$= \omega + (\alpha+\beta)h(t-1) + \alpha\left[\varepsilon^2(t-1) - h(t-1)\right]$$

$$= \frac{\omega}{1-(\alpha+\beta)} + \alpha\sum_{i=0,t-1}(\alpha+\beta)^i v(t-1-i). \tag{24}$$

Comparing Equations (23) and (24), we observe that the first two terms of Equation (23) are equivalent to the Garch conditional variance. If we term the Garch volatility given by the right-hand side of Equation (24) as $h_{garch}(t)$, we can rewrite Equation (23) as

$$h(t) = h_{garch}(t) + \delta\sigma_1^2(t) +$$
$$\delta\sum_{i=1,t-1}(\alpha+\beta)^i\sigma_1^2(t-i).$$

Thus Equation (22) is equivalent to the estimation equation

$$h(t) = h_{garch}(t) + \delta\sigma_1^2(t) + \sum_{i=1,t-1}\delta_i\sigma_1^2(t-i),$$

with the constraints $\delta_i = \delta(\alpha+\beta)^i$ for all $i = 1,\ldots,t-1$.

If the lagged implied volatility is uninformative, its coefficient will be zero. However, our constraints do not allow a zero coefficient. Specifically, if α and β are significant and the current implied volatility contains some volatility information (δ is significantly different from zero), then the δ_is cannot be zero.

Thus these constraints provide a joint test of the significance of current and multiple lagged implied volatilities with a specific lag structure. However, since this joint test does not directly address the current implied volatility, it cannot test the information content of this volatility. Furthermore, it yields a downwardly biased estimate for δ. If the Arch and Garch coefficients are not significantly affected, we can approximate the magnitude of this bias. Let h_m be the sample unconditional variance. At the maximum of the likelihood function, the expected conditional variance (evaluated at the estimated parameters) should be fairly close to the sample unconditional variance. Similarly, the expected value of the implied volatility should be proportional to the sample unconditional variance. Denoting this proportionality factor as g, for parameters estimated from Equation (21) (ω, α, β, and δ), we find

$$h_m = \frac{\omega}{1-(\alpha+\beta)} + \delta g h_m.$$

Note that the unconditional variance under a Garch(1, 1) model is equal to

$$\frac{\omega}{1-(\alpha+\beta)}.$$

Conversely, using parameters estimated from Equations (22) or (23) (ω, α, β, and δ^*) provides

$$h_m = \frac{\omega}{1-(\alpha+\beta)} + \delta^* gh_m\left[1-(\alpha+\beta)^T\right]\frac{\omega}{1-(\alpha+\beta)}$$

where T is the number of observations.

If the number of observations is large enough and the Arch and Garch parameters are not significantly affected by specification choice, we can identify the relationship between δ^* and δ:

$$\delta^* = \delta(1-\alpha-\beta).$$

Thus, if $\alpha + \beta = 0.8$, a Day and Lewis (1992) δ estimate could be as small as 20% of the true δ. Of course the actual bias also depends on the effect of the specification on the estimates of a and b. In fact, the Day and Lewis (1992) approach will probably yield a downward biased β. In their article, Day and Lewis (1992) estimate β to be negative, implying a very unusual lag structure.

To correct for this bias we eliminate the implicit lagged implied volatility terms. Consider the following equation:

$$\begin{aligned} h(t) &= h_{garch}(t) + \delta\sigma_1^2(t) \\ &= \frac{\omega}{1-(\alpha+\beta)} + \\ &\quad \alpha\sum\nolimits_{i=0,t-1}(\alpha+\beta)^i v(t-1-i) + \delta\sigma_1^2(t). \end{aligned}$$

Rewriting this equation in autoregressive form, with L as the lag operator creates

$$h(t) = \frac{\omega}{1-(\alpha+\beta)} + \frac{\alpha}{1-(\alpha+\beta)L}v(t-1) + \delta\sigma_1^2(t).$$

Multiplying both sides by $1 - (\alpha + \beta)L$ and rearranging terms yields the corrected test equation:

$$\begin{aligned} h(t) &= \omega + \beta h(t-1) + \alpha\varepsilon^2(t-1) \\ &\quad \delta\sigma_1^2(t) - \delta(\alpha+\beta)\sigma_1^2(t-1). \end{aligned} \qquad (25)$$

Equation (25) yields an unbiased method for testing the information content of the current implied volatility. If the market is informationally efficient and the option pricing model is valid, $\sigma_1(t)^2$ incorporates all current and past information. Thus the Arch terms, $h(t - 1)$ and $\varepsilon(t - 1)^2$ should provide no added explanatory power for $h(t)$. However, if α and β are significant, then either the market is not informationally efficient or the option pricing model is misspecified.

In addition to the Day and Lewis (1992)-type tests based on Equation (22), we have also performed tests based on the bias-corrected Equation (25) and the corresponding equations for the GJR and hybrid models.

To conduct our predictive test, we derive the test equation by replacing the implied volatility in Equation (20) by its one-period lagged counterpart:

$$\begin{aligned} h(t) &= h_{garch}(t) + \delta\sigma_1^2(t-1) \\ &= \frac{\omega}{1-(\alpha+\beta)} + \\ &\quad \alpha\sum\nolimits_{i=0,t-1}(\alpha+\beta)^i v(t-1-i) + \delta\sigma_1^2(t-1). \end{aligned}$$

We can rewrite this equation as

$$\begin{aligned} h(t) &= \omega + \beta h(t-1) + \alpha\varepsilon^2(t-1) + \\ &\quad \delta\sigma_1^2(t-1) - \delta(\alpha+\beta)\sigma_1^2(t-2). \end{aligned} \qquad (26)$$

Equation (26) compares the one-period-ahead implied volatility forecast to the Garch forecast. For testing the HJM model and the information content of the implied volatility, this test is cleaner than a multiperiod forecast comparison, which requires a dynamic implied volatility model. This model becomes complicated if the HJM model is not correct. Furthermore, multiperiod comparisons require computation of the multiperiod expected average volatility from the Garch model using numerical integration. This computation introduces additional numerical errors. None the less, for completeness, we perform a multiperiod forecast comparison similar to that of Canina and Figlewski (1993), which we report below.

Empirical results comparing historical forecasts with implied volatilities

In this section we analyse the results of the empirical tests developed in the previous section.

CONTEMPORANEOUS IMPLIED VOLATILITY

We first estimate Equations (22) and (25) with the current implied volatility (see Table 3 for Garch results). From Table 3 we see that implied volatilities from all five HJM models are strongly significant. However, the Day-Lewis equation coefficient is significantly weaker. In fact, the coefficient of the implied volatility term (δ) in our persistence-corrected equation is at least

Table 3. Implied volatility and Garch models

	log L	Constant ω	h_{t-1} β	ε^2_{t-1} α	σ^2_{1t} δ
Variance equation without persistence adjustment (Day-Lewis approach) $h_t = \omega + \beta h_{t-1} + \alpha\varepsilon^2_{t-1} + \delta\sigma^2_{1t}$					
Ho-Lee model implied volatility					
Coefficient	1563.2	0.000	0.838	0.050	0.08
t-statistic		0.0	16.3	3.2	2.4
Courtadon model implied volatility					
Coefficient	1565.2	0.000	0.662	0.042	0.234
t-statistic		0.0	4.4	2.1	2.1
Linear proportional model implied volatility					
Coefficient	1576.9	0.000	0.780	0.025	0.251
t-statistic		–1.5	11.2	1.8	2.9
Cox-Ingersoll-Ross model implied volatility					
Coefficient	1564.9	0.000	0.807	0.047	0.120
t-statistic		–0.5	11.3	2.8	2.2
Vasicek model implied volatility					
Coefficient	1576.0	0.000	0.733	0.029	0.283
t-statistic		–0.3	6.9	1.8	2.3
Variance equation with persistence adjustment $h_t = \omega + \beta h_{t-1} + \alpha\varepsilon^2_{t-1} + \delta\sigma^2_{1t} - \delta(\beta + \alpha)\sigma^2_{1t-1}$					
Ho-Lee model implied volatility					
Coefficient	1563.9	0.000	0.860	0.039	0.725
t-statistic		0.0	17.6	2.8	6.1
Courtadon model implied volatility					
Coefficient	1567.8	0.000	0.863	0.036	0.795
t-statistic		0.0	4.4	2.1	2.1
Linear proportional model implied volatility					
Coefficient	1566.3	0.000	0.788	0.030	0.854
t-statistic		1.4	6.9	1.9	9.9
Cox-Ingersoll-Ross model implied volatility					
Coefficient	1566.4	0.000	0.858	0.040	0.805
t-statistic		–0.2	16.8	2.7	6.3
Vasicek model implied volatility					
Coefficient	1569.9	0.000	0.766	0.022	1.04
t-statistic		0.7	4.5	1.5	9.3

This table reports the maximum likelihood parameter estimates for the coefficients of HJM implied volatility and Garch-style historical volatility in the variance equation. Several HJM volatility functions are tested. The implied volatility is tested in the equation in two ways. The first is based on Day and Lewis (1992) and the second corrects for an implicit persistence structure for the lagged implied volatility in Day and Lewis; r_t is the spot interest rate, ε_t is the interest rate shock, σ_{1t} is the implied volatility, and h_t is the volatility at date t.

three times its corresponding value from the uncorrected equation. For example, in the CIR case, the coefficient increases from 0.12 to 0.805 after the correction. As expected, the Day-Lewis and Lamoureux-Lastrapes implicit lag structure creates an underestimate of the effect of the implied volatility.

When computing implied volatility with the Ho-Lee, Courtadon, or the CIR models, we find that the squared residual term, $\varepsilon_2(t - 1)$ (which represents the Arch effect), is strongly significant. However, it is only marginally significant for the HJM linear proportional model and marginally insignificant for the Vasicek model. Thus the HJM linear proportional and Vasicek models capture the spot rate volatility better than the Garch models. Since the Vasicek and linear proportional HJM models permit the volatility of different maturity rates to be different, the term structure of interest rate volatility seems important in explaining interest rate volatilities.

In Table 4 we report the results of comparing the GJR specification with the implied volatility in our persistence corrected equation. Note that the Arch terms are insignificant for both the Vasicek (1977) and the linear proportional HJM model. Interestingly the implied volatility captures the asymmetric response effect, making the asymmetric response term insignificant even in equations with significant Arch terms.

Although the Garch/GJR parameter, β, is significant in Table 4, there is no Garch effect when the α parameter is insignificant. We recall that Equation (25) is equivalent to

$$h(t) = \frac{\omega}{1-(\alpha+\beta)} + \frac{\alpha}{1-(\alpha+\beta)L}\left[\varepsilon^2(t-1) - h(t-1)\right] + \delta\sigma_1^2(t), \qquad (27)$$

where L is the lag operator. When α is zero, the second term in the above equation drops out, leaving multiple optima that correspond to different values of ω and β that yield the same value for $\omega/(1 - \beta)$. In this case, since we cannot estimate β, we also cannot interpret its standard error.

In our test of implied volatility, a significant interaction effect for interest rates and previous period stocks implies an inefficient implied volatility forecast. Recall that our results with the hybrid models using historical data indicate a strong interaction term in Table 2. By testing whether the implied volatility from simple volatility models captures this interaction effect we can provide a more powerful test of the interaction hypothesis.

To test for an interaction effect, we add $r(t - 1)\varepsilon^2(t - 1)$ and $r(t - 1)$ into Equation (25) to obtain

$$h(t) = \omega + \beta h(t-1) + \alpha\varepsilon^2(t-1) + \phi r(t-1)\varepsilon^2(t-1) + \gamma r(t-1) + \delta\sigma_1^2(t) - \delta(\alpha+\beta)\sigma_1^2(t-1). \qquad (28)$$

With Equation (28) we can evaluate the information content of implied volatility relative to the mixed Garch and Courtadon models. Specifically, a significant ϕ coefficient suggests an interaction effect between the Garch term and the interest rate level, whereas a significant γ coefficient indicates misspecification of the sensitivity of volatility to the interest rate level. The test equation using the mixed GJR and Courtadon model as the benchmark is

$$h(t) = \omega + \beta h(t-1) + \alpha\varepsilon^2(t-1) + \phi r(t-1)\varepsilon^2(t-1) + \gamma r(t-1) + \alpha\_\eta^2(t-1) + \delta\sigma_1^2(t) - \delta(\alpha+\beta)\sigma_1^2(t-1). \qquad (29)$$

For conciseness, only the results with Equation (29) are reported in Table 5. The results with Equation (28) are similar.

To test our mixed GJR and CIN models, we replace $r(t-1)$ with $\sqrt{r(t-1)}$ in Equation (29):

$$h(t) = \omega + \beta h(t-1) + \alpha\varepsilon^2(t-1) + \phi\sqrt{r(t-1)}\varepsilon^2(t-1) + \gamma\sqrt{r(t-1)} + \alpha\_\eta^2(t-1) + \delta\sigma_1^2(t) - \delta(\alpha+\beta)\sigma_1^2(t-1). \qquad (30)$$

Considering both $r(t-1)$ and $\sqrt{r(t-1)}$, we can also test to see if the functional form of the volatility dependence on interest rate levels is misspecified. These results are also reported in Table 5.

Notice that the coefficient for the Garch term $\varepsilon^2(t-1)$ in all cases is negative. It is also negative in the estimates with the Garch model in Equation (28) (results not reported). However, note that the total impact of a shock to volatility under Equation (30) is $[\alpha + \phi r(t-1)]\varepsilon^2(t-1)$. Hence, even if α is negative, the total impact is still positive as long as $\alpha + \phi r(t-1)$ is positive, a condition that is always satisfied in our estimation. As the interest rate is expressed as a percentage, the product of $r(t-1)$ and ϕ dominates α. Further, the estimated implied volatility coefficient is significantly lower than with only the Garch/GJR terms (see Tables 3 and 4). This

Table 4. Implied volatility and GJR volatility

	log L	Constant ω	h_{t-1} β	ε^2_{t-1} α	σ^2_{1t} δ	η^2_{t-1} $\alpha\_$
Ho-Lee model implied volatility						
Coefficient	1563.8	0.000	0.870	0.038	0.712	–0.006
t-statistic		0.1	19.0	2.3	5.6	–0.3
Courtadon model implied volatility						
Coefficient	1567.7	0.000	0.869	0.038	0.793	–0.008
t-statistic		–0.1	18.1	2.2	6.0	–0.4
Linear proportional model implied volatility						
Coefficient	1567.1	0.000	0.776	0.016	0.888	0.019
t-statistic		1.1	5.3	1.0	9.3	0.7
Cox-Ingersoll-Ross model implied volatility						
Coefficient	1566.1	0.000	0.871	0.036	0.741	–0.005
t-statistic		–0.1	18.5	2.2	5.9	–0.3
Vasicek model implied volatility						
Coefficient	1569.9	0.000	0.764	0.016	0.950	0.007
t-statistic		0.9	4.0	1.0	8.5	0.3

This table reports the maximum likelihood parameter estimates for the coefficients of the HJM implied volatility and GJR historical volatility terms in the variance equation. Several different HJM volatility specifications are tested. The variance equation is corrected for the implicit lag structure of implied volatility in the Day and Lewis (1992) approach; r_t is the spot interest rate, ε_t is the interest rate shock, σ_{1t} is the implied volatility and h_t is the volatility at date t.

Variance equation estimated:

$h_t = \omega + \beta h_{t-1} + \alpha\varepsilon^2_{t-1} + \delta\sigma^2_{1t} - \delta(\beta+\alpha)\sigma^2_{1t-1} + \alpha\_\eta^2_{t-1}$

when $\eta_{t-1} = \max[0, -\varepsilon_{t-1}]$

Table 5. Implied volatility and mixed GJR/interest rate dependent models

Implied volatility versus mixed GJR and Courtadon model

$h_t = \omega + \beta h_{t-1} + \alpha\varepsilon^2_{t-1} + \delta\sigma^2_{1t} - \delta(\beta+\alpha)\sigma^2_{1t-1} + \phi J_{t-1} + \gamma r_{t-1} + \alpha\_\eta^2_{t-1} + \phi r_{t-1}\eta^2_{t-1}$

where $J_{t-1} = r_{t-1}\varepsilon^2_{t-1}$ and $\eta_{t-1} = \max[0, -\varepsilon_{t-1}]$

	log L	Constant ω	h_{t-1} β	ε^2_{t-1} α	σ^2_{1t} δ	J_{t-1} ϕ	r_{t-1} γ	η^2_{t-1} $\alpha\_$
Ho-Lee model implied volatility								
Coefficient	1568.5	0.000	0.840	–0.026	0.349	0.012	0.000	–0.26
t-statistic		1.0	14.4	–0.7	3.3	2.0	–0.3	–1.1
Courtadon model implied volatility								
Coefficient	1570.4	0.000	0.844	–0.022	0.446	0.010	0.000	–0.022
t-statistic		1.5	13.1	–0.6	3.4	1.8	–1.1	–1.0
Linear proportional model implied volatility								
Coefficient	1576.9	0.000	0.806	–0.048	0.672	0.012	0.000	–0.018
t-statistic		31.7	10.0	–1.5	7.2	2.5	–0.4	–0.9
Cox-Ingersoll-Ross model implied volatility								
Coefficient	1569.2	0.000	0.848	–0.029	0.400	0.010	0.000	–0.017
t-statistic		1.3	13.0	–0.7	3.3	1.8	–0.7	–0.8
Vasicek model implied volatility								
Coefficient	1575.3	0.000	0.823	–0.037	0.737	0.012	0.000	–0.027
t-statistic		2.3	13.3	–1.3	5.5	2.9	–2.2	–1.4

Implied volatility versus mixed GJR and CIR model

$h_t = \omega + \beta h_{t-1} + \alpha\varepsilon^2_{t-1} + \delta\sigma^2_{1t} - \delta(\beta+\alpha)\sigma^2_{1t-1} + \phi C_{t-1} + \gamma\sqrt{r_{t-1}} + \alpha\_\eta^2_{t-1} + \phi\sqrt{r_{t-1}}\eta^2_{t-1}$

where $C_{t-1} = \sqrt{r_{t-1}}\varepsilon^2_{t-1}$ and $\eta_{t-1} = \max[0, -\varepsilon_{t-1}]$

	log L	Constant ω	h_{t-1} β	ε^2_{t-1} α	σ^2_{1t} δ	C_{t-1} ϕ	$\sqrt{r_{t-1}}$ γ	η^2_{t-1} $\alpha\_$
Ho-Lee model implied volatility								
Coefficient	1568.1	0.000	0.847	–0.079	0.269	0.049	0.000	–0.16
t-statistic		0.7	14.6	–1.1	2.8	1.8	–0.3	–0.7
Courtadon model implied volatility								
Coefficient	1570.3	0.000	0.830	–0.085	0.365	0.053	0.000	–0.023
t-statistic		1.5	12.2	–1.2	3.2	1.8	–1.3	–1.0
Linear proportional model implied volatility								
Coefficient	1577.4	0.000	0.832	–0.072	0.619	0.040	0.000	–0.014
t-statistic		0.5	10.2	–1.3	5.0	1.7	–0.4	–0.7
Cox-Ingersoll-Ross model implied volatility								
Coefficient	1569.3	0.000	0.834	–0.080	0.338	0.049	0.000	–0.019
t-statistic		1.0	12.1	–1.1	3.1	1.7	–0.7	–0.8
Vasicek model implied volatility								
Coefficient	1576.8	0.000	0.819	–0.082	0.657	0.046	0.000	–0.021
t-statistic		1.6	10.4	–1.5	4.7	2.0	–1.5	–1.1

This table reports the maximum likelihood parameter estimates for the coefficients of the persistence corrected HJM implied volatility and historical volatility terms, which include the GJR terms, interest rate levels, and the interaction between the interest rate level and stocks to the interest rate in the variance equation; r_t is the spot interest rate, ε_t is the interest rate shock, σ_{1t} is the implied volatility, and h_t is the volatility at date t.

Table 6. Predictive power of lagged implied volatility versus Garch and GJR

Lagged implied volatility versus Garch. Variance equation:

$h_t = \omega + \beta h_{t-1} + \alpha\varepsilon^2_{t-1} + \delta\sigma^2_{1t-1} - \delta(\beta + \alpha)\sigma^2_{1t-2}$

	log L	Constant ω	h_{t-1} β	ε^2_{t-1} α	σ^2_{1t-1} δ
Ho-Lee model implied volatility					
Coefficient	1563.8	0.000	0.860	0.044	0.772
t-statistic		–0.2	18.3	3.0	5.5
Courtadon model implied volatility					
Coefficient	1567.9	0.000	0.867	0.037	0.859
t-statistic		–0.6	17.1	2.7	6.4
Linear proportional model implied volatility					
Coefficient	1560.7	0.000	0.795	0.043	0.765
t-statistic		1.7	8.4	2.2	5.9
Cox-Ingersoll-Ross model implied volatility					
Coefficient	1566.2	0.000	0.864	0.038	0.808
t-statistic		–0.5	17.3	2.8	6.0
Vasicek model implied volatility					
Coefficient	1563.5	0.000	0.767	0.038	0.915
t-statistic		1.3	6.6	2.0	6.8

Lagged implied volatility versus GJR. Variance equation:

$h_t = \omega + \beta h_{t-1} + \alpha\varepsilon^2_{t-1} + \delta\sigma^2_{1t} - \delta(\beta + \alpha)\sigma^2_{1t-2} + \phi C_{t-1} + \alpha\_\eta^2_{t-1}$

where $\eta_{t-1} = \max[0, -\varepsilon_{t-1}]$

	log L	Constant ω	h_{t-1} β	ε^2_{t-1} α	σ^2_{1t-1} δ	η^2_{t-1} $\alpha\_$
Ho-Lee model implied volatility						
Coefficient	1563.6	0.000	0.874	0.040	0.729	–0.008
t-statistic		0.0	19.6	2.4	5.2	–0.4
Courtadon model implied volatility						
Coefficient	1568.1	0.000	0.867	0.046	0.913	–0.014
t-statistic		–0.5	18.1	2.4	5.5	–0.8
Linear proportional model implied volatility						
Coefficient	1561.0	0.000	0.849	0.022	0.766	0.003
t-statistic		1.6	11.4	1.5	6.3	0.2
Cox-Ingersoll-Ross model implied volatility						
Coefficient	1566.4	0.000	0.864	0.046	0.858	–0.013
t-statistic		–0.4	17.9	2.5	5.3	–0.7
Vasicek model implied volatility						
Coefficient	1563.5	0.000	0.768	0.031	0.898	0.011
t-statistic		1.3	6.4	1.6	6.5	0.4

This table reports the maximum likelihood parameter estimates for the coefficients of the persistence corrected lagged HJM implied volatility and the Garch and GJR historical volatility terms in the variance equation; r_t is the spot interest rate, ε_t is the interest rate shock, σ_{1t} is the implied volatility, and h_t is the volatility at date t.

decline is more significant for the Ho and Lee, Courtadon, and CIR models, which also do not perform well under previous Garch tests.

As in Table 4, the asymmetry term in the GJR specification is insignificant. Further, the interest rate level is also insignificant. But the interaction terms $J(t-1)] = r(t-1)\varepsilon^2(t-1)$ and $C(t-1) = \sqrt{r(t-1)}\varepsilon^2(t-1)$ are significant. Therefore both the interest rate level and the Garch term $\varepsilon^2(t-1)$ seem to affect interest rate volatility only through the interaction term. That is, when interest rates are low, shocks to the interest rate lead to smaller volatility increases than when they are high. As this behaviour is not completely captured by any of the HJM models, they are not informationally efficient.

So far we have used the current period's implied volatility to forecast the realised volatility and to test to see if historical information provides additional explanatory power. However, even though the volatility forecast from the contemporaneous implied volatility can be improved using historical information, we also want to determine the forecasting ability of lagged implied volatilities relative to the Garch and GJR forecasts.

PREDICTIVE POWER OF LAGGED IMPLIED VOLATILITY

To compare the predictive ability of Garch forecasts with implied volatility we consider the effect of lagged implied volatility in the persistence corrected variance equation. As it does not contain current information, the lagged implied volatility permits more significant Arch terms. Thus we can use this test to judge the forecast usefulness of lagged implied volatility.

In Table 6 we report results for the Garch/GJR forecasts and HJM implied volatilities. As with the current implied volatility, the Arch coefficient for $\varepsilon^2(t-1)$ is strongly significant for the Ho and Lee, Courtadon, and CIR models. However, this parameter is insignificant for the HJM linear proportional and Vasicek models with the GJR benchmark and only marginally significant with the Garch benchmark. Thus these two models capture spot rate volatility better than the Garch/GJR models do.

To study the interaction effect in the Garch/GJR equation in conjunction with the lagged implied volatility, we replace $\sigma_1^2(t)$ with $\sigma_1^2(t-1)$ and $\sigma_1^2(t-1)$ with $\sigma_1^2(t-2)$ in Equations (29) and (30). The results are reported in Table 7. As with the current implied volatility, parameters for the Garch, interest rate level, and the asymmetric response term are insignificant. However, the interaction terms are still significant for both the linear proportional HJM model and the Vasicek model. Further, these terms significantly reduce the implied volatility coefficients. For example, by including the interaction terms, the Vasicek implied volatility coefficient declines from about 0.7 in Table 5 to about 0.5 in

Table 7. Preditive power of implied volatility relative to mixed GJR models

Lagged implied volatility versus mixed GJR and Courtadon models

$h_t = \omega + \beta h_{t-1} + \alpha\varepsilon^2_{t-1} + \delta\sigma^2_{1t-1} - \delta(\beta+\alpha)\sigma^2_{1t-2} + \phi J_{t-1} + \gamma r_{t-1} + \alpha\_\eta^2_{t-1}$

where $J_{t-1} = r_{t-1}\varepsilon^2_{t-1}$ and $\eta_{t-1} = \max[0, -\varepsilon_{t-1}]$

	log L	Constant ω	h_{t-1} β	ε^2_{t-1} α	σ^2_{1t-1} δ	J_{t-1} ϕ	r_{t-1} γ	η^2_{t-1} $\alpha\_$
Ho-Lee model implied volatility								
Coefficient	1567.2	0.000	0.861	0.002	0.394	0.008	0.000	–0.26
t-statistic		0.2	17.5	0.1	2.9	1.6	0.4	–1.2
Courtadon model implied volatility								
Coefficient	1569.7	0.000	0.865	–0.007	0.520	0.007	0.000	–0.019
t-statistic		1.3	15.3	–0.2	3.1	1.5	–1.1	–0.9
Linear proportional model implied volatility								
Coefficient	1571.1	0.000	0.855	–0.042	0.572	0.011	0.000	–0.010
t-statistic		1.4	13.4	–1.2	4.1	2.0	–0.8	–0.5
Cox-Ingersoll-Ross model implied volatility								
Coefficient	1568.6	0.000	0.855	–0.012	0.418	0.009	0.000	–0.022
t-statistic		1.0	14.8	–0.3	3.0	1.6	–0.4	–1.0
Vasicek model implied volatility								
Coefficient	1571.2	0.000	0.837	–0.042	0.614	0.012	0.000	–0.020
t-statistic		2.1	13.5	–1.3	4.0	2.5	–1.7	–1.0

Lagged implied volatility versus mixed GJR and CIR model

$h_t = \omega + \beta h_{t-1} + \alpha\varepsilon^2_{t-1} + \delta\sigma^2_{1t-1} - \delta(\beta+\alpha)\sigma^2_{1t-2} + \phi C_{t-1} + \gamma\sqrt{r_{t-1}} + \alpha\_\eta^2_{t-1}$

where $C_{t-1} = \sqrt{r_{t-1}}\varepsilon^2_{t-1}$ and $\eta_{t-1} = \max[0, -\varepsilon_{t-1}]$

	log L	Constant ω	h_{t-1} β	ε^2_{t-1} α	σ^2_{1t} δ	C_{t-1} ϕ	$\sqrt{r_{t-1}}$ γ	η^2_{t-1} $\alpha\_$
Ho-Lee model implied volatility								
Coefficient	1566.9	0.000	0.852	–0.065	0.275	0.042	0.000	–0.13
t-statistic		0.6	14.3	–0.9	2.5	1.5	–0.2	–0.6
Courtadon model implied volatility								
Coefficient	1569.2	0.000	0.843	–0.044	0.419	0.036	0.000	–0.020
t-statistic		1.1	13.3	–0.7	2.7	1.4	–1.0	–0.9
Linear proportional model implied volatility								
Coefficient	1572.8	0.000	0.819	–0.107	0.462	0.054	0.000	–0.010
t-statistic		1.2	10.6	–1.7	3.9	2.1	–0.8	–0.5
Cox-Ingersoll-Ross model implied volatility								
Coefficient	1568.5	0.000	0.843	–0.064	0.347	0.044	0.000	–0.020
t-statistic		0.9	13.2	–0.9	2.7	1.6	–0.6	–0.9
Vasicek model implied volatility								
Coefficient	1573.1	0.001	0.829	–0.109	0.504	0.058	0.000	–0.015
t-statistic		1.8	12.2	–1.7	3.5	2.2	–1.7	–0.7

This table reports the maximum likelihood parameter estimates for the coefficients of the persistence corrected lagged HJM implied volatility and historical volatility terms, which include the GJR terms, interest rate levels, and the interaction between the interest rate level and stocks to the interest rate in the variance equation; r_t is the spot interest rate, ε_t is the interest rate shock, σ_{1t} is the implied volatility, and h_t is the volatility at date t.

Table 7. This decline is even more significant for the single parameter models (Ho and Lee, Courtadon, and CIR).

A ROBUSTNESS CHECK WITH MULTIPERIOD VOLATILITY FORECASTS

So far we have studied the forecast ability of HJM implied volatility models relative to historical volatility models for one-period-ahead forecasts. However, as the implied volatility is computed from longer maturity options, it also contains information about longer period volatility. We check the robustness of our results and assess multiperiod forecast ability with a simple test described below. To differentiate between the Arch and interaction effects, we construct volatility forecasts using the moving average of the realised volatility due to each of these terms over the last 20 business days. These tests are based on Canina and Figlewski's (1993) use of the realised historical volatility (estimated by the moving average of squared shocks) to forecast the future realised volatility. We also include terms to represent shock asymmetry and interaction effects.

The historical volatility forecasts are proxied by the variables:

- Arch term (lagged realised volatility):

$$V_{\varepsilon t} = \frac{1}{19}\sum_{i=1}^{20}\varepsilon^2_{t+1-i}.$$

- Asymmetric shocks:

$$V_{\eta t} = \frac{1}{19}\sum_{i=1}^{20}\max\left[0, \varepsilon^2_{t+1-i}\right].$$

- Interaction terms:

$$V_{Ct} = \frac{1}{19}\sum_{i=1}^{20} r_{t+1-i}\varepsilon^2_{t+1-i} \text{ or } \frac{1}{19}\sum_{i=1}^{20}\sqrt{r_{t+1-i}}\,\varepsilon^2_{t+1-i}.$$

The realised volatility over the next 20 business days is proxied by the mean of the squared shocks. Therefore our test equation becomes

$$h_{t,t+20} = \frac{1}{19}\sum_{i=1}^{20}\varepsilon^2_{t+1+i} = \omega + \alpha V_{\varepsilon t} + \gamma r(t) + \alpha\_V_{\eta t} + \phi V_{Ct} + \delta\sigma_1^2(t), \quad (31)$$

where $h_{t,t+20}$ is the realised volatility between time t and t + 20. Table 8 overleaf presents the results of this test. In Table 9 we report results using $\sqrt{r(t)}$ as a rate level proxy and incorporating an interaction term. Note that the reported t-statistics are corrected for heteroskedasticity and serial correlation for up to the twentieth order using the approach of Newey and West (1987).

The results of our multiperiod tests coincide with the single-period forecast results. With all of the HJM models, the implied volatility plays a dominant role in explaining the realised volatility. We see the most significant results for models that permit a term structure of volatility (the Vasicek and linear proportional volatility models). In fact, for these models, the coefficient of the implied volatility is not significantly different

Table 8. Forecasting realised volatility over the next 20 days using current and past shocks, the interest rate level and the implied volatility

Dependent variable: $\Sigma_{i=1,20}\varepsilon^2_{t-1}/19$ (realised volatility)

	Independent variables						
	Constant	$V_{\varepsilon t}$	$V_{\eta t}$	V_{Jt}	r_t	σ^2_{1t}	R^2
Estimate	0.004	0.281	–0.128				0.050
t-statistic	6.68	4.02	–0.99				
Estimate	0.003	–0.949	0.150	0.109	0.000		0.177
t-statistic	1.20	–2.85	1.00	3.38	1.22		
Implied volatility from the Ho-Lee model							
Estimate	0.002	–0.941	0.185	0.099	0.000	0.357	0.192
t-statistic	0.94	–2.82	1.29	2.97	0.74	1.33	
Estimate	0.002					0.753	0.129
t-statistic	1.31					3.53	
Implied volatility from the Courtadon model							
Estimate	0.003	–0.926	0.176	0.095	0.000	0.530	0.207
t-statistic	1.31	–2.71	1.24	2.79	0.18	1.93	
Estimate	0.002					0.808	0.175
t-statistic	1.60					4.49	
Implied volatility from the linear proportional model							
Estimate	0.002	–0.840	0.097	0.084	0.000	0.714	0.242
t-statistic	0.91	–2.40	0.67	2.40	0.65	3.79	
Estimate	0.002					0.929	0.190
t-statistic	3.83					5.88	
Implied volatility from the Cox-Ingersoll-Ross model							
Estimate	0.003	–0.934	0.182	0.097	0.000	0.443	0.199
t-statistic	1.09	–2.77	1.28	2.88	0.48	1.62	
Estimate	0.002					0.793	0.154
t-statistic	1.36					4.04	
Implied volatility from the Vasicek model							
Estimate	0.003	–0.755	0.065	0.074	0.000	0.802	0.246
t-statistic	1.07	–2.12	0.44	2.04	0.40	3.69	
Estimate	0.002					0.971	0.211
t-statistic	3.23					5.72	

This table presents the results of regressing the 20-day moving realised volatility on the implied volatility, the interest rate level, the lagged realised volatility, the lagged asymmetric shock effect and the lagged effect due to the interaction between the shocks and interest rate levels; r_t is the spot interest rate; ε_t is the interest rate shock and h_t is the volatility at date t. The t-statistics reported are the Newey-West heteroskedasticity and serial correlation consistent t-statistics (for up to the 20th order).

Variable definitions:
$V_{\varepsilon t} = \Sigma_{i=1,20}\varepsilon^2_{t+1-i}/19$ (lagged realised volatility)
$V_{\eta t} = \Sigma_{i=1,20}\max(0,-\varepsilon^2_{t+1-i})^2/19$ (asymmetric shock effect)
$V_{Jt} = \Sigma_{i=1,20}r_{t+1-i}\varepsilon^2_{t+1-i}/19$ (shock and interest rate interaction effect)

from 1. Overall, whereas the realised historical volatility, interest rate level, and asymmetric volatility are all insignificant, the interaction term is still quite significant.

Conclusions and economic implications

This article offers several important conclusions. First, in contrast to earlier studies on the information content of implied volatility from equity options (Canina and Figlewski, 1993; Day and Lewis, 1992; Lamoureux and Lastrapes, 1993 and others), we find that HJM implied volatility from Eurodollar futures options explains most of the realised interest rate volatility. Our test equation corrects for some biases in Day and Lewis (1992) and Lamoureux and Lastrapes (1993). Since the transaction costs for arbitrage activity are significantly lower for Eurodollar futures options than for OEX options or individual stock options, this market is more efficient. Therefore the implied volatility is more likely to reflect the market's ex ante expectation of the future volatility in the Eurodollar upturns market. Our findings support this expectation, using several volatility models to minimise specification errors.

Second, based on the historical time series of interest rates, we find that the Garch persistence terms and the GJR asymmetric shock terms are highly significant. Specifically, interest rate volatility increases more with shocks that increase the interest rate (decrease bond prices) than with shocks that decrease the rate (increase bond prices). Both these effects are captured by the implied volatility from the different HJM models. They are no longer significant once we incorporate the implied volatility into the volatility forecast equation.

Third, the Vasicek (1977) and linear proportional volatility models perform better than the other implied volatility models. The implied volatility from these two models explains most of the time variation in realised volatility. These two models permit the volatility of different points of the term structure to be different. Volatility of short-term rates is significantly different from that of even one-year forward rates. Incorporating the implied volatility from these two models in the volatility equation, we find that the interest rate level, the Garch term, and the asymmetric volatility effect are insignificant.

Fourth, using the hybrid models as historical volatility benchmarks, we find that the HJM models fail to capture the interaction between rate shocks and rate levels in determining realised volatility. The impact of an interest rate shock on volatility is significantly lower when interest rates are low than when they are high. Further, the implied volatility coefficient drops significantly when we include these interaction terms. This drop is more significant for the Ho and Lee, Courtadon, and CIR implied volatilities. Although the importance of the implied volatility in the linear proportional and Vasicek models is reduced, these models still explain a dominant portion of the time variation in volatility.

The interaction effect exists under all volatility models we examine. As the Eurodollar futures options market providers low arbitrage costs in an efficient market setting, it is unlikely that our results reflect market frictions.

Fifth, we have also examined the predictive ability of implied volatility by using lagged implied volatility in our tests. The results are weaker but still consistent with the current implied volatility results.

Finally, we find that implied volatility has significant explanatory power even over monthly horizons. In fact, historical volatility terms representing Arch and asymmetric shock effects provide no additional explanatory power. None the less, even in monthly tests, the interaction term is still significant. Once again, models that permit a term structure of volatility yield better explanatory power.

These results have several important economic implications. First, our results are much more optimistic regarding the usefulness of option pricing models than those from recent studies on equity options. They also help us identify interest rate models for pricing contingent claims. Even for options based on forward rates of maturity of one year or less, we need to specify a term structure of volatility.

Second, we can use the interaction effect results to improve pricing and hedging strategies based on interest rate models. For example, after a large shock in a low interest rate period, we should price and hedge options with a lower volatility than we do during high interest rate periods. This differential impact is not captured by implied volatility measures/models.

Finally, our results can be used to optimally combine the implied volatility from HJM models with historical volatility terms (incorporating the interaction effect) in a volatility forecast equation. These volatility forecasts are important for determining the risk premia in equilibrium asset pricing models.

Table 9. Forecasting realised volatility over the next 20 days using current and past shocks, the square root of the interest rate level and the implied volatility

Dependent variable: $\Sigma_{i=1,20}\varepsilon^2_{t+1}/19$ (realised volatility)

	Independent variables						
	Constant	$V_{\varepsilon t}$	$V_{\eta t}$	V_{Jt}	$\sqrt{r_t}$	σ^2_{1t}	R^2
Estimate	0.004	0.286	–0.133				0.050
t-statistic	6.700	4.059	–1.021				
Estimate	0.002	–1.777	0.113	0.615	0.002		0.167
t-statistic	0.334	–3.290	0.761	3.684	0.973		
Implied volatility from the Ho-Lee model							
Estimate	0.002	–1.684	0.158	0.555	0.001	0.397	0.187
t-statistic	0.418	–3.108	1.135	3.195	0.479	1.489	
Estimate	0.002					0.753	0.129
t-statistic	1.307					3.526	
Implied volatility from the Courtadon model							
Estimate	0.004	–1.617	0.151	0.523	0.000	0.572	0.203
t-statistic	0.889	–2.934	1.086	2.952	–0.094	2.132	
Estimate	0.002					0.808	0.175
t-statistic	1.604					4.486	
Implied volatility from the linear proportional model							
Estimate	0.002	–1.462	0.068	0.468	0.001	0.738	0.237
t-statistic	0.433	–2.566	0.479	2.577	0.423	3.911	
Estimate	0.002					0.929	0.190
t-statistic	3.831					5.880	
Implied volatility from the Cox-Ingersoll-Ross model							
Estimate	0.003	–1.652	0.156	0.539	0.000	0.485	0.194
t-statistic	0.625	–3.030	1.126	3.080	0.211	1.797	
Estimate	0.002					0.793	0.154
t-statistic	1.362					4.036	
Implied volatility from the Vasicek model							
Estimate	0.003	–1.285	0.037	0.407	0.000	0.831	0.243
t-statistic	0.629	–2.186	0.262	2.141	0.173	3.807	
Estimate	0.002					0.971	0.211
t-statistic	3.234					5.721	

This table presents the results of regressing the 20-day moving realised volatility on the implied volatility, the square root of the interest rate level, the lagged realised volatility, the lagged asymmetric shock effect and the lagged effect due to the interaction between the shocks and interest rate levels; r_t is the spot interest rate; ε_t is the interest rate shock and h_t is the volatility at date t. The t-statistics reported are the Newey-West heteroskedasticity and serial correlation consistent t-statistics (for up to the 20th order).

Variable definitions:

$V_{\varepsilon t} = \Sigma_{i=1,20}\varepsilon^2_{t+1-i}/19$ (lagged realised volatility)

$V_{\eta t} = \Sigma_{i=1,20}\max(0,-\varepsilon^2_{t+1-i})^2/19$ (asymmetric shock effect)

$V_{Jt} = \Sigma_{i=1,20}\sqrt{r_{t+1-i}}\varepsilon^2_{t+1-i}/19$ (shock and interest rate interaction effect)

1 *This conclusion is not true, however, for the implied volatility models. Since we will use options of different maturities, each of the five volatility models will yield a different implied volatility estimate for the spot rate.*

2 *London interbank offered rate. This is the rate offered on three-month deposits in the London interbank market.*

3 *Caps and floors are essentially linear combinations of Eurodollar futures options and have much longer maturities; they are significantly less liquid than Eurodollar options.*

4 *Note that this conclusion is not true for the implied volatility estimation since we use options of all maturities to estimate the volatility of a single rate.*

BIBLIOGRAPHY

Amin, K. and A. Morton, 1994, "Implied Volatility Functions in Arbitrage-Free Term-Structure Models", *Journal of Financial Economics* 35, pp. 141-80.

Bollerslev, T., 1986, "Generalized Autoregressive Conditional Heteroskedasticity", *Journal of Econometrics* 31, pp. 307-27.

Bollerslev, T., 1987, "A Conditional Heteroskedastic Time Series Model for Speculative Prices and Rates of Return", *Review of Economics and Statistics* 69, pp. 542-7.

Bollerslev, T., R. Chou and K. Kroner, 1992, "Arch Modeling in Finance: A Review of the Theory and Empirical Evidence", *Journal of Econometrics* 52, pp. 5-60; reprinted as Chapter 2 of the present volume.

Brace, A., D. Gatarek and M. Musiela, 1995, "The Market Model of Interest Rate Dynamics", Working paper, University of New South Wales.

Brenner, R., R. Harjes and K. Kroner, 1993, "Another Look at Alternative Models of the Short-Term Interest Rate", Working paper, University of Arizona.

Canina, L. and S. Figlewski, 1993, "The Informational Content of Implied Volatility", *Review of Financial Studies*, 3, pp. 659-82; reprinted as Chapter 13 of the present volume.

Chiras, D., P. and S. Manaster, 1978, "The Informational Content of Option Prices and a Test of Market Efficiency", *Journal of Financial Economics* 6, pp. 259-82.

Courtadon, G., 1982, "The Pricing of Options on Default-Free Bonds", *Journal of Financial and Quantitative Analysts* 17, pp. 75-100.

Cox, J., J. Ingersoll and S. Ross, 1985, "A Theory of the Term Structure of Interest Rates", *Econometrica* 53, pp. 385-407.

Day, T. E. and C. Lewis, 1992, "Stock Market Volatility and the Information Content of Stock Index Options", *Journal of Econometrics* 52, 267-87.

Engle, R., D. Lilien and R. Robins, 1987, "Estimating Time Varying Risk Premia in the Term Structure: The Arch-M Model", *Econometrica* 55, pp. 391-407.

Engle, R. and V. Ng, 1993, "Measuring and Testing the Impact of News on Volatility", *Journal of Finance*, 48, pp. 1749-78.

Engle, R., V. Ng and M. Rothschild, 1990, "Asset Pricing with a Factor Arch Covariance Structure: Empirical Estimates for Treasury Bills", *Journal of Econometrics* 45, pp. 213-38.

Gallant, A. R., P. Rossi and G. Tauchen, 1992, "Stock Prices and Volume", *Review of Financial Studies* 5, pp. 199-242.

Glosten, I., R. Jagannathan and D. Runkle, 1993, "On the Relationship Between the Expected Value and the Volatility of the Nominal Excess Return on Stocks", *Journal of Finance* 48, pp. 1779-802.

Heath, D., R. Jarrow, and A. Morton, 1992, "Bond Pricing and the Term-Structure of Interest Rates: A New Methodology", *Econometrica* 60, pp. 77-105.

Ho, R. and S. Lee, 1986, "Term-Structure Movements and Pricing Interest Rate Contingent Claims", *Journal of Finance* 41, pp. 1011-29.

Jarrow, N. and G. Oldfield, 1981, "Forward Contracts and Futures Contracts", *Journal of Financial Economics* 9, pp. 373-82.

Koedijk, K., F. Nissen, P. Schotman, and Wolff, 1994, "The Dynamics of Short-Term Interest Rate Volatility Reconsidered," Working paper, University of Limburg, Maastricht, The Netherlands.

Lamoureux, C. and W. Lastrapes, 1993, "Forecasting Stock-Return Variance: Toward an Understanding of Stochastic Implied Volatilities", *Review of Financial Studies* 6, pp. 293-326.

Latane, H.A., and R. Rendleman, 1976, "Standard Deviations of Stock Price Ratios Implied in Options Prices", *Journal of Finance* 31, pp. 369-81.

Longstaff, F. and E. Schwartz, 1992, "Interest Rate Volatility and the Term Structure: A Two-Factor General Equilibrium Model", *Journal of Finance* 47, pp. 1259-82.

Nelson, D., 1990, "Conditional Heteroskedasticity in Asset Returns: A New Approach", *Econometrica* 59, pp. 347-70.

Newey, W.K. and K.D. West, 1987, "A Simple, Positive, Semi-Definite Heteroskedasticity and Autocorrelation Consistent Covariance Matrix", *Econometrica* 55, pp. 703-8.

Pagan, A. and G.W. Schwert, 1990, "Alternative Models for Conditional Stock Volatility", *Journal of Econometrics* 45, pp. 267-90.

Schwert, W., 1990, "Stock Volatility and the Crash of '87", *Review of Financial Studies* 3, pp. 77-102.

Vasicek, O., 1977, "An Equilibrium Characterization of the Term-Structure," *Journal of Financial Econometrics* 5, pp. 177-88.

INTERRELATED INTERNATIONAL MARKETS: PRICE AND VOLATILITY SPILLOVERS

Introduction

Robert Jarrow

This section considers whether price and volatility shocks in one country influence the price and volatilities elsewhere – issues known as price and volatility "spillovers". These spillovers can be determined using multivariate Garch procedures (as discussed in Section I). The insights they provide have implications for both portfolio management and VAR computations.

The first step is to document mean return and volatility persistence in various stock markets. This is the purpose of the first paper, by Panayiotis Theodossiou and Unro Lee, who study the "within country" relation of the mean and volatility of returns for 10 different nations: Australia, Belgium, Canada, France, Italy, Japan, Switzerland, the UK, the US, and Germany.

Theodossiou and Lee examine weekly stock market returns of various indexes from the period January 1976 to December 1991, and so including the market crash of October 1987. They then fit a univariate Garch-M model to each country, with three different specifications for the mean (linear, square root, and logarithmic). Their estimates are based on maximum likelihood estimation, with a conditional normal distribution.

Perhaps surprisingly, the results are similar for all 10 countries. Volatility persistence exists, in various degrees, throughout the different stock markets. No relationship is found between the expected returns and the volatility of returns in any of the countries studied. But serial correlation of returns is found in some – Australia, Belgium, Canada, France and Italy.

The similarity of the results suggests that the various markets are integrated – a suspicion confirmed by the following four papers. Panayiotis Theodossiou, Emel Kahya, Gregory Koutmos and Andreas Christofi study the behaviour of the mean, volatility and correlation structure of stock market returns in the US, Japan and the UK in the period before and after the October 1987 crash, from May 1984 to October 1994. As in the previous paper, weekly returns (Friday closing prices) are used for the various market indexes: US (S&P 500), Japan (Topix) and UK (FTSE100). This reduces any downward bias in correlations resulting from non-overlapping trading horizons within a day.

Theodossioiu, Kahya, Koutmos and Christofi fit a trivariate Garch with structural dummies (using maximum likelihood estimation) to account for the crash in October 1987. Their results are quite interesting. For mean returns, spillovers exist from the US and Japan to the UK. It turns out that positive returns in the US in one week imply positive returns in the UK the week after. In contrast, positive returns in Japan in one week lead to negative returns in Britain in the next. No other spillovers are evidenced.

For volatilities, high volatility persistence is shown to be present in the US and Japan, but not in the UK. Spillovers seem to occur from the US to the UK, and from Japan to the UK, but not in the reverse direction.

There appears to be a minimal shift in trends pre- and post-crash. The volatility in the US has decreased, but is unchanged in Japan and the UK. The correlation between the UK and Japan has decreased, but all the other correlations remain the same.

This evidence confirms the strong interaction between the various markets. Another study which backs this up is by G. Geoffrey Booth, Tae-Hwy Lee and Yiuman Tse. Their paper analyses the relationship between Nikkei 225 stock index futures traded on three international exchanges: the OSE (Osaka Securities Exchange), the Simex (Singapore International Monetary Exchange) and the CME (Chicago Mercantile Exchange). The OSE and Simex futures contracts are traded almost simultaneously, while the CME contracts are traded when the former are closed.

Booth, Lee and Tse examine daily open and close futures prices for the time period December 1990 to May 1994. They start by investigating the futures volatility during trading and non-trading hours. (As we saw in Section II, there is evidence of differing volatilities between trading and non-trading hours.) The results are fascinating. The trading time variances on the OSE and Simex are greater than their non-trading time variances, but the opposite is true for the CME, where non-trading time variance is larger. This observation is consistent with the belief that the relevant information concerning the Nikkei 225 is released during Japanese business hours and not when the CME is open.

To investigate this data further, Booth, Lee and Tse model the return processes of these three contracts as a cointegrated system. The results show that the three markets are cointegrated with one common stochastic trend. A variance decomposition and impulse control analysis clarifies the lead/lag relationship that exists across the markets. The results shown are consistent with the notion that the three markets follow each other in a natural progression; the last market traded influences the next market to open – a common sense result.

In the next paper in this section Booth, together with Teppo Martikainen and Yiuman Tse, investigates the price and volatility spillovers among the Danish, Norwegian, Swedish and Finnish stock markets. The various stock market indexes in each country are considered: KFX (Denmark), OBX (Norway), OMX (Sweden) and FOX (Finland). As the trading hours for the four markets are nearly the same, daily closing prices are employed from the period May 1988 to June 1994.

Consistent with previous studies, the individual return series for these four stock market indexes are non-normal (with excess kurtosis and skewness) and they exhibit Arch effects. Consequently, a multivariate Egarch model (with a conditional student-t distribution) is fitted to the data. Maximum likelihood estimation is used.

The results show that prices in all markets depend on their own past values. The price spillovers between markets appear to be as follows: Sweden spills over to Finland, and Norway spills over to both Denmark and Sweden. Finland and Denmark do not spill over to any other market. That is, two-way price spillovers do not appear to occur.

As expected, volatilities are persistent in all markets. And volatility spillovers do exist. The evidence suggests that Sweden spills over to Norway and Finland, and Finland spills over to Sweden. No other spillovers occur.

Asymmetric volatility spillovers are also investigated. Tests for asymmetry show that the four markets are more sensitive to bad news (shocks) in the other markets than they are to good news. Again, this evidence is consistent with an integrated and efficient international market place.

The last paper in this section, by Yiuman Tse and G. Geoffrey Booth, investigates the fixed income markets, looking at the volatility spillovers between US and Eurodollar interest rates. It is well known that these rates are highly correlated (see Figure 1 of the paper). The question here is whether the volatilities of these two rates are related as well.

Daily closing prices of the three-month US T-bill and the three-month Eurodollar futures are considered. The time period covered is March 1982 to February 1994. First a common volatility test is employed. This is a two-step procedure. To start with, both rate processes are tested for Arch, which is shown to be true. The series is then tested for a common factor. A common factor Arch specification is rejected. The reason for this is an asymmetry in the evolution of the two rate processes. It appears that the rates are close substitutes in normal times, but in adverse times, they move differently.

Thus, Tse and Booth fit a bivariate Egarch model (with a conditional normal density) which allows for asymmetry. A lagged change in the TED spread (difference between the Eurodollar and T-bill rate) is also included in the conditional variance equation. The data supports this model. The model was also extended to include cross-market spillover parameters, however these were found to be insignificant from zero, indicating that no cross-market spillover exists.

Taken together, the papers in this section all tell a similar story. The markets for stocks and fixed income securities are integrated across different countries and times. There is a well-developed and efficient global market for risk. This integration – spillovers in returns and volatilities – is important for both portfolio and risk management.

For portfolio managers, this whole area has implications for international diversification. Spillovers imply that international diversification is less than expected or believed. For risk managers, it has implications for the computation of value-at-risk. VAR calculations need to include spillovers, otherwise their estimates will be biased low (too much implicit diversification). The introduction of these spillovers into portfolio and risk management tools awaits subsequent research.

16

Relationship between Volatility and Expected Returns across International Stock Markets*

Panayiotis Theodossiou and Unro Lee
Rutgers University, Camden; University of the Pacific

Several papers have examined the intertemporal relationship between stock market volatility (risk) and expected returns in the US. The findings of these papers, however, have been inconclusive. Pindyck (1984) and Chou (1988) assert that much of the decline in stock prices during the 1970s is directly related to the increase in volatility. Bollerslev, Engle, and Wooldridge (1988) report that the conditional volatility significantly affects expected returns. Poterba and Summers (1986), French, Schwert, and Stambaugh (1987), and Baillie and DeGennaro (1990) find a weak relationship between stock market volatility and expected returns.

In light of the fact that most of these studies have used the variance or the standard deviation of returns and a linear framework to model the relationship between volatility and expected returns, such disparities in the results lend credence to the notion that perhaps other measures of volatility or different factional specifications between volatility and expected returns need to be considered, eg Baillie and DeGennaro (1990). Moreover, these studies have focused on the US market and there is no comprehensive study dealing with a large set of major international stock markets.

The objective of this paper is to provide additional insight into the nature of stock market volatility and its relation to expected returns for 10 industrialised countries. These countries are Australia, Belgium, Canada, France, Italy, Japan, Switzerland, the United Kingdom, the United States, and (West) Germany. For this purpose we use the generalised autoregressive conditional heteroskedasticity in the mean (Garch-M) model and test three different factional specifications for the conditional variance and expected market returns relationship. That is, we consider the linear, the square root, and the log-linear specifications. In addition, we impose no restrictions on the lag-structure of the Garch-M model, since smaller capitalisations markets may exhibit higher order lag-structures for the conditional mean and/or conditional variance of returns than the single-lag specification used in studies for the US, eg, Chou (1988) and Akgiray (1989).

Significant conditional heteroskedasticity is found to be present in the return series of all 10 markets, indicating the presence of volatility clustering, that is, the tendency of large stock price changes to be followed by large stock price changes, but unpredictable sign. No relationship is found between conditional volatility and expected returns in any of the 10 national stock markets. Stock prices for markets of Australia, Belgium, Canada, France, and Italy violate the martingale model.

The organisation of the chapter is as follows: the next section elaborates on the Garch-M methodology; the third section discusses the sample and the results. A summary of the findings is presented in the final section.

Garch-M model for stock market returns

The Garch model proposed by Engle (1982) and generalised by Bollerslev (1986) has been used to study the stochastic behaviour of several financial time series and, in particular, to explore the changing behaviour of volatility over time; see Bollerslev, Chou, and Kroner (1992) for an exten-

* *This paper was first published in the* Journal of Business Finance & Accounting, *Vol 22, No 2 (1995). It is reprinted with the permission of Blackwell Publishers.*

sive literature review. Numerous empirical applications to stock return data for the US have appeared in recent finance literature. The Garch-M model, introduced by Engle, Lilien and Robins (1987), explicitly links the conditional variance to the conditional mean of returns and provides a framework to study the relationship between market risk and expected returns.[1] With Garch models, the conditional mean and volatility of stock returns are assumed to be predictable using past available information at a given point in time, such as past returns and past volatility measures.

Let μ_t and σ_t^2 denote the conditional mean and conditional variance of stock returns in each market during period t based on the information set Φ_{t-1}, where Φ_{t-1} includes available information at time $t - 1$ relevant to the formation of μ_t and σ_t^2. The conditional mean of market returns is specified as a function of past returns and the conditional variance of returns. That is

$$\mu_t = \beta_0 + \beta_1 R_{t-1} + \ldots + \beta_k R_{t-k} + g(\sigma_t^2 \delta) \qquad (1)$$

where R_{t-1} and β_s, for $s = 1,\ldots,k$, denote past returns and their respective autoregressive coefficients, and $g(\sigma_t^2,\delta)$ denotes a function that links the conditional variance to the conditional mean. Statistically significant values for β_ss indicate that the conditional mean is influenced by past returns and that future returns are predictable using past information. The latter is in direct violation of the random walk and the martingale models for stock prices.[2]

The factional forms for $g(\sigma_t^2,\delta)$ considered include the linear ($g(\sigma_t^2,\delta) = \delta\sigma_t^2$), the square root ($g(\sigma_t^2,\delta) = \delta\sigma_t$), and the logarithmic ($g(\sigma_t^2,\delta) = \delta \log(\sigma_t^2)$) specifications. Merton (1973) shows that the conditional variance of returns will be linearly related to expected (mean) returns if there is a representative investor with a log-utility function. Merton's model postulates a positive relationship between variance of returns and expected returns, ie $\delta > 0$. Moreover, under the linear specification the parameter δ can be interpreted as a relative risk aversion coefficient. The square root specification is in line with the standard CAPM model, which assumes a positive-linear relationship between the standard deviation of returns and expected returns. The choice of the logarithmic specification is based on empirical grounds since it often provides a better fit to financial data, eg Engle, Lilien, and Robins (1987).

The conditional variance of returns is specified as a linear function of past volatility shocks (ε_{t-s}^2, for $s = 1,\ldots,r$) and past conditional variances (σ_{t-s}^2, for $s = 1,\ldots,q$). That is:

$$\sigma_t^2 = \alpha_0 + a_1\varepsilon_{t-1}^2 + \ldots + \alpha_p\varepsilon_{t-p}^2 + \gamma_1\sigma_{t-1}^2 + \ldots + \gamma_q\sigma_{t-q}^2 \qquad (2)$$

where ε_{t-s} represents a market innovation or an unexpected shock and is calculated using the difference between the return of period $t - s$ and its conditional mean, ie $\varepsilon_{t-s} \equiv R_{t-s} - \mu_{t-s}$. To ensure positive conditional variances, all parameters for (2) are restricted to non-negative values. For $q = 0$ the Garch(p, q)-M model truncates to that of an Arch(p)-M model.

Equation (2) assumes that past volatility shocks have a positive but decreasing impact on future market volatility and it is consistent with the actual volatility pattern of stock markets during stable and unstable periods. During stable periods shocks are expected to be small, resulting in low levels of market volatility, whereas in unstable periods shocks are expected to be large resulting in high levels of market volatility. In this respect, the conditional variance equation "emulates" the tendency for volatility clustering - the tendency of large (small) stock price changes to be followed by large (small) stock price changes of unpredictable sign (eg Mandelbrot (1963), Fama (1965)).

Under normality, the sample log-likelihood function of market returns for each country, omitting the constants, is equal to

$$L(\theta) = (-1/2)\sum_{t=1}^{T}\left\{\log(\sigma_t^2) + \varepsilon_t^2 / \sigma_t^2\right\} \qquad (3)$$

where θ is a vector that includes the parameters for the conditional mean and conditional variance equations. The maximum likelihood estimates for θ are obtained by maximising $L(\theta)$ with respect to θ subject to the non-negativity constraints for the conditional variance parameters.[3]

Empirical results

DATA AND PRELIMINARY STATISTICS

The data include weekly aggregate stock market returns for Australia, Belgium, Canada, France, Italy, Japan, Switzerland, the United Kingdom, the United States and (West) Germany and span the period January 16, 1976, to December 27, 1991 (833 observations). These were obtained from the Barron's National Business and Financial Weekly. Barron's regularly publishes data for stock market indices of major industrialised countries. The indices are based on Friday's closing prices expressed in local currencies and do not include dividends. Table 1 presents the names and exchanges for these indices, The returns in each market (R_t) are expressed in percentages. These are computed by multiplying the first difference of the natural logarithm of stock market indices by 100. That is $R_t = 100 \times [\log(P_t) - \log(P_{t-1})]$, where P_t is the level of the price index at time t. Some of the indices have been rebased during the sampling period. Therefore, before calculating the returns, each of the indices is adjusted to a single base.

A graphical inspection of the return series shows that they exhibit frequent spikes and increased magnitude during several periods, therefore supporting the notion that they are non-linear processes (figures available upon request).

Table 2 reports several descriptive statistics for the return series. These include the mean, the standard deviation of returns, and the measures for skewness (m_3) and kurtosis (m_4). The sample means of all return series are statistically greater than zero at the at the 5% level except for Italy, Germany, and Switzerland. Judging from the sample standard deviations, the Italian stock market appears to be the most volatile. The statistics m_3 and m_4 are the standard measures of skewness and kurtosis, respectively. Under the null hypothesis of normality for the return series, m_3 and m_4 are asymptotically distributed as $m_3 \sim N(0,6/T)$ and $m_4 \sim N(3,24/T)$, where T is the number of observations. Statistically significant skewness is present in the stock market return series of all countries except Australia, Italy, and the United

Table 1. National stock market indices

Country	Exchange	Index
Australia	Sydney	All ordinaries
Belgium	Brussels	General
Canada	Toronto	TSE 300
France	Paris	Agefi
Italy	Milan	MIN
Japan	Tokyo	Topix
Switzerland	Zurich	Swiss Bank Corporation
UK	London	Financial Times 500
US	New York	Standard & Poor's 500
(West) Germany	Frankfurt	Commerzbank

Table 2. Preliminary statistics for weekly stock market returns

Countries	Mean	Standard deviation	Skewness (m_3)	Kurtosis (m_4)
Australia	0.2485 (3.21)*	2.2336	–0.0353 (–0.42)	6.8928 (40.2)*
Belgium	0.2278 (3.38)*	1.9466	0.8031 (–9.46)*	6.5492 (38.6)*
Canada	0.1609 (2.20)*	2.1142	–0.3914 (–4.61)*	6.1470 (36.2)*
France	0.2141 (2.68)*	2.2994	–0.3184 (–3.75)*	1.9769 (11.6)*
Italy	0.1546 (1.39)	3.2206	–0.1416 (–1.67)	3.6494 (21.5)*
Japan	0.1920 (2.80)*	1.9789	–0.7847 (–9.24)*	6.2171 (36.6)*
Switzerland	0.0704 (1.07)	1.8955	–1.4240 (–16.8)*	11.5461 (68.0)*
UK	0.2387 (2.68)*	2.5743	0.0088 (0.10)	1.2193 (7.18)*
US	0.1746 (2.41)*	2.0867	–0.4637 (–5.47)*	2.9243 (17.2)*
Germany	0.0941 (1.26)	2.1638	–0.6898 (–8.13)*	2.8127 (16.6)*

Data cover the period January 16, 1976 to December 27, 1991, and include 833 weekly observations for returns. Returns are expressed in percentages. Parentheses include the t-values for the estimates.
* Statistically significant at the 5% level.

Table 3. Autocorrelation coefficients for weekly stock market returns

Autocorrelation coefficients	Countries Australia	Belgium	Canada	France	Italy	Japan	Switzerland	UK	US	Germany
ρ(1)	0.0991	0.1833	0.1272	0.1477	–0.0143	0.0331	0.1197	–0.0038	0.0033	0.0974
ρ(2)	0.0742	0.1689	0.0020	0.0951	0.0689	0.0725	0.1465	0.0160	0.0433	0.1098
ρ(3)	0.0412	0.0294	0.0451	0.0026	0.0533	0.0137	–0.0029	0.0095	–0.0293	0.0393
ρ(4)	0.0350	0.0456	0.0141	0.0389	0.0873	–0.0198	0.0203	0.0285	0.0098	0.0160
ρ(5)	0.0585	0.0526	–0.0203	–0.0257	–0.0320	0.0194	0.0079	–0.0277	–0.0290	0.0056
ρ(6)	–0.0616	0.0385	0.0494	0.0233	0.0094	0.0551	0.0722	0.0017	0.0503	–0.0380
ρ(7)	–0.0421	0.0080	–0.0416	0.0314	–0.0139	–0.0155	0.0043	–0.0558	0.0256	–0.0060
ρ(8)	–0.0295	–0.0153	–0.0435	–0.0604	0.0425	–0.0184	0.0251	0.0046	–0.0310	0.0264
ρ(9)	–0.0785	–0.0153	–0.0092	–0.0225	0.0237	0.0472	–0.0389	–0.0236	0.0204	–0.0342
ρ(10)	–0.0108	–0.1370	–0.0691	–0.0501	0.0267	–0.0366	–0.0537	–0.0491	–0.0948	0.0257
ρ(11)	–0.0372	–0.0970	–0.0333	0.0007	–0.0593	–0.460	–0.0445	–0.0097	–0.0051	0.0355
ρ(12)	–0.0134	–0.0653	0.0354	0.0467	0.0339	0.0151	–0.0557	–0.0542	–0.0351	0.0144
Q(12)	30.18*	85.87*	26.95*	36.40*	21.56*	14.16	43.29*	9.35	15.59	24.17*
$Q^2(12)$	188.61*	33.53*	36.06*	128.21*	88.00*	256.81*	103.01*	65.70*	131.83*	284.64*

Parentheses include the t-values for the estimates.
Q(12) and $Q^2(12)$ are the 12th lag Ljung-Box test statistics applied to the return and squared return series.
*Statistically significant at the 5% level.

Kingdom. Statistically significant kurtosis is present in all return series.[4]

Table 3 presents the autocorrelation coefficients of the return series and the Ljung-Box portmanteau test statistics of the return and squared return series for $k = 12$ lags, denoted by $Q(k)$ and $Q^2(k)$, respectively. The $Q(k)$ and $Q^2(k)$ statistics test for kth-order serial correlation of the return and squared return series, respectively. Under the null hypothesis of serial independence, both statistics follow the chi-squared distribution with $k = 12$ degrees of freedom.

A visual inspection of the autocorrelation coefficients shows that higher-order autocorrelations are small and decaying, indicating that the return series are stationary over time. The $Q(12)$ statistics for Australia, Belgium, Canada, France, Italy, Switzerland, and Germany are statistically significant indicating the presence of serial correlation in the stock market return series (first moment dependencies) of these countries. The $Q^2(k)$ statistics are all highly significant indicating the presence of serial correlation in the squared return series (conditional heteroskedasticity). The latter depicts that stock market returns exhibit strong second moment dependencies and therefore cannot be modelled as white noise linear processes, eg AR or ARMA processes. The results, however, for the first moment dependencies can be misleading because the test statistics do not explicitly account for the heteroskedastic behaviour of stock returns.

Garch-M models

The identification of the optimal lag-structure of the conditional mean and conditional variance equations of the Garch-M model for each country is accomplished by means of the log-likelihood ratio test. The robustness of each model is assessed using the Ljung-Box statistics of the standardised residual and squared standardised residuals of the models. F-tests are also used to test for correct specification of the conditional variance equations.

Tables 4–6 respectively present the "best" Garch-M models for the linear, square root, and logarithmic specifications of the conditional mean equations.

Interestingly, the results for the three specifications are similar. Significant first-moment dependencies (serial correlation) are present in the market return series for Australia, Belgium, Canada, France, and Italy. The conditional mean return equations for Australia and Canada are best represented by a first-order autoregressive process and a second-order autoregressive process best represents those for Belgium, France, and Italy. These results violate the martingale model for stock prices. No serial correlation is observed in the return series for markets of Japan, Switzerland, the UK, the US, and Germany. No significant relationship is found between the conditional variance of returns and expected returns in any of the ten national markets. All δ coefficients for the three specifications of the conditional mean equations are statistically insignificant.

Conditional heteroskedasticity (volatility) of stock market returns is present in all countries. Stock market volatility in Australia is best represented by a Garch(1,0) or an Arch(1) model. Thus, conditional variance of the returns in Australia during one week is influenced only by volatility shocks during the previous week. Stock market volatility in the remaining markets is best represented by a low-order Garch(1,1) process – ie is a function of past volatility shocks and past conditional variances from the previous week. Contrary to Australia's situation, volatility shocks in these markets tend to persist for more than one week. The highest volatility persistence is found in Germany's market and the lowest volatility persistent, besides Australia, is found in the US market. The half-life of a volatility shock, calculated as the $\log(0.5)/\log(\alpha_1 + \gamma_1)$, is 34.84 weeks for Germany's market and 6.46 weeks for the US market.

Second moment dependencies of the return series are in direct violation of the random walk model for stock prices; see Lo and Mackinlay (1988) for additional discussion and tests on the random walk model. However, such dependencies are in line with the martingale model, provided that stock market return series are not serially correlated. In this respect, stock prices in Australia, Belgium, Canada, France, and Italy are not martingale processes.

Next we evaluate the robustness of the results using a series of misspecification tests. The Ljung-Box test statistics of the series of standardised and squared standardised residuals, denoted by $Q(12)$ and $Q^2(12)$, are lower than their critical values at the 5% level for all 10 countries. Correct specification of the conditional variance equations also requires that $E(\varepsilon_t | \Phi_{t-1}) = \sigma_t^2$ for each market. To test the latter condition, we regress $(\varepsilon_t^2/\sigma_t^2 - 1)$ on $1/\sigma_t^2$ and $\varepsilon_{t-1}^2/\sigma_{t-1}^2, \ldots, \varepsilon_{t-5}^2/\sigma_{t-5}^2$, and test the null hypothesis that the coefficients of all the explanatory variables are equal to zero against the alternative hypothesis that at least

Table 4. Garch-M models for weekly stock market returns: linear specification

$$\mu_t = \beta_0 + \beta_1 R_{t-1} + \beta_2 R_{t-2} + \delta\,\sigma_t^2$$
$$\sigma_t^2 = \alpha_0 + \alpha_1 \varepsilon_{t-1}^2 + \gamma_1\,\sigma_{t-1}^2$$

Parameter estimates	Countries									
	Australia	Belgium	Canada	France	Italy	Japan	Switzerland	UK	US	Germany
β_0	0.2251	0.0365	0.0810	0.2945	0.0099	0.2140	0.1767	0.1306	0.0983	0.0678
	(1.41)	(0.25)	(0.47)	(1.46)	(0.04)	(2.17)	(1.74)	(0.49)	(0.44)	(0.60)
β_1	0.1742	0.1603	0.1357	0.1355	−0.0136					
	(4.00)*	(4.01)*	(3.43)*	(3.64)*	(−0.37)					
β_2		0.1276		0.0785	0.0812					
		(2.98)*		(2.01)*	(2.03)*					
δ	0.0067	0.0427	0.0157	−0.0152	0.0099	0.0156	−0.0229	0.0203	0.0260	0.0056
	(0.21)	(0.95)	(0.37)	(−0.36)	(0.38)	(0.50)	(−0.65)	(0.49)	(0.47)	(0.19)
α_0	3.5104	0.3496	0.2269	0.3174	0.8145	0.1773	0.2530	0.3210	0.4315	0.1042
	(18.7)*	(3.46)*	(5.23)*	(2.79)*	(4.67)*	(4.15)*	(3.83)*	(2.09)*	(2.76)*	(2.38)*
α_1	0.2485	0.1419	0.0694	0.0808	0.0969	0.1716	0.2071	0.0747	0.0966	0.1087
	(9.02)*	(8.49)*	(7.68)*	(4.82)*	(6.22)*	(7.13)*	(6.60)*	(3.67)*	(5.13)*	(6.67)*
γ_1		0.7666	0.8808	0.8565	0.8245	0.7947	0.7487	0.8774	0.8024	0.8717
		(18.1)*	(52.6)*	(24.7)*	(30.8)*	(31.4)*	(17.6)*	(24.8)*	(16.9)*	(39.1)*
Log*L*	−1798.18	−1670.58	−1762.82	−1830.92	−2113.48	−1647.89	−1638.56	−1948.09	−1761.72	−1741.69
L-ratio	97.02*	31.01*	59.04*	58.03*	74.93*	142.81*	103.66*	42.09*	50.62*	78.77*
Q(12)	13.56	15.64	6.49	10.05	13.42	14.00	19.50	13.47	9.11	17.77
$Q^2(12)$	18.52	5.00	14.96	11.77	13.03	3.89	3.85	12.94	8.33	9.10
F-value	1.43	0.34	0.37	0.74	1.38	0.21	0.45	0.34	0.62	0.69

μ_t and σ_t^2 denote the conditional mean and conditional variance of returns, R_t, in each market. ε_t^2 denotes the market volatility shocks, where $\varepsilon_t = R_t - \mu_t$.
Parentheses include the t-values for the estimates.
Log*L* is the Log-likelihood function evaluated at the maximum.
L-ratio is Log-likelihood ratio statistics, testing for conditional heteroskedasticity.
Q(12) and $Q^2(12)$ are the 12th lag Ljung-Box test statistics applied to the original and squared standardised residuals.
F-values test for correct specification of the conditional variance equations.
*Statistically significant at the 5% level.

Table 5. Garch-M models for weekly stock market returns: squared root specification

$$\mu_t = \beta_0 + \beta_1 R_{t-1} + \beta_2 R_{t-2} + \delta\,\sigma_t$$
$$\sigma_t^2 = \alpha_0 + \alpha_1 \varepsilon_{t-1}^2 + \gamma_1\,\sigma_{t-1}^2$$

Parameter estimates	Countries									
	Australia	Belgium	Canada	France	Italy	Japan	Switzerland	UK	US	Germany
β_0	0.0989	−0.2040	−0.0419	0.4162	−0.0937	0.0722	0.1226	−0.0496	−0.1319	−0.0798
	(1.19)	(−0.64)	(−0.12)	(0.96)	(−0.17)	(0.33)	(0.54)	(−0.09)	(−0.26)	(−0.33)
β_1	0.1743	0.1596	0.1354	0.1353	−0.0136					
	(3.99)*	(3.98)*	(3.43)*	(3.63)*	(−0.37)					
β_2		0.1272		0.0783	0.0810					
		(2.96)*		(2.00)*	(2.02)*					
δ	0.0754	0.2177	0.0955	−0.0909	0.0655	0.1140	−0.0032	0.1247	0.1700	0.0956
	(0.31)	(1.17)	(0.51)	(−0.44)	(0.36)	(0.85)	(−0.02)	(0.55)	(0.67)	(0.71)
α_0	3.5118	0.3494	0.2275	0.3165	0.8149	0.1794	0.2589	0.3198	0.4344	0.1052
	(18.7)*	(3.46)*	(5.23)*	(2.79)*	(4.66)*	(4.13)*	(3.90)*	(2.09)*	(2.76)*	(2.41)*
α_1	0.2479	0.1426	0.0696	0.0808	0.0970	0.1706	0.2145	0.0747	0.0972	0.1099
	(8.98)*	(8.53)*	(7.70)*	(4.82)*	(6.22)*	(7.12)*	(6.76)*	(3.67)*	(5.26)*	(6.81)*
γ_1		0.7661	0.8805	0.8567	0.8244	0.7948	0.7419	0.8775	0.8011	0.8704
		(18.1)*	(52.6)*	(24.8)*	(30.8)*	(31.4)*	(17.5)*	(24.9)*	(16.9)*	(39.3)*
Log*L*	−1798.15	−1670.33	−1762.76	−1830.89	−2113.49	−1647.46	−1638.89	−1948.05	−1761.60	−1741.39
L-ratio	96.83*	71.74*	67.89*	63.37*	77.30*	181.83*	103.66*	41.85*	50.62*	137.32*
Q(12)	13.68	15.71	6.47	10.05	13.39	13.12	19.69	13.46	9.12	17.72
$Q^2(12)$	18.55	4.97	14.97	11.78	13.03	3.86	4.02	12.92	8.33	9.36
F-value	1.43	0.35	0.37	0.74	1.38	0.19	0.45	0.34	0.64	0.73

μ_t and σ_t^2 denote the conditional mean and conditional variance of returns, R_t, in each market. ε_t^2 denotes the market volatility shocks, where $\varepsilon_t = R_t - \mu_t$.
Parentheses include the t-values for the estimates.
Log*L* is the Log-likelihood function evaluated at the maximum.
L-ratio is Log-likelihood ratio statistics, testing for conditional heteroskedasticity.
Q(12) and $Q^2(12)$ are the 12th lag Ljung-Box test statistics applied to the original and squared standardised residuals.
F-values test for correct specification of the conditional variance equations.
*Statistically significant at the 5% level.

Table 6. Garch-M models for weekly stock market returns: logarithmic specification

$$\mu_t - \beta_0 + \beta_1 R_{t-1} + \beta_2 R_{t-2} + \delta \log(\sigma_t^2) \quad \sigma_t^2 = \alpha_0 + \alpha_1 \varepsilon_{t-1}^2 + \gamma_1 \sigma_{t-1}^2$$

Parameter estimates	Countries									
	Australia	Belgium	Canada	France	Italy	Japan	Switzerland	UK	US	Germany
β_0	0.1296	–0.0766	–0.0210	0.3957	–0.1260	0.1394	0.0676	–0.0754	–0.1004	–0.0712
	(0.27)	(–3.95)*	(–0.08)	(1.12)	(–0.19)	(1.25)	(0.60)	(–0.14)	(–0.27)	(–0.48)
β_1	0.1736	0.1591	0.1351	0.1351	–0.0137					
	(3.40)*	(3.96)*	(3.43)*	(3.62)*	(–0.37)					
β_2		0.1266		0.0782	0.0809					
		(2.95)*		(2.01)*	(2.01)*					
δ	0.0874	0.2377	0.1277	–0.1168	0.0809	0.1359	0.0614	0.1878	0.2278	0.1520
	(0.26)	(1.34)	(0.66)	(–0.49)	(0.35)	(1.15)	(0.49)	(0.63)	(0.82)	(1.16)
α_0	3.5159	0.3495	0.2282	0.3161	0.8172	0.1779	0.2623	0.3181	0.43614	0.1055
	(18.7)*	(3.47)*	(5.23)*	(2.80)*	(4.65)*	(4.07)*	(3.93)*	(2.08)*	(2.77)*	(2.43)*
α_1	0.2465	0.1432	0.0699	0.0808	0.0971	0.1697	0.2195	0.0749	0.0976	0.1105
	(8.95)*	(8.55)*	(7.71)*	(4.82)*	(6.21)*	(7.11)*	(6.93)*	(3.67)*	(5.34)*	(6.93)*
γ_1		0.7655	0.8801	0.8568	0.8241	0.7959	0.7373	0.8777	0.8003	0.8698
		(18.1)*	(52.5)*	(24.8)*	(30.7)*	(31.5)*	(17.4)*	(25.0)*	(16.9)*	(39.6)*
Log*L*	–1798.16	–1670.11	–1762.70	–1830.86	–2113.49	–1647.20	–1638.77	–1948.00	–1761.48	–1740.92
L-ratio	97.87*	87.89*	68.97*	66.94*	78.49*	203.94*	149.66*	42.24*	63.31*	165.35*
Q(12)	13.67	15.81	6.46	10.03	13.38	13.09	19.55	13.43	9.15	17.46
$Q^2(12)$	18.54	5.00	15.00	11.81	13.02	3.88	4.22	12.91	8.32	9.42
F-value	1.41	0.35	0.37	0.74	1.38	0.19	0.47	0.34	0.65	0.74

μ_t and σ_t^2 denote the conditional mean and conditional variance of returns, R_t, in each market. ε_t^2 denotes the market volatility shocks, where $\varepsilon_t = R_t - \mu_t$.
Parentheses include the *t*-values for the estimates.
Log*L* is the Log-likelihood function evaluated at the maximum.
L-ratio is Log-likelihood ratio statistics, testing for conditional heteroskedasticity.
Q(12) and $Q^2(12)$ are the 12th lag Ljung-Box test statistics applied to the original and squared standardised residuals.
F-values test for correct specification of the conditional variance equations.
*Statistically significant at the 5% level.

one coefficient is different from zero. The F-statistics for the 10 regressions are below their 5% level critical value of $F_{6,818} = 2.10$; therefore, they support the hypothesis of correct specification for the conditional variance equations.

Summary and concluding remarks

This chapter presents new evidence on the stochastic behaviour of weekly stock market returns and the relationship between stock market volatility and expected returns for ten industrialised countries using the Garch-M model. The countries are Australia, Belgium, Canada, France, Italy, Japan, Switzerland, the United Kingdom, the United States and (West) Germany. Three alternative specifications for the relationship between conditional variance and expected stock market returns are tested. These include square root, logarithmic, and linear specifications.

Strong conditional heteroskedasticity is found to be present in the return series of all markets, indicating the presence of volatility clustering. No relationship is found between expected returns and conditional volatility of returns in any of the 10 markets. Significant serial correlation is also present in the return series for markets of Australia, Belgium, Canada, France, and Italy; thus prices in these markets are incompatible with the martingale model.

The stochastic properties of international stock market returns have important implications for market equilibrium models, such as the international CAPM model and the pricing of options written on stock market indices. These models are based on the assumption that stock prices follow the random walk or its continuous time counterpart, the Brownian motion. These assumptions are clearly violated for international stock prices. In this respect, it is important to identify and more fully understand these properties in order to use them to develop or modify existing models so that they provide better approximations of reality.

1 *Chou (1988) finds that the Garch-M model is more reliable than two-stage least squares models used by Pindyck (1984), Poterba and Summers (1986) and French, Schwert and Stambaugh (1987) to examine the relationship between expected returns and volatility.*

2 *The random walk and martingale models assume that stock price changes are unpredictable, ie they are serially uncorrelated. In addition, the random walk model assumes that the variance of price changes is homoskedastic. Thus, conditional heteroskedasticity is only compatible with the martingale model.*

3 *See Bollerslev (1986) for details on the estimation of the*

likelihood function. Normality has been a popular parametric specification for the sample likelihood function (eg, Engle, 1982; and Akgiray, 1989). Other parametric specifications include the student's t distribution (eg, Bollerslev, 1987; and Baillie and Bollerslev,1989) and the generalised exponential distribution (eg Nelson, 1991).

4 *It is possible that the conditional distribution is normal even though unconditional normality is rejected.*

BIBLIOGRAPHY

Akgiray, V., 1989, "Conditional Heteroskedasticity in Time Series of Stock Returns: Evidence and Forecasts", *Journal of Business* 62, pp. 55-80.

Baillie, R.T., and T. Bollerslev, 1989, "The Message in Daily Exchange Rates: A Conditional Variance Tale", *Journal of Business and Economics Statistics* 7, pp. 297-305.

Baillie, R.T., and R.P. DeGennaro, 1990, "Stock Returns and Volatility", *Journal of Financial and Quantitative Analysis*, 23, pp. 203-14.

Bollerslev, T., 1986, "Generalized Autoregressive Conditional Heteroscedasticity", *Journal of Econometrics* 31, pp. 307-27.

Bollerslev, T., 1987, "A Conditional Heteroscedastic Time Series Model for Speculative Prices and Rates of Returns", *Review of Economics and Statistics*, 69, pp. 542-7.

Bollerslev, T., R.Y. Chou and K.F. Kroner, 1992, "ARCH Modeling in Finance: A Review of Theory and Empirical Evidence", *Journal of Econometrics* 52, pp. 5-59; reprinted as chapter 2 of the present volume.

Bollerslev, T., R.F. Engle and J.M. Wooldridge, 1988, "A Capital Asset Pricing Model with Time Varying Covariance", *Journal of Political Economy* 96, pp. 116-31.

Chou, R.Y., 1988, "Volatility Persistence and Stock Valuations: Some Empirical Evidence Using Garch", *Journal of Applied Econometrics* 3, pp. 279-94.

Engle, R.F., 1982, "Autoregressive Conditional Heteroskedasticity with Estimates of the Variance of UK Inflation", *Econometrica* 50, pp. 987-1008.

Engle, R.F., D.M. Lilien and R.P. Robins, 1987, "Estimating Time Varying Risk Premia in the Term Structure: The ARCH-M Model", *Econometrica* 55, pp. 391-407.

Fama, E.F., 1965, "The Behavior of Stock Market Prices", *Journal of Business* 38, pp. 34-105.

French, K.R., G.W. Schwert and R.E. Stambaugh, 1987, "Expected Stock Returns and Volatility", *Journal of Financial Economics* 19, pp. 3-29.

Koutmos, G., U. Lee and P. Theodossiou, 1994, "Time-Varying Betas and Volatility Persistence in International Stock Markets", *Journal of Economics and Business* 46, pp. 101-12.

Lo, A., and G. MacKinlay, 1988, "Stock Market Prices do not Follow the Random Walks: Evidence from a Simple Specification Test", *Review of Financial Studies* 1, pp. 41-66.

Mandelbrot, B., 1963, "The Variation of Certain Speculative Prices", *Journal of Business* 36, pp. 394-419.

Merton, R.C., 1973, "An Intertemporal Capital Asset Pricing Model", *Econometrica* 41, pp. 867-87.

Nelson, D., 1991, "Conditional Heteroskedasticity in Asset Returns: A New Approach", *Econometrica* 45, pp. 347-70.

Pindyck, R., 1984, "Risk, Inflation and the Stock Market", *American Economic Review* 74, pp. 335-51.

Poterba, J., and L. Summers, 1986, "The Persistence of Volatility and Stock Market Fluctuations", *American Economic Review* 76, pp. 1142-51.

Volatility Reversion and Correlation Structure of Returns in Major International Stock Markets*

Panayiotis Theodossiou, Emel Kahya, Gregory Koutmos and Andreas Christofi
Rutgers University-Camden; Fairfield University; Monmouth University

This paper investigates the stochastic behaviour of weekly stock-market returns in the US, Japan, and the UK during the period 1984 to 1994. The analysis is carried out using an augmented version of Bollerslev's (1990) multivariate generalised autoregressive conditional heteroskedasticity (Garch) model with structural dummies to test for differences in the mean, volatility, and covariance structure of returns during the pre- and post-October 1987 crash periods. In addition, the paper explores the issue of the volatility reversion and time-varying behaviour of correlation structure of returns in these markets. Mean spillovers exist from the US and Japan to the UK. The magnitude of these spillovers is, however, low. Volatility spillovers exist from the US and, to a lesser extent, from Japan to the UK. Mean returns in all three markets and volatility in Japan and the UK are the same during the two periods, while volatility in the US is lower during the post-crash period. With the exception of the correlation of returns between Japan and the UK, which has doubled since the October 1987 crash, the remaining correlations are statistically similar during the two periods. Simulations performed indicate that volatility is reverting in the sense that, when it departs from its long-run equilibrium level, it tends to revert back to that level.

The growing globalisation of international stock markets raises questions as to: the nature and transmission mechanism of innovations and volatility shocks from one market to the others (mean and volatility spillovers); and whether volatility and correlations of returns in these markets have increased in recent years and, in particular, after the October 1987 international stock market crash.

A better understanding of these relationships can be useful to investors for developing new trading rules, establishing risk-hedging strategies, and rebalancing portfolios. Moreover, an increased contemporaneous correlation structure of returns has serious implications for international investors because it reduces the benefits derived from international portfolio diversification.

Several papers have investigated the transmission mechanism of stock price innovations (mean spillovers) across international stock markets. Eun and Shim (1989) and Koch and Koch (1991) find that stock market innovations in the US are rapidly transmitted to the rest of the world, whereas innovations in other national

* *This paper was first published in* The Financial Review, *Vol 32, No 2 (1997).*

markets have a very low impact on stock prices in the US. Similar findings are documented by Fischer and Palasvirta (1990) and Becker, Finnerty, and Gupta (1990). Von Furstenberg and Jeon (1989) find that correlations of stock market returns for the US, Japan, the UK, and Germany have doubled since the October 1987 crash.

Hamao, Masulis, and Ng (1990) and Theodossiou and Lee (1993) use multivariate extensions of the Garch model and test simultaneously for mean and volatility spillovers across major national stock markets. Multivariate Garch models allow for interaction effects within the conditional mean and conditional variance of two or more series and, as such, they provide a suitable framework to study the transmission mechanism of mean and volatility shocks across different markets. Unlike univariate Garch models, these models have not been used much because their estimation is cumbersome. Univariate Garch models have been used mainly to study the time-series behaviour of US stock market returns, eg Akgiray (1989), Baillie and DeGennaro (1990), Schwert (1990), and Schwert and Seguin (1990); exchange rates, eg Hsieh (1988, 1989), Baillie and Bollerslev (1989), Bollerslev (1990), Akgiray and Booth (1990), and Koutmos and Theodossiou (1994); and precious metals, eg Akgiray et al. (1991).[1]

Hamao, Masulis, and Ng (1990) document significant price volatility spillovers from the stock market of the US to Japan and the UK, and from the UK to Japan. In addition to these markets, Theodossiou and Lee (1993) consider the national stock markets of Germany and Canada. They find statistically significant volatility spillovers from the US to all four stock markets, from the UK to the Canadian stock market and from the German to the Japanese stock market. Interestingly, there are no volatility spillovers from the Canadian stock market to the other four markets. Moreover, volatility spillovers from the US to the German market and from the German market to the Japanese market are weak.

This chapter extends the work of Hamao, Masulis, and Ng (1990) and Theodossiou and Lee (1993) by investigating the issue of volatility reversion and behaviour of mean, volatility, and correlation structure of stock market returns in the US, Japan, and the UK during the pre- and post-October 1987 crash periods. The analysis is carried out using an augmented version of Bollerslev's (1990) model with structural dummies and more recent data. Estimates of the models are obtained simultaneously using the maximum likelihood estimation (MLE) method.[2] In addition, the behaviour of the correlation structure of returns over time is investigated using a state-space model based on the Kalman filter statistical method. The issue of increased correlations of returns is re-examined because Von Furstenberg and Jeon's (1989) findings may reflect transitory changes in the correlation structure of returns following the crash (their sample covers one year prior and one year after the crash). Moreover, their analysis does not take into account the time-varying volatility and volatility spillovers in these markets.

The chapter focuses on the stock markets of the US, Japan, and UK because they are the largest and most influential in the world, and other national stock markets are expected to have a small or no impact on them. The analysis is performed on weekly rather than daily or intra-daily data, because weekly data provide more accurate estimates of the mean and volatility spillovers, and contemporaneous correlations of returns in international stock markets with non-overlapping trading hours, such as the New York Stock Exchange (NYSE), the London Stock Exchange (LSE), and Tokyo Stock Exchange (TSE).

The paper is organised as follows: The second section discusses the data and presents some preliminary results. The third section elaborates on Bollerslev's multivariate Garch model and its estimation and presents some of the major findings. The fourth section explores the issue of reverting volatility. The fifth section investigates the state-space behaviour of the correlation structure of returns over time, and the sixth section presents a summary of the results and concluding remarks.

Data and preliminary findings

The data include weekly stock market returns for the US, Japan, and the UK and cover the period May 4, 1984 to October 21, 1994. The stock market returns for each country are computed using the formula $R_{i,t} = 100 * [\log(P_{i,t}) - \log(P_{i,t-1})]$, where $P_{i,t}$ is the level of the stock price index for country i based on Friday's closing prices, and i = US, JP, and UK. The indices are the S&P500 for the US, the Topix for Japan, and the FTSE100 for the UK

The remainder of this section explains the reasons for using weekly data. For this purpose, consider a 24-hour time chart of the operating hours of the three stock exchanges based on New York Eastern Standard Time.

1. Operating hours of the TSE, LSE and NYSE in New York EST

TSE 7pm _ _ _ _ _ _ _ _ 1am			
	LSE 4am _ _ _ _ _ _ _ _ _ _ 11am		
		NYSE 9am _ _ _ _ _ _ _ 4pm	
4pm _ 4pm			

The Tokyo market opens at 19.00 and closes at 01.00, the London market opens at 04.00 and closes at 11.00, and the New York market opens at 09.00 and closes at 16.00 Eastern Standard Time. Note that Tokyo and London are respectively 15 hours and 5 hours ahead of New York. The time overlap between daily (ie, close to close) US returns and daily Japanese returns is nine hours, between daily US returns and daily UK returns is 19 hours, and between daily Japanese returns and daily UK returns is 14 hours. The degree of overlap is measured by the ratio of time overlap to time frequency of returns. For the US and Japan it is 0.375 (= 9/24), for the US and the UK it is 0.7917 (= 19/24) and for Japan and the UK it is 0.5833 (= 14/24). Clearly, daily returns in these markets are not contemporaneous.

Because of imperfect overlapping, the pairwise correlations of daily returns in the three markets are expected to be biased downwards. Moreover, lag values of daily stock market returns and volatility shocks in the US and the UK are expected to exhibit a statistically significant relationship with current daily returns and volatility in the UK (US only) and Japan giving credence to the assertion of mean and volatility spillovers from the US to Japan and the UK and from the UK to Japan, when, in fact, such spillovers are not present. The downward bias in correlations and the size of spillover coefficients are expected to be smaller and insignificant for lower-frequency, such as the weekly, data.[3] A formal mathematical and empirical analysis of the above issues can be found in Kahya (1997).

Table 1 presents preliminary statistics for the three weekly stock market return series. The mean weekly returns are 0.1971% for the US, 0.1084% for Japan, and 0.1808% for the UK and, except for the US, they are statistically insignificant (5% level). The respective annual compounded figures are 10.78%, 5.80%, and 9.85%. The unconditional variance of returns for the US is 4.07, for Japan is 6.57 and for the UK it is 5.43. The distributions of returns in all three markets are negatively skewed and leptokurtic relative to

Table 1. Preliminary statistics on weekly return series

Statistics	US	Japan	UK
Mean	0.1971	0.1084	0.1808
	(2.27)*	(0.99)	(1.81)
Variance	4.0708	6.5696	5.4258
Skewness	–1.6304*	–0.4013*	–2.2581*
Kurtosis	13.43	3.52	24.02
KS	0.0619	0.0622	0.0554
Q(26)	33.58*	35.48*	46.43*
$Q^2(26)$	27.52	114.68*	7.92

The data cover the period May 4, 1984 to October 21, 1994, and include 544 weekly observations. Returns are expressed in percentages. Parentheses include the t-values for the estimates.
* Statistically significant at the 5% level.
KS is the Kolmogorov-Smirnov D statistics for testing normality. Q(26) and $Q^2(26)$ are the Ljung-Box test statistics for the returns and squared returns series, calculated using 26 lags. Their critical value at the 5% level is 32.89 (26 d.f.).

the normal distribution. The Kolmogorov-Smirnov (KS) statistics verify that the return series are not normally distributed. The Ljung-Box (LB) statistics show that the return series for all three countries and the squared return series for Japan are serially correlated.

Testing for mean and volatility spillovers

MULTIVARIATE GARCH MODEL

The existence of mean and volatility spillovers in the three national stock markets is investigated using a trivariate Garch model with structural dummies. The dummies are used to test for differential behaviour of the mean, volatility and correlation structure of returns during the pre- and post-October 1987 stock market crash periods. In this paper, the pre-crash period is May 4, 1984 to October 15, 1987, and the post-crash period is October 23, 1987, to October 21, 1994. The model is described by the following equations:

$$R_{i,t} = \mu_{i,t} + \varepsilon_{i,t}$$
$$= m_i + m_{C,i}C_t + \beta_{1,i}R_{t-1} + \beta_{2,i}R_{t-2} + \varepsilon_{i,t} \qquad (1)$$

$$\sigma^2_{i,t} = v_i + v_{C,i}C_t + \alpha_i\eta_{t-1} + \gamma_i\sigma^2_{i,t-1} \qquad (2)$$

$$\sigma_{i,j,t} = \left(\rho_{i,j} + \delta_{i,j}C_t\right)\sigma_{i,t}\sigma_{j,t} \qquad (3)$$

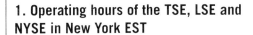

for i,j = US, JP, and UK, where $\mu_{i,t} \equiv E(R_{i,t} | \Phi_{t-1})$ and $\sigma^2_{i,t} \equiv Var(R_{i,t} | \Phi_{t-1})$ are the conditional mean and conditional variance of returns in market i based on past information, Φ_{t-1}; $\sigma_{ij,t} \equiv Cov(R_{i,t}, R_{j,t} | \Phi_{t-1})$ is the conditional covariance of returns in markets i and j; $\rho_{i,j}$ is the contemporaneous correlation; $\delta_{i,j}$ is a pre-crash deviation from $\rho_{i,j}$; and C_t is a dummy variable that takes the value of 1 for the pre-crash period and the value of 0 for the post-crash period.

The conditional means of returns in the three markets are specified as a VAR(2) process;[4] that is, a function of past returns from all three markets, $R_{t-s} = [R_{US,t-s}, R_{JP,t-s}, R_{UK,t-s}]'$ for s = 1 and 2. The autoregressive coefficients $\beta_{s,i} = [\beta_{s,i,US}, \beta_{s,i,JP}, \beta_{s,i,UK}]$, for i = US, JP, and UK, are indicative of mean spillovers from one market to the others. Specifically, statistically significant values for $\beta_{s,i,j}$ indicate that current returns in market i are influenced by their own past values. Statistically significant $\beta_{s,i,j}$ values, for $i \neq j$, indicate that current returns in market i are influenced by past returns in market j; ie, there are mean spillovers from market j to market i. The error term $\varepsilon_{i,t}$ represents innovations (shocks) in market i during week t.

The conditional variance of returns in each market is specified as a linear function of past volatility shocks from the three markets, represented by a vector of past squared innovations $\eta_{t-1} = [\varepsilon^2_{US,t-1}, \varepsilon^2_{JP,t-1}, \varepsilon^2_{UK,t-1}]'$ and their own past conditional variance $\sigma^2_{i,t-1}$. The conditional variance equation provides a means of exploring the transmission of volatility shocks from one market to the others (volatility spillovers). Let $\alpha_i = [\alpha_{i,US}, \alpha_{i,JP}, \alpha_{i,UK}]$. Then, statistically significant values for $\alpha_{i,j}$ indicate that volatility in market i is influenced by its own volatility shocks (own-volatility spillovers). Statistically significant $\alpha_{i,j}$ values for $i \neq j$ imply that current volatility in market i is influenced by past volatility shocks in market j, ie, there are volatility spillovers from market j to market i. Note that the estimated parameters for $\sigma^2_{i,t}$ are restricted to non-negative values because of the non-negativity property of the conditional variances.

The dummy variable C_t is included in equations (1)–(3) to test for differences in the conditional mean, conditional variance, and conditional covariance of returns during the pre- and post-crash periods. Note that the intercepts of the conditional mean and conditional variance equations of returns in each market are $m_i + m_{C,i}$ and $v_i + v_{C,i}$ for the pre-crash period and m_i and v_i for the post-crash period. Similarly, the correlations of returns are $\rho_{i,j} + \delta_{i,j}$ for the pre-crash period and $\rho_{i,j}$ for the post-crash period. The parameters $m_{C,i}$, $v_{C,i}$, and $\delta_{i,j}$ represent deviations from their respective post-crash values. Significant negative deviations indicate that the respective measures are lower during the pre-crash period.

Estimation and empirical findings

Parameter estimates for equations (1)–(3) are obtained by maximising the sample log-likelihood function

$$L(\theta) = -(1/2)\sum_{t=1}^{T}\left(\log\left|\Sigma_t\right| + \varepsilon_t'\Sigma_t^{-1}\varepsilon_t\right) \quad (4)$$

with respect to the parameter vector $\theta = (m_i, m_{C,i}, \beta_{1,i}, \beta_{2,i}, v_i, v_{C,i}, \alpha_i, \gamma_i, \rho_{i,j}, \delta_{i,j})$, where $\Sigma_t \equiv Cov(R_t | \Phi_{t-1})$ is the conditional variance-covariance matrix of the returns, $R_t = (R_{US,t}, R_{JP,t}, R_{UK,t})'$, $\varepsilon_t = R_t - \mu_t$ is a vector of market innovations, and $\mu_t \equiv E(R_t | \Phi_{t-1})$. The diagonal elements of Σ_t include the conditional variances $\sigma^2_{i,t}$, and the cross-diagonal elements include the conditional covariances $\sigma_{i,j,t}$. Standard errors and t-statistics for the estimates are obtained from the model's information matrix. The identification of the lag-structure of the model is accomplished using log-likelihood ratio tests as well as various diagnostic tests on the residuals of the model presented in the next section. The estimated parameters of the model are presented in Table 2.

Panel A of Table 2 presents the estimates for the conditional mean equations of returns. The results for the first lag-values indicate statistically significant mean-spillovers from the US and Japan to the UK. The spillover coefficients from the US to the UK is 0.1836, implying that positive returns in the US during one week cause positive returns in the UK during the next week. The spillover coefficient from Japan to the UK is −0.099 implying that negative returns in Japan during one week are followed by positive returns in the UK.

All autoregressive coefficients for the second lag-values of returns are statistically insignificant at the 5% level using univariate tests. However, the inclusion of second lags in the model can be justified using log-likelihood ratio tests as well as univariate diagnostic tests on the model's residuals. Conditional mean return parameters for a model with the dummy variable C_t are not reported because they are statistically insignificant at both the univariate and multivariate level (results available upon request).

Panel B of Table 2 presents the results for the conditional variance equations. These confirm the presence of significant conditional heteroskedasticity in the stock market returns of all three countries. The coefficients g_i for past conditional variances are large and highly significant, indicating high-volatility persistence. Significant own-volatility spillovers are present in the US and Japan only. The own-volatility spillover coefficient for the US is 0.1881, for Japan is 0.2316, while for the UK is 0, due to the non-negativity constraint for the conditional variances. The volatility spillover coefficient from the US to the UK is 0.2557 and from Japan to the UK is 0.0486. These findings imply that conditional volatility in the UK is triggered from the US, and to a lesser extent from Japan.

The coefficient for the pre-crash dummy is positive and statistically significant for the US only (5% level), indicating that volatility in the US has decreased during the post-crash period. Panel C of Table 2 presents the unconditional variances of returns during the pre- and post-crash periods. During the pre-crash period, volatility in the US is 4.2182; in Japan, 4.1041; and in the UK, 4.1856. The respective figures for the post-crash period are 3.4785, 7.1819, and 3.9612. The formula used to calculate these figures is presented in the next section. Note that only volatility in the US is statistically different during the two periods.

Panel D of Table 2 presents the contemporaneous correlations of returns. The correlation of returns for the US and Japan is 0.3668, for the US and the UK, it is 0.5276, and for Japan and the UK, it is 0.3952. Their respective deviations during the pre-crash period are all negative. However, only the deviation for Japan and the UK is statistically significant at the 5% level, indicating that the correlation of returns in Japan and the UK is smaller during the pre-crash period. The latter correlation for the pre- and post-crash periods is 0.1449 and 0.3952, respectively.

Various model specification tests performed on the standardised residuals, the squared standardised residuals, and cross products of the standardised residuals, indicate that the conditional mean and conditional variance equations of the multivariate Garch model are correctly specified (eg Bollerslev (1990), pp. 501–2, for more details). Results are available from the authors upon request.

Table 2. Multivariate Garch model estimates

Panel A: Conditional mean equations			
	$\mu_{US,t}$	$\mu_{JP,t}$	$\mu_{UK,t}$
Intercept	0.2963	0.2825	0.2590
	(3.99)*	(2.78)*	(2.67)*
$R_{US,t-1}$	−0.1296	0.1370	0.1836
	(−2.21)*	(1.93)	(2.37)*
$R_{JP,t-1}$	−0.0276	0.0031	−0.0990
	(−0.73)	(0.06)	(−2.10)
$R_{UK,t-1}$	0.0522	−0.0654	−0.0036
	(1.12)	(−1.18)	(−0.06)
$R_{US,t-2}$	0.0412	0.0420	0.1021
	(0.76)	(0.69)	(1.60)
$R_{JP,t-2}$	0.0181	0.0519	0.0037
	(0.49)	(0.93)	(0.08)
$R_{UK,t-2}$	−0.0305	−0.0967	0.0449
	(−0.72)	(−1.69)	(0.93)
Panel B: conditional variance equations			
	$\sigma^2_{US,t}$	$\sigma^2_{JP,t}$	$\sigma^2_{UK,t}$
Intercept	0.6206	0.7858	1.2106
	(3.63)*	(2.41)*	(3.45)*
C_t	0.5135	−0.4182	0.3221
	(2.36)*	(−1.88)	(1.01)
$\varepsilon^2_{US,t-1}$	0.1881	0.0695	0.2557
	(3.54)*	(1.35)	(4.17)*
$\varepsilon^2_{JP,t-1}$	0.0000	0.2316	0.0486
	(0.00)	(3.91)*	(2.77)*
$\varepsilon^2_{UK,t-1}$	0.0510	0.0000	0.0000
	(1.66)	(0.00)	(0.00)
$\sigma^2_{US,t-1}$	0.5619		
	(8.72)*		
$\sigma^2_{JP,t-1}$		0.6380	
		(7.57)*	
$\sigma^2_{UK,t-1}$			0.4438
			(4.15)*
Panel C: unconditional variances of returns			
	σ^2_{US}	σ^2_{JP}	σ^2_{UK}
Pre-crash	4.2182	4.1041	4.1856
Post-crash	3.4785	7.1819	3.9612
Panel D: contemporaneous correlations and pre-crash deviations			
i,j	**US, JP**	**US, UK**	**JP, UK**
$\rho_{i,j}$	0.3668	0.5276	0.3952
	(7.34)*	(12.5)*	(8.32)*
$\delta_{i,j}$	−0.0643	−0.1255	−0.2453
	(−0.69)	(−1.70)	(−2.32)*

The conditional mean of returns $\mu_{i,t}$ is specified as a linear function of past returns from all three markets $R_{j,t-s}$, where i,j = US, JP, and UK, and s = 1,2. Note that $R_{i,t} = \mu_{i,t} + \varepsilon_{i,t}$, where the error term $\varepsilon_{i,t}$ represents a market innovation. The conditional variance of returns $\sigma^2_{i,t}$ is specified as a linear function of past volatility shocks, measured by $\varepsilon^2_{j,t-1}$, its own past conditional variance $\sigma^2_{i,t-1}$, and a dummy variable C_t. C_t takes the value of 1 for the pre-crash period (May 4, 1984 to October 15, 1987) and the value of 0 for the post-crash period (October 23, 1987 to October 21, 1994). Some of the estimated parameters of the conditional variance equations are assigned the values of 0 because of the non-negativity constraints for the conditional variances. The unconditional variances are calculated using equation (6). The correlation of returns in markets i and j during the pre-crash period is $\rho_{i,j} + \delta_{i,j}$ and during the post-crash period is $\rho_{i,j}$. Parentheses include the t-values for the estimates.

* Statistically significant at the 5% level.

Volatility reversion

The previous findings document that stock market volatility in the US, Japan, and the UK depends on past volatility shocks and past conditional variances and, as such, is time varying. An issue that needs to be addressed is whether volatility in these markets is reverting. That is, when it departs from its long-run equilibrium level, measured by the unconditional variance of returns, it does tend to revert back to that level.[5] This is equivalent to saying that volatility shocks are transitory and have no permanent impact on future volatility.

The reminder of this section presents an analytical framework for testing the hypothesis of reverting volatility. For this purpose, the conditional variance equations of returns are put into their vector form

$$\sigma_t^2 = \nu + \nu_C C_t + \alpha\eta_{t-1} + \gamma\sigma_{t-1}^2, \qquad (5)$$

where $\sigma_t^2 = [\sigma_{t,US}^2, \sigma_{t,JP}^2, \sigma_{t,UK}^2]'$ is a 3×1 vector of conditional variances; $\nu = [\nu_{US}, \nu_{JP}, \nu_{UK}]'$ and $\nu_C = [\nu_{C,US}, \nu_{C,JP}, \nu_{C,UK}]'$ are 3×1 vectors of intercepts and pre-crash deviations for the intercepts related to the dummy variable C_t; $\alpha = [\alpha_{US}', \alpha_{JP}', \alpha_{UK}']'$ is a 3×3 matrix of spillover coefficients; $\eta_{t-1} = [\varepsilon_{US,t-1}^2, \varepsilon_{JP,t-1}^2, \varepsilon_{UK,t-1}^2]'$, $\gamma = \mathrm{diag}(\gamma_{US}, \gamma_{JP}, \gamma_{UK})$ is a 3 x 3 diagonal matrix.

It easily can be shown that the unconditional variance of returns, $\sigma^2 \equiv E(\sigma_t^2)$, is equal to:

$$\sigma^2 = (I - \alpha - \gamma)^{-1}(\nu + \nu_C C_t), \qquad (6)$$

where I is a 3×3 identity matrix. The latter requires that σ_t^2 is a stationary process, which is met when the roots of the polynomial $\det(I - \gamma z) = 0$ lie outside the complex unit circle, where det denotes the determinant of the matrix $(I - \alpha z)$ and z denotes the roots of the polynomial. Note that this requirement for stationarity is similar to that of a multivariate autoregressive-moving average process, eg Judge et al. (1985), pp. 656–9.[6] Moreover, the Arch component $\alpha\eta_{t-1}$ of equation (5) would be invertible. Consequently, the conditional variance σ_t^2 could be expressed as a geometric function of past conditional variances σ_{t-s}^2, for $s = 1,\ldots,\infty$, if the roots of $\det(I - \alpha z) = 0$ lie outside the complex unit circle.

Substituting $(\nu + \nu_C C_t) = (I - \alpha - \gamma)\sigma^2$ from equation (6) into equation (5) gives:

$$\sigma_t^2 = \sigma^2 + \alpha(\eta_{t-1} - \sigma^2) + \gamma(\sigma_{t-1}^2 - \sigma^2). \qquad (7)$$

This equation models conditional volatility at a given point in time as a function of past volatility shocks, η_{t-1}, and past conditional variances σ_{t-1}^2, both expressed in deviations from their respective means σ^2. Under stationarity, the above equation can be expressed as an infinite order Arch process

$$\sigma_t^2 = \sigma^2 + \alpha(\eta_{t-1} - \sigma^2) + \gamma\alpha(\eta_{t-2} - \sigma^2)$$
$$+\gamma^2\alpha(\eta_{t-3} - \sigma^2) + \ldots + \gamma^\infty\alpha(\eta_{t-\infty} - \sigma^2). \qquad (8)$$

This specification expresses conditional volatility in the three markets as a "multivariate" geometric function of past volatility shocks $(\eta_{t-s} - \sigma^2)$, for $s = 1,2,\ldots,\infty$. Due to stationarity, the impact of past volatility shocks on future volatility is expected to decline geometrically with time. In the limit, past volatility shocks have a zero impact on future volatility, ie $\lim_{s\to\infty}\gamma^s\alpha = 0$. Moreover, equation (8) indicates that above-average volatility shocks, ie $(\eta_{t-s} - \sigma^2) > 0$, during one period generally result in larger volatility during the next period. However, the impact of such shocks on future volatility is expected to decline over time. Under normal conditions, volatility will level down to its mean value. The opposite is true for below-average volatility shocks.

Based on the previous parameter estimates of the conditional variance equations, the length of the roots of the polynomial $\det(I - \gamma z) = 0$ are found to be 1.5673, 1.7796, and 2.2531. These roots are greater than 1, providing support to the hypothesis of stationary conditional variances. Moreover, the roots of the polynomial $\det(I - \alpha z) = 0$ are 3.8327, 4.7430, and 19.2711, providing support to the hypothesis of inevitability of the Arch component of the conditional variance.

To further assess the validity of the above results, the distribution of the minimum length root for each polynomial is approximated using 10,000 samples of randomly generated parameters for α and γ. The random parameters, denoted by $\tilde{\alpha}$ and $\tilde{\gamma}$, are generated by adding a random component to their respective MLE estimators. That is, $\tilde{\alpha}_{i,j} = \hat{\alpha}_{i,j} + se(\hat{\alpha}_{i,j})\xi_{i,j}$ and $\tilde{\gamma}_i = \hat{\gamma}_i + se(\hat{\gamma}_i)\xi_i$ where $\hat{\alpha}_{i,j}$ and $\hat{\gamma}_i$ are the MLE estimators for $\alpha_{i,j}$ and γ_i, $se(\hat{\alpha}_{i,j})$ and $se(\hat{\gamma}_i)$ are the standard errors of the estimators obtained from the information matrix, $\xi_{i,j}$ and ξ_i are randomly generated Gaussian errors with zero mean and unit variance, and i,j = US, JP, and UK. Interestingly, the minimum roots for each polynomial and all samples are greater than 1, providing strong support to the hypotheses of stationarity and inevitability of the Arch component of the conditional variance equations. Specifically, the minimum and maximum of the minimum length root for the polynomial $\det(I - \gamma z) = 0$ are 1.0664 and 2.3626, respectively, and for the polynomial $\det(I - \alpha z) = 0$ they are 2.236 and 3.7232 respectively.

State-space behaviour of correlation structure

The time-varying behaviour of the correlation of returns in the three markets is also explored using the Kalman filter technique. Under the Kalman filter technique, the cross product of standardised residuals, $z_{i,j,t} \equiv \varepsilon_{i,t}\varepsilon_{j,t}/(\sigma_{i,t}\sigma_{j,t})$, is specified as:

$$z_{i,j,t} = \rho_{i,j,t} + u_{i,j,t} \qquad (9)$$

where $\rho_{i,j,t}$, for $i \neq j$, is a state-space (time-varying) contemporaneous correlation of returns in markets i and j, and $u_{i,j,t}$ is a white-noise process with mean zero and variance equal to $\sigma^2_{u,i,j}$ for i,j = US, JP and UK. The behaviour of $\rho_{i,j,t}$ is described by the following transition equation:

$$\rho_{i,j,t} = \rho_{i,j} + \theta_{i,j}\left(\rho_{i,j,t-1} - \rho_{i,j}\right) + \upsilon_{i,j,t} \qquad (10)$$

where $\upsilon_{i,j,t}$, is a white-noise process with zero mean and variance $\sigma^2_{\upsilon,i,j}$, and $\rho_{i,j}$ is the unconditional mean of $\rho_{i,j,t}$. The parameter $\theta_{i,j}$ describes the state-space behaviour of the correlation of returns in markets i and j. For $\theta_{i,j} = 0$, then $\rho_{i,j,t} = \rho_{i,j} + \upsilon_{i,j,t}$, and the correlation deviates around its mean value of $\rho_{i,j}$ in a random (i.i.d.) fashion. For $|\theta_{i,j}| < 1$, the process deviates around its mean in a systematic fashion determined by the sign and size of the coefficient $\theta_{i,j}$. If, however, $\theta_{i,j} = 1$ the correlation coefficient is a random-walk process. The latter two cases (ie $\theta_{i,j} \neq 0$) imply that the constant correlation assumption of the multivariate Garch model is violated.

The Kalman filter technique is applied to data for both the pre- and post-crash periods. The estimated transition equations of the correlation coefficients for the pre-crash period are:

$$\hat{\rho}_{US,JP,t} = \underset{(2.55)^*}{0.2591} - \underset{(-0.003)}{0.0008}(\hat{\rho}_{US,JP,t-1} - 0.2591)$$

$$\hat{\rho}_{US,UK,t} = \underset{(2.36)^*}{0.3373} - \underset{(-0.08)}{0.0743}(\hat{\rho}_{US,UK,t-1} - 0.3373)$$

$$\hat{\rho}_{JP,UK,t} = \underset{(2.55)^*}{0.1036} + \underset{(1.08)}{0.0126}(\hat{\rho}_{JP,UK,t-1} - 0.1036)$$

while for the post-crash period:

$$\hat{\rho}_{US,JP,t} = \underset{(4.08)^*}{0.3379} + \underset{(0.99)}{0.0008}(\hat{\rho}_{US,JP,t-1} - 0.2591)$$

$$\hat{\rho}_{US,UK,t} = \underset{(5.41)^*}{0.4956} + \underset{(0.63)}{0.0637}(\hat{\rho}_{US,UK,t-1} - 0.4956)$$

$$\hat{\rho}_{JP,UK,t} = \underset{(4.38)^*}{0.3556} + \underset{(0.31)}{0.0445}(\hat{\rho}_{JP,UK,t-1} - 0.3556).$$

Note that the parameters θ_{ij} for all six transition equations are statistically insignificant, lending support to the assumption that the correlation structure of returns is not time-varying. These results are in line with the constant correlation multivariate Garch model.

Summary and concluding remarks

This chapter investigates the stochastic behaviour of weekly stock market returns in the US, Japan, and the UK for the period 1984 to 1994. The analysis is carried out using an augmented version of Bollerslev's (1990) multivariate Garch model with structural dummies to test for differences in the behaviour of the mean, volatility, and covariance structure of returns during the pre- and post-October 1987 crash periods. In addition, the paper explores the issue of volatility reversion and investigates the time-varying behaviour of the correlation structure of returns in these markets, using the Kalman filter statistical method.

Statistically significant mean-spillovers exist from the US and Japan to the UK. The magnitude of these spillovers is, however, low. Significant conditional heteroskedasticity is present in the returns series of all three markets. Volatility spillovers exist from the US and, to a lesser extent, from Japan to the UK. Significant own-volatility spillovers are present in the US and Japan, but not in the UK. The latter results imply that conditional volatility in the UK is imported from abroad, and predominantly from the US. These findings are in general agreement with those of Hamao, Masulis, and Ng (1990) and Theodossiou and Lee (1993).

The behaviour of mean returns and volatility during the pre- and post-crash periods is statistically the same in all three markets, except for volatility in the US, which is lower during the post-crash period. The correlations of returns for the US with Japan and the UK are the same during the pre- and post-crash periods. However, the correlation of returns between Japan and the UK is more than twice as large during the post-crash period, indicating a higher degree of integration between the two markets.

Simulations performed show that volatility in all three markets is reverting in the sense that, when it departs from its long-run equilibrium level, it tends to revert back to that level. Volatility reversion also implies that past volatility shocks have a transitory impact on future volatility in that their impact diminishes over time. This suggests that regulatory agencies do not have to take long-range measures to reduce the impact of large volatility shocks on future volatility in these markets.

Kalman filter tests applied on the cross-product of standardised residuals of the multivariate Garch model indicate that the contemporaneous correlations of returns in the three markets are not time varying. This suggests that deviations of correlations from their mean values are random and, therefore, the assumption of constant correlation imposed on the Garch model is valid. These findings are in general agreement with the conclusions reached by Philippatos, Christofi, and Christofi (1983), although the latter authors have used different methodology and samples.

Moreover, a constant correlation structure implies that increased co-movements in the stock indices that are observed after market corrections are due to changes in the covariance structure of returns rather than the correlation structure. In particular, the increased magnitude of volatility is offset by an equivalent change in the covariance structure, leaving the correlations unaffected.

1 *An extensive literature review of Garch applications in finance is provided in Bollerslev, Chou, and Kroner (1992).*

2 *See Bollerslev (1990) for the details. Hamao, Masulis, and Ng (1990) use a two-step procedure to estimate the parameters of the model. In step one, they estimate univariate Garch models to obtain residuals for each of the return series. In stage two, they use the squared residuals as explanatory variables in the conditional variance of each series and, via univariate MLE, they obtain estimates for the volatility spillover coefficients. This approach provides unbiased but inefficient estimates relative to the simultaneous estimation technique used in this paper.*

3 *The degree of overlapping for weekly returns in the US and in Japan is 0.9107 (= 153/168); in the US and the UK, 0.9702 (= 163/168); and in Japan and the UK, 0.9405 (= 158/168).*

4 *Previous papers have found no linkage between conditional mean and conditional variance of stock market returns, eg Baillie and DeGennaro (1990) and Theodossiou and Lee (1993, 1995).*

5 *The concept of volatility reversion is an extension of that of mean reversion to the variance of stock returns, eg, Poterba and Summers (1988) for the concept of mean reversion.*

6 *This condition for stationarity is the same as* $\det[I - \gamma z] \neq 0$ *for* $|z| \leq 1$, *stated in Judge et al (1985) p. 657. Note that stationarity implies that the process is not integrated Garch.*

BIBLIOGRAPHY

Akgiray, V., 1989, "Conditional Heteroskedasticity in Time Series of Stock Returns: Evidence and Forecasts", *Journal of Business* 62, pp. 55-80.

Akgiray, V., and G.G. Booth, 1990, "Modeling the Stochastic Behavior of Canadian Foreign Exchange Rates", *Journal of Multinational Financial Management* 1, pp. 43-71.

Akgiray, V., G.G. Booth, J.J. Hatem, and C. Mustafa, 1991, "Conditional Dependence in Precious Metal Prices", *The Financial Review* 26, pp. 367-86.

Baillie, R.T., and T. Bollerslev, 1989, "The Message in Daily Exchange Rates: A Conditional Variance Tale", *Journal of Business and Economics Statistics* 7, pp. 297-305.

Baillie, R.T., and R.P. DeGennaro, 1990, "Stock Returns and Volatility", *Journal of Financial and Quantitative Analysis* 25, pp. 203-14.

Becker, K.G., J.E. Finnerty and M. Gupta, 1990, "The Intertemporal Relation Between the US and Japanese Stock Markets", *Journal of Finance* 45, pp. 1297-306.

Bollerslev, T., 1990, "Modelling the Coherence in Short-Run Nominal Exchange Rates: A Multivariate Generalized Arch Approach", *Review of Economics and Statistics* 72, pp. 498-505.

Bollerslev, T., R. Chou and K.F. Kroner, 1992, "Arch Modeling in Finance: A Review of Theory and Empirical Evidence", *Journal of Econometrics* 52, pp. 5-59; reprinted as Chapter 2 of the present volume.

Eun, C.S., and S. Shim, 1989, "International Transmission of Stock Market Movements", *Journal of Financial and Quantitative Analysis* 24, pp. 241-56.

Fischer, K.P., and A.P. Palasvirta,1990, "High Road to Global Marketplace: The International Transmission of Stock Fluctuations", *The Financial Review* 25, pp. 371-94.

Hamao, Y., R.W. Masulis and V. Ng, 1990, "Correlation in Price Changes Across International Stock Markets", *Review of Financial Studies* 3, pp. 281-307.

Hsieh, D.A., 1988, "The Statistical Properties of Daily Foreign Exchange Rates: 1974-1983", *Journal of International Economics* 24, pp.129-45.

Hsieh, D.A.,1989, "Modeling Heteroskedasticity in Foreign Exchange Rates", *Journal of Business and Economics Statistics* 7, pp. 307-17.

Judge, G.G., W.E. Griffiths, R. Carter Hill, H. Lütkepohl and T-C. Lee, 1985, *The Theory and Practice of Econometrics*, Second Edition, New York: John Wiley.

Kahya, E., 1997, "Correlations of Returns in Non-Contemporaneous Markets", *Multinational Finance Journal* 1 (2), pp. 18-29.

Koch, P.D., and T.W. Koch, 1991, "Evolution in Dynamic Linkage Across Daily National Stock Indexes", *Journal of International Money and Finance* 10, pp. 231-51.

Koutmos, G., and P. Theodossiou, 1994, "Time-Series Properties and Predictability of Greek Exchange Rates", *Managerial and Decision Economics* 15, pp. 159-67.

Philippatos, G.C., A. Christofi and P. Christofi, 1983, "The Inter-Temporal Stability of International Stock Market Relationships: Another View", *Financial Management* 12, pp. 63-9.

Poterba, J.M., and L.H. Summers, 1988, "Mean Reversion

in Stock Prices: Evidence and Implications", *Journal of Financial Economics* 22, pp. 27-59.

Schwert, W.G., 1990, "Stock Volatility and the Crash of '87," *Review of Financial Studies* 3, pp. 77-102.

Schwert, W.G., and P.J. Seguin, 1990, "Heteroskedasticity in Stock Returns", *Journal of Finance* 45, pp. 1129-55.

Theodossiou, P., and U. Lee, 1993, "Mean and Volatility Spillovers Across Major National Stock Markets: Further Empirical Evidence", *Journal of Financial Research* 16, pp. 337-50.

Theodossiou, P., and U. Lee, 1995, "Relationship Between Volatility and Expected Returns Across International Stock Markets", *Journal of Business, Finance, and Accounting* 21, pp. 289-300; reprinted as Chapter 16 of the present volume.

Von Furstenberg, G.M., and B. N. Jeon, 1989, "International Stock Price Movements: Links and Messages", *Brookings Papers on Economic Activity* 1, pp. 125-79.

18

International Linkages in the Nikkei Stock Index Futures Markets*

G. Geoffrey Booth, Tae-Hwy Lee and Yiuman Tse

Louisiana State University; University of California, Riverside; Binghamton University

This paper analyses the linkages and information transmission of similar Nikkei stock index futures contracts traded on three international exchanges, the OSE, SIMEX, and CME. Comparisons between the trading and nontrading time variances within individual markets and across markets indicate that relevant information is revealed during the trading hours of the OSE and SIMEX, but not the CME. An approach of variance decomposition and impulse response functions exploring the common stochastic trend in the cointegration system is employed. The common factor is found to be simply driven by the last trading market in the 24-hour trading sequence. Specifically, each market, while it is trading, impounds all the information that will affect other markets, and rides on the common stochastic trend. Granger- causality also runs from the market(s) that is placed in the last trading order within 24 hours in the vector error correction model but this causal relationship is shorter than one day. On balance, the three markets are informationally efficient on a daily basis.

Nikkei 225 futures are now the most actively traded stock index futures contracts in the world, though their trading history is shorter than other stock index futures contracts. This paper investigates the international transmission mechanism in three Nikkei 225 futures markets contained in the Osaka, Singapore, and Chicago exchanges. Bacha and Vila (1994) document that the introduction of Nikkei futures has no significant effect on the volatility in the Japanese stock market. Bacha and Vila (1993) report no evidence of lead-lag relationship between the Nikkei futures traded on the Chicago exchange and those traded on the Osaka and Singapore markets. Nevertheless, no previous paper has explored the common stochastic trend within the cointegration system of these three futures markets. A better understanding of the transmission mechanism by using this approach may provide investors with more efficient strategies for hedging or speculating the risk associated with Japanese stocks.

The Nikkei Stock Average (NSA) comprises 225 top-rated Japanese companies listed in the First Section of the Tokyo Stock Exchange (TSE), which is the largest stock market in the world in terms of both of the value of listed stocks and daily trading volume. In September 1986, the Singapore International Monetary Exchange (SIMEX) introduced futures contracts on the NSA. After two years, in September 1988, Nikkei futures started trading in the Osaka Securities Exchange (OSE) following financial reforms in Japan. One of the most dramatic changes in

**This paper was first published in the* Pacific-Basin Finance Journal, *Vol. 4 (1996). It is reprinted with kind permission of Elsevier Science - NL, Sara Burgerhartstraat 25, 1055 KV Amsterdam, The Netherlands. The authors would like to thank S. Ghon Rhee and two anonymous referees for useful comments and suggestions.*

recent years in the US markets has been the increase in market value of non-US equities. In response to the increasing demand for diversification and risk management among US pension funds, mutual funds, and institutional and individual traders, in September 1990, the Chicago Mercantile Exchange (CME) began trading futures contracts on the NSA. Since that time, Nikkei futures at the CME have become the second largest (next to S&P 500) equity index contract traded in the US.[1] Moreover, the interrelationship between the Nikkei futures at the SIMEX and CME is strengthened by the mutual offset arrangement between them.[2]

Although Nikkei futures at the OSE was launched later than the SIMEX, they are currently more actively traded at the OSE. The 1993 annual trading volume in value of Nikkei futures traded at the OSE was ¥170 trillion ($1.5 trillion), and was about three times that traded on the SIMEX and 30 times that traded on the CME. These three Nikkei futures markets differ in several aspects. In particular,

- the OSE is more regulated and has much higher transaction costs (commissions, margins, and price limits) than the other two markets (Bacha and Vila, 1994);
- the SIMEX and CME use open outcry auctions with a large number of brokers-dealers, while the OSE adopts the computer-assisted trading system without a designated market maker;
- the OSE has a greater proportion of investors who are large institutional investors and corporations;
- the CME contracts is dollar denominated, while the SIMEX and OSE contracts are denominated in yen; and
- the contract size and settlement dates are different (Bacha and Vila, 1993).

Hereafter, for simplicity, OSE, SIMEX, and CME are used to represent the corresponding Nikkei futures, and results are presented in this order, which is in the descending order of trading volume.

In Tokyo time, the OSE trades from 9:00am to 3:00pm (6 hours) with a lunch break from 11:00 am to 12:30pm, the SIMEX trades from 9:00am to 3:15pm (6.25 trading hours), and the CME trades from 10:20pm to 5:15am (7.25 trading hours).[3] Thus, the OSE and SIMEX futures contracts are traded almost simultaneously, except for the two-hour lunch break at the OSE and the last 15 minutes at the SIMEX, while the contracts at the CME are traded exclusively when the former markets and the spot market (NSA) are closed. More importantly, two possible orderings of the trading sequence within 24 hours can be constructed among these three futures markets. Note that on a calendar basis, the OSE and SIMEX open earlier than the CME. Denote t as the trading day index. Sequence 1 represents the trading sequence as the usual way with the CME as the last trading market within a 24-hour interval, ie, $\{OSE_t, SIMEX_t\}$ and CME_t. Sequence 2 represents the trading sequence with the CME as the *first* trading market, ie, CME_t and $\{OSE_{t+1}, SIMEX_{t+1}\}$. The importance of these two trading sequences is evinced subsequently.

Comparing the trading and nontrading time variances, the OSE and SIMEX markets are found to be more volatile when they are trading. In contrast, the Chicago market is more volatile when it is closed. These results are consistent with the notion that relevant information is revealed during the Japanese business hours and the trading hours of the NSA spot market, which are also the trading hours of the OSE and SIMEX. Moreover, the nontrading (trading) variance of the CME is close to the trading (nontrading) variances of the OSE and SIMEX. These results suggest that the three markets are driven by the same kind of information. The three Nikkei futures are shown to be cointegrated with a single stochastic trend. However, none of the markets Granger-cause the other two markets on a daily basis. Instead, causality runs from the last trading market(s) in the 24-hour trading sequence but this causal relationship is shorter than one day. The impulse responses and the fractions of forecast error variances in each market attributed to the common stochastic trend are computed. Employing an approach that explores this common factor and allowing for the nonsynchronous trading problem among markets, the paper shows that the common factor is simply driven by the last trading market(s) in the 24-hour trading sequence. These results suggest informational efficiency on a daily basis: the responses of all markets to an innovation to the common factor are fully settled within a day. Moreover, the paper provides some weak evidence that the tighter regulations and higher transaction costs of the OSE market may impede the information transmission mechanism in the market.

Data and summary statistics

Daily open and close futures prices of nearest contracts until the maturity month for the period after three months of the introduction of Nikkei futures at the CME – December 3, 1990 to May

18, 1994 (900 observations) – are obtained from Commodity Systems, Inc (CSI). When trading day data are not available due to holidays, the index price is assumed to stay the same as the previous trading day.[4] Moreover, logarithmic transformation for the futures price is adopted.

Table 1 summarises the descriptive statistics of close-to-close futures price changes. Comparing the variance, skewness, and kurtosis, it shows that they give similar results – all futures price changes exhibit slightly positive skewness, and moderately "heavy-tailed" (with respect to the normal distribution), and the variances are almost the same. The last result implies that the markets incorporate information at the same speed, assuming that variances are directly related to information flow (Ross, 1989). The Ljung-Box Q-statistics show that all futures price changes are not significantly autocorrelated. The strong Arch effects (Engle, 1982) are indicated by the Langrange multiplier Arch tests. Together with insignificant means, the statistics suggest a martingale process with Garch (Bollerslev, 1986) innovations in the Nikkei futures markets. Not surprisingly, Table 1 also indicates that the futures price changes of the three markets are highly correlated, with SIMEX and OSE having a correlation coefficient of greater than 0.9 and with the other two coefficients being approximately the same.

Table 1. Sample statistics of yield changes ($close_t – close_{t-1}$)
December 3, 1990–May 18, 1994 (900 observations). Asymptotic p-values are contained in parentheses

	ΔOSE	ΔSIMEX	ΔCME
Mean	-1.57×10^{-4}	-1.57×10^{-4}	-1.48×10^{-4}
	(0.743)	(0.764)	(0.778)
Median	0.00	0.00	0.00
Variance (σ^2)	2.10×10^{-4}	2.46×10^{-4}	2.10×10^{-4}
Skewness	0.112	0.201	0.201
	(0.170)	(0.014)	(0.014)
Excess kurtosis	0.697	2.47	2.47
	(<0.001)	(<0.001)	(0.001)
Ljung-Box Q-stat, Q(12)	8.82	9.82	17.6
	(0.718)	(0.632)	(0.130)
LM Arch(12) test	74.9	52.9	62.4
	(<0.001)	(<0.001)	(<0.001)
Correlation coefficients			
ΔOSE		0.912	0.764
ΔSIMEX			0.818

Volatility during trading and nontrading hours

Numerous papers report that return variance for stocks are higher during trading than nontrading hours. See, for example, Fama (1965), Oldfield and Rogalaski (1980), and French and Roll (1986) for US stock markets, Barclay *et al* (1990) and Chang *et al* (1993) for Japanese markets, and Chan and Chan (1993) for Hong Kong markets. Three hypotheses have been proposed for this phenomenon:

- greater amounts of public information revealed;
- more private information released; and
- a greater level of noise during trading hours.

Specifically, if return volatility is mainly derived from private information and noise trading, return volatility is related to trading activities when the market is open. However, if volatility is caused by the release of public information, volatilities during trading and nontrading hours are only related to the information flow instead of trading activities.

Comparisons between trading and nontrading time variances within individual markets and across markets may shed some light on the information, either private or public, transmission mechanism among the three Nikkei futures markets. Since relevant information is likely to be revealed during the Japanese business hours and the trading hours of the NSA spot market, which are also the trading hours of the OSE and SIMEX, volatilities of trading hours of these two markets are expected to be higher than those of nontrading hours. The opposite should be true for the CME, ie the nontrading time variance is higher, because the nontrading hours of the CME overlap the trading hours of the OSE and SIMEX. Of particular interest, the paper compares the nontrading (trading) time variance of the CME market with the trading (nontrading) time variances of the other two markets. If these three markets are driven by the same kind of information, the nontrading (trading) time variance per hour of the CME should be close to the trading (nontrading) time variances per hour of the OSE and SIMEX markets.

EMPIRICAL RESULTS

Table 2 Panel A demonstrates that the trading time (open-to-close) variance per hour, σ_T^{2*}, of ΔCME (0.041) is much smaller than those of ΔOSE (0.232) and ΔSIMEX (0.322). In contrast, in Panel B, the Chicago market gives the greatest nontrading time (close-to-open) variance per hour, σ_N^{2*}. The per hour trading and nontrading time variance ratios, $\sigma_T^{2*}/\sigma_N^{2*}$, are presented in Panel C. Panels B and C report both of the results when the weekends and holidays are included and when they are not included. Since the week-

Table 2. A comparison of trading time (open-to-close) variances, σ_T^2, and nontrading time (close-to-open) variances, σ_N^2

	ΔOSE	ΔSIMEX	ΔCME
Panel A: Trading time variances (10^{-4})			
Total variance, σ_T^2	1.39	2.01	0.298
Variance per hour, σ_T^{2*},σ_T^2/(no of trading hours)	0.232	0.322	0.041
Panel B: Nontrading time variances (10^{-4})			
Total variance, σ_N^2			
With weekends and holidays	0.708	0.707	2.25
No weekends and holidays	0.555	0.490	2.12
Variance per hour, σ_N^{2*},σ_N^2/(no of trading hours)			
With weekends and holidays	0.039	0.040	0.134
No weekends and holidays	0.031	0.028	0.126
Panel C: Trading time and nontrading time variance ratio			
Total variance ratio, σ_T^2/σ_N^2			
With weekends and holidays	1.96	2.84	0.132
No weekends and holidays	2.50	4.10	0.141
Variance per hour ratio, $\sigma_T^{2*}/\sigma_N^{2*}$			
With weekends and holidays	5.95	8.05	0.306
No weekends and holidays	7.19	11.50	0.325
Panel D: Bartlett's test statistic for homogeneity of variance[a]			
H_0: σ_T^{2*} of ΔCME = σ_N^{2*} of ΔSIMEX		0.223 (0.64)	
H_0: σ_T^{2*} of ΔCME = σ_N^{2*} of ΔOSE		0.030 (0.86)	
H_0: σ_N^{2*} of ΔCME = σ_T^{2*} of ΔSIMEX		164.5 (<0.001)	
H_0: σ_N^{2*} of ΔCME = σ_T^{2*} of ΔOSE		56.6 (<0.001)	

[a] The Bartlett's test statistic has an approximate $\chi^2(1)$ distribution under the null hypothesis of equal variances. Asymptotic p-values are contained in parentheses.

Table 3. Augmented Dickey-Fuller and Phillips-Perron root tests

	OSE	SIMEX	CME
ADF (no trend)	–1.547	–1.531	–1.500
ADF (with trend)	–1.661	–1.697	–1.648
Phillips-Peron (no trend)	–1.598	–1.628	–1.553
Phillips-Peron (with trend)	–1.726	–1.718	–1.598

The statistics are computed with one lag for the ADF tests and one nonzero autocovariance in Newey and West (1987) correction for the Phillips-Peron tests. The lag length is selected by the AIC and similar results are given for higher lags up to 20. The critical values for both statistics, which are asymptotically equivalent, are available in Fuller (1976, p. 373). The 5% critical values are –2.86 (no trend) and –3.41 (with trend).

ends and holidays do not affect the results qualitatively as shown, only the results with the weekends and holidays are discussed. The results show that the trading time variances are greater than the nontrading time variances in the Osaka and Singapore markets with the ratios of 5.95 and 8.05, respectively; but the opposite is true for the Chicago market with a ratio of 0.306. The results are consistent with aforementioned argument that the relevant information is released in Japanese business hours.

It is worth noting that although noise trading may explain the low trading time variance of the CME (the trading volume of which is much smaller than the OSE and SIMEX), it cannot describe the high nontrading time variance of the CME. Moreover, the trading volume of the OSE is three times of that of the SIMEX, but the trading time variance per hour of the OSE is smaller. These results are consistent with Bacha and Vila (1994), who find that the intradaily variance using daily high/low prices is higher at the SIMEX Nikkei futures market for the period September 1986 to August 1991. Examining why the trading time variance of the OSE is smaller than that of the SIMEX is beyond the scope of the paper. Bacha and Vila (1994), however, point out that these results may be caused by the tighter regulation and high transaction costs and the two-hour lunch break of the OSE.[5]

Of particular interest, the first two rows of Panel D show that the trading variance per hour, σ_T^{2*}, of ΔCME (0.041) is statistically equal to the nontrading variance per hour, σ_N^{2*}, of ΔOSE and ΔSIMEX (both 0.04). Moreover, the magnitude of σ_N^{2*} of ΔCME (0.134) is close to σ_T^{2*} of ΔOSE (0.223) and ΔSIMEX (0.322), though the last two rows of Panel D indicate that σ_N^{2*} of ΔCME is statistically different from both of them. As mentioned before, the nontrading (trading) hours of the CME overlap the trading (nontrading) hours of the OSE and SIMEX. These results not only further support the argument that information is revealed during the trading hours of the OSE and SIMEX, but also imply that these three markets are driven by the same kind of information.

Unit root and cointegration

Table 3 presents the unit root results using the augmented Dickey-Fuller (ADF) (Dickey and Fuller, 1979; and 1981) tests and the Phillips-Perron (PP) (Phillips, 1987; and Phillips and Perron, 1988) tests.[6] Both tests do not reject the null hypothesis of unit roots. These results show that OSE_t, $SIMEX_t$, and CME_t can be characterised as I(1) processes and, accordingly, they can wander extensively. Since these three futures contracts are very similar, their futures prices should move together and should not diverge from each other in the long run. Cointegration, which can describe the existence of this equilibrium (or stationary) relationship among nonstationary series, is used to analyse the information transmission of the three futures markets. The theory of cointegration is fully developed in Granger (1986) and Engle and Granger (1987).

Johansen (1988, 1991) has developed the maximum likelihood estimator for a cointegrated system. Let $Y_t \equiv (OSE_t\ SIMEX_t\ CME_t)'$; n = the number of variables in the system, three in this case. If Y_t is cointegrated, it can be generated by a vector error correction model (VECM):

$$\Delta Y_t = \mu + \sum_{i=1}^{k-1} G_i \Delta Y_{t-i} + G_k Y_{t-1} + \varepsilon_t, \quad (1)$$

where μ is a 3×1 vector of drift, G's are 3×3 matrices of parameters, and ε_t is a 3×1 white noise vector. The Johansen trace test statistic of the null hypothesis that there are at most r cointegrating vectors $0 \leq r \leq n$, and thus $(n - r)$ common stochastic trends is

$$\text{trace} = -(T - nk) \sum_{i=r+1}^{n} \ln\left(1 - \hat{\lambda}_i\right), \quad (2)$$

where $\hat{\lambda}_i$'s are the $n - r$ smallest squared canonical correlations of Y_{t-1} with respect to ΔY_t corrected for lagged differences and T is the sample size actually used for estimation. Following the correction suggested by Reinsel and Ahn (1992), $(T - nk)$ instead of T is used in equation (2) (and equations (3) and (4) below). The Johansen maximum eigenvalue (λ_{max}) test statistic of the null hypothesis that there are r cointegrating vectors against $r + 1$ is

$$\lambda_{max} = -(T - nk) \ln\left(1 - \hat{\lambda}_{r+1}\right), \quad (3)$$

where $\hat{\lambda}_{r+1}$ is the $(r + 1)$th greatest squared canonical correlation.

The results of the Johansen (1991) cointegration tests are reported in Table 4. It demonstrates that the futures prices of the three markets are cointegrated with $r = 2$, indicating that there is one common stochastic trend. The lag length k equal to 2 (i.e., one lag of ΔY_t) in the VECM (1) is chosen by the Schwarz information criteria (SIC) (results not reported). Reimers (1991) finds that the SIC does well in selecting k and the residual diagnostics shown in the table indicate that the residuals from each equation in the VECM are not significantly autocorrelated. Results reported in this paper are qualitatively the same for k = 3 to 6; the lag length chosen by AIC is 6.

Table 5 reports the cointegration results of every two markets in a bivariate system, (OSE_t,$SIMEX_t$), (OSE_t,CME_t), and ($SIMEX_t$, CME_t). Significant cointegration results reported in Panel A are obtained in each bivariate system. Moreover, Panel B presents the results of the hypotheses that the cointegrating vectors for the error correction terms are $(1 - \alpha)'$ with $\alpha = 1$, ie, the futures price differentials. These results will be used below. The hypothesis testing H_0: $\alpha = 1$ against H_a: $\alpha \neq 1$ in Panel B follows Johansen (1991), and the test statistic is given as

$$Q_H = (T - nk) \sum_{i=1}^{r} \ln\left[\left(1 - \hat{\lambda}_i^*\right) / \left(1 - \hat{\lambda}_i\right)\right], \quad (4)$$

Table 4. Johansen cointegration tests

	Trace	Critical values at the 1% level	λ_{max}	Critical values at the 1% level
r = 2	2.30	11.65	2.30	11.65
r = 1	327.5[a]	23.52	325.2[a]	19.19
r = 0	712.0	37.22	384.5[a]	25.75

Residual diagnostics

	OSE	SIMEX	CME
p-values of Ljung-box Q(12) test	0.704	0.215	0.16

[a] Significant at the 1% level.

Table 5. Johansen tests and cointegrating vectors for bivariate systems

	(OSE, SIMEX)	(OSE,CME)	(SIMEX,CME)
Panel A: Johansen tests			
Trace			
r = 1	2.19	2.30	2.35
r = 0	388.0[a]	356.6[a]	329.7[a]
λ_{max}			
r = 1	2.29	2.30	2.35
r = 0	385.7[a]	354.3[a]	327.5[a]
Panel B: Cointegrating vectors, $(1 - \alpha)'$			
$\hat{\alpha}$	1.00	0.99	0.99
p-value of H_0: $\hat{\alpha} = 1$	(0.99)	(0.99)	(0.99)

[a] Significant at the 1% level.

where λ_i^* and λ_i are the eigenvalues associated with the H_0 and H_a specifications. In these bivariate cointegration systems, $r = 1$ and Q_H is distributed asymptotically as a $\chi^2(1)$. The null hypothesis that $\alpha = 1$ is not rejected in each case.

Variance decomposition and impulse response analysis

Variance decomposition and impulse response analysis put forth in Sims (1980) have been widely used to examine how much movement in one market can be explained by innovations in different markets and how rapidly the price movements in one market are transmitted to other markets. (See Eun and Shim (1989) and Jeon and Furstenberg (1990), for the international transmission of stock market movements, and Booth *et al* (1993), for stock index futures markets.) This paper following King *et al* (1991) explores the common factor within the cointegration system. The cumulative impulse functions of Nikkei futures prices and the fractions of the forecast error variances attributed to the shocks to the common factor are computed. Note that the shock is innovation to the common factor, instead of each individual series as the usual way done in the conventional VAR literature. Since a common factor naturally exists among markets for similar products, this approach may provide a more in-depth analysis of international transmission mechanism for Nikkei futures markets.

IDENTIFICATION OF THE COMMON STOCHASTIC TREND

Since there is only one common factor in $Y_t \equiv (OSE_t\ SIMEX_t\ CME_t)'$, Y_t may be considered to be generated from the following common factor representation

$$Y_t = Y_0 + \mu t + Jq_t + \tilde{Y}_t, \qquad (5)$$

where $Y_0 = (OSE_0\ SIMEX_0\ CME_0)'$, μ is a 3×1 vector of drift, $J = (1\ 1\ 1)'$, q_t is the scalar $I(1)$ common stochastic trend, and Y_t is a 3×1 vector of $I(0)$ transitory components.

Let $\xi_{1t} = \Delta q_t$. The response of Y_t to the shock ξ_{1t}, ie, $\partial Y_t / \partial \xi_{1,t-l}$ for $l = 0, 1, 2, \ldots$, is computed as follows. From equation (5),

$$\lim_{l \to \infty} \partial Y_t / \partial \xi_{1,t-1} = J, \qquad (6)$$

as $q_t = \Delta^{-1}\xi_{1t}$. Thus the long-run multiplier of ξ_{1t} is unity. Since ξ_{1t} is the innovation process to the common permanent component, it may be considered the permanent shock. The fractions of forecast error variances of ΔY_t due to the permanent shock which yields information about the relative importance of the common stochastic trend in each series are also estimated.

The VECM (1) is estimated and transformed to a vector moving average (VMA) model

$$\Delta Y_t = \mu + C(L)\varepsilon_t, \qquad (7)$$

where $C(L)$ is a 3×3 matrix polynomial in the lag operator L, and $E\varepsilon_t\varepsilon_t' = \Sigma_\varepsilon$. Since there is only one common factor in Y_t, $C(1)$ is of rank 1 and there exists a 3×1 vector D such that $C(1) = JD'$.

To identify the common stochastic trend qt, some identifying restrictions are imposed.

Table 6. Forecast error varianced decomposition

Horizon	ΔOSE_t	$\Delta SIMEX_t$	ΔCME_t
Panel A: Sequence 1 - $\{OSE_t, SIMEX_t\} \rightarrow CME_t$			
1	0.8264	0.8493	0.9924
2	0.7315	0.7488	0.9894
3	0.7297	0.7474	0.9882
4	0.7297	0.7473	0.9882
5	0.7297	0.7473	0.9882
10	0.7297	0.7473	0.9882
50	0.7297	0.7473	0.9882
Panel B: Sequence 2 - $CME_t \rightarrow \{OSE_{t+1}, SIMEX_{t+1}\}$			
1	0.9737	0.9818	0.1162
2	0.9318	0.9765	0.7008
3	0.9307	0.9728	0.7000
4	0.9305	0.9728	0.6993
5	0.9305	0.9728	0.6993
10	0.9305	0.9728	0.6993
50	0.9305	0.9728	0.6993

Rewrite equation (7) as

$$\Delta Y_t = \mu + \Gamma(L)\xi_t, \qquad (8)$$

where $\Gamma(L) = C(L)\Gamma_0$, Γ_0^{-1} exists, and $\xi_t = \Gamma_0^{-1}\varepsilon_t$. As $\Gamma(1) = C(1)\Gamma_0 = JD'\Gamma_0$ is of rank one, and Γ_0 may be chosen so that

$$\Gamma(1) = \begin{pmatrix} 1 & 0 & 0 \\ 1 & 0 & 0 \\ 1 & 0 & 0 \end{pmatrix}. \qquad (9)$$

Accordingly, if $\xi_t = (\xi_{1t}\ \xi_{2t}\ \xi_{3t})'$, ξ_{1t} is the persistent shock with the long-run multiplier J while ξ_{2t} and ξ_{3t} are transitory shocks with the long-run multiplier equal to 0. Since $C(L)\varepsilon_t = \Gamma(L)\xi_t$ and $C(L)\varepsilon_t = \Gamma(1)\xi_t$, it can be shown that $\xi_{1t} = D'\varepsilon_t$ and $E\xi_{1t}^2 = D'\Sigma_\varepsilon D$. The impulse response associated with ξ_{1t} are given by the first column of $\Gamma(L)$ and can be computed according to King *et al* (1991).

EMPIRICAL RESULTS

As previously mentioned, two possible orderings of trading sequence exist. Consider Sequence 1 with the CME being the last trading market within a 24-hour interval. The percentage of the forecast error variances of ΔY_t attributed to innovations ξ_{1t} in the common stochastic trend is presented in Panel A of Table 6. In computing these, the permanent shock is assumed to be uncorrelated with the transitory shocks, i.e., $E\xi_{1t}\xi_{2t} = E\xi_{1t}\xi_{3t} = 0$. The point estimates suggest that at the end of a 50-day horizon, 99% of the forecast error variance in ΔCME, 73% in ΔOSE, and 75% in $\Delta SIMEX$ can be attributed to innovations in the common stochastic trend, ξ_{1t}. Even at the end of a one-day horizon, the innovations in the common factor explain 99% of the fluctuations in ΔCME, but only 83% and 85% in ΔOSE and $\Delta SIMEX$, respectively.

The impulse responses of Y_t to an innovation to the common stochastic trend are reported in Table 7. In response to a shock generated at day 0 (the same day), all markets fully respond in day 1 (next day). Specifically, at day 0, the Chicago market responds 108%, the Osaka market 83%, and the Singapore market 93%. Note that the long-run multiplier of the permanent shock is unity as shown in equation (6), ie

$$\lim_{l \to \infty} \partial Y_{it} / \partial \xi_{1,t-1} = 1, \qquad (10)$$

where y_{it} is OSE_t, $SIMEX_t$, or CME_t.

These results, both variance decomposition and impulse response function, may imply that the common factor is mainly derived from the Chicago market, and the Chicago market drives the information transmission mechanism among markets, assuming that the common factor impounds all the long-run information. Nevertheless, these results are shown to be simply induced by the nonsynchronous trading problem by comparing the results of Sequence 2 reported in Panel B of Tables 6 and 7. In Sequence 2, the CME trades earlier than the OSE and SIMEX within a 24-hour interval, ie the OSE and SIMEX are the last trading markets in the trading sequence. Panel B of Table 6 shows that the percentages of the forecast error variance attributed by ξ_{1t} at the end of 50 days and one day drop substantially to 70% and 12%, respectively. Oppositely, ξ_{1t} accounts for higher than 90% either at the end of 50 days and one day for both OSE and SIMEX. Analogous results are also obtained for the impulse responses. For Sequence 2, Panel B of Table 7 shows that at day 0, the Chicago market responds only 16% to an innovation to the common stochastic trend, while both the OSE and SIMEX responds higher than 90%. In essence, the common factor is more likely to be derived from the OSE and SIMEX (particularly the latter, see discussion below) because even in Sequence 1, the forecast error variance decomposition (at day 1 and 5) and responses to innovation to the common factor (at day 0) are larger than 80% for the OSE and SIMEX.

A more detailed comparison between the results of OSE and SIMEX warrants further discussion. The percentage of forecast error variance decomposition and responses to innovation to the common factor is higher for the SIMEX either in Sequences 1 or 2: about 2% higher in the forecast error variance decomposition, and 10% higher in the response to ξ_{1t}. Hence, the SIMEX responds to the common stochastic trend more quickly than the OSE. These comparisons may suggest that the tighter regulation and higher transaction of the OSE may reduce the informational efficiency of the market, though the evidence is not conclusive. It is also worth mentioning that the SIMEX is closed 15 minutes later than the OSE, and therefore, the OSE close price may incorporate less information than the OSE. Nevertheless, investigating whether these market microstructure aspects will affect the informational efficiency of the OSE is beyond the scope of the paper and reserved for future research.

On balance, results from Sequences 1 and 2 demonstrate that whichever is the last trading market(s) in the 24-hour trading sequence is the "dominant" market driving the common factor. Put in another way, none of the three markets can be described as the main source of information flow. Instead, each trading market is informationally efficient, on a daily basis, and embodies all the relevant information. These results also suggest that the markets are driven by the same information mechanism that flows around each trading market. It is worth mentioning that these results are consistent with the results obtained in a previous section. This section merely indicates that information is revealed during the nontrading hours of the Chicago market; here the results demonstrate that the Chicago market, as well as the other two markets, incorporates all the information when there is information flow.

Table 7. Responses to innovation to the common factor

Horizon	ΔOSE_t	$\Delta SIMEX_t$	ΔCME_t
Panel A: Sequence 1 - $\{OSE_t, SIMEX_t\} \rightarrow CME_t$			
0	0.8285	0.9305	1.0807
1	0.9994	1.0337	1.0131
2	1.0033	0.9946	0.9973
3	1.0001	0.9985	0.9981
4	1.0007	1.0001	0.9982
5	1.0011	1.0001	0.9980
10	1.0011	1.0001	0.9980
50	1.0011	1.0001	0.9980
Panel B: Sequence 2 - $CME_t \rightarrow \{OSE_{t+1}, SIMEX_{t+1}\}$			
0	0.9213	1.0328	0.1562
1	0.9813	0.9992	1.0203
2	1.0078	0.9994	0.9593
3	0.9982	0.9977	0.9951
4	1.0080	1.0009	0.9944
5	1.0010	1.0008	0.9979
10	1.0011	1.0009	0.9980
50	1.0011	1.0009	0.9980

Granger causality among markets

This section explicitly investigates the directions of Granger causality among the futures prices of the three markets by estimating the following VECM.

$$\begin{aligned}\Delta OSE_s = {} & a_1 + \beta_{11}(OSE_{s-1} - SIMEX_{s-1}) \\ & + \beta_{12}(OSE_{s-1} - CME_{s-1}) + b_{11}\Delta OSE_{s-1} \\ & + b_{12}\Delta SIMEX_{s-1} + b_{13}\Delta CME_{s-1} + \varepsilon_{1s}\end{aligned} \tag{11a}$$

$$\begin{aligned}\Delta SIMEX_s = {} & a_2 + \beta_{21}(SIMEX_{s-1} - OSE_{s-1}) \\ & + \beta_{22}(SIMEX_{s-1} - CME_{s-1}) \\ & + b_{21}\Delta OSE_{s-1} + b_{22}\Delta SIMEX_{s-1} \\ & + b_{23}\Delta CME_{s-1} + \varepsilon_{2s}\end{aligned} \tag{11b}$$

$$\begin{aligned}\Delta CME_s = {} & a_3 + \beta_{31}(CME_{s-1} - OSE_{s-1}) \\ & + \beta_{32}(CME_{s-1} - SIMEX_{s-1}) \\ & + b_{31}\Delta OSE_{s-1} + b_{32}\Delta SIMEX_{s-1} \\ & + b_{33}\Delta CME_{s-1} + \varepsilon_{3s}\end{aligned} \tag{11c}$$

Table 8. Estimation of VECM

	ΔOSE		ΔSIMEX		ΔCME	
Panel A: Sequence 1 (OSE_t, $SIMEX_t \rightarrow CME_t$)						
α_i	-5.5×10^{-4}	(−0.24)	0.2×10^{-4}	(0.047)	-0.3×10^{-4}	(−0.051)
β_{i1}	−0.120	(−0.73)	−0.161	(−0.88)	−0.210	(−1.08)
β_{i2}	-0.650^{b}	(−6.49)	-0.727^{b}	(−6.22)	0.078	(0.37)
b_{i1}	−0.039	(−0.38)	−0.086	(−0.63)	−0.046	(−0.30)
b_{i2}	−0.013	(−0.11)	0.000	(0.00)	−0.010	(−0.06)
b_{i3}	0.035	(0.48)	0.074	(0.88)	0.018	(0.20)
Panel B: Sequence 2 ($CME_t \rightarrow OSE_{t+1}$, $SIMEX_{t+1}$)						
α_i	-4.4×10^{-4}	(−0.93)	1.46×10^{-4}	(0.28)	-0.9×10^{-4}	(0.37)
β_{i1}	-0.500^{b}	(−2.76)	-0.451^{a}	(−2.06)	-0.269^{a}	(−2.56)
β_{i2}	−0.009	(−0.10)	0.013	(0.13)	-0.589^{b}	(−5.69)
b_{i1}	−0.148	(−1.22)	−0.199	(−1.28)	−0.054	(−1.11)
b_{i2}	0.138	(1.16)	0.172	(1.11)	0.191	(3.77)
b_{i3}	0.038	(0.98)	0.034	(0.75)	−0.027	(−1.59)

a Significant at the 5% level. b Significant at the 1% level.

where β_{ij}, i = 1, 2, or 3 and j = 1 or 2, are the parameters for the two error correction terms of each equation.[7] Note that the subscript s refers to the index of trading-market series in each of the two 24-hour trading sequences instead of the calendar trading day denoted by t. That is, for Sequence 1 with the CME as the last trading market within a particular 24-hour trading hour, s is the same as t for each market. But for Sequence 2, s corresponds to t + 1 for the OSE and SIMEX. The cointegrating vector of the error correction terms are (1 – 1)′ as verified by the results shown in Table 5.

Results of Sequences 1 and 2 are respectively presented in Panels A and B of Table 8. First of all, none of the own- and cross-market lagged futures price change terms are significant in Panels A and B. Therefore, the causal relationship discussed below only derives from the disequilibrium errors, ie the error correction terms. Panel A shows that the error correction terms including CME_{s-1} in the ΔOSE and ΔSIMEX models (β_{12} and β_{22} in equations (11a) and (11b), respectively) are strongly significant at any conventional significance level, but both error correction terms in the ΔCME model (β_{31} and β_{32} in equation (11c)) are insignificant with t-statistics = -1.08 and -0.37. Simply based on this result, it is interpreted that CME unidirectionally Granger-causes OSE and SIMEX. Nonetheless, these results are shown to be induced by the problem of nonsynchronous trading discussed in the previous section. When the OSE are SIMEX are the last trading markets as in Sequence 2, Panel B demonstrates that both error correction terms in the ΔCME model are now significant, and the error correction term including $SIMEX_{s-1}$ (β_{32}) has a larger (in magnitude) coefficient and t-statistics than that including OSE_{s-1} (β_{31}). In contrast, the error corrections terms including CME_{s-1} in both the ΔOSE and ΔSIMEX are insignificant. Moreover, the significant error correction terms incorporating $SIMEX_{s-1}$ in the ΔOSE model (β_{11} with t-statistic = -2.76) and OSE_{s-1} in the ΔSIMEX model (β_{21} with t-statistic = -2.06) indicate a bidirectional Granger causality relationship between the OSE and SIMEX.

In sum, none of the markets Granger-cause the other two on a daily basis. Causality possibly runs from the last trading market(s) in the sequence but this causal relationship is shorter than one day. The results of Sequence 2 also evince a bidirectional Granger causality between the OSE and SIMEX on a daily basis.

Conclusions

This paper investigates the international transmission of information in Nikkei 225 stock index futures markets. Comparing the trading and nontrading time variances, it is found that, in contrast to the other two markets, the nontrading time variance of the Chicago market is higher than the trading time variance. These results are consistent with the notion that relevant information is released during the Japanese business hours. Moreover, the nontrading (trading) variance per hour of the Chicago is close to the trading (nontrading) variance per hour of the OSE and SIMEX. These results suggest that the three markets are driven by the same kind of information. Futures prices of three markets are shown to be cointegrated with a single stochastic trend. However, none of the markets Granger-cause the other two markets on a daily basis. Instead, causality runs from the last trading market(s) in the 24-hour trading sequence but this causal relationship is shorter than one day.

An approach exploring the variance decomposition and impulse response functions of the Nikkei futures series is employed to examine the common stochastic trend in the cointegration system. All markets respond to the shock generated from the common factor rapidly. Comparing the results with two different orderings of the trading sequence, each trading market is evinced to impound all of the relevant information. In this way, none of the three markets can be considered the main source of information flow, and each trading market is informationally efficient. Some weak evidence suggests that the SIMEX responds to the common factor more quickly than the OSE, although the trading volume of the

OSE dominates the other two markets. Nevertheless, future research examining the influences of different market microstructures, ie tighter regulations and higher transaction costs of the OSE, on the market efficiency may provide a better understanding of international transmission of information among the Nikkei futures markets.

1 *Source:* An introduction to Nikkei stock average futures and options, *Chicago Mercantile Exchange Publication.*

2 *The mutual offset arrangement means that Nikkei futures positions established at the CME may be offset at the SIMEX, and vice versa.*

3 *More precisely, the OSE was closed at 3:15pm before February 1992.*

4 *Results reported are qualitatively the same if these 73 different trading days are deleted.*

5 *Bacha and Vila (1993) also suggest that the existence of intraday price limit and the absence of a market maker in the OSE may make it less efficient in processing information.*

6 *Consider the series* $\{xt\}$. *The ADF tests are based on the following OLS regression:*

$$\Delta x_t = c_0 + c_1 x_{t-1} + c_2 t + \sum_{i=1}^{p} \theta_i x_{t-i} + e_t,$$

with the null hypothesis H_0: $c_1 = 0$. *The Phillips-Perron tests involve computing the following OLS regressions:*

$$x_t = \mu^* + v_1^* x_{t-1} + \varepsilon_t^*$$

$$x_t = \mu + v_2(t - T/2) + v_1 x_{t-1} + \varepsilon_1,$$

with H_0: $v_1^* = 1$.

7 *If only one error correction term that incorporates all the three markets is included in the VECM, collinearity may be induced because the system contains two cointegration vectors.*

BIBLIOGRAPHY

Bacha, O., and A.F. Vila, 1994, "Futures markets, regulation and volatility: The case of the Nikkei stock index futures markets", *Pacific-Basin Finance Journal* 2, pp. 201–25.

Bacha, O., and A.F. Vila, 1993, "Lead-lag relationships in a multi-market context: The Nikkei stock index futures markets", in *Frontiers in Finance*, Routledge Press-UK.

Barclay, M.J., R. Litzenberger and J.B. Warner, 1990, "Private information, trading volume and stock return variances", *Review of Financial Studies* 3, pp. 233–53.

Bollerslev, T., 1986, "Generalized autoregressive conditional heteroskedasticity", *Journal of Econometrics* 31, pp. 309–28.

Booth, G.G., M. Chowdhury and T. Martikainen, 1993, "The international transmission of information in stock index futures markets", Working Paper, Louisiana State University.

Chan, K., and Y.C. Chan, 1993, "Price volatility in the Hong Kong stock market: A test of the information and trading noise hypothesis", *Pacific Basin Finance Journal* 1, pp. 189–202.

Chang, R.P., T. Fukuda, S.G. Rhee and M. Takano, 1993, "Interday and intraday return behavior of the TOPIX", *Pacific Basin Finance Journal* 1, pp. 67–95.

Dickey, D.A., and W.A. Fuller, 1979, "Distribution of the estimators for autoregressive time series with a unit root", *Journal of the American Statistical Association* 74, pp. 427–31.

Dickey, D.A., and W.A. Fuller, 1981, "Likelihood ratio statistics for autoregressive time series with a unit root", *Econometrica* 49, pp. 1057–72.

Engle, R.F., 1982, "Autoregressive conditional heteroskedasticity with estimates of the variance of U.K. inflation", *Econometrica* 50, pp. 987–1008.

Engle, R.F., and C.W.J. Granger, 1987, "Cointegration and error correction: Representation, estimation, and testing", *Econometrica* 55, pp. 251–76.

Eun, C.S., and S. Shim, 1989, "International transmission of stock market movements", *Journal of Financial and Quantitative Analysis* 24, pp. 241–56.

Fama, E., 1965, "The behavior of stock market prices", *Journal of Business* 38, pp. 34–105.

French, K.R., and R. Roll, 1986, "Stock return variances: The arrival of information and the reaction of traders", *Journal of Financial Economics* 17, pp.5–26.

Fuller, W.A., 1976, *Introduction to Statistical Time Series*, Wiley, New York.

Granger, C.W.J., 1986, "Developments in the study of cointegrated economic variables", *Oxford Bulletin of Economics and Statistics* 48, pp. 213–28.

Jeon, B., and G.M. von Furstenberg, 1990, "Growing international co-movements in stock price indexes", *Quarterly Review of Economics and Business* 30, pp. 15–30.

Johansen, S., 1988, "Statistical analysis of cointegration vectors", *Journal of Economic Dynamics and Control* 12, pp. 231-54.

Johansen, S., 1991, "Estimation and hypothesis testing of cointegration vectors in Gaussian vector autoregressive models", *Econometrica* 59, pp. 1551-80.

King, R.G., C.I. Plosser, J.H. Stock and M.W. Watson, 1991, "Stochastic trends and economic fluctuations", *American Economic Review* 81, pp. 819-40.

Newey, W.K., and K.D. West, 1987, "A simple positive semi-definite, heteroskedasticity and autocorrelation consistent covariance matrix", *Econometrica* 55, pp. 703-8.

Oldfield, S., and R. Rogalaski, 1980, "A theory of common stock returns over trading and nontrading periods", *Journal of Finance* 35, pp. 729-51.

Phillips, P. C. B., 1987, "Time series regression with a unit root", *Econometrica* 55, pp. 277-301.

Phillips, P.C.B., and P. Perron, 1988, "Testing for a unit root in time series regression", *Biometrika* 75, pp. 335-46.

Reimers, H.E., 1991, *Comparisons of tests for multivariate cointegration*, Deutsche Bundesbank, Frankfurt.

Reinsel, G.C., and S.K. Ahn, 1992, "Vector autoregressive models with unit roots and reduced rank structure: estimation, likelihood ratio test, and forecasting", *Journal of Time Series Analysis* 13, pp. 353-75.

Ross, S., 1989, "Information and volatility: The no-arbitrage martingale approach to timing and resolution irrelevancy", *Journal of Finance* 44, pp. 1-17.

Sims, C., 1980, "Macroeconomics and reality", *Econometrica* 48, pp. 1-48.

19

Price and Volatility Spillovers in Scandinavian Stock Markets*

G. Geoffrey Booth, Teppo Martikainen and Yiuman Tse
Louisiana State University; Helsinki School of Business and Economics; Binghamton University

New evidence is provided on price and volatility spillovers among the Danish, Norwegian, Swedish, and Finnish stock markets. The impact of good news (market advances) and bad news (market retreats) is described by a multivariate Exponential Generalised Autoregressive Conditionally Heteroskedastic (Egarch) model. Volatility transmission is asymmetric, spillovers being more pronounced for bad than good news. Significant price and volatility spillovers exist but they are few in number.

Advanced computer technology and improved world-wide processing of news have made the international financial transactions easier and less expensive than ever before. At the same time the liberalisation of capital movements and the securitisation of stock markets have further improved the possibilities for national stock markets to react rapidly to new information from international markets. Nevertheless, although the international comovements between stock markets appear to have increased in recent years, the observed relationships are still lower than might be expected based on the recent trends in financial markets. Roll (1992) investigates the reasons for the observed low relationships between different stock markets. He suggests that these may at least partly be because of:

- differences in the way in which the indexes are constructed, chiefly some indexes being more diversified than the others,
- differences in industrial structures, and
- differences in exchange rate behaviour and policies.

The purpose of this paper is to provide new evidence on the price and volatility spillovers among four Scandinavian (Nordic) stock markets: Copenhagen, Denmark; Oslo, Norway; Stockholm, Sweden; and Helsinki, Finland.[1] The task is accomplished by applying a multivariate extension of Nelson's (1991) Exponential Generalised Autoregressive Conditionally Heteroskedastic (Egarch) model to daily stock price data spanning an approximate six-year period. An Egarch model makes it possible to investigate the asymmetric impact of good news (market advances) and bad news (market retreats) on the volatility transmission among the four markets.[2] The need for this approach, as opposed to the now common Garch specification, is underscored by Bae and Karolyi (1994) and Koutmos and Booth (1995), who collectively report that the volatility transmission between US, UK and Japanese stock markets is asymmetric. The analysis extends Mathur and Subrahmanyam (1990), who investigate interdependencies among the four markets using VAR models on 1974–85 monthly stock returns.

Investigation of the spillover relationships among Scandinavian stock markets is beneficial because these markets jointly provide an environment where the differences in the three aspects pointed out by Roll (1992) are small. By way of illustration, consider the following. First, there is strong economic cooperation among the Scandinavian countries. The Nordic Council, a

* *This paper was first published in the* Journal of Banking & Finance, *Vol. 21 (1997). It is reprinted with the permission of Elsevier Science - NL, Sara Burgerhartstraat 25, 1055 KV Amsterdam, The Netherlands. Teppo Martikainen was visiting Louisiana State University when this research was initially undertaken. He acknowledges the financial support from The Finnish Academy of Sciences to support the visit. The authors are grateful to Swedish and Finnish Options Markets and Copenhagen, Helsinki and Oslo Stock Exchanges for providing the data as well as to Jenny and Antti Wihuri Foundation for their generous financial support.*

prominent organ for the Scandinavian group, serves as the focal point for regional coordination and unification (see Christiansen and Elling, (1993)). Second, the tax systems, currency systems and exchange rate policies of the four Scandinavian markets are closely related. As an example, in 1983 the Nordic countries developed the world's first multilateral tax treaty. This treaty was revised in 1990 and is described by Anderson *et al* (1991). Third, in addition to substantial relationships with common international trading partners (the US, the UK and Germany), there is significant trade among the Nordic countries themselves (Monsen and Wallace (1995)). Fourth, the Nordic countries have followed German law when developing their company acts and accounting systems. Thus, as Monsen and Wallace (1995) point out, tax legislation has strongly influenced accounting legislation in these countries. Fifth, the Danish, Norwegian, Swedish and Finnish exchanges currently cooperate in several ways. For instance, efforts are made to harmonise security regulations, construct and maintain similar market architecture, and calculate compatible market indexes.

Scandinavian stock markets

The Scandinavian stock markets followed the world-wide trend in the 1980s to deregulate. Despite deregulation, however, the market value of listed stocks relative to GDP has remained relatively low in Scandinavia. An important development in the Scandinavian markets is the increased level of foreign ownership in recent years. While the foreign ownership was typically limited to a minority interest in most Scandinavian firms, the abolition of foreign ownership restrictions has increased foreign ownership considerably.[3] In October 1994, the proportions of foreign ownership in different stock exchanges were Sweden 26%, Finland 30%, Norway 31%, and Denmark 10%.[4]

Table 1 provides basic statistics for the four Scandinavian markets in 1990–94. As can be seen, the market value of the stocks listed in Sweden is more than half of the total market value of all firms listed in the Scandinavian markets. Stockholm is also the largest market when measured by the trading volume. Helsinki and Oslo are the two smallest markets. Copenhagen has the largest number of listed firms.[5]

Trading is electronic on all the Scandinavian stock markets. In Oslo the trading is centralised with brokers present at the exchange, but in the other three markets it is decentralised. The Scandinavian markets have adapted the Continuous Limit Order Book trading system, which resembles the Continuous Automatic Trading System (CATS) employed, for instance, by the Toronto, Paris and Brussels exchanges. In Norway and Denmark, derivative instruments are traded on the stock exchange, but in Finland and Sweden they trade on separate options markets. Since the Scandinavian countries are geographically close, three are within one time zone and one, Finland, is located in the eastern adjacent time zone. As a consequence, the trading hours for the markets are about the same (see Table 2). For instance, three of the exchanges close at the same time and one closes 30 minutes earlier, Denmark being the exception.

The Nordic markets actively cooperate in many areas. Actions have been taken to harmonise the Nordic regulations governing stock market activities and securities trading. The harmonising process has been strengthened, because the Scandinavian countries have gradually implemented European Union (EU) regulations in a number of fields, including securities trading. In January 1995 Sweden and Finland became members of the EU, which Denmark had previously joined. Norway, however, has not yet become an official member. Further, in 1992 the Scandinavian stock exchanges entered into an agreement concerning the joint distribution of price and turnover statistics.

To strengthen the cooperation of Scandinavian stock exchanges further, at the initiative of the Copenhagen Stock Exchange, the Scandinavian stock exchanges are considering the possibility of creating a joint Scandinavian securities market. One obvious reason for the establishment of a joint Scandinavian market is

Table 1. Market value and trading volume in Scandinavian markets 1990–94

	1990	1991	1992	1993	1994
Market value, year-end (ECU billion)					
Denmark	28	34	30	36	38
Norway	19	16	15	25	30
Sweden	68	73	63	90	97
Finland	17	11	10	21	31
Scandinavian turnover (%)					
Denmark	25	27	32	27	20
Norway	30	22	9	19	13
Stockholm	36	47	46	45	57
Finland	9	4	13	9	10
Number of listed firms (year-end)					
Denmark	268	280	268	260	252
Norway	121	112	123	131	146
Sweden	132	127	118	112	114
Finland	77	65	63	58	65

Sources: Helsinki and Stockholm Stock Exchanges.

Table 2. Stock market indexes used in the study

Market	Trading hours	Index	Details of the index construction
Denmark	9.00am–3.30pm	KFX	A basic portfolio of top 25 stocks in terms of turnover in market value is selected in November each year. Of these an active portfolio of 20 stocks with the highest market value is selected by the Copenhagen Stock Exchange. Value-weighted.
Norway	10.00am–4.00pm	OBX	Top 25 shares in terms of share turnover during the half a calendar year. The composition of the index comes up for review at the beginning of June and December by the Oslo Stock Exchange. Value-weighted.
Sweden	10.00am–4.00pm	OMX	Top 25 stocks in terms of turnover in market value. The composition of the index comes up for review at the beginning of June and December by the Swedish Option Market. Value-weighted.
Finland	9.00am–4.00pm	FOX	Top 25 shares in terms of median trading during the half a calendar year. The composition of the index comes up for review at the beginning of February and August by the Finnish Options Market. Value-weighted.

All trading hours are in Swedish time in January 1994.

that it would offer the advantage of a sizeable home market for Scandinavian firms and investors, improving competitiveness and making Scandinavian stocks more attractive to foreign traders and investors. Externally, the market would be viewed as a single market in which it would be possible to trade all Scandinavian securities through the investor's usual Scandinavian broker, who may or may not be of Scandinavian origin. As mentioned in the 1992 Annual Report of the Copenhagen Stock Exchange, the creation of new market is based on the synergistic premise that a combined market is greater than the sum of its component markets.

Data description and preliminary statistics

There are different types of spillover environments. At one end of the spectrum are markets whose trading hours do not overlap. At the other end are markets whose trading hours perfectly coincide with each other. The first type requires that only trading time returns be considered. This is because the presence of perfect nonsynchronous trading may cause dependencies to exist that are not the result of information transmission. Since the second type is characterised by simultaneous (synchronous) trading, either trading time or daily returns can be used. Recent spillover investigations of the nonsynchronous trading environment using open-to-close returns include Hamao, Masulis and Ng (1990), Bae and Karolyi (1994) and Koutmos and Booth (1995). Close-to-close returns have been used by Koutmos and Tucker (1996) and Huang, Masulis and Stoll (1996) to analyse spillovers between spot and futures market and by Karolyi (1995) to investigate the spillover between the stock indexes of the US and Canada. All of these latter market pairs trade almost simultaneously.

The KFX, OBX, OMX and FOX indexes are used to proxy the stock price behaviour of Denmark, Norway, Sweden and Finland, respectively. Table 2 describes these indexes in more detail and documents that they are similarly constructed. Since the four markets trade virtually simultaneously, the raw data consist of 1,574 daily observations of the natural logarithms of the closing values of the price indexes for each market for the period beginning May 2, 1988 and ending June 30, 1994. The data begin after the October 1987 worldwide stock market crash because of the observed subsequent increase in international comovements of stock prices. May 2 was selected as the beginning date because this date marks the creation of the FOX index, the asset underlying the Finnish Option Market's stock index futures contracts.

Summary statistics of the continuously compounded returns on the four market indexes are reported in Table 3.[6] The excess kurtosis and skewness measures for all the return series indicate that these distributions are not normal.

Table 3. Descriptive statistics of returns

	Denmark	Norway	Sweden	Finland
Mean (10^{-4})	3.96	3.23	4.45	0.19
	(0.021)	(0.364)	(0.157)	(0.949)
Variance (10^{-4})	0.468	2.010	1.560	1.440
Skewness	–0.472	–0.327	0.270	0.301
	(0.000)	(0.000)	(0.000)	(0.000)
Excess kurtosis	6.97	9.43	6.51	2.88
	(0.000)	(0.000)	(0.000)	(0.000)
First order autocorrelation coefficients	0.248	0.105	0.157	0.257
Diebold Q*(16) test	69.6	21.4	34.2	99.58
	(0.000)	(0.105)	(0.004)	(0.000)
ARCH(16) LM test	68.1	84.6	128.9	89.1
	(0.000)	(0.000)	(0.000)	(0.000)
Correlation coefficients				
Denmark	1.000	0.340	0.341	0.226
Norway		1.000	0.498	0.211
Sweden			1.000	0.273
Finland				1.000

P-values are in parentheses. The null hypotheses for the mean, skewness and excess kurtosis are that they are zero. The Diebold Q* statistic tests for zero autocorrelation in the first 16 lags. For the Arch LM test, the null hypothesis is that Arch effects are not present in the first 16 lags.

Moreover, applications of the Diebold Q* (Diebold, 1988) and Arch Lagrange Multiplier (LM) tests (Engle, 1982) indicate that each market's returns strongly depend on their past values and exhibit strong Arch effects, supporting the earlier findings by Frennberg and Hansson (1993) and Booth, Chowdhury and Martikainen (1994), among others, for Swedish and Finnish markets, respectively. The Arch effects may explain (at least partially) the observed thicker-than-normal distributional tails. The pairwise correlation coefficients between the markets are all positive, the largest being associated with Sweden and the smallest with Finland.

Since previous studies among major world stock markets suggest that they may be cointegrated (see for example, Jeon and Chiang (1991) and Kasa (1992)), the Johansen *trace* and λ max tests (see Johansen, (1991)) for multivariate and Geweke and Porter-Hudak (1983) tests for fractional cointegration were conducted. Moreover, the Arch common volatility test developed by Engle and Kozicki (1993) was used to test whether the Scandinavian markets share the same volatility process. The results, available from the authors upon request, provide no evidence of cointegration or common volatility. The lack of cointegration indicates that if price spillovers exist, they are short-run in nature. Moreover, not detecting the presence of common volatility is equivalent to finding that the unexpected component of returns for each market is idiosyncratic. This means that volatility spillovers, if they exist, should be modelled as pairwise phenomena.

Price and volatility spillovers among markets

Suppose $R_{i,t}$, $i = 1, \ldots, 4$ (ie 1 = Denmark, 2 = Norway, 3 = Sweden, and 4 = Finland) is the return for market i at time t. Ω_{t-1} is the information set available at time $t-1$. μ_{it}, σ^2_{it} and $\sigma_{i,j,t}$ are the conditional mean, conditional variance, and conditional covariance, respectively. ε_{it} is the innovation ($\varepsilon_{it} = R_{it} - \mu_{it}$), and z_{it} represents the standardised innovation ($z_{it} = \varepsilon_{it}/\sigma_{it}$). An Egarch model depicting price and volatility spillovers among the four markets may be formulated as:[7]

$$R_{it} = \beta_{i0} + \sum_{j=1}^{4} \beta_{ij} R_{j,t-1} + \varepsilon_{it}, \text{ for } i = 1, \ldots, 4 \text{ and} \qquad (1)$$
$$\varepsilon \big| \Omega_{t-1} \sim \text{Student - } t(0, H_t, v);$$

$$\sigma^2_{it} = \exp\left\{ \alpha_{i0} + \sum_{j=1}^{4} \alpha_{ij} f_j(z_{j,t-1}) + \gamma_i \ln\left(\sigma^2_{i,t-1}\right) \right\}, \qquad (2)$$

$$f_j(z_{j,t-1}) = |z_{j,t-1}| - E(|z_{j,t-1}|) + \delta_j z_{j,t-1}, \qquad (3)$$
$$\text{for } j = 1, \ldots, 4;$$

$$\sigma_{ijt} = \rho_{ij}\sigma_{it}\sigma_{jt}, \text{ for } i, j = 1, \ldots, 4 \text{ and } i \neq j; \qquad (4)$$

where $E(|z_{it}|) = (2/\pi)^{1/2}(\Gamma(v-1)/2)/\Gamma(v/2)$, and H is the conditional matrix of the error vector, ε_t. Following Bollerslev (1987) and Baillie and Bollerslev (1989), the Student t-distribution is used to account for the possible excess kurtosis displayed by the residuals after accounting for the Arch effect. Baillie and Bollerslev (1995) point out that using the Student t-distribution to accomplish this task is appropriate, provided that the estimated degree-of-freedom parameter v is larger than 4 (ie $1/v < 0.25$).

The model is estimated by maximising the log-likelihood function:

$$L(\theta) = \sum_{t=1}^{T} l_t(\theta), \qquad (5)$$

where

$$l_t(\theta) = \Gamma[(n+v)/2] / \left[\Gamma(v/2)\pi(v-2)^{n/2}\right] |H_t|^{-1/2}$$
$$\times \left[1 + 1/(v-2)(\varepsilon_t' H_t^{-1} \varepsilon_t)\right]^{-(n+v)/2} \qquad (6)$$

with n the number of variables (ie 4) and θ the parameter vector of the model. Estimation is accomplished using the algorithm developed by Berndt *et al* (1974) with no parameter restrictions.

Table 4 reports the Ljung-Box statistics for 24th-order serial correlation in the level and squared standardised residuals as well as the asymmetry test statistics (sign bias, negative size, positive size and joint tests) developed by Engle and Ng (1993). The latter are included because the findings by Engle and Ng suggest that the

Table 4. Diagnostic checking

	Denmark	Norway	Sweden	Finland
P-values of Ljung-Box Q(24) statistics				
z_{jt}	0.463	0.604	0.464	0.035
z_t	0.999	0.999	0.999	0.978
$z_{1t}z_{jt}$, $j>1$		0.999	0.999	0.999
$z_{2t}z_{jt}$, $j>2$			0.999	0.999
$z_{3t}z_{4t}$				0.786
P-values of the Engle and Ng (1993) diagnostic test				
Sign bias test	0.909	0.122	0.045	0.072
Negative size bias test	0.810	0.974	0.814	0.075
Positive size bias test	0.580	0.086	0.569	0.524
Joint test	0.874	0.236	0.448	0.249

Ljung-Box test may not have much power in detecting misspecifications related to the asymmetric effects. Both the Ljung-Box and the asymmetry checks indicate that the estimated model fits the data very well. Only the own market linear dependence for Finland and the sign bias test for Sweden marginally fail the diagnostic checks at the 5% significance level.

Table 5 provides maximum likelihood estimates of equation (1). The table shows that prices in all markets are dependent on their own past values, as indicated by β_{ij}, $i = j$. The strongest linear dependencies are observed in Denmark and Finland. Linear dependencies may be due to time-varying risk premia or to some form of market inefficiency (see, for example, Fama, (1991)). Coefficients β_{ij}, $i \neq j$, measure the extent of the price spillover between markets. These coefficients indicate that while Sweden and Norway spill over to other markets, Finland and Denmark do not. Norway price spills over to Denmark and Sweden, and Sweden price spills over to Finland. Not a single pair of markets indicate a two-way price spillover, indicating the lack of a feedback effect.

Equation (2) specifies a conditional variance process for market i that permits its own past standardised innovations as well as past cross market standardised innovations to exert an asymmetric impact on its volatility. The parameter values of α_{ij}, $i = j$, indicate that volatilities in each market are dependent on their own past innovations. Similar to returns, this dependence is highest in Denmark and Finland. Coefficients α_{ij}, $i \neq j$, measure the extent of volatility spillovers between markets. Based on these estimates, Swedish volatility spills over to Norway and Finland. Finnish volatility spills over to Sweden, thereby creating a bidirectional effect between these two markets.

The persistence of volatility implied by Equation (2) is measured by γ_i. The γ values in Table 5 are all significantly less than one, a result that is necessary for the unconditional variance to be finite. Persistence is strongest in Finland and least in Denmark. This characteristic may be best interpreted by using the half-life concept, which measures the time it takes a shock to reduce its impact by one half. For Finland the half-life is 18.2 days. The corresponding measure for Denmark is 3.3 days. Norway and Sweden fall in the middle of these extremes.

Asymmetry in volatility transmission is modelled by Equation (3) and can be conveniently examined using its derivatives:

Table 5. Models for price and volatility spillover[a]

	Denmark (i=1)	Norway (i=2)	Sweden (i=3)	Finland (i=4)
Price spillover parameters				
β_{i0}	0.000	0.000	0.000	–0.000
	(2.00)	(1.30)	(2.51)	(–1.43)
β_{i1} (Denmark)	0.298	–0.058	–0.045	0.028
	(11.7)	(–1.26)	(–1.15)	(0.87)
β_{i2} (Norway)	0.038	0.152	0.048	0.033
	(3.45)	(5.77)	(2.25)	(1.93)
β_{i3} (Sweden)	0.017	0.008	0.128	0.084
	(1.28)	(0.28)	(4.81)	(3.78)
β_{i4} (Finland)	0.004	0.015	–0.103	0.277
	(0.32)	(0.58)	(–0.45)	(11.7)
Volatility spillover parameters				
α_{i0}	–2.04	–0.653	–0.606	–0.400
	(–5.15)	(–4.41)	(–5.25)	(–4.86)
α_{i1} (Denmark)	0.245	–0.008	0.011	–0.053
	(7.30)	(–0.37)	(0.37)	(–1.95)
α_{i2} (Norway)	0.006	0.108	0.013	–0.029
	(0.15)	(3.37)	(0.45)	(–1.06)
α_{i3} (Sweden)	0.060	0.079	0.180	0.082
	(1.38)	(2.78)	(5.23)	(2.64)
α_{i4} (Finland)	0.061	0.047	0.065	0.272
	(1.45)	(1.71)	(2.14)	(7.76)
Other parameters and statistics				
γ_i	0.812	0.932	0.941	0.963
	(21.5)	(57.4)	(78.7)	(113.2)
Half-life	3.3	9.9	11.4	18.2
δ_i	0.051	–0.358	–0.316	–0.196
	(0.68)	(–2.21)	(–2.61)	(–3.07)
Relative asymmetry	1.00	2.12	1.92	1.49
ρ_{i1} (Denmark)		0.283	0.301	0.153
		(11.0)	(11.9)	(5.26)
ρ_{i2} (Norway)			0.392	0.154
			(16.3)	(5.41)
ρ_{i2} (Sweden)				0.217
				(7.95)
1/v	0.152			
	(16.5)			

[a] See equations 1–4

t-statistics contained within parentheses. Half-life for market i equals $\ln(.5)/\ln\gamma_i$. Relative asymmetry for market i equals $|-1+\delta_i|/(1+\delta_i)$. This statistic is greater than one, equal to one and less than one for negative asymmetry, symmetry, and positive asymmetry, respectively. The statistic for Denmark is set equal to one because δ_i is not significant. Half-life for market i equals $\ln(.5)/\ln \gamma_i$. v is common to all models. Since $1/v < 0.25$, the Baillie and Bollerslev (1995) criterion for the appropriateness of using the Student-t distribution is satisfied.

$$\partial f_j(z_{jt}) / \partial z_{jt} = \begin{Bmatrix} 1 = \delta_j, & \text{for } z_j > 0 \\ -1 + \delta_j, & \text{for } z_j < 0 \end{Bmatrix}. \qquad (7)$$

The size effect is measured by $|z_{jt}| - E(|z_{jt}|)$, and the corresponding sign effect given by $\delta_j z_{jt}$. If δ_j is negative (positive), a negative z_{jt} tends to reinforce (mitigate) the size effect. The relative magnitude of asymmetry may be quantified by comparing the right-hand side of Equation (7) when $z_j < 0$ and $z_j > 0$. The results in Table 5 indicate asymmetry in three of the four markets, Denmark being the exception. For Norway, Sweden and Finland, negative innovations increase volatility considerably more than positive innovations. These findings suggest that Scandinavian stock markets are sensitive to news originating from other markets more strongly when the news is "bad" than when the news is "good". Numerically, bad news for Norway, Sweden and Finland have 2.12, 1.92 and 1.49

times the impact of good news, respectively.

Following Bollerslev (1990), Ng (1991), and others, Equation (4) specifies a conditional time invariant covariance, which is a strong economic assumption in rapidly changing markets. Nevertheless, the assumption does substantially reduce the number of parameters to be estimated. Bollerslev (1990) indicates that the assumption is warranted if the cross products of the standardised residuals are not serially correlated. Moreover, Baillie and Bollerslev (1990) suggest that if the assumption is appropriate all of the estimated correlation coefficients will be statistically significant. As reported in Tables 4 and 5, both of these suggested conditions are met.

Conclusion

This paper uses an extended multivariate Egarch model to investigate the dynamic interaction of four Scandinavian stock markets for the period May 2, 1988 to June 30, 1994. The investigation of price and volatility spillovers among Swedish, Danish, Norwegian, and Finnish markets is motivated by the ongoing discussions on the establishment of a joint Scandinavian Stock Market among the Scandinavian countries, as well as the high level of current cooperation between the Scandinavian stock exchanges and their economies.

The results of this study indicate that each of the four markets is well described by an Egarch model with autoregressive returns. Each market's returns and volatilities are strongly dependent on their own past values. The linear dependencies may be due to the presence of time-varying risk premia or to some form of market inefficiency. They may also be the result of infrequent trading of the stocks contained in each index. Volatility behaviour represents the often observed phenomenon of volatility clustering. With the exception of Denmark, their volatilities respond more strongly to bad news (market retreats) than good news (market advances).

The results of this study also indicate that these four markets are, at best, weakly related to each other. Of the 12 possible pairwise effects, there are three price spillovers and three volatility spillovers, with two of the latter creating a feedback effect. Both Swedish price and volatility spill over to Finland, and there is some support for Finnish volatility spilling over to Sweden. These spillovers may well reflect the longstanding economic and cultural ties between these two countries.

In sum, it appears that if an integrated market is to be attained, it will be necessary to do more than harmonise regulations and provide access to price screens. One option is to merge the extant Nordic exchanges, an action that has been seriously discussed by these exchanges for the last few years. Such a merger would create the fourth largest stock market in Europe, after those in London, Paris and Frankfurt. Another is to exploit the recent EU directive on investment services, which permits brokerage firms in one country to conduct business on another country's exchange – that is, brokerage firms could be encouraged to hold seats on all four exchanges. These firms should include not only Scandinavian brokers, but also brokers from the major international markets. Indeed, such actions are already taking place.

1 *The fifth Scandinavian stock market, Iceland, is excluded because it is still in the process of being established. In 1994, only 24 shares were listed in this market and the annual turnover of stocks was ECU16 million.*

2 *This asymmetry referred to as the leverage effect is documented for individual stocks in several countries. See, for example, Cheung and Ng (1992) for the US; Koutmos (1992) for Canada, France and Japan; and Poon and Taylor (1992) for the UK.*

3 *Bergström* et al *(1993) and Booth* et al *(1994) describe and provide an analysis on Swedish and Finnish foreign ownership restrictions, respectively.*

4 *In Denmark the figure of foreign ownership is not directly available, but this figure is based on the estimates provided by the representatives of the Copenhagen Stock Exchange.*

5 *The number of listed foreign firms is very small in Scandinavian countries. In 1994 Copenhagen had 10, Oslo 14 and Stockholm 10 foreign listed firms. In Helsinki all listed firms were domestic.*

6 *When trading does not occur in some markets because of holidays, missing prices are replaced by previous prices. Results are qualitatively the same if these 51 days are deleted instead.*

7 *Also an Egarch-MA(1) model similar to French* et al *(1987) was estimated. The results that are obtainable from the authors upon request indicate that inclusion of the MA (1) term does not materially change the results.*

BIBLIOGRAPHY

Anderson, E., N. Mattson, A. Michelsen and F. Zimmer, 1991, *The Nordic tax law*, Tano, Sweden.

Bae, K.-H., and G.A. Karolyi, 1994, "Good news, bad news and international spillovers of stock return volatility between Japan and the U.S.", *Pacific-Basin Finance Journal* 2, pp. 405–38.

Baillie, R.T., and T. Bollerslev, 1989, "The message of daily exchange rates", *Journal of Business & Economic Statistics* 7, pp. 287–305.

Baillie, R.T., and T. Bollerslev, 1990, "A multivariate generalized ARCH approach to modeling risk premia in the forward foreign exchange rate", *Journal of International Money and Finance* 9, pp. 309–24.

Baillie, R.T., and T. Bollerslev, 1995, "On the interdependence of international asset markets", in: R. Aggarwal and D. C. Schrim, eds., *Global portfolio diversification*, Academic Press, San Diego, pp. 19–27.

Bergström, C., K. Rydqvist and P. Sellin, 1993, "Asset pricing with inflow and outflow constraints: Theory and evidence from Sweden", *Journal of Business Finance and Accounting* 20, pp. 865–79.

Berndt, E.K., H.B. Hall, R.E. Hall and J.A. Hausman, 1974, "Estimation and inference in nonlinear structural models", *Annals of Economic and Social Measurement* 4, pp. 653–66.

Bollerslev, T., 1987, "A conditional heteroskedastic time series model for speculative prices and rates of return", *Review of Economics and Statistics* 69, pp. 542–7.

Bollerslev, T., 1990, "Modelling the coherence in short-run nominal exchange rates: A multivariate generalized ARCH model", *Review of Economics and Statistics* 72, pp. 498–505.

Booth, G.G., M. Chowdhury and T. Martikainen, 1994, "The effect of foreign ownership restrictions on stock price dynamics", *Weltwirtschaftliches Archiv* 130, pp. 730–46.

Cheung, Y.-W., and L.K. Ng, 1992, "Stock price dynamics and firm size: An empirical investigation", *Journal of Finance* 47, pp. 1985–97.

Christiansen, M., and J. Elling, 1993, *European financial reporting*, Routledge, Denmark.

Diebold, F.X., 1988, *Empirical modeling of exchange rate dynamics*, Springer-Verlag, New York.

Engle, R.F., 1982, "Autoregressive conditional heteroskedasticity with estimates of the variance of U.K. inflation", *Econometrica* 50, pp. 987–1008.

Engle, R.F. and S. Kozicki, 1993, "Testing for common features", *Journal of Business & Economic Statistics* 11, pp. 369–80.

Engle, R.F., and V.K. Ng, 1993, "Measuring and testing the impact of news on volatility", *Journal of Finance* 48, pp. 1749–78.

Frennberg, P., and B. Hansson, 1993, "Testing the random walk hypothesis on Swedish stock prices: 1919-1990", *Journal of Banking and Finance* 17, pp. 175–91.

Fama, E.F., 1991, "Efficient capital markets: II", *Journal of Finance* 46, pp. 1575–617.

French, K.R., G.W. Schwert and R. Stambaugh, 1987, "Expected stock returns and volatility", *Journal of Financial Economics* 19, pp. 3–29.

Geweke, J., and S. Porter-Hudak, 1983, "The estimation and application of long memory time series models", *Journal of Time Series Analysis* 4, pp. 221–38.

Hamao, Y., R.W. Masulis, and V. Ng, 1990, "Correlations in price changes and volatility across international stock markets", *Review of Financial Studies* 3, pp. 281–307.

Huang, R., R.W Masulis and H. Stoll, 1996, "Energy shocks and financial markets", *Journal of Futures Markets* 6, pp. 1–28.

Jeon, B.N., and T.C. Chiang, 1991, "A system of stock prices in world stock exchanges: Common stochastic trends for 1975-1990", *Journal of Economics and Business* 43, pp. 329–85.

Johansen, S., 1991, "Estimation and hypothesis testing of cointegration vectors in Gaussian vector autoregressive models", *Econometrica* 59, pp. 1551–80.

Karolyi, G.A., 1995, "A multivariate GARCH model of international transmissions of stock returns and volatility: The case of the United States and Canada", *Journal of Business and Economic Statistics* 13, pp. 11–25.

Kasa, K., 1992, "Common stochastic trends in international stock markets", *Journal of Monetary Economics* 29, pp. 95–124.

Koutmos, G., 1992, "Asymmetric volatility and risk return tradeoff in foreign stock markets", *Journal of Multinational Financial Management* 2, pp. 27–43.

Koutmos, G., and G.G. Booth, 1995, "Asymmetric volatility transmission in international stock markets", *Journal of International Money and Finance* 14, pp. 747–62.

Koutmos, G., and M. Tucker, 1996, "Temporal relationships and dynamic interactions between spot and futures stock markets", *Journal of Futures Markets* 16, pp. 55–70.

Mathur, I., and V. Subrahmanyam, 1990, "Interdependencies among the Nordic and U.S. stock markets", *Scandinavian Journal of Economics* 92, pp. 587–97.

Monsen, N. and W.A. Wallace, 1995, "Evolving financial

reporting practices: A comparative study of the Nordic countries' harmonization efforts", *Contemporary Accounting Research* 11, pp. 973-97.

Nelson, D., 1991, "Conditional heteroskedasticity in asset returns: A new approach", *Econometrica* 59, pp. 347-70.

Ng, L., 1991, "Tests of the CAPM with time-varying covariances: A multivariate GARCH approach", *Journal of Finance* 46, pp. 1507-21.

Poon, S-H., and S.J. Taylor, 1992, "Stock returns and volatility: An empirical study of the U.K. stock market", *Journal of Banking and Finance* 16, pp. 37-59.

Roll, R., 1992, "Industrial structure and the comparative behavior of international stock market indices", *Journal of Finance* 47, pp. 3-41.

20

Common Volatility and Volatility Spillovers between US and Eurodollar Interest Rates:

Evidence from the Futures Market*

Yiuman Tse and G. Geoffrey Booth
Binghamton University; Louisiana State University

US Treasury bill and Eurodollar futures are employed to investigate volatility spillovers between US and Eurodollar interest rates. This paper shows that both interest rates follow a Garch process but they do not share a common volatility factor. A bivariate Egarch model that allows for the asymmetric volatility influence of the interest rate differential between markets (the TED spread), as well as that of the domestic market, is used to analyse the volatility spillovers between markets. Results show that the lagged TED spread change is the driving force of the volatility process.

Examining the causal relationship between interest rate changes in the US (domestic) and Eurodollar (external) markets is essential to the understanding of international financial market integration. One aspect of concern has been the influence of domestic dollar denominated asset returns on comparable external dollar returns. Research analysing this relationship has been done since the 1960s (see, among others, Hendershott (1967); Kaen, Helms, and Booth (1983); Swanson (1988); Fung and Isberg (1992); and Tse and Booth (1995)). Nevertheless, all previous research investigates the relationship between US and Eurodollar interest rates via the first moment of the series. Ross (1989), however, argued that the variance of price changes is related directly to the rate of flow of information. Hence, previous studies ignoring the volatility mechanism may not offer a thorough understanding of the information transmission process. In this paper, Treasury bill and Eurodollar futures are employed to investigate the volatility spillovers between US and Eurodollar interest rates.

In other international financial markets, recent works have focused their attention on examining how news from one international market influences other markets' volatility process (see, for exmple, Engle, Ito, and Lin (1990) for currency markets, and Hamao, Masulis, and Ng (1990) for stock markets). Engle and Susmel (1993) explicitly addressed the issue of a common component driving the volatility in international stock markets. Using the common volatility test developed by Engle and Kozicki (1993), they find that some international markets have the same volatility process. By the same token, analysing whether US and Eurodollar interest rates share a common volatility feature leads to a better a understanding of interest rate linkages and the nature of the interest rate risks faced by banks. Some preliminary statistics seem to support the hypothesis

* *This paper was first published in the* Journal of Economics and Business, *Vol. 48 (1996). It is reprinted with kind permission from Elsevier Science - NL, Sara Burgerhartstraat 25, 1055 KV Amsterdam, The Netherlands. The authors thank three anonymous referees for useful suggestions and comments.*

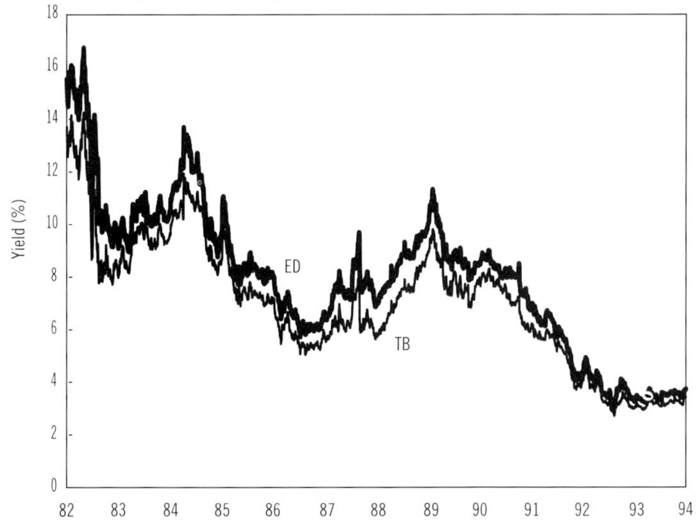

1. Daily TB and ED yields

that Treasury bill and Eurodollar futures share the same contemporaneous volatility process, which follows a Garch process. However, this hypothesis is rejected by the common volatility test of Engle and Kozicki (1993).

The idea that the interest rate differential, namely the TED spread, between Eurodollar and Treasury bill futures yields reflects the soundness of the international financial market is widely accepted among practitioners and academics. (See, for example, Siegel and Siegel (1989), and Edwards and Ma (1992)). Specifically, events that jeopardise the solvency of the banking system tend to widen the spread. Evidence of this relationship is provided by Slentz (1987) who analyses the incident of Continental Illinois Bank and its effects on the TED spread. Nevertheless, no previous paper has explicitly incorporated this idea into information transmission or volatility spillover models. This paper documents that a highly volatile TED spread indicates a state of uncertainty. Accordingly, if the spread changes substantially on a particular day, Treasury and Eurodollar futures will also change in either direction in the following day. A bivariate Egarch model that allows for asymmetric volatility influence of the TED spread, as well as that of the domestic market, is used to analyse the volatility spillovers between markets. Results shows that the lagged TED spread change is the driving force of the volatility spillover mechanism.

Table 1. Descriptive statistics of yield changes

	ΔTB	ΔED
Mean (10^{-2})	–0.596 (0.002)	–0.761 (0.000)
Variance	0.011	0.012
Skewness	–1.212 (0.000)	–0.983 (0.000)
Excess kurtosis	15.39 (0.000)	9.551 (0.000)
LM Arch(8) test, $\chi^2(8)$	269.8 (0.000)	331.5 (0.000)
Pearson correlation coefficient		
Yield changes	0.905	
Yield change squares	0.882	

P values are in parentheses

Data and preliminary statistics

Daily closing index prices of the three-month US Treasury bill and Eurodollar futures March 1, 1982 to February 22, 1994 (3,032 observations) are collected from Commodity Systems, Inc. (CSI). The nearest contract, which is actively traded, is used until the first trading day of the expiration months, and first differences are taken before rolling over the contracts. Because both the Treasury bill and Eurodollar futures are traded at the International Monetary Market (IMM), a division of the Chicago Mercantile Exchange, the problem of nonsynchronous trading did not appear. Hereafter, TB (or x_1) and ED (or x_2) are used to represent the Treasury bill and Eurodollar futures, respectively.

Unlike Treasury bills, which are sold on discount, Eurodollar time deposits pay add-on interest. To compare them on an equal basis, the implied discount yield of TB futures and the implied add-on yield of ED futures are converted into the bond equivalent yield.[1] Nonetheless, results presented through the paper were qualitatively the same when the originally implied yields are used. Furthermore, to ensure that the interpretation of test statistics was not distorted by the large sample size used in this paper, the significance level adopted was 1%, unless otherwise specified. (See Zellner (1984), for a detailed explanation of this issue.)

Figure 1 demonstrates the comovements of TB and ED yields, and visually supports the notion that they move together. Both TB and ED yield changes exhibit negative skewness and leptokurtosis as shown in Table 1. The significant results of the Engle's (1982) Lagrange multiplier Arch test suggests that TB and ED follow the Arch-type processes. The large positive correlation of yield changes between TB and ED (0.91) provides evidence that they are close substitutes. Moreover, the correlation of yield change squares (0.88) indicates that these two interest rates are related through their volatility processes. This latter issue is the main concern of this paper.

The augmented Dickey-Fuller (ADF) (Dickey and Fuller (1979); (1981)) and Phillips-Perron (Phillips (1987); and Phillips and Perron (1988)) tests were used to test for unit roots. Table 2 shows that both of the interest rates and the TED spread, ED minus TB, have a unit root. The result showing that the TED spread has a unit root is not consistent with the conventional wisdom that there is a long-run relationship between TB and ED. However, Booth and Tse (1995), using the Geweke and Porter-Hudak (1983) (GPH) test, report that the TED spread is a fractionally integrated series, $I(d)$, with $d = 0.75$ for the same period examined. This means that TB and ED are fractionally cointegrated, indicating an equilibrium relationship with the deviations from equilibrium being highly persistent. (See Cheung and Lai (1993), and Baillie and Bollerslev (1994) for a detailed description of fractional cointegration.) Accordingly, the TED spread behaves more like an $I(1)$ than an $I(0)$ series. The first differences of the yields and the TED spread, therefore, are employed in the volatility spillover models analysed later.

Table 2. Augmented Dickey-Fuller and Phillips-Perron unit root tests

	TB	ED	TED
ADF1	−2.506	−2.493	−2.673
ADF2	−2.924	−2.999	−3.462
PP1	−2.145	−2.092	−2.724
PP2	−2.771	−2.721	−3.675

ADF and PP denote the augmented Dickey-Fuller test and the Phillips-Perron test statistics, respectively. ADF1 and PP1 were computed with a constant term; and ADF2 and PP2, with a constant and a linear trend. The statistics were computed with 20 lags for the ADF tests and 20 nonzero autocovariances in Newey-West (1987) correction. Results are robust for 10 and 30 lags; the hypothesis that a unit root in each series is not rejected. The critical values using the 1% level are −3.43 (no trend) and −3.96 (with trend) for both statistics, which are asymptotically equivalent, are available in Fuller (1976).

Common volatility

Engle and Kozicki (1993) introduced a class of statistical tests for the hypothesis that some feature that is present in each of the markets is common to all of them. A common feature is detected by a test that finds linear combinations of returns with no feature. The common feature that is investigated in this paper is the common volatility process, which is related to the information transmission mechanism.

The common volatility test by Engle and Kozicki (1993) is used to assess the validity of a simple one-factor Arch model. This test is based on the result that series y_{1t}, y_{2t}, ..., y_{pt} with Arch features have a common Arch factor if there exists at least one no-Arch portfolio. In other words, for a common factor to obtain, there should exist a linear combination of y_{it}, ie

$$\sum_{i=1}^{P} w_i y_{it}, \tag{1}$$

where $w_i (w_1 = 1$ and $w_{i>1} \neq 0)$ is the weight of y_{it} that displays no Arch features as measured by the Lagrange multiplier statistic. Therefore, if TB and ED have a one-factor model representation for yield changes with a time-varying variance, a linear combination of the TB and ED yield changes that does not exhibit time-varying variance can be constructed; ie the factor is eliminated. Operationally, testing whether there is a portfolio that has a constant variance exhibiting no Arch errors (while individual series contains Arch) is equivalent to testing the validity of the simple model. For a detailed analytical description see Diebold and Nerlove (1989) and Engle and Susmel (1993).

The common feature test has two steps. First, both series are tested for the Arch feature. Second, if Arch effects are found in both series, then the test for common Arch is undertaken. The first step showing the Arch effects in TB and ED yield changes are previously reported in Table 1. Then the portfolio formed by the linear combination of ΔTB_t and ΔED_t, ie $\Delta TB_t + w_2 \Delta ED_t$, showing no Arch is found by iteration of the weight w_2. Lagged squared yield changes $((\Delta x_{i,t-k})^2, i = 1,2)$ and lagged cross-product of yield changes $(\Delta x_{1,t-k} \Delta x_{2,t-k})$ of order 8, ie $k = 1,...,8$, and a constant are used as instrumental variables; results are robust for the orders of 4 and 16. Engle and Kozicki (1993) show that the minimum Lagrange multiplier statistic, $LM = TR^2$, is distributed as χ^2 with degrees of freedom = $3 \times 8 - 1 = 23$. For $-3 \leq w_2 < 3$ excluding $w_2 = 0$, the smallest LM is found to be 492.4 (with $w_2 = 2.70$), which is still significant at any conventional level. Therefore, a single factor does not exist. In other words, TB and ED do not share the same contemporaneous volatility process, assuming that the common feature follows Arch. In sum, the common volatility test gives contradictory results with the preliminary correlation results in the previous section.[2]

TED spread and volatility spillovers

ECONOMIC INTUITION AND PRELIMINARY RESULTS

The TED spread and spread change are plotted in Figure 2. The spread is always positive, because Eurodollar deposits are obligations of major commercial banks and are not government guaranteed against default like Treasury bills.

2. TED spread and spread change

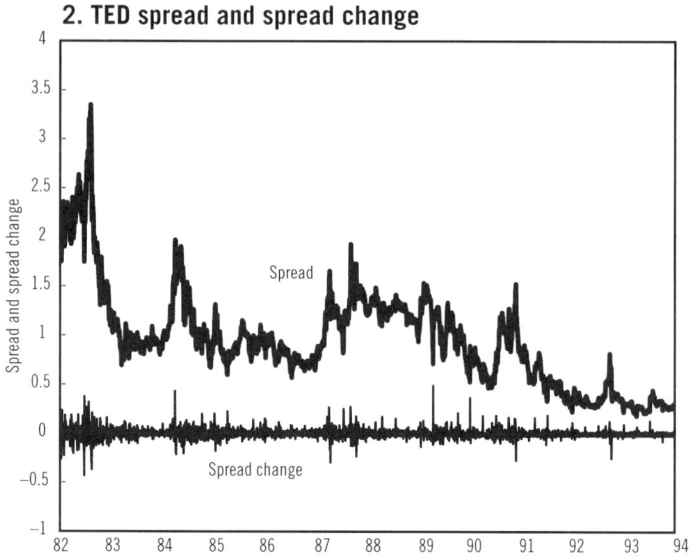

Accordingly, the TED spread may be considered a quality spread, which reflects the risk premium of holding a Eurodollar deposit versus a Treasury bill. Figure 2 illustrates several upward and downward spikes in the spread series. These spikes, revealing important international financial market changes, are made more obvious by observing the spread change in the figure.

A review of the dynamical behaviour of the TED spread during the sample period provides anecdotal evidence supporting the notion that the TED spread reflects the soundness of the international financial markets. To wit: during the second half of 1982 the United States was emerging from a recession. On August 18, 1982, investors appeared to speculate that interest rates would be decreased to encourage economic recovery. As a result the stock market soared and the TED spread plunged. On the next day, however, rumours swept financial markets that one or more major US banks faced problems in their loan exposure in the Mexican peso. The rumor triggered a so-called "flight to quality" for the greater safety of government instruments such as Treasury bills; consequently, the TED spread jumped. After remaining at a high level for two more months, the spread dropped, particularly on October 7, 1982, as a result of declining interest rates and an easing of the Federal Reserve's monetary policy.[3] On May 24, 1984, the spread surged again in response to the rumours of funding problems among US banks after the de facto failure of Continental Illinois Bank. The spread then dropped because of the subsequent FDIC rescue. The spread remained low until May 19, 1987 when Citicorp announced that it would take a $2.5 billion loss and investors, consequently, rushed to buy the shortest-term and highest-quality securities, three-month Treasury bills. This surge was followed by the well-known stock market crash (Black Monday) on October 19, 1987, when investors feared that epidemic defaults among securities and futures traders might endanger the bank solvency. Because no important international news happened during the next three years, the TED spread became less volatile. Then in January 1991, the eruption of the Persian Gulf War jolted the world's financial markets, and the TED spread rose substantially. But on January 17, 1991, speculation that US-led forces in the Gulf War were headed for a quick victory convinced some investors that the war would be brief and that there might not be any major damage to Middle East oil facilities. Therefore, the ED yields and the spread that had been rising because of the war declined substantially. Afterwards, the spread was fairly stable except for the spike on November 16, 1992. On that day, the weak market fundamentals were aggravated by Japan's political scandal; Tokyo stock prices, as well as other major international stock prices, dropped broadly.

Table 3. Correlations between the lagged TED spread changes and yield change squares

	Δx_{it}	
	TB	ED
Corr $[(\Delta x_{it})^2,(\Delta x_{j,t-1})^2]$	0.166	0.122
Corr $[(\Delta x_{it})^2,(\Delta x_{j,t-1})^2]$	0.102	0.162
Corr $[(\Delta x_{it})^2,\lvert\Delta TED_{t-1}\rvert^2]$	0.319	0.247
Corr $[(\Delta x_{it})^2,\Delta TED_{t-1}]$	0.138	0.094

i = 1 and j = 2 and vice versa.

In summary, the above suggests that events that jeopardise the economy, especially the solvency of the banking system, tend to widen the spread. A highly volatile TED spread indicates a state of uncertainty; accordingly, if the spread changes substantially on a particular day, TB and ED will also change in either direction in the following day. Moreover, because the spread increases in response to bad economic news, the conditional variance of TB and ED yield changes should be increased more by an increase than by an decrease in the spread.

Table 3 provides some evidence that the lagged TED spread change squares, $(\Delta TED_{t-1})^2$, and the *lagged* absolute value of the TED spread changes, $\lvert\Delta TED_{t-1}\rvert$, which are proxies for volatility, are related to the *current* TB and ED yield change squares, $(\Delta x_{it})^2$, i = 1 or 2. Comparing the first three rows of Table 3 to the second two rows indicates that the correlation coefficients between $(\Delta x_{it})^2$ and $(\Delta TED_{t-1})^2$ and $|\Delta TED_{t-1}|$ are not only positive but also noticeably higher than between $(\Delta x_{i,t-1})^2$ and $(\Delta x_{j,t-1})^2$, $i = 1$ and $j = 2$ and vice versa. Moreover, the last row reporting the positive correlation between $(\Delta x_{it})^2$ and $(\Delta TED_{t-1})^2$ evinces the above-mentioned asymmetric volatility influence of the TED spread.

Indisputably, TB and ED are close substitutes and move in the same direction according to common economic fundamentals during *normal economic situations*. However, during an abnormal environment such as wars, TB and ED may move in an opposite direction and the TED spread becomes wider (narrower) if the situation gets worse (better). During the entire period examined, TB and ED moved in an opposite direction on 195 days; more than 70% of these 195 days happened two weeks before or after the erratic events discussed in the last section. Moreover, ED fluctuated more than TB during these events.

As an example, consider the aforementioned Persian Gulf War in more detail. ED yields increased by 29 basis points from January 2, 1991 to January 16, 1991. During the same period of time, TB yields decreased moderately by nine basis points. In contrast, on January 17, 1991, the date that US-led forces joined the war, the ED yield fell by 13 points because of the elimination of the war premium which had been established in the market, while the TB yield rose by 14 points as a result of so-called "yield curve trades," ie selling short-term bills and using the proceeds to buy long-term bonds.

This example demonstrates that during erratic periods, TB and ED respond differently because the risk premium between them dominates economic fundamentals. This explains why TB and ED may not have a common volatility (Garch) process (see footnote 2). Moreover, a significant increase or decrease in the TED spread reveals a state of uncertainty and, therefore, induces volatility to both yields. Evidence showing the effect of TED spread change on the volatility mechanism between TB and ED is presented in the following subsection.

ASYMMETRIC VOLATILITY MODEL: BIVARIATE EGARCH

To capture the asymmetric impact of innovation on volatility σ_t^2, Nelson (1991) developed the exponential Garch (Egarch) model of the form

$$\ln(\sigma_t^2) = \varphi_0 + \varphi_1\left(|u_{t-1}| - E|u_{t-1}| + \theta u_{t-1}\right) + \varphi_2 \ln(\sigma_{t-1}^2), \quad (2)$$

where u_t is the standardised residual and $E|u_t| = (2/\pi)^{1/2}$ for conditional normal distributions. He showed that the asymmetric volatility parameter θ is significantly negative for modelling the stock market index volatility, suggesting that the variance tends to rise (fall) when the past innovation is negative (positive) in accordance with the empirical evidence for stock returns. From this perspective, θ should be positive in the current study as an increase in the interest rate corresponds to a decrease in the bond price.

The volatility spillover mechanism is analysed by the following bivariate Egarch model:

$$\Delta x_{it} = c_{i0} + c_{i1}\Delta x_{i,t-1} + c_{i2}\Delta x_{j,t-1} + \varepsilon_{it}, \quad (3a)$$

$i = 1$ and $j = 2$ and vice versa,

$$\varepsilon_t \equiv \begin{pmatrix} \varepsilon_{1t} \\ \varepsilon_{2t} \end{pmatrix} \Bigg| \psi_{t-1} \sim N(0, H_t), H_t \equiv \begin{pmatrix} \sigma_{1t}^2 & \sigma_{12,t} \\ \sigma_{12,t} & \sigma_{2t}^2 \end{pmatrix}, \quad (3b)$$

$$\ln(\sigma_{it}^2) = \varphi_{i0} + \varphi_{i1}\left(|u_{i,t-1}| - E|u_{i,t-1}| + \theta u_{i,t-1}\right) + \varphi_{i2}\ln(\sigma_{i,t-1}^2) + \delta_{i1}|\Delta TED_{t-1}| + \delta_{i2}\Delta TED_{t-1}, \quad (3c)$$

$i = 1$ or 2

$$\sigma_{12,t} = \rho\sigma_{1t}\sigma_{2t} + \gamma_1|\Delta TED_{t-1}| + \gamma_2\Delta TED_{t-1}, \quad (3d)$$

where $u_{i,t-1} \equiv \varepsilon_{i,t-1}/\sigma_{i,t-1}$ and ψ_{t-1} is the information set at $t - 1$. The model is jointly estimated by maximising the following log-likelihood function

$$L(\Theta) = -\frac{1}{2}\sum_{t=1}^{T}\left(\ln|H_t| + \varepsilon_t' H_t^{-1}\varepsilon_t\right), \quad (4)$$

where Θ is the parameter vector of the model. The BFG numerical optimisation algorithm in RATS 4.2 with robust standard errors was used. A similar Garch model with no asymmetric volatility is employed by Ng and Pirrong (1994). In the context of industrial metals, they report that the lagged-squared spread had a significant effect on the variances of both spot and forward returns and on the correlation between these returns.

The conditional mean equation (3a) of Δx_{it}, includes a lagged Δx_i and a lagged Δx_j. The former acounts for the potential autoregressive behaviour of Δx_{it}, and the latter was added to allow for mean spillover. The conditional variance equation (3c), was constructed by adding $\delta_{i1}|\Delta TED_{t-1}|$ and $\delta_{i2}\Delta TED_{t-1}$ to equation (2). Respectively, these terms represent the magnitude (symmetric) effect and the sign (asymmetric) effect of the lagged

Table 4. Volatility spillover bivariate Egarch models

$$\Delta x_{it} = c_{i0} + c_{i1}\Delta x_{i,t-1} + c_{i2}\Delta x_{j,t-1} + \varepsilon_{it}, \quad i = 1 \text{ and } j = 2 \text{ and vice versa,}$$

$$\varepsilon_t \equiv \begin{pmatrix} \varepsilon_{1t} \\ \varepsilon_{2t} \end{pmatrix} \Bigg| \psi_{t-1} \sim N(0,H_t), H_t \equiv \begin{pmatrix} \sigma^2_{1t} & \sigma_{12,t} \\ \sigma_{12,t} & \sigma^2_{2t} \end{pmatrix},$$

$$\ln(\sigma^2_{it}) = \varphi_{i0} + \varphi_{i1}\left(|u_{i,t-1}| - E|u_{i,t-1}| + \theta u_{i,t-1}\right) + \varphi_{i2}\ln(\sigma^2_{i,t-1}) + \delta_{i1}|\Delta TED_{t-1}| + \delta_{i2}\Delta TED_{t-1}, \quad i = 1 \text{ or } 2$$

$$\sigma_{12,t} = \rho\sigma_{1t}\sigma_{2t} + \gamma_1|\Delta TED_{t-1}| + \gamma_2\Delta TED_{t-1},$$

	ΔTB		ΔED	
c_{i0}	−0.002	(−2.17)	−0.003*	(−3.73)
c_{i1}	0.084*	(2.73)	−0.058*	(−2.67)
c_{i2}	−0.003	(−0.13)	−0.024	(0.97)
φ_{i0}	−0.210*	(−6.48)	−0.212*	(−6.76)
φ_{i1}	0.096*	(7.94)	0.092*	(8.02)
θ_i (or θ_j)	0.358*	(3.14)	0.373*	(3.70)
φ_{i2}	0.966*	(187.4)	0.966*	(194.1)
δ_{i1}	1.676*	(6.76)	1.754*	(6.91)
δ_{i2}	1.007*	(5.24)	0.732*	(3.60)
ρ		0.917*	(189.3)	
γ_1		−0.002*	(−2.89)	
γ_2		−0.001	(−1.38)	
$L(\Theta)$		14856.9		
		Diagnostic checking: P values of test statistics		
Ljung-Box Q(12) statistics				
u_{it}		0.902		0.638
u^2_{it}		0.289		0.509
$u_{1t}u_{2t}$			0.431	
Engle and Ng (1993) asymmetric tests				
Sign bias test		0.258		0.351
Negative size bias test		0.108		0.936
Positive size bias test		0.067		0.132
Joint test		0.182		0.441

Asymptotic robust t statistics in parentheses. * Significant at the 1% level.

TED spread change. Both δ_{i1} and δ_{i2} should be positive in theory: a change in the TED will increase the volatility of yield changes, and a positive change has a greater impact. Finally, in the conditional correlation equation (3d), ρ is the conditional correlation between ΔTB_t and ΔED_t when the TED spread does not change at $t-1$, ie $\Delta TED_{t-1} = 0$. As illustrated by the previous Gulf War example, the conditional covariance (and correlation) between ΔTB_t and ΔED_t should decline as the lagged TED spread fluctuates greatly (size effect), a "signal" of instability in the international financial markets. Hence, γ_1 and γ_2 should be both negative.

Table 4 presents the results of the volatility spillover Egarch model. As the mean spillover parameters c_{i2} in equation (3a) are found to be insignificant, neither market mean spills over into the other. As expected, the asymmetric volatility parameters Θ_i of domestic markets are significantly positive for both yield changes. Being consistent with the theory of asymmetric volatility influences of ΔTED_{t-1}, for either of the ΔTB_t and ΔED_t conditional variance equation (3c), δ_{i1} and δ_{i2} are positive. Not surprisingly, ρ in equation (3d) is 0.91 and significant at any conventional levels due to the fact that TB and ED yields are moving in response to the same fundamentals except during erratic events. Also, as presumed, γ_1 is significantly negative, but γ_2 is not significantly different from zero.[4] The diagnostic checking of the residuals indicates little evidence of misspecification. The Ljung-Box Q-statistics of the standardised residuals, u_{it}, and their squares, and the cross product standardised residuals, $u_{it}u_{jt}$ are all insignificant. The insignificant results of Engle and Ng's (1993) asymmetric diagnostic tests (namely, sign bias, negative bias, positive bias, and joint tests) further indicate that the model estimated is well-specified.

Therefore, the volatility spillover mechanism between markets is reasonably described by the bivariate Egarch model, which shows that the lagged TED change is the driving factor for the volatility process. In particular, a large lagged change of the spread suggests a state of uncertainty as reflected by a higher conditional variance of yield changes, and, consequently, implies an increase in risk premium of Eurodollar deposits over Treasury bills. These influences are greater when the change is positive than when it is negative. To examine the robustness of the estimates over time, the model was estimated for the subperiods March 1982 to September 1987, and January 1988 to February 1994. The former two subperiods reflect the environment before and after the world-wide stock market crash of October 1987, respectively.[5] The beginning of the third period roughly corresponds to a change in Federal Reserve monetary targets (see footnote 3). Results (available upon request) for all the subperiods are similar to those of the whole period.

Although the above model demonstrates the volatility effects of the spread on both TB and ED, the model is restrictive in the sense that it does not incorporate cross-market volatility spillovers. To allow for these cross-market spillovers from market j to i, equation (3c) is modified by including the term $k_i(|u_{j,t-1}| - E|u_{j,t-1}| + \theta_j u_{j,t-1})$ as follows:

$$\begin{aligned}\ln(\sigma^2_{it}) = {} & \varphi_{i0} + \varphi_{i1}\left(|u_{i,t-1}| - E|u_{i,t-1}| + \theta_i u_{i,t-1}\right) \\ & + \varphi_{i2}\ln(\sigma^2_{i,t-1}) + \delta_{i1}|\Delta TED_{t-1}| + \delta_{i2}\Delta TED_{t-1} \\ & + k_i\left(|u_{j,t-1}| - E|u_{j,t-1}| + \theta_j u_{j,t-1}\right),\end{aligned} \quad (5)$$

$i = 1$ and $j = 2$ and vice versa. Table 5 shows that both of the cross-market spillover parameters k_i (from TB to ED and vice versa) are insignificant even at the 10% level, while the other parameters are qualitatively the same as the previous Egarch model. Moreover, the p-value of the likelihood ratio test, testing the joint hypothesis that $k_{\Delta TB} = k_{\Delta ED} = 0$ is 0.456. Hence, the cross-market volatility spillover effects are insignificant.

Table 5. Volatility spillover bivariate Egarch models (with cross-market spillover)

$$\Delta x_{it} = c_{i0} + c_{i1}\Delta x_{i,t-1} + c_{i2}\Delta x_{j,t-1} + \varepsilon_{it}, \quad i = 1 \text{ and } j = 2 \text{ and vice versa,}$$

$$\varepsilon_t \equiv \begin{pmatrix} \varepsilon_{1t} \\ \varepsilon_{2t} \end{pmatrix} \Bigg| \psi_{t-1} \sim N(0, H_t), H_t \equiv \begin{pmatrix} \sigma_{1t}^2 & \sigma_{12,t} \\ \sigma_{12,t} & \sigma_{2t}^2 \end{pmatrix},$$

$$\ln(\sigma_{it}^2) = \varphi_{i0} + \varphi_{i1}\left(|u_{i,t-1}| - E|u_{i,t-1}| + \theta_i u_{i,t-1}\right) + \varphi_{i2}\ln(\sigma_{i,t-1}^2)$$
$$+\delta_{i1}|\Delta TED_{t-1}| + \delta_{i2}\Delta TED_{t-1} + k_i\left(|u_{j,t-1}| - E|u_{j,t-1}| + \theta_j u_{j,t-1}\right), \quad i = 1 \text{ or } 2$$

$$\sigma_{12,t} = \rho\sigma_{1t}\sigma_{2t} + \gamma_1|\Delta TED_{t-1}| + \gamma_2\Delta TED_{t-1},$$

	ΔTB		ΔED	
c_{i0}	–0.002*	(–3.12)	–0.003*	(–4.67)
c_{i1}	0.084	(2.83)	–0.056	(1.84)
c_{i2}	–0.005	(–0.16)	–0.022	(0.73)
φ_{i0}	–0.208*	(–5.01)	–0.197*	(–5.87)
φ_{i1}	0.097*	(2.83)	0.082*	(4.00)
θ_i (or θ_j)	0.348*	(2.93)	0.344*	(3.41)
φ_{i2}	0.967*	(143.6)	0.968*	(180.2)
δ_{i1}	1.658*	(5.12)	1.626*	(5.81)
δ_{i2}	0.996*	(3.21)	0.811*	(3.36)
k_i	0.004	(0.15)	0.014	(0.65)
ρ		0.918*	(198.0)	
γ_1		–0.002*	(–2.98)	
γ_2		–0.001	(–1.19)	
$L(\Theta)$		14857.2		

Asymptotic robust t statistics in parentheses. * Significant at the 1% level.

Conclusions

Using US Treasury bill and Eurodollar futures daily data, this paper has analysed the causal relationship via the volatility spillover mechanism between US and Eurodollar interest rates. Although some preliminary statistics seem to support the hypothesis that TB and ED share the same volatility process, which follows a GARCH process, this hypothesis is rejected by the common volatility test of Engle and Kozicki (1993). A further examination indicates that during erratic periods, TB and ED responded differently (even moving in opposite directions) because the risk premium between them dominates economic fundamentals.

A bivariate Egarch model that allows for asymmetric volatility influence of the TED spread, as well as that of the domestic market, was used to model the volatility spillovers between markets. The model shows that the lagged TED spread change is the driving force of the volatility process, a finding that is robust to allowing for cross-market volatility spillovers. The reason is that, when the TED spread is highly volatile, the financial market is in a state of uncertainty, and, accordingly, the (conditional) variance of interest rates increases. In particular, a large change of the spread implies an increase in risk premium of Eurodollar deposits over Treasury bills. These influences are greater when the change is positive than when it is negative, suggesting asymmetric volatility spillovers from the TED spread changes.

These findings have important implications for the interest rate risk management strategies of large international banks as these banks are generally active in the TB and ED markets. In particular, these strategies should not only explicitly recognise that interest rate volatility is time varying, but should also consider that the dynamics of this risk are, to some extent, predictable by the spread between these two interest rates.[6] Enacting such strategies should enable banks to deal more effectively with government oversight initiatives such as the Federal Reserve's risk-based capital requirements as well as those proposed by the BIS Basle Committee on Banking Supervision.

1 *The following formulas convert a discount yield and an add-on yield to a bond equivalent yield (BEY): Discount yield:* BEY = 365 × yield/[365-yield × days to maturity]; Add-On yield: BEY = 365/360 × yield = (100-index price)/100.

2 *Note that the result showing no common volatility factor may be induced by the restrictive model specifications imposed in Engle and Kozicki's (1993) common volatiltiy test. Particularly, shared volatility at lags, which is empirically of interest, is not allowed or tested in the model. See the comments by Ericcson (1993) for detailed discussion.*

3 *On October 6, 1982, the Federal Reserve shifted from focusing on nonborrowed reserves to targeting borrowed reserves. The increased volatility of money growth during the nonborrowed reserves period 1979–82 raised the degree of perceived uncertainty with regard to standard economic measures, such as interest rates and output (Friedman (1983)).*

4 *Although γ_1 is statistically significant, the economic impact of $|\Delta TED_{t-1}|$ on $\sigma_{12,t}$ is small as its elasticity (evaluated at the means) is only 6×10^{-5}.*

5 *Several studies report that the crash changed the structure of international movements between financial markets (see,*

for example, Malliaris and Urrutia (1992) and Arshanapalli and Doukas (1993) among others). Note that both TB and ED experienced the greatest (absolute) yield changes on October 19, 1987, for the total sample.

6 *A comparison of various interest rate volatility forecasting techniques is provided by Boudoukh et al (1995). Included in the comparison are Garch, MDE (multivariate non-parametric density estimation), and JP Morgan's RiskMetrics.*

BIBLIOGRAPHY

Arshanapalli, B., and J. Doukas, 1993, "International Stock Markets Linkages: Evidence form the Pre and Post-October 1987 Period", *Journal of Banking and Finance* 17, pp.193-208.

Baillie, R.T., and T. Bollerslev, 1994, "Cointegration, fractional cointegration, and exchange rate dynamics", *Journal of Finance* 49, pp.737-45.

Booth, G.G., and Y. Tse, 1995, "Long memory in interest rate futures markets: A fractional cointegration analysis ", *Journal of Futures Markets* 15, pp. 573-84.

Boudoukh, J., M. Richardson and R.Whitelaw, 1995, "The Stochastic Behaviour of Interest Rates", Working Paper, Stern School of Business, New York University, New York.

Cheung, Y.W. and K.S. Lai, 1993, "A fractional cointegration analysis of purchasing power parity", *Journal of Business and Economics* 11, pp.103-12.

Dickey, D.A., and Fuller, W.A., 1979, "Distribution of the estimators for autoregressive time series with a unit root", *Journal of the American Statistical Association* 74, pp.427-31.

Dickey, D.A., and W.A. Fuller, 1981, "Likelihood ratio statistics for autoregressive time series with a unit root", *Econometrica* 49, pp.1057-72.

Diebold, F.X., and M. Nerlove, 1989, "The dynamic of exchange rate volatility: A multivariate latent factor ARCH model", *Journal of Applied Econometrics* 4, pp.1-21.

Edwards, F.R., and C.W. Ma, 1992, *Futures & Options*, New York: McGraw-Hill.

Engle, R.F., 1982, "Autoregressive conditional heteroskedasticity with estimates of the variance of United Kingdom inflation", *Econometrica* 50, pp.987-1007.

Engle, R.F., T. Ito, and W.L. Lin, 1990, "Meteor showers or heat waves? Heteroskedastic intra- daily volatility in the foreign exchange market", *Econometrica* 58, pp.525-42.

Engle, R.F., and S. Kozicki, 1993, "Testing for common features", *Journal of Business & Economic Statistics* 11, pp. 369-80.

Engle, R.F., and V.K. Ng, 1993, "Measuring and testing the impact of news on volatility", *Journal of Finance* 48, pp. 1749-778.

Engle, R.F., and R. Susmel, 1993, "Common volatility in international equity markets", *Journal of Business & Economic Statistics* 11, pp.167-76.

Ericsson, N.R., 1993, "Comment: Testing for common features", *Journal of Business & Economics Statistics* 11, pp.380-3.

Friedman, M., 1983, "Lessons from the 1979-82 monetary policy experiment", *Journal of Money, Credit Banking* 15, pp. 339-43.

Fuller, W.A., 1976, *Introduction to Statistical Time Series*. New York: Wiley, New York.

Fung, H.K., and S.C. Isberg, 1992, "The international transmission of Eurodollar and US Interest Rates: A cointegration analysis", *Journal of Banking and Finance* 16, pp.757-69.

Geweke, J.F., and S. Porter-Hudak, 1983, "The estimation and application of long memory time series models", *Journal of Time Series Analysis* 1, pp.221-38.

Hamao, Y., R. Masulis, and V. Ng, 1990, "Corrections in price change and volatility cross international stock markets", *Review of Financial Studies* 3, pp.281-308.

Hendershott, P.H., 1967, "The structure of international interest rates: The US treasury bill rate and the Eurodollar deposit rate", *Journal of Finance* 22, pp.455-65.

Kaen, F.R., B.P. Helms, and G.G. Booth, 1983, "The integration of Eurodollar and U.S. money market interest rates in the futures market", *Weltwirtschaftliches Archiv* 119, pp.601-15.

Malliaris, A.G., and J.L Urrutia, 1992, "The international crash of October 1987: Causality tests", *Journal of Financial and Quantitative Analysis* 27, pp.353-64.

Nelson, D.B., 1991, "Conditional heteroskedasticity in asset returns: A new approach", *Econometrica* 59, pp.347-70.

Newey, W.K., and K.D. West, 1987, "A simple positive semi-definite, heteroskedasticity and autocorrelation consistent covariance matrix", *Econometrica* 55, pp.703-08.

Ng, V.K., and S.C. Pirrong, 1994, "Fundamentals and volatility: Storage, spreads, and the dynamics of metals prices", *Journal of Business* 67, pp.203-30.

Phillips, P., 1987, "Time series regression with a unit root", *Econometrica* 55, pp.277-301.

Phillips, P., and P. Perron, 1988, "Testing for unit root in time series regression", *Biometrika* 75, pp.335-46.

Ross, S., 1989, "Information and volatility: The no-arbitrage martingale approach to timing and resolution irrelevancy", *Journal of Finance* 44, pp.1-17.

Siegel, D.R., and D.F. Siegel, 1989, *Futures Markets*. The Dryden Press.

Slentz, J., 1987, "The TED spread", *Market Perspective*, Chicago Mercantile Exchange 5, pp.1-4.

Swanson, P.E., 1988, "The international transmission of interest rates: A note on causal relationships between short-term external and domestic US dollar returns", *Journal of Banking and Finance* 12, pp.563-73.

Tse, Y., and G.G. Booth, 1995, "The Relationship between U.S. and Eurodollar interest rates: Evidence from the futures markets", *Weltwirtschaftliches Archiv* 131, pp. 28-46.

Zellner, A., 1984, *Basic Issues in Econometrics*, Chicago: University of Chicago Press.

STOCHASTIC VOLATILITY MODELS: THE NEXT GENERATION?

Introduction

Robert Jarrow

Given what we have seen about volatility in Sections I–IV of this book, it is obvious that volatilities are stochastic. This implies that the standard Black–Scholes formula, when used as the theory suggests – with historic volatilities and delta hedging for replication – will provide poor pricing and hedging.

Nonetheless, the Black–Scholes formula is used in practice. But it is used in a modified fashion. To make the formula more useful for pricing, it is calibrated to the market price through the use of implicit volatilities. And to make it more useful for hedging, delta hedging is augmented by both gamma and vega hedging. Of course, gamma and vega hedging are inconsistent with the underlying model, but since these ad hoc adjustments work, they are used.

My interpretation of this evidence is simply this – the Black–Scholes formula, with these modifications, is approximating a more complex option pricing model with stochastic volatility. But what model? This is the question this section partially addresses by considering the next generation of stochastic volatility option pricing models. Their empirical validation awaits subsequent research.

The first paper, by Larry Eisenberg and Robert Jarrow, reviews the stochastic volatility option pricing models using the perspective of the martingale measure pricing technology. Three classes of models are discussed. First, complete market models are analysed, where a complete market is defined as one where delta hedging in the stock alone can replicate the option. Complete market models include, as special cases, the Black–Scholes (trivial case) and the CEV model.

Second, incomplete market models are discussed. Here, without adding additional traded assets, equilibrium notions must be used uniquely to specify an option's price. This class of models includes the models of Hull and White or Wiggins (see the paper for the references). It also includes the (continuous time analogues) models proposed by the three remaining papers discussed in this section.

Third, this paper discusses a class of models where an additional traded asset (in addition to the stock) completes the market and thereby uniquely determines the option's price. An example is provided where the additional traded asset is a market index. The option's price for this example is shown to be a weighted average of Black–Scholes values.

In contrast to the third approach in Eisenberg and Jarrow, the next papers provide option pricing models using the incomplete market approach. Using this method, delta hedging in the stock alone cannot replicate the option. Consequently, the option's price must rely on some equilibrium notion or the specification of a risk premium or market price of risk to determine a price uniquely.

The paper by Elias Stein and Jeremy Stein develops an option pricing model where the stock's volatility follows an arithmetic Ornstein–Uhlenbeck (or AR(1)) process with mean reversion. A closed-form solution is derived for a European call option (an approximate formula is also provided). The solution depends upon the market price of risk, assumed to be a constant. Simulated comparisons between the Black–Scholes prices and this new formula are provided. The asymptotic properties of the model are also explored.

Steven Heston's article develops an option pricing model where the stock price follows a square root process in the volatility, and where the volatility itself follows an Ornstein–Uhlenbeck process. The market price of risk is assumed to be proportional to the stock's volatility. A closed-form solution for a European call is obtained using a characteristic function approach. Heston shows how to apply his model to both bond options and currency options. An analytic (and numerical) comparison between his model and the Black-Scholes formula is provided.

The last paper, by Jin-Chuan Duan, generates an option pricing model when the stock price follows a discrete time Garch (p,q) process. The formula is derived under a locally risk-neutral valuation relationship (LRNVR). Sufficient conditions for the satisfaction of the LRNVR process are provided. The option's delta and delta hedging are also discussed. Finally, a numerical comparison is provided between a Garch(1,1) process option model and the Black-Scholes formula.

These papers provide new models, all of which are shown to explain the known biases in the Black-Scholes model. The empirical validation and differentiation of these models awaits subsequent research.

The above models are most useful for pricing (vanilla) calls and puts, taking as given the underlying stock price process. But with the expansion in the trading of exotic options (non-vanilla), another class of models is useful, something foreshadowed by the third approach discussed by Eisenberg and Jarrow. This new class of models takes as given the strike and/or maturity structure of vanilla calls or puts. Exotic options are then priced off these curves. This class of models is discussed in the next section.

21

Option Pricing with Random Volatilities in Complete Markets*

Larry Eisenberg and Robert Jarrow
Risk Engineering Company; Cornell University

This article presents the theory of option pricing with random volatilities in complete markets. As such, it makes two contributions. First, the newly developed martingale measure technique is used to synthesise results dating from Merton (1973) through Eisenberg (1985, 1987). This synthesis illustrates how Merton's formula, the CEV formula, and the Black–Scholes formula are special cases of the random volatility model derived herein. The impossibility of obtaining a self-financing trading strategy to duplicate an option in incomplete markets is demonstrated. This omission is important because option pricing models are often used for risk management, which requires the construction of synthetic options. Second, we derive a new formula, which is easy to interpret and easy to program, for pricing options given a random volatility. This formula (for a European call option) is seen to be a weighted average of Black–Scholes values, and is consistent with recent empirical studies finding evidence of mean-reversion in volatilities.

Much of the existing literature on pricing options with random volatilities is for complete markets (see Merton, 1973; Cox and Ross, 1976; Eisenberg, 1985, 1987; Johnson and Shanno, 1987; and Scott, 1987). Notable exceptions are the analyses by Wiggins (1987), Hull and White (1987), and Stein and Stein (1991). There are two advantages to maintaining complete markets when pricing options: simplicity and the ability to construct a synthetic option. Simplicity is important for practical implementation, as it is very difficult to identify a usable, yet realistic general equilibrium model for pricing assets. In addition, the equilibrium based pricing models of Wiggins (1987), Hull and White (1987), and Stein and Stein (1991) do not provide a procedure for constructing synthetic options. The ability to construct a synthetic option position is essential for modern risk management techniques. Given these advantages, the purpose of this article is to extend the insights of Eisenberg (1985, 1987) and Johnson and Shanno (1987) by utilising the newly developed martingale measure techniques to investigate the pricing of options with random volatilities in complete markets.

A synthesis of the existing techniques for random volatility option pricing, in the context of this new methodology, is developed below. To provide this synthesis, a general model for random volatility stock price dynamics is postulated. Using this process as a frame of reference, the restrictions necessary to obtain Merton's (1973) complete markets model are detailed. Merton's model includes, as special cases, the well-known Black–Scholes and CEV option pricing models. A discussion of why synthetic options cannot be constructed using the stock and bond alone, without these restrictions, is provided. We show

* *This paper was first published in the* Review of Quantitative Finance and Accounting, *Vol. 4 (1994). It is reprinted with the permission of Kluwer Academic Publishers. Helpful comments from an anonymous referee are greatly appreciated.*

how the introduction of an additional traded asset, imperfectly correlated to the stock, can complete the market. This asset could be a market index or a derivative security on the stock. General valuation formulas and the procedure for constructing synthetic options are discussed. This technique, in its most abstract form, can also be used to price options given any two sources of risk.

To illustrate the general theory, we provide an example that should prove useful in practical applications. This example is for a stock whose random volatility exhibits both mean reversion and is correlated to the instantaneous random returns on a market index like the S&P 500. This stochastic process is consistent with recent empirical evidence regarding the form of the volatility process; see Merville and Pieptea (1989) for supporting evidence.[1] An easily computed expression for a European option is provided. The option's value is seen to be a weighted average of Black-Scholes values.

The complete markets economy

We consider a continuous trading economy with the trading interval $[0,\tau]$ for $\tau < +\infty$. We are given a probability space (Ω, F, P) and two standard independent Brownian motions $\{W_1(t), W_2(t): t \in [0,\tau]\}$ initialised at zero. We denote the augmented[2] filtration generated by $\{W_1(t), W_2(t): t \in [0,\tau]\}$ as $\{F_t: t \in [0,\tau]\}$ where $F = F_\tau$. Let $E(\cdot)$ denote expectation with respect to the probability P.

Initially, two assets trade: a stock with a random volatility and a money market account. For convenience, we assume that the spot rate of interest is constant and equal to $r > 0$. This assumption is easily relaxed along the lines of Heath, Jarrow, Morton (1992) and it is not crucial to the subsequent analysis. The traded money market account, therefore, earns interest at this rate (r), ie

$$B(t) = \exp\{rt\} \text{ for } t \in [0,\tau]. \qquad (1)$$

The stock price process has no cash dividends and is given by

$$S(t,\omega) = S(0)\exp\Big\{\int_0^t \mu(y,\omega)dy - (1/2)\int_0^t \sigma^2(y,\omega)dy + \int_0^t \sigma(y,\omega)dW_1(y)\Big\} \qquad (2)$$

where $S(0)$ is a strictly positive constant, the volatility and drift coefficients $(\sigma(y,\omega), \mu(y,\omega))$ are both predictable with respect to $\{F_t: t \in [0,\tau]\}$, and satisfy

$$\int_0^\tau |\mu(y,\omega)|dy < +\infty \text{ a.e. } P, \int_0^\tau \sigma^2(y,\omega)dy < +\infty \text{ a.e. } P,$$

with $P(\sigma(t,\omega) > 0 \text{ for all } t \in [0,\tau]) = 1$.

In its stochastic differential form, this can be written as (omitting the dependence on $\omega \in \Omega$)[3]:

$$dS(t) = S(t)\big[\mu(t)dt + \sigma(t)dW_1(t)\big]. \qquad (3)$$

This stock price process has a random volatility because $\sigma(t, \omega)$ is functionally dependent (through $\omega \in \Omega$) on the information set generated by both Brownian motions $\{W_1(t), W_2(t): t \in [0, \tau]\}$. Special cases of (3) are of some interest. If $\sigma(t, \omega)$ is set equal to a fixed positive constant independent of $\omega \in \Omega$, then (3) yields the Black-Scholes economy. Alternatively, if $\sigma(t, \omega)$ is a deterministic function of time (t), the current stock price $(S(t))$, and independent of the second Brownian motion $(W_2(t))$, then we get Merton's (1973) economy (of which the constant elasticity of variance (CEV) process is a special case (see Jarrow and Rudd, (1983)).

From the perspective of option pricing theory, however, the interesting aspect of (3) is due to the fact that both the volatility and drift coefficients can depend on the path of the second Brownian motion $\{W_2(t): t \in [0, \tau]\}$. Without this additional dependence, and given some mild integrability conditions, the above economy is easily shown to be complete.[4] As this subcase has already been adequately investigated by Merton (1973), we restrict our attention to the more complicated, but realistic, situation. For the remainder of the paper, we assume that both $\mu(t)$ and $\sigma(t)$ depend nontrivially on the information set generated by $\{W_2(t): t \in [0, \tau]\}$.

Under the above structure, we claim that the economy is incomplete. To see this intuitively, suppose that the volatility has the stochastic differential:[5]

$$d\sigma(t) = \pi(t)dt + \sum_{i=1}^{2} \beta_i(t)dW_i(t). \qquad (4)$$

Given this characterisation of the volatility process and expression (2), two independent sources of randomness are seen to influence the stock's value at a future date $\{W_1(t), W_2(t)\}$. Thus, to create a synthetic option, we need the ability to hedge these two risks. But, as there is only one traded asset, the stock, this is impossible.[6]

To value contingent claims, we would like to utilise the equivalent martingale measure to construct the risk neutral present value operator.[7] In incomplete markets, not all contingent claims can be synthetically constructed, and these nonredundant claims cannot be uniquely priced by arbitrage arguments alone. To solve this nonuniqueness problem, equilibrium pricing arguments can be invoked, for example see Hull and White (1987) or Wiggins (1987). Instead, following Eisenberg (1985, 1987), to complete the market we allow trading in an additional asset whose time t price $A(t)$ satisfies the following stochastic process:

$$A(t,\omega) = A(0)\exp\Big\{\int_0^t \alpha(y,\omega)dy - \sum_{i=1}^{2}\int_0^t (1/2)\eta_i(y,\omega)^2 dy + \sum_{i=1}^{2}\int_0^t \eta_i(y,\omega)dW_i(y)\Big\} \quad (5)$$

where $A(0)$ is a strictly positive constant, the drift and volatility coefficients $\alpha(y, \omega)$, $\eta_i(y, \omega)$ for $i = 1,2$ are predictable $\{F_t: t \in [0, \tau]\}$, and satisfy

$$\int_0^\tau |\alpha(y,\omega)|dy < +\infty \text{ a.e. } P,\ \int_0^\tau \eta_i(y,\omega)^2 dy < +\infty \text{ a.e. } P,$$

for $i = 1,2$ with $P(\eta_i(y,\omega) \neq 0$ for all $t \in [0, \tau]) = 1$.

In a differential form,

$$dA(t) = A(t)\Big[\alpha(t)dt + \sum_{i=1}^{2}\eta_i(t)dW_i(t)\Big]. \quad (6)$$

The asset's price process is similar to that given for the stock in (3). Note however, that the second Brownian motion influences this asset's price dynamics through a nonzero volatility coefficient (η_2). The first volatility coefficient (η_1) could be zero.

The asset $A(t)$ could be a market index,[8] like the S&P 500, or a contingent claim issued against the stock, like a call option. The first example is emphasised below. The second example is similar to that used in Jones (1984) for jump-diffusion processes. The subsequent mathematics is identical for either of these two cases. Indeed, (5) allows the asset to have random volatilities, which is implied by either of these two examples. These two examples are by no means exhaustive. In fact, any asset correlated with both the stock ($S(t)$) and the volatility ($\sigma(t)$) is acceptable.

Intuitively, since there are now two random shocks $\{W_1(t), W_2(t): t \in [0,\tau]\}$ and two imperfectly correlated traded risky assets ($S(t)$, $A(t)$) to hedge these risks, the markets should be complete. This is, in fact, the case as the next proposition shows.

PROPOSITION 1 (COMPLETE MARKETS)
Define

$$\phi_1(t) \equiv -(\mu(t) - r)/\sigma(t) \quad (7)$$

and

$$\phi_2(t) \equiv -[\alpha(t) - r/\eta_2(t)] - [\eta_1(t)\phi_1(t)/\eta_2(t)]. \quad (8)$$

If

$$\int_0^\tau \phi_1(t)^2 dy < +\infty \text{ a.e. } P$$

and

$$\int_0^\tau \phi_2(t)^2 dt < +\infty \text{ a.e. } P,$$

$$E\Big(\exp\Big\{\sum_{i=1}^{2}\int_0^\tau \phi_i(t)dW_i(t) - (1/2)\sum_{i=1}^{2}\int_0^\tau \phi_i(t)^2 dt\Big\}\Big) = 1,$$

$$E\Big(\exp\Big\{\int_0^\tau (\phi(t) + \sigma(t))dW_1(t) + \int_0^\tau \phi_2(t)dW_2(t) - (1/2)\int_0^\tau (\phi_1(t) + \sigma(t))^2 dt - (1/2)\int_0^\tau \phi_2(t)^2 dt\Big\}\Big) = 1,$$

$$E\Big(\exp\Big\{\sum_{i=1}^{2}\int_0^\tau (\phi_i(t) + \eta_i(t))dW_i(t) - (1/2)\sum_{i=1}^{2}\int_0^\tau (\phi_i(t) + \eta_i(t))^2 dt\Big\}\Big) = 1;$$

then there exists a unique probability $\tilde{P}$ defined by

$$d\tilde{P}/dP = \exp\Big\{\sum_{i=1}^{2}\int_0^\tau \phi_i(t)dW_i(t) - (1/2)\sum_{i=1}^{2}\int_0^\tau \phi_i(t)^2 dt\Big\} \quad (9)$$

such that both $\{S(t)/B(t): t \in [0, \tau]\}$ and $\{A(t)/B(t): t \in [0, \tau]\}$ are $\tilde{P}$ martingales with respect to $\{F_t: t \in [0, \tau]\}$.
Proof. See Appendix. Q.E.D.

This proposition states that under the stated hypotheses, there exists a unique equivalent martingale measure for this economy. The two stochastic processes $\phi_1(t)$ and $\phi_2(t)$ defined in expressions (7) and (8) correspond to the market prices of risk associated with the two Brownian motions $W_1(t)$ and $W_2(t)$, respectively. These quantities are the unique solutions to the well-known arbitrage-free restrictions:

$$\mu(t) - r = -\phi_1(t)\,\sigma(t)$$
$$\alpha(t) - r = -\phi_1(t)\,\eta_1(t) - \phi_2(t)\,\eta_2(t). \quad (10)$$

These arbitrage-free restrictions guarantee that the excess return on the stock and the asset must be linearly related to the market prices of risk times the sensitivity of the stock and the asset to each of these risks. These restrictions are needed in a crucial step in the proof of this proposition (see the Appendix).

The first four conditions of this proposition guarantee that the market price of risk processes are well-behaved. By a result from Harrison and Pliska (1981), the uniqueness of the equivalent martingale measure implies that markets are complete. Hence, any contingent claim can be synthetically constructed using a self-financing trading strategy in the stock S(t) and index A(t).

A useful corollary to this proposition is obtained by invoking Girsanov's Theorem (see Karatzas and Shreve (1988)), which asserts that

$$\tilde{W}_i(t) = W_i(t) - \int_0^t \phi_i(y)dy \text{ for } i = 1, 2 \qquad (11)$$

are independent, standard Brownian motions on the stochastic basis $\{(\Omega, F, \tilde{P}), F_t: t \in [0,\tau]\}$. The corollary is that there exists a risk neutral transformation of the original economy where both the stock and asset earn the risk free rate. This transformation is obtained by substituting (11) into expressions (3), (6) along with expression (10), ie:

$$dS(t) = S(t)\left[rdt + \sigma(t)d\tilde{W}_1(t)\right]$$

and

$$dA(t) = A(t)\left[rdt + \sum_{i=1}^{2}\eta_i(t)d\tilde{W}_i(t)\right]. \qquad (12)$$

Since the markets are complete, given any contingent claim $\{C(t): t \in [0, \tau]\}$ with a random payoff X at time t, which is F measurable and satisfying $\tilde{E}(X^2) < +\infty$, its time t price is:

$$C(t) = \tilde{E}\left(X / B(\tau)\right)B(t). \qquad (13)$$

For example, if the contingent claim is a European call option on the stock S(t) with exercise price $K > 0$ and maturity date τ, then $X = \max[S(\tau) - K, 0]$ and

$$C(t) = \tilde{E}\left(\max\left[S(\tau) - K, 0\right] / B(\tau) \middle| F_t\right)B(t). \qquad (14)$$

Substitution of expression (12) into expression (14) yields:

$$C(t) = \tilde{E}\left(\max\left(S(\tau)e^{-1/2\int_t^\tau \sigma^2(y)dy + \int_t^\tau \sigma(y)d\tilde{W}_1(y)} - Ke^{-r(\tau-t)}, 0\right)\right| \qquad (15)$$

The difficulty in evaluating expression (15) is in the fact that both $\int_t^\tau \sigma(y)d\tilde{W}_1(y)$ and $\int_t^\tau \sigma^2(y)dy$ are random with unknown distributions. The distribution for $\int_t^T \sigma(y)d\tilde{W}_1(y)$ and $\int_t^T \sigma^2(y)dy$ could be obtained via Monte Carlo simulation, given fixed specifications for the volatility coefficients $\sigma(y)$. Alternatively, for practical applications we can compute expression (15) for specified $(\sigma(y))$ by using a multinomial tree along the lines of Madan, Milne, and Shefrin (1989). With a specification of $\sigma(y)$, the multinomial approximation of $\int_t^T \sigma(y)d\tilde{W}_1(y)$ and $\int_t^T \sigma^2(y)dy$ can be explicitly computed. We now illustrate this procedure with an example.

Creating a synthetic option using a market index

This section illustrates the general analysis of the preceding section using an example. The example itself, however, is of considerable independent interest as it is selected based on recent empirical evidence relating to the form of the volatility process.

Merville and Pieptea (1989) investigated the volatilities of 25 optioned stocks and the futures index over the 10-year period 1975–85. Using implicit volatilities from Black-Scholes models, they find evidence consistent with the belief that stock volatilities follow a mean-reverting diffusion process with noise. Stein and Stein (1991) argue that the noise component could be due to a misspecification from using the Black-Scholes model to approximate a random volatility option model. (See Jarrow and Wiggins, 1989 for a related discussion). Consequently, Stein and Stein (1991) ignore the noise term and concentrate on only the diffusion component. We will do likewise. Last, Merville and Pieptea also show that changes in volatilities are correlated across stocks. As we choose our volatility process to be correlated to a market index, different stock volatilities will be correlated with each other and this condition is satisfied as well (see footnote 1). The process we specify reflects these observations.

Let the stochastic process for the stock's volatility be:[9]

$$d\sigma(t) = \left(\bar{\sigma} - \gamma\,\sigma(t)\right)dt + \sigma(t)\beta_2 dW_2(t) \qquad (16)$$

where $\sigma(0)$, $\bar{\sigma}$, γ, and β_2 are strictly positive constants, and

$$\int_0^\tau \left[\bar{\sigma} - \gamma\sigma(y)\right]^2 dy < +\infty \text{ a.e. P.}$$

Expression (16) has four notable features. The first is that the volatility follows a mean reverting process with a long-run value of $\bar{\sigma}$. This is consistent with Merville and Pieptea (1989). The second is that the volatility coefficient of the volatility is proportional to (β_2), a constant. Given the restrictions on the other parameters of the volatility process, non-negative β_2 implies non-negative volatilities. This is an improvement over the process employed in Stein and Stein (1991), who allow volatilities to be negative with positive probability. Third, the randomness in the stock's volatility is correlated with the index (A(t)) through the second Brownian motion $\{W_2(t): t \in [0,\tau]\}$. If other volatilities follow similar processes, then they will be correlated to each other through the $dW_2(t)$ term. This is consistent with the evidence in Merville and Pieptea (1989). Interpreting A(t) as a market index, (16) then states that the stock's volatility is correlated with the market index (through the first Brownian motion $W_1(t)$). Fourth, the first Brownian motion does not influence the volatility's dynamics. The consequence of which is that $\{\sigma(s): s \leq t\}$ is independent of the information set generated by the first Brownian motion $\{W_1(s): s \leq t\}$. If we assume that the market prices of risk, $\phi_1(t)$ and $\phi_2(t)$, are constants, then $\{\sigma(s): s \leq t\}$ is also independent of the information set generated by the risk adjusted Brownian motion $\{\tilde{W}_1(s): s \leq t\}$. This simplifies the valuation formula (15) considerably. We impose this restriction upon the model.

Consider a European type call option on the stock (S(t)) with exercise price K and maturity date τ. By (15), its time 0 value is:

$$C(0) = \tilde{E}\left(\tilde{E}\left[\max\left(S(0)e^{-1/2\int_t^\tau \sigma^2(y)dy + \int_t^\tau \sigma(y)d\tilde{W}_1(y)} - Ke^{-r\tau}, 0\right) \middle| \{\sigma(t): t \in [0,\tau]\}\right]\right). \qquad (17)$$

Conditional on $\{\sigma(t): t \in [0,\tau]\}$ (or equivalently $\{\tilde{W}_2(s): t \in [0,\tau]\}$), the inner conditional expectation generates the well-known Black-Scholes formula. A simplification yields:

$$C(0) = \int_0^\infty \left[S(0)\Phi(h) - Ke^{-r\tau}\Phi(h - v)\right]dF(v) \qquad (18)$$

where

$$h = \left(\log\left(S(0)/Ke^{-r\tau}\right) + (1/2)v^2\right)/v$$
$$v^2 = \int_0^\tau \sigma^2(u)du,$$

and F(v) is the distribution function for v.

The call's value is thus a weighted average of Black-Scholes values, each with a differing "modified" volatility (v).[10] The weights of the differing "modified" volatilities (v) correspond to the likelihood of each occurring (dF(v)). This call value differs from that obtained in Stein and Stein (1991) only to the extent that the distribution dF(v) differs.[11] The distribution for F(v) is unknown, yet it can be shown to depend upon the parameters $(\sigma(0), \bar{\sigma}, \gamma, \beta_2; \phi_2)$.[12] To see this, (16) is used to rewrite v^2 as:

$$v^2 = \sigma(0)^2\int_0^\tau \exp\left\{\int_0^y \left(2\left(\bar{\sigma}/\sigma(u) - \gamma\right) - \beta_2^2 + 2\beta_2\phi_2\right)du + 2\beta_2\tilde{W}_2(y)\right\}dy. \qquad (19)$$

Using (19), it is easy to see that as $-\phi_2$ increases, everything else constant, call values decline. Thus, as investors become more risk averse, call values decline. As the underlying volatility increases (σ(0) increases) or if its long-run value is expected to increase ($\bar{\sigma}$ increases), call values increase.

To obtain the distribution for the "modified" volatility (v), one can perform a Monte Carlo simulation on (19), and use the resulting distribution to compute (18). More importantly, because markets are complete, there is a dynamic trading strategy in the stock and market index {S(t), A(t)} that creates the synthetic call. This trading strategy can be obtained via a multinomial lattice approximation to the stochastic system involving {S(t), A(t), σ(t)}. The option's "deltas" can then be obtained using the standard procedures. (See Madan, Milne, Shefrin (1989)).

Stein and Stein (1991) observe that at-the-money Black-Scholes values are "nearly linear" in volatility. For out-of-the-money options, however, an increase in the volatility of the volatility increases the value of the option. Note that this is a different effect than increasing the current volatility, and it generates the well-known "smile" in implied volatilities. Thus, Stein and Stein argue that their random volatility model is consistent with the observed "smile" in implied volatilities. These arguments also apply to our pricing formula as it is similarly an average of Black-Scholes prices.

Conclusion

This paper presents the theory of option pricing with random volatilities in complete markets. Its contribution is two-fold. First, it extends and synthesises the existing literature by using the newly developed martingale measure technique. Second, it provides an example where a computable solution for a European call option is obtainable. This example may prove useful in practical applications.

Appendix

PROPOSITION A1
If both $\mu(y,\omega)$, $\sigma(y,\omega)$ are predictable with respect to $\{F_t^1: t \in [0,\tau]\}$, and suitably integrable (to be made precise in the proof) then the market is complete.

Proof. Using the result stated in the text from Harrison and Pliska (1981) or Jarrow and Madan (1991), we show that there exists a unique equivalent probability measure $\tilde{P}^1$ on (Ω, F_t^1) making $S(t)/B(t)$ a $\tilde{P}^1$-martingale. The definition of $\tilde{P}^1$ and F_t^1 are given in footnote 2.

(Existence)
Define

$$\phi_1(t) \equiv \frac{\mu(t) - r}{\sigma(t)}$$

and

$$Z_1(t) \equiv \exp\left\{\int_0^\tau \phi_1(t)dW_1(t) - (1/2)\int_0^\tau \phi_1^2(t)dt\right\}.$$

Assume $E(Z_1(\tau)) = 1$ and $E(Z_1(\tau)S(\tau)/S(0)B(\tau)) = 1$. These are the integrability conditions.

Define $\tilde{P}^1(A) = \int_A Z_1(\tau)dP^1$. The first two integrability conditions make $\tilde{P}^1$ a probability on F_t^1. The third makes $S(t)/B(t)$ a $\tilde{P}^1$ martingale with respect to $\{F_t^1: t \in [0,\tau]\}$.

(Uniqueness)
The volatility matrix (a scalar) $\sigma(y)$ is nonsingular for all $t \in [0,\tau]$ a.e. P. By Jarrow and Madan (1991), $\tilde{P}^1$ is unique. Q.E.D.

PROPOSITION A2 (INCOMPLETE MARKETS)
Define $\phi_1(t) \equiv -(\mu(t) - r)/\sigma(t)$.
Let

$$\int_0^\tau \phi_1^2(t)dt < +\infty \text{ a.e.}$$

For any predictable process $\{\phi_2(t): t \in [0, \tau]\}$ such that

$$\int_0^\tau \phi_2^2(t)dt < +\infty \text{ a.e.},$$

$$E\left(\exp\left\{\sum_{i=1}^{2}\int_0^\tau \phi_i(t)dW_i(t) - (1/2)\sum_{i=1}^{2}\int_0^\tau \phi_i^2(t)dt\right\}\right) = 1,$$

and

$$E\Big(\exp\Big\{\int_0^\tau \phi_1(t) + \sigma(t)dW_1(t) + \int_0^\tau \phi_2(t)dW_2(t) - (1/2)$$
$$\int_0^\tau (\phi_1(t) + \sigma(t))^2 dt - (1/2)\int_0^\tau \phi_2(t)^2 dt\Big\}\Big) = 1,$$

then $\tilde{P}(\phi_2)$ defined by

$$d\tilde{P}(\phi_2)/dP \equiv$$
$$\exp\left\{\sum_{i=1}^{2}\int_0^\tau \phi_i(t)dW_i(t) - (1/2)\sum_{i=1}^{2}\int_0^\tau \phi_i^2(t)dt\right\}$$

is an equivalent probability measure making $\{S(t)/B(t): t \in [0,\tau]\}$ a martingale with respect to $\{F_t: t \in [0,\tau]\}$.

Proof. The statement of proposition A2 identifies the candidates for equivalent martingale probability measures. We show that each of these make $S(t)/B(t)$ a $\tilde{P}(\phi_2)$ martingale with respect to $\{F_t: t \in [0,\tau]\}$.

Note that the first two conditions in the hypothesis guarantee that $\tilde{P}(\phi_2)(\Omega) = 1$.

Next, define $L(t) \equiv (d\tilde{P}(\phi_2)/dP) \mid F_t)$. It is well known that $S(t)/B(t)$ is a P martingale if and only if $S(t)L(t)/B(t)$ is a P martingale. We show this latter condition.

Writing out $S(t)L(t)/B(t)$ yields

$$S(t)L(t)/B(t)S(0) =$$
$$\exp\Big\{\int_0^t(\mu(y) - r)dy - (1/2)\int_0^t \sigma^2(y)dy + \int_0^t \sigma(y)dW_1(y)$$
$$+\sum_{i=1}^{2}\int_0^t \phi_i(y)dW_i(y) - (1/2)\sum_{i=1}^{2}\int_0^t \sigma_i^2(y)dy\Big\}$$
$$= \exp\Big\{\int_0^t[\phi_1(y) + \sigma(y)]dW_1(y) + \int_0^t \phi_2(y)dW_2(y)$$
$$-(1/2)\int_0^t[\phi_1(y) + \sigma(y)]^2 dy - (1/2)\int_0^t \phi_2(y)^2 dy\Big\}$$
$$\bullet \exp\left\{\int_0^t(\mu(y) - r)dy + \int_0^t \phi_1(y)\sigma(y)dy\right\}.$$

By the definition of $\phi_1(t)$, the second term is equal to 1. The remaining expression is a nonnegative supermartingale. The third condition in the hypothesis guarantees that it is a martingale. Q.E.D.

Proof of proposition 1 The first two conditions following expressions (7) and (8) in the text yield that $\tilde{P}(\Omega) = 1$. Define $L(t) \equiv (d\tilde{P}/dP) \mid Ft$.

(Existence)
We show that $S(t)L(t)/B(t)$ and $A(t)L(t)/B(t)$ are P martingales.

The identical argument as in proposition A.2 shows $S(t)L(t)/B(t)$ is a P martingale. Next, we write (after algebra)

$$A(t)L(t)/B(t)S(0) =$$
$$\exp\Big\{-(1/2)\sum_{i=1}^{2}\int_0^t[\phi_1(y) + \eta_i(y)]^2 dy +$$
$$\sum_{i=1}^{2}\int_0^t[\phi_1(y) + \eta_i(y)]dW_i(y)\Big\}$$
$$\exp\left\{\int_0^t(\alpha(y) - r)dy + \sum_{i=1}^{2}\int_0^t \phi_i(y)\eta_i(y)dy\right\}.$$

By the definition of ϕ_2, the second term in this product is 1. The remaining expression is a non-negative supermartingale. The fourth condition in the hypothesis guarantees that this is a martingale.

(Uniqueness)
The volatility matrix

$$\begin{pmatrix} \sigma(t) & 0 \\ \eta_1(t) & \eta_2(t) \end{pmatrix}$$

is non-singular for all $t \in [0,\tau]$ a.e. P, by the assumptions that both $\sigma(t)$ and $\eta_2(t)$ are nonzero. By Jarrow and Madan (1991), P is unique.

1 *Among the findings reported by Merville and Pieptea is standard deviations of both individual stocks and the market, as measured by implied standard deviations using non-random variance option pricing models, exhibit mean-reversion with arithmetic rather than geometric Brownian motion. They also report that these implied standard deviations have a noise component and that changes in individual stock-return standard deviations are correlated with changes in the standard deviation of the returns to the market.*

2 *The filtration is augmented to be* P*-complete and right continuous. For subsequent footnotes, we denote the augmented filtration generated by* $\{W_1(t): t \in [0,\tau]\}$ *as* $\{F_t^1: t \in [0,\tau]\}$. *The restriction of* P *to* F_t^1 *is denoted by* P^1 *as well.*

3 *This stock price process could be generalised to*

$$dS(t) = S(t)[\mu(t)dt + \sigma_1(t)dW_1(t) + \sigma_2(t)dW_2(t)]$$

where $\sigma_1(t)$ *and* $\sigma_2(t)$ *are random and satisfy the same measurability and integrability conditions imposed on* $\sigma(t)$. *The subsequent mathematics follows in an identical fashion. In the text, we concentrate on the simpler expression (3) for expositional clarity.*

4 *See Appendix, proposition A1.*

5 *Necessary and sufficient conditions for this are that:*
$\sigma_1(t)$ *is a semi-martingale; and*
its bounded variation component is absolutely continuous with respect to Lebesgue measure. The proof of this statement follows from the martingale representation theorem.

6 *Formally, to prove this assertion, we use a well-known result from Harrison and Pliska (1981) or Jarrow and Madan (1991). The result is: given the existence of a probability measure* $\tilde{P}$ *equivalent to* P, *making* $\{S(t)/B(t): t \in [0, t]\}$ *a* $\tilde{P}$*-martingale with respect to* $\{F_t: t \in [0, t]\}$*; then the economy is complete if and only if* $\tilde{P}$ *is unique. We show that there exists a continuum of non-unique equivalent martingale measures in proposition A2 of the Appendix.*

7 *Letting* X *be* F_τ *measurable, the risk neutral present value operator is defined to be* $\tilde{E}(X/B(\tau))$ *where* $\tilde{E}(\cdot)$ *is expectation with respect to the equivalent martingale probability measure* $\tilde{P}$.

8 *To see that* A(t) *could be a market index, let there be m traded stocks with prices* $s_i(t)$ *for* $i = 1, 2, \ldots, m$. *Let*

$S(t) \equiv s_1(t)$ *and*

$$A(t) \equiv \sum_{i=1}^{m} N_i(t)s_i(t) \text{ with } N_i(t) > 0 \text{ and } \sum_{i=1}^{m} dN_i(t)s_i(t) = 0.$$

Let
$Z_i(t)$ $i = 1, \ldots, m$ *be independent Brownian motions, and let*

$$ds_i(t) = s_i(t)[\mu_i(t)dt + \sigma_i(t)dZ_i(t)] \textit{ for all } i.$$

Then,

$$dA(t) \equiv \sum_{i=1}^{m} N_i(t)s_i(t)\mu_i(t)dt + \sum_{i=1}^{m} N_i(t)s_i(t)\sigma_i(t)dZ_i(t).$$

Define

$$dW_1(t) \equiv dZ_1(t) \text{ and}$$
$$dW_2(t) \equiv \sum_{i=2}^{m} N_i(t)s_i(t)\sigma_i(t)dZ_i(t) / \sum_{i=2}^{m} N_i(t)^2 s_i^2(t)\sigma_i^2(t)$$

then

$$dS(t) = S(t)\left[\mu(t)dt + \sigma(t)dW_1(t)\right] \text{ and}$$
$$dA(t) \equiv \sum_{i=1}^{m} N_i(t)s_i(t)\mu_i(t)dt + N_1(t)S(t)\sigma(t)dW_1(t) + \left[\sum_{i=2}^{m} N_i(t)^2 s_i^2(t)\sigma_i^2(t)\right]dW_2(t)$$

which satisfy (3) and (6). This example could be extended to allow correlation across the various stocks. Indeed, just let $Z_i(t)$ *be correlated for* $i = 1, \ldots, m$. *This, in turn, will induce a correlation across* $dW_1(t)$ *and* $dW_2(t)$. *An orthogonalisation at this point returns us to the process in footnote 3 and (6).*

9 *The volatility process in (16) could be modified to that used in Stein and Stein (1991), ie,*

$$d\sigma(t) = [\bar{\sigma} - \gamma\sigma(t)dt + \beta_2 dW_2(t).$$

Their process allows negative volatilities with positive probability. In this case (18) still applies, but the distribution dF(v) *differs, and is given in Stein and Stein (1991); (11)).*

10 *The form of this expression is not new; see Hull and White (1987) or Stein and Stein (1991).*

11 *See footnote 9.*

12 *Even though there are complete markets, the option price still depends on the second market price of risk* ϕ_2. *This result is due to the transformation of the volatility process (16) to that process which holds under the risk adjusted Brownian motion* $dW_2(t) = d\tilde{W}_2(t) + \phi_2 dt$.

BIBLIOGRAPHY

Cox, J., and S. Ross, 1976, "The Valuation of Options for Alternative Stochastic Processes", *Journal of Financial Economics* 3, pp. 145-66.

Eisenberg, L., 1985, "Random Variance Option Pricing and Spread Valuation", Working paper, University of Illinois.

Eisenberg, L., 1987, Random Variance Option Pricing, Ph.D. thesis, University of Pennsylvania.

Harrison, J. M., and S. Pliska, 1981, "Martingales and Stochastic Integrals in the Theory of Continuous Trading", *Stochastic Processes and Their Applications* 11, pp. 215-60.

Heath, D., R. Jarrow and A. Morton, 1992, "Bond Pricing and the Term Structure of Interest Rates: A New Methodology for Contingent Claims Valuation", *Econometrica* 6 (1), pp. 77-105.

Hull, J., and A. White, 1987, "The Pricing of Options on Assets with Stochastic Volatilities", *Journal of Finance* 42, pp. 271-301.

Jarrow, R., and D. Madan, 1991, "A Characterisation of Complete Security Markets on a Brownian Filtration", *Mathematical Finance* 1(3), pp. 31-44.

Jarrow, R., and A. Rudd, 1983, *Option Pricing*, Homewood, Illinois: Richard Irwin.

Jarrow, R., and J. Wiggins, 1989, "Option Pricing and Implicit Volatilities: A Review and a New Perspective", *Journal of Economic Surveys* 3, pp. 59-81.

Johnson, H., and D. Shanno, 1987, "Option Pricing When the Variance is Changing", *Journal of Financial and Quantitative Analysis* 22, pp. 143-53.

Jones, E. P., 1984, "Option Arbitrage and Strategy with Large Price Changes", *Journal of Financial Economics* 13, pp. 91-113.

Karatzas, I., and S. Shreve, 1988, *Brownian Motion and Stochastic Calculus*, New York: Springer-Verlag.

Madan, D., F. Milne and H. Shefrin, 1989, "The Multinomial Option Pricing Model and Its Brownian and Poisson Limits", *The Review of Financial Studies* 2(2), pp. 251-66.

Merton, R., 1973, "Theory of Rational Option Pricing", *Bell Journal of Economics and Management Science* 4, pp. 141-83.

Merville, L., and D. Pieptea, 1989, "Stock-Price Volatility, Mean-Reverting Diffusion, and Noise", *Journal of Financial Economics* 24, pp. 193-214.

Scott, L., 1987, "Option Pricing When Variance Changes Randomly: Theory, Estimation, and An Application", *Journal of Financial and Quantitative Analysis* 22, pp 419-38.

Stein, E., and J. Stein, 1991, "Stock Price Distributions with Stochastic Volatility: An Analytic Approach", *The Review of Financial Studies* 4(4), pp. 727-52.

Wiggins, J., 1987, "Option Values Under Stochastic Volatility: Theory and Empirical Estimates", *Journal of Financial Economics* 19, pp. 351-72.

22

Stock Price Distributions with Stochastic Volatility:

An Analytic Approach*

Elias M. Stein and Jeremy C. Stein

Princeton University; Massachusetts Institute of Technology

We study the stock price distributions that arise when prices follow a diffusion process with a stochastically varying volatility parameter. We use analytic techniques to derive an explicit closed-form solution for the case where volatility is driven by an arithmetic Ornstein-Uhlenbeck (or AR1) process. We then apply our results to two related problems in the finance literature: (i) options pricing in a world of stochastic volatility, and (ii) the relationship between stochastic volatility and the nature of "fat tails" in stock price distributions.

In this article, we study the stock price distributions that arise when prices follow a diffusion process with a stochastically varying volatility parameter, as described in the following two equations:

$$dP = \mu P dt + \sigma P dz_1 \tag{1}$$

and

$$d\sigma = -\delta(\sigma - \theta)dt + k dz_2, \tag{2}$$

where P is the stock price, σ is the "volatility" of the stock, k, μ, δ, and θ are fixed constants, and dz_1 and dz_2 are two independent Wiener processes. Thus, the model is one where volatility is governed by an arithmetic Ornstein-Uhlenbeck (or AR1) process, with a tendency to revert back to a long-run average level of θ. We use analytic techniques (related to the heat equation for the Heisenberg group) to derive a closed-form solution for the distribution of stock prices in this case.

Our primary interest in doing so is to generate an options pricing formula that is appropriate for the case where volatility follows an autoregressive stochastic process. A large and growing literature suggests that this case is empirically relevant. Although the empirical literature offers many different models for time-varying volatility, of which the AR1 is but one example, the AR1 model provides a natural starting point for the types of questions we address here.[1] It is parsimonious enough that the analysis is tractable, yet (as we argue in more detail below) it captures many of the documented features of volatility data.

Recently, interesting papers by Johnson and Shanno (1987), Wiggins (1987), and Hull and White (1987) have also examined options pricing in a world where stock price dynamics are similar to those given by (1) and (2). The first two papers use numerical methods to determine options prices. In the third, Hull and White solve explicitly for the options price by using a Taylor expansion about $k = 0$ (ie about the point where volatility is nonstochastic). It is not clear that such an expansion provides a good approximation to options prices when k is significantly greater than zero. Furthermore, Hull and White only apply this series solution for the case $\delta = 0$. (They use numerical methods to study the case of nonzero δ.)

---

* *This paper was first published in* The Review of Financial Studies, *Vol. 4, No.4 (1991). It is reprinted with permission of Oxford University Press. The authors thank Ron Henderson for invaluable research assistance, and also thank Michael Brennan, Peter Freund, Ken Froot, Bruce Petersen, Dan Stroock, and an anonymous referee for helpful comments and discussions.*

Although our closed-form solution is quite cumbersome, it is composed entirely of elementary mathematical functions. Consequently, it s readily and directly applied on a desktop computer. We are thus able to avoid using more burdensome numerical methods, or any assumptions about k being close to zero. Also, our method is capable of handling a nonzero mean reversion parameter δ, which should be valuable, given the empirical evidence that volatility is strongly mean-reverting.

In addition to deriving an exact closed-form solution for the stock price distribution, we also use analytic techniques to develop an approximation to the distribution. The approximation has the advantage of being even less computationally demanding than the exact solution. For most parameter values, we also find that the approximation is reasonably accurate - it leads to options prices close to those obtained with the exact formula.

A by-product of analysis is that it allows us to draw a direct link between the parameters of the volatility process and the extent to which stock price distributions have "fat tails" compared to the log-normal distribution. (See, for example, Fama (1963, 1965) and Mandlebrot (1963)). We are able to show explicitly how the shape of stock price distributions depends on the parameters of our Equation (2), thereby tracing fat tails back to their "primitive origins," the constants δ, θ, and k.[2]

The remainder of the paper is organised as follows. Our principal results for exact and approximate stock price distributions are presented below. We then apply these results to options pricing. Using the empirical literature on stochastic volatility as a guide, we select a range of "reasonable" parameter values and compare the prices generated by our model to Black-Scholes (1973) prices. We then explore the connection between our model's parameters and the degree to which stock price distributions over different time horizons have fat tails. Finally, we conclude and discuss some possible extensions of our work.

The problems studied in this article require a substantial amount of mathematical analysis. In order not to interfere with the presentation of the main ideas, most of it is omitted from the text. The Appendices contain a brief review of the important derivations. Further details is available from the authors on request.

Before proceeding, we ought to comment on our assumption that volatility is driven by an arithmetic process, which raises the possibility that σ can become negative. This formulation is equivalent to putting a reflecting barrier at $\sigma = 0$ in the volatility process, since σ enters everywhere else in squared fashion. Although this is not a very natural feature, geometric models for σ are much less analytically tractable.[3] Furthermore, as we argue below, any objections to the arithmetic process are more theoretical than practical. For a wide range of relevant parameter values, the probability of actually reaching the point $\sigma = 0$ is so small as to be of no significant consequence.

Exact and approximate stock price distribution

THE CLOSED-FORM EXACT SOLUTION

An explicit, closed-form solution for the stock price distribution corresponding to (1) and (2) is presented below. As a normalisation, we set the initial stock price, P_0, equal to unity.

We start by defining the following new variables:

$$A \equiv -\delta / k^2, \quad B = \theta\delta / k^2, \quad C = -\lambda / k^2 t. \tag{3}$$

A and B are simply functions of our primitive parameters; C also contains λ, which is a dummy variable to be used in defining an integral expression below.

Next, we define

$$a \equiv \left(A^2 - 2C\right)^{1/2}, \quad b \equiv -A / a, \tag{4}$$

$$L \equiv -A - a\left(\frac{\sinh(ak^2t) + b\cosh(ak^2t)}{\cosh(ak^2t) + b\sinh(ak^2t)}\right), \tag{5}$$

$$M \equiv B\left\{\frac{b\sinh(ak^2t) + b^2\cosh(ak^2t) + 1 - b^2}{\cosh(ak^2t) + b\sinh(ak^2t)} - 1\right\}, \tag{6}$$

$$\begin{aligned} N \equiv\ & \frac{a-A}{2a^2}\left[a^2 - AB^2 - B^2a\right]k^2t + \frac{B^2\left[A^2 - a^2\right]}{2a^3} \\ & \times\left\{\frac{(2A+a) + (2A-a)e^{2ak^2t}}{\left(A + a + (a-A)e^{2ak^2t}\right)}\right\} \\ & + \frac{2AB^2\left[a^2 - A^2\right]e^{ak^2t}}{a^3\left(A + a + (a-A)e^{2ak^2t}\right)} \\ & - \frac{1}{2}\log\left\{\frac{1}{2}\left(\frac{A}{a} + 1\right) + \frac{1}{2}\left(1 - \frac{A}{a}\right)e^{2ak^2t}\right\}, \end{aligned} \tag{7}$$

and

$$I = \exp\left(L\sigma_0^2 / 2 + M\sigma_0 + N\right). \tag{8}$$

Notice that I, in addition to being a function of the primitive parameters δ, θ, k, t, and σ_0, also depends on the dummy variable λ. We denote this relationship by writing I as $I(\lambda)$. We now write down an expression for the stock price distribution in two steps. First, we define $S_0(P,t)$ as the time t stock price distribution in the special case where the stock price drift $\mu = 0$. It is given by

$$S_0(P,t) = (2\pi)^{-1} P^{-3/2} \times \int_{\eta=-\infty}^{\infty} I\left(\left(\eta^2 + \frac{1}{4}\right)\frac{t}{2}\right) e^{i\eta \log P} d\eta. \quad (9)$$

The time t stock price distribution for the more general case of a nonzero μ, which we denote simply by $S(P,t)$, is then

$$S(P,t) = e^{-\mu t} S_0\left(Pe^{-\mu t}\right). \quad (10)$$

Although the formula for $S(P,t)$ is complicated, it is composed entirely of elementary functions and requires only a single integration. Also, note that $S(P,t)$ is a conditional distribution, conditional upon the current stock price and current volatility – more comprehensive notation would involve writing this distribution as $S(P,t \mid P_0,\sigma_0)$.

AN APPROXIMATE SOLUTION

In some cases, it may be useful to have a somewhat simpler approximation to $S(P,t)$. In order to derive such an approximation, we note that our exact distribution can always be expressed as an average of lognormal distributions, averaged via a mixing distribution. (This is proved in Appendix A.) That is,

$$S(P,t) = \int L(\sigma) m_t(\sigma) d\sigma, \quad (11)$$

where $L(\sigma)$ is a lognormal with the same mean as $S(P,t)$ and volatility σ, and $m_t(\sigma)$ is a mixing distribution. The t subscript on $m_t(\sigma)$ emphasises the fact that the mixing distribution depends on the time horizon.

Our approximation technique works by approximating this mixing distribution $m_t(\sigma)$. In Appendix C, we show that $m_t(\sigma)$ can be well approximated (in a sense we make precise) by $\hat{m}_t(\sigma)$, which has the simple form

$$\hat{m}_t(\sigma) = \rho e^{-\alpha\sigma^2} e^{-\beta/\sigma^2}, \quad (12)$$

where the parameters ρ, α, and β are defined in Appendix C. With $\hat{m}_t(\sigma)$ in hand, our approximate stock price distribution $\hat{S}(P, t)$ is given by

$$\hat{S}(P,t) = \int L(\sigma) \hat{m}_t(\sigma) d\sigma. \quad (13)$$

Application to options pricing

In this section, we apply our results to the pricing of European stock options. It can be shown that, given our assumptions, the price of an option F must satisfy the partial differential equation

$$\tfrac{1}{2}\sigma^2 P^2 F_{pp} + rPF_p - rF + F_t + \tfrac{1}{2}k^2 F_{\sigma\sigma} + F_\sigma\left[-\delta(\sigma-\theta) - \phi k\right] = 0. \quad (14)$$

Here ϕ denotes the market price of the stock's volatility risk and r is the riskless interest rate. The presence of ϕ in (14) reflects the fact that with stochastic volatility, one cannot use arbitrage arguments to eliminate investor risk preferences from the options pricing problem, because the volatility σ is itself not a traded asset.[4]

As we demonstrate below, our analytic results allow us to solve (14) both in the case where ϕ is zero, as well as in the case where ϕ is a nonzero constant. Before doing so, however, it is worth noting when either of these two assumptions can be justified in the context of a specific equilibrium model. Wiggins (1987) contains a thorough discussion of the equilibrium determinants of ϕ, drawing on the results of Cox, Ingersoll, and Ross (1985). Wiggins points out that, in general, ϕ need not be constant, and indeed may not be expressible in a closed form. However, he goes on to identify some interesting special cases that obtain when there is a representative consumer with log utility.

With log utility, $\phi = 0$ if the option in question is an option on the market portfolio. Somewhat more generally, Wiggins argues that log utility also leads to a constant (though possibly nonzero) ϕ for individual stocks, so long as the following underlying moments themselves remain constant: the standard deviation of the market portfolio, and the pairwise correlation coefficients between the individual stock's returns, its volatility, and the return on the market portfolio. These results imply that the assumption of a constant ϕ can indeed be compatible with a fully specified (but somewhat restrictive) equilibrium model. In the case where $\phi = 0$, the pricing equation simplifies to

$$\tfrac{1}{2}\sigma^2 P^2 F_{pp} + rPF_p - rF + F_t + \tfrac{1}{2}k^2 F_{\sigma\sigma} + F_\sigma\left[-\delta(\sigma-\theta)\right] = 0. \quad (14')$$

Equation (14′) does not depend on risk preferences. Thus, in a world where $\phi = 0$, we can calculate the option price by assuming that risk neutrality prevails. This implies that the price of a European call is given by

$$F_0 = e^{-rt}\int_{P=K}^{\infty}[P-K]S(P,t|\delta,r,k,\theta)dP. \quad (15)$$

The subscript 0 on F emphasises the fact that (15) applies only to the case where $\phi = 0$. The stock price distribution S(P,t) in this equation is generated using the parameters δ, k, and θ, along with the assumption that the stock's drift equals the riskless rate r. Thus, the mean of S(P,t) in (15) is equal to P_0e^{rt}.[5]

Now consider the somewhat more general case of a nonzero but constant ϕ. From a comparison of (14) and (14′), it is apparent that if the solution to (14′) is given by (15), then the solution to (14) must be given by

$$F = e^{-rt}\int_{P=K}^{\infty}[P-K]S(P,t|\delta,r,k,\hat{\theta}), \quad (16)$$

where $\hat{\theta} = \theta - \phi k/\delta$. Therefore, in addition to setting the stock price drift to r, we also modify the parameter θ to account for the effect of volatility risk on options prices. When the volatility risk premium ϕ is positive, $\hat{\theta}$ is lower than θ, and options prices are lower, all else being equal.

Before presenting some sample options prices, we briefly discuss two practical issues. The first concerns the calibration of the model – that is, the choice of appropriate parameter values. The second concerns the implementation of the model on a computer.

CALIBRATING THE MODEL

In order to choose reasonable values for the parameters θ, k, and δ, we draw on the existing empirical literature on the time-series properties of volatility, focusing upon those articles that use an AR1 model for volatility. While an AR1 model cannot be expected to fit the data as well as a less parsimonious one, there is some evidence that suggests it does quite a good job, at least for aggregate stock indices. For example, Stein (1989) finds that when modelling the implied volatility of S&P 100 index options, the corrected R^2 from an AR1 model is the same as that from a model that includes eight lags. Using a different data set, Poterba and Summers (1986) also come to the conclusion that an AR1 model provides a good description of the time-series behaviour of volatility.[6]

A related concern is the appropriateness of using an arithmetic versus geometric specification for the volatility process. However, note that Stein (1989) finds no evidence of skewness in the implied volatilities of S&P 100 index options, concluding that it is reasonable to model the volatility process in levels. In addition, empirically reasonable parameter values imply a very small probability that an arithmetic volatility process will ever reach zero.

Two studies are used as principal sources for parameter values, those of Stein (1989) and Merville and Pieptea (1989). Both studies use options-implied volatilities as their data, rather than relying on volatilities estimated from stock price returns. The former focuses on S&P 100 index options, while the latter looks primarily at 25 individual stocks.[7]

Using data from 1983 to 1987, Stein (1989) finds that index volatility averages between about 15% and 20%, depending on the sample period. The half-life of a volatility shock is approximately one month for the entire sample, corresponding to a δ of 8. However in some subsamples, the half-life is as short as two weeks, corresponding to a δ of 16.[8] Estimates of k range from 0.15 to 0.30.

The individual stocks examined by Merville and Pieptea (1989) have (not surprisingly) higher average implied volatilities than the index, generally ranging between about 25% and 35%. Mean reversion is typically stronger than with the index, with a median value of δ in the range of 14, and several individual observations over 20. The parameter k also tends to be higher, often exceeding 0.4 and, in some cases, 0.5.[9] There appears to be a cross-sectional correlation between δ and k: those stocks that have higher ks also often have higher δs.

It is straightforward to demonstrate that the unconditional standard deviation of volatility, denoted by $s_u(\sigma)$, is given by

$$s_u(\sigma) = k/(2\delta)^{1/2}. \quad (17)$$

This formula allows one to calculate the unconditional probability of obtaining values of σ less than zero with the arithmetic AR1 process. For example, a typical set of parameter values for an individual stock would be $\theta = 0.30$, $\delta = 16$, $k = 0.4$. This implies that the standard deviation of volatility is 0.07, or less than one fourth of its mean. Clearly, the probability of observing a negative σ is extremely small. Other configurations of the parameters lead to similar conclusions, as it is difficult to generate reasonable examples where the unconditional probability of a negative σ exceeds 1% or 2%.

COMPUTATIONAL CONSIDERATIONS

The techniques involved in computing prices numerically based on the pricing formulas are neither complex nor particularly costly in terms of computer resources. The code used to produce the results presented here, essentially a collection of numerical integration routines, was written by Ron Henderson in the "C" programming language and was implemented by him on a Silicon Graphics Iris 4D 240 GTX workstation. At the heart of the computations is a Romberg integration routine with some slight modifications to truncate an integral over infinity to some finite region containing enough information to produce accurate results. Romberg integration was chosen over several other candidate schemes (ie quadrature formulas) because of its robustness and ability to adjust to a widely varying integrand.

Our program was able to generate options prices for most parameter values in less than one minute, and in many cases, in less than 15 seconds. Using the approximate distributions instead of the exact ones reduced the amount of computation by a factor that varied between about 10 and 100. It may also be possible to streamline the computation of prices based on the exact distributions. One alternative to the current approach would be to use a fast Fourier transform (FFT) in the calculations. This would effectively reduce the two integrations now involved to a single real FFT and a summation, and could bring computational "cost" to a level comparable to that required to evaluate the Black-Scholes formula numerically. We are currently pursuing this possibility.

SAMPLE OPTIONS PRICES

Options prices based on the exact stock price distributions $S(P,t)$ are presented in Table 1 overleaf. The table is divided into 10 panels, labelled A-J. Each panel looks at seven strike prices and three maturities (one month, three months, and six months) - a total of 21 options. For each option, three numbers are calculated: the Black-Scholes price, a "new" price corresponding to our exact distribution, and the Black-Scholes, implied volatility associated with the new price.

The panels cover a broad range of the parameter values discussed above. (In all cases, we set $\phi = 0$ and $r = \ln(1.1) = 9.53\%$.) Panels A–C encompass the values that appear to characterise stock index options, setting $\theta = \sigma_0 = 0.20$ and allowing δ to range from 4 to 16, while k ranges from 0.10 to 0.30. The subsequent panels examine higher values of volatility and k that seem appropriate for options on individual stocks. In D-F, $\theta = \sigma_0 = 0.25$ and k ranges from 0.20 to 0.40. In G-I, $\theta = \sigma_0 = 0.35$ and k ranges from 0.40 to 0.60. Finally, in panel J, we consider a case where initial volatility differs from its long-run mean, replicating all the parameters of panel F except setting $\sigma_0 = 0.35$, rather than its long-run mean of 0.25.

Several observations emerge from the table. First, stochastic volatility exerts an upward influence on all options prices. Whenever $\sigma_0 = \theta$, the new price exceeds the Black-Scholes price for the same θ. Second, stochastic volatility is "more important" for away-from-the-money options than for at-the-money options, in the sense that the implied volatilities corresponding to the new prices exhibit a U-shape as the strike price is varied. Implied volatility is lowest at-the-money, and rises as the strike price moves in either direction.

The concept of the mixing distribution for σ provides a useful heuristic device for understanding these effects. Given (11), one can always represent our "new" price as an average of Black-Scholes prices with different σs, weighted by the mixing distribution $m_t(\sigma)$. Intuitively, the difference between the Black-Scholes and new prices should depend both on the mean of the distribution $m_t(\sigma)$ as well as on its dispersion.

As it turns out, the Black-Scholes formula is very close to linear in volatility for at-the-money options. This suggests that, for these options, all that should matter (loosely speaking) is the mean of the mixing distribution. Now, even when $\sigma_0 = \theta$, it is not the case that the mean of the mixing distribution equals θ. For example, when volatility evolves deterministically over time, the mean of the mixing distribution is given by the square root of the average value of σ^2 over the life of the option. [See (A2) in Appendix A]. By Jensen's inequality, this is greater than the average value of σ. A similar (though more complex) logic also applies for the case when volatility is stochastic. This "mean of the mixing distribution effect" (roughly) explains the implied volatilities seen at the money.

For away-from-the-money options, there is a second effect. For these options, the Black-Scholes formula is convex in volatility. Thus, for a fixed mean of the mixing distribution, these options are more valuable when the mixing distribution has more dispersion. This "dispersion of the mixing distribution effect" explains the U-shape in implied volatilities mentioned above.

Table 1 shows that the overall impact on options prices can be economically significant, especially when the options are out-of-the-money and the parameter k is allowed to take on large

Table 1. Comparison of Black-Scholes and new prices

Strike	1 month			3 months			6 months		
	Black-Scholes	New	Implied volatility	Black-Scholes	New	Implied volatility	Black-Scholes	New	Implied volatility
A				$(\sigma = 0.20, \theta = 0.20, \delta = 4.00, k = 0.10)$					
90	10.76	10.77	0.2023	12.55	12.57	0.2024	15.12	15.16	0.2025
95	6.20	6.20	0.2009	8.50	8.52	0.2013	11.34	11.38	0.2017
100	2.71	2.71	0.2003	5.23	5.24	0.2008	8.14	8.18	0.2013
105	0.83	0.84	0.2006	2.90	2.91	0.2008	5.58	5.62	0.2012
110	0.17	0.18	0.2015	1.44	1.46	0.2013	3.66	3.69	0.2013
115	0.02	0.03	0.2029	0.65	0.67	0.2021	2.29	2.33	0.2017
120	0.00	0.00	0.2050	0.26	0.28	0.2032	1.38	1.42	0.2022
B				$(\sigma = 0.20, \theta = 0.20, \delta = 8.00, k = 0.20)$					
90	10.76	10.77	0.2070	12.55	12.60	0.2060	15.12	15.20	0.2056
95	6.20	6.21	0.2029	8.50	8.55	0.2037	11.34	11.44	0.2044
100	2.71	2.72	0.2011	5.23	5.28	0.2025	8.14	8.24	0.2037
105	0.83	0.85	0.2020	2.90	2.95	0.2025	5.58	5.68	0.2035
110	0.17	0.19	0.2048	1.44	1.50	0.2035	3.66	3.76	0.2037
115	0.02	0.03	0.2088	0.65	0.70	0.2054	2.29	2.40	0.2043
120	0.00	0.00	0.2133	0.26	0.31	0.2077	1.38	1.48	0.2052
C				$(\sigma = 0.20, \theta = 0.20, \delta = 16.00, k = 0.30)$					
90	10.76	10.78	0.2103	12.55	12.61	0.2073	15.12	15.22	0.2066
95	6.20	6.23	0.2046	8.50	8.57	0.2051	11.34	11.46	0.2058
100	2.71	2.73	0.2021	5.23	5.31	0.2041	8.14	8.28	0.2053
105	0.83	0.86	0.2033	2.90	2.98	0.2041	5.58	5.73	0.2052
110	0.17	0.20	0.2073	1.44	1.52	0.2050	3.66	3.80	0.2053
115	0.02	0.04	0.2127	0.65	0.72	0.2067	2.29	2.43	0.2057
120	0.00	0.00	0.2187	0.26	0.32	0.2088	1.38	1.50	0.2063
D				$(\sigma = 0.25, \theta = 0.25, \delta = 4.00, k\ 0.20)$					
90	10.88	10.90	0.2550	13.03	13.10	0.2558	15.94	16.05	0.2565
95	6.56	6.58	0.2521	9.26	9.32	0.2536	12.44	12.56	0.2550
100	3.28	3.29	0.2510	6.19	6.24	0.2525	9.45	9.56	0.2541
105	1.31	1.33	0.2515	3.88	3.93	0.2525	6.99	7.10	0.2538
110	0.41	0.43	0.2534	2.28	2.35	0.2535	5.03	5.15	0.2541
115	0.10	0.12	0.2563	1.26	1.33	0.2552	3.54	3.66	0.2548
120	0.02	0.03	0.2598	0.66	0.73	0.2574	2.42	2.56	0.2559
E				$(\sigma = 0.25, \theta = 0.25, \delta = 8.00, k = 0.30)$					
90	10.88	10.91	0.2589	13.03	13.13	0.2585	15.94	16.09	0.2588
95	6.56	6.59	0.2539	9.26	9.36	0.2558	12.44	12.61	0.2574
100	3.28	3.30	0.2520	6.19	6.28	0.2545	9.45	9.63	0.2566
105	1.31	1.34	0.2530	3.88	3.97	0.2545	6.99	7.17	0.2563
110	0.41	0.45	0.2563	2.28	2.38	0.2557	5.03	5.22	0.2566
115	0.10	0.13	0.2610	1.26	1.37	0.2578	3.54	3.72	0.2572
120	0.02	0.03	0.2665	0.66	0.76	0.2604	2.42	2.61	0.2582

(but plausible) values. For example, in panel H, where $\sigma_0 = \theta = 0.35$, $\delta = 8$, and $k = 0.50$, our model prices a three-month option with a 120 strike at 2.10, or 11.7% more than its Black-Scholes price of 1.88. The new price corresponds to an implied volatility of 36.5%. Even larger proportional effects can be observed with cheaper options. A one-month option with a 120 strike has a new price of 0.25, which is 31.6% more than its Black-Scholes price of 0.19, and which corresponds to an implied volatility of 36.9%.

In Table 2 overleaf, the approximate prices (based on the approximate distribution $\hat{S}(P,t)$) are compared to the exact new prices. Black-Scholes prices are also included as a benchmark for comparison.[10] In Table 2, the same parameter values are used as in panel F of Table 1, and the results are representative of those seen with other parameter values. As the table shows, the approximate prices are quite close to the exact prices for away-from-the-money options. For example, at a maturity of three months and a strike price of 120, the approximate price is 0.75, as compared to an exact price of 0.76 and a Black-Scholes price of 0.66. In other words, the approximation error is roughly one tenth of the error incurred in using Black-Scholes.

According to this criterion, the approximation technique works somewhat less well at-the-money, although it still outperforms Black-Scholes substantially. At a maturity of three

Table 1 continued

	1 month			3 months			6 months		
Strike	Black-Scholes	New	Implied volatility	Black-Scholes	New	Implied volatility	Black-Scholes	New	Implied volatility
F					($\sigma = 0.25, \theta = 0.25, \delta = 16.00, k = 0.40$)				
90	10.88	10.92	0.2608	13.03	13.13	0.2587	15.94	16.09	0.2587
95	6.56	6.61	0.2553	9.26	9.37	0.2567	12.44	12.62	0.2579
100	3.28	3.31	0.2530	6.19	6.30	0.2557	9.45	9.65	0.2575
105	1.31	1.35	0.2541	3.88	4.00	0.2558	6.99	7.20	0.2573
110	0.41	0.46	0.2579	2.28	2.40	0.2566	5.03	5.24	0.2575
115	0.10	0.14	0.2632	1.26	1.38	0.2581	3.54	3.74	0.2578
120	0.02	0.04	0.2693	0.66	0.76	0.2601	2.42	2.61	0.2584
G					($\sigma = 0.35, \theta = 0.35, \delta = 4.00, k = 0.40$)				
90	11.34	11.39	0.3588	14.31	14.48	0.3619	17.93	18.25	0.3650
95	7.44	7.48	0.3545	10.95	11.10	0.3587	14.83	15.15	0.3628
100	4.42	4.45	0.3529	8.13	8.27	0.3572	12.12	12.43	0.3616
105	2.36	2.40	0.3537	5.87	6.01	0.3572	9.80	10.11	0.3612
110	1.13	1.18	0.3565	4.12	4.28	0.3586	7.83	8.16	0.3616
115	0.49	0.54	0.3606	2.82	3.00	0.3610	6.20	6.55	0.3626
120	0.19	0.24	0.3657	1.88	2.08	0.3642	4.87	5.23	0.3641
H					($\sigma = 0.35, \theta = 0.35, \delta = 8.00, k = 0.50$)				
90	11.34	11.41	0.3612	14.31	14.50	0.3629	17.93	18.25	0.3650
95	7.44	7.50	0.3516	10.95	11.12	0.3602	14.83	15.17	0.3636
100	4.42	4.47	0.3540	8.13	8.30	0.3588	12.12	12.47	0.3629
105	2.36	2.41	0.3550	5.87	6.04	0.3588	9.80	10.15	0.3626
110	1.13	1.20	0.3584	4.12	4.31	0.3600	7.83	8.20	0.3629
115	0.49	0.56	0.3634	2.82	3.02	0.3622	6.20	6.57	0.3635
120	0.19	0.25	0.3694	1.88	2.10	0.3649	4.87	5.24	0.3645
I					($\sigma = 0.35, \theta = 0.35, \delta = 16.00, k = 0.60$)				
90	11.34	11.41	0.3615	14.31	14.48	0.3616	17.93	18.20	0.3628
95	7.44	7.51	0.3567	10.95	11.12	0.3599	14.83	15.13	0.3622
100	4.42	4.48	0.3548	8.13	8.31	0.3592	12.12	12.44	0.3618
105	2.36	2.42	0.3557	5.87	6.05	0.3592	9.80	10.13	0.3617
110	1.13	1.20	0.3589	4.12	4.31	0.3599	7.83	8.17	0.3618
115	0.49	0.56	0.3637	2.82	3.01	0.3611	6.20	6.53	0.3621
120	0.19	0.25	0.3694	1.88	2.06	0.3628	4.87	5.19	0.3626
J					($\sigma = 0.35, \theta = 0.25, \delta = 16.00, k = 0.40$)				
90	11.34	11.14	0.3129	14.31	13.42	0.2832	17.93	16.33	0.2715
95	7.44	7.07	0.3097	10.95	9.78	0.2817	14.83	12.93	0.2709
100	4.42	3.95	0.3085	8.13	6.79	0.2811	12.12	10.00	0.2705
105	2.36	1.92	0.3091	5.87	4.50	0.2811	9.80	7.56	0.2704
110	1.13	0.82	0.3111	4.12	2.85	0.2817	7.83	5.61	0.2705
115	0.49	0.32	0.3143	2.82	1.74	0.2828	6.20	4.08	0.2708
120	0.19	0.11	0.3182	1.88	1.02	0.2842	4.87	2.91	0.2713

The "new" price corresponds to the equations $dP = \mu P\,dt + \sigma P\,dz_1$ and $d\sigma = -\delta(\sigma - \theta)dt + k\,dz_2$. For all entries, $P = 100$, the riskless rate $r = 9.53\%$, and the volatility risk premium $\phi = 0$. The Black-Scholes price corresponds to the nonstochastic volatility setting where $\delta = k = 0$.

months and a strike price of 100, the approximate price is 6.34, as compared to an exact price of 6.30 and a Black-Scholes price of 6.19. In this case, the approximation error is about one third of the error incurred with Black-Scholes.[11]

Asymptotic behaviour of stock price distributions

In this section, we explore the connection between the parameters of the process driving σ and the degree to which stock price distributions have fat tails. In discussing fat tails, we focus primarily on the asymptotic shape of stock price distributions, and on the related question of what moments of the distribution exist.[12] We begin by stating the following definition.

Definition. Two functions $F(z)$ and $G(z)$ are *asymptotically equivalent* as $z \to \infty$ (or as $z \to 0$) if $\log F(z)/\log G(z) \to 1$ as $z \to \infty$ (or as $z \to 0$). This will be denoted as $F(z) \cong G(z)$.

Because we are looking at asymptotic behaviour, the reflecting barrier assumption inherent in the arithmetic process of (2) will not colour our conclusions. The existence of a reflecting barrier at $\sigma = 0$ may lead to unnatural implications about the movements of σ when it is close to zero. However, all that is important for the asymptotics is the nature of σs movements when it is large (ie how quickly can σ move toward infinity?).

To see this point heuristically, note that we are looking at processes for σ of the form

Table 2. Comparison of exact and approximate prices

($\sigma = 0.25$, $\theta = 0.25$, $\delta = 16.00$, $k = 0.40$)

Strike	Black-Scholes	New	Approximation
1 month			
90	10.88	10.92	10.91
95	6.56	6.61	6.61
100	3.28	3.31	3.34
105	1.31	1.35	1.37
110	0.41	0.46	0.45
115	0.10	0.14	0.12
120	0.02	0.04	0.03
3 months			
90	13.03	13.13	13.13
95	9.26	9.37	9.39
100	6.19	6.30	6.34
105	3.88	4.00	4.04
110	2.28	2.40	2.43
115	1.26	1.38	1.38
120	0.66	0.76	0.75
6 months			
90	15.94	16.09	16.10
95	12.44	12.62	12.65
100	9.45	9.65	9.68
105	6.99	7.20	7.23
110	5.03	5.24	5.28
115	3.54	3.74	3.76
120	2.42	2.61	2.63

The "new" price corresponds to the equations $dP = \mu P\,dt + \sigma P\,dz_1$ and $d\sigma = -\delta(\sigma - \theta)dt + k\,dz_2$. For all entries, $P = 100$, the riskless rate $r = 9.53\%$, and the volatility risk premium $\phi = 0$. The "approximate" price corresponds to the approximation technique described in the text. The Black-Scholes price corresponds to the nonstochastic volatility setting where $\delta = k = 0$.

$$d\sigma = a(\sigma)dt + b(\sigma)dz. \tag{18}$$

The asymptotic nature of stock price distributions will be determined by the limiting behaviour of $a(\sigma)$ and $b(\sigma)$ as σ gets large. Thus, the noteworthy difference between an arithmetic and a geometric Brownian motion model for σ is that in the former $b(\sigma)$ remains constant as σ gets larger, while in the latter it increases indefinitely with σ. The fact that $b(\sigma)$ is also constant for small σ may be an unrealistic aspect of arithmetic Brownian motion, but it does not affect asymptotic stock price distributions - a more reasonable process that had $b(\sigma)$ shrinking for small σ but remaining bounded for large σ would lead to the same basic conclusions.

Once the stock price distributions are given, their asymptotic order can be recovered using a well-known technique called Laplace's method, or the theory of stationary real phase. (For a complete description, see Erdelyi (1956, pp. 36-38)). The derivations are outlined in Appendix D, where we also make the heuristic argument above more precise. Here we simply present and discuss our results.

The benchmark for comparison is the lognormal distribution $L(\sigma)$. Its asymptotic order is given by

$$L(\sigma) \cong \exp\left(-(\log P)^2 / 2\sigma^2 t\right)$$
$$\text{as } P \to 0 \text{ or } P \to \infty. \tag{19}$$

Thus, the relative thinness of the tails of the lognormal is reflected in the rapid decrease of the exponential as P goes to zero or infinity.

In comparison, the stochastic volatility distributions studied here have asymptotic behaviour that can be written as

$$S(P,t) \cong P^{-\gamma} \text{ as } P \to \infty, \tag{20}$$

$$S(P,t) \cong P^{-1+\gamma} \text{ as } P \to 0. \tag{21}$$

The exponent γ is given by

$$\gamma = \tfrac{3}{2} + \tfrac{1}{2}\left(1 + 4/t\bar{t}\right)^{1/2}, \tag{22}$$

where

$$\bar{t} = k^2 t / \left(v^2 + t^2\delta^2\right).$$

and $v = v(t\delta)$ is the smallest positive root of the equation $\cos v + (t\delta/v)\sin v = 0$. The variable v always lies between $\pi/2$ and π, and $v = \pi/2$ when $\delta = 0$.

Several observations follow from (20)-(22). First, and most obviously, the asymptotic behaviour of stock price distributions, which might be termed "power behaviour," implies slower rates of decrease (ie fatter tails) than the lognormal. This power behaviour is compatible with the generalised beta distribution (GB2) introduced by Bookstaber and McDonald (1987) to fit stock return data. In particular, an inspection of their formula (1a) (p. 403) shows that our parameter γ is essentially equivalent to unity plus the product of their parameters a and q. They note that no moments of order equal to or higher than aq will exist; analogously, it can be shown in our models that no moments of order equal to or greater than $(\gamma - 1)$ will exist for stock price distributions. For example, when $\gamma \leq 3$, the distribution will not have a well-defined variance.

Next, it is easy to verify that in our model γ always exceeds 2, and can exceed 3, depending on the values of the parameters. Thus, for this model, stock prices sometimes have a well-defined variance.[13]

Equation (22) implies that γ approaches infinity as t or k goes to zero. When σ follows an arithmetic process, decreasing its end-of-horizon variance makes stock price tails thinner, and higher and higher moments exist.

If $\delta = 0$, there is no mean reversion in σ, and γ approaches 2 as t or k goes to infinity. Thus, if the horizon is very long, so that there is a great deal of variance in the ultimate value of σ, the stock price distribution gets very fat-tailed, losing all its higher order moments up to and including the variance.

In contrast, where there is a nonzero mean reversion coefficient δ, γ approaches a number that is strictly greater than 2 as t goes to infinity. The greater is δ, the larger is this limiting γ. Intuitively, a nonzero δ bounds the end-of-horizon variance for σ away from infinity, no matter how long the horizon. Consequently, the limiting case of $\gamma = 2$ is never approached, even for very large values of t.

The implications of the model with a positive δ appears to accord closely with the empirical findings of Bookstaber and McDonald (1987). They note that while one- and five-day stock returns have significantly fatter tails than lognormals of the same variance, returns over longer horizons (eg, 250 days) are much better described by a lognormal distribution. This observation, taken together with our analytical results, would seem to provide indirect support for the hypothesis that volatility follows a stationary process.[14] If volatility were nonstationary, then our results would lead one to expect long-horizon returns that look substantially fatter-tailed than lognormals.

Conclusion

We have used analytic techniques to derive both exact and approximate stock price distributions for the case where stock price dynamics are given by (1) and (2). Our results have enabled us to develop closed-form options pricing formulas that incorporate important aspects of the time-series properties of volatility, as well as to sketch some links between these time-series properties and the extent to which stock price distributions have fat tails.

Although our approximation technique appears to work relatively well in pricing options (particularly those away from the money), one might question its usefulness, given that the exact formula can itself be quite easily implemented. However, it should be noted that our basic approximation methodology may be helpful in attacking more general models than the one studied here, where exact solutions prove less tractable.

Consider, for example, a constant elasticity of volatility (CEV) generalisation of (1), that is,

$$dP = rPdt + \sigma P^{j} dz_1, \qquad (1')$$

where $0 < j < 1$. This extension, when combined with (2), captures other empirically relevant aspects of volatility, including the tendency for percentage returns to be more volatile when prices are low. We do not know whether a tractable exact solution exists for stock price distributions generated by (1′) and (2).

However, it would appear that we can apply a variant of our approximation technique. The logic is as follows. Suppose we know the stock price distribution corresponding to just (1′) with σ fixed.[15] It can be shown that an analogue to (11) holds in that our desired exact distribution for the stochastic volatility case can be represented as a mixture of fixed σ CEV distributions. The mixing distribution is somewhat more complicated than $m_t(\sigma)$, but has a similar form. This suggests that even if we cannot solve for the exact distribution as readily as above, we may be able to use the same method of approximation. As in (13), we might use a simple substitute for the mixing distribution to generate an approximate stock price distribution.

In this vein, it should be noted that our method of approximating $m_t(\sigma)$ can probably be refined, by allowing $\hat{m}_t(\sigma)$ to be less tightly parameterised and thereby fitting more of the characteristics of $m_t(\sigma)$. Such refinement may prove worthwhile for addressing the sorts of problems described above.

Appendix A

DERIVATION OF FORMULA FOR S

We now sketch the derivations of the results presented above. Our first observation is that the distribution of prices generated by the two stochastic equations (1) and (2) is a mixture of lognormal distributions. We begin by making this precise.

If we solve (1), with σ fixed and $\mu = 0$, the resulting distribution of prices is the lognormal $L(\sigma)$, given by

$$L(\sigma) = \left(2\pi t\sigma^2 P^2\right)^{-1/2} \exp\left(\frac{-\left(\log P + t\sigma^2/2\right)^2}{2t\sigma^2}\right). \quad (A1)$$

It is easy to show that if σ is not constant, but a deterministic function $\sigma(t)$, the distribution of prices is given by $L(\alpha(t))$, where

$$\alpha(t) = \left(\frac{1}{t}\int_0^t \sigma^2(s)ds\right)^{1/2}. \quad (A2)$$

That is, in this case, prices are still lognormally distributed, with a variance that corresponds to the *average* σ^2 over the time interval.

In the case where $\sigma(t)$ is stochastic, and by (2) is given by an AR1 process, we can write $\sigma = \sigma_\omega(t)$, where ω is the point in the probability space that labels the stochastic path. By the reasoning above, each path ω implies a price distribution $L(\alpha_w(t))$, where

$$\alpha_\omega(t) = \left(\frac{1}{t}\int_0^t \sigma_\omega^2(s)ds\right)^{1/2}. \quad (A3)$$

The desired price distribution S is simply the expectation of $L(\alpha_w(t))$ so that

$$S = E_\omega\left\{L\left(\alpha_\omega(t)\right)\right\}. \quad (A4)$$

We now focus on the random variable $\alpha_\omega(t)$. Let $m_t(\sigma)d\sigma$ be its distribution function so that

$$\mathrm{Prob}_\omega\left\{b > \alpha_\omega(t) > a\right\} = \int_a^b m_t(\sigma)d\sigma. \quad (A5)$$

This implies that, for any function F,

$$E_\omega\left(F\left(\alpha_\omega(t)\right)\right) = \int F(\sigma)m_t(\sigma)d\sigma.$$

Therefore, (A4) implies

$$S = \int L(\sigma)m_t(\sigma)d\sigma. \quad (A6)$$

This is the claim that was stated in (11) - that is, our desired distribution is a mixture of lognormals, averaged via the mixing distribution $m_t(\sigma)$. This conclusion holds generally for the type of stochastic equations we consider in this article, and not just the particular example at hand. (See, for example, Hull and White (1987)).

It is clear that what we need to understand next is the mixing distribution $m_t(\sigma)$. The key to this is the formula for the "moment generating function,"

$$I(\lambda) = E_\omega\left(e^{-\lambda\alpha_\omega^2(t)}\right) = \int_0^\infty e^{-\lambda\sigma^2} m_t(\sigma)d\sigma,$$

which is given by the lemma below.

Lemma. For all $\lambda \geq 0$, the function $I(\lambda)$ is given by (8), where the quantities appearing in its definition are given by (3)-(7).

The proof of the lemma will be described in Appendix B. In the special case where the parameters are $\sigma_0 = 0$, $\delta = 0$, and $\theta = 0$,

$$I(\lambda) = \left[\cosh(2\lambda)^{1/2} kt^{1/2}\right]^{-1/2}. \quad (A7)$$

This formula goes back to Cameron and Martin (1944).

With the lemma in hand, the exact formula can now be derived from (A1) and (A6) using the Fourier transform formula for $g(\xi)$ and the inversion formula for $f(x)$:

$$g(\xi) = \int_{-\infty}^{\infty} e^{ix\xi} f(x)dx, \quad (A8)$$

$$f(x) = (2\pi)^{-1}\int_{-\infty}^{\infty} e^{-ix\xi} g(\xi)d\xi. \quad (A9)$$

We define $f(x) = P \cdot S(P,t)$, with the change of variables $x = \log P$. Using (A6), this yields the following definition of $f(x)$:

$$f(x) = \int \left(2\pi t\sigma^2\right)^{-1/2} \exp\left(\frac{-\left(x + t\sigma^2/2\right)^2}{2t\sigma^2}\right) m(\sigma)d\sigma. \quad (A10)$$

Now we apply the Fourier transform formula (A8) to $f(x)$ to obtain

$$g(\xi) = \int m(\sigma)\left\{\int \left(2\pi t\sigma^2\right)^{-1/2} \times \exp\left(\frac{-\left(x + t\sigma^2/2\right)^2}{2t\sigma^2}\right) e^{ix\xi}dx\right\}d\sigma. \quad (A11)$$

The term in braces is the Fourier transform of

$$\left(2\pi t\sigma^2\right)^{-1/2} \exp\left(\frac{-\left(x + t\sigma^2/2\right)^2}{2t\sigma^2}\right),$$

which equals $\exp(-(\xi^2 + i\xi)\sigma^2 t/2)$. [This is a standard fact about Fourier transforms, as illustrated in Wiener (1933, p. 50).] Therefore, Equation (A11) can be rewritten as

$$g(\xi) = \int m(\sigma) \exp\left(-(\xi^2 + i\xi)\frac{\sigma^2 t}{2}\right) d\sigma. \quad \text{(A12)}$$

Now recall that $I(\lambda)$ is defined as

$$I(\lambda) = \int_0^\infty e^{-\lambda\sigma^2} m(\sigma) d\sigma.$$

This definition means that (A12) can be reexpressed as

$$g(\xi) = I\left((\xi^2 + i\xi)t/2\right). \quad \text{(A13)}$$

We now apply the Fourier inversion formula (A9) to (A13) yielding

$$f(x) = (2\pi)^{-1} \int e^{-ix\xi} I\left((\xi^2 + i\xi)\frac{t}{2}\right) d\xi. \quad \text{(A14)}$$

We then make the change of variables $\xi = \eta - i/2$ in the above formula, also performing the indicated shift of contours in the complex plane. Since $\xi^2 + i\xi = \eta^2 + 1/4$, this becomes

$$f(x) = (2\pi)^{-1} e^{-x/2} \int e^{-ix\eta} I\left(\left(\eta^2 + \frac{1}{4}\right)\frac{t}{2}\right) d\eta. \quad \text{(A15)}$$

When we recall our definitions $f(x) = P \cdot S_0(P,t)$ and $x = \log P$, Equation (A15) becomes Equation (9), which is the exact distribution formula for $S_0(P,t)$. This completes the derivation.

Appendix B

PROOF OF THE LEMMA

According to the Feynman-Kac formula [see, for example, Durrett (1984, pp. 229-34) and Freidlin (1985, pp. 117-26)), for suitable functions c we have

$$E\left(\exp\left(\int_0^t c(\sigma(s)) ds\right)\right) = u(\sigma_0, t), \quad \text{(B1)}$$

where $\sigma(t)$ is the AR1 process given by

$$d\sigma = -\delta(\sigma - \theta)dt + k\, dz_2, \quad \text{(B2)}$$

with $\sigma(0) = \sigma_0$, and u is the solution of

$$\frac{1}{2}k^2 \frac{\partial^2 u(x,t)}{\partial x^2} - \delta(x - \theta)\frac{\partial u(x,t)}{\partial x} + c(x)u(x,t) = \frac{\partial u(x,t)}{\partial t}, \quad \text{(B3)}$$

with the initial condition $u(x,0) \equiv 1$.

In our case, we are dealing in effect with the situation that arises when $c(x) = -\lambda x^2$. With that choice of the function c, we have

$$u(\sigma_0, t) = E\left(\exp\left(-\lambda \int_0^t \sigma^2(s) ds\right)\right) = I(\lambda t).$$

Therefore,

$$u(\sigma_0, t) = I(\lambda t). \quad \text{(B4)}$$

To simplify the presentation we now relabel the parameters above so that our problem is reduced to that of solving the differential equation

$$\frac{1}{2}\frac{\partial^2 U(x,t)}{\partial x^2} + (Ax + B)\frac{\partial U(x,t)}{\partial x} + Cx^2 U(x,t) = \frac{\partial U(x,t)}{\partial t}, \quad \text{(B5)}$$

with the initial condition $U(x, 0) \equiv 1$.

It can be shown theoretically that this problem always has a solution of the form

$$U(x,t) = \exp\left(L_1 x^2/2 + M_1 x + N_1\right), \quad \text{(B6)}$$

where L_1, M_1, and N_1 are suitable functions of t. Once we know that $U(x,t)$ is of the above form, we can explicitly determine L_1, M_1, and N_1 by direct computation. The result is the following proposition.

Proposition. Equation (B5) has a solution (B6), where the functions L_1, M_1, and N_1 are given by the formulas (5), (6), and (7), with $k = 1$. In these formulas, we have used the definition $a = (A^2 - 2C)^{1/2}$ and $b = -A/a$.

Finding a solution to (B5) with the functional form of (B6) is equivalent to solving three differential equations that determine L_1, M_1, and N_1. These are

$$\frac{1}{2}\cdot\frac{dL_1(t)}{dt} = C + \frac{1}{2}\left(L_1(t)\right)^2 + AL_1(t), \quad \text{(B7)}$$

$$\frac{dM_1(t)}{dt} = L_1(t)M_1(t) + BL_1(t) + AM_1(t), \quad \text{(B8)}$$

$$\frac{dN_1(t)}{dt} = \frac{1}{2}\left(M_1(t)\right)^2 + \frac{1}{2}L_1(t) + BM_1(t). \quad \text{(B9)}$$

The initial condition $U(x, 0) \equiv 1$ is equivalent to the initial conditions $L_1(0) = 0$, $M_1(0) = 0$, and $N_1(0) = 0$.

The solution of (B7) is given by (5) (with k set equal to 1). Next, with $L_1(t)$ known, one solves (B8). The solution is given by (6) (again, with $k = 1$). Finally, with L_1 and M_1 known, one solves (B9), and its solution is given by (7), with $k = 1$. To check that (B6) is indeed a solution [with L_1,

M_1, and N_1 given by (5)-(7)] is a straightforward but tedious task. It also has been checked using the computer program Mathematica for symbolic manipulation.

Finally, to determine $I(\lambda)$ from these considerations, we first replace t by k^2t in the formulas for L_1, M_1, and N_1, giving us the function L, M, and N, respectively. We also set $A = -\delta/k^2$, $B = \theta\delta/k^2$, and $C = -\lambda/k^2$ and, because of (B4), replace λ by λ/t and x by σ_0. The result is the substitution (3) and the formula

$$I(\lambda) = \exp\left(L\sigma_0^2/2 + M\sigma_0 + N\right). \qquad \text{(B10)}$$

The lemma stated in Appendix A is therefore proved.

Appendix C

THE MIXING DISTRIBUTION AND APPROXIMATE MIXING DISTRIBUTION

There are three significant asymptotic characteristics of the mixing distribution $m_t(\sigma)$. The first is that

$$m_t(\sigma) \cong e^{-\sigma^2/2\bar{t}}, \text{ as } \sigma \to \infty, \qquad \text{(C1)}$$

where

$$\bar{t} = k^2t / \left(v^2 + t^2\delta^2\right) \qquad \text{(C2)}$$

and $v = v(t\delta)$ is the smallest positive root of the equation $\cos v + (t\delta/v)\sin v = 0$ $(\pi/2 \le v < \pi)$.

We shall prove here that if $m_t(\sigma) \cong e^{-\alpha\sigma^2}$, for some fixed α, as $\sigma \to \infty$, then indeed $\alpha = 1/2\bar{t}$ as claimed in (C1). To see this, consider $I(\lambda)$, which equals $\int_0^\infty e^{-\lambda\sigma^2}\cdot m_t(\sigma)d\sigma$, as noted above. This integral converges when $\lambda \ge 0$, and actually also does so for some negative values of λ, if $m_t(\sigma) \cong e^{-\alpha\sigma^2}$, as $\sigma \to \infty$. In fact, the first negative value below which the integral $I(\lambda)$ diverges is exactly $\lambda = -\alpha$. Now if we examine the formula (8) (also (3)-(7)) giving the exact value of $I(\lambda)$, we see that this singularity occurs at exactly that value of λ for which $\cosh(ak^2t) + b\sinh(ak^2t) = 0$. Now recall that $a = (A^2 - 2C)^{1/2}$, $b = -A/2$, with $A = -\delta/k^2$, $C = -\lambda/k^2t$. Making the indicated substitutions gives $\alpha = 1/2\bar{t}$, with $\bar{t}$ as in (C2).

The second important fact about the mixing distribution is that it decreases very rapidly as $\sigma \to 0$. More precisely,

$$m_t(\sigma) \le c_1 e^{-c_2/\sigma^2}, \text{ as } \sigma \to 0, \qquad \text{(C3)}$$

for two positive constants c_1 and c_2. This is a consequence of a corresponding rapid decrease of $I(\lambda)$ as $\lambda \to \infty$. This decrease is given by

$$I(\lambda) \le e^{-c_3\lambda^{1/2}}, \text{ as } \lambda \to \infty, \qquad \text{(C4)}$$

for some positive constant c_3. This in turn follows directly from an examination of the formula for the term N entering in the definition of $I(\lambda)$. The formula for N is a sum of four terms. The first and fourth terms contribute essentially $at/2 - at = -at/2$, for large values of λ, while the second and third terms contribute negligible quantities. Since $a = (A^2 - 2C)^{1/2}$, which is essentially $(2\lambda/k^2)^{1/2}$, when λ is large, the conclusion (C4) is established.

Since

$$\int_0^\infty e^{-\lambda\sigma^2} m_t(\sigma)d\sigma \le e^{-c_3\lambda^{1/2}},$$

it follows that, for each s,

$$\int_0^s m_t(\sigma)d\sigma \le e^{\lambda s^2} e^{-c_3\lambda^{1/2}}. \qquad \text{(C5)}$$

Now in the above, choose λ so that $\lambda s^2 = ½c_3\lambda^{1/2}$. Thus,

$$\int_0^s m_t(\sigma)d\sigma \le e^{-(c_3/2)\lambda^{1/2}} = e^{-(c_3/2)^2 s^{-2}},$$

which asserts that the claimed estimate (C3) holds on the average, at least. The fact that the full estimate (C3) holds is proved by a more refined version of this argument.

The third important fact about the mixing distribution we want to point out is that

$$\int_0^\infty \sigma^2 m_t(\sigma)d\sigma = -I'(0), \qquad \text{(C6)}$$

so that the mean of σ^2 with respect to the mixing distribution is easily determinable from the function $I(\lambda)$. Equation (C6) follows immediately from the definition

$$I(\lambda) = \int_0^\infty e^{-\lambda\sigma^2} m_t(\sigma)d\sigma.$$

The above observations concerning the mixing distribution $m_t(\sigma)$ suggest that we can approximate the distribution $m_t(\sigma)$ by a simpler one, $\hat{m}_t(\sigma)$, which has the form

$$\hat{m}_t(\sigma) = \rho e^{-\alpha\sigma^2} e^{-\beta/\sigma^2}, \qquad \text{(C7)}$$

where α, β, and ρ are parameters that are picked in order to obtain the best fit with $m_t(\sigma)$.

Intuitively, the form for $\hat{m}_t(\sigma)$ is chosen because the factor $e^{-\alpha\sigma^2}$ matches the asymptotic behaviour of $m_t(\sigma)$ at infinity given by (C1), and the factor $e^{-\beta/\sigma^2}$ matches the decay of $m_t(\sigma)$, as $\sigma \to 0$, given by (C3).

As we have said, we choose $\alpha = 1/2\bar{t}$, in accordance with (C1). Next, β and ρ are determined by the requirements that $\int_0^\infty \hat{m}_t(\sigma)d\sigma = 1$, and, like (C6), that $\int_0^\infty \sigma^2\hat{m}_t(\sigma)d\sigma = -I'(0)$.

These requirements give

$$\beta = [-\alpha^{1/2}I(0) - 1/2\alpha^{1/2}]^2, \quad \rho = (2/\sqrt{\pi})\cdot e^{2\alpha^{1/2}\beta^{1/2}}\cdot\alpha^{1/2}. \qquad \text{(C8)}$$

Appendix D

FAT TAILS

The asymptotic formula $S(P) \cong P^{-\gamma}$, $P \to \infty$ (and the corresponding formula $S(P) \cong P^{-1+\gamma}$, $P \to 0$) given in (20) and (21) can be derived by using Laplace's method for finding asymptotics of integrals with real phase functions. (For a description of this method, see Erdelyi (1956, pp. 36–38) and Hsu (1951).)

We use the identity (A6) and the asymptotic formula (C1). As is easily seen, this implies that $S(P,t) \cong \bar{S}(P,t)$, where

$$\bar{S}(P,t) = \int_0^\infty e^{A(x,\sigma)} B(x,\sigma)\, d\sigma, \qquad \text{(D1)}$$

and

$$A(x,\sigma) = -\left(x + t\sigma^2/2 - rt\right)^2 / 2t\sigma^2 - \sigma^2/2\bar{t}, \qquad \text{(D2)}$$

$$B(x,\sigma) = \left(2\pi t\sigma^2 e^{2x} 2\pi\bar{t}\right)^{-1/2} \qquad \text{(D3)}$$

with $x = \log P$.

We are interested in the asymptotics as $x \to \pm\infty$. Now it is not difficult to see that the main contribution to the integral (D1) when x is large occurs for large values of σ (with $|x|$ and σ^2 being roughly of the same order of magnitude). Thus, if we disregard terms of negligible size in $A(x,\sigma)$, we can simplify matters and replace $A(x,\sigma)$ by $\bar{A}(x,\sigma)$, where

$$\bar{A}(x,\sigma) = -\left(x + t\sigma^2/2\right)^2 / 2t\sigma^2 - \sigma^2/2\bar{t}. \qquad \text{(D4)}$$

According to the recipe of stationary phase, the asymptotic behaviour of this integral is given by

$$\frac{e^{\bar{A}(x,\sigma^*)}}{\left|\bar{A}''(x,\sigma^*)\right|^{1/2}} \cdot B(x,\sigma^*), \qquad \text{(D5)}$$

where σ^* is the critical point of $\bar{A}(x,\sigma)$ as a function of σ, that is

$$\left.\frac{\partial \bar{A}(x,\sigma)}{\partial\sigma}\right|_{\sigma=\sigma^*} = 0.$$

The value of σ^* is readily determined, and substituting it in (D5) leads to the formulas in the text.

1 *Empirical articles that model volatility as an AR1 process include Poterba and Summers (1986), Stein (1989), and Merville and Pieptea (1989). (The latter allows the AR1 process to be displaced by white noise.) Alternative models include the Arch model of Engle (1982) and its descendants such as Bollerslev (1986), Engle and Bollerslev (1986), and Engle, Lilien, and Robins (1987). [See also French, Schwert, and Stambaugh (1987) and Schwert (1987, 1989).]*

2 *There are analogous results in the literature for different models of volatility. For example, Praetz (1972) and Blattberg and Gonedes (1974) show that if σ^2 follows an inverted gamma distribution, then prices are distributed as a log t [see also Clark (1973)]. Engle (1982) computes the kurtosis of an Arch process as an explicit function of the Arch parameters.*

3 *While we have been able to solve a model where σ follows a geometric random walk (and the results are considerably more computationally cumbersome than those reported here), we have been unable to make any progress on the case where σ follows a geometric Ornstein-Uhlenbeck process. Since mean reversion appears to be one of the most important empirical characteristics of volatility, the practical usefulness of the geometric random walk model is unclear.*

4 *Very similar expressions appear in Wiggins (1987) and Hull and White (1987). In particular, our PDE is a simplification of Wiggins' equation (8) (p. 355) to the case where dz_1 and dz_2 are uncorrelated and where s follows an arithmetic, rather than geometric, process. Our model is not as general as Wiggins' because we have been unable to apply our analytic techniques when dz_1 and dz_2 are correlated. However, it may be possible to capture the tendency for volatility and stock prices to move together even without assuming an instantaneous correlation between dz_1 and dz_2. This might be accomplished in our framework by using a constant-elasticity-of-volatility generalisation of Equation (1).*

5 *Hull and White produce a similar result (equation (6), p. 283) also by effectively assuming that $\phi = 0$.*

6 *Using implied volatilities for individual stocks, Merville and Pieptea (1989) argue that a better fit is obtained by allowing the AR1 process to be displaced by white noise. One plausible interpretation is that "true" volatility follows an AR1, but that their implied volatilities contain significant white noise measurement errors.*

7 *It should be noted that the implied volatilities used in these studies are generated from pricing models that assume nonstochastic volatility. If volatility is in reality stochastic, then the implied volatilities will be subject to measurement error, and any parameter estimates derived from them may be biased. However, as Stein (1989) argues, any such biases are likely to be extremely small. This is because variation in measurement errors for a given option are dwarfed by variations in the level of volatility. (Table 1 provides some intuition for how the measurement error on a given option changes with a change in the level of volatility.) Moreover, the parameter values used below are only intended to give a rough, "ballpark" idea of the relevant magnitude. We do not intend to suggest that they represent the best possible statistical estimates.*

8 *These estimates of the half-life of stock index volatility are broadly consistent with those seen in a number of other studies using a variety of other empirical formulations.*

9 *Merville and Pieptea (1989) do not present k directly, since they are not exactly estimating an AR1 process. However, it is straightforward to recombine their parameter*

estimates to calculate what k *would have been had they specified their empirical model as an AR1. In particular,* $k = \sigma_D/(1 - NVR)^{1/2}$, *where the variables are defined in their Table 4 (p. 205).*

10 *By comparing the errors incurred with our approximation technique to the errors incurred with the Black-Scholes formula, one can get a rough idea of how useful the approximation technique is relative to the "default" option of not modelling stochastic volatility at all.*

11 *The fact that there are larger errors at-the-money suggests that our approximate distribution does a better job of matching the tails of the true distribution than it does of matching the central part of the true distribution. Clearly, a more complete analysis would involve a detailed comparison (perhaps via simulation) of the approximate and true distributions. Our aim is not so much to make a strong case for the use of the particular approximation described here, especially since the exact formula is relatively easily implemented. Rather, we believe that the general method of approximation is instructive - as we explain, it may be of practical relevance in more complicated models whose exact solutions prove elusive.*

12 *Empirical studies often quantify fat tails by computing an estimate of the kurtosis, or fourth moment of the distribution. Unfortunately, such higher moments do not always converge for our theoretical stochastic volatility distributions, so we are unable to make a direct comparison in this regard.*

13 *In contrast, we can show that a geometric process for* σ *leads to "hyper-fat" tails - a* γ *of 2 and an unbounded variance for any nonzero values of* t *and* k.

14 *The question of whether volatility contains a unit root has been the subject of a great deal of direct testing. Schwert (1987) provides a detailed discussion of the issues that arise in such direct testing for stationarity.*

15 *Cox and Ross (1976) provide a closed-form solution for this distribution in the case where* $j = \frac{1}{2}$.

BIBLIOGRAPHY

Black, F., and M. Scholes, 1973, "The Pricing of Options and Corporate Liabilities", *Journal of Political Economy* 81, pp. 637-54.

Blattberg, R. C., and N. J. Gonedes, 1974, "A Comparison of the Stable and Student Distributions as Statistical Models for Stock Prices", *Journal of Business* 47, pp. 244-80.

Bollerslev, T., 1986, "Generalised Autoregressive Conditional Heteroskedasticity", *Journal of Econometrics* 31, pp. 307-28.

Bookstaber, R.M., and J.B. McDonald, 1987, "A General Distribution for Describing Security Price Returns", *Journal of Business* 60, pp. 401-24.

Cameron, R.H., and W.T. Martin, 1944, "The Wiener Measure of Hilbert Neighbourhoods in the Space of Real Continuous Functions", *Journal of Mathematical Physics* 34, pp. 195-209.

Clark, P.K., 1973, "A Subordinate Stochastic Process Model with Finite Variance for Speculative Prices", *Econometrica* 41, pp. 135-55.

Cox, J.C., and S.A. Ross, 1976, "The Valuation of Options for Alternative Stochastic Processes", *Journal of Financial Economics* 3, pp. 145-66.

Cox, J.C., J.E. Ingersoll, and S.A. Ross, 1985, "An Intertemporal General Equilibrium Model of Asset Prices", *Econometrica* 33, pp. 363-84.

Durrett, R., 1984, *Brownian Motion and Martingales in Analysis*, Wadsworth, Belmont, Calif.

Engle, R.F., 1982, "Autoregressive Conditional Heteroskedasticity with Estimates of the Variance of United Kingdom Inflation", *Econometrica* 50, pp. 987-1007.

Engle, R.F., and T. Bollerslev, 1986, "Modeling the Persistence of Conditional Variances", *Econometric Reviews* 5, pp. 1-50.

Engle, R.F., D.M. Lilien, and R.D. Robins, 1987, "Estimating Time Varying Risk Premia in the Term Structure: The ARCH-M Model", *Econometrica* 55, pp. 391-407.

Erdelyi, A., 1956, *Asymptotic Expansions*, Dover, New York.

Fama, E.F., 1963, "Mandlebrot and the Stable Paretian Hypothesis", *Journal of Business* 36, pp. 420-29.

Fama, E.F., 1965, "The Behavior of Stock Market Prices", *Journal of Business* 38, pp. 34-105.

Freidlin, M., 1985, *Functional Integration and Partial Differential Equations*, Princeton University Press, Princeton, NJ.

French, K.R., G.W. Schwert, and R.F. Stambaugh, 1987, "Expected Stock Returns and Volatility", *Journal of Financial Economics* 19, pp. 3-29.

Hsu, L.C., 1951, "On the Asymptotic Evaluation of a Class of Integrals Involving a Parameter", *American Journal of Mathematics* 73, pp. 625-34.

Hull, J., and A. White, 1987, "The Pricing of Options on Assets with Stochastic Volatilities", *Journal of Finance* 42, pp. 281-300.

Johnson, H., and D. Shanno, 1987, "Option Pricing When the Variance is Changing", *Journal of Financial and Quantitative Analysis* 22, pp. 143-51.

Mandelbrot, B., 1963, "The Variation of Certain Speculative Prices", *Journal of Business* 36, pp. 394-419.

Merville, L.H., and D.R. Pieptea, 1989, "Stock Price Volatility, Mean-Reverting Diffusion, and Noise", *Journal of Financial Economics* 24, pp. 193-214.

Poterba, J.M., and L.H. Summers, 1986, "The Persistence of Volatility and Stock Market Fluctuations", *American Economic Review* 76, pp. 1142-51.

Praetz, P.D., 1972, "The Distribution of Share Price Changes", *Journal of Business* 45, pp. 49-55.

Schwert, G.W., 1987, "Effects of Model Specification on Tests for Unit Roots in Macroeconomic Data", *Journal of Monetary Economics* 20, pp. 73-103.

Schwert, G.W., 1989, "Why Does Stock Market Volatility Change Over Time?", *Journal of Finance* 44, pp. 1115-53.

Stein, J., 1989, "Overreactions in the Options Market", *Journal of Finance* 44, pp. 1011-23.

Wiener, N., 1933, *The Fourier Integral and Certain of Its Applications*, Cambridge University Press, Cambridge, UK.

Wiggins, J.B., 1987, "Option Values Under Stochastic Volatility: Theory and Empirical Estimates", *Journal of Financial Economics* 19, pp. 351-72.

A Closed-Form Solution for Options with Stochastic Volatility with Applications to Bond and Currency Options*

Steven L. Heston
Washington University in St Louis

This chapter uses a new technique to derive a closed-form solution for the price of a European call option on an asset with stochastic volatility. The model allows arbitrary correlation between volatility and spot-asset returns. The chapter introduces stochastic interest rates and shows how to apply the model to bond options and foreign currency options. Simulations show that correlation between volatility and the spot asset's price is important for explaining return skewness and strike-price biases in the Black-Scholes (1973) model. The solution technique is based on characteristic functions, and can be applied to other problems.

Many plaudits have been aptly used to describe Black and Scholes' (1973) contribution to option-pricing theory. Despite subsequent development of option theory, the original Black-Scholes formula for a European call option remains the most successful and widely used application. This formula is particularly useful because it relates the distribution of spot returns to the cross-sectional properties of option prices. In this paper I generalise the model while retaining this feature.

Although the Black-Scholes formula is often quite successful in explaining stock option prices (Black and Scholes (1973)), it does have known biases (Rubinstein (1985)). Its performance is also substantially worse on foreign currency options (Melino and Turnbull (1990, 1991); Knoch (1992)). This is not surprising as the Black-Scholes model makes the strong assumption that (continuously compounded) stock returns are normally distributed with known mean and variance. Since the Black-Scholes formula does not depend on the mean spot return, it cannot be generalised by allowing the mean to vary. The variance assumption is somewhat dubious, however. Motivated by this theoretical consideration, Scott (1987), Hull and White (1987), and Wiggins (1987) have generalised the model to allow stochastic volatility. Melino and Turnbull (1990, 1991) report that this approach is successful in explaining the prices of currency options. These papers have the disadvantage that their models do not have closed-form solutions and require extensive use of numerical techniques to solve two-dimensional partial differential equations. Eisenberg and Jarrow (1991) and Stein and Stein (1991) assume that volatility is uncorrelated with the spot asset and use an average of Black-Scholes formula values over different volatility paths. As this approach assumes that

* *This paper was first published in* The Review of Financial Studies, *Vol. 6, No. 2 (1993). It is reprinted with permission of Oxford University Press. I thank Hans Knoch for computational assistance. I am grateful for the suggestions of Hyeng Keun (the referee) and for comments by participants at a 1992 National Bureau of Economic Research seminar and the Queen's University 1992 Derivative Securities Symposium. Any remaining errors are my responsibility.*

volatility is uncorrelated with spot returns, however, it cannot capture important skewness effects that arise from such correlation. This chapter offers a model of stochastic volatility that is not based on the Black–Scholes formula. It provides a closed-form solution for the price of a European call option when the spot asset is correlated with volatility, and it adapts the model to incorporate stochastic interest rates. Thus, the model can be applied to bond options and currency options.

Stochastic volatility model

We begin by assuming that the spot asset at time t follows the diffusion

$$dS(t) = \mu S\,dt + \sqrt{v(t)}S dz_1(t), \qquad (1)$$

where $z_1(t)$ is a Wiener process. If the volatility follows an Ornstein–Uhlenbeck process (eg used by Stein and Stein 1991)

$$d\sqrt{v(t)} = -\beta\sqrt{v(t)}dt + \delta dz_2(t), \qquad (2)$$

then Ito's lemma shows that the variance, $v(t)$ follows the process

$$dv(t) = \left[\delta^2 - 2\beta v(t)dt + 2\delta\sqrt{v(t)}dz_2(t)\right]. \qquad (3)$$

This can be written as the familiar square root process (used by Cox, Ingersoll, and Ross (1985))

$$dv(t) = \kappa\left[\theta - v(t)\right]dt + \sigma\sqrt{v(t)}dz_2(t), \qquad (4)$$

where $z_2(t)$ has correlation ρ with $z_1(t)$. For simplicity at this stage we assume a constant interest rate r. Therefore, the price at time t of a unit discount bond which matures at time $t + \tau$ is

$$P(t, t+\tau) = e^{-r\tau}. \qquad (5)$$

These assumptions are still insufficient to price contingent claims because we have not yet made an assumption that gives the "price of volatility risk". Standard arbitrage arguments (Black and Scholes (1973); Merton (1973)) demonstrate that the value of any asset, $U(S,v,t)$ (including accrued payments) must satisfy the partial differential equation (PDE)

$$\frac{1}{2}vS^2\frac{\partial^2 U}{\partial S^2} + \rho\sigma\, vS\frac{\partial^2 U}{\partial S\partial v} + \frac{1}{2}\sigma^2 v\frac{\partial^2 U}{\partial v^2} + rS\frac{\partial U}{\partial S}$$
$$+\left\{\kappa\left[\theta - v(t)\right] - \lambda(s,v,t)\right\}\frac{\partial U}{\partial v} - rU + \frac{\partial U}{\partial t} = 0. \qquad (6)$$

The unspecified term $\lambda(S,v,t)$ represents the "price of volatility risk" and must be independent of the particular asset. Lamoureux and Lastrapes (1992) present evidence that this term is nonzero for equity options. To motivate the choice of $\lambda(S,v,t)$, we note that in Breeden's (1979) consumption-based model

$$\lambda(s,v,t)dt = \gamma\,\mathrm{Cov}\left[dv, dC/C\right], \qquad (7)$$

where $C(t)$ is the consumption rate and γ is the relative risk aversion of an investor. Consider the consumption process, which emerges in the (general equilibrium) Cox, Ingersoll, Ross (1985) model

$$dC(t) = \mu_c v(t)C\,dt + \sigma_c\sqrt{v(t)}C\,dz_3(t), \qquad (8)$$

where consumption growth has constant correlation with the spot-asset return. This generates a risk premium proportional to $v, \lambda(S,v,t) = \lambda v$. Although we will use this form of the risk premium, the pricing results are obtained by arbitrage and do not depend on the other assumptions of the Breeden (1979) or Cox, Ingersoll, Ross (1985) models. However, we note that the model is consistent with conditional heteroskedasticity in consumption growth as well as in asset returns. In theory, the parameter λ could be determined by one volatility-dependent asset, and then used to price all other volatility-dependent assets.[1]

A European call option with strike price K and maturing at time T satisfies the PDE (6) subject to the following boundary conditions:

$$\begin{aligned}
&U(S,v,T) = \mathrm{Max}(0, S-K),\\
&U(0,v,t) = 0,\\
&\frac{\partial U}{\partial S}(\infty, v, t) = 1,\\
&rS\frac{\partial U}{\partial S}(S,0,t) + \kappa\theta\frac{\partial U}{\partial v}(s,0,t) - rU(S,0,t)\\
&+U_t(S,0,t) = 0,\\
&U(S,\infty,t) = S.
\end{aligned} \qquad (9)$$

By analogy with the Black–Scholes formula, we guess a solution of the form

$$C(S,v,t) = SP_1 - KP(t,T)P_2, \qquad (10)$$

where the first term is the present value of the spot asset upon optimal exercise, and the second term is the present value of the strike price payment. Both of these terms must satisfy the original partial differential Equation (6). It is convenient to write them in terms of the logarithm of the spot price

$$x = \ln[S]. \qquad (11)$$

Substituting the proposed solution (10) into the original PDE (6) shows that P_1 and P_2 must satisfy the PDEs

$$\frac{1}{2}v\frac{\partial^2 P_j}{\partial x^2}+\rho\sigma v\frac{\partial^2 P_j}{\partial x\partial v}+\frac{1}{2}\sigma^2 v\frac{\partial^2 P_j}{\partial v^2}$$
$$+(r+u_j v)\frac{\partial P_j}{\partial x}+(a_j-b_j v)\frac{\partial P_j}{\partial v}+\frac{\partial P_j}{\partial t}=0 \quad (12)$$

for j = 1,2, where

$$u_1=½, u_2=-½, a=\kappa\theta,$$
$$b_1=\kappa+\lambda-\rho\sigma, b_2=\kappa+\lambda.$$

In order for the option price to satisfy the terminal condition in Equation (9), these PDEs (12) are subject to the terminal condition

$$P_j(x,v,T;\ln[K])=1_{(x\geq\ln[K])}. \quad (13)$$

Thus, they may be interpreted as "adjusted" or "risk neutralised" probabilities (see Cox and Ross 1976). The Appendix explains that when x follows the stochastic process

$$dx(t)=[r+u_j v]dt+\sqrt{v(t)}dz_1(t),$$
$$dv=(a_j-b_j v)dt+\sigma\sqrt{v(t)}dz_2(t), \quad (14)$$

where the parameters u_j, a_j and b_j are defined as before, then P_j is the conditional probability that the option expires in the money:

$$P_j(x,v,T;\ln[K])=$$
$$\Pr[x(T)\geq\ln[K]|x(t)=x, v(t)=v]. \quad (15)$$

The probabilities are not immediately available in closed form. However, the Appendix shows that their characteristic functions, $f_1(x,v,T;\phi)$ and $f_2(x,v,T;\phi)$ respectively, satisfy the same PDEs in (12), subject to the terminal condition:

$$f_j(x,v,T;\phi)=e^{i\phi x}. \quad (16)$$

The characteristic function solution is

$$f_j(x,v,t;\phi)=e^{C(T-t;\phi)+D(T-t;\phi)v+i\phi x}, \quad (17)$$

where

$$C(\tau;\phi)=r\phi i\tau+\frac{a}{\sigma^2}\left\{(b_j-\rho\sigma\phi i+d)\tau-2\ln\left[\frac{1-ge^{d\tau}}{1-g}\right]\right\},$$

$$D(\tau;\phi)=\frac{b_j-\rho\sigma\phi i+d}{\sigma^2}\left[\frac{1-e^{d\tau}}{1-ge^{d\tau}}\right],$$

and

$$g=\frac{b_j-\rho\sigma\phi i+d}{b_j-\rho\sigma\phi i-d},$$

$$d=\sqrt{(\rho\sigma\phi i-b_j)^2-\sigma^2(2u_j\phi i-\phi^2)}.$$

One can invert the characteristic functions to get the desired probabilities

$$P_j(x,v,T;\ln[K])=$$
$$\frac{1}{2}+\frac{1}{\pi}\int_0^\infty \mathrm{Re}\left[\frac{e^{-i\phi\ln[K]}f_j(x,v,T;\phi)}{i\phi}\right]d\phi. \quad (18)$$

The integrand in Equation (18) is a smooth function that decays rapidly, and presents no difficulties.[2]

Equations (10), (17), and (18) give the solution for European call options. In general, one cannot eliminate the integrals in Equation (18), even in the Black–Scholes case. However, they can be evaluated in a fraction of a second on a microcomputer by using approximations similar to the standard ones used to evaluate cumulative normal probabilities.[3]

Bond options, currency options and other extensions

One can incorporate stochastic interest rates into the option pricing model, following Merton (1973) and Ingersoll (1990). In this manner, one can apply the model to options on bonds or on foreign currency. This section outlines these generalisations to show the broad applicability of the stochastic volatility model. These generalisations are equivalent to the model of the previous section, except that certain parameters become time-dependent to reflect the changing characteristics of bonds as they approach maturity.

To incorporate stochastic interest rates, we modify equation (1) to allow time dependence in the volatility of the spot asset

$$dS(t)=\mu_S S\,dt+\sigma_S(t)\sqrt{v(t)}S dz_1(t). \quad (19)$$

This equation is satisfied by discount bond prices in the Cox, Ingersoll and Ross (1985) model and multiple factor models of Heston (1990). Although the results of this section do not depend on the specific form of σ_S, if the spot asset is a discount bond, then σ_S must vanish at maturity in order for the bond price to reach par with probability 1. The specification of the drift term, μ_S, is unimportant because it will not affect option prices. We specify analogous dynamics for the bond price

$$dP(t;T)=\mu_P P(t;T)\,dt$$
$$+\sigma_P(t)\sqrt{v(t)}P(t;T)dz_2(t). \quad (20)$$

Note that for parsimony, we assume that the variance of both the spot asset and the bond are determined by the same variable $v(t)$. In this model, that the valuation equation is

$$\frac{1}{2}\sigma_S(t)^2 vS^2\frac{\partial^2 U}{\partial S^2}+\sigma_P^2(t)\,vP^2\frac{\partial^2 U}{\partial P^2}+\frac{1}{2}\sigma^2 v\frac{\partial^2 U}{\partial v^2}$$
$$+\rho_{SP}\sigma_S(t)\sigma_P(t)vSP\frac{\partial^2 U}{\partial S\,\partial P}+\rho_{Sv}\sigma_S(t)\sigma vS\frac{\partial^2 U}{\partial S\,\partial v}$$
$$+\rho_{Pv}\sigma_P(t)\sigma vP\frac{\partial^2 U}{\partial P\,\partial v}+rS\frac{\partial U}{\partial S}+rP\frac{\partial U}{\partial P}$$
$$+\left\{\kappa\left[\theta-v(t)\right]-\lambda v\right\}\frac{\partial U}{\partial v}-rU+\frac{\partial U}{\partial t}=0, \qquad (21)$$

where ρ_{xy} denotes the correlation between stochastic processes x and y. Proceeding with the substitution (10) exactly as in the previous section shows that the probabilities P_1 and P_2 must satisfy the PDE:

$$\frac{1}{2}\sigma_x(t)^2 v\frac{\partial^2 P_j}{\partial x^2}+\rho_{xv}(t)\sigma_x(t)\,\sigma v\frac{\partial^2 P_j}{\partial x\partial v}$$
$$+\frac{1}{2}\sigma^2 v\frac{\partial^2 P_j}{\partial v^2}+u_j(t)v\frac{\partial P_j}{\partial x}+$$
$$\left(a_j-b_j(t)v\right)\frac{\partial P_j}{\partial v}+\frac{\partial P_j}{\partial t}=0, \qquad (22)$$

for j = 1,2, where

$$x=\ln\left[\frac{S}{P(t;T)}\right],$$
$$\sigma_x(t)^2=\tfrac{1}{2}\sigma_S(t)^2-\rho_{SP}\sigma_S(t)\sigma_P(t)+\tfrac{1}{2}\sigma_P^2(t),$$
$$\rho_{xv}(t)=\frac{\rho_{Sv}\sigma_S(t)\sigma-\rho_{Py}\sigma_P(t)\sigma}{\sigma_x(t)\sigma},$$
$$u_1(t)=\tfrac{1}{2}\sigma_x(t)^2,\ u_2(t)=-\tfrac{1}{2}\sigma_x(t)^2,$$
$$a=\kappa\theta$$
$$b_1(t)=\kappa+\lambda-\rho_{Sv}\sigma_S(t)\sigma,$$
$$b_2(t)=\kappa+\lambda-\rho_{Pv}\sigma_P(t)\sigma.$$

Note that equation (22) is equivalent to equation (12) with some time-dependent coefficients. The availability of closed-form solutions to equation (22) will depend on the particular term structure model (eg the specification of $\sigma_x(t)$). In any case, the method used in the Appendix shows the characteristic function takes the form of equation (17), where the functions $C(\tau)$ and $D(\tau)$ satisfy certain ordinary differential equations. The option price is then determined by equation (18). While the functions $C(\tau)$ and $D(\tau)$ might not have closed-form solutions for some term structure models, this represents an enormous reduction compared to solving equation (21) numerically.

One can also apply the model when the spot asset S(t) is the dollar price of foreign currency. We assume that the foreign price of a foreign discount bond, F(t;T), follows dynamics analogous to the domestic bond in equation (20)

$$dF(t;T)=\mu_P F(t;T)\,dt$$
$$+\sigma_P(t)\sqrt{v(t)}F(t;T)dz_2(t). \qquad (23)$$

For clarity, we denote the domestic interest rate by r_D, and the foreign interest rate by r_F. Following the arguments in Ingersoll (1990), the valuation equation is

$$\frac{1}{2}\sigma_S(t)^2 vS^2\frac{\partial^2 U}{\partial S^2}+\sigma_P^2(t)\,vP^2\frac{\partial^2 U}{\partial P^2}$$
$$+\frac{1}{2}\sigma_F^2(t)vF^2\frac{\partial^2 U}{\partial F^2}+\frac{1}{2}\sigma^2 v\frac{\partial^2 U}{\partial v^2}$$
$$+\rho_{SP}\sigma_S(t)\sigma_P(t)vSP\frac{\partial^2 U}{\partial S\,\partial P}$$
$$+\rho_{SP}\sigma_S(t)\sigma_F(t)vSF\frac{\partial^2 U}{\partial S\,\partial F}$$
$$+\rho_{SP}\sigma_P(t)\sigma_F(t)vPF\frac{\partial^2 U}{\partial P\,\partial F}$$
$$+\rho_{Sv}\sigma_S(t)\sigma vS\frac{\partial^2 U}{\partial S\,\partial v}+\rho_{Pv}\sigma_P(t)\sigma vP\frac{\partial^2 U}{\partial P\,\partial v}$$
$$+\rho_{Fv}\sigma_F(t)\sigma vF\frac{\partial^2 U}{\partial F\,\partial v}$$
$$+r_D S\frac{\partial U}{\partial S}+r_D P\frac{\partial U}{\partial P}+r_F F\frac{\partial U}{\partial F}$$
$$+\left\{\kappa\left[\theta-v(t)\right]-\lambda v\right\}\frac{\partial U}{\partial v}-rU+\frac{\partial U}{\partial t}=0. \qquad (24)$$

Solving this five-variable partial differential equation numerically would be completely infeasible. But one can use Garman and Kohlhagen's (1983) substitution analogous to Equation (10)

$$C(S,v,t)=SF(t,T)P_1-KP(t,T)P_2. \qquad (25)$$

The probabilities P_1 and P_2 must satisfy the PDE

$$\frac{1}{2}\sigma_x(t)^2 v\frac{\partial^2 P_j}{\partial x^2}+\rho_{xv}(t)\sigma_x(t)\,\sigma v\frac{\partial^2 P_j}{\partial x\partial v}$$
$$+\frac{1}{2}\sigma^2 v\frac{\partial^2 P_j}{\partial v^2}+u_j(t)v\frac{\partial P_j}{\partial x}+$$
$$\left(a_j-b_j(t)v\right)\frac{\partial P_j}{\partial v}+\frac{\partial P_j}{\partial t}=0, \qquad (26)$$

for j = 1,2, where

$$x=\ln\left[\frac{SF(t;T)}{P(t;T)}\right],$$
$$\sigma_x(t)^2=\tfrac{1}{2}\sigma_S(t)^2+\tfrac{1}{2}\sigma_P^2(t)+\tfrac{1}{2}\sigma_F^2(t)$$
$$-\rho_{SP}\sigma_S(t)\sigma_P(t)+\rho_{SF}\sigma_S(t)\sigma_F(t)$$
$$-\rho_{PF}\sigma_P(t)\sigma_F(t),$$
$$\rho_{xv}(t)=\frac{\rho_{Sv}\sigma_S(t)\sigma-\rho_{Pv}\sigma_P(t)\sigma+\rho_{Fv}\sigma_F(t)\sigma}{\sigma_x(t)\sigma},$$
$$u_1(t)=\tfrac{1}{2}\sigma_x(t)^2,\ u_2(t)=-\tfrac{1}{2}\sigma_x(t)^2,$$
$$a=\kappa\theta$$

$$b_1(t) = \kappa + \lambda - \rho_{Sv}\sigma_S(t)\sigma - \rho_{Fv}\sigma_F(t)\sigma,$$
$$b_2(t) = \kappa + \lambda - \rho_{Pv}\sigma_P(t)\sigma.$$

Once again, the characteristic function has the form of Equation (17), where $C(\tau)$ and $D(\tau)$ depend on the specification of $\sigma_x(t)$, $\rho_{xv}(t)$, and $b_j(t)$ (see Appendix 1).

Although the stochastic interest rate models of this section are tractable, they would be more complicated to estimate than the simpler model of the previous section. For short-maturity options on equities, any increase in accuracy would probably be outweighed by the estimation error introduced by implementing a more complicated model. As option maturities extend beyond one year, however, the interest rate effects can become more important (Knoch 1992). The more complicated models illustrate how the stochastic volatility model can be adapted to a variety of applications. For example, one could value US options by adding on the early exercise approximation of Barone-Adesi and Whalley (1987). The solution technique has other applications too. See the Appendix for application to Stein and Stein's (1991) model (with correlated volatility) and see Bates (1992) for application to jump-diffusion processes.

Effects of the stochastic volatility model options prices

In this section I examine the effects of stochastic volatility on option prices and contrast results with the Black-Scholes model. Many effects are related to the time-series dynamics of volatility. For example, a higher variance $v(t)$ raises the prices of all options, just as it does in the Black-Scholes model. In the risk neutralised pricing probabilities, the variance follows a square-root process

$$dv(t) = \kappa^*\left[\theta^* - v(t)\right]dt + \sigma\sqrt{v(t)}\,dz_2(t), \quad (27)$$

where

$$\kappa^* = \kappa + \lambda$$

and

$$\theta^* = \kappa\theta(\kappa + \lambda).$$

We analyse the model in terms of this risk-neutralised volatility process instead of the "true" process of equation (4), because the risk-neutralised process exclusively determines prices.[4] The variance drifts toward a long-run mean of θ^*, with mean-reversion speed determined by κ^*. Hence, an increase in the average variance, θ^*, increases the prices of options. The mean reversion then determines the relative weights of the current variance and the long-run variance on option prices. When mean reversion is positive, the variance has a steady-state distribution (Cox, Ingersoll, and Ross 1985) with mean θ^*. Therefore, spot returns over long periods will have asymptotically normal distributions, with variance per unit of time given by θ^*. Consequently, the Black-Scholes model should tend to work well for long-term options. However, it is important to realise that the implied variance θ^* from option prices may not equal the variance of spot returns given by the "true" process (4). This difference is caused by the risk premium associated with exposure to volatility changes. As equation (27) shows, whether θ^* is larger or smaller than the true average variance θ depends on the sign of the risk premium parameter λ. One could estimate θ^* and other parameters by using values implied by option prices. Alternatively, one could estimate θ and κ from the true spot price process. One could then estimate the risk premium parameter λ by using average returns on option positions that are hedged against the risk of changes in the spot asset.

The stochastic volatility model can conveniently explain properties of option prices in terms of the underlying distribution of spot returns. Indeed, this is the intuitive interpretation of the solution (10), since P_2 corresponds to the risk-neutralised probability that the option expires in the money. To illustrate effects on option prices, we shall use the default parameters in Table 1.[5] For comparison, we shall use the Black-Scholes model with a volatility parameter that matches the (square root of the) variance of the spot return over the life of the option.[6] This

Table 1. Default parameters for simulation of option prices

$$dS(t) = \mu S\,dt + \sqrt{v(t)}S\,dz_1(t), \quad (1)$$
$$dv(t) = \kappa^*\left[\theta^* - v(t)\right]dt + \sigma\sqrt{v(t)}\,dz_2(t), \quad (27)$$

Parameter	Value
Mean reversion	$\kappa^* = 2$
Long-run variance	$\theta^* = .01$
Current variance	$v(t) = .01$
Correlation of $z_1(t)$ and $z_2(t)$	$\rho = 0$
Volatility of volatility parameter	$\sigma = .1$
Option maturity	.5 year
Interest rate	$r = 0$
Strike price	$K = 100$

1. Conditional probability density of the continuously compounded spot return over a six-month horizon

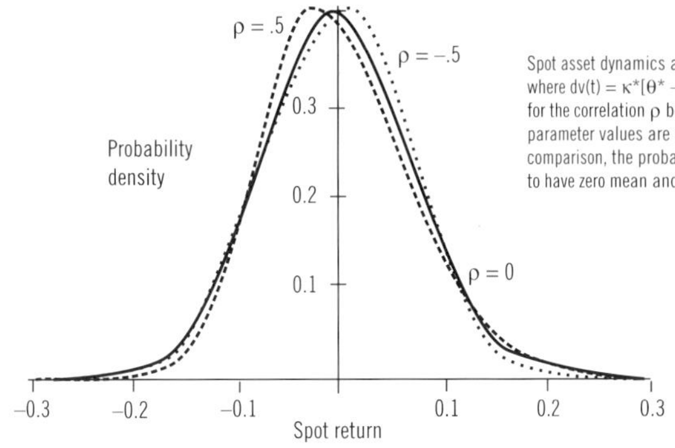

Spot asset dynamics are $dS(t) = \mu S dt + \sqrt{v(t)}\, S\, dz_1(t)$, where $dv(t) = \kappa^*[\theta^* - v(t)]dt + \sigma\sqrt{v(t)}\, dz_2(t)$. Except for the correlation ρ between z_1 and z_2 shown, parameter values are shown in Table 1. For comparison, the probability densities are normalised to have zero mean and unit variance.

2. Option prices from the stochastic volatility model minus Black-Scholes values with equal volatility to option maturity

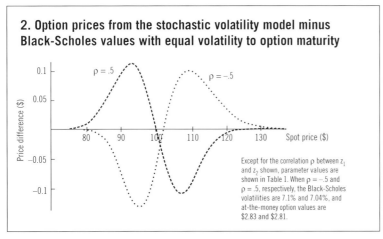

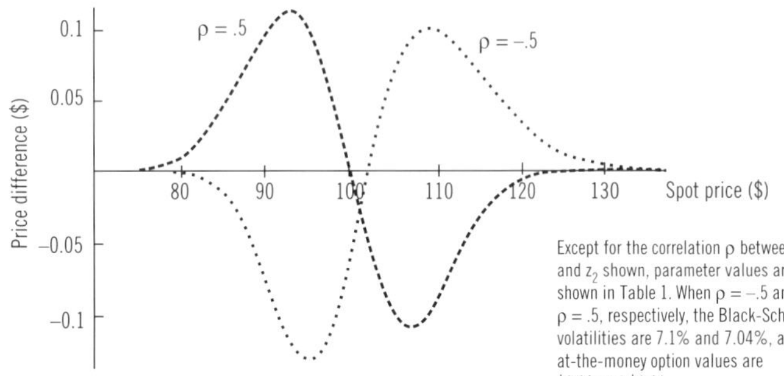

Except for the correlation ρ between z_1 and z_2 shown, parameter values are shown in Table 1. When ρ = –.5 and ρ = .5, respectively, the Black-Scholes volatilities are 7.1% and 7.04%, and at-the-money option values are $2.83 and $2.81.

3. Conditional probability density of the continuously compounded spot return over a six-month horizon

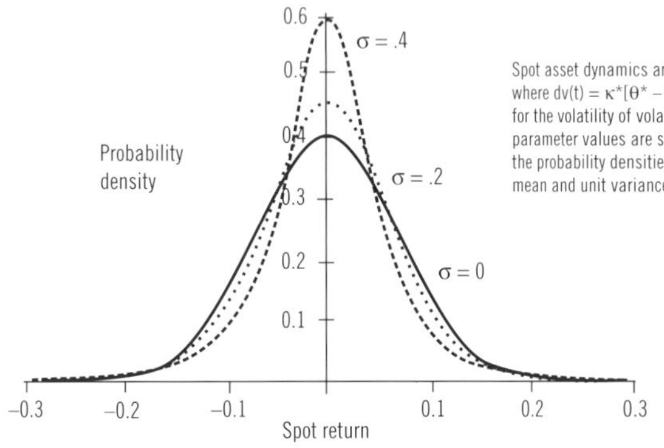

Spot asset dynamics are $dS(t) = \mu S dt + \sqrt{v(t)}\, S\, dz_1(t)$, where $dv(t) = \kappa^*[\theta^* - v(t)]dt + \sigma\sqrt{v(t)}\, dz_2(t)$. Except for the volatility of volatility parameter σ shown, parameter values are shown in Table 1. For comparison, the probability densities are normalised to have zero mean and unit variance.

4. Option prices from the stochastic volatility model minus Black-Scholes values with equal volatility to option maturity

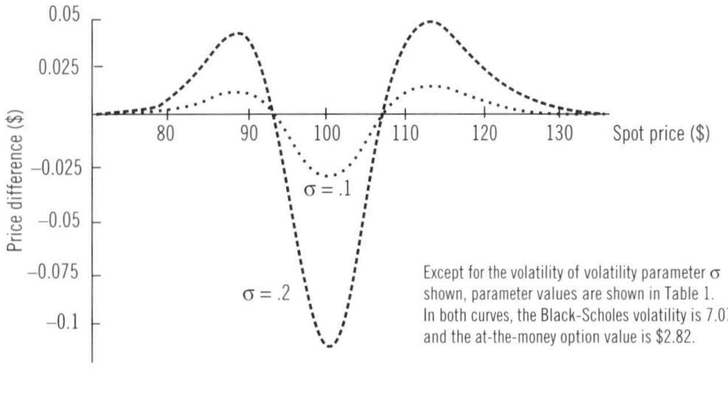

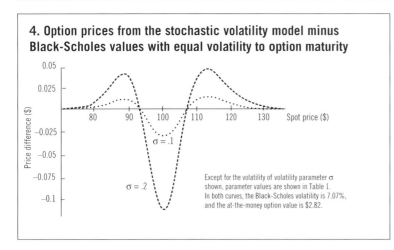

Except for the volatility of volatility parameter σ shown, parameter values are shown in Table 1. In both curves, the Black-Scholes volatility is 7.07%, and the at-the-money option value is $2.82.

normalisation focuses attention on the effects of stochastic volatility on one option relative to another by equalising "average" option model prices across different spot prices. The correlation parameter ρ positively affects the skewness of spot returns. Intuitively, a positive correlation results in high variance when the spot asset rises, and this "spreads" the right tail of the probability density. Conversely, the left tail is associated with low variance and is not spread out. Figure 1 shows how a positive correlation of volatility with the spot return creates a fat right tail and a thin left tail in the distribution of continuously compounded spot returns.[7] Figure 2 shows that this increases the prices of out-of-the-money options and decreases the prices of in-the-money options, relative to the Black–Scholes model with comparable volatility. Intuitively, out-of-the-money call options benefit substantially from a fat right tail and pay little penalty for an increased probability of an average or slightly below average spot return. A negative correlation has completely opposite effects. It decreases the prices of out-of-the-money options relative to in-the-money options.

The parameter σ controls the volatility of volatility. When σ is zero, the volatility is deterministic and continuously compounded spot returns have a normal distribution. Otherwise, σ increases the kurtosis of spot returns. Figure 3 shows how this creates two fat tails in the distribution of spot returns. As Figure 4 shows, this has the effect of raising far-in-the-money and far-out-of-the-money option prices, and lowering near-the-money prices. Note however, that there is little effect on skewness nor on the overall pricing of in-the-money options relative to out-of-the-money options.

These simulations show that the stochastic volatility model can produce a rich variety of pricing effects compared with the Black–Scholes model. The effects just illustrated assumed that variance was at its long-run mean, θ*. In practice, the stochastic variance will drift above and below this level, but the basic conclusions should not change. An important insight from the analysis is the distinction between the effects of stochastic volatility *per se* and the effects of correlation of volatility with the spot return. If volatility is uncorrelated with the spot return, then increasing the volatility of volatility (σ) increases the kurtosis of spot returns, not the skewness. In this case, random volatility is associated with increases in the prices of far-from-the-money options relative to near-the-money options. In contrast, the correlation of volatility with the spot return produces skewness. And positive skewness is associated with increases in the prices of out-of-the-money options relative to in-the-money options. It is therefore essential to choose properly the correlation of volatility with spot returns as well as the volatility of volatility.

Conclusions

This chapter presented a closed-form solution for options on assets with stochastic volatility. The model is versatile enough to describe stock options, bond options, and currency options. As the figures illustrate, the model can impart almost any type of bias to option prices. In particular, it links these biases to the dynamics of the spot price and the distribution of spot returns. Conceptually, one can characterise the option models in terms of the first four moments of the spot return (under the risk-neutral probabilities). The Black–Scholes (1973) model shows that the mean spot return does not affect option prices at all, whereas variance has a substantial effect. Therefore, the pricing analysis of this paper controls for the variance when comparing option models with different skewness and kurtosis. The Black–Scholes formula produces option prices virtually identical to the stochastic volatility models for at-the-money options. One could interpret this as saying that the Black–Scholes model performs quite well. Alternatively, all option models with the same volatility are equivalent for at-the-money options. As options are usually traded near the money, this explains some of the empirical support for the Black–Scholes model. Correlation between volatility and the spot price is necessary to generate skewness. Skewness in the distribution of spot returns affects the pricing of in-the-money options relative to out-of-the money options. Without this correlation, stochastic volatility only changes the kurtosis. Kurtosis affects the pricing of near-the-money versus far-from-the-money options.

With a proper choice of parameters, the stochastic volatility model appears to be a very flexible and promising description of option prices. It presents a number of testable restrictions, since it relates option-pricing biases to the dynamics of spot prices and the distribution of spot returns. Knoch (1992) has successfully used the model to explain currency option prices. The model may eventually explain other option phenomena. For example, Rubinstein (1985) found option biases that changed through time. There is also some evidence that implied volatilities from options prices do not seem properly related to future volatility. The model makes it feasible to examine these puzzles and to investigate other features of option pricing. Finally, the solution technique itself can be applied to other problems, and is not limited to stochastic volatility or diffusion problems.

Appendix

DERIVATION OF THE CHARACTERISTIC FUNCTIONS

This appendix derives the characteristic functions in (17), and shows how to apply the solution technique to other valuation problems. Suppose that $x(t)$ and $v(t)$ follow the (risk-neutral) processes in (15). Consider any twice-differentiable function $f(x,v,t)$, which is a conditional expectation of some function of x and v at a later date, T, $g(x(T),v(T))$:

$$f(x,v,t) = E\left[g\left(x(T),v(T)\right)\middle|x(t)=x,v(t)=v\right]. \qquad (A1)$$

Ito's lemma shows

$$df = \left(\frac{1}{2}v\frac{\partial^2 f}{\partial x^2} + \rho\sigma v\frac{\partial^2 f}{\partial x\,\partial v} + \frac{1}{2}\sigma^2 v\frac{\partial^2 f}{\partial v^2} + \left(r+u_j v\right)\frac{\partial f}{\partial x} + \left(a-b_j v\right)\frac{\partial f}{\partial t}\right)dt + \left(r+u_j v\right)\frac{\partial f}{\partial x}dz_1 + \left(a-b_j v\right)\frac{\partial f}{\partial v}dz_2. \qquad (A2)$$

By iterated expectations, we know that f must be a martingale

$$E\left[df\right] = 0. \qquad (A3)$$

Applying this to (A2) yields the Fokker–Planck forward equation

$$\frac{1}{2}v\frac{\partial^2 f}{\partial x^2} + \rho\sigma v\frac{\partial^2 f}{\partial x\,\partial v} + \frac{1}{2}\sigma^2 v\frac{\partial^2 f}{\partial v^2} + \left(r+u_j v\right)\frac{\partial f}{\partial x} + \left(a-b_j v\right)\frac{\partial f}{\partial v} + \frac{\partial f}{\partial t} = 0. \qquad (A4)$$

See Karlin and Taylor (1975) for more details. Equation (A1) imposes the terminal condition

$$f(x,v,T) = g(x,v). \qquad (A5)$$

This equation has many uses. If $g(x,v) = \delta(x - x_0)$, then the solution is the conditional probability density at time t that $x(T) = x_0$. If $g(x,v) = 1_{\{x\geq \ln[K]\}}$, then the solution is the conditional probability at time t that $x(T)$ is greater than $\ln[K]$. Finally, if $g(x,v) = e^{i\phi x}$, then the solution is the characteristic function. For properties of characteristic functions see Feller (1966) or Johnson and Kotz (1970).

To solve for the characteristic function explicitly, we guess the functional form

$$f(x,v,t) = \exp\left[C(T-t) + D(T-t)v + i\phi x\right]. \quad (A6)$$

This "guess" exploits the linearity of the coefficients in the PDE (A2). Following Ingersoll (1989, p. 397), one can substitute this functional form into the PDE (A2) to reduce it to two ordinary differential equations

$$-\frac{1}{2}\sigma^2\phi^2 + \rho\sigma\phi iD + \frac{1}{2}D^2 + u_j\phi i - b_jD + \frac{\partial D}{\partial t} = 0,$$

$$r\phi i + aD + \frac{\partial C}{\partial t} = 0, \quad (A7)$$

subject to

$$C(0) = 0, \quad D(0) = 0.$$

These equations can be solved to produce the solution in the text.

One can apply the solution technique of this chapter to other problems where the characteristic functions are known. For example, Stein and Stein [1991] specify a stochastic volatility model of the form

$$d\sqrt{v(t)} = \left[\alpha - \beta\sqrt{v(t)}\right]dt + \delta\, dz_2(t). \quad (A8)$$

Using Ito's lemma, the process for the variance is

$$dv(t) = \left[\delta^2 + 2\alpha\sqrt{v} - 2\beta v\right]dt + 2\delta\sqrt{v(t)}\, dz_2(t). \quad (A9)$$

Although Stein and Stein (1991) assume that the volatility process is uncorrelated with the spot asset, one can generalise this to allow $z_1(t)$ and $z_2(t)$ to have constant correlation. The solution method of this paper applies directly except that the characteristic functions take the form

$$f_j(x,v,t;\phi) = \exp\left[C(t-t) + D(T-t)v + E(T-t)\sqrt{v} + \phi x\right]. \quad (A10)$$

Bates (1992) provides additional applications of the solution technique to mixed jump-diffusion processes.

1 *This is analogous to extracting an implied volatility parameter in the Black-Scholes model.*

2 *Note that characteristic functions always exist; Kendall and Stuart (1977) establish that the integral converges.*

3 *Note that when evaluating multiple options with different strike prices, one need not recompute the characteristic functions when evaluating the integral in Equation (18).*

4 *This occurs for exactly the same reason that the Black-Scholes formula does not depend on the mean stock return. See Heston (1992) for a theoretical analysis that explains when parameters drop out of option prices.*

5 *These parameters roughly correspond to Knoch's (1992) estimates with yen and Deutschmark currency options, assuming no risk premium associated with volatility. However, the mean-reversion parameter is chosen to be more reasonable.*

6 *This variance can be determined using the characteristic function.*

7 *This illustration is motivated by Jarrow and Rudd (1982) and Hull (1989).*

BIBLIOGRAPHY

Barone-Adesi, G., and R.E. Whalley, 1987, "Efficient Analytic Approximation of American Option Values", *Journal of Finance* 42, pp. 301-20.

Bates, D.S., 1992, "Jumps and Stochastic Processes Implicit in PHLX Foreign Currency Options", Working paper, Wharton School, University of Pennsylvania.

Black, F., and M. Scholes, 1972, "The Valuation of Option Contracts and a Test of Market Efficiency", *Journal of Finance* 27, pp. 399-417.

Black, F., and M. Scholes, 1973, "The Valuation of Options and Corporate Liabilities", *Journal of Political Economy* 81, pp. 637-54.

Breeden, D.T., 1979, "An Intertemporal Asset Pricing Model With Stochastic Consumption and Investment Opportunities", *Journal of Financial Economics* 7, pp. 265-96.

Cox, J.C., J.E. Ingersoll and S.A. Ross, 1985, "A Theory of the Term Structure of Interest Rates", *Econometrica* 53, pp. 385-408.

Cox, J.C., and S.A. Ross, 1976, "The Valuation of Options for Alternative Stochastic Processes", *Journal of Financial Economics* 3, pp.145-66.

Eisenberg, L.K., and R.A. Jarrow, 1991, "Option Pricing With Random Volatilities in Complete Markets", *Review of Quantatitive Finance and Accounting* 4, pp. 5-17; reprinted as Chapter 21 of the present volume.

Feller, W., 1966, *An Introduction to Probability Theory and Its Applications*, Volume 2, Wiley & Sons, New York.

Garman M.B., and S.W. Kohlhagen, 1983, "Foreign Currency Option Values", *Journal of International Money and Finance* 2, pp. 231-7.

Heston, S.L., 1990, "Testing Continuous Time Models of the Term Structure of Interest Rates", PhD Dissertation, Carnegie Mellon University Graduate School of Industrial Administration.

Heston, S.L., 1992, "Invisible Parameters in Option Prices", Working Paper, Yale School of Organization and Management.

Hull, J.C., 1989, *Options, Futures, and Other Derivative Instruments*, Prentice-Hall, Englewood Cliffs, New Jersey.

Hull, J.C., and A. White, 1987, "The Pricing of Options on Assets with Stochastic Volatilities", *Journal of Finance* 42, pp. 281-300.

Ingersoll, J.E., 1989, *Theory of Financial Decision Making*, Rowman & Littlefield, Totowa, New Jersey.

Ingersoll, J.E., 1990, "Contingent Foreign Exchange Contracts with Stochastic Interest Rates", Working paper, Yale School of Organization and Management.

Jarrow, R.A., and A. Rudd, 1982, "Approximate Option Valuation for Arbitrary Stochastic Processes", *Journal of Financial Economics* 10, pp. 347-69.

Johnson, N.L., and S. Kotz, 1970, *Continuous Univariate Distributions*, Houghton Mifflin, New York.

Karlin, S., and H.M. Taylor, 1975, *A First Course in Stochastic Processes*, Academic Press, New York.

Kendall, M., and Alan Stuart, 1977, *The Advanced Theory of Statistics*, Volume 1, Macmillan Publishing Co., Inc., New York.

Knoch, Hans J., 1992, "The Pricing of Foreign Currency Options With Stochastic Volatility", PhD Dissertation, Yale School of Organisation and Management.

Lamoureux, C.G., and W.D. Lastrapes, 1993, "Forecasting Stock-Return Variance: Toward an Understanding of Stochastic Implied Volatilities", *Review of Financial Studies* 6, 2, pp. 293-6; reprinted as Chapter 14 of the present volume.

Melino, A., and S. Turnbull, 1991, "The Pricing of Foreign Currency Options", *Canadian Journal of Economics* 24, pp. 251-81.

Melino, A., and S. Turnbull, 1990, "The Pricing of Foreign Currency Options With Stochastic Volatility", *Journal of Econometrics* 45, pp. 239-65.

Merton, R.C., 1973, "Theory of Rational Option Pricing", *Bell Journal of Economics and Management Science* 4, pp. 141-83.

Ross, S.A., 1987, "Finance", in John Eatwell, Murray Milgate and Peter Newman (eds), *The New Palgrave A Dictionary of Economics*, Macmillan Press Limited, London.

Rubinstein, M., 1985, "Nonparametric Tests of Alternative Option Pricing Models Using All Reported Trades and Quotes on the 30 Most Active CBOE Option Classes from August 23, 1976 through August 31, 1978", *Journal of Finance* 40, pp. 455-80.

Scott, L.O., 1987, "Option Pricing When the Variance Changes Randomly: Theory, Estimation, and an Application," *Journal of Financial and Quantitative Analysis* 22, pp. 419-38.

Stein, E.M.. and J.C. Stein, 1991, "Stock Price Distributions with Stochastic Volatility: An Analytic Approach," *Review of Financial Studies* 4, pp. 727-52; reprinted as Chapter 22 of the present volume.

Wiggins, J.B., 1987, "Option Values Under Stochastic Volatilities", *Journal of Financial Economics* 19, pp. 351-72.

24

The Garch Option Pricing Model*

Jin-Chuan Duan
Hong Kong University of Science and Technology

This paper develops an option pricing model and its corresponding delta formula in the context of the generalized autoregressive conditional heteroskedastic (Garch) asset return process. The development utilises the locally risk-neutral valuation relationship (LRNVR). The LRNVR is shown to hold under certain combinations of preference and distribution assumptions. The Garch option pricing model is capable of reflecting the changes in the conditional volatility of the underlying asset in a parsimonious manner. Numerical analyses suggest that the Garch model may be able to explain some well-documented systematic biases associated with the Black-Scholes model.

Following the seminal work of Black and Scholes (1973) and Merton (1973), the option literature has developed into an important area of research. The heteroskedasticity of assets returns has attracted considerable attention. The option pricing models that deal with heteroskedasticity include the constant-elasticity-of-variance model by Cox (1975), the jump-diffusion model by Merton (1976), the compound option model by Geske (1979) and the displaced diffusion model by Rubinstein (1983). As opposed to the aforementioned models, Hull and White (1987) proposed a bivariate diffusion model for pricing options on assets with stochastic volatilities. In their model, an exogenous process is assumed to govern the evolution of asset volatilities. Other stochastic volatility option models similar to that of Hull and White include Johnson and Shanno (1987), Scott (1987), Wiggins (1987) and Stein and Stein (1991). The bivariate diffusion option pricing models all require conditions stronger than no arbitrage. Empirically, these models face the difficulty that the variance rate is not observable.

This article develops a pricing model for options on an asset whose continuously compounded returns follow the generalised autoregressive conditional heteroskedastic (Garch) process. The Garch process of Bollerslev (1986) and its variants have gained increasing prominence for modelling financial time series in recent years.[1] This article is an attempt to link this powerful econometric model with the contingent pricing literature. The Garch option pricing model has three distinctive features. First, the Garch option price is a function of the risk premium embedded in the underlying asset. This contrasts with the standard preference-free option pricing result. Second, the Garch option pricing model is non-Markovian.[2] In the option pricing literature, the underlying asset value is usually assumed to follow a diffusion process. The standard approach is thus of the Markovian nature. Third, the Garch option pricing model can potentially explain some well-documented systematic biases associated with the Black-Scholes model. These biases include underpricing of out-of-the-money options (see Black (1975); and Gultekin *et al* (1982), underpricing of options on low volatility securities (see Black and Scholes (1972); Gultekin *et al* (1982); and Whaley, (1982)), underpricing of short-maturity option (see Black (1975); and Whaley (1982)), and the U-shaped implied volatility curve in relation to exercise price (see Rubinstein (1985); and Sheikh (1991)). The Garch option pricing model also subsumes the Black-Scholes model because the homoskedastic asset return process is a special case of the Garch model.

* *This paper was first published in* Mathematical Finance, *Vol. 5, No.1 (1995). It is reprinted with permission of Blackwell Publishers.*

THE GARCH OPTION PRICING MODEL

The Garch process was used by Engle and Mustafa (1992) to study options and their implied conditional volatilities. The first attempt to provide a rigorous theoretical foundation for option pricing in the Garch framework can be found in Duan (1990). In this early attempt, the risk-neutral valuation relation was incorrectly applied to option pricing in the Garch framework. Subsequently, Satchell and Timmermann (1992) and Amin and Ng (1993) proposed option pricing models in the Garch framework which yield results invalidating the risk-neutral valuation relationship.[3] Both models assume joint lognormality for the asset return and the state price density. In contrast to the standard result, the option price becomes a function of the expected return on the underlying asset.

The development of the Garch option pricing model in this article differs from the previous models by exploring the extension of the risk-neutralisation in Rubinstein (1976) and Brennan (1979). Due to the complex nature of the Garch process, a generalised version of risk-neutralisation, referred to as the locally risk-neutral valuation relationship (LRNVR), is called for. The LRNVR differs from its conventional counterpart in the aspect of variances. The LRNVR stipulates that the one-period ahead conditional variance is invariant with respect to a change to the risk-neutralised pricing measure. This is important because, in the context of the Garch process, the unconditional variance or any conditional variance beyond one period is not invariant to the change in measures caused by risk-neutralisation. It is shown that the LRNVR holds under some familiar combinations of preference and distribution assumptions. With the LRNVR, the asset return process under the risk-neutralised pricing measure differs from the conventional Garch process in an interesting way. The conditional variance process in the Garch model of Bollerslev (1986) is known to be governed by the chi-square innovation. Local risk-neutralisation alters the conditional variance process. Under the risk-neutralised pricing measure, the conditional variance process continues to have the same form except the innovation is governed by the non-central chi-square random variable and the non-centrality parameter equals the unit risk premium for the underlying asset.

The remainder of the article is organised as follows. The section below provides a description of the Garch logarithmic asset returns and the definition of the LRNVR. Three sufficient conditions under which the LRNVR holds are laid out. The asset return process under the risk-neutralised pricing measure is also derived in this section. Then some general comparisons are made between the Garch option pricing model and the Black-Scholes formula. A Monte Carlo simulation method is then used to examine the Garch option pricing model numerically. We then present the conclusion of the article.

The Garch option pricing model

Consider a discrete-time economy and let X_t be the asset price at time t. Its one-period rate of return is assumed to be conditionally lognormally distributed under probability measure P. That is,

$$\ln\frac{X_t}{X_{t-1}} = r + \lambda\sqrt{h_t} - \frac{1}{2}h_t + \varepsilon_t, \qquad (1)$$

where ε_t has mean zero and conditional variance h_t under measure P; r is the constant one-period risk-free rate of return (continuously compounded) and λ the constant unit risk premium. Under conditional lognormality, one plus the conditionally expected rate of return equals $\exp(r + \lambda\sqrt{h_t})$. It thus suggests that λ can be interpreted as the unit risk premium.

We further assume that ε_t follows a Garch (p,q) process of Bollerslev (1986) under measure P. Formally,

$$\varepsilon_t \big| \phi_{t-1} \sim N(0,h_t), \text{ under measure } P. \qquad (2)$$
$$h_t = \alpha_0 + \sum_{i=1}^{q}\alpha_i\varepsilon_{t-i}^2 + \sum_{i=1}^{p}\beta_i h_{t-i},$$

where ϕ_t is the information set (σ-field) of all information up to and including time t; $p \geq 0$, $q \geq 0$; $\alpha_0 > 0$, $\alpha_i \geq 0$, $i = 1, ..., q$; $\beta_i \geq 0$, $i = 1, ..., p$. In words, the conditional variance is a linear function of the past squared disturbances and the past conditional variances. Clearly, h_t is ϕ_t-predictable. The option pricing results to be developed in this section rely on conditional normality. Using an alternative specification for h_t such as the Egarch of Nelson (1991) or that of Glosten *et al* (1993) will not change the basic option pricing results as long as conditional normality remains in place.

To ensure covariance stationarity of the Garch (p,q) process, $\Sigma_{i=1}^{q}\alpha_i + \Sigma_{i=1}^{p}\beta_i$ is assumed to be less than 1.[4] The Garch process specified in (1) and (2) reduces to the standard homoskedastic lognormal process in the Black-Scholes model if $p = 0$ and $q = 0$. This ensures that the Black-Scholes model is a special case.

In order to develop the Garch option pricing model, the conventional risk-neutral valuation relationship has to be generalised to accommodate heteroskedasticity of the asset return process. We thus introduce a generalised version of this principle below.

DEFINITION
A pricing measure Q is said to satisfy the Locally Risk-Neutral Valuation Relationship (LRNVR) if measure Q is mutually absolutely continuous with respect to measure P, $X_t/X_{t-1} \mid \phi_{t-1}$ distributes lognormally (under Q),

$$E^Q\left(X_t / X_{t-1} \middle| \phi_{t-1}\right) = e^r,$$

and

$$Var^Q\left(\ln(X_t / X_{t-1}) \middle| \phi_{t-1}\right) = Var^P\left(\ln(X_t / X_{t-1}) \middle| \phi_{t-1}\right)$$

almost surely with respect to measure P.

In the above definition of the LRNVR, the conditional variances under the two measures are required to be equal. This is desirable because one can observe and hence estimate the conditional variance under P. This property and the fact that the conditional mean can be replaced by the risk-free rate yield a well-specified model that does not locally depend on preferences. Local risk-neutralisation is, however, insufficient for eliminating the preference parameters. Under our model setup, it is nevertheless strong enough to reduce all preference consideration to the unit risk premium, λ. This assertion will be proved in theorem 1. In the definition, the conditional variance equality is an almost sure relationship. Since Q is absolutely continuous with respect to P, the almost sure relationship under P also holds true under Q. In the case of a homoskedastic lognormal process, ie $p = 0$ and $q = 0$, the conditional variances become the same constant and the LRNVR reduces to the conventional risk-neutral valuation relationship.

Rubinstein (1976) and Brennan (1979) proved that, under some combinations of preferences and distributions, the risk-neutral valuation relationship holds. In the following theorem, we prove the validity of the LRNVR under similar conditions.

THEOREM 1
If the representative agent is an expected utility maximiser and the utility function is time separable and additive, then the LRNVR holds under any of the following three conditions:
(i) the utility function is of constant relative risk aversion and changes in the logarithmic aggregate consumption are distributed normally with constant mean and variance under measure P;
(ii) the utility function is of constant absolute risk aversion and changes in the aggregate consumption are distributed normally with constant mean and variance under measure P;
(iii) the utility function is linear.
PROOF See Appendix.

The constant mean and variance assumption for the aggregate consumption process in (i) and (ii) of theorem (1) ensures that the implied interest rate is constant. Hence this guarantees the consistency with the constant interest rate assumption made earlier. Although it is possible to develop the model with stochastic interest rates, the resulting model will become considerably more complicated. The constant interest rate assumption allows for the comparison with the Black-Scholes model solely in the dimension of heteroskedasticity. It is worth noting that the condition in (ii) of theorem (1) permits the aggregate consumption to become negative.

The implication of the LRNVR is presented in the following theorem.[5]

THEOREM 2
The LRNVR implies that, under pricing measure Q,

$$\ln\frac{X_t}{X_{t-1}} = r - \frac{1}{2}h_t + \xi_t, \tag{3}$$

where

$$\xi_t \middle| \phi_{t-1} \sim N(0, h_t)$$

and

$$h_t = \alpha_0 + \sum_{i=1}^{q} \alpha_i\left(\xi_{t-i} - \lambda\sqrt{h_{t-i}}\right)^2 + \sum_{i=1}^{p} \beta_i h_{t-i}.$$

PROOF See Appendix

Theorem 2 implies that the form of the Garch (p,q) process remains largely intact with respect to local risk-neutralisation. The conditional variance process under the risk-neutralised pricing measure, is not a Garch process. The variance innovation is governed by q non-central chi-square random variables with one degree of freedom, whereas the Garch process under P can be seen as the process governed by q central chi-square innovations. The common non-centrality parameter for the conditional variance process under Q is the unit risk premium λ. To see this, one needs to factor out $\sqrt{h_{t-i}}$ from the terms inside the parentheses and recognise that $\xi_{t-i}/\sqrt{h_{t-i}}$ is a standard normal random variable under measure Q. Theorem 2 suggests that the unit risk premium, λ, influences the conditional variance process globally although the risk has been locally neutralised under the pricing measure Q. In other words, local risk-neutralisation is not equivalent to global risk-neutralisation. The need to distinguish between local and global risk-neutralisations disappears when the coefficients governing the variance innovation equal zero.

If an alternative Garch specification for asset returns is chosen, say the Egarch process, a result similar to theorem 2 can immediately be obtained. Whenever the variable ε_t appears in the conditional variance equation, it should be replaced by $\xi_t - \lambda\sqrt{h_t}$ with everything else remaining unchanged. Although the pricing results are tailored specifically for the Garch process of Bollerslev (1986), they are applicable, after minor modifications, to other asset return specifications.

Pricing contingent payoffs requires temporally aggregating one-period asset returns to arrive at a random terminal asset price at some future point of time. The terminal asset price is derived in the following corollary.

COROLLARY 1

$$X_T = X_t \exp\left[(T-t)r - \frac{1}{2}\sum_{s=t+1}^{T} h_s + \sum_{s=t+1}^{T} \xi_s\right]. \quad (4)$$

PROOF Follows immediately from Theorem 2.

The asset price, discounted at the risk-free rate, possesses the martingale property. The importance of the martingale property for the theory of contingent claim pricing was first established by Harrison and Kreps (1979), and later elaborated by Harrison and Pliska (1981).

COROLLARY 2 The discount asset price process $e^{-rt}X_t$ is a Q-martingale.
PROOF See Appendix.

Under the Garch (p,q) specification, a European call option with exercise price K maturing at time T has the time-t value equal to

COROLLARY 3

$$C_t^{GH} = e^{-(T-t)r} E^Q\left[\max(X_T - K, 0) \middle| \phi_t\right]. \quad (5)$$

Under the Garch (p,q) specification, ϕ_t is the σ-field generated by $\{X_t, \varepsilon_t, \ldots, \varepsilon_{t-q+1}, h_t, \ldots, h_{t-p+1}\}$. A substantial simplification of the information set can be obtained if one restricts the model to the popular Garch (1,1) specification. For the Garch (1,1) model, X_t and h_{t+1} together serve as the sufficient statistics for ϕ_t. In other words, the Garch (1,1) is not a univariate Markov process, but can be stated as a bivariate Markov process. The Garch (1,1) option pricing model explicitly reflects the state of the underlying asset price in two dimensions: price level and conditional volatility. This added dimension enables the model price to reflect high or low variance of the underlying asset when the state of the economy changes.

One important use of the option pricing model is delta hedging. The delta of an option is the first partial derivative of the option price with respect to the underlying asset price. To use such a technique in the Garch framework, one must first derive the corresponding delta formula. Denote the Garch option delta at time t by Δ_t^{GH}. The following result is in order.

COROLLARY 4

$$\Delta_t^{GH} = e^{-(T-t)r} E^Q\left[\frac{X_T}{X_t} 1_{\{X_T \geq K\}} \middle| \phi_t\right], \quad (6)$$

where $1_{\{X_T \geq K\}}$ is an indicator function.
PROOF See Appendix.

For a European put, its price and delta can be derived using the put-call parity relationship.

It can be shown that the Garch option price and delta reduce to their Black-Scholes counterparts when the underlying process is homoskedastic. The analytic solution for the Garch option price in (5) or delta in (6) is not available because the conditional distribution over more than one period cannot be analytically derived. A control-variate Monte Carlo simulation method can nevertheless be used to compute the Garch option price and delta.

Comparison of the Garch (1,1) option pricing model and the Black-Scholes model

In this section, we compare the Black-Scholes model with the Garch option pricing model. Since the Garch (1,1) model is the most commonly used Garch process, our discussion for the remainder of this paper will be restricted to the Garch (1,1) model.

Although the homoskedastic process used by the Black-Scholes model is a special case of the Garch process, the interpretation of the Black-Scholes model in the Garch framework is considerably more complicated. Under the incorrect assumption of homoskedasticity when the real governing process is heteroskedastic, risk-neutralisation must be of a global nature to maintain model consistency. This incorrect assumption thus requires the asset volatility to remain unchanged with respect to risk-neutralisation. Using the Black-Scholes model when the underlying process follows a Garch process should therefore be regarded as employing the stationary variance of the Garch asset return process in the Black-Scholes formula.

The following theorem characterises some properties of the Garch process after local risk-neutralisation. It suggests that a correct use of local risk neutralisation will alter some key characteristics of the Garch process.

THEOREM 3
Under pricing measure Q, if

$$|\lambda| < \sqrt{(1-\alpha_1-\beta_1)/\alpha_1},$$

then
(i) the stationary variance of ξ_t equals $\alpha_0[1-(1+\lambda^2)\alpha_1-\beta_1]^{-1}$;
(ii) ξ_t is leptokurtic;
(iii) $Cov^Q(\xi_t/\sqrt{h_t}, h_{t+1}) = -2\lambda\alpha_0\alpha_1[1-(1+\lambda^2)\alpha_1-\beta_1]^{-1}$.
PROOF See Appendix.

As stated earlier, the stationary variance of the Garch return process, under the original probability measure P, is $\alpha_0(1-\alpha_1-\beta_1)^{-1}$. It is also true that the conditional variance is uncorrelated with the lagged asset return under measure P. By Theorem 3, local risk-neutralisation induces an increase in the stationary variance to $\alpha_0[1-\alpha_1(1+\lambda^2)-\beta_1]^{-1}$. It also causes the conditional variance to be negatively (positively) correlated with the lagged asset return if the risk premium λ is positive (negative).

As stated earlier, the Black-Scholes option price in the Garch framework should be interpreted as using an incorrect assumption of homoskedasticity and hence an incorrect unconditional standard deviation for the risk-neutralised asset return process. Specifically, the Black-Scholes call option price and delta can be written as

$$C_t^{BS} = X_t N(d_t) - e^{-(T-t)r} K\, N\left(d_t - \sigma\sqrt{T-t}\right), \quad (7)$$

$$\Delta_t^{BS} = N(d_t), \quad (8)$$

where

$$d_t = \frac{\ln(X_t/K) + (r+\sigma^2/2)(T-t)}{\sigma\sqrt{T-t}}$$

and

$$\sigma^2 = \alpha_0(1-\alpha_1-\beta_1)^{-1}.$$

Loosely speaking, the difference between the Garch option price and its Black-Scholes counterpart can be regarded as using two different levels of asset return volatility. A closer examination of these two models reveals something that is considerably more complicated. The initial conditional variance for a Garch process is unlikely to be equal to the unconditional variance σ^2. Even if the initial conditional variance is set at the unconditional variance of the original asset return process, local risk-neutralisation implies that the conditional variance under pricing measure Q will revert to an unconditional variance higher than σ^2. Since the conditional volatility is negatively (or positively) correlated with the lagged asset return, the reverting behavior is also different from the one usually associated with the standard Garch model.

Since the risk-neutralised Garch process is still leptokurtic, it will be more likely for an out-of-the-money option to finish in the money. This implies that the Garch option price will be higher than its Black-Scholes counterpart. Leptokurtosis also implies that an in-the-money option is more likely to finish out of the money. This does not, however, imply lower Garch option prices for in-the-money options when compared to their Black-Scholes counterparts. This is true because there must be an offsetting increase in probability at the higher value end to make in-the-money options attain even higher values. Other than these general observations, the comparison between these two option pricing models can only be made numerically.

Numerical results and discussion

Monte Carlo simulation is used in the computation of the Garch option prices and deltas. Use of the Monte Carlo method to compute option prices can be traced back to Boyle (1977). It is a convenient method for the Garch option pricing model because the distribution for the temporally aggregated asset return cannot be derived analytically. To simulate the risk-neutralised Garch (1,1) asset returns for pricing options at time t, we recognise that the asset price X_t and the conditional volatility h_{t+1} can together serve as sufficient statistics. A control-variate technique is employed to improve the efficiency of the Garch option price and delta estimators. The control variables are the Black-Scholes price and delta described above.

Table 1. S&P 100 index call option pricing biases as a percentage of the Black-Scholes price for different maturities, exercise prices and conditional volatilities[a]

		B-S	Garch								
			$\sqrt{h_1}/\sigma = 0.8$			$\sqrt{h_1}/\sigma = 1.0$			$\sqrt{h_1}/\sigma = 1.2$		
Maturity	s/x	Price	Price	% bias	sd	Price	% bias	sd	Price	% bias	sd
	.80	.1027	.6892	571.2200	107.9300	.9495	824.7200	115.4700	1.6164	1474.2000	142.6000
	.90	18.2380	16.4340	−9.8893	1.6291	20.9300	14.7600	1.7680	26.9050	47.5210	2.0957
	.95	89.7900	75.4490	−15.9710	.4722	86.0280	−4.1893	.5102	99.2440	10.5290	.5855
T = 30	1.00	276.1100	251.5200	−8.9036	.1916	266.7500	−3.3897	.2058	284.3400	2.9828	.2339
	1.05	600.4100	583.9500	−2.7423	.1047	596.1300	−.7131	.1106	610.4400	1.6694	.1251
	1.10	1027.9000	1023.6000	−.4244	.0697	1030.2000	.2164	.0730	1037.9000	.9668	.0826
	1.20	2001.0000	2002.0000	.0518	.0417	2003.5000	.1240	.0442	2004.2000	.1628	.0498
	.80	13.0160	14.3700	10.4070	2.9874	15.7590	21.0770	3.0099	18.3170	40.7310	3.6271
	.90	118.5400	109.5700	−7.5685	.6037	116.0600	−2.0913	.6240	123.3200	4.0344	.6763
	.95	257.7900	241.3500	−6.3774	.3419	251.0200	−2.6268	.3533	259.9500	.8347	.3802
T = 90	1.00	478.0000	458.2200	−4.1371	.2180	468.9000	−1.9038	.2242	477.8600	−.0291	.2403
	1.05	779.6800	761.8800	−2.2836	.1531	772.3500	−.9402	.1572	780.4200	.0950	.1676
	1.10	1152.2000	1140.0000	−1.0631	.1159	1149.4000	−.2502	.1185	1155.6000	.2900	.1260
	1.20	2036.6000	2034.4000	−.1080	.0775	2040.5000	.1955	.0788	2042.3000	.2836	.0837
	.80	66.4460	65.8050	−.9638	1.1575	68.3570	2.8763	1.1727	71.6500	7.8323	1.2052
	.90	261.3000	252.5100	−3.3625	.4560	257.0900	−1.6128	.4642	264.6500	1.2818	.4730
	.95	438.1700	425.4700	−2.8984	.3213	431.7000	−1.4777	.3260	440.5700	.5483	.3332
T = 180	1.00	675.5400	661.5100	−2.0766	.2389	668.5000	−1.0419	.2420	677.9400	.3553	.2481
	1.05	970.4900	957.8900	−1.2987	.1866	964.2900	−.6391	.1886	973.6500	.3257	.1936
	1.10	1318.0000	1308.9000	−.6910	.1515	1313.9000	−.3147	.1526	1322.5000	.3437	.1567
	1.20	2133.4000	2131.7000	−.0764	.1088	2134.7000	.0637	.1098	2139.7000	.2959	.1128

[a] The riskless rate is fixed at 0%. The results are obtained using 50,000 Monte Carlo simulation runs. The values under "sd" are the standard deviations of percentage biases from Monte Carlo simulation. Prices are reported as 10,000 times.

The general characteristics of the Garch option pricing model in comparison to the Black-Scholes formula are reflected in Table 1 and Table 2. The options used to generate these tables are the S&P 100 index calls of European style.[6] The S&P 100 index options are known to be most actively traded contracts. The Garch-M model specified in (1) and (2) with $p = 1$ and $q = 1$ is fitted to the S& P 100 daily index series from January 2, 1986 to December 15, 1989. The estimated parameter values are $\alpha_0 = 1.524 \times 10^{-5}$, $\alpha_1 = 0.1883$, $\beta_1 = 0.7162$ and $\lambda = 7.452 \times 10^{-3}$, respectively. The Garch parameter values together imply that the annualised (based on 365 days) stationary standard deviation is 24.13%. The risk-free rate is fixed at 0% to make easier the interpretation of in-the-money or out-of-the-money options. The exercise price is set at \$1. The relative index values, denoted by s/x, range from 0.8 to 1.2. Fifty thousand simulation runs are carried out for a given set of Garch option prices corresponding to different s/x ratios.

The Garch option pricing model provides an opportunity for examining the impacts of the initial conditional variance on the price of an option. Intuitively, if the conditional volatility of the underlying asset at the time of option valuation is high (low), all options written on this asset should be relatively more (less) valuable. With the conditional variance incorporated, the Garch option pricing model is expected to generate an important flexibility for valuing options in a frequently-changing market. To shed light on the effect of conditional volatility, three levels of initial conditional standard deviations are studied. They are the stationary level, 20% below the stationary level and 20% above, respectively.

The Black-Scholes model is known to underprice out-of-money options (see Black (1975); and Gultekin *et al* (1982)). As compared to the Garch option prices, Table 1 reveals that the Black-Scholes model can underprice or overprice an out-of-the-money option depending on the level of its initial conditional volatility. For deep out-of-the-money options, the Black-Scholes always underprices. Since the Garch conditional variance process is known to generate low-variance states more frequently, underpricing by the Black-Scholes model is expected to be the norm rather than the exception. The Black-Scholes model is also known to underprice short-maturity options (see Black (1975); and Whaley, (1982)). For out-of-the-money options, one can see this pattern present in Table 1. Moreover, the underpricing of the Black-Scholes model for out-of-the money options becomes more pronounced when the maturity of an option is shortened. The comparison of the Garch option delta with its Black-Scholes counterpart is presented in Table 2. The results, by and large, exhibit patterns similar to the price comparison.

Rubinstein (1985) documented empirically that implied volatilities of traded options exhibit a systematic pattern with respect to different

Table 2. S&P 100 index call option delta biases as a percentage of the Black-Scholes delta for different maturities, exercise prices and conditional volatilities[a]

		B-S	Garch								
			$\sqrt{h_1}/\sigma = 0.8$			$\sqrt{h_1}/\sigma = 1.0$			$\sqrt{h_1}/\sigma = 1.2$		
Maturity	s/x	Delta	Delta	% bias	sd	Delta	% bias	sd	Delta	% bias	sd
	.80	.0007	.0020	184.3500	29.0140	.0027	272.3800	33.5170	.0046	539.6500	44.5830
	.90	.0684	.0530	−22.4570	1.0397	.0622	−9.0391	1.0702	.0750	9.7047	1.1575
	.95	.2399	.2089	−12.8980	.4158	.2210	−7.8541	.4050	.2372	−1.1100	.4154
T = 30	1.00	.5138	.5130	−.1601	.1868	.5132	−.1153	.1899	.5170	.6285	.2029
	1.05	.7703	.7975	3.5301	.1240	.7874	2.2281	.1213	.7745	.5491	.1250
	1.10	.9211	.9385	1.8921	.0762	.9288	.8464	.0772	.9177	−.3643	.0801
	1.20	.9962	.9955	−.0721	.0260	.9937	−.2514	.0307	.9914	−.4832	.0341
	.80	.0358	.0334	−6.5577	1.8009	.0362	1.0530	1.8323	.0401	12.0250	1.8802
	.90	.2063	.1905	−7.6792	.5089	.1966	−4.7120	.5061	.2022	−1.9943	.5184
	.95	.3564	.3443	−3.4015	.3156	.3491	−2.0481	.3184	.3522	−1.1825	.3278
T = 90	1.00	.5239	.5227	−.2320	.2155	.5236	−.0472	.2171	.5213	−.4955	.2196
	1.05	.6798	.6880	1.2196	.1560	.6860	.9132	.1570	.6844	.6841	.1616
	1.10	.8038	.8161	1.5333	.1192	.8131	1.1571	.1192	.8081	.5426	.1208
	1.20	.9431	.9492	.6469	.0683	.9448	.1824	.0700	.9426	−.0550	.0714
	.80	.1090	.1035	−5.0268	.8782	.1026	−5.8582	.8926	.1083	−.6324	.9165
	.90	.2957	.2862	−3.2014	.4103	.2904	−1.7819	.4071	.2928	−.9889	.4123
	.95	.4137	.4089	−1.1624	.2959	.4114	−.5567	.2970	.4144	.1457	.3004
T = 180	1.00	.5338	.5354	.3002	.2267	.5343	.0881	.2270	.5345	.1298	.2311
	1.05	.6453	.6505	.8056	.1805	.6485	.5044	.1772	.6472	.2994	.1794
	1.10	.7412	.7489	1.0406	.1424	.7472	.8101	.1418	.7442	.3999	.1433
	1.20	.8771	.8844	.8278	.0954	.8819	.5436	.0964	.8787	.1785	.0981

[a] The riskless rate is fixed at 0%. The results are obtained using 50,000 Monte Carlo simulation runs. The values under "sd" are the standard deviations of percentage biases from Monte Carlo simulation.

maturities and exercise prices. Sheikh (1991) analysed S&P 100 index calls and arrived at a conclusion similar to that of Rubinstein. These findings suggest a U-shape implied volatility phenomenon, when the Black-Scholes model is used to invert the market prices of traded options. In Figure 1 and Figure 2, we use the Black-Scholes formula to invert the Garch option prices. Three implied volatility graphs corresponding to three different option maturities are plotted. The implied volatilities produced in this way also exhibit a U-shaped pattern.

Rubinstein (1985) and Sheikh (1991) also analysed the effect of the time to maturity on the implied volatility relationship. They reported that, for at-the-money calls, the longer the time to maturity, the higher is the option's implied volatility. They also reported that a reversal occurs over a different time period. Figure 1 presents the results for the case of low initial conditional volatility, ie 20% below the stationary level. The implied volatility for the shortest-maturity option is clearly the lowest. When the initial conditional volatility is high, ie 20% above the stationary level, the resulting pattern is different and is shown in Figure 2. The implied volatility of the shortest-maturity option is now the highest for the at-the-money option. Since the estimated parameter values imply a model that is close to the integrated Garch asset return process, the conditional volatility must exhibit a strong clustering phenomenon. The Garch conditional variance process is also known to be asymmetrical and skewed to the lower end. These two facts together imply that the likelihood of observing

1. Low conditional volatility and its effect on the annualised implied volatility of the Garch option price

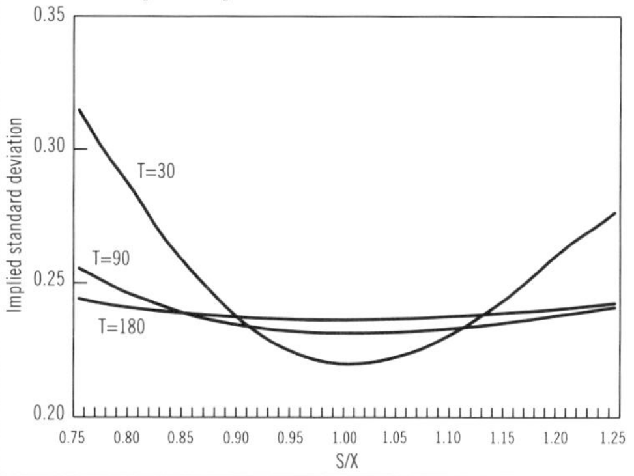

2. High conditional volatility and its effect on the annualised implied volatility of the Garch option price

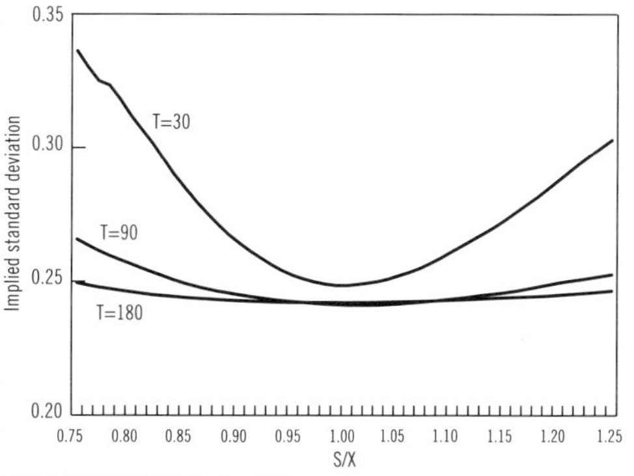

an extended low-variance state is higher than others. For at-the-money calls, the longer-maturity option should frequently have a higher implied volatility with occasional periods of reversal. The reversal phenomenon reported by Rubinstein (1985) and Sheikh (1991) is therefore not too surprising, and indeed lends support to the Garch option pricing model.

Conclusion

This paper develops a Garch option pricing model using local risk-neutralisation. The Garch option pricing model has a number of desirable features and presents a real possibility of correcting the pricing biases associated with the Black-Scholes model. The ultimate test of the model, however, must be its empirical performance. Since the empirical technology for the Garch process has been well developed, a reasonable test of the model can therefore be designed and executed without too much difficulty.

Market prices for traded options are readily available. The Garch option pricing model presents a possibility of inferring implied Garch parameters from the market data. These inferred parameter values can be used in a spirit very similar to the implied volatility of the Black-Scholes model. Calculating the implied Garch parameters with Monte Carlo simulation is, however, computationally demanding. To make the task manageable, one has to develop a numerical approximation procedure for computing the Garch option price. Analytically approximating the distribution function of the terminal asset price under the locally risk-neutralised pricing measure seems a promising approach.

Finally, using the Garch option pricing model in delta hedging adds another dimension of flexibility to the process of dynamic hedging. In a low-variance state, the Garch delta hedging calls for a smaller option position, relative to the Black-Scholes model, whereas it calls for a larger position in a high-variance state. This additional dynamic feature may prove to be materially beneficial for risk management.

Appendix

PROOF OF THEOREM 1

Let $U(C_t)$ and C_t denote the utility function and the aggregate consumption at time t, respectively. The parameter ρ is used to denote the impatience factor. The standard expected utility maximisation argument leads to the following Euler equation:

$$X_{t-1} = E^P\left[e^{-\rho}\frac{U'(C_t)}{U'(C_{t-1})}X_t \middle| \phi_{t-1}\right].$$

To organise the proof, two intermediate lemmas are useful. Let $Y_t = \nu + Z_t$ where ν is the constant mean and Z_t distributes normally with zero mean and constant variance under P. Define a measure Q by $dQ = e^{(r-\rho)T + \sum_{s=1}^{T} Y_s} dP$. It is clear that measure Q is mutually absolutely continuous with respect to measure P.

LEMMA A.1 If $X_{t-1} = E^P(e^{-\rho+Y_t} X_t \mid \phi_{t-1})$, then Q is a probability measure and, for any ϕ_t-measurable random variable W_t, $E^Q(W_t \mid \phi_{t-1}) = E^P(W_t e^{(r-\rho)+Y_t} \mid \phi_{t-1})$.

Proof of the lemma

$$\int 1 dQ = E^P\left(e^{(r-\rho)T+\sum_{s=1}^{T} Y_s}\middle|\phi_0\right)$$

$$= E^P\left[e^{(r-\rho)(T-1)+\sum_{s=1}^{T-1} Y_s} e^r E^P\left(e^{-\rho+Y_T}\middle|\phi_{T-1}\right)\middle|\phi_0\right]$$

$$= E^P\left[e^{(r-\rho)(T-1)+\sum_{s=1}^{T-1} Y_s}\middle|\phi_0\right].$$

The last equality is due to

$$E^P\left(e^{-\rho+Y_T}\middle|\phi_{T-1}\right) = e^{-r},$$

which is, of course, implied by the assumption of the lemma. Continuing the process, one obtains

$$\int 1 dQ = 1$$

which confirms that Q is a probability measure. The second half of the lemma follows from the Radon-Nikodym Theorem and the law of iterated expectations.

LEMMA A.2 If $X_{t-1} = E^P(e^{-\rho+Y_t} X_t \mid \phi_{t-1})$, then
(a) $X_t/X_{t-1} \mid \phi_{t-1}$ distributes lognormally under measure Q;
(b) $E^Q(X_t/X_{t-1} \mid \phi_{t-1}) = e^r$; and
(c) $Var^Q(\ln(X_t/X_{t-1}) \mid \phi_{t-1}) = Var^P(\ln(X_t/X_{t-1}) \mid \phi_{t-1})$ almost surely with respect to measure P.

Proof of the lemma

Using Lemma A.1, part (b) is easily verified.

$$E^Q\left(\frac{X_t}{X_{t-1}}\middle|\phi_{t-1}\right) = E^P\left(\frac{X_t}{X_{t-1}}e^{(r-\rho)+Y_t}\middle|\phi_{t-1}\right)$$
$$= \frac{e^r}{X_{t-1}}E^P\left(X_t e^{-\rho+Y_t}\middle|\phi_{t-1}\right)$$
$$= e^r.$$

To prove (a) and (c), we consider the conditional moment generating function of $W_t \equiv \ln(X_t/X_{t-1})$ under Q:

$$E^Q\left(e^{cW_t}\middle|\phi_{t-1}\right) = E^P\left(e^{cW_t+(r-\rho)+Y_t}\middle|\phi_{t-1}\right).$$

Let $\mu_t = E^P(\ln(X_t/X_{t-1}) \mid \phi_{t-1})$. Since under measure P, $W_t \mid \phi_{t-1} \sim N(\mu_t, h_t)$ and Y_t is ϕ_{t-1}-conditionally normal, it follows that $Y_t = \alpha + \beta W_t + U_t$, where W_t and U_t are independent. Thus,

$$E^Q\left(e^{cW_t}\middle|\phi_{t-1}\right) = e^{\alpha+(r-\rho)}E^P\left(e^{(\beta+c)W_t+U_t}\middle|\phi_{t-1}\right)$$
$$= e^{\alpha+(r-\rho)+E\left(U_t^2|\phi_{t-1}\right)/2}E^P\left(e^{(\beta+c)W_t}\middle|\phi_{t-1}\right)$$
$$= e^{\alpha+(r-\rho)+E\left(U_t^2|\phi_{t-1}\right)/2+\beta\mu_t+\beta^2h_t/2+(\mu_t+\beta h_t)c+c^2h_t/2}.$$

Let $c = 0$ and use the fact that $E^Q(1 \mid \phi_{t-1}) = 1$ to yield

$$E^Q\left(e^{cW_t}\middle|\phi_{t-1}\right) = e^{(\mu_t+\beta h_t)c+c^2h_t/2}.$$

This in turn implies

$$\ln\frac{X_t}{X_{t-1}}\middle|\phi_{t-1} \sim N(\mu_t+\beta h_t, h_t)$$

under measure Q. So, the proofs for both (a) and (c) are complete.

With Lemma A.2 in place, the first two assertions in the theorem can be proved if, under measure P, logarithmic marginal rate of substitution can be expressed as the sum of a constant and a normally distributed disturbance with zero mean and constant variance.

(i) $\ln(U'(C_t)/U'(C_{t-1})) = (\lambda_1 - 1)\ln(C_t/C_{t-1})$ where λ_1 is the constant relative risk-aversion coefficient. Since $\ln(C_t/C_{t-1})$ distributes normally under P, the result is immediately established.

(ii) $\ln(U'(C_t)/U'(c_{t-1})) = -\lambda_2(C_t - C_{t-1})$ where λ_2 is the constant absolute-risk-aversion coefficient. The assertion is true because $C_t - C_{t-1}$ distributes normally under P.

The statement (iii) of Theorem 1 trivially holds because the ratio of marginal utilities equals one. Note that, under any of the above assumptions, the implied interest rate is constant. This thus ensures the consistency with the constant interest rate assumption made in the article.

PROOF OF THEOREM 2

Since $X_t/X_{t-1} \mid \phi_{t-1}$ distributes lognormally under measure Q, it can be ritten as

$$\ln\frac{X_t}{X_{t-1}} = \nu_t + \xi_t,$$

where ν_t is the conditional mean and ξ_t is a Q-normal random variable. The conditional mean of ξ_t equals zero and its conditional variance is to be determined. First, we prove that $\nu_t = r - ½h_t$

$$E^Q\left(\frac{X_t}{X_{t-1}}\middle|\phi_{t-1}\right) = E^Q\left(e^{\nu_t+\xi_t}\middle|\phi_{t-1}\right)$$
$$= e^{\nu_t+h_t/2}$$

where

$h_t = \text{Var}^P(\ln(X_t/X_{t-1}) \mid \phi_{t-1}) = \text{Var}^Q(\ln(X_t/X_{t-1}) \mid \phi_{t-1})$ by the LRNVR. Since $E^Q(X_t/X_{t-1} \mid \phi_{t-1}) = e^r$ by the LRNVR, it follows that $\nu_t = r - ½h_t$. It remains to prove that h_t can indeed be expressed as stated in Theorem 2.2. By the preceding result and equation (1), $r + \lambda\sqrt{h_t} - ½h_t + \varepsilon_t = r - ½h_t + \xi_t$. This implies that $\varepsilon_t = \xi_t - \lambda\sqrt{h_t}$. Substituting ε_t into the conditional variance equation yields the desirable result.

PROOF OF COROLLARY 2

The proof follows from Corollary 1 and the fact that ξ_t is conditionally normal with mean zero and variance h_t under Q.

PROOF OF COROLLARY 4

Define

$$Y_{t,T} \equiv (T-t)r - ½\sum_{s=t+1}^{T} h_s + \sum_{s=t+1}^{T}\xi_s.$$

By Corollaries 1 and 3

$$C_t(X_t) = e^{-(T-t)r}E^Q\left[\max\left(X_t e^{Y_{t,T}} - K, 0\right)\middle|\phi_t\right].$$

Note that we have dropped the superscript, GH, to simplify the notation and added the argument X_t to reflect that the option price at time t is a function of X_t. Consider an arbitrary $h > 0$ and compute the following quantity:

$$C_t(X_t+h) - C_t(X_t)$$
$$= e^{-(T-t)r}E^Q\left[\max\left[(X_t+h)e^{Y_{t,T}} - K, 0\right] - \max\left(X_t e^{Y_{t,T}} - K, 0\right)\middle|\phi_t\right]$$
$$= e^{-(T-t)r}\int_{-\infty}^{\infty}\left\{\max\left[(X_t+h)e^y - K, 0\right] - \max\left(X_t e^y - K, 0\right)\right\}dF\left(y|\phi_t\right),$$

where $F(y \mid \phi_t)$ denotes the conditional distribution function of $Y_{t,T}$ under measure Q. Using the fact that $h > 0$, the above quantity can be further simplified to

$$e^{-(T-t)r}\int_{\ln(K/X_t)}^{\infty} he^y dF(y|\phi_t) + e^{-(T-t)r}$$
$$\int_{\ln(K/(X_t+h))}^{\ln(K/X_t)}\left[(X_t+h)e^y - K\right]dF(y|\phi_t).$$

Since

$$\frac{1}{h}\int_{\ln(K/(X_t+h))}^{\ln(K/X_t)}\left[(X_t+h)e^y - K\right]dF(y|\phi_t) \to 0$$

as $h \to 0$, we have

$$\frac{1}{h}\left[C_t(X_t+h) - C_t(X_t)\right] \to e^{-(T-t)r}\int_{\ln(K/X_t)}^{\infty} e^y dF(y|\phi_t).$$

A similar argument can be constructed for $h < 0$ to arrive at the same result. Together, we have

$$\Delta_t = e^{-(T-t)r}\int_{\ln(K/X_t)}^{\infty} e^y dF(y|\phi_t)$$
$$= e^{-(T-t)r}E^Q\left[\frac{X_T}{X_t}1_{\{X_T \geq K\}}|\phi_t\right].$$

PROOF OF THEOREM 3

(i) Define $z_t = \xi_t/\sqrt{h_t} - \lambda$, $G_i = G_{i-1}(\alpha_1 z_{t-i}^2 + \beta_1)$, and $G_0 = 1$. It follows from (3) with $p = 1$ and $q = 1$ that

$$h_t = \alpha_0 + \alpha_1\left(\xi_{t-1} - \lambda\sqrt{h_{t-1}}\right)^2 + \beta_1 h_{t-1}$$
$$= \alpha_0 + h_{t-1}\left(\alpha_1 z_{t-1}^2 + \beta_1\right)$$
$$= h_0\prod_{i=1}^{t}\left(\alpha_1 z_{t-i}^2 + \beta_1\right) + \alpha_0\left[1 + \sum_{k=1}^{t-1}\prod_{i=1}^{k}\left(\alpha_1 z_{t-i}^2 + \beta_1\right)\right]$$
$$= h_0 G_t + \alpha_0\sum_{k=0}^{t-1} G_k.$$

Since z_t^2, for any t, is a non-central chi-square random variable with the degrees of freedom 1 and the non-centrality parameter λ, $E^Q(z_t^2 | \phi_0) = 1 + \lambda^2$. Thus, for $t > k$,

$$E^Q(G_k|\phi_0) = E^Q\left[G_{k-1}\left(\alpha_1 z_{t-k}^2 + \beta_1\right)|\phi_0\right]$$
$$= E^Q(G_{k-1}|\phi_0)E^Q\left(\alpha_1 z_{t-k}^2 + \beta_1|\phi_0\right)$$
$$= E^Q(G_{k-1}|\phi_0)\left[\alpha_1(1+\lambda^2) + \beta_1\right]$$
$$= \left[\alpha_1(1+\lambda^2) + \beta_1\right]^k.$$

This in turn implies that

$$E^Q(h_t|\phi_0) = h_0\left[\alpha_1(1+\lambda^2) + \beta_1\right]^t$$
$$+\alpha_0\sum_{k=0}^{t-1}\left[\alpha_1(1+\lambda^2) + \beta_1\right]^k.$$

The stationary variance can be computed by letting $t \to \infty$. The condition of the theorem ensures that $|\alpha_1(1 + \lambda^2) + \beta_1| < 1$, and implies that

$$E^Q(h_t) = \alpha_0\sum_{k=0}^{\infty}\left[\alpha_1(1+\lambda^2) + \beta_1\right]^k$$
$$= \alpha_0\left[1 - \alpha_1(1+\lambda^2) - \beta_1\right]^{-1}.$$

(ii) By the definition of z_t, we have $E^Q(z_t^4 | \phi_0) = 3 + 6\lambda^2 + \lambda^4$. For any $t > k$,

$$E^Q(G_k^2|\phi_0) = E^Q\left[G_{k-1}^2\left(\alpha_1 z_{t-k}^2 + \beta_1\right)^2|\phi_0\right]$$
$$= E^Q(G_{k-1}^2|\phi_0)E^Q\left[\left(\alpha_1 z_{t-k}^2 + \beta_1\right)^2|\phi_0\right]$$
$$= E^Q(G_{k-1}^2|\phi_0)$$
$$\left[\alpha_1^2(3+6\lambda^2+\lambda^4) + 2\alpha_1\beta_1(1+\lambda^2) + \beta_1^2\right]$$
$$= \left[\alpha_1^2(3+6\lambda^2+\lambda^4) + 2\alpha_1\beta_1(1+\lambda^2) + \beta_1^2\right]^k.$$

Define $u = \alpha_1^2(3 + 6\lambda^2 + \lambda^4) + 2\alpha_1\beta_1(1 + \lambda^2) + \beta_1^2$ and $v = \alpha_1(1 + \lambda^2) + \beta_1$. It can be easily verified that $u = v^2 + 2(1 + 2\lambda^2)\alpha_1^2$ and $u > v$. For $k > j$,

$$E^Q(G_k G_j|\phi_0) = E^Q\left[G_j^2\prod_{i=j}^{k}\left(\alpha_1 z_{t-2k+i}^2 + \beta_1\right)|\phi_0\right]$$
$$= E^Q(G_j^2|\phi_0)E^Q\left[\prod_{i=j}^{k}\left(\alpha_1 z_{t-2k+i}^2 + \beta_1\right)|\phi_0\right]$$
$$= u^j v^{k-j}.$$

Thus,

$$E^Q(h_t^2|\phi_0) = h_0^2 E^Q(G_t^2|\phi_0) + 2\alpha_0 h_0\sum_{k=0}^{t-1}E^Q(G_t G_k|\phi_0)$$
$$+\alpha_0^2 E^Q\left[\left(\sum_{k=0}^{t-1}G_k\right)^2|\phi_0\right]$$
$$= h_0^2 u^t + 2\alpha_0 h_0\sum_{k=0}^{t-1}u^k v^{t-k}$$
$$+\alpha_0^2\left[\sum_{k=0}^{t-1}u^k + 2\sum_{k=0}^{t-1}\sum_{j=0}^{k-1}u^j v^{k-j}\right]$$
$$= h_0^2 u^t + 2\alpha_0 h_0\frac{v(u^t - v^t)}{u - v}$$
$$+\alpha_0^2\left[\frac{1-u^t}{1-u} + 2\frac{v}{u-v}\left(\frac{1-u^t}{1-u} - \frac{1-v^t}{1-v}\right)\right].$$

It follows that, as $t \to \infty$,

$$E^Q(h_t^2|\phi_0) \to \begin{cases} \frac{(1+v)\alpha_0^2}{(1-u)(1-v)} & \text{for } u < 1, \\ \infty & \text{for } u \geq 1. \end{cases}$$

The random variable ξ_t is leptokurtic if $E^Q(\xi_t^4) > 3[E^Q(\xi_t^2)]^2$. Recall that h_t is ϕ_{t-1}-measurable and $\xi_t/\sqrt{h_t}$ is a standard normal random variable.

$$E^Q(\xi_t^4) = E^Q\left[E^Q(\xi_t^4|\phi_{t-1})\right]$$
$$= E^Q\left\{h_t^2 E^Q\left[\left(\xi_t/\sqrt{h_t}\right)^4|\phi_{t-1}\right]\right\}$$
$$= 3E^Q(h_t^2).$$

The random variable ξ_t is clearly leptokurtic when $u \geq 1$. For $u < 1$,

$$E^Q(\xi_t^4) = 3\frac{(1+v)\alpha_0^2}{(1-u)(1-v)} = 3\frac{1-v^2}{1-u}\left[E^Q(\xi_t^2)\right]^2.$$

Since $v < u$ and $u < 1$, it follows that $(1 - v^2)/(1 - u) > 1$ and the proof is complete.

(iii) Using the conditional variance process in (3) with $p = 1$ and $q = 1$, the product of ξ_t and h_{t+1} can be written as

$$\frac{\xi_t}{\sqrt{h_t}}h_{t+1} = \alpha_0\frac{\xi_t}{\sqrt{h_t}} + \alpha_1\frac{\xi_t}{\sqrt{h_t}}\left(\xi_t - \lambda\sqrt{h_t}\right)^2 + \beta_1\frac{\xi_t}{\sqrt{h_t}}h_t.$$

Thus,

$$E^Q\left(\frac{\xi_t}{\sqrt{h_t}}h_{t+1}\middle|\phi_{t-1}\right) = \alpha_1 E^Q\left[\frac{\xi_t}{\sqrt{h_t}}\left(\xi_t - \lambda\sqrt{h_t}\right)^2\middle|\phi_{t-1}\right] = -2\lambda\alpha_1 h_t$$

and

$$\begin{aligned}\mathrm{Cov}^Q\left(\frac{\xi_t}{\sqrt{h_t}}, h_{t+1}\right) &= E^Q\left(\frac{\xi_t}{\sqrt{h_t}}, h_{t+1}\right)\\ &= E^Q\left[E^Q\left(\frac{\xi_t}{\sqrt{h_t}}, h_{t+1}\middle|\phi_{t-1}\right)\right]\\ &= E^Q(-2\lambda\alpha_1 h_t)\\ &= -2\lambda\alpha_0\alpha_1\left[1-(1+\lambda^2)\alpha_1-\beta_1\right]^{-1}.\end{aligned}$$

1 *The Garch process is a generalised version of the Arch by Engle (1982). The Garch (1,1) model was independently proposed by Taylor (1986).*

2 *The only Markovian Garch process is Garch (0,1) or Arch (1). It is well known that a non-Markovian univariate process can be converted into a Markovian vector process through a change in dimension. The statement should thus be understood with the usual interpretation.*

3 *Satchell and Timmermann's (1992) model was developed independently of Duan (1990). Amin and Ng (1993), on the other hand, developed their model along the line of Duan (1990) and pointed out a critical error in Theorem 2 of Duan (1990) and some subsequent versions.*

4 *See Theorem 1 of Bollerslev (1986). If the sum equals 1 in the case of the Garch(1,1) process, the process is referred to as the integrated Garch process. Nelson (1990) showed that the Igarch process is stationary and ergodic although the variance is unbounded. In fact, the Garch process may still be strictly stationary if the sum of α_is and β_is is greater than 1. The sufficient and necessary condition for its strict stationarity is related to the top Lyapunov exponent of a particular sequence of random matrices (see Bougerol and Picard, 1992).*

5 *The author is grateful to an anonymous reviewer for pointing out an error in an earlier version of this paper. The same error was also noted in Amin and Ng (1993).*

6 *Strictly speaking, the Garch option pricing model with the assumptions made in the article to ensure a constant interest rate can only be used for the valuation of individual equity options. The market portfolio (the S&P 100 index) is expected to be highly correlated with aggregate consumption. The market portfolio's return will therefore not follow a Garch process. The numerical results in this section should therefore be interpreted as if the estimated parameter values are for individual stocks. The author appreciates this comment made by an anonymous reviewer.*

BIBLIOGRAPHY

Amin, K., and V. Ng, 1993, "ARCH Processes and Option Valuation", Unpublished Manuscript, University of Michigan.

Black, F., 1975, "Fact and Fantasy in the Use of Options", *Financial Analysts Journal*, 31, pp. 36–41 and 61–72.

Black, F., and M. Scholes, 1973, "The Pricing of Options and Corporate Liabilities", *Journal of Political Economy*, 81, pp. 637-59.

Black, F., and M. Scholes, 1972, "The Valuation of Option Contracts and a Test of Market Efficiency", *Journal of Finance*, 27, pp. 399–417.

Bollerslev, T., 1986, "Generalized Autoregressive Conditional Heteroskedasticity", *Journal of Econometrics*, 31, pp. 307–27.

Bougerol, P., and N. Picard, 1992, "Stationarity of GARCH Processes and of Some Nonnegative Time Series", *Journal of Econometrics* 52, pp. 115–27.

Boyle, P., 1977, "Options: a Monte Carlo Approach", *Journal of Financial Economics* 4, pp. 323–38.

Brennan, M., 1979, "The Pricing of Contingent Claims in Discrete Time Models", *Journal of Finance*, 34, pp. 53–68.

Cox, J., 1975, "Notes on Option Pricing I: Constant Elasticity of Variance Diffusions", Unpublished Manuscript, Stanford University.

Duan, J.-C., 1990, "The GARCH Option Pricing Model," Unpublished Manuscript, McGill University.

Engle, R., 1982, "Autoregressive Conditional Heteroskedasticity with Estimates of the Variance of UK Inflation", *Econometrica*, 50, pp. 987–1008.

Engle, R., and C. Mustafa, 1992, "Implied ARCH Models from Options Prices", *Journal of Econometrics* 52, pp. 289-311.

Geske, R., 1979, "The Valuation of Compound Options", *Journal of Financial Economics* 7, pp. 63-81.

Glosten, L., R. Jagannathan and D. Runkle, 1993, "Relationship Between the Expected Value and the Volatility of the Nominal Excess Return on Stocks", *Journal of Finance*, 48, 5, pp. 1779-801

Gultekin, B., R. Rogalski and S. Tinic, 1982, "Option Pricing Model Estimates: Some Empirical Results", *Financial Management* 11, pp. 58-69.

Harrison, M., and D. Kreps, 1979, "Martingales and Arbitrage in Multiperiod Securities Markets", *Journal of Economic Theory* 20, pp. 381-408.

Harrison, M., and S. Pliska, 1981, "Martingales and Stochastic Integrals in the Theory of Continuous Trading", *Stochastic Processes and Their Applications* 11, p. 215-60.

Hull, J., and A. White, 1987, "The Pricing of Options on Assets with Stochastic Volatilities", *Journal of Finance* 42, pp. 281-300.

Johnson, H., and D. Shanno, 1987, "Option Pricing When the Variance is Changing", *Journal of Financial and Quantitative Analysis* 22, pp. 143-51.

Merton, R., 1976, "Option Pricing When Underlying Stock Returns are Discontinuous", *Journal of Financial Economics* 3, pp. 125-44.

Merton, R., 1973, "The Theory of Rational Option Pricing", *Bell Journal of Economics and Management Science* 4, pp. 141-83.

Nelson, D., 1991, "Conditional Heteroskedasticity in Asset Returns: A New Approach", *Econometrica* 59, pp. 347-70.

Nelson, D., 1990, "Stationarity and Persistence in the GARCH(1,1) Model", *Econometric Theory* 6, pp. 318-34.

Rubinstein, M., 1985, "Nonparametric Tests of Alternative Option Pricing Models Using All Reported Trades and Quotes on the 30 Most Active CBOE Option Classes from August 23, 1976 through August 31, 1978", *Journal of Finance* 40, pp. 455-80.

Rubinstein, M., 1983, "Displaced Diffusion Option Pricing", *Journal of Finance* 38, pp. 213-17.

Rubinstein, M., 1976, "The Valuation of Uncertain Income Streams and the Pricing of Options", *Bell Journal of Economics and Management Science* 7, pp. 407-25.

Satchell, S., and A. Timmermann, 1992, "Option Pricing with GARCH", Unpublished Manuscript, Birkbeck College, University of London.

Scott, L., 1987, "Option Pricing When the Variance Changes Randomly: Theory, Estimation, and an Application", *Journal of Financial and Quantitative Analysis* 22, pp. 419-38.

Sheikh, A., 1991, "Transaction Data Tests of S&P 100 Call Option Pricing", *Journal of Financial and Quantitative Analysis* 26, pp. 459-75.

Stein, E., and J. Stein, 1991, "Stock Price Distributions with Stochastic Volatility: An Analytic Approach", *Review of Financial Studies* 4, pp. 727-52; reprinted as Chapter 22 of the present volume.

Taylor, S., 1986, *Modelling Financial Time Series* Wiley, New York.

Whaley, R., 1982, "Valuation of American Call Options on Dividend-Paying Stocks", *Journal of Financial Economics* 10, pp. 29-58.

Wiggins, J., 1987, "Option Values Under Stochastic Volatility: Theory and Empirical Estimates", *Journal of Financial Economics* 19, pp. 351-72.

SMILES, SKEWS AND STOCHASTIC VOLATILITIES

Introduction

Robert Jarrow

This section looks at short cuts and new computational approaches for incorporating implied volatility (strike) smiles and (maturity) skews into option valuation, and at ways of using stochastic volatilities in risk analysis and risk management.

The first paper, by Emanuel Derman, Iraj Kani and Neil Chriss, concerns a new computational approach for incorporating smiles and skews into implied trees. An implied tree is a lattice in which the stochastic process's parameters are inverted, so that a given strike and maturity structure of option prices is matched by the theoretical values generated from the tree. Derman, Kani and Chriss generalise the standard implied binomial tree to a trinomial tree; that is, from a tree containing two branches at each node to one containing three. This added flexibility is useful for overcoming common difficulties encountered with implied binomial trees, such as the inability to match inconsistent (arbitrage violating) option prices, or the danger of obtaining implausible (discontinuous) local volatilities and distributions for the evolution of the stock price process.

Derman, Kani and Chriss start with a review, and then give a detailed description of their new theory for building a trinomial tree. This includes an analysis for incorporating a maturity-based implied volatility skew. They end with an excellent numerical example, useful for checking the new technique and understanding how the method works in practice.

Rather than developing a new option valuation formula as we saw in Section V, Charles Corrado and Tie Su give us a short cut for stochastic volatility option pricing. They have developed a procedure for incorporating an implied volatility smile into option prices, by applying the Jarrow and Rudd approximation (based on an Edgeworth series expansion) for extending the Black-Scholes formula to include random volatilities.

Corrado and Su illustrate this procedure using intraday prices of S&P 500 index options for the month of December 1993. First, they document the implied volatility smile bias in the Black-Scholes values. Then they apply the Jarrow and Rudd approximation, which modifies the Black-Scholes value to account for differences in skewness and kurtosis from the constant volatility process that the Black-Scholes model assumes. As expected, the Jarrow and Rudd model performs well when compared to Black-Scholes, flattening the volatility skew and producing more stable volatility estimates. The pricing of deep in-the-money and deep out-of-the-money options is significantly improved. Hedging differences between the two approaches are also discussed.

The next two papers investigate the use of stochastic volatilities in risk analysis and risk management. Robert Engle and Joshua Rosenberg explore the hedging of options in discrete time when the underlying asset's return follows a Garch-t process (a student-t distribution for the conditional density). Given that option prices can no longer be determined by arbitrage alone, some equilibrium argument must be invoked. Engle and Rosenberg use Monte Carlo simulation assuming risk neutrality under a constant interest rates assumption to price European options, as well as to compute hedge ratios and other greeks.

The technique is illustrated with price observations for four underlying assets: the S&P500 index, the Treasury bond futures index, a weighted exchange rate index, and a crude oil futures index. A Garch model is fitted for each underlying asset, using daily returns from June 1983 to May 1994 and maximum likelihood estimation.

Engle and Rosenberg compare Garch deltas to Black–Scholes deltas and Garch gammas to Black–Scholes gammas. They note substantial differences between them; Garch gammas, for example, are generally higher. The implication of these results is that with stochastic volatility models, delta neutral and gamma neutral portfolios will be misspecified unless the proper Garch quantities are employed.

The final paper, by Robert Whaley, shows how futures and options on the Chicago Board Options Exchange (CBOE) market volatility index (VIX) can be used for risk management. The VIX index is based on the implied volatilities of eight near-the-money, nearby and second nearby OEX options (options on the S&P 100 index), and so provides a good measure of a market volatility. The details of its construction are contained within the paper.

Whaley first explains how volatility index options and/or volatility index futures can be used to hedge the vega (volatility) risk in a portfolio of options. Second, he shows how volatility derivatives can also be used to hedge the vega risk of an individual option, if it is largely due to changes in market volatility. As such, this paper demonstrates the usefulness of the CBOE market volatility index futures and options contracts for eliminating volatility risk from a trader's option position.

25

Implied Trinomial Trees of the Volatility Smile*

Emanuel Derman, Iraj Kani and Neil Chriss
Goldman Sachs; Martingale Technologies

In options markets where there is a significant or persistent volatility smile, implied tree models can ensure the consistency of exotic options prices with the market prices of liquid standard options. Implied trees can be constructed in a variety of ways. Implied binomial trees are minimal: they have just enough parameters - node prices and transition probabilities - to fit the smile. Trinomial trees inherently have more parameters than binomial trees. We can use these additional parameters to choose conveniently the "state space" of all node prices in the trinomial tree, and let only the transition probabilities be constrained by market options prices. This freedom of state space provides a flexibility that is sometimes advantageous in matching trees to smiles. A judiciously chosen state space is needed to obtain a reasonable fit to the smile. We discuss a simple method for building "skewed" state spaces which fit typical index option smiles rather well.

Binomial trees are perhaps the most commonly used machinery for options pricing. A standard Cox-Ross-Rubinstein (CRR) (1979) binomial tree consists of a set of nodes, representing possible future stock prices, with a constant logarithmic spacing between these nodes. This spacing is a measure of the future stock price volatility, itself assumed to be constant in the CRR framework.

In the continuous limit, a CRR tree with an "infinite" number of time steps to expiration represents a continuous risk-neutral evolution of the stock price with constant volatility. Option prices computed using the CRR tree will converge to the Black-Scholes (1973) continuous-time results in this limit.

The constancy of volatility in the Black-Scholes theory and its corresponding binomial framework cannot easily be reconciled with the observed structure of implied volatilities for traded options. In most index options markets, the implied Black-Scholes volatilities vary with both strike and expiration. This variation, known as the implied volatility "smile," is currently a significant and persistent feature of most global index option markets. But the constant local volatility assumption in the Black-Scholes theory and the CRR tree leads to the absence of a volatility smile, at least as long as market frictions are ignored.

Implied tree theories extend the Black-Scholes theory to make it consistent with the shape of the smile.[1] They achieve this consistency by extracting an implied evolution for the stock price in equilibrium from market prices of liquid standard options on the underlying stock. Implemented discretely, implied binomial trees are constructed so that local volatility (or spacing) varies from node to node, making the tree flexible, so that market prices of all standard options can be matched. There is a unique implied binomial tree that fits option prices in any market, because binomial trees have the min-

* *This paper was first published in* The Journal of Derivatives, *Summer (1996). Reprinted with permission from Institutional Investor, Inc.. To order a subscription, or for other information, please call (212) 224 3185. The authors are grateful to Barbara Dunn for her careful review of this manuscript and to Alex Bergier for his helpful comments.*

imal number of parameters, just enough to match the smile.[2]

The uniqueness of implied binomial trees is usually desirable. Sometimes, however, it becomes disadvantageous, because the uniqueness leaves little room for compromise or adjustment when the mechanism of matching tree parameters to market options prices runs into difficulties. These difficulties can arise from inconsistent and/or arbitrage-violating market options prices, which make a consistent tree impossible.

Or, difficulties can arise in a more qualitative sense that, even though the constructed tree is consistent, its local volatility and probability distributions are jagged and implausible. In these cases, one prefers to obtain trees whose local distributions are more plausible, even though they may not match every single market options price.[3]

One way to make implied tree structures more flexible is to consider using implied trinomial (or multinomial) trees. These trees inherently possess more parameters than binomial trees. In the continuous limit, these parameters are superfluous and have no effect, and many different multinomial trees can all converge to the same continuous evolution process. But, for a finite number of tree periods, the parameters in any particular tree can be tuned to impose plausible smoothness constraints on the local distributions, and some trees may be more appropriate than others.

1. Schematic representation of standard CRR binomial tree and implied binomial tree

(a)

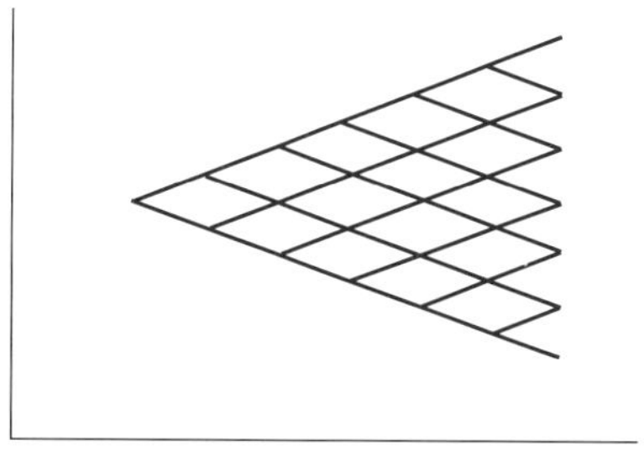

(b)

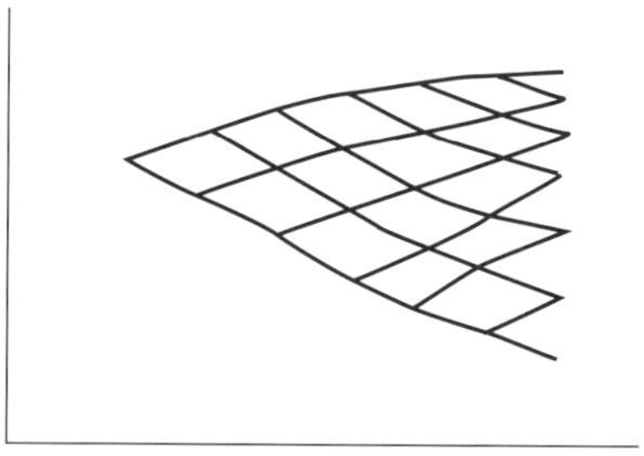

The use of trinomial trees for building implied models has been suggested by Dupire (1994). The extra parameters in trinomial trees give us the freedom to choose the price (that is, the location in "price space") at each node in the tree. This freedom to pre-specify the "state space" can be quite advantageous if used judiciously.

After an appropriate choice of the state space has been made, the transition probabilities can be iteratively calculated to ensure that all European standard options (with strikes and maturities coinciding with the tree nodes) will have theoretical values which match their market prices. We will show the equations to perform the iteration are very similar to those derived for implied binomial trees.

Implied theories

Implied theories assume that the stock (or index) price follows a process whose instantaneous (local) volatility $\sigma(S,t)$ varies only with spot price and time.[4] Under this assumption, since all uncertainty in the local volatility is derived from uncertainty in the stock price, we can hedge options using the stock, and so, as in the traditional Black-Scholes theory, valuation remains preference-free.

To do this we need to know the functional form of the local volatility function. It has been shown by Derman and Kani (1994), and separately by Dupire (1994) and Rubinstein (1994), that in principle we can determine the local volatility function directly from the market prices of liquid options.

Once the local volatility function is determined, all future evolution of the stock price S is known. We can price any option using this evolution process, secure in the knowledge that our pricing model is completely consistent with the prices of all liquid options with the same underlier. Therefore, implied theories provide us with a method for moving directly from the market option prices to the underlying equilibrium price process.

An understanding of the logic behind implied trinomial trees is necessary as a starting point for the construction of implied trinomial trees. An implied binomial tree is a discrete version of a continuous evolution process that fits current options prices, in much the same way as the standard CRR binomial tree is a discrete version of the Black-Scholes constant volatility process.[5]

Figure 1 shows a schematic representation of an implied binomial tree compared to a standard CRR tree. The node spacing is constant throughout a standard CRR tree; in an implied binomial tree it varies with market level and time, as specified by the local volatility function $\sigma(S,t)$.

We use induction to build an implied tree with levels Δt apart. Assume the first n levels that match the implied volatilities of all options with all strikes out to that time period have already been constructed. Figure 2 shows the nth level of the tree at time t_n, with n implied tree nodes and their already known stock prices s_i. All notation is the same as in Derman and Kani (1994), which describes the tree construction in greater detail.

We want to determine the nodes of the $(n + 1)$th level at time t_{n+1}. There are $n + 1$ nodes to fix, with $n + 1$ corresponding unknown stock prices S_i. Figure 2 shows the ith node at level n. It has a known stock price s_i and evolves into an "up" node with price S_{i+1} and a "down" node with price S_i at level $n + 1$, where the forward price corresponding to s_i is $F_i = s_i e^{(r-\delta)}\Delta t$, where r is the riskless interest rate, and δ is the continuously compounded dividend yield.

We call p_i the probability of making a transition into the up node. We call λ_i the Arrow-Debreu price at node (n,i); it is computed by forward induction as the sum over all paths, from the root of the tree to node (n,i), of the product of the risklessly-discounted transition probabilities at each node in each path leading to node (n,i). All λ_i at level n are known, because earlier tree nodes and their transition probabilities have already been implied out to level n.

There are $2n + 1$ parameters that define the transition from the nth to the $(n + 1)$th level of the tree, namely the $n + 1$ stock prices S_i and the n transition probabilities p_i. We need to determine them using the smile.

We imply the nodes at the $(n + 1)$th level by using the tree to calculate the theoretical values of $2n$ known quantities - the values of n forwards and n options, all expiring at time t_{n+1} - and requiring that these theoretical values match the interpolated market values. This provides $2n$ equations for these $2n + 1$ parameters. We use the one remaining degree of freedom to make the centre of our tree coincide with the centre of the standard CRR tree that has constant local volatility.

The implied binomial tree is risk-neutral. Consequently, the expected value, one period later, of the stock at any node (n,i) must be its known forward price. This leads to the equation

$$F_i = p_i S_{i+1} + (1 - p_i) S_i \qquad (1)$$

where F_i is known. There are n of these forward equations, one for each i.

2. Constructing the (n+1)th level of the implied binomial tree

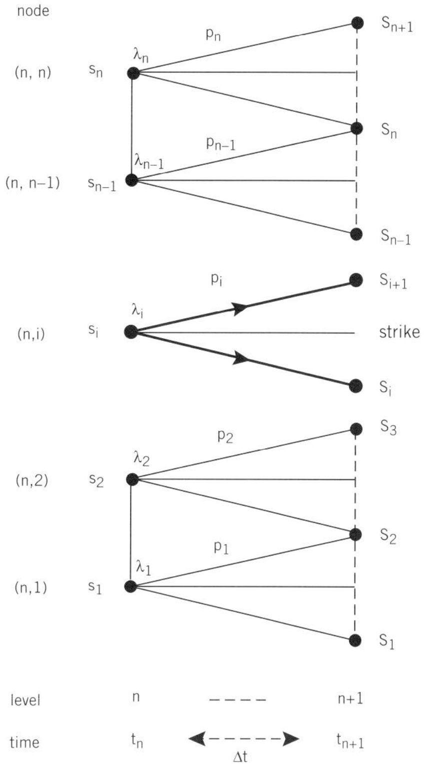

The second set of equations expresses the values of the n independent options, one for each strike s_i equal to the known stock prices at the nth level, that expire at the $(n + 1)$th level.[6] Let $C(s_i,t_{n+1})$ and $P(s_i,t_{n+1})$, respectively, be the known market values for a call and put struck today (ie at t_0) at s_i and expiring at t_{n+1}. We know the values of each of these calls and puts from interpolating the smile curve at time t_{n+1}. Then

$$C(K,t_{n+1}) = e^{-r\Delta t}\sum_{j=1}^{n}\left\{\lambda_j p_j + \lambda_{j+1}(1 - p_{j+1})\right\} \times \max(S_{j+1} - K, 0).$$

When the strike K equals s_i, the contribution from the transition to the first in-the-money up node can be separated from the other contributions, which, using (1), can be rewritten in terms of the known Arrow-Debreu prices, the known stock prices s_i, and the known forwards F_i, so that

$$e^{r\Delta t}C(s_i,t_{n+1}) = \lambda_i p_i (S_{i+1} - s_i) + \sum_{j=i+1}^{n}\lambda_j (F_j - s_i). \qquad (2)$$

Since we know both F_i and $C(s_i,t_{n+1})$ from the smile, we can simultaneously solve (1) and (2) for S_{i+1} and the transition probability p_i in terms of S_i and other quantities known from the previously determined levels.

$$S_{i+1} = \frac{S_i\left[e^{r\Delta t}C(s_i, t_{n+1}) - \Sigma\right] - \lambda_i s_i(F_i - S_i)}{\left[e^{r\Delta t}C(s_i, t_{n+1}) - \Sigma\right] - \lambda_i(F_i - S_i)} \quad (3)$$

$$p_i = \frac{F_i - S_i}{S_{i+1} - S_i} \quad (4)$$

where Σ denotes the sum

$$\sum_{j=i+1}^{n} \lambda_j(F_j - s_i).$$

We can use these equations iteratively to find the S_{i+1} and p_i for all nodes above the centre of the tree, starting from the known central node. In this way we imply the upper half of each level.

In a similar way we can fix all the nodes below the central node at this level by using known put prices. The analogous formula that determines a lower node's stock price from a known upper one is

$$S_i = \frac{S_{i+1}\left[e^{r\Delta t}P(s_i, t_{n+1}) - \Sigma\right] + \lambda_i s_i(F_i - S_{i+1})}{\left[e^{r\Delta t}P(s_i, t_{n+1}) - \Sigma\right] + \lambda_i(F_i - S_{i+1})} \quad (5)$$

where here Σ denotes the sum

$$\sum_{j=1}^{i-1} \lambda_j(s_i - F_j)$$

over all nodes below the one with price s_i at which the put is struck. If you know the value of the stock price at the central node, equations (4) and (5) can be used to find, node by node, the values of the stock prices and transition probabilities at all the lower nodes.

By repeating this process at each level, we can use the smile to find the transition probabilities and node values for the entire tree. If we do this for small enough time steps between successive levels of the tree, using interpolated call and put values from the smile curve, we obtain a good discrete approximation to the implied risk-neutral stock evolution process.

Aside from the choice of the central trunk, the implied binomial tree is uniquely determined from forward and option prices. As mentioned above, sometimes we desire more flexibility in setting up the theory discretely. The need for flexibility reflects the common-sense feeling that, to be considered plausible, the local volatilities, transition probabilities and probability distributions generated by the implied tree should vary as smoothly as possible with market level and time across the tree.

This is particularly important when the available options market prices are inaccurate because they reflect bids made at an earlier market level, or are inefficient because of various market frictions that may not be included in the model. In these cases we would prefer to start by using "smooth" trees for valuing and hedging complex options.

3. Single time step of a trinomial tree

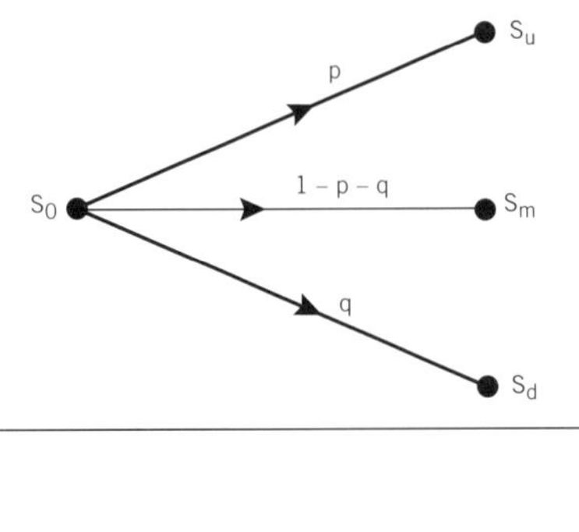

Trinomial trees

One way to introduce more flexibility is to use trinomial (or higher multinomial) tree structures for building implied tree models. Trinomial trees provide another discrete representation of stock price movement, analogous to binomial trees.[7]

Figure 3 illustrates a single time step in a trinomial tree. The stock price at the beginning of the time step is S_0. During this time step the stock price can move to one of three nodes: with probability p to the *up* node, value S_u; with probability q to the *down* node, value S_d; and with probability $1 - p - q$ to the middle node, value S_m. At the end of the time step, there are five unknown parameters: the two probabilities p and q, and the three node prices S_u, S_m and S_d.

In a risk-neutral trinomial tree, the expected value of the stock at the end of the period must be its known forward price, $F_0 = S_0 e^{(r-\delta)}\Delta t$, where δ is the dividend yield. Therefore:

$$pS_u + qS_d + (1 - p - q)S_m = F_0. \quad (6)$$

If the stock price volatility during this time period is σ, then the node prices and transition probabilities satisfy:

$$p(S_u - F_0)^2 + q(S_d - F_0)^2 + (1 - p - q)(S_m - F_0)^2 = F_0^2\sigma^2\Delta t + O(\Delta t). \quad (7)$$

where $O(\Delta t)$ denotes terms of higher order than Δt. Different discretisations of risk-neutral trinomial trees have different higher order terms in (7).

Of the five parameters needed to fix the whole tree, (6) and (7) provide only two constraints, and so we have three more parameters than are necessary to satisfy them. By contrast, for implied binomial trees, all unknown parameters were determined by the constraints. As a result, we can construct many "economically equivalent" trinomial trees which, in the limit as the time spacing becomes very small, represent the same continuous theory.

Appendix A discusses a few different ways for building constant volatility trinomial trees. When volatilities are not constant, a common method is to choose the stock prices at every node and attempt to satisfy the two constraints through the choice of the transition probabilities.

This method of initially choosing the state space of prices for the trinomial tree, and then solving for the transition probabilities, is familiar in most applications of the finite-difference method. We must make a judicious choice of the state space in order to ensure that the transition probabilities remain between 0 and 1, a necessary condition for the discrete world represented by the tree to preclude arbitrage.

Figure 4 gives schematic representations for both standard and implied trinomial trees. The standard trinomial tree represents a constant volatility world and is constructed out of a regular mesh. The implied trinomial tree has an irregular mesh conforming to the variation of local volatility with level and time across the tree.

To fix the nodes and probabilities, we need the forward prices and option prices corresponding to strikes and expiration at all tree nodes. In contrast to the construction of an implied binomial tree, here we have total freedom over the choice of the state space of an implied trinomial tree. In choosing a state space, we eliminate three of the five unknown parameters corresponding to the evolution of each node (see Figure 3), leaving only the transition probabilities to solve for.

4. Schematic representation of standard trinomial tree and implied trinomial tree

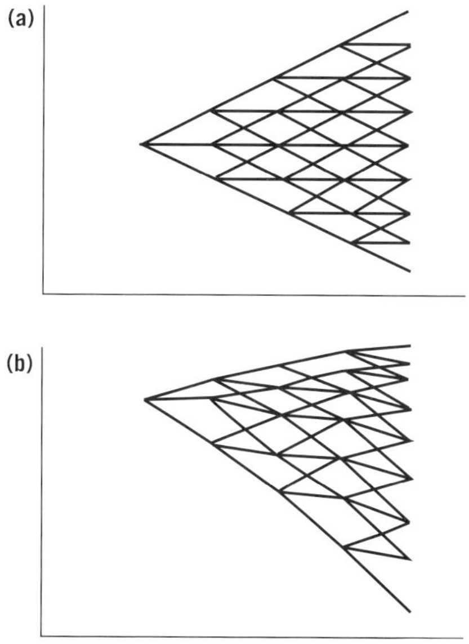

5. Transition probabilities from nth to (n+1)th level of an implied trinomial tree

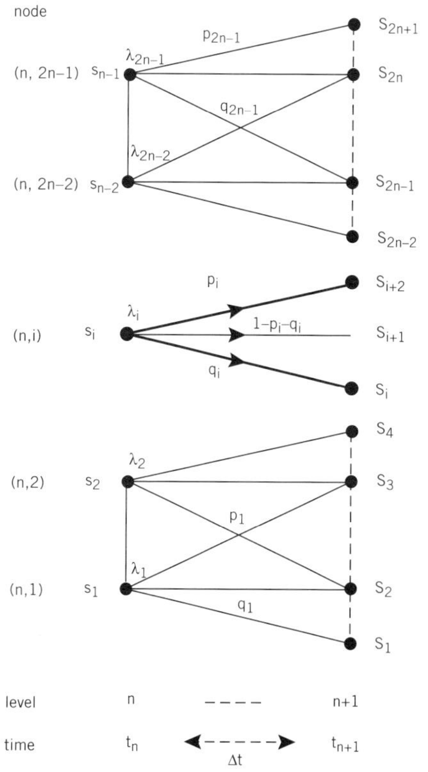

Constructing the implied trinomial tree

We will construct our implied trinomial tree model in two stages. First, we judiciously choose a state space, ie specify the position of every tree node. Next, knowing the location of every node, we use market forward and option prices to calculate the transition probabilities between the nodes.

Suppose that we have already fixed the state space of the implied trinomial tree. Figure 5 shows the nth and $(n + 1)$th levels of the tree. We will use induction to infer the transition probabilities p_i and q_i for all tree nodes (n,i) at each tree level n. Our notation and treatment follows the Derman and Kani (1994) binomial tree construction.

Since the implied trinomial tree is risk-neutral, the expected value of the stock at the node (n,i) at the later time t_{n+1}, must be the known forward price of that node. This gives one relationship between the unknown transition probabilities and known stock and forward prices:

$$p_i S_{i+2} + (1 - p_i - q_i)S_{i+1} + q_i S_i = F_i. \qquad (8)$$

Let $C(S_{i+1},t_{n+1})$ and $P(S_{i+1},t_{n+1})$, respectively, denote today's market price for a standard call and put option struck at S_{i+1} and expiring at time t_{n+1}. We obtain the values of these options by interpolating the smile surface at various strike and time points corresponding to the implied tree nodes.

The trinomial tree value of a call option struck at K and expiring at t_{n+1} is the sum over all nodes $(n + 1,j)$ of the discounted probability of reaching that node multiplied by the call payoff there. Hence

$$C(K,t_{n+1}) = e^{-r\Delta t}\sum_{j=1}^{2n+2}\times \left\{\lambda_{j-2}p_{j-2} + \lambda_{j-1}\left(1 - p_{j-1} - q_{j-1}\right) + \lambda_j q_j\right\} \max\left(S_j - K, 0\right) \qquad (9)$$

where $\lambda_j = 0$ for $j < 0$ and $j > 2n - 1$. If we set the strike K to the value S_{i+1}, the stock price at the node $(n + 1,i + 1)$, then we can rearrange the terms and use (9) to write the call price in terms of known Arrow-Debreu prices, known stock prices, known forward prices, and a contribution from up-transition probability p_i to the first in-the-money node:

$$e^{r\Delta t}C(S_{i+1},t_{n+1}) = \lambda_i p_i\left(S_{i+2} - S_{i+1}\right) + \sum_{j=i+1}^{2n}\lambda_j\left(F_j - S_{i+1}\right). \qquad (10)$$

The only unknown in (10) is the transition probability p_i, since the stock prices are already fixed by the choice of state space, and the option price $C(S_{i+1},t_{n+1})$ and the forward prices F_i are known from the smile. We can solve this equation for p_i:

$$p_i = \frac{e^{r\Delta t}C(S_{i+1},t_{n+1}) - \sum_{j=i+1}^{2n}\lambda_j\left(F_j - S_{i+1}\right)}{\lambda_i\left(S_{i+2} - S_{i+1}\right)}. \qquad (11)$$

6. State space of a trinomial tree with constant volatility of 15%

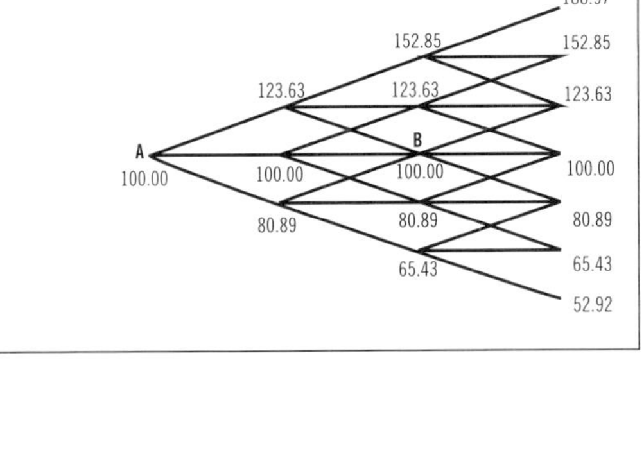

Using (8) we can solve for the down transition probability q_i:

$$q_i = \frac{F_i - p_i\left(S_{i+2} - S_{i+1}\right) - S_{i+1}}{S_i - S_{i+1}}. \qquad (12)$$

We use put option prices $P(S_{i+1},t_{n+1})$ to determine the transition probabilities from all the nodes below (and including) the centre node $(n + 1,n)$ at time t_n. This leads to the equation

$$q_i = \frac{e^{r\Delta t}P(S_{i+1},t_{n+1}) - \sum_{j=1}^{i-1}\lambda_j\left(S_{i+1} - F_j\right)}{\lambda_i\left(S_{i+1} - S_i\right)} \qquad (13)$$

for q_i and, using (8), the following equation for p_i:

$$p_i = \frac{F_i + q_i\left(S_{i+1} - S_i\right) - S_{i+1}}{S_{i+2} - S_{i+1}} \qquad (14)$$

We can now use (7) to find the local volatility σ at each node.

A detailed example

To illustrate the construction of an implied trinomial tree, we assume that the current index level is 100, the dividend yield is 5% per year, and the annually compounded riskless interest rate is 10% for all maturities. We also assume that implied volatility of an at-the-money European call is 15%, for all expirations, and that implied volatility increases (decreases) 0.5 percentage points with every 10 point drop (rise) in the strike price. To keep our example simple, we choose the state space of our implied trinomial model to coincide with nodes of a three-year, three-period, 15% (constant) volatility CRR-type, trinomial tree, as shown in Figure 6.

The method used to construct this state space is described in Figure 14(a) in Appendix A. The first node, at time $t_0 = 0$, is labelled A in Figure 6 and it has a price $S_A = 100$, equal to today's spot price. All the central nodes $(i + 1,i)$ in this tree also have the same price as this node. The next three nodes, at time $t_1 = 1$, have prices $S_1 = 80.89$, $S_2 = 100$ and $S_3 = 123.63$, respectively. These values are found using the equation

$$S_{1,3} = S\exp\left(\mp\sigma\sqrt{2\Delta t}\right)$$

as discussed in Appendix A.

We can determine the up and down transition probabilities p_A and q_A, corresponding to node A, using (13) and (14) with $e^{r\Delta t} = 1.1$ and $\lambda_A = 1.0$. Then

$$q_A = \frac{1.1P(S_2,t_1) - \Sigma}{1.0(100 - 80.89)}.$$

$P(S_2,t_1)$ is the calculated value of a put option, struck at $S_2 = 100$ and expiring one year from now. From the smile, the implied volatility of this option is 15%. We calculate its price using a constant volatility discrete trinomial tree with the same state space, and find it to be \$3.091. The summation term Σ in the numerator is zero in this case because there are no nodes with price higher than S_3 at time t_1. Combining these we find $q_A = 0.178$.

The one-period forward price corresponding to node A is $F_A = Se^{(r-\delta)\Delta t} = 104.50$. Equation (14) then gives the value of p_A:

$$p_A = \left(104.5 + 0.178(100 - 80.89) - 100.00\right) / \left(123.63 - 100.00\right) = 0.334.$$

Since probabilities add to 1, the middle transition probability is equal to $1 - p_A - q_A = 0.488$.

The Arrow-Debreu prices corresponding to each of the three nodes at time t_1 are defined to be the (total) discounted probabilities that the stock price reaches at that node. For these nodes the Arrow-Debreu prices turn out to be just the transition probabilities divided by $e^{r\Delta t}$. The implied local volatility at node A is calculated using (7):

$$\sigma_A = \left[0.334(123.63 - 104.5)^2 + 0.488(100 - 104.5)^2 + 0.178(80.89 - 104.5)^2\right]^{1/2} = 14.6\%.$$

The difference between the 14.6% implied local volatility and the 15% implied volatility assumed for this option arises from the higher order terms in (7), and will vanish as the time spacing approaches zero.

As another example let us look at node B in year 2 of Figure 6. The stock price at this node is $S_B = 123.63$, whose forward price one period later is $F_B = 129.19$. From this node, the stock can move to one of three future nodes at time $t_3 = 3$, with prices $S_4 = 100$, $S_5 = 123.63$ and $S_6 = 152.85$. We can apply (10) and (11) to find the up and down transition probabilities from this node.

Then using $\lambda_B = 0.292$ we find

$$p_B = \frac{1.1C(S_5,t_3) - \Sigma}{0.292(152.85 - 123.63)}.$$

The value of a call option, struck at 123.63 and expiring at Year 3 is $C(S_5,t_3) = \$4.947$, corresponding to the implied volatility of 13.81% interpolated from the smile. There is a single node above node B whose forward price $F_5 = 159.73$ contributes to the summation term Σ, giving $\Sigma = 0.0825 \times (159.73 - 123.63) = 2.978$. Putting this back into the above equation we find $p_B = 0.289$. The down transition probability q_B is then calculated as

$$q_B = \frac{129.19 - 0.289(152.86 - 123.63) - 123.63}{100 - 123.63} = 0.122.$$

Also from (7) we find the implied local volatility at this node is $\sigma_B = 13.6\%$.

Figure 7 shows the full solution to the problem, including the implied transition probabilities, Arrow-Derbreu prices, and local volatilities for every node.

7. Up- and down-transition probability trees, Arrow-Debreu and local volatility tree

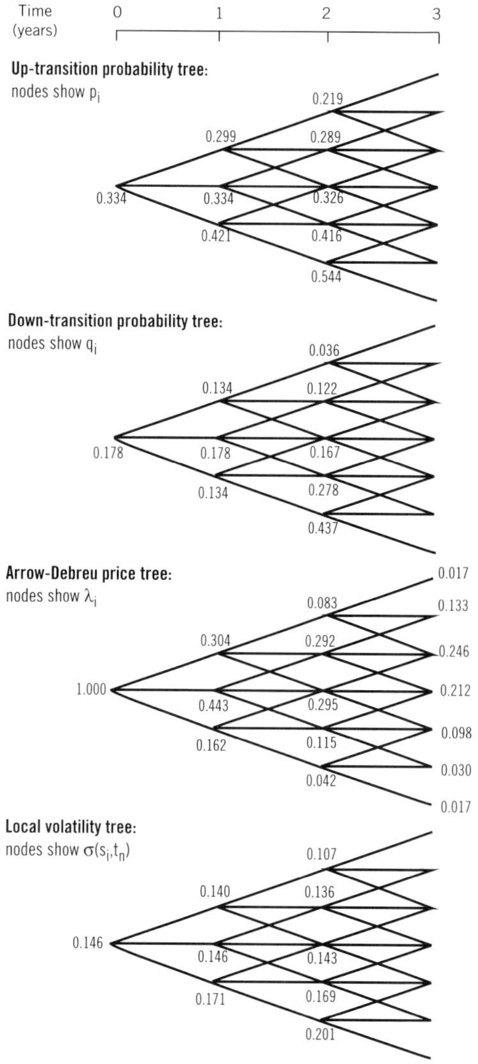

WHAT CAN GO WRONG?

The transition probabilities in (11)-(14) for any node must lie between 0 and 1. Otherwise the implied tree allows riskless arbitrages, which are

8. Negative transition probabilities for any node whose forward price does not lie between S_i and S_{i+2}

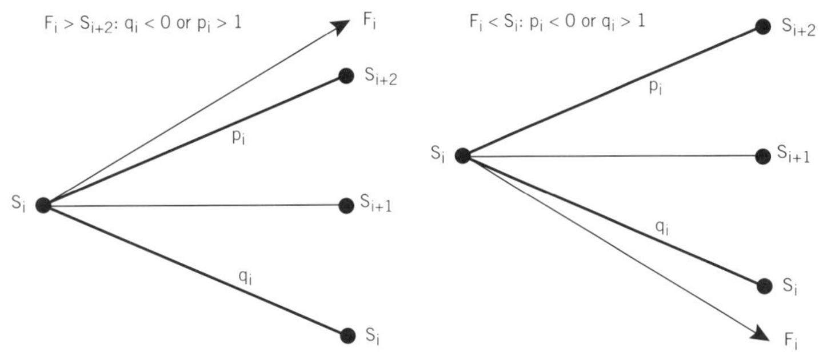

inconsistent with rational options prices.

For implied trinomial trees, there are two possible causes for negative probability at a node. First, the forward price F_i of a node (n,i) may fall outside the range S_i to S_{i+2} as illustrated in Figure 8. In that case, the forward condition of (8) cannot be satisfied with all transition probabilities lying between 0 and 1.

It is usually not difficult to avoid these types of situations by making an appropriate choice for the state space of the trinomial tree. We must make sure that our choice of state space does not allow any violations of the forward price condition, as shown in Figure 8.

The second cause of having negative probabilities relates to the magnitude of local volatility at an implied tree node. For instance, an especially large (small) value for the call option $C(S_{i+1},t_{n+1})$ in (11) would imply a large (small) value of local volatility at s_i. Having fixed the position of all the nodes, it may not be possible to obtain such extreme values of local volatility with probabilities between 0 and 1.

In these cases we must discard the option price which produces the unacceptable probabilities, and replace it with another option price of our choice. In doing so, we must maintain the forward condition at every node of the tree. This is always possible when we are working with a state space in which the forward price violations of Figure 8 do not occur, as our next example illustrates.

For our second example, we assume that the implied volatility of an at-the-money European call is 15% and that implied volatility increases (decreases) one percentage point with every 10 point drop (rise) in the strike price. This skew is twice as steep as in our previous example. Using the same state space (ie the 15% constant-volatility CRR-type trinomial tree) as used in Figure 6, we now find negative transition probabilities at nodes A, B and C of Figure 9.

9. Replacing negative probabilities

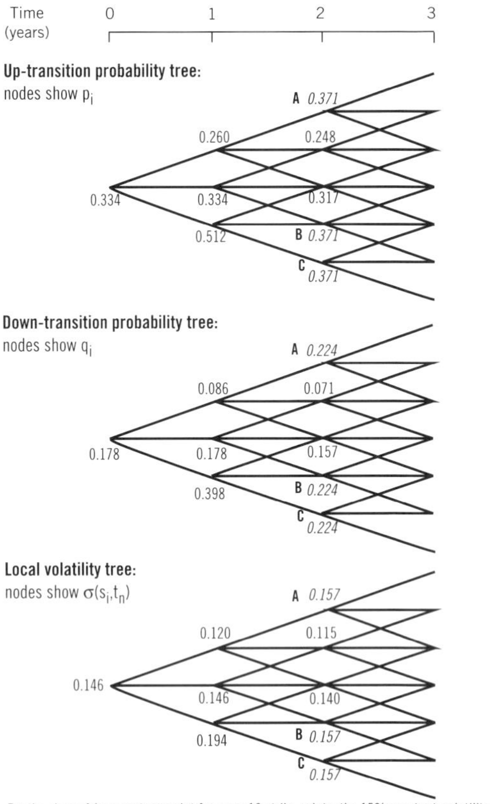

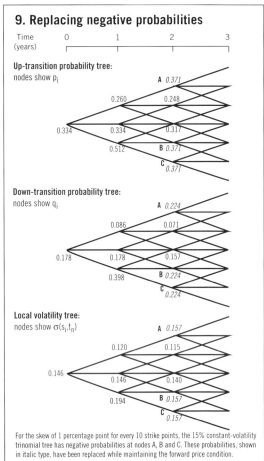

For the skew of 1 percentage point for every 10 strike points, the 15% constant-volatility trinomial tree has negative probabilities at nodes A, B and C. These probabilities, shown in italic type, have been replaced while maintaining the forward price condition.

There are an infinite number of ways of replacing negative probabilities with probabilities lying between 0 and 1 so as to satisfy the forward condition. For example, since we work with state spaces where the forward price condition $S_i < F_i < S_{i+2}$ holds at every tree node, we can always choose the value of middle transition probability to be zero (essentially reducing the node to a binomial node) and set the up and down transition probabilities to $p_i = (F_i - S_i)/(S_{i+2} - S_i)$ and $q_i = 1 - p_i$ respectively.

In Figure 9 we use an alternative method of correcting negative probabilities where, if $S_{i+1} < F_i < S_{i+2}$, we set

$$p_i = \frac{1}{2}\left[\frac{F_i - S_{i+1}}{S_{i+2} - S_{i+1}} + \frac{F_i - S_i}{S_{i+2} - S_i}\right]$$

and

$$q_i = \frac{1}{2}\left[\frac{S_{i+2} - F_i}{S_{i+2} - S_i}\right]$$

and, if $S_i < F_i < S_{i+1}$, we set

$$p_i = \frac{1}{2}\left[\frac{F_i - S_i}{S_{i+2} - S_i}\right]$$

and

$$q_i = \frac{1}{2}\left[\frac{S_{i+2} - F_i}{S_{i+2} - S_i} + \frac{S_{i+1} - F_i}{S_{i+1} - S_i}\right].$$

In either case the middle probability is equal to $1 - p_i - q_i$.

CONSTRUCTING THE STATE SPACE FOR THE IMPLIED TRINOMIAL TREE

Regular state spaces with uniform mesh sizes are usually adequate for constructing implied trinomial tree models when implied volatility varies slowly with strike and expiration. But if volatility varies significantly with strike or time to expiration, it may be necessary to choose a state space whose mesh size (or node spacing) changes significantly with time and stock level.

Figure 10 shows a more appropriate choice of state space in which the negative probabilities in the above example do not occur and there is no need for probability correction. This state space is "skewed," with spacing between the nodes at the same time point decreasing with stock level. This helps the state space fit the market's negative volatility skew better. The results are shown in Figure 11.

The implied trinomial tree model constructed using this skewed state space has no negative probabilities, fits the option market prices accurately, and generates reasonably smooth values for local volatility at different stock and time points.

One way to construct trinomial state spaces with proper skew and term structure is to build it in the following two stages:

❑ First, assume all interest rates (and dividends) are zero and build a regular trinomial lattice with constant time spacing Δt and logarithmic level spacing ΔS. Any constant volatility trinomial tree corresponding to a typical market implied volatility is an example of this type of lattice (see Appendix A). Then modify Δt at different times and, subsequently, ΔS at different stock levels until the lattice captures the basic term-and skew- structures of local volatility in the market.

❑ Next, if there are forward price violations in any of the nodes, in the sense of Figure 8, rescale all the node prices along the forward curve by multiplying all node prices in the zero-rate tree at time t_i by the growth factor $e^{(r-\delta)t_i}$.[8] This effectively removes all forward price violations.

Figure 12 shows the steps described above. Panel A depicts a regular state space with equal time and price steps. In the state space of Panel B, the time steps increase with time (corresponding to annualised local volatility that falls over

10. Skewed choice for state space of implied trinomial tree model for second example

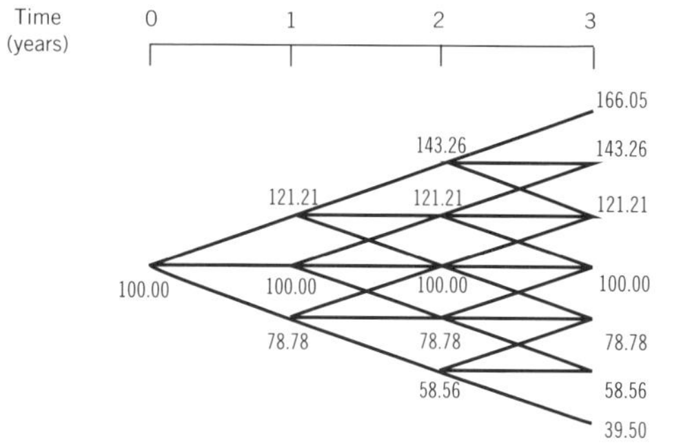

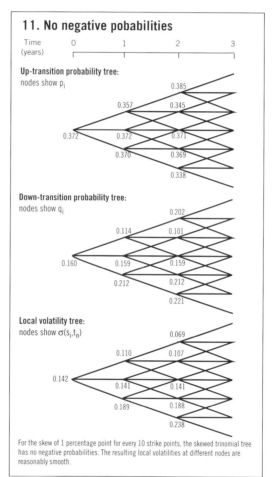

11. No negative pobabilities

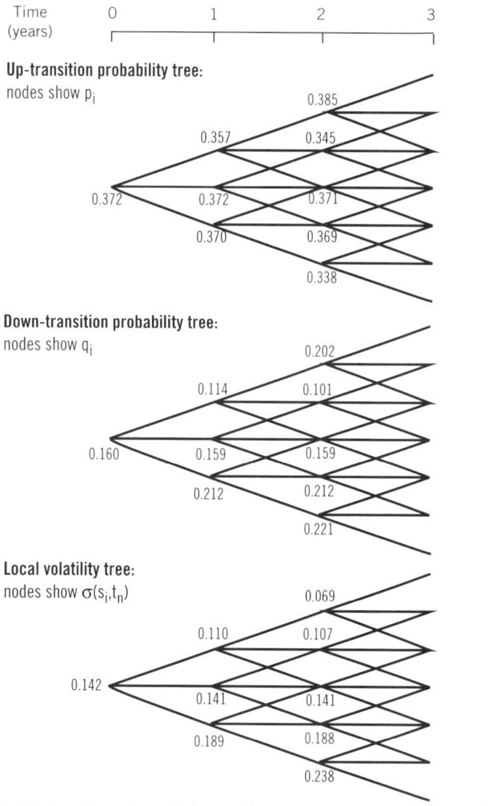

For the skew of 1 percentage point for every 10 strike points, the skewed trinomial tree has no negative probabilities. The resulting local volatilities at different nodes are reasonably smooth.

12. Constructing state space of implied trinomial tree model

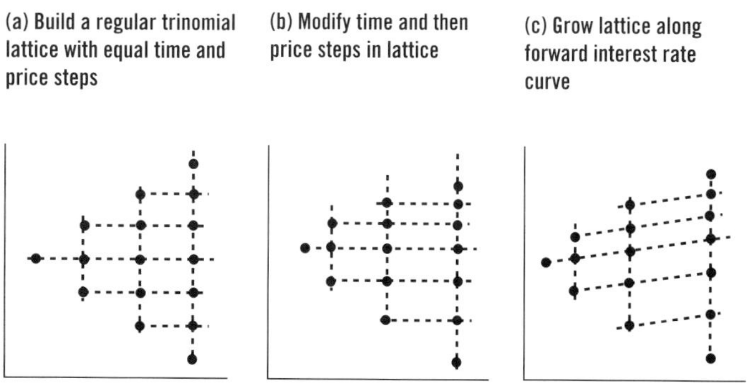
(a) Build a regular trinomial lattice with equal time and price steps
(b) Modify time and then price steps in lattice
(c) Grow lattice along forward interest rate curve

time), and price steps decrease with stock price (corresponding to volatility that increases as stock prices fall). In Panel C, the forward growth factor has been applied to all the nodes to ensure that no forward price violations remain. The resulting state space in this figure is more suitable for a market with significant (inverted) term-structure and (negative) skew-structure. Some of the details of this type of construction are provided in Appendix B.

We must point out that, no matter what choice of state space is made, we may not be able to fit all market options prices with probabilities lying between zero and one. In that case, as long as our choice does not violate the forward price condition at any node, we choose to replace the option prices that produce these negative probabilities.

In this way, even though we give up fitting the option price at some of the implied tree nodes, we fit the forward prices with transition probabilities which lie between zero and one at every node. Generally, the fewer ad hoc corrections we introduce in our implied tree, the better it will fit the smile.

We have described some simple choices for correcting unacceptable transition probabilities. Other types of replacement strategies may involve keeping local volatilities or distributions as smooth as possible across the tree nodes. One strategy is to try fitting the probabilities to the local volatility at the previous node before applying a more naive correction like those discussed. Other more complicated strategies require use of optimisation over the set of possible corrections and are more difficult to implement.

Using implied trinomial trees

Once an implied trinomial tree has been constructed to match the volatility smile, it can be used in the same way as standard binomial or trinomial trees. Hedge ratios of standard options can be calculated, as well as other sensitivity ratios such gamma and theta by comparing option values at different nodes on the same tree. By imposing different boundary conditions, exotic options (such as barrier options) can be valued consistent with the smile.

Appendix A

CONSTRUCTING CONSTANT-VOLATILITY TRINOMIAL TREES

There are several methods for constructing constant volatility trinomial trees that can serve as initial state spaces for implied trees. The different methods described here will all converge to the same theory, ie the constant-volatility Black-Scholes theory, in the continuous limit. In this sense, we can view them as equivalent discretisations of the constant volatility diffusion process.

Figure 13 shows two common methods for building binomial trees. There are in general an

infinite number of (equivalent) binomial trees, all representing the same discrete constant volatility world, due to freedom in the choice of overall growth of the price at tree nodes (not to be confused with the stock's risk-neutral growth rate). If we multiply all the node prices of a binomial tree by some constant (and reasonably small) growth factor, we will end up with another binomial tree which has different (positive) probabilities but represents the same continuous theory.

The familiar Cox-Ross-Rubinstein (CRR) binomial tree has the property that all nodes with same spatial index have the same price. This makes CRR tree look regular in both spatial and temporal directions.

The Jarrow-Rudd (JR, 1983) binomial tree has the property that all probabilties are equal to 1/2. This property makes the JR tree a natural discretisation for the Brownian motion. The JR tree does not grow precisely along the forward risk-free interest rate curve, but we can just as easily construct binomial trees which have this property.[9]

We have even more freedom when it comes to building constant volatility trinomial trees. Figure 14 illustrates three methods for doing so. The first two are based on the fact that we can view two steps of a binomial tree in combination as a single step of a trinomial tree. Panel A uses a CRR-type binomial tree to do so, while Panel B

13. Two equivalent methods for building a constant-volatility binomial tree

$S_u = Se^{\sigma\sqrt{\Delta t}}$
$S_d = Se^{-\sigma\sqrt{\Delta t}}$
$p = (S_F - S_d)(S_u - S_d) = 1/2$

$S_u = Se^{(r-\sigma^2/2)\Delta t+\sigma\sqrt{\Delta t}}$
$S_d = Se^{r-\sigma^2/2)\Delta t-\sigma\sqrt{\Delta t}}$
$p = (S_F - S_d)(S_u - S_d) = 1/2$

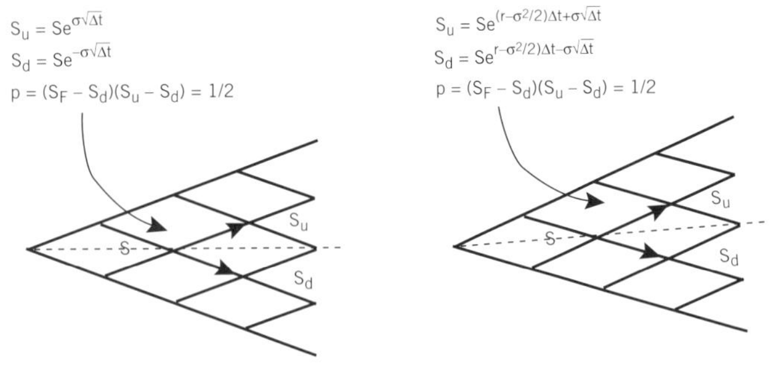

14. Three equivalent methods for building constant-volatility trinomial trees with spacing Δt

(a) Combining two steps of a CRR binomial tree

$$S_u = Se^{\sigma\sqrt{2\Delta t}}$$
$$S_m = S$$
$$S_d = Se^{-\sigma\sqrt{2\Delta t}}$$
$$p = \left(\frac{e^{r\Delta t/2} - e^{-\sigma\sqrt{\Delta t/2}}}{e^{\sigma\sqrt{\Delta t/2}} - e^{-\sigma\sqrt{\Delta t/2}}}\right)^2$$
$$q = \left(\frac{e^{\sigma\sqrt{\Delta t/2}} - e^{r\Delta t/2}}{e^{\sigma\sqrt{\Delta t/2}} - e^{-\sigma\sqrt{\Delta t/2}}}\right)^2$$

(b) Combining two steps of a JR binomial tree

$$S_u = Se^{(r-\sigma^2/2)\Delta t+\sigma\sqrt{2\Delta t}}$$
$$S_m = Se^{(r-\sigma^2/2)\Delta t}$$
$$S_d = Se^{(r-\sigma^2/2)\Delta t-\sigma\sqrt{2\Delta t}}$$
$$p = 1/4$$
$$q = 1/4$$

(c) Equal-probability tree

$$S_u = Se^{(r-\sigma^2/2)\Delta t+\sigma\sqrt{3\Delta t}}$$
$$S_m = Se^{(r-\sigma^2/2)\Delta t}$$
$$S_d = Se^{(r-\sigma^2/2)\Delta t-\sigma\sqrt{3\Delta t}}$$
$$p = 1/3$$
$$q = 1/3$$

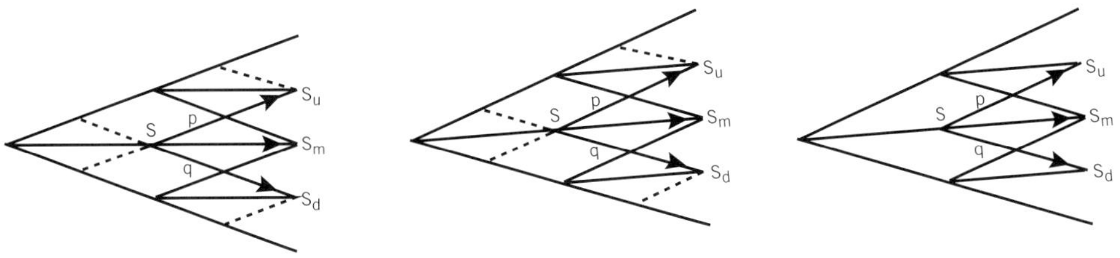

uses a JR-type binomial tree.

To construct other kinds of trinomial trees, we can apply a variety of criteria, all of which may be equally reasonable.[10] For example, Panel C is based on the requirement that all three transition probabilities be equal (to 1/3) for all the tree nodes. Another common choice of probabilities, which we have not described here but is simple to construct, is $p = q = 1/6$.

Appendix B

CONSTRUCTING SKEWED TRINOMIAL STATE SPACES

If there is significant term or skew structure in implied volatilities, we need to build a trinomial state space with irregular mesh size to accommodate better the variations of the local volatilities with time and level. One obstacle to achieving this is the fact that often we do not a priori know what the local volatility function looks like, although there are exceptions.

For example, if there is a significant term-structure but little skew-structure in the market, then local volatility is mostly a function of time.[11] On the other hand, if there is a large skew-structure but insignificant term-structure in the implied volatilities, then we know that local volatility is mostly a function of the level.[12]

Assume that interest and dividend rates are zero for now. Consider the term-structure case first. Here local volatility is some function of time $\sigma(t)$. We can introduce the notion of scaled time $\tilde{t}$ as

$$t = c\int_0^{\tilde{t}} \sigma^2(u)du$$

for some constant c. Differentiating both sides of this equation, we can write an equivalent non-linear equation describing $\tilde{t}$ in terms of t:

$$\tilde{t} = \frac{1}{c}\int_0^{t} \frac{1}{\sigma^2\left[\tilde{t}(u)\right]}du.$$

Using the scaled time in place of standard time transforms the stock evolution process to a constant volatility (Black-Scholes) process.[13] We can choose the constant c so that the rescaled and physical times coincide at some fixed future time T, eg $\tilde{t}(T) = T$. In this case

$$c = T\Bigg/\left(\int_0^{T} \sigma^2(u)du\right) = \frac{1}{T}\int_0^{t} \frac{1}{\sigma^2\left[\tilde{t}(u)\right]}du.$$

In the discrete-time world of a multinomial tree, with known (equally spaced) time points $t_0 = t_1,\ldots,t_n = T$, we want to find unknown scaled times $\tilde{t}_0 = \tilde{t}_1,\ldots,\tilde{t}_n = T$, such that $\sigma^2(\tilde{t}_i)\Delta\tilde{t}_i$ is the same constant for all times $\tilde{t}_i$. This guarantees that the tree will recombine.

One way to do this is by iteratively searching for solutions of discrete-time analogues of the second set of earlier (non-linear) relations:

$$\tilde{t}_k = \frac{T\sum_{i=1}^{k}\frac{1}{\sigma^2(\tilde{t}_i)}}{\sum_{i=1}^{n}\frac{1}{\sigma^2(\tilde{t}_i)}};\ k = 1,\ldots,n.$$

Next consider the skew-structure. Assume that local volatility is some function $\sigma(S)$ of the level. This assumption is roughly valid when implied volatilities have little or no term-structure. We define the scaled stock price $\tilde{S}$ using the equation:[14]

$$\tilde{S} = S_0 \exp\left[c\int_{S_0}^{S}\frac{1}{x\sigma(x)}dx\right]$$

for some constant c.

The scaled stock price has a constant volatility equal to c.[15] A reasonable discrete representation of scaled stock price movements can be given by a constant-volatility tree. Inverting this equation, we can convert the discrete nodal values of $\tilde{S}$ to discrete values of S. In the resulting S-tree, the spacing between nodes varies with the level, corresponding to the similar variation in local volatility. We can choose the constant c to represent the at-the-money or some other typical value of local volatility.

For any fixed time period, if $\tilde{S}_i$ denote the nodal values of scaled stock price, the corresponding stock price values can be found by solving the discrete version of the above equation. For nodes which lie above the central node this gives:

$$S_k = S_{k-1} + \frac{1}{c}\sigma(S_{k-1})S_{k-1}\log\frac{\tilde{S}_k}{\tilde{S}_{k-1}}$$

and for those below it gives:[16]

$$S_{k-1} = S_k - \frac{1}{c}\sigma(S_k)S_k\log\frac{\tilde{S}_k}{\tilde{S}_{k-1}}.$$

Again we can set the constant c to the at-the-money or any other reasonable value of local volatility.[17]

In general, if local volatility is in the form of a product of some function of time and some function of stock price, ie if local volatility function is "separable", then we can perform the scaling transformations on time and stock price independently. As a result we will obtain state spaces which can accommodate a term-structure with a constant skew-structure superimposed on it.

A simple example of this is when local volatility has a constant elasticity of variance (CEV) form:

$$\sigma(S,t) = \sigma_0(t)\left(\frac{S}{S_0}\right)^{\gamma}.$$

Here $\sigma_0(t)$ represents the at-the-money term structure and γ is a constant skew or elasticity parameter. Most equity options markets have time-varying skew structures. Despite this, with judicious choices for term-structure and skew parameters and using the procedure outlined above, we can create a state space which fits any particular options market rather well. Non-zero interest rates and dividends can also be incorporated in this state space by growing all the nodes with an appropriate growth factor, as discussed above.

1 *See Derman and Kani (1994).*

2 *Strictly speaking, the implied trinomial tree is unique to a user-specified central tree trunk. In the continuous limit where there are an infinite number of nodes at each time step, this choice becomes irrelevant.*

3 *To be honest, we point out that no one really knows all the market options prices needed to find the price and transaction probabilities at every tree node. In practice, there are market quotes for a discrete set of commonly traded strikes and expirations, and market participants interpolate or extrapolate implied volatilities to other points.*

4 *This process is an extension of the constant volatility lognormal process, as described by the stochastic differential equation:*

$$\frac{dS}{S} = r(t)dt + \sigma(S,t)dZ$$

where $r(t)$ is the risk-free rate of interest at time t, $\sigma(S,t)$ is the local volatility assumed to depend only on the future time t and future spot price S, and dZ is the standard Wiener process.

5 *See Derman and Kani (1994). For a review of implied binomial tree models, see also Chriss (1996).*

6 *There are only n independent options because puts and calls with the same strike are related through put-call parity, which holds in our model because the implied tree is constrained to value all forwards correctly.*

7 *Trinomial and binomial trees approach the same continuous-time theory as the number of periods in each allowed to grow without limit. Despite their similarity, one kind of tree may sometimes be more convenient than another.*

8 *It may not be necessary to rescale the nodes precisely along the forward-rate curve. Any sufficiently large growth*

factor that removes forward price violations of the types described in Figure 8 will be sufficient.

9 *In a recombining constant-volatility binomial tree,* S_u *and* S_d *have the general form:*

$$S_u = Se^{\pi\Delta t + \sigma\sqrt{\Delta t}}$$

and

$$S_d = Se^{\pi\Delta t - \sigma\sqrt{\Delta t}}$$

for any reasonable number π.

10 *In a recombining constant-volatility trinomial tree,* S_u, S_m *and* S_d *have the general form:*

$$S_u = Se^{\pi\Delta t + \phi\sigma\sqrt{\Delta t}},\ S_m = Se^{\pi\Delta t}$$

and

$$S_d = S_d = Se^{\pi\Delta t - \phi\sigma\sqrt{\Delta t}}$$

for $\phi > 1$ *and any reasonable value of* π.

11 *If* $\Sigma = \Sigma(T)$ *is implied volatility for expiration* T, *then local volatility at time* $t = T$ *is given by the relation* $\sigma^2(T) = d[T\Sigma^2(T)]/dT$.

12 *If* $\Sigma = \Sigma_0 + b(K - K_0)$ *is implied volatility at for the strike price* K, *then the local volatility at level* K *in the vicinity of* K_0 *is roughly given by the relation* $\sigma = \Sigma_0 + 2b(K - K_0)$.

13 *Define a new stock price variable* $\tilde{S}$ *by the relation* $\tilde{S}(t) = S(\tilde{t})$ *and also Brownian motion* $\tilde{Z}$ *by*

$$\frac{1}{\sqrt{c}}\tilde{Z}\left(c\int_0^t \sigma^2(u)du\right) = \int_0^t \sigma(u)dZ(u).$$

Note that the term in parentheses on the left-hand side refers to a point in time at which $\tilde{Z}$ *is evaluated. Then, using the definition of scaled time we find:*

$$\frac{d\tilde{S}(t)}{\tilde{S}(t)} = \frac{d\left[S(\tilde{t})\right]}{S(\tilde{t})} = \sigma(\tilde{t})d\left[Z(\tilde{t})\right] = \frac{1}{\sqrt{c}}d\left[\tilde{Z}\left(c\int_0^{\tilde{t}} \sigma^2(u)du\right)\right] = \frac{1}{\sqrt{c}}d\tilde{Z}(t).$$

Hence the new stock price variable evolves with constant volatility $1/\sqrt{c}$.

14 *See Nelson and Ramaswamy (1990).*

15 *Starting from the stochastic equation* $dS/S = \sigma(S)dZ$ *and using Itô's lemma*

$$d\log\tilde{S} = -\frac{c}{2}(\sigma + \sigma' S)dt + cdZ.$$

There is an induced drift from the variation of the local volatility function with level. Starting from a constant-volatility state space, the discrete-world trinomial (or higher multinomial) implementations can accommodate this drift through the choice of transition probabilities, given small enough drift or short enough time step.

16 *To guarantee positivity of stock prices, we can use alternative relations:*

$$S_k = S_{k-1}e^{\frac{\sigma(S_k)}{c}\log\frac{\tilde{S}_k}{\tilde{S}_{k-1}}} \text{ and } S_{k-1} = S_k e^{\frac{\sigma(S_k)}{c}\log\frac{\tilde{S}_k}{\tilde{S}_{k-1}}}$$

for nodes above and below the central nodes, respectively. These relations have the further advantage that when volatility is constant (and equal to c*) the* S *and* $\tilde{S}$ *trees will be identical.*

17 *Choosing somewhat larger volatilities increases the spacing between the nodes and often improves the ability of the tree top fit option prices. A similar situation occurs in explicit finite-difference lattices where increasing the price spacing relative to time spacing increases the stability of the solutions.*

BIBLIOGRAPHY

Black, F., and M. Scholes, 1973, "The Pricing of Options and Corporate Liabilities", *Journal of Political Economy* 81, pp. 637–59.

Chriss, N., 1996, *Black-Scholes and Beyond: Modern Options Pricing*, Irwin Professional Publishing, Burr Ridge, Illinois.

Cox, J.C., S.A. Ross and M. Rubinstein, 1979, "Option Pricing: A Simplified Approach", *Journal of Financial Economics* 7, pp. 229–63.

Derman, E., and I. Kani, 1994, "Riding on a Smile", *Risk* 7 no 2, pp. 32–9.

Dupire, B., 1994, "Pricing with a Smile", *Risk* 7 no 1, pp. 18–20.

Jarrow, R., and A. Rudd, 1983, *Option Pricing*, Dow Jones-Irwin Publishing, Homewood, Illinois.

Nelson, D.B., and K. Ramaswamy, 1990 "Simple Binomial Processes as Diffusion Approximations in Financial Models", *Review of Financial Studies* 3, pp. 393–430.

Rubinstein, M.E., 1994 "Implied Binomial Trees", *Journal of Finance* 69, pp. 771–818.

Implied Volatility Skews and Stock Index Skewness and Kurtosis implied by S&P 500 Index Option Prices

Charles J. Corrado and Tie Su
University of Missouri; University of Miami

The Black-Scholes option pricing model is used to value a wide range of option contracts. It often prices deep in-the-money and deep out-of-the-money options inconsistently, a phenomenon we refer to as a volatility "skew" or "smile." This paper applies an extension of the Black-Scholes model developed by Jarrow and Rudd to an investigation of S&P 500 index option prices. Non-normal skewness and kurtosis in option-implied distributions of index returns are found to contribute significantly to the phenomenon of volatility skews.

The Black-Scholes (1973) option pricing model provides the foundation of modern option pricing theory. In actual application, however, the model often inconsistently prices deep in-the-money and deep out-of-the-money options. Options professionals call this effect the volatility "skew" or "smile."

A volatility skew is the anomalous pattern that results from calculating implied volatilities across a range of strike prices. Typically, the skew pattern is systematically related to the degree to which the options are in or out of the money. This phenomenon is not predicted by the Black-Scholes model, since volatility is a property of the underlying instrument, and the same implied volatility value should be observed across all options on the same instrument.

The Black-Scholes model assumes that stock prices are lognormally distributed, which implies in turn that stock log-prices are normally distributed. Hull (1993) and Natenburg (1994) point out that volatility skews are a consequence of empirical violations of the normality assumption.

In this paper, we investigate volatility skew patterns embedded in S&P 500 index option prices. We adapt a method developed by Jarrow and Rudd (1982) to extend the Black-Scholes formula to account for non-normal skewness and kurtosis in stock returns. This method fits the first four moments of a distribution to a pattern of empirically observed option prices. The mean of this distribution is determined by option pricing theory, but an estimation procedure is employed to yield implied values for the standard deviation, skewness and kurtosis of the distribution of stock index prices.

Non-normal skewness and kurtosis in stock returns

It is widely known that stock returns do not always conform well to a normal distribution. As a simple examination, we separately compute the mean, standard deviation, and coefficients of skewness and kurtosis of monthly S&P 500 index returns in each of the seven decades from 1926 through 1995. In Table 1, Panel A reports statistics based on arithmetic returns, and Panel B reports statistics based on log-relative returns.

* *This paper was first published in* The Journal of Derivatives, *Summer (1997). Reprinted with permission from Institutional Investor, Inc. To order a subscription, or for other information, please call (212) 224 3185.*

Table 1. Historical S&P 500 index return statistics 1926–95

Decade	Mean (%)	Standard deviation (%)	Skewness	Kurtosis
Panel A: arithmetic returns				
1926–35	7.4	35.1	0.77	7.50
1936–45	5.8	22.4	−0.55	7.15
1946–55	10.1	13.5	−0.28	3.02
1956–65	7.8	11.7	−0.52	3.37
1966–75	2.1	15.9	0.23	4.08
1976–85	9.5	14.1	0.30	3.67
1986–95	11.8	14.9	−1.19	9.27
1986–95*	14.0	13.0	−0.04	4.06
Panel B: log-relative returns				
1926–35	1.4	34.5	−0.02	6.23
1936–45	3.2	22.9	−1.12	8.30
1946–55	9.2	13.5	−0.39	3.22
1956–65	7.1	11.7	−0.62	3.43
1966–75	0.9	15.9	0.03	3.90
1976–85	8.5	13.9	0.15	3.63
1986–95	10.6	15.2	−1.67	11.92
1986–95*	13.0	12.9	−0.20	4.05

Means and standard deviation are annualised. 95% confidence intervals for normal sample skewness and kurtosis coefficients are ±4.38 and 3 ± 0.877, respectively.
* Indicates exclusion of October 1987 crash–month return.

Arithmetic returns are calculated as $P_t/P_{t-1} - 1$, and log-relative returns are calculated as $\log(P_t/P_{t-1})$, where P_t denotes the index value observed at the end of month t.

The returns series used to compute statistics reported in Table 1 do not include dividends. We choose returns without dividends because dividends paid out over the life of a European-style option do not accrue to the optionholder. Thus European-style S&P 500 index option prices are properly determined by index returns that exclude any dividend payments.

The Black-Scholes model assumes that arithmetic returns are lognormally distributed, or equivalently, that log-relative returns are normally distributed. All normal distributions have a skewness coefficient of zero and a kurtosis coefficient of 3. All lognormal distributions are positively skewed with kurtosis always greater than 3 (see Stuart and Ord, 1987).

We have two observations to make about Table 1. First, reported coefficients of skewness and kurtosis show significant deviations from normality occurring in the first two decades (1926–35 and 1936–45) and the most recent decade (1986–95) of this 70-year period.

Statistical significance is assessed by noting that population skewness and kurtosis for a normal distribution are 0 and 3, respectively. Also, variances of sample coefficients of skewness and kurtosis from a normal population are $6/n$ and $24/n$, respectively. For each decade, $n = 120$ months, which is sufficiently large to invoke the central limit theorem and to assume that sample coefficients are normally distributed.

Thus, 95% confidence intervals for a test of index return normality are given by $\pm 1.96 \times \sqrt{6/120} = \pm 0.438$ for sample skewness and $3 \pm 1.96 \times \sqrt{24/120} = 3 \pm 0.877$ for sample kurtosis. For statistics computed from log-relative returns, sample skewness and kurtosis values outside these confidence intervals indicate statistically significant departures from normality. For statistics obtained from arithmetic returns, a negative sample skewness value outside the appropriate confidence interval indicates a statistically significant departure from lognormality.

Second, statistics reported for the decade 1986–95 are sensitive to the inclusion of the October 1987 return when the S&P 500 index fell by -21.76%. Including the October 1987 return yields log-relative skewness and kurtosis coefficients of -1.67 and 11.92, respectively, which deviate significantly from a normal specification. Excluding the October 1987 return yields skewness and kurtosis coefficients of -0.20 and 4.05, which are not significant deviations from normality.

The contrasting estimates of S&P 500 index return skewness and kurtosis in the decade 1986-95 raise an interesting empirical issue regarding the pricing of S&P 500 index options. Specifically, do post-crash option prices embody an ongoing market perception of the possibility of another market crash similar to that of October 1987?

If post-crash option prices contain no memory of the crash, then the near-normal skewness and kurtosis obtained by omitting the October 1987 return suggest that the Black-Scholes model should be well-specified. If post-crash option prices "remember" the crash, however, we expect to see non-normal skewness and kurtosis in the option-implied distribution of stock returns similar to the sample skewness and kurtosis obtained by including the October 1987 return.

Jarrow-Rudd skewness- and kurtosis-adjusted model

The Jarrow-Rudd (1982) option pricing model provides a useful analytic tool to examine the contrasting hypotheses. They propose a method to value European style options when the underlying security price at option expiration follows a distribution F known only through its moments. They derive an option pricing formula from an Edgeworth series expansion of the security price distribution F about an approximating distribution A.

Their simplest option pricing formula is the following expression for an option price:

$$C(F) = C(A) - e^{rt}\,\frac{\kappa_3(F) - \kappa_3(A)}{3!}\frac{da(K)}{dS_t} + e^{-rt}\,\frac{\kappa_4(F) - \kappa_4(A)}{4!}\frac{d^2a(K)}{dS_t^2} + \varepsilon(K). \qquad (1)$$

The left-hand side term $C(F)$ denotes a call option price based on the unknown price distribution F. The first right-hand side term $C(A)$ is a call price based on a known distribution A, followed by adjustment terms based on the cumulants $\kappa_j(F)$ and $\kappa_j(A)$ of the distributions F and A, respectively, and derivatives of the density of A. The density of A is denoted by $a(S_t)$, where S_t is a random stock price at option expiration. These derivatives are evaluated at the strike price K. The remainder $\varepsilon(K)$ continues the Edgeworth series with terms based on higher order cumulants and derivatives.

Cumulants are similar to moments. In fact, the first cumulant is equal to the mean, and the second cumulant is equal to the variance. The Jarrow-Rudd model uses third and fourth cumulants. The relationship between third and fourth cumulants and moments for a distribution F are: $\kappa_3(F) = \mu_3(F)$ and $\kappa_4(F) = \mu_4(F) - 3\mu_2^2(F)$, where μ_2^2 is the squared variance, and μ_3, μ_4 denote third and fourth central moments (Stuart and Ord, 1987, p.87). Thus the third cumulant is the same as the third central moment, and the fourth cumulant is equal to the fourth central moment less three times the squared variance.

Jarrow and Rudd (1982) suggest that with a good choice for the approximating distribution A, higher order terms in the remainder $\varepsilon(K)$ are likely to be negligible. In essence, the Jarrow-Rudd model relaxes the strict distributional assumptions of the Black-Scholes model without requiring an exact knowledge of the true underlying distribution.

Because of its pre-eminence in option pricing theory and practice, Jarrow-Rudd suggest the lognormal distribution as a good approximating distribution. When the distribution A is lognormal, $C(A)$ becomes the familiar Black-Scholes call price formula.

In notation followed throughout, the Black-Scholes call price formula is stated in Equation (2), where S_0 is a current stock price, K is a strike price, r is an interest rate, t is the time until option expiration, and the parameter σ^2 is the instantaneous variance of the security log-price.

$$C(A) = S_0N(d_1) - Ke^{-rt}N(d_2) \qquad (2)$$

$$d_1 = \frac{\log(S_0/K) + (r + \sigma^2/2)t}{\sigma\sqrt{t}}$$

$$d_2 = d_1 - \sigma\sqrt{t}$$

Evaluating the lognormal density $a(S_t)$ and its first two derivatives at the strike price K yields the expressions:

$$a(K) = \left(K\sigma\sqrt{t2\pi}\right)^{-1}\exp(-d_2^2/2)$$

$$\frac{da(K)}{dS_t} = \frac{a(K)\left(d_2 - \sigma\sqrt{t}\right)}{K\sigma\sqrt{t}}$$

$$\frac{d^2a(K)}{dS_t^2} = \frac{a(K)}{K^2\sigma^2t}\times\left[\left(d_2 - \sigma\sqrt{t}\right)^2 - \sigma\sqrt{t}\left(d_2 - \sigma\sqrt{t}\right) - 1\right]. \qquad (3)$$

The risk-neutral valuation approach adopted by Jarrow and Rudd (1982) implies equality of the first cumulants of F and A, ie $\kappa_1(F) = \kappa_1(A) = S_0e^{rt}$. This is equivalent to the equality of the means of F and A, as the first cumulant of a distribution is its mean.

Also, the call price in Equation (1) corresponds to Jarrow-Rudd's first option price approximation method. This method selects an approximating distribution that equates second cumulants of F and A, ie $\kappa_2(F) = \kappa_2(A)$. This is equivalent to the equality of t.

Dropping the remainder term $\varepsilon(K)$, the Jarrow-Rudd option price in Equation (1) is conveniently restated as

$$C(F) = C(A) + \lambda_1Q_3 + \lambda_2Q_4 \qquad (4)$$

where the terms λ_j and Q_j, j = 1, 2, above are defined as follows:

$$\lambda_1 = \gamma_1(F) - \gamma_1(A)$$

$$Q_3 = -\left(S_0e^{rt}\right)^3\left(e^{\sigma^2t} - 1\right)^{3/2}\frac{e^{-rt}}{3!}\frac{da(K)}{dS_t} \qquad (5a)$$

$$\lambda_2 = \gamma_2(F) - \gamma_2(A)$$

$$Q_4 = \left(S_0e^{rt}\right)^4\left(e^{\sigma^2t} - 1\right)^2\frac{e^{-rt}}{4!}\frac{d^2a(K)}{dS_t^2}. \qquad (5b)$$

In Equation (5), $\gamma_1(F)$ and $\gamma_1(A)$ are skewness coefficients for the distributions F and A, respectively. Similarly, $\gamma_2(F)$ and $\gamma_2(A)$ are excess kurtosis coefficients. Skewness and excess kurtosis coefficients are defined in terms of cumulants as follows (Stuart and Ord (1987, p.107)).

$$\gamma_1(F) = \frac{\kappa_3(F)}{\kappa_2^{3/2}(F)} \qquad \gamma_2(F) = \frac{\kappa_4(F)}{\kappa_2^2(F)} \tag{6}$$

is used to simplify the algebraic expression, coefficients of skewness and excess kurtosis for the lognormal distribution A are defined as

$$\gamma_1(A) = 3q + q^3$$
$$\gamma_2(A) = 16q^2 + 15q^4 + 6q^6 + q^8. \tag{7}$$

For example, when $\sigma = 15\%$ and $t = 0.25$, then skewness is $\gamma_1(A) = 0.226$ and excess kurtosis is $\gamma_2(A) = 0.091$. Notice that skewness is always positive for the lognormal distribution.

Non-lognormal skewness and kurtosis for $\gamma_1(F)$ and $\gamma_2(F)$ defined in Equation (6) give rise to implied volatility skews. To illustrate this effect, we generate option prices according to the Jarrow-Rudd option price in Equation (4) using parameter values $\lambda_1 = -0.5$, $\lambda_2 = 3$, $S_0 = 450$, $\sigma = 20\%$, $t = 3$ months and $r = 4\%$, and strike prices ranging from 400 to 500. Implied volatilities are then calculated for each skewness- and kurtosis-impacted option price using the Black-Scholes formula.

The resulting volatility skew is plotted in Figure 1, where the horizontal axis measures strike prices, and the vertical axis measures implied standard deviation value. While the true volatility value is $\sigma = 20\%$, Figure 1 reveals that implied volatility is greater than true volatility for deep in-the-money options, but less than true volatility for deep out-of-the-money options.

Figure 2 shows an empirical volatility skew obtained from S&P 500 index call option price quotes recorded on December 2, 1993 for options expiring in February 1994. The horizontal axis measures option moneyness as the percentage difference between a dividend-adjusted stock index level and a discounted strike price. Positive (negative) moneyness corresponds to in-the-money (out-of-the-money) options with low (high) strike prices.

The vertical axis measures implied standard deviation values. Solid marks represent implied volatilities calculated from observed option prices using the Black-Scholes formula. Hollow marks represent implied volatilities calculated from observed option prices using the Jarrow-Rudd formula.

The Jarrow-Rudd formula uses a single skewness parameter and a single kurtosis parameter across all price observations. The skewness parameter and the kurtosis parameter are estimated by a procedure described in the empirical results section below. There are actually 1,354 price quotes used to form this graph, but the number of visually distinguishable dots is smaller.

Figure 2 reveals that Black-Scholes implied volatilities range from about 17% for the deepest in-the-money options (positive moneyness) to about 9% for the deepest out-of-the-money options (negative moneyness). By contrast, Jarrow-Rudd implied volatilities are all close to 12-13% regardless of option moneyness. Comparing Figure 2 with Figure 1 reveals that the Black-Scholes implied volatility skew for these S&P 500 index options is consistent with negative skewness in the distribution of S&P 500 index prices.

1. Implied volatility skew

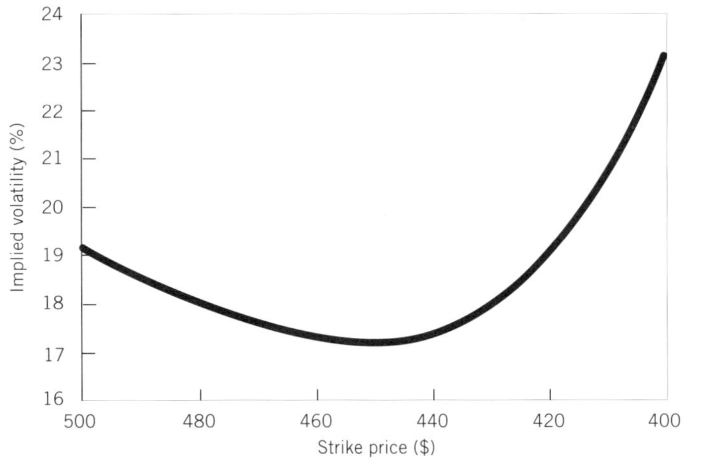

2. Implied volatilities (SPX: Dec 12, 1993)

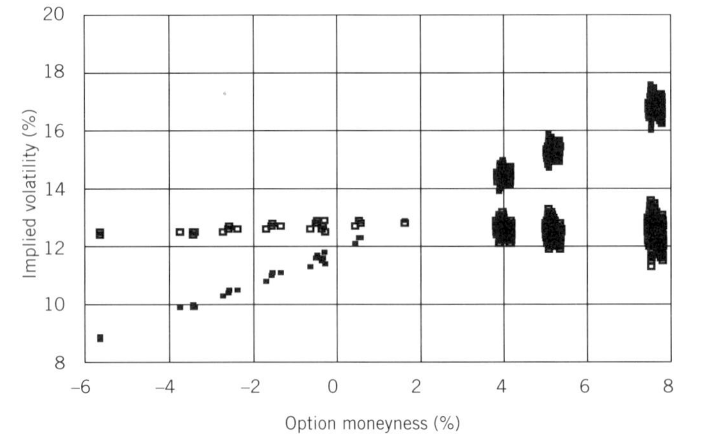

Data sources

We base this study on the market for S&P 500 index options at the Chicago Board Options Exchange (CBOE), the SPX contracts. Rubinstein (1994) argues that this market best approximates conditions required for the Black-Scholes model, although Jarrow and Rudd (1982) point out that a stock index distribution is a convolution of its component distributions. Therefore, when the Black-Scholes model is the correct model for individual stocks it is only an approximation for stock index options.

Intraday price data come from the Berkeley Options Data Base of CBOE options trading. S&P 500 index levels, strike prices and option maturities also come from the Berkeley data base. To avoid bid-ask bounce problems in transaction prices, we take option prices as midpoints of CBOE dealers' bid-ask price quotations. The risk free interest rate is taken as the US Treasury bill rate for a bill maturing closest to option contract expiration. Interest rate information is culled from the *Wall Street Journal*.

Since S&P 500 index options are European style, we use Black's (1975) method to adjust index levels by subtracting present values of dividend payments made before each option's expiration date. Daily S&P 500 index dividends are collected from the *S&P 500 Information Bulletin*.

Following data screening procedures in Barone-Adesi and Whaley (1986), we delete all option prices under $0.125, and all transactions listed as occurring before 9:00am. Obvious outliers are also purged from the sample; including recorded option prices lying outside well-known no-arbitrage option price boundaries (Merton, 1973).

Empirical results

We first assess the out-of-sample performance of the Black-Scholes option pricing model without adjusting for skewness and kurtosis. Specifically, using option prices for all contracts within a given maturity series observed on a given day, we estimate a single implied standard deviation using Whaley's (1982) simultaneous equations procedure.

We then use this implied volatility as an input to the Black-Scholes formula to calculate theoretical option prices corresponding to all actual option prices within the same maturity series observed on the following day. Thus, theoretical option prices for a given day are based on a prior-day, out-of-sample implied standard deviation estimate. We then compare these theoretical prices with the actual market prices observed that day.

Next, we assess the skewness- and kurtosis-adjusted Black-Scholes option pricing formula developed by Jarrow and Rudd (1982) using an analogous procedure. Specifically, on a given day we estimate a single implied standard deviation, a single skewness coefficient, and a single excess kurtosis coefficient using an expanded version of Whaley's (1982) simultaneous equations procedure.

We then use these three parameter estimates as inputs to the Jarrow-Rudd formula to calculate theoretical option prices corresponding to all option prices within the same maturity series observed on the following day. Thus, these theoretical option prices for a given day are based on prior-day, out-of-sample implied standard deviation, skewness, and excess kurtosis estimates. We then compare these theoretical prices with the actual market prices.

BLACK-SCHOLES OPTION PRICING MODEL

The Black-Scholes formula specifies five inputs: a stock price, a strike price, a risk free interest rate, an option maturity and a return standard deviation. The first four inputs are directly observable market data. Since the return standard deviation is not directly observable, we estimate a return standard deviation implied by option prices using Whaley's (1982) simultaneous equations procedure.

This procedure yields a Black-Scholes implied standard deviation (BSISD) that minimises the sum of squares:

$$\min_{BSISD} \sum_{j=1}^{N} \left[C_{OBS,j} - C_{BS,j}(BSISD) \right]^2 \qquad (8)$$

where N denotes the number of price quotations available on a given day for a given maturity series, C_{OBS} represents a market-observed call price, and $C_{BS}(BSISD)$ specifies a theoretical Black-Scholes call price based on the parameter BSISD.

Using a prior-day BSISD estimate, we calculate theoretical Black-Scholes option prices for all contracts in a current-day sample within the same maturity series. We then compare these theoretical Black-Scholes option prices with their corresponding market-observed prices.

Table 2 summarises results for S&P 500 index call option prices observed in December 1993 for options expiring in February 1994. To save space, we list in the stub only even-numbered dates within the month. Column 1 lists the number of price quotations available on each date. The Black-Scholes implied standard deviation (BSISD) used to calculate theoretical prices for each date is reported in column 2.

To assess differences between theoretical and observed prices, the next-to-last column gives

Table 2. Comparison of Black-Scholes prices and observed prices of S&P 500 options

Date	Number of price observations	Implied standard deviation (%)	Average observed call price (%)	Average observed bid-ask spread (%)	Proportion of theoretical prices outside bid-ask spread (%)	Average absolute deviation of theoretical price from spread boundaries ($)
Dec 2, 1993	1,354	15.29	2,862.74	67.87	59.68	48.98
Dec 6, 1993	1,667	14.94	3,113.35	67.26	56.63	54.14
Dec 8, 1993	956	14.77	3,012.24	59.95	62.03	40.53
Dec 10, 1993	2,445	14.56	2,962.24	61.60	60.00	32.87
Dec 14, 1993	3,100	15.14	3,003.08	68.75	66.58	37.46
Dec 16, 1993	1,944	14.55	2,754.71	61.79	78.65	59.65
Dec 20, 1993	115	10.66	1,453.04	55.76	91.30	194.51
Dec 22, 1993	199	9.93	1,203.78	45.63	99.50	117.83
Dec 28, 1993	166	9.07	608.45	27.52	83.13	46.56
Dec 30, 1993	242	9.86	1,339.86	51.32	94.63	65.18
Average	1,218	12.88	2,231.35	56.75	75.21	69.77

Black-Scholes implied standard deviations (BSISD) estimated from prior-day option price observations. Current-day theoretical Black-Scholes option prices calculated using prior-day volatility parameter estimate. Prices stated on a per contract basis, ie, 100 times quote price.

the proportion of theoretical Black-Scholes option prices lying outside their corresponding bid-ask spreads, either below the bid price or above the asked price. The last column shows the average absolute deviation of theoretical prices from spread boundaries for those prices lying outside their bid-ask spreads.

Specifically, for each theoretical option price lying outside its corresponding bid-ask spread, we compute an absolute deviation according to:

$$\max\left[C_{BS}(BSISD) - Ask, Bid - C_{BS}(BSISD)\right].$$

This absolute deviation statistic measures deviations of theoretical option prices from observed bid-ask spreads.

Finally, the two middle columns list day-by-day averages of observed call prices and day-by-day averages of observed bid-ask spreads. Since option contracts are indivisible, all prices are stated on a per-contract basis, which for SPX options is 100 times a quoted price.

The last row in Table 2 lists column averages for all variables. For example, the average number of daily price observations is 1,218, with an average contract price of $2,231.35, and an average bid-ask spread of $56.75. The average implied standard deviation is 12.88%. The average proportion of theoretical Black-Scholes prices lying outside their corresponding bid-ask spreads is 75.21%, with an average deviation of $69.77 for those observations lying outside a spread boundary.

The average price deviation of $69.77 per contract for observations lying outside a spread boundary is slightly larger than the average bid-ask spread of $56.75. Price deviations are larger for deep in-the-money and deep out-of-the-money options, however.

For example, Table 2 shows that the Black-Scholes implied standard deviation (BSISD) estimated using Whaley's simultaneous equations procedure on December 2 option prices is 15.29%, while Figure 2 reveals that contract-specific Black-Scholes implied volatilities range from about 18% for deep in-the-money options to about 8% for deep out-of-the-money options.

Given December 2 SPX input values (S = \$459.65, r = 3.15%, t = 78 days), a deep in-the-money option with a strike price of 430 yields call contract prices of \$3,635.76 and \$3,495.68, respectively, from volatility values of 18% and 15.29%. Similarly, a deep out-of-the-money option with a strike price of 490 yields call contract prices of \$46.02 and \$395.13, respectively, from volatility values of 8% and 15.29%. These prices correspond to contract price deviations of \$140.08 for deep in-the-money options and \$349.11 for deep out-of-the-money options. These deviations are significantly larger than the average deviation of \$56.75 per contract.

Price deviations of the magnitude described above indicate that CBOE market makers quote deep in-the-money (out-of-the-money) call option prices at a premium (discount) compared to Black-Scholes prices, although the Black-Scholes formula is a useful first approximation to these option prices.

SKEWNESS- AND KURTOSIS-ADJUSTED JARROW-RUDD MODEL

To examine the improvement in pricing accuracy obtained by adding skewness- and kurtosis-adjustment terms, in the second set of estimation procedures, on a given day within a given option maturity series, we simultaneously estimate a single return standard deviation, a single skewness parameter, and a single kurtosis parameter by

Table 3. Comparison of skewness- and kurtosis-adjusted Black-Scholes prices and observed prices of S&P 500 options

Date	Number of price observations	Implied standard deviation (%)	Implied skewness (ISD)	Implied kurtosis (IKT)	Proportion of theoretical prices outside bid-ask spread (%)	Average absolute deviation of theoretical price from spread boundaries ($)
Dec 2, 1993	1,354	12.70	−1.57	4.33	17.73	8.60
Dec 6, 1993	1,667	11.90	−1.54	5.19	23.10	15.15
Dec 8, 1993	956	12.12	−1.36	5.68	6.59	17.22
Dec 10, 1993	2,445	11.58	−1.44	4.72	8.06	10.37
Dec 14, 1993	3,100	12.06	−1.46	5.73	11.03	8.15
Dec 16, 1993	1,944	12.04	−1.58	5.32	12.65	14.18
Dec 20, 1993	115	11.42	−2.13	5.86	62.61	28.27
Dec 22, 1993	199	11.06	−2.22	6.12	72.86	30.82
Dec 28, 1993	166	10.55	−1.91	5.21	50.60	12.36
Dec 30, 1993	242	10.75	−1.62	5.77	53.31	13.42
Average	1,218	11.62	−1.68	5.39	31.85	15.85

Implied standard deviation (ISD), skewness (ISK), and kurtosis (IKT) estimated from prior-day option price observations. Current-day theoretical Black-Scholes option prices calculated using out-of-sample parameter estimates.

minimising the following sum of squares with respect to the arguments ISD, L_1, and L_2, respectively:

$$\min_{ISD,L_1,L_2} \sum_{j=1}^{N} \left[C_{OBS,j} - \left(C_{BS,j}(ISD) + L_1Q_3 + L_2Q_4\right)\right]^2. \quad (9)$$

The coefficients L_1 and L_2 estimate the parameters λ_1 and λ_2, respectively, defined in (5), where the terms Q_3 and Q_4 are also defined. These daily estimates yield implied coefficients of skewness (ISK) and kurtosis (IKT) calculated as follows, where $\gamma_1(A)$ and $\gamma_2(A)$ are defined in (7):

$$ISK = L_1 + \gamma_1\left[A(ISD)\right]$$
$$IKT = 3 + L_2 + \gamma_2\left[A(ISD)\right].$$

Thus ISK estimates the skewness parameter $\gamma_1(F)$ and IKT estimates the kurtosis parameter $3 + \gamma_2(F)$.

Substituting estimates of ISD, L_1, and L_2 into (4) yields skewness- and kurtosis-adjusted Jarrow-Rudd option prices, ie C_{JR}, expressed as the following sum of a Black-Scholes option price plus adjustments for skewness and kurtosis deviations from lognormality:

$$C_{JR} = C_{BS}(ISD) + L_1Q_3 + L_2Q_4. \quad (10)$$

Equation (10) yields theoretical skewness- and kurtosis-adjusted Black-Scholes option prices from which we compute deviations of theoretical prices from market-observed prices.

Table 3 summarises results for the same S&P 500 index call option prices used to compile Table 2. Consequently, the stub lists the same even-numbered dates and column 1 the same number of price quotations given in Table 2.

To assess the out-of-sample forecasting power of skewness- and kurtosis-adjustments, the implied standard deviation (ISD), implied skewness coefficient (ISK), and implied kurtosis coefficient (IKT) for each date are estimated from prices observed on the trading day immediately prior to each date listed in column 1. For example, the first row of Table 3 lists the date December 2, 1993, but columns 3–5 report that day's standard deviation, skewness and kurtosis estimates obtained from December 1 prices. Thus, out-of-sample parameters ISD, ISK and IKT reported correspond to one-day lagged estimates.

We use these one-day lagged values of ISD, ISK and IKT to calculate theoretical skewness- and kurtosis-adjusted Black-Scholes option prices according to (10) for all price observations on the even-numbered dates listed. In turn, these theoretical prices based on out-of-sample ISD, ISK and IKT values are then used to compute daily proportions of theoretical prices outside bid-ask spreads and daily averages of deviations from spread boundaries. Column averages are reported in the last row of Table 3.

All daily skewness coefficients are negative, with a column average of −1.68. Daily kurtosis coefficients average 5.39. These option-implied coefficients may be compared with sample coefficients reported in Table 1 for the decade 1986–95.

For example, option-implied skewness of −1.68 is comparable to log-relative return skewness of −1.67 and arithmetic return skewness of −1.19 calculated by including the October 1987 return, but option-implied kurtosis of 5.39 is less extreme than arithmetic return kurtosis of 9.27 and log-relative return kurtosis of 11.92 calculated including the October 1987 return. This appears to suggest that any memory of the October 1987 crash embodied in S&P 500 option prices is more strongly manifested by negative option-implied skewness than option-implied excess kurtosis.

The next-to-last column of Table 3 lists the proportion of skewness- and kurtosis-adjusted prices lying outside their corresponding bid-ask spread boundaries. The column average proportion is 31.85%. The last column lists average absolute deviations of theoretical prices from bid-ask spread boundaries for only those prices lying outside their bid-ask spreads. The column average contract price deviation is $15.85, which is about one-fourth the size of the average bid-ask spread of $69.77 reported in Table 2.

Moreover, Table 3 reveals that implied volatilities from skewness- and kurtosis-adjusted option prices (hollow markers) are unrelated to option moneyness. In turn, this implies that the corresponding price deviations are also unrelated to option moneyness.

Comparison of implied volatility values in Tables 2 and 3 suggests that the implied volatility series obtained using the Jarrow-Rudd model is smoother than the series obtained using the Black-Scholes model. Indeed, the average absolute value of daily changes in implied volatility is 0.42% for the Jarrow-Rudd model, less than half the larger 0.91% of the Black-Scholes model. Using a matched-pairs t-test on absolute values of daily changes in implied volatilities for both models, we obtain a t-value of 4.0, indicating a significantly smoother time series of implied volatilities from the Jarrow-Rudd model. Thus the Jarrow-Rudd model not only flattens the implied volatility skew, it also produces more stable volatility estimates.

The empirical results will vary slightly depending on the assumed interest rate. If the assumed rate is too low, implied standard deviation estimates will be biased upwards. Likewise, if the assumed rate is too high, implied volatility estimates will be biased downward.

We follow standard research practice, and use Treasury bill rates, which may understate the true cost of funds to option market participants. For example, Treasury bill repurchase (repo) rates likely better represent the true cost of borrowed funds to securities firms. For individual investors, the broker call money rate would better represent the true cost of funds.

To assess the robustness of our results to the assumed interest rate, we repeat all empirical analyses leading to Tables 2 and 3 using Treasury bill repurchase rates and broker call money rates. On average, repurchase rates were seven basis points higher than Treasury bill rates in December 1993. Call money rates were on average 196 basis points higher.

Average daily Black-Scholes implied standard deviations are 12.81% using repurchase rates and 10.72% using call money rates. These are lower than the 12.88% average implied volatility reported in Table 2. Using repurchase rates for the Jarrow-Rudd model yields an average daily implied volatility of 11.55%, and using call money rates yields an average volatility of 9.69%. Both are lower than the 11.62% average implied volatility reported in Table 3.

Using repurchase rates yields an average daily skewness coefficient of –1.66 and an average daily kurtosis coefficient of 5.34, while using call money rates yields an average daily skewness coefficient of –1.11 and an average daily excess kurtosis coefficient of 3.46. These are smaller in magnitude than the average skewness of –1.68 and average kurtosis of 5.39 reported in Table 3. Yet whichever interest rate is used to measure the cost of funds to S&P 500 options market participants, the option-implied distributions of S&P 500 returns are still noticeably non-normal.

Overall, we conclude that skewness- and kurtosis-adjustment terms added to the Black-Scholes formula significantly improve pricing accuracy for deep in-the-money or deep out-of-the-money S&P 500 index options. Furthermore, these improvements are obtainable from out-of-sample estimates of skewness and kurtosis.

Of course, there is an added cost, in that two additional parameters must be estimated. But this cost is slight, because once the computer code is in place, the additional computation time is trivial on modern computers.

Hedging implications of the Jarrow-Rudd model

To explore the Jarrow-Rudd model's implications for hedging strategies using options, we derive formulas for an option's delta and gamma based on the model. Delta is used to calculate the number of contracts needed to form an effective hedge based on options. Gamma states the sensitivity of a delta-hedged position to stock price changes. By definition, delta is the first partial derivative of an option price with respect to the underlying stock price. Similarly, gamma is the second partial derivative.

Taking first and second derivatives of the Jarrow-Rudd call option price formula yields these delta and gamma formulas, where the variables λ_j and Q_j were defined earlier in (5).

$$\text{Delta: } \frac{\partial C}{\partial S_0} = N(d_1) + \lambda_1\left(\frac{3}{S_0}\right)Q_3 + \lambda_2\left(\frac{4}{S_0}\right)Q_4 \quad (11a)$$

$$\text{Gamma: } \frac{\partial^2 C}{\partial S_0^2} = n(d_1)\left(S_0\sigma\sqrt{t}\right)^{-1} + \lambda_1\left(\frac{6}{S_0^2}\right)Q_3 + \lambda_2\left(\frac{12}{S_0^2}\right)Q_4. \quad (11b)$$

The first terms on the right-hand sides of (11a) and (11b) are the delta and gamma for the Black-Scholes model. Adding the second and third terms yields the delta and gamma for the Jarrow-Rudd model.

Table 4 illustrates how a hedging strategy based on the Jarrow-Rudd model might differ from a hedging strategy based on the Black-Scholes model. In this example, S&P 500 index options are used to delta-hedge a hypothetical $10 million stock portfolio with a beta of one. The example assumes an index level of S_0 = $700, an interest rate of r = 5%, a dividend yield of y = 2%, and a time until option expiration of t = 0.25. For the volatility parameter in the Black-Scholes model, we use the average implied volatility of 12.88% reported in Table 2. For the Jarrow-Rudd model, we use the average implied volatility of 11.62% along with the average skewness and kurtosis values of $\lambda_1 = -1.68$ and $\lambda_2 = 5.39$ reported in Table 3.

Strike prices range from 660 to 750 in increments of 10. For each strike price, the BS and JR columns list the number of S&P 500 index option contracts needed to delta-hedge the assumed $10 million stock portfolio, according to the Black-Scholes and the Jarrow-Rudd models.

In both cases, numbers of contracts required are computed as follows, where the option contract size is 100 times the index level (Hull, 1993).

Table 4 reveals that for in-the-money options a delta-hedge based on the Black-Scholes model specifies a greater number of contracts than a delta-hedge based on the Jarrow-Rudd model. But for out-of-the-money options, a delta-hedge based on the Jarrow-Rudd model requires more contracts (except in one case).

Table 4. Number of option contracts needed to delta-hedge $10 million stock portfolio with beta of one

In-the-money options			Out-of-the-money options		
Strike	(BS)	(JR)	Strike	(BS)	(JR)
660	167	161	710	303	302
670	179	173	720	370	377
680	197	190	730	465	486
690	221	215	740	601	651
700	256	250	750	802	900

Index level S_0 = $700, interest rate r = 5%, dividend yield y = 2%, time until option expiration t = 0.25, Black-Scholes (BS) model assumes volatility of σ = 12.88%. Jarrow-Rudd (JR) model assumes σ = 11.62%, and skewness and kurtosis parameters of $\lambda_1 = -1.68$ and $\lambda_2 = 5.39$.

Differences in the number of contracts specified by each model are greatest for out-of-the-money options. For example, in the case of a delta-hedge based on options with a strike price of 740, the Black-Scholes model specifies 601 contracts while the Jarrow-Rudd model specifies 651 contracts.

Summary and conclusion

We have empirically tested an expanded version of the Black-Scholes (1973) option pricing model developed by Jarrow and Rudd (1982) that accounts for skewness and kurtosis deviations from lognormality in stock price distributions. The Jarrow-Rudd model was applied to estimate coefficients of skewness and kurtosis implied by S&P 500 index option prices.

We find significant negative skewness and positive excess kurtosis in the option-implied distribution of S&P 500 index prices. This observed negative skewness and positive excess kurtosis induces a volatility smile when the Black-Scholes formula is used to calculate option-implied volatilities across a range of strike prices.

By adding skewness and kurtosis-adjustment terms developed in the Jarrow-Rudd model, the volatility smile is effectively flattened. We conclude that skewness- and kurtosis-adjustment terms added to the Black-Scholes formula significantly improve accuracy and consistency for pricing deep in-the-money and deep out-of-the-money options.

BIBLIOGRAPHY

Barone-Adesi, G., and R.E. Whaley, 1986, "The Valuation of American Call Options and the Expected Ex-Dividend Stock Price Decline", *Journal of Financial Economics* 17, pp. 91-111.

Black, F., and M. Scholes, 1973, "The Pricing of Options and Corporate Liabilities", *Journal of Political Economy* 81, pp. 637-59.

Black, F., 1975, "Fact and Fantasy in the Use of Options", *Financial Analysts Journal* 31, pp. 36-72.

Hull, J.C., 1993, *Options, Futures, and Other Derivative Securities*, Englewood Cliffs, N.J.: Prentice Hall.

Jarrow, R., and A. Rudd, 1982, "Approximate Option Valuation for Arbitrary Stochastic Processes", *Journal of Financial Economics* 10, pp. 347-69.

Merton, R.C., 1973, "The Theory of Rational Option Pricing", *Bell Journal of Economics and Management Science* 4, pp. 141-83.

Natenburg, S., 1994, *Option Volatility and Pricing*, Chicago: Probus Publishing.

Rubinstein, M., 1994, "Implied Binomial Trees", *Journal of Finance* 49, pp. 771-818.

Stuart, A., and J.K. Ord, 1987 *Kendall's Advanced Theory of Statistics*, New York: Oxford University Press.

Whaley, R.E., 1982 "Valuation of American Call Options on Dividend Paying Stocks", *Journal of Financial Economics* 10, pp. 29-58.

Garch Gamma*

Robert F. Engle and Joshua V. Rosenberg
University of California at San Diego; Stern School of Business, New York University

This paper addresses the issue of hedging option positions when the underlying asset exhibits stochastic volatility. By parameterising the volatility process as Garch, and using risk-neutral valuation, we approximate hedging parameters (delta and gamma) using Monte Carlo simulation. We estimate hedging parameters for options on the Standard & Poor's (S&P) 500 index, a bond futures index, a weighted foreign exchange rate index, and an oil futures index. We find that Black-Scholes and Garch deltas are similar for the options considered, whereas Garch gammas are significantly higher than Black-Scholes gammas for all options. For near-the-money options, Garch gamma hedge ratios are higher than Black-Scholes hedge ratios when hedging a long-term option with a short-term option. Away from the money, Garch gamma hedge ratios are lower than Black-Scholes.

Constructing a hedge for an options position involves minimising exposure to factors that influence the option price. The primary risk factors for an option are changes in the price and volatility of the underlying asset. This chapter explores the hedging of options when trading occurs in discrete time, and volatility follows a stochastic process in which the magnitude of recent price changes provides information about future volatility.

Initially, consider the problem of hedging under the Black and Scholes (1973) assumptions of continuous trading and constant volatility over the life of the option. In deriving their option-pricing formula, Black and Scholes use the linear relationship between the change in the option price and the change in the underlying price over an infinitesimal unit of time. This means that a perfect dynamic hedge for an options position can be formed by selling short a given number (delta) of shares of the underlying. If volatility is deterministic, but not constant, Merton (1973) shows that a perfect hedge can be formed if average variance is used in the Black-Scholes equation.

Assuming that hedging occurs in discrete time complicates the process. Boyle (1977) shows that if continuous trading is possible but hedging occurs in discrete time, option and underlying price behaviour are no longer perfectly correlated. The option price response to large underlying price changes is convex, so that a delta hedge is no longer riskless. The second derivative of the Black-Scholes formula with respect to the underlying price, gamma, measures this characteristic.

In this case, in addition to the underlying asset, hedging an option position requires a hedging instrument correlated with convexity. Possible candidates for additional hedging instruments are options on the same underlying asset with a different strike or with a different maturity.

Relaxing the assumption of deterministic volatility presents additional challenges. Under stochastic volatility, the option price will respond to random changes in volatility as well as random changes in the underlying price. Thus, an option hedge requires a hedging instrument correlated with the random change in volatility. Again, the natural hedging instrument is an option on the same underlying with some other difference in contract specification.

It is now clear that hedging an option position in discrete time under stochastic volatility will require the underlying and at least one additional option. Once the Black-Scholes assumptions

* *This paper was first published in* The Journal of Derivatives, *Summer (1995). Reprinted with permission from Institutional Investor Inc. To order a subscription, or for other information, please call (212) 224 3185.*

have been relaxed, however, the problem of option pricing must be re-examined.

There is a substantial literature concerning pricing options under stochastic volatility in continuous time. Johnson and Shanno (1987), Scott (1987), Wiggins (1987) and Hull and White (1987a) derive option pricing formulas when the underlying asset follows a diffusion with stochastic variance. Except for Wiggins, all these researchers invoke risk-neutral pricing and estimate option prices using Monte Carlo techniques. More recently, Ball and Roma (1994), Stein and Stein (1991) and Heston (1993) find closed-form solutions for option prices in continuous time for various stochastic volatility processes.

Option pricing in discrete time has received substantial attention too. Rubinstein (1976) shows that the Black–Scholes formula can be derived in discrete time, with the standard Black–Scholes assumptions, assuming that the underlying price and consumption are jointly lognormal. Brennan (1979), Lee, Rao and Auchmuty (1981) and Stapleton and Subrahmanyam (1984) derive option-pricing results in discrete time in a more general framework.

Amin and Ng (1993) and Duan (1995) address the issue of option pricing in discrete time under stochastic volatility. Duan finds an equivalent martingale measure that can be used for risk-neutral pricing in the Garch-in-mean model under certain restrictions on preferences and distributions. Amin and Ng derive an option-pricing formula under systematic stochastic volatility.

As trading intervals shrink, we could view our discrete time problem as an approximation to continuous time and invoke the assumptions given in previous research for risk-neutral valuation in continuous time. Alternatively, we could apply the discrete time results under the assumption that there is no risk premium for volatility and according to the preference and distribution restrictions given in Duan. In either case, we assume that if there is a leverage effect (ie correlations between price changes and volatility changes) it is small enough so that risk-neutral pricing is an acceptable approximation.

As there is generally not a closed-form solution to the option pricing problem under stochastic volatility, we use Monte Carlo simulation to price options, and finite differences to estimate hedge ratios. Polynomial functions are fitted to estimated hedge ratios to give a closed form.

We select the Garch-t components with leverage model developed by Engle and Lee (1993) as a particularly appealing representation of the volatility process. The Garch components with leverage model nests the Garch(1,1) and Garch-t models (in which the stochastic innovations are assumed to follow a Student t distribution) developed by Bollerslev (1986, 1987). It explicitly accounts for the relationship between the magnitude of recent price changes and volatility, incorporates relatively complex dynamics in mean reversion, and allows for an asymmetric effect of "bad news" on volatility. The leverage effect follows the model developed by Glosten, Jagannathan and Runkle (1993).

The Garch hedging parameters we estimate differ from Black–Scholes hedging parameters because Garch parameters incorporate the interrelationships among underlying price changes, volatility, and the option price. For instance, Engle and Rosenberg (1994) show that, for at-the-money options, Garch gamma is a weighted average of Black–Scholes gamma and vega. Under Garch, a large price shock affects the option price through convexity and through an increase in volatility. In addition, Garch delta incorporates the direct effect on the option price of an underlying price change and the indirect effect of an increase in volatility that follows "bad news".

Option hedging tests

The issue of hedging options positions has been examined in several contexts. Galai (1983) analyses the returns from delta-hedged positions for options on individual stocks traded on the CBOE. The Black–Scholes model, with volatility held constant, is found to be unable to explain the observed average option returns. This suggests that there may be missing factors that drive the option price, such as stochastic volatility.

Hull and White (1987b) consider the problem of hedging non-exchange-traded foreign currency options with exchange-traded options and the underlying currency. They derive a general model in continuous time with delta, gamma and vega hedge parameters. In simulations and tests of hedging currency options on the Philadelphia Stock Exchange, they find that delta-gamma hedging works best under "fairly constant implied standard deviation" (p 147) and short times to maturity, whereas delta-vega hedging works best in the opposite situation.

The primary problem with their empirical tests is pricing of the non-exchange-traded options. They price these options by

Black-Scholes evaluated at the implied standard deviation of the exchange-traded option. Observed differences between quoted and Black-Scholes prices, especially for away-from-the-money options, make this a tenuous assumption.

It is also unclear that the implied volatilities are substitutable between options with a different maturity and strike prices as the implied volatilities may reflect option-specific mispricing as well as volatility information. In addition, the simulations that agree with these empirical results rely on a volatility process that is independent of underlying prices.

Engle and Rosenberg (1998) test the effectiveness of Garch gammas in hedging medium-term at-the-money S&P 500 index options with short-term at-the-money options. Delta-Garch-gamma hedges outperform Black-Scholes delta hedges and delta-vega hedges derived from an autoregressive volatility model. Garch gammas differ from those in this study because they are derived analytically from an approximate stochastic volatility option-pricing formula, using a Garch components model with no leverage. The analytic gammas, however, are known to be close to the Monte Carlo simulated gammas for at-the-money options. This article also models in-the-money and out-of-the-money hedge parameters, for which simulation is essential.

Problems with using option-pricing formulas derived from arbitrage-based arguments are examined by Figlewski (1989). He finds evidence from simulations that transaction costs, market imperfections and discrete rebalancing make it possible only to establish bounds, not to determine a unique option price. In this case, option hedge ratios are not well defined.

Moreover, in a study of the 30 most actively traded individual stock options on the CBOE, Figlewski and Freund (1994) find evidence that gamma and theta risks are priced. This suggests that risk-neutral pricing may be an inadequate approximation for deriving hedge parameters.

Discretely rebalanced hedges, as opposed to continuously rebalanced hedges, present additional complications. Robins and Schachter (1994) show that a Black-Scholes delta hedge is not a variance-minimising hedge over a non-instantaneous time interval. Gilster (1990) shows that hedges rebalanced over a long period of time may exhibit systematic risk. Chen and Johnson (1985) as well as Wolf, Castelino and Francis (1987) derive hedging parameters for mispriced options.

Methodology

Our basic approach is to estimate an underlying asset price process as Garch-t components with leverage, and then approximate hedging parameters for options on this asset using Monte Carlo simulation. Initially, it is useful to discuss the specification of the Garch model. The Garch model reflects many of the observed dynamics of asset returns volatility including short- and long-run mean reversion and asymmetric effects of underlying price movements on volatility. It is specified as follows:

$$\ln(r_t) = e_t; \quad e_t = z_t\sigma_t \tag{1}$$

$$\sigma_t^2 = q_t + \alpha\left(e_{t-1}^2 - q_{t-1}\right) + \delta\left(D_{t-1}e_{t-1}^2 - 0.5q_{t-1)}\right) + \beta\left(\sigma_{t-1}^2 - q_{t-1}\right) \tag{2}$$

where $D_{t-1} = 1$ if $e_{t-1} < 1$, 0 otherwise.

$$q_t = \omega + \rho q_{t-1} + \phi\left(e_{t-1}^2 - \sigma_{t-1}^2\right) \tag{3}$$

$$z_t \sim \text{standardised Student - t}(\nu). \tag{4}$$

In this model, log prices follow a random walk with time-varying volatility, and volatility is related to its own lags as well as lag returns. At time t, ρ is the underlying return, z is the random shock, σ is the conditional standard deviation, and q is the conditional volatility trend. Note that while our focus is on volatility as an input to an option-pricing model, the Garch framework models the evolution of variance. In what follows we typically refer to the Garch variance as "volatility" for convenience.

Of the parameters, α reflects the effect of a shock on the temporary component of volatility, δ captures the asymmetric effect of "bad news" on volatility, β reflects the influence of the prior day's volatility forecast, ρ measures the persistence of the long-term component, and ϕ represents the effect of a shock on the long-run component. Shocks are selected from a standardised Student-t distribution with ν degrees of freedom, where ν is estimated so as to emulate the observed leptokurtosis in many financial returns' time series.

Engle and Lee (1993) show that the Garch components model is equivalent to a Garch (2,2) model. In fact, with ρ and ϕ equal to zero, the components model simplifies to a Garch (1,1) model. We take advantage of this simplification in our estimation process, when the components' parameters are statistically insignificant.

Several simplifying assumptions are made for

GARCH GAMMA

option-valuation purposes. We suppose that conditions necessary to invoke risk-neutral valuation are satisfied. Options are all assumed to be European. We also assume that futures prices are unaffected by marking to market, uncertain delivery dates and the quality option. Finally, interest rates are assumed to be constant, whereas dividends are assumed to be deterministic.

We then apply risk-neutral valuation in a straightforward way for the different types of options. Merton (1973) generalises Black–Scholes to options on assets with a known dividend yield. This methodology is used to price S&P 500 index options. Black (1976) shows that options on futures can be valued as standard options with the dividend yield set equal to the risk-free rate. This method is applied for options on oil and bond futures indices.

Garman and Kohlhagan (1983) and Grabbe (1983) show that foreign exchange options can be valued as standard options with the dividend yield replaced by the foreign risk-free rate. We use this result as well.

We approximate hedging parameters by simulating the effect of an underlying price shock on the option price. The option price is evaluated using risk-neutral valuation as given by Equation (5). That is, the option price is the present value of the expected payoff of the option, where the expectation is taken with respect to the probability distribution of terminal prices given by the Garch components process, with drift equal to the risk-free rate.

The distribution of terminal underlying prices is approximated using Monte Carlo simulation of the asset price path under the Garch volatility process as given by Equation (6). Fifty-thousand terminal prices are generated and the antithetic variate technique is used to improve the efficiency of the option price estimate.

$$\begin{aligned} & C_1(S_1,\sigma_1^2,q_1,T) \\ & \overset{RNVR}{=} e^{-rT}E\{\max[0,S_T-K]|S_1,\sigma_1^2,q_1,T\} \\ & \overset{CLT}{\cong} \hat{C}_1(S_1,\sigma_1^2,q_1,T) \\ & = \frac{1}{N}e^{-rt}\sum_{j=1}^{N}\{\max[0,S_{T,j}-K]|S_1,\sigma_1^2,q_1,T\} \end{aligned} \quad (5)$$

$$S_{t,j} = \exp^{r_f - \frac{\sigma^2_{t,j}}{2} + e_{t,j}\sigma_{t,j}} S_{t-1,j}; \quad (6)$$

$\sigma^2_{t,j}$ are generated by Garch $(\alpha,\beta,\delta,\rho,\phi,\nu)$
$e_{t,j}$ ~ standardised Student-t (ν), j = 1...50,000.
In (5) the first equality, labelled $\overset{RNVR}{=}$ is due to a risk-neutral valuation relation, whereas the second, labelled $\overset{CLT}{=}$ results from the central limit theorem.

The initial volatility forecasts, σ_1^2 and q_1 are set equal to the unconditional variance as a default case. The implication is that volatility is currently at its long-run level. Changing the initial variance will affect the hedging parameters, since average volatility will depend on the maturity of the option.

The hedging problem in discrete time involves neutralising the option portfolio to a change in today's underlying price. The first derivative of today's option price with respect to today's underlying price does not depend on yesterday's price in a Black–Scholes world because returns carry no information about volatility, however the price yesterday does have useful information.

In Equations (7) and (8), the finite difference estimate of the first and second derivatives of option prices at time 1 are given and both S_0 and S_1 are listed as arguments.

$$\begin{aligned} \Delta_{GARCH} &= \frac{\partial C_1(S_0,S_1,\sigma_1^2,q_1,T)}{\partial S_1} \\ &\cong \frac{\hat{C}_1(S_0,S_0+\varepsilon,\sigma_1^2,q_1,T)-\hat{C}_1(S_0,S_0-\varepsilon,\sigma_1^2,q_1,T)}{2\varepsilon}. \end{aligned} \quad (7)$$

$$\begin{aligned} \Gamma_{GARCH} &= \frac{\partial^2 C_1(S_0,S_1,\sigma_1^2,q_1,T)}{\partial S_1^2} \\ &\cong \frac{\hat{C}_1(S_0,S_0+\varepsilon,\sigma_1^2,q_1,T)-2\hat{C}_1(S_0,S_0,\sigma_1^2,q_1,T)}{\varepsilon^2} + \\ & \frac{+\hat{C}_1(S_0,S_0-\varepsilon,\sigma_1^2,q_1,T)}{\varepsilon^2} \end{aligned} \quad (8)$$

$$\varepsilon = 0.1\sigma_1 * S_0.$$

Equations (7) and (8) are estimated using an initial index price of 10,000 with ε set to a one-tenth standard deviation price shock.

The polynomial function in (9) is fitted to the simulated hedge ratios using least squares, with one function for each moneyness. The final hedge ratios are given by the fitted values from the estimated function in Equation (10):

$$\begin{aligned} \log(\Gamma(S_0,T,K)) = \hat{a} + \hat{b}T + \hat{c}T^{\frac{1}{2}} + \hat{d}T^{-\frac{1}{2}} + \\ \hat{e}T^{-1} + \hat{f}T^{-2} + \hat{g}T^{-3} + \varepsilon_{T,K}. \end{aligned} \quad (9)$$

$$\begin{aligned} & \hat{\Gamma}(S_0,T,K) = \\ & \exp\left(\hat{a} + \hat{b}T + \hat{c}T^{\frac{1}{2}} + \hat{d}T^{-\frac{1}{2}} + \hat{e}T^{-1} + \hat{f}T^{-2} + \hat{g}T^{-3}\right). \end{aligned} \quad (10)$$

As we mentioned earlier, under Garch volatility, the response of the option price to volatility changes is incorporated directly in Garch delta and gamma. Thus, we do not estimate a separate vega parameter.

Estimation of Garch models

Garch models are estimated for four underlying assets: the S&P 500 index, a Treasury bond futures index, a weighted exchange rate index and a crude oil futures index. For each underlying asset we have a daily returns time series of 2,114 observations over the period from June 1983 through mid-May 1994 from the Datastream database. The data were provided by Salomon Brothers. The oil and bond futures index prices are taken from contracts rolled on the first day of the expiration month. The weighted foreign exchange index prices are from an index developed by the Bank of England. Table 1 lists the sample statistics for the index log returns.

As expected, all of the series exhibit substantial departures from normality. In particular, normality is rejected for all series at the 0.001 level using the Kolmogorov D test. All the series exhibit excess kurtosis, while the oil futures and the S&P 500 index exhibit substantial negative skewness. All mean log returns are within four basis points of zero, while there are large differences in volatility. The oil futures series is the most volatile with a daily standard deviation of 2.8%, more than five times greater than the foreign exchange index standard deviation of 0.5%.

There is evidence for autocorrelation in the log returns of the S&P 500 and the oil futures index, and marginal evidence in the bond futures index. According to the standardised log returns, however, no series exhibits autocorrelation. All of the series show strong autocorrelation in their squared returns, which is an indication of Garch-type heteroskedasticity.

We used maximum likelihood estimation to estimate one Garch model for each log return series where the log returns are assumed to be Student-t with ν degrees of freedom. Table 2 (overleaf) reports the parameter estimates for each model along with Ljung-Box statistics. In some models, insignificant variables are excluded in the final estimation. When components parameters are not significant, the model is estimated as a Garch (1,1) and the parameters should be interpreted accordingly.

Garch-t components models provide the best fit for the S&P 500 and the oil futures index volatility, whereas a Garch(1,1)-t model is best for the bond futures and exchange rate index volatility. The leverage effect (measured by the parameter δ) is marginally significant in the bond futures model using robust t-statistics. It is insignificant in the S&P 500 model. Engle and Lee (1993), however, find the S&P 500 leverage effect to be significant in a model estimated over a longer time period, so we include it in our model. There is strong evidence that the underlying shocks are non-normal as $1/\nu$ is significantly greater than zero for all models.

Estimation of hedge parameters

Using the Monte-Carlo finite difference technique described above, we approximate Garch delta and gamma for options on the Standard & Poor's 500 index, a bond futures index, a weighted foreign exchange rate index, and an oil futures index. Hedge parameters are estimated for moneynesses ranging from 0.8 to 1.2 and for maturities of 1 to 250 days. Garch deltas are not reported but are discussed below.

There are several notable characteristics of Garch deltas. First, Garch deltas are very close to Black–Scholes deltas for at-the-money options, except when there is a strong leverage effect.

Table 1. Data summary

Sample statistics for daily log returns

	Number of observations	Mean	Standard deviation	Skewness	Kurtosis	Kolmogorov normality test p-value	Ljung-Box (15) on log returns	Ljung-Box (15) on squared log returns
S&P 500 index	2,114	0.0003	0.0109	–6.34	145.60	0.001	36.33	80.19
Bond futures index	2,114	0.0001	0.0070	–0.07	5.25	0.001	25.78	553.88
Exchange rate index	2,114	–0.0002	0.0051	0.11	4.45	0.001	23.54	108.87
Oil futures index	2,114	–0.0005	0.0283	–3.30	58.14	0.001	58.32	59.50

Sample statistics for daily standardised log returns (using estimated Garch model)

	Number of observations	Mean (in units of standard deviation)	Standard deviation	Skewness	Kurtosis	Kolmogorov normality test p-value	Ljung-Box (15) on standardised log returns	Ljung-Box (15) on squared standardised log returns
S&P 500 index	2,114	0.04	1.06	–1.12	12.22	0.001	14.21	5.06
Bond futures index	2,114	0.01	1.00	–0.19	4.46	0.001	22.75	14.96
Exchange rate index	2,114	–0.03	0.99	0.06	4.35	0.001	20.99	9.32
Oil futures index	2,114	–0.02	1.00	–0.68	8.84	0.001	9.91	12.23

Ljung-Box (15) 5% critical value = 25.

Table 2. Estimation of Garch models: maximum likelihood estimates with t-distribution as the underlying density – 2,114 observations (June 7, 1986–May 12, 1994)

S&P index log returns; Garch-t components model	Coefficient	Standard error	t-stat	Robust standard error	Robust t-stat
ω	6.00E-07	2.00E-07	3.00	1.13E-06	0.53
α	0.0000	0.0221	0.00	0.0255	0.00
β	0.7615	0.0615	12.39	0.2267	3.36
δ	0.1236	0.0347	3.56	0.1916	0.65
φ	0.0154	0.0059	2.62	0.0137	1.12
ρ	0.9891	0.0031	315.57	0.0046	213.65
1/ν	0.1935	0.0177	10.95		
T-bond futures index log returns; Garch(1,1)-t model	**Coefficient**	**Standard error**	**t-stat**	**Robust standard error**	**Robust t-stat**
ω	3.56E-07	1.69E-07	2.10	2.43E-06	0.15
α	0.0236	0.0088	2.67	0.0095	2.49
β	0.9574	0.0092	103.68	0.0092	104.50
δ	0.0245	0.0116	2.10	0.0127	1.92
1/ν	0.1626	0.0240	6.77		
Weighted foreign exchange rate index log returns; Garch(1,1)-t model	**Coefficient**	**Standard error**	**t-stat**	**Robust standard error**	**Robust t-stat**
ω	8.61E-07	3.58E-07	2.40	1.18E-06	0.73
α	0.0495	0.0122	4.05	0.0124	3.99
β	0.9190	0.0221	41.67	0.0197	46.72
1/ν	0.1550	0.0248	6.25		
Crude oil futures index log returns; Garch(1,1)-t model	**Coefficient**	**Standard error**	**t-stat**	**Robust standard error**	**Robust t-stat**
ω	7.21E-06	2.40E-06	3.01	2.88E-05	0.25
α	0.0787	0.0321	2.45	0.0348	2.26
β	0.7149	0.1314	5.44	0.1460	4.90
φ	0.0985	0.0226	4.36	0.0331	2.97
ρ	0.9953	0.0082	121.73	0.0142	70.31
1/ν	0.2311	0.0232	9.95		

Second, out-of-the-money options have higher Garch deltas and in-the-money options have lower Garch deltas than Black-Scholes. All Garch deltas, however, are close to Black-Scholes deltas, with the maximum difference being 0.12 for the oil futures options. For foreign exchange, bond futures and S&P500 index options, the maximum differences are 0.02, 0.07, and 0.03 respectively.

Garch gammas are reported for options on each index in Table 3. The formulas in each table can be used for either calls or puts, for any risk-free or dividend rate, and various combinations of index levels and strike prices. Each table corresponds to an underlying index, and each column corresponds to an option's moneyness (S′/K′). The column gives the coefficients for the hedge parameter equation, so that the hedge parameters can be calculated using Equation (10).

1. Black-Scholes gamma

Out-of-the-money options (risk-free rate = 0, dividends = 0, sigma = 0.74% daily)

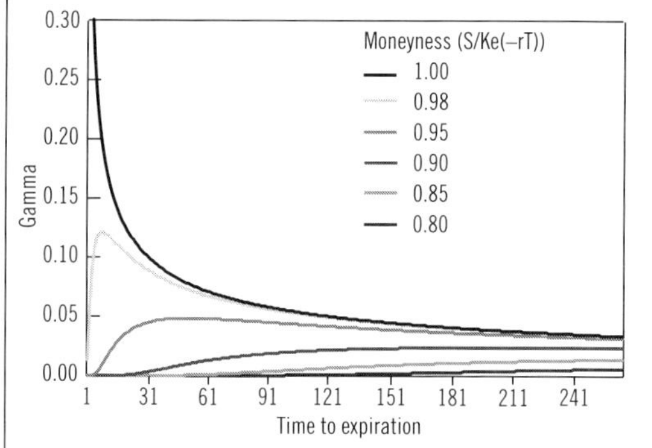

2. Garch gamma (smoothed)

Out-of-the-money options estimated for options on the S&P 500 index (risk-free rate = 0, dividends = 0, $\text{sigma}_1 = \sqrt{q_1}$ = 0.74% daily)

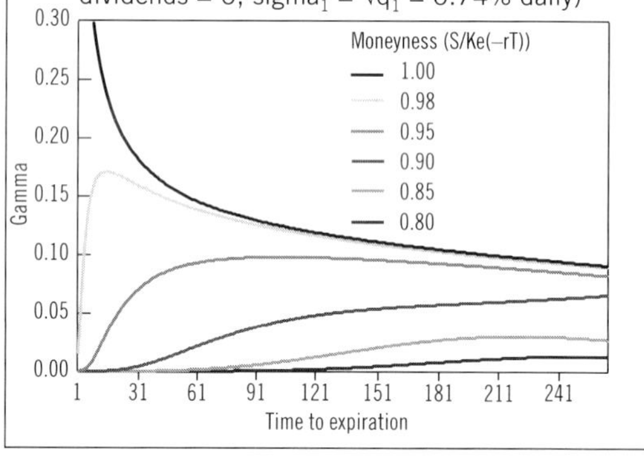

There are substantial differences between Black-Scholes and Garch gammas. These result in even larger differences in gamma hedge ratios. Figures 1 and 2 display gammas for out-of-the-money options on the S&P 500 derived from Black-Scholes and Garch. Garch gammas are higher than Black-Scholes gammas because they reflect the dual impact of the second-order effects of an underlying price shock.

First, as in Black-Scholes, the underlying price shock has a positive second-order effect on the options price and, second, the underlying price shock increases future volatility, which further increases the option price. Garch gammas also decay more slowly, since the decline of convexity as maturity increases is partly offset by the increase in the sensitivity of the option price to a volatility shock as maturity increases. For substantially away-from-the-money options, both Black-Scholes and Garch gammas approach zero.

Table 4 reports the Black-Scholes and Garch gamma hedge ratios for hedging a near-the-money long-term option on the S&P 500 index with a short-term option having the same strike price, assuming no dividends and a risk-free rate

Table 3. Garch gammas

Garch gamma for options on the S&P 500 index (estimated for one $100 option)

$$\text{Garch gamma} = 100 / (\text{current index level}) \times \exp(-qT) \times \left[\exp\left(a + bT + c\sqrt{T} + d/\sqrt{T} + e/T + f/T^2 + g/T^3\right)\right]$$

T = number of trading days until maturity; r = domestic risk-free rate of interest; q = dividend yield
Coefficients are chosen from table below using column S′/K′
S′ = exp(–qT) current index level; K′ = exp(–rT) strike price

Coefficient	S′/K′ 1.20	1.15	1.10	1.05	1.02	1.00	0.98	0.95	0.90	0.85	0.80
a	1.943	–2.164	–2.985	0.853	–2.845	–2.805	–2.492	–4.151	18.558	–11.346	–52.025
b	0.000	–0.009	–0.007	0.006	–0.003	–0.002	–0.001	–0.005	0.034	–0.053	–0.122
c	–0.119	0.188	0.159	–0.250	0.047	0.033	0.003	0.135	–1.423	1.440	4.344
d	–67.212	–29.966	–6.735	–13.697	6.260	6.562	5.795	15.806	–126.824	–33.888	165.451
e	115.481	31.437	–21.193	8.070	–11.456	–7.106	–11.899	–61.808	185.480	96.339	–237.589
f	–110.942	–5.342	49.192	–14.229	4.989	4.989	6.215	94.303	–145.829	–133.325	200.393
g	51.641	–3.356	–27.637	10.727	–0.993	–1.942	–1.786	–53.490	60.790	71.642	–89.671

Garch gamma for options on a T-bond futures index (estimated for one $100 option)

$$\text{Garch gamma} = 100 / (\text{current index level}) \times \exp(-rT) \times \left[\exp\left(a + bT + c\sqrt{T} + d/\sqrt{T} + e/T + f/T^2 + g/T^3\right)\right]$$

T = number of trading days until maturity; r = domestic risk-free rate of interest; q = dividend yield
Coefficients are chosen from table below using column S′/K′
S′ = current index level – present value of expected coupon payments; K′ = strike price

Coefficient	S′/K′ 1.20	1.15	1.10	1.05	1.02	1.00	0.98	0.95	0.90	0.85	0.80
a	–46.694	–16.195	26.575	1.183	–1.142	–1.703	–1.042	11.406	–2.159	–57.295	–50.400
b	–0.130	–0.071	0.036	0.002	–0.001	–0.003	–0.001	0.024	–0.043	–0.142	–0.079
c	4.330	2.035	1.603	0.156	–0.004	0.050	–0.010	–0.955	0.959	5.008	3.517
d	125.029	–20.132	–193.330	–13.264	–0.063	1.867	–0.276	–66.033	–84.679	180.888	182.390
e	–155.280	83.541	330.044	–31.732	–9.133	1.100	–9.320	53.109	186.247	–253.696	–290.170
f	102.560	–131.416	–326.586	86.591	2.046	–2.739	2.113	15.277	–227.343	206.868	278.062
g	–39.018	73.052	155.761	–51.837	2.177	1.604	2.461	–22.049	117.836	–90.846	–133.555

Garch gamma for options on a weighted foreign exchange rate index (estimated for one $100 option)

$$\text{Garch gamma} = 100 / (\text{current index level}) \times \exp(-r_f T) \times \left[\exp\left(a + bT + c\sqrt{T} + d/\sqrt{T} + e/T + f/T^2 + g/T^3\right)\right]$$

T = number of trading days until maturity; r_f = foreign risk-free rate of interest; r_d = domestic risk-free rate of interest
Coefficients are chosen from table below using column S′/K′
S′ = exp($-r_f$T) current index level; K′ = exp($-r_d$T) strike price

Coefficient	S′/K′ 1.20	1.15	1.10	1.05	1.02	1.00	0.98	0.95	0.90	0.85	0.80
a	–46.386	–12.319	28.112	3.388	–0.169	0.155	–0.171	3.935	18.128	–26.078	–37.319
b	–0.108	–0.049	0.050	0.009	0.002	0.003	0.002	0.010	0.025	–0.074	–0.061
c	3.826	1.402	–2.062	–0.409	–0.145	–0.175	–0.146	–0.444	–1.198	2.406	2.548
d	140.928	–26.898	–188.507	–23.898	–3.052	–4.531	–2.704	–26.888	–147.028	38.563	118.743
e	–198.426	83.759	308.590	1.999	–2.857	8.837	–4.474	4.012	247.956	–22.996	–182.620
f	162.141	–120.971	–290.759	20.997	–1.343	–8.010	2.794	25.086	–240.657	–18.158	168.180
g	–71.189	65.885	135.378	11.294	2.067	3.720	–0.822	–14.920	113.576	17.139	–78.694

Garch gamma for options on a crude oil futures index (estimated for one $100 option)

$$\text{Garch gamma} = 100 / (\text{current index level}) \times \exp(-rT) \times \left[\exp\left(a + bT + c\sqrt{T} + d/\sqrt{T} + e/T + f/T^2 + g/T^3\right)\right]$$

T = number of trading days until maturity; r = domestic risk-free rate of interest
Coefficients are chosen from table below using column S′/K′
S′ = current index level; K′ = strike price

Coefficient	S′/K′ 1.20	1.15	1.10	1.05	1.02	1.00	0.98	0.95	0.90	0.85	0.80
a	1.181	–0.238	–0.235	–0.537	–0.273	–0.415	–0.534	–0.918	–0.705	0.019	0.724
b	0.009	0.005	0.005	0.004	0.004	0.004	0.004	0.003	0.003	0.005	0.006
c	–0.330	–0.212	–0.201	–0.168	–0.185	–0.174	–0.160	–0.127	–0.150	–0.207	–0.255
d	–18.977	–10.974	–11.141	–9.797	–11.156	–10.337	–9.915	–7.900	–8.431	–12.430	–17.323
e	18.028	7.931	14.165	16.062	19.921	18.562	17.840	12.769	8.149	9.171	12.424
f	–16.519	–6.639	–16.882	–17.116	–20.228	–18.092	–18.026	–13.931	–9.293	–8.156	–6.804
g	8.497	3.316	8.972	8.215	9.794	8.689	8.647	6.654	4.714	4.469	2.711

Table 4. Comparison of hedge ratios: hedging longer-term contract with shorter-term contract (same strike)

Black-Scholes gamma hedge ratios (risk-free rate = 0, sigma = 0.74% daily, dividends = 0)

	Moneyness (S/Ke^{-rT})										
Maturities	1.20	1.15	1.10	1.05	1.02	1.00	0.98	0.95	0.90	0.85	0.80
40:20	>1,000	59.16	5.39	1.29	0.78	0.71	0.77	1.22	8.49	367.50	>1,000
60:20	>1,000	211.27	8.65	1.29	0.65	0.53	0.65	1.19	15.88	>1,000	>1,000
80:20	>1,000	382.60	10.51	1.23	0.57	0.50	0.57	1.13	20.81	>1,000	>1,000
100:20	>1,000	532.71	11.51	1.17	0.52	0.45	0.52	1.07	23.87	>1,000	>1,000
120:20	>1,000	653.16	12.03	1.11	0.48	0.41	0.47	1.01	25.71	>1,000	>1,000
140:20	>1,000	746.51	12.27	1.06	0.44	0.38	0.44	0.96	26.79	>1,000	>1,000
160:20	>1,000	817.80	12.33	1.01	0.42	0.35	0.41	0.91	27.38	>1,000	>1,000
180:20	>1,000	871.80	12.30	0.97	0.39	0.33	0.39	0.87	27.66	>1,000	>1,000
200:20	>1,000	912.44	12.21	0.93	0.37	0.32	0.37	0.84	27.73	>1,000	>1,000
220:20	>1,000	942.77	12.08	0.90	0.36	0.30	0.35	0.81	27.66	>1,000	>1,000
240:20	>1,000	965.13	11.92	0.87	0.34	0.29	0.34	0.78	27.49	>1,000	>1,000

Garch simulated gamma hedge ratios estimated for the S&P 500 index (risk-free rate = 0, h1 = q1 = 0.74% daily, dividends = 0)

	Moneyness (S/Ke^{-rT})										
Maturities	1.20	1.15	1.10	1.05	1.02	1.00	0.98	0.95	0.90	0.85	0.80
40:20	4.47	3.87	2.80	1.45	0.90	0.79	0.90	1.63	7.24	5.26	1.41
60:20	10.52	7.75	4.31	1.59	0.84	0.69	0.82	1.84	16.80	17.70	3.29
80:20	18.27	11.94	5.49	1.62	0.79	0.64	0.76	1.91	25.39	42.08	7.85
100:20	26.86	15.98	6.37	1.61	0.75	0.60	0.72	1.92	31.61	78.76	17.05
120:20	35.64	19.65	7.02	1.58	0.71	0.57	0.68	1.91	35.71	123.92	32.80
140:20	44.21	22.80	7.46	1.55	0.68	0.54	0.65	1.88	38.37	170.84	55.81
160:20	52.29	25.38	7.74	1.51	0.66	0.52	0.63	1.84	40.17	212.23	84.56
180:20	59.74	27.38	7.89	1.48	0.63	0.50	0.60	1.80	41.56	242.26	115.11
200:20	66.50	28.83	7.92	1.45	0.61	0.48	0.58	1.75	42.83	257.73	142.08
220:20	72.55	29.78	7.87	1.43	0.58	0.46	0.56	1.70	44.20	258.32	160.38
240:20	77.89	30.26	7.74	1.41	0.56	0.45	0.55	1.65	45.80	245.95	166.84

of zero. For near-the-money hedges, Garch gamma hedge ratios are significantly higher than Black-Scholes hedge ratios due to the slower decay of Garch gamma.

For instance, under Black-Scholes assumptions, gamma hedging one 60-day at-the-money option contract requires 0.58 20-day contracts. On the other hand, using Garch gammas, 0.69 20-day contracts are needed. In contrast, for away-from-the-money options, Garch hedge ratios are lower than Black-Scholes hedge ratios.

As with Black-Scholes gammas, Garch gammas are sensitive to the level of volatility. Figure 3 compares Garch gamma for S&P 500 index options with different maturities and three different levels for the initial variance. The initial variance is set equal to the unconditional variance, indicating a flat expected term structure of volatility, 50% below the unconditional variance, which indicates an upward-sloping expected term structure of volatility, and 50% above the unconditional variance, indicating a downward-sloping expected term structure of volatility.

3. Garch gamma

Estimated for near-the-money options on the S&P 500 index at initial volatility = 0.52% (upward-sloping term structure); 0.74% (flat term structure); 0.91% (downward-sloping term structure)

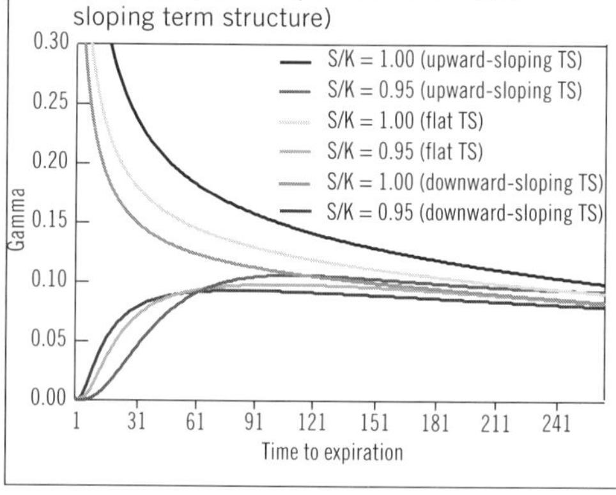

Figure 3 indicates that changing the term structure shape affects the gammas less than moneyness, but it does have an important impact. This indicates that new Garch gammas should be estimated at the current volatility level, if volatility is away from its long-term mean.

Conclusion

This paper develops a methodology for estimating option hedge parameters when the underlying asset exhibits stochastic volatility. We find substantial evidence for Garch-type stochastic volatility in four index returns time-series and estimate Garch delta and gamma using Monte-Carlo simulation and finite differences. Garch deltas are similar to Black-Scholes deltas, whereas Garch gammas and gamma hedge ratios are quite different. This suggests that there is potential for more effective option gamma-hedging by accounting for the relationship between price changes and volatility. In particular, it is possible that incorporating Garch volatility into option models will enhance hedge performance.

BIBLIOGRAPHY

Amin, K.I., and V.K. Ng, 1993, "Option Valuation with Systematic Stochastic Volatility", *Journal of Finance* 48, pp. 881-910.

Ball, C., and A. Roma, 1994, "Stochastic Volatility Option Pricing", *Journal of Financial and Quantitative Analysis* 29, pp. 589-607.

Black, F., 1976, "The Pricing of Commodity Contracts", *Journal of Financial Economics* 3, pp. 167-179.

Black, F. and M. Scholes, 1973, "The Pricing of Options and Corporate Liabilities", *Journal of Political Economy* 81, pp. 637-54.

Bollerslev, T., 1986, "Generalized Autoregressive Conditional Heteroskedasticity", *Journal of Econometrics* 31, pp. 307-27.

Bollerslev, T., 1987, "A Conditionally Heteroskedastic Time Series Model for Speculative Prices and Rates of Return", *Review of Economics and Statistics* pp. 542-7.

Boyle, P.P., 1977, "Options: A Monte Carlo Approach", *Journal of Financial Economics*, 4, pp 323-38.

Brennan, M., 1979, "The Pricing of Contingent Claims in Discrete-Time Models," *Journal of Finance* 34, pp. 53-68.

Chen, N.P. and H. Johnson, 1985, "Hedging Options", *Journal of Financial Economics* 14, pp. 317-21.

Duan, J.C., 1995, "The Garch Option Pricing Model", *Mathematical Finance* 5, pp. 13-32; reprinted as Chapter 24 of the present volume.

Engle, R.F., and G. Lee, 1998, "Testing the Volatility Term Structure using Option Hedging Criteria", Working Paper, New York University Stern School of Business.

Figlewski, S., 1989 "Options Arbitrage in Imperfect Markets", *Journal of Finance* 44, pp. 1289-1311.

Figlewski, S., and S. Freund, 1994, "The Pricing of Convexity, Risk and Time Decay in Options Markets", *Journal of Banking and Finance* 18, pp. 73-91.

Galai, D., 1983, "The Components of the Return from Hedging Options against Stocks", *Journal of Business* 56, pp. 45-54.

Garman, M.B., and S.W. Kohlhagen, 1983, "Foreign Currency Option Values", *Journal of International Money and Finance* 2, pp. 231-7.

Gilster, J.E. Jr, 1990, "The Systematic Risk of Discretely Rebalanced Option Hedges", *Journal of Financial and Quantitative Analysis* 25, pp. 507-16.

Glosten, L.R., R. Jagannathan and D.E. Runkle, 1993, "On the Relation Between the Expected Value and the Volatility of the Nominal Excess Return on Stocks", *Journal of Finance* 48, pp. 1779-801.

Grabbe, J.O., 1983, "The Pricing of Call and Put Options on Foreign Exchange", *Journal of International Money and Finance* 2, pp. 239-53.

Heston, S.L., 1993, "A Closed-Form Solution for Options with Stochastic Volatility with Applications to Bond and Currency Options", *Review of Financial Studies* 6, pp. 327-43; reprinted as Chapter 23 of the present volume.

Hull, J., and A. White, 1987a, "Hedging the Risks from Writing Foreign Currency Options", *Journal of International Money and Finance* 6, pp. 131-52.

Hull, J., and A. White, 1987b, "The Pricing of Options on Assets with Stochastic Volatilities", *Journal of Finance* 42, pp. 143-51.

Johnson, H., and D. Shanno, 1987, "Option Pricing when the Variance is Changing", *Journal of Financial and Quantitative Analysis* 22, pp. 143-51.

Lee, W.Y., R.K.S. Rao and J.F.G. Auchmuty, 1981, "Option Pricing in a Lognormal Securities Market with Discrete Trading", *Journal of Financial Economics* 9, pp. 75-101.

Merton, R.C., 1973, "Theory of Rational Option Pricing", *Bell Journal of Economics and Management Science* 4, pp.141-83.

Robins, R.P., and B. Schachter, 1994, "An Analysis of the Risk in Discretely Rebalanced Option Hedges and Delta-Based Techniques", *Management Science* 40, pp. 798-808.

Rubinstein, M., 1976, "The valuation of Uncertain Income Streams and the Pricing of Options", *Bell Journal of Economics and Management Science* 7, pp. 407-25.

Scott, L.O., 1987, "Option Pricing when the Variance Changes Randomly: Theory, Estimation and an Application", *Journal of Financial and Quantitative Analysis* 22, pp. 419-38.

Stapleton, R.C., and M.G. Subrahmanyam, 1984, "The Valuation of Multivariate Contingent Claims in Discrete Time Models", *Journal of Finance* 39, pp. 207-28.

Stein, E.M., and J.C. Stein, 1991, "Stock Price Distributions with Stochastic Volatility - An Analytic Approach", *Review of Financial Studies* 4, pp. 727-52;

reprinted as Chapter 22 of the present volume.

Wiggins, J.B., 1987, "Option Values under Stochastic Volatility: Theory and Empirical Estimates," *Journal of Financial Economics* 19, pp. 351–72.

Wolf, A., M. Castelino and J.C. Francis, 1987, "Hedging Mispriced Options", *Journal of Futures Markets* 7, pp. 147–56.

Derivatives on Market Volatility:

Hedging Tools Long Overdue*

Robert E. Whaley
Duke University

The Chicago Board Options Exchange Market Volatility Index, based on the implied volatilities of OEX options, provides not only a reliable estimate of short-term stock market volatility but also a volatility "standard" upon which futures and options contracts can be written. This paper shows how volatility derivatives can be used to provide a simple, cost-effective means for hedging the market volatility risk of portfolios that contain options or securities with option-like features. Market volatility derivatives should prove to be valuable risk management tools for option market makers, portfolio insurers, and covered call writers.

The Chicago Board Options Exchange Market Volatility Index (ticker symbol VIX), which is based on the implied volatilities of eight different OEX option series, represents a market consensus forecast of stock market volatility over the next 30 calendar days. The Volatility Index can help the investment community in at least two important ways.

First, it provides a reliable estimate of expected short-term stock market volatility.[1] Expected market volatility is a critical piece of information to many investment decisions; the asset allocation decision is one. Second, it offers a market volatility "standard" upon which derivative contracts may be written. Such a standard must be based on a highly liquid underlying security market. In the case of VIX, the underlying security market is the OEX options market – by far the most active index option market in the United States.

1. Proportion of total number of index options traded in the US in 1992

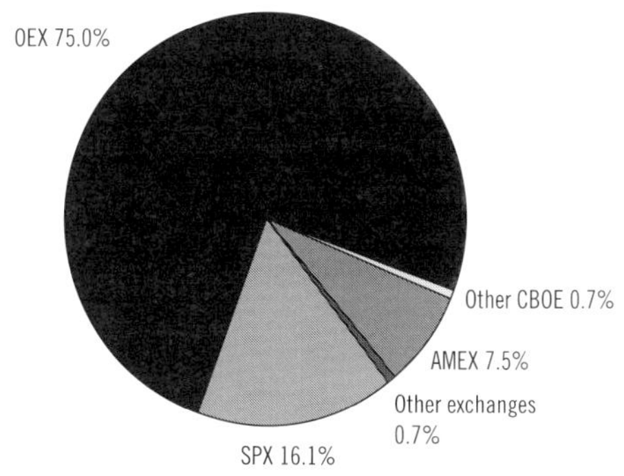

Source: Chicago Board Options Exchange

Figure 1 shows that OEX options accounted for 75% of the total number of index option contracts traded domestically in 1992. Average daily trading volume for OEX calls was 120,475, for puts 125,302.[2] Because it is based on the implied volatilities from the prices of highly active OEX options, VIX provides an up-to-the-minute account of new information affecting market volatility.

The purpose of this paper is to show how futures and options contracts on the CBOE Market Volatility Index may be used to manage the volatility risk exposure of portfolios containing options or securities with option-like features. Following some basic description, we show how to measure a portfolio's volatility risk and how that risk exposure can be managed using exchange-traded index options as well as

* *This paper was first published in* The Journal of Derivatives, *Vol. 1 (1993). Reprinted with permission from Institutional Investor, Inc. To order a subscription, or for other information, please call (212) 224 3185. This research was supported by the Futures and Options Research Center at Duke University. Discussions with Stephen Figlewski, Jeff Fleming, Joseph Levin, Barbara Ostdiek, and Tom Smith were useful in developing this paper.*

the volatility derivatives. Volatility derivatives are shown to be more effective and less expensive.

CBOE market volatility index

The CBOE Market Volatility Index is based upon the implied volatilities of eight near-the-money nearby and second nearby OEX options.[3] To maintain consistency in the composition of VIX, the Volatility Index is constructed so that, at any given time, it represents the implied volatility of a hypothetical at-the-money OEX option with thirty calendar days to expiration. (A detailed description of VIX construction appears in the appendix.)

The at-the-money distinction is important for two reasons. First, it means that the index is based on the most actively traded OEX option series, which are the at-the-money series. Second, it means that the volatility index moves approximately linearly with volatility-induced movements in the underlying OEX option prices.[4] Because there is almost no convexity in the relation between changes in implied volatility and changes in option prices for at-the-money options, the hedging effectiveness of volatility index derivatives is maximised.

The 30-calendar day distinction is also important. Fleming, Ostdiek, and Whaley (1995) document that short-term OEX options tend to have higher implied volatilities than longer-term options. While the explanation for this relation is unclear,[5] maintaining a constant time to expiration minimises the effect that this consideration may have on the Volatility Index level.

Figure 2 shows the levels of the CBOE Market Volatility Index at the close of trading each Wednesday during the five year period January 1988- December 1992. Also included in the figure is the level of the S&P 100 stock index (OEX). The figure is interesting in a number of respects.

2. Levels of VIX and OEX at the close of trading each Wednesday: 1988–92

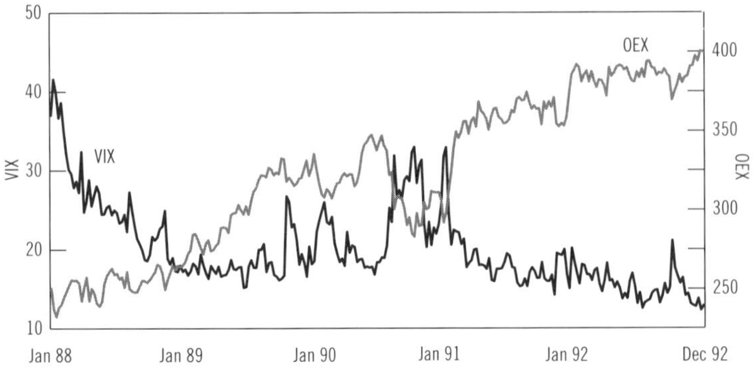

First, VIX generally declined over the period. At the beginning of 1988, the market was coming off the October 1987 market crash when the level of VIX exceeded 150%. As investors regained confidence in the future prospects of equities, the level of expected market volatility tapered off slowly. By the end of 1992, the level of VIX was below 15%.

Second, expected market volatility experienced periodic jumps. These jumps are not without explanation. The jump in late 1989, for example, is the "mini-crash" resulting from the UAL restructuring failure. The jump in mid-1990 occurs with Iraq's invasion of Kuwait; the jump in early 1991 corresponds to UN forces attacking Iraq; and the jump in November 1992 reflects uncertainty about the US presidential election.

Unexpected economic and political news causes investors to expect increased future volatility, and to bid up the prices of OEX options relative to the value of the underlying OEX index. VIX is merely reflecting the market's current thinking about expected volatility.

Third, VIX and OEX tend to move in opposite directions. This stands to reason. If expected market volatility increases, investors will demand a higher rate of return on stocks, and hence stock prices will fall.

The inverse correlation between VIX and OEX will not be perfect, however, because the volatility horizons in the two security valuations are different.[6] For stocks, the relevant expected volatility is the volatility over the life of the stock, which presumably is infinite. For options, it is generally short-term expected volatility that is important.

Managing volatility risk exposure

For traders whose portfolios contain options or securities with option-like features, the two most important risk exposures are:

❑ what happens if the underlying security price changes unexpectedly; and

❑ what happens if the expected volatility changes.

We first show how portfolio managers can measure these risks by computing the delta and the vega of their option portfolios; we then demonstrate how these risks can be managed dynamically using derivative contracts. In particular, we show that volatility derivatives provide the most direct and inexpensive means of hedging volatility risk.

The analysis requires a number of simplifying assumptions. First, we assume that the option portfolio consists entirely of European-style options written on the stock index portfolio. The stock index portfolio has a current level, S, a constant proportional dividend yield rate, δ, and a volatility rate σ. The riskless rate of interest, r, is constant. All index option prices are assumed to obey the Merton (1973) constant proportional dividend yield option valuation formula.

Second, we assume that there exist futures contracts on the volatility of the stock index portfolio (ie on the "volatility index"), and that the volatility futures price F equals the underlying volatility index level.[7]

Third, we assume that there exist European-style options on the volatility index. The volatility index has a current level V ($\equiv \sigma$, the volatility rate of the stock index portfolio as defined above) and a volatility rate σ_V. The prices of the volatility options are assumed to obey the Black (1976) futures option valuation formula.

In assuming that the option values follow the Merton (1973) and Black (1976) formulas, we are assuming implicitly that the stock index level and the volatility index level follow independent log-normal diffusion processes. All these assumptions can be relaxed in order to be more precise in measuring and managing volatility risk.

MEASURING RISK EXPOSURES

The most important determinants of option value are the underlying security price and the volatility rate. The effect of an unexpected change in the price of the underlying security on option value is measured by the option's delta.

A European-style call option on a stock index is valued by the equation,

$$c = e^{-\delta T} S N(d_1) - X e^{-rT} N(d_2), \tag{1}$$

where

$$d_1 = \frac{\ln(S/X) + (r - \delta + 0.5\sigma^2)T}{\sigma\sqrt{T}}, \tag{1A}$$

and

$$d_2 = d_1 - \sigma\sqrt{T}, \tag{1B}$$

where X is the exercise price of the index option, T is the time to expiration, N is the cumulative normal probability, and all other notation is as previously defined. The change in the option value with respect to a change in the index level is therefore

$$\text{Delta}_c = e^{-\delta T} N(d_1) > 0. \tag{2}$$

A European-style index put option is valued by the equation,

$$p = X e^{-rT} N(-d_2) - e^{-\delta T} S N(-d_1), \tag{3}$$

and has a delta of

$$\text{Delta}_p = -e^{-\delta T} N(-d_1) < 0. \tag{4}$$

For portfolio risk management, individual option deltas are not as important as the delta of the overall portfolio. To compute the net delta of an index option portfolio, we multiply the delta of each option series by the number of contracts held, and then sum across all option series. That is,

$$\text{Net portfolio delta} = \sum_{i=1}^{n} \text{Delta}_i \times \text{Number of contracts}_i \tag{5}$$

where n is the number of different option series in the portfolio. (For ease of exposition, we treat an option as applying to a single share. In practice, expressions such as (5) would have to be multiplied by the contract multiple, eg 100, in the case of OEX options.)

The effect of a change in the volatility parameter on option value is measured by the option's vega. If index call and put options are valued using (1) and (3) respectively, the vegas of the call and put options are equal and have the form,[8]

$$\text{Vega}_c = \text{Vega}_p = S e^{-\delta T} n(d_1)\sqrt{T} < 0, \tag{6}$$

where $n(d_1)$ is the normal density function evaluated at d_1, that is,

$$n(d_1) \equiv \frac{1}{\sqrt{2\pi}} e^{-\delta_1^2/2}.$$

Both the index call and put increase in value as volatility increases. This stands to reason, because an increase in volatility means that there is a greater probability of a large index move during the life of the option. The net vega of an index option portfolio is the sum of the weighted volatility exposures of the individual option series; that is,

$$\text{Net portfolio vega} = \sum_{i=1}^{n} \text{Vega}_i \times \text{Number of contracts}_i \tag{7}$$

AN ILLUSTRATION

The hedging problem in this illustration is that faced by an index option market maker who, in the course of business during a trading day, acquires a large option position and does not unwind the position by the close of trading.

Table 1. Hypothetical portfolio held by index option market maker at close of trading

Quantity	Call/put	Exercise price	Days to expiration	Price	Delta	Vega	Theta
A. Unhedged portfolio							
–50	C	390	30	15.29	0.689	0.403	
–100	C	400	60	13.52	0.530	0.642	
–75	P	400	60	12.21	–0.465	0.642	
–100	P	405	60	14.84	–0.526	0.642	
Net portfolio position with hedge				–4,516.25	0.025	–196.700	
B. Hedged portfolio using index put option only							
448	P	395	30	6.52	–0.390	0.439	0.136
Total hedge position				2,920.96	–174.720	196.672	60.928
Net portfolio position with hedge				–1,595.29	–174.695	–0.028	
C. Hedged portfolio using index call and put options							
233	P	395	30	6.52	–0.390	0.439	0.136
209	C	405	30	7.18	0.436	0.451	0.158
Total hedge position				3,019.78	0.254	196.546	64.710
Net portfolio position with hedge				–1,496.47	0.279	–0.154	
D. Hedged portfolio using volatility futures							
197	F			20.00		1.000	
Total hedge position						197.000	
Net portfolio position with hedge				–4,516.25	0.025	0.300	
E. Hedged portfolio using volatility call							
364	C	20	30	1.71		0.541	0.028
Total hedge position				622.44		196.924	10.192
Net Portfolio position with hedge				–3,893.81	0.025	0.224	

The index portfolio's level is assumed to be 400, its volatility rate is 20%, and its dividend yield rate is 3%. The volatility index level is assumed to be 20%, and the volatility rate of the volatility index is 75%. The interest rate is 5%.

Holding the option position overnight exposes the market maker to unexpected overnight changes both in the index level and in volatility.[9]

To begin, we set the parameters of the problem and measure the market maker's portfolio risk exposures. Suppose that at the close of trading the market maker is holding the portfolio of short index option positions listed in Panel A of Table 1. The fact that the market maker is short in all four option series means that net the market maker is short market volatility. (Recall that option value increases with the volatility rate.)

To measure the volatility risk exposure, we compute the net vega of the portfolio,

$$\text{Net portfolio vega} = 0.403(-50) + 0.642(-100) + 0.642(-75) + 0.642(-100) = -196.700.$$

This value implies that, if volatility increases by 100 basis points overnight,[10] the option portfolio value will fall by about \$197, more than 4% of the portfolio value.

To measure the price risk exposure, we compute the net delta of the market maker's portfolio,

$$\text{Net portfolio delta} = 0.689(-50) + 0.530(-100) - 0.465(-75) - 0.526(-100) = 0.025.$$

The portfolio is "delta-neutral". If the index level rises unexpectedly by a dollar, the portfolio will increase in value by only two cents.

HEDGING VOLATILITY RISK EXPOSURE USING INDEX OPTIONS

In the absence of market volatility derivatives, volatility risk can be hedged using index options. In the illustration, the market maker is short volatility. To negate this exposure, the market maker can buy either index calls or puts, since both calls and puts increase in value with volatility. Since the portfolio's current net vega is -196.700, the net vega of the purchased index options must equal 196.700.

Suppose that an index put with an exercise price of 395 and a time to expiration of thirty days is available. Its price, delta, and vega are shown in Panel B of Table 1. To eliminate volatility exposure using the 395 put, the market maker must buy

$$n_p = \frac{196.700}{0.439} = 448$$

contracts. The cost of the options is \$2,920.96. After the hedge is in place, the net vega of the portfolio is -0.028 so the market maker is now "vega-neutral" .

Unfortunately, the purchase of a single index option series to hedge volatility risk has the undesired consequence of changing the market maker's delta exposure. After the puts are purchased, the option portfolio has a net delta of -174.695, as shown in Panel B. This means that if the stock index level increases by one point overnight, the portfolio value will drop by nearly 11%. In all likelihood, the market maker will find this delta exposure unacceptable.

To hedge volatility risk without changing delta risk, at least two index options must be used. The most natural way to hedge this risk is to use "volatility spreads". Volatility spreads consist of buying calls and puts in such a way that the incremental delta value is near zero. We assume that the market maker has the opportunity to buy not only the 395 put with thirty days to expiration but also a 405 call with thirty days to expiration. Panel C of Table 1 shows both options.

To find the optimal number of calls and puts to buy, we must solve a simultaneous system of equations. First, since the unhedged portfolio is approximately delta-neutral, we want the net delta of the newly purchased options to be zero:

$$n_p Delta_p + n_c Delta_c = 0.$$

Second, since the unhedged portfolio has a net vega of -196.700, the net vega of the newly purchased calls and puts should be 196.700:

$$n_p Delta_p + n_c Delta_c = 196.700.$$

By solving this system of two equations with two unknowns, we find that $n_p \approx 233$ and that $n_c \approx 209$, as is shown in Panel C. The total cost of buying these options is $3,019.78. After the hedge is in place, the net delta exposure is 0.279, and the net vega exposure is -0.154, which means the portfolio, for all intents and purposes, is both delta-neutral and vega-neutral. The effective cost of using this hedge is the erosion in the option's value overnight.

The theta of an option is the change in option value with respect to a change in the option's remaining time to expiration. The theta values of the 395 put and the 405 call are also shown in Panel C. The net theta of the purchased index options is 64.710, which means that, holding other factors constant, the value of the hedge options will drop by approximately $64.71 overnight (ie one day for computation purposes).

To gauge the effectiveness of the volatility hedge, we compare the percentage change in the unhedged portfolio value to the percentage change in the hedge portfolio value when the volatility rate changes unexpectedly overnight.

Figure 3 shows that the unhedged portfolio has considerable volatility risk. If the volatility rate increases from 20% at the close of trading to 24% by the following morning, the portfolio value falls by more than 20%.

The hedged portfolio, on the other hand, is

3. Percent gain/loss in value of portfolio for unexpected change in market volatility

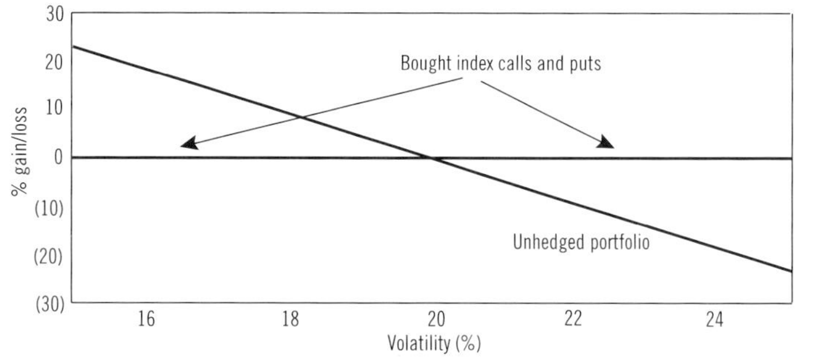

4. Percent gain/loss in value of portfolio for unexpected change in market volatility

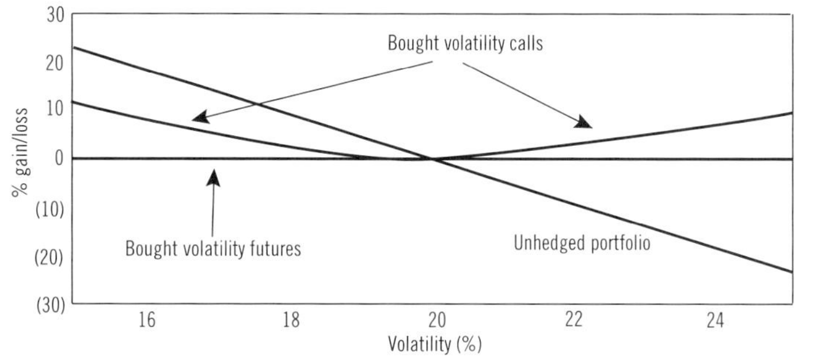

relatively immune to shifts in the volatility rate. Overnight shifts in the volatility rate as high as 500 basis points in either direction do not have an appreciable effect on portfolio value.[11]

HEDGING VOLATILITY RISK EXPOSURE USING VOLATILITY FUTURES

Hedging the market maker's vega risk exposure using volatility futures is straightforward. Since the net vega exposure of the market maker's portfolio is -196.700, the portfolio value will decrease by $196.700 for each 100 basis points of volatility increase. Since the price of volatility futures moves directly with volatility, a 100-basis point increase in the volatility rate elicits a $1.00 increase in the futures price. Hence, the optimal number of volatility futures to buy is 197.

Panel D of Table 1 shows the net effect of buying 197 volatility futures contracts. Since there is no cost in establishing the futures position, the portfolio value remains at $4,516.25. After the futures are purchased, the net vega of the portfolio is reduced to 0.300. The net delta of the portfolio, however, remains unchanged. Volatility derivatives, unlike index options, do not affect the delta exposure of the index option portfolio.

Figure 4 contrasts the percentage change of the unhedged portfolio with the percentage change of the hedged portfolio including the volatility futures as volatility changes. As the figure shows, the hedged portfolio value remains relatively constant over the 1,000-basis point volatility range considered.

HEDGING VOLATILITY RISK EXPOSURE USING VOLATILITY OPTIONS

Hedging the market maker's vega risk exposure using volatility options is nearly as straightforward as using volatility futures. The only difference is that the value of a volatility option does not move quite as quickly as volatility futures in response to volatility changes.

To quantify the rate of change, we need to compute the volatility option's delta. To do so, we apply the Black (1976) futures option valuation framework.[12] The valuation equation for a European-style call option on the volatility index is

$$c = e^{-rT}\left[VN(d_1) - XN(d_2)\right], \tag{8}$$

where

$$d_1 = \frac{\ln(V/X) + 0.5\sigma_V^2 T}{\sigma_V\sqrt{T}}, \tag{8A}$$

and

$$d_2 = d_1 - \sigma_V\sqrt{T}, \tag{8B}$$

so the delta value of a volatility call option is

$$\text{Delta}_{c_V} = e^{-rT}N(d_1) > 0. \tag{9}$$

The valuation equation for a European-style put option on the volatility index is

$$p = e^{-rT}\left[XN(-d_2) - VN(-d_1)\right], \tag{10}$$

with a delta value of

$$\text{Delta}_{p_V} = -e^{-rT}N(-d_1) < 0. \tag{11}$$

To set the volatility hedge for the market maker's portfolio, we simply divide the index option portfolio's volatility risk by the volatility option's delta, since the delta (rather than the vega) for a volatility option measures the option's sensitivity to volatility changes.

In the illustration, the unhedged portfolio has a net vega of -196.700. Suppose the market maker has the opportunity to buy volatility index calls with an exercise price of 20 and a time to expiration of thirty days. The optimal number of volatility calls to buy is

$$n_{c_V} = \frac{196.700}{0.541} = 36.$$

Panel E of Table 1 summarises this hedge. The total cost of purchasing the volatility calls is \$622.44. With the purchase of the calls, the net portfolio vega is reduced to 0.224. Again, the net delta remains at 0.025 since volatility derivatives do not alter price risk exposure.

To gauge the effectiveness of the volatility option hedge relative to the volatility futures hedge, reconsider Figure 4. While the volatility futures hedge is immune to large shifts in volatility, the volatility option hedge provides an interesting convexity in which the market maker's profits increase in the event that volatility either rises or falls sharply. This convexity is not without cost, however. The volatility options are expected to erode in value by about \$10.19 overnight.

SUMMARY

Using volatility derivatives to manage market volatility risk offers at least two advantages over index option contracts. First, the hedge is simpler to implement. Using index options to hedge requires at least two different option series, while using volatility derivatives requires only one.

Second, volatility derivatives are less expensive. Using volatility futures, the hedge costs nothing. Using volatility options, the hedge costs only a small fraction of a similar hedge created using index options.[13]

In demonstrating the hedging mechanics of volatility derivatives, we made a number of simplifying assumptions regarding index option and volatility option valuation. Many of these assumptions can and should be relaxed in order to make option valuation and hence risk measurement more precise.

With respect to index option valuation, for example, the assumption that the dividends on the index portfolio are paid at a constant, proportional rate is unreliable.[14] The valuation methodology should account for discrete cash dividends on the underlying index.

In addition, OEX option contracts - the most active index options currently traded - are American-style, so the early exercise premium must be valued.[15] With respect to volatility option valuation, we assumed that the volatility options are European-style. If volatility options are American-style, other valuation methods must be used.[16]

We also made fundamental assumptions regarding the dynamics of stock index level and volatility index level movements. We assume that both the stock index and the volatility index follow separate lognormal diffusion processes and that the increments to the two processes are independent of each other. There is evidence instead that suggests market volatility is mean-reverting. There is also evidence that shows that stock index level movements and market volatility movements are inversely correlated. (See Figure 2.) Capturing these behaviours should lead to more precise option valuation,[17] more precise risk measurement, and hence greater hedging effectiveness using volatility index derivatives.

Hedging individual stock volatility

Market volatility derivatives can be used not only for index option portfolio volatility risk management but also for volatility risk management of any portfolio that has option-like securities whose values are sensitive to the economic climate in the stock market. We can demonstrate empirically that the movements in individual stock volatility are driven largely by movements in market volatility. Among other things, this implies that the volatility risk of options on individual stocks, as well as rights, warrants, and any convertible security issued by a firm, can be hedged using volatility derivatives.

To estimate the relation between stock volatility and market volatility, we collected return data for New York Stock Exchange and American Stock Exchange stocks from the Center for Research in Security Prices (CRSP) daily return file. Only stocks with continuous returns during the entire sixty-month period (January 1986 to December 1990) are included in the sample. The total number of stocks is 1,118.

Next, we compute the return standard deviation for each stock in each month using the stock's daily returns,

$$\mathrm{Vol}_{i,t} = \sqrt{\frac{\sum_{t=1}^{T}\left(R_{i,t} - \bar{R}_i\right)^2}{T-1}}$$

where T is the number of days in the month. In addition, the return standard deviation of the S&P 100 index portfolio was computed each month.

Finally to assess the degree to which changes in individual stock volatility are explained by changes in market volatility, we regress monthly stock volatility changes, $\Delta\mathrm{Vol}_{i,t}$ on monthly market volatility changes, $\Delta\mathrm{Vol}_{m,t}$

$$\Delta\mathrm{Vol}_{i,t} = a + b\Delta\mathrm{Vol}_{m,t} + e_{i,t},$$

for each stock in the sample.[18] A summary of the regression results is reported in Table 2.

Table 2 shows a number of interesting results. First, across all 1,118 stocks included in the sample, the average correlation between monthly stock volatility and market volatility changes is 0.644. This suggests that derivative contracts on market volatility can provide a reasonable, but not exceptional, hedge of individual stock volatility on average.

A problem with considering these composite results, however, is that there is considerable measurement error in the estimates of monthly volatility for the individual stocks, particularly for those stocks that do not trade frequently. (Recall that the estimates of volatility are based only on the daily returns of a single month - approximately 22 days.) The volatility estimates for inactive stocks will tend to be more noisy, undermining the estimated relation between individual stock volatility movements and movements in market volatility.

To examine the consequences of this bias, we consider only the 500 most active (ie highest trading volume) stocks. The regression results indicate that measurement error is indeed a problem. The average slope coefficient increases from 0.7991 in the full sample to 0.9210 for the 500 most active stocks, and the average correlation between the volatility changes also increases from 0.644 to 0.743.

Finally, we examine the estimated relation for selected stocks. During the sample period, IBM, XON, and GE had the greatest number of shares traded of any of the stocks in the sample. The results of their regressions are also included in Table 2.

The degree of correlation between the stock volatility movements and market volatility movements for these stocks is extremely high. For IBM, the correlation is 0.949, for XON, 0.942, and for GE, 0.936. Among other things, this suggests that the volatility risk exposure of contingent claims on any of these stocks can be managed very effectively using derivative contracts on the CBOE Market Volatility Index.

Table 2. Regression estimates of changes in stock volatility on changes in S&P 100 market volatility

Sample	Statistic	$\hat{a}$	$t(\hat{a})$	$\hat{b}$	$t(\hat{b})$	Corr
All stocks	Mean	0.0029	0.09	0.7991	7.86	0.644
(n = 1,118)	Median	0.0010	0.07	0.7681	7.11	0.686
Most active stocks	Mean	0.0017	0.08	0.9210	10.12	0.743
(n = 500)	Median	0.0008	0.06	0.9002	9.68	0.788
Individual stocks						
IBM		−0.0015	−0.24	0.9440	22.64	0.949
XON		−0.0007	−0.08	1.1225	21.26	0.942
GE		−0.0004	−0.06	0.8624	20.11	0.936

Individual stock and market volatilities are computed each month using daily stock returns. The sample contains all NYSE and AMEX stocks that have continuous return data during the period January 1986–December 1990. The regression equation is $\Delta\mathrm{Vol}_{i,t} = a + b\Delta\mathrm{Vol}_{m,t} + e_{i,t}$ where $\Delta\mathrm{Vol}_{i,t}$ and $\Delta\mathrm{Vol}_{m,t}$ are the changes in individual stock and S&P 100 market volatility, respectively.

Summary

The marketplace will undoubtedly benefit from derivative contracts on the CBOE Market Volatility Index. Any portfolio consisting of options or securities with option-like features has volatility risk, which can be managed using volatility derivatives that are simpler and less expensive to implement than existing approaches.

To illustrate the use of volatility derivatives, we used the portfolio of an index option market maker. The job of a market maker is to stand ready to transact, which may involve accumulating a sizable option position. If this portfolio is held overnight, the market maker is exposed to volatility risk. With the advent of markets for volatility derivatives, this risk can be hedged, and market makers may pass on their cost savings to the investment public in the form of lower bid/ask spreads.

Option market makers are not the only beneficiaries of volatility index derivative markets, however. Portfolio insurers can use short-term, exchange-traded index options to create synthetic long-term portfolio insurance, as long as they can buy volatility futures or volatility calls to lock in the level of market volatility when the short-term option portfolio is rolled over. Other users may be covered call option writers, who may face substantial losses if market volatility increases unexpectedly. Volatility derivatives would provide option writers an effective means of hedging their volatility risk exposure.

Nor is the set of beneficiaries limited to hedgers. Market research may produce predictions not only about the direction of the market movements but also about volatility of those movements. Volatility derivatives provide speculators with a means of trading volatility and profiting from superior market volatility prediction skills.

Appendix

COMPOSITION OF CBOE MARKET VOLATILITY INDEX (VIX)

The CBOE Market Volatility Index (VIX) is constructed from the implied volatilities of the eight near-the-money, nearby, and second nearby OEX option series. The implied volatilities are weighted in such a manner that VIX represents the implied volatility of a hypothetical thirty-calendar day (22-trading day), at-the-money OEX option. This appendix describes the VIX construction, beginning with the valuation method and data used to compute eight individual OEX option implied volatilities and ending with the algorithm used to combine the individual implied volatilities to generate the level of VIX.

IMPLIED VOLATILITY COMPUTATION

To compute an implied volatility, three types of information are required:

- an option valuation model;
- the values of the model's determinants (except for volatility); and
- an observed option price.

OEX option valuation is based on the Black-Scholes (1973)/Merton (1973) assumption regarding the dynamics of security price movements. Because the OEX options are American-style, and because the underlying index portfolio pays discrete cash dividends, the option valuation problem is analytically intractable (ie no option valuation equation can be derived), and a valuation approximation is necessary. The approximation method used to compute the OEX option implied volatilities is the cash-dividend-adjusted, Cox-Ross-Rubinstein (1979) binomial method described in Harvey and Whaley (1992).[19]

Second, the option model's determinants are the current index value, the option's exercise price and time to expiration, the riskless rate of interest, and the amount and timing of the anticipated cash dividends paid during the option's life. In generating the historical VIX series, the actual cash dividends paid during the option life are used as the proxy for anticipated dividends. The source of the dividend data is Harvey and Whaley (1992) prior to June 1988 and the S&P 100 Information Bulletin thereafter, through December 1992.

With VIX now computed on a real-time basis, the anticipated daily cash dividends of the S&P 100 index portfolio must be forecast. The dividend forecasts are obtained from a time sharing data service contracted by the CBOE.

The interest rate is the effective yield on a T-bill whose maturity most closely matches the option expiration, except where the option time to expiration is less than 30 days, in which case the T-bill with 30 days to maturity is used. The source of the T-bill bid/ask discounts used in the construction of the VIX historical series is *The Wall Street Journal*.

Of the remaining option determinants, exercise price and time to expiration are known. The reported OEX index level is used as a proxy for the current OEX index value. The reported index level is appended to each option transaction/quote record at the time the trade/quote is entered into the CBOE's Market Data Retrieval (MDR) system.

The distinction between "reported OEX index level" and "current OEX index value" is subtle but important. The reported OEX index level is computed throughout the trading day and is based on last transaction prices of the 100 index stocks. Since stocks do not trade continuously, reported levels of stock indexes, particularly broad-based indexes such as the S&P 100, are always "stale" indicators of actual index portfolio values.

When the market rises quickly during the trading day, for example, OEX option price movements lead movements in the reported OEX index because OEX options trade more frequently than does the "average" stock in the S&P 100 portfolio. This means that if an implied volatility is computed using an OEX call (put) price the implied volatility is upward- (downward-) biased because the reported OEX index is lower than its true (but as yet unobserved) value.[20] Since the upward (downward) bias of the call implied volatility is approximately equal to the downward (upward) bias of the put implied volatility, the effect of the infrequent trading of stocks in the index can be and is mitigated within the VIX construction by averaging the call and put implied volatilities.

Third, the CBOE records both transaction and bid/ask price quotes in its MDR system. In both cases, the contemporaneous reported OEX index level is appended to the data record at the instant the option information is recorded. In constructing VIX, the midpoint of the bid/ask price quote is used as the option price in the implied volatility computation. This is done for two reasons.

First, bid/ask price quotes are entered instantly into the MDR system as they are heard by quote reporters stationed at various points in the OEX trading pit. OEX option transactions, on the other hand, are entered in different ways. Some transactions are entered manually when the trade ticket is received by a transaction reporter. For these transactions, there is a short delay in recording the option trade, so the trade price and the reported index level recorded on the transaction record are not synchronous.

Other transactions are entered electronically. The CBOE's Retail Automatic Execution System (RAES), for example, is available for certain option series. RAES automatically executes buy (sell) orders of ten contracts or fewer at the prevailing ask (bid) price. For these transaction records, the trade price and the index level are synchronous.

If the trade price and index level are not synchronous, implied volatilities based on transaction record information will have error. While the size of the error is probably small, its effect is unpredictable because the delay between the time the trade occurs and the time it is entered into the MDR system may differ across options (eg RAES versus non-RAES) and across varying levels of market activity.

Second, using the midpoint of the bid/ask price quotes eliminates the bouncing between bid and ask price levels (and hence computed implied volatilities) observed in the sequence of option transactions.[21]

Finally, it should be noted that VIX is based on trading days. If the time to expiration of the option is measured in calendar days, the implied volatility would be a volatility rate per calendar day. This means, among other things, that the return variance of the OEX index over a weekend (from Friday close to Monday close) should be three times greater than it is over any other pair of adjacent trading days during the week (say, Monday close to Tuesday close).

Empirically, this is simply not true. Volatility over the weekend is approximately the same as it is for other trading days.[22] For this reason, each (calendar-day) implied volatility rate is transformed to a trading-day basis in the following manner. First, according to the number of calendar days to expiration, N_c, the number of trading days, N_t, is computed as

$$N_t = N_c - 2 \times \text{int}(N_c / 7). \qquad \text{(A1)}$$

An option with eight calendar days to expiration, for example, has six trading days to expiration.

Second, the implied volatility rate is multiplied by the ratio of the square root of the number of calendar days to the square root of the number of trading days, that is,

$$\sigma_t = \sigma_c \left(\frac{\sqrt{N_c}}{\sqrt{N_t}} \right), \qquad \text{(A2)}$$

where $\sigma_t(\sigma_c)$ is the trading-day (calendar-day) implied volatility rate.[23, 24]

INDEX CONSTRUCTION

The CBOE Market Volatility Index is constructed from the implied volatilities of the eight near-the-money, nearby, and second nearby OEX option series. The nearby OEX series are defined as the series with the shortest time to expiration but with at least eight calendar days to expiration.[25] The second nearby OEX series are the series of the adjacent contract month.

To explain the index construction, we denote the OEX option exercise price just below the current index level, S, as X_l and the exercise price just above the current index level as X_u. The implied volatilities of the nearby and second nearby OEX options are thus:

	Nearby contract (1) Call	Nearby contract (1) Put	Nearby contract (2) Call	Nearby contract (2) Put
$X_l(< S)$	$\sigma_{c,1}^{X_l}$	$\sigma_{p,1}^{X_l}$	$\sigma_{c,2}^{X_l}$	$\sigma_{p,2}^{X_l}$.
$X_u(\geq S)$	$\sigma_{c,1}^{X_u}$	$\sigma_{p,1}^{X_u}$	$\sigma_{c,2}^{X_u}$	$\sigma_{p,2}^{X_u}$

The first step in computation of the index level is to average the call and put implied volatilities in each of the four categories of options, that is,

$$\sigma_1^{X_l} = \left(\sigma_{c,1}^{X_l} + \sigma_{p,1}^{X_l}\right)/2 \tag{A3A}$$

$$\sigma_2^{X_l} = \left(\sigma_{c,2}^{X_l} + \sigma_{p,2}^{X_l}\right)/2 \tag{A3B}$$

$$\sigma_1^{X_u} = \left(\sigma_{c,1}^{X_u} + \sigma_{p,1}^{X_u}\right)/2 \tag{A3C}$$

$$\sigma_2^{X_u} = \left(\sigma_{c,2}^{X_u} + \sigma_{p,2}^{X_u}\right)/2. \tag{A3D}$$

Recall that the averaging mitigates the effects that the staleness of the reported stock index level may have on computation of individual call and put option implied volatilities.

Next, interpolate between the nearby implied volatilities and the second nearby implied volatilities to create "at-the-money" implied volatilities. More specifically,

$$\sigma_1 = \sigma_1^{X_l}\left(\frac{X_u - S}{X_u - X_l}\right) + \sigma_1^{X_u}\left(\frac{S - X_l}{X_u - X_l}\right) \tag{A4A}$$

$$\sigma_2 = \sigma_2^{X_l}\left(\frac{X_u - S}{X_u - X_l}\right) + \sigma_2^{X_u}\left(\frac{S - X_l}{X_u - X_l}\right). \tag{A4B}$$

Finally, interpolate (or, occasionally, extrapolate) between the nearby and second nearby implied volatilities to create a 30-calendar day (30 - 2 × int(30/7) ≡ 22-trading day) implied volatility. If N_{t_1} is the number of trading days to expiration of the nearby contract, and N_{t_2} is the number of trading days of the second nearby contract, the CBOE Market Volatility Index is

$$VIX = \sigma_1\left(\frac{N_{t_2} - 22}{N_{t_2} - N_{t_1}}\right) + \sigma_2\left(\frac{22 - N_{t_1}}{N_{t_2} - N_{t_1}}\right). \tag{A5}$$

1 *In theory, the volatility implied by an OEX option price is an estimate of the expected volatility over the remaining life of the option. Empirical research assessing how well OEX implied volatility predicts future realised market volatility includes, Canina and Figlewski (1993); Fleming (1993); and Fleming, Ostdiek, and Whaley (1995). Fleming, Ostdiek, and Whaley find that the level of VIX is an accurate predictor of subsequently realised market volatility.*

2 *These data were provided by Eileen Smith of the Chicago Board Options Exchange.*

3 *Other types of volatility indexes have also been proposed. Brenner and Galai (1989), for example, argue that a volatility index could also be constructed from historical volatility or from some weighted combination of implied and historical volatility measures. Even if a combination predicts future realised volatility more accurately than either measure by itself, including a historical volatility component in the volatility index will reduce the degree of correlation between changes in the volatility index and changes in the implied volatilities (or, equivalently, changes in option premiums), and thereby undermine the hedging effectiveness of volatility index derivatives.*

4 *Feinstein (1989) shows that the Black-Scholes option valuation formula is approximately linear in volatility for at-the-money options.*

5 *One possible explanation is that there is more speculation in the options market when option time premiums are small. Another is that the option valuation model is misspecified.*

6 *Indeed, with perfect negative correlation between the changes of VIX and OEX, volatility index derivatives would serve no purpose.*

7 *That is, the cost of carrying the volatility index is assumed to be zero.*

8 *Aside from the fact that vegas are equal for call and put options with the same terms, it is important to recognise that the option's sensitivity to volatility is greatest where the options are approximately at-the-money. Vega, as defined by (6), depends on the normal density* $n(d_1)$. *The normal density is maximised where* $d_1 = 0$, *which, according to (1A), happens where* $S = X$.

9 *The dynamic hedge framework applied in this section is drawn from Stoll and Whaley (1993, Chapter 12).*

10 *A basis point is 1/100th of 1%.*

11 *The figure ignores the cost of the hedge.*

12 *There is an implicit assumption that it is possible to cre-*

ate a riskless hedge between the volatility option and the underlying volatility index. While on first appearance the volatility index would seem to be a statistical artifact and not a traded asset, buying and selling the volatility index can be accomplished using the eight OEX options that constitute the volatility index. See the appendix for details of the index construction.

13 *In our illustration, the cost of the overnight hedge using volatility options was less than 16% (≡ 10.192/64.710) of the cost of using index options.*

14 *Harvey and Whaley (1992) demonstrate how misleading an assumption of a constant dividend yield can be in valuing OEX options.*

15 *Fleming and Whaley (1993) show how to value the interest income/cash dividend and wildcard early exercise features of the OEX options.*

16 *To value American-style options on the volatility index under the assumption that the volatility index follows a lognormal diffusion process, the quadratic approximation in Whaley (1986) can be used.*

17 *Hull and White (1987), Scott (1987), Wiggins (1987), and Stein and Stein (1991) consider different models of stochastic volatility and their effects on option valuation. Ball (1993) reviews this work. Grunbichler and Longstaff (1993) discuss volatility option valuation where volatility is assumed to follow a mean-reverting process.*

18 *A similar analysis could be performed by regressing the movements of stock option implied volatilities on movements in the CBOE Market Volatility Index.*

19 *This valuation method accounts for the interest income/cash dividend motives for exercising OEX options early but does not account for the sequence of end-of-day wildcard options embedded in the OEX option contract. Fleming and Whaley (1993) show how to value the wildcard feature of OEX options. Although the wildcard privilege may contribute significantly to the overall option value, the wildcard premiums for the at-the-money call and put with the same expiration are approximately equal, and the size of the wildcard premium is approximately linear in time to expiration, This means that the Volatility Index, which is designed to be the implied volatility of a constant 30-day, at-the-money OEX option, is slightly upward-biased (because the wildcard privilege is not valued), but is not influenced more heavily by calls or puts, nor does it change systematically through time as the times to expiration of the component options grow short.*

20 *Ideally one would like to use the true OEX index value in the implied volatility computation. Since such an index value is unavailable, proxies must be considered. An ideal proxy would be the price of an actively traded futures contract on the OEX index, but the S&P 100 index futures market is now long defunct. Another possibility is the actively traded S&P 500 futures, although over long periods of time, the basis between the S&P 100 and S&P 500 cash indexes changes as small- (large-) capitalisation stocks fall in and out of favour.*

21 *Fleming, Ostdiek, and Whaley (1996) face this issue in examining the intraday price movements of OEX options and price movements of the underlying index portfolio stocks.*

22 *Using all stocks on the New York Stock Exchange and the American Stock Exchange during the period 1963 through 1982, French and Roll (1986) estimate that weekend return variance is only 10.79% greater than trading day return variance. For the quintile of highest market capitalisation stocks (which includes all of the S&P 100 stocks), the weekend return variance is only 8.2% higher.*

23 *The logic underlying this transformation is that total volatility over the option's remaining life is the same, whether time to expiration is measured using calendar days or ending days. If time to expiration is measured in calendar days, the implied volatility is the volatility rate per calendar day, and total volatility over the option's remaining life is* $\sigma_c\sqrt{N_c}$. *If the volatility rate over the weekend is the same as for other trading days, the weekend must be treated like a trading day, and the volatility must be adjusted to a trading day basis. Since we know total volatility over the life of the option is* $\sigma_c\sqrt{N_c}$, *we can find the volatility rate per trading day by setting the total volatility equal to* $\sigma_t\sqrt{N_t}$ *and solving for* σ_t. *Note that this procedure is not the same as computing the implied volatility by simply inserting the number of trading days to expiration directly into the option valuation method. The option' s time to expiration parameter affects valuation not only through total volatility (which, as has been argued, is best measured using trading days) but also through the expected rate of price appreciation in the index level over the option' s life and through the length of time over which the option's expected cash is discounted to the present (both of which are more appropriately measured using calendar days).*

24 *Fleming, Ostdiek, and Whaley (1995) show that this transformation to the volatility rate removes day-of the-week seasonality in the OEX implied volatility computed on a calendar-day basis. Intuitively, the market values OEX options as if the volatility over the weekend is the same as for any other trading day. When one examines the movement of implied volatility (computed using calendar days) from Friday close to Monday close, the volatility race increases, holding other factors constant, because the number of days to expiration in the option's life has been reduced by three instead of one.*

25 *The volatility of implied OEX volatilities increases dramatically during the last week of trading. To avoid the spurious effect that this behaviour would have on a volatility index, such options are not used.*

BIBLIOGRAPHY

Ball, C.A., 1993, "A Review of Stochastic Volatility Models with Applications to Option Pricing". Working paper, Owen Graduate School of Management, Vanderbilt University.

Black, F., 1976, "The Pricing of Commodity Contracts", *Journal of Financial Economics* 3, pp. 167-79.

Black, F., and M. Scholes, 1973, "The Pricing of Options and Corporate Liabilities", *Journal of Political Economy* 81, pp. 637-59.

Brenner, M., and D. Galai, 1989, "New Financial Instruments for Hedging Changes in Volatility", *Financial Analysts Journal*, July/August, pp. 61-5.

Canina, L., and S. Figlewski, 1993, "The Information Content of Implied Volatility", *Review of Financial Studies* 6, No.3, pp. 659-81; reprinted as Chapter 13 of the present volume.

Cox, J.C., S.A. Ross, and M. Rubinstein, 1979, "Option Pricing: A Simplified Approach", *Journal of Financial Economics* 7, pp. 229-63.

Feinstein, S., 1989, "The Black-Scholes Formula is Nearly Linear in Sigma for At-The-Money Options; Therefore Implied Volatilities from At-The-Money Options are Virtually Unbiased". Unpublished manuscript, Federal Reserve Bank of Atlanta.

Fleming, J., 1993, "The Quality of Volatility Forecast from S&P 100 Index Option Prices". Working paper, Futures and Options Research Center, Duke University.

Fleming, J., B. Ostdiek, and R. Whaley, 1993, "Predicting Stock Market Volatility: A New Measure". *Journal of Futures Markets* 15, pp. 265-302.

Fleming, J., B. Ostdiek, and R. Whaley, 1996, "Trading Costs and the Relative Rates of Price Discovery in the Stock, Futures and Options Markets", *Journal of Futures Markets* 16, pp. 353-87.

Fleming, J., and R.E. Whaley, 1993, "Binomial Valuation of Wildcard Options", *Journal of Finance* 49, pp. 215-36.

French, K.R., and R. Roll, 1986, "Stock Return Variances: The Arrival of Information and the Reaction of Traders", *Journal of Financial Economics* 17, pp. 5-26.

Grunbichler, A., and F. Longstaff, 1993, "Valuing Options on Volatility". Working paper, University of California at Los Angeles.

Harvey, C.R., and R. E. Whaley, 1992, "Dividends and S&P 100 Index Option Valuation", *Journal of Futures Markets* 12, pp. 125-37.

Hull, J., and A. White, 1987, "The Pricing of Options on Assets with Stochastic Volatilities", *Journal of Finance* 42, pp. 281-300.

Merton, R.C., 1973, "The Theory of Rational Option Pricing", *Bell Journal of Economics and Management Science* 4, pp. 141-83.

Scott, L.O., 1987, "Option Pricing When the Variance Changes Randomly: Theory, Estimation, and an Application", *Journal of Financial and Quantitative Analysts* 22, pp. 419-38.

Stein, E.M., and C.J. Stein, 1991, "Stock Price Distributions with Stochastic Volatility: An Analytical Approach", *Review of Financial Studies* 4, pp. 727-52; reprinted as Chapter 22 of the present volume.

Stoll, H.R., and R.E. Whaley, 1993, *Futures and Options: Theory and Applications*. Cincinnati: South-Western Publishing Co.

Whaley, R.E., 1986, "Valuation of American Futures Options: Theory and Empirical Tests", *Journal of Finance* 41, pp. 127-50.

Wiggins, J.B.,1987, "Option Values Under Stochastic Volatility: Theory and Empirical Tests", *Journal of Financial Economics* 19, pp. 351-72.

A PRACTITIONER'S PERSPECTIVE: WHAT'S AHEAD?

Introduction

Robert Jarrow

The other sections of this book contain papers that have been previously published and met the test of time in an often arduous publication process. By contrast, the papers in this section are appearing here for the first time. All of outstanding quality, they were invited from practitioners to give us a sense of the way ahead. What new models or techniques are on the horizon? Where is stochastic volatility option pricing research going?

The first paper, by Peter Carr and Dilip Madan, studies various trading strategies that can be used to speculate on the volatility of futures prices. They start by investigating static trading strategies, showing how to construct a portfolio whose value equals the variance of the futures price over the investment interval. Carr and Madan demonstrate how delta neutral hedging using the Black–Scholes model generates a profit/loss that depends on the difference between the realised volatility and the inputted (assumed) volatility in the delta hedge. They then show how to generate a dynamic portfolio whose pay out generates the volatility of the underlying futures price, over some interval, but only if the futures price remains in some corridor (interval). These trading strategies are very simple and should prove useful for traders wishing to hedge or speculate on volatility.

The second paper by Bruno Dupire is a widely read, but previously unpublished, piece on how to modify the Black–Scholes methodology to incorporate both implied volatility strike smiles and maturity skews into pricing and hedging. Dupire starts by explaining how to incorporate maturity skews by making the volatility dependent on time. As he points out, this modification can be traced back to Merton's original paper of 1973. He then shows how to incorporate strike smiles by making the volatility a function of the stock price. The details of this inversion procedure are new. This procedure is, in fact, the continuous time analogue of the implied binomial tree. Finally, Dupire provides a useful discretisation for implementing his model. Much of subsequent stochastic volatility literature has followed from the insights originally developed in this paper.

In Dupire's paper, the market is complete in the stock and riskless investment. This follows because the stock's volatility is a deterministic function of the stock price and time chosen to match a strike and maturity structure of standard calls. Emanuel Derman and Iraj Kani show how this approach can be generalised to include stochastic volatilities in an incomplete market, depending upon a finite number of factors. The market is completed, however, by trading in a finite number of calls in addition to the stock and riskless investment.

This innovative paper applies the Heath–Jarrow–Morton technology to the forward volatility surface, a two-dimensional surface (the two dimensions are strike and maturity) derived from standard call option prices. The purpose of this paper is to price exotic options, given an arbitrage-free evolution of the underlying forward volatility surface. The mathematics are clearly explained in the paper. A trinomial lattice representation is provided for practical implementation, and examples are provided to illustrate the computations. The approach in this paper is such that, by specialising the stochastic structure imposed, all the previous models discussed in this book can be considered as special cases. This paper is the modelling approach of the future in the area of stochastic volatilities.

29

Towards a Theory of Volatility Trading

Peter Carr and Dilip Madan
Morgan Stanley; University of Maryland

We review three methods which have emerged for trading realised volatility. The first method involves taking static positions in options, such as straddles, while the second method involves delta-hedging an option position. If the investor is successful in hedging away the price risk, then a prime determinant of the profit or loss from this strategy is the difference between the realised volatility and the anticipated volatility used in pricing and hedging the option. The final method involves buying or selling a "vol swap". This contract pays the buyer the difference between the realised volatility and the fixed swap rate determined at the outset of the contract. We also uncover the link between volatility contracts and some recent work on local volatility.

Much research has been directed towards forecasting the volatility[1] of various macroeconomic variables such as stock indexes, interest rates and exchange rates. However, comparatively little research has been directed towards the optimal way to invest given a view on volatility. This absence is probably due to the belief that volatility is difficult to trade.

For this reason, a small literature has emerged which advocates the development of volatility indexes and the listing of financial products whose payoff is tied to these indexes. For example, Gastineau (1977) and Galai (1979) propose the development of option indexes similar in concept to stock indexes. Brenner and Galai (1989) propose the development of realised volatility indexes and the development of futures and options contracts on these indexes. Similarly, Fleming, Ostdiek and Whaley (1993) describe the construction of an implied volatility index (the VIX), while Whaley (1993) proposes derivative contracts written on this index. Brenner and Galai (1993,1996) develop a valuation model for options on volatility using a binomial process, while Grunbichler and Longstaff (1993) instead assume a mean reverting process in continuous time.

In response to this hue and cry, some volatility contracts have been listed. OMLX, the London-based subsidiary of the Swedish exchange OM, launched volatility futures at the beginning of 1997. The Deutsche Terminbörse (DTB) recently launched its own futures based on its already established implied volatility index. Thus far, the volume in these contracts has been disappointing.

One possible explanation for this outcome is that volatility can already be traded by combining static positions in options on price with dynamic trading in the underlying. Neuberger (1990) showed that by delta-hedging a contract paying the log of the price, the hedging error accumulates to the difference between the realised variance and the fixed variance used in the delta-hedge. The contract paying the log of the price can be created with a static position in options, as shown in Breeden and Litzenberger (1978).

Independently of Neuberger, Dupire (1993)

We thank the participants of presentations at Boston University, the NYU Courant Institute, M.I.T., Morgan Stanley, and the Risk 1997 Congress. We would also like to thank Marco Avellaneda, Joseph Cherian, Stephen Chung, Emanuel Derman, Raphael Douady, Bruno Dupire, Ognian Enchev, Chris Fernandes, Marvin Friedman, Iraj Kani, Keith Lewis, Harry Mendell, Lisa Polsky, John Ryan, Murad Taqqu, Alan White, and especially Robert Jarrow for useful discussions. They are not responsible for any errors.

showed that a calendar spread of two such log-contracts pays the variance between the two maturities, and developed the notion of forward variance. Following Heath, Jarrow and Morton (HJM, 1992), Dupire modelled the evolution of the term structure of this forward variance, thereby developing the first stochastic volatility model in which the market price of volatility risk does not require specification, even though volatility is imperfectly correlated with the price of the underlying.

The primary purpose of this paper is to review three methods which have emerged for trading realised volatility. The first method involves taking static positions in options. The classic example is that of a long position in a straddle, since the value usually[2] increases with a rise in volatility. The second involves delta-hedging an option position; if the investor is successful in hedging away the price risk, then a prime determinant of the profit or loss from this strategy is the difference between the realised volatility and the anticipated volatility used in pricing and hedging the option. The final method involves buying or selling an over-the-counter contract whose payoff is an explicit function of volatility. The simplest example of this is a vol swap, which pays the buyer the difference between the realised volatility[3] and the fixed swap rate determined at the outset of the contract.[4]

A secondary purpose of this paper is to uncover the link between volatility contracts and some recent path-breaking work by Dupire (1996) and by Derman, Kani, and Kamal (DKK 1997). By restricting the set of times and price levels for which returns are used in the volatility calculation, one can synthesise a contract which pays off the "local volatility", ie the volatility which will be experienced should the underlying be at a specified price level at a specified future date. These authors develop the notion of forward local volatility, which is the fixed rate the buyer of the local vol swap pays at maturity in the event that the specified price level is reached. Given a complete term and strike structure of options, the entire forward local volatility surface can be backed out from the prices of options. This surface is the two dimensional analogue of the forward rate curve central to the HJM analysis. Following HJM, these authors impose a stochastic process on the forward local volatility surface and derive the risk-neutral dynamics of this surface.

The outline of this paper is as follows. The next section looks at trading realised volatility via static positions in options. The theory of static replication using options is reviewed in order to develop some new positions for profiting from a correct view on volatility. The subsequent section shows how dynamic trading in the underlying can alternatively be used to create or hedge a volatility exposure. We then look at over-the-counter volatility contracts as a further alternative for trading volatility. The section shows how such contracts can be synthesised by combining static replication using options with dynamic trading in the underlying asset. A fifth section draws a link between these volatility contracts and the work on forward local volatility pioneered by Dupire and DKK. The final section summarises and suggests some avenues for future research.

Trading realised volatility via static positions in options

The classic position for gaining exposure to volatility is to buy an at-the-money[5] straddle. Since at-the-money options are frequently used to trade volatility, the implied volatility from these options is widely used as a forecast of subsequent realised volatility. The widespread use of this measure is surprising, since the approach relies on a model which itself assumes that volatility is constant.

This section derives an alternative forecast, which is also calculated from market prices of options. In contrast to implied volatility, the forecast does not assume constant volatility, or even that the underlying price process is continuous. Instead, our forecast uses the market prices of options of all strikes. In order to develop the alternative forecast, the next subsection reviews the theory of static replication using options developed in Ross (1976) and Breeden and Litzenberger (1978). We then apply this theory to determine a model-free forecast of subsequent realised volatility.

STATIC REPLICATION WITH OPTIONS

Consider a single period setting in which investments are made at time 0 with all payoffs being received at time T. In contrast to the standard intertemporal model, we assume that there are no trading opportunities other than at times 0 and T. We assume that there is a futures market in a risky asset (a stock index, for example) for delivery at some date $T' \geq T$.

We also assume that markets exist for European-style futures options[6] of all strikes. While the assumption of a continuum of strikes is far from standard, it is essentially the analogue of the standard assumption of continuous trading. Just as the latter assumption is frequently made as a reasonable approximation to an environment where investors can trade frequently, our assumption is a reasonable approximation when there are a large but finite number of option strikes (such as S&P 500 futures options).

It is widely recognised that this market structure allows investors to create any smooth function $f(F_T)$ of the terminal futures price by taking a static position at time 0 in options.[7] Appendix A shows that any twice differentiable payoff can be re-written as:

$$f(F_T) = f(\kappa) + f'(\kappa)\left[(F_T - \kappa)^+ - (\kappa - F_T)^+\right] + \int_0^\kappa f''(K)(K - F_T)^+ dK + \int_\kappa^\infty f''(K)(F_T - K)^+ dK. \quad (1)$$

The first term can be interpreted as the payoff from a static position in $f(\kappa)$ pure discount bonds, each paying one dollar at T. The second term can be interpreted as the payoff from $f'(\kappa)$ calls struck at κ less $f'(\kappa)$ puts, also struck at κ. The third term arises from a static position in $f''(K)dK$ puts at all strikes less than κ. Similarly, the fourth term arises from a static position in $f''(K)dK$ calls at all strikes greater than κ.

In the absence of arbitrage, a decomposition similar to (1) must prevail among the initial values. Let V_0^f and B_0 denote the initial values of the payoff and the pure discount bond respectively. Similarly, let $P_0(K)$ and $C_0(K)$ denote the initial prices of the put and the call struck at K respectively. Then the no arbitrage condition requires that:

$$V_0^f = f(\kappa)B_0 + f'(\kappa)\left[C_0(\kappa) - P_0(\kappa)\right] + \int_0^\kappa f''(K)P_0(K)dK + \int_\kappa^\infty f''(K)C_0(K)dK. \quad (2)$$

Thus, the value of an arbitrary payoff can be obtained from bond and option prices. Note that no assumption was made regarding the stochastic process governing the futures price.

AN ALTERNATIVE FORECAST OF VARIANCE

Consider the problem of forecasting the variance of the log futures price relative

$$\ln\left(\frac{F_T}{F_0}\right).$$

For simplicity, we refer to the log futures price relative as a return, even though no investment is required in a futures contract. The variance of the return over some interval $[0,T]$ is of course given by the expectation of the squared deviation of the return from its mean:

$$\mathrm{Var}_0\left\{\ln\left(\frac{F_T}{F_0}\right)\right\} = E_0\left\{\ln\left(\frac{F_T}{F_0}\right) - E_0\left[\ln\left(\frac{F_T}{F_0}\right)\right]\right\}^2. \quad (3)$$

It is well known that futures prices are martingales under the appropriate risk-neutral measure. When the futures contract marks to market continuously, then futures prices are martingales under the measure induced by taking the money market account as numeraire. When the futures contract marks to market daily, then futures prices are martingales under the measure induced by taking a daily rollover strategy as numeraire, where this strategy involves rolling over pure discount bonds with maturities of one day. Thus, given a mark-to-market frequency, futures prices are martingales under the measure induced by the rollover strategy with the same rollover frequency.

If the variance in (3) is calculated using this measure, then

$$E_0\left[\ln\left(\frac{F_T}{F_0}\right)\right]$$

can be interpreted as the futures[8] price of a portfolio of options which pays off

$$f_m(F) \equiv \ln\left(\frac{F_T}{F_0}\right)$$

at T. The spot value of this payoff is given by (2) with κ arbitrary and

$$f_m''(K) = \frac{-1}{K^2}.$$

Setting $\kappa = F_0$, the futures price of the payoff is given by:

$$\mathcal{F} \equiv E_0\left[\ln\left(\frac{F_T}{F_0}\right)\right] = -\int_0^{F_0} \frac{1}{K^2}\hat{P}_0(K,T)dK - \int_{F_0}^\infty \frac{1}{K^2}\hat{C}_0(K,T)dK,$$

where $\hat{P}_0(K,T)$ and $\hat{C}_0(K,T)$ denote the initial futures price of the put and the call respectively, both for delivery at T. This futures price is initially negative[9] due to the concavity (negative time value) of the payoff.

Similarly, the variance of returns is just the futures price of the portfolio of options which pays off

$$f_v(F_T) = \left\{\ln\left(\frac{F_T}{F_0}\right) - \mathcal{F}\right\}^2$$

at T (see Figure 1 overleaf). The second deriva-

1. Payoff for variance of return ($F_0 = 1$; $\mathcal{F} = -0.09$)

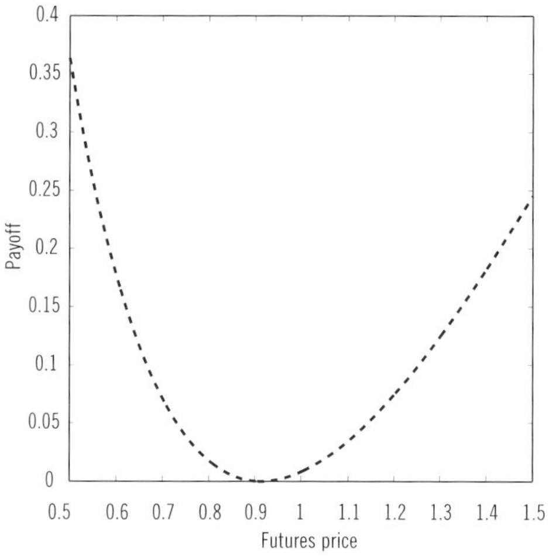

tive of this payoff is

$$f_v''(K) = \frac{2}{K^2}\left[1 - \ln\left(\frac{K}{F_0}\right) + \mathcal{F}\right].$$

This payoff has zero value and slope at $F_0e^{\mathcal{F}}$. Thus, setting $\kappa = F_0e^{\mathcal{F}}$, the futures price of the payoff is given by:

$$\mathrm{Var}_0\left\{\ln\left(\frac{F_T}{F_0}\right)\right\} = \int_0^{F_0e^{\mathcal{F}}} \frac{2}{K^2}\left[1 - \ln\left(\frac{K}{F_0}\right) + \mathcal{F}\right]\hat{P}_0(K,T)dK$$
$$+\int_{F_0e^{\mathcal{F}}}^{\infty} \frac{2}{K^2}\left[1 - \ln\left(\frac{K}{F_0}\right) + \mathcal{F}\right]\hat{C}_0(K,T)dK. \quad (4)$$

At time 0, this futures price is an interesting alternative to implied or historical volatility as a forecast of subsequent realised volatility.

However, in common with any futures price, this forecast is a reflection of both statistical expected value and risk aversion. Consequently, by comparing this forecast with the *ex post* outcome, the market price of variance risk can be inferred. We will derive a simpler forecast of variance below, under more restrictive assumptions (principally price continuity).

When compared to an at-the-money straddle, the static position in options used to create f_v has the advantage of maintaining sensitivity to volatility as the underlying moves away from its initial level. Unfortunately, like straddles, these contracts can take on significant price exposure once the underlying moves away from its initial level. An obvious solution to this problem is to delta-hedge with the underlying. We now consider this alternative.

Trading realised volatility by delta-hedging options

The static replication results of the last section made no assumption whatsoever about the price process or volatility process. In order to apply delta-hedging with the underlying futures, we now assume that investors can trade continuously, that interest rates are constant, and that the underlying futures price process is a continuous semi-martingale. Note that we maintain our previous assumption that the volatility of the futures follows an arbitrary unknown stochastic process. While one could specify a stochastic process and develop the correct delta-hedge in such a model, such an approach is subject to significant model risk since one is unlikely to guess the correct volatility process. Furthermore, such models generally require dynamic trading in options, which is costly in practice. Consequently, in what follows we leave the volatility process unspecified and restrict dynamic strategies to the underlying alone. Specifically, we assume that an investor follows the classic replication strategy specified by the Black model, with the delta calculated using a constant volatility σ_h. Since the volatility is actually stochastic[10], the replication will be imperfect and the error results in either a profit or a loss realised at the expiration of the hedge.

To uncover the magnitude of this P&L, let $V(F,t;\sigma)$ denote the Black model value of a European-style claim given that the current futures price is F and the current time is t.

Note that the last argument of V is the volatility used in the calculation of the value. In what follows, it will be convenient to have the attempted replication occur over an arbitrary future period (T,T') rather than over $(0,T)$. Consequently, we assume that the underlying futures matures at some date $T'' \geq T'$.

We suppose that an investor sells a European-style claim at T for the Black model value $V(F_T,T;\sigma_h)$ and holds

$$\frac{\partial V}{\partial F}(F_t,t;\sigma_h)$$

futures contracts over (T,T').

Since futures contracts are costless, applying Itô's lemma to $V(F_t,t;\sigma_h)e^{r(T'-t)}$ gives:

$$V(F_{T'},T';\sigma_h) = V(F_T,T;\sigma_h)e^{r(T'-T)} + \int_T^{T'} e^{r(T'-T)}\frac{\partial V}{\partial F}(F_t,t;\sigma_h)dF_t$$
$$+\int_T^{T'} e^{r(T'-T)}\left[-rV(F_t,t;\sigma_h) + \frac{\partial V}{\partial t}(F_t,t;\sigma_h)\right]dt$$
$$+\int_T^{T'} e^{r(T'-T)}\frac{\partial^2 V}{\partial F^2}(F_t,t;\sigma_h)\frac{F_t^2}{2}\sigma_t^2 dt. \quad (5)$$

Now, by definition, $V(F,t;\sigma_h)$ solves the Black partial differential equation subject to a terminal condition:

$$-rV(F_t,t;\sigma_h)+\frac{\partial V}{\partial t}(F_t,t;\sigma_h)=-\frac{\sigma_h^2F^2}{2}\frac{\partial^2 V}{\partial F^2}(F_t,t;\sigma_h), \quad (6)$$

$$V(F,T';\sigma_h)=f(F). \quad (7)$$

Substituting (6) and (7) in (5) and rearranging gives:

$$f(F_{T'})+\int_T^{T'}e^{r(T'-t)}\frac{F_t^2}{2}\frac{\partial^2 V}{\partial F^2}(F_t,t;\sigma_h)(\sigma_h^2-\sigma_t^2)dt=$$
$$V(F_T,T;\sigma_h)e^{r(T'-T)}+\int_T^{T'}e^{r(T'-t)}\frac{\partial V}{\partial F}(F_t,t;\sigma_h)dF_t. \quad (8)$$

The right hand side is clearly the terminal value of a dynamic strategy comprising an investment at T of $V(F_T,T;\sigma_h)$ dollars in the riskless asset and a dynamic position in

$$\frac{\partial V}{\partial F}(F_t,t;\sigma_h)$$

futures contracts over the time interval (T,T'). Thus, the left hand side must also be the terminal value of this strategy, indicating that the strategy misses its target $f(F_{T'})$ by:

$$P\&L=\int_T^{T'}e^{r(T'-t)}\frac{F_t^2}{2}\frac{\partial^2 V}{\partial F^2}(F_t,t;\sigma_h)(\sigma_h^2-\sigma_t^2)dt. \quad (9)$$

So, when a claim is sold for the implied volatility σ_h at T, the instantaneous P&L from delta-hedging it over (T,T') is

$$\frac{F_t^2}{2}\frac{\partial^2 V}{\partial F^2}(F_t,t;\sigma_h)(\sigma_h^2-\sigma_t^2),$$

which is the difference between the hedge variance rate and the realised variance rate, weighted by half the dollar gamma. Note that the P&L (hedging error) will be zero if the realised instantaneous volatility σ_t is constant at σ_h. It is well known that claims with convex payoffs have non-negative gammas:

$$\frac{F_t^2}{2}\frac{\partial^2 V}{\partial F^2}(F_t,t;\sigma_h)\geq 0$$

in the Black model. For such claims (options, for example), a loss results if the hedge volatility is always less than the true volatility ($\sigma_h<\sigma_t$ for all t in $[T,T']$), regardless of the path. Conversely, if the claim with a convex payoff is sold for an implied volatility σ_h which dominates[11] the subsequent realised volatility at all times, then delta-hedging at σ_h using the Black model delta guarantees a positive P&L.

When compared with static options positions, delta hedging appears to have the advantage of being insensitive to the price of the underlying. However, (9) indicates that the P&L at T' does depend on the final price as well as on the price path. An investor with a view on volatility alone would like to immunise the exposure to this path. One solution is to use a stochastic volatility model to conduct the replication of the desired volatility dependent payoff.

However, as mentioned previously, this requires specifying a volatility process and employing dynamic replication with options. A better solution is to choose the payoff function $f(\cdot)$, so that the path dependence can be removed or managed. For example, Neuberger recognised that if $f(F)=2\ln F$, then

$$\frac{\partial^2 V}{\partial F^2}(F_t,t;\sigma_h)=e^{-r(T'-t)}\frac{-2}{F_t^2}$$

and thus from (9), the P&L at T' is the payoff of a variance swap $\int_T^{T'}(\sigma_t^2-\sigma_h^2)dt$. This volatility contract and others related to it are explored below.

Trading realised volatility by using volatility contracts

This section shows that several interesting volatility contracts can be manufactured by taking options positions and then delta-hedging them at zero volatility. Accordingly, suppose we set $\sigma_h=0$ in (8) and negate both sides:

$$\int_T^{T'}\frac{F_t^2}{2}f''(F_t)\sigma_t^2dt=f(F_{T'})-f(F_T)-\int_T^{T'}f'(F_t)dFt. \quad (10)$$

The left hand side is a payoff at T' based on both the realised instantaneous volatility σ_t^2 and the price path. The dependence of this payoff on f arises only through f'', and accordingly, we will henceforth only consider payoff functions f which have zero value and slope at a given point κ. The right hand side of (10) depends only on the price path and results from adding the following three payoffs:

❑ The payoff from a static position in options maturing at T' paying $f(F_{T'})$ at T'

❑ The payoff from a static position in options maturing at T paying $-e^{r(T'-T)}f(F_T)$ and future-valued to T'

❑ The payoff from maintaining a dynamic position in $-e^{r(T'-t)}f'(F_T)$ futures contracts over the time interval (T,T') (assuming continuous marking-to-market and that the margin account balance earns interest at the riskfree rate).

Thus, the payoff on the left-hand side can be achieved by combining a static position in options with a dynamic strategy in futures. The dynamic strategy can be interpreted as an attempt to create the payoff $-f(F_{T'})$ at T', con-

Table 1

Description of payoff	$f''(F_t)$	Payoff at T'
Variance over future period	$\frac{2}{F_t^2}$	$\int_T^{T'} \sigma_t^2 dt$
Future corridor variance	$\frac{2}{F_t^2} 1[F_t \in (\kappa - \Delta\kappa, \kappa + \Delta\kappa)]$	$\int_T^{T'} 1[F_t \in (\kappa - \Delta\kappa, \kappa + \Delta\kappa)]\sigma_t^2 dt$
Future variance along strike	$\frac{2}{\kappa^2}\delta(F_t - \kappa)$	$\int_T^{T'} \delta(F_t - \kappa)\sigma_t^2 dt$

ducted under the false assumption of zero volatility. Since realised volatility will be positive, an error arises, and the magnitude of this error is given by

$$\int_T^{T'} \frac{F_t^2}{2} f''(F_t)\sigma_t^2 dt,$$

which is the left side of (10).

The payoff $f(\cdot)$ can be chosen so that when its second derivative is substituted into this expression, the dependence on the path is consistent with the investor's joint view on volatility and price. In this section, we consider the following three second derivatives of payoffs at T' and work out the $f(\cdot)$ which leads to them (see Table 1).

CONTRACT PAYING FUTURE VARIANCE

Consider the following payoff function $\phi(F)$ (see Figure 2):

$$\phi(F) \equiv 2\left[\ln\left(\frac{\kappa}{F}\right) + \frac{F}{\kappa} - 1\right], \qquad (11)$$

where κ is an arbitrary finite positive number. The first derivative is given by:

$$\phi'(F) = 2\left[\frac{1}{\kappa} - \frac{1}{F}\right]. \qquad (12)$$

Thus, the value and slope both vanish at $F = \kappa$. The second derivative of ϕ is simply:

$$\phi''(F) = \frac{2}{F^2}. \qquad (13)$$

Substituting (11) to (13) into (10) results in a relationship between a contract paying the realised variance over the time interval (T, T') and three payoffs based on price:

$$\int_T^{T'} \sigma_t^2 dt = 2\left[\ln\left(\frac{\kappa}{F_{T'}}\right) + \frac{F_{T'}}{\kappa} - 1\right] - 2\left[\ln\left(\frac{\kappa}{F_T}\right) + \frac{F_T}{\kappa} - 1\right] - 2\int_T^{T'}\left[\frac{1}{\kappa} - \frac{1}{F_t}\right]dF_t. \qquad (14)$$

The first two terms on the right hand side arise from static positions in options. Substituting (13) into (2) implies that for each term, the required

2. Payoff to delta hedge to create contract paying variance ($\kappa = 1$)

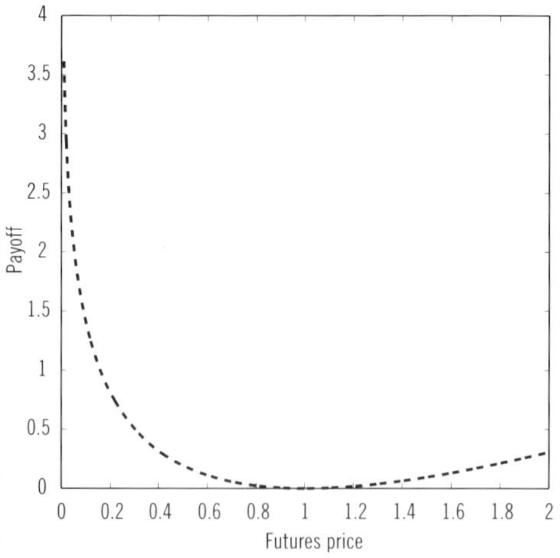

position is given by:

$$2\left[\ln\left(\frac{\kappa}{F}\right) + \frac{F}{\kappa} - 1\right] = \int_0^{\kappa} \frac{2}{K^2}(K - F)^+ dK + \int_{\kappa}^{\infty} \frac{2}{K^2}(F - K)^+ dK. \qquad (15)$$

Thus, to create the contract paying $\int_T^{T'}\sigma_t^2 dt$ at T', at $t = 0$, the investor should buy options at the longer maturity T' and sell options at the nearer maturity T. The initial cost of this position is given by:

$$\int_0^{\kappa} \frac{2}{K^2} P_0(K, T')dK + \int_{\kappa}^{\infty} \frac{2}{K^2} C_0(K, T')dK - e^{-r(T'-T)}\left[\int_0^{\kappa} \frac{2}{K^2} P_0(K, T)dK + \int_{\kappa}^{\infty} \frac{2}{K^2} C_0(K, T)dK\right]. \qquad (16)$$

When the nearer maturity options expire, the investor should borrow to finance the payout of

$$2e^{-r(T'-T)}\left[\ln\left(\frac{\kappa}{F_T}\right) + \frac{F_T}{\kappa} - 1\right].$$

The investor should also start a dynamic strategy in futures, holding

$$2e^{-r(T'-t)}\left[\frac{1}{\kappa} - \frac{1}{F_t}\right].$$

futures contracts for each $t \in [T, T']$. The net payoff at T' is:

$$2\left[\ln\left(\frac{\kappa}{F_{T'}}\right) + \frac{F_{T'}}{\kappa} - 1\right] - 2\left[\ln\left(\frac{\kappa}{F_T}\right) + \frac{F_T}{\kappa} - 1\right] - 2\int_T^{T'}\left[\frac{1}{\kappa} - \frac{1}{F_t}\right]dF_t = \int_T^{T'}\sigma_t^2 dt,$$

as required. Since the initial cost of achieving this payoff is given by (16), an interesting forecast $\hat{\sigma}^2_{T,T'}$ of the variance between T and T′ is given by the future value of this cost:

$$\hat{\sigma}^2_{T,T'} = e^{rT'}\int_0^{\kappa}\frac{2}{K^2}P_0(K,T')dK + \int_{\kappa}^{\infty}\frac{2}{K^2}C_0(K,T')dK$$
$$-e^{rT}\left[\int_0^{\kappa}\frac{2}{K^2}P_0(K,T)dK + \int_{\kappa}^{\infty}\frac{2}{K^2}C_0(K,T)dK\right].$$

In contrast to implied volatility, this forecast does not use a model in which volatility is assumed to be constant. However, in common with any forward price, this forecast is a reflection of both statistical expected value and risk aversion. Consequently, by comparing this forecast with the ex-post outcome, the market price of volatility risk can be inferred.

CONTRACT PAYING FUTURE CORRIDOR VARIANCE

We now generalise to a contract which pays the "corridor variance", defined as the variance calculated using only the returns at times for which the futures price is within a specified corridor. In particular, consider a corridor $(\kappa - \Delta\kappa, \kappa + \Delta\kappa)$ centred at some arbitrary level κ and with width $2\Delta\kappa$. Suppose that we wish to generate a payoff at T′ of $\int_T^{T'} 1[F_t \in (\kappa - \Delta\kappa, \kappa + \Delta\kappa)]\sigma_t^2 dt$. Thus, the variance calculation is based only on returns at times in which the futures price is inside the corridor.

Consider the following payoff $\phi_{\Delta\kappa}(\cdot)$:

$$\phi_{\Delta\kappa}(F) \equiv 2\left[\ln\left(\frac{\kappa}{\underline{\bar{F}}}\right) + F\left(\frac{1}{\kappa} - \frac{1}{\underline{\bar{F}}}\right)\right],$$

where:

$$\underline{\bar{F}}_t \equiv \max\left[\kappa - \Delta\kappa, \min(F_t, \kappa + \Delta\kappa)\right] \quad (17)$$

is the futures price floored at $\kappa - \Delta\kappa$ and capped at $\kappa + \Delta\kappa$ (see Figure 3).

From inspection, the payoff $\phi_{\Delta\kappa}(\cdot)$ is the same as ϕ defined in (11), but with F replaced by $\underline{\bar{F}}$. The new payoff is shown in Figure 4. This payoff is actually a generalisation of (11), since

$$\lim_{\Delta\kappa \uparrow \infty} \underline{\bar{F}}_t = F.$$

For a finite corridor width, the payoff $\phi_{\Delta\kappa}(F)$ matches $\phi(F)$ for futures prices within the corridor.

Consequently, like $\phi(F)$, $\phi_{\Delta\kappa}(F)$has zero value and slope at $F = \kappa$. However, in contrast to $\phi(F)$, $\phi_{\Delta\kappa}(F)$ is linear outside the corridor with the lines chosen so that the payoff is continuous and differentiable at $\kappa \pm \Delta\kappa$. The first derivative of (17) is given by:

3. Capped and floored futures price ($\kappa = 1$, $\Delta\kappa = 0.5$)

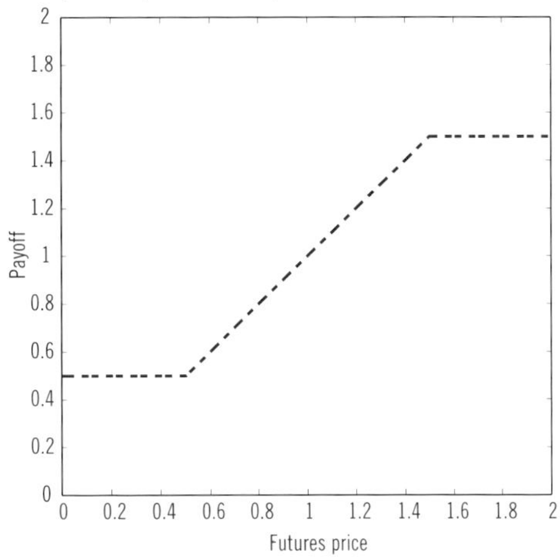

4. Trimming the log payoff ($\kappa = 1$, $\Delta\kappa = 0.5$)

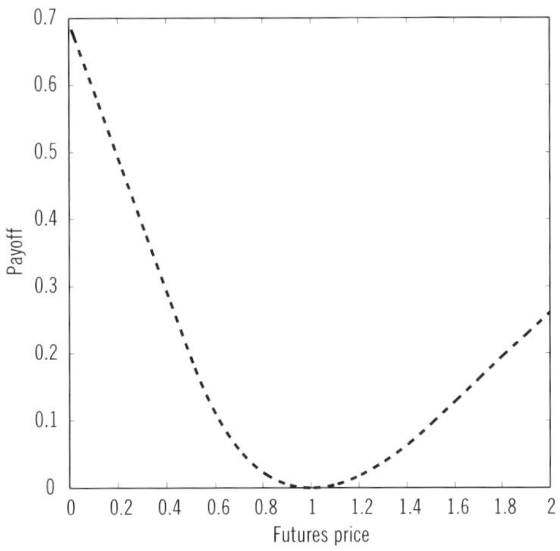

$$\phi'_{\Delta\kappa}(F) = 2\left[\frac{1}{\kappa} - \frac{1}{\underline{\bar{F}}}\right], \quad (18)$$

while the second derivative is simply:

$$\phi''_{\Delta\kappa}(F) = \frac{2}{F^2}1\left[F \in (\kappa - \Delta\kappa, \kappa + \Delta\kappa)\right]. \quad (19)$$

Substituting (17) to (19) into (10) implies that the volatility-based payoff decomposes as:

$$\int_T^{T'} \sigma_t^2 1\left[F_T \in (\kappa - \Delta\kappa, \kappa + \Delta\kappa)\right]dt =$$
$$2\left[\ln\left(\frac{\kappa}{\underline{\bar{F}}_{T'}}\right) + F_{T'}\left(\frac{1}{\kappa} - \frac{1}{\underline{\bar{F}}_{T'}}\right)\right]$$
$$-2\left[\ln\left(\frac{\kappa}{\underline{\bar{F}}_T}\right) + F_T\left(\frac{1}{\kappa} - \frac{1}{\underline{\bar{F}}_T}\right)\right] - 2\int_T^{T'}\left[\frac{1}{\kappa} - \frac{1}{\underline{\bar{F}}_t}\right]dF_t.$$

The payoff function $\phi_{\Delta\kappa}(\cdot)$ has no curvature outside the corridor and consequently, the static positions in options needed to create the first two terms will not require strikes set outside the corridor. Thus, to create the contract paying the future corridor variance, $\int_T^{T'} \sigma_t^2 1[F_t \in (\kappa - \Delta\kappa, \kappa + \Delta\kappa)]dt$ at T′, the investor should initially only buy and sell options struck within the corridor, for an initial cost of:

$$\int_{\kappa-\Delta\kappa}^{\kappa} \frac{2}{K^2} P_0(K,T')dK + \int_{\kappa}^{\kappa+\Delta\kappa} \frac{2}{K^2} C_0(K,T')dK$$
$$-e^{-r(T'-T)}\left[\int_{\kappa-\Delta\kappa}^{\kappa} \frac{2}{K^2} P_0(K,T)dK + \int_{\kappa}^{\kappa+\Delta\kappa} \frac{2}{K^2} C_0(K,T)dK\right].$$

At t = T, the investor should borrow to finance the payout of

$$2e^{-r(T'-T)}\left[\ln\left(\frac{\kappa}{\underline{\overline{F}}_T}\right) + F_T\left(\frac{1}{\kappa} - \frac{\kappa}{\underline{\overline{F}}_T}\right)\right]$$

from having initially written the T maturity options. The investor should also start a dynamic strategy in futures, holding

$$-2e^{-r(T'-t)}\left[\frac{1}{\kappa} - \frac{\kappa}{\underline{\overline{F}}_t}\right]$$

futures contracts for each $t \in [T,T']$. This strategy is semi-static in that no trading is required when the futures price is outside the corridor. The net payoff at T′ is:

$$2\left[\ln\left(\frac{\kappa}{\underline{\overline{F}}_{T'}}\right) + F_{T'}\left(\frac{1}{\kappa} - \frac{1}{\underline{\overline{F}}_{T'}}\right)\right] - 2\left[\ln\left(\frac{\kappa}{\underline{\overline{F}}_{T}}\right) + F_{T}\left(\frac{1}{\kappa} - \frac{1}{\underline{\overline{F}}_{T}}\right)\right]$$
$$-2\int_T^{T'}\left[\frac{1}{\kappa} - \frac{1}{\underline{\overline{F}}_t}\right]dF_t = \int_T^{T'} \sigma_t^2 1\left[F_t \in (\kappa - \Delta\kappa, \kappa + \Delta\kappa)\right]dt,$$

as desired.

CONTRACT PAYING FUTURE VARIANCE ALONG A STRIKE

In the last subsection, only options struck within the corridor were used in the static options position, and dynamic trading in the underlying futures was required only when the futures price was in the corridor. We shrink the width of the corridor of the last subsection down to a single point and examine the impact on the volatility based payoff and its replicating strategy. In order that this payoff have a non-negligible value, all asset positions oulined in the subsection above must be re-scaled by

$$\frac{1}{2\Delta\kappa}.$$

Thus, the volatility-based payoff at T′ would instead be

$$\int_T^{T'} \frac{1\left[F_t \in (\kappa - \Delta\kappa, \kappa + \Delta\kappa)\right]}{2\Delta\kappa} \sigma_t^2 \, dt.$$

By letting $\Delta\kappa \downarrow 0$, the variance received can be completely localised in the spatial dimension to $\int_T^{T'} \delta(F_t - \kappa)\sigma_t^2 dt$, where $\delta(\cdot)$ denotes a Dirac delta function.[12] Recalling that only options struck within the corridor are used to create the corridor variance, the initial cost of creating this localised cash flow is given by the following ratioed calendar spread of straddles:

$$\frac{1}{\kappa^2}\left[V_0(\kappa,T') - e^{-r(T'-T)}V_0(\kappa,T)\right],$$

where $V_0(\kappa,T)$ is the initial cost of a straddle struck at κ and maturing at T:

$$V_0(\kappa,T) \equiv P_0(\kappa,T) + C_0(\kappa,T).$$

As usual, at t = T, the investor should borrow to finance the payout of

$$\frac{|F_T - \kappa|}{\kappa^2}$$

from having initially written the T maturity straddle. The appendix proves that the dynamic strategy in futures initiated at T involves holding

$$-\frac{e^{-r(T'-t)}}{\kappa^2}\operatorname{sgn}(F_t - \kappa)$$

futures contracts, where sgn(x) is the sign function:

$$\operatorname{sgn}(x) \equiv \begin{cases} -1 & \text{if } x < 0; \\ 0 & \text{if } x = 0; \\ 1 & \text{if } x > 0. \end{cases}$$

When T = 0, this strategy reduces to the initial purchase of a straddle maturing at T′, initially borrowing $e^{-rT'}|F_0 - \kappa|$ dollars and holding

$$-\frac{e^{-r(T'-t)}}{\kappa^2}\operatorname{sgn}(F_t - \kappa)$$

futures contracts for $t \in [0,T']$. The component of this strategy involving borrowing and futures is known as the stop-loss start-gain strategy, previously investigated by Carr and Jarrow (1990). By the Tanaka-Meyer formula[13] the difference between the payoff from the straddles and this dynamic strategy is known as the local time of the futures price process. Local time is a fundamental concept in the study of one dimensional stochastic processes. Fortunately, a straddle combined with a stop-loss start-gain strategy in the underlying provides a mechanism for synthesising a contract paying off this fundamental concept. The initial time value of the straddle is the market's (risk-neutral) expectation of the local time. By comparing this time value with the ex-post outcome, the market price of local time risk can be inferred.

Connection to recent work on stochastic volatility

The last contract examined above represents the limit of a localisation in the futures price. When a continuum of option maturities is also available, we may additionally localise in the time dimension, as in recent work by Dupire (1996) and DKK (1997). Accordingly, suppose we further rescale all the asset positions described in the last subsection above by $1/\Delta T$ where $\Delta T \equiv T' - T$. The payoff at T' would instead be:

$$\int_T^{T'} \frac{\delta(F_t - \kappa)}{\Delta T} \sigma_t^2 dt.$$

The cost of creating this position would be:

$$\frac{1}{\kappa^2}\left[\frac{V_0(\kappa, T') - e^{-r(T'-T)} V_0(\kappa, T)}{\Delta T}\right].$$

By letting $\Delta T \downarrow 0$, one gets the beautiful result of Dupire (1996) that

$$\frac{1}{\kappa^2}\left[\frac{\partial V_0}{\partial T}(\kappa, T) + rV_0(\kappa, T)\right]$$

is the cost of creating the payment $\delta(F_T - \kappa)\sigma_T^2$ at T. As Dupire showed, the forward local variance can be defined as the number of butterfly spreads paying $\delta(F_T - \kappa)$ at T that must be sold in order to finance the above option position initially. A discretised version of this result can be found in DKK (1997). We could go on to impose a stochastic process on the forward local variance as in Dupire (1996) and in DKK. These authors derive conditions on the risk-neutral drift of the forward local variance, allowing replication of price or volatility-based payoffs using dynamic trading in only the underlying asset and a single option.[14] In contrast to earlier work on stochastic volatility, the form of the market price of volatility risk need not be specified.

Summary and suggestions for future research

We reviewed three approaches for trading volatility. While static positions in options do generate exposure to volatility, they also generate exposure to price. Similarly, a dynamic strategy in futures alone can yield a volatility exposure, but it always has a price exposure as well. By combining static positions in options with dynamic trading in futures, payoffs related to realised volatility can be achieved which either have no exposure to price, or which have an exposure contingent on certain price levels being achieved in specified time intervals.

Under certain assumptions, we were able to price and hedge certain volatility contracts without specifying the process for volatility. The principle assumption made was that of price continuity. Under this assumption, a calendar spread of options emerges as a simple tool for trading the local volatility (or local time) between the two maturities. It would be interesting to see if this insight survives the relaxation of the critical assumption of price continuity. It would also be interesting to consider contracts which pay nonlinear functions of realised variance or local variance. Finally, it would be interesting to develop contracts on other statistics of the sample path such as the Sharpe ratio, skewness, covariance, correlation, and so on. In the interests of brevity, such inquiries are best left for future research.

Appendix A

SPANNING WITH BONDS AND OPTIONS

For any payoff $f(F)$, the sifting property of a Dirac delta function implies:

$$\begin{aligned} f(F) &= \int_0^\infty f(K)\delta(F-K)dK \\ &= \int_0^\kappa f(K)\delta(F-K)dK + \int_\kappa^\infty f(K)\delta(F-K)dK, \end{aligned}$$

for any nonnegative κ. Integrating each integral by parts implies:

$$\begin{aligned} f(F) = {} & f(K)1(F<K)\Big|_0^\kappa - \int_0^\kappa f'(K)1(F<K)dK \\ & + f(K)1(F \geq K)\Big|_\kappa^\infty + \int_\kappa^\infty f'(K)1(F \geq K)dK. \end{aligned}$$

Integrating each integral by parts once more implies:

$$\begin{aligned} f(F) = {} & f(\kappa)1(F<K) - f'(K)(K-F)^+\Big|_0^\kappa + \int_0^\kappa f''(K)(K-F)^+ dK \\ & + f(\kappa)1(F \geq K) - f'(K)(F-K)^+\Big|_\kappa^\infty + \int_\kappa^\infty f''(K)(F-K)^+ dK \\ = {} & f(\kappa) + f'(\kappa)\left[(F-\kappa)^+ - (\kappa - F)^+\right] \\ & + \int_0^\kappa f''(K)(K-F)^+ dK + \int_\kappa^\infty f''(K)(F-K)^+ dK. \end{aligned}$$

Appendix B

DERIVATION OF FUTURES POSITION WHEN SYNTHESISING CONTRACT PAYING FUTURE VARIANCE ALONG A STRIKE

Recall that all asset positions were normalised by multiplying by

$$\frac{1}{2\Delta\kappa}.$$

Thus in particular, the futures position of

$$-2e^{-r(T'-t)}\left[\frac{1}{\kappa}-\frac{\kappa}{\underline{\bar{F}}_t}\right]$$

contracts in the subsection titled "Contract paying future corridor variance" is changed to

$$-\frac{e^{-r(T'-t)}}{\Delta\kappa}\left[\frac{1}{\kappa}-\frac{\kappa}{\underline{\bar{F}}_t}\right]$$

contracts in the subsection titled "Contract paying future variance along a strike".

More explicitly, the number of contracts held is given by

$$\begin{cases} -\dfrac{e^{-r(T'-t)}}{\Delta\kappa}\left[\dfrac{1}{\kappa}-\dfrac{\kappa}{\kappa-\Delta\kappa}\right] & \text{if } F_t \le \kappa-\Delta\kappa; \\ -\dfrac{e^{-r(T'-t)}}{\Delta\kappa}\left[\dfrac{1}{\kappa}-\dfrac{1}{F_t}\right] & \text{if } F_t \in (\kappa-\Delta\kappa, \kappa+\Delta\kappa); \\ -\dfrac{e^{-r(T'-t)}}{\Delta\kappa}\left[\dfrac{1}{\kappa}-\dfrac{\kappa}{\kappa+\Delta\kappa}\right] & \text{if } F_t \ge \kappa+\Delta\kappa. \end{cases}$$

Now, by Taylor's series:

$$\frac{1}{\kappa-\Delta\kappa}=\frac{1}{\kappa}+\frac{1}{\kappa^2}\Delta\kappa+O\left(\Delta\kappa^2\right)$$

and:

$$\frac{1}{\kappa+\Delta\kappa}=\frac{1}{\kappa}-\frac{1}{\kappa^2}\Delta\kappa+O\left(\Delta\kappa^2\right).$$

Substitution implies that the number of futures contracts held is given by:

$$\begin{cases} -\dfrac{e^{-r(T'-t)}}{\Delta\kappa}\left[-\dfrac{1}{\kappa^2}\Delta\kappa+O\left(\Delta\kappa^2\right)\right] & \text{if } F_t \le \kappa-\Delta\kappa; \\ -\dfrac{e^{-r(T'-t)}}{\Delta\kappa}\left[\dfrac{1}{\kappa}-\dfrac{1}{F_t}\right] & \text{if } F_t \in (\kappa-\Delta\kappa, \kappa+\Delta\kappa); \\ -\dfrac{e^{-r(T'-t)}}{\Delta\kappa}\left[\dfrac{1}{\kappa^2}\Delta\kappa+O\left(\Delta\kappa^2\right)\right] & \text{if } F_t \ge \kappa+\Delta\kappa. \end{cases}$$

Thus, as $\Delta\kappa \downarrow 0$, the number of futures contracts held converges to

$$-\frac{e^{-r(T'-t)}}{\kappa^2}\operatorname{sgn}(F_t-\kappa)$$

where $\operatorname{sgn}(x)$ is the sign function:

$$\operatorname{sgn}(x) \equiv \begin{cases} -1 & \text{if } x<0; \\ 0 & \text{if } x=0; \\ 1 & \text{if } x>0. \end{cases}$$

1 *In this article, the term "volatility" refers to either the variance or the standard deviation of the return on an investment.*

2 *Jagannathan (1984) shows that in general options need not be increasing in volatility.*

3 *For marketing reasons, these contracts are usually written on the standard deviation, despite the focus of the literature on spanning contracts on variance.*

4 *This contract is actually a forward contract on realised volatility, but is nonetheless termed a swap.*

5 *Note that in the Black model, the sensitivity to volatility of a straddle is actually maximised at slightly below the forward price.*

6 *Note that listed futures options are generally American-style. However, by setting* $T' = T$, *the underlying futures will converge to the spot at* T *and so the assumption is that there exists European-style spot options in this special case.*

7 *This observation was first noted in Breeden and Litzenberger (1978) and established formally in Green and Jarrow (1987) and Nachman (1988).*

8 *Options do trade futures-style in Hong Kong. However, when only spot option prices are available, one can set* $T' = T$ *and calculate the mean and variance of the terminal spot under the forward measure. The variance is then expressed in terms of the forward prices of options, which can be obtained from the spot price by dividing by the bond price.*

9 *If the futures price process is a continuous semi-martingale, then Itô's lemma implies that*

$$E_0\left[\ln\left(\frac{F_T}{F_0}\right)\right]=-E_0\frac{1}{2}\int_0^T\sigma_t^2dt,$$

where σ_t *is the volatility at time* t.

10 *In an interesting paper, Cherian and Jarrow (1997) show the existence of an equilibrium in an incomplete economy where investors believe the Black Scholes formula is valid even though volatility is stochastic.*

11 *See El Karoui, Jeanblanc-Picque, and Shreve (1996) for the extension of this result to the case when the hedger uses a delta-hedging strategy assuming that volatility is a function of stock price and time. Also see Avellaneda et al (1995; 1996) and Lyons (1995) for similar results.*

12 *The Dirac delta function is a generalised function characterised by two properties:*

1. $\delta(x) = \begin{cases} 0 & \text{if } x \neq 0 \\ \infty & \text{if } x = 0 \end{cases}$

2. $\int_{-\infty}^{\infty} \delta(x)dx = 1.$

See Richards and Youn (1990) for an accessible introduction to such generalised functions.

13 *See Karatzas and Shreve (1988), p. 220.*

14 *When two Brownian motions drive the price and the forward local volatility surface, any two assets whose payoffs are not colinear can be used to span.*

BIBLIOGRAPHY

Avellaneda, M., A. Levy, and A. Paras, 1995, "Pricing and Hedging Derivative Securities in Markets with Uncertain Volatilities", *Applied Mathematical Finance* 2, pp. 73–88.

Avellaneda, M., A. Levy, and A. Paras, 1996, "Managing the Volatility Risk of Portfolios of Derivative Securities: The Lagrangian Uncertain Volatility Model", *Applied Mathematical Finance* 3, pp.21–52.

Breeden, D., and R. Litzenberger, 1978, "Prices of State Contingent Claims Implicit in Option Prices,", *Journal of Business* 51, pp. 621–51.

Brenner, M., and D. Galai, 1989, "New Financial Instruments for Hedging Changes in Volatility", *Financial Analyst's Journal*, July-August, pp. 61–5.

Brenner, M., and D. Galai, 1993, "Hedging Volatility in Foreign Currencies", *Journal of Derivatives*, Fall, pp. 53–9.

Brenner, M., and D. Galai, 1996, "Options on Volatility", in *Option Embedded Bonds*, ed. I. Nelken, Irwin: Chicago, pp.273–86.

Carr P., and R. Jarrow, 1990, "The Stop-Loss Start-Gain Strategy and Option Valuation: A New Decomposition into Intrinsic and Time Value", *Review of Financial Studies* 3, pp. 469–92.

Carr P., and D. Madan, 1997, "Optimal Positioning in Derivative Securities", Working paper, Morgan Stanley.

Cherian, J., and R. Jarrow, 1998, "Options Markets, Self-fulfilling Prophecies and Implied Volatilities", *Review of Derivatives Research* forthcoming.

Derman E., I. Kani, and M. Kamal, 1997, "Trading and Hedging Local Volatility", *Journal of Financial Engineering* 6, No.3, pp. 233–68.

Dupire B., 1993, "Model Art", *Risk*, Sept., pp. 118–20.

Dupire B., 1996, "A Unified Theory of Volatility", Working paper, Paribas.

El Karoui, N., M. Jeanblanc-Picque, and S. Shreve, 1996, "Robustness of the Black and Scholes Formula", Working paper, Carnegie Mellon University.

Fleming, J., B. Ostdiek, and R. Whaley, 1993, "Predicting Stock Market Volatility: A New Measure", Working paper, Duke University.

Galai, D., 1979, "A Proposal for Indexes for Traded Call Options", *Journal of Finance* 34, 5, pp. 1157–72.

Gastineau, G., 1977, "An Index of Listed Option Premiums", *Financial Analyst's Journal*, 33 (3), pp. 70–5.

Green, R.C., and R.A. Jarrow, 1987, "Spanning and Completeness in markets with Contingent Claims", *Journal of Economic Theory* 41, pp. 202–10.

Grunbichler A., and F. Longstaff, 1993, "Valuing Options on Volatility", Working paper, UCLA.

Heath, D., R. Jarrow, and A. Morton, 1992, "Bond Pricing and the Term Structure of Interest Rates: A New Methodology for Contingent Claim Valuation", *Econometrica* 66, pp. 77–105.

Jagannathan R., 1984, "Call Options and the Risk of Underlying Securities", *Journal of Financial Economics*, 13, No. 3, pp. 425–34.

Karatzas, I., and S. Shreve, 1988, *Brownian Motion and Stochastic Calculus*, Springer Verlag, NY.

Lyons, T., 1995, "Uncertain Volatility and the Risk-free Synthesis of Derivatives", *Applied Mathematical Finance* 2, pp. 117–33.

Nachman, D., 1988, "Spanning and Completeness with Options", *Review of Financial Studies* 3, 31, pp. 311–28.

Neuberger, A., 1990, "Volatility Trading", Working paper, London Business School.

Richards, J.I., and H.K. Youn, 1990, *Theory of Distributions: A Non-technical Introduction*, Cambridge University Press.

Ross, S., 1976, "Options and Efficiency", *Quarterly Journal of Economics*, February, pp. 75–89.

Whaley, R., 1993, "Derivatives on Market Volatility: Hedging Tools Long Overdue", *Journal of Derivatives*, Fall, pp. 71–84; reprinted as Chapter 28 of the present volume.

30

Pricing and Hedging with Smiles*

Bruno Dupire
Nikko Financial Products

Black-Scholes volatilities implied from market prices exhibit a strike pattern, commonly termed the volatility "smile", as well as a term structure. This non-constancy of volatility contradicts the assumptions of the model, and leads to the unpleasant situation where a single spot process has many supposedly constant but yet distinct volatilities. We show how to reconcile these seemingly incompatible assumptions with a single hypothesis on the spot process - instantaneous volatility is a deterministic function of spot and time. This has the merit of preserving one-dimensionality and completeness. The process is used to price exotic options and hedge them robustly with standard European options.

Option pricing consists, after specifying a model and estimating its parameters, of deriving option prices as a function of these parameters. If the market model is complete, the prices will be unique. A typical example is given by the Black-Scholes model, which gives us options prices as a function of a parameter called volatility. In fact, we often have to invert this relationship, for what we know is the price of the option, given by the market. This then gives us the implied value of the parameter.

If the model were good, this implied value would be the same for all option market prices - but in reality, we know that it is not so. Implied Black-Scholes volatilities strongly depend on the maturity and the strike of the European option under scrutiny. If the implied volatilities of at-the-money options on the Nikkei are 20% for a maturity of six months and 18% for a maturity of one year, we are in the uncomfortable situation of assuming that the Nikkei vibrates with a constant volatility of 20% for six months, and, at the same time, that the very same index vibrates with a constant volatility of 18% for one year!

It is easy to solve this paradox by allowing volatility to be time-dependent, as Merton (1973) long ago suggested. The Nikkei would first exhibit an instantaneous volatility of 20% and subsequently a lower one, computed by a forward relationship to accommodate the one-year volatility. We now have one unique process, compatible with the two option prices. From the term structure of implied volatilities we can infer a time-dependent instantaneous volatility, for the former is the quadratic mean of the latter. The spot process S is then governed by the following stochastic differential equation:

$$\frac{dS}{S} = r(t)dt + \sigma(t)dW$$

where r is the instantaneous forward rate implied from the yield curve.

Some Wall Street houses incorporate this temporal information in their discretisation schemes in order to price American or path-dependent options.

However, the dependence of implied volatility on the strike, for a given maturity (the smile effect) is trickier. Many researchers have attempted to enrich the Black-Scholes model in order to compute a theoretical "smile". Unfortunately they have to introduce a non-traded source of risk (jumps in the case of Merton (1976) and stochastic volatility in the case of Hull and White (1987)), so they lose the completeness of the model. And completeness is

* *This paper was first reproduced in the proceedings of AFFI Conference (La Baule, June 1993). At the time of writing the author was head of derivatives research at Paribas Capital Markets. I am happy to mention fruitful conversations with Nicole El Karoui, Marc Yor, Emmanuel Bocquet and my colleagues at Paribas. All errors are indeed mine.*

of the highest value, since it allows for arbitrage pricing and for hedging.

This paper considers the following issue: is it possible to build a spot process which:

- is compatible with the observed smiles at all maturities?
- keeps the model complete?

Or, more precisely, given the prices of European calls of all strikes K and maturities T: C(K,T), is it possible to find a risk neutral process for the spot in the form of a diffusion,

$$\frac{dS}{S} = r(t)dt + \sigma(S,t)dW$$

where the instantaneous volatility σ is a deterministic function of the spot and of the time?

This would nicely extend the Black-Scholes model and take full advantage of its diffusion setting, without increasing the dimension of uncertainty at the same time. It would give us the features of a one-factor model to explain all European option prices. We could then also price and hedge any American or path-dependent option[1], enabling us to answer questions such as "how to hedge a forward start option?", "what is the smile of Asian options?" or "which strike to use to hedge the volatility risk on the intermediate date of a compound option?"

The problem

If the spot price follows a one dimensional diffusion process, then the model is complete and option prices can be computed by discounting an expectation with respect to a so-called "risk neutral" probability. The discounted spot has no drift but retains the same diffusion coefficient.

More precisely, path-dependent options are priced as the discounted expected value of their terminal payoff over all possible paths. In the case of European options, it boils down to an expectation over the terminal values of the spot (which can be seen as bundling the paths which end at a same point and associating with it the probability of those paths). It follows that knowing the prices of all path-dependent options is equivalent to knowing the full (risk-neutral) diffusion process of the spot, while knowing all European option prices merely amounts to knowing the laws of the spot at different times, conditional on its current value.

The full diffusion contains much more information than the conditional laws, as distinct diffusions may generate identical conditional laws. However, if we restrict ourselves to risk-neutral diffusions, the ambiguity is removed and we can retrieve the unique risk-neutral diffusion from the conditional laws. This result is interesting on its own, but we will exploit its consequences in terms of hedging as well.

A diffusion from prices

In this section, we address the problem of existence, uniqueness and construction of a diffusion process compatible with observed option prices, in a continuous time setting. For the sake of clarity, we assume that the interest rate is 0.

FROM PRICES TO DISTRIBUTIONS

For a given maturity T, the collection $C(K,T)_K$ of option prices of different strikes yields the risk-neutral density function φ_T of the spot at time T through the relationship:

$$C(K,T) = \int_0^{\infty} (x-K)^{+} \varphi_T(x)dx$$

which we differentiate twice with respect to K to obtain:

$$\varphi_T(K) = \frac{\partial^2 C}{\partial K^2}(K,T).$$

If we start from (S_0,T_0), we have $\varphi_{T_0}(K) = \delta_{S_0}(K)$ for $C(K,T_0) = (S_0 - K)^+$.

We are then left with an interesting stochastic problem (with the notation (x,t) instead of (K,T)): knowing all the densities conditional on an initial fixed (x_0,t_0), is there a unique diffusion process which generates these densities?

The converse problem is well known: from the coefficients a and b (satisfying slow growth assumption) of the diffusion:

$$dx = a(x,t)dt + b(x,t)dW$$

we can deduce the conditional distributions φ_t thanks to the Fokker-Planck (or forward Kolmogorov) equation (define $f(x,t) \equiv \varphi_t(x)$):

$$\frac{1}{2}\frac{\partial^2(b^2 f)}{\partial x^2} - \frac{\partial(af)}{\partial x} = \frac{\partial f}{\partial t}.$$

However, a diffusion is more informative than the distributions it generates. It is easy to exhibit two distinct diffusions which generate the same distributions. For instance, with $x_0 = 0$, $t_0 = 0$:

$$dx = -\lambda x dt + \mu dW$$

and

$$dx = \mu e^{-\lambda t} dW$$

lead to the same Gaussian distribution for each t, with a mean equal to 0, and a variance equal to

$$\frac{\mu^2}{2\lambda}\left(1 - e^{-2\lambda t}\right).$$

However, if we restrict ourselves to risk-neutral diffusions, we can recover, up to technical regularity assumptions, a unique diffusion process from the $f(x,t)$. The interest rate being 0, we only pay attention to martingale diffusions (ie $a = 0$), which in the case of our counterexample rules out the first candidate.

FROM DISTRIBUTIONS TO THE DIFFUSION

The Fokker-Planck equation then takes the simple form (now f is known and b is the unknown!):

$$\frac{1}{2}\frac{\partial^2(b^2 f)}{\partial x^2} = \frac{\partial f}{\partial t}$$

As f can be written as

$$\frac{\partial^2 C}{\partial x^2}$$

we obtain, after changing the order of derivatives:

$$\frac{1}{2}\frac{\partial^2(b^2 f)}{\partial x^2} = \frac{\partial^2}{\partial x^2}\left(\frac{\partial C}{\partial t}\right).$$

Integrating twice in x for a constant t gives:

$$\frac{1}{2}b_{\alpha,\beta}^2 f = \frac{\partial C}{\partial t} + \alpha(t)x + \beta(t).$$

We assume that[2]

$$\lim_{x\to+\infty}\frac{\partial C}{\partial t} = 0.$$

The two integration constants, α and β, are actually zero because the lower limit of the LHS as x goes to infinity is 0.[3] This means that

$$\frac{1}{2}b^2 f = \frac{\partial C}{\partial t}$$

is the only possible candidate. Remembering that

$$f = \frac{\partial^2 C}{\partial x^2}$$

we get:

$$\frac{1}{2}b^2\frac{\partial^2 C}{\partial x^2} = \frac{\partial C}{\partial t}. \quad (1)$$

Both derivatives are positive by arbitrage (butterfly for the convexity and conversion for the maturity). The definite candidate is then (we may impose it is positive)

$$b(x,t) = \sqrt{\frac{2\frac{\partial C}{\partial t}(x,t)}{\frac{\partial^2 C}{\partial x^2}(x,t)}}. \quad (2)$$

To ensure it is admissible (that is, it satisfies the slow growth condition), we impose:

$$\frac{\partial C}{\partial t} \le x^2\frac{\partial^2 C}{\partial x^2}$$

for large x. This makes sense: diffusions cannot generate *everything*. For instance, let us consider a diffusion process with a binary (martingale) jump at a fixed time t^*. The call prices it generates will increase sharply at time t^* and cannot be reproduced by a diffusion; such kinks must be ruled out.

Going back to the spot process, we indeed obtain the instantaneous volatility by

$$\sigma(S,t) = \frac{b(S,t)}{S}.$$

Reminding that x actually denotes the strike, we can rewrite (1) as:

$$\frac{1}{2}b^2\frac{\partial^2 C}{\partial K^2} = \frac{\partial C}{\partial T}.$$

This equation has the same flavour as, but is distinct from, the classical Black-Scholes partial differential equation. It involves derivatives of option prices computed today, in contrast with Black-Scholes PDE which involves, for a fixed option, derivatives with respect to the current time and value of the spot. This equation can be used to compute option prices if b is known.

Discretisation

It is indeed possible to compute b numerically from the relation (2) obtained from the continuous time and price analysis, and to discretise the associated spot process with explicit recombining binomial (Nelson & Ramaswamy (1990)) or trinomial (Hull & White (1990)) schemes. However, we prefer to present a construction which uses a common interest rate model fitting technique: forward induction. See Jamshidian (1991) and Hull & White (1992) for more details.

It is actually quite easy to find a set of coefficients which correctly prices options, since degrees of freedom are superabundant in comparison with the constraints. The situation is analogous to the one encountered in the continuous case, where various diffusions could generate the same densities. However, imposing the martingale condition (risk-neutrality) leads to uniqueness. In the discrete time setting, the martingale condition expressed at each node gives additional constraints. This extra structure is a key point in our pricing/hedging approach but existence and uniqueness are generally not achieved by a simplistic discretisation. The trinomial one nicely meets these requirements.

We build a trinomial tree with equally spaced time steps and a price step consistent with the likeliest volatility. Weights will be assigned to the connections, which means that the discounted probability of each path can be computed, allowing us to value any path-dependent option. In many cases the complexity of the computation can be reduced.

At each discrete date, all profiles consisting of continuous piecewise linear functions with break points located at inner nodes of the tree are asked to be correctly priced by the tree. At the nth step, the aforementioned space is of dimension $2n + 1$, for any such profile is uniquely characterised by the value it takes on the $2n + 1$ nodes. It contains the zero-coupon, the asset itself and all calls (and puts) whose strikes are the inner nodes. To each node we associate an Arrow-Debreu profile whose value is 1 on this node and 0 on the others.

A node is labelled (n,i) with n denoting the time step and i the price step. Its associated Arrow-Debreu price is noted $A(n,i)$ and the weight of the connection between nodes (n,i) and $(n+1,j)$, $j = i-1$, i, or $i+1$ is noted $w(n,i,j)$. The weights are computed through the tree in a forward fashion.

We can exploit two types of relations:

❑ forward relations, which relate the Arrow-Debreu price of a node to the Arrow-Debreu prices of its immediate predecessors.

❑ standard backward relations, which link the value of a contingent claim at a node to its value at the immediate successors. We apply this relation to two simple claims: one unit of the numeraire and one unit of the spot, both to be received one time step later.

The generic step of the algorithm is as follows:

❑ Compute $w(n,i,i-1)$ from $A(n+1,i-1)$, $A(n,i)$, $A(n,i-1)$, $A(n,i-2)$, $w(n,i-1,i-1)$ and $w(n,i-2,i-1)$.

Compute $w(n,i,i)$ and $w(n,i,i+1)$ from the forward discount factors of the cash and the spot.

Hedging

Knowing the whole process allows for the pricing of path-dependent options (by Monte Carlo methods) and American options (by dynamic programming). It also allows for hedging through an equivalent spot position because the sensitivity of the options with respect to the spot can be computed: knowing the full process, it is possible to shift the initial value and to infer the process which starts from this new value and the new price it incurs. Delta hedging can then be achieved, which will be effective throughout the life of the option if the spot behaves according to the inferred process.

But it probably won't, which leads us to a more sophisticated method of hedging. We can build a robust hedge which will be efficient, even if the spot does not behave according to the instantaneous inferred volatilities of the diffusion process.

The idea is to associate to every contingent claim X a portfolio of European options which will be tangent to it, in the sense that it will change in value identically up to the first order for changes in the volatility manifold $\sigma(K,T)_{K,T}$.

We proceed as follows: a local move of the volatility manifold around (K_0,T_0) will lead to a new diffusion process, hence to a new value of X. We can then compute the sensitivity of X to a change of volatility $\sigma(K_0,T_0)$ and the equivalent $C(K_0,T_0)$ position. Repeating for all (K,T), we obtain a spectrum of sensitivities $\mathrm{Vega}(K,T)_{K,T}$ and the associated (continuous) portfolio of $C(K,T)$, which can be seen as a projection of X on the $C(K,T)_{K,T}$. This portfolio will behave up to the first order as X, even if the market evolves transgressing the induced forward volatilities computed above.

Conclusion

This paper has two main findings. On the theoretical side, it shows that it is possible under certain conditions to recover from the conditional laws a full diffusion process whose drift is imposed. This means that we can induce a unique diffusion process from option prices observed in the market.

On the practical side, it tells how to elaborate a sound pricing for path-dependent and American options. Moreover, it finely assesses the risk of such options by performing a risk analysis along both strikes and maturities. This rightly enables the full integration of these options in a book of standard European options – a key point for many financial institutions.

1 *Even for European options, the knowledge of the whole process is compulsory for hedging.*

2 *This is somewhat reasonable since*

$$\lim_{x \to +\infty} C(x) = 0$$

3 *Otherwise, there would be a strictly positive real* γ *bounding from below* b^2f *which is in turn lesser than* v^2x^2f *for a non-negative* v *due to the slow growth assumption, so*

$$xf \geq \frac{\gamma}{v^2 x}$$

which contradicts the fact that f *has a finite expectation (equal to* x_0*).*

BIBLIOGRAPHY

Black, F., and M. Scholes, 1973, "The Pricing of Options and Corporate Liabilities", *Journal of Political Economy* 81, pp. 637-54.

Breeden, D., and R. Litzenberger, 1978, "Prices of State-Contingent Claims Implicit in Option Prices," *Journal of Business* 51, pp. 621-51.

Duffie, D., 1988, *Security Markets, Stochastic Models*. San Diego: Academic Press.

Dupire, B., 1992, "Arbitrage Pricing with Stochastic Volatility", Proceedings of AFFI Conference in Paris, June 1992.

El Karoui, N., R. Myneni, R. Viswanathan, 1992, "Arbitrage Pricing and Hedging of Interest Rates Claims with State Variables," Working paper, Université de Jussieu, Paris VI.

Harrison, J. M., and D. Kreps, 1979, "Martingales and Arbitrage in Multiperiod Securities Markets", *Journal of Economic Theory* 20, pp. 381-408.

Harrison, J. M., and S. Pliska, 1981, "Martingales and Stochastic Integrals in the Theory of Continuous Trading", *Stochastic Processes and their Applications* 11, pp. 215-60.

Hull, J., and A. White, 1987, "The Pricing of Options on Assets with Stochastic Volatilities", *The Journal of Finance* 3, pp. 281-300.

Hull, J., and A. White, 1990, "Valuing Derivative Securities Using the Explicit Finite Difference Method", *Journal of Financial and Quantitative Analysis* 25, pp. 87-100.

Hull, J., and A. White, 1992, "One Factor Interest-Rate Models and the Valuation of Interest-Rate Contingent Claims," Working paper, University of Toronto.

Jamshidian, F., 1991, "Forward Induction and Construction of Yield Curve Diffusion Models," *Journal of Fixed Income* 1.

Karatzas, I., and , S. E. Shreve, 1988, *Brownian Motion and Stochastic Calculus*, Springer-Verlag, New-York.

Merton, R., 1973, "The Theory of Rational Option Pricing," *Bell Journal of Economics and Management Science* 4, pp. 141-83.

Merton, R., 1976, "Option Pricing when Underlying Stock Returns are Discontinuous," *Journal of Financial Economics* 3, pp. 124-44.

Nelson, D., and K. Ramaswamy, 1990, "Simple Binomial Processes as Diffusion Approximations in Financial Models," *The Review of Financial Studies* 3, pp. 393-430.

31

Stochastic Implied Trees:

Arbitrage Pricing with Stochastic Term and Strike Structure of Volatility

Emanuel Derman and Iraj Kani
Goldman Sachs; Martingale Technologies

In this paper we present an arbitrage pricing framework for valuing and hedging contingent equity index claims in the presence of a stochastic term and strike structure of volatility. Our approach to stochastic volatility is similar to the Heath-Jarrow-Morton (HJM) approach to stochastic interest rates. Starting from an initial set of index options prices and their associated local volatility surface, we show how to construct a family of continuous time stochastic processes which define the arbitrage-free evolution of this local volatility surface through time. The no-arbitrage conditions are similar to, but more involved than, the HJM conditions for arbitrage-free stochastic movements of the interest rate curve. They guarantee that even under a general stochastic volatility evolution the initial options prices, or their equivalent Black-Scholes implied volatilities, remain fair. We introduce stochastic implied trees as discrete implementations of our family of continuous time models. The nodes of a stochastic implied tree remain fixed as time passes. During each discrete time step the index moves randomly from its initial node to some node at the next time level, while the local transition probabilities between the nodes also vary. The change in transition probabilities corresponds to a general (multifactor) stochastic variation of the local volatility surface. Starting from any node, the future movements of the index and the local volatilities must be restricted so that the transition probabilities to all future nodes are simultaneously martingales. This guarantees that initial options prices remain fair. On the tree, these martingale conditions are effected through appropriate choices of the drift parameters for the transition probabilities at every future node, in such a way that the subsequent evolution of the index and of the local volatility surface do not lead to riskless arbitrage opportunities among different option and forward contracts or their underlying index. Stochastic implied trees can be used to value complex index options, or other derivative securities with payoffs that depend on index volatility, even when the volatility surface is both skewed and stochastic. The resulting security prices are consistent with the current market prices of all standard index options and forwards, and with the absence of future arbitrage opportunities in the framework. The calculated options values are independent of investor preferences and the market price of index or volatility risk. Stochastic implied trees can also be used to calculate hedge ratios for any contingent index security in terms of its underlying index and all standard options defined on that index.

STOCHASTIC IMPLIED TREES

The Black-Scholes theory of options pricing (Black and Scholes, 1973) assumes that stock prices are stochastic and vary lognormally, but that future stock volatilities, interest rates and dividend yields are known and deterministic. The theory is based on the exclusion of arbitrage: an option's payoff can be replicated by that of a time-varying portfolio of stock and riskless bonds, and must therefore at any time have the same value as the portfolio. The most compelling consequence of this *arbitrage-free* approach is that options values are *preference-free:* investors of all risk preferences can agree on the unique fair value of an option. This transcendent quality of the theory has led to its great practical success, spawning more than two decades of intensive research that extended it to other underlyers and relaxed its basic assumptions so as to better match the observed behaviour of options markets and underlyers. The current generation of models, even though they treat underlyers more realistically and can be calibrated to prevailing options market prices, are still based on an arbitrage-free approach, admitting no arbitrage opportunities in their theoretical framework.

The history of interest rate options pricing illustrates this development. Original models were simple adaptations of the Black-Scholes formula with bonds, rather than stocks, as the underlyers. Today, most interest rate options pricing models assume interest rates themselves are stochastic and mean-reverting, allow for several stochastic factors, and can be calibrated to observed initial bond prices (and their volatilities), while constraining future interest-rate evolution to be arbitrage-free. These models fall into two basic families. *Equilibrium* models[1] consider interest rate processes depending on one or more state variables and are derived from general equilibrium arguments. The market prices of risk are then derived from associated characteristics of the yield curve (such as level, slope, curvature, etc.) or bond prices. In general these models are not calibrated to all current bond prices, and may therefore contain initial arbitrage violations. *Arbitrage-free* models, in contrast, are calibrated to all initial bond prices and also admit no future arbitrage violations. They achieve this in two different ways. The first class[2] use stochastic interest rate processes that automatically generate arbitrage-free future scenarios, and equip the process with enough parameters to be forcibly calibrated to the initial traded bond prices. The second class[3] instead, start with exogenously specified stochastic processes for bond prices or forward rates. They then derive constraints on the evolution of bond prices or forward rates so that no future arbitrages occur.

The history of stochastic volatility modelling is shorter but still similar to the history of stochastic interest rates. Existing stochastic volatility models fall into two basic families. *Complete-market*[4] models specify conditions under which the financial market is complete in the presence of the volatility risk. They posit (if necessary) hypothetical traded volatility instruments that can be used to hedge the volatility risk and complete the market. Contingent claim prices in these models depend critically on the price dynamics of the volatility instruments and may also implicitly depend on the market price(s) of volatility risk. *Equilibrium* models[5] tend to assume (rather than derive) some parametric form for the stochastic evolution of the index and its volatility in equilibrium, and then derive implicit options valuation formulas which depend on the parameters of the process. The traded options prices are then inverted for the unknown parameters.

Complete-market models can be somewhat arbitrary and sometimes unnatural because of the specific assumptions they make about the hypothetical volatility instruments. The equilibrium volatility models have the drawback that the choice of the parametric form for the underlying stochastic processes remains largely arbitrary. In addition, it is usually difficult to invert complex and non-linear options prices to obtain the parameters. Finally, *ad hoc* specification of the market prices of risk can lead to violations of arbitrage.[6]

In this paper we propose a new arbitrage-based approach to contingent claims valuation with stochastic volatility[7], similar to the Heath-Jarrow-Morton (HJM) methodology for stochastic interest rates.[8] We begin with a continuous time economy with multiple factors. We work with local (forward) volatilities, instead of implied volatilities (or option prices), imposing an exogenous stochastic structure on the local volatility surface. The primacy of the local volatility surface in our work is analogous to that of the forward rate curve in the HJM framework. Our model takes as given the initial local volatility surface and posits a general multi-factor continuous

We thank Indrajit Bardhan, Peter Carr, Michael Kamal and Joseph Zou for helpful conversations. We are also grateful to Barbara Dunn for her careful review of the manuscript.

time stochastic process for its evolution across time. To ensure that this process is consistent with an arbitrage-free economy we characterise the conditions which guarantee absence of explicit arbitrage opportunities (at any future time) among the various option (and futures) contracts defined and traded on the underlying index. Under these conditions markets are complete and contingent claim valuation is preference-free. Unfortunately, in contrast to the HJM conditions, here the arbitrage-free conditions are complex and non-linear (integral) equations, which are difficult to use in their continuous form.

We then introduce *stochastic implied trees* as a discrete-time framework where the volatility surface undergoes multi-factor (arbitrage-free) stochastic variations. Here we work with trinomial stochastic implied trees.[9] The location of the nodes in this kind of tree are fixed but the transition probabilities vary stochastically as time changes and index level moves. As time evolves, the index level moves randomly from node to node while local volatilities (and concurrently the transition probabilities) fluctuate stochastically across the tree. Starting from any initial node, the future movements of the index and the local volatility surface must be restricted so that total transition probabilities to all future nodes are simultaneously martingales. On the tree, these martingale conditions can be satisfied by making an appropriate choice of the *drift parameter* for every future node. In the discrete time framework defined by the stochastic implied tree, this process step-by-step guarantees absence of arbitrage opportunities among different option (and forward) contracts and the underlying index.

We draw extensively on the analogy between interest rates and volatility throughout this paper. We begin by reviewing the concept of the local (forward) volatility surface and the *effective theory* of volatility which it defines. The local volatility surface is the options world analogue of the forward interest rate curve. Standard option prices calculated using today's local volatility surface match their market prices, just as the bond prices calculated from today's forward rate curve match their market prices. The dynamics of standard option prices, as defined by today's local volatility surface, albeit arbitrage-free, is based on the assumption of non-stochastic volatility, as portrayed by the static (non-random) nature of the local volatility surface. This *effective dynamics* of option prices is analogous to the deterministic, but arbitrage-free, bond price dynamics which result from a static forward rate curve. To allow *stochastic dynamics* we introduce exogenous stochastic structure on the effective theory. This is to say that we allow general (multi-factor) fluctuations of the local volatility surface as time and spot index level change. We impose dynamical conditions which explicitly guarantee absence of arbitrage among standard options, forwards and the underlying index. This process will augment an effective theory of volatility to a full *stochastic theory* of volatility in a manner which is the hallmark of the HJM approach to stochastic interest rates.

Local volatility surface: the effective theory of volatility

We can think of local volatility $\sigma_{K,T}$ as the market's consensus estimate of instantaneous volatility at the future market level K and future time T. Local volatilities corresponding to different future market levels and times together comprise the *local volatility surface*. The local volatility surface indicates the fair value of future index volatility at future market levels and times as implied by the spectrum of available standard option (and forward contract) prices.

The relationship between the local volatilities and option prices (or implied volatilities) in the options world is analogous to the relationship between the forward rates and bond prices (or yield-to-maturities) in the fixed income world. We can calculate the forward interest rates f_T corresponding to the future times T from the spectrum of zero-coupon bond prices B_T with different maturities T, using a well-known formula

$$f_T = -\frac{1}{B_T}\frac{dB_T}{dT}. \quad (1)$$

Similarly, we can calculate the local volatility $\sigma_{K,T}$ corresponding to the future market level K and time T from the spectrum of standard option prices $C_{K,T}$, with different strikes K and maturities T, using the formula

$$\sigma^2_{K,T} = 2\frac{\left\{\frac{\partial C_{K,T}}{\partial T} + (r-\delta)K\frac{\partial C_{K,T}}{\partial K} + \delta C_{K,T}\right\}}{K^2\frac{\partial^2 C_{K,T}}{\partial K^2}}. \quad (2)$$

The riskfree discount rate r and the dividend yield δ in (2) are both assumed to be constant. Also, the quantities which we will discuss throughout this paper are usually evaluated at a specific times t or spot prices S, and contain

1. In an effective theory defined by a static forward rate curve, short rate follows the instantaneous forward rates

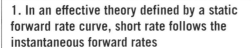

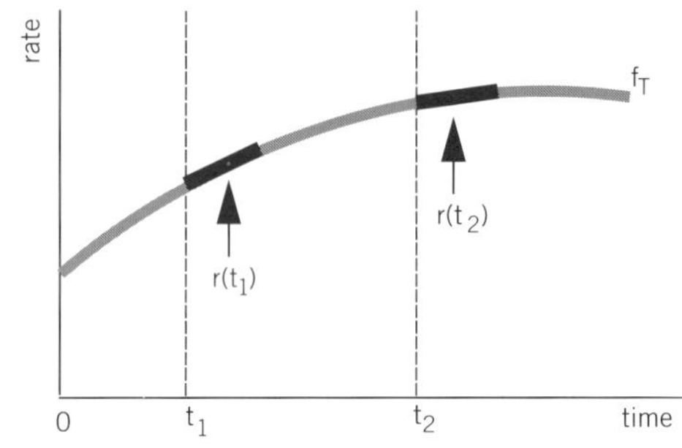

other explicit or implicit (deterministic or stochastic) parameters which we may omit for brevity. For example, the quantities in (1) and (2) are evaluated at the present time and spot price, hence $f_T = f_T(t_0)$, $\sigma_{K,T} = \sigma_{K,T}(t_0,S_0)$ etc.

Equation (1) often serves as a general definition for forward rates, regardless of the specific nature of the interest rate process. It can be shown[10] that under very general assumptions, forward rates are risk-adjusted expectations of future short rates

$$f_T = E^{(T)}\left[r(T)\right]. \tag{3}$$

The expectation $E^{(T)}[\ldots]$ is performed at the present time and with respect to a measure known as the *T-maturity forward risk-adjusted measure*. The precise description of this measure is not necessary for our purposes here. The only thing to remember is that (1) gives us a direct way for extracting these expectations of future short rates from the traded bond prices. Similarly, it can be shown that local volatilities are risk-adjusted expectations of future instantaneous volatilities. More precisely, local variance $\sigma^2_{K,T}$ is a risk-adjusted expectation of future instantaneous variance of $\sigma^2(T)$ at time T as

$$\sigma^2_{K,T} = E^{(K,T)}\left[\sigma^2(T)\right]. \tag{4}$$

Here the expectation $E^{(K,T)}[\ldots]$ is performed at the present time and market level, and with respect to a new measure which we call the *K-strike and T-maturity forward risk-adjusted measure*, as described in Appendix A. Again the precise details about the measure are unimportant at this point, only that these expectations can be directly extracted from the market prices of standard options, as given by (2).

A static (non-random) local volatility surface defines an *effective theory* of volatility in the same way as a static forward rate curve defines an effective theory for interest rates. In an effective theory, specific expectations (or *integrals*) of some or all of the underlying stochastic variables are extracted from the current prices of the traded assets, and are subsequently assumed to remain unchanged as time evolves. The effective dynamics which results is based on some of the sources of uncertainty being "effectively" integrated out of the full stochastic theory. Let us briefly review the interest rate case first.

THE EFFECTIVE INTEREST RATE THEORY

In the effective interest rate setting, the forward rate curve is evaluated from the available bond prices at time t_0, and is assumed to remain unchanged thereafter as time t evolves, thus for all $t \geq t_0$:

$$f_T(t) = f_T. \tag{5}$$

As Figure 1 illustrates, this procedure integrates all sources of interest rate stochasticity out of the original theory, and therefore, the effective dynamics of the rates in the effective theory is completely deterministic. As physical time t elapses, the spot rate (or short rate) $r(t)$ rolls along the static forward rate curve, coinciding with the forward rate at time t:

$$r(t) = f_t. \tag{6}$$

The dynamics of zero-coupon bond prices is also deterministic and is described by a simple *backward equation*:

$$\left(\frac{d}{dt} - f_t\right)B_T(t) = 0. \tag{7}$$

This equation, with the aid of (6), shows that the asset price dynamics in the effective theory is *local* and arbitrage-free. Equation (7) is also the dual of the *forward equation* satisfied by the zero-coupon bond prices:

$$\left(\frac{d}{dT} + f_T\right)B_T(t) = 0. \tag{8}$$

The forward equation is merely a restatement of (1), and holds by the definition of the forward rates regardless of specific assumptions concerning the behaviour of interest rates.

The backward equation describes propagation *forward* in physical time, for a fixed maturity. More precisely, it relates the prices of a T-maturity bond at different time points t, with earlier times in terms of the later ones. This is best understood by introducing the *forward propagator* (or *forward Green's function*) $p_{t,t'}$, which relates bond prices at times t and t', with

$t \le t'$, for any T-maturity bond, through a simple relationship:

$$B_T(t) = p_{t,t'} B_T(t'). \quad (9)$$

The forward propagator $p_{t,t'}$ describes bond price evolution forward in physical time, as illustrated by Figure 2(a). It satisfies the backward and forward differential equations with boundary conditions $p_{t,t'} = 1$:

$$\left(\frac{d}{dt} - f_t\right)p_{t,t'} = 0; \left(\frac{d}{dt'} + f_{t'}\right)p_{t,t'} = 0 \quad (10)$$

and for any $t \le \tilde{t} \le t'$, the composition relation:

$$p(t,t') = p(t,\tilde{t})p(\tilde{t},t'). \quad (11)$$

Similarly, the forward equation describes propagation *backward* in maturity time, for a fixed physical time. More precisely, it relates the prices of bonds with different maturities T, but at a fixed time t, with longer maturity bonds in terms of the shorter maturity ones. The *backward propagator*[11] $\phi_{T,T'}$ relates zero-coupon bond prices of maturities T and T′, with, at any fixed time t, using the relation

$$B_T(t) = \phi_{T,T'} B_{T'}(t). \quad (12)$$

The backward propagator $\phi_{T,T'}$ describes bond price evolution backward in maturity time, as depicted by Figure 2(b). It also satisfies the forward and backward equations with boundary conditions $\Phi_{T,T} = 1$:

$$\left(\frac{d}{dT} + f_T\right)\phi_{T,T'} = 0; \left(\frac{d}{dT'} - f_{T'}\right)\phi_{T,T'} = 0 \quad (13)$$

and, for any $T' \le \tilde{T} \le t$, the composition relation

$$\phi_{T,T'} = \phi_{T,\tilde{T}}\phi_{\tilde{T},T'}. \quad (14)$$

2. Forward propagator describes the evolution of bond prices forward in physical time. Backward propagator describes evolution of bond prices backward in maturity time

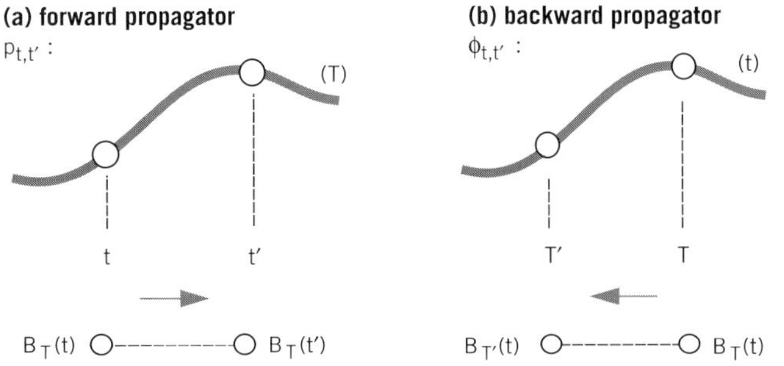

3. In an effective theory represented by a static local volatility surface, instantaneous volatility σ(t) at time t follows the local volatility at time t and index price S_t

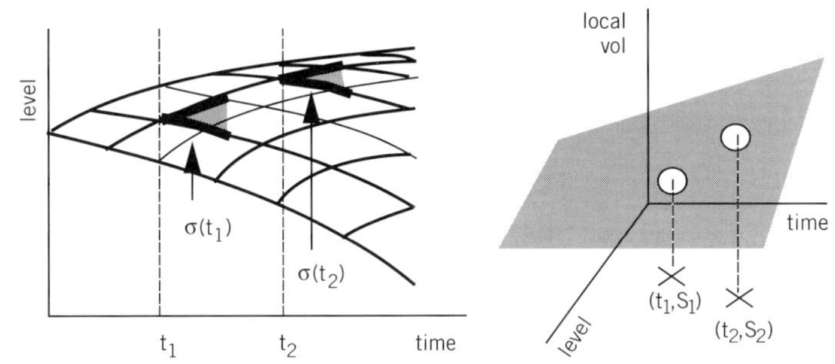

THE EFFECTIVE VOLATILITY THEORY

In the effective volatility setting, the local volatility surface is calculated using the spectrum of available option prices (and futures) at time t_0, and is assumed to remain unchanged thereafter as time t and index price S change:

$$\sigma_{K,T}(t,S) = \sigma_{K,T}. \quad (15)$$

This procedure amounts to averaging out all sources of stochastic volatility, leaving the index price uncertainty as the only source of uncertainty left within the theory. The resulting effective dynamics only depends on the index price and time and, as a function of these variables, is deterministic. As the physical time t elapses and index price S moves, the instantaneous volatility σ(t) follows along the local volatility surface, as depicted in Figure 3, coinciding with the local volatility at time t and level S:

$$\sigma(t) = \sigma_{t,S_t}. \quad (16)$$

This is consistent with an equilibrium (effective) index price process described by the stochastic differential equation:

$$\frac{dS_t}{S_t} = \mu_t dt + \sigma_{t,S_t} dZ_t \quad (17)$$

where μ_t is the index's expected return and dZ_t is the standard Wiener measure at time t. In this process the instantaneous volatility is a known (deterministic) function of time t and index price S_t. Implied tree models are the discrete frameworks for implementing the (effective) dynamics represented by (17). The dynamics of standard option prices in the effective theory is described by the *backward equation*:

$$\left(\frac{\partial}{\partial t} + (r-\delta)S\frac{\partial}{\partial S} + \frac{1}{2}\sigma^2_{S,t}S^2\frac{\partial^2}{\partial S^2} - r\right)C_{K,T}(t,S) = 0. \quad (18)$$

Since the only remaining source of uncertainty is the index price, the standard options are completely hedgeable (using index as the hedge) within the effective theory. Equations (16) and

4. Forward propagator describes the evolution of standard prices in physical time and index price. Backward propagator describes the evolution of option prices in maturity time and strike price

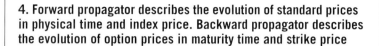

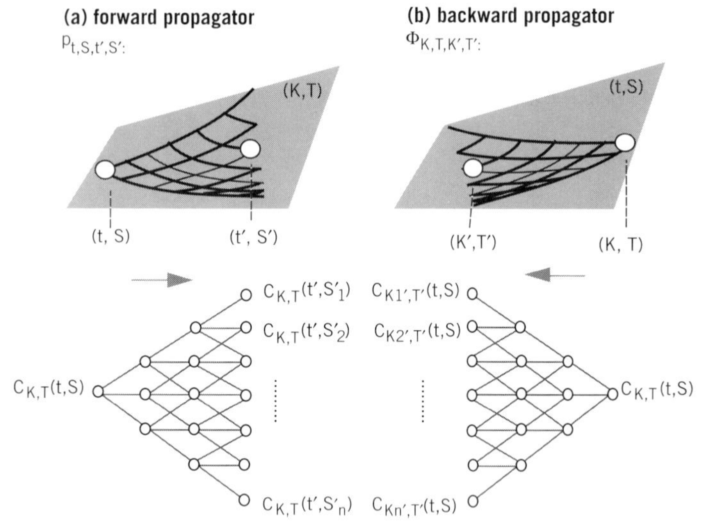

(18) then show that the option price dynamics in this theory is arbitrage-free. Equation (18) is also the dual of the *forward equation* satisfied by the standard option prices:

$$\left(\frac{\partial}{\partial T}+(r-\delta)K\frac{\partial}{\partial K}-\frac{1}{2}\sigma^2_{K,T}K^2\frac{\partial^2}{\partial K^2}+\delta\right)C_{K,T}(t,S)=0. \quad (19)$$

This forward equation is the same as (2) and holds by the definition of local volatility, regardless of any specific assumptions about the behaviour of volatility.

The *forward propagator* $p_{t,S,t',S'}$ describes the relationship between the option prices at the two points (t, S) and (t′, S′), with $t \leq t'$, for any K-strike and T-maturity standard option, through the relation

$$C_{K,T}(t,S)=\int_0^\infty p_{t,S,t',S'}C_{K,T}(t',S')dS'. \quad (20)$$

The forward propagator $p_{t,S,t',S'}$ describes option price evolution forward in time and index price, as illustrated by Figure 4a. We can define the forward transition probability density function $p(t,S,t',S')$ in terms of the forward propagator as $p(t,S,t',S') = e^{r(t'-t)}p_{t,S,t',S'}$. It describes the total probability that the index price will reach level S′ at time t′, given that the index price at time t is S. The mathematical properties of $p_{t,S,t',S'}$ and $p(t,S,t',S')$ are discussed in Appendix B.

The *backward propagator* $\Phi_{K,T,K',T'}$ describes the relationship between prices of two standard options corresponding to strike-maturity pairs (K,T) and (K′,T′), with $T' \leq T$, at a fixed time t and index price S, as

$$C_{K,T}(t,S)=\int_0^\infty \Phi_{K,T,K',T'}C_{K',T'}(t,S)dK'. \quad (21)$$

As Figure 4b illustrates, we can also define the effective theory backward transition probability density function $\Phi(K,T,K',T')$ in terms of the backward propagator as $\Phi(K,T,K',T') = e^{\delta(T-T')}\Phi_{K,T,K',T'}$. Appendix B discusses some of the mathematical properties of $\Phi_{K,T,K',T'}$ and $\Phi(K,T,K',T')$.

We can use (17), either by performing simulations or by using implied tree methods, to price and hedge complex options, with the knowledge that the standard options initially used to derive the local volatility surface will have model prices which match their market values. In spite of this calibration, if the volatility has a substantial stochastic behaviour, the prices and hedge ratios of most options with path-dependent or volatility-dependent payoffs will not be accurately represented by the effective theory results. The reason is simply that effective theory results are based on the assumption that local volatilities are static or, equivalently, that the instantaneous volatility is substantially a function of the market level (and time). This is a good assumption in situations where the volatility exhibits strong correlation to the market level and, hence, can be viewed predominantly as a function of it. For most equity index option markets, for example, this more or less holds, specially for shorter dated options. On the contrary, in the currency options markets or in longer dated equity (and most other) options markets, the volatility is predominantly stochastic and the effective theory of static local volatilities is not valid. We must therefore move towards a full stochastic framework by allowing general multi-factor stochastic variations of the volatility surface.

Towards a stochastic theory of volatility

To allow for stochastic dynamics we must introduce exogenous stochastic structure on the effective theory. In general, there are few restrictions on the choice of this structure. One important restriction, which is the cornerstone of the arbitrage framework, is the absence of any explicit future arbitrage opportunities in the final stochastic theory. Another restriction is how close the number or the behaviour of the stochastic factors are to what is empirically observed. For now, we will consider very general (but sufficiently regular) stochastic structures and discuss the conditions which must be imposed upon them to guarantee the absence of arbitrage. Let us briefly examine the stochastic interest rate theory first.

THE STOCHASTIC INTEREST RATE THEORY

Figure 5 illustrates the dynamics of the forward rates in the stochastic framework. Here, the forward rate curve is allowed to fluctuate stochastically with several independent stochastic factors represented by Brownian motions $W^i, i = 1,\ldots,N$, with factor volatilities $\vartheta^i_T(t)$ generally depending on both maturity T and time t, according to the stochastic differential equation:

$$df_T(t) = \alpha_T(t)dt + \sum_{i=1}^{n} \vartheta^i_T(t)dW^i_T. \quad (22)$$

In the family of processes described by (22), the volatility coefficients $\vartheta^i_T(t)$ reflect the sensitivities of specific maturity forward rates to the random shocks introduced by the Brownian motions W^i. These coefficients are left unrestricted, except for mild measurability and integrability conditions, and can depend on the past histories of the Brownian motions W^i. The drift coefficients $\alpha_T(t)$ must also satisfy mild measurability and integrability conditions, but must be further constrained by the no-arbitrage requirement.

The *spot rate* at time t, r(t), is the instantaneous forward rate at time t, ie $r(t) = f_t(t)$. The stochastic integral equation satisfied by the spot rate is found by integrating (22) and evaluating the result at T = t. It is given by

$$r(t) = f_t(0) + \int_0^t \alpha_t(u)du + \sum_{i=1}^{n} \int_0^t \vartheta^i_t(u)dW^i_u. \quad (23)$$

It has been argued by Heath, Jarrow and Morton that there will be no explicit arbitrage opportunities in the theory defined by (23) if (and only if) the drift coefficients are of the form:

$$\alpha_T(t) = \sum_{i=1}^{n} \vartheta^i_T(t)\left(\int_t^T \vartheta^i_u(t)du + \lambda^i(t)\right). \quad (24)$$

Here $\lambda^i(t)$, i = 1,…,n, denote the *market prices of risk*, which cannot explicitly depend on maturity T but are otherwise arbitrary. Under these conditions, they have shown that markets are complete and contingent claims prices are independent of the market prices of risk.

THE STOCHASTIC VOLATILITY THEORY

Our goal is to introduce a similar stochastic structure on the local volatility surface. To do so, we allow the surface to undergo stochastic fluctuations with several independent stochastic factors, $W^0, W^1,\ldots,W^n$, based on the following stochastic differential equation[12]:

$$d\sigma^2_{K,T}(t,S) = \alpha_{K,T}(t,S)dt + \sum_{i=1}^{n} \theta^i_{K,T}(t,S)dW^i_t. \quad (25)$$

The family of processes of (25) defines a multifactor dynamics for the local volatility surface, as illustrated by Figure 6. These processes can be integrated, starting from a fixed (non-random) initial local volatility surface $\sigma_{K,T}(0,S_0)$ at time t = 0, as

$$\sigma^2_{K,T}(t,S_t) = \sigma^2_{K,T}(0,S_0) + \int_0^t \alpha_{K,T}(u,S_u)du + \sum_{i=1}^{n} \int_0^t \theta^i_{K,T}(u,S_u)dW^i_u. \quad (26)$$

The factor volatility $\theta^i_{K,T}(t,S)$ reflects the sensitivity of local volatilities $\sigma_{K,T}(t,S)$, across the whole surface, to the shock introduced by the Brownian motion W^i. Except for mild measurability and integrability conditions,[13] the family of factor volatilities are unrestricted, generally depending on time and index price, and on the factors or their past histories.

The spot volatility (or instantaneous volatility) at time t, σ(t), is the instantaneous local volatility at time t and level S_t, ie

5. In a stochastic interest rate theory spot rate r(t) follows the instantaneous forward rate $f_t(t)$

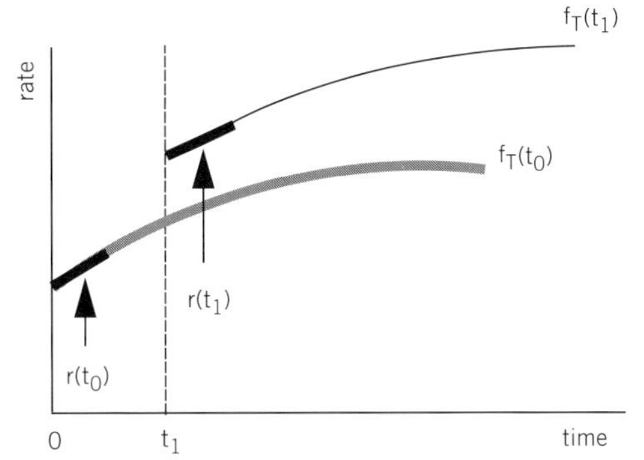

6. In a stochastic volatility theory instantaneous volatility σ(t) follows the local volatility $\sigma_{S_t,t}(t,S_t)$ at time t and index price S_t

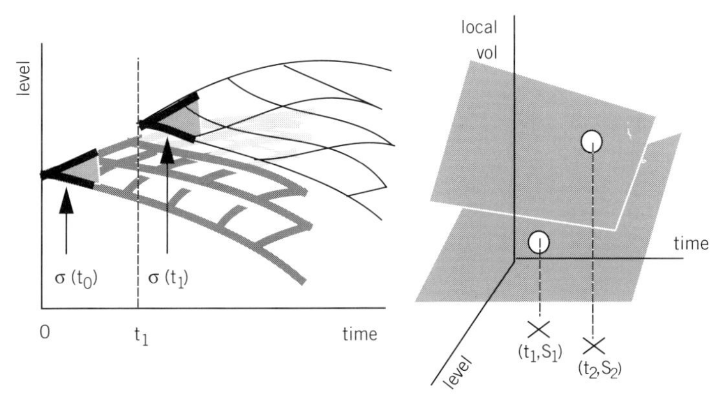

$$\sigma(t) = \sigma_{S_t,t}(t,S_t). \tag{27}$$

It describes the variability of index price return process, as given by the differential equation

$$\frac{dS_t}{S_t} = \mu_t dt + \sigma(t)dW_t^0 \tag{28}$$

or its integral form

$$S_t = S_0 + \int_0^t \mu_u S_u du + \int_0^t \sigma(u)S_u dW_u^0 \tag{29}$$

where μ_t is the index's expected return. Setting $T = t$ and $K = S_t$ in (26) we find the stochastic integral equation satisfied by the spot volatility as

$$\sigma^2(t) = \sigma^2_{t,S_t}(0,S_0) + \int_0^t \alpha_{t,S_t}(u,S_u)du + \sum_{i=1}^{n} \int_0^t \theta^i_{t,S_t}(u,S_u)dW_u^i. \tag{30}$$

The drift coefficients $\alpha_{K,T}(t,S)$ must also satisfy mild measurability and integrability conditions, but they must be further restricted by the requirement that the stochastic theory described by (28) and (30) disallows explicit arbitrage opportunities among the standard options, forwards and their underlying index. This is similar to the HJM arbitrage conditions on the spot rate process. Let us briefly examine (a variation of) the HJM argument below.

THE HJM CONDITIONS AND THE STOCHASTIC THEORY OF INTEREST RATES

The bond price dynamics corresponding to the forward rate process of (85) is, by applying Ito's lemma, described by the stochastic integral equation

$$dB_T(t) = r(t)B_T(t)dt + \int_t^T \frac{\delta B_T(t)}{\delta f_u(t)} df_u(t)du + \frac{1}{2}\int_t^T\int_t^T \frac{\delta^2 B_T(t)}{\delta f_u(t)\delta f_{u'}(t)} df_u(t)df_{u'}(t)du du'. \tag{31}$$

7. Sensitivity of the forward and backward propagators $p_{t,t'}$ and $\phi_{T,T'}$ to the sudden changes of the forward rate f_u

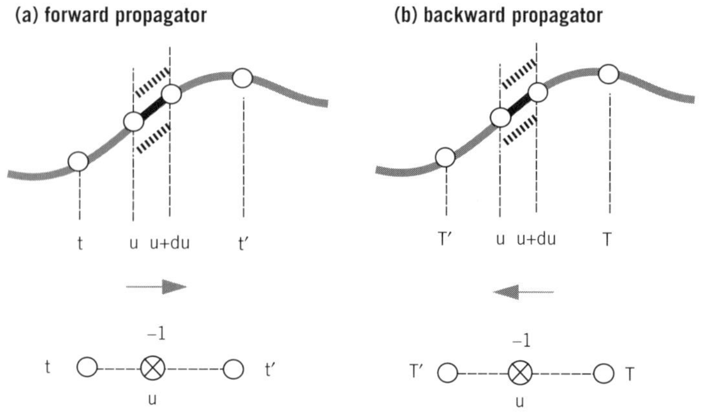

The symbol $\delta/\delta f_u$ here denotes the variational (or functional) derivative with respect to the function f evaluated at u. The first term in this equation describes precisely the effective theory bond price dynamics restricted to the fixed forward rate curve $f_T(t)$ at time t. The next two terms describe the bond price dynamics resulting from the stochastic variations of the effective theory (defined by $f_T(t)$) during the next infinitesimal time interval dt.

It follows from the definition of the forward rates (1) that the price of a T-maturity zero-coupon bond with unit face, at time t, is given by

$$B_T(t) = \exp\left(-\int_t^T f_u(t)du\right). \tag{32}$$

From this expression it is simple to see that for any u ($t \le u \le T$):

$$\frac{\delta B_T(t)}{\delta f_u(t)} = -B_T(t). \tag{33}$$

Another way of seeing this is by noticing how the forward and backward propagators, $p_{t,t'}$ and $\Phi_{T,T'}$, corresponding to an otherwise fixed (non-random) forward rate curve, respond to sudden changes of a specific forward rate f_u along the curve. It is simple to see that $p_{t,t'}$ satisfies the following relation, as depicted in Figure 7a:

$$\frac{\delta p(t,t')}{\delta f_u} = -p(t,u)p(u,t') = -p(t,t') \tag{34}$$

and, as shown in Figure 7b, that $\phi_{T,T'}$ satisfies the relation:

$$\frac{\delta \phi_{T,T'}}{\delta f_u} = -\phi_{T,u}\phi_{u,T'} = -\phi_{T,T'}. \tag{35}$$

These relations combined, respectively, with (9) and (12), again lead to (33). Similarly, we can show that for $t \le u \le u' \le T$ the second order variational derivatives are given by:

$$\frac{\delta^2 B_T(t)}{\delta f_u(t)\delta f_{u'}(t)} = B_T(t). \tag{36}$$

The special f_u-independent form of variational relations (33)–(36) can be directly attributed to the special form of the functional relationship between the zero-coupon bond prices and the forward rates as described by (32). This feature underlies the special simplicity of no-arbitrage conditions in the HJM framework.

Using (22), (33) and (36) inside (31) we find

$$\frac{dB_T(t)}{B_T(t)} = r(t)dt - \sum_{i=1}^{n}\left(\int_t^T \vartheta^i_u(t)du\right)dW_t^i - \left(\int_t^T \left[\alpha_u(t) - \sum_{i=1}^{n}\vartheta^i_u(t)\int_t^u \vartheta^i_v(t)dv\right]du\right)dt. \tag{37}$$

If the drift coefficients $\alpha_T(t)$ satisfy the no-arbitrage conditions of (24) for some set of market prices of risk $\lambda^i(t)$, then (37) shows that in terms of the equivalent measure $d\overline{W}^i = dW^i + \lambda^i dt$, defined by the Brownian motions,

$$\overline{W}^i_t = W^i_t + \int_0^t \lambda^i(u)\,du,\ i = 1,\ldots,n$$

the dynamics of zero-coupon bond prices is:

$$\frac{dB_T(t)}{B_T(t)} = r(t)dt - \sum_{i=1}^{n}\left(\int_t^T \vartheta^i_u(t)du\right)d\overline{W}^i_t. \quad (38)$$

Therefore, $\{d\overline{W}^i;\ i = 1,\ldots,n\}$ defines an equivalent martingale measure under which the rescaled bond prices

$$B_T(t)\exp\left(-\int_0^t r(u)du\right)$$

for all maturities T are jointly martingale. Under this measure the interest rate contingent claims prices are independent of the market prices of risk and, hence, remain preference-free.

The no-arbitrage conditions and the stochastic theory of volatility

The standard option prices $C_{K,T}(t,S)$ are functionals of the local volatilities at time t and market level S, just as bond prices $B_T(t)$ are functionals of the forward rates at time t. As a result, the dynamical variations of the local volatility surface induce corresponding dynamical variations of the standard option prices. During a time interval dt, the index price moves and the local volatilities also change. We can think of the local volatility changes as comprised of two components. A predictable component, due to movements of time and index price restricted to the static local volatility surface $\sigma_{K,T}(t,S)$ at time t and level S, and a non-predictable (stochastic) component due to dynamic fluctuations away from this surface. It is somewhat simpler, but entirely equivalent, to work with the transition probabilities, instead of option prices. The transition probability, $P_{K,T}(t,S)$, describes the total probability that the index price will reach level K at time T, given that the index price at time t is S, when both the index price and volatility are stochastic. It is related to the option prices $C_{K,T}(t,S)$ through a general and well-known[14] formula:

$$P_{K,T}(t,S) = e^{r(T-t)}\frac{\partial^2}{\partial K^2}C_{K,T}(t,S). \quad (39)$$

The dynamical evolution of transition probabilities $P_{K,T}(t,S)$ based on the local volatility process of (26) is given by the stochastic integral equation:

$$dP_{K,T} = \Bigg[\left(\frac{\partial P_{K,T}}{\partial t} + \mu(t)S\frac{\partial P_{K,T}}{\partial S} + \frac{1}{2}\sigma^2(t)S^2\frac{\partial^2 P_{K,T}}{\partial S^2}\right)dt +$$
$$\sigma(t)S\frac{\partial P_{K,T}}{\partial S}dW^0(t)\Bigg]_{(t,S)} + \int_t^T\int_0^\infty \frac{\delta P_{K,T}}{\delta\sigma^2_{K',T'}}d\sigma^2_{K',T'}dK'dT' +$$
$$\frac{1}{2}\int_t^T\int_t^T\int_0^\infty\int_0^\infty \frac{\delta^2 P_{K,T}}{\delta\sigma^2_{K',T'}\delta\sigma^2_{K'',T''}}d\sigma^2_{K',T'}d\sigma^2_{K'',T''}dK'dK''dT'dT''. \quad (40)$$

All the probability and local volatility expressions in this equation are evaluated at (t,S). The first term describes the effective dynamics of the transition probabilities $P_{K,T}(t,S)$ restricted to the fixed local volatility surface $\sigma_{K,T}(t,S)$, prevailing at time t and level S. The bracket symbol, $[\ldots]_{(t,S)}$, therefore, expresses the fact that in this term the future volatility is a deterministic function of the future time T and market level K, given by $\sigma_{K,T}(t,S)$ viewed as function of these two variables. The next two terms describe the dynamical variations of the transition probabilities resulting from the stochastic fluctuations of the local volatility surface during the next instant of time dt.

Contrary to (32), in general there are no explicit expressions describing the functional relationship between option prices and local volatilities. Therefore, we can not directly compute the variational derivatives in (40). Instead, we can look at the variations of the forward and backward transition probabilities with respect to the specific local volatilities. As shown in Appendix C and illustrated in Figure 8, the forward transition probability $p(t,S,t',S')$, associated with the non-random local volatility surface $\sigma_{K,T}(t,S)$ prevailing at time t and spot price S, has the following variational derivative with respect to the local volatility $\sigma_{v,u}(t,S)$ on the surface, corresponding to future maturity u and market level v:

$$\frac{\delta p(t,S,t',S')}{\delta\sigma^2_{v,u}} = \frac{1}{2}p(t,S,u,v)v^2\frac{\partial^2}{\partial v^2}p(u,v,t',S'). \quad (41)$$

This relation holds for any u in the range $t \le u \le t'$, otherwise the variational derivative is equal to zero. Similarly, the backward transition probability $\Phi(K,T,K',T')$ satisfies, for $T' \le u \le T$, the relation

$$\frac{\delta\Phi(K,T,K',T')}{\delta\sigma^2_{v,u}} = \frac{1}{2}\Phi(K,T,v,u)v^2\frac{\partial^2}{\partial v^2}\Phi(v,u,K',T') \quad (42)$$

and zero otherwise. Using (21) and (39), the standard option prices $C_{K,T}(t,S)$ and transition probabilities $P_{K,T}(t,S)$ satisfy similar relationships for $t \le u \le T$:

$$\frac{\delta C_{K,T}(t,S)}{\delta\sigma^2_{v,u}} = \frac{1}{2}e^{-\delta(T-u)}\Phi(K,T,v,u)v^2\frac{\partial^2}{\partial v^2}C_{v,u}(t,S) \quad (43)$$

8. Sensitivity of the forward and backward transition probabilities p(t,S,t′,S′) and Φ(K,T,K′,T′) to the sudden changes of the local volatility $\sigma_{v,u}$

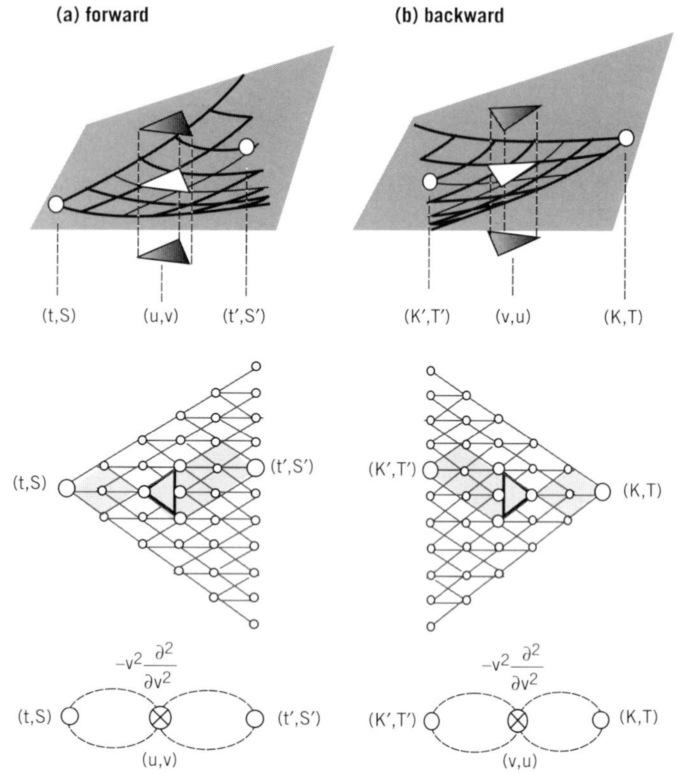

9. Second order variational derivatives of the forward and backward transition probabilities p(t,S,t′,S′) and Φ(K,T,K′,T′) with respect to the local volatilities

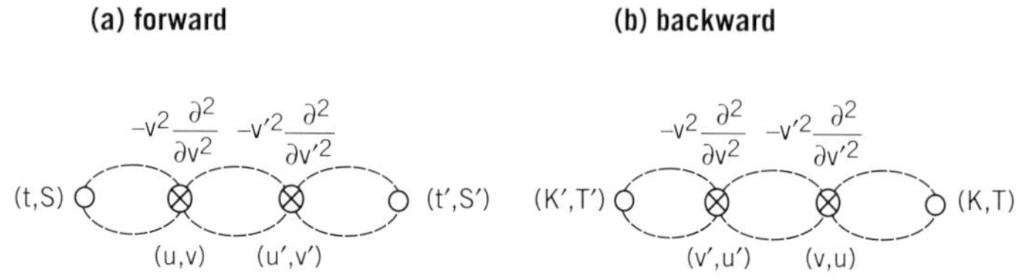

and

$$\frac{\delta P_{K,T}(t,S)}{\delta\sigma^2_{v,u}} = \frac{1}{2}p(t,S,u,v)v^2\frac{\partial^2}{\partial v^2}p(u,v,T,K) \quad (44)$$

in which the effective transition probabilities p(...) and Φ(...) correspond to the static local volatility surface $\sigma_{K,T}(t,S)$ prevailing at time t and market level S. In arriving at (43) and (44) we have also used the following identities:

$$P_{K,T}(t,S) = p(t,S,T,K) \quad (45)$$

$$p(t,S,T,K) = e^{r(T-t)}\frac{\partial^2}{\partial K^2}C_{K,T}(t,S) \quad (46)$$

$$\Phi(K,T,S,t) = e^{\delta(T-t)}\frac{\partial^2}{\partial S^2}C_{K,T}(t,S). \quad (47)$$

As discussed in Appendix B, these identities are all consequences of the fact that the effective theory associated with $\sigma_{K,T}(t,S)$ embodies all the information necessary for pricing standard options of all strikes and maturities correctly.

Taking the variational derivatives of both sides of (41) and (42) with respect to the local volatility $\sigma_{v',u'}$ we find the second order variational derivatives as

$$\frac{\delta p(t,S,t',S')}{\delta\sigma^2_{v,u}\delta\sigma^2_{v',u'}} = \frac{1}{4}p(t,S,u,v)v^2 \frac{\partial^2}{\partial v^2}p(u,v,u',v')v'^2\frac{\partial^2}{\partial v'^2}p(u',v',t',S') \quad (48)$$

for any $t \le u \le u' \le t'$, and

$$\frac{\delta\Phi(K,T,K',T')}{\delta\sigma^2_{v,u}\delta\sigma^2_{v',u'}} = \frac{1}{4}\Phi(K,T,v,u)v^2 \frac{\partial^2}{\partial v^2}\Phi(v,u,v',u')v'^2\frac{\partial^2}{\partial v'^2}\Phi(v',u',K',T') \quad (49)$$

for $T' \le u' \le u \le T$. Figure 9 gives a graphical depiction of these identities. The standard option prices $C_{K,T}(t,S)$ and transition probabilities $P_{K,T}(t,S)$ satisfy similar relationships for $t \le u \le u' \le T$:

$$\frac{\delta C_{K,T}(t,S)}{\delta\sigma^2_{v,u}\delta\sigma^2_{v',u'}} = \frac{1}{4}e^{-\delta(T-u')}\Phi(K,T,v,u)v^2 \frac{\partial^2}{\partial v^2}\Phi(v,u,v',u')v'^2\frac{\partial^2}{\partial v'^2}C_{v',u'}(t,S) \quad (50)$$

$$\frac{\delta P_{K,T}(t,S)}{\delta\sigma^2_{v,u}\delta\sigma^2_{v',u'}} = \frac{1}{4}p(t,S,u,v)v^2 \frac{\partial^2}{\partial v^2}p(u,v,u',v')v'^2\frac{\partial^2}{\partial v'^2}p(u',v',t,K). \quad (51)$$

Using these relations, Appendix D proves that (40) leads to

$$dP_{K,T} = \sigma(t)S\frac{\partial P_{K,T}}{\partial S}d\overline{W}^0 + \sum_{i=1}^{n}\int_t^T\int_0^\infty \frac{\delta P_{K,T}}{\delta\sigma^2_{K',T'}}\sigma^2_{K',T'}\theta^i_{K',T'}dK'dT'd\overline{W}^i \quad (52)$$

if and only if, for any S, K and $t \le T$, the drift functions $\alpha_{K,T}(t,S)$ satisfy the following *no-arbitrage conditions*

$$\alpha_{K,T}(t,S) = -\sum_{i=0}^{n}\theta^i_{K,T}(t,S)\left\{\frac{1}{p(t,S,T,K)}\int_t^T\int_0^\infty \theta^i_{K',T'}(t,S)p(t,S,T',K')K'^2 \frac{\partial^2}{\partial K'^2}p(T',K',T,K)dK'dT' - \Pi^i\right\} \quad (53)$$

where Π^i for $i = 1,\ldots,n$ are arbitrary but independent of K and T, and where the equivalent measure $\{\bar{W}^i\}$ is defined by

$$d\bar{W}^0 = dW^0 + \frac{(\mu(t) - r + \delta)}{\sigma(t)} dt;$$

$$d\bar{W}^i = dW^i + \Pi^i dt. \qquad (54)$$

The quantities Π^i denote the *market prices of risk* associated with the volatility risk factors W^i, $i = 1,\dots,n$, while $\mu(t) - r + \delta/\sigma(t)$ is the market price of risk associated with the index price risk factor W^0. Equation (52) shows that under the no-arbitrage conditions the measure $\{d\bar{W}^i;\ i = 1,\dots,n\}$ is an *equivalent martingale measure*, with respect to which the rescaled index price and rescaled option prices for all strikes and maturities are simultaneously martingales.

These no-arbitrage conditions in the present case are significantly more involved than the HJM no-arbitrage conditions described in the previous section. The basic reason is that local volatilities span a (two-dimensional) surface on which (forward and backward) propagation depends, in a rather complicated and non-linear manner, on the structure of local volatilities across the whole surface. This is evident by the apparent complexity of (44) and (51) as compared to the simplicity of the corresponding Equations (33) and (36) in the interest rate framework. It is, therefore, rather difficult to use the no-arbitrage conditions for stochastic volatility in their continuous form directly.

In the next section we introduce *stochastic implied trees* as a discrete-time framework for describing arbitrage-free stochastic variations of the local volatility surface.

10. Schematic illustration of the dynamics of the index price and local volatility surface in a stochastic volatility theory

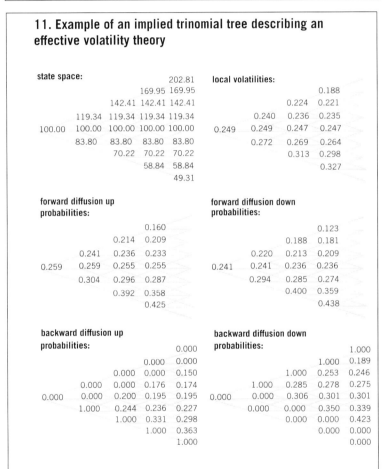

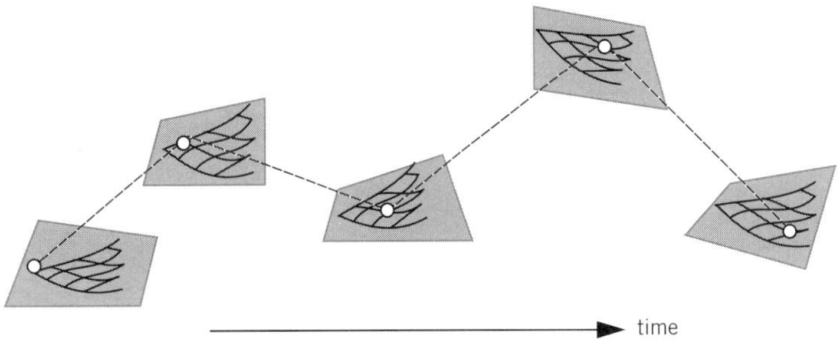

11. Example of an implied trinomial tree describing an effective volatility theory

state space:

				202.81
			169.95	169.95
		142.41	142.41	142.41
	119.34	119.34	119.34	119.34
100.00	100.00	100.00	100.00	100.00
	83.80	83.80	83.80	83.80
		70.22	70.22	70.22
			58.84	58.84
				49.31

local volatilities:

			0.188
		0.224	0.221
	0.240	0.236	0.235
0.249	0.249	0.247	0.247
	0.272	0.269	0.264
		0.313	0.298
			0.327

forward diffusion up probabilities:

			0.160
		0.214	0.209
	0.241	0.236	0.233
0.259	0.259	0.255	0.255
	0.304	0.296	0.287
		0.392	0.358
			0.425

forward diffusion down probabilities:

			0.123
		0.188	0.181
	0.220	0.213	0.209
0.241	0.241	0.236	0.236
	0.294	0.285	0.274
		0.400	0.359
			0.438

backward diffusion up probabilities:

				0.000
			0.000	0.000
		0.000	0.000	0.150
	0.000	0.000	0.176	0.174
0.000	0.000	0.200	0.195	0.195
	1.000	0.244	0.236	0.227
		1.000	0.331	0.298
			1.000	0.363
				1.000

backward diffusion down probabilities:

				1.000
			1.000	0.189
		1.000	0.253	0.246
	1.000	0.285	0.278	0.275
0.000	0.000	0.306	0.301	0.301
	0.000	0.000	0.350	0.339
		0.000	0.000	0.423
			0.000	0.000
				0.000

Stochastic implied trees

Figure 10 gives a schematic illustration of the dynamics in a stochastic volatility theory. As the physical time moves forward, the index price changes and, simultaneously, all local volatilities on the volatility surface undergo multi-factor stochastic variations.

To provide a more quantitative description of this stochastic dynamics we choose to work within a discrete-time framework described by a stochastic implied tree. These trees are extensions of the standard (non-stochastic) implied trees, which are used to describe effective volatility models (see Derman, Kani and Chriss (1996)). Figure 11 shows an example of a one-year, five-period standard implied trinomial tree which is calibrated to a market where at-the-money implied volatility is 25% and there is an implied volatility skew of 0.5% point per 10 strike points. In an implied trinomial tree the location of the nodes, or the *state space*, is more or less arbitrarily. Once the state space is fixed, however, the transition probabilities at different nodes are determined from the requirement that standard options and forwards with strike prices coinciding with those nodes and maturing at different periods of the tree all have prices using the tree which match their market prices. Since local volatility at any node depends on the nodal levels and the transition probabilities to the nearby nodes, the local volatilities at different nodes are also determined in this way.

Stochastic implied trinomial trees are extensions of the implied trinomial tree in which the

12. In a stochastic implied tree, as the index moves from node A to node B in a single time step, the local volatilities and transition probabilities, for every node on the future subtree beginning at node B, vary stochastically with multiple stochastic factors

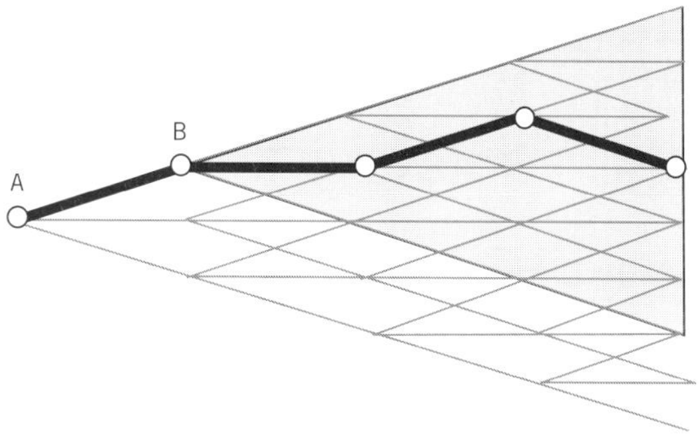

13. During a time step Δt, the total transition probability $P_{K,T}$ will move to one of M values $P^{(i)}_{K,T}$, i = 1,...,M, as index price moves randomly to one of the nearby nodes and the local volatility surface assumes one of N possible configurations

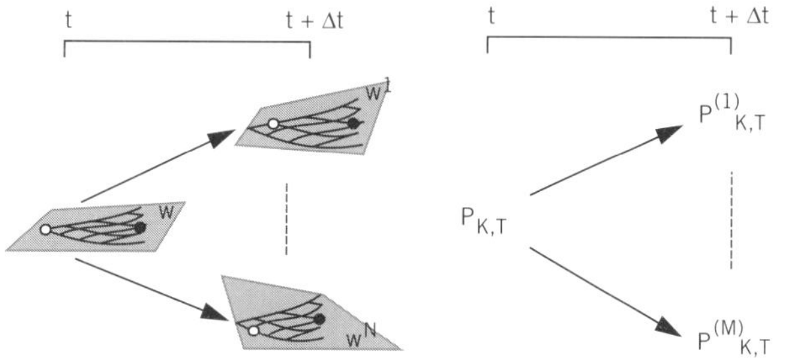

transition probabilities are, in addition, allowed to vary stochastically, with several stochastic factors, as time elapses and index level moves. The index level is allowed to move randomly from node to node, while the local volatilities, and simultaneously the transition probabilities corresponding to the future nodes, all vary stochastically across the tree. This behaviour is shown in Figure 12.

Starting from any initial node, the possible future movements of the local volatility surface must be restricted to guarantee absence of any arbitrage opportunities in the discrete theory represented by the stochastic implied tree. As discussed earlier, this is equivalent to the requirement that the total transition probabilities to all future nodes be simultaneously martingales on the tree. This is also the same as the requirement that all rescaled standard option prices be simultaneously martingales on the tree. As Figure 13 shows, during the time interval Δt, the spot price will move randomly (by amount ΔS) to one of the nearby nodes and, at the same time, the local volatility surface will assume one of its N possible configurations, $w^1,\ldots,w^N$. As a result, the total transition probability $P_{K,T}(t,S)$ to any given future node (K,T) also moves to one of its several possible values $P^{(i)}_{K,T}(t + \Delta t, S + \Delta S)$, $i = 1,\ldots,M$, during this time interval. To guarantee no-arbitrage, $P_{K,T}$ must be a martingale (fair game), that is it must equal the expectation , under some (equivalent) measure, of its future values $P^{(i)}_{K,T}$ for all the future nodes (K,T) on the tree.

OUR NOTATION IN DISCRETE TIME

To make positivity manifest, it is more convenient to redefine the drift and volatility functions in (25) as $\alpha_{K,T} \to \alpha_{K,T}\sigma^2_{K,T}$ and $\theta^l_{K,T} \to \theta^l_{K,T}\sigma^2_{K,T}$, $l = 0,\ldots,n$, and begin by discretising the following continuous-time differential equation:

$$\frac{d\sigma^2_{K,T}(t,S)}{\sigma^2_{K,T}(t,S)} = \alpha_{K,T}(t,S)dt + \sum_{l=1}^{n}\theta^l_{K,T}(t,S)dW^l_t. \qquad (55)$$

We let the integer pair (i,j) label the node (t_i,S_j) describing the current location (ie (t,S)) of the index at the ith step of the simulation. We also let the pair (n,m) label the future node (t_n,S_m) corresponding to the future time and level (ie (T,K)). Then the discrete form of (55) can be written as

$$\Delta\sigma^2_{m,n}(i,j) = \sigma^2_{m,n}(i,j)\left[\alpha_{m,n}(i,j)\Delta t_i + \sum_{l=0}^{n}\theta^l_{m,n}(i,j)\,\Delta W^l_i\right]. \qquad (56)$$

The vector $(\Delta W^0_i, \Delta W^1_i,\ldots,\Delta W^n_i)$ is random and is drawn, at time i, from the sample space of the increments of n independent Brownian motions W^l.

The volatility parameters are pre-specified but the drift parameters must be determined from the no-arbitrage requirements that the total probabilities of arriving at the future node (n,m) from the (fixed) initial node (i,j) must be jointly martingales for all future nodes (n,m). As we shall argue below, these martingale conditions are precise enough to completely determine all the drift parameters step by step during the simulation process.

A stochastic implied tree simulation begins with the construction of a trinomial implied tree calibrated to today's prices of standard options and forwards. The simulation begins at the node (0,0) of this tree. During the first simulation step the drift parameters $\alpha_{m,n}(0,0)$, for all future nodes (m,n), are determined from the martingale conditions on the total probabilities $p_{m,n}(0,0)$. Figure 14 illustrates that the drift parameter $\alpha_{0,0}(0,0)$ is determined from the martingale condition for $P_{1,2}(0,0)$. This also guarantees that the transition probabilities $P_{1,1}(0,0)$ and $P_{1,0}(0,0)$

are martingales. The reason is that these probabilities are constrained by two extra conditions which must hold irrespective of the specific behaviour of the local volatilities:

$$P_{1,0}(0,0) + P_{1,1}(0,0) + P_{1,2}(0,0) = 1$$
$$P_{1,0}(0,0)S_{1,0} + P_{1,1}(0,0)S_{1,1} + P_{1,2}(0,0)S_{1,2}$$
$$= S_{0,0}e^{(r-\delta)(t_1-t_0)}. \qquad (57)$$

The first condition is the normalisation condition, requiring that the sum of the three total transition probabilities at time t_1 must be unity. The second is the forward condition, requiring that the t_1-maturity forward price at time t_0 must match its risk-neutral value.

In a similar way, the three drift parameters $\alpha_{1,2}(0,0)$, $\alpha_{1,1}(0,0)$ and $\alpha_{1,0}(0,0)$ are determined from the martingale conditions of the three total transition probabilities $P_{2,4}(0,0)$, $P_{2,3}(0,0)$ and $P_{2,2}(0,0)$. The remaining transition probabilities $P_{2,1}(0,0)$ and $P_{2,0}(0,0)$ will then also be martingales due to the normalisation and forward conditions at time t_2. In this way all drift parameters $\alpha_{m,n}(0,0)$ will be determined during the first simulation step. Finally, to complete this step we draw a random vector $(\Delta W_0^0, \Delta W_0^1, \ldots, \Delta W_0^n)$ from the sample space of the increments of W^i at time t_0, and use this vector to simultaneously arrive at a (random) new location for the index price and new values for all future local volatilities. Equation (56) is used directly with $i = j = 0$ to calculate the new local volatility values from this choice of the random vector. As for the index price, we use the random number ΔW_0^0 to determine which of the three possible future nodes (ie (1,2), (1,1) or (1,0)) does the index price move to during time interval Δt. Figure 15 gives one simple possible method for doing this, starting from an arbitrary initial node (i,j). First ΔW_i^0 is renormalised to represent a uniformly-distributed random number between 0 and 1. Let $P_u(i,j)$, $P_m(i,j)$ and $P_d(i,j)$ denote the one period transition probabilities, prevailing at time t_i and index price S_j, from the node (i,j) to the up, middle and down nodes at time t_{i+1}. We then compare our random number with these three probabilities. If it is smaller than $P_d(i,j)$, we move the index price to the down node. On the other hand, if the random number is greater than the sum $P_u(i,j) + P_m(i,j)$, we allow the index price to move to the up node. In every other case we move the index price to the middle node at the next time period.

We can continue this procedure, step-by-step, for any point (i,j) along a simulated path through

14. The drift parameter $\alpha_{0,0}(0,0)$ in a stochastic implied tree is determined from a martingale condition on the total transition proability $P_{1,2}(0,0)$

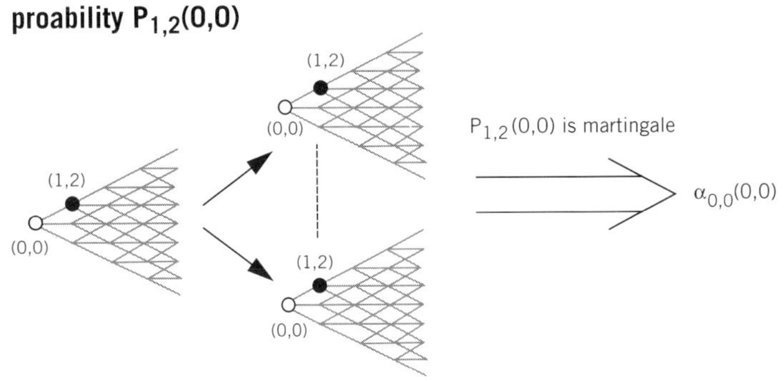

15. Determining which node the index price will go to during one simulation step using the renormalised random number ΔW_i^0

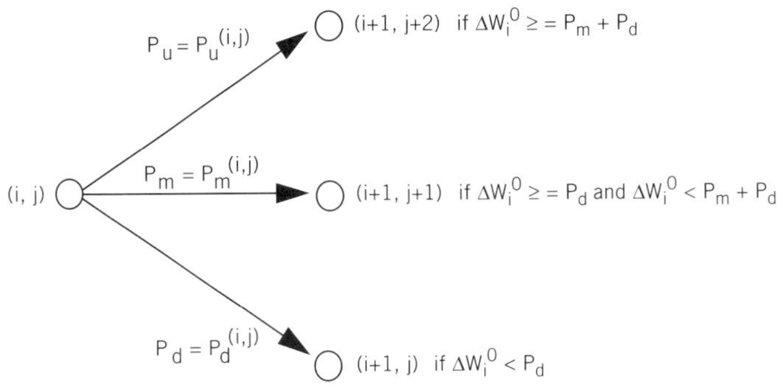

the stochastic implied tree. First, all the drift parameters $\alpha_{m,n}(i,j)$ are determined from the martingale conditions on $P_{m,n}(i,j)$. Appendix E gives the necessary details for doing this calculation. Subsequently, these drift parameters are used to generate arbitrage-free (random) movements of the future local volatility surface as the index price moves randomly forward across the tree. We can generate many such sample paths through the tree. Along each path, the movements of the index price and the local volatility surface are random realisations of an arbitrage-free dynamics, which step-by-step guarantees absence of arbitrage opportunities among different standard option (and forward) contracts and their underlying index within the discrete time framework of the stochastic implied tree.

A SIMPLE EXAMPLE

Consider a one-factor stochastic volatility model with a lognormal volatility of volatility structure, as described by the following pair of stochastic differential equations:

$$\frac{dS}{S} = \mu dt + \sigma dW^0$$
$$\frac{d\sigma_{K,T}^2}{\sigma_{K,T}^2} = \alpha_{K,T}dt + \theta dW^1$$

where $\sigma(t) = \sigma_{t,S_t}(t,S_t)$. For the purpose of this example we take the volatility coefficient θ to be constant, so that the factor W^1 has the interpretation of a simultaneous constant (proportional) shift in all local volatilities. All the other quantities can depend on t, S, factors W^0 and W^1 or their past values. More specifically, we consider a one-year, five-period example with the initial term and strike structure of volatility given by an at-the-money implied volatility of 20% and a constant skewness of 0.5% per 10 strike points. For instance, initially a 80 strike option of any maturity has implied volatility of 21%. Let the risk-free discount rate be equal to 10%, dividend yield 5% and the volatility (of volatility) parameter θ = 30%. We choose the state space of the stochastic implied trinomial tree to be the same as a standard (CRR-type) trinomial tree with constant volatility of 20%. Figure 16 shows this state space. It also shows the local volatilities and total transition probabilities, corresponding to various nodes of this tree, at the initial time $t = 0$. As we expect, local volatilities increase as the index level decreases roughly twice as fast as implied volatilities. Also the probability distribution is skewed (around the forward price) towards the lower index levels. The first step toward the construction of the stochastic implied tree is to determine the drift coefficients $\alpha_{m,n}(0,0)$ at time $t_0 = 0$. Appendix E gives the formulas for directly calculating these coefficients, which are shown in Figure 17. We can justify the numbers by examining what can happen to the total transition probabilities during the next time interval Δt. All local volatilities will simultaneously move, with probability of 1/2, to their up values, $\sigma^{(u)}_{m,n}(0,0)$, or their down values, $\sigma^{(d)}_{m,n}(0,0)$, as given by

$$\sigma^{(u,d)}_{m,n}(0,0) =$$

$$\sigma_{m,n}(0,0)\exp\left\{\left(\alpha_{m,n}(0,0) - \frac{1}{2}\theta^2\right)\Delta t \pm \theta\sqrt{\Delta t}\right\}$$

with $\alpha_{m,n}(0,0)$ given in Figure 17. As a result, all transition probabilities also change across the tree, simultaneously moving to their up values, $p^{(u)}_{m,n}(0,0)$, or to their down values, $p^{(d)}_{m,n}(0,0)$, each with probability of 1/2. Figure 18 shows that with the present choice of drift coefficients the initial total probabilities are precisely equal to the average value of their up and down values. To complete the step 1 we draw a pair of independent random numbers between 0 and 1, say (0.853, 0.612). Since 0.853 is greater than the

16. The state space of a stochastic implied tree, the local volatility surface and the total probability distribution on the tree at the initial time t = 0

state space:

				176.06
			152.85	152.85
		132.69	132.69	132.69
	115.19	115.19	115.19	115.19
100.00	100.00	100.00	100.00	100.00
	86.81	86.81	86.81	86.81
		75.36	75.36	75.36
			65.43	65.43
				56.80

local vols $\sigma_{m,n}(0,0)$:

			0.155
		0.180	0.177
	0.191	0.189	0.188
0.199	0.199	0.197	0.197
	0.218	0.215	0.211
		0.251	0.240
			0.263

total probs $P_{m,n}(0,0)$:

				0.003
			0.016	0.037
		0.071	0.112	0.135
	0.275	0.281	0.267	0.251
1.000	0.493	0.376	0.311	0.271
	0.232	0.206	0.197	0.182
		0.066	0.070	0.083
			0.026	0.028
				0.011

17. The first step of the stochastic implied tree construction consists of determining all the drift coefficients $\alpha_{m,n}(0,0)$ at time $t_0 = 0$, from the martingale conditions for the total probabilities $P_{m,n}(0,0)$

step 1

local vols $\sigma_{m,n}(0,0)$:

			0.155
		0.180	0.177
	0.191	0.189	0.188
0.199	0.199	0.197	0.197
	0.218	0.215	0.211
		0.251	0.240
			0.263

total probs $P_{m,n}(0,0)$:

				0.003
			0.016	0.037
		0.071	0.112	0.135
	0.275	0.281	0.267	0.251
1.000	0.493	0.376	0.311	0.271
	0.232	0.206	0.197	0.182
		0.066	0.070	0.083
			0.026	0.028
				0.011

drifts $\alpha_{m,n}(0,0)$:

			-0.381
		-0.298	-0.194
	-0.184	-0.037	0.009
-0.044	0.139	0.072	0.063
	-0.232	-0.051	-0.043
		-0.369	-0.195
			-0.452

choose a random vector $(\Delta W^0, \Delta W^1)$-> (up,up)

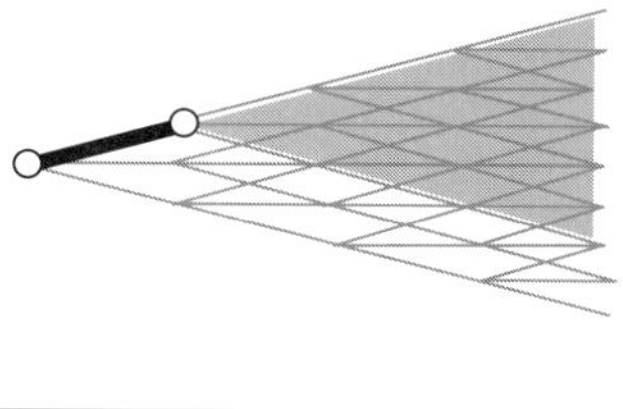

sum of prevailing down and middle probabilities, 0.493 + 0.232 = 0.725, as discussed in Figure 15 we move the index to the node (1,2). Also, since 0.612 is greater than 1/2 we move all local volatilities to their up values, before we begin the next simulation step. The second step of the simulation is precisely the same as step 1, except confined to the subtree that begins at the node (1,2). As shown in Figure 19, again the martingale conditions on the total probabilities $P_{m,n}(1,2)$ are used to solve for the drift coefficients $\alpha_{m,n}(1,2)$ at time $t_1 = 0.25$, and then these coefficients, together with a pair of random numbers, are used to determine jointly the new values for the index price and the future local volatilities. Steps 3 and 4 are also quite similar and their results have been shown in Figures 20 and 21, respectively.

In this example, we chose a simple two-state (up and down) representation for the stochastic movements of the local volatility surface during the time step Δt. We could instead choose any equivalent representation of the same process with m states, for any integer $m > 1$. There are an infinite number of equivalent representations for any choice of m. If the model is well-behaved, these discrete representations should all converge to the same continuous-time process as goes to zero. However, a representation with a large number of states may converge substantially faster than the two-state representation we chose here. Table 1 shows the calibration results for a 50,000 path simulation on the five-period tree described above.

The fourth and fifth columns give, respectively, the standard (non-stochastic) implied trinomial tree and the stochastic implied tree results for a series of standard European-style call and put options used to calibrate the trees. The results are seen to agree well.

18. Up- and down-values of local volatilities and total transition probabilities correspondingto the first simulation step

up local vols $\sigma^{(u)}_{m,n}(0,0)$:

			0.161
		0.192	0.194
	0.210	0.215	0.216
0.226	0.237	0.231	0.230
	0.236	0.244	0.240
		0.264	0.262
			0.270

down local vols $\sigma^{(d)}_{m,n}(0,0)$:

			0.120
		0.142	0.144
	0.156	0.159	0.160
0.168	0.175	0.171	0.170
	0.175	0.181	0.178
		0.195	0.194
			0.200

up total probs $P^{(u)}_{m,n}(0,0)$:

				0.005
			0.027	0.055
		0.103	0.142	0.154
	0.343	0.278	0.243	0.220
1.000	0.346	0.303	0.256	0.226
	0.311	0.209	0.197	0.175
		0.107	0.089	0.102
			0.046	0.042
				0.021

down total probs $P^{(d)}_{m,n}(0,0)$:

				0.001
			0.006	0.018
		0.038	0.082	0.116
	0.206	0.284	0.291	0.282
1.000	0.640	0.448	0.367	0.315
	0.154	0.203	0.198	0.190
		0.026	0.051	0.063
			0.006	0.014
				0.001

average total probs $(P^{(u)}_{m,n}(0,0) + P^{(d)}_{m,n}(0,0))/2$:

				0.003
			0.016	0.037
		0.071	0.112	0.135
	0.275	0.281	0.267	0.251
1.000	0.493	0.376	0.311	0.271
	0.232	0.206	0.197	0.182
		0.066	0.070	0.083
			0.026	0.028
				0.011

19. During step 2 of the simulation, the drift coefficients $\alpha_{m,n}(1,2)$ at time $t_1 = 0.25$, are determined from the martingale conditions for the total probabilities $P_{m,n}(1,2)$

step 2

local vols $\sigma_{m,n}(1,2)$:

		0.161
	0.192	0.194
0.210	0.215	0.216
	0.231	0.230
		0.240

total probs $P_{m,n}(1,2)$:

			0.015
		0.077	0.129
	0.301	0.296	0.271
1.000	0.436	0.336	0.273
	0.363	0.205	0.193
		0.085	0.089
			0.030

drifts $\alpha_{m,n}(1,2)$:

		-0.299
	-0.186	-0.017
-0.044	0.189	0.051
	-0.229	0.016
		-0.365

choose a random vector $(\Delta W^0, \Delta W^1)$-> (middle,down)

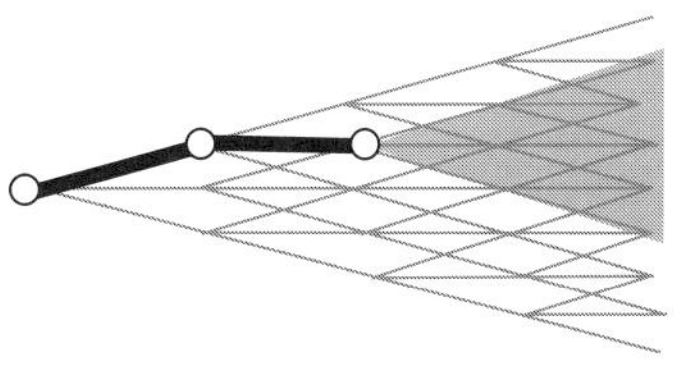

20. During step 3 of the simulation, the drift coefficients $\alpha_{m,n}(2,3)$ at time $t_2 = 0.50$, are determined from the martingale conditions for the total probabilities $P_{m,n}(2,3)$

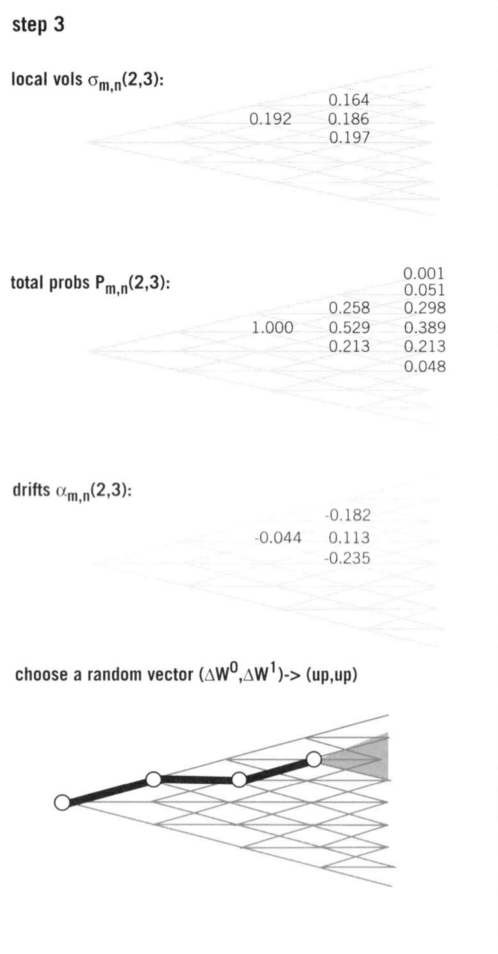

21. During step 4 of the simulation, the drift coefficients $\alpha_{m,n}(3,5)$ at time $t_3 = 0.75$, are determined from the martingale conditions for the total probabilities $P_{m,n}(3,5)$

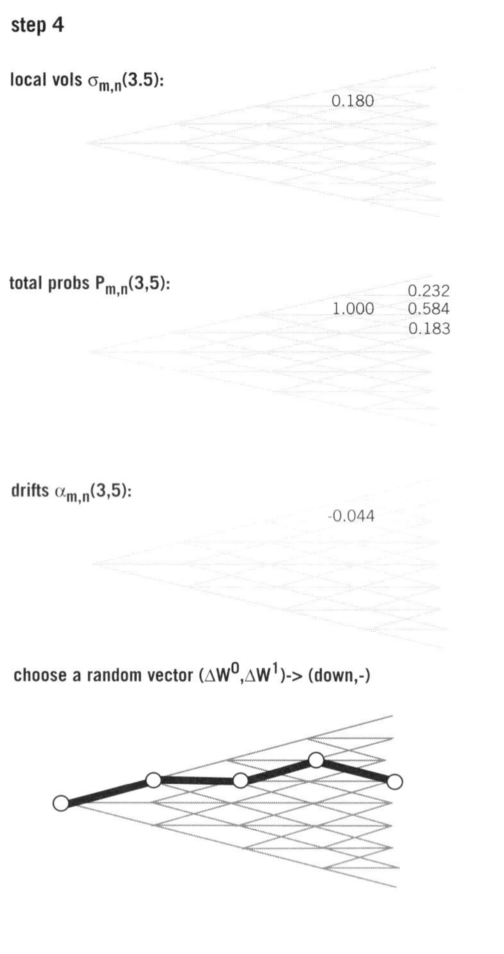

Table 1. Calibration results of a 50,000-path simulation on a one-year, five-period stochastic implied tree

Strike price	Option type	Black-Scholes price	Standard implied tree price	Stochastic implied tree price
130	call	1.142	1.118	1.176
120	call	2.629	2.764	2.775
110	call	5.332	5.529	5.556
100	call	9.628	9.395	9.432
90	put	2.452	2.566	2.556
80	put	0.840	0.936	0.928
70	put	0.202	0.244	0.230

CAVEAT:

Since the location of the nodes (ie the state space) of the stochastic implied trinomial tree is fixed throughout, it may not be possible to fit very large local volatilities, which may occur at various nodes and at different times during the simulation, with transition probabilities which lie between 0 and 1. In such cases, we must overwrite the unacceptable transition probabilities (or, equivalently, the local volatilities) at those nodes.[15] Even though this overwrite procedure makes for an imperfect calibration to the initial smile (and, theoretically, a violation of arbitrage), it must be diligently adhered to, in order to keep the simulation process meaningful. We can define overwrite ratio as the number of overwrites per future node, per simulation path. In the previous example, the overwrite ratio for five periods and 50,000 paths is found to be 2.7%, indicating that only a relatively small portion of the calculated local volatilities have been overwritten.

PRICING OF SOME CONTRACTS WITH PAYOFFS BASED ON REALISED VOLATILITY

Consider a *realised variance forward contract*,[16] defined as a forward contract on the realised variance of index returns, Σ^2, with strike price K and payoff ($\Sigma^2 - K$) at the contract maturity. Table 2 shows the valuation results for a one-year realised variance contract with zero strike price, using 20-period, 10,000-path stochastic implied tree simulations with four different volatility of volatility parameters θ = 0%, 20%, 30%, 50%. To make the results more clear, we choose a flat initial volatility smile with a constant implied volatility of 20% for all standard European options. Also the discount rate and dividend yield are both chosen to be zero.

It is clear from this table that the price of a realised variance forward contract is independent of the volatility of volatility parameter, and is what one would expect from a *static* 20% flat initial implied volatility surface. In fact, it can be shown that under very general conditions (see footnote 14) the price of this forward contract depends only on the initial volatility surface and not on the specific stochastic aspects of the volatility process. More precisely, its price equals the discounted value of the expected (equilibrium) total index return variance during the life of the contract. As discussed earlier, this expectation is fully embodied in today's local volatility surface. Therefore, we are able to price this forward contract by using an effective theory (θ = 0), as the second column in the table indicates. This is quite analogous to our ability to price index forwards contracts using the static initial forward curve without any specific knowledge of the stochastic behaviour of the future index prices, or to price straight bonds using the initial yield curve with no specific knowledge of the behaviour of future interest rates.

Now consider a *realised variance (call) option contract* with strike price K whose payoff at maturity is given by $\mathrm{Max}(\Sigma^2 - K, 0)$. Table 3 shows the valuation results for one-year realised variance call options with different strike prices, under precisely the same conditions as before.

According to this table the price of a realised variance option contract increases with the volatility of volatility parameter. This result should be expected as most options prices increase when their price becomes more volatile. Furthermore, like most options, the pricing and hedging of a realised variance option contract depends crucially on our choice of the stochastic volatility model.

Hedging the index and volatility risks in stochastic volatility models

Appendix D gives conditions for the existence and uniqueness of an equivalent martingale measure in multi-factor stochastic volatility models. Under these conditions the markets are complete and, given a contingent claim C, there exists an admissible self-financing trading strategy (Harrison and Pliska (1981)) involving the index S, the money market account B, and (any) n different standard options $C_i = C_{K_i,T_i}$, $i = 1,\ldots,n$, which replicate this contingent claim:

Table 2. Price of a zero-strike realised variance forward contract for different values of the volatility of volatility parameter

θ	0%	20%	30%	50%
price	399.81	400.37	401.10	400.69

Table 3. Prices of realised variance call option contracts with different strike prices and volatility of volatility parameters

K\θ	0%	20%	30%	50%
400	0.00	48.336	65.784	95.742
500	0.00	14.745	31.221	56.096
600	0.00	3.391	11.780	25.211
700	0.00	0.203	1.682	4.654

$$N_B B + N_S S + \sum_{i=1}^{n} N_i C_i = C \quad \text{a.e.}$$

This replication strategy is dynamical, so that the hedge ratios N_B, N_S and N_i, $i = 1,\ldots,n$, are in general functions of time and other dynamical variables.

To find the hedge ratios N_S and N_i we must separately move the index price S and introduce n independent shocks W^i (possibly corresponding to the n independent factors) to the initial local volatility surface, and subsequently reprice the contingent claim and the n hedge standard options. For the simple model in our examples, we find these hedge ratios from solving the following system of equations

$$\begin{bmatrix} 1 & \partial C_1 / \partial S \\ 0 & \partial C_1 / \partial W^1 \end{bmatrix} \begin{bmatrix} N_S \\ N_1 \end{bmatrix} = \begin{bmatrix} \partial C / \partial S \\ \partial C / \partial W^1 \end{bmatrix}.$$

This system has a unique solution if the sensitivity matrix on the right hand side is non-singular. This is true if $\partial C_1/\partial W^1 > 0$, ie when the sensitivity of the option to a parallel shift in the local volatility surface is positive. This condition holds for any standard option with non-zero strike price.

22.

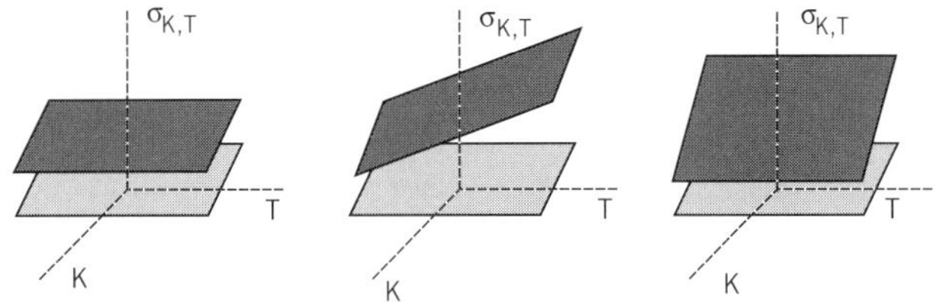

More realistic stochastic volatility models

In the previous example, all instantaneous changes of the volatility surface are caused by a single source of randomness, a *parallel shift factor*. However, empirical analyses[17] of the daily changes of the volatility surface for index options reveals other important sources of randomness. A more realistic stochastic volatility model may be, for example, given by the following pair of stochastic differential equations:

$$\frac{dS}{S} = \mu dt + \sigma dW^0$$

$$\frac{d\sigma^2_{K,T}(t,S)}{\sigma^2_{K,T}(t,S)} = \alpha_{K,T}(t,S)dt + \theta_1 dW^1 + \theta_2 e^{-\lambda(T-t)}dW^2 + \theta_3 e^{-\eta(K-S)}dW^3$$

where $\sigma(t) = \sigma_{t,S_t}(t,S_t)$ and θ_1, θ_2, θ_3, λ, η are all constants. The first factor has the same interpretation as before, whereas the second and third factors may be interpreted as the *term structure factor* and *skewness factor*, respectively. The shocks to the local volatility surface resulting from these factors are shown in Figure 22.

Conclusion

In this paper we discussed an arbitrage pricing approach to contingent claims valuation with stochastic volatility similar to the Heath-Jarrow-Morton (HJM) methodology for stochastic interest rates. We began with a continuous time economy with multiple factors, and posited a general multi-factor continuous time stochastic process for the evolution of the local volatility surface. We characterised the conditions which guarantee absence of arbitrage opportunities among the various option and forward contracts defined on the underlying index. Under these conditions markets are complete and contingent claim valuation is preference-free. However, these no-arbitrage conditions are non-linear and difficult to use in their continuous form. We then introduced the stochastic implied tree as a discrete-time framework for implementing our family of models. Starting from any initial node, we can guarantee absence of future arbitrages by choosing appropriate drift parameters for every future node. This procedure guarantees arbitrage-free future movements of the index and local volatility surface in the discrete-time world defined by the stochastic implied tree. We can use stochastic implied trees to price contingent claims with payoffs which depend on the index and index volatility, when the volatility surface is skewed and stochastic. The resulting contingent claim prices are independent of the market prices of risk. They are also consistent with the current market prices of all standard options and forwards defined on the underlying index and with the absence of any future arbitrage opportunities.

Appendix A

EXPECTATION DEFINITIONS OF LOCAL VOLATILITY

This appendix provides expectation definitions for local volatility. It begins with (2) as the definition of local volatility and derives the expectation relationships between local volatilities and future instantaneous volatilities, given the assumption that the equivalent martingale measure (risk-neutral measure) exists.

Under the equivalent martingale measure, the index price evolution is given by the stochastic differential equation

$$\frac{dS_t}{S_t} = (r-\delta)dt + \sigma_t dZ_t \qquad (A1)$$

where the riskless discount rate r and continuously compounded dividend yield δ are assumed to be constant, σ_t is the instantaneous volatility at time t and $Z = \bar{W}^0$ is a standard Brownian motion under this measure, as discussed in the text. Let $E = E_{t,S}$ denote the expectation corresponding to this measure, given the information available at time t (with the index level at $S = S_t$). Aside from the spot index level, the information at time t generally includes the past index levels, the values of the n (independent) stochastic factors W^i (governing the stochastic behaviour of volatility) and their past histories. Under the equivalent martingale measure rescaled option prices are martingales. Therefore, the price, $C_{K,T}(t,S)$, at time t and market level S of a standard European-style (call) option, with strike K and maturity T, with terminal value $C_{K,T}(T,S_T) = (S_T - K)^+$ is given by

$$C_{K,T}(t,S) = -e^{-r(T-t)}E\left[(S_T - K)^+\right]. \quad (A2)$$

Differentiating this equation once with respect to K gives

$$\frac{\partial C_{K,T}}{\partial K} = -e^{-r(T-t)}E\left[\theta(S_T - K)\right] \quad (A3)$$

where $\theta(.)$ is the *Heaviside* function. Differentiating twice with respect to K gives

$$\frac{\partial^2 C_{K,T}}{\partial K^2} = +e^{-r(T-t)}E\left[\delta(S_T - K)\right] \quad (A4)$$

where $\delta(.)$ is the Dirac delta function. Lastly, differentiating with respect to T gives

$$\frac{\partial C_{K,T}}{\partial T} = -rC_{K,T} + e^{-r(T-t)}\frac{\partial}{\partial T}E\left[(S_T - K)^+\right]. \quad (A5)$$

A formal application of Ito's lemma to the option's terminal payoff leads to the identity

$$d(S_T - K)^+ = \theta(S_T - K)dS_T + \frac{1}{2}\sigma_T^2 S_T^2 \delta(S_T - K)dT. \quad (A6)$$

Taking expectations of both sides of this equation and using (A1) leads to

$$dE\left[(S_T - K)^+\right] = (r - \delta)E\left[S_T\theta(S_T - K)\right]dT + \frac{1}{2}E\left[\sigma_T^2 S_T^2 \delta(S_T - K)\right]dT. \quad (A7)$$

The first term in this expression can be rewritten as

$$E\left[S_T\theta(S_T - K)\right] = E\left[(S_T - K)^+\right] + KE\left[\theta(S_T - K)\right]. \quad (A8)$$

Inserting this relation and multiplying both sides of (A7) by the discount factor $e^{-r(T-t)}$, and using (A2) and (A3) we obtain

$$e^{-r(t-t)}\frac{\partial}{\partial T}E\left[(S_T - K)^+\right] = (r - \delta)\left\{C_{K,T} - K\frac{\partial C_{K,T}}{\partial K}\right\} + \frac{1}{2}e^{-r(T-t)}K^2 E\left[\sigma_T^2\delta(S_T - K)\right]. \quad (A9)$$

Replacing this expression for the last term in (A5) gives

$$\frac{\partial C_{K,T}}{\partial T} = -(r - \delta)K\frac{\partial C_{K,T}}{\partial K} - \delta C_{K,T} + \frac{1}{2}e^{-r(T-t)}K^2 E\left[\sigma_T^2\delta(S_T - K)\right]. \quad (A10)$$

Finally, using conditional expectations we can write

$$E\left[\sigma_T^2\delta(S_T - K)\right] = E\left[\sigma_T^2 | S_T = K\right]\cdot E\left[\delta(S_T - K)\right] \quad (A11)$$

which together with (A4), can be inserted back into (A10) to arrive at

$$E\left[\sigma_T^2 | S_T = K\right] = 2\frac{\left\{\frac{\partial C_{K,T}}{\partial T} + (r - \delta)K\frac{\partial C_{K,T}}{\partial K} + \delta C_{K,T}\right\}}{K^2\frac{\partial^2 C_{K,T}}{\partial K^2}}. \quad (A12)$$

The right hand side of this equation is precisely the definition of the local variance $\sigma_{K,T}^2(t,S)$, as defined in (2). It follows that

$$\sigma_{K,T}^2(t,S) = E\left[\sigma_T^2 | S_T = K\right] = \frac{E\left[\sigma_T^2\delta(S_T - K)\right]}{E\left[\delta(S_T - K)\right]}. \quad (A13)$$

The local variance $\sigma_{K,T}^2(t,S)$ is, therefore, the conditional expectation of the instantaneous variance of index returns at the future time T, contingent on index level S_T being equal to K. If the instantaneous index volatility is only a function of the spot index level and time, ie if $\sigma_t = \sigma(S_t,t)$ then

$$\sigma_{K,T}^2(t,S) = E\left[\sigma_T^2 | S_T = K\right] = E\left[\sigma^2(S_T,T) | S_T = K\right] = \sigma^2(K,T). \quad (A14)$$

Since the right hand side is independent of t and S, in this case the local volatility surface remains *static* as time evolves and index level S changes. This situation corresponds to an *effective theory* where all sources of volatility uncertainty, other than the future time T and the future index level K, are effectively averaged out of the theory, leaving an effective volatility which is only a function of T and K.

In the general stochastic setting the dynamics of local volatilities is described by the stochastic differential equation

$$\frac{d\sigma_{K,T}^2(t,S)}{\sigma_{K,T}^2(t,S)} = \alpha_{K,T}(t,S)dt + \sum_{i=0}^{n}\theta_{K,T}^i(t,S)d\overline{W}_t^i. \quad (A15)$$

As discussed in the text, $\overline{W}^i$, $i = 0,\ldots,n$, are independent Brownian motions under the equivalent martingale measure and the volatility coefficients $\theta_{K,T}^i$ are some given functions of time t, index level S and factor values W_t^i, or the past histories of these variables. The drift coefficients $\alpha_{K,T}(t,S)$ have similar dependencies, but are constrained by the requirement of no-arbitrage. In an effective theory $d\sigma^2_{K,T}(t,S) = 0$ for all values of t and S, as seen by (A14), thus the drift and volatility coefficients are all identically equal to zero.

The denominator on the right hand side of (A13) is the total transition probability (see (39)):

$$P_{K,T}(t,S) = E\left[\delta(S_T - K)\right]. \tag{A16}$$

Since $P_{K,T}$, for all values of K and T, are jointly martingales under the equivalent martingale measure, the stochastic differential equation governing their evolution has the form

$$\frac{dP_{K,T}(t,S)}{P_{K,T}(t,S)} = \sum_{i=0}^{n} \zeta^i_{K,T}(t,S)\,d\overline{W}^i_t. \tag{A17}$$

The numerator on the right hand side of (A13) is also a martingale under this measure. Therefore, by taking differentials of both sides of this equation and applying Ito's lemma we find that

$$\alpha_{K,T} + \sum_{i=0}^{n} \zeta^i_{K,T}\theta^i_{K,T} = 0. \tag{A18}$$

Let us define a new measure, $d\hat{W}^i = d\overline{W}^i - \zeta^i_{K,T}dt$, specifically depending on K and T. From (A15) and (A18), we observe that under this new measure local variance $\sigma^2_{K,T}$ is a martingale, ie

$$\frac{d\sigma^2_{K,T}(t,S)}{\sigma^2_{K,T}(t,S)} = \sum_{i=0}^{n} \theta^i_{K,T}(t,S)\,d\hat{W}^i_t. \tag{A19}$$

We call this measure the *K-strike and T-maturity forward risk-adjusted measure* in analogy with T-maturity forward risk-neutral measure in interest rates (see Jamshidian (1993)). Letting $E^{(K,T)}[\ldots]$ denote expectations with respect to this new measure, we can write (A13) as

$$\sigma^2_{K,T} = E^{(K,T)}\left[\sigma^2_T\right]. \tag{A20}$$

Therefore, in the K-strike and T-maturity forward risk-adjusted measure the local variance $\sigma^2_{K,T}$ is the expectation of future spot variances σ^2_T at time T. This is analogous to the similar situation in the interest rate world where the forward rate f_T is the T-maturity forward risk-adjusted expectation of the future spot rates at time T.

Appendix B

MATHEMATICS OF EFFECTIVE THEORIES

In this appendix we describe several mathematical relationships satisfied by the propagators, transition probabilities and the standard option prices in the effective volatility theories.

The forward propagator $p_{t,S,t',S'}$ in an effective volatility theory describes the (standard) option price evolution forward in time and index price. It satisfies the same backward equation as option prices, a dual forward equation and the boundary condition $p_{t,S,t',S'} = \delta(S - S')$ for all time t. Alternatively we can work with the forward transition probability density function, $p(t,S,t',S')$, which is defined in terms of the forward propagator as $p(t,S,t',S') = e^{r(t'-t)}p_{t,S,t',S'}$. The forward transition probability, with boundary condition $p(t,S,t',S') = \delta(S - S')$, satisfies the following backward equation

$$\left(\frac{\partial}{\partial t} + (r-\delta)S\frac{\partial}{\partial S} + \frac{1}{2}\sigma^2_{S,t}S^2\frac{\partial^2}{\partial S^2}\right)p(t,S,t',S') = 0 \tag{B1}$$

and its dual forward equation

$$\frac{\partial}{\partial t'}p(t,S,t',S') + (r-\delta)\frac{\partial}{\partial S'}\left(S'p(t,S,t',S')\right) - \frac{1}{2}\frac{\partial^2}{\partial S'^2}\left(\sigma^2_{S',t'}S'^2p(t,S,t',S')\right) = 0 \tag{B2}$$

and, for any $t \le \tilde{t} \le t'$, the Chapman-Kolmogorov relation

$$p(t,S,t',S') = \int_0^\infty p(t,S,\tilde{t},\tilde{S})\,p(\tilde{t},\tilde{S},t',S')\,d\tilde{S}. \tag{B3}$$

The forward transition probability (propagator) relates prices of a standard option, with fixed strike K and maturity T, at different time and market levels according to

$$C_{K,T}(t,S) = e^{-r(T-t)}\int_0^\infty p(t,S,t',S')C_{K,T}(t',S')\,dS'. \tag{B4}$$

Differentiating this relation twice and evaluating it at $t' = T$ leads to

$$p(t,S,T,K) = e^{r(T-t)}\frac{\partial^2}{\partial K^2}C_{K,T}(t,S). \tag{B5}$$

Similarly, the backward propagator $\Phi_{K,T,K',T'}$ describes option price evolution backward in maturity time and strike price. It satisfies the same forward equation as the option prices, its dual backward equation, and the boundary condition $\Phi_{K,T,K',T'} = \delta(K - K')$ for all T. Alternatively we can work with the backward transition probability density function, $\Phi(K,T,K',T')$, which is defined in terms of the backward propagator as $\Phi(K,T,K',T') = e^{\delta(T-T')}\Phi_{K,T,K',T'}$. The backward transition probability density function, with the boundary condition $\Phi(K,T,K',T') = \delta(K - K')$, satisfies the following forward equation

$$\left(\frac{\partial}{\partial T} + (r-\delta)K\frac{\partial}{\partial K} - \frac{1}{2}\sigma^2_{K,T}K^2\frac{\partial^2}{\partial K^2}\right)\Phi(K,T,K',T') = 0 \tag{B6}$$

its dual backward equation

$$\frac{\partial}{\partial T'}\Phi(K,T,K',T') + (r-\delta)\frac{\partial}{\partial K'}\left(K'\Phi(K,T,K',T')\right) + \frac{1}{2}\frac{\partial^2}{\partial K'^2}\left(\sigma^2_{K',T'}K'^2\Phi(K,T,K',T')\right) = 0 \quad \text{(B7)}$$

and, for any $T' \le \tilde{T} \le T$, the Chapman-Kolmogorov relation

$$\Phi(K,T,K',T') = \int_0^\infty \Phi(K,T,\tilde{K},\tilde{T})\Phi(\tilde{K},\tilde{T},K',T')d\tilde{K}. \quad \text{(B8)}$$

The backward transition probability (propagator) relates prices of standard options, with different strikes and maturities, at a fixed time t, $t \le T' \le T$, and market level S according to

$$C_{K,T}(t,S) = e^{-\delta(T-T')}\int_0^\infty \Phi(K,T,K',T')C_{K',T'}(t,S). \quad \text{(B9)}$$

Differentiating this relation twice and evaluating it at $T' = t$ leads to

$$\Phi(K,T,S,t) = e^{\delta(T-t)}\frac{\partial^2}{\partial S^2}C_{K,T}(t,S). \quad \text{(B10)}$$

Appendix C

LOCAL VOLATILITY VARIATIONAL FORMULAS IN EFFECTIVE VOLATILITY THEORIES

In this appendix we derive variational formulas describing sensitivity of the transition probabilities (propagators) to a specific local volatility on the volatility surface. We work within the context of effective theories, (formally) changing the local volatility corresponding to a single future time and market level, while leaving all other local volatilities unchanged.

We begin by studying the relationship between transition probabilities and local volatilities in a discrete time setting. We then take the continuous-time limit by letting the spacing go to zero. Consider one period forward transition probabilities p^*_u, p^*_m and p^*_d, from the index level S^* at time t^* to the three nearby index levels S^*_u, S^*_m and S^*_d at time $t^* + \Delta t^*$, as shown in Figure 23.

Let $F^* = S^* e^{(r-\delta)\Delta t^*}$ denote the one-step forward price and $\sigma^* = \sigma_{S^*,t^*}$ the local volatility, corresponding to the initial node (t^*,S^*). The three transition probabilities in Figure 23 add up to 1, and are further constrained by the forward and volatility conditions, ie

$$p^*_u + p^*_m + p^*_d = 1 \quad \text{(C1)}$$

$$p^*_u S^*_u + p^*_m S^*_m + p^*_d S^*_d = F^* \quad \text{(C2)}$$

$$p^*_u (S^*_u - F^*)^2 + p^*_m (S^*_m - F^*)^2 + p^*_d (S^*_d - F^*)^2 = F^{*2}\sigma^{*2}\Delta t^*. \quad \text{(C3)}$$

We can solve these expressions for transition probabilities in terms of the local volatility. The results are

$$p^*_u = \frac{(F^* - S^*_m)(F^* - S^*_d)}{(S^*_u - S^*_m)(S^*_u - S^*_d)} + \frac{F^{*2}}{(S^*_u - S^*_m)(S^*_u - S^*_d)}\sigma^{*2}\Delta t^* \quad \text{(C4)}$$

$$p^*_d = \frac{(F^* - S^*_m)(F^* - S^*_u)}{(S^*_m - S^*_d)(S^*_u - S^*_d)} + \frac{F^{*2}}{(S^*_m - S^*_d)(S^*_u - S^*_d)}\sigma^{*2}\Delta t^* \quad \text{(C5)}$$

and $p^*_m = 1 - p^*_u - p^*_d$.

Now consider the forward transition probability $p(t,S,t',S')$, describing the total probability that starting with the level S at time t the index will move to the level S' at the future time t', in the effective theory context. We can isolate the sensitivity of this transition probability to a specific local volatility σ_{S^*,t^*}, corresponding to the future time $t \le t^* \le t'$ and future market level S^*, using the Chapman-Kolmogorov relation of (B3). In discrete-time this contribution is isolated in Figure 24.

Figure 24 describes the following decomposition of the total transition probability:

23.

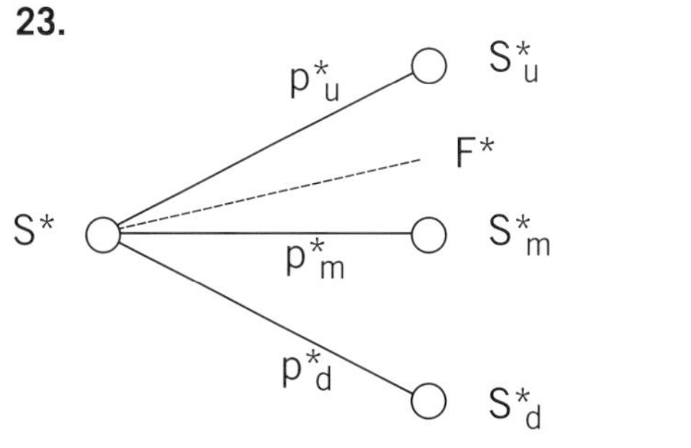

24.

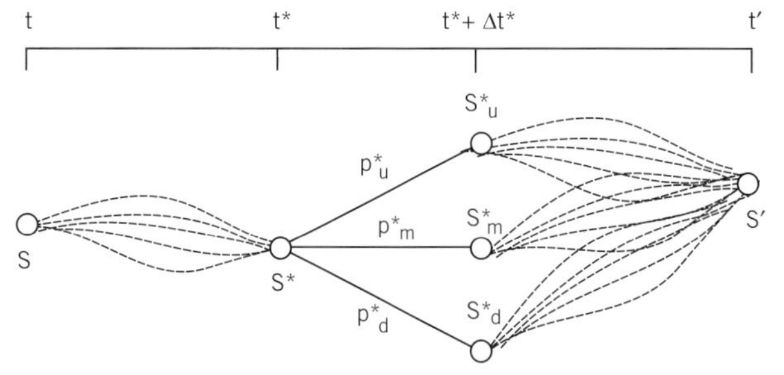

25.

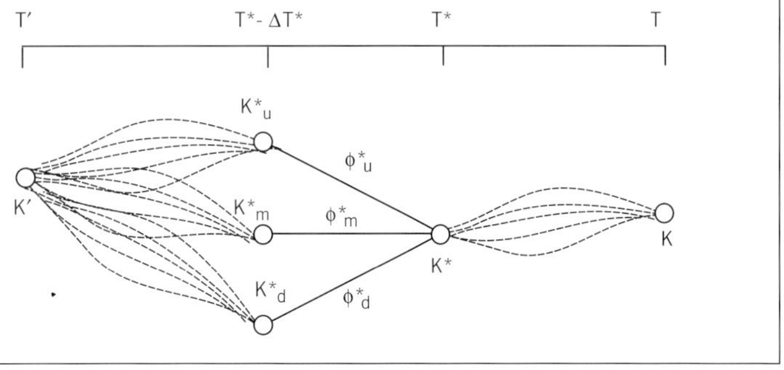

$$p(t,S,t',S') = p(t,S,t^*,S^*)p^*_u\, p(t^*+\Delta t^*,S^*_u,t',S') + p(t,S,t^*,S^*)p^*_m\, p(t^*+\Delta t^*,S^*_m,t',S') + p(t,S,t^*,S^*)p^*_d\, p(t^*+\Delta t^*,S^*_d,t',S') + \text{terms with no sensitivity to } \sigma_{S^*,t^*}. \quad \text{(C6)}$$

Taking the variational derivative with respect to $\sigma^2_{S^*,t^*}$ gives

$$\frac{\delta p(t,S,t',S')}{\delta\sigma^2_{S^*,t^*}} = p(t,S,t^*,S^*)\left(\frac{\delta p^*_u}{\delta\sigma^2_{S^*,t^*}}\right)p(t^*+\Delta t^*,S^*_u,t',S') + p(t,S,t^*,S^*)\left(\frac{\delta p^*_m}{\delta\sigma^2_{S^*,t^*}}\right)p(t^*+\Delta t^*,S^*_m,t',S') + p(t,S,t^*,S^*)\left(\frac{\delta p^*_d}{\delta\sigma^2_{S^*,t^*}}\right)p(t^*+\Delta t^*,S^*_d,t',S'). \quad \text{(C7)}$$

From (C4) and (C5), and ignoring $o(\Delta t^*)$ terms, we have

$$\frac{\delta p^*_u}{\delta\sigma^2_{S^*,t^*}} = \frac{S^{*2}}{(S^*_u - S^*_m)(S^*_u - S^*_d)} \sim \frac{1}{2}\left(\frac{S^*}{\Delta S^*}\right)^2 \quad \text{(C8)}$$

$$\frac{\delta p^*_d}{\delta\sigma^2_{S^*,t^*}} = \frac{S^{*2}}{(S^*_m - S^*_d)(S^*_u - S^*_d)} \sim \frac{1}{2}\left(\frac{S^*}{\Delta S^*}\right)^2 \quad \text{(C9)}$$

$$\frac{\delta p^*_m}{\delta\sigma^2_{S^*,t^*}} = -\left(\frac{\delta p^*_u}{\delta\sigma^2_{S^*,t^*}} + \frac{\delta p^*_d}{\delta\sigma^2_{S^*,t^*}}\right) \sim -\left(\frac{S^*}{\Delta S^*}\right)^2. \quad \text{(C10)}$$

where we used the approximation $S^*_u - S^*_m \sim S^*_m - S^*_d = \Delta S^*$. Inserting these relations back in (C7) leads to

$$\frac{\delta p(t,S,t',S')}{\delta\sigma^2_{S^*,t^*}} = \frac{1}{2}p(t,S,t^*,S^*)S^{*2} \{p(t^*+\Delta t^*,S^*+\Delta S^*,t',S') - 2p(t^*+\Delta t^*,S^*,t',S') + p(t^*+\Delta t^*,S^*-\Delta S^*,t',S')\}/(\Delta S^*)^2. \quad \text{(C11)}$$

In the limit $\Delta S \to 0$ we find the desired result

$$\frac{\delta p(t,S,t',S')}{\delta\sigma^2_{S^*,t^*}} = \frac{1}{2}p(t,S,t^*,S^*)S^{*2}\frac{\partial^2}{\partial S^{*2}}p(t^*,S^*,t',S'). \quad \text{(C12)}$$

Similarly, the variational derivative of the backward transition probability $\Phi(K,T,K',T')$ to the local volatility σ_{K^*,T^*} with $T' \le T^* \le T$ is found using Figure 25 and can be written as

$$\frac{\delta\Phi(K,T,K',T')}{\delta\sigma^2_{K^*,T^*}} = \frac{1}{2}\Phi(K,T,K^*,T^*)K^{*2}\frac{\partial^2}{\partial K^{*2}}\Phi(K^*,T^*,K',T'). \quad \text{(C13)}$$

Appendix D

THE NO-ARBITRAGE CONDITIONS AND THE EXISTENCE OF THE EQUIVALENT MARTINGALE MEASURE IN STOCHASTIC VOLATILITY THEORIES

This appendix presents a proof of the no-arbitrage drift conditions of Equation (53). We also make the usual assumptions about the regularity, measurability and integrability of various quantities. A more rigorous treatment will need to address these issues.

Let us begin with Equation (40) in the text, describing the stochastic process followed by the total transition probability $P_{K,T}(t,S)$ in a stochastic volatility theory:

$$dP_{K,T} = \left[\left(\frac{\partial P_{K,T}}{\partial t} + \mu(t)S\frac{\partial P_{K,T}}{\partial S} + \frac{1}{2}\sigma^2(t)S^2\frac{\partial^2 P_{K,T}}{\partial S^2}\right)dt + \sigma(t)S\frac{\partial P_{K,T}}{\partial S}dW^0(t)\right]_{(t,S)} + \int_t^T\int_0^\infty \frac{\delta P_{K,T}}{\delta\sigma^2_{K',T'}}d\sigma^2_{K',T'}dK'dT' + \frac{1}{2}\int_t^T\int_t^T\int_0^\infty\int_0^\infty \frac{\delta^2 P_{K,T}}{\delta\sigma^2_{K',T'}\delta\sigma^2_{K'',T''}}d\sigma^2_{K',T'}d\sigma^2_{K'',T''}dK'dK''dT'dT''.$$

The first term describes differential changes of the transition probability restricted to the effective theory defined by the (non-random) local volatility surface $\sigma_{K,T}(t,S)$ prevailing at time t and market level S. Restricted to this surface, $P_{K,T}(t,S)$ coincides with the effective theory total transition probability $p(t,S,K,T)$ and the instantaneous volatility $\sigma(t)$ coincides with the local volatility $\sigma_{t,S}$. Therefore, in view of (B1), the following backward equation holds:

$$\left[\frac{\partial P_{K,T}}{\partial t} + (r-\delta)S\frac{\partial P_{K,T}}{\partial S} + \frac{1}{2}\sigma^2(t)S^2\frac{\partial^2 P_{K,T}}{\partial S^2}\right]_{(t,s)} = 0.$$

Using this expression, Equations (25) and (C12), and some manipulations, we arrive at

$$dP_{K,T} = \sigma(t)S\frac{\partial P_{K,T}}{\partial S}\left[dW^0(t) + \frac{\mu(t)-r+\delta}{\sigma(t)}dt\right] + \sum_{i=1}^n\left(\int_t^T\int_0^\infty \frac{\delta P_{K,T}}{\delta\sigma^2_{K',T'}}\theta^i_{K',T'}dK'dT'\right)dW^i_t + \left(\int_t^T\int_0^\infty \frac{\delta P_{K,T}}{\delta\sigma^2_{K',T'}}\left[\alpha_{K',T'}(t,S) + \sum_{i=1}^n\theta^i_{K',T'}(t,S)\right.\right.$$

$$\left\{\frac{1}{p(t,S,T',K')}\times\int_t^{T'}\int_0^{\infty}\theta^i_{K'',T''}(t,S)p(t,S,T'',K'')K''^2\right.$$

$$\left.\left.\left.\frac{\partial^2}{\partial K''^2}p(T'',K'',T',K')dK''dT''\right\}\right]dK'dT'\right).$$

Note that the effective theory transition probabilities $p(..)$ implicitly depend on t and S, whether or not they contain these variables explicitly.

Now assume that the drift parameters $\sigma_{K,T}(t,S)$ satisfy the following relations with $\Pi^0 = 0$ and (so far) arbitrary functions Π^i, $i = 1, .., n$:

$$\alpha_{K,T} = -\sum_{i=0}^{n}\theta^i_{K,T}(t,S)\left\{\frac{1}{p(t,S,T,K)}\int_t^{T'}\int_0^{\infty}\theta^i_{K',T'}(t,S)\right.$$

$$\left.p(t,S,T',K')K'^2\frac{\partial^2}{\partial K'^2}p(T',K',T,K)dK'dT' - \Pi^i\right\}.$$

Then we can define a new measure $\{d\overline{W}^i,\ i = 0,\dots,n\}$ by

$$d\overline{W}^i_t = dW^i_t + \Pi^i_t dt \quad (i = 0,\dots,n);$$

$$\Pi^0 = \frac{\mu(t) - r + \delta}{\sigma(t)}$$

in terms of which we have

$$dP_{K,T} = \sigma(t)S\frac{\partial P_{K,T}}{\partial S}d\overline{W}^0 +$$

$$\sum_{i=1}^{n}\left(\int_t^{T}\int_0^{\infty}\frac{\delta P_{K,T}}{\delta\sigma^2_{K',T'}}\theta^i_{K',T'}dK'dT'\right)d\overline{W}^i_t.$$

The measure $\{d\overline{W}^i,\ i = 0,\dots,n\}$ is an equivalent martingale probability measure. Applying the arguments of Harrison and Kreps (1979) we can show that this equivalent martingale measure is unique if (and only if) the market prices of risk Π^i, $i = 0,\dots,n$, remain independent of strike price K and maturity T. Under these conditions the markets are complete and contingent claims valuation follows the standard methods of Harrison and Pliska (1989) and remains independent of market prices of risk.

We may choose to include $W^0 = Z$, the index price's source of uncertainty among the factors affecting local volatilities so that the stochastic variations of the local volatility surface can directly depend on the index price changes. In this case, we have (see (26)):

$$\frac{d\sigma^2_{K,T}(t,S)}{\sigma^2_{K,T}(t,S)} = \alpha_{K,T}(t,S)dt + \sum_{i=0}^{n}\theta^i_{K,T}(t,S)dW^i_t.$$

Here the local volatility function $\theta^0_{K,T}$ reflects the sensitivity of local volatilities to the shocks introduced by the Brownian motion W^0. We can then show that the no-arbitrage conditions for the drift functions $\alpha_{K,T}(t,S)$ in this case are given by

$$\alpha_{K,T}(t,S) = -\sum_{i=0}^{n}\theta^i_{K,T}(t,S)\left\{\frac{1}{P(t,S,K,T)}\right.$$

$$\int_t^{T}\int_0^{\infty}\theta^i_{K',T'}(t,S)P(t,S,T',K')$$

$$\left.\times K'^2\frac{\partial^2}{\partial K'^2}P(T',K',T,K)dK'dT' - \Pi^i\right\}$$

$$-\frac{\theta^0_{K,T}(t,S)}{P(t,S,K,T)}\sigma_{(t)}S(t)\frac{\partial}{\partial S}P(t,S,K,T).$$

Appendix E

COMPUTING DRIFT PARAMETERS IN ARBITRAGE-FREE STOCHASTIC VOLATILITY THEORIES

This appendix derives formulas for calculating drift parameters from the no-arbitrage conditions in stochastic volatility theories. We work in the discrete time context of the stochastic implied trinomial trees and show how to inductively calculate the arbitrage-free drift parameters for all future nodes from the martingale conditions on the total transition probabilities to the neighbouring nodes at the next time step.

We begin our analysis at the $(i + 1)$th step of the simulation, at time t_i, with index level at node (i,j) of the stochastic implied tree. Our objective is to calculate the arbitrage-free drift parameters $\alpha_{m,n}(i,j)$, to all future nodes (n, m) at future times t_n for $n \geq i$. We calculate the drift parameter $\alpha_{m,n}(i,j)$ iteratively, using the results of the previous iteration steps and the condition that the total transition probability $P_{m+2,n+1}(i,j)$, from the node (i,j) to the node $(n + 1, m + 2)$, is a martingale under all possible future movements of the local volatility surface. This situation is shown in Figure 26.

Figure 26 shows the subtree which starts at the initial node (i,j). All the future movements of the index and local volatilities will be confined to the nodes of this subtree. Our iteration for calculating drift parameters $\alpha_{m,n}(i,j)$ for all subtree nodes begins with the calculation of the drift parameter at the initial node, $\alpha_{j,i}(i,j)$, and continues forward to subsequent time steps beginning with the highest node at each time step.

To make matters simple, for now let us assume that the only possible movements of the local volatility surface during the next instant Δt are up or down (proportionately), with some

26.

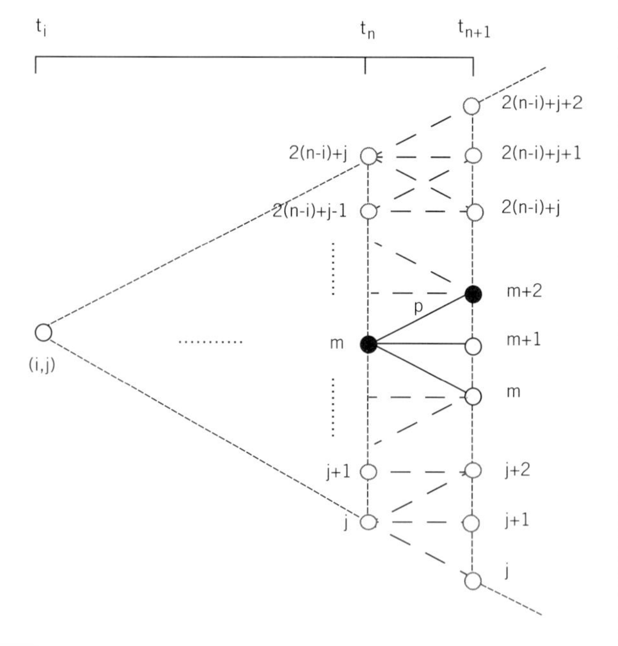

constant volatility θ, as in our example in the text, ie

$$\sigma^{(u,d)}_{m,n}(i,j) = \sigma_{m,n}(i,j)\exp\left\{\left(\alpha_{m,n}(i,j) - \frac{1}{2}\theta^2\right)\Delta t \pm \theta\sqrt{\Delta t}\right\}.$$

Suppose that we have calculated the drift parameters for every node before time t_n, and also for every node at time t_n which lies above the node (n,m), shown in bold in the figure. We must now calculate $\alpha_{m,n}(i,j)$ from the previously known quantities and the martingale condition on the total probability $P_{m+2,n+1}(i,j)$, of arriving at the node $(n + 1,\ m + 2)$ at the next time step. We can decompose the contributions to this probability into two components as follows:

$$P_{m+2,n+1}(i,j) = P_{m,n}(i,j)\mathbf{p} + \Lambda_{m,n}(i,j).$$

As in the figure, $\mathbf{p}$ denotes the one period up transition probability from the node (n,m) to the node $(n + 1,\ m + 2)$. The first term describes the contribution of the node (n,m) to the total transition probability, stemming from all the paths which go through this node before arriving at $(n + 1,\ m + 2)$. The second term describes the contribution of all the nodes lying above the node (n,m) to this transition probability.

Consider now the next instant Δt in time where all future local volatilities will simultaneously move either to their up state, $\sigma^{(u)}_{m,n}(i,j)$, or to their down state $\sigma^{(d)}_{m,n}(i,j)$. Since transition probabilities are direct functions of local volatilities, then all probabilities will also simultaneously move to their up or down states, ie

$$P^{(u,d)}_{m+2,n+1}(i,j) = P^{(u,d)}_{m,n}(i,j)\mathbf{p}^{(u,d)} + \Lambda^{(u,d)}_{m,n}(i,j).$$

The quantities $P^{(u,d)}_{m,n}(i,j)$ and $\Lambda^{(u,d)}_{m,n}(i,j)$ depend on drift parameters and other quantities known from the previous iteration steps, but $\mathbf{p}^{(u,d)}$ remain unknown as they depend on the unknown drift parameter $\alpha_{m,n}(i,j)$. We have previously discussed the structure of this dependence in Equations (C4) and (C5). The one period transition probability $\mathbf{p}$ depends linearly on the local variance $\sigma^2_{m,n}(i,j)$, ie $\mathbf{p} = A + B\sigma^2_{m,n}(i,j)$, with coefficients A and B depending only on the position of the nodes, which are fixed and known. Hence

$$\mathbf{p}^{(u,d)} = A + B\sigma^{(u,d)2}_{m,n}(i,j) =$$

$$A + B\sigma_{m,n}(i,j)\exp\left\{2\left(\alpha_{m,n}(i,j) - \frac{1}{2}\theta^2\right)\Delta t \pm 2\theta\sqrt{\Delta t}\right\}.$$

Using this and previous relations, we can now determine the unknown drift parameter $\alpha_{m,n}(i,j)$ from the martingale condition for the (known) total probability $P_{m+2,n+1}(i,j)$:

$$\begin{aligned}
P_{m+2,n+1}(i,j) &= \frac{1}{2}\left\{P^{(u)}_{m+2,n+1}(i,j) + P^{(d)}_{m+2,n+1}(i,j)\right\} \\
&= \frac{1}{2}\left\{P^{(u)}_{m,n}(i,j)\mathbf{p}^{(u)} + P^{(d)}_{m,n}(i,j)\mathbf{p}^{(d)} + \Lambda^{(u)}_{m,n}(i,j) + \Lambda^{(d)}_{m,n}(i,j)\right\} \\
&= \frac{1}{2}\left\{\left[P^{(u)}_{m,n}(i,j) + P^{(d)}_{m,n}(i,j)\right]A + \Lambda^{(u)}_{m,n}(i,j) + \Lambda^{(d)}_{m,n}(i,j)\right\} + \\
&\quad \frac{1}{2}B\sigma^2_{m,n}(i,j)e^{-\theta^2\Delta t}\left[P^{(u)}_{m,n}(i,j)e^{2\theta\Delta t} + P^{(d)}_{m,n}(i,j)e^{-2\theta\Delta t}\right] \\
&\quad \exp\left\{2\alpha_{m,n}(i,j)\Delta t\right\}.
\end{aligned}$$

Therefore the desired formula is

$$\alpha_{m,n}(i,j) =$$

$$\left(\log\left[\frac{P_{m+2,n+1}(i,j) - \frac{1}{2}\left\{\left[P^{(u)}_{m,n}(i,j) + P^{(d)}_{m,n}(i,j)\right]A + \Lambda^{(u)}_{m,n}(i,j) + \Lambda^{(d)}_{m,n}(i,j)\right\}}{\frac{1}{2}B\sigma^2_{m,n}(i,j)e^{-\theta^2\Delta t}\left[P^{(u)}_{m,n}(i,j)e^{2\theta\sqrt{\Delta t}} + P^{(d)}_{m,n}(i,j)e^{-2\theta\sqrt{\Delta t}}\right]}\right]\right) / (2\Delta t).$$

This result can be readily extended to the cases where the local volatility surface can move to any number (more than two) of possible states during a time step, has multiple stochastic factors, or has factor volatilities which are more complicated functions of time, market level, factor values or their past histories.

1 *See, for example, Cox, Ingersoll, and Ross (1985).*

2 *See, for example, Vasicek (1977), Black, Derman and Toy (1990).*

3 *See, for example, Ho and Lee (1986), Heath-Jarrow and Morton (1992).*

4 *See, for example, Merton (1973), Cox and Ross (1976), Johnson and Shanno (1987), Eisenberg and Jarrow (1994).*

5 *See, for example, Wiggins (1987), Hull and White (1987), Stein and Stein (1991).*

6 *See Cox, Ingersoll and Ross (1985), Heath, Jarrow and Morton (1992).*

7 *Presented in Risk Advanced Mathematics for Derivatives Conference, New York, December 1997.*

8 *For attempts in this direction see, for example, Dupire (1993) and Dupire in the Proceedings of Risk Derivatives Conference, Brussels, February 1997.*

9 *See Derman, Kani and Chriss (1996), Kani, Derman and Kamal (1996).*

10 *See, for example, Jamshidian (1993).*

11 *The forward and backward propagators for a static yield curve are both simply equal to the discount function ie*

$$p_{u,v} = \phi_{u,v} = \exp\left(-\int_u^v f_\tau d\tau\right).$$

12 *The variable* S *in the expression for local volatility* $\sigma_{K,T}(t,S)$ *is included for notational purposes and does not imply dependence solely on the spot level. In fact, local volatilities generally depend on the entire history of the index price other stochastic factors. Aside from time* t *and index price* S*, all other variables have been explicitly omitted from expressions for local volatilities, drifts and factor volatilities.*

13 *The factor volatility functions* $\theta^i_{K,T}(t,S)$ *are assumed to be positive, adapted and jointly measurable with respect to the Borel* σ*-algebra restricted to* $0 \le t \le T \le T^*$*, for some fixed maximum time* T^**. They must also satisfy*

$$\int_0^T \left(\theta^i_{K,T}\right)^2 (u,S_u)\,du < \infty, i = 0,\ldots,n,$$

to assure regularity of spot volatility process, and certain additional integrability conditions to assure regularity of the standard option price processes.

14 *See Breeden and Litzenberger (1978).*

15 *This also occurs in the standard implied trees. See, for instance, Derman, Kani and Chriss (1996).*

16 *See also* Investing in Volatility, *Derman et al (1996).*

17 *To be presented in an upcoming Quantitative Strategies Research Note.*

BIBLIOGRAPHY

Black, F., and M. Scholes, 1973, "The Pricing of Options and Corporate Liabilities", *Journal of Political Economy* 81, pp. 637-54.

Black, F., E. Derman and W. Toy, 1990, "A One-Factor Model of Interest Rates and Its Application to Treasury Bond Options", *Financial Analysts Journal*, 817 pp. 33-9.

Breeden, D., and R. Litzenberger, 1978, "The Pricing of State-Contingent Claims Implicit in Option Prices", *Journal of Business* 51, pp. 621-51.

Cox, J., J.E. Ingersoll and S. Ross, 1985, "A Theory of the Term Structure of Interest Rates", *Econometrica* 53, No. 2, pp. 385-407.

Cox. J., and S. Ross, 1976, "The Valuation of Options for Alternative Stochastic Processes", *Journal of Financial Economics* 3, pp. 145-66.

Cox, J., S. Ross and M. Rubinstein, 1979, "Option Pricing: A Simplified Approach", *Journal of Financial Economics* 7, pp. 229-63.

Derman, E., and I. Kani, 1994, "Riding on a Smile", *Risk* 7, No. 2, pp. 32-9.

Derman, E., I. Kani and N. Chriss, 1996, "Implied Trinomial Trees of the Volatility Smile", *Journal of Derivatives* 3, No. 4 pp. 7-22.

Dupire, B., 1993, "Model Art", *Risk* 6, No. 9, pp. 118-24.

Dupire, B., 1994, "Pricing with a Smile", *Risk* 7, No. 1, pp. 18-20.

Eisenberg L., and R. Jarrow, 1994, "Option Pricing With Random Volatilities in Complete Markets", *Review of Quantitative Finance and Accounting* 4, pp. 5-17; reprinted as Chapter 21 of the present volume.

Harrison, J. M., and D. Kreps, 1979, "Martingales and Arbitrage in Multiperiod Securities Markets", *Journal of Economic Theory* 20, pp. 381-408.

Harrison, J.M., and S. Pliska, 1981, "Martingales and Stochastic Integrals in the Theory of Continuous Trading",. *Stochastic Processes and Their Applications* 20, pp. 215-60.

Heath, D., R. Jarrow and A. Morton, 1992, "Bond Pricing and The Term Structure of Interest Rates: A New Methodology for Contingent Claims Valuation", *Econometrica* 60, No. 1, pp. 77-105.

Ho, T. S. Y., and S. B. Lee, 1986, "Term Structure Movements and Pricing Interest Rate Contingent Claims", *Journal of Finance* 41, No. 5, pp. 1011-29.

Hull, J., and A. White, 1987, "The Pricing of Options on Assets With Stochastic Volatilities", *Journal of Finance* 42, pp. 271-301.

Jamshidian, F., 1993, "Option and Futures Evaluation with Deterministic Volatilities", *Mathematical Finance* 3, No. 2, pp. 149-59.

Johnson, H., and D. Shanno, 1987, "Option Pricing When Variance is Changing", *Journal of Financial and Quantitative Analysis* 22, pp. 143-53.

Kani, I., E. Derman and M. Kamal, 1996, "Trading and Hedging Local Volatility", *Quantitative Strategies Research Notes*, Goldman Sachs & Co.

Merton, R., 1973, "Theory of Rational Option Pricing", *Bell Journal of Economics and Management Science* 4, pp. 141-83.

Rubinstein, M.E., 1994, "Implied Binomial Trees", *Journal of Finance* 69, pp. 771-818.

Stein, E., and J. Stein, 1991, "Stock Price Distribution With Stochastic Volatility: An Analytical Approach", *Review of Financial Studies* 4, No. 4, pp. 727-52.

Vasicek, O.A., 1977, "An Equilibrium Characterization of the Term Structure", *Journal of Financial Economics* 5, pp. 177-88.

Wiggins, J., 1987, "Option Values Under Stochastic Volatility: Theory and Empirical Estimates", *Journal of Financial Economics* 19, pp. 351-72.

INDEX

INDEX

INDEX